The Works of Art of the Corporation of London

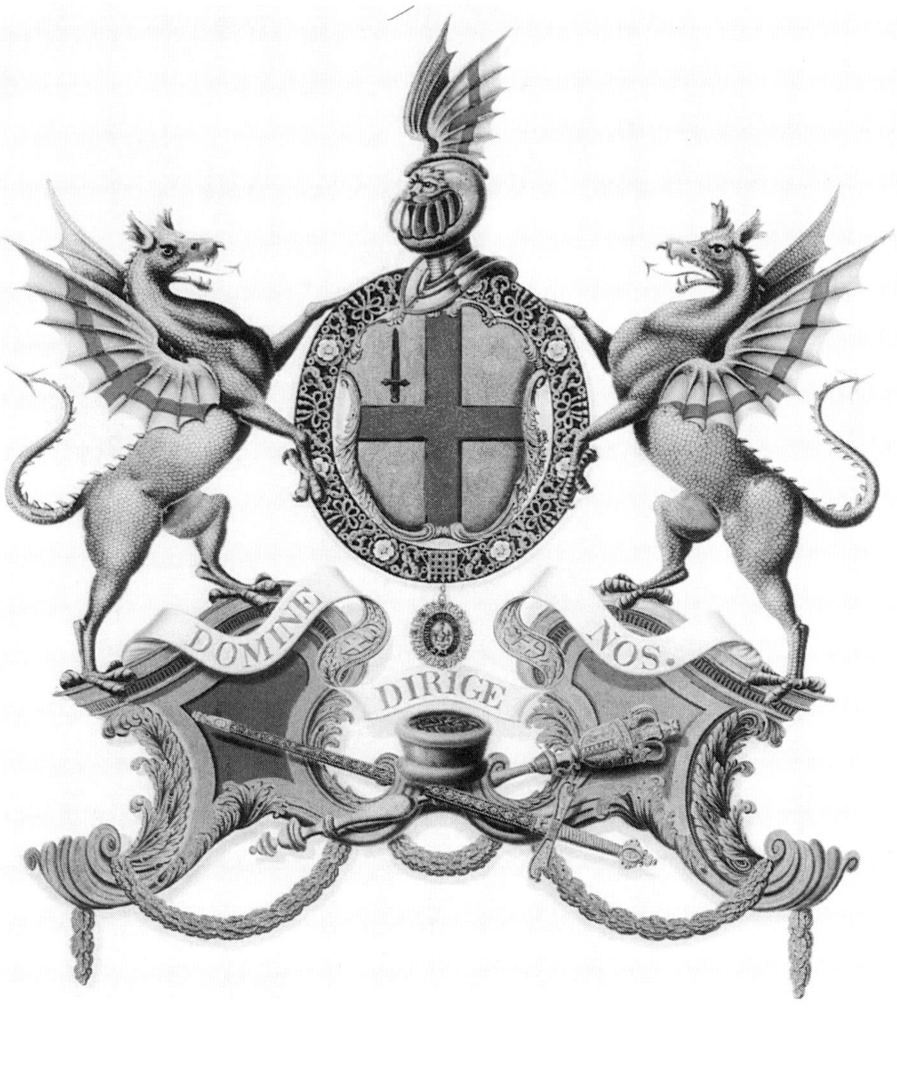

Anon
The Coat of Arms of the Corporation of London
acc. no. 1364
watercolour on vellum: $22\frac{1}{2} \times 21$ in.
Presented by J. Harvey Hull, 1947

The Works of Art of the Corporation of London

A catalogue of paintings, watercolours, drawings, prints and sculpture

Compiled by Vivien Knight

Curator of the Permanent Collection,

Guildhall Art Gallery

Woodhead-Faulkner
Cambridge

Published by Woodhead-Faulkner Limited
Fitzwilliam House, 32 Trumpington Street,
Cambridge CB2 1QY, England
and
27 South Main Street,
Wolfeboro, NH 03894-2069, USA

First published 1986

British Library Cataloguing in Publication Data

City of London. *Corporation*
The works of art of the Corporation of London: a catalogue of paintings, watercolours, drawings, prints and sculpture
1. Guildhall Art Gallery—Catalogs
I. Title II. Knight, Vivien
708.2′12 N1033

ISBN 0-85941-379-9

Designed by Jane Norman
Typeset and printed by BAS Printers Limited

Contents

Preface

The publication of this catalogue is a significant event in various respects. Firstly, its timing is particularly appropriate – Guildhall Art Gallery was opened to the public in 1886, and it is specially pleasurable that this catalogue was prepared in the centenary year. While the Gallery itself was the victim of enemy action in 1941, most items survived and the collection again began to expand. So while the bricks and mortar of the original Gallery are no longer with us, we still celebrate the centenary in the knowledge that the spirit of Guildhall Art Gallery lives on in the Corporation's extensive collection of works.

It is also significant to record that the last complete catalogue of the Corporation's collection was published in 1910, with a supplement in 1924. Today's catalogue shows a collection which has grown enormously since the early part of the century, even allowing for wartime losses. A new and comprehensive catalogue is therefore an overdue and important publishing event, which will make available to the art world a considerable amount of information in a convenient form.

There is one major omission. The catalogue does not include the collection of works by Sir Matthew Smith, which was bequeathed to the Corporation by Mrs Mary Keene. The Smith collection is so substantial in itself that it was not possible to record it here. Indeed it stands as a unique part of the City's holdings in its own right, and it is hoped that in the future a separate catalogue of our works by Sir Matthew Smith will appear.

The interest of Woodhead-Faulkner in publishing this catalogue is greatly appreciated, and this has proved to be a constructive partnership between the Corporation and a commercial publisher. It is hoped that the many institutions and professionals in the art world, and indeed anyone interested in what by any definition is an important collection of works, will find this catalogue of great value.

Although many have been involved in this production, I would specially acknowledge the hard work and dedication of our Curator of the Permanent Collection, Vivien Knight. In her monumental task of compiling the catalogue and writing a most informative introduction, she has performed a worthwhile public service for which many will be grateful.

Melvyn Barnes
Guildhall Librarian and Director of Libraries
and Art Galleries

Acknowledgements

Photographic acknowledgements

David Clarke
Cranfield Institute of Technology
Michael England
Jonathan Morris-Ebbs
Godfrey New
Nick Warwick
W. W. Winter Ltd.

Author's acknowledgements

I am extremely grateful to Clare Signy for arranging all the new photography necessary for this catalogue, assisted by Jan Speirs. Jan Speirs also catalogued the John Gilbert and Anna Lea Merritt material, and with Sara Eckersley and Gillian Keay prepared the indexes. Tony Ward gave valuable assistance, and Sara Eckersley and Gillian Keay undertook collation and proof reading. Dave Clarke, Mike England, Jonathan Morris-Ebbs and Nick Warwick undertook the bulk of the photography, often under difficult circumstances and at short notice. Irene Pollock and the staff of Guildhall Library have been, as always, helpful and informative, as have Ralph Hyde and the Print Room staff. Thanks also to my husband Jim for his tolerance.

Historical Introduction

The Corporation of London began to purchase and commission paintings and sculpture during the 17th century, primarily as an expression of the City's appreciation of royal favours and its loyalty to the Crown, its gratitude to the naval and military heroes of famous British victories, and as a record of important civic events and City personages. To these were added numerous gifts and bequests, and of the items included in this catalogue more than half have entered the collection by this means. By 1879 the City's collection was so large that a Curator was appointed, reporting to the City Lands Committee. The influential City of London Society of Artists was founded in the same year under the presidency of the Lord Mayor, Sir Francis Wyatt Truscott, with the aims of establishing a permanent art gallery in the City and of exhibiting the work of contemporary local artists. In 1884 the Society was allowed to hold its fourth exhibition in the empty Court of Queen's Bench next to Guildhall, and in 1885 the Court of Common Council asked the Library Committee to report on 'the desirability and practicability of establishing a City of London Art Gallery, for the reception and exhibition of Works of Art belonging to the Corporation, or which may be presented from time to time'. On 30 July the Committee replied:

> It appears to your Committee that the Paintings, Busts and Engravings at Guildhall, would of themselves form the nucleus of a Gallery of no ordinary interest, and it may reasonably be anticipated that, if the proposed Gallery were established, valuable contributions by way of gift or bequest would from time to time be received.
>
> Seeing that other Corporations, such as Liverpool, Manchester, Leeds, &c., have adopted a course similar to that now contemplated and have established Galleries that have proved eminently successful, it appears to us that a Gallery in connection with the Corporation of London would, in the increased taste for Art now prevalent, be exceedingly attractive and instructive, especially if the Corporation become, as is very probable, the recipient of such bequests or presentations as have other municipalities.

The disused Court of Queen's Bench was immediately allocated for the new Art Gallery with the intention – never pursued – of finding better permanent space elsewhere at Guildhall in the future, and the Gallery opened to the public in April 1886. Its Secretary (later Director), Alfred Temple, was responsible only for the items located within the Gallery, and works located elsewhere at Guildhall continued in the care of the Curator. On his death in 1896 Temple was appointed to his duties, carrying out the dual roles of Director of the Art Gallery and Curator of Works of Art until 1920. In March of that year the Court of Common Council resolved that the office of Curator and that of Director of the Art Gallery be merged, so that a single individual was responsible for all works of art belonging to the Corporation, regardless of where they were located. The combined office was under the control of the Library Committee. Following Temple's death in 1928 the positions of Director of the Art Gallery and Librarian were merged.

There are several areas in which the Corporation's collection is now particularly strong. It includes a large number of civic, especially mayoral, portraits, although of the latter only two were commissioned by the Corporation (those of Alderman Boydell, Lord

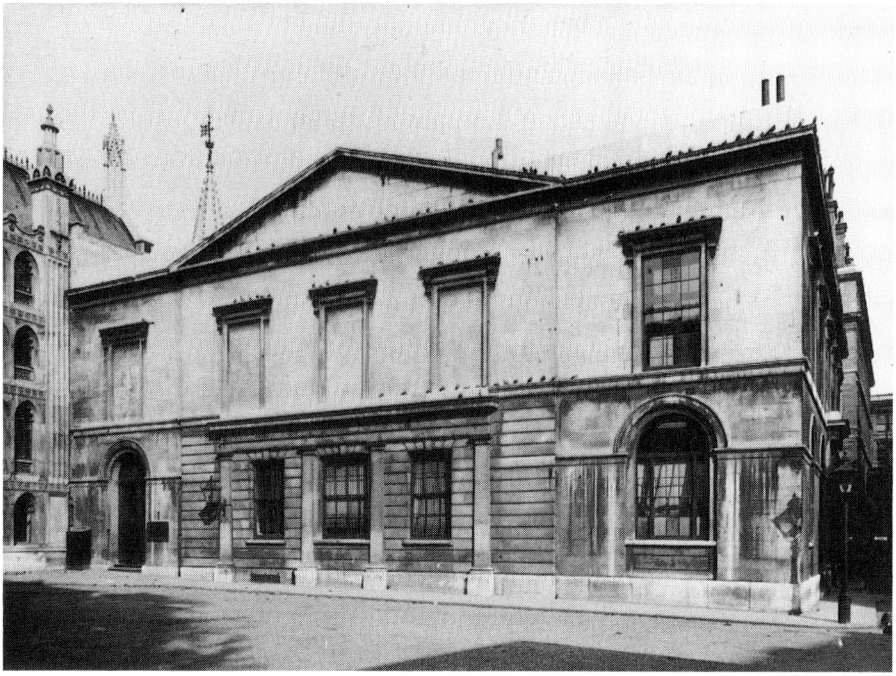

Guildhall Art Gallery, photographed on 22 September 1912 (coll: Guildhall Library, Print Room)

Mayor 1790, and Dame Mary Donaldson, Lord Mayor 1983–4). Paintings commemorating civic events include *The Ceremony of Administering the Mayoralty Oath to Nathaniel Newnham, 1782* by William Miller, Paton and Wheatley's *The Lord Mayor's Procession by Water to Westminster, 1789*, and *Queen Victoria's Procession to Guildhall, 1837* by J. H. Nixon, as well as more recent large paintings by Frank O. Salisbury and Terence Cuneo. A large section of the collection illustrates the changing topography of London from the 17th century to the present day, and includes works by Samuel Scott, William Marlow and Jan Vorsterman. A further major aspect comprises large holdings of 19th century landscape, marine and genre pictures, most of which have been acquired through gift or bequest. The most important of these was Charles Gassiot's bequest in 1902 of his large collection which included Constable's large-scale oil sketch *Salisbury Cathedral from the Meadows* (although because it had been overpainted Gassiot knew it as a different composition; the picture's true appearance was not revealed until 1951), and works by Landseer, David Roberts, William Dyce and J. E. Millais. Gassiot's taste was conservative and more avant-garde works did not enter the collection for some years (by which time, of course, they were no longer considered to be so): Viscount Bearsted presented *The Woodman's Daughter* by Millais in 1921, as well as G. F. Watts' *Ariadne in Naxos* in 1918 and *The Music Lesson* by Lord Leighton in 1925. *La Ghirlandata* by Rossetti and a painting based on one of Rossetti's poems, *The Blessed Damozel* by Byam Shaw, were purchased by the Gallery in 1927. In 1921 Sir George Touche presented Poynter's *Israel in Egypt*, a spectacular success when it was shown at the Royal Academy in 1867, and the same donor, with Sir Francis Agar and Sir Charles (later Viscount) Wakefield, presented *The Eve of St Agnes*, an early work by William Holman Hunt, in 1924. William Shakespeare Burton's most famous painting, *The Wounded Cavalier*, was bought from its private owner by Alfred Temple in haste and from his own pocket, in order to forestall the curators of two provincial galleries; Temple was later reimbursed his £750 by a body of subscribers which included Wakefield, who continued to be a generous benefactor both to the Art Gallery and to Guildhall Library. The Gallery's own newly-acquired Purchase Fund was used for the first time in 1902, when two contemporary paintings, *The River Bank* by Arnesby Brown and Henry Scott Tuke's *Ruby, Gold and Malachite*, were purchased from the Royal Academy Exhibition; H. H. La Thangue's *Mowing Bracken* was bought from the Exhibition in 1903.

Since the Second World War, collecting policy has been directed primarily towards acquiring works of London interest. However, the collection has been fortunate in continuing to receive many gifts and bequests, which have introduced a wide variety of other subjects. Notable among such gifts was that made in 1944 by Lady Wakefield in accordance with her late husband's wishes, including works by Lely, Nicolas Maes and John Opie; Mrs Mary Keene's donation in 1973 of more than 1,000 works by Sir Matthew Smith transformed the Corporation's 20th-century holdings; and most recently, Miss Helen Guiterman's gift in 1985 of 103 oils, watercolours, prints and drawings by a variety of artists included only six London subjects.

The Corporation appears to have commissioned its first paintings in 1670. The Great Fire of London broke out on 2 September 1666, and in February 1667 a Court was appointed to arbitrate in the disputes arising from the chaos of obliterated buildings and property boundaries. Consisting of the Justices of the Courts of King's Bench and Common Pleas and the Barons of the Exchequer, the Commission sat at Clifford's Inn until 20 September 1672. On 19 April 1670 the Court of Aldermen ordered that 'their pictures be taken by a skillfull hand & kept in some public place of the City for a greatfull memoriall of this good office'.[1] The artists recommended to the Court were 'Mr. Houseman' (probably Jacob Huysmans), 'Mr. Hales' (probably John Hayles) and John Michael Wright, who received the commission; George Vertue recorded that 'Sr Peter Lily was to have done them but he would not wait upon the Judges in the City to Paint them wherefore Wright had them to do'.[2] Lely did receive the commission resulting from a further resolution of the court in September 1670, 'that good peeces or pictures be obtained of his Majesty and His Royall Highnesse the Duke of Yorke & that the same be placed where the Judges are intended to be in the Guildhall as some remembrance of their Royall Favoures and encouragements to the worke of rebuilding the Citty'.[3]

Fourteen portraits of Fire Judges by Wright and Lely's portraits of Charles II and James, Duke of York were hanging in the Great Hall by the end of 1671, the lower part of the windows having been blocked up to accommodate them. On 14 December the 'Committee formerly appointed to treat and agree for the Pictures of his Majesty, his Royall Highnesse the Duke of Yorke the Lord Keeper and ye Judges' reported to the Court of Aldermen:

> Wee have agreed with Mr. Lilly for the Pictures of the King and Duke of Yorke to pay him one hundred pounds And for the Pictures of the Lord Keeper and Judges which were done by Mr. Wright Wee have agreed to allow him XXXVI li per picture, which for the 14 Pictures amounts to £504, although his comon price hath alwayes been £40 for pictures of whole length and for these hee demanded more in regard of his extraordinary expences in painting the same upon Bed Tickin (which are usually done upon Canvas) and priming them on both sides double for strength and Substance, Also Mr. Wright the Herald Painters Bill for Painting the Judges Coates of Armes and inscriptions of their names at Xs a peece amounts to £6.10s [*sic*] And Wee also certifye that Wee agreed with Mrs. Ashfeild and Mrs. Flushier for doing the frames of the Judges Pictures (with the Iron worke) at £12 a peece and £15 a peece for the Kings and Duke of Yorkes, eight of the Judges were done by Mrs. Ashfeild which amounts to £96 and five by Mrs. Flushier which with the other two amounts to £90 (besides one formerly paid for to Mr. Norris) And Mr. Man hath also expended £5.14.10 in and about the setting upp of the said Pictures & other

expences relating thereunto All which persons Wee humbly recomend to bee paid by Order of this honoble Court.[4]

Wright was paid for three further portraits in November 1672, receiving the commission for another picture on the same day; a fifth portrait was ordered in 1674 and three more in 1675, bringing the total to 22. When John Evelyn saw those already completed on 31 July 1673 he noted in his Diary that 'most of them are very like the Persons they are made to represent, though I never tooke Write to be any considerable artist'.[5]

Six more royal portraits were commissioned during the next century: William III and Queen Mary by Jan Van der Vaardt (1682), Queen Anne by John Closterman (1702), George I by Sir Godfrey Kneller (1716) and George II and Queen Caroline by Charles Jervas (1727); these were followed by portraits of George III and Queen Caroline by Allan Ramsay, presented by the King in 1764 and Sir Joshua Reynolds' portrait of Sir Charles Pratt, commissioned by the Corporation in the same year.

In 1778 the City's Surveyor, George Dance, was ordered to provide estimates for the repair of the pictures in Guildhall, many of which, despite restoration in the past, were in a dilapidated condition. He noted that 'the Portrait of George the first is so much decayed and torn as not to be capable of repair',[6] and the following year the Court of Common Council heard that all the pictures, now removed from Guildhall to the neighbouring Chapel, were 'in a dirty condition and some by age and dampness totally destroyed';[7] John Nichols recorded that 'when Guildhall was repaired in 1779, all the portraits (except the modern ones) were in so bad a condition that it became a matter of doubt whether they were to be restored to their places or committed to the flames'.[8]

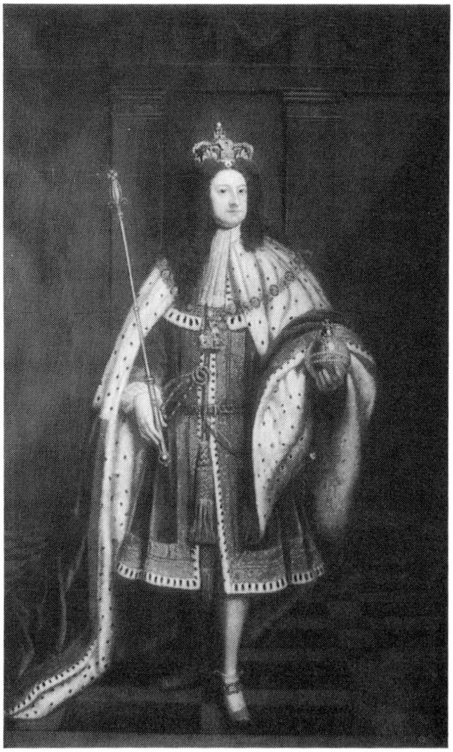

Sir Godfrey Kneller, *King George I*, oil on canvas: 95 × 58 in., commissioned by the Corporation 1716, destroyed 29 December 1940

It being decided to save the pictures, estimates for restoration were obtained, and Spiridione Roma was selected to carry out the work. A portrait and history painter, Roma had already undertaken restoration of paintings for various Livery Companies in the City. According to the *Gentleman's Magazine*, his cleaning process:

> appeared to be dissolving the varnish and dirt which adhered to the painting, and which he removed with a small ivory scraper without any injury to the body of colour on the canvas. . . . He could never be prevailed on to commit his recipe for his composition of the liquid he used in picture-cleaning to paper . . . and as he always worked at home under lock and key, it is to be feared his knowledge, whatever it was, perished with him.[9]

Roma's work on the Guildhall portraits was done not at his home but at Goldsmiths' Hall. Having received the commission in June 1779, he worked extremely rapidly and delivered his final account in July 1780:

> Having cleaned, repaired and perfectly restored 19 whole length paintings of Judges and having with infinite labour tooke every one of them out of the stretching frame and firmly secured to each of them an entire new back of canvas and strongly prepared the same with new cement of colour in oil against damp . . . at £5 each, £95.0.0 . . . Having cleaned repaired and perfectly restored seven pictures of Kings and Queens six of whom was entirely destroyed and having put to them a new back of canvass with the same preservative against damp . . . at £5 each, £35.0.0 . . . The eighth picture of Kings is George the first and the only truly rarity of this kind in this kingdom that exists now and will exist longer than any picture in Guildhall or any other Hall in this great Metropolis, being many score of small pieces put together again and completely reduced to one for which the least demand can be made is one hundred guineas but to this Honble Committee I charge only £14.[10]

It is difficult to imagine the appearance of the latter picture, but Roma's biographer in the *Gentleman's Magazine* confirms that:

> many of these paintings were certainly in very bad condition, and cost him much labour to repair, particularly that of George the first, which he exhibited in shattered fragments of an inch square, and which he perfectly restored to its original state. At the conclusion of this work he was involved in a long contest with the Corporation regarding payment.[11]

All the portraits were rehung in Guildhall, but in 1803 it was noted that:

> the constant exposure to which every article in the Hall is liable, of damp in winter and dust in summer, with a constant and fresh supply of smoke, condensed in this very centre of the city, accounts for the deplorable state of the paintings in 1779. Indeed, they are almost reduced to the same pitiable condition again (24 years later).[12]

Closterman's portrait of Queen Anne and Lely's of Charles II and the Duke of York had presumably decayed completely or have been otherwise lost by 1827, since they do not appear in the catalogue of works of art at Guildhall published in that year. Kneller's portrait of George I survived until December 1940 when it was destroyed by enemy action. The 22 Fire Judge portraits were subjected to crude retouching on several occasions, and when Sir George Scharf saw them hanging in the Old Council Chamber in 1893 he stated that 'as the result of frequent cleans and repairs in former times, very little of the original manipulation of Wright remains to be seen'.[13] The portraits were later hung in Guildhall Art Gallery but in 1939 they were removed for safety to the Crypt beneath the Great Hall. Already in a poor and flaking condition they were there badly soaked and stained by the water used to extinguish the conflagration overhead when Guildhall was burnt out on the night of 29 December 1940. In January they were removed to storage in the country, continuing to deteriorate for the next 10 years. During this period they were examined by a number of restorers, one of whom explained:

> They have been so crudely and heavily repainted that the original work is completely obscured. It is my opinion that many years ago a grossly incompetent person was entrusted with the cleaning, and being unable to remove the old varnishes successfully, considerable damage was done to the original paint film. To conceal the damage caused by the scouring, they were equally crudely repainted. There is every possibility that beneath the old varnishes and repainting there will be original work intact. . . .[14]

Possibly much of Spiridione Roma's 'restoration' had consisted of such crude scouring and overpainting; at the very least his techniques may have been irreversible, and these, coupled with Wright's own closely woven bed ticking, double primed and impervious, may have contributed to later difficulties in cleaning and the arrest of flaking. In 1945 the portrait of Sir Matthew Hale received treatment, but in February 1946 the General Purposes Committee of the Court of Aldermen stated that they had no strong feelings that the portraits should be rehung and consequently no wish that they should be restored. Although further estimates were received in 1949 and 1950 the Library Committee also decided against restoration and in 1951 it was resolved to dispose of all but two of the series. The National Portrait Gallery and the National Gallery of Scotland were among those offered canvases, but both institutions declined the offer on account of their size and poor condition. Seven canvases were donated to the Courtauld Institute for the purpose of conservation research and their frames were sold to a firm of period framers; one portrait was presented to the Association of Fire Loss Adjustors, nine to the various Inns of Court and three, cut down, to individuals as gifts.

The full length (94 × 58 in.) portrait of Sir Charles Pratt, Chief Justice of the Common Pleas had been commissioned from Sir Joshua Reynolds in 1764. In common with his usual practice, only the head appears definitely to be by Reynolds, the painting of the drapery and the background probably being left largely to assistants. In 1777 the City Lands Committee ordered the picture to be returned to Reynolds for repair; it was restored again on several later occasions and extensively retouched, but by 1968 it was flaking badly and needed lining. In view of the picture's size, and the fact that only the head was probably by Reynolds, it was decided not to commit the £294 estimated as the cost of full restoration and the picture was cut down to a more manageable size.

A more satisfactory solution has recently been achieved in the case of John Singleton Copley's very large canvas, *The Defeat of the Floating Batteries at Gibraltar, September 1782.* The painting was commissioned in 1783 to commemorate the victory of the British and their Hanoverian allies over the French and Spanish, when Gibraltar's garrison under General Sir George Augustus Eliott (later Lord Heathfield) succeeded in routing the battering ships which supplemented the land forces laying siege to the Rock. Several Spanish ships caught fire from the British shot and exploded, and on 14 September the dawn revealed:

> numbers of men . . . in the midst of the flames, crying out for pity and help; others floating upon pieces of timber, exposed to an equal, though less dreadful danger, from the opposite element. Even those in the ships where the fire had yet made less progress, expressed in their looks, gestures and words, the deepest distress and despair; and were no less urgent in imploring assistance.[15]

British fire was halted and rescue of the stricken Spanish seamen began. It was not until

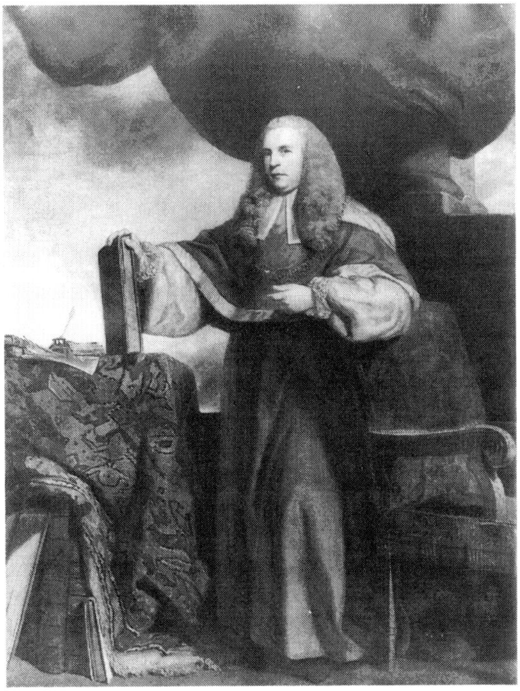

Sir Joshua Reynolds, *Sir Charles Pratt*, oil on canvas: 94 × 58 in., commissioned by the Corporation 1764; the picture before it was cut down

October, when a large relief fleet under Lord Howe pierced the blockade, that the siege was fully ended.

In February 1783 the Court of Common Council decided to record its respect and gratitude to the British officers through an 'Historical Painting', and in March Copley received the commission. Many changes were made to his original plan and the picture was not completed until 1791, when it was exhibited in Green Park with a pendant by Dominic Serres depicting the Relief of Gibraltar. Copley's canvas represents:

> the Victory of the Garrison, and in the moment of their triumph, a display of humanity, that highly exalts the British Character; it is composed of three large groups; that on the right contains the Portraits of the principal British and Hanoverian Officers, of the size of life, who are assembled on the Rampart (the Action being over) to view the dreadful scene which ensued from the battering ships being set on fire. LORD HEATHFIELD on horseback, in conversation with GENERALS BOYD, DE LA MOTTE and GREEN; pointing to SIR ROGER CURTIS, and a detachment of British Seamen, who, at the hazard of their own lives, are rescuing their vanquished enemies from destruction. Several of the seamen are seen at the stern of one of the battering Ships, striking the Spanish Ensign; whilst others generously relieve a number of the unfortunate Spaniards from a sinking wreck; . . . The third group occupy the centre, where a number of the enemy are represented in extreme distress, endeavouring to escape from a floating battery that is enveloped in flames. At a distance is a view of the Camp of the Allied Army, and the headquarters of the Duke de Crillon.[16]

The painting was eventually hung in the Common Council Chamber in 1794, but by this time relations between Copley and the Corporation were strained; he was unable to persuade the Court to pay him any more than the 1,000 guineas which had originally been agreed, and of the 300 guineas allowed him in 1794 for expenses he was ordered to repay Alderman Boydell 200 guineas, which had been advanced in order for Copley to travel to Hanover to take the German officers' portraits. The painting was transferred to Guildhall Art Gallery in 1886 and hung there until 1941 when it was evacuated to the country. After the Gallery's destruction by bombing, many attempts were made to rehouse it, but no wall large enough to accommodate it could be found either at Guildhall or in any other institution. The picture remained rolled up in store, and there were fears that its deteriorated condition would prevent economic restoration. Fortunately, when remedial work to arrest further damage was being carried out by the Area Museums Service in 1984, it was discovered that despite splits caused by poor rolling, the paint surface was sound and easily cleaned, and at the time of writing the canvas is undergoing complete restoration at the Conservation Studio of the Historic Buildings and Monuments Commission. The original carved frame is also in excellent condition, and on completion it is hoped that the picture may be hung in the proposed new Guildhall Art Gallery.

One of the earliest gifts to the Corporation appears to have been Sir James Thornhill's series of paintings in the Aldermen's Court Room. References in the minutes of the Court of Aldermen, and in the notes made by the Committee appointed by them in July 1725 to arrange the refurbishment of the Court Room, are very brief; unlike the plasterer, City's painter, upholsterer and clockmaker, Thornhill seems to have submitted no bill for his work, and was by contrast rewarded by the Aldermen with an expensive gift. On 20 July 1725 the Furniture Committee was told that 'Sr. J. Thornhill would paint something for ye oval'[17] – that is, the central space in the Court Room ceiling. His work was presumably in place by April 1727 when the Court of Aldermen ordered the Chamberlain to give the Lord Mayor 200 guineas 'to be by His Lordship Disposed of in plate or otherwise as His Lordship shall think proper to be presented to Sir James Thornhill, Knt., as the gift of this Court'.[18] On 24 June the Lord Mayor reported that the gold cup he had had made cost £225 7s., and the Common Cryer was 'ordered

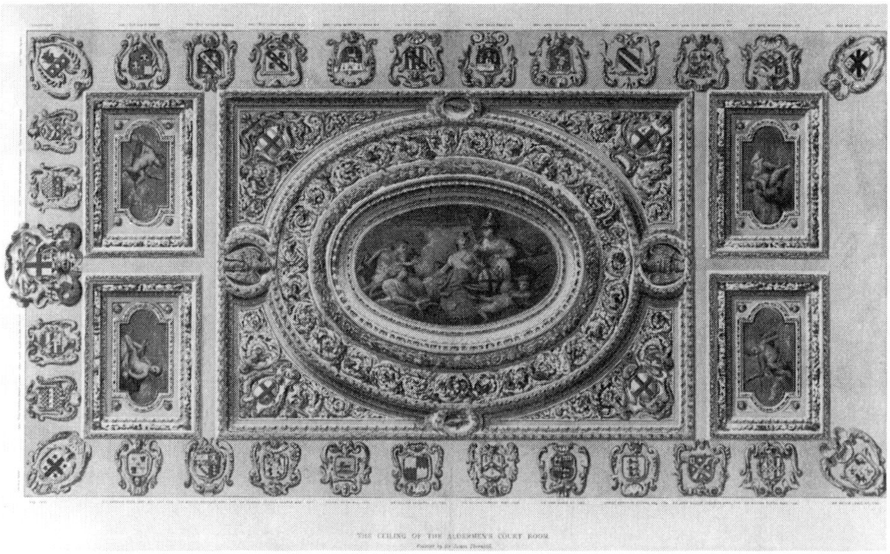

Thornhill's ceiling in the Aldermen's Court Room. *c.*1880 chromo-lithograph (coll: Guildhall Library, Print Room)

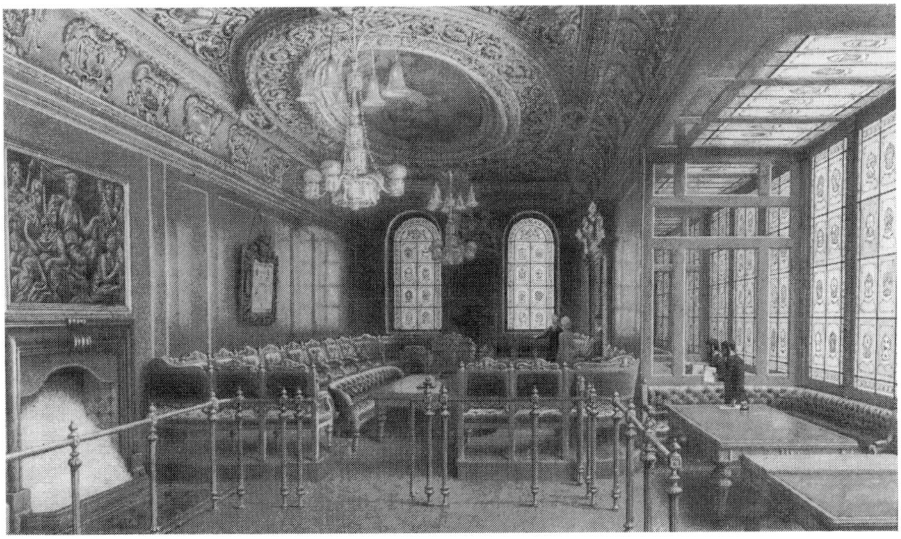

The Aldermen's Court Room in 1884. Chromo-lithograph, (coll: Guildhall Library, Print Room) Thornhill's *Justice Embracing Mercy, with Liberty, Piety, Truth, Loyalty and Concord* is on the chimney breast, and *London, Pallas Athene, Peace and Plenty* is just visible in the decorative plasterwork of the ceiling

to present the said Gold cup the first opportunity to Sir James Thornhill'.[19] Thornhill's scheme consisted of an oval canvas depicting personifications of London, Civic Wisdom (represented by Pallas Athene), Peace and Plenty, flanked by four smaller canvases of putti representing Prudence, Justice, Temperance and Fortitude. These were set into decorative painted and gilded plasterwork. A further monochrome canvas placed on the chimney breast as an overmantel represented Justice, Mercy, Truth, Piety, Liberty, Loyalty and Concord. In addition, Thornhill supplied three further allegorical paintings in grisaille. They have been described in the past as overdoors, but it is not known whether they were ever hung in the Aldermen's Court Room. Each measuring 60 × 96 in., they were housed in the Art Gallery from 1886 but by 1924 they had been removed to the City of London Mental Asylum. They were returned to Guildhall in 1952 but were considered to have deteriorated beyond economic repair, and no records of their subject or appearance survive. The overmantel was removed to the Art Gallery in 1939 and was there destroyed by enemy action in 1941; a sheet of studies for it exists in Guildhall Library Print Room. The ceiling canvases are the only part of the scheme to have survived, having spent the war in store outside London, but they were not replaced in the ceiling when the Court Room was rebuilt after the war.

A second decorative scheme, the gift of Alderman John Boydell, consisted of life-size figures of Providence, Happiness, Innocence and Wisdom, executed in fresco on the pendentives beneath the dome of the Common Council Chamber by John Francis Rigaud. Boydell seems to have misunderstood the nature of fresco, a medium which is extremely durable provided the climate is dry, but he explained the reason for his choice in his *Description*, published before the figures were completed:

> It has been the general opinion that fresco painting was not practicable in this country, on account of the dampness of the climate, but it is for that very reason that it ought to be adopted in preference to any other, as it absorbs the dampness of the walls and gives a passage to the moisture, which by that means evaporates freely, whereas oil painting offers a resistance to it, and is forced at last to detach, blister and fall off, as every painted wall will demonstrate.[20]

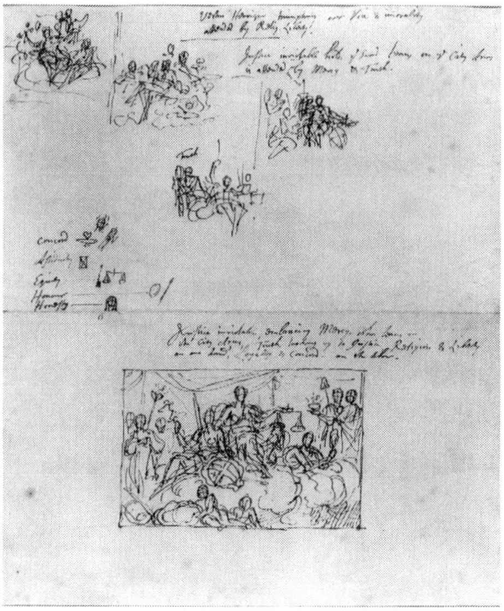

Sir James Thornhill, Studies for *Justice embracing Mercy, with Liberty, Piety, Truth, Loyalty and Concord* (*c.*1725) pen and ink: $14\frac{1}{8} \times 11\frac{5}{8}$ in. (coll: Guildhall Library, Print Room)

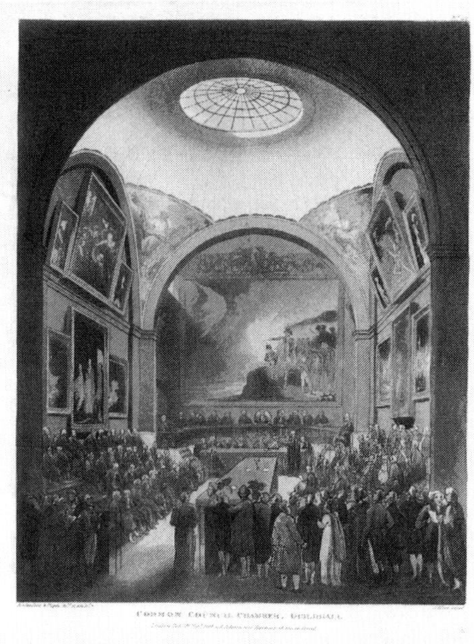

The Common Council Chamber, 1808. Aquatint by Rowlandson and Pugin (coll: Guildhall Library, Print Room)
On the walls are paintings presented by Alderman Boydell, with Rigaud's frescoes *Providence* (left) and *Wisdom* (right) visible on the pendentives beneath the dome. Copley's *Defeat of the Floating Batteries* hangs at the end of the room

But Boydell's confidence in the medium was misplaced. A month after their completion in October 1794 the paintings still were not dry due, thought Rigaud, to 'the situation of the dome which does not allow a free circulation of air'.[21] Further, they were 'spotted and black in many places with the flesh colours rather too brown'. While Rigaud suspected the freshness of the lime used in the surface plaster, the real fault probably lay in the poor quality of the rough plastering beneath, a mixture of chalk, plaster of Paris and coal ashes, which was not completely dry when the artist's own fine surface plaster was applied. Apart from anything else, the Chamber, like the Great Hall, was cold and damp, and when the decayed frescoes were painted over in 1814 as part of a general refurbishment, there was some discussion about installing a stove to warm Members during meetings (although none about the fate of the frescoes themselves). Two paintings of putti in distemper, also commissioned from Rigaud by Boydell, had also disappeared long before the Chamber was finally demolished in 1908. No record of their appearance survives, but the collection contains Rigaud's four oil sketches for the main figures and engravings published by Boydell and presented by him *c.*1799. The failure of the scheme was a great disappointment to both artist and patron. In his diary Rigaud wrote of Boydell:

> He understood nothing of the nature of Fresco, and I am still at a loss to account for his choosing it. I sometimes imagine that it was a mistake, and that he wanted something else. He thought that he would see every day something to admire and to bring people to see, as it went on. He appeared quite dejected after the first week, and still more in a fortnight, when he saw it look so very dark; coming two or three

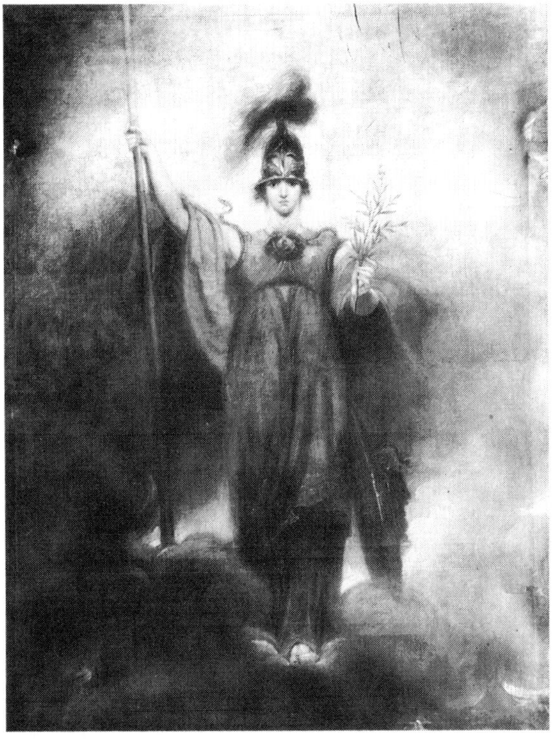

Richard Westall, *Minerva,* (1794) oil on canvas: 120 × 84 in., presented by Alderman Boydell, 1794; destroyed 10 May 1941

times a day in expectation of seeing some change. Under these circumstances, and having a great interest in presenting to the City something worth accepting, I think it a great instance of goodness that he let me proceed and did not stop me while there was still time to substitute something else.

Fortunately for Boydell, his fresco scheme was only part of a much larger gift to the Corporation. Between *c.*1792 and *c.*1800 he presented thirty further works, most of which hung in the Common Council Chamber, and in 1794 he published his *Description of Several Pictures Presented to the Corporation of the City of London by John Boydell, Alderman of the Ward of Cheap, and Placed in the Common Council Chamber of the City . . . for the Benefit of the Servants who shew the Pictures.* There he explained his motives for the gift:

First, to show my respect for the Corporation and my fellow-citizens. Secondly, to give pleasure to the public, and Foreigners in general. Thirdly, to be of service to the Artists, by shewing their works to the greatest advantage; and, Fourthly, for the mere purpose of pleasing myself. The poor, and all in the inferior stations of life may profit by the advice which many of the subjects in this collection will impart to them. . . . When the whole is completed and arranged, I hope and trust, it will convince my Fellow-Citizens of the utility of the Arts; not only in affording pleasure to all who view them, but in their moral influence on their mind, by holding forth affecting and impressive examples of great and good actions.

Specially commissioned for the Chamber was Robert Smirke's uplifting subject *Conjugal Affection, or, Industry and Prudence* (a subject which Boydell seems originally to have conceived as a series of pictures). He also commissioned paintings of 'the great and glorious actions, of departed Heroes, or of our own present commanders by sea and land, that have exerted themselves to the Honour and advantage of our King and country';[22] as well as portraits of Marquis Cornwallis by Copley, Lord Nelson by Beechey and Lord Duncan by Hoppner, Boydell also commissioned portraits of the heroes of the siege and relief of Gibraltar, neither of which now remains in the collection. James Northcote's portrait of Lord Howe decayed and was replaced with a copy by

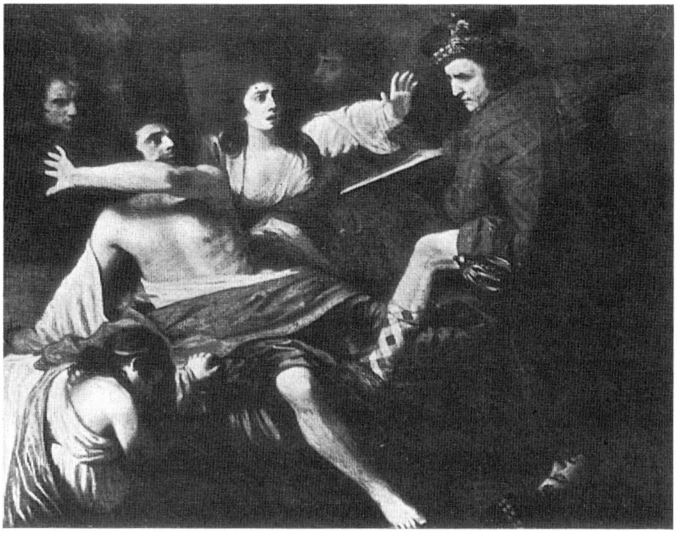

John Opie, *The Assassination of James I of Scotland* (1786) oil on canvas: 68 × 82 in., presented by Alderman Boydell *c.*1794; destroyed 10 May 1941

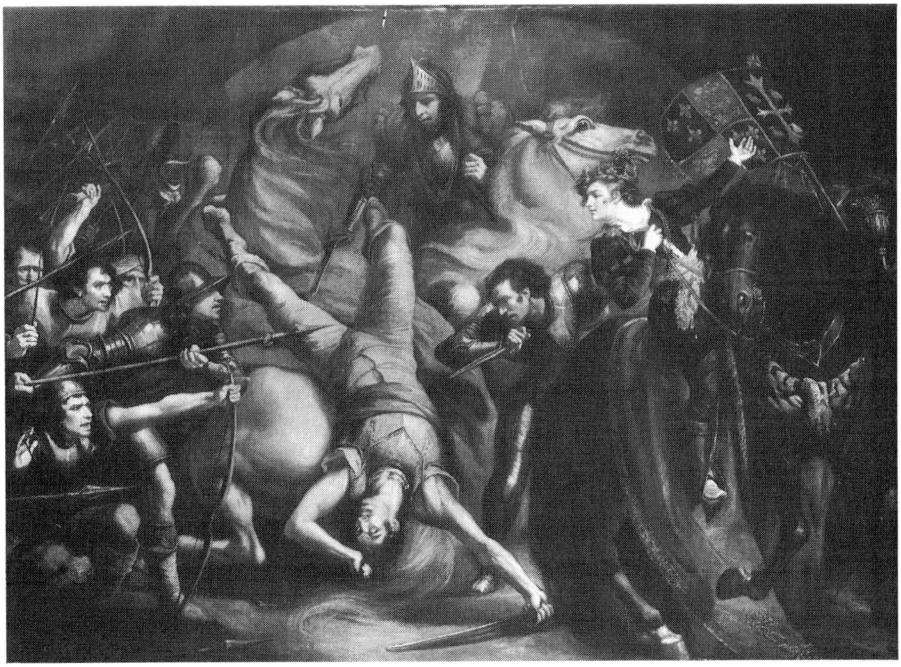

James Northcote, *The Death of Wat Tyler* (1787), oil on canvas: 108 × 147 in., presented by Alderman Boydell 1793; destroyed 29 December 1940

George Kirtland of the picture by Gainsborough Dupont at Trinity House. More regrettable was the loss of the portrait of Lord Heathfield by Sir Joshua Reynolds, which Boydell had evidently delighted in placing in the Common Council Chamber, and which he had described as 'the most Capital Portrait ever Painted by this Master'.[23] Sometime after the Alderman's death in 1804, his nephew and business partner Josiah Boydell, removed the picture from the Chamber, and a copy was substituted. On 31 May 1809 the original was sent for sale to the European Museum and in June it was purchased by Sir Thomas Lawrence. Joseph Farington, who had helped in its sale, explained:

> The original picture of Lord Heathfield wd. have perished had it remained hung upon a damp wall. The copy from it was openly made by another artist, & touched on by Boydell, and shown at the Shakespeare Gallery. Sir George Beaumont saw it and doubted some parts, the rest He thought had an original look. The original was hung at His House at Hampstead & was there seen by the Common Council. . . . Should the City claim it it must be given up.[24]

As the picture is now in the National Gallery, the option of reclaiming it is unfortunately no longer available. A number of other paintings presented by Boydell were destroyed in the Second World War, including Smirke's *Conjugal Affection* and large canvases by Northcote, Westall, Hamilton and Opie.

In 1793 Boydell had suggested to the Court of Common Council that the Mansion House's Egyptian Hall, then in a ruinous condition and used as a lumber room, be adapted as a gallery for paintings and sculpture. His idea had not been adopted, but by 1853 the Egyptian Hall had been restored to use, and the Court began to commission for it a series of statues from leading contemporary sculptors. The idea arose following consideration of the marble busts by John Francis which the sculptor had been exhibiting at Mansion House; in 1852 the Court of Common Council agreed to purchase four, of Queen Victoria, Prince Albert, the Duke of Wellington and the Duke of Kent. (The two royal busts remain at the House, but those of Wellington and Kent were stored in the cellar beneath the Art Gallery and destroyed there in 1941.) In September 1852 the Court agreed to the City Architect's suggestion that marble statues representing passages from the English poets be commissioned for the Egyptian Hall; a sub-committee was formed and on 20 October Bunning recommended that a deputation make studio visits to select suitable sculptors. The £700 payable for each statue of a subject from poetry or from British history was to include the preparation of a statuette one-quarter the size of the finished figure. Eleven sculptors were visited and a selection made by ballot; statuettes were viewed by the Committee, and the first commissions were given in March 1853 to Edward Hodges Baily, John Henry Foley, William Calder Marshall, John Graham Lough and Patrick MacDowell. Frederick Thrupp's design for *Timon of Athens* was approved on 18 May. In September 1855 further studio visits took place and in February 1856 commissions were given to Edward William Wyon, Henry Weekes, Edward Hodges Baily and Joseph Durham. Foley received an additional commission in March. The final commissions were given in 1861 to Edward Bowring Stephens, Susan Durant, James Sherwood Westmacott and Joseph Durham. All the figures had been received by September 1863. Four of the statuettes, transferred to the City Surveyor's office, were destroyed in 1940, and that for Foley's *Egeria* was discovered to be missing from the Mansion House in 1978. The other maquettes and all the full-size figures all remain in situ at the House.

Meanwhile the collection housed at Guildhall continued to grow by purchase, gift and bequest until it was resolved in 1885 to house a proportion of it in a public art gallery, opened in April 1886. At first the Gallery had no purchase budget but, as had been hoped, the altruistic nature of the scheme immediately attracted presentations of works of art; the first large bequest was received in 1888 when a former City businessman, William Dunnett, left his large and miscellaneous collection to the Gallery. In its first four years of life the Gallery attracted 154,000 visitors, but it was the popular success of Alfred Temple's ambitious Loan Exhibitions, mounted between 1890 and 1907, that was probably responsible for attracting subsequent gifts and bequests. In his memoirs Temple later recorded that the 288 works owned by the Corporation at the Gallery's establishment had increased by 1916 to 937, 'the additional 649, with the exception of about 30, having come into the Corporation's possession by gift or bequest, estimated at a value of about £114,000'.[25] The first major gift was received in 1893, when Sir John Gilbert decided to distribute some of his paintings among public collections; he was advised to include Guildhall in the gift by Lord Leighton, who felt that Temple's exhibitions 'indicated a vitality in the City in regard to art which could not be too warmly encouraged'.[26] The first curator to arrive at Gilbert's home, Temple selected five oil paintings and 43 watercolours and drawings; the City expressed its gratitude for the artist's generosity by awarding Gilbert an honorary Freedom. In 1903 a further 53 works were bequeathed by the artist's brother George.

Temple was indefatigable in pursuing acquisitions for the Gallery. It was only as a result of his persuasion that Charles Gassiot eventually decided to bequeathe 127 19th-century oil paintings to the City, having originally, after the death of his heir, thought of leaving them to the Tate Gallery or of selling them at Christie's. Temple had argued 'were your pictures at the Guildhall your name, for all time, would have far greater prominence than if it were identified with probably a selection of them at the Tate Gallery'[27]; when Gassiot died in 1902, only four paintings were left to the Tate, and the rest, valued by Agnews' at £84,000, were put on display at Guildhall at the end of the year.

Gassiot wished his collection to be displayed together for the public benefit, but although the Gallery had been enlarged in 1890 and 1901, *The Times* predicted:

The difficulty of the Corporation will be to find room for it in their existing galleries, and the problem of more space will become acute. We imagine many members will regret the short-sighted policy which led the Common Council to alienate the fine site upon the Embankment, a portion of which would have provided an ideal site for an art gallery.[28]

It was presumably this site which Temple had had in mind in June 1891, when he and Lord Leighton devised a plan to bring Henry Tate's proposed National Gallery of British Art within the precincts of the City. Temple explained in his memoirs:

> The scheme was that the Corporation of London might be induced to place at the disposal of the Government a piece of ground adjoining the Temple Gardens, and fronting the Victoria Embankment, just on the threshold as it were, but not within, the busy life of the City, one of the chief conditions being that the Corporation should be so identified with the institution as to have a strong representation on the Board of Control. The site was unique for the purpose, and Leighton saw it at once. Its market value approached £200,000. Sir Henry Tate (then Mr. Henry Tate) was to transfer his offer to erect the building and present his collection of pictures to the Corporation, who with the Government were then to proceed to constitute the governing body.[29]

Although Temple expected Tate to make a formal offer to the Corporation, he preferred to deal with the Government rather than a municipal body and accepted the Government's offer of the site at Millbank instead. Temple was disappointed, for he had secured from wealthy livery companies the promise of grants totalling £34,000 towards the purchase of contemporary art, but only provided the new gallery were located within the City. However, in view of the rise of the Tate Gallery to its present status and the decline in the fortunes of Guildhall Art Gallery, Tate's decision seems in retrospect to have been wisely made. In 1897 Temple was offered the chance to become the Tate Gallery's first Keeper, but he declined because the Treasury would not allow him also to retain his position as Director of Guildhall Art Gallery. He later explained:

> I conceived that the duties attaching to the position at the Tate Gallery would not occupy my entire time once the pictures were arranged on the walls, and that I should be able efficiently to deal with the work at the Guildhall . . . I was not a little actuated by the scope for action which the Guildhall Art Gallery presented when placed beside the appointment in question, in which I could discern only a very limited field for activity.[30]

The 'scope for action' referred to Temple's series of loan exhibitions. In 1890 the Gallery had been enlarged, and the first exhibition, of Flemish, Dutch and British pictures, was mounted to inaugurate the new structure. 109,383 visitors were recorded, and this figure was more than doubled during the exhibition in 1892. In 1894 the Gallery opened for the first time on a Sunday, and Temple described how:

> Guildhall Yard and the adjacent streets presented an unusual spectacle; people crowding in, the patient queue reaching to Basinghall Street round to Gresham Street, and almost to the Bank of England. It was the prelude to all the museums and galleries in London being opened to the public on Sunday afternoons.[31]

The Spanish exhibition of 1901 was so popular that it was extended for four weeks beyond its original three months; 3,000 visitors per day were recorded and a Spanish edition of the catalogue was published. Opening the exhibition of English and French 18th-century pictures in 1902, the Lord Mayor said that Temple 'had the entire confidence of the Corporation, and but for his tact and artistic judgement the exhibition

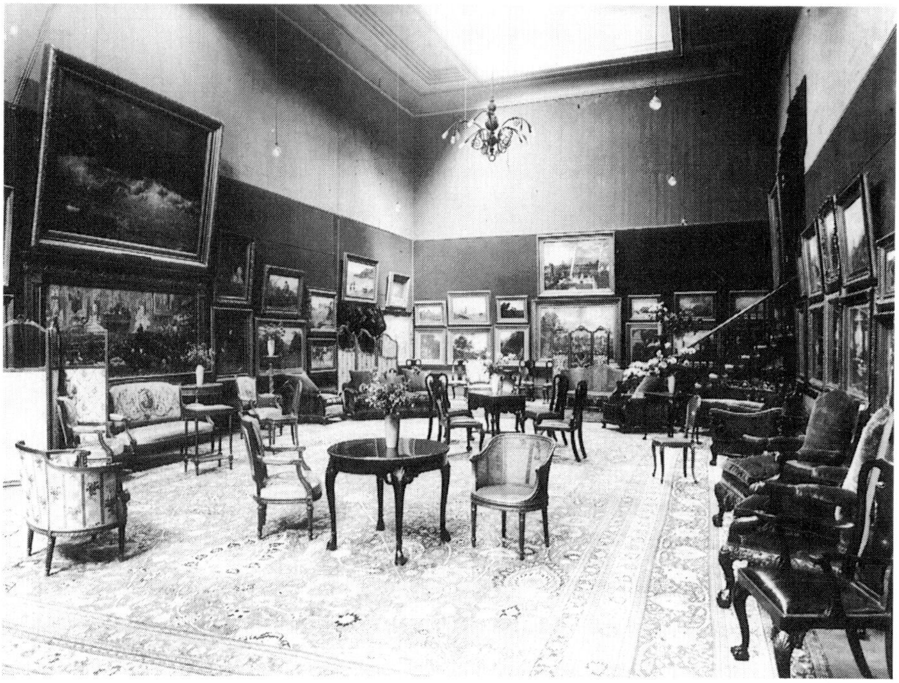

Interior of Guildhall Art Gallery, 1917 (coll: Guildhall Library, Print Room)

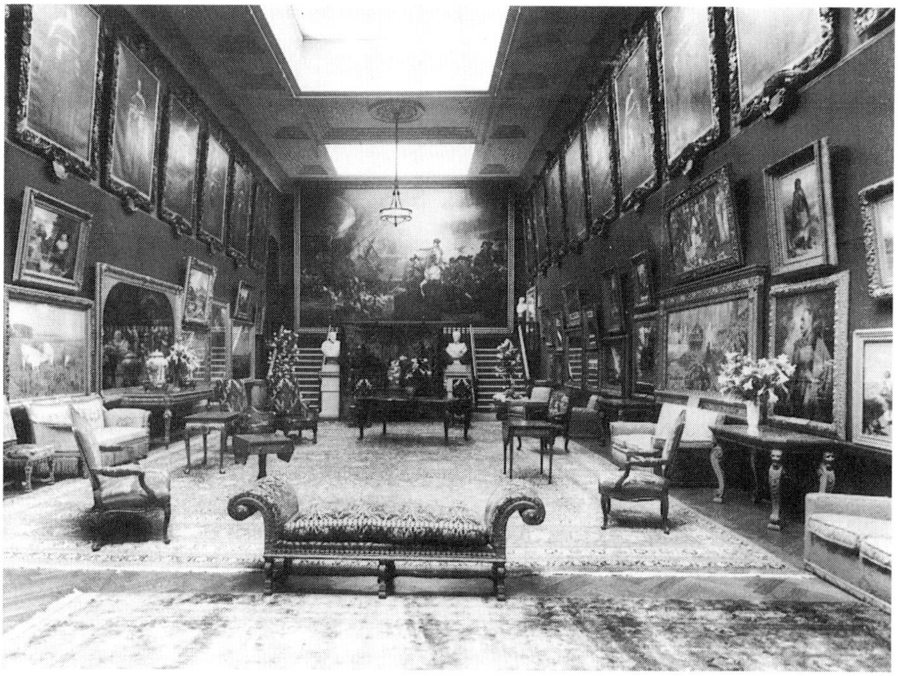

Interior of Guildhall Art Gallery *c.*1930, with Copley's *Defeat of the Floating Batteries* at the end of the room and John Michael Wright's series of the Fire Judges' portraits high on the side walls (coll: Guildhall Library, Print Room)

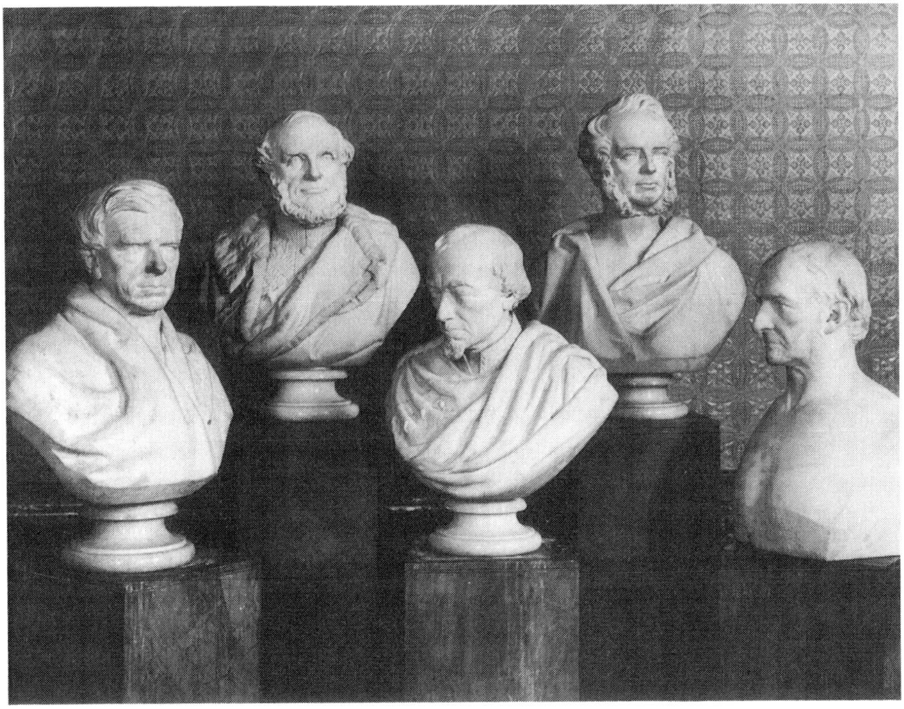

Five busts commissioned by the Corporation between 1867 and 1883; all destroyed in the raid of 29 December 1940. From left to right: *Lord Brougham* (G. G. Adams), *Lord Russell* (C. B. Birch), *Lord Beaconsfield* (R. Belt), *Lord Palmerston* (J. Durham) and *William Gladstone* (T. Woolner)

could hardly have been got together'.[32] It must therefore have been a shock to Temple when the Corporation decided in 1907 to discontinue the series of exhibitions, which had so far attracted almost three million visitors to the Gallery. When no exhibition had been held in 1905, the *Morning Advertiser* had described the missing event as:

> one of the really good things, from the artistic point of view, of which London in recent years has been able to boast, one of the few things indeed that kept Cockneydom from hanging its head in shame before the artistic enthusiasms of such provincial towns as Manchester, Leeds and Liverpool. One can, in fact, hardly calculate the amount of good which these exhibitions at the Guildhall have done since their institution in 1890. . . . Starting out to educate the clerk, the Corporation have found themselves the promoters of one of the most successful and widely and deservedly popular shows in the country. They have created a welcome taste for art in an enormous public, which they have now suddenly determined to starve.[33]

The Gallery was again enlarged in 1923 but in 1925 the Library Committee complained that space was still inadequate and that many pictures were outhoused. Only a proportion of the Corporation's whole collection was displayed in the Art Gallery, and a large number of items, particularly marble and plaster busts and small pictures from the Dunnett bequest, were placed in offices and other areas of Guildhall. On the outbreak of war in 1939 many paintings were removed to the country, but more than 300 works were lost through the air raids of 29 December 1940 and 10 May 1941, when the Gallery itself was destroyed. Among the losses were large paintings from the Boydell gift and a number of sculptures which could not be moved. Many other items were so badly damaged by fire and water that they were written off after the war and still more were simply never traced. Almost before the losses could be fully comprehended the Library Committee began to plan the Gallery's post-war policy. On 18 October 1943, a special Sub-Committee heard from the Chairman that:

> the situation in London is entirely different from that of any provincial city. In London we have the National Gallery, the National Portrait Gallery, the Tate Gallery, the Victoria and Albert Museum, etc..with none of which can the Corporation hope to compete. . . . On the other hand the Corporation has already the nucleus of what might become a first class specialised collection which would attract visitors from all over the world.

It was accordingly resolved that future acquisitions should consist mainly of works of London interest: topographical pictures, ceremonial subjects and portraits and genre pictures illustrative of London social life.

In 1944 a temporary interior was erected within the shell of the ground floor facade of the Art Gallery – all that now remained – with the expectation that rebuilding would take place very shortly. Although the collection could not be permanently displayed, selections were henceforward exhibited at regular intervals and major loan exhibitions were again arranged; the Gallery also housed, as it had done occasionally before the war, exhibitions mounted by other organisations such as the Royal Drawing Society. The original aims of the City of London Society of Artists were recalled in the City of London Art Exhibitions and the Lord Mayor's Art Award, from which many pictures of London interest were purchased for the collection.

Restrictions on local government spending in the 1970s prevented the rebuilding of the Gallery as part of the Guildhall Reconstruction Scheme Phase V, and the 'temporary' structure continued to house this programme of exhibitions until 1977, when it was ended because of inadequate environmental and security conditions and financial stringencies. The Gallery has since housed only temporary exhibitions arranged by art societies and similar bodies. Certain paintings have been on long-term display in the old Guildhall Library and its environs, but it has been necessary to store a large number of works. In order to relieve the pressure on inadequate storage space, the practice begun before the war of loaning pictures within Corporation departments has greatly expanded. Access to the collection has thus necessarily been by appointment only. Loans to exhibitions organised by other galleries and two temporary exhibitions held at Barbican Art Gallery in 1982–3 and 1984 have allowed the public to see pictures to which access has otherwise generally been restricted. In 1985 the Court of Common Council decided that the site of the Art Gallery on the east side of Guildhall Yard should at last be redeveloped. The proposed new building will serve a variety of functions, and at the time of writing full consideration is being given to the inclusion of facilities for the display of the Corporation's collection, together with conservation and workshop areas and environmentally-controlled picture stores. The whole scheme, yet to be finalised in detail, will take several years to reach fruition.

Notes

[1] Corporation of London Records Office (CLRO), Repertory of the Court of Aldermen, 75, fo. 160, 19 April 1670

[2] Vertue Notebooks, *Walpole Society*, vol. XVIII, p. 44

[3] CLRO, Repertory of the Court of Aldermen, 75, fo. 316, 28 September 1670

[4] Ibid., 77, fo. 43, 14 December 1671. Walpole (*Anecdotes*) recorded that Wright was paid £60 per portrait rather than the £36 specified above. 'Mr. Wright the Herald Painter' was the artist's brother

[5] John Evelyn's *Diary*, 31 July 1673

[6] CLRO, City Lands Committee, Journal, vol. 70, fo. 119, 30 September 1778

[7] CLRO, Court of Common Council, Journal, 67, fo. 266b, 4 June 1779

[8] John Nichols in 'London's Gratitude', 1783, quoted by Sir George Scharf in 'Portraits of the Judges at the Guildhall', *Archaeological Journal*, vol. L, 1893, p. 271
[9] *Gentleman's Magazine*, August 1789, p. 701
[10] CLRO, City Lands Committee, Journal, vol. 72, fo. 96, 26 July 1780
[11] *Gentleman's Magazine*, op. cit., pp. 701–02
[12] Quoted by Scharf, op. cit., p. 272
[13] Ibid.
[14] Guildhall Art Gallery, artists' files, letter from William Drown, restorer, to the Librarian, 27 April 1943
[15] 'History of Europe', Chapter 10, *Annual Register . . . for the year 1782*, p. 238
[16] Description of the painting, with a key to the principal portraits; printed by B. McMillan, Bow Street, Covent Garden, n.d. (?*c.*1791)
[17] CLRO, Alchin Box S/CXL No. 11
[18] CLRO, Repertory of the Court of Aldermen, 131, fo. 203, 18 April 1727
[19] Ibid., ff. 342–3, 24 June 1727
[20] Alderman John Boydell, *A Description of Several Pictures Presented to the Corporation of the City of London by John Boydell, Alderman of the Ward of Cheap, and Placed in the Common-Council Chamber of the City . . . for the Benefit of the Servants who shew the Pictures*, 1794
[21] This and succeeding extracts from Rigaud's diary are from 'Facts and Recollections of the XVIIIth Century in a Memoir of John Francis Rigaud Esq. R.A. by Stephen Dutilh Rigaud', MS held in the Beinecke Library, Yale University; transcribed and edited by William Pressly, *Walpole Society*, Vol. L. pp. 1–164
[22] Guildhall Library MS 198, Boydell's draft for his speech delivered to the Court of Common Council on 31 October 1793
[23] Boydell, *Description . . .*, 1794; see also his draft notes in *supra*
[24] Joseph Farington, *Diary*, 29 June 1809
[25] A. G. Temple, *Guildhall Memories*, 1918, p. 87
[26] Ibid., p. 118
[27] Ibid., p. 243
[28] *The Times*, 30 May, 1902, p. 7
[29] Temple, op. cit., p. 110
[30] Ibid., pp. 174–5
[31] Ibid., p. 137
[32] *The Times*, 12 April, 1902, p. 12
[33] Quoted by Temple, op. cit., pp. 297–8

The Catalogue

Note to readers

The catalogue is arranged in two sections. The first deals with paintings, watercolours, drawings and prints, the second covers sculpture. Each section is arranged alphabetically by artist and thereafter in order of date. A name index listing artists, engravers, sitters and donors will be found at the end of the volume, followed by an index of named places depicted.

Paintings, Watercolours, Drawings and Prints

Lemuel Francis Abbott (1760–1802)

acc. no. 61
Samuel, First Viscount Hood (?c.1794)

oil on canvas: 56 × 46 in.
Presented by Alderman John Boydell after 1794

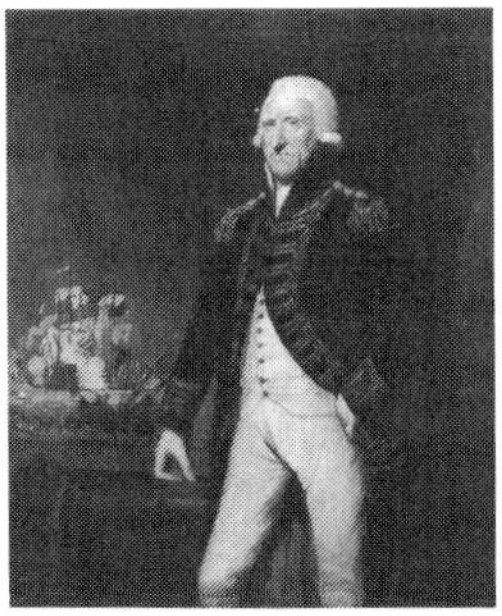

Joseph Adam (*fl.* 1858–80)

acc. no. 264
Burnham Beeches

oil on canvas: 31 × 50 in.
signed: *J Adam*
Purchased, 1882

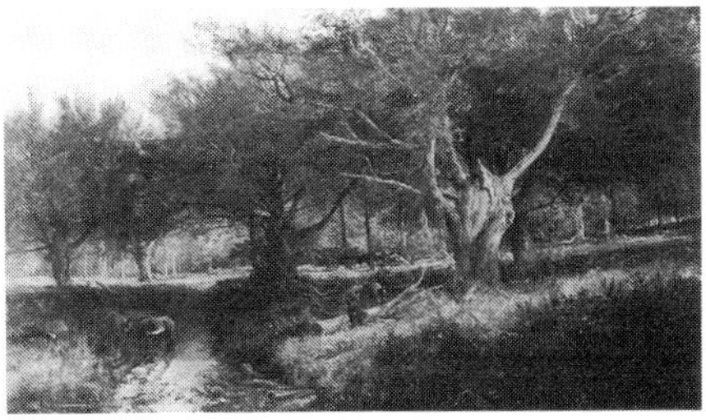

José Aguiar (b.1895)

acc. no. 1591
La Pescadera

oil on paper laid on hardboard: 32¾ × 40 in.
signed: *José Aguiar*
Presented by the Lord Mayor of Madrid, 1960

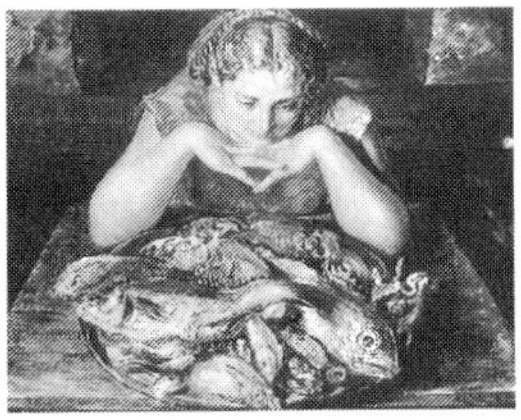

M. Alabaster (20th C)

acc. no. 1782
Lower Thames Street Looking West (*c.*1967)

oil on hardboard: 26¾ × 19¾ in.
signed: *ALABASTER*
Purchased from the artist, 1967

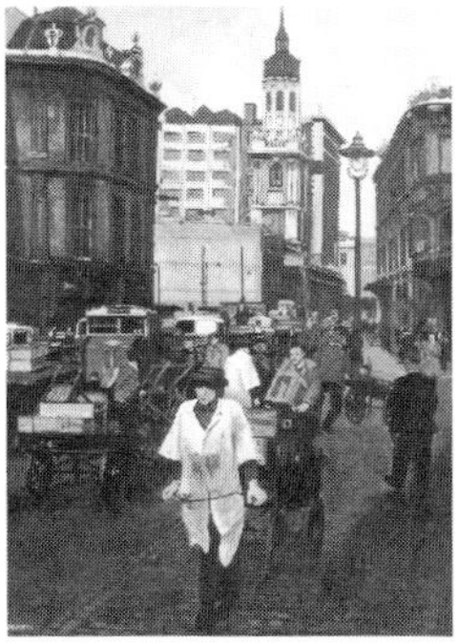

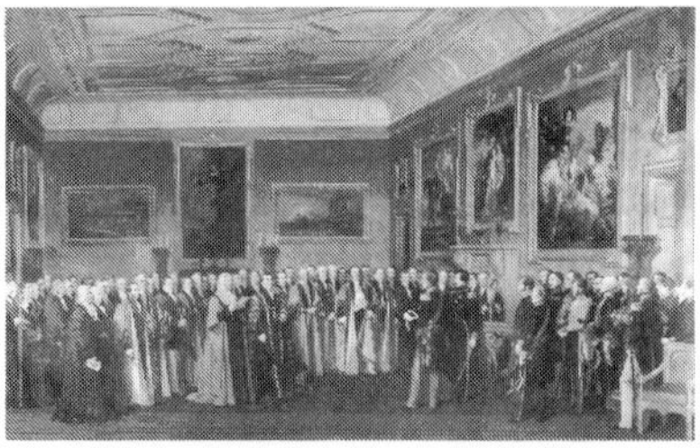

Jean Alaux (1786–1864)

acc. no. 2164
The Lord Mayor presenting an Address of Congratulation to H.M. Louis Philippe at Windsor Castle, October 1844 (1847)

oil on canvas: 90 × 143 in.
signed and dated: *Alaux 1847*
Purchased from the Galerie Marcus, Paris, 1975

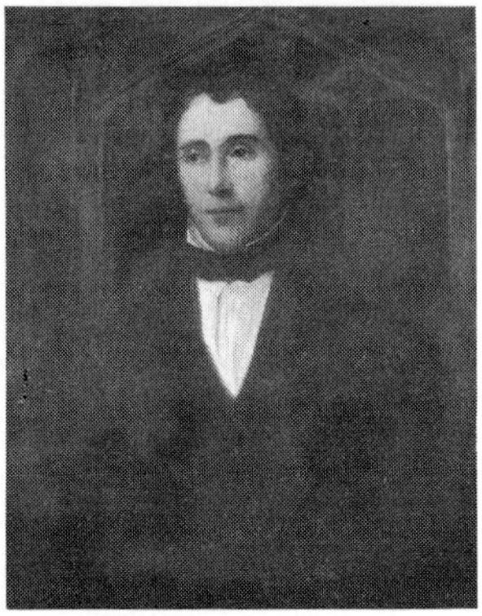

Joseph William Allen (1803–52)

acc. no. 106
Warren Stormes Hale, Founder of the City of London School

oil on canvas: 29 × 25 in.
Presented by the artist, 1841

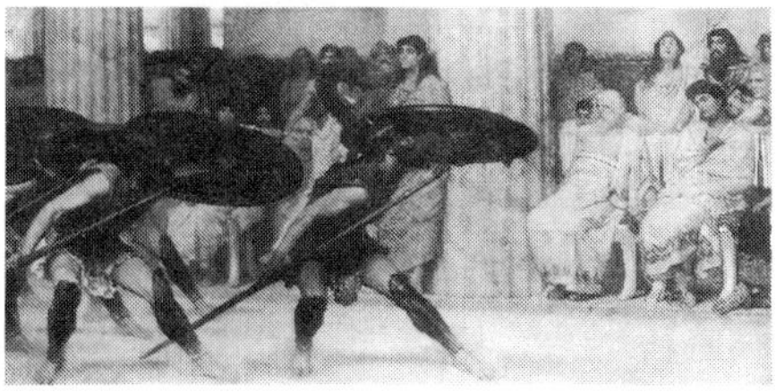

Sir Lawrence Alma-Tadema (1836–1912)

acc. no. 637
The Pyrrhic Dance (1869)

oil on panel: 16 × 32 in.
signed and dated: *1869. L Alma-Tadema*
Bequeathed by Charles Gassiot, 1902

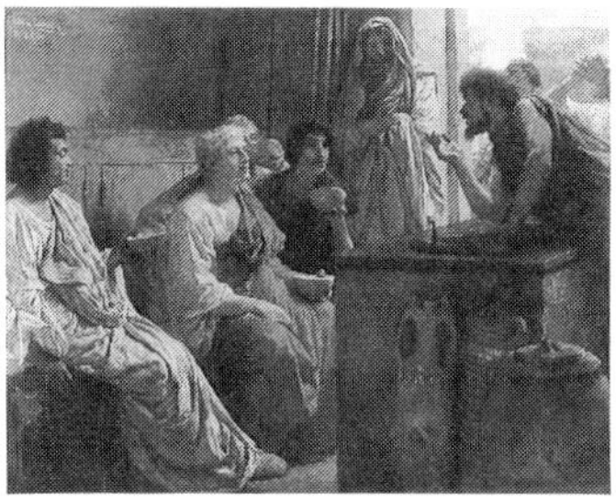

acc. no. 1513
The Wine Shop (1869–74)

oil on panel: 15 × 19 in.
inscribed: *OP LXXIV*
Bequeathed by Cecil French, 1954

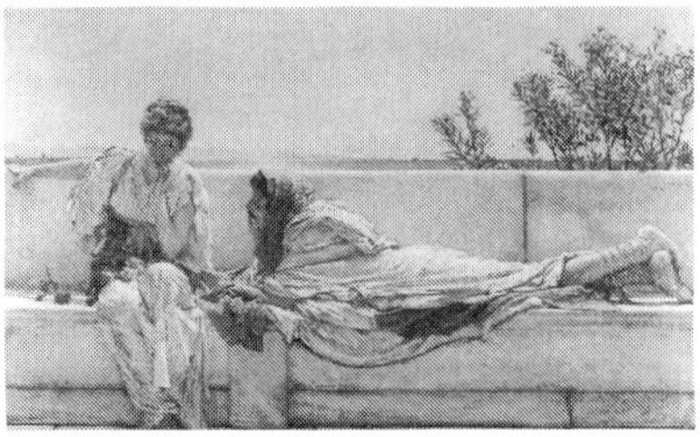

acc. no. 638
Pleading (1876)

oil on canvas laid on panel: $8\frac{1}{2}$ × 14 in.
signed and inscribed: *L. Alma-Tadema OP CLXVII*
Bequeathed by Charles Gassiot, 1902

William Anderson (1757–1837)

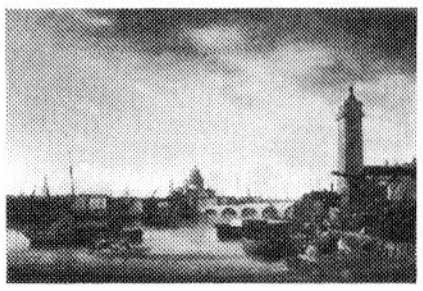

acc. no. 1596
Blackfriars Bridge and the City from Lambeth
oil on canvas: $27\frac{3}{4} \times 38$ in.
Purchased from E. Stacy-Marks Ltd., 1960

after George Henry Andrews (1816–98) by Robert Carrick (*fl.* 1850s)

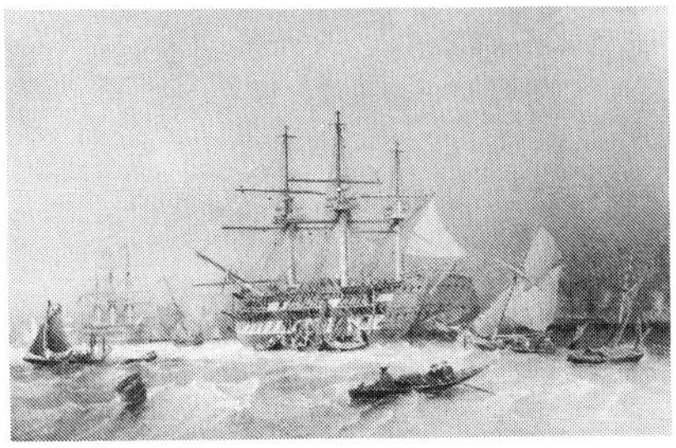

acc. no. 1424
The Old School, 1755: Eight Months to India (1855)
lithograph: $16 \times 23\frac{7}{8}$ in.
lettered: *PAINTED BY G.H. ANDREW.* (sic) *T.G. DUTTON, LITH. / DAY & SON, LITH^{RS}. TO THE QUEEN. / LONDON. PUBLISHED BY LLOYD BROTHERS & C^{O}. 22 LUDGATE HILL, OCT^{R}. 8TH 1855 / NEW YORK WILLIAMS STEVENS WILLIAMS & C^{O}. 359 BROADWAY / THE NEW SCHOOL, 1855 / SIXTY DAYS TO AUSTRALIA.*
Presented by Captain and Alderman R. S. Hewett, 1951

after George Henry Andrews (1816–98) by T. G. Dutton (*fl.* 1842–73)

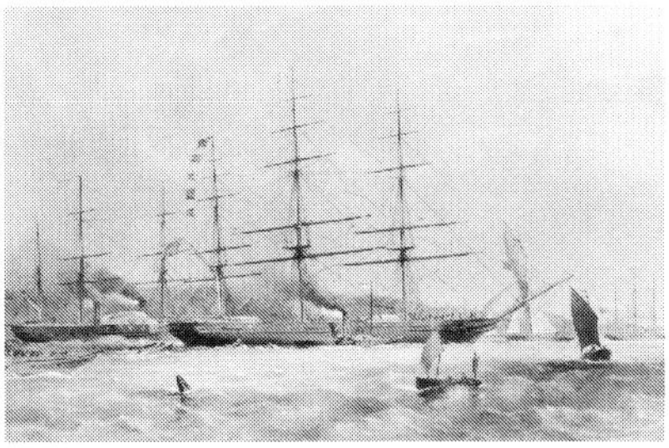

acc. no. 1425
The New School, 1855: Sixty Days to Australia (1855)
lithograph: $16 \times 23\frac{7}{8}$ in.
lettered: *PAINTED BY G.H. ANDREW.* (sic) *T.G. DUTTON, LITH. / DAY & SON, LITH^{RS}. TO THE QUEEN. / LONDON. PUBLISHED BY LLOYD BROTHERS & C^{O}. 22 LUDGATE HILL, OCT^{R}. 8TH 1855 / NEW YORK WILLIAMS STEVENS WILLIAMS & C^{O}. 359 BROADWAY / THE NEW SCHOOL, 1855 / SIXTY DAYS TO AUSTRALIA.*
Presented by Captain and Alderman R. S. Hewett, 1951

Richard Ansdell (1815–85)

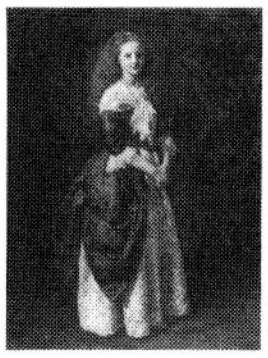

acc. no. 687
Dog with Wild Duck
oil on canvas: 15×18 in.
signed: *R.A.*
Bequeathed by Charles Gassiot, 1902

James Archer (1823–1904)

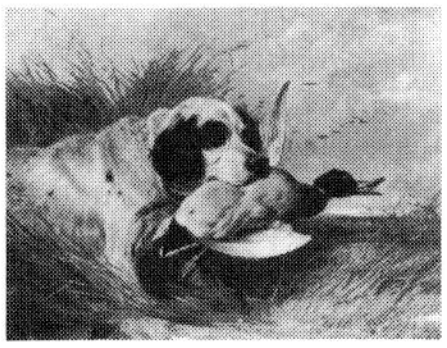

acc. no. 639
My Great Grandmother (1865)
oil on canvas: 24×18 in.
signed (mono) and dated: *JA 1865*
Bequeathed by Charles Gassiot, 1902

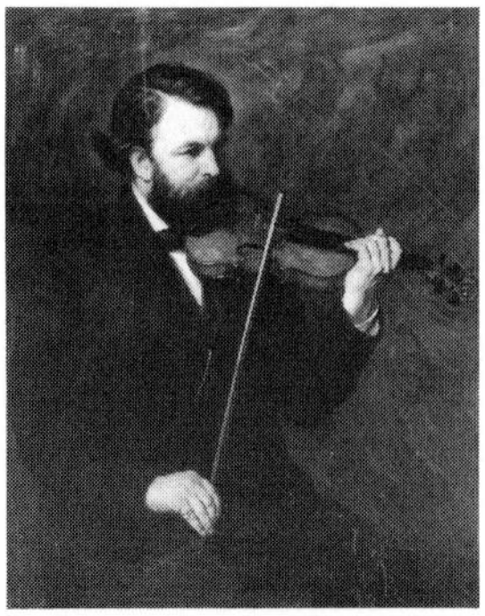

acc. no. 894
Doctor Joseph Joachim (1876)
oil on canvas: 50 × 39 in.
dated: *1876*
Presented by Dr. W. H. Cummings, 1910

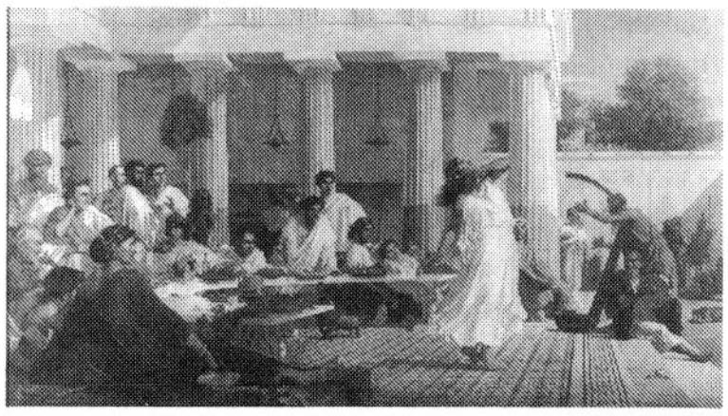

Edward Armitage (1817–96)
acc. no. 587
Herod's Birthday Feast (1868)
oil on canvas: 61 × 109 in.
signed and dated: *E. ARMITAGE / 1868*
Presented by the artist, 1894

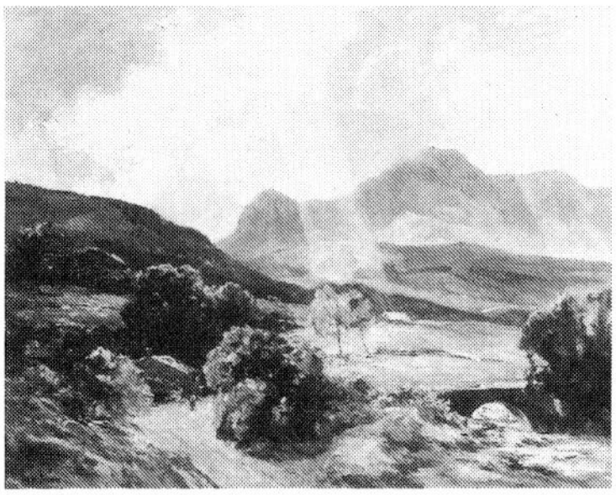

Francis Abel William Taylor Armstrong (1849–1920)
acc. no. 1050
Cader Idris (1918)
oil on canvas: $40\frac{1}{2}$ × 50 in.
signed and dated: *Armstrong / '18*
Presented by the artist's daughter, Miss Isabel Armstrong, 1926

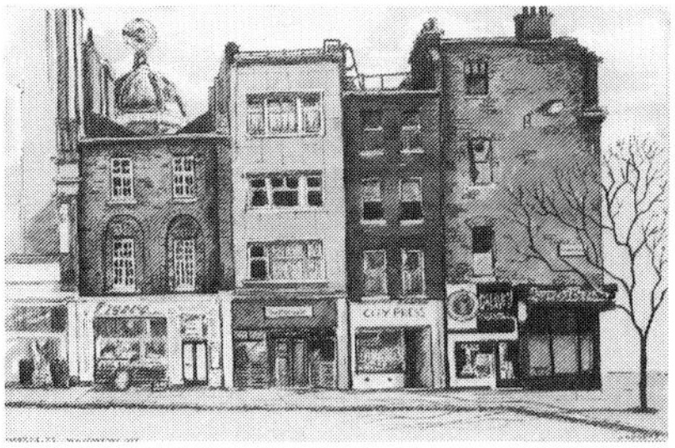

Sydney Arrobus (b.1901)
acc. no. 2207
Moorfields, New Year's Day 1977
watercolour: $13\frac{1}{2}$ × $21\frac{1}{2}$ in.
signed: *ARROBUS* and inscribed:
MOORFIELDS NEW YEAR'S DAY 1977
Purchased from the artist, 1977

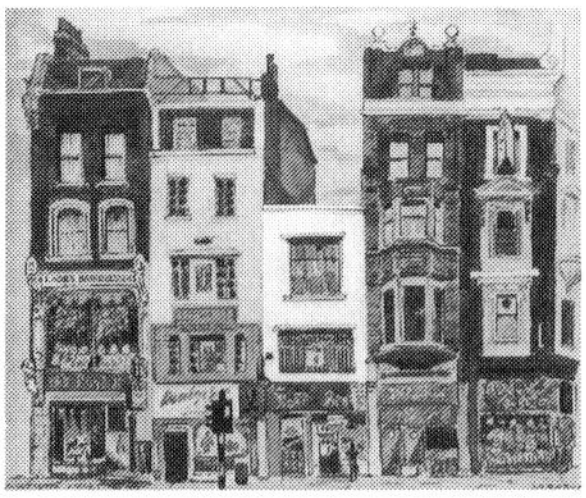

acc. no. 2211
Bishopsgate, February 1977
watercolour: $12\frac{1}{4}$ × 15 in.
signed: *ARROBUS* and inscribed:
BISHOPSGATE STREET FEB 1977
Purchased from the artist, 1977

John Henry Frederick Bacon (1868–1914)

acc. no. 636
The City Imperial Volunteers in Guildhall on their Return from South Africa, October 29 1900 (1902)
oil on canvas: 46 × 99 in.
Presented by C. W. Bartholomew, 1902

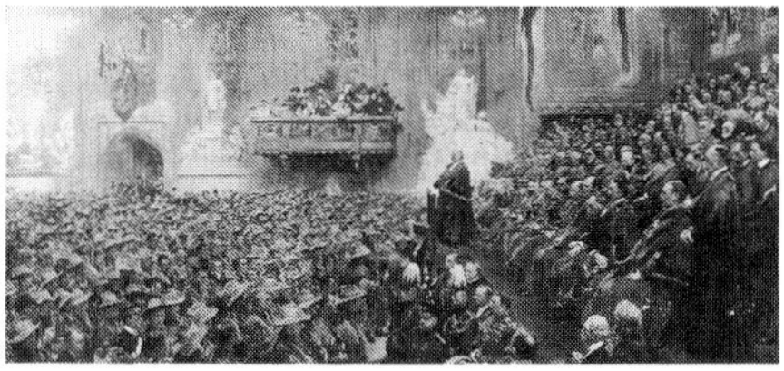

acc. no. 1544
Study for the Portrait of Sir Walter Wilkin in acc. no. 636
black and coloured chalks on brown paper: $19\frac{1}{4} \times 15\frac{1}{2}$ in.
signed and inscribed: *right of Sir H. Knight / J.H. Bacon*
Presented by H. F. Hippach, 1957

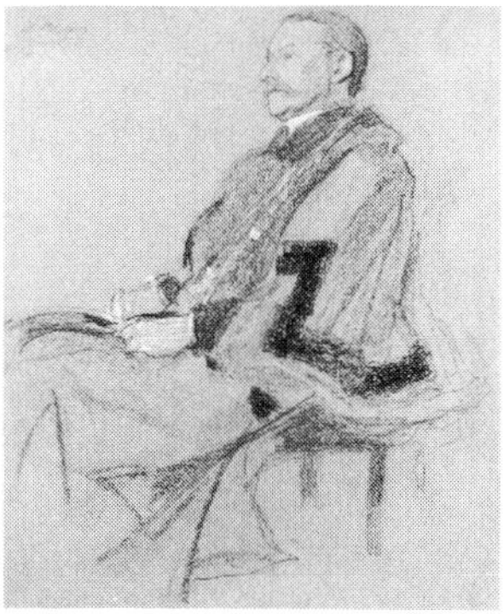

acc. no. 1690
Study for the Portrait of Sir John Johnson Runtz in acc. no. 636
black and coloured chalks on brown paper: 19 × 15 in.
signed and inscribed: (three illegible words) *4 seats from the L. Mayor. / Sir J.J. Runtz / Study for the CIV picture in Guildhall. / John HF Bacon*
Presented by A. S. Grant, 1963

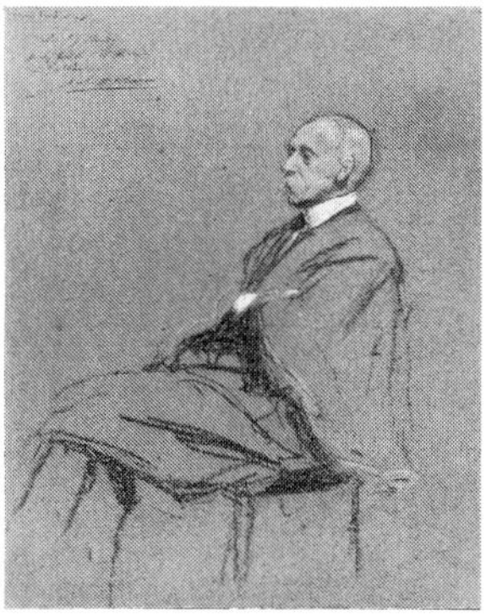

acc. no. 1363
The City Imperial Volunteers in Guildhall, 1900 (1902)
photogravure, laid on canvas: 20 × 36 in. (sight)
signed: *John H. Bacon* and *Henry MacKinnon / Comm.*
Published by C. W. Faulkner & Co. 1902
Presented by S. Harvey Hull, 1947

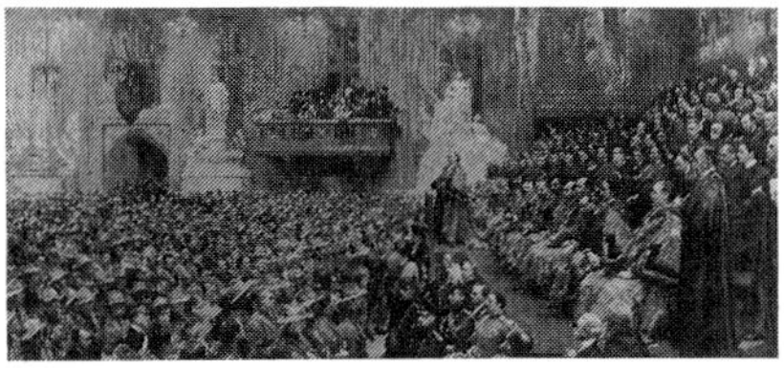

acc. no. 977
The City Imperial Volunteers in Guildhall, 1900
chromolithograph: $15\frac{1}{2} \times 34$ in. (sight)
Presented by Lady Newton, 1915

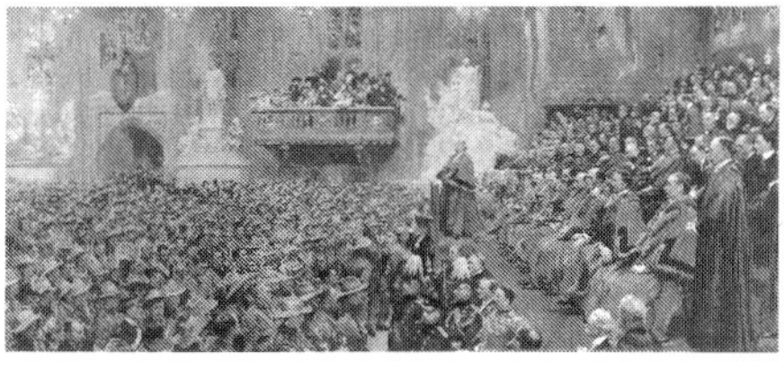

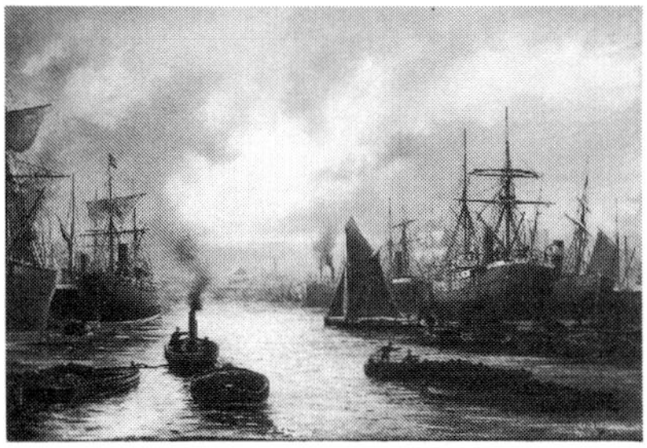

W. J. Baker (*fl.* mid–late 19th C)

acc. no. 1734
The Pool of London (1892)

oil on canvas: $19\frac{1}{2} \times 27$ in.
signed (mono) and dated: *WJB '92*
Bequeathed by F. J. Whittingham, 1948

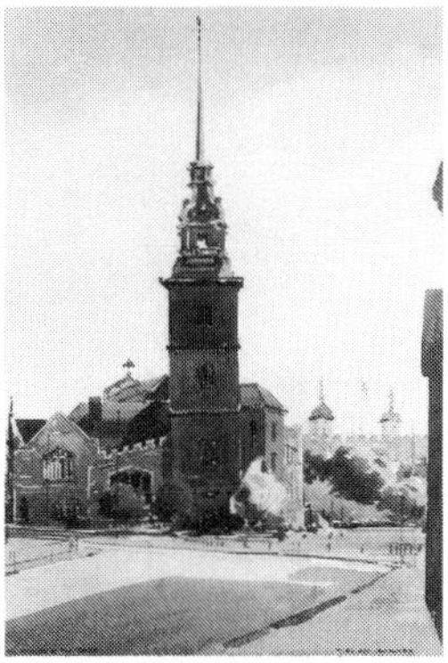

William Barnes (b.1916)

acc. no. 1859
All Hallows by the Tower (1970)

watercolour: $18\frac{1}{4} \times 12\frac{3}{8}$ in.
signed: *WILLIAM BARNES* and inscribed: *ALL HALLOWS BY THE TOWER.*
Purchased from the artist, 1971

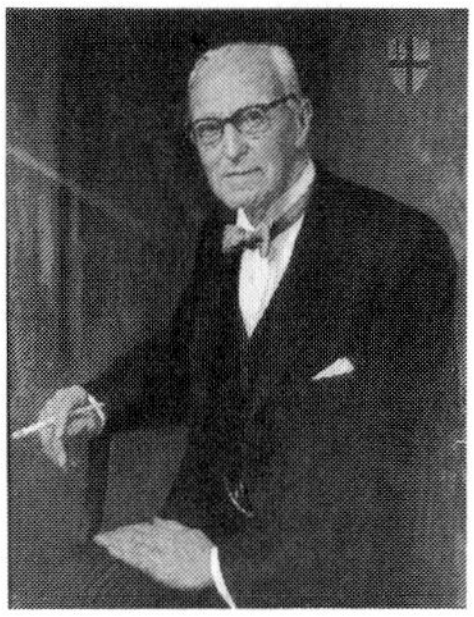

Howard Barron (b.1900)

acc. no. 1934
Sir Frank Newson Smith, Lord Mayor 1943

oil on canvas: 36×28 in.
signed: *Howard Barron*
Presented by the sitter's son, Deputy Sir John Newson-Smith, 1972

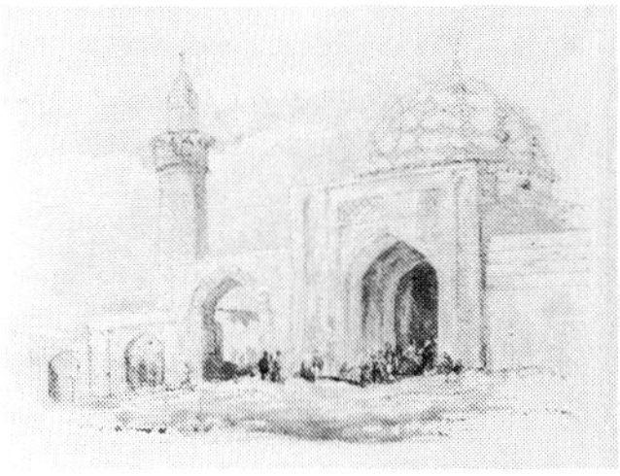

attributed to William Henry Bartlett (1809–54)

acc. no. 3558
Mecca Gate, Jerusalem

pencil and watercolour: $6\frac{3}{4} \times 8\frac{1}{8}$ in.
Presented by Miss Helen Guiterman, 1985

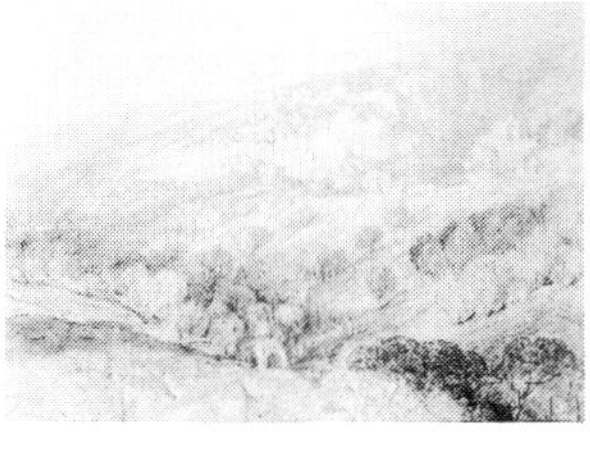

acc. no. 3553
View of Jerusalem

watercolour: $6\frac{1}{4} \times 8\frac{3}{4}$ in.
Presented by Miss Helen Guiterman, 1985

F. Barucco (*fl.* 1864–66)

acc. no. 262
General Garibaldi (1864)

oil on canvas: 24 × 20 in.
signed and dated: *F. Barucco 1864 / London*
Presented by Sir John Bennett, 1882

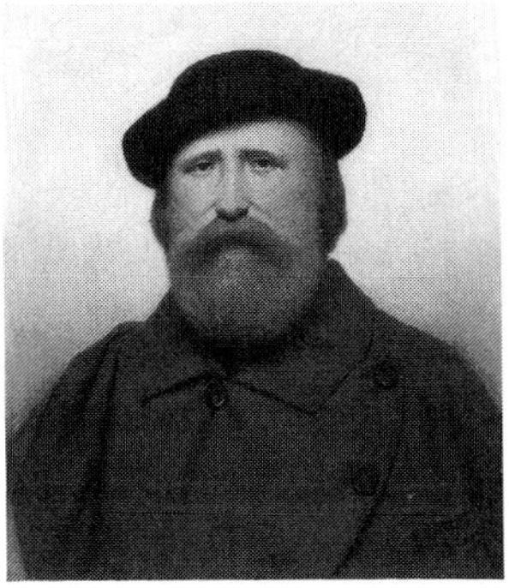

Reginald Bass (20th C)

acc. no. 1719
Sir Winston Leaves the City (1965)

oil on canvas: 18 × 48 in.
signed and dated: *REGINALD BASS – 1965*
Purchased from the artist, 1965

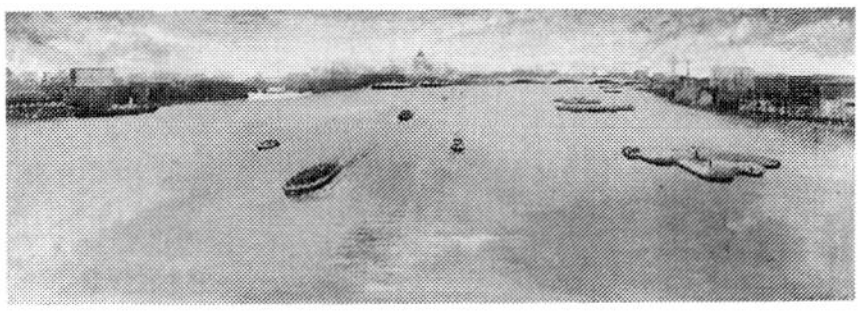

Charles Baxter (1809–79)

acc. no. 641
The Pretty Peasant (1838)

oil on canvas: 14 × 12 in.
signed and dated: *C.B. 1838*
Bequeathed by Charles Gassiot, 1902

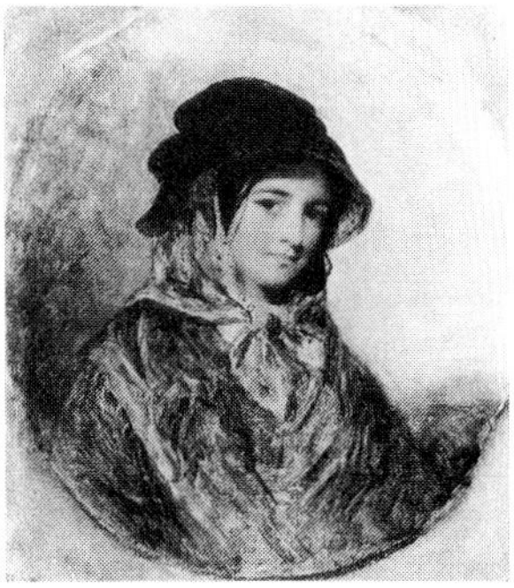

acc. no. 640
The Fair Friend (*c.*1840)

oil on millboard: 18 × 16 in.
Bequeathed by Charles Gassiot, 1902

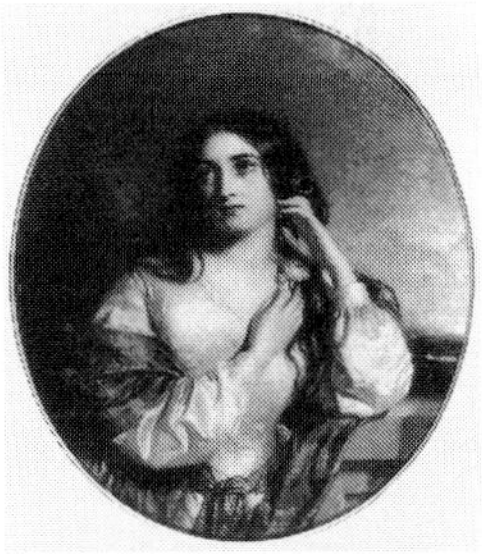

Richard Beavis (1824–96)

acc. no. 298
Dutch Schuyts Beating out of the Scheldt

oil on canvas: 18 × 24 in.
signed: *Beavis*
Presented by J. H. Skilbeck, 1886

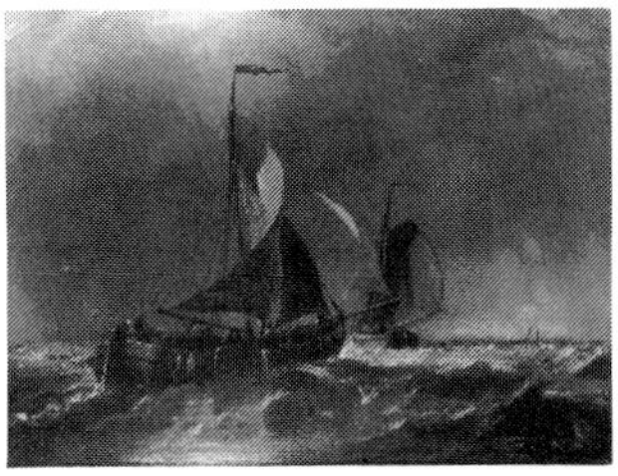

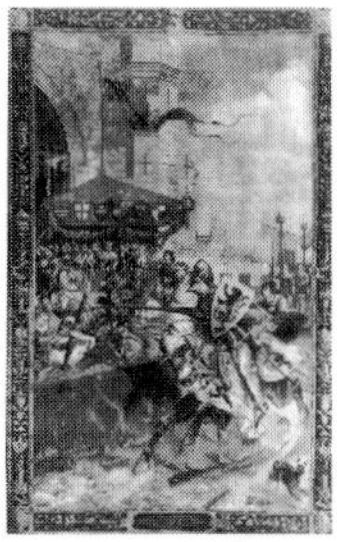

acc. no. 338
The Solemn Joust on London Bridge, between David de Lyndsays, Earl of Crawford and Lord John de Welles, Ambassador of Richard II (1886)

tapestry, executed by the Windsor Tapestry Works: 114 × 68 in.
signed and dated in the panel: *RBeavis 1886*
Commissioned by the Corporation, 1885

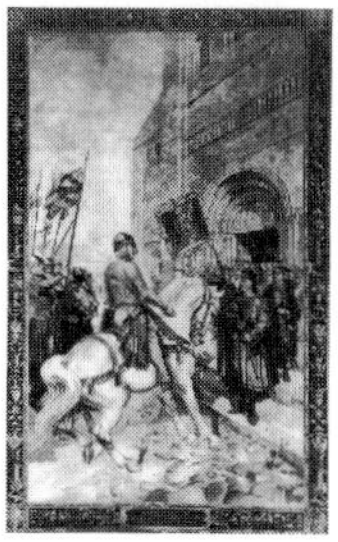

acc. no. 336
Robert Fitzwalter receiving the City's Banner from the Lord Mayor on the Steps of St. Paul's Cathedral (1887)

tapestry, executed by the Windsor Tapestry Works: 114 × 68 in.
signed in the panel: *R. Beavis*
Commissioned by the Corporation, 1885

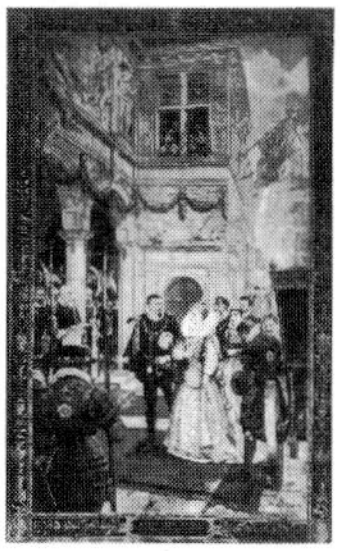

acc. no. 340
Queen Elizabeth Received by Sir Thomas Gresham on the Opening of the Royal Exchange, 1571 (1887)

tapestry, executed by the Windsor Tapestry Works: 114 × 68 in.
signed and dated in the panel: *RBeavis 1887*
Commissioned by the Corporation, 1885

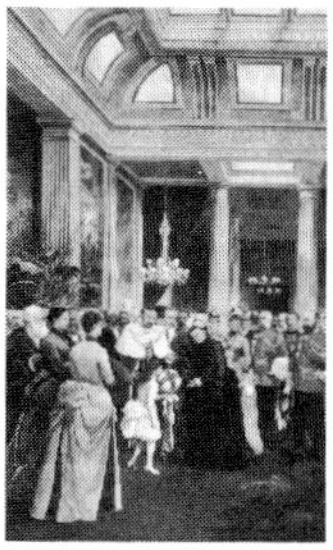

acc. no. 342a
The Visit of Queen Victoria to the Mansion House, May 14 1887 (1889)

pencil and watercolour heightened with white, backed onto canvas: 114 × 68 in.
signed and dated in reverse: *R. Beavis 1888/9*
Commissioned by the Corporation, 1888

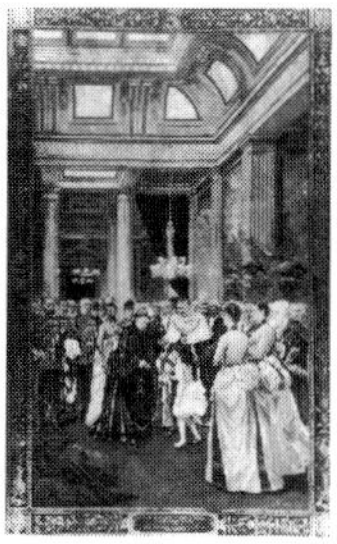

acc. no. 342
The Visit of Queen Victoria to the Mansion House, May 14 1887 (1890)
tapestry executed at the Windsor Tapestry Works: 114 × 68 in.
signed in the panel: *RBeavis*
Commissioned by the Corporation, 1888

Sir William Beechey (1753–1839)

acc. no. 58
Admiral John Jervis, Earl St. Vincent (*c.*1801)
oil on canvas: 56 × 47 in.
Presented by Alderman John Boydell, *c.*1801

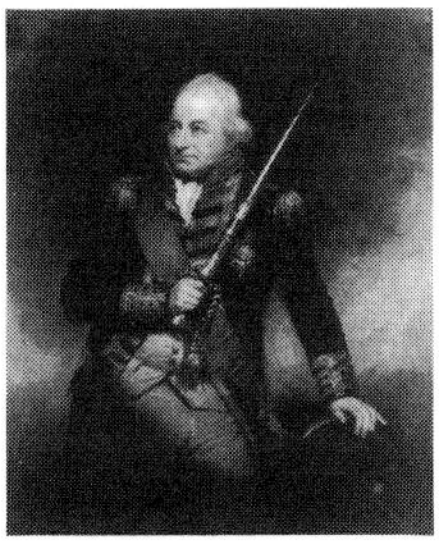

acc. no. 62
Viscount Nelson (1801)
oil on canvas: 55 × 46 in.
Presented by Alderman John Boydell, 1801

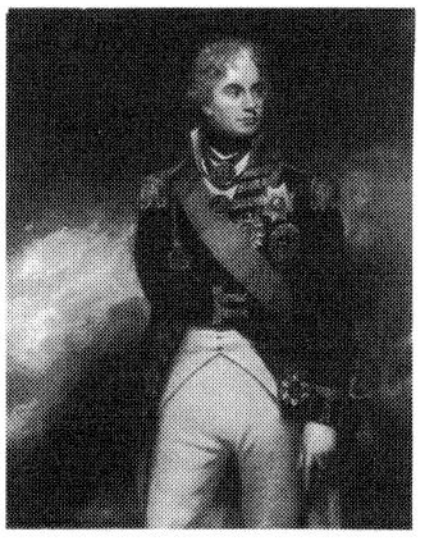

acc. no. 82
Alderman John Boydell (1801)
oil on canvas: 116 × 93 in.
Commissioned by the Corporation, 1800

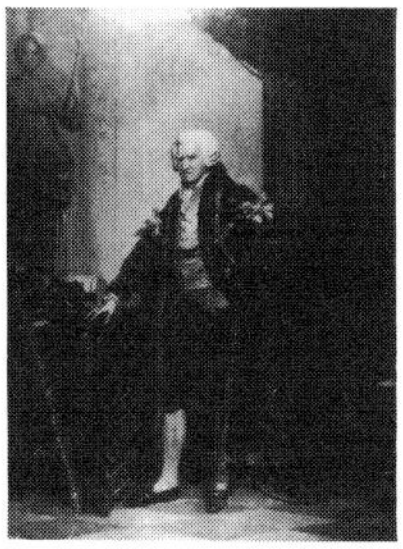

acc. no. 109
Sir William Staines, Lord Mayor 1800
(exh. 1803)
oil on canvas: 50 × 40 in.
Presented by Mrs. Maria Weybridge, 1843

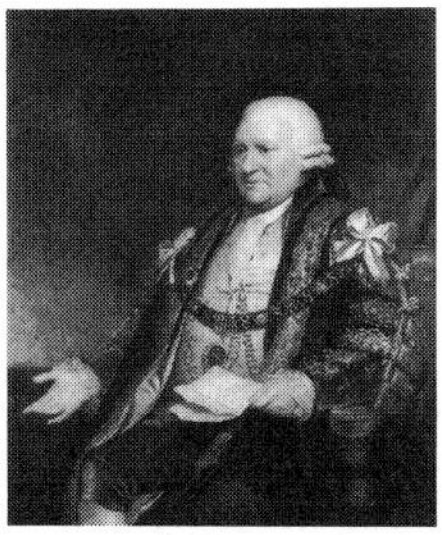

William Beetham (*fl.* 1834–53)

acc. no. 579
James Anderton CC
oil on canvas: 44 × 34 in.
Presented by R. Malcolm Kerr, 1893

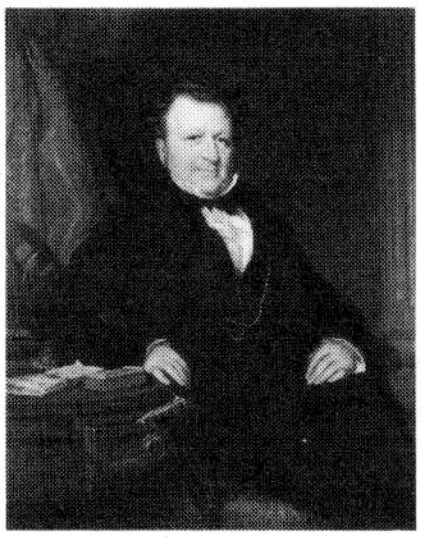

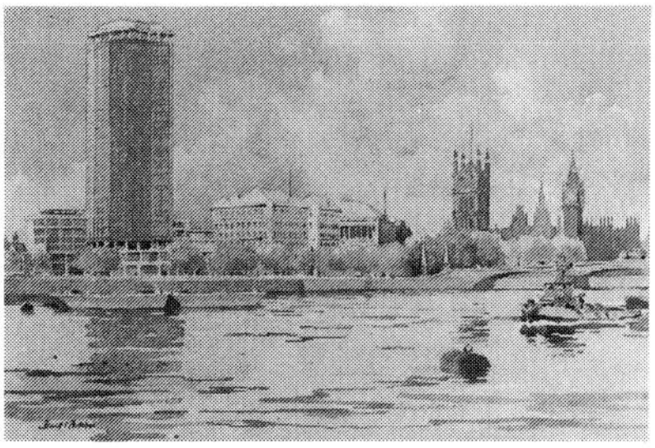

Frank C. Belcher (20th C)

acc. no. 2200
The Changing Scene at Millbank

watercolour: 12 × 17 in.
signed: *Frank C. Belcher*
Purchased from Mrs. F. Belcher, 1976

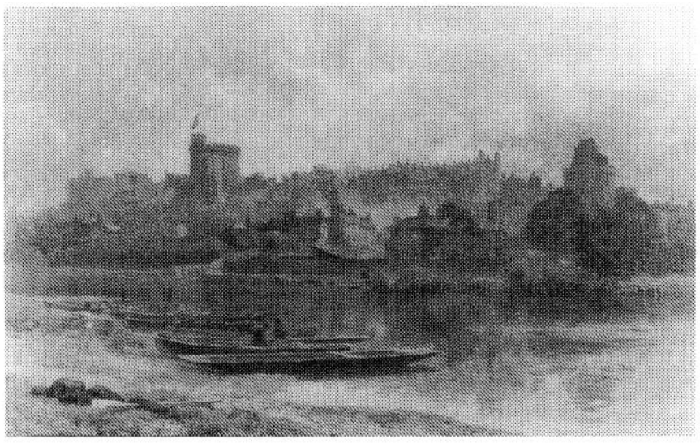

Newton Benett (1854–1914)

acc. no. 972
Windsor Castle in the Gloom

watercolour: $10\frac{1}{2} \times 16\frac{1}{4}$ in.
inscribed on label on verso: *NEWTON BENETT / St Andrews – Lyme Regis. Dorset / 2. Windsor in Gloom. / 11.*
Presented by William C. Benett, 1915

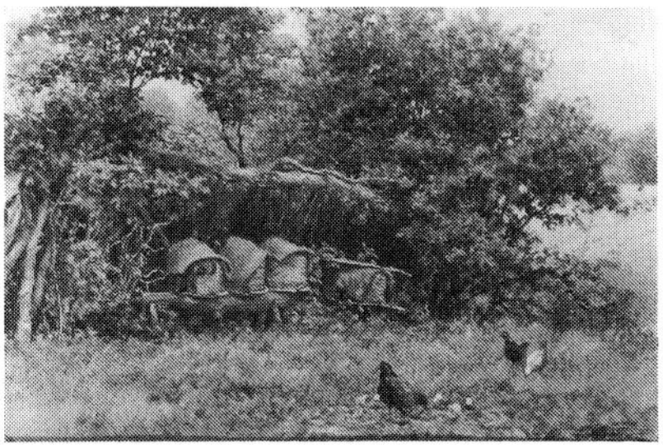

Acc. no. 973
Bee Hives

watercolour: $10 \times 14\frac{1}{2}$ in.
Presented by Miss Sarah Benett, 1915

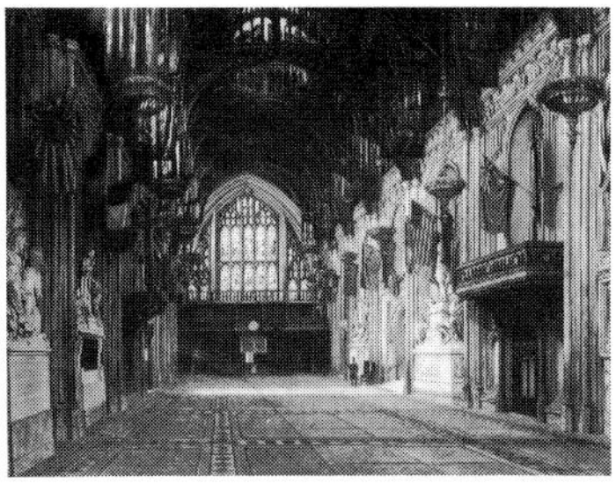

Daisy Radcliffe Beresford (*fl.* from 1904, d.1939)

acc. no. 1344
Interior of the Great Hall, Guildhall (1921)

oil on canvas: $28\frac{1}{4} \times 36\frac{1}{4}$ in.
signed and dated: *D. Radcliffe Beresford 1921*
Bequeathed by Deputy Charles Newell, 1946

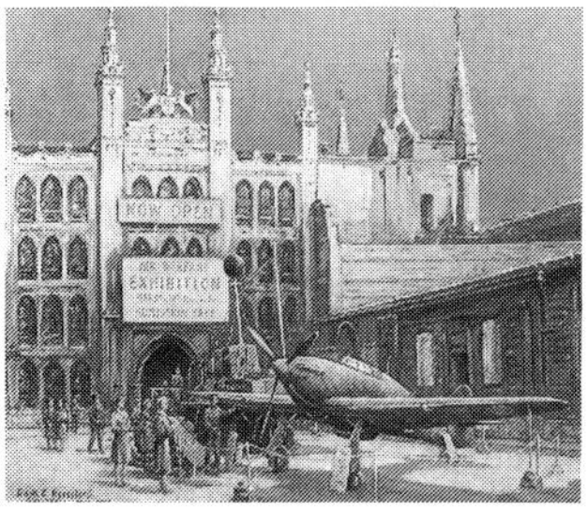

Frank Ernest Beresford (1881–1967)

acc. no. 1579
A Hurricane at Guildhall (1943)

oil on canvas: 20 × 24 in.
signed and dated: *Frank E Beresford /GUILDHALL March 1943*
Presented by the artist, 1960

attributed to Thomas Best (*fl.* 1834–39)

acc. no. 3563
A Cavalry Charge

watercolour: $5\frac{3}{8} \times 11\frac{3}{4}$ in.
signed: *T Best* (?)
Presented by Miss Helen Guiterman, 1985

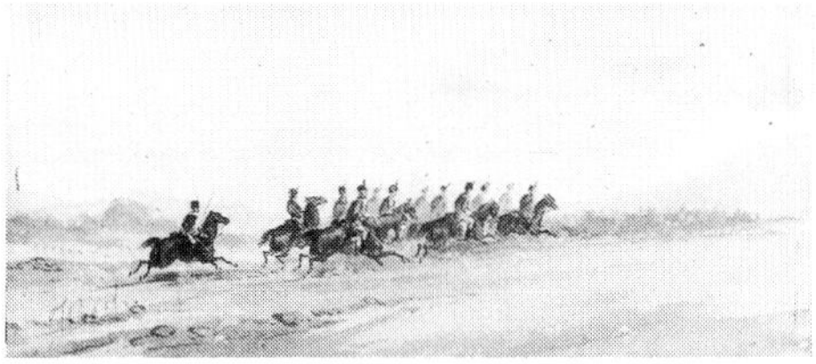

attributed to John Bettes (d. *c.*1570)

acc. no. 1005
Sir Thomas Exmewe, Lord Mayor 1517

oil on panel: $21\frac{1}{4} \times 17$ in.
Presented by the Hon. Mrs. Laurence Brodrick, 1919

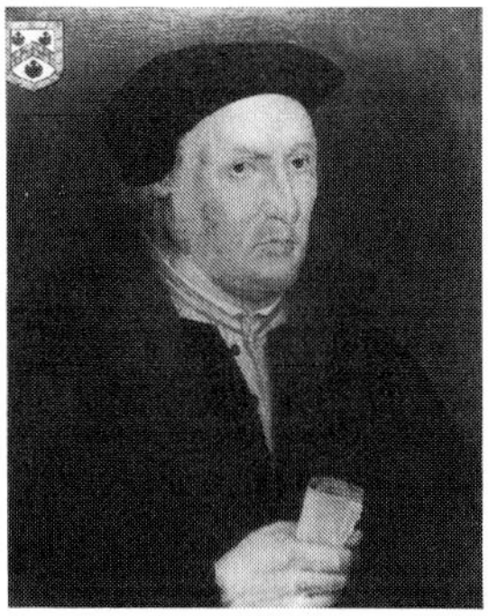

Edward Bird (1772–1819)

acc. no. 330
The Poacher (1813)

oil on panel: 18×24 in.
signed: *E.BIRD A.R.A.*
Presented by William Rome, 1887

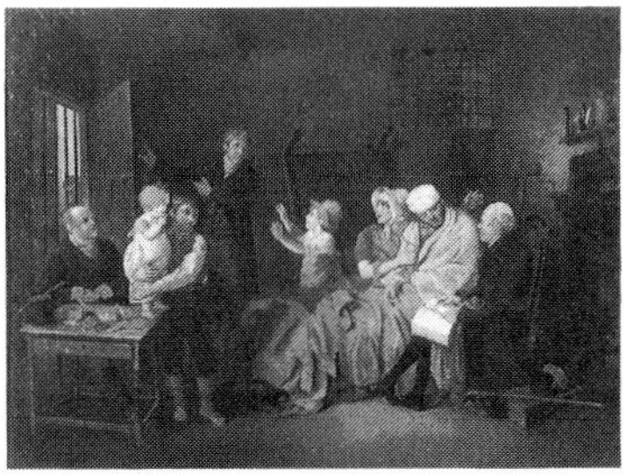

Nigella Bittleston (20th C)

acc. no. 1711
The Cat in Whittington Gardens (1965)

oil on canvas: $14 \times 18\frac{1}{2}$ in.
Purchased from the artist, 1965

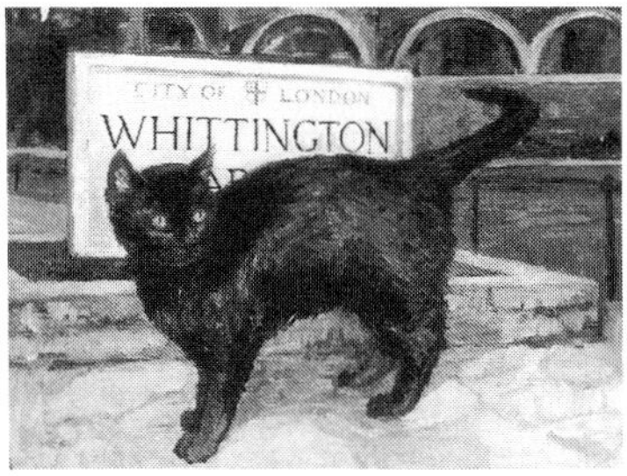

Pamela Blake (20th C)

acc. no. 1641
The George and Vulture (1961)
ink and bodycolour: $14\frac{3}{4} \times 21\frac{3}{4}$ in.
signed and dated: *PB 61*
Purchased from the artist, 1962

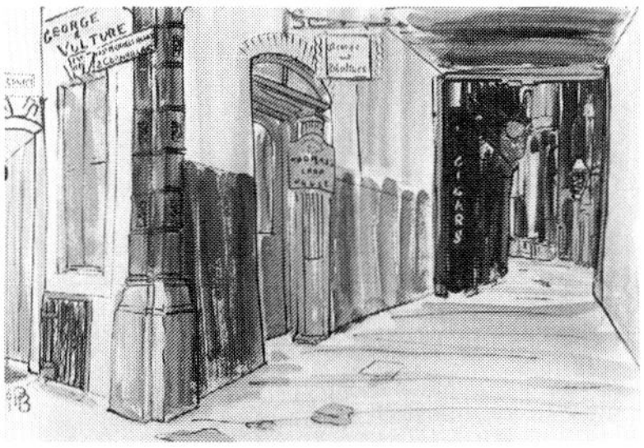

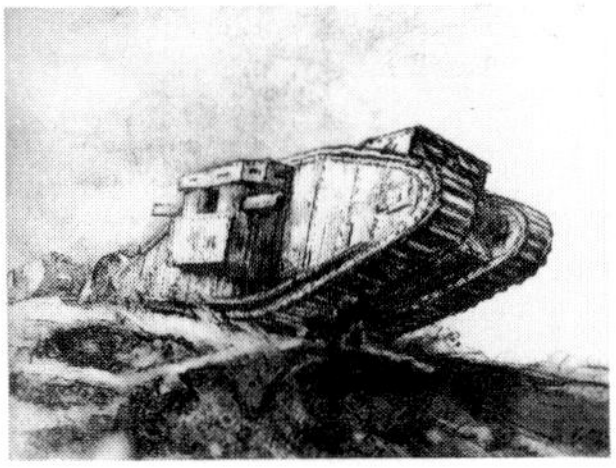

Sir Muirhead Bone (1876–1953)

acc. no. 1012
A British Tank

lithograph: 27 × 20 in.
signed in the plate: *M Bone*; signed in the margin: *Muirhead Bone* and inscribed: *To the Lord Mayor and Corporation of the City of London, / a memento of the War Savings Campaign, 1917–8.*
Presented by the artist, 1921

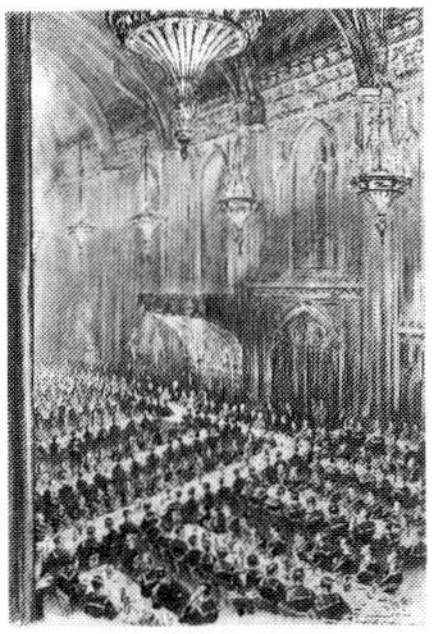

acc. no. 1355
Luncheon at Guildhall to the Officers and Men of HMS 'Ajax' and 'Exeter', February 23 1940

pencil, black chalk and grey wash heightened with white: 20 × 13½ in.
signed, dated and inscribed: *Muirhead Bone / Guildhall. London. / 23 Feb. 1940*
Allocated by the War Artists Advisory Committee, 1947

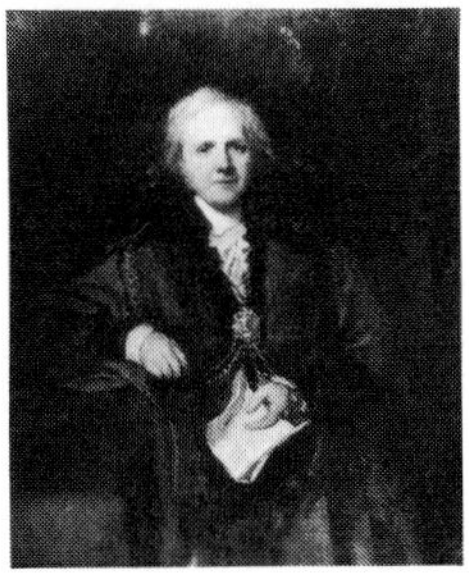

Sir William Boxall (1800–79)

acc. no. 974
William Cubitt

oil on canvas: 50 × 40 in.
Presented by Lord Ashcombe, 1915

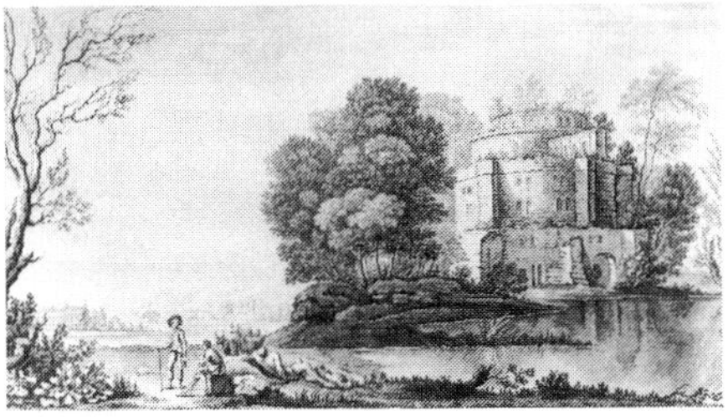

John Boydell (1719–1804)

acc. no. 1413
Imaginary Landscape with a Fantastic Castle (1745)

pen and grey ink and wash: 9 × 15½ in.
signed and dated: *John Boydell delin. 1745*
Purchased, 1950

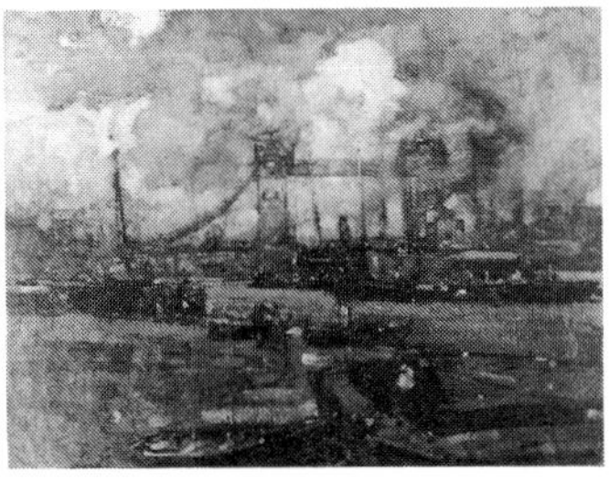

Sir Frank Brangwyn (1867–1956)

acc. no. 860
*Tower Bridge c.*1905

oil on canvas: 25 × 30½ in.
signed: *Fr. BRANGWYN*
Presented by Alderman Sir Charles, later Lord, Wakefield, 1908

acc. no. 861
The Lord Mayor's Show in Olden Days (*c.*1905)
oil on canvas: $20\frac{1}{2} \times 24\frac{1}{2}$ in.
signed: *FB*
Presented by Alderman Sir Charles, later Lord, Wakefield, 1908

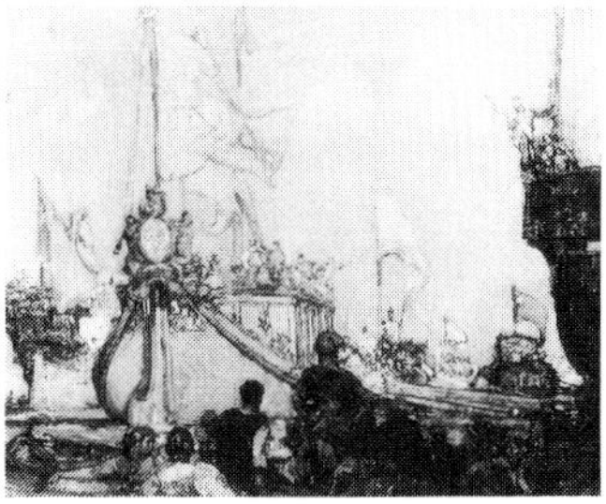

acc. no. 937
Arab Fruit Carriers (*c.*1908)
lithograph: 17×22 in.
signed in the plate: *FB.* and in the margin: *Frank Brangwyn*
Presented by Miss Evelyn P. McGhee, 1912

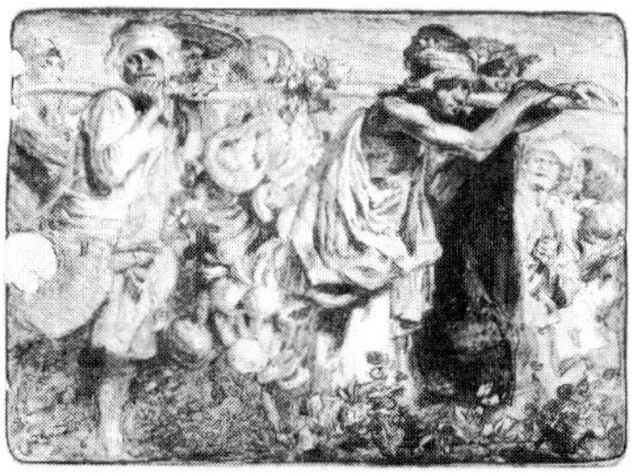

acc. no. 1349
The Monument (1912)
etching: $28 \times 17\frac{7}{8}$ in.
signed: *Frank Brangwyn*
Purchased, 1946

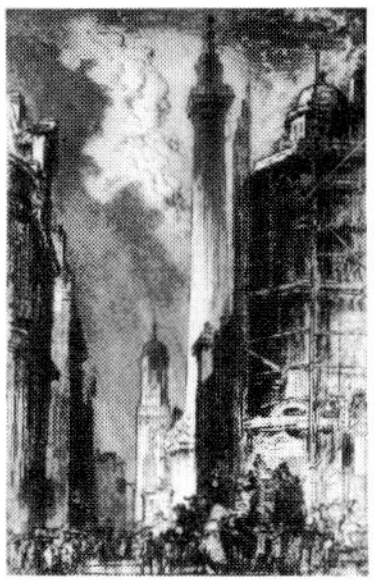

acc. no. 2326
The Abbey of St. Leonard, Tours (1912)
watercolour heightened with white over pencil: $21\frac{1}{2} \times 27\frac{3}{4}$ in.
signed, dated and inscribed: *FB. L'ILE BOUCHARD 1912*
Bequeathed by the Comtesse de Trémereuc, 1983

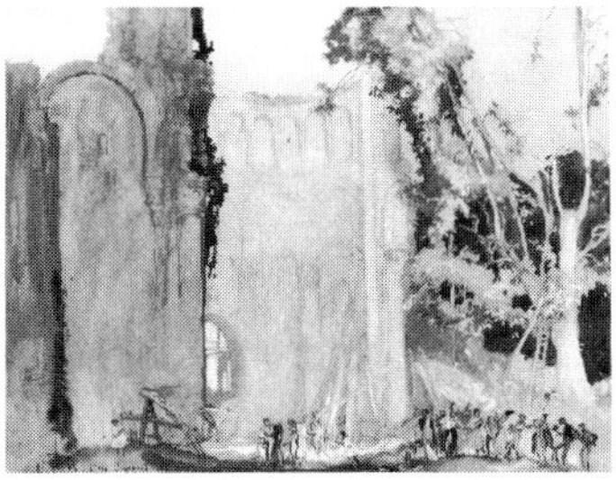

acc. no. 2325
Le Pont de Vernay, Airvault, Deux-Sèvres (*c.*1913)
watercolour: $21\frac{1}{2} \times 27\frac{3}{4}$ in.
signed: *FB.*
Bequeathed by the Comtesse de Trémereuc, 1983

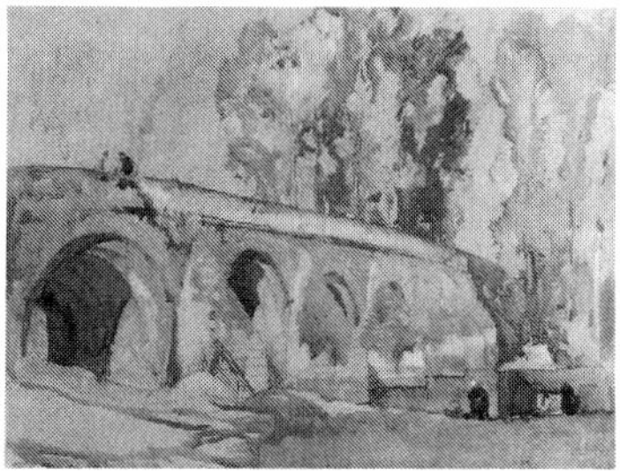

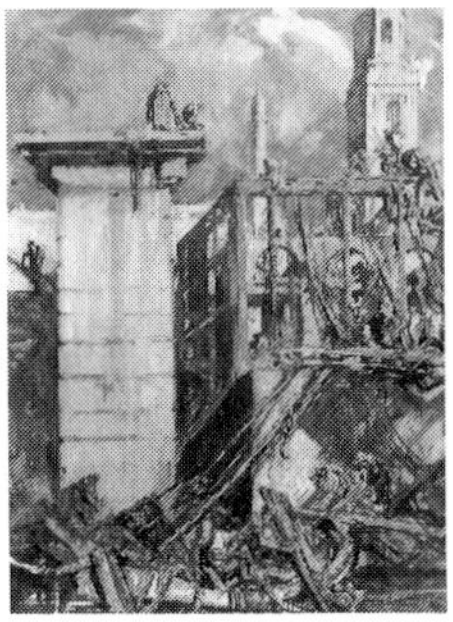

acc. no. 1508
Demolition of Fresh Wharf, London Bridge, 1924
watercolour and bodycolour: $30 \times 21\frac{3}{4}$ in.
signed (mono): *FB*
Presented by F. C. Lewis, 1954

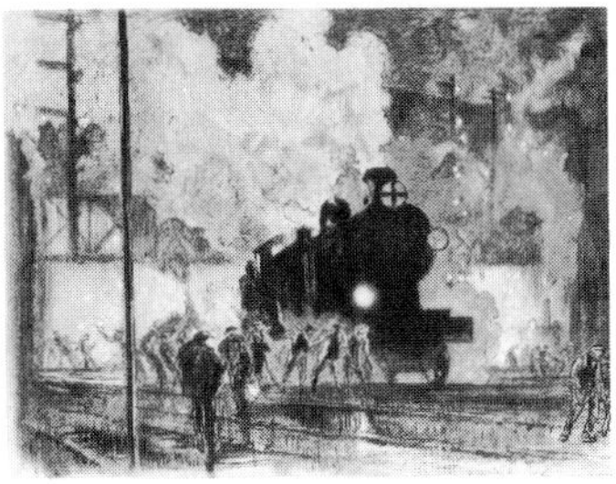

acc. no. 1514
The Railway Station (King's Cross)
lithograph: $22\frac{7}{8} \times 30\frac{1}{4}$ in.
signed: *Frank Brangwyn*
Presented by the Guild of Freemen, 1954

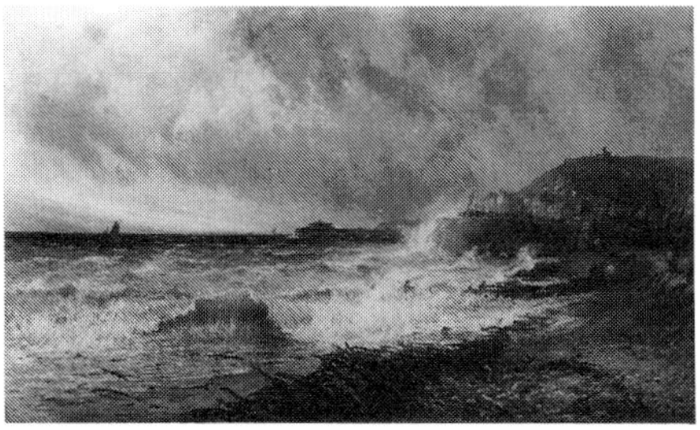

Gustave de Breanski (*c.*1856–98)

acc. no. 299
Hastings (1884)
oil on canvas: 30 × 50 in.
signed and dated: *Gustave de Breanski/ 1884*
Presented by Graham King, 1886

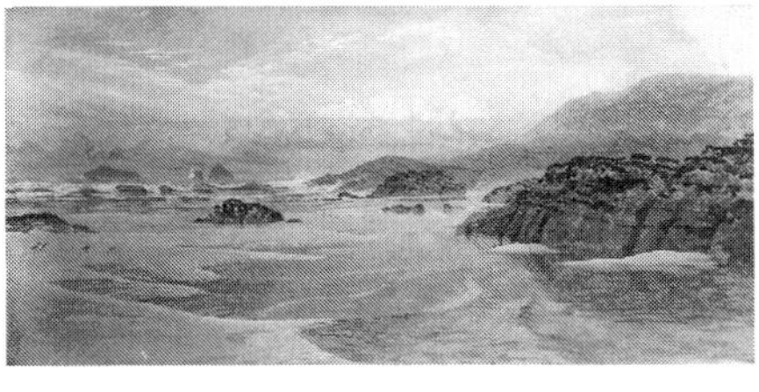

John Brett (1830–1902)

acc. no. 991
Echoes of a Far-Off Storm (1890)
oil on canvas: 42 × 84 in.
signed and dated: *John Brett 1890*
Presented by Sir Thomas Devitt, 1918

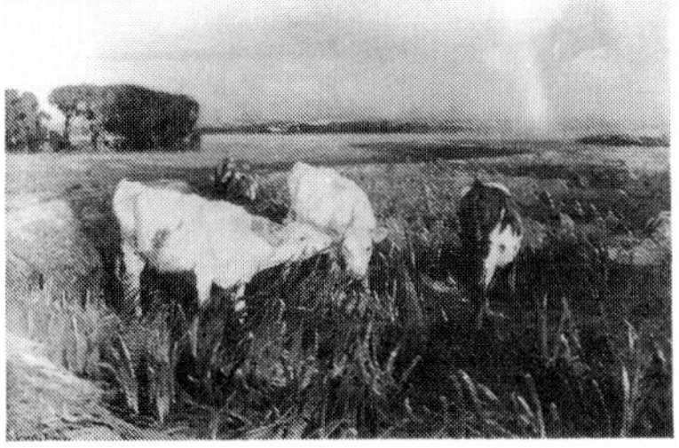

Sir John Alfred Arnesby Brown (1866–1955)

acc. no. 634
The River Bank (1902)
oil on canvas: 50 × 72 in.
signed: *Arnesby Brown*
Purchased from the artist, 1902

Mather Brown (1761–1831)

acc. no. 1735
Peter Mellish, Sheriff 1798–99

oil on canvas: 48 × 40 in.
Presented by the Worshipful Company of Butchers, 1966

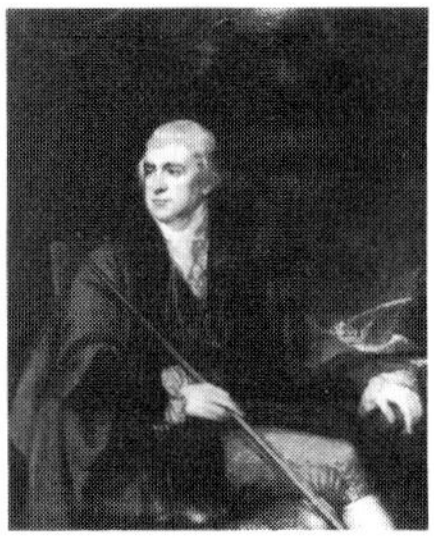

acc. no. 241
Sir John Eamer, Lord Mayor, 1801

oil on canvas: 94 × 58 in.
Bequeathed by Mrs. Claxson, 1873

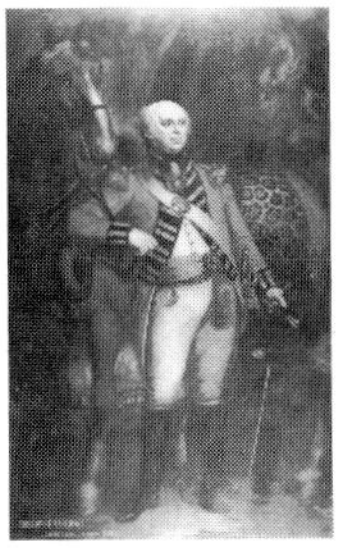

Alexander Joshua Caleb Bryce (1868–1940)

acc. no. 1622
St. Paul's from Bankside (1924)

watercolour: $13\frac{1}{2} \times 9\frac{5}{8}$ in.
signed and dated: *A J C Bryce / '24*; inscribed on verso: *Alexander J.C. Bryce / 4 Nevern Road / London SW5. / Title / St Paul's. London / price 120 dollars*
Presented by Mrs. A. Bryce, 1961

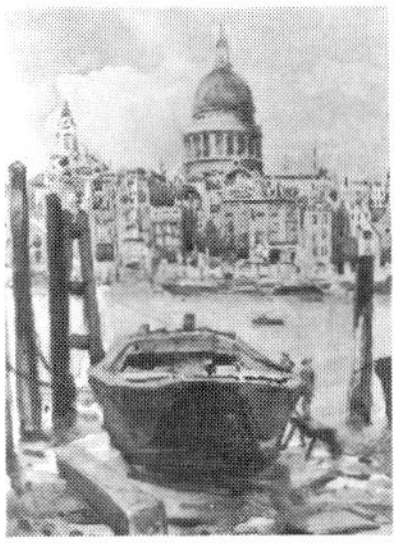

Herbert Ashwin Budd (1881–1950)

acc. no. 1380
Francis Richard Dale, Headmaster of the City of London School 1929–1950 (1949)

oil on canvas: $41\frac{1}{2} \times 31\frac{1}{2}$ in.
signed and dated: *H.A. BUDD / 49*
Presented by the John Carpenter Club, 1949

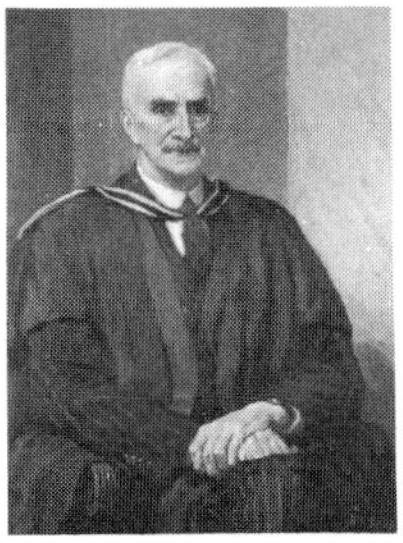

Henry T. Bulmer (19th C)

acc. no. 3541
Portrait of a Young Man (1837)

pencil, watercolour and bodycolour: $6\frac{1}{2} \times 4\frac{3}{4}$ in.
signed and dated: *Henry T. Bulmer del. / 1837*
Presented by Miss Helen Guiterman, 1985

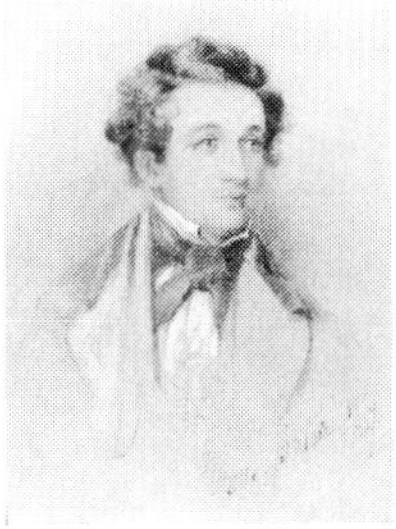

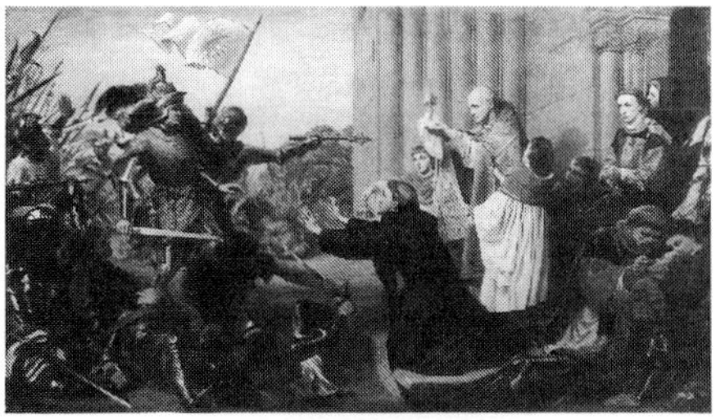

Richard Burchett (1815–75)

acc. no. 600
Sanctuary (Edward IV and Lancastrian Fugitives at Tewkesbury Abbey) (1867)
oil on canvas: 61 × 108 in.
Bequeathed by E. J. Brett, 1895

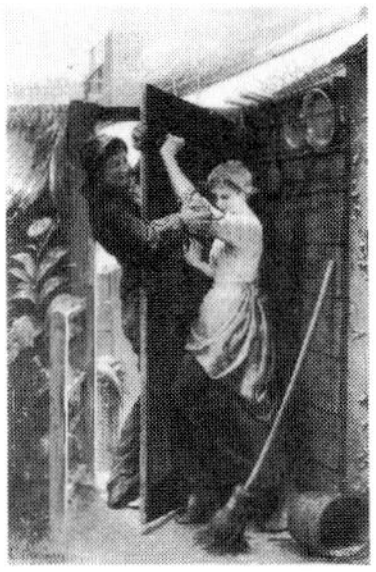

Hendricus-Jacobus Burgers (1834–99)

ac. no. 694
Sailor with a Crab (1874)
oil on canvas: 33 × 22 in.
signed and dated: *H.J. Burgers / Paris 1874*
Bequeathed by Charles Gassiot, 1902

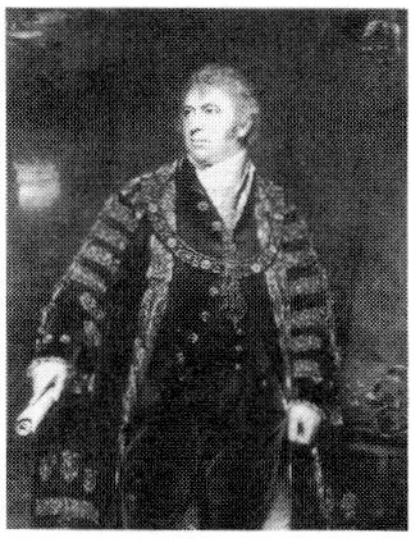

Benjamin Burnell (1769–1828)

acc. no. 1387
Harvey Christian Combe, Lord Mayor 1799 (1800)
oil on canvas: 52 × 48 in.
Purchased from Montague Marcusson, 1948

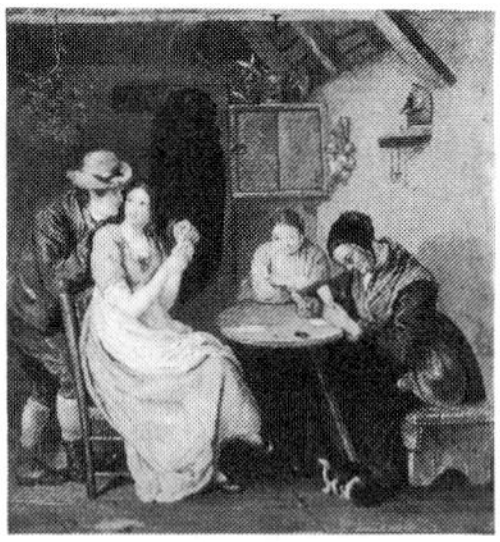

John Burnett (1784–1868)

acc. no. 1034
The Card Players
oil on panel: $18\frac{3}{4} \times 17\frac{3}{8}$ in.
signed: *John Birnet* (sic)
Presented by Lord Bearsted, 1924

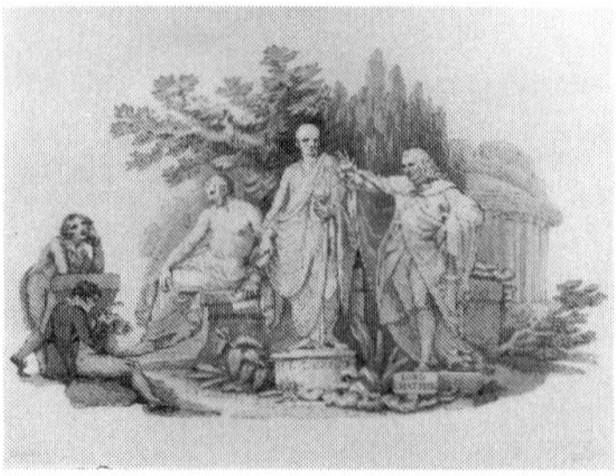

Edward Francis Burney (1760–1848)

acc. no. 497
Two Youths Contemplating Statues of Demosthenes, Cicero and Pitt (design for title page of 'Elegant Extracts: or Useful and Entertaining Passages in Prose', 1790)
pen and grey ink and watercolour: $4\frac{5}{8} \times 3$ in.
Presented by Felix Joseph, 1890

acc. no. 496
Adam and Eve Expelled from Eden (*c.*1799)

pen and ink and grey wash: $6\frac{3}{4} \times 4\frac{1}{4}$ in.
inscribed: *In either hand the hast'ning angel caught Our ling'ring Parents, – / PARADISE LOST. BOOK XII verse 636*
Presented by Felix Joseph, 1890

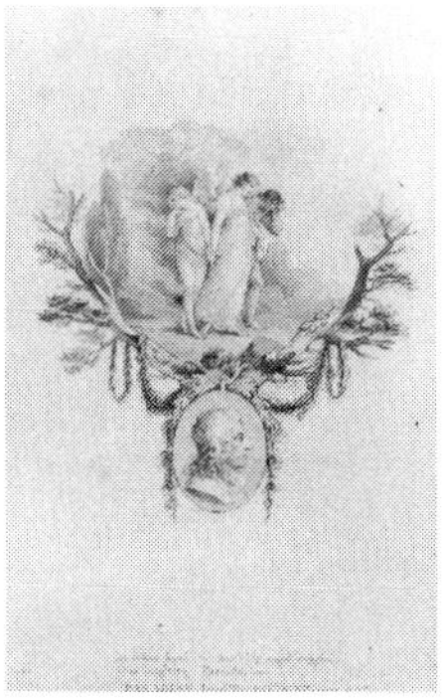

acc. no. 501
Satan and Beelzebub in Hell (*c.*1799)

pen and grey ink and grey wash: $6\frac{5}{8} \times 4\frac{1}{4}$ in.
inscribed: *Then with expanded wings he steers his flight. / PARADISE LOST. Book I. v.225.*
Presented by Felix Joseph, 1890

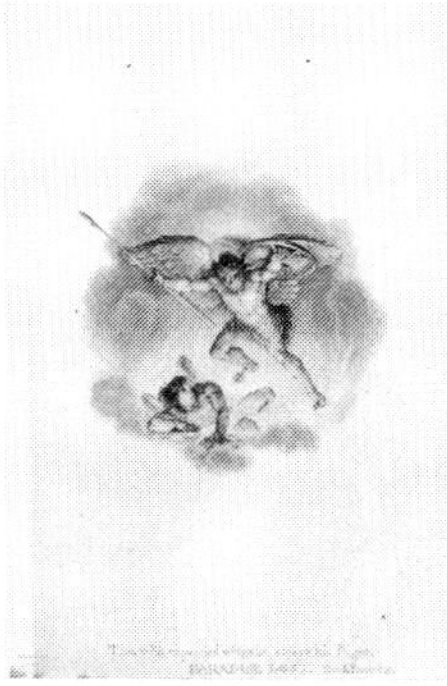

acc. no. 495
The Evening Milkmaid

pen and grey ink and watercolour: $4\frac{1}{4} \times 3\frac{1}{4}$ in.
Presented by Felix Joseph, 1890

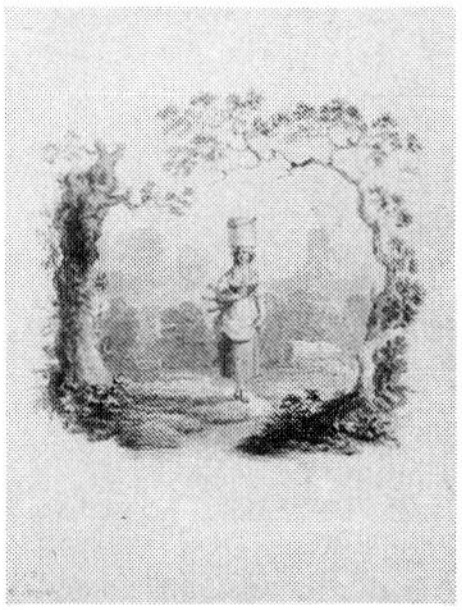

acc. no. 498
Genius bearing the Soul Aloft

pen and grey ink and watercolour: $4\frac{5}{8} \times 3$ in.
Presented by Felix Joseph, 1890

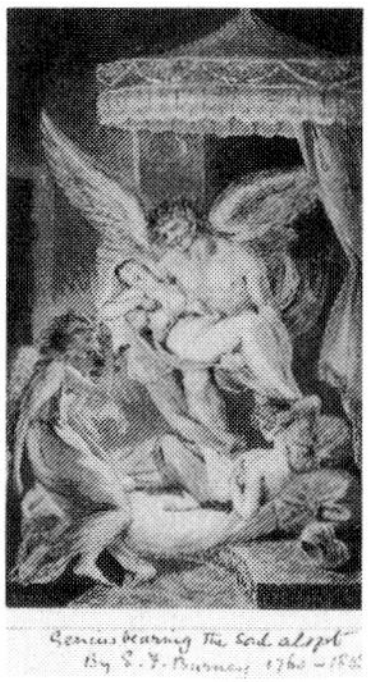

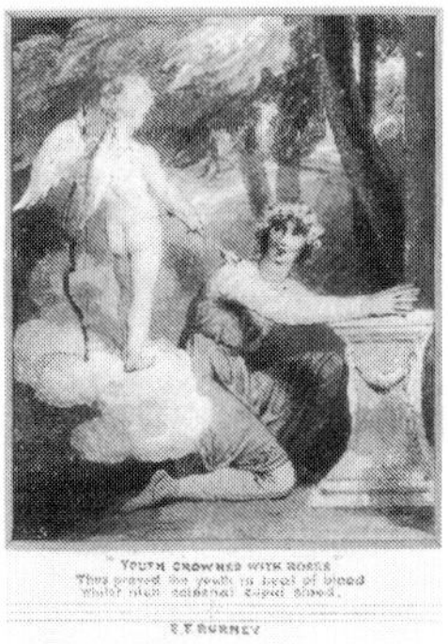

acc. no. 499
Youth Crowned with Roses

pen and grey ink and watercolour: $4 \times 3\frac{1}{4}$ in.
Presented by Felix Joseph, 1890

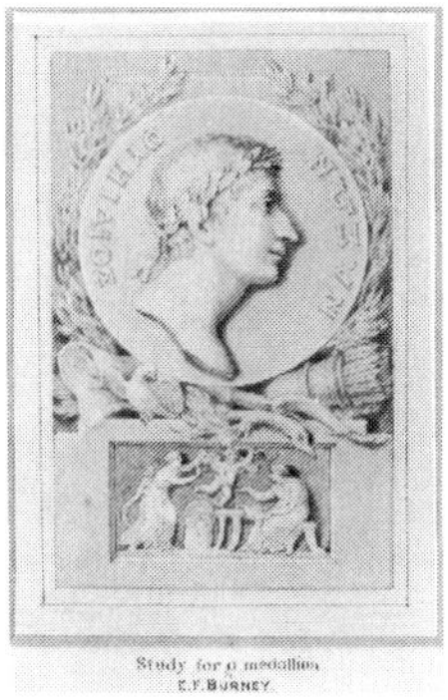

acc. no. 500
A Bas-Relief to Ovid

pen and grey ink and grey and blue wash: $5 \times 3\frac{3}{8}$ in.
Presented by Felix Joseph, 1890

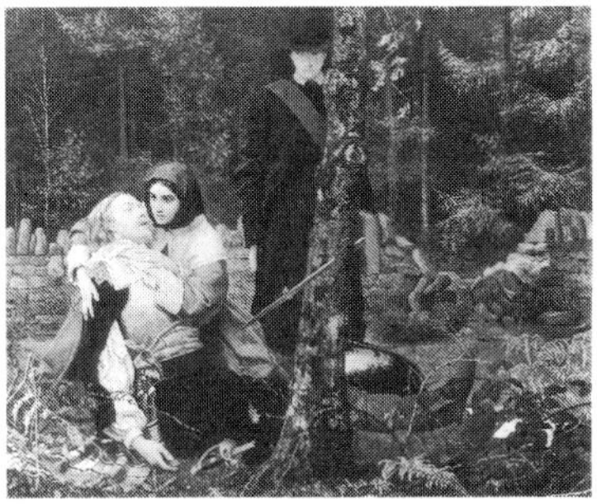

William Shakespeare Burton (1824–1916)

acc. no. 927
The Wounded Cavalier (1855)

oil on canvas: 35×41 in.
Presented by a body of subscribers, 1911

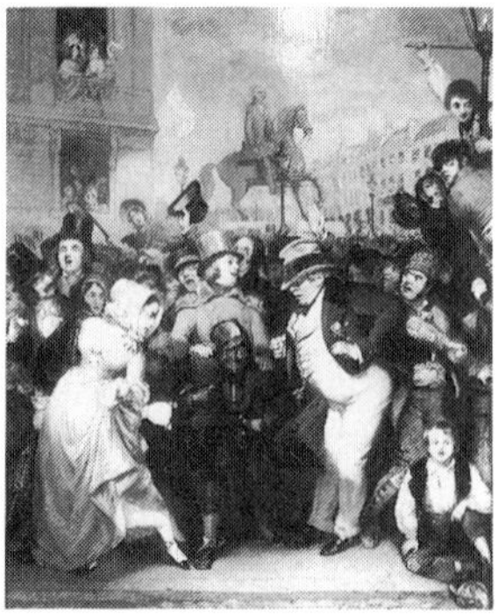

Robert William Buss (1804–74)

acc. no. 1306
The Crowd (1847)

oil on canvas: $30\frac{1}{2} \times 25\frac{1}{2}$ in.
signed and dated: *RWBuss. 1847*
Purchased, 1944

Alec Butson (20th C)

acc. no. 2206
The 'British Sailor', Greenwich (1976)

watercolour: 14 × 19 in.
signed and dated: *Alec Butson '76*
Purchased from the artist, 1977

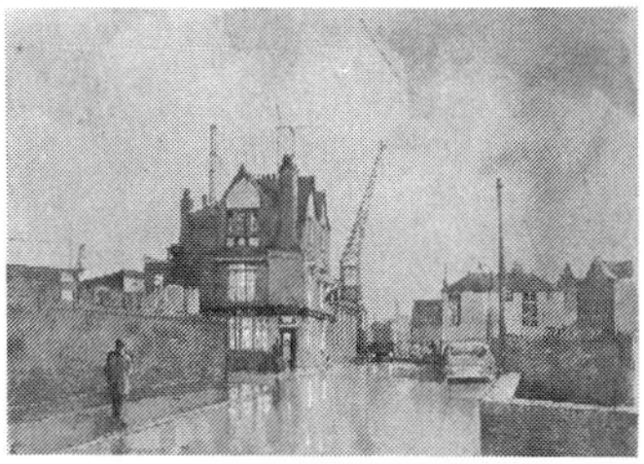

William Callow (1812–1908)

acc. no. 1885
Abbeville (1841)

pencil: 10 × 15 in.
dated: *Abbeville / Sept 30th 41*
Presented by Miss Helen Guiterman, 1985

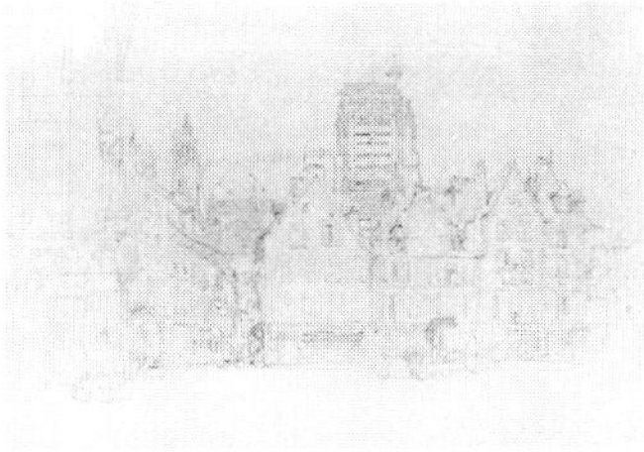

acc. no. 2252
The Rathaus, Hanover (1852)

pencil: $13\frac{7}{8}$ × 10 in.
inscribed: *The Building all Brick/ Rathaus Hanover / Aug. 31. 1852*
Presented by Miss Helen Guiterman, 1985

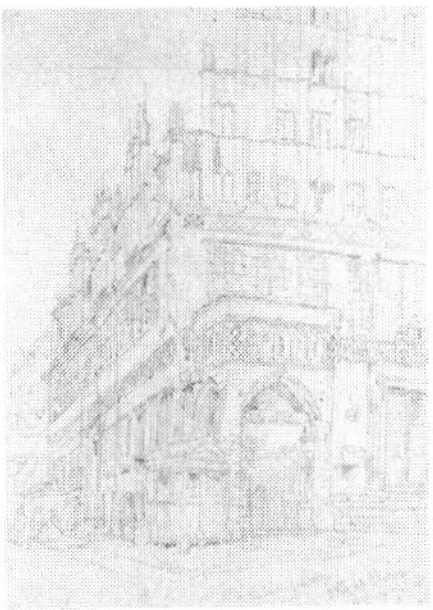

acc. no. 2253
Lisieux, France (?1854)

pencil: $13\frac{3}{4}$ × $9\frac{7}{8}$ in.
inscribed and dated: *The aux Fevres.*(?)*Lisieux / August 22 1854* (?)
Presented by Miss Helen Guiterman, 1985

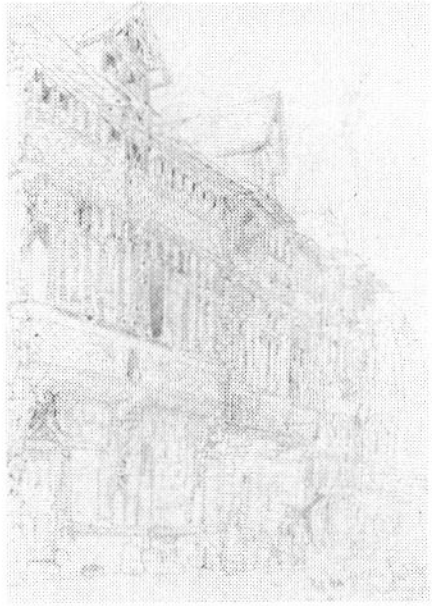

Reginald Henry Campbell (b.1877)

acc. no. 1353
The Rt. Hon. H.H. Asquith (1921)

oil on canvas: 47 × 39 in.
signed and dated: *R.H. CAMPBELL / 1921*
Presented to the City of London School by the John Carpenter Club, *c.*1937

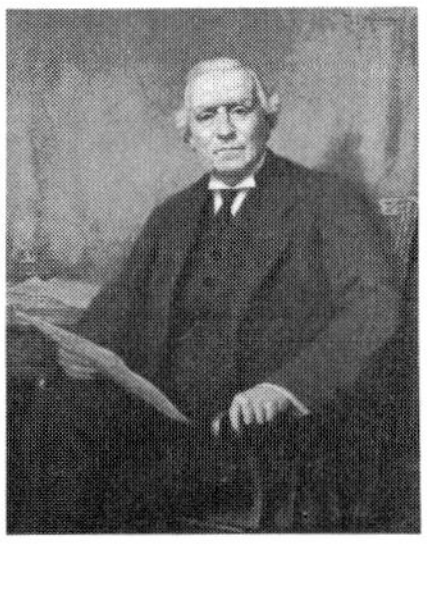

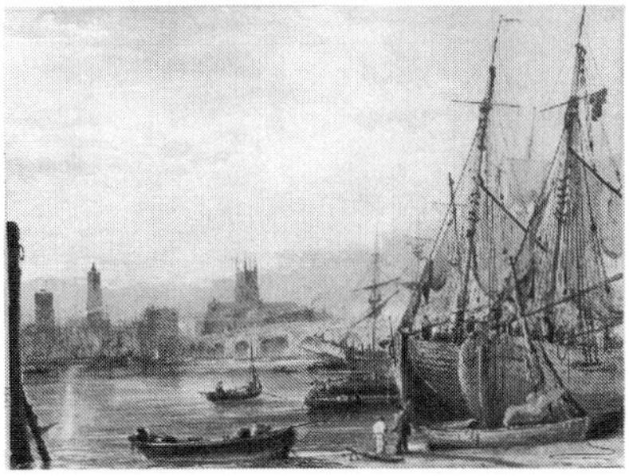

attributed to George Bryant Campion (1796–1870)

acc. no. 1693
Old London Bridge and Southwark (*c.*1830)
watercolour: $13\frac{1}{2} \times 17\frac{3}{4}$ in.
Purchased from F. T. Sabin, 1964

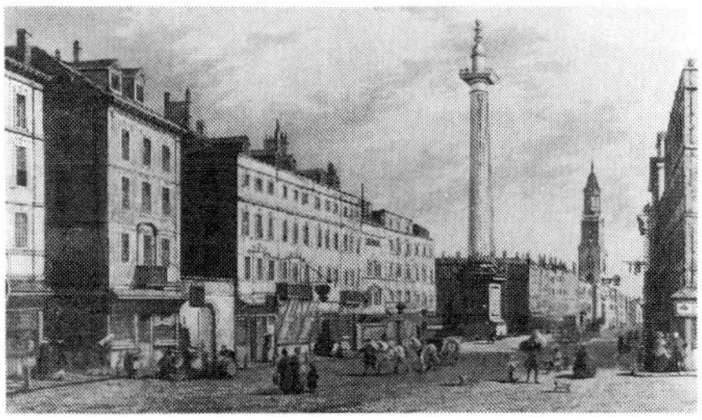

after Canaletto (18th C)

acc. no. 1013
The Monument from Gracechurch Street
oil on canvas: $30 \times 49\frac{1}{2}$ in.
Presented by Oscar C. Berry, 1921

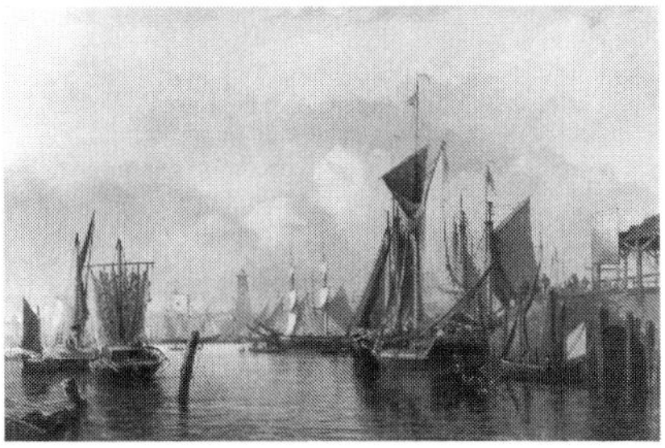

John Wilson Carmichael (1800–68)

acc. no. 1811
Billingsgate Wharf (1852)
oil on canvas: 24×36 in.
signed and dated: *J.W. Carmichael / 1852*
Purchased from the Cooling Galleries, 1969

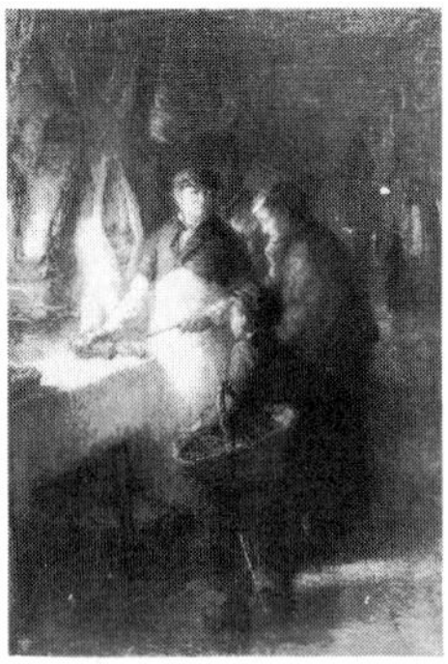

Hugh Carter (1837–1903)

acc. no. 834
Hard Times
oil on canvas: 34×24 in.
signed: *H. Carter*
Presented by the artist's widow, 1904

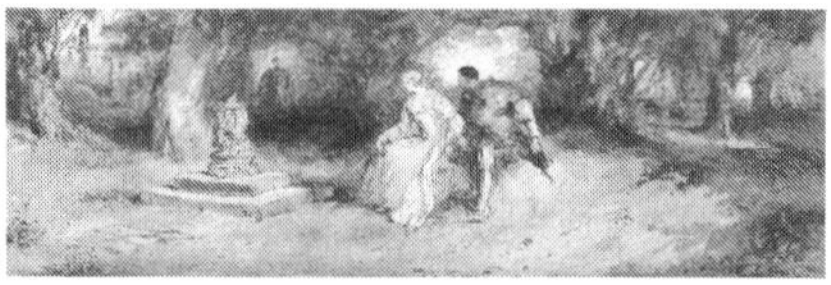

Charles Cattermole (1832–1900)

acc. no. 2256
Lovers Beside a Sundial (1885)
watercolour: $5\frac{3}{4} \times 17\frac{5}{8}$ in.
signed and dated: *Chas Cattermole 85*
Presented by Miss Helen Guiterman, 1985

Christopher Chamberlain (20th C)

acc. no. 1637
Sea Coal Lane (1962)

oil on board: 28 × 36 in.
signed and dated: *C. Chamberlain '62*
Purchased from the artist, 1962

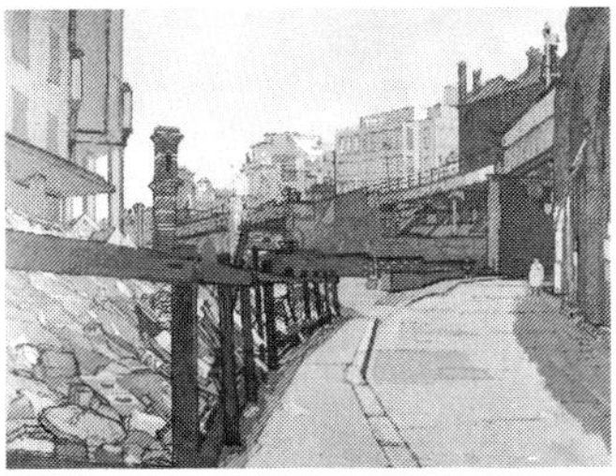

Trevor Chamberlain (b.1933)

acc. no. 1892
Swilling Down, Billingsgate Market (*c.*1971)

oil on canvas: $29\frac{7}{8} \times 19\frac{7}{8}$ in.
signed: *Trevor Chamberlain RSMA NS*
Purchased from the artist, 1971

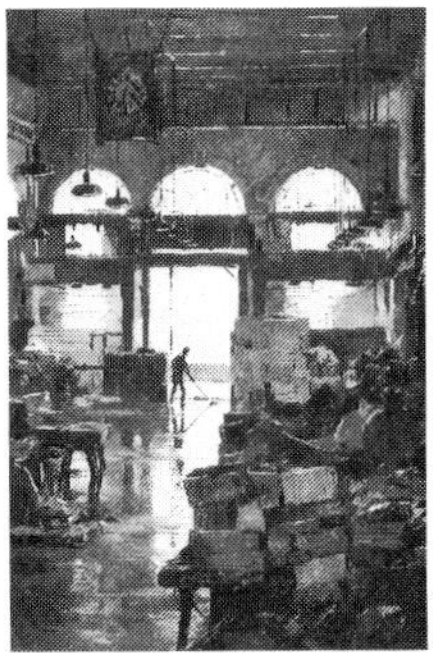

Clifford Charman (b.1910)

acc. no. 2209
Street of Shadows, Greenwich (*c.*1977)

oil on canvas: $29 \times 35\frac{1}{2}$ in.
Purchased from the artist, 1977

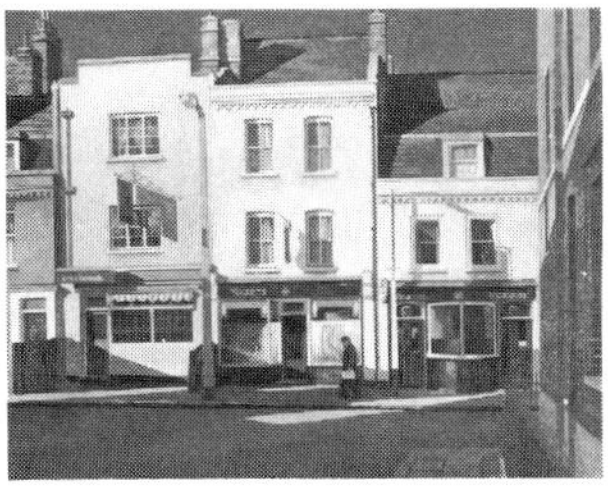

G. Chaumont (19th C)

acc. no. 1593
The South Bank, with Waterloo Bridge (1847)

watercolour heightened with white:
$11\frac{5}{8} \times 18\frac{3}{8}$ in.
signed: *G. Chaumont*; inscribed on verso: *Waterloo Bridge / Seen from and / Near Somerset House / London 1847* and in a different hand: *G. Chaumont / 1847 Waterloo Bridge*
Purchased from F. T. Sabin, 1960

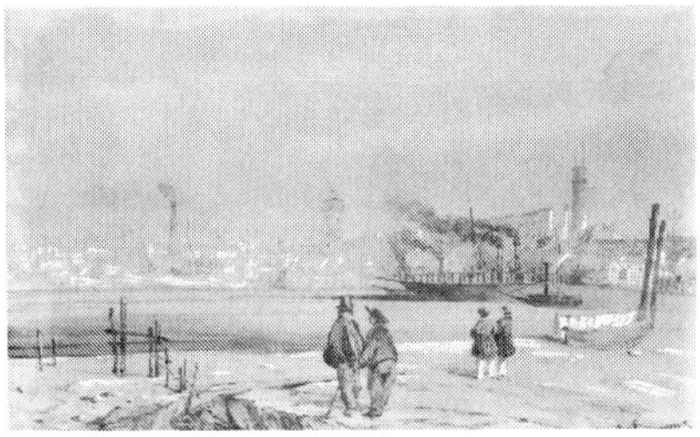

acc. no. 1594
Waterloo Bridge, Looking towards the City (1847)

watercolour heightened with white:
$11\frac{5}{8} \times 18\frac{3}{8}$ in.
signed: *G. Chaumont*; inscribed on verso: *Waterloo Bridge / Somerset House and / S. Paul 1847* and in a different hand: *G. Chaumont/ 1847 / Waterloo Bridge*
Purchased from F. T. Sabin, 1960

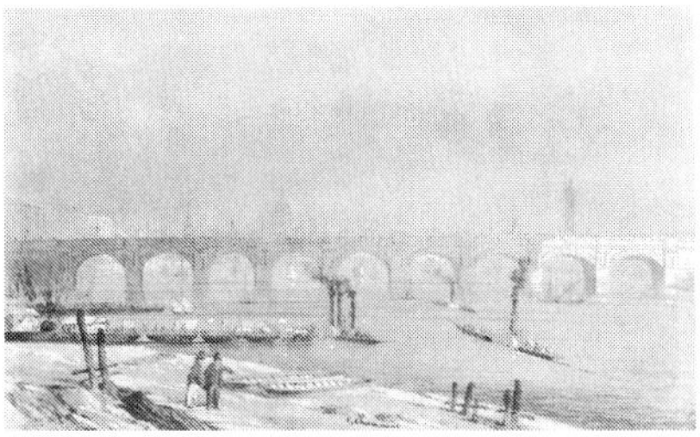

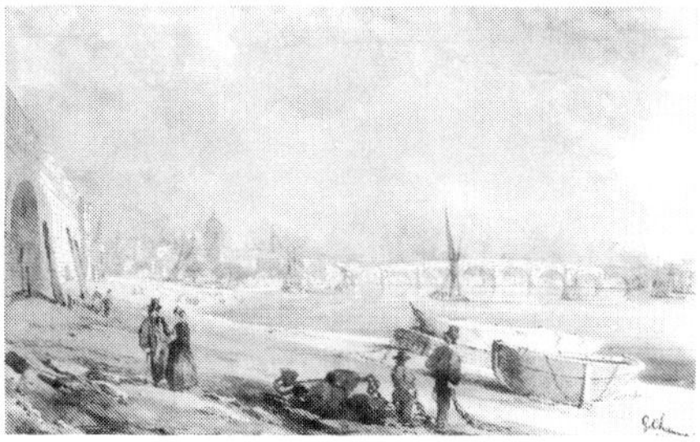

acc. no. 1595
Blackfriars Bridge and the City (1847)

watercolour heightened with white: $11\frac{3}{4} \times 18\frac{1}{2}$ in.
signed: *G. Chaumont*; inscribed on verso: *Blackfriar's Bridge / Somerset House and / S. Paul / London 1847* and in a different hand: *G. Chaumont / 1847*
Purchased from F. T. Sabin, 1960

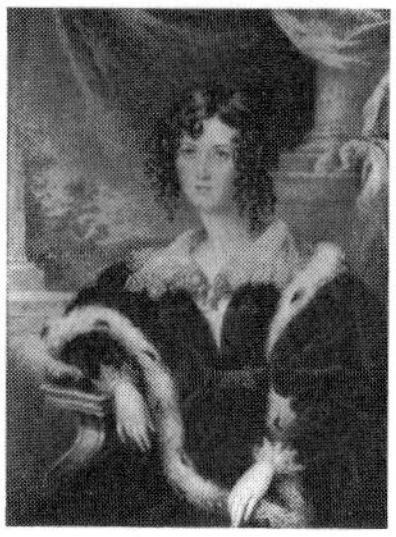

James Warren Childe (1780–1862)

acc. no. 847
Mary Ann Paton (1831)

watercolour on ivory: $7 \times 5\frac{1}{4}$ in.
signed: *Childe*
Presented by the sitter's son, Robert Wood, 1907

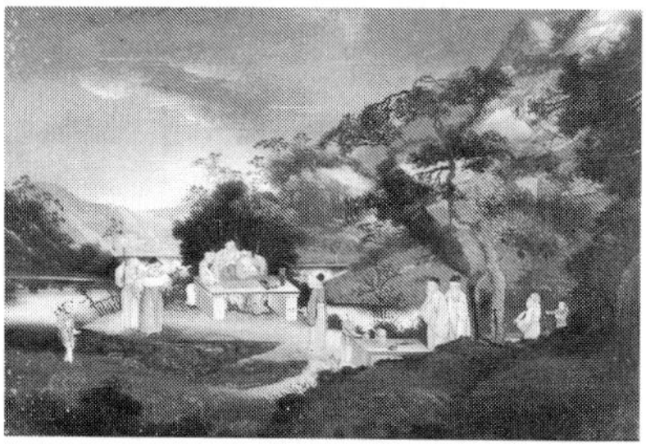

Chinese School

The following eight works were presented by Miss P Flinders Baldwin in 1924.

acc. no. 1060h
Scholars in a Garden (*c.*1800)

mirror painting on glass: $17\frac{3}{4} \times 25\frac{3}{4}$ in. (sight)

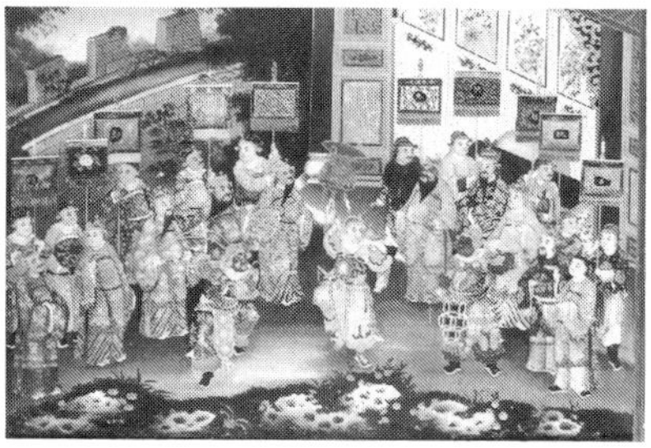

acc. no. 1060a
Unidentified Scene (19th C)

mirror painting on glass: 24 × 33 in. (sight)

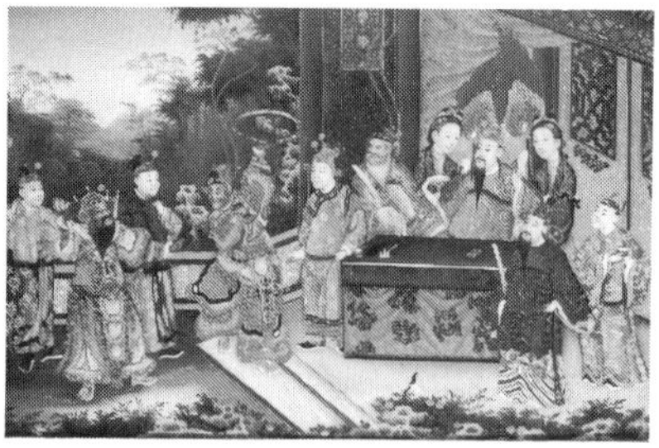

acc. no. 1060b
Unidentified Scene (19th C)

mirror painting on glass: $17\frac{1}{2} \times 25\frac{1}{4}$ in. (sight)

acc. no. 1060c
Unidentified Scene (19th C)
mirror painting on glass: $17\frac{1}{2} \times 25\frac{1}{2}$ in. (sight)

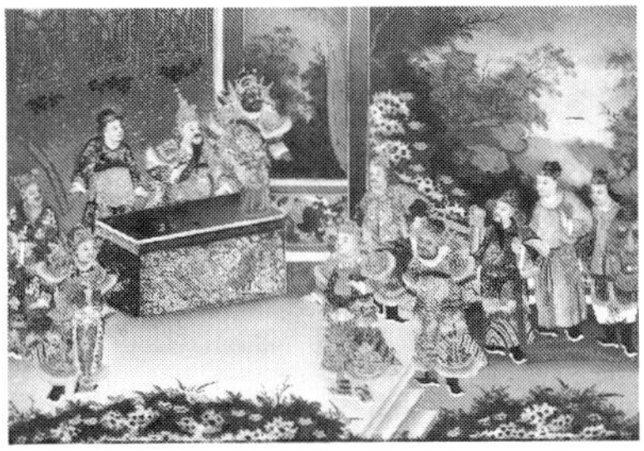

acc. no. 1060d
Unidentified Scene (19th C)
mirror painting on glass: 24 × 33 in. (sight)

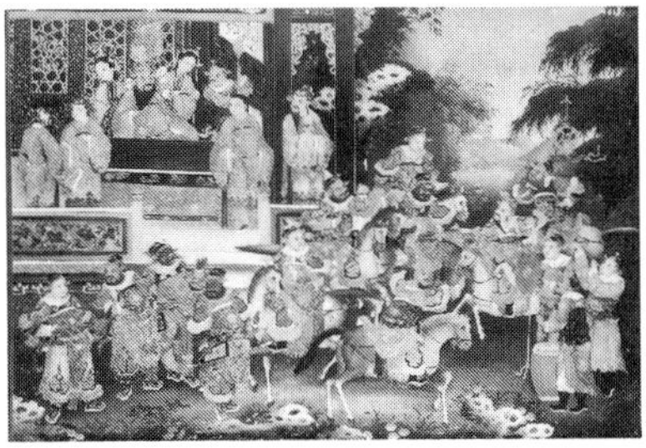

acc. no. 1060e
Unidentified Scene (19th C)
mirror painting on glass: $17\frac{5}{8} \times 25\frac{1}{2}$ in. (sight)

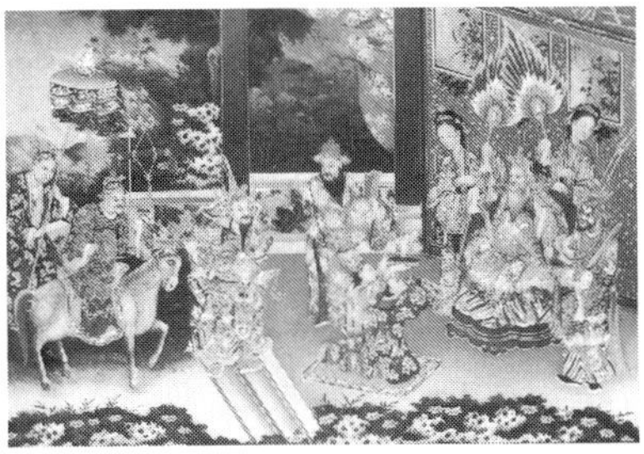

acc. no. 1060f
Unidentified Scene (19th C)
mirror painting on glass: $16 \times 22\frac{1}{2}$ in. (sight)

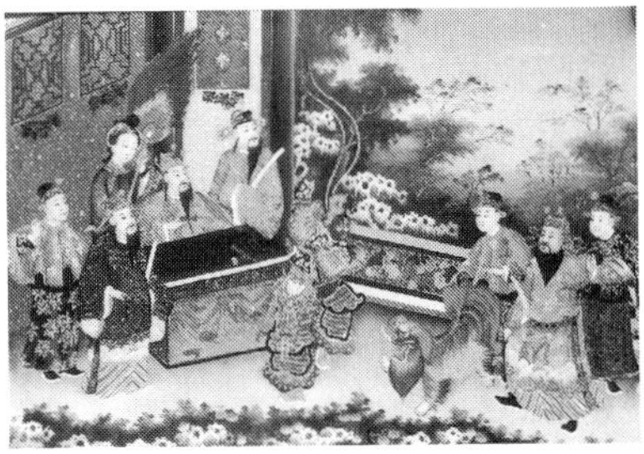

acc. no. 1060g
Unidentified Scene (19th C)
mirror painting on glass: $16 \times 22\frac{1}{2}$ in. (sight)

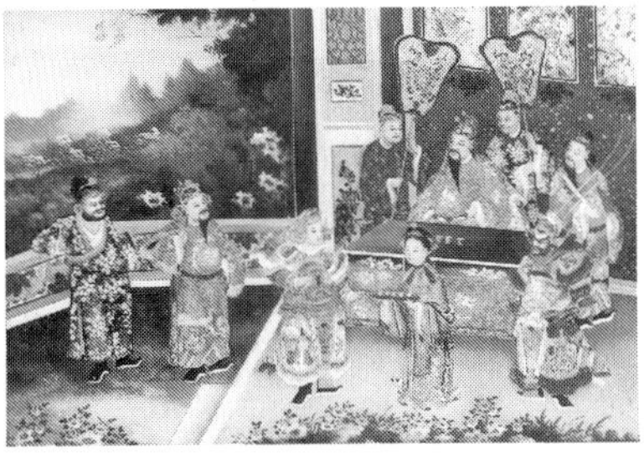

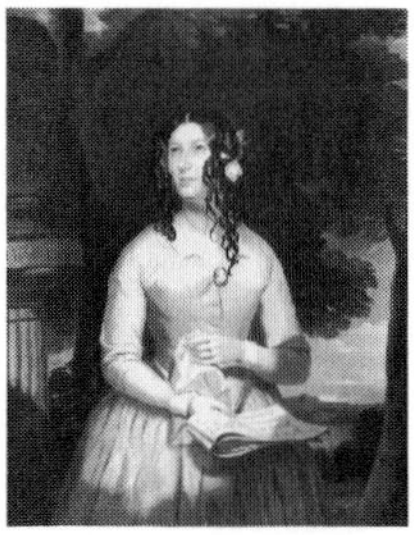

Samuel Chinn (*fl.* 1833–48)

acc. no. 893
Mary Ann Paton (1848)

oil on canvas: 50 × 40 in.
dated: *1848*
Presented by Dr. W. H. Cummings, 1910

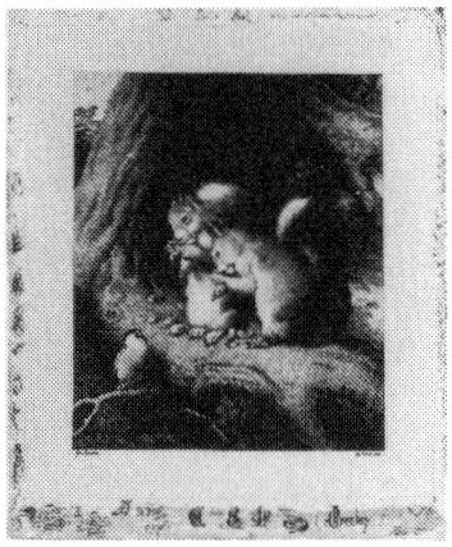

John Chumley (19th C) after Landseer

acc. no. 329
A Piper and a Pair of Nutcrackers (1871)

pen and ink: $9\frac{3}{4} \times 8\frac{3}{8}$ in. (sight)
signed: *John Chumley* and dated: *14 Febr. Y. 1871*; inscribed in the border with doodles and signatures and the dates *14 Febr. Y. / 5 April* and *Feb. 2nd*
Presented by the artist, 1886

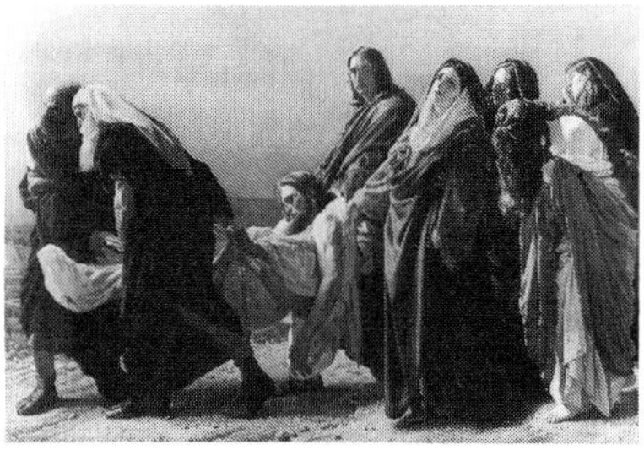

Antonio Ciseri (1821–91)

acc. no. 1022
The Entombment (1883)

oil on canvas: 74 × 108 in.
signed: *A Ciseri F* and dated: *1883*
Presented by Lady Newton, 1922

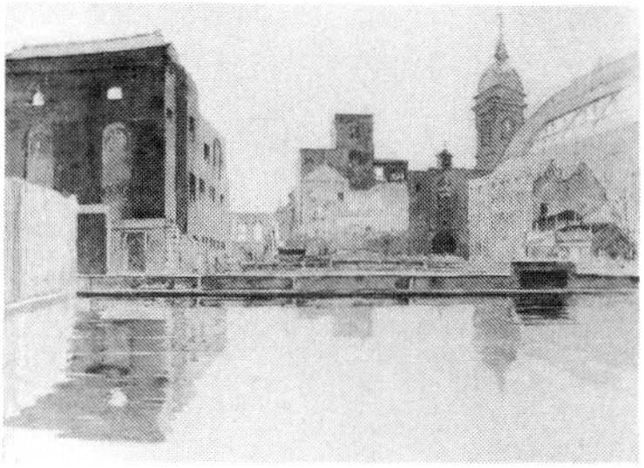

L. Clarke (20th C)

acc. no. 1283
All Hallows the Less Churchyard and Water-tank, Looking South (1943)

watercolour and black chalk: $12\frac{7}{8} \times 17$ in.
signed (mono): *LC.* and signed and dated: *L. CLARKE / FEB / 1943*
Presented by the artist (?) 1944

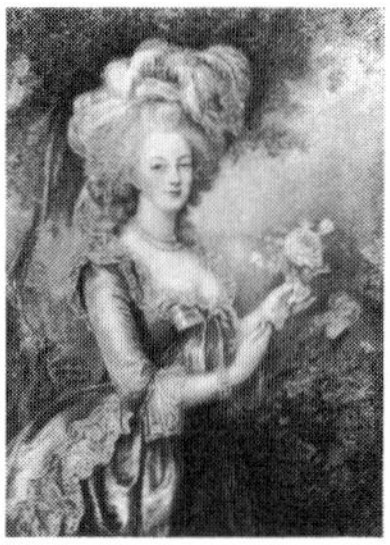

Louisa Campbell Clarke (*fl.* 1887–1907) after Mme Vigée Lebrun

acc. no. 857
Marie Antoinette

watercolour on ivory: $11 \times 8\frac{1}{4}$ in.
Presented by the artist, 1907

William Clerihew (*c.*1814–*c.*1880)

acc. no. 3534
Point Sikree Gully, Rajmahal Hills (1843)
watercolour: $2\frac{7}{8} \times 9\frac{1}{2}$ in.
inscribed and dated on mount: *Point Sikree Gully Rajmahal Hills / 1st Sept. 1843*
Presented by Miss Helen Guiterman, 1985

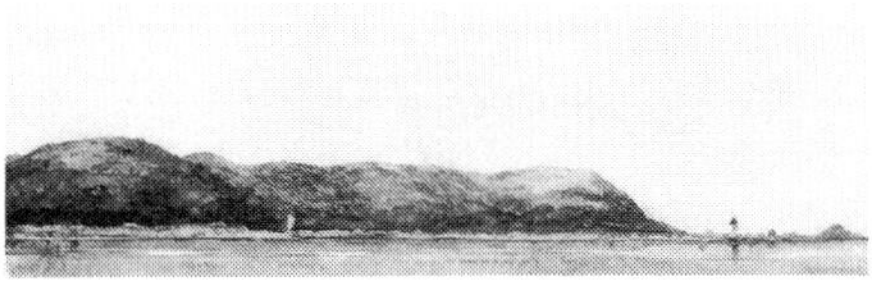

acc. no. 3535
Rajmahal Hills from Above (1843)
watercolour: $3 \times 9\frac{7}{8}$ in.
inscribed on mount: *Rajmahal Hills from Above. 4th Sept. 1843*
Presented by Miss Helen Guiterman, 1985

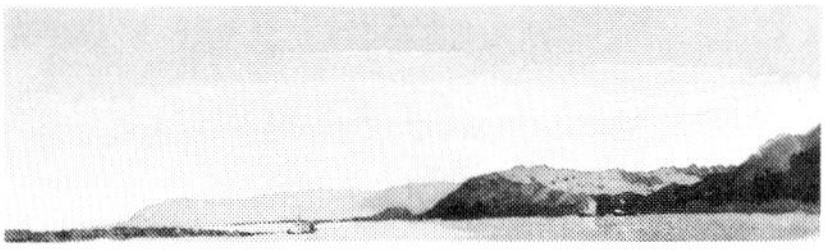

acc. no. 3533
View South West of Cairo (1851)
pencil and wash heightened with white: 7 × 10 in.
inscribed and dated: *South West of Cairo / 25th April 1851*
Presented by Miss Helen Guiterman, 1985

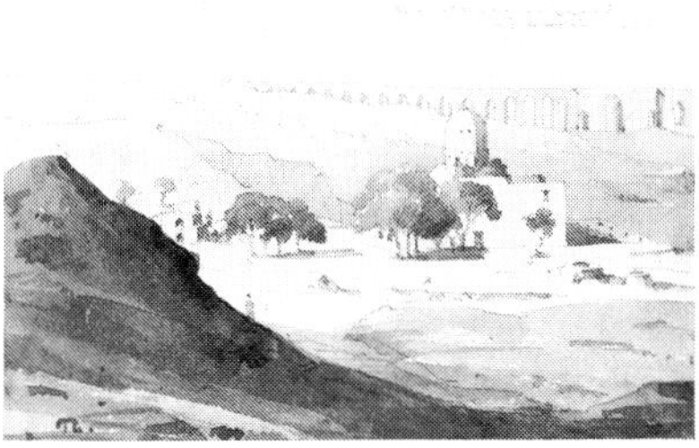

attributed to John Cleveley (1747–86)

acc. no. 1696
Naval Dockyard, Deptford
oil on canvas: 28 × 36 in.
Purchased at Christie's 3.7.1964 (37)

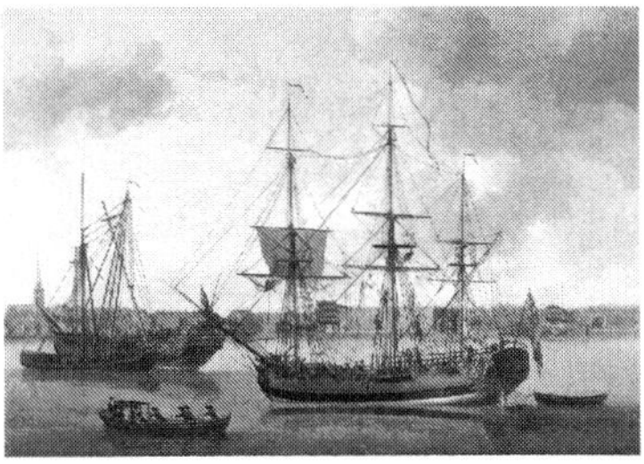

Robert Cleveley (1747–1809)

acc. no. 1614
Billingsgate at High Water (?1772)
watercolour: $30 \times 52\frac{1}{2}$ in.
signed and dated: *Cleveley 1772* (?)
Purchased from F. T. Sabin, 1960

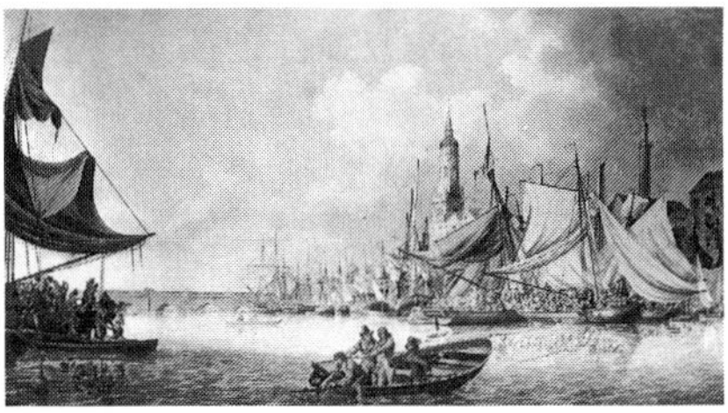

George Clint (1770–1854)

acc. no. 1026
Banquet given by the Corporation to the Prince Regent, the Emperor of Russia and the King of Prussia, June 18 1814
oil on canvas: 50 × 75 in.
Presented by Sir William Dunn, 1923

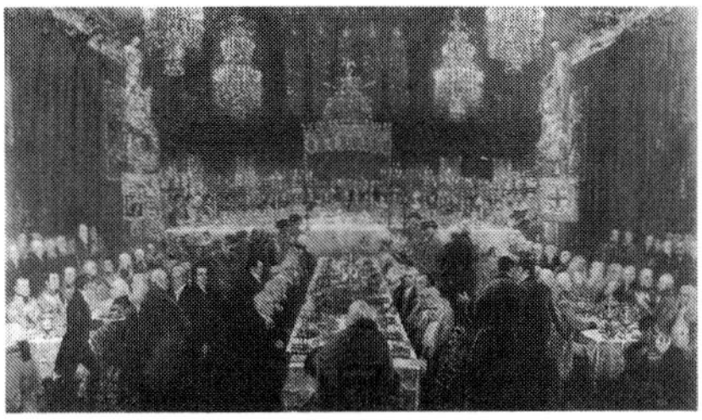

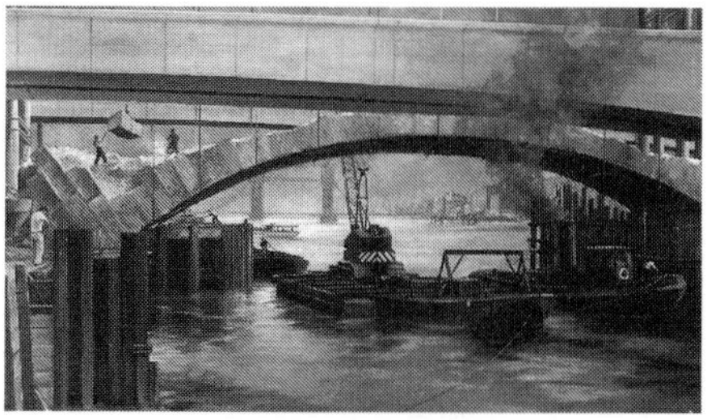

Gordon Close (20th C)

acc. no. 1896
Old London Bridge Makes Way for the New (1971)

oil on canvas: 24 × 40 in.
Purchased from the artist, 1972

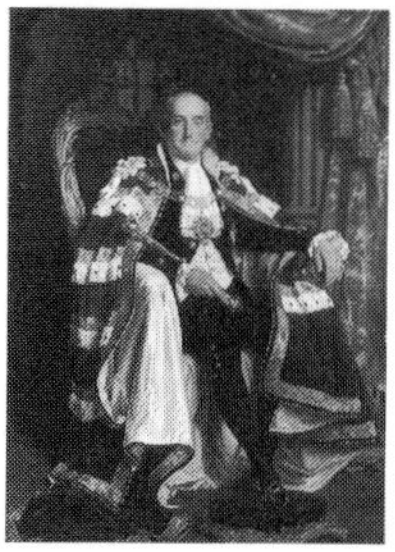

Maurice Frederick Codner (1888–1958)

acc. no. 1373
Sir George Broadbridge, Lord Mayor 1936

oil on canvas: 71 × $48\frac{1}{2}$ in.
signed: *Maurice CODNER*
Presented by the sitter, 1947

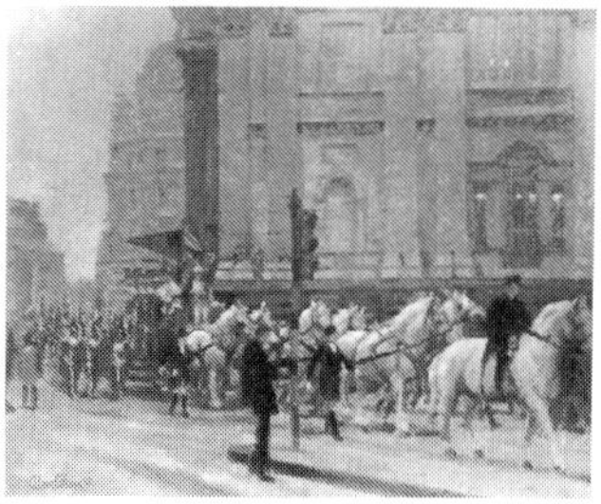

Alex Cohen (20th C)

acc. no. 1807
Starting the Lord Mayor's Show (1968)

oil on hardboard: $24\frac{3}{4}$ × 30 in.
signed and dated: *Alex Cohen 68*
Purchased from the artist, 1969

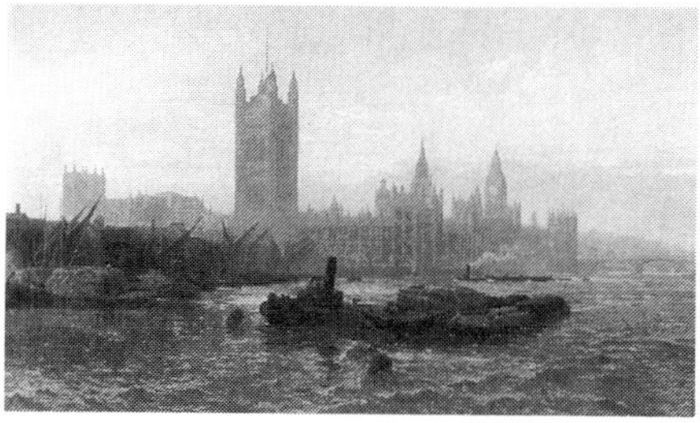

George Vicat Cole (1833–93)

acc. no. 1729
The Palace of Westminster (1892)

oil on canvas: 50 × 84 in.
signed (mono) and dated: *VC 1892*
Purchased from M. Newman, 1966

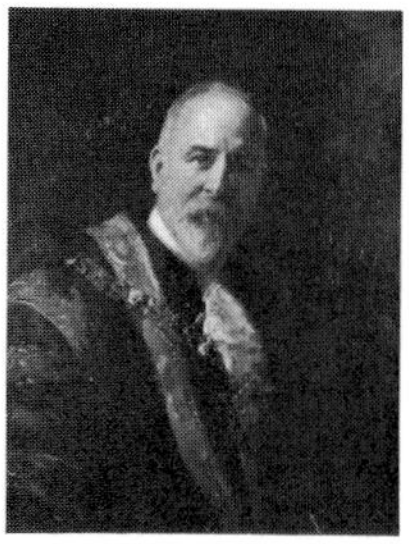

Philip Tennyson Cole (*fl.* 1880–1930)

acc. no. 846
Sir William Treloar, Lord Mayor 1906 (1907)

oil on canvas, cut down to: 36 × 28 in.
Presented by Sir William Dunn, 1907

Rex Vicat Cole (1870–1940)

acc. no. 1099
Demolition of St. Olave's Tooley Street, 1927
oil on canvas: 37 × 46 in.
signed: *REX VICAT COLE*
Presented by Miss Margaret Chigwell, 1935

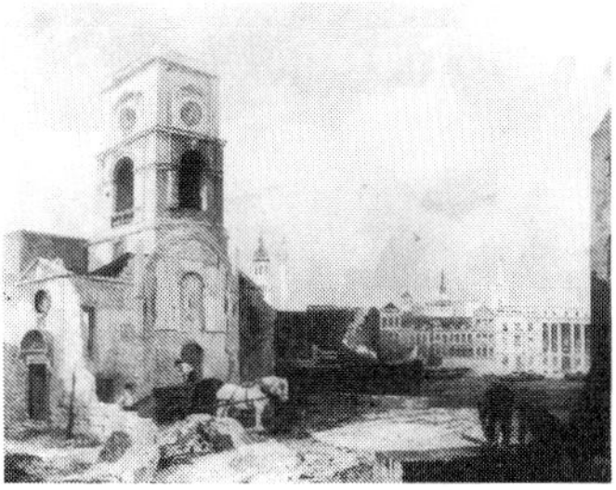

The Hon. John Collier (1850–1934)

acc. no. 577
Clytemnestra (1882)
oil on canvas: 94 × 58 in.
signed and dated: *John Collier 1882*
Presented by Mrs. Mary Harrison, 1893

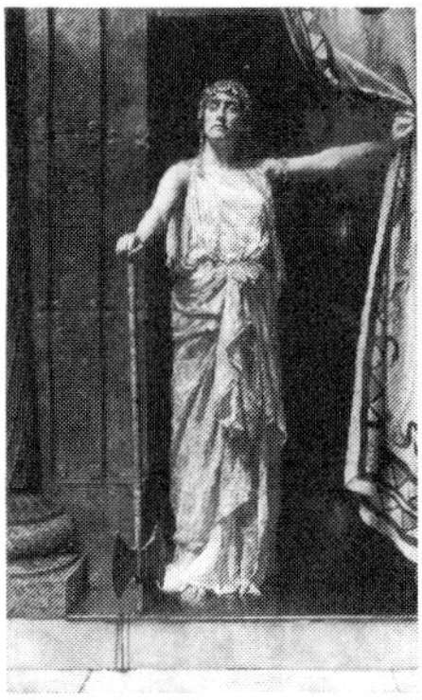

acc. no. 1025
Sir George Williams, Founder of the Y.M.C.A. (1888)
oil on canvas: 82 × 44 in.
signed: *John Collier*
Presented by the sitter's son, Howard Williams, 1923

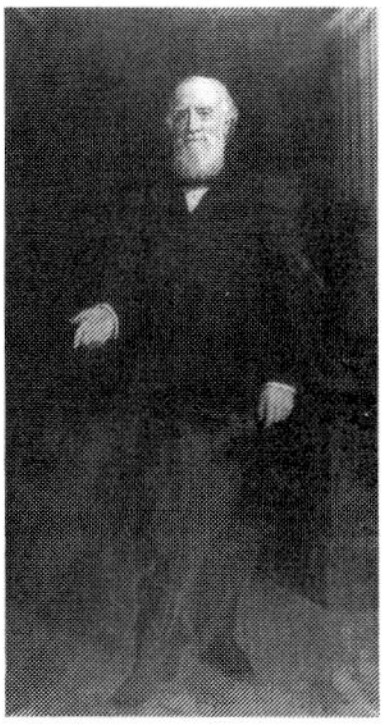

acc. no. 1237
Sir Charles Hall, Recorder of London (1895)
oil on canvas: 50 × 40 in.
signed: *John / Collier* and inscribed: *RIGHT HON SIR CHARLES HALL / KCMO QC MP / RECORDER OF LONDON*
Presented by Lady Holland, 1939

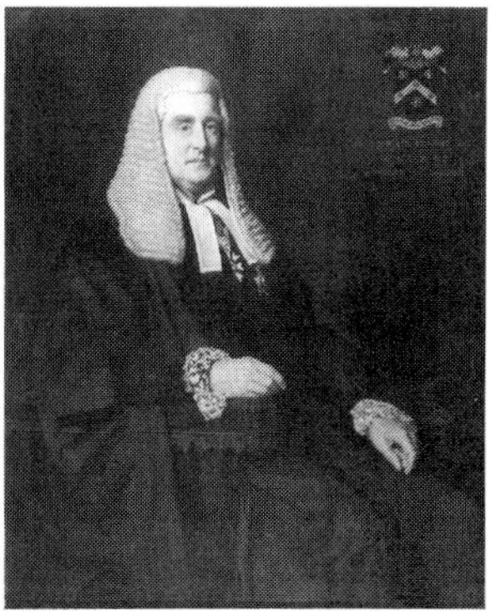

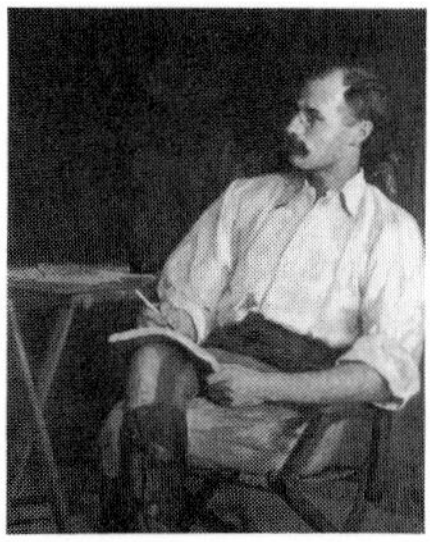

acc. no. 772
George Warrington Steevens, War Correspondent (1900)

oil on canvas: 46 × 36 in.
signed and dated: *John Collier / 1900*
Presented to the City of London School by some of his friends, 1900

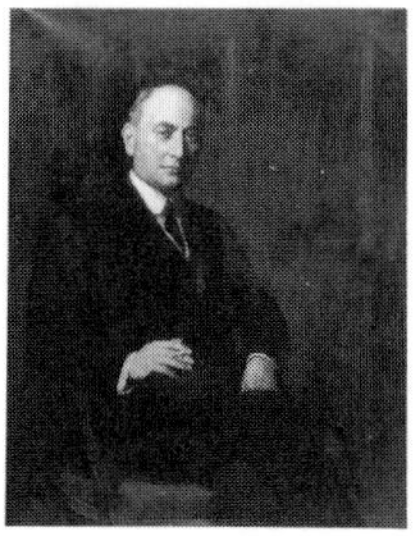

acc. no. 1284
Sir Landon Ronald, Principal of Guildhall School of Music 1910–1938

oil on canvas: $49\frac{1}{2} \times 39\frac{1}{2}$ in.
signed and dated: *John Collier / 1928*
Presented by a body of subscribers, chiefly Lady Hodder-Williams in memory of her husband, Sir J. E. Hodder-Williams, to the Guildhall School of Music, *c.*1928

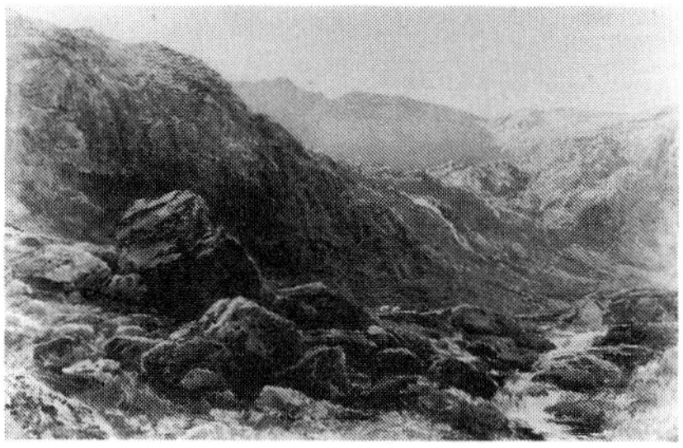

Thomas Collier (1840–91)

acc. no. 889
Llanberis Pass (1875)

watercolour: 15 × 23 in.
signed and dated: *T. Collier 1875*
Bequeathed by James Thomas Slater, 1909

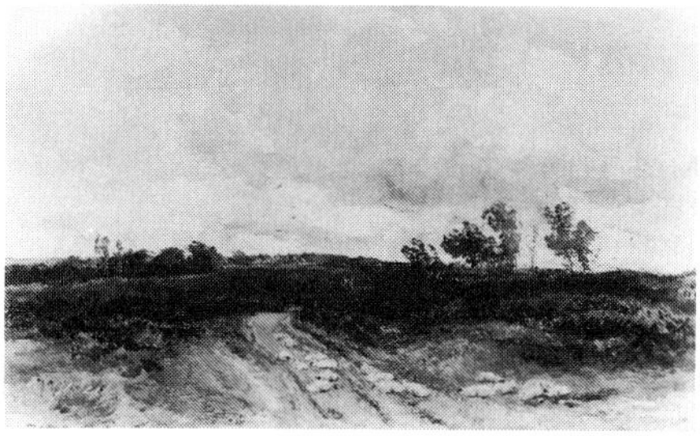

acc. no. 890
Moorland Scene (1878)

watercolour: $11\frac{1}{2} \times 19$ in.
signed and dated: *T. Collier 1878*
Bequeathed by James Thomas Slater, 1909

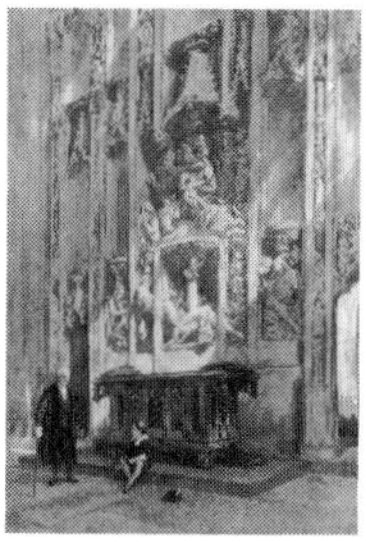

William Collingwood (1819–1903)

acc. no. 1990
Christchurch, Hants. (1851)

watercolour: $19\frac{1}{2} \times 13\frac{1}{2}$ in.
signed, dated and inscribed: *Christ Church, Hants. / W. Collingwood 1851*
Presented by Miss Helen Guiterman, 1985

William Collins (1788–1847)

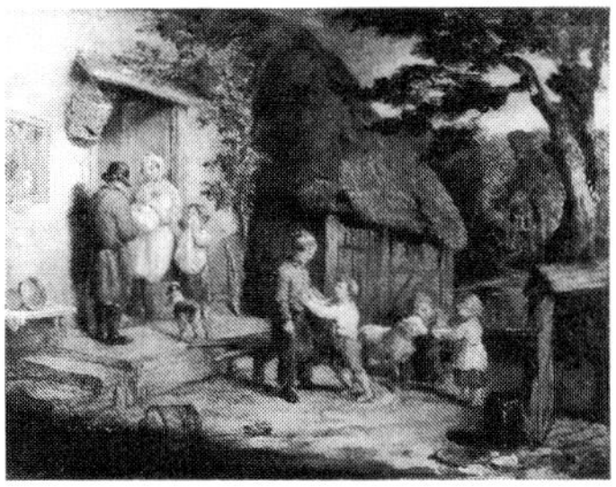

acc. no. 644
The Pet Lamb (*c.*1813)

oil on canvas: 14 × 17½ in.
Bequeathed by Charles Gassiot, 1902

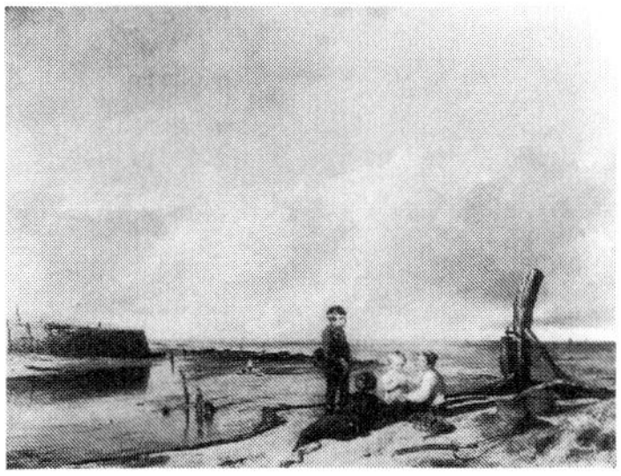

acc. no. 645
Shrimp Boys at Cromer (1815)

oil on canvas: 34 × 44½ in.
signed: *W Collins*
Bequeathed by Charles Gassiot, 1902

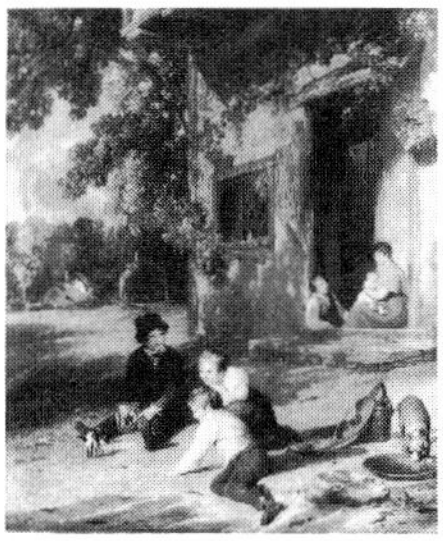

acc. no. 648
The Kitten Deceived (1816)

oil on canvas: 30½ × 25½ in.
signed and dated: *W Collins / 1816*
Bequeathed by Charles Gassiot, 1902

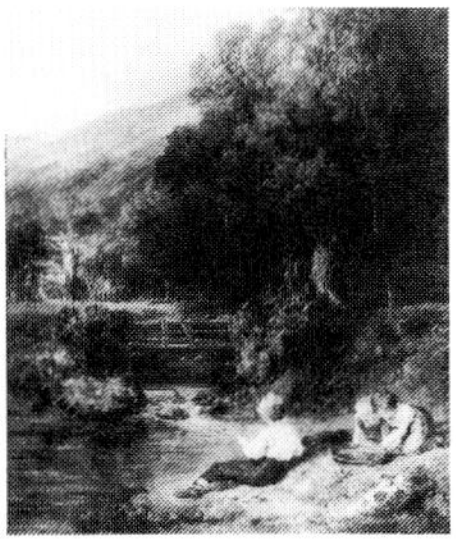

acc. no. 646
Borrowdale (?1821)

oil on canvas: 30 × 25 in.
signed and dated: *W. Collins 1821* (?)
Bequeathed by Charles Gassiot, 1902

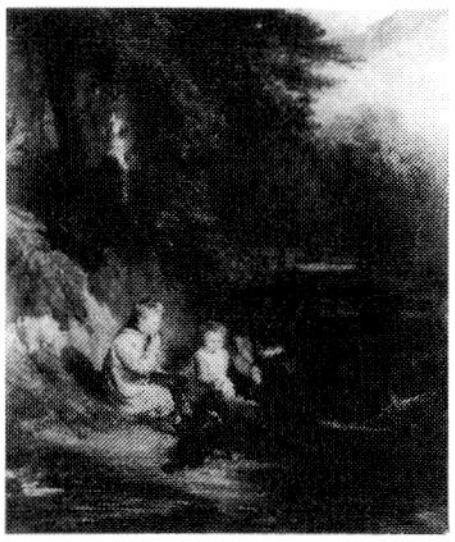

acc. no. 647
The Nutting Party (1831)

oil on canvas: 27 × 23 in.
Bequeathed by Charles Gassiot, 1902

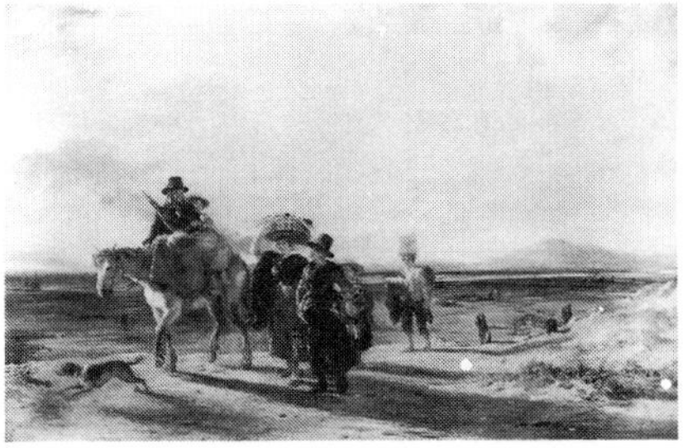

acc. no. 643
Barmouth Sands (Welsh Peasants Crossing the Sands to Market) (1835)
oil on canvas: $28\frac{1}{2} \times 42$ in.
signed and dated: *W Collins / 1835*
Bequeathed by Charles Gassiot, 1902

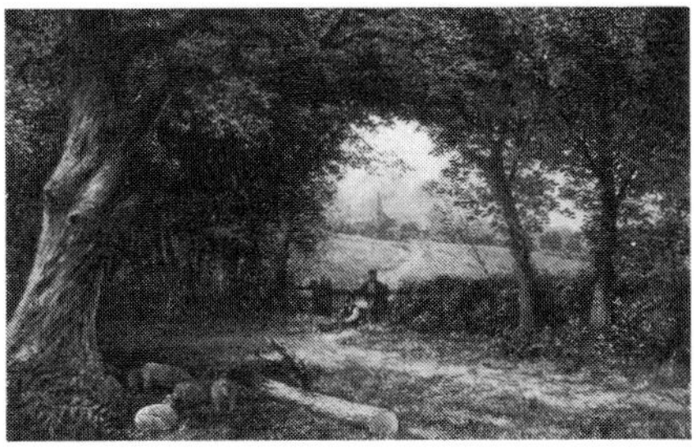

Alfred Conquest (*fl.* 1880–1904)

acc. no. 1731
Surrey Landscape (?1881)
oil on canvas: $19\frac{3}{4} \times 30$ in.
signed and dated: *A. Conquest 1881* (?)
Transferred from the Mayor's Court, 1966

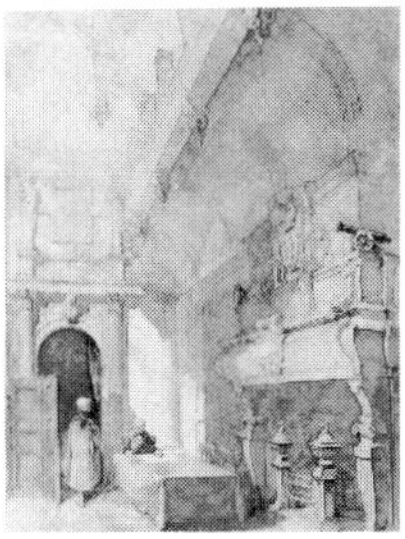

Alfred Charles Conrade (1863–1955)

acc. no. 3555
Salle-à-Manger, Charterhouse (1913)
pencil and watercolour: $11\frac{1}{2} \times 8\frac{3}{4}$ in.
signed and dated: *A.C. CONRADE 1913.* and *CONRAD . . .* (?); inscribed on verso: *43 London / Salle-ă-Manger, Charterhouse.*
Presented by Miss Helen Guiterman, 1985

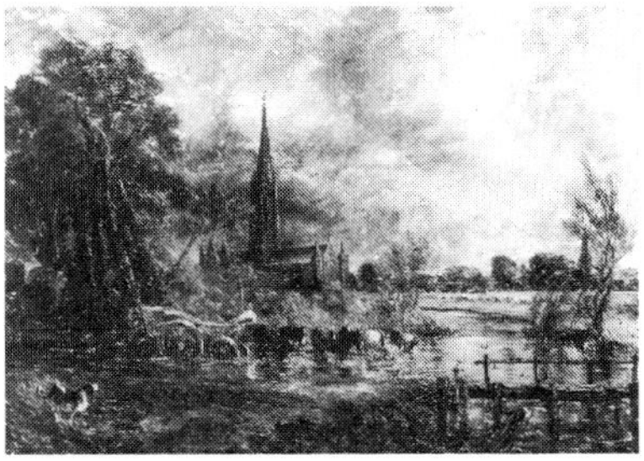

John Constable (1776–1837)

acc. no. 649
Salisbury Cathedral from the Meadows (1829–30)
oil on canvas: $53\frac{1}{2} \times 74$ in.
Bequeathed by Charles Gassiot, 1902

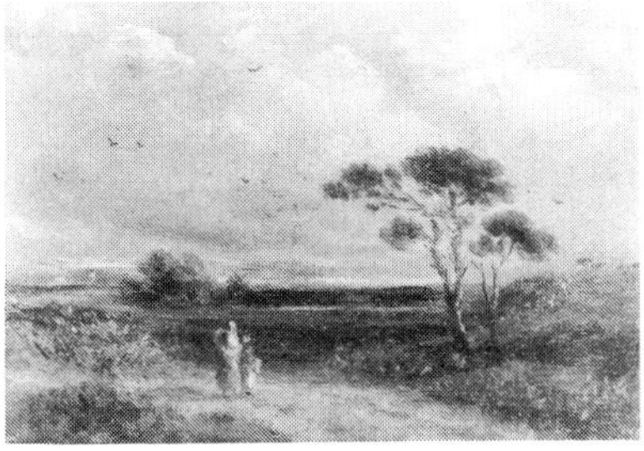

follower of John Constable (19th C)

acc. no. 650
Near East Bergholt
oil on canvas: $7 \times 9\frac{1}{2}$ in.
Bequeathed by Charles Gassiot, 1902

attributed to Lionel Bicknell Constable (1828–87)

acc. no. 651
Landscape with Windmill

oil on paper on millboard: $9\frac{1}{4} \times 14\frac{1}{2}$ in.
Bequeathed by Charles Gassiot, 1902

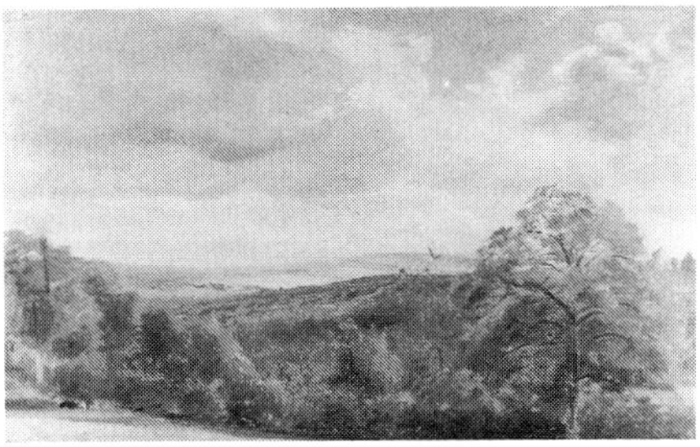

Alan D. Cooke (20th C)

acc. no. 1852
August Morning, Remarkables Range, Lake Wakatipu (1970)

oil on hardboard: 24 × 30 in.
signed and dated: *ALAN D COOKE '70*
Presented by the City of Dunedin, New Zealand, 1970

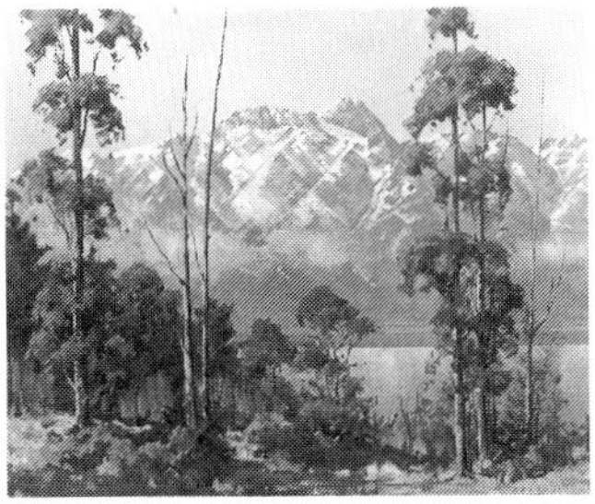

Cecil Cooke (20th C)

acc. no. 1808
The Heart of the City (1969)

oil on canvas: 25 × 30 in.
signed: *Cecil Cooke*
Purchased from the artist, 1969

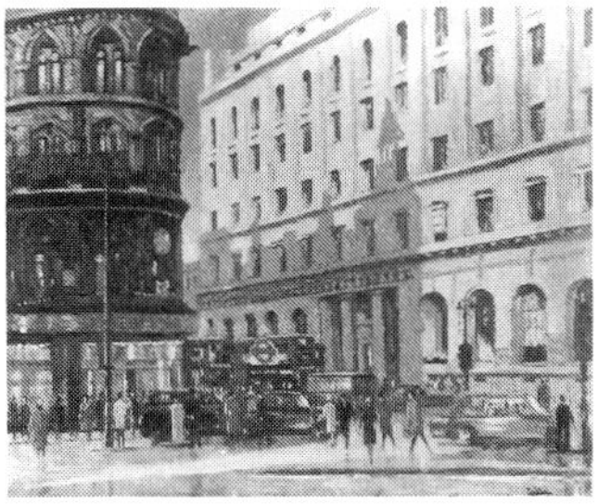

Edward William Cooke (1811–80)

acc. no. 653
Salerno (1849)

oil on canvas: 24 × 39 in.
signed and dated: *E W Cooke. 1849*
Bequeathed by Charles Gassiot, 1902

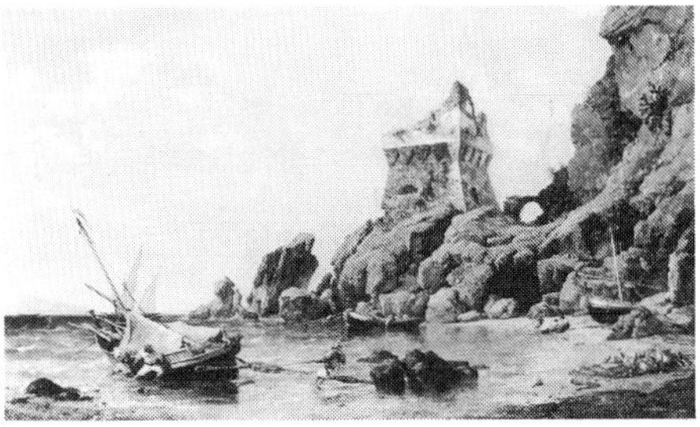

acc. no. 652
Dutch Pincks, Scheveningen (1860)

oil on canvas: $26\frac{1}{2} \times 42\frac{1}{2}$ in.
signed and dated: *E.W. COOKE ARA. 1860.*
Bequeathed by Charles Gassiot, 1902

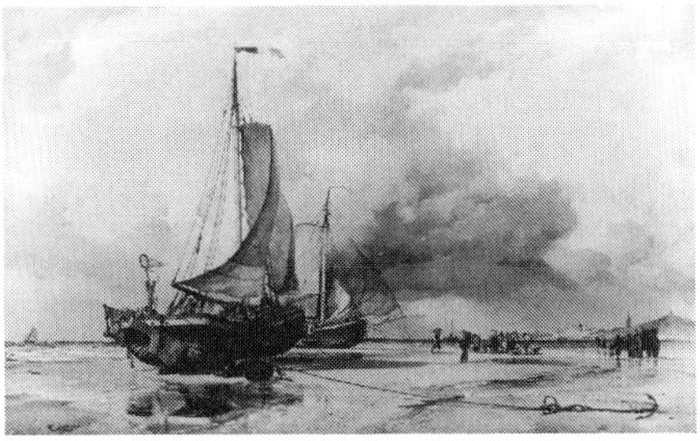

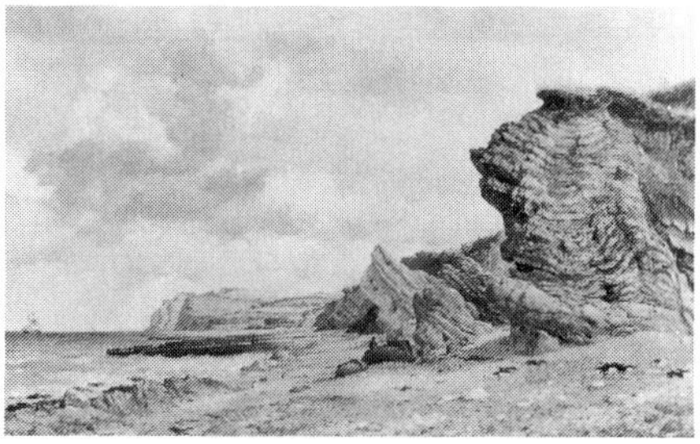

acc. no. 1658
Triassic Cliffs, Blue Anchor, North Somerset (1866)

oil on canvas: $16\frac{1}{2} \times 26$ in.
signed: *E.W. Cooke.*
Presented by John Byram, 1963

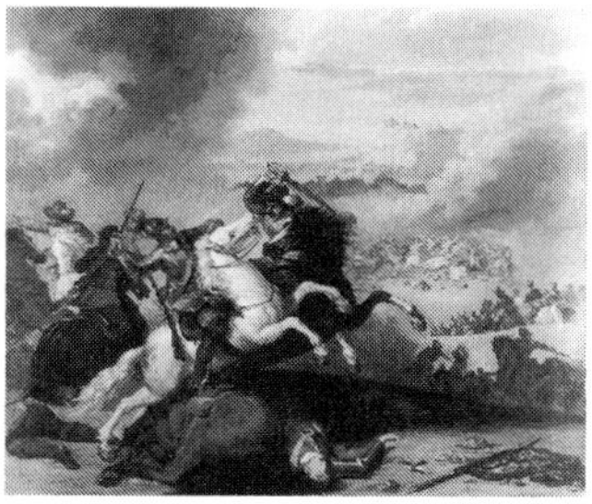

attributed to Abraham Cooper (1787–1868)

acc. no. 433
Battle Piece

oil on canvas: 14×16 in.
Bequeathed by William Dunnett, 1888

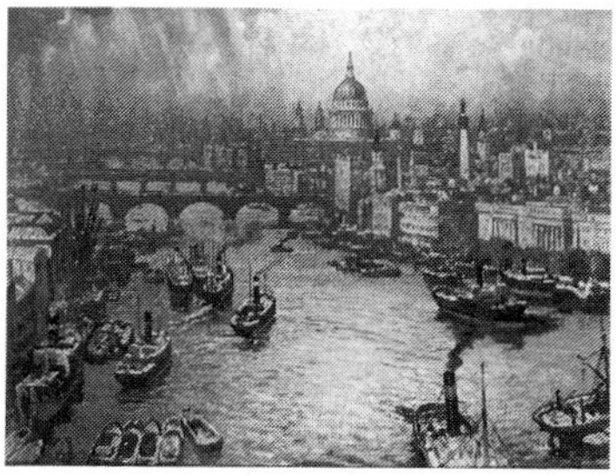

Alfred Egerton Cooper (1883–1974)

acc. no. 1908
The Pool of London (1913)

oil on canvas: 28×36 in.
signed and dated: *A.E. COOPER / 1913*
Purchased from the Churchill Gallery, 1972

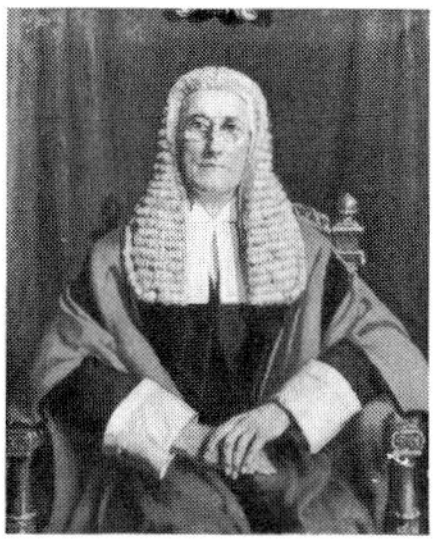

acc. no. 1492
Sir Gerald Dodson

oil on canvas: $40\frac{3}{8} \times 33\frac{3}{4}$ in.
signed: *AE COOPER*
Presented by the sitter, 1952

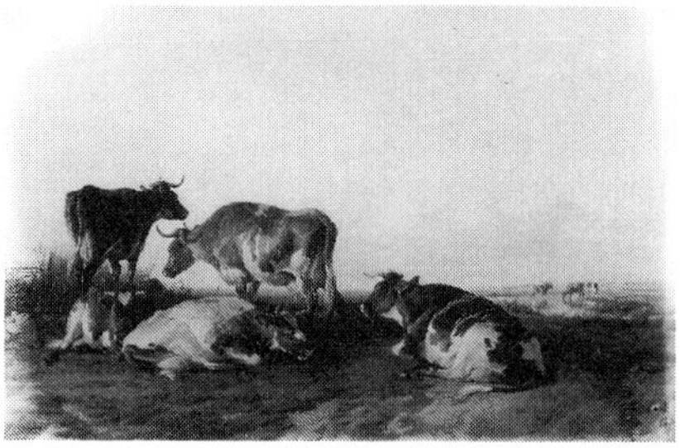

Thomas Sidney Cooper (1803–1902)

acc. no. 655
Landscape and Cattle (1868)

oil on canvas: 24×36 in.
signed and dated: *T. Sidney. Cooper / 1868*
Bequeathed by Charles Gassiot, 1902

acc. no. 355
Landscape and Cattle
watercolour: 13 × 17 in.
Bequeathed by William Dunnett, 1888

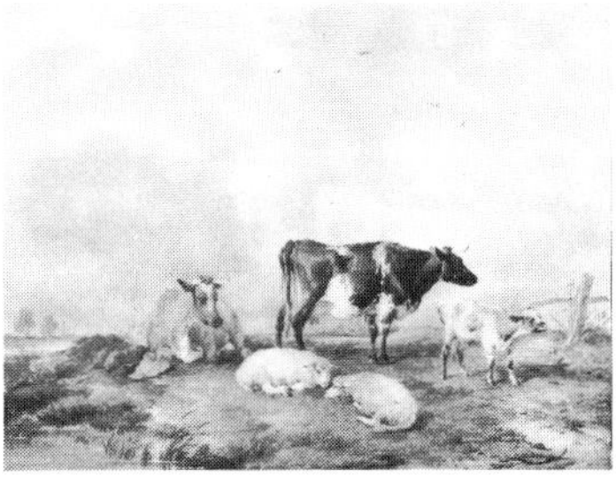

acc. no. 656
Canterbury Meadows
oil on panel: 10 × 8 in.
Bequeathed by Charles Gassiot, 1902

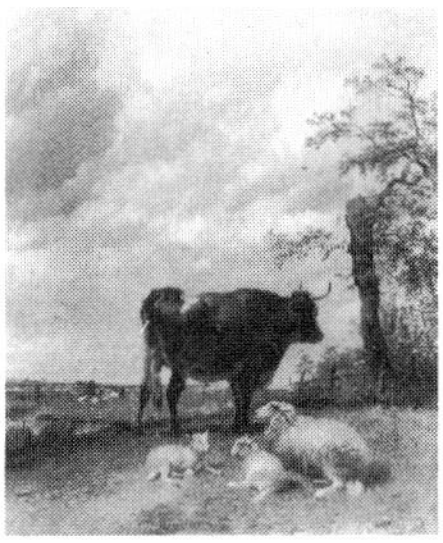

Sir Arthur Stockdale Cope (1857–1940)

acc. no. 1382
Sir Joseph Cockfield Dimsdale, Lord Mayor 1901 (1902)
oil on canvas: 90 × 64 in.
Presented by the sitter's grandson, Sir John Holdsworth Dimsdale, 1948

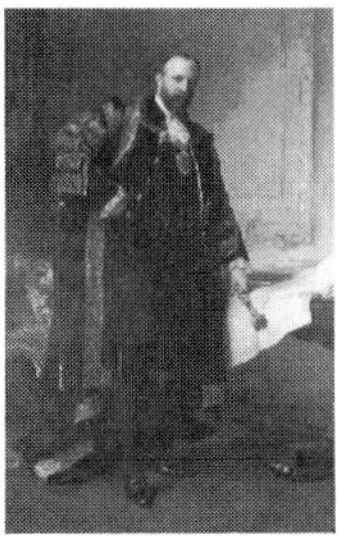

John Singleton Copley (1738–1815)

acc. no. 43
The Defeat of the Floating Batteries at Gibraltar, September 1782 (1783–1791)
oil on canvas: 214 × 297 in.
Commissioned by the Corporation, 1783

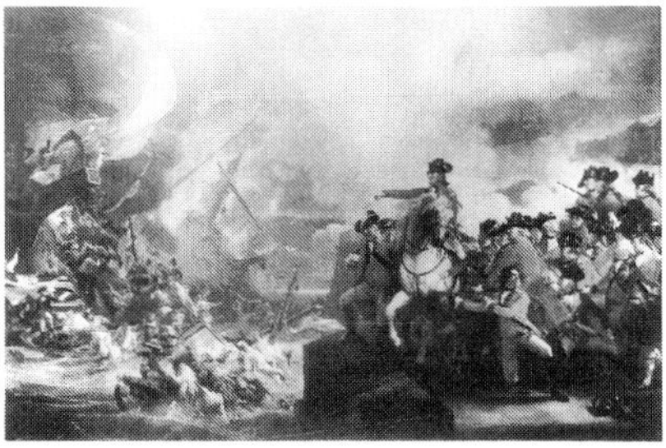

acc. no. 59
Charles, 2nd Earl and 1st Marquis Cornwallis (*c.*1795)
oil on canvas: 57 × 45 in.
Presented by Alderman Boydell, 1795

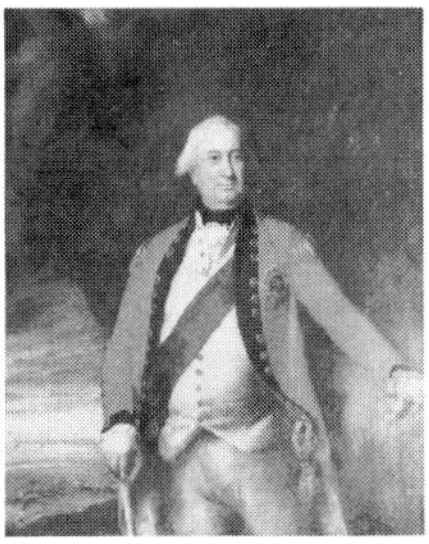

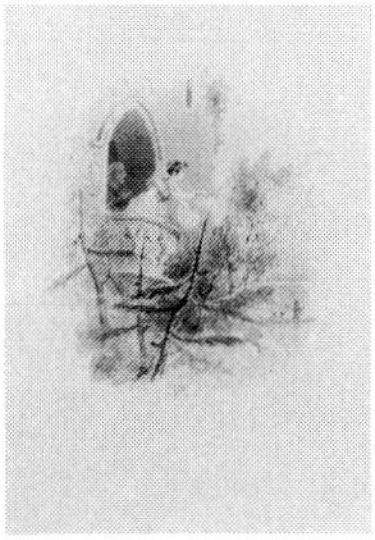

Henry Corbould (1787–1844)

The following seven drawings were presented by Felix Joseph in 1890.

acc. no. 488
Julia waving a Greeting to Udolph (illustration to Thomas Campbell's 'Theodric')

pen and grey ink and wash: $4\frac{7}{8} \times 3\frac{1}{8}$ in. (whole sheet)

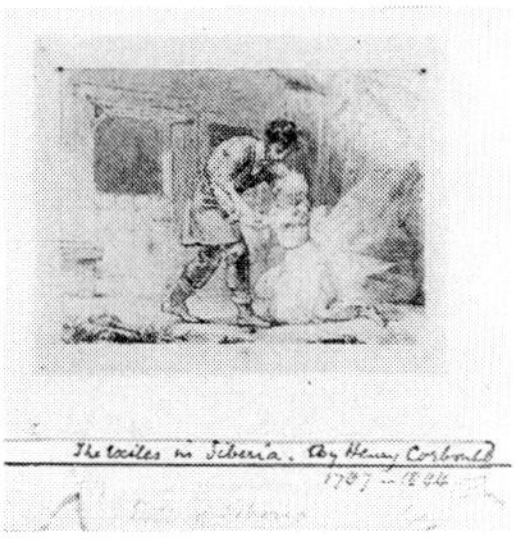

acc. no. 489
The Exiles in Siberia

pen and grey ink and wash: $2\frac{1}{4} \times 1\frac{3}{4}$ in. (size of image)

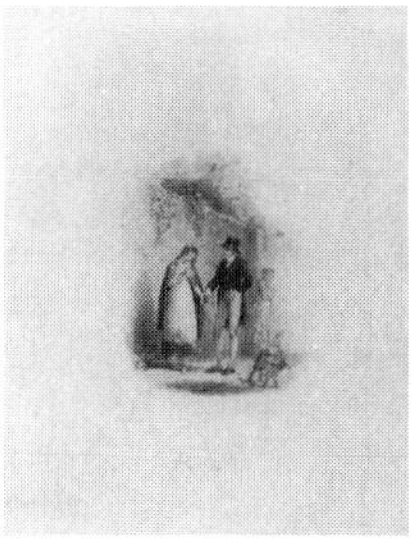

acc. no. 490
A Gentleman giving Alms to a Beggar Girl

pen and grey ink and wash, slightly touched with white: $5\frac{7}{8} \times 4\frac{1}{4}$ in. (whole sheet)

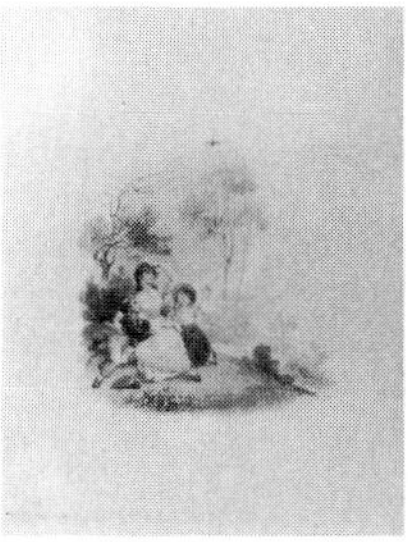

acc. no. 491
Children Looking at a Bird

pen and grey ink and wash: $5\frac{3}{8} \times 4\frac{1}{8}$ in. (whole sheet)

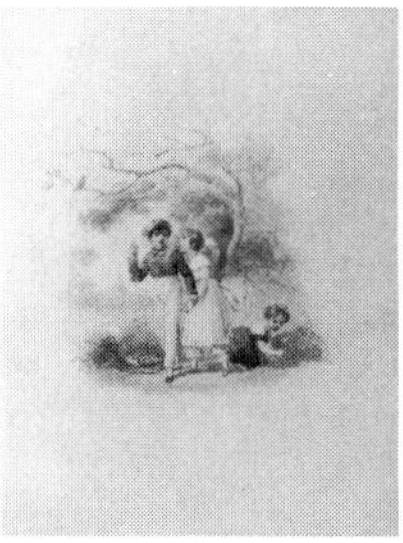

acc. no. 492
Hark! the Nightingale

pen and grey ink and wash, slightly touched with white: $4\frac{3}{4} \times 3\frac{3}{4}$ in. (whole sheet)

acc. no. 493
Fitz-James and the dying Blanche of Devan (illustration to Sir Walter Scott's 'The Lady of the Lake')
pen and grey ink and wash: $4\frac{7}{8} \times 4\frac{1}{8}$ in. (whole sheet)

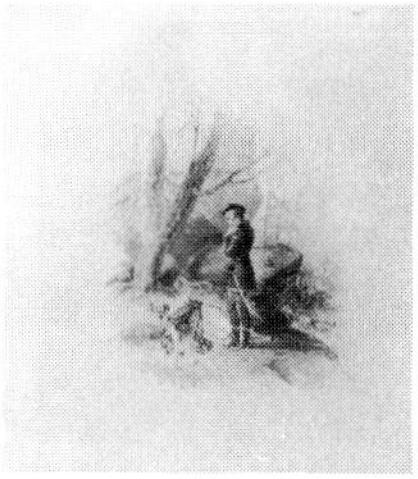

acc. no. 494
Rachel mourns the Dying Robert (Crabbe's 'Tales of the Hall', Book XXI)
grey wash heightened with white: $2\frac{3}{4} \times 2\frac{1}{4}$ in.

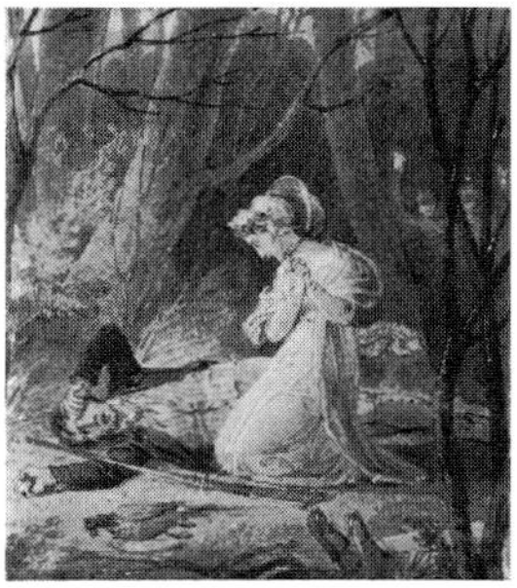

attributed to Henry Corbould (1787–1844)
(accessioned *c.*1890, source unknown)

acc. no. 1449
The Marriage at Cana
grey ink and wash: 5 × 4 in. (whole sheet)
inscription trimmed at top, and further numbered: *N° 1.*

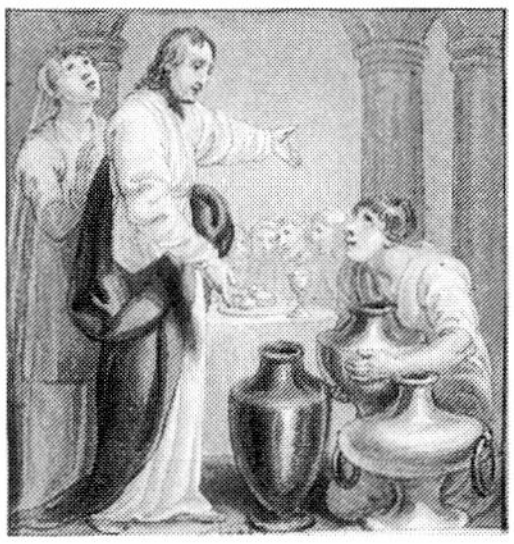

acc. no. 1450
The Miraculous Draught of Fishes
grey ink and wash: $4\frac{3}{4} \times 4\frac{1}{4}$ in. (whole sheet)
inscribed: *N° 2*

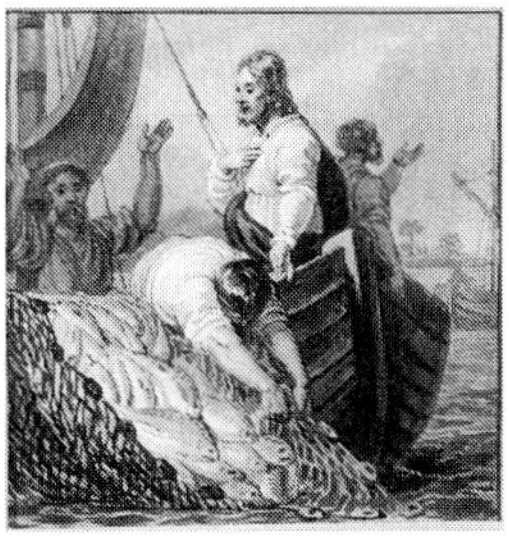

acc. no. 1451
Christ and the Rich Man with the Dying Son
grey ink and wash: $4\frac{3}{4} \times 4\frac{1}{4}$ in. (whole sheet)
inscribed: *N° 3*

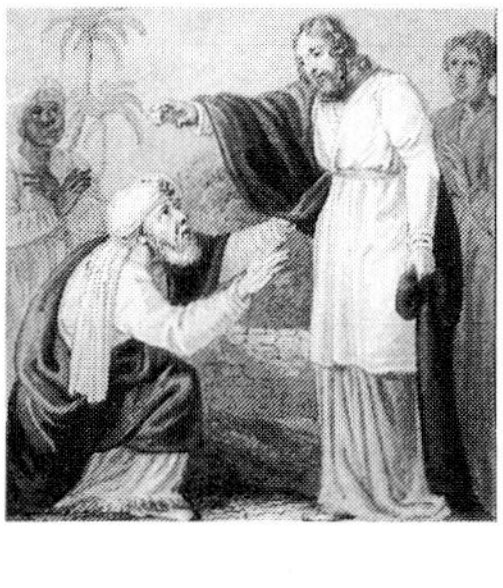

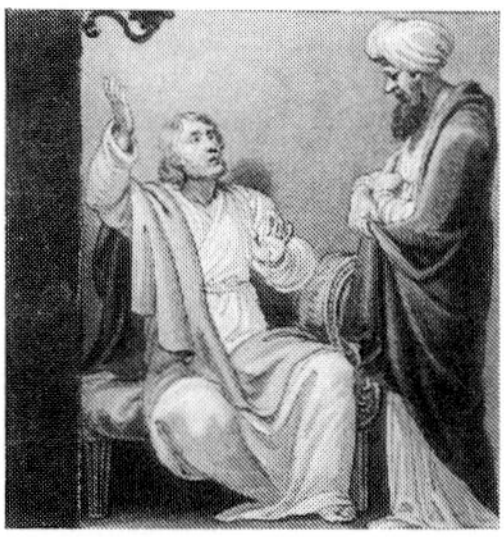

acc. no. 1452
Christ Preaching

grey ink and wash: $5 \times 4\frac{1}{4}$ in. (whole sheet)
inscribed: *N° 4*

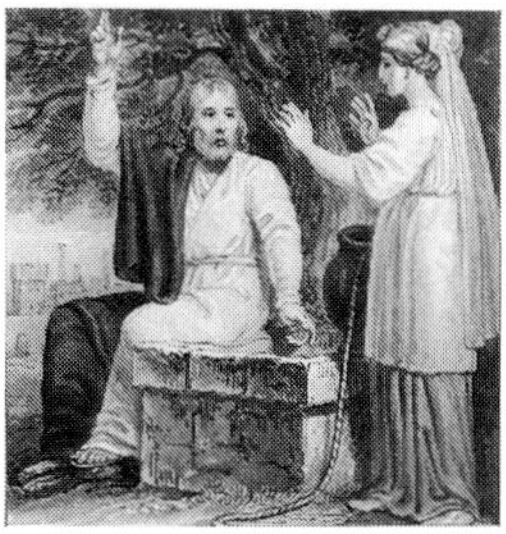

acc. no. 1453
Christ and the Woman of Samaria

grey ink and wash: $4\frac{3}{4} \times 4\frac{1}{4}$ in. (whole sheet)
inscribed: *N° 5*

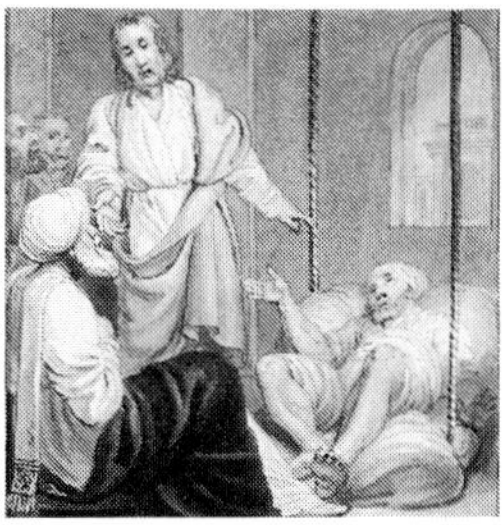

acc. no. 1454
Christ healing the Paralysed Man let Down by Ropes

grey ink and wash: $5 \times 4\frac{1}{4}$ in. (whole sheet)
inscribed: *N° 6.* and (in a different hand): *14*

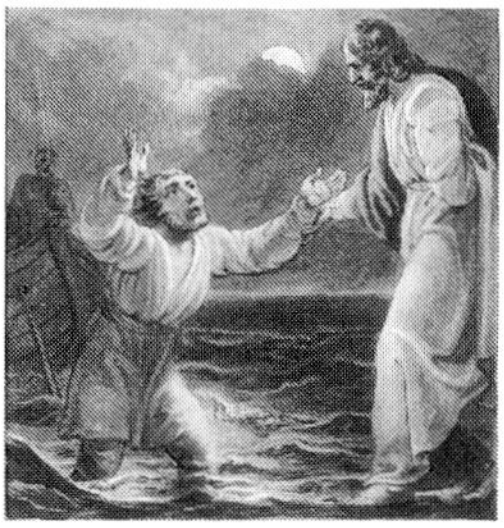

acc. no. 1455
Christ Walking on the Water

grey ink and wash: 5×4 in. (whole sheet)
inscribed: *N° 7.*

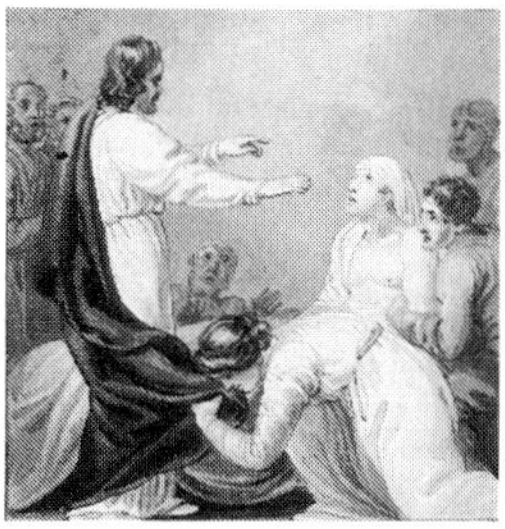

acc. no. 1456
Christ Healing a Sick Man

grey ink and wash: $4\frac{7}{8} \times 4\frac{1}{4}$ in.
inscribed: *N° 8* and (in a different hand): *16*

acc. no. 1457
The Raising of Jairus's Daughter
grey ink and wash: $4\frac{3}{4} \times 4\frac{1}{4}$ in. (whole sheet)
inscribed: *N° 9*

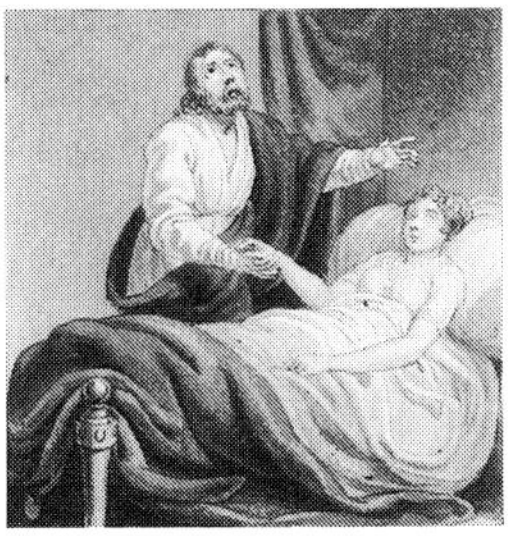

acc. no. 1458
Salome with the head of John the Baptist
grey ink and wash: $4\frac{3}{4} \times 4\frac{1}{8}$ in. (whole sheet)
inscribed: *N° 10*

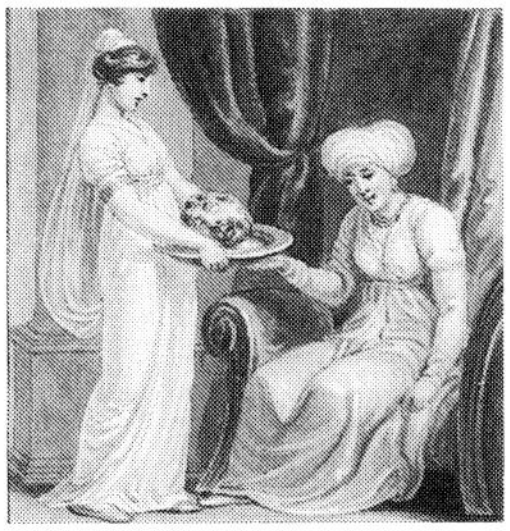

acc. no. 1459
The Miracle of the Loaves and Fishes
grey ink and wash: $4\frac{5}{8} \times 3\frac{7}{8}$ in. (whole sheet)
inscribed: *N° 11* and (in a different hand): *19*

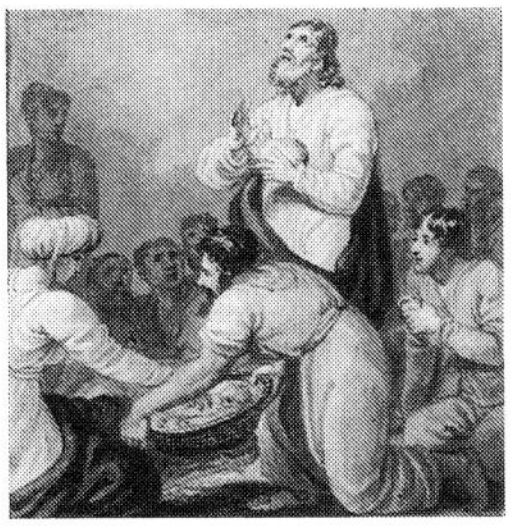

acc. no. 1460
Christ and the Children
grey ink and wash: $4\frac{3}{8} \times 4$ in. (whole sheet)
inscribed: *N° 12.*

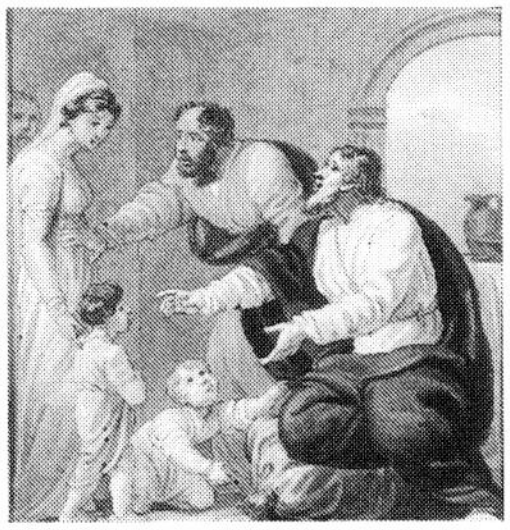

acc. no. 1461
Christ with Martha and Mary
grey ink and wash: $5 \times 4\frac{3}{8}$ in. (whole sheet)
inscribed: *N° 13.*

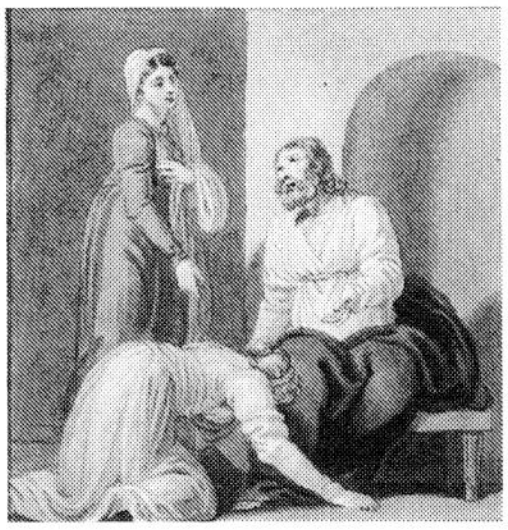

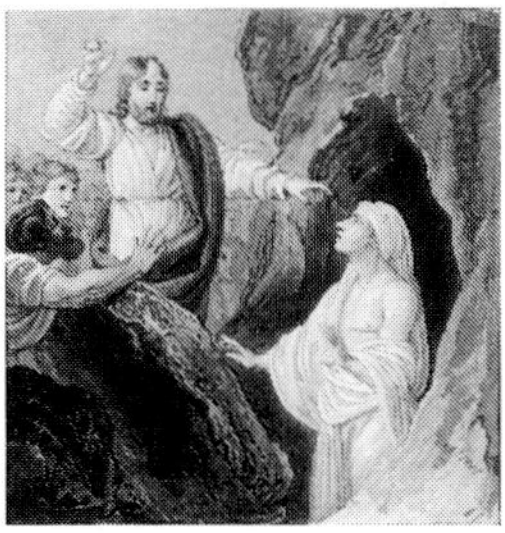

acc. no. 1462
Christ Raising Lazarus from the Tomb
grey ink and wash: $5\frac{1}{8} \times 4\frac{3}{8}$ in. (whole sheet)
inscribed: *N° 14*

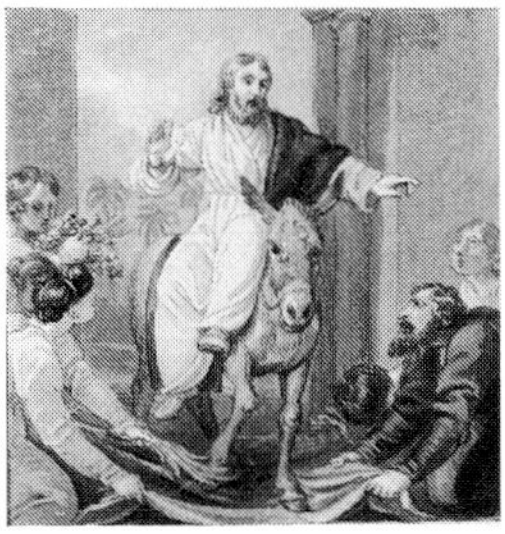

acc. no. 1463
Christ entering Jerusalem
grey ink and wash: $5 \times 4\frac{1}{4}$ in.
inscribed: *N° 15.*

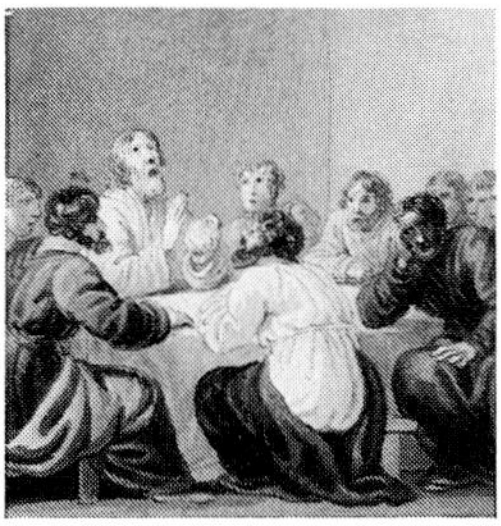

acc. no. 1464
The Last Supper
grey ink and wash: $4\frac{5}{8} \times 4\frac{1}{8}$ in.
inscribed: *N° 16.*

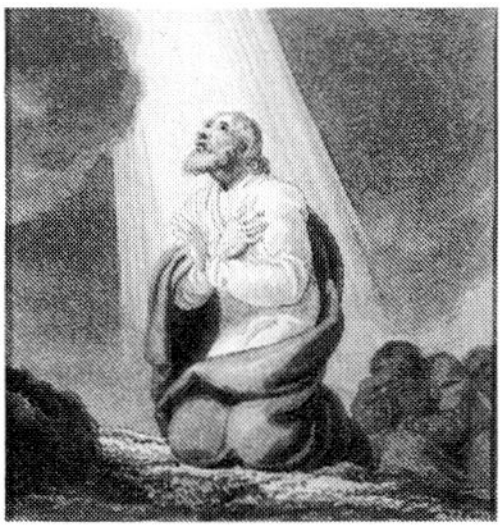

acc. no. 1465
The Agony in the Garden
grey ink and wash: $4\frac{5}{8} \times 4\frac{1}{4}$ in.
inscribed: *N° 17.*

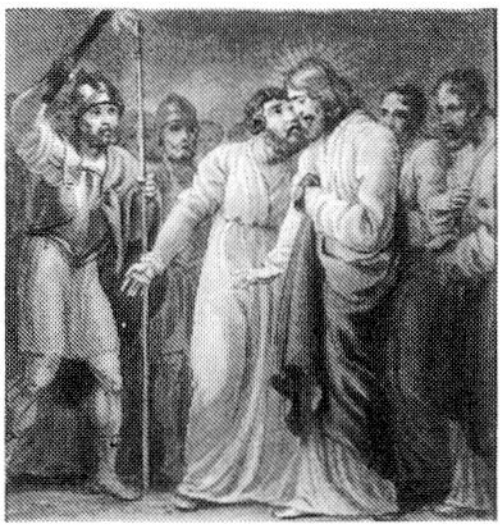

acc. no. 1466
The Betrayal of Christ
grey ink and wash: $4\frac{1}{2} \times 4$ in. (whole sheet)
inscribed: *N° 18.*

acc. no. 1467
The Mocking of Christ
grey ink and wash: $4\frac{3}{8} \times 3\frac{7}{8}$ in. (whole sheet)
inscribed: *N° 19.*

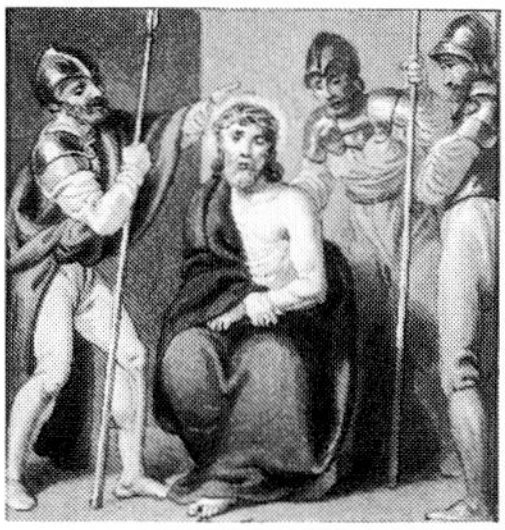

acc. no. 1468
The Crucifixion
grey ink and wash: $4\frac{1}{2} \times 4$ in. (whole sheet)
inscribed: *N° 20*

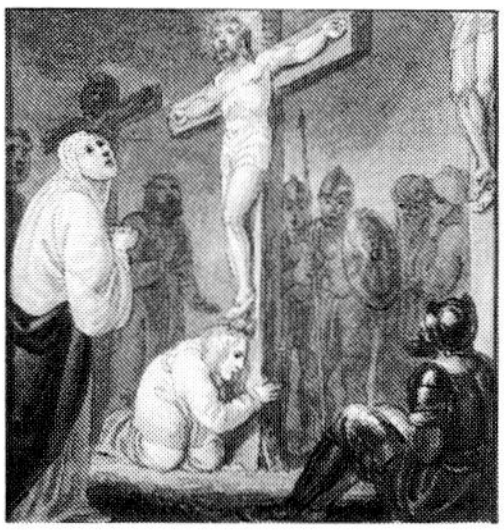

acc. no. 1469
The Sealing of the Sepulchre
grey ink and wash: $4\frac{1}{2} \times 4$ in. (whole sheet)
inscribed: *N° 21*

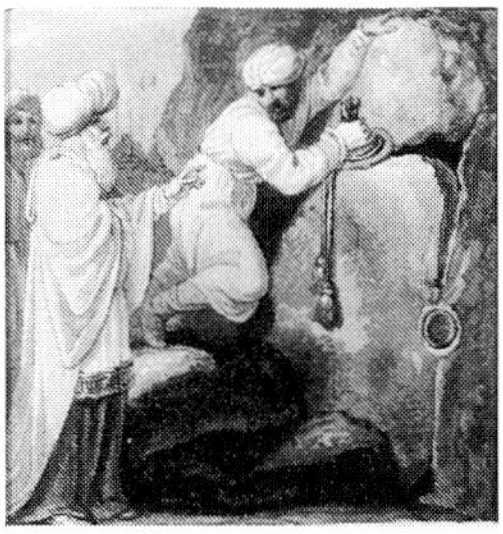

acc. no. 1470
The Resurrection
grey ink and wash: $4\frac{5}{8} \times 4\frac{1}{4}$ in. (whole sheet)
inscribed: *N° 22*

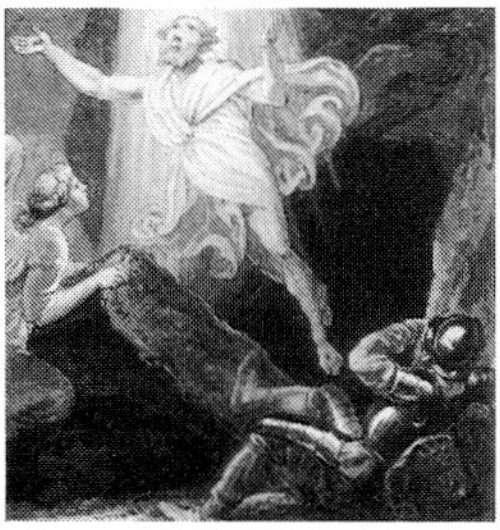

acc. no. 1471
Christ and St. Thomas
grey ink and wash: $4\frac{3}{4} \times 4$ in. (whole sheet)
inscribed: *N° 23*

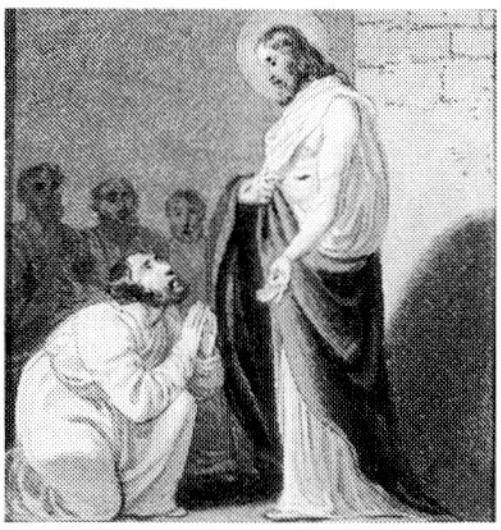

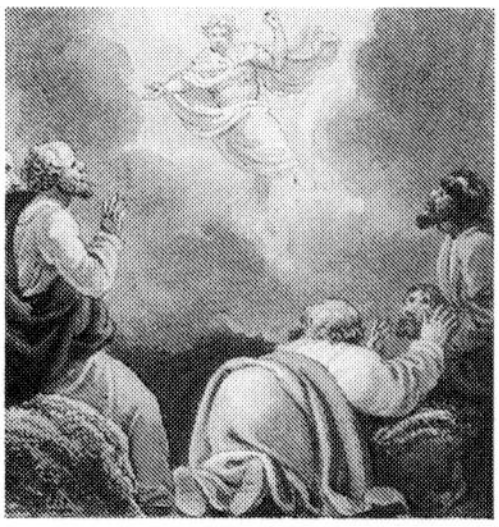

acc. no. 1472
The Ascension

grey ink and wash: $4\frac{3}{4} \times 4\frac{1}{8}$ in. (whole sheet)
inscribed: *N° 24.*

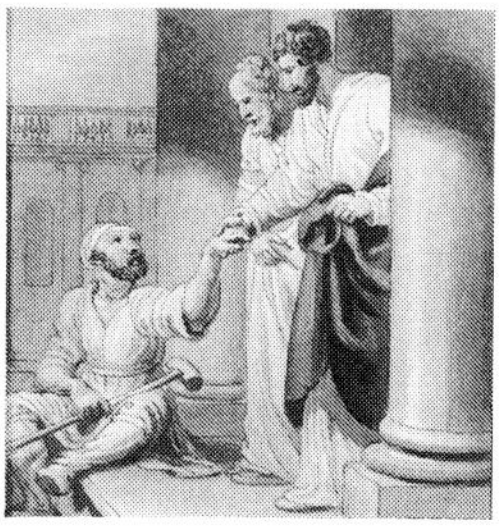

acc. no. 1473
Peter and John with the Beggar at the Beautiful Gate

grey ink and wash: $4\frac{7}{8} \times 4\frac{1}{4}$ in. (whole sheet)
inscribed: *N° 25.*

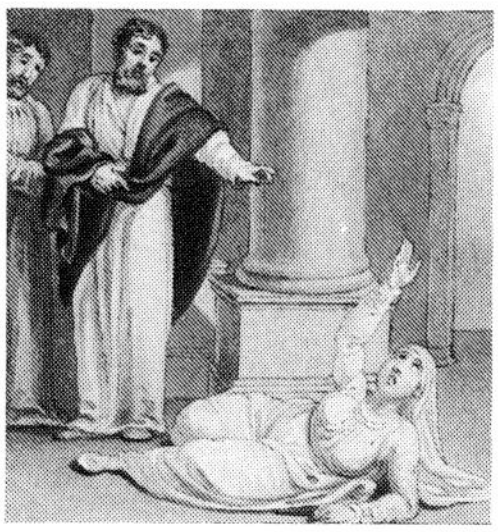

acc. no. 1474
Peter and Sapphira, Wife of Ananias

grey ink and wash: $5 \times 4\frac{1}{2}$ in. (whole sheet)
inscribed: *N° 26*

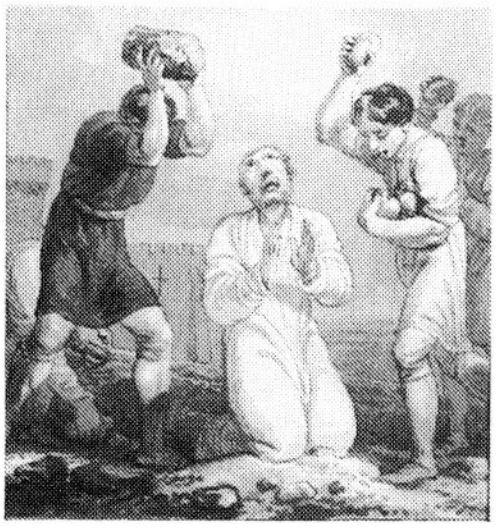

acc. no. 1475
The Stoning of St. Stephen

grey ink and wash: $4\frac{7}{8} \times 4\frac{1}{4}$ in. (whole sheet
inscribed: *N° 27*

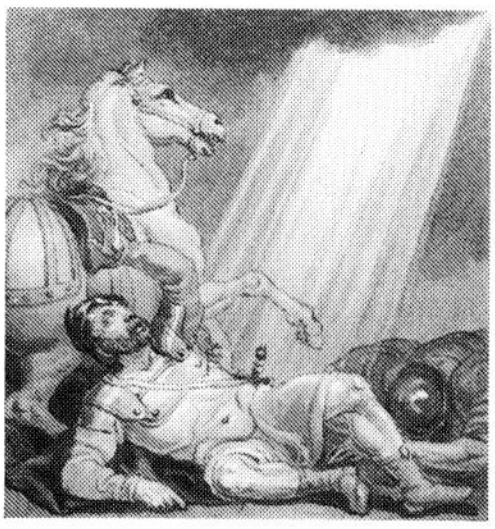

acc. no. 1476
The Conversion of Saul

grey ink and wash: $4\frac{3}{4} \times 4\frac{1}{4}$ in.
inscribed: *N° 28*

acc. no. 1477
The Angel appearing to Cornelius
grey ink and wash: $4\frac{7}{8} \times 4\frac{1}{4}$ in. (whole sheet)
inscribed: *Nº 29*

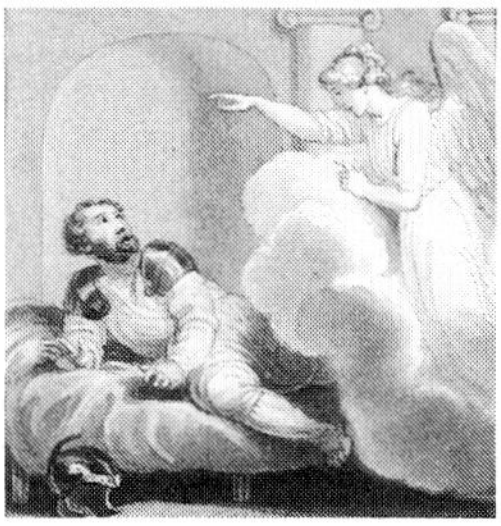

acc. no. 1478
The Blinding of Elymas
grey ink and wash: $4\frac{7}{8} \times 4\frac{1}{8}$ in. (whole sheet)
inscribed: *Nº 30*

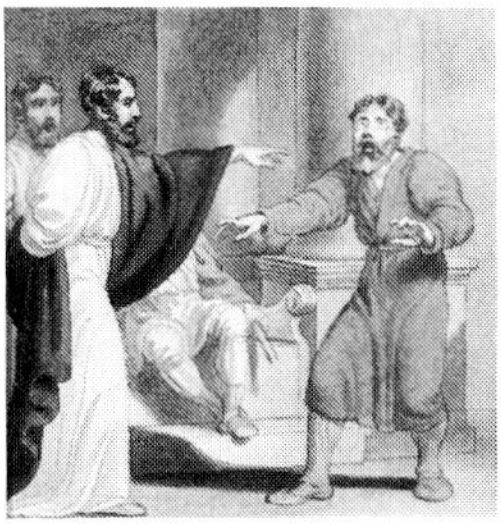

acc. no. 1479
St Peter healing the Cripple at Lystra
grey ink and wash: $4\frac{1}{2} \times 4\frac{1}{4}$ in. (whole sheet)
inscribed: *Nº 31*

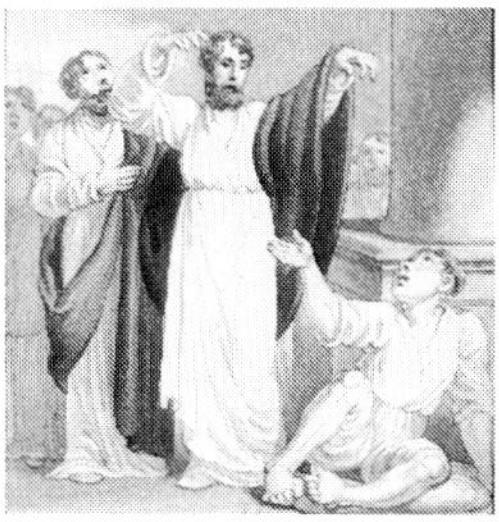

acc. no. 1480
St Paul before the Governor of Caesarea, Felix, and his Wife, Drusilla
grey ink and wash: $4\frac{5}{8} \times 4\frac{1}{8}$ in. (whole sheet)
inscribed: *Nº 32*

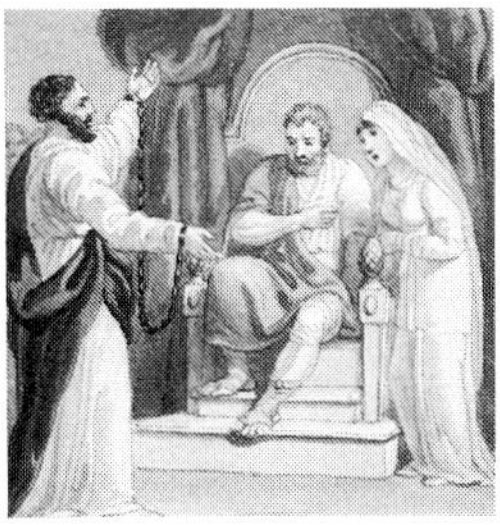

attributed to a Member of the Corbould family (19th C)
(accessioned *c.* 1890, source unknown)

acc. no. 1481
The Annunciation
grey ink and wash: $3\frac{7}{8} \times 3\frac{3}{4}$ in.
inscribed: *33*

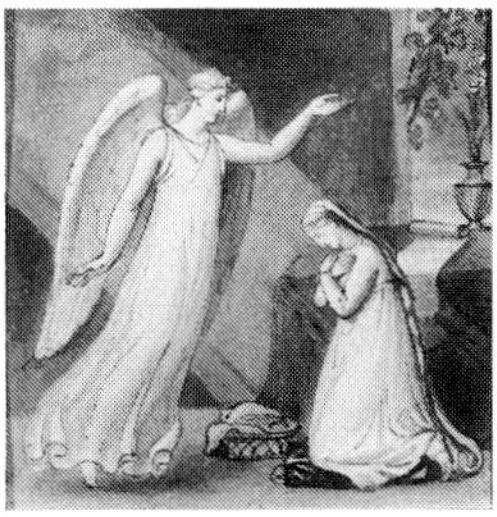

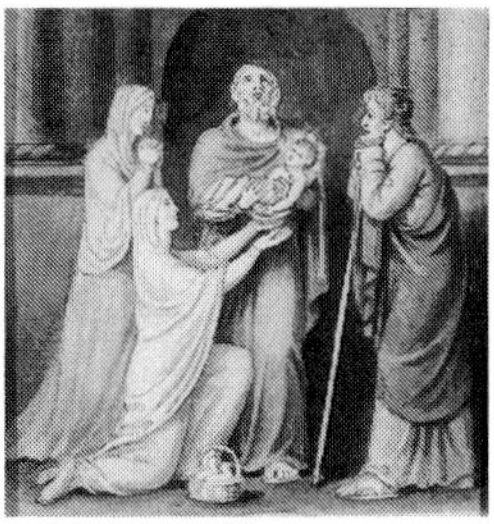

acc. no. 1482
The Presentation in the Temple
grey ink and wash: $3\frac{3}{4} \times 3\frac{3}{4}$ in.
inscribed: *34* and *S Mary, Simeon* and *J*(oseph)

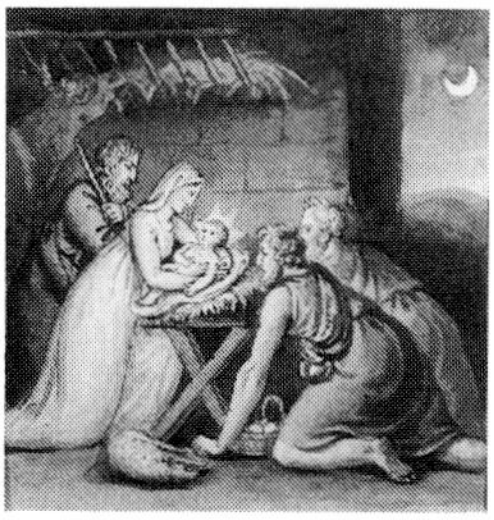

acc. no. 1483
The Nativity
grey ink and wash: $3\frac{7}{8} \times 3\frac{5}{8}$ in.
inscribed: *35*

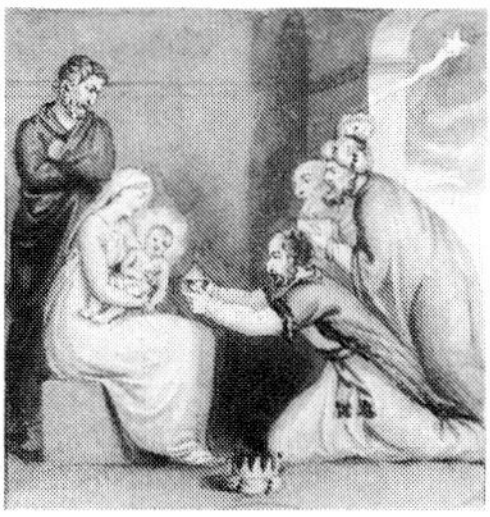

acc. no. 1484
The Adoration of the Magi
grey ink and wash: $3\frac{7}{8} \times 3\frac{5}{8}$ in.
inscribed: *36*

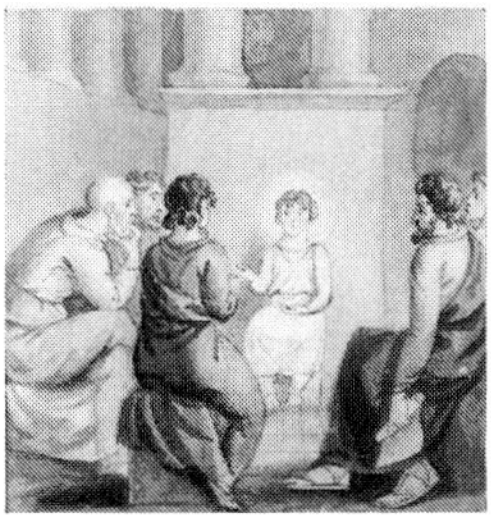

acc. no. 1485
The Child Jesus in the Temple
sepia and grey ink and wash: $3\frac{3}{4} \times 3\frac{3}{4}$ in.
inscribed: *37*

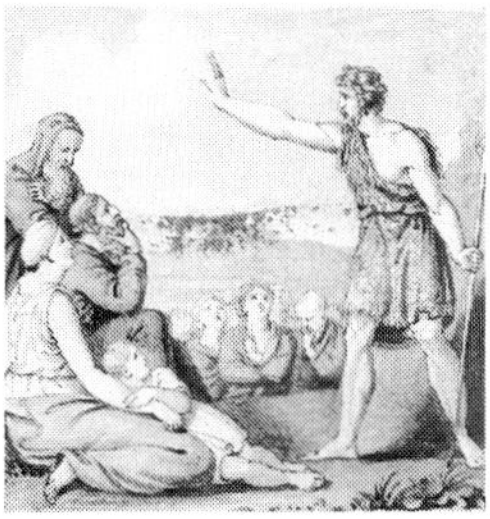

acc. no. 1486
St. John the Baptist preaching
sepia and grey ink and wash: $3\frac{7}{8} \times 3\frac{5}{8}$ in.
inscribed: *38*

acc. no. 1487
Christ in the Garden with Angels
grey ink and wash: 4 × $3\frac{3}{4}$ in.
inscribed: *39*

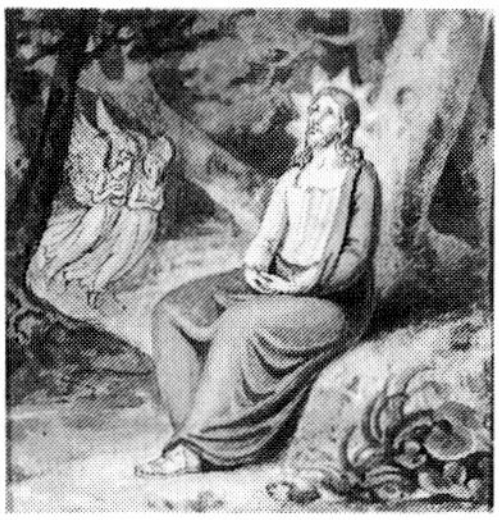

acc. no. 1488
A King offering his Crown to a Roman General
grey wash: $3\frac{1}{8}$ × 3 in. (sight)

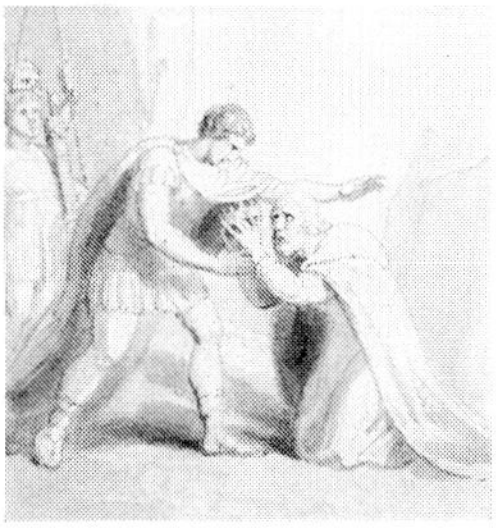

acc. no. 1489
A King setting alight his own Pyre
grey wash: $3\frac{1}{8}$ × 3 in. (sight)

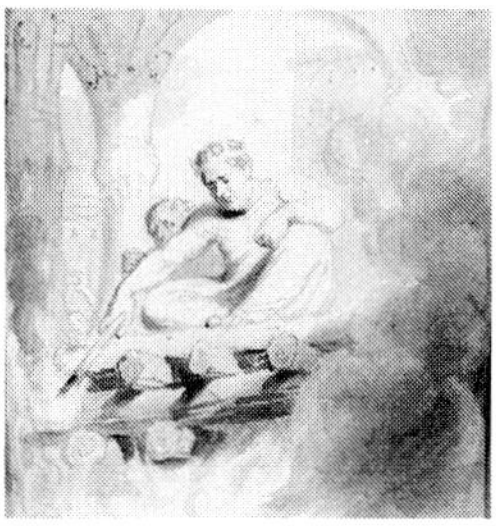

acc. no. 1490
The Death of Absalom
grey wash: $3\frac{1}{8}$ × 3 in. (sight)

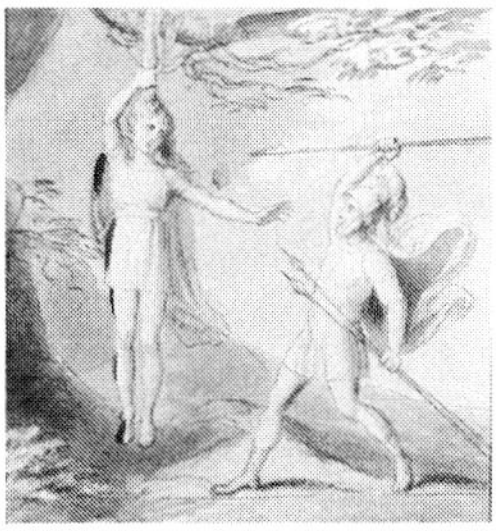

acc. no. 1491
An Angel appearing to a Praying Man
grey wash: $3\frac{1}{8}$ × 3 in. (sight)

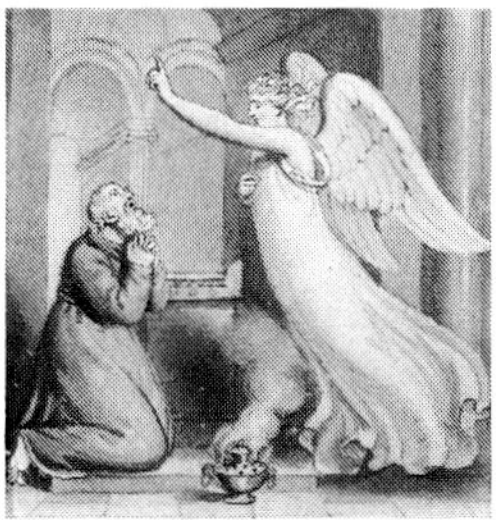

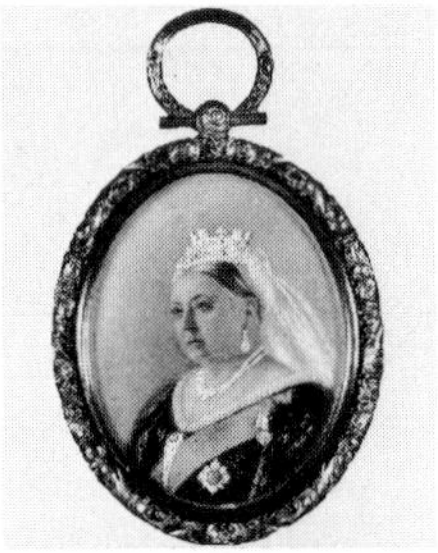

Eveline M. Corbould-Ellis (*fl.* 1896–1932)

acc. no. 608
Queen Victoria, Empress of India (*c.*1896)
watercolour on ivory: $2\frac{1}{8} \times 1\frac{5}{8}$ in.
signed: *E. Corbould-Ellis.*
Presented by H. Homewood Crawford, 1897

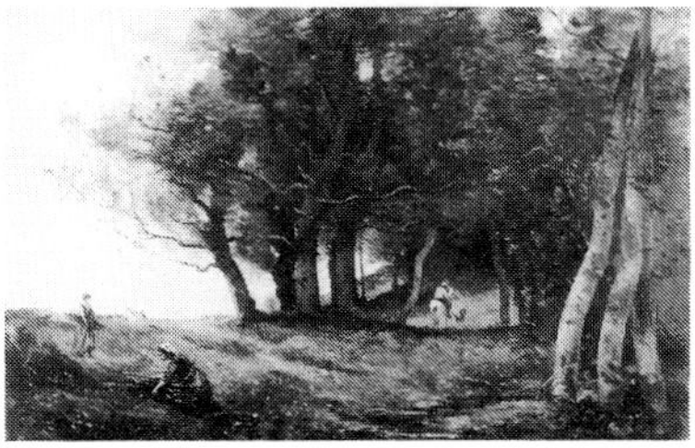

after Jean-Baptiste-Camille Corot (1796–1875)

acc. no. 1041
The Wood Gatherers (after 1875)
oil on canvas: 28 × 39 in.
bears signature: *COROT*
Presented by G. N. Stevens, 1925

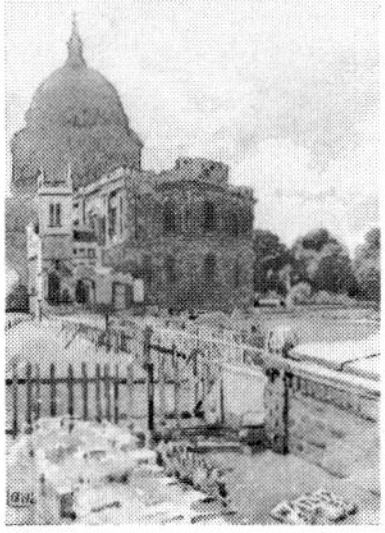

Richard Cowie (*fl.* 1939–47)

acc. no. 1826
Ruins at the East End of St. Paul's Cathedral (1947)
watercolour: $14\frac{3}{4} \times 11$ in.
signed: *LCOWIE* (sic)
Presented by Miss Gertrude Malcolm-Wood, 1969

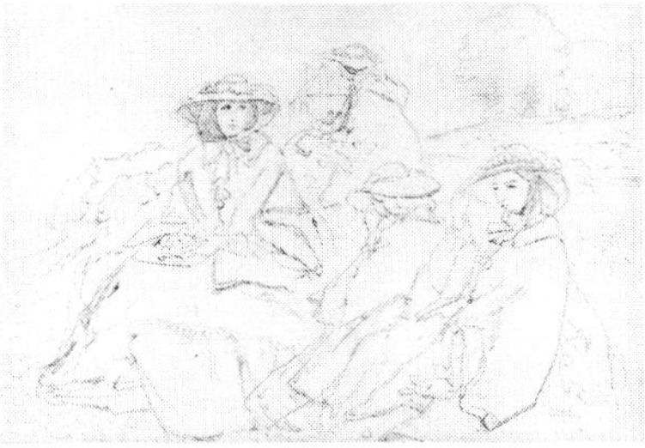

attributed to David Cox (1783–1859)

acc. no. 3547
Ladies Seated in a Meadow
pencil: $10\frac{1}{4} \times 14$ in.
Presented by Miss Helen Guiterman, 1985

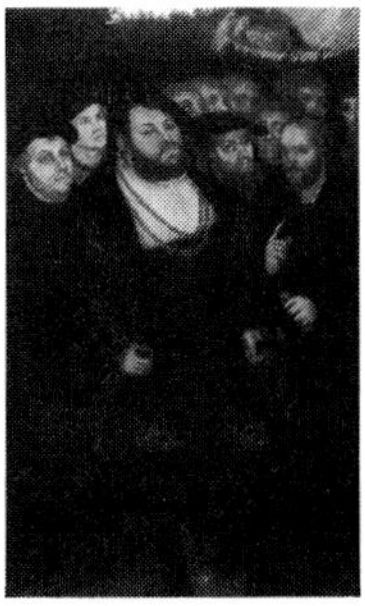

after Lucas Cranach the Elder (?16th C)

acc. no. 162
John Frederic the Magnanimous with a Group of Reformers
oil on canvas: 25 × 16 in.
Presented by Thomas Adderley, 1856

Walter Crane (1845–1915)

acc. no. 976
Design for a Stained Glass Window: St Cecilia (1898)
watercolour and bodycolour: $22\frac{1}{2} \times 7\frac{5}{8}$ in.
signed and dated: *Walter Crane. May / 1898*; inscribed: *SKETCH. DESIGN. 1½" SCALE. FOR. WINDOW. IN. TER. AA. Ch*
Presented by Miss Evelyn P. McGhee, 1915

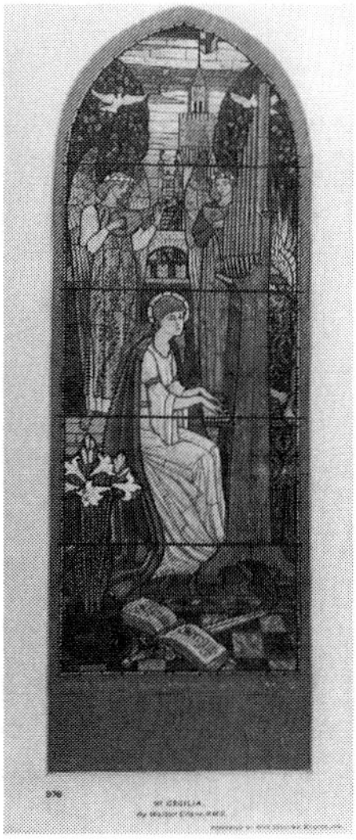

Edmund Thornton Crawford (1806–85)

acc. no. 849
A Dutch Hay Barge
watercolour: $6\frac{1}{4} \times 9$ in.
signed and dated: *E.J. Crawford / 1870*
Presented by R.H. Wood, 1907

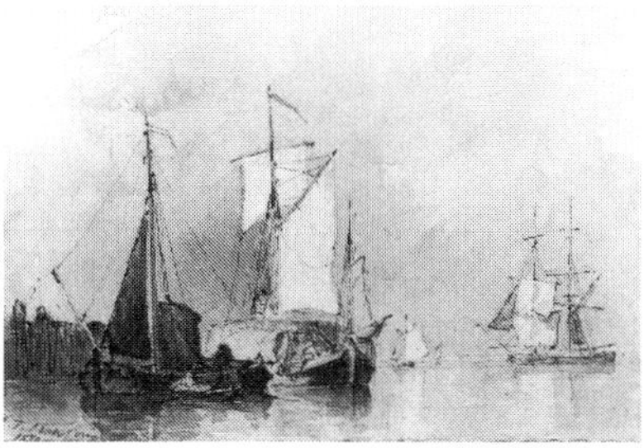

H. H. Cresswell (20th C)

acc. no. 1783
Panorama of the Thames from Westminster Bridge to Tower Bridge
watercolour in eight sections: $8\frac{3}{4} \times 211\frac{5}{8}$ in. overall
each section signed: *H.H. Cresswell*
Purchased from the Old Bailey Boutique, 1967

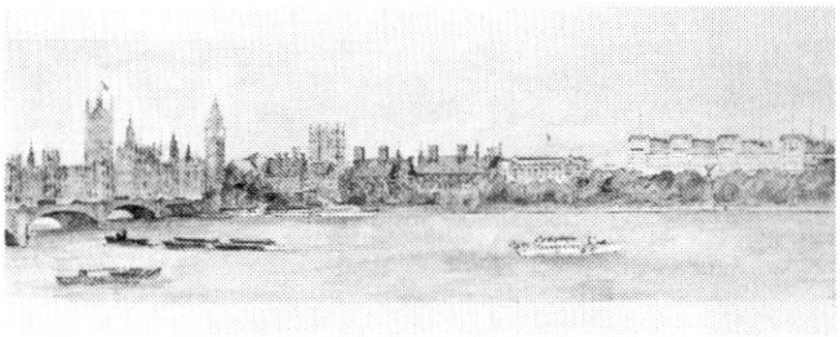

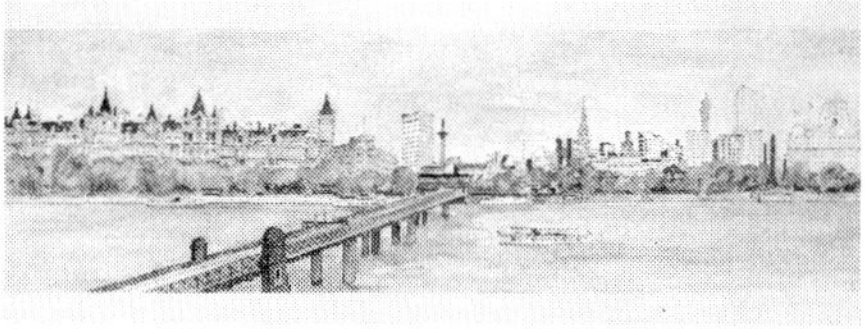

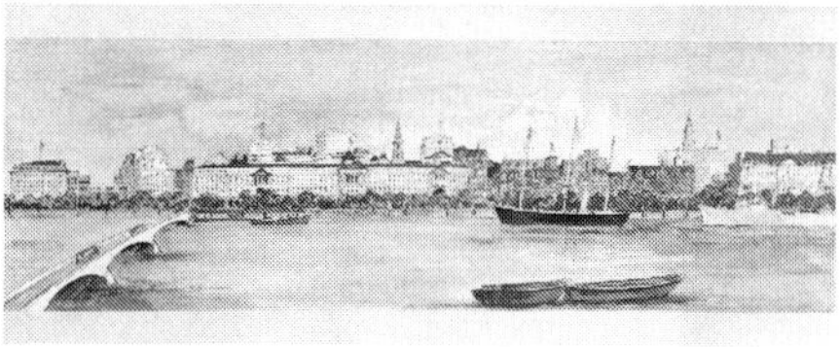

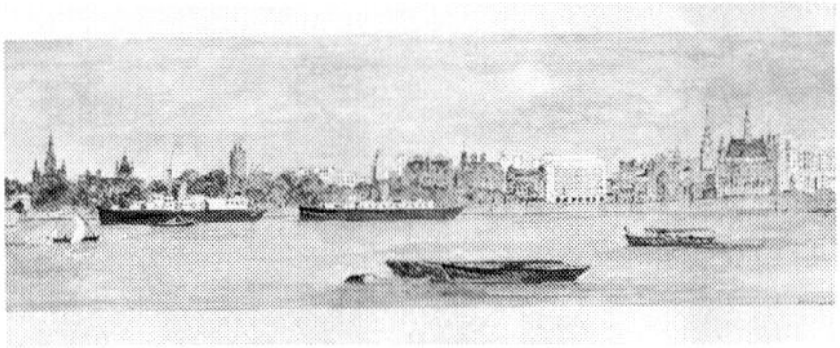

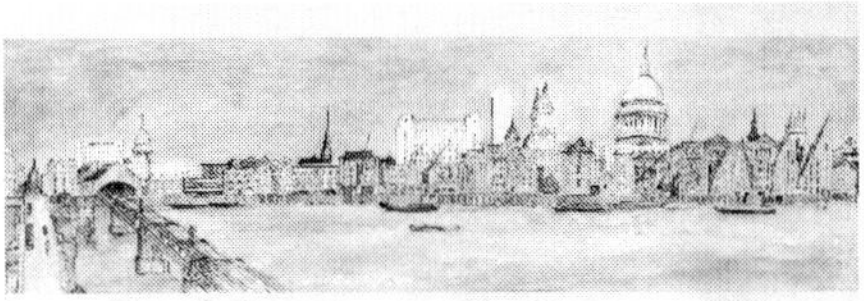

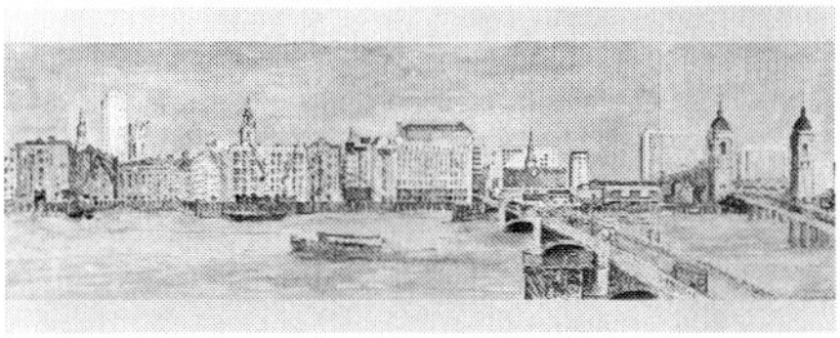

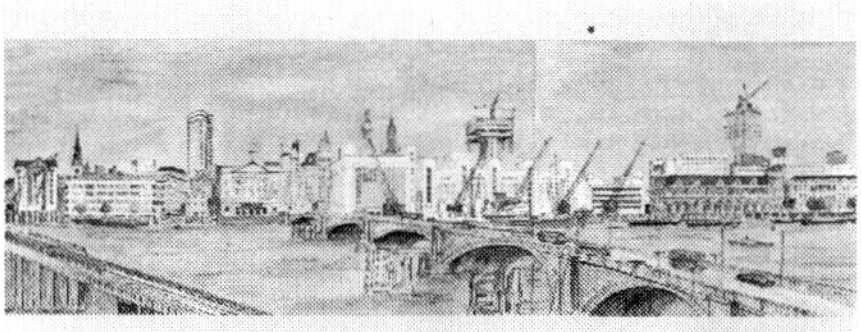

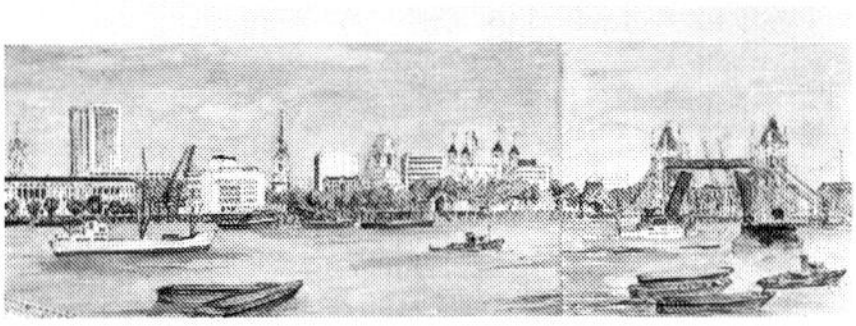

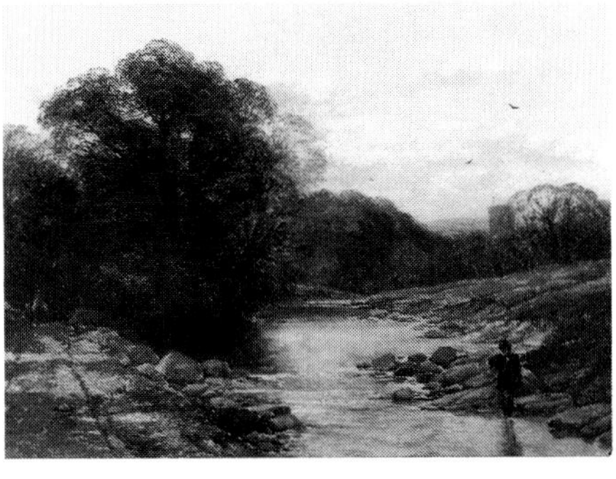

Thomas Creswick (1811–69)

acc. no. 657
A Sylvan Stream

oil on canvas: 9 × 12 in.
signed: *T.C.*
Bequeathed by Charles Gassiot, 1902

acc. no. 658
Evening

oil on canvas: 9 × 12 in.
signed: *T.C.*
Bequeathed by Charles Gassiot, 1902

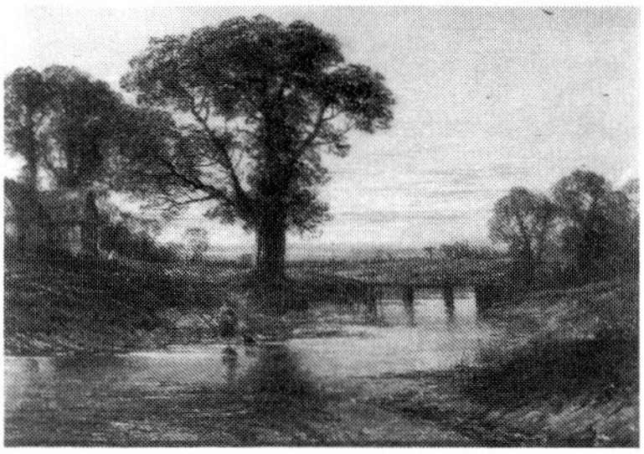

Isaac Cruikshank (1756/7–1810/11)

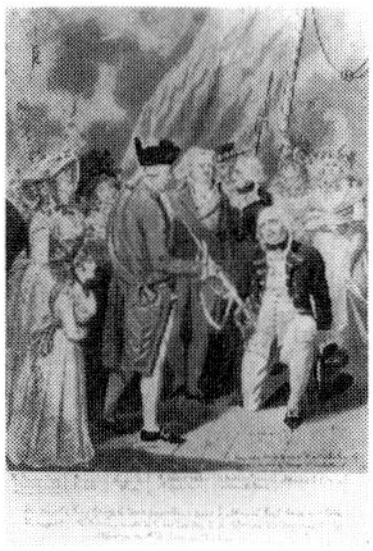

acc. no. 243
George III presenting a Sword to Admiral Earl Howe (*c.*1794)

pen and ink and watercolour: 13 × 10 in.
inscribed: *Designed and Drawn by Isaac Cruikshank – the Father of Isaac Robert & George Cruikshank*; inscribed and signed verso: *His Majesty Presenting ~~the~~ / an / Elegant Sword / to Admiral Earl Howe, as a token of his respe*^{t} */ for the Services rendered his country in the Glorious ac* (tion) */ with the French Fleet on the 1*st *of June 1794 / No. 344 / Published ––––––––– / Cruikshank Sen*^{r} *Del*^{t}
Presented by John Robert Taylor, 1875

Charles Ernest Cundall (1890–1971)

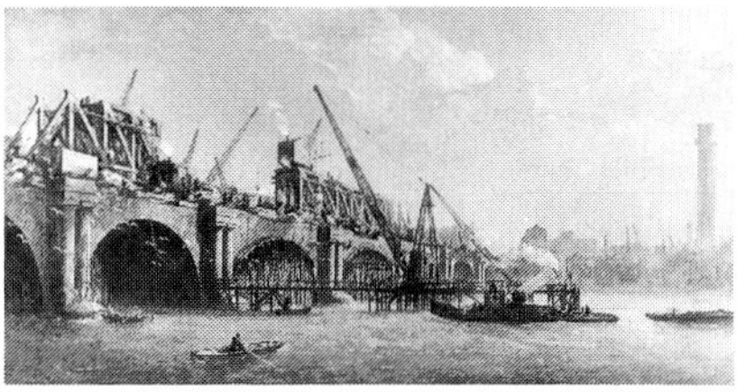

acc. no. 1253
The Demolition of Waterloo Bridge

oil on canvas: $33\frac{1}{4}$ × 50 in.
signed and dated: *Charles Cundall 1935*
Presented by Lady Wakefield, 1943

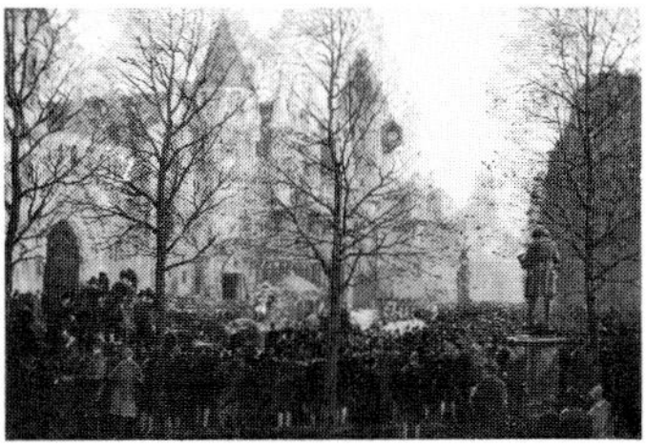

acc. no. 1354
The Lord Mayor's Procession arriving at the Law Courts, 1926

oil on canvas: $31\frac{1}{2}$ × 39 in.
signed: *C. Cundall*
Presented by E. Holroyd Pearce K.C. 1947

Terence Tenison Cuneo (b.1907)

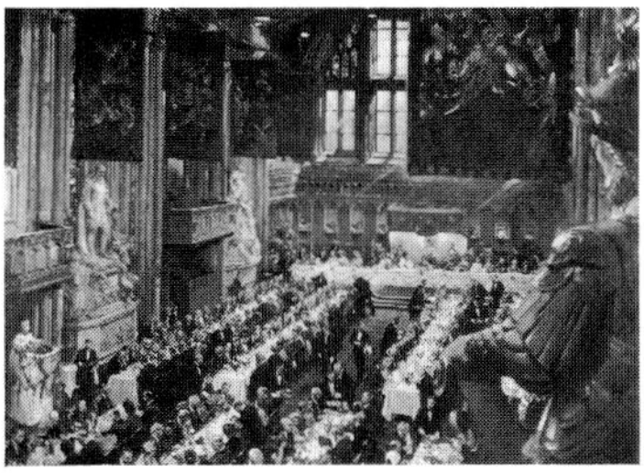

acc. no. 1507
The Coronation Luncheon to Her Majesty Queen Elizabeth II in Guildhall, 12 June 1953

oil on canvas: $66\frac{1}{2}$ × $84\frac{1}{2}$ in.
signed and dated: *·CUNEO· / DECEMBER / 1953*
Presented by Sir Sidney Fox, 1954

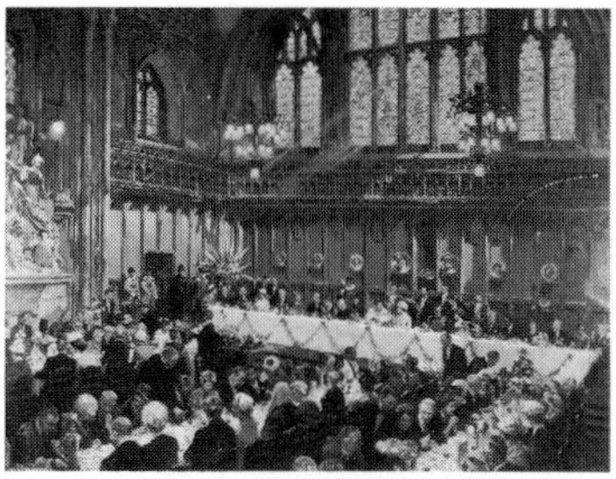

acc. no. 1624
Luncheon in Guildhall to Her Majesty the Queen and the Duke of Edinburgh, 10 March 1961
oil on canvas: $77\frac{3}{4} \times 101\frac{3}{4}$ in.
signed and dated: *TERENCE·CUNEO· / NOVEMBER 1961*
Commissioned by the Corporation, 1961

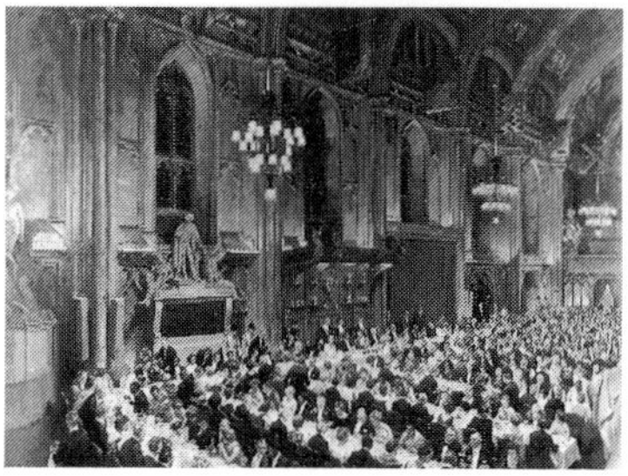

acc. no. 1827
The Commonwealth Prime Ministers' Banquet, January 13 1969
oil on canvas: 72×96 in.
signed and dated: *TERENCE·CUNEO· / SEPTEMBER·1969·*
Commissioned by the Corporation, 1969

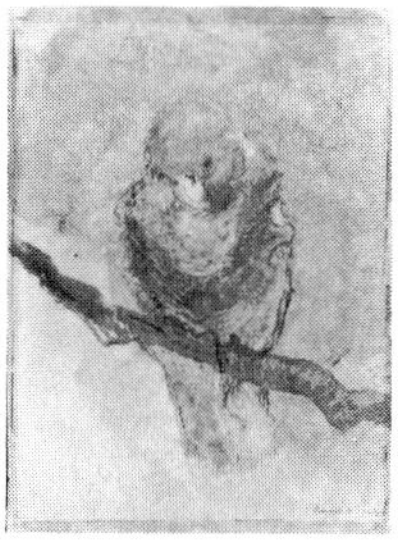

Vera Cuningham (1897–1955)

acc. no. 3603
Green Parakeet (1947)
ink and watercolour: $11\frac{1}{2} \times 5\frac{7}{8}$ in.
signed and dated: *Cuningham 1947*
Presented by Miss Helen Guiterman, 1985

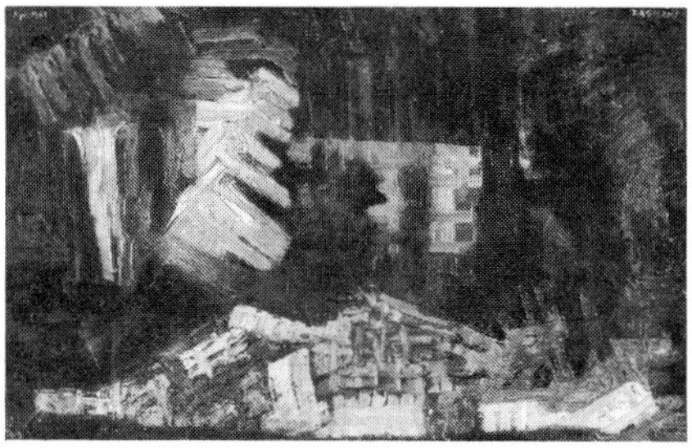

Arnold Daghani (b.1909)

acc. no. 1667
Blitz, 1940 (1963)
oil on paper: $12\frac{5}{8} \times 20\frac{1}{8}$ in.
signed and dated: *DAGHANI Apr. 1963*
Presented by the artist, 1963

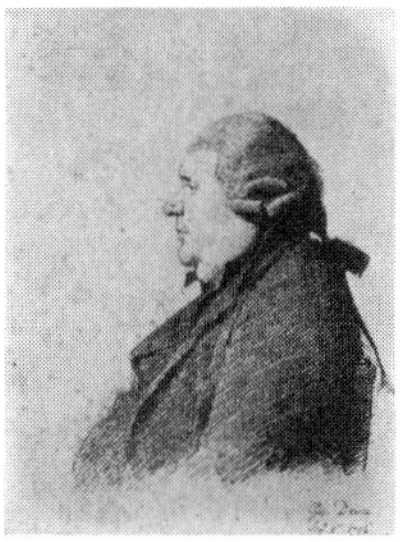

George Dance (1740–1825)

acc. no. 621
William Rix, Town Clerk (1796)
pencil, touched with red chalk: $9\frac{7}{8} \times 7\frac{1}{2}$ in.
signed and dated: *Geo. Dance / Sept. 8th 1796*
Presented by Colonel J. L. Rutley, 1900

acc. no. 620
Richard Clark, Chamberlain of London (1798)
pencil: $9\frac{7}{8} \times 7\frac{1}{2}$ in.
signed and dated: *Geo. Dance / Nov.r 2.d 1798*
Presented by Colonel J. L. Rutley, 1900

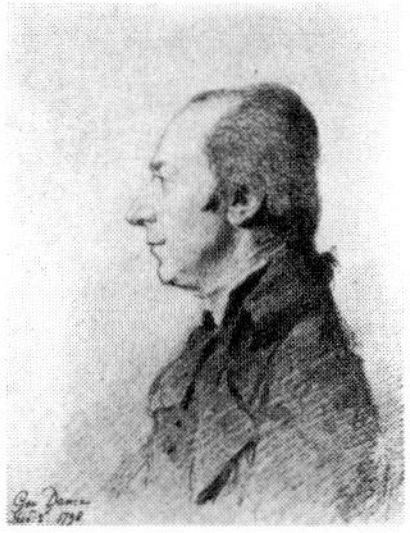

Nathaniel Dance (1735–1811)
acc. no. 108
Sir Robert Kite, Lord Mayor 1766
oil on canvas: 56 × 47 in.
Presented by Major-General Sir James Cockburn, 1843

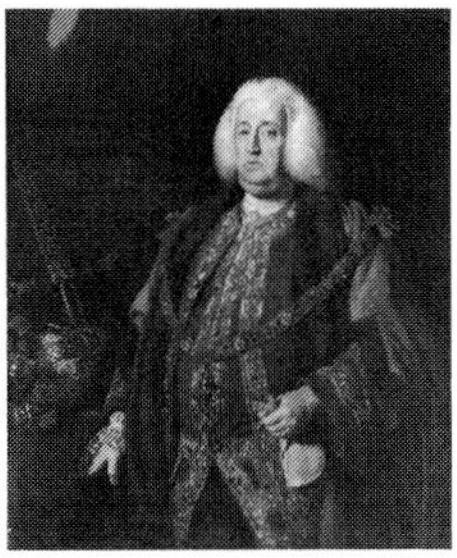

acc. no. 1238
George Dance
oil on canvas: $38 \times 29\frac{1}{2}$ in.
Presented by Lord Bearsted through the N.A.-C.F., 1934

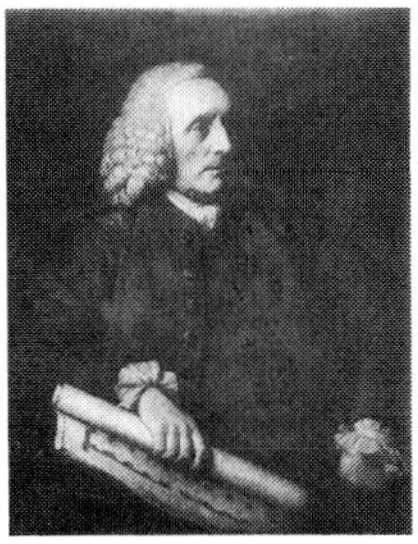

Bartholomew Dandridge (1691–c.1755)
acc. no. 1860
John Barber, Lord Mayor 1732
pencil: $15\frac{1}{2} \times 10\frac{1}{2}$ in.
inscribed: *Excise Bill* and *John Barber Esquire / Alderman of Castle Baynard Ward / Lord Mayor of London AD 1732*
Purchased from Dr. Bonavia, 1971

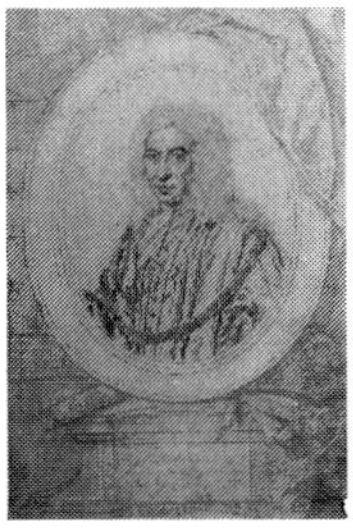

William Daniell (1769–1837)
acc. no. 88
Banquet at Guildhall to the Prince Regent, the Czar of Russia and the King of Prussia, June 18 1814
oil on canvas: 21 × 20 in.
Commissioned by the Corporation, 1815

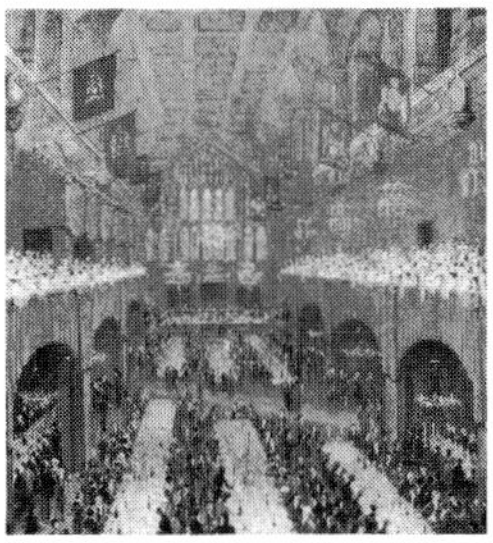

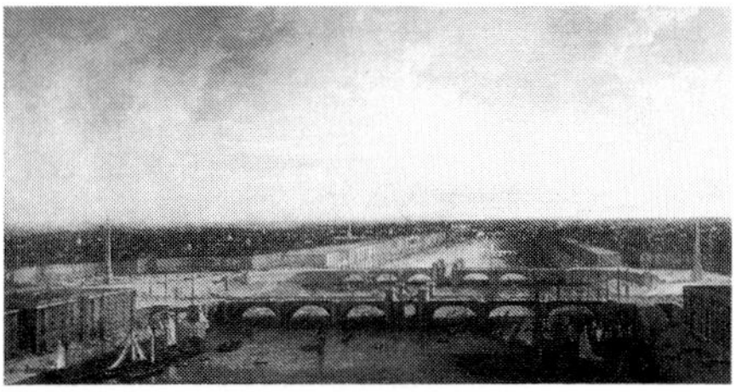

acc. no. 1378
George Dance's Design for London Bridge (1802)
oil on canvas: $36\frac{1}{4} \times 71\frac{1}{2}$ in.
Bequeathed by Miss M. S. Dance, 1948

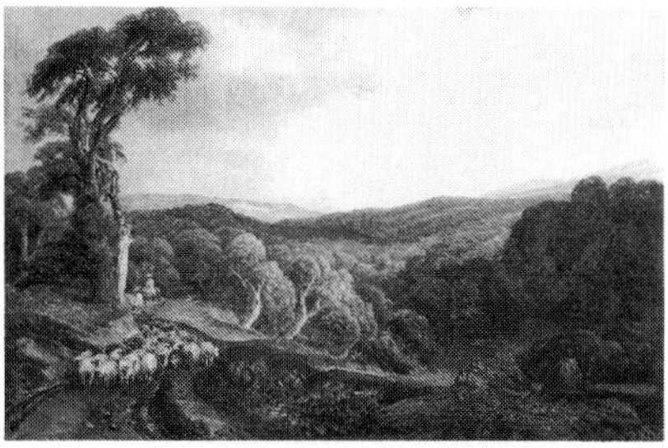

A. A. Deans (20th C)

acc. no. 1666
Lake Tekapo (1963)
oil on hardboard: $17\frac{1}{2} \times 25$ in.
signed and dated: *A.A. Deans 1963*
Presented by the City of Christchurch, NZ, 1963

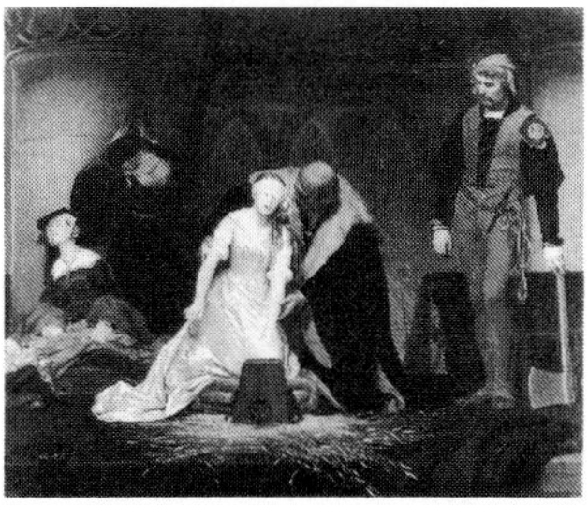

Paul Delaroche (1797–1856)

acc. no. 1052
The Execution of Lady Jane Grey (*c.*1834)
oil on canvas: 18 × 21 in.
Presented by Horace J. Cropper, 1926

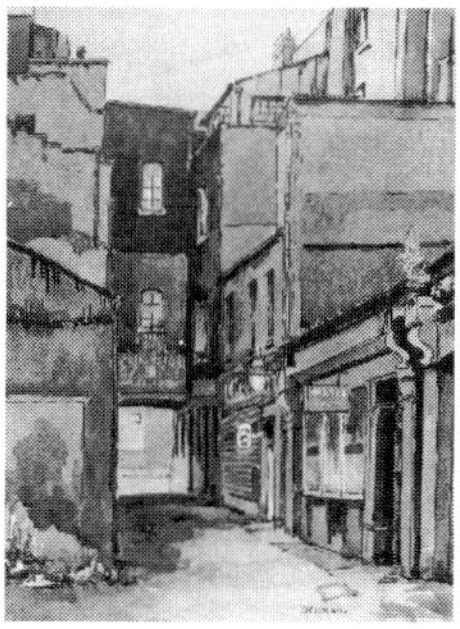

Gladys Denman (20th C)

acc. no. 2205
The Star Inn, Aldersgate Street (*c.* 1977)
watercolour: 14 × 10 in.
signed: *DENMAN*
Purchased from the artist, 1977

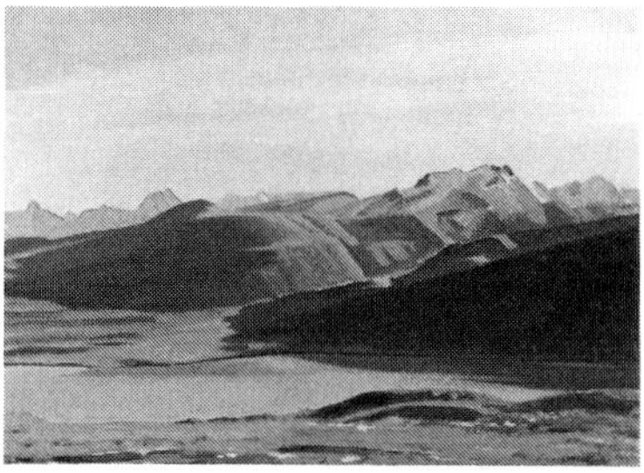

Peter De Wint (1784–1849)

acc. no. 1346
Near Lowther Castle
watercolour over pencil, on paper laid on canvas: $28\frac{1}{4} \times 42\frac{3}{4}$ in.
Presented by Miss T. A. C. Durning Lawrence, 1946

John Robert Dicksee (1817–1905)

acc. no. 157
Warren Stormes Hale, Originator and Chairman of the City of London Freemen's Orphans' School (1853)

oil on canvas: 56 × 44 in.
signed and dated: *J.R. Dicksee 1853*
Presented by the artist, 1856

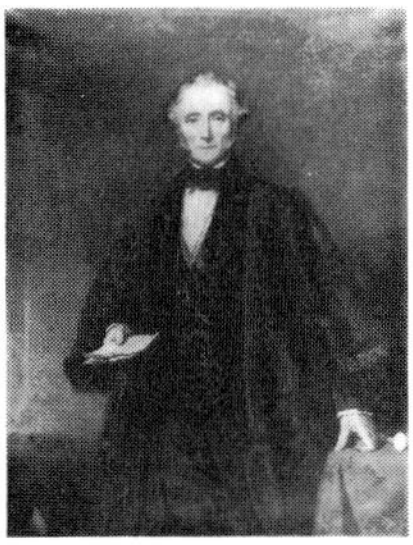

acc. no. 173
Richard Lambert Jones (?c.1862)

oil on canvas: 44 × 34 in.
Purchased, 1862

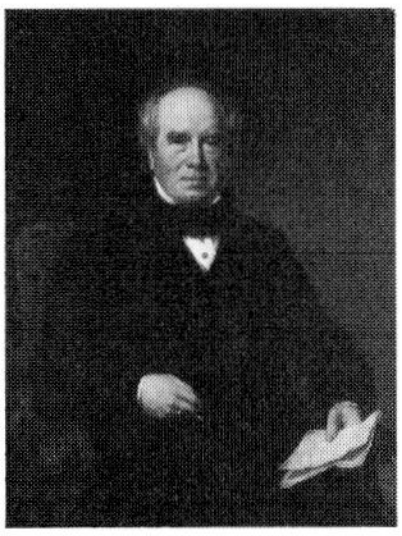

acc. no. 280
John Laird Mair, Lord Lawrence (1863)

oil on canvas: 40 × 32 in.
signed and dated: *J.R. Dicksee / 1863*
Presented by the artist, 1883

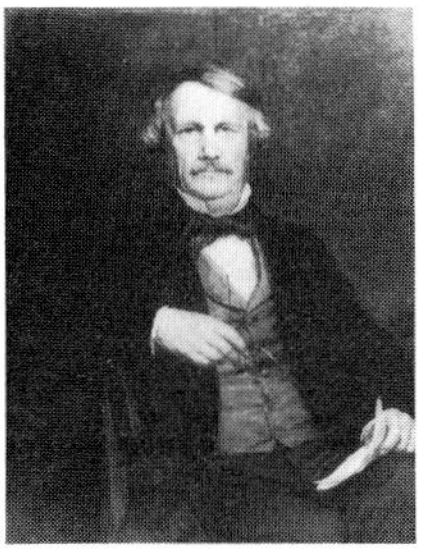

acc. no. 3633
Man with Spectacles (?c.1860s)

oil on canvas: 24 × 20 in.
signed (mono) *JRD*
Found in store 1985, source and method of acquisition unknown

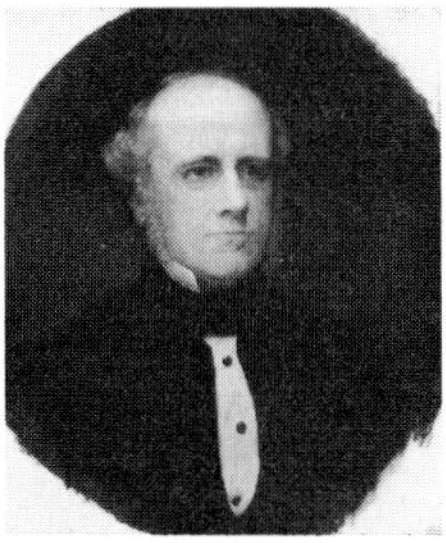

acc. no. 263
Sir N.E. Knight, Lord Mayor 1882 (1883)

oil on canvas: 56 × 45 in.
signed and dated: *John R^t Dicksee 1883*
Presented to the City of London School by Old Pupils, 1883

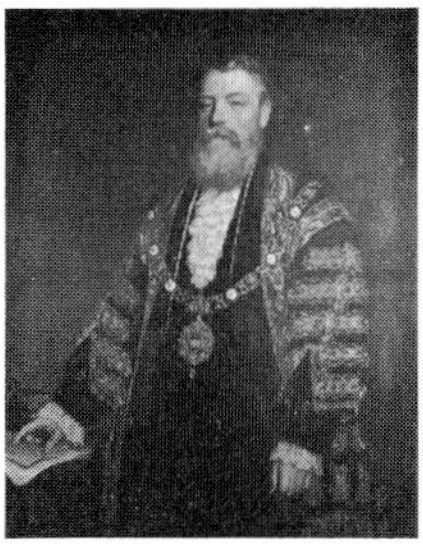

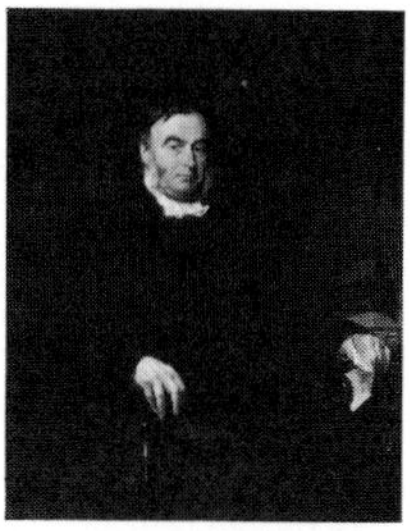

acc. no. 517
The Rev. Joseph Harris, Master at the City of London School (1891)

oil on canvas: 56 × 44 in.
Presented by Old Pupils and Colleagues, 1891

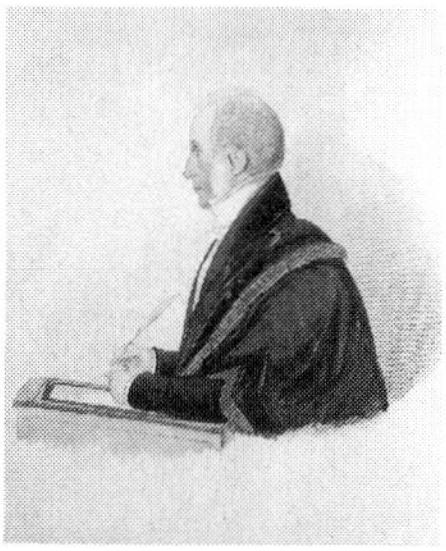

Richard Dighton (1795–1880)

acc. no. 1510
Samuel Wilson, Lord Mayor 1838

pencil, pen and ink and watercolour: $6\frac{1}{8}$ × 5 in.
signed on verso: *Richard Dighton / 6 St Michael's Terrace / Pimlico*
and inscribed: *Aldn Wilson*
Purchased from Stabley Crowe, 1954

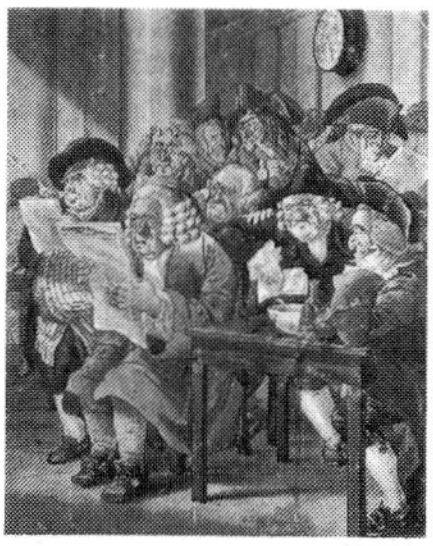

Robert Dighton (*c.*1752–1814)

acc. no. 1255
Stock-Jobbers Extraordinary (*c.*1795)

pen and ink and watercolour: $12\frac{1}{4}$ × $9\frac{3}{4}$ in.
Purchased from Mr. Yakovleff, 1943

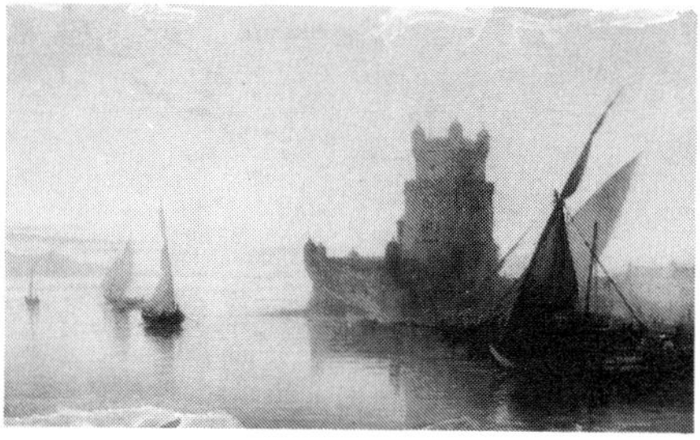

Frank Dillon (1823–1909)

acc. no. 919
View near Lisbon (?1850)

oil on canvas: 28 × 42 in.
Presented by Walter Morrison, 1911

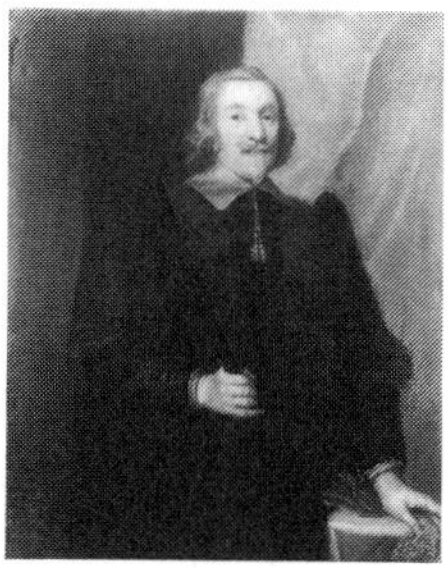

ascribed to William Dobson (1610–46)

acc. no. 1072
Isaac Pennington, Lord Mayor 1642

oil on canvas: $41\frac{1}{2}$ × $33\frac{1}{2}$ in.
inscribed: *Isaac Pennington / Alderman / of London / MDCXLVIII.* and *Elected/ Lord Mayor / XXIX Septr / MDCXLII.*
Purchased, 1931

Joseph Josiah Dodd (1809–80)

acc. no. 1618
Old London Bridge in 1745 (1846)
watercolour: 23 × 29 in.
Presented by Commander Wise, 1955

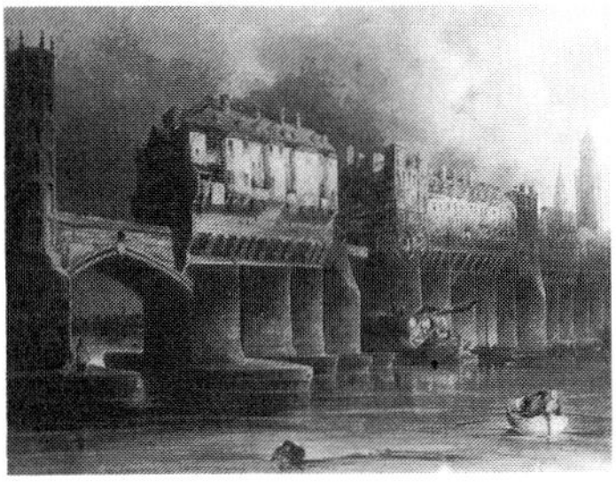

Robert Dodd (1748–1816) after Richard Paton (1717–91)

acc. no. 66
Lord Rodney Breaking the French Line off Dominica, April 12 1782
oil on canvas: 47 × 70 in.
Presented by Alderman John Boydell, 1793

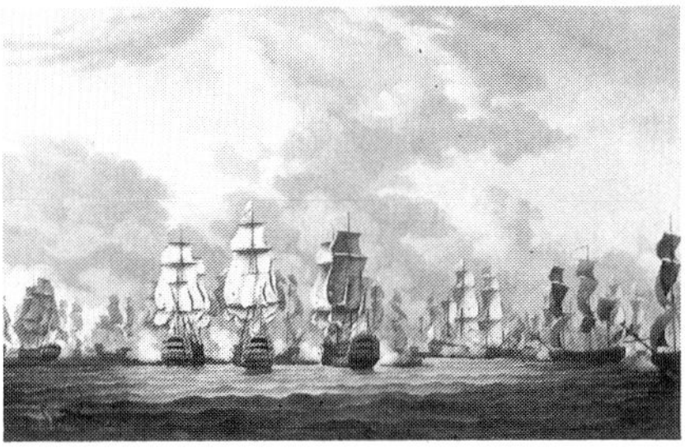

acc. no. 67
The Victory of Lord Rodney over the French Fleet off Dominica, April 12 1782
oil on canvas: 47 × 70 in.
Presented by Alderman John Boydell, 1793

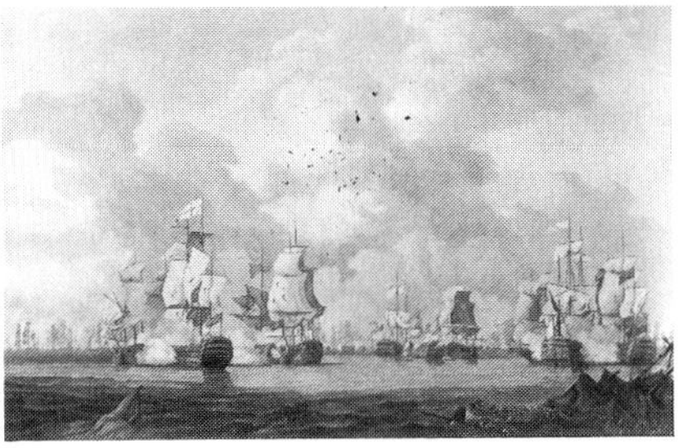

Antony Dracup (20th C)

acc. no. 2264
Bow Lane Looking South (1971)
watercolour: 19 × 14 in.
signed and dated: *Antony Dracup / Dec 1971*
Purchased from the artist, 1981

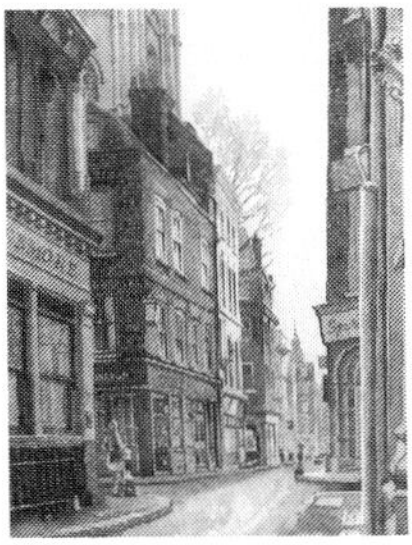

William Dring (b.1904)

acc. no. 1386
Presentation of the Freedom of the City to H.R.H. the Princess Elizabeth, 1947 (1948)
oil on canvas: $71\frac{1}{2} \times 95\frac{1}{4}$ in.
signed and dated: *William Dring 48*
Presented by Sir W. Bracewell-Smith, 1948

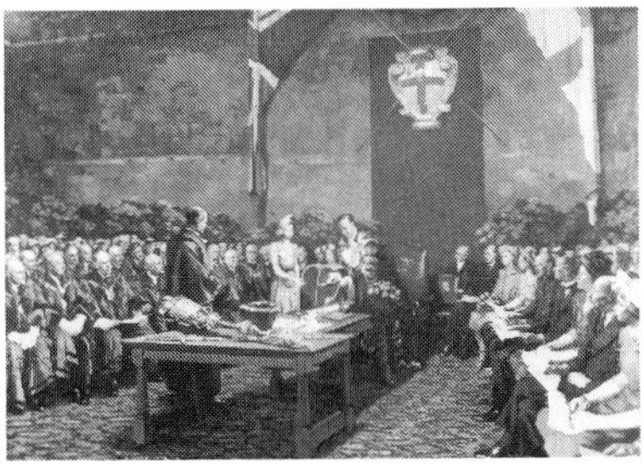

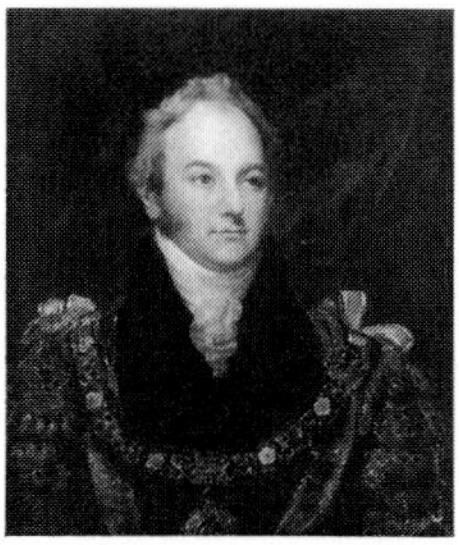

Samuel Drummond (1765–1844)

acc. no. 161
Sir Claudius Stephen Hunter, Lord Mayor 1811 (1813)

oil on canvas: 30 × 25 in.
Purchased, 1856

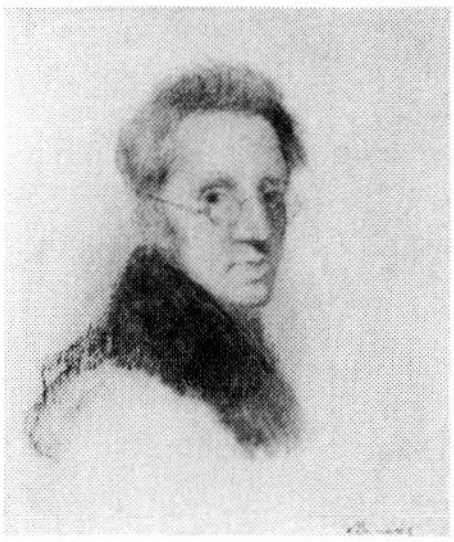

acc. no. 3538
Man with Spectacles

coloured chalks: $6\frac{3}{4} \times 5\frac{5}{8}$ in.
signed: *S Drummond*
Presented by Miss Helen Guiterman, 1985

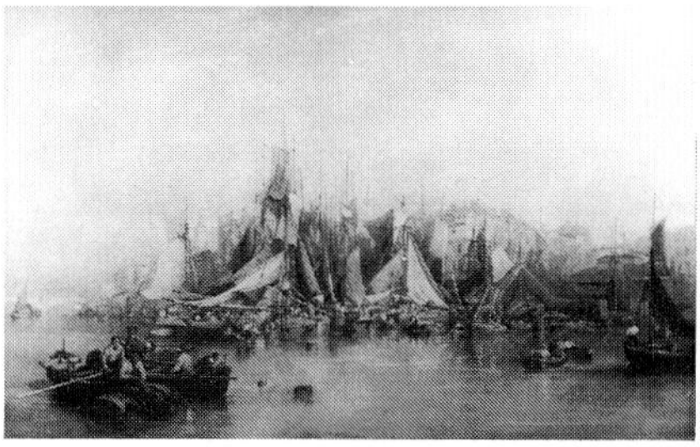

Edward Duncan (1803–82)

acc. no. 1644
Billingsgate, First Day of Oysters, Early Morning (1843)

watercolour: $27\frac{7}{8} \times 44\frac{1}{4}$ in.
signed and dated: *E.DUNCAN 1843*
Purchased from F. T. Sabin, 1962

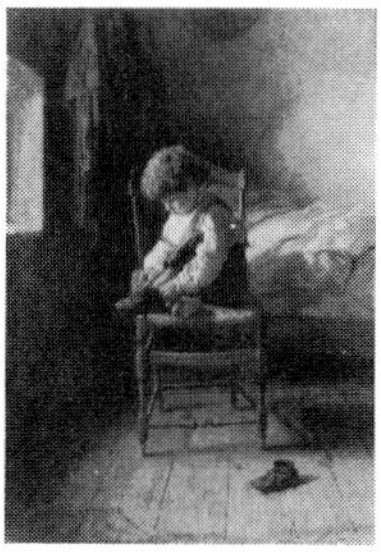

Théophile-Emmanuel Duverger (1821–?1901)

acc. no. 659
Alone

oil on panel: 10 × 7 in.
signed: *DUVERGER*
Bequeathed by Charles Gassiot, 1902

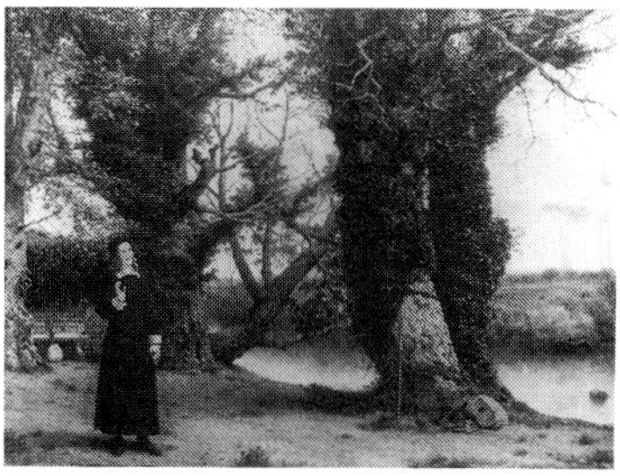

William Dyce (1806–64)

acc. no. 660
George Herbert at Bemerton (1860)

oil on canvas: 34 × 44 in.
Bequeathed by Charles Gassiot, 1902

acc. no. 661
Henry VI at Towton (1860)

oil on panel: $14\frac{1}{2} \times 20$ in.
Bequeathed by Charles Gassiot, 1902

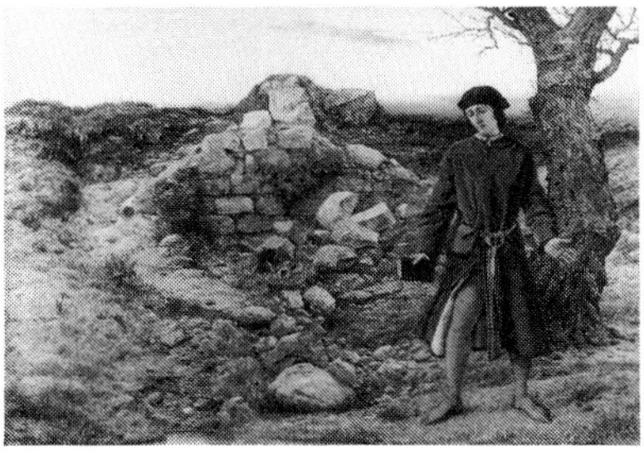

after The Hon. Miss Emily Eden (1797–1869) by Lowes Cato Dickinson (1819–1908)

acc. no. 3576
A Fakeer (1844)

lithograph: $20\frac{3}{4} \times 14\frac{5}{8}$ in.
lettered: *FAKEER ATTACHED TO THE SUITE OF THE GOVERNOR GENERAL IN CAMP*
Presented by Miss Helen Guiterman, 1985

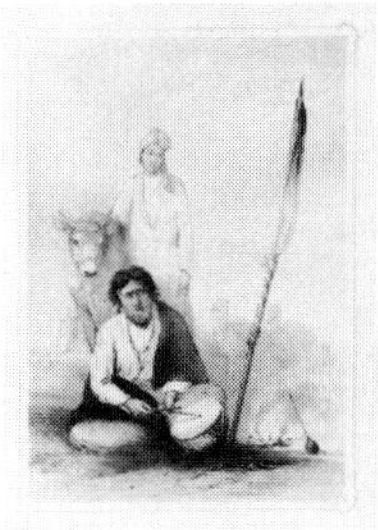

acc. no. 3577
A Young Hill Raja (1844)

lithograph: $20\frac{3}{4} \times 14\frac{5}{8}$ in.
lettered: *A YOUNG HILL RAJA*
Presented by Miss Helen Guiterman, 1985

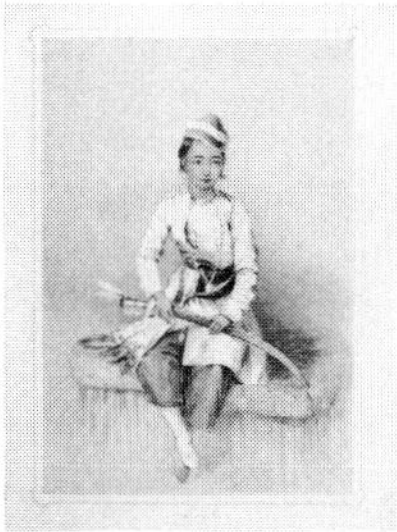

acc. no. 3578
A Zemindar and a Puthan (1844)

lithograph: $20\frac{3}{4} \times 14\frac{5}{8}$ in.
lettered: *A ZEMINDAR OR FARMER OF THE UPPER PROVINCES AND A PUTHAN, A FAMOUS WRESTLER*
Presented by Miss Helen Guiterman, 1985

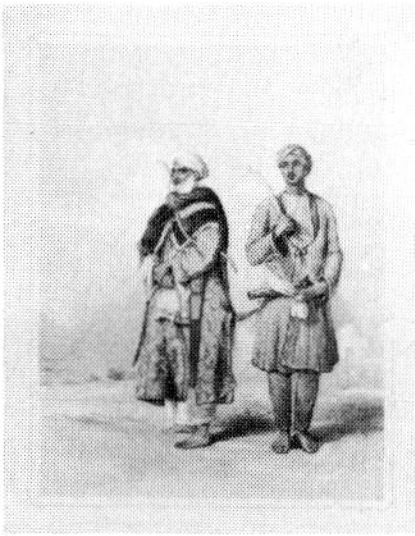

acc. no. 3579
Akalees (1844)

lithograph: $20\frac{3}{4} \times 14\frac{5}{8}$ in.
lettered: *AKALEES*
Presented by Miss Helen Guiterman, 1985

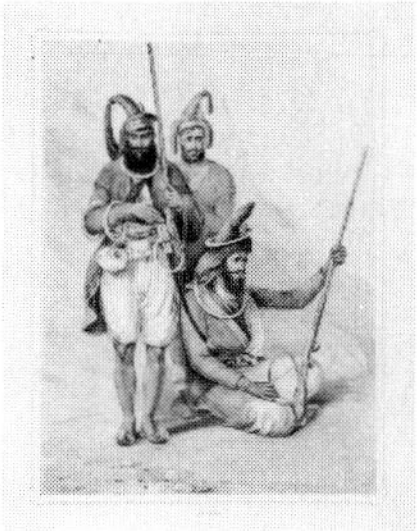

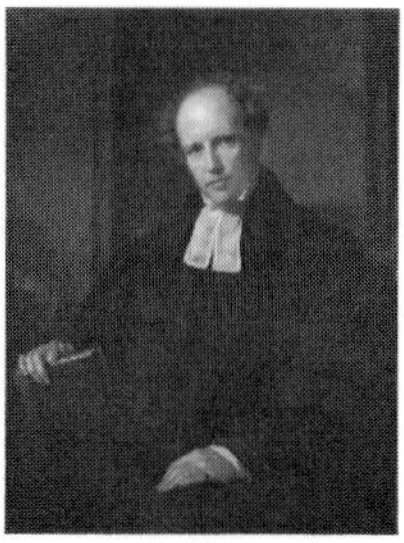

Eden Upton Eddis (1812–1901)

acc. no. 1634
Dr. George Ferris Whidborne Mortimer, Headmaster of the City of London School
oil on canvas: $42\frac{1}{2} \times 34$ in.
Presented to the City of London School by Brian M. Clarke, 1961

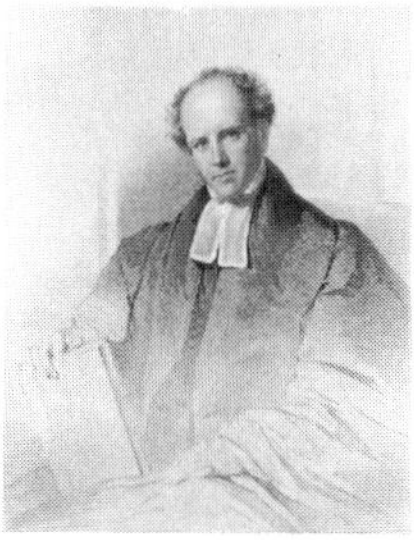

after Eden Upton Eddis (1812–1901)

acc. no. 2212
Dr. G.F.W. Mortimer, Headmaster of the City of London School
lithograph: $13 \times 10\frac{1}{4}$ in.
Found at the City of London School 1977, source and date of acquisition unknown

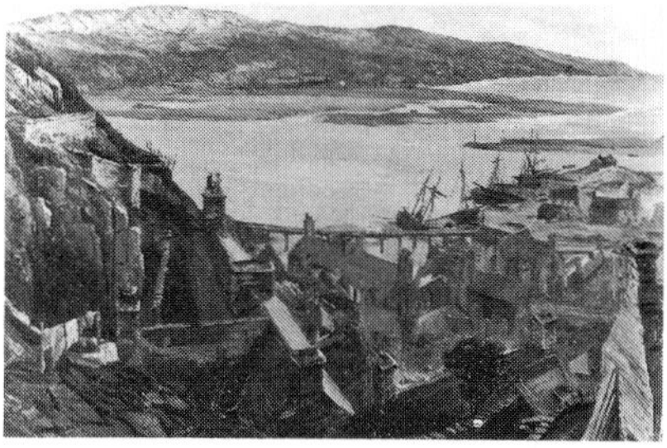

Edwin Edwards (1823–79)

acc. no. 838
Barmouth
oil on canvas: $14 \times 21\frac{1}{4}$ in.
signed: *Edwin Edwards*
Presented by Mrs. Edwards, 1905

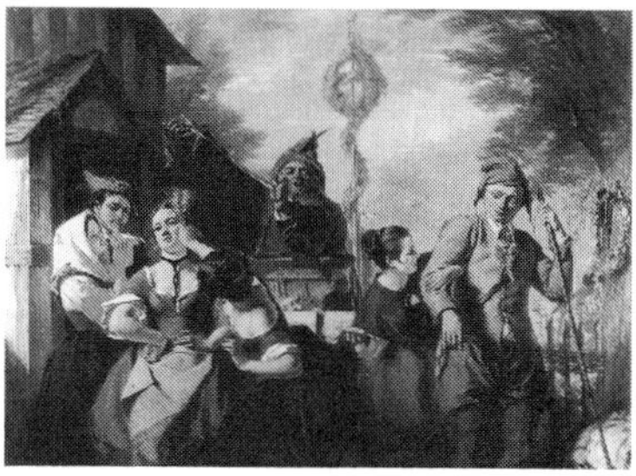

Augustus Leopold Egg (1816–63)

acc. no. 662
Scene from 'The Winter's Tale' (1845)
oil on canvas: 34×46 in.
signed and dated: *Augustus Egg 1845*
Bequeathed by Charles Gassiot, 1902

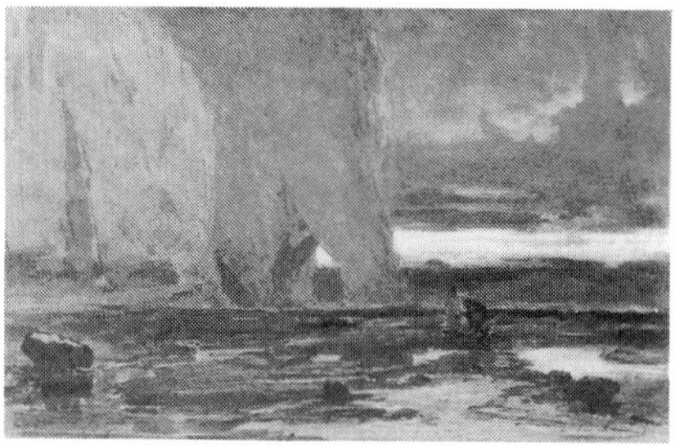

Edwin Ellis (1841–95)

acc. no. 3531
Beach and Cliffs
watercolour: $14\frac{1}{2} \times 21\frac{1}{2}$ in.
signed: *E ELLIS*
Presented by Miss Helen Guiterman, 1985

Noel Ellis (b.1917)

acc. no. 2208
St Mary's Parish Church, Battersea (1976)

screenprint: 13 × 16 in.
signed, dated and inscribed: *"Battersea Parish Church: St Mary's (by the river)" Noel Ellis 1976*
Purchased from the artist, 1977

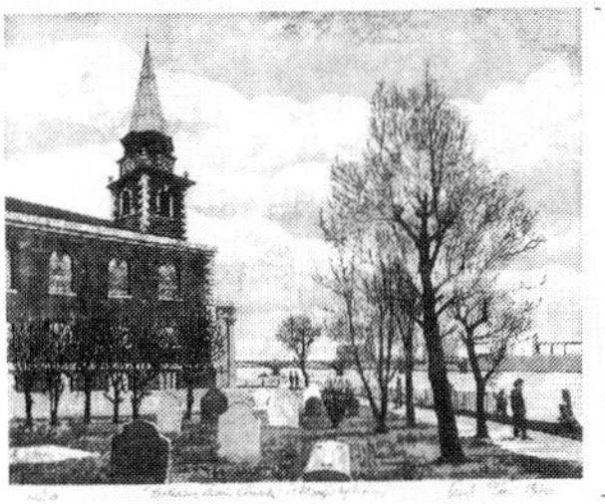

Alfred Edward Emslie (1848–1918)

acc. no. 604
Alderman William Lawrence, Sheriff 1849
(*c.*1849)

oil on canvas: 50 × 38 in.
signed: *A E Emslie*
Bequeathed by the sitter's son, Alderman Sir William Lawrence, 1897

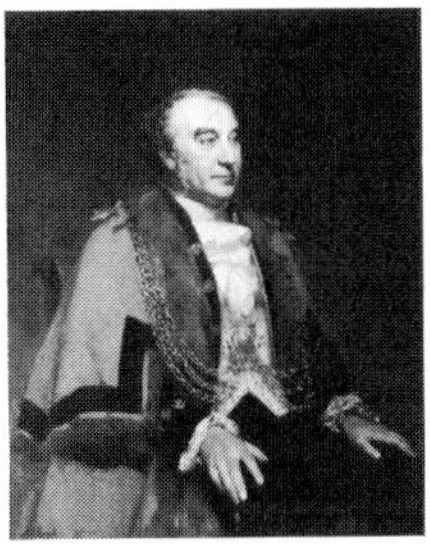

acc. no. 997
A Sonata of Beethoven

oil on canvas: 62 × 46 in.
signed: *A E EMSLIE*
Presented to the Guildhall School of Music by the artist's widow, Mrs. Rosalie Emslie, 1919

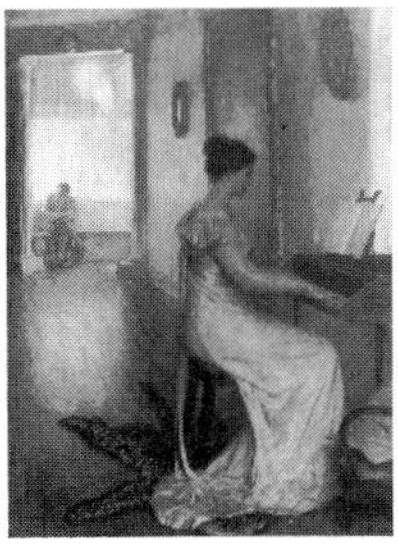

Ignacio Garcia Ergüin (20th C)

acc. no. 2213
Bilbao (1977)

oil on canvas: 12½ × 15½ in.
signed and dated: *Garcia Erguin 77*
Presented by Deputy Stanley Edward Cohen, 1977

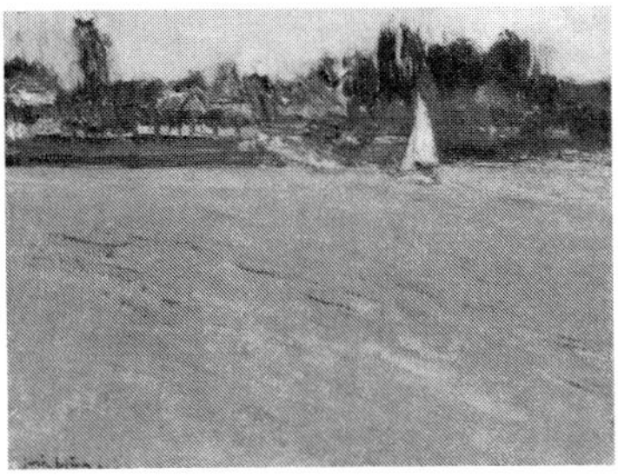

Thomas Faed (1826–1900)

acc. no. 664
Too Young to be Married (1869)

oil on canvas: 10½ × 8½ in.
signed and dated: *Faed 1869*
Bequeathed by Charles Gassiot, 1902

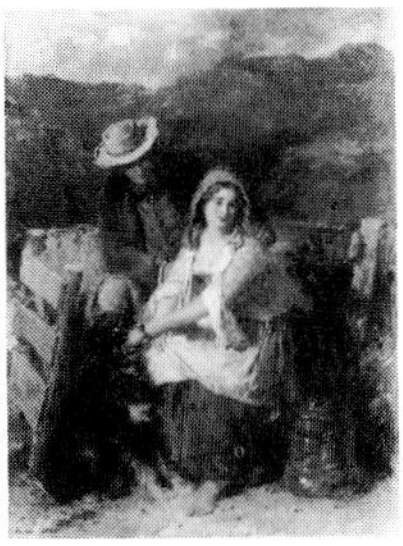

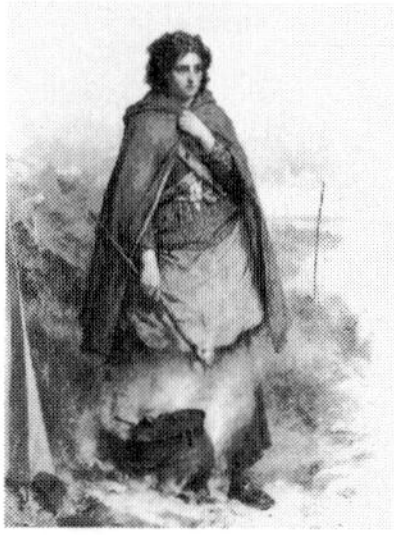

acc. no. 666
A Highland Gipsy (1870)
oil on canvas: $10\frac{1}{2} \times 8\frac{1}{2}$ in.
signed and dated: *Thomas Faed 1870*
Bequeathed by Charles Gassiot, 1902

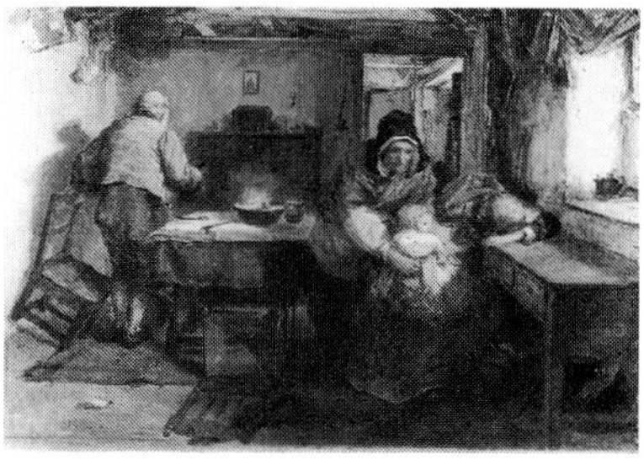

acc. no. 667
Forgiven (1874)
oil on canvas: 14 × 19 in.
signed: *Thomas Faed*
Bequeathed by Charles Gassiot, 1902

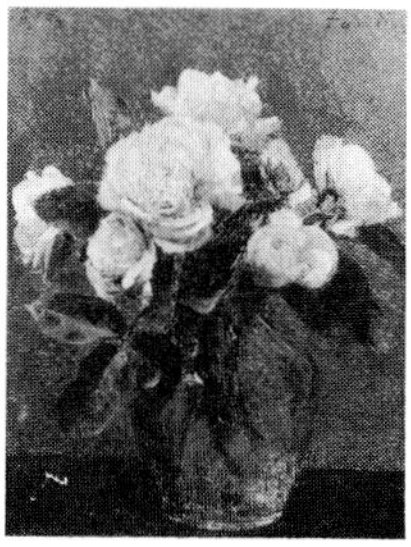

Henri Fantin-Latour (1836–1904)
acc. no. 882
White Roses in a Glass Vase (1875)
oil on canvas: $10\frac{1}{2} \times 9\frac{1}{2}$ in.
signed: *Fantin* and dated: *1875*
Bequeathed by James Thomas Slater, 1909

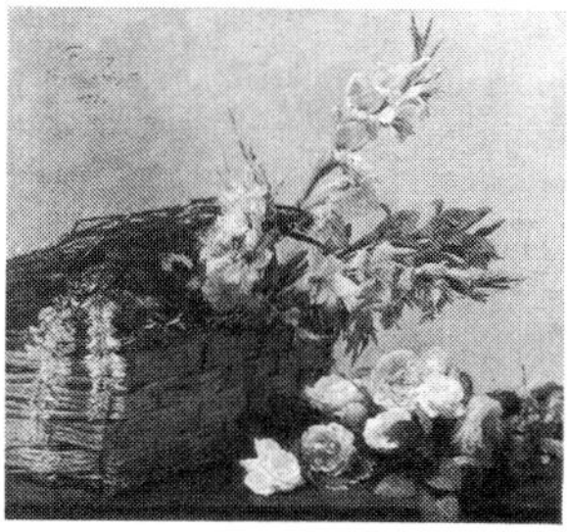

acc. no. 881
Gladioli and Roses (1880)
oil on canvas: 24 × 26 in.
signed, dated and inscribed: *Fantin/Buré – Sept./1880*
Bequeathed by James Thomas Slater, 1909

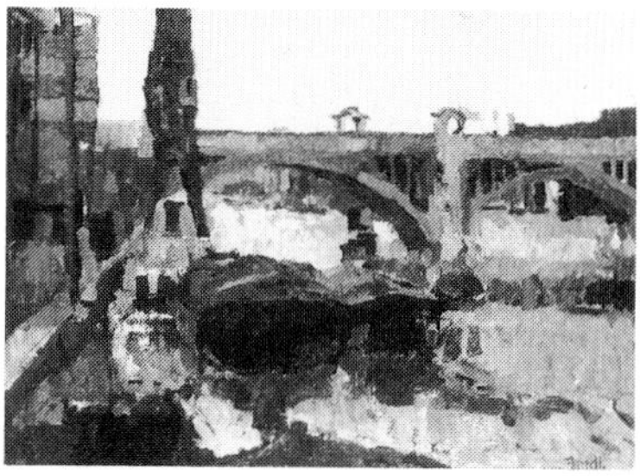

Patrick J. Farrell (20th C)
acc. no. 1715
Southwark Bridge
oil on canvas: 30 × 40 in.
signed: *Farrell*
Purchased from the artist, 1965

after James Fergusson (1808–86) by Thomas Colman Dibdin (1810–93)

acc. no. 3580
Kannari, Interior of a Small Vihara (published 1845)

lithograph: $22\frac{1}{8} \times 15$ in.
lettered: *KANNARI / T.C. DIBDIN DEL & LITH M & N HANHART IMP / INTERIOR OF SMALL VIHARA / FROM A SKETCH BY JAS. FERGUSSON ESQR. / PUBLISHED BY JOHN WEALE, 59, HIGH HOLBORN*
Presented by Miss Helen Guiterman, 1985

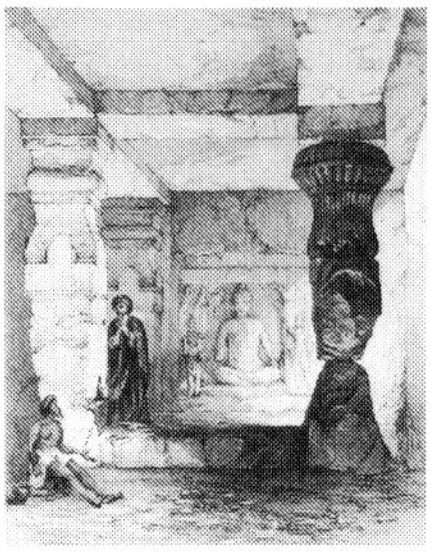

acc. no. 3581
Kannari, Exterior of Great Chaitya Cave (published 1845)

lithograph: $15 \times 22\frac{1}{8}$ in.
lettered: *KANNARI, T.C. DIBDIN DEL & LITH M & N HANHART IMP / EXTERIOR OF GREAT CHAITYA CAVE / FROM A SKETCH BY JAS. FERGUSSON ESQR. / PUBLISHED BY JOHN WEALE, / 59 HIGH HOLBORN*
Presented by Miss Helen Guiterman, 1985

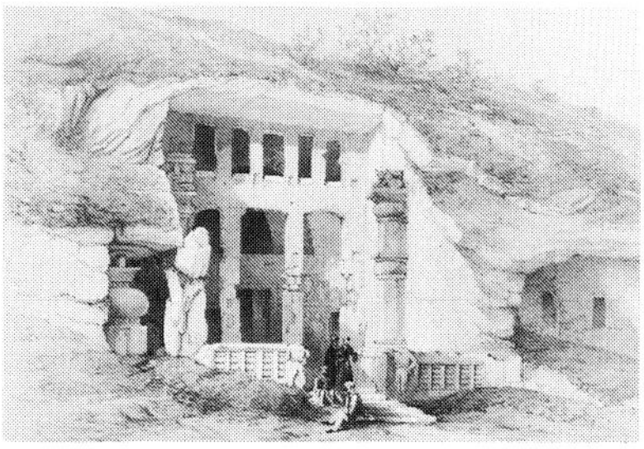

acc. no. 3582
Kannari, Exterior of Great Chaitya Cave (another impression)

similar to acc. no. 3581

acc. no. 3583
Ajunta, Vihara Cave No. 7 (published 1845)

lithograph: $15 \times 21\frac{7}{8}$ in.
lettered: *AJUNTA / T.C. DIBDIN DEL & LITH M & N HANHART IMP / VIHARA CAVE NO. 7 / FROM A SKETCH BY JAS. FERGUSSON ESQR.*
Presented by Miss Helen Guiterman, 1985

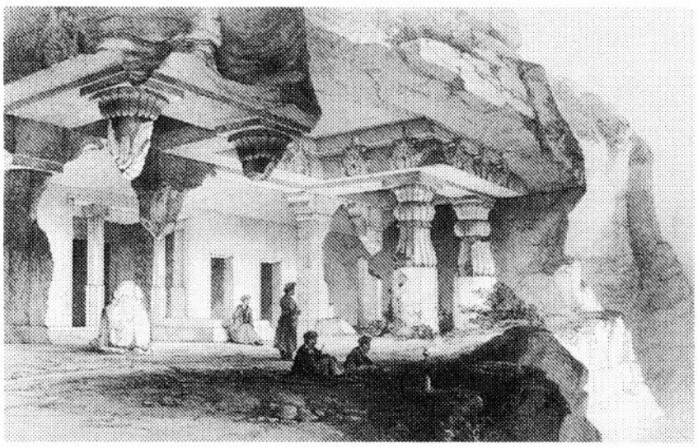

acc. no. 3585
Karli, Entrance of Great Chaitya Cave (published 1845)

lithograph: $15 \times 21\frac{3}{4}$ in.
lettered: *KARLI / T.C. DIBDIN, DEL & LITH M & N HANHART IMP / ENTRANCE OF GREAT CHAITYA CAVE. / FROM A SKETCH BY JAS. FERGUSSON ESQR. PUBLISHED BY JOHN WEALE, 59, HIGH HOLBORN*
Presented by Miss Helen Guiterman, 1985

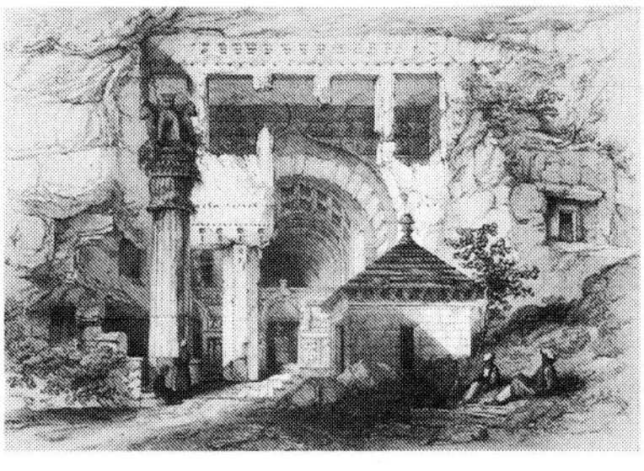

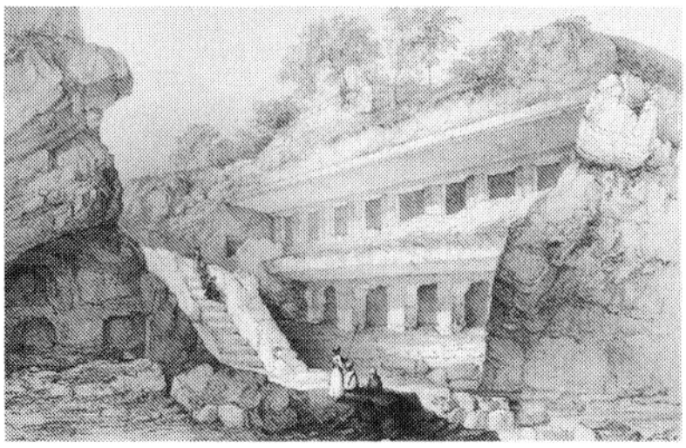

acc. no. 3586
Kannari, View of Durbar Cave (published 1845)
lithograph: 15 × 22 in.
lettered: *KANNARI / T C DIBDIN DEL & LITH M & N HANHART IMP / VIEW OF DURBAR CAVE / FROM A SKETCH BY JA^{S} FERGUSSON ESQ^{R} / PUBLISHED BY JOHN WEALE, 59, HIGH HOLBORN*
Presented by Miss Helen Guiterman, 1985

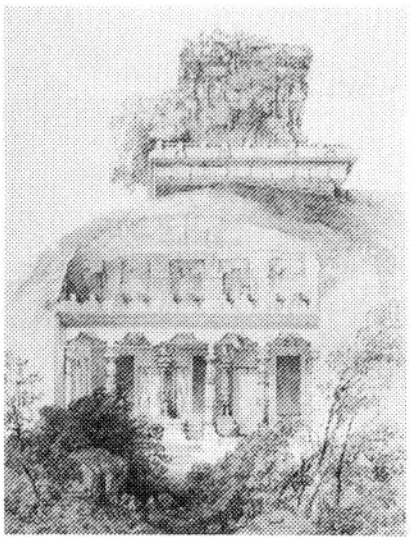

acc. no. 3588
Cave with Structural Vimana, Mahavellipore (published 1845)
lithograph: $21\frac{7}{8} \times 14\frac{7}{8}$ in.
lettered: *MAHAVELLIPORE / PLATE XVII / T.C. DIBDIN DEL & LITH M & N HANHART IMP / CAVE WITH STRUCTURAL VIMANA / FROM A SKETCH BY JA^{S} FERGUSSON ESQ^{R} / PUBLISHED BY JOHN WEALE, 59, HIGH HOLBORN.*
Presented by Miss Helen Guiterman, 1985

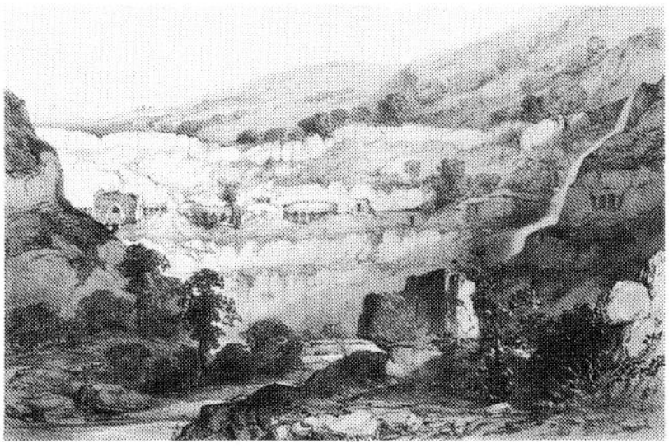

acc. no. 3589
General Views of Caves, Ajunta (published 1845)
lithograph: $15\frac{1}{8} \times 21\frac{7}{8}$ in.
signed in the plate: *T C Dibdin / 1844*
lettered: *AJUNTA / PLATE II / T.C. DIBDIN DEL & LITH M & N HANHART IMP / GENERAL VIEW OF CAVES COMPRISING CAVES N^{O} 21 & 26 / FROM A SKETCH BY JA^{S} FERGUSSON ESQ^{R} / PUBLISHED BY JOHN WEALE 59 HIGH HOLBORN*
Presented by Miss Helen Guiterman, 1985

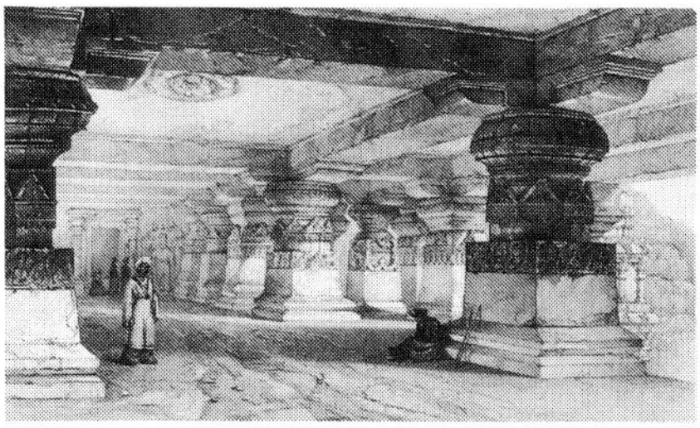

acc. no. 3590
Interior of Lanka, Ellora (published 1845)
lithograph: 15 × 22 in.
lettered: *ELLORA / PLATE XVI / T.C. DIBDIN DEL & LITH. M & N HANHART IMP. / INTERIOR OF LANKA / FROM A SKETCH BY JA^{S} FERGUSSON ESQ^{R} / PUBLISHED BY JOHN WEALE, 59, HIGH HOLBORN.*
Presented by Miss Helen Guiterman, 1985

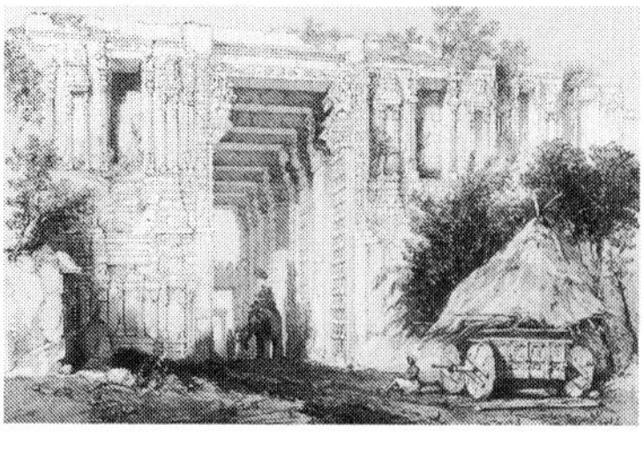

acc. no. 3584
Gateway at Seringham (published 1852)
lithograph: $14\frac{7}{8} \times 22\frac{1}{8}$ in.
lettered: *DRAWN & LITH^{D} BY T.C. DIBDIN, FROM A SKETCH BY J. FERGUSSON ESQ^{E} PRINTED BY M & N HANHART / Pl. 23. GATEWAY AT SERINGHAM. / PUBLISHED BY J. HOGARTH 5, HAYMARKET.*
Presented by Miss Helen Guiterman, 1985

acc. no. 3587
Temple of Sri Rama, Combaconum (published 1852)

lithograph: $14\frac{3}{4} \times 22$ in.
lettered: *DRAWN & LITHD. BY T.C. DIBDIN. FROM A SKETCH BY J. FERGUSSON ESQE. PRINTED BY M & N HANHART / Pl. 20. TEMPLE OF SRI RAMA, COMBACONUM / PUBLISHED BY J. HOGARTH, 5, HAYMARKET*
Presented by Miss Helen Guiterman, 1985

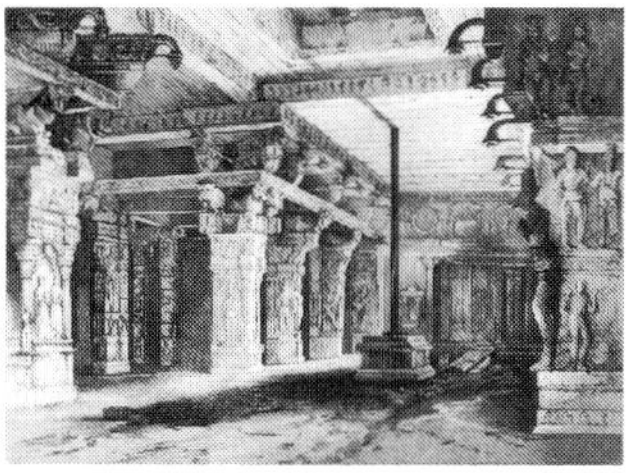

Sidney G. Ferris (20th C)

acc. no. 1789
St. Paul's from the South-East, 1966

watercolour on paper: $14\frac{1}{4} \times 19$ in.
signed: *SIDNEY FERRIS*
Purchased from the Furneaux Gallery, 1968

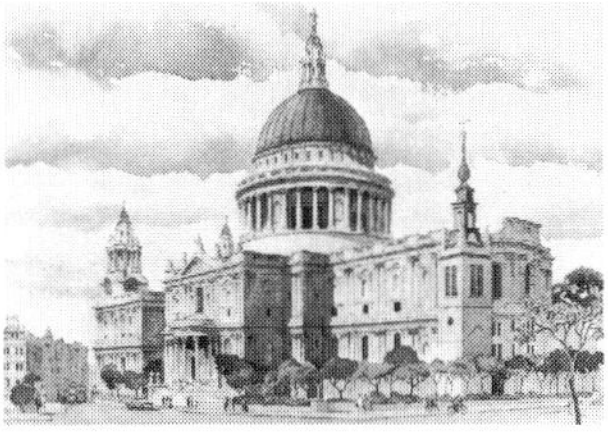

Sir Luke Fildes (1843–1927)

acc. no. 1774
Naomi (1914)

oil on canvas: $25\frac{1}{2} \times 19\frac{1}{2}$ in.
signed and dated: *Luke Fildes/1914.*
Presented by L. V. Fildes, 1967

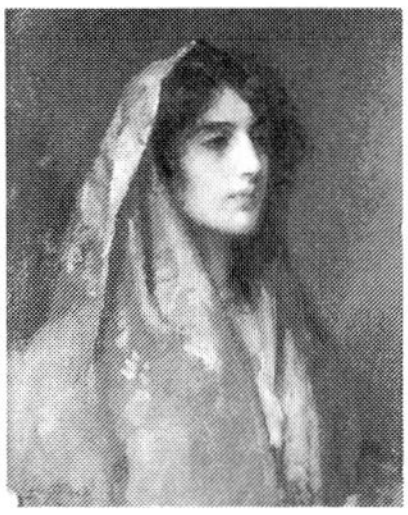

Mario da Fiori (1603–73) – see Mario Nuzzi

John Austen Fitzgerald (1832–1906)

acc. no. 518
Study of a Nude Woman

oil on canvas: 18×9 in.
Presented by Graham King, 1891

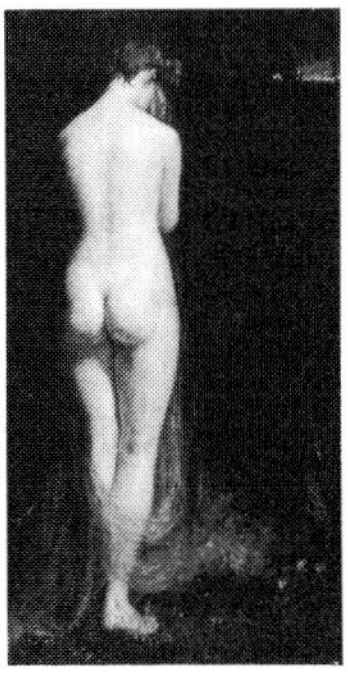

Dennis Flanders (b.1915)

acc. no. 1371
All Hallows, Lombard Street (1938)

pen and ink with watercolour: $15\frac{1}{2} \times 21\frac{1}{2}$ in.
signed and dated: *Dennis Flanders '38.*
Purchased from Colnaghi's 1947

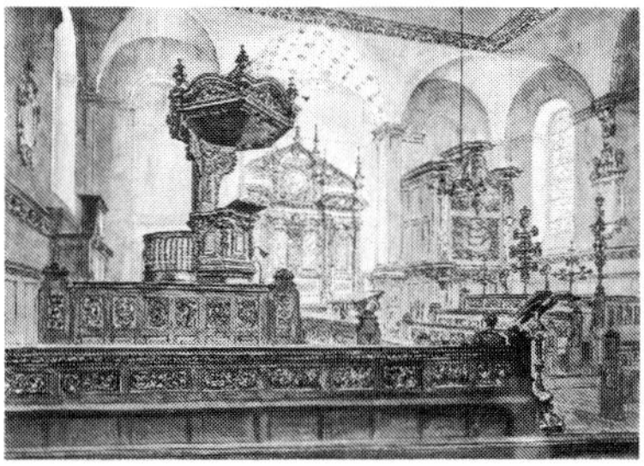

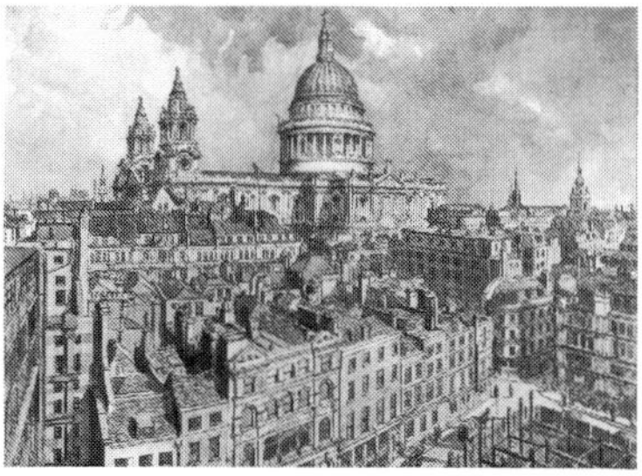

acc. no. 1370
St. Paul's and Doctors' Commons (1939)

pen and wash: $16\frac{1}{8} \times 21\frac{1}{2}$ in.
signed: *Dennis Flanders*
Purchased from Colnaghi's, 1947

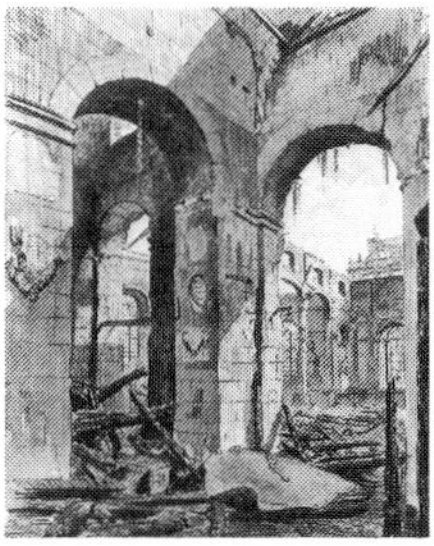

acc. no. 1356
Ruins of St. Lawrence Jewry (1941)

watercolour: $17\frac{1}{2} \times 14$ in.
signed and dated: *Dennis Flanders / Feb. 41.*
Allocated by the War Artists Advisory Committee, 1947

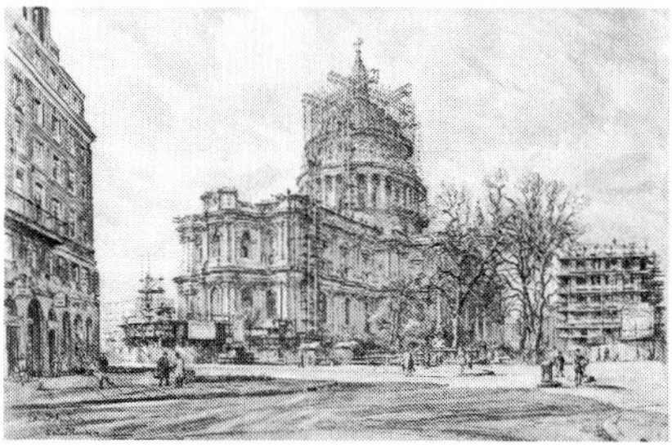

acc. no. 1773
St. Paul's: Scaffolding around the Dome

pen and watercolour: $13\frac{3}{4} \times 21\frac{1}{2}$ in.
signed twice: *Dennis Flanders*
Purchased from the artist, 1967

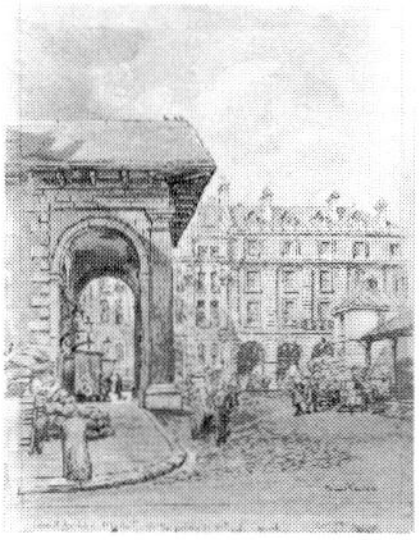

acc. no. 1897
Covent Garden (1971)

watercolour: $13\frac{1}{4} \times 10\frac{5}{8}$ in.
signed: *Dennis Flanders* and inscribed: *Covent Garden Market, with the portico of St. Paul's Church*
Purchased from the artist, 1972

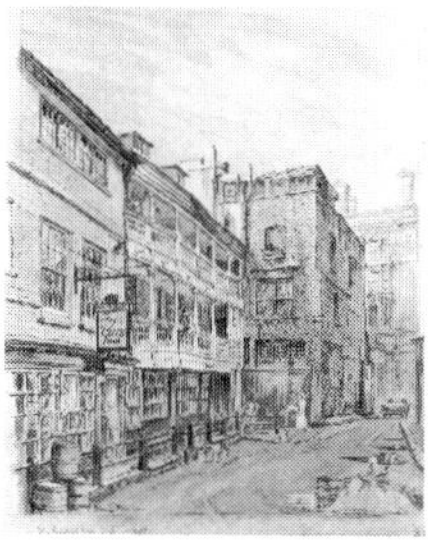

acc. no. 1899
'The George' Inn, Southwark (1971)

watercolour: $15\frac{1}{8} \times 11\frac{1}{2}$ in.
signed: *Dennis Flanders* and inscribed: *The George Inn, Southwark*
Purchased from the artist, 1972

acc. no. 1996
Christ Church, Newgate (1972)
watercolour: $12\frac{1}{2} \times 17\frac{1}{2}$ in.
signed: *Dennis Flanders*
Purchased from the artist, 1974

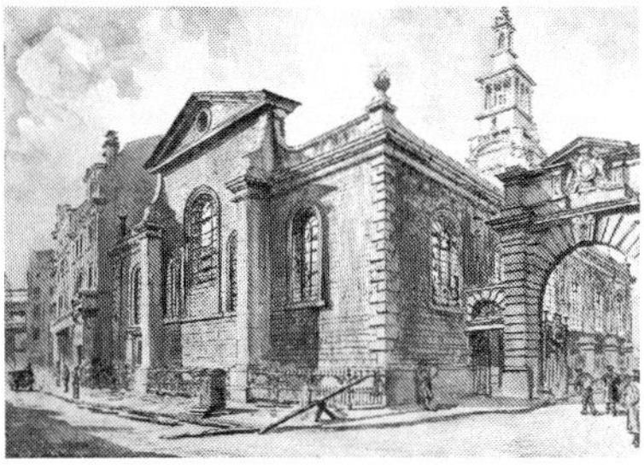

acc. no. 2161
The Guildhall (?1972)
watercolour: $13 \times 16\frac{1}{2}$ in.
signed: *Dennis Flanders*
Purchased from the artist, 1975

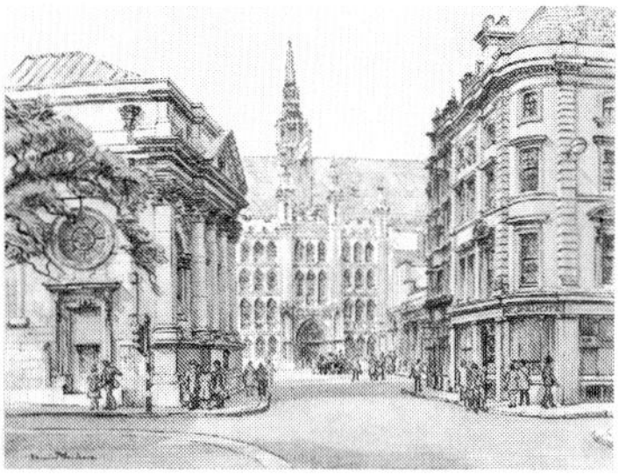

acc. no. 2190
Salters' Hall before 1824 (after Thomas Hosmer Shepherd)
watercolour: $13\frac{3}{4} \times 9\frac{1}{4}$ in.
signed: *D.F. (after Shepherd)*
Purchased from the artist, 1975

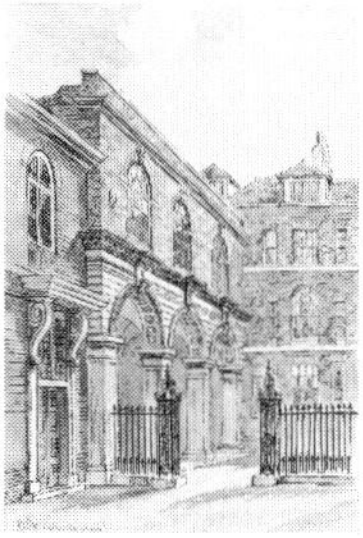

after John Flaxman (1755–1826)

acc. no. 3564
Maria Sharpe
pencil: $8\frac{3}{8} \times 6\frac{5}{8}$ in.
inscribed on label attached to verso: *Mrs. Sharpe d.1806 / Henry's Mother / Copy from Flaxman / Sister of Samuel Rogers – Poet*
Presented by Miss Helen Guiterman, 1985

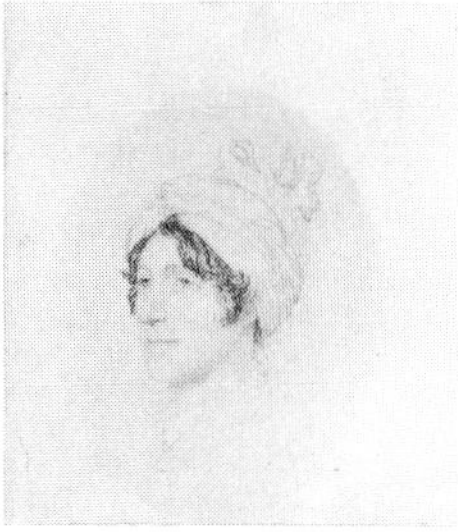

Elizabeth A. Forbes (1859–1912)

acc. no. 949
On a Fine Day (1903)
oil on canvas: 39×58 in.
signed: *EA FORBES.*
Presented by Stanhope Forbes, 1913

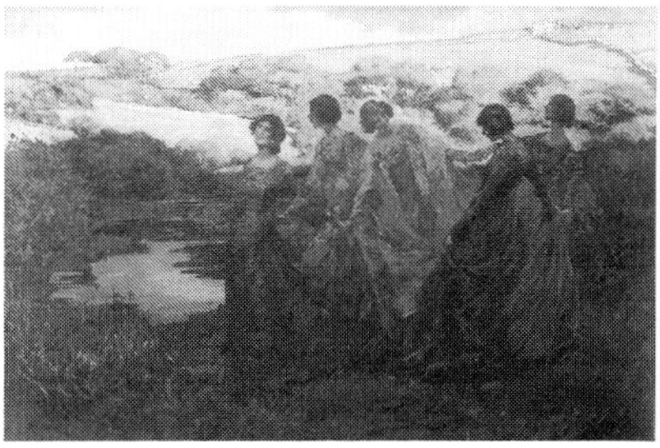

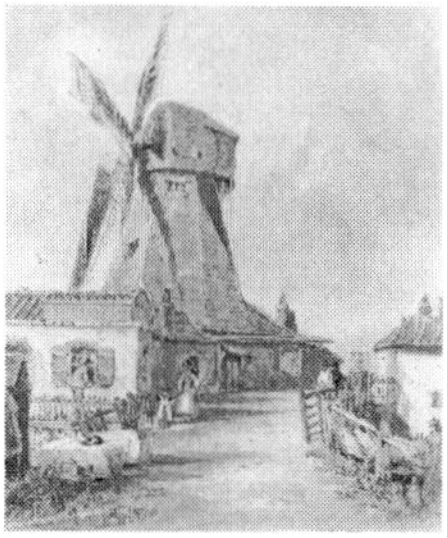

L. G. Ford (19th C)

acc. no. 2258
Millwall in 1843

watercolour: $9\frac{5}{8} \times 8\frac{1}{4}$ in.
inscribed: *Mill Wall / in 1843*
Presented by Miss Helen Guiterman, 1985

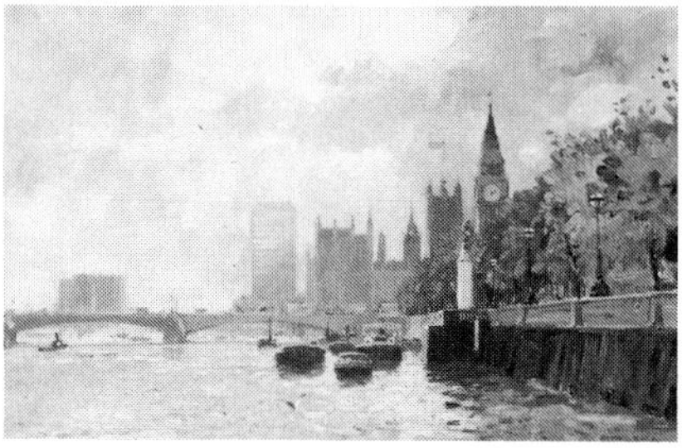

Marcus Ford (20th C)

acc. no. 1736
Westminster from the Embankment (1966)

oil on canvas: 24 × 36 in.
signed *MARCUS FORD*
Purchased from the artist, 1966

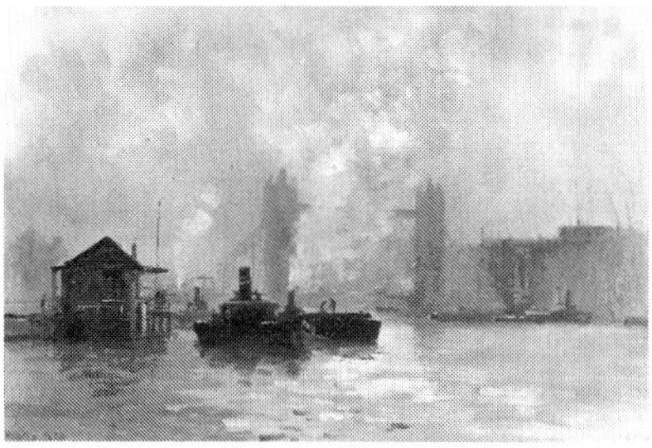

acc. no. 1834
Tower Bridge

oil on canvas: $24 \times 35\frac{1}{2}$ in.
signed: *MARCUS FORD*
Purchased from the artist, 1970

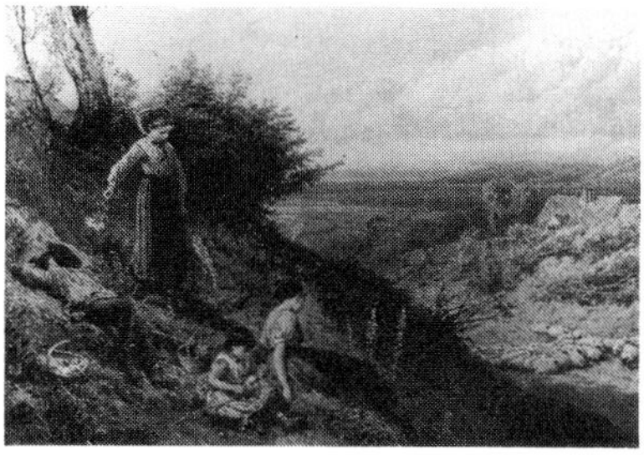

Myles Birket Foster (1825–99)

acc. no. 886
The Hillside (Gathering Foxgloves)

watercolour: 12 × 17 in.
signed in monogram: *BF*; inscribed on verso *The Hill Side or Gathering Fox Gloves*
Bequeathed by James Thomas Slater, 1909

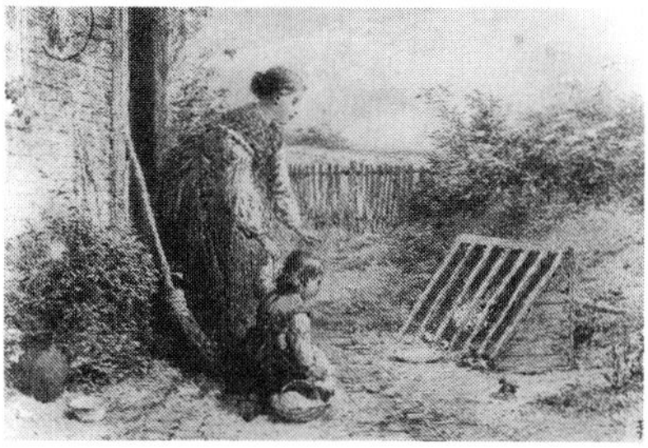

acc. no. 887
The Hencoop

watercolour: 7 × 10 in.
signed in monogram: *BF*
Bequeathed by James Thomas Slater, 1909

acc. no. 1043
Richmond Bridge
watercolour: $4 \times 5\frac{1}{4}$ in.
signed in monogram: *BF*
Presented by Sir William Lancaster, 1926

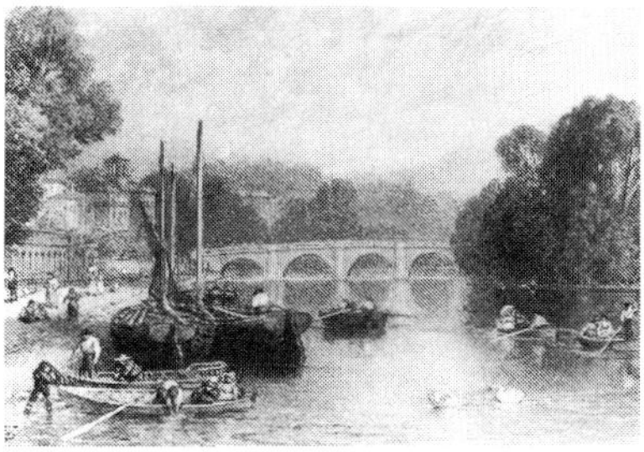

acc. no. 1347
Seascape
watercolour: $6\frac{1}{4} \times 8\frac{3}{4}$ in.
signed in monogram: *BF*
Presented by Miss T. A. C. Durning-Lawrence, 1946

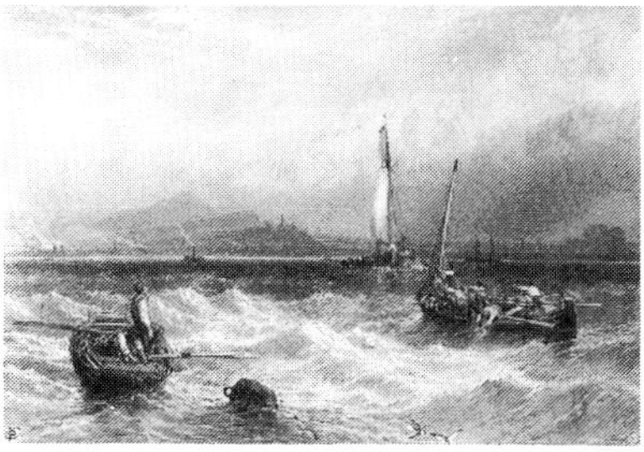

acc. no. 1497
A Girl driving Cattle across a Stream
watercolour: 5×7 in.
signed in monogram: *BF*
Bequeathed by John E. S. Dallas, 1953

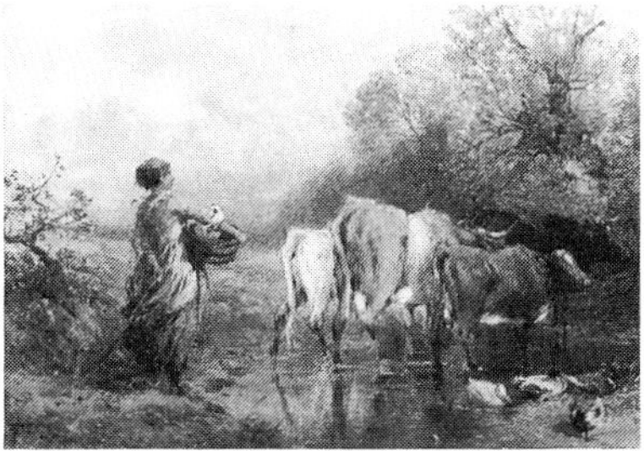

Derek Fowler (b.1919)

acc. no. 1726
Dr. Arthur Willoughby Barton (1965)
oil on canvas: 40×30 in.
signed: *Derek Fowler*
Presented to the City of London School by the John Carpenter Club, 1965

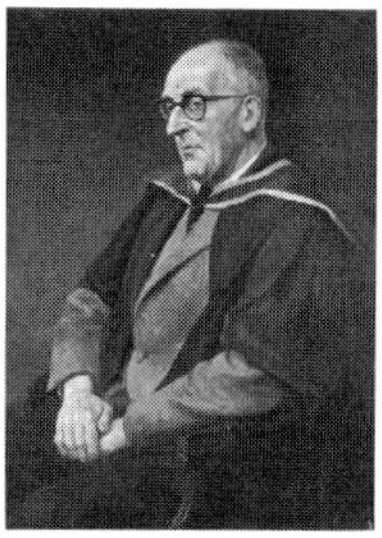

acc. no. 1935
Warren Stormes Hale, Founder of the City of London School and Lord Mayor 1864 (1972)
oil on canvas: 40×30 in.
signed: *Derek Fowler*
Commissioned by the City of London School, 1972

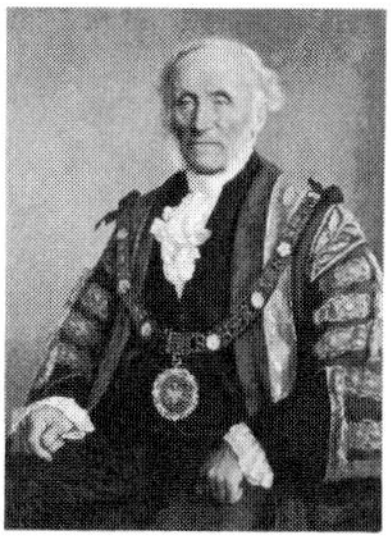

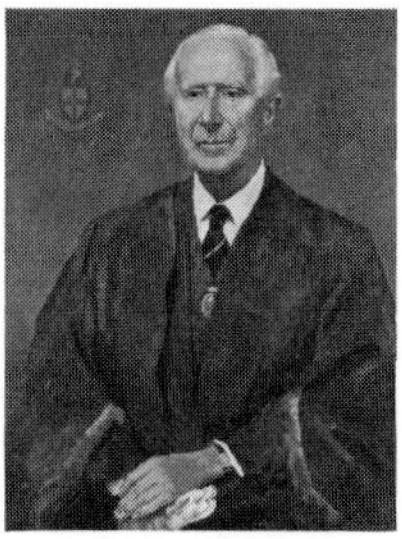

acc. no. 2273
Deputy Alexander George Coulson (1980)

oil on canvas: 36 × 28 in.
signed and dated: *Derek Fowler 1980*
Presented to the City of London School by the John Carpenter Club, 1980

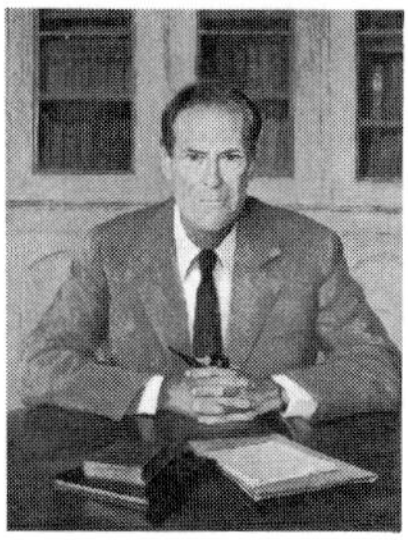

acc. no. 3414
James Boyes, Headmaster of the City of London School (1983)

oil on canvas: 38 × 30½ in.
signed: *Derek Fowler*
Presented to the School by the sitter, 1983

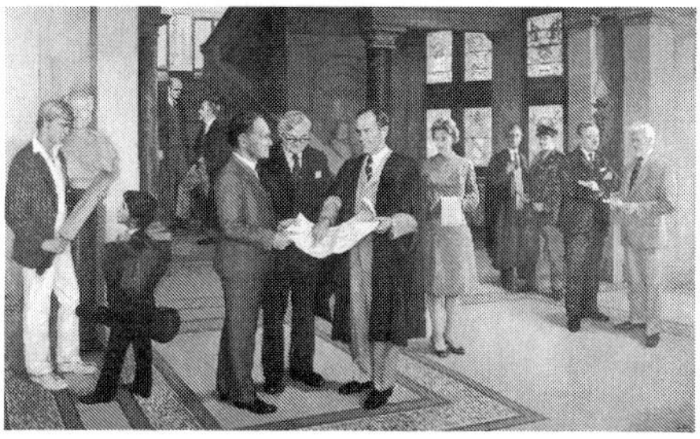

acc. no. 3511
The Chairman, Deputy Chairman, Headmaster, other Members of Staff and Pupils in the Entrance Hall of the Old City of London School, Victoria Embankment (1985)

oil on canvas: 79 × 127 in.
signed and dated: *Derek Fowler. / 1985*
Commissioned by the Board of Governors of the City of London School, 1984

Hubert Andrew Freeth (1912–86)

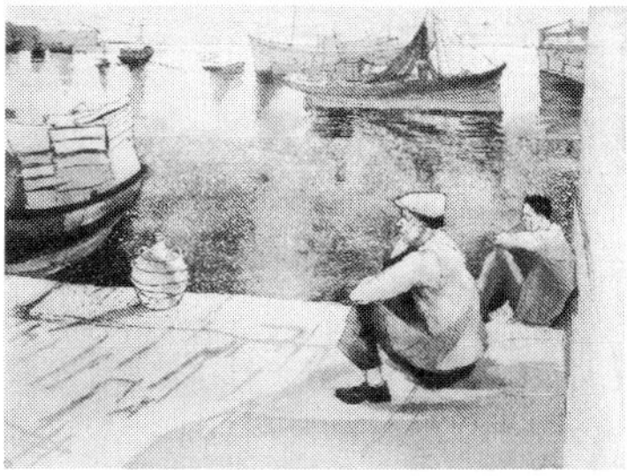

acc. no. 3556
Fishermen at Algeciras (1959)

etching and aquatint: 8⅞ × 11⅞ in. (plate)
signed: *H.A. Freeth.* and inscribed: *Fishermen at Algeciras*
Presented by Miss Helen Guiterman, 1985

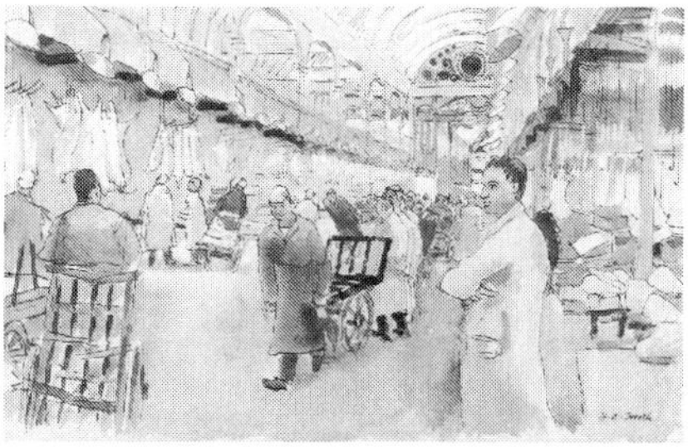

acc. no. 1794
Smithfield Market: Interior of the Meat Market (1968)

pen and ink and watercolour: 11 × 17 in.
signed: *H.A. Freeth*
Purchased from the artist, 1968

acc. no. 1795
Smithfield Market: Interior of the Meat Market (1968)

pen and ink and watercolour: 11 × 17 in.
signed: *H.A. Freeth*
Purchased from the artist, 1968

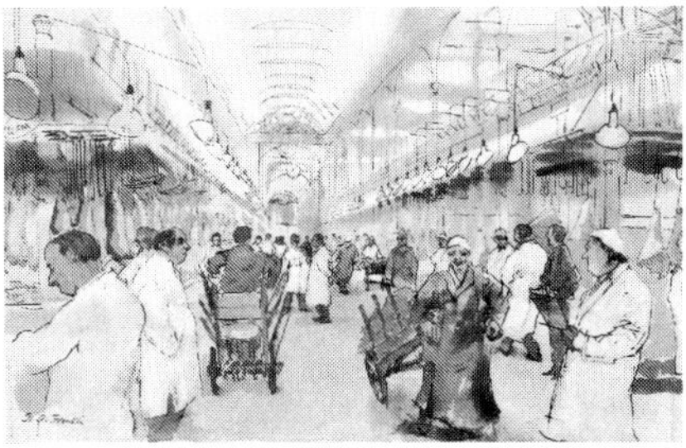

acc. no. 1796
Smithfield Market: Unloading Meat from Vans (1968)

pen and ink and watercolour: 11 × 17 in.
signed: *H.A. Freeth* and inscribed on label formerly attached to verso: *Smithfield Market / No 5 / Price 25 guineas / framed*
Purchased from the artist, 1968

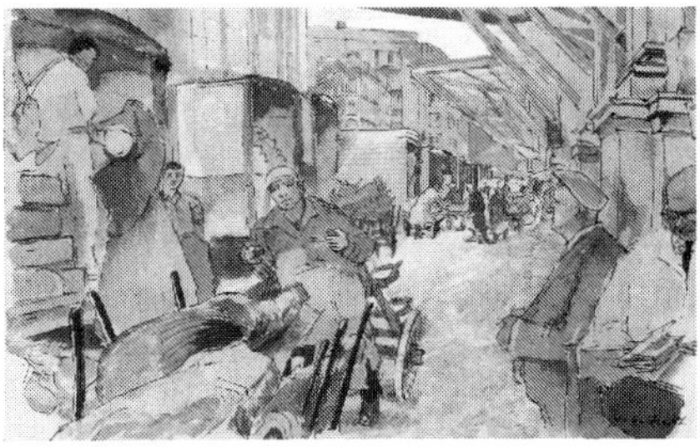

acc. no. 1797
Smithfield Market: Grand Avenue (1968)

pen and ink and watercolour: 17 × 11 in.
signed: *H.A. Freeth*
Purchased from the artist, 1968

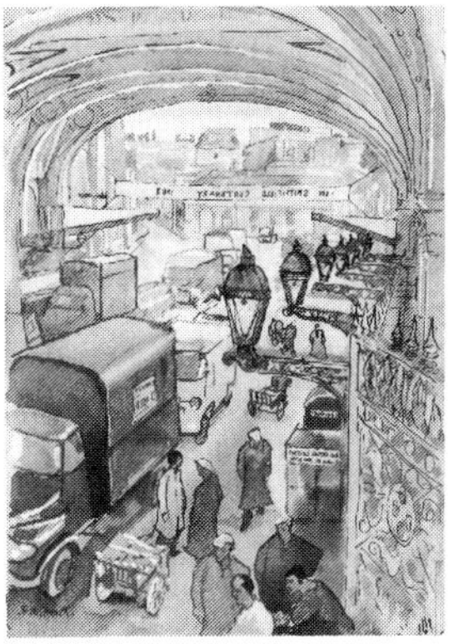

acc. no. 1798
Smithfield Market: Interior of the Meat Market (1968)

pen and ink and watercolour: $10\frac{3}{4} \times 16\frac{3}{4}$ in.
signed: *H.A. Freeth*
Purchased from the artist, 1968

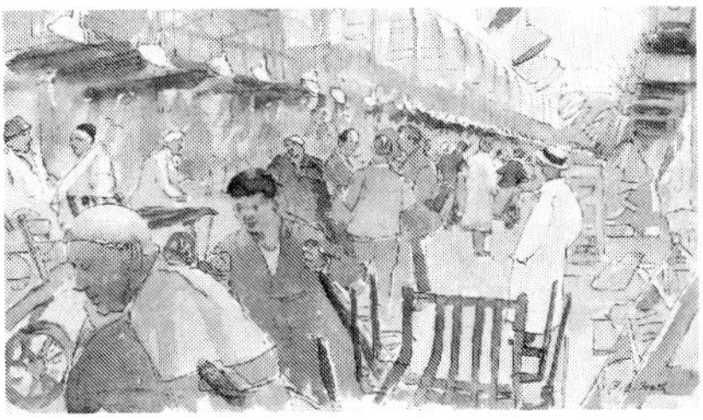

acc. no. 1963
Smithfield Centenary: Meat Porters' Race (1968)

pen and ink and watercolour: $10\frac{1}{2} \times 16\frac{1}{2}$ in.
signed: *H.A. Freeth*
Purchased from the Butchers' Company, 1973

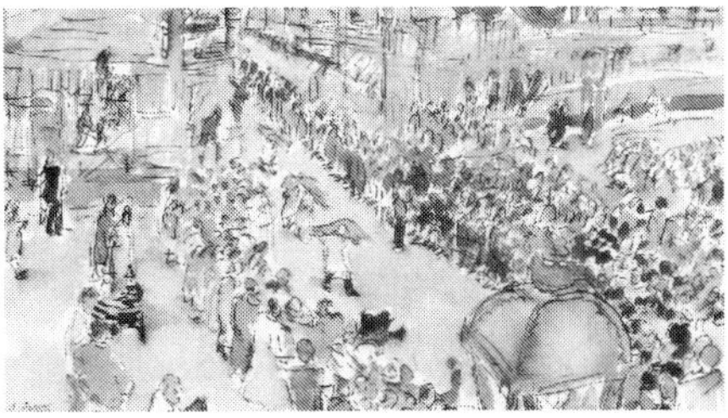

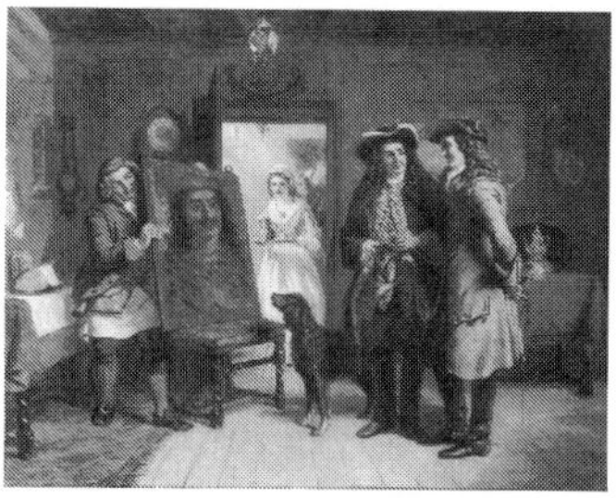

William Powell Frith (1819–1909)

acc. no. 663
Sir Roger de Coverley and Addison with 'The Saracen's Head' – a Scene from 'The Spectator' (1867)

oil on canvas: 15 × 18 in.
signed and dated: *W.P. Frith 1867*
Bequeathed by Charles Gassiot, 1902

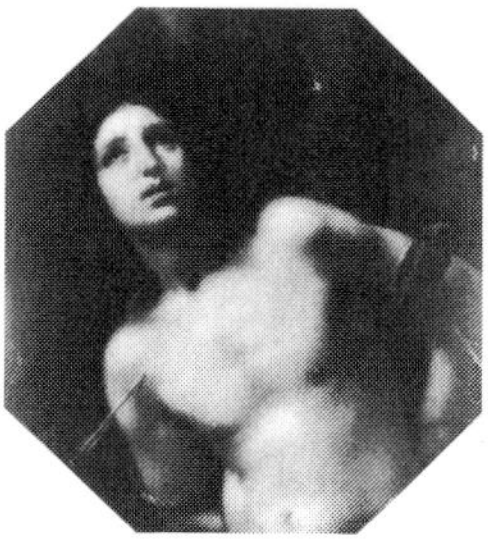

attributed to Francesco Furini (1604–46)

acc. no. 359
St. Sebastian

oil on canvas: 32 × 29 in. (octagonal)
Bequeathed by William Dunnett, 1888

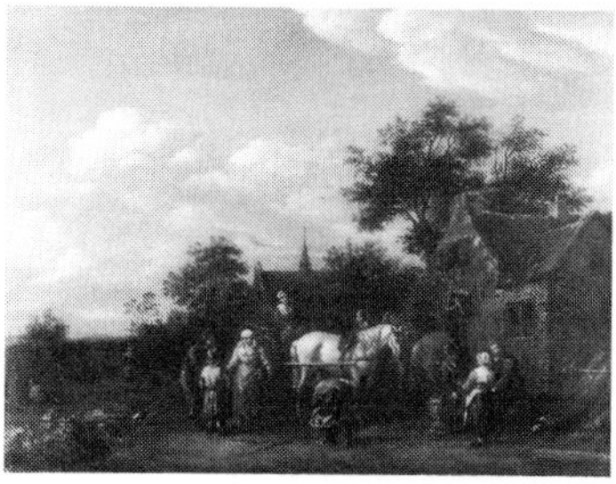

Barent Gael (1650–1703)

acc. no. 351
A Farrier's Shop

oil on canvas: 22 × 17 in.
signed: *B. Gael*
Bequeathed by William Dunnett, 1888

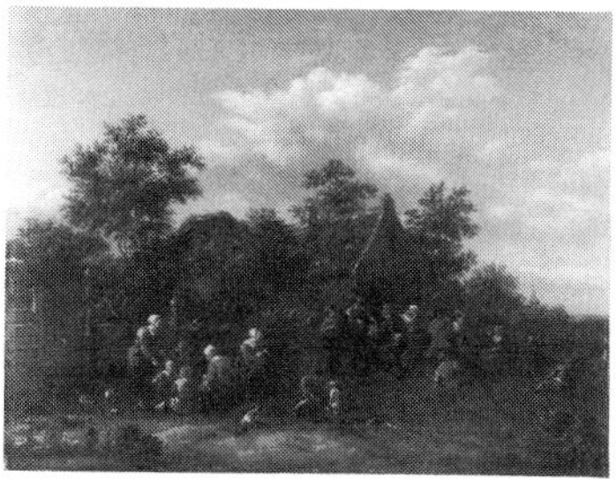

acc. no. 352
A Village Festival

oil on canvas: 22 × 17 in.
Bequeathed by William Dunnett, 1888

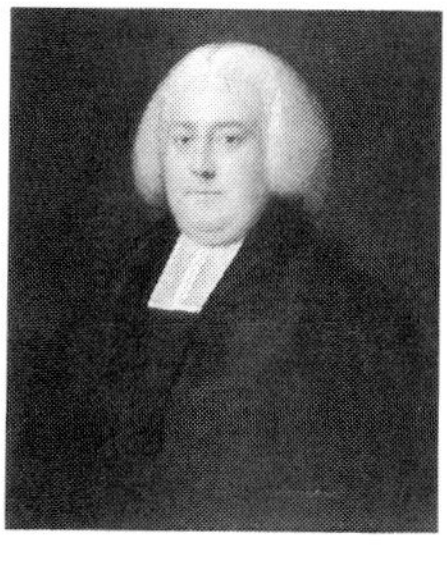

Thomas Gainsborough (1727–88)

acc. no. 1297
The Rev. Henry Burrough

oil on canvas: 30 × 25 in.
Presented by Lady Wakefield, 1944

Baldomero Galofre Y Gimenez (1849–1902)

acc. no. 983
The Market Place, Granada (1884)
oil on canvas: 6 × 10 in.
signed and dated: *B. GALOFRE. ROMA / 84.*
Presented by H. S. E. Vanderpant, 1916

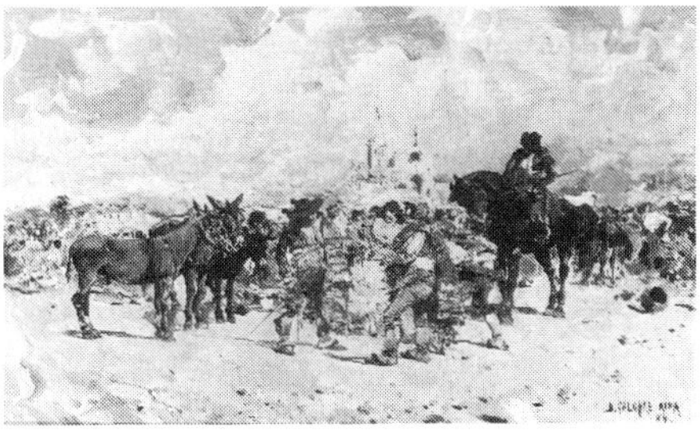

Arthur Paine Garratt (b.1873–?)

acc. no. 1326
St. Bride's Fleet Street (1908)
oil on panel: $9\frac{1}{2} \times 13\frac{1}{4}$ in.
signed: *ARTHUR GARRATT*
Presented by the artist, 1945

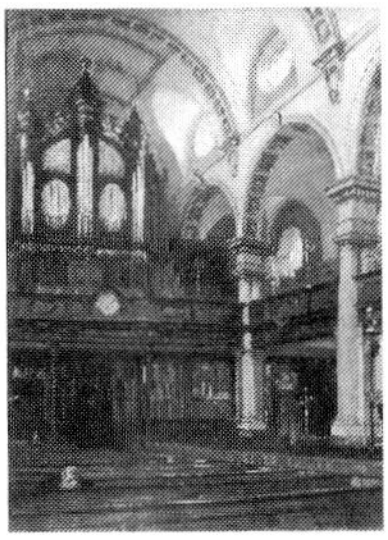

acc. no. 1327
St. Catherine Cree (1908)
oil on panel: $13\frac{1}{2} \times 9\frac{3}{4}$ in.
signed: *ARTHUR GARRATT*
Presented by the artist, 1945

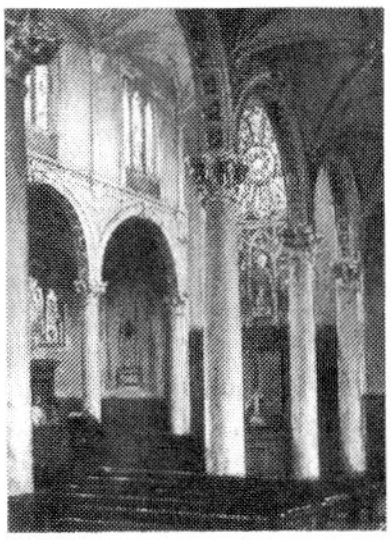

acc. no. 1328
John Stow's Monument in St. Andrew Undershaft (1908)
oil on panel: $13\frac{1}{2} \times 10$ in.
signed: *ARTHUR GARRATT*
Presented by the artist, 1945

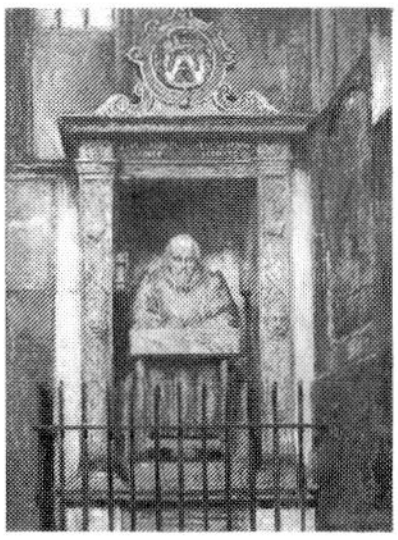

acc. no. 1329
Crypt of St. Mary le Bow (1908)
oil on panel: $13\frac{1}{4} \times 9\frac{3}{4}$ in.
signed: *ARTHUR GARRATT*
Presented by the artist, 1945

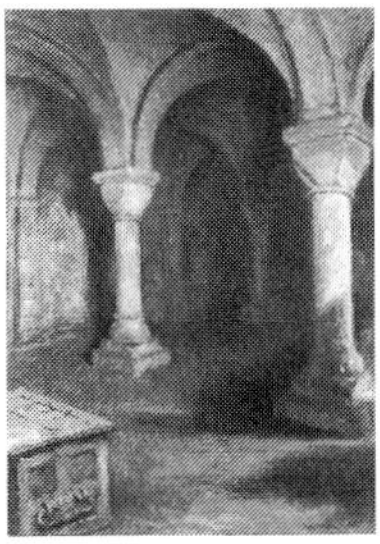

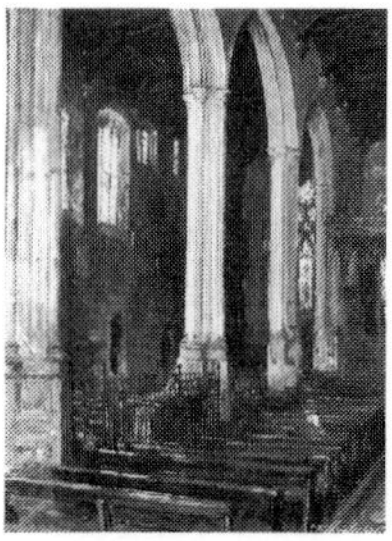

acc. no. 1330
St. Helen Bishopsgate (1908)

oil on panel: 13½ × 10 in.
signed: *ARTHUR GARRATT*
Presented by the artist, 1945

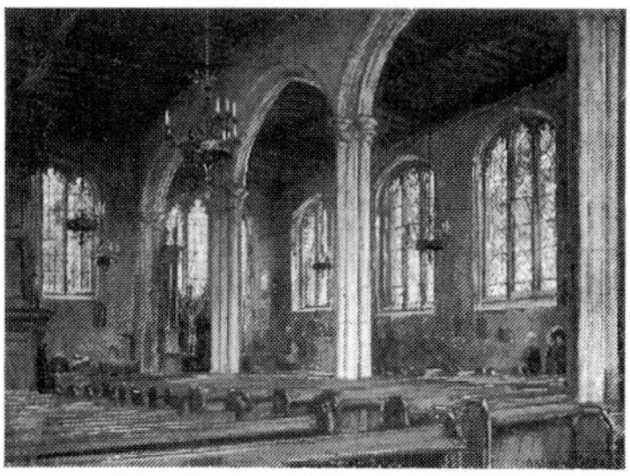

acc. no. 1331
St. Peter ad Vincula (1908)

oil on panel: 10 × 13½ in.
signed: *ARTHUR GARRATT*
Presented by the artist, 1945

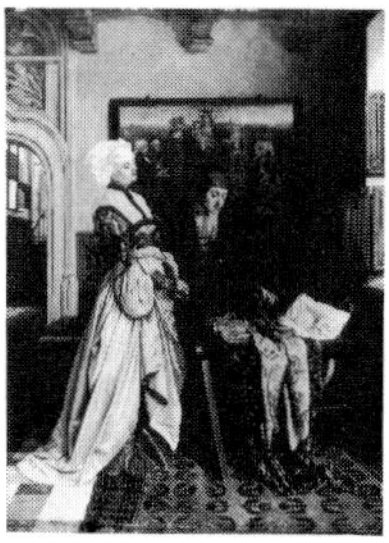

Willem Geets (b.1838–1919)

acc. no. 668
Charles V and Jeanne Vandergeynst at the Cradle of their Daughter Marguerite (1870)

oil on panel: 27½ × 20½ in.
signed and dated: *W. Geets/1870*
Bequeathed by Charles Gassiot, 1902

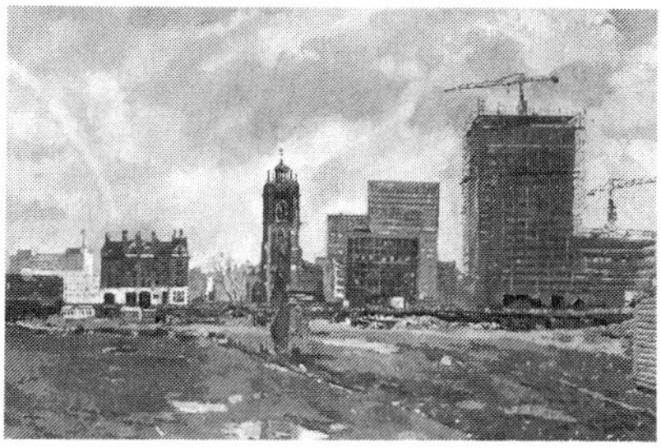

David Ghilchik (d.1972)

acc. no. 1941
Out of the Ruins at Cripplegate (1962)

oil on canvas: 24 × 36 in.
signed and dated: *Ghilchik / '62*
Purchased from the artist, 1973

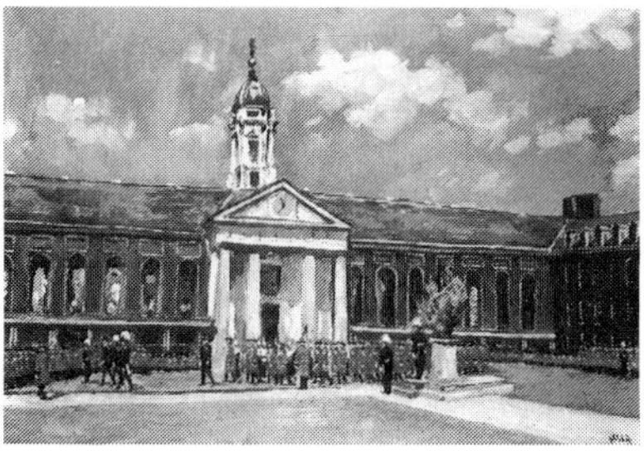

acc. no. 1856
Oak Apple Day, Royal Hospital, Chelsea (1970)

oil on canvas: 20 × 28 in.
signed: *Ghilchik*
Purchased from the artist, 1971

Dennis Gilbert (b.1922)

acc. no. 1995
Trafalgar Square
pastel: 21 × 29 in.
Purchased from the artist, 1974

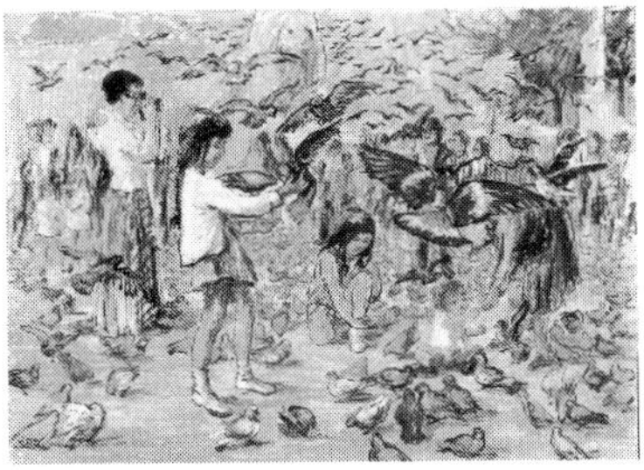

Sir John Gilbert (1817–97)

acc. no. 816a
Shoreham Church (1844)
pencil and watercolour: $6\frac{3}{4}$ × 10 in.
inscribed and dated: *Shoreham Church / 24th June 1844*
Bequeathed by George Gilbert, 1903

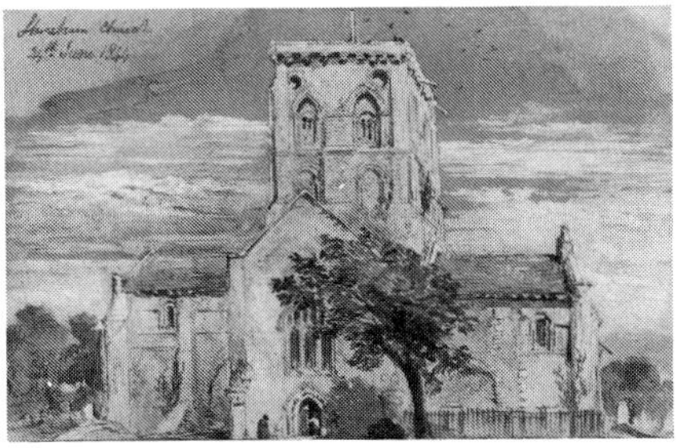

acc. no. 816b
Interior of Shoreham Church (1844)
watercolour over pencil: $6\frac{3}{4}$ × 10 in.
inscribed and dated: *Shoreham Church / 24th June 1844*
Bequeathed by George Gilbert, 1903

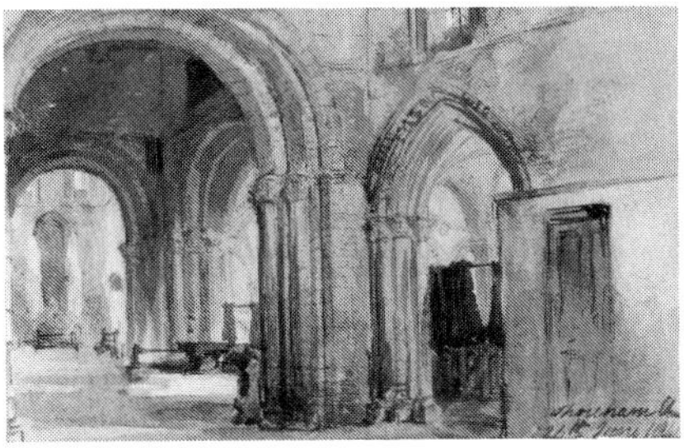

acc. no. 553
Rochester (1845)
watercolour: $13\frac{5}{8}$ × 10 in. (sight)
inscribed and dated: *Rochester / July 19th 1845*
Presented by the artist, 1893

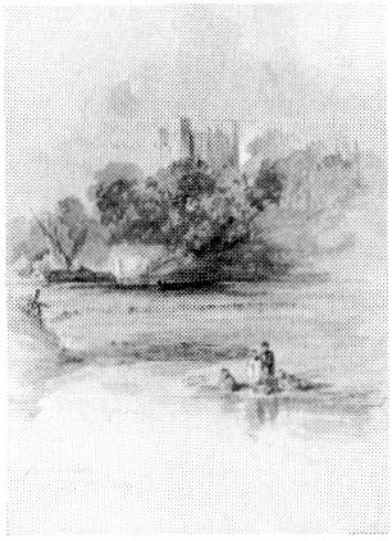

acc. no. 804
Melrose Abbey (1845)
watercolour: 10 × 14 in. (sight)
inscribed and dated: *Melrose Abbey / September 29th 1845*
Bequeathed by George Gilbert, 1903

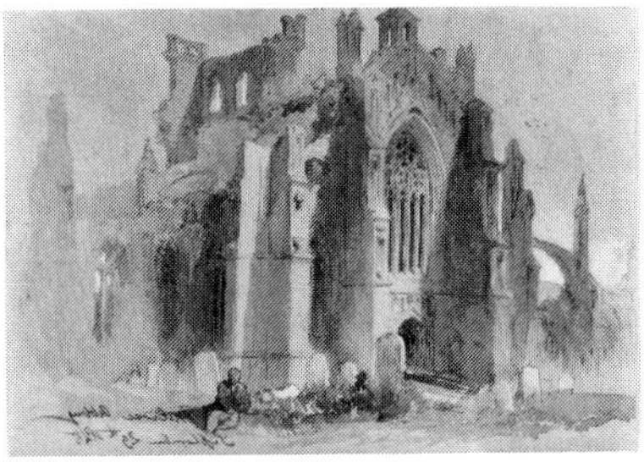

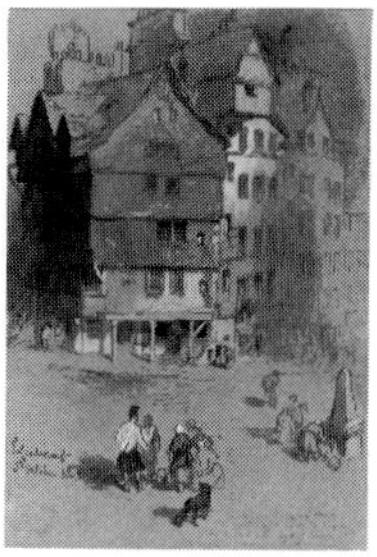

acc. no. 557
Edinburgh (1845)

pencil and watercolour: $13\frac{3}{4} \times 9\frac{5}{8}$ in.
dated: *Edinburgh / 3rd October 1845* and inscribed: *Sir George McKenzies House / commonly called bloody McKenzie / Lord Advocate in the reign of Charles 2nd / so called for his persecution of the Covenanters*
Presented by the artist, 1893

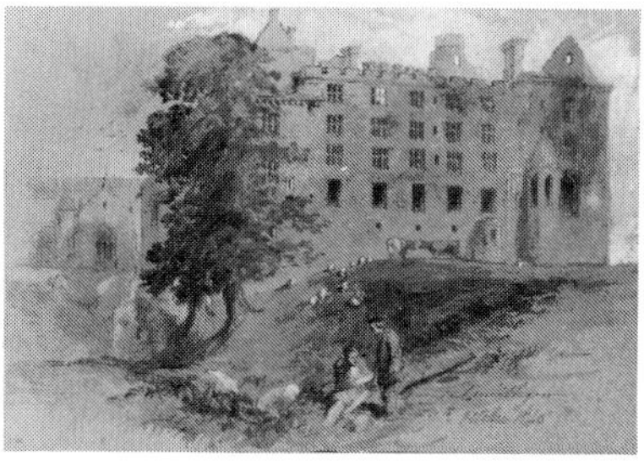

acc. no. 808
Linlithgow Castle (1845)

pencil and watercolour: 10×14 in.
inscribed and dated: *Linlithgow / 9th October 1845*
Bequeathed by George Gilbert, 1903

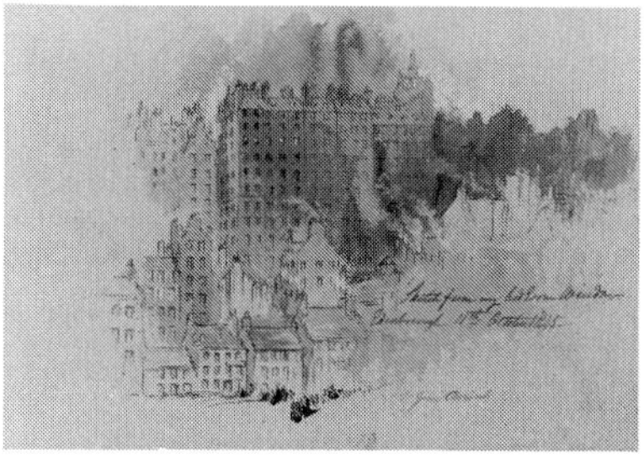

acc. no. 554
Edinburgh from the Artist's Bedroom (1845)

pencil and watercolour: $9\frac{5}{8} \times 13\frac{3}{4}$ in.
inscribed and dated: *Sketch from my bedroom window / Edinburgh 11th October 1845 / S. Giles Church*
Presented by the artist, 1893

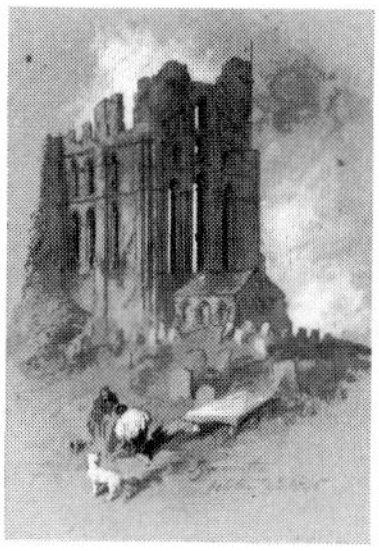

acc. no. 799
Tynemouth (1845)

pencil and watercolour: 14×10 ins.
inscribed and dated: *Tynemouth/October 14th 1845*
Bequeathed by George Gilbert, 1903

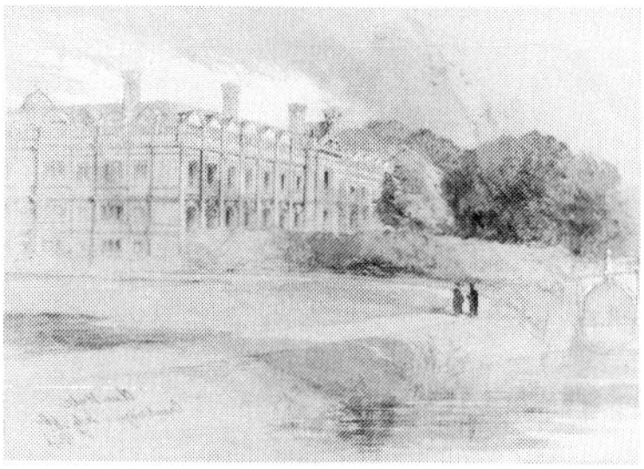

acc. no. 551

Clare Hall, Cambridge (1846)
pencil and watercolour, heightened with white: $9\frac{3}{4} \times 13\frac{3}{4}$ in.
inscribed and dated: *Clare Hall/Cambridge – July 16th/1846*
Presented by the artist, 1893

acc. no. 549
Cambridge (1846)

pencil, brown wash and watercolour: 7 × 9¾ in.
inscribed and dated: *Cambridge 16th July 1846*
Presented by the artist, 1893

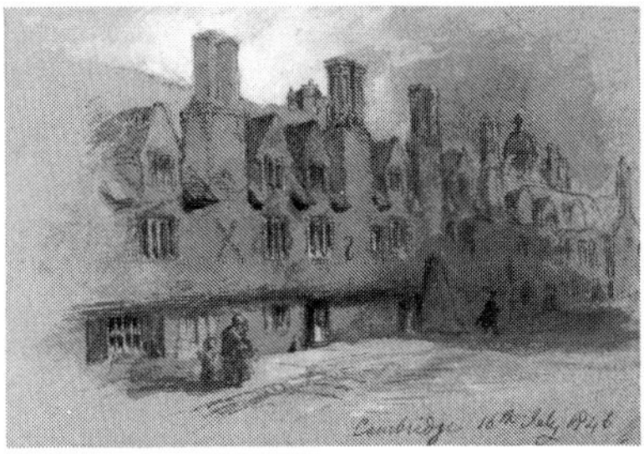

acc. no. 802
Norwich Cathedral (1846)

pencil and watercolour: 9⅞ × 13⅞ in.
inscribed and dated: *Norwich Cathedral/July 17 1846*
Bequeathed by George Gilbert, 1903

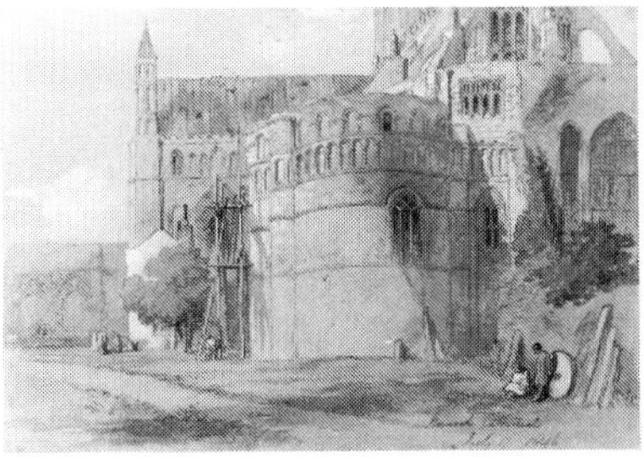

acc. no. 546
Ghent (1846)

watercolour over pencil heightened with white: 6⅜ × 9½ in.
inscribed and dated: *Ghent/24th August 1846*
Presented by the artist, 1893

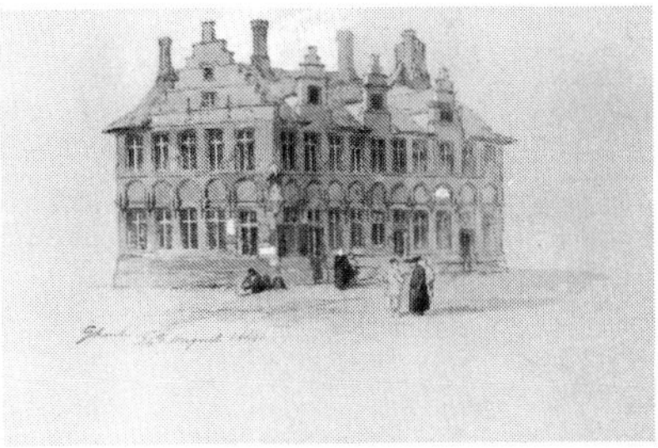

acc. no. 544
The Belfry, Ghent (1846)

pen and ink and watercolour: 13⅜ × 9½ in.
inscribed and dated : *The Belfry Tower/Ghent/ August 25th 1846/The date of this Tower/is 1183*
Presented by the artist, 1893

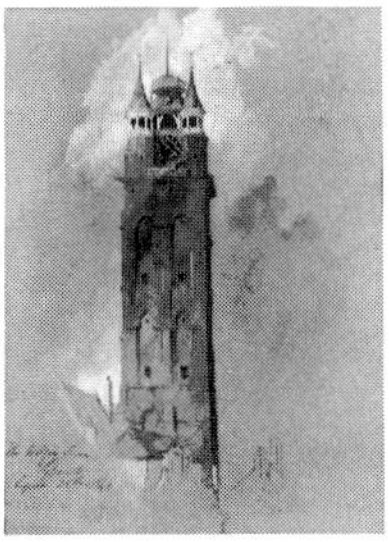

acc. no. 545
Ghent (?1846)

pencil, brown wash and watercolour: 7 × 9⅜ in.
inscribed: *Ghent*
Presented by the artist, 1893

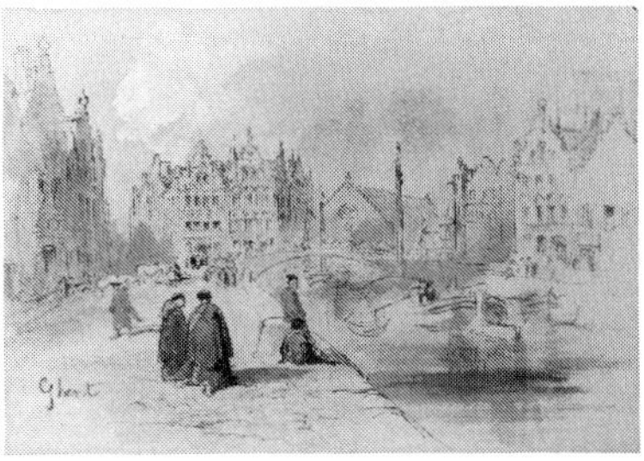

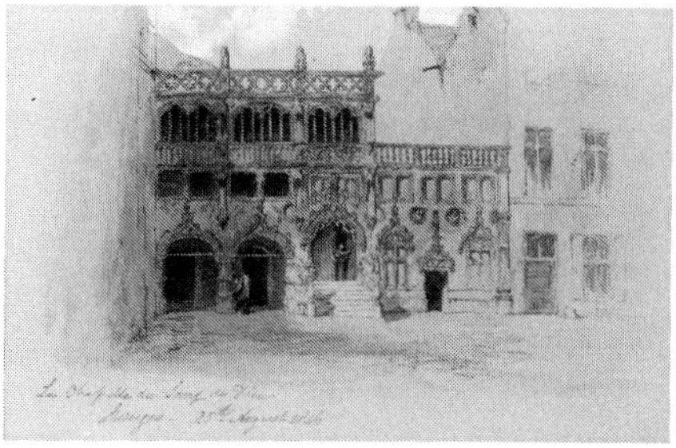

acc. no. 547
La Chapelle du Sang de Dieu, Bruges (1846)
brown ink and watercolour: $6\frac{1}{4} \times 9\frac{3}{8}$ in.
inscribed and dated: *La Chapelle du Sang de Dieu / Bruges – 25th August 1846*
Presented by the artist, 1893

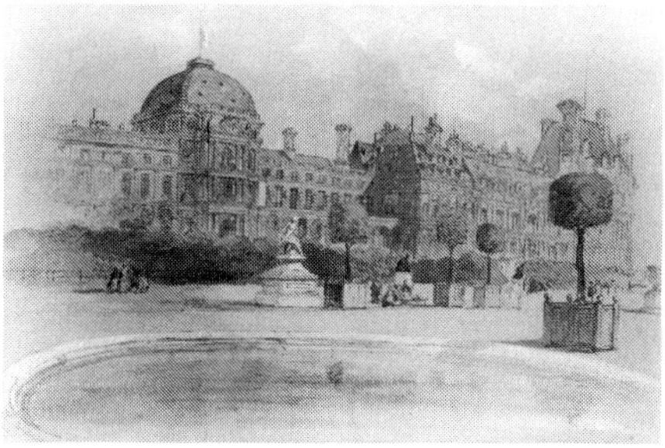

acc. no. 803
The Tuileries, Paris (1846)
watercolour: 10×14 in.
inscribed and dated: *The Tuileries – 2nd Sept 1846*
Bequeathed by George Gilbert, 1903

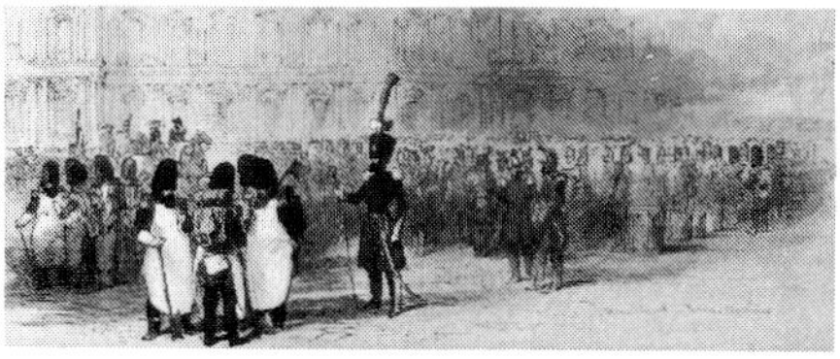

acc. no. 569
The National Guard on Parade at The Tuileries (?1846)
pen and ink and watercolour over pencil: $5\frac{3}{4} \times 13\frac{1}{2}$ in.
inscribed: *National Guard – Parade – Tuileries*
Presented by the artist, 1893

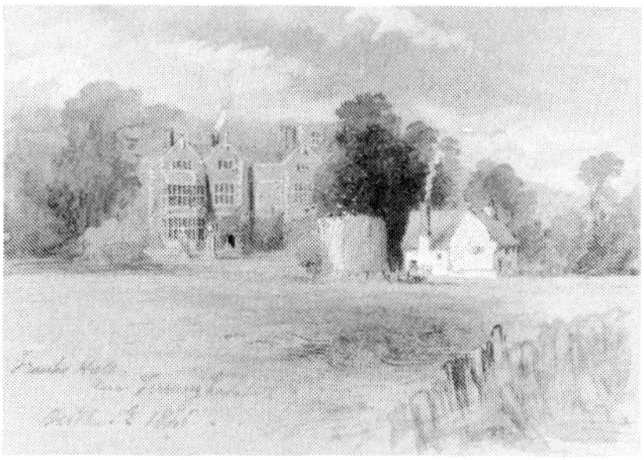

acc. no. 548
Frank's Hall near Farningham (1846)
watercolour, heightened with white: 7×10 in. (sight)
inscribed and dated: *Franks Hall. / near Farningham / October 1st 1846*
Presented by the artist, 1893

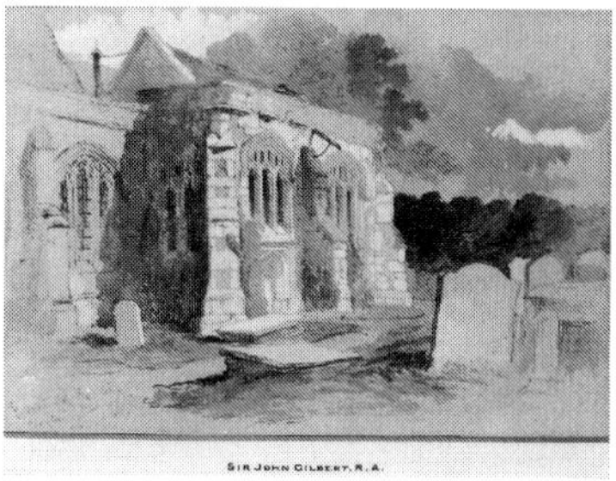

acc. no. 550
Beddington Church, Surrey (1847)
pen and ink, pencil and watercolour, heightened with white: $6\frac{7}{8} \times 9\frac{7}{8}$ in.
inscribed and dated: *Beddington Church / Croydon, Surrey / 9th July 1847* and with colour and other notes
Presented by the artist, 1893

acc. no. 566
Othello and Desdemona before the Senate (1847)

black and grey wash with traces of pencil, heightened with white: $7 \times 9\frac{1}{2}$ in.
inscribed and dated: *Othello / 1847*
Presented by the artist, 1893

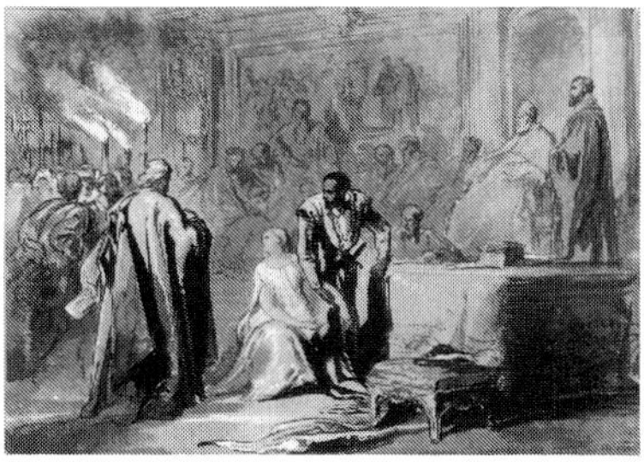

acc. no. 552
The Devil's Dyke (1848)

pencil and watercolour, heightened with white: $6\frac{7}{8} \times 9\frac{3}{4}$ in.
inscribed and dated: *The Devils Dyke / August 10th 1848*
Presented by the artist, 1893

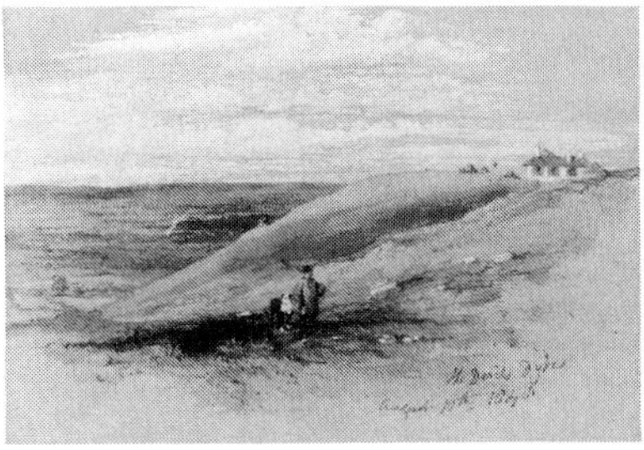

acc. no. 558
Lewes, Sussex (1848)

watercolour with traces of pencil: 7×10 in.
inscribed and dated: *Lewes / Aug^st 11th 1848.*
Presented by the artist, 1893

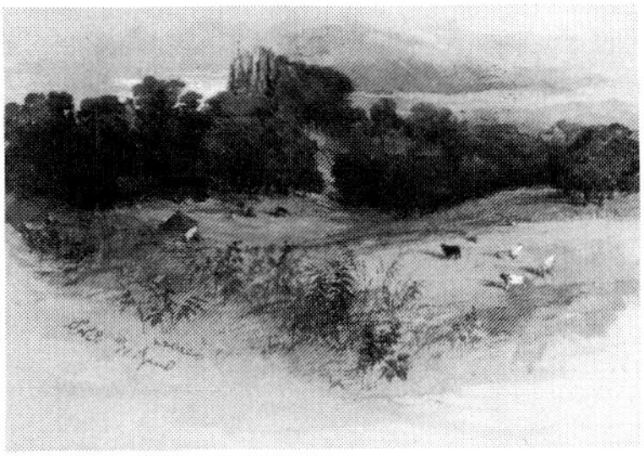

acc. no. 573
Mounted Escort at St. James's Palace (1848)

pen and ink and watercolour: $6 \times 13\frac{1}{4}$ in.
inscribed and dated: *St James' Palace / Drawing Room / Nov 1848*
Presented by the artist, 1893

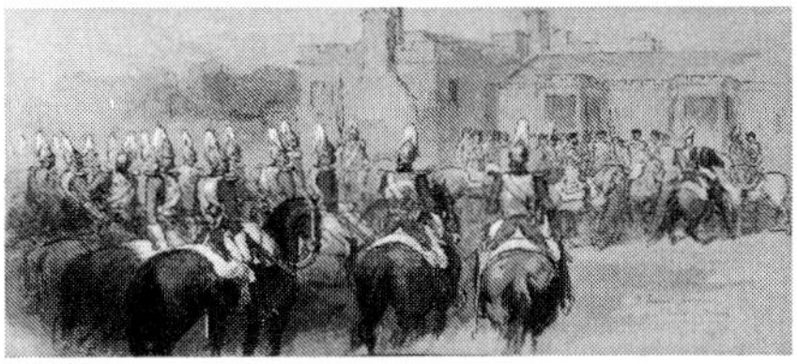

acc. no. 1702
Black Girl with Fruit (?1849)

pencil and watercolour: $16\frac{3}{4} \times 11$ in.
Bequeathed by Captain Dyer through Miss M. Dyer, 1965

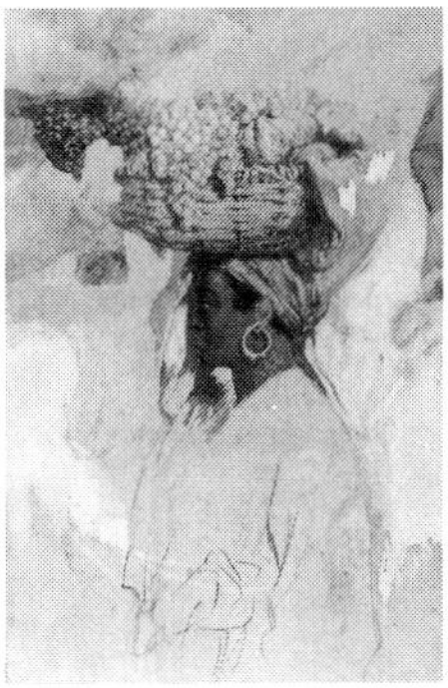

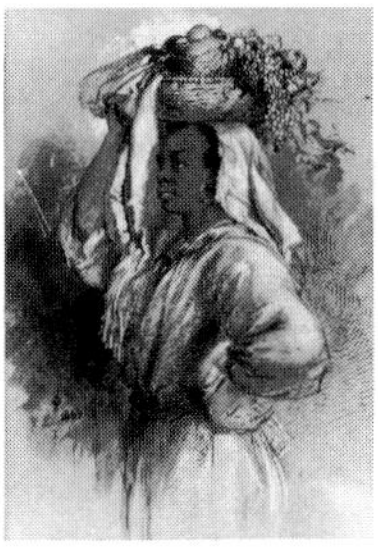

acc. no. 1701
Black Girl with Fruit (1849)
watercolour: $13 \times 9\frac{1}{4}$ in.
signed (mono) and dated: *JG / 1849*
Bequeathed by Captain Dyer through Miss M. Dyer, 1965

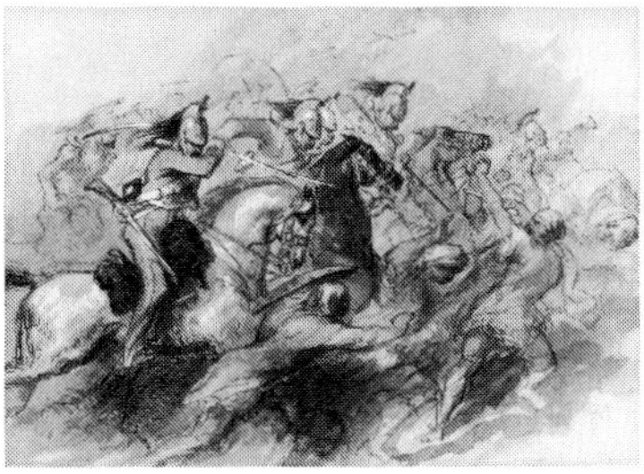

acc. no. 570
A Cavalry Charge (1849)
pen and ink and watercolour: $8\frac{3}{4} \times 12$ in.
signed (reversed mono) and dated: *JG / 1849*
Presented by the artist, 1893

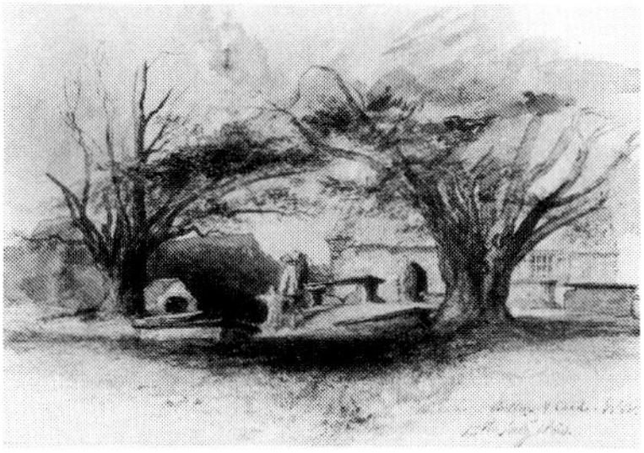

acc. no. 807
The Church, Bettws-y-Coed (1850)
pencil and watercolour: 10×14 in.
inscribed and dated: *The Church – Bettws. y Coed NW / 15th July 1850*
Bequeathed by George Gilbert, 1903

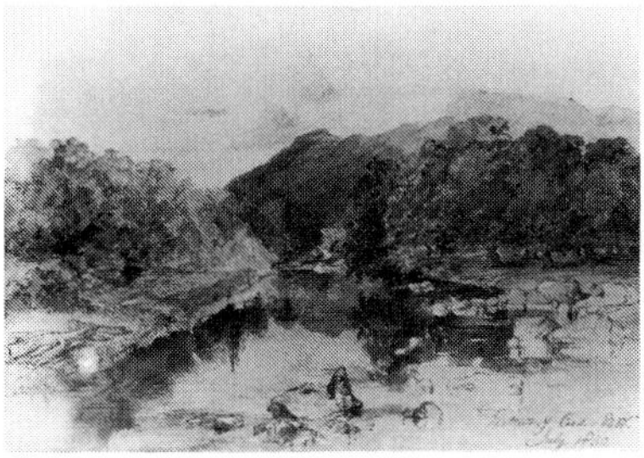

acc. no. 809
The Stream, Bettws-y-Coed (1850)
watercolour: 10×14 in.
inscribed and dated: *Bettws. Y Coed. NW. / July 1850*
Bequeathed by George Gilbert, 1903

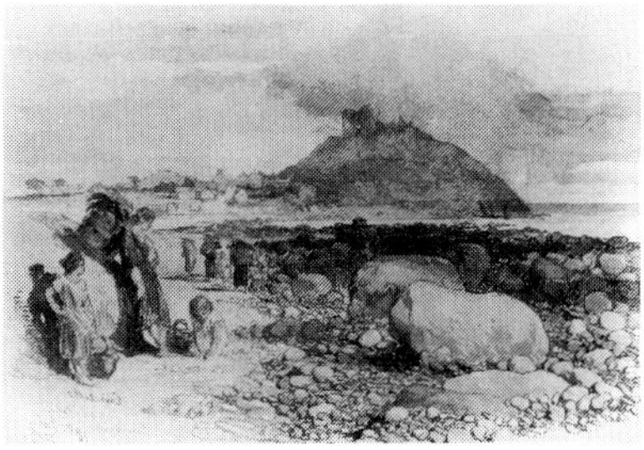

acc. no. 810
Criccieth Castle from the Shore (1850)
watercolour: 10×14 in.
inscribed and dated: *Criccieth / Crileth / Cricketh 18th July / 1850*
Bequeathed by George Gilbert, 1903

acc. no. 805
Harlech Castle from the Ramparts (1850)

pen and ink and watercolour: 10 × 14 in.
inscribed and dated: *Harlech Castle / from the Ramparts / 19th July / 1850*
Bequeathed by George Gilbert, 1903

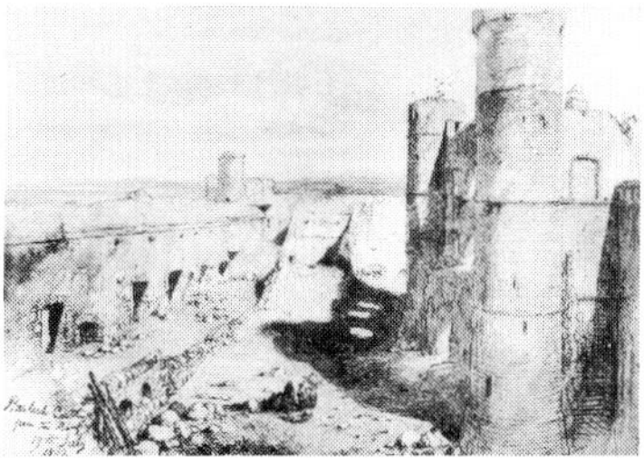

acc. no. 562
Hudibras in the Stocks (1850)

pencil and pen and ink, heightened with white: $6\frac{7}{8} \times 9\frac{7}{8}$ in.
inscribed and dated: *Hudibras in the stocks / 1850*
Presented by the artist, 1893

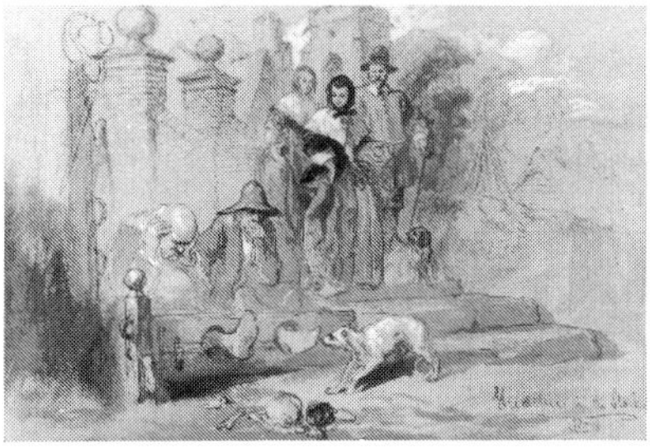

acc. no. 568
French Cavalry (1851)

pen and ink and watercolour with traces of pencil: $7 \times 9\frac{3}{4}$ in.
dated: *Jan 1851*
Presented by the artist, 1893

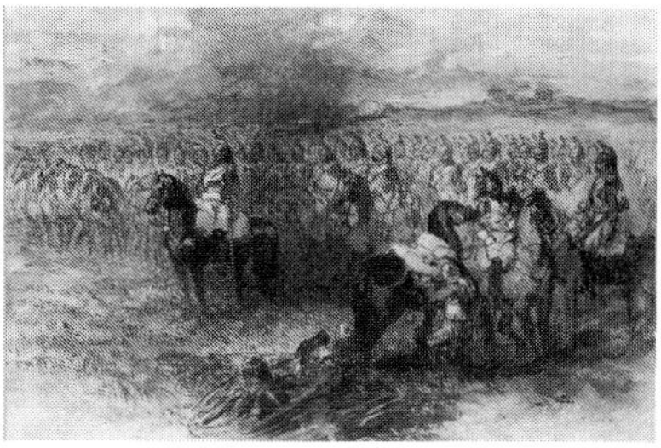

acc. no. 780
The Destruction of Job's Flock (1851)

oil on canvas: $49 \times 53\frac{1}{2}$ in.
Bequeathed by George Gilbert, 1903

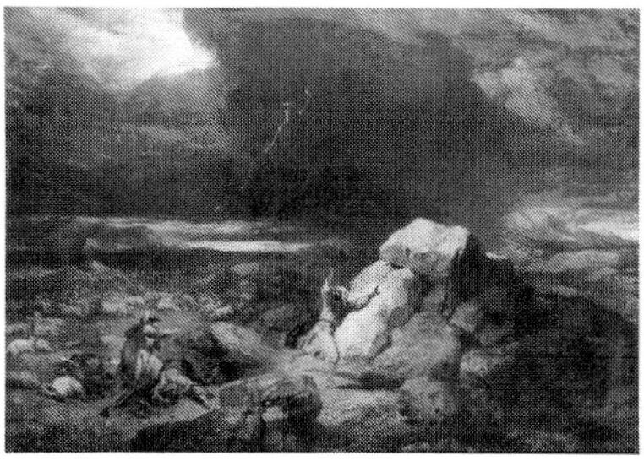

acc. no. 818a
The Sea near Hastings (1853)

watercolour: $6\frac{7}{8} \times 9\frac{3}{4}$ in.
inscribed and dated: *Hastings / July 1853*
Bequeathed by George Gilbert, 1903

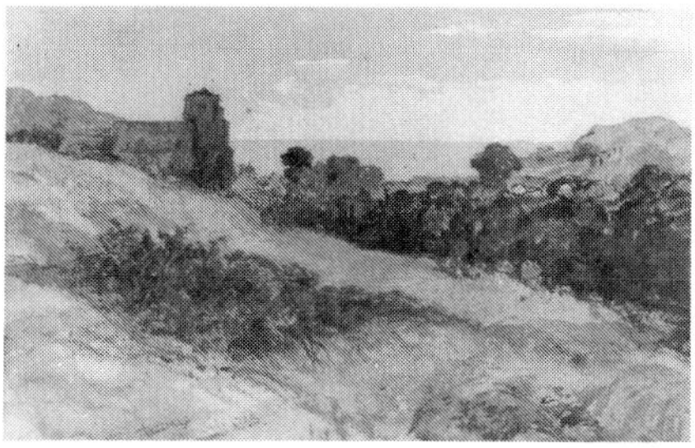

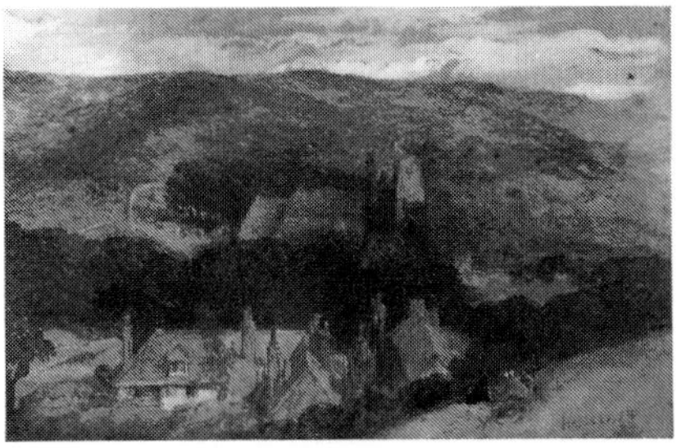

acc. no. 818b
View at Hastings (1853)
watercolour: $6\frac{5}{8} \times 9\frac{3}{4}$ in.
inscribed and dated: *Hastings / July 1853*
Bequeathed by George Gilbert, 1903

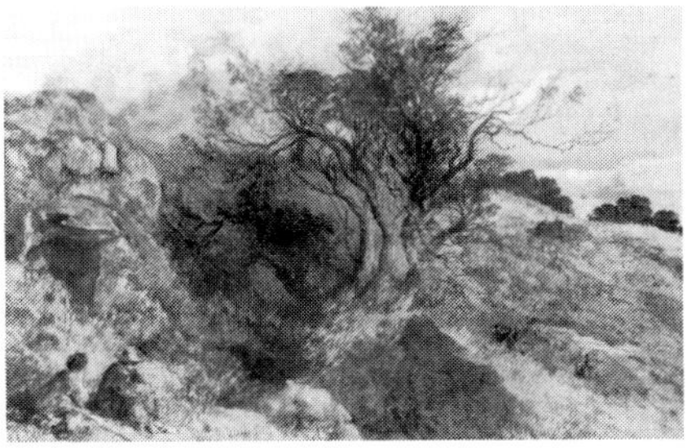

acc. no. 817a
Pevensey (?1853)
pencil and watercolour: 7×10 in.
Bequeathed by George Gilbert, 1903

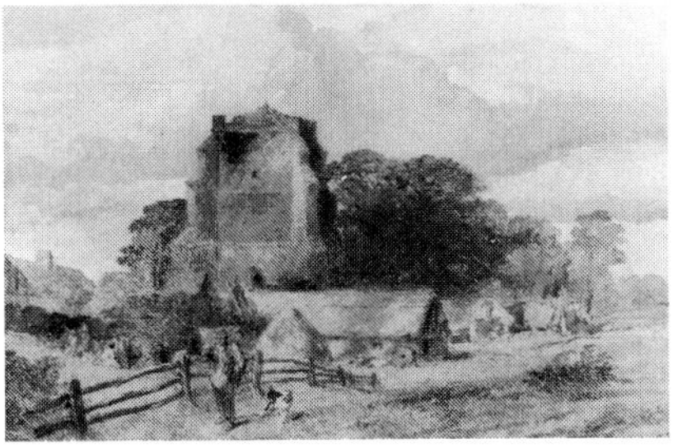

acc. no. 817b
Westham Church near Pevensey
pencil and watercolour: 7×10 in.
inscribed and dated: *PEVENSEY. / 1853*
Bequeathed by George Gilbert, 1903

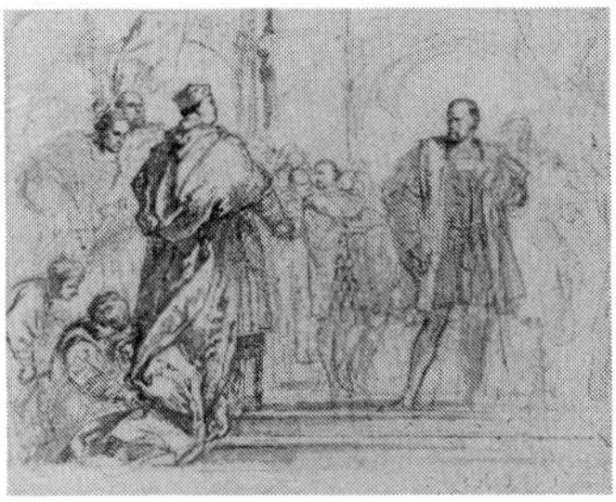

acc. no. 559
Wolsey and Buckingham (*c.*1856–59)
pencil and grey wash: $5\frac{1}{4} \times 6\frac{5}{8}$ in.
inscribed: *3 Lords*
Presented by the artist, 1893

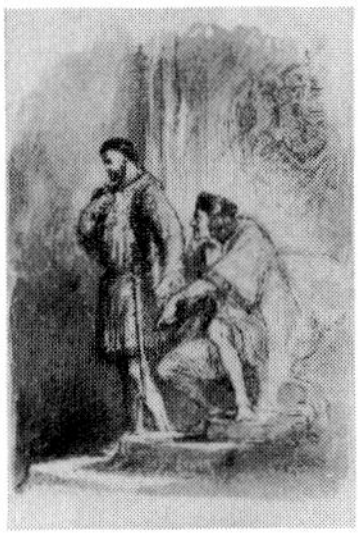

acc. no. 560
Richard III (*c.*1856–59)
pencil, pen and ink and grey wash: $8\frac{5}{8} \times 5\frac{7}{8}$ in.
inscribed: *P543*
Presented by the artist, 1893

acc. no. 561
The Arrest of Lord Hastings (*c.*1856–59)

pen and ink, grey wash strengthened with black and white, with traces of pencil: $5\frac{1}{2} \times 8\frac{1}{4}$ in.
inscribed: *Lord Hastings / Richard of Gloucester*
Presented by the artist, 1893

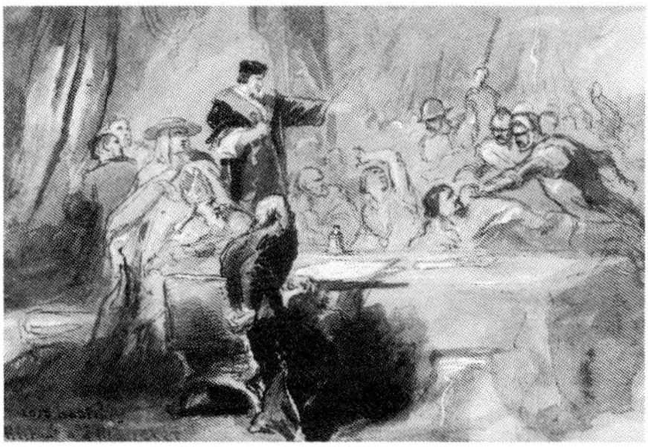

acc. no. 824a
Sir Andrew Aguecheek writes a Challenge (1859)

Brown ink, pencil and watercolour: $6 \times 8\frac{5}{8}$ in.
signed and dated: *John Gilbert 1859*
Bequeathed by George Gilbert, 1903

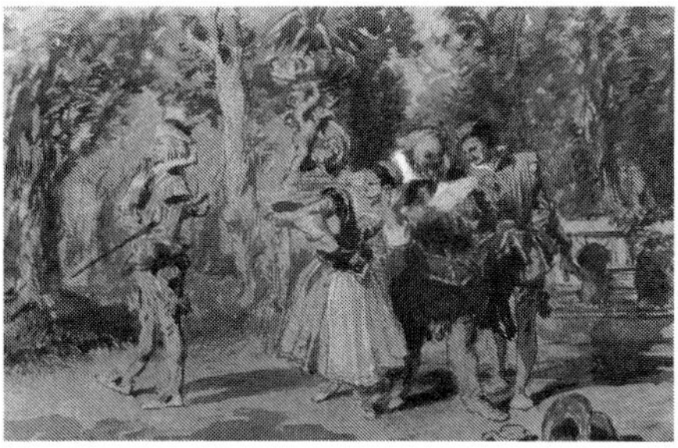

acc. no. 824b
The Banquet at Lucentio's House (1859)

pencil and watercolour: $5\frac{1}{4} \times 7\frac{1}{2}$ in.
signed and dated: *J Gilbert 1859*
Bequeathed by George Gilbert, 1903

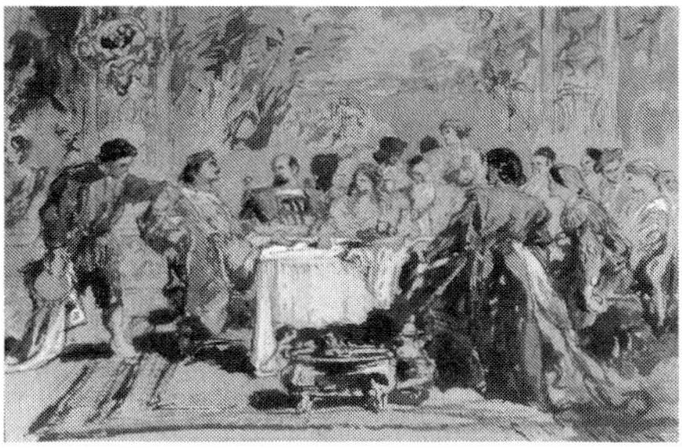

acc. no. 787
Cedric's Toast (?*c.*1859)

watercolour: 24×29 in.
Bequeathed by George Gilbert, 1903

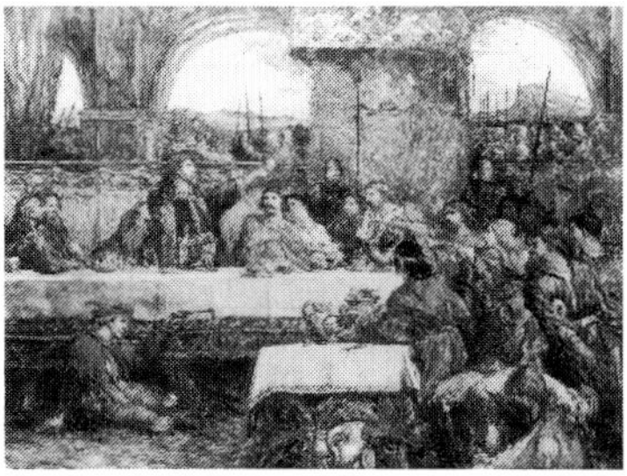

acc. no. 1703b
Lord Clyde and Staff at Volunteer Review, Brighton (1862)

pencil, pen and ink, bodycolour and wash: $4\frac{1}{2} \times 13\frac{1}{2}$ in.
inscribed, dated and signed: *Lord Clyde / and staff* and *Volunteer Review at Brighton / April 21st. 1862 / J.G.*
Bequeathed by Captain Dyer through Miss M. Dyer, 1965

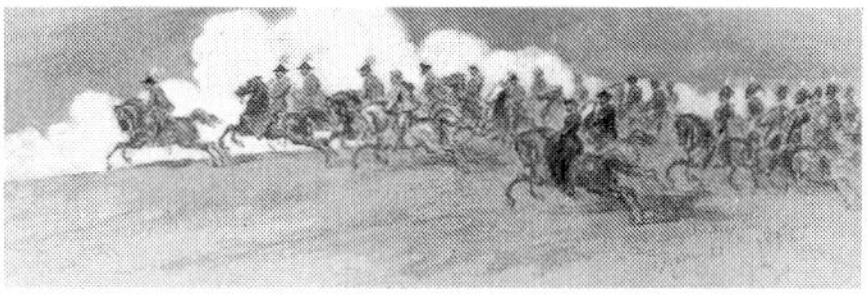

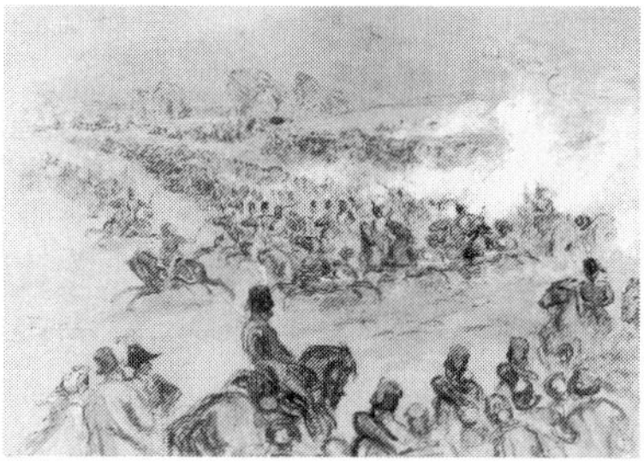

acc. no. 1703a
Review on Woolwich Common before the Prince of Wales (1863)

pencil, watercolour and bodycolour: $9\frac{3}{4} \times 13\frac{1}{2}$ in.
inscribed, dated and signed: *Woolwich / June 1863 / J.G.*
Bequeathed by Captain Dyer through Miss M. Dyer, 1965

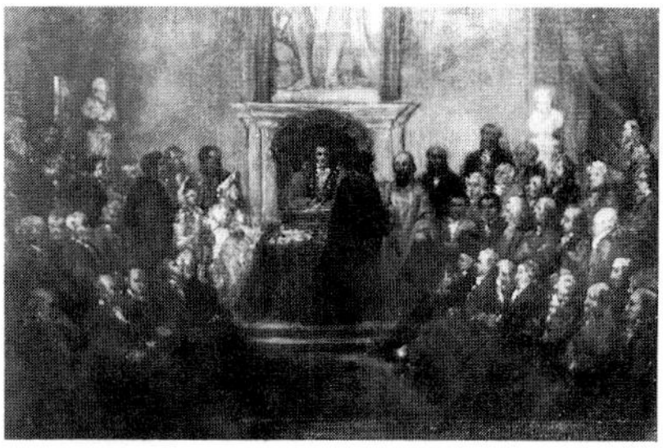

acc. no. 1313
Presentation of the Freedom of the City to General Garibaldi, April 20 1864

oil on canvas: 11×16 in.
Purchased, 1944

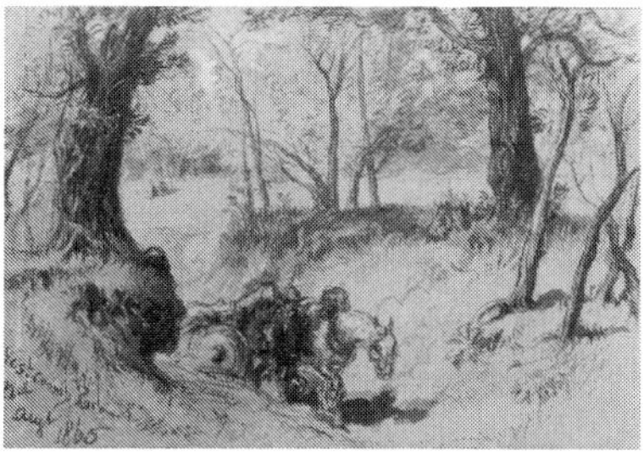

acc. no. 821b
Westcomb Park (1865)

pencil and watercolour: $4\frac{3}{4} \times 6\frac{3}{4}$ in.
inscribed and dated: *Westcomb Park / 21st / Aug 1865*
Bequeathed by George Gilbert, 1903

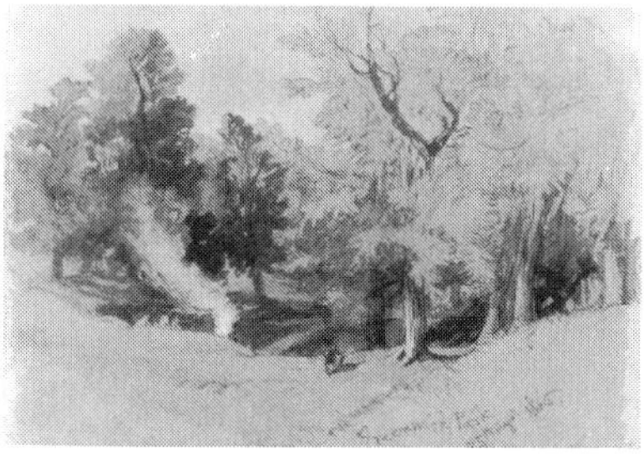

acc. no. 821a
Greenwich Park (1865)

pencil and watercolour: $4\frac{5}{8} \times 6\frac{5}{8}$ in.
inscribed and dated: *Greenwich Park / 25th Augst 1865*
Bequeathed by George Gilbert, 1903

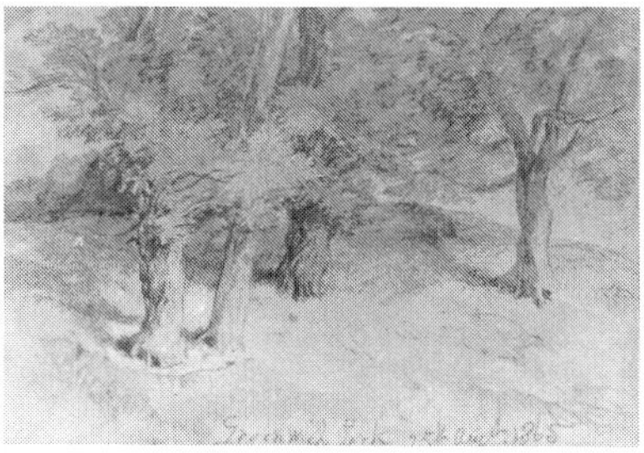

acc. no. 821c
Greenwich Park (1865)

pencil and watercolour: $4\frac{3}{4} \times 6\frac{3}{4}$ in.
inscribed and dated: *Greenwich Park 25th Augst. 1865*
Bequeathed by George Gilbert, 1903

acc. no. 826c
Hastings (1865)

pencil and wash: $4\frac{3}{4} \times 6\frac{5}{8}$ in.
inscribed and dated: *Hastings / 5th Septr 1865. six o. clock / AM*
Bequeathed by George Gilbert, 1903

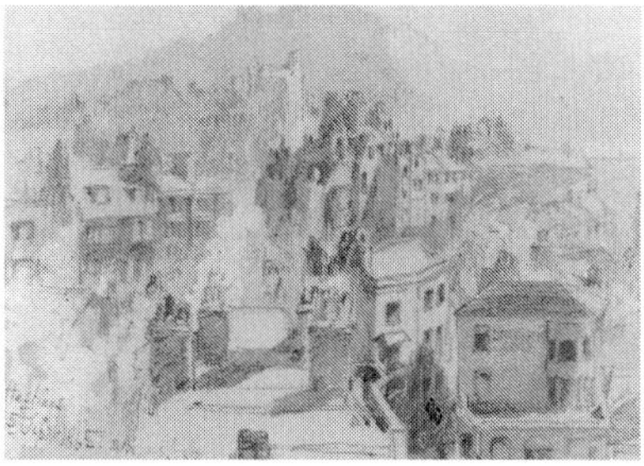

acc. no. 826b
Ecclesbourne (1865)

pencil and wash: $4\frac{5}{8} \times 6\frac{5}{8}$ in.
inscribed and dated: *Ecclesbourne / 5th Septr. 1865*
Bequeathed by George Gilbert, 1903

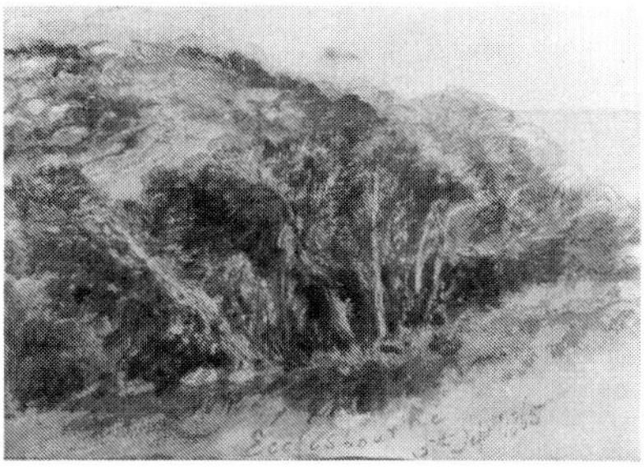

acc. no. 826f
Pevensey Castle (1865)

pencil, ink and watercolour: $4\frac{3}{4} \times 6\frac{3}{4}$ in.
inscribed and dated: *Pevensey Castle / 6th Septr 1865*
Bequeathed by George Gilbert, 1903

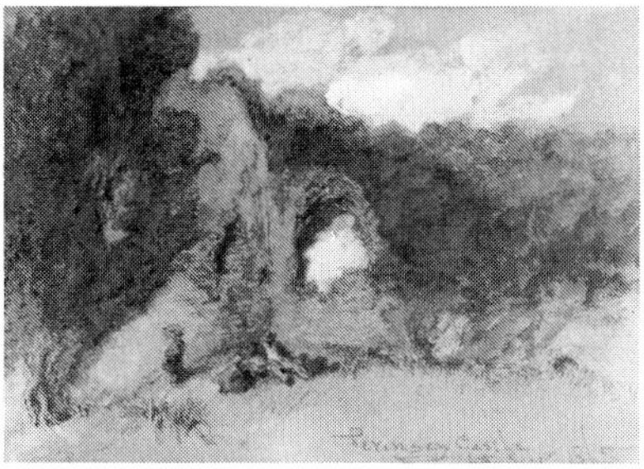

acc. no. 826d
Winchelsea (1865)

pencil and wash: $4\frac{5}{8} \times 6\frac{3}{4}$ in.
inscribed and dated: *Winchelsea / 7th Septr 1865*
Bequeathed by George Gilbert, 1903

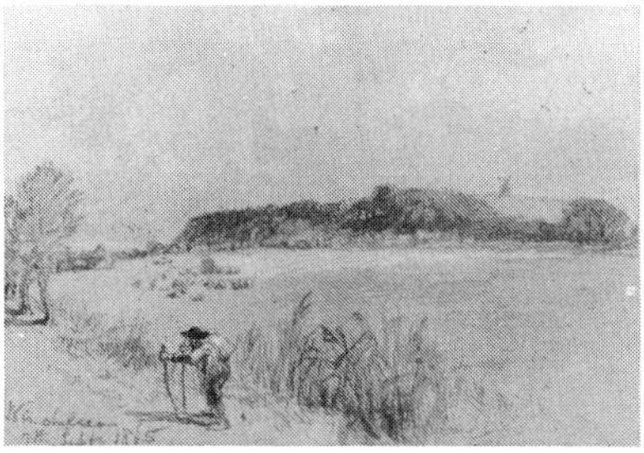

acc. no. 795
Winchelsea (?1865)

watercolour: $8\frac{3}{4} \times 16$ in.
inscribed and signed (mono) *Winchelsea JG*
Bequeathed by George Gilbert, 1903

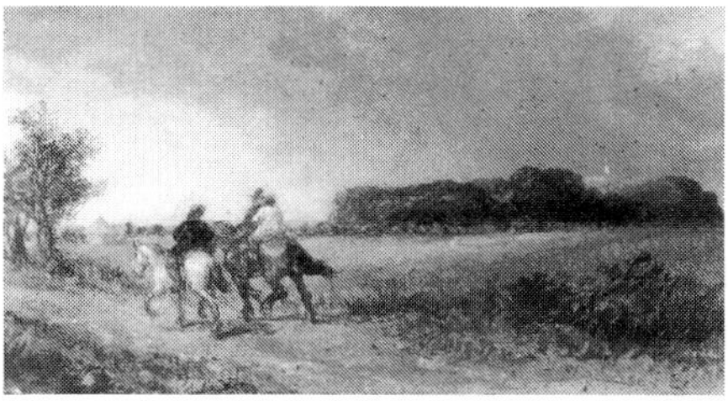

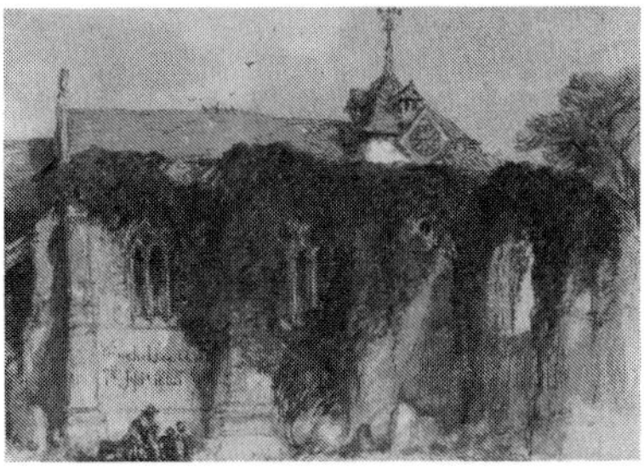

acc. no. 826g
Winchelsea Church (1865)

ink, pencil and watercolour: $4\frac{5}{8} \times 6\frac{5}{8}$ in.
inscribed and dated: *Winchelsea Church / 7th Septr 1865*
Bequeathed by George Gilbert, 1903

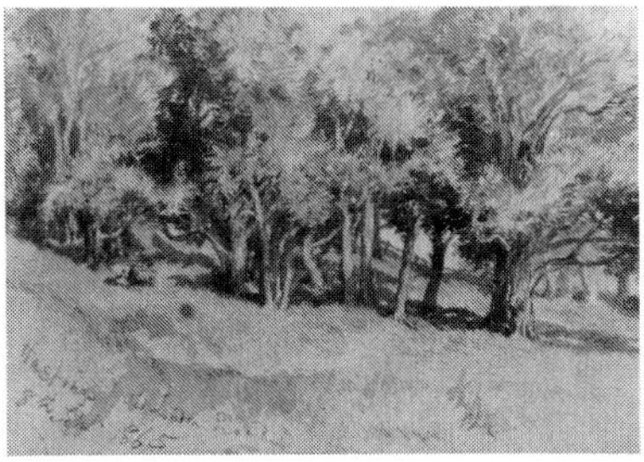

acc. no. 826a
Clump of Trees at Hastings (1865)

pencil and waterclour: $4\frac{5}{8} \times 6\frac{3}{4}$ in.
inscribed and dated: *Hastings. Old London Road / 8th Septr 1865.*
Bequeathed by George Gilbert, 1903

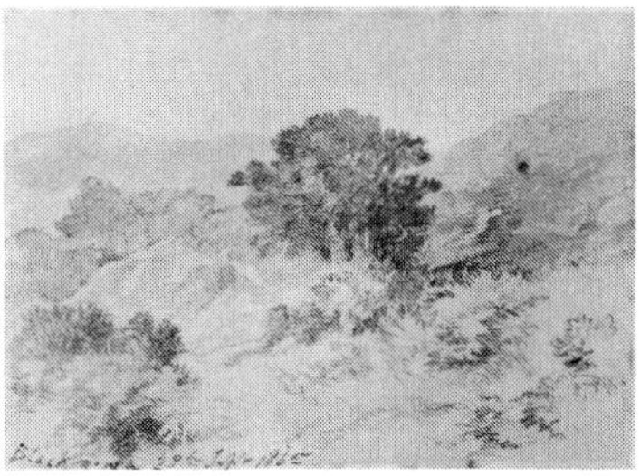

acc. no. 826e
Blackdown (1865)

pencil and watercolour: $4\frac{1}{2} \times 6\frac{5}{8}$ in.
inscribed and dated: *Blackdown 28th Sept 1865*
Bequeathed by George Gilbert, 1903

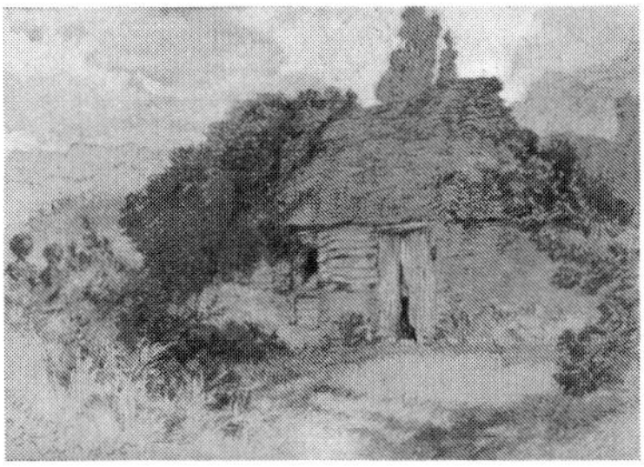

acc. no. 826h
Derelict Cottage at Rundhurst (1865)

pencil and watercolour: $4\frac{5}{8} \times 6\frac{3}{4}$ in.
inscribed and dated: *Rundhurst / 28th Sept 1865*
Bequeathed by George Gilbert, 1903

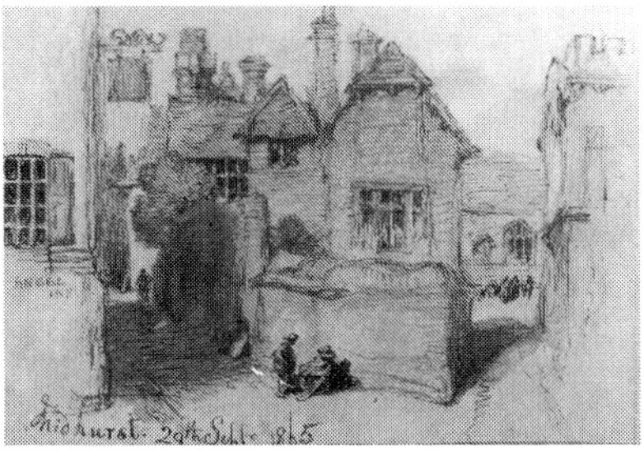

acc. no. 821f
The Angel Inn, Midhurst (1865)

pencil, ink and watercolour: $4\frac{5}{8} \times 6\frac{5}{8}$ in.
inscribed: *ANGEL / INN* and *Midhurst 29th Sept 1865*
Bequeathed by George Gilbert, 1903

acc. no. 821e
Cowdray House, near Midhurst

pencil and watercolour: $4\frac{5}{8} \times 6\frac{5}{8}$ in.
inscribed and dated: *Cowdray House / 29th Septr 1865*
Bequeathed by George Gilbert, 1903

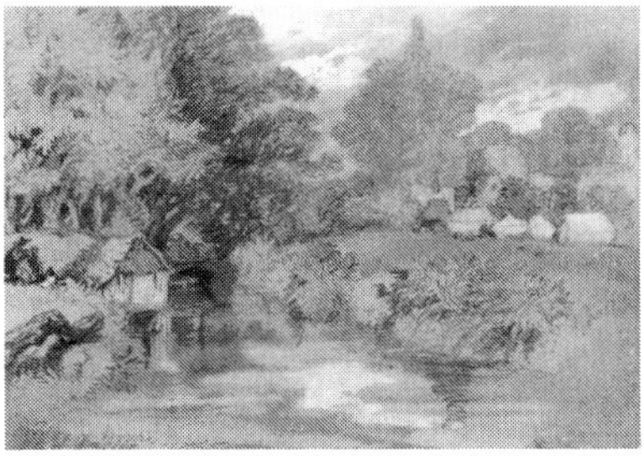

acc. no. 821i
Haslemere, Surrey (1865)

ink, pencil and wash, heightened with white: $4\frac{5}{8} \times 6\frac{3}{4}$ in.
inscribed and dated: *Hazlemere Surrey / 29th Sept 1865*
Bequeathed by George Gilbert, 1903

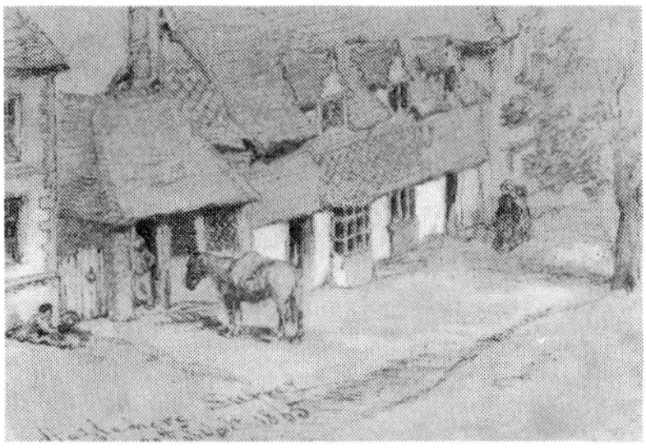

acc. no. 821h
Hampton Court Palace (1868)

pencil, ink and watercolour: $4\frac{5}{8} \times 6\frac{5}{8}$ in.
inscribed and dated: *Hampton Court Palace / Augst. 14th 1868*
Bequeathed by George Gilbert, 1903

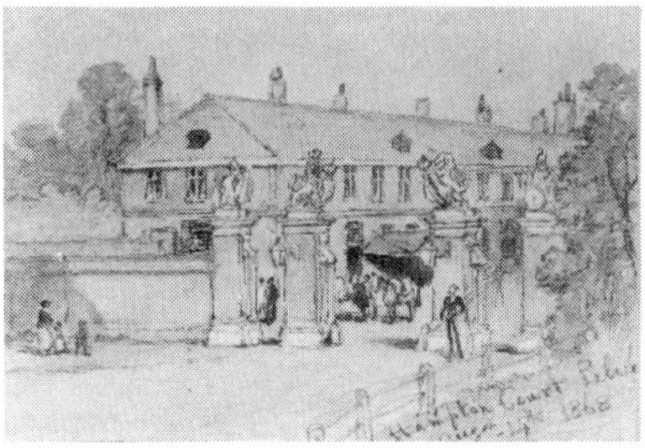

acc. no. 820b
Charles I Leaving Westminster Hall after his Trial

pencil, ink and watercolour heightened with white: $6\frac{3}{4} \times 9\frac{1}{2}$ in.
signed (mono) and dated: *JG / 1870* and inscribed: *King Charles Ist. leaving Westminster Hall after sentance* (sic) *of Death had been passed. Size of Picture 6ft × 4ft*
Bequeathed by George Gilbert, 1903

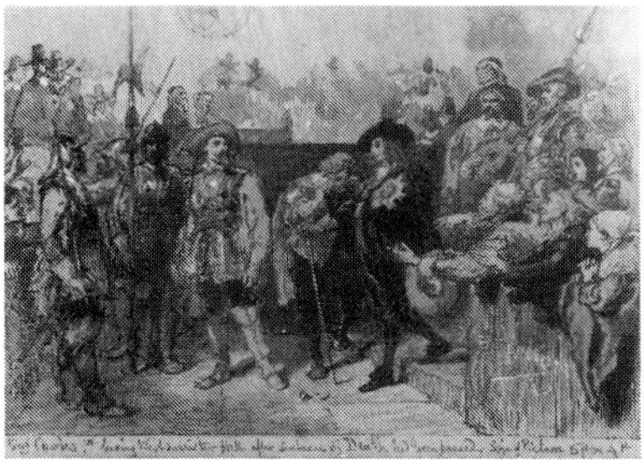

acc. no. 821d
Haslemere, Surrey (1871)

pencil and brown ink: $4\frac{5}{8} \times 6\frac{5}{8}$ in.
inscribed and dated: *Haselemere / 30th August 1871*
Bequeathed by George Gilbert, 1903

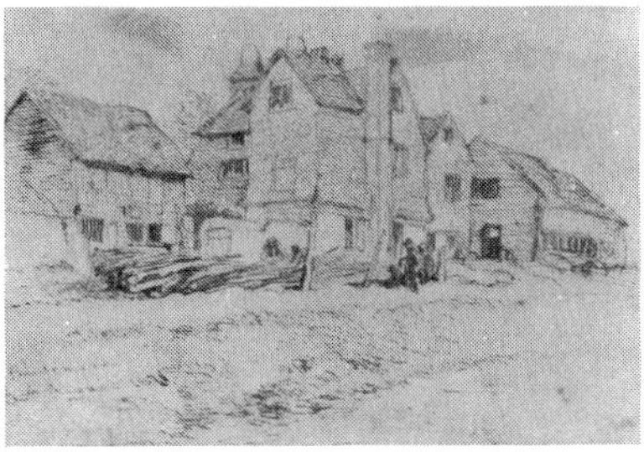

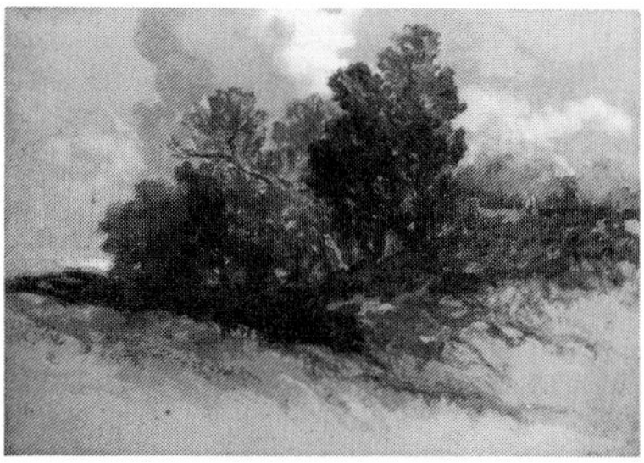

acc. no. 555
Wraysbury, Buckinghamshire (1872)

watercolour over pencil: $9\frac{3}{4} \times 13\frac{3}{4}$ in.
inscribed, dated and signed (mono): *Wraysbury Bucks / April 1872 / JG*
Presented by the artist, 1893

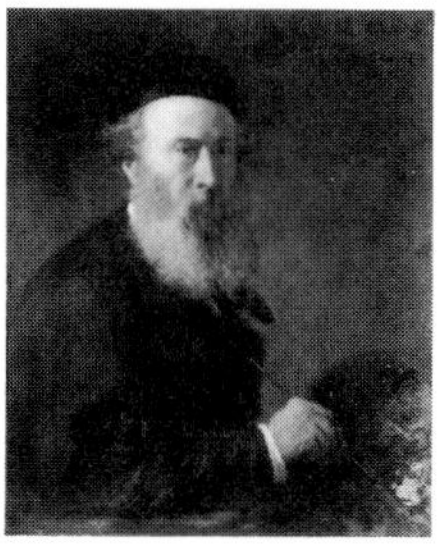

acc. no. 774
Self Portrait (1872)

oil on canvas: $29\frac{3}{4} \times 25$ in.
signed, inscribed and dated: *John Gilbert. Painted by / himself for his friend / James Christie / 1872*
Bequeathed by George Gilbert, 1903

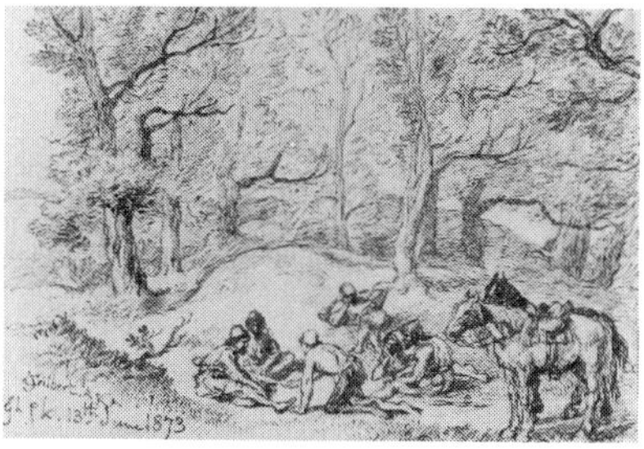

acc. no. 819c
Greenwich Park (1873)

pencil and brown ink: $4\frac{3}{4} \times 6\frac{5}{8}$ in.
signed, inscribed and dated: *JGilbert ARA / Gh Pk 13th June 1873*
Bequeathed by George Gilbert, 1903

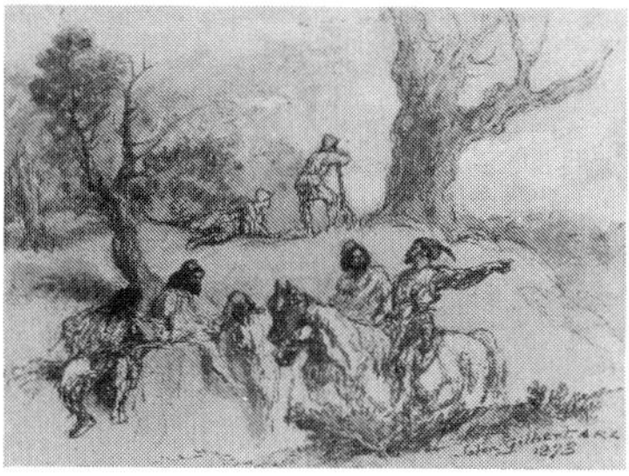

acc. no. 820a
Banditti (1873)

watercolour: $6\frac{3}{4} \times 5\frac{1}{8}$ in.
signed and dated: *John Gilbert ARA 1873*
Bequeathed by George Gilbert, 1903

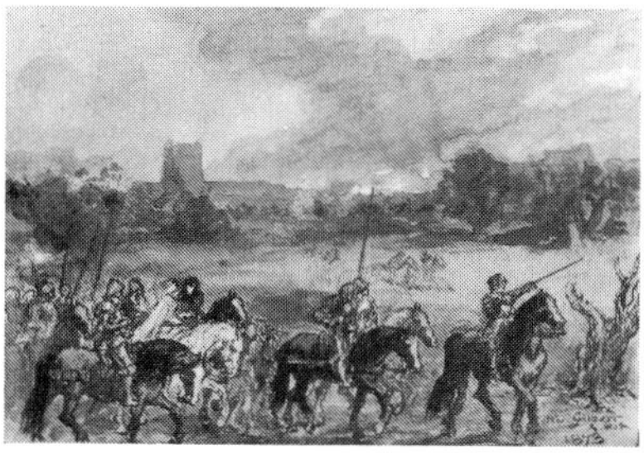

acc. no. 819a
Queen Margaret of Anjou taken Prisoner after the Battle of Tewkesbury (1873)

pencil and watercolour: $4\frac{7}{8} \times 6\frac{7}{8}$ in.
signed and dated: *John Gilbert / A.R.A / 1873*
Bequeathed by George Gilbert, 1903

acc. no. 819b
Winchelsea (1874)

watercolour: $9\frac{3}{4} \times 6\frac{3}{4}$ in.
inscribed, signed and dated: *Winchelsea JG 1874*
Bequeathed by George Gilbert, 1903

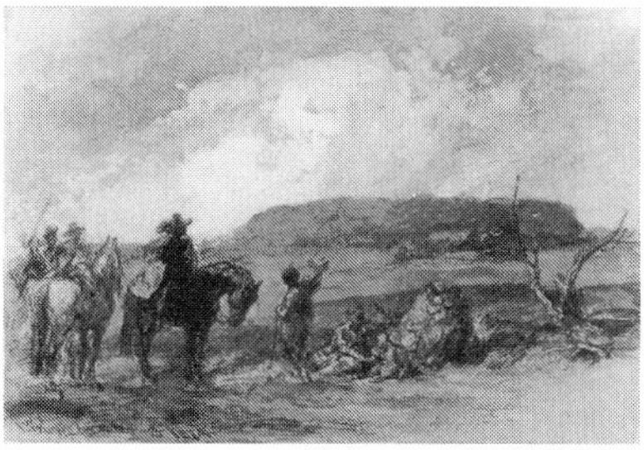

acc. no. 820c
On the March (1874)

ink, pencil and watercolour: $4\frac{3}{4} \times 6\frac{3}{4}$ in.
signed and dated: *JG / June 18th 1874*
Bequeathed by George Gilbert, 1903

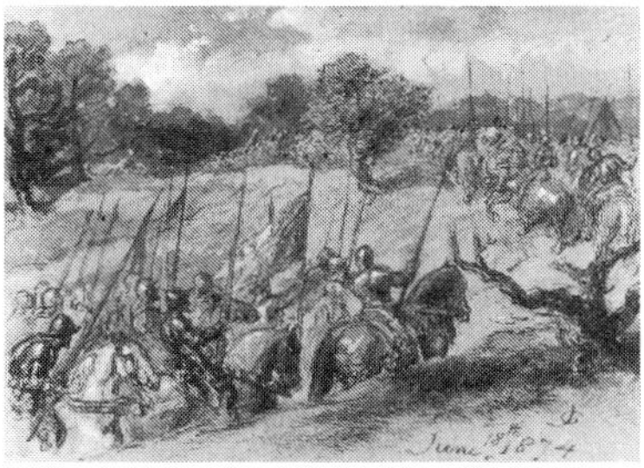

acc. no. 1700
Portrait of an Elderly Lady, supposed to be the Artist's Mother (1874)

oil on canvas: $25\frac{1}{2} \times 20\frac{1}{2}$ in.
signed (mono) and dated: *JG / July 1874*
Bequeathed by Captain Dyer through Miss M Dyer, 1965

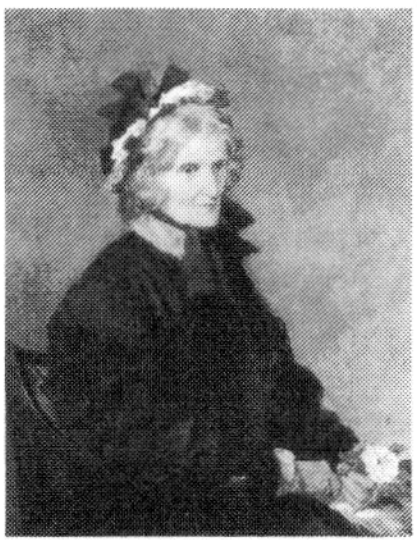

acc. no. 783
Queen Margaret of Anjou taken Prisoner after the Battle of Tewkesbury

oil on canvas: $49\frac{1}{4} \times 65$ in.
signed and dated: *John Gilbert ARA 1875*
Bequeathed by George Gilbert, 1903

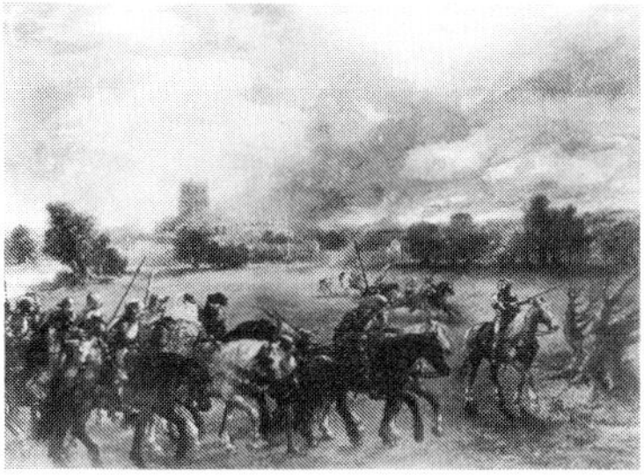

acc. no. 563
The Guide (1875)

pencil and watercolour heightened with white: $6\frac{3}{4} \times 9\frac{7}{8}$ in.
dated: *July 1875*
Presented by the artist, 1893

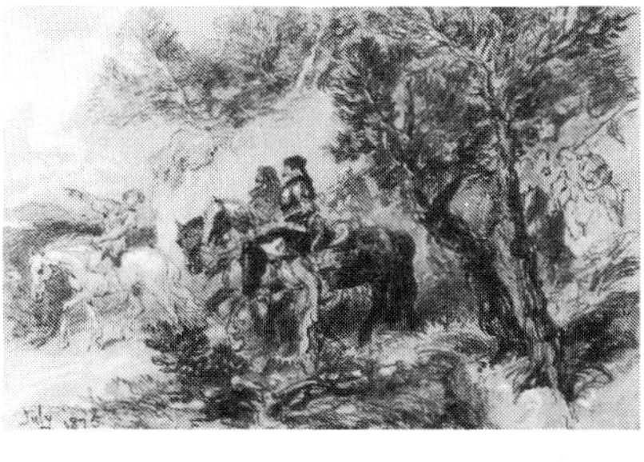

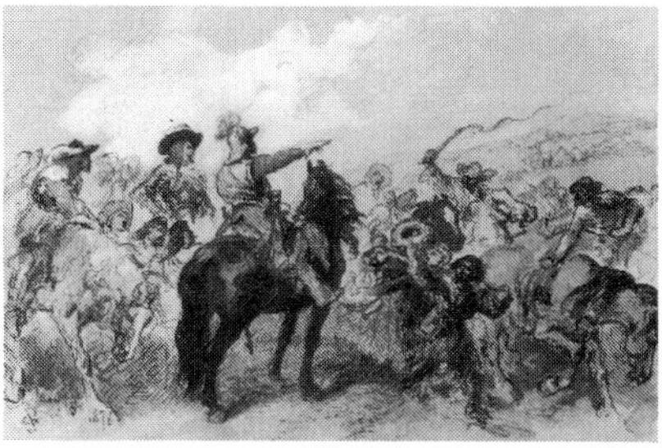

acc. no. 567
Horsemen in the Time of Charles I (1876)
pen and ink and watercolour over pencil: $6\frac{3}{4} \times 9\frac{7}{8}$ in.
signed (mono) and dated: *JG May 10th 1876*
Presented by the artist, 1893

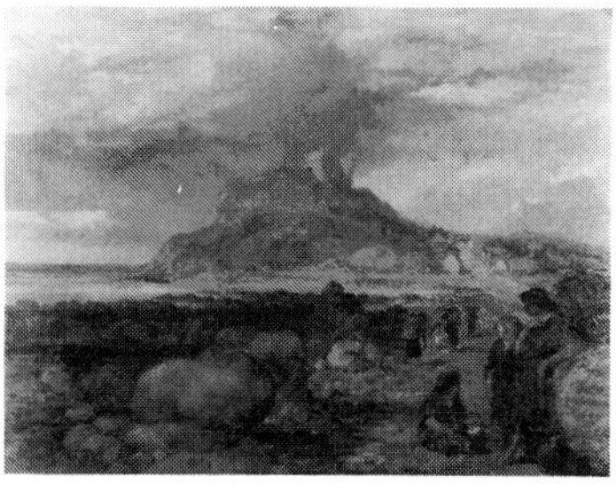

acc. no. 777
Criccieth Castle (1878)
oil on canvas: $27\frac{1}{2} \times 36$ in.
signed and dated: *JG / 1850 / 1878*
Bequeathed by George Gilbert, 1903

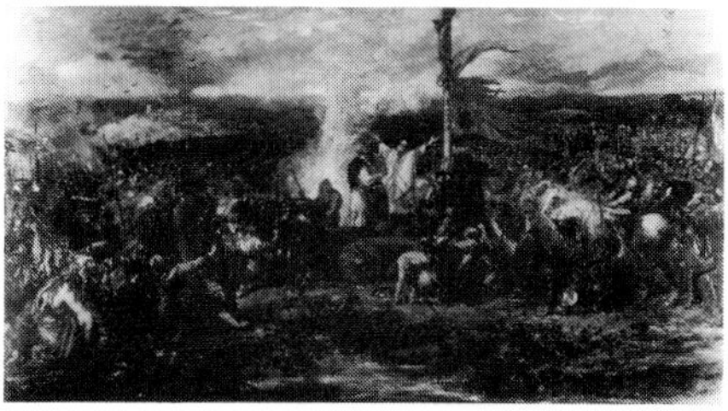

acc. no. 537
The Battle of the Standard, Northallerton (1880)
watercolour: 42 × 60 in.
signed and dated: *John Gilbert RA / 1879–80*
Presented by the artist, 1893

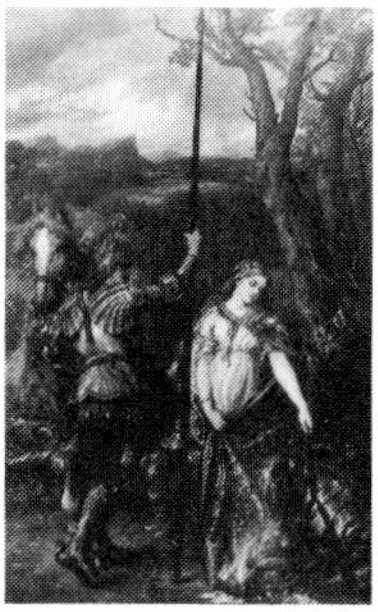

acc. no. 526
Fair St. George (1881)
oil on canvas: 96 × 60 in.
signed (mono) and dated: *JG 1880–1*
Presented by the artist, 1893

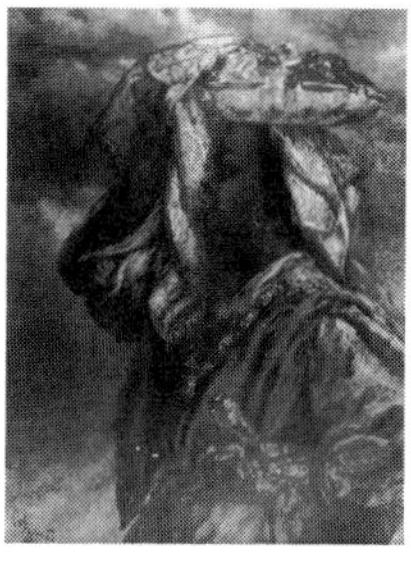

acc. no. 779
Black Girl Carrying Fruit (1882)
oil on canvas: 49 × 36 in.
signed (mono) and dated: *JG / Repainted / 1882*
Bequeathed by George Gilbert, 1903

acc. no. 1705b
Study for 'The Head of the Procession' (c.1882)

pen and ink: $12\frac{3}{8} \times 7\frac{3}{8}$ in.
signed: *John Gilbert* and inscribed: *The head of the Procession / J. Gilbert* and *2.B. M R / 5 feet* × *2. 9in* and *delete accidental ink spots*
Bequeathed by Captain Dyer through Miss M. Dyer, 1965

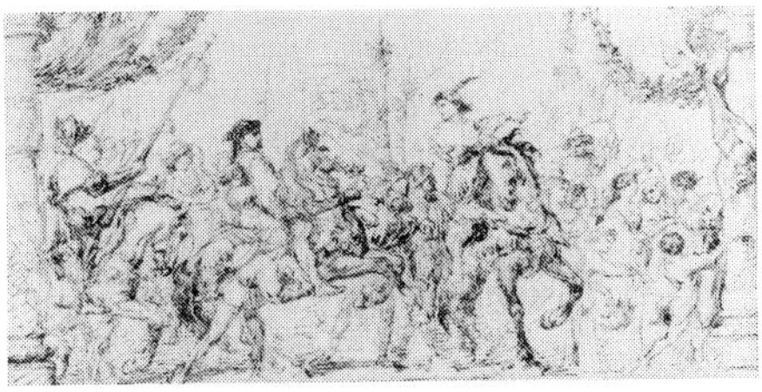

acc. no. 1704f
St John Preaching in the Wilderness (1883)

pen and ink: $7\frac{1}{2} \times 9\frac{1}{2}$ in.
signed and dated: *John Gilbert / 1883*
Bequeathed by Captain Dyer through Miss M. Dyer, 1965

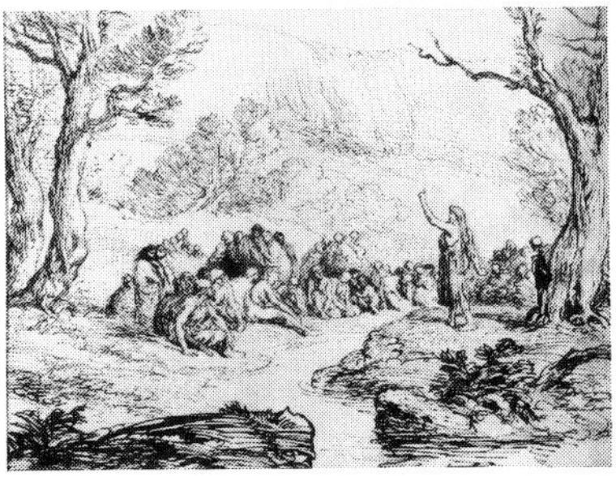

acc. no. 1705c
Young Man with a Book (1883)

pen and ink: $8\frac{3}{8} \times 7\frac{1}{4}$ in.
signed (mono) and dated: *JG 1883*
Bequeathed by Captain Dyer through Miss M. Dyer, 1965

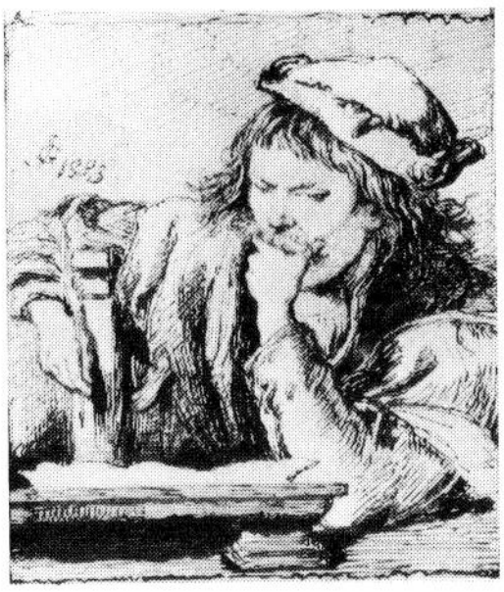

acc. no. 572
Landscape with a Horse and Cart (1883)

watercolour: $9 \times 15\frac{1}{2}$ in.
signed (mono) and dated: *JG 1883*
Presented by the artist, 1893

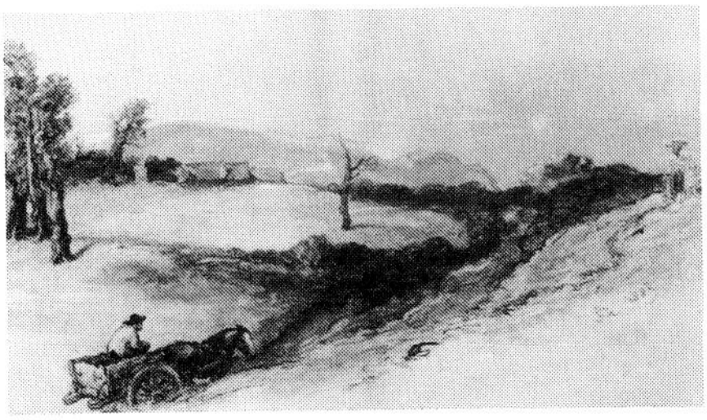

acc. no. 1704d
Timon and Apemantus (1883)

pen and ink: $5\frac{3}{4} \times 7\frac{1}{4}$ in.
signed on verso: *Sir John Gilbert* and inscribed: *Timon and Apemantus / Timon of Athens. Act 4. Scene 3. / 30* × *24* and: $4\frac{1}{4}$ *ins*
Bequeathed by Captain Dyer through Miss M. Dyer, 1965

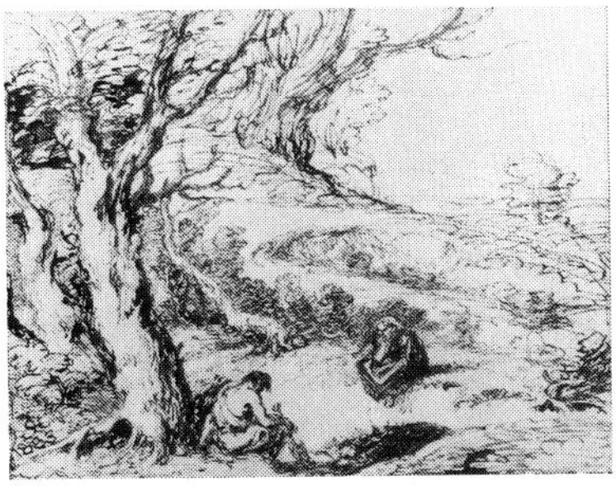

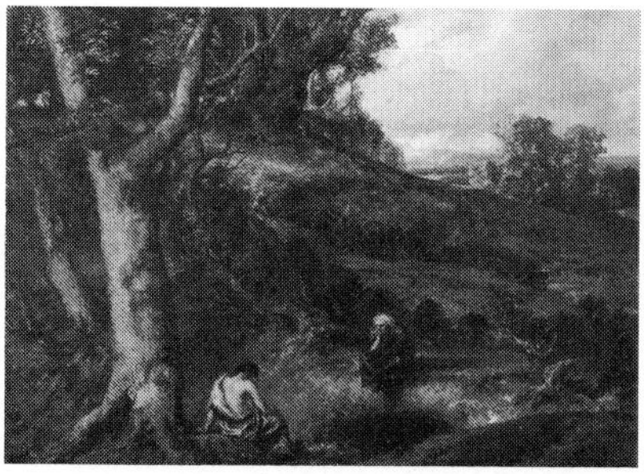

acc. no. 786
Timon and Apemantus (1883)
watercolour: $24\frac{1}{2} \times 30$ in.
signed (mono) and dated: *JG / 1883*
Bequeathed by George Gilbert, 1903

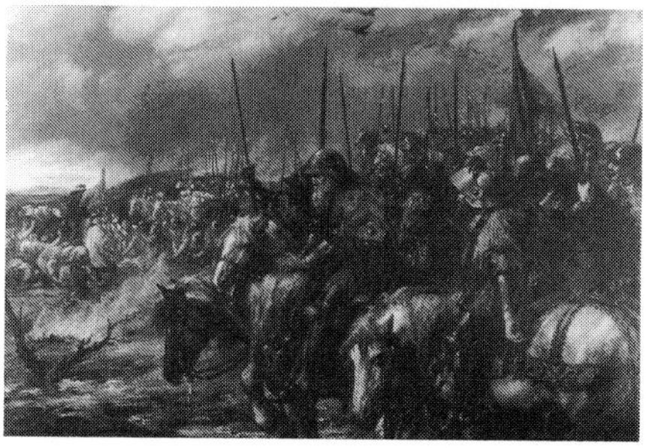

acc. no. 528
Morning of the Battle of Agincourt (1884)
oil on canvas: 48×66 in.
signed (mono) and dated: *JG 1883.4*
Presented by the artist, 1893

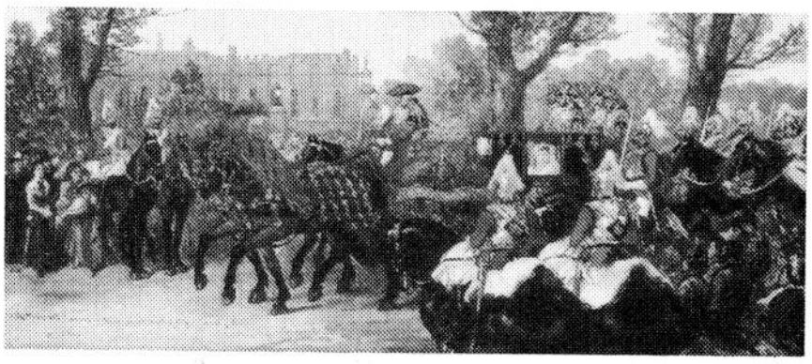

acc. no. 543
The Prince and Princess of Wales going to a 'Drawing Room' at St. James's Palace (1884)
watercolour heightened with white: 15×36 in.
signed (mono) and dated: *JG 1884* and inscribed: *The Prince and Princess of Wales going to Her Majesty's Drawing Room. / St James's Palace.*
Presented by the artist, 1893

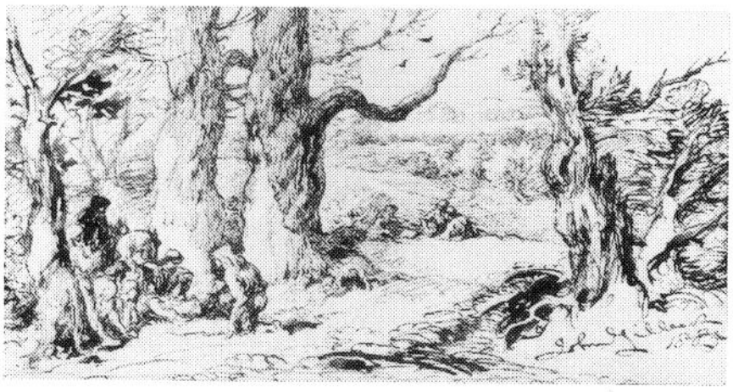

acc. no. 1704e
Study for 'Landscape with Banditti Gambling' (1885)
pen and ink: $5\frac{1}{4} \times 10\frac{1}{4}$ in.
signed and dated: *John Gilbert / 1885*; signed and inscribed on verso: *Banditti / 3ft.5 in × 1ft 8 in / John Gilbert*
Bequeathed by Captain Dyer through Miss M. Dyer, 1965

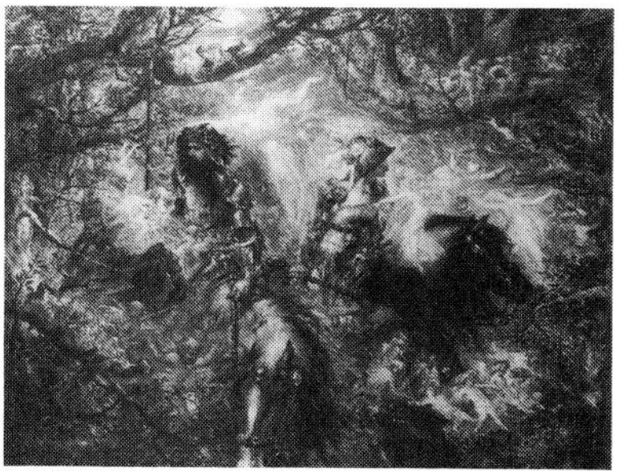

acc. no. 531
The Enchanted Forest (1886)
watercolour: 44×50 in.
signed (mono) and dated: *JG 1885.6*
Presented by the artist, 1893

acc. no. 801
Under the Greenwood Tree (1886)

watercolour: 21 × $14\frac{1}{4}$ in.
signed (mono) and dated: *JG 1886* and inscribed in margin: *Under the Greenwood Tree*
Bequeathed by George Gilbert, 1903

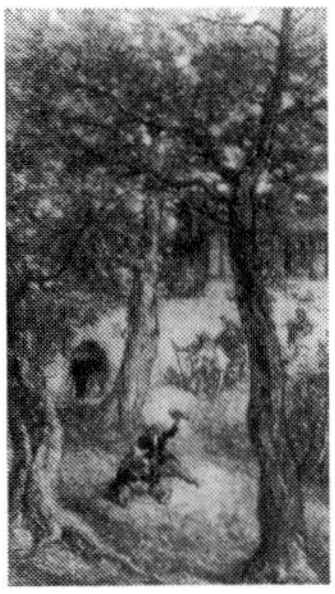

acc. no. 527
Sir Lancelot du Lac (1886)

oil on canvas: 36 × 48 in.
signed (mono) and dated: *JG / 1886*
Presented by the artist, 1893

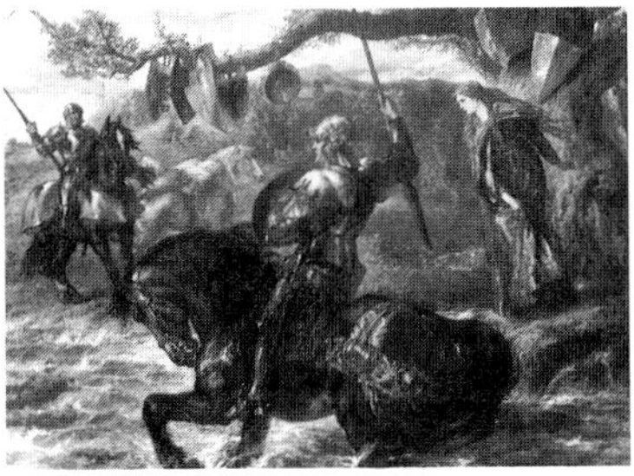

acc. no. 781
A Standard Bearer (?1886)

oil on canvas: 60 × 33 in.
signed (mono) and dated *JG / 1886* (?)
Bequeathed by George Gilbert, 1903

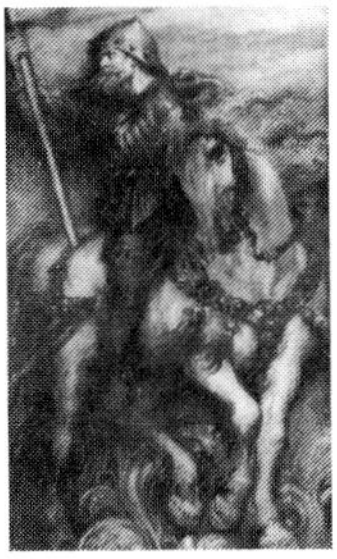

acc. no. 1705e
Cardinal Wolsey in procession to Westminster Hall (1887)

pen and ink: 5 × $10\frac{1}{8}$ in.
signed and dated: *John Gilbert 1887.* and inscribed: *Wolsey Cardinal and Chancellor / John Gilbert* and *size – 5 feet × 2ft 9 in 2.B.L.* and *Title of Picture / Cardinal Wolsey Chancellor of England on his progress to Westminster Hall*
Bequeathed by Captain Dyer through Miss M. Dyer, 1965

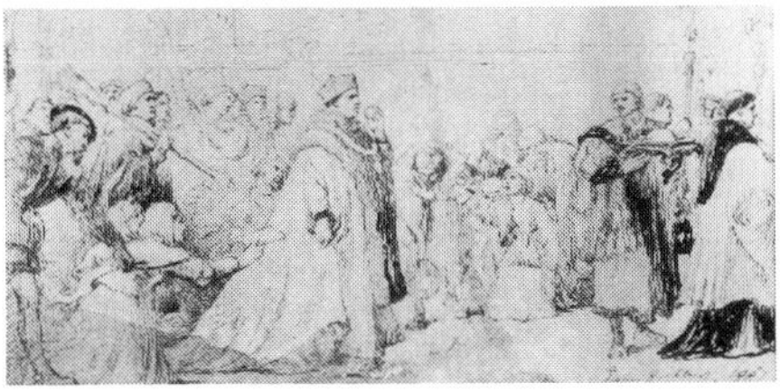

acc. no. 535
Cardinal Wolsey, Chancellor of England, on his Progress to Westminster Hall (1887)

watercolour: 36 × 60 in.
signed and dated: *JG 1886.7*
Presented by the artist, 1893

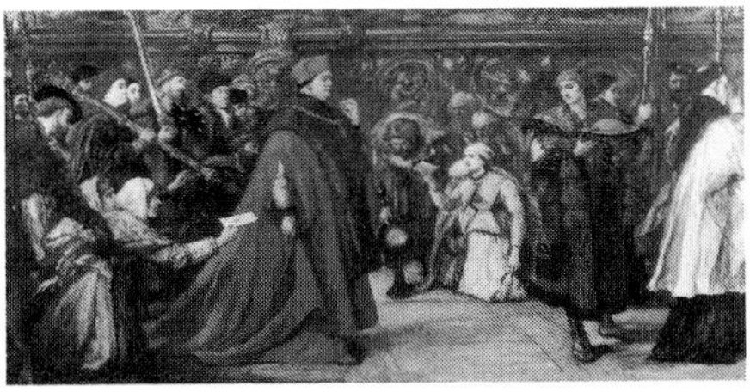

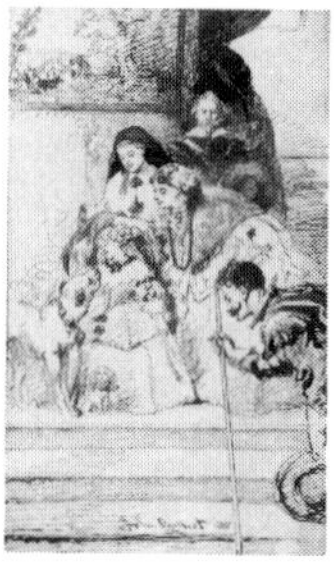

acc. no. 1705d
A Spanish Infanta (1888)

pen and ink: $5\frac{1}{4} \times 10\frac{1}{4}$ in.
signed and dated: *John Gilbert 1888* and inscribed and signed on verso: *Title* / (A) *Spanish Infanta.* / *Size 3ft × 2ft.* / *JGilbert*
Bequeathed by Captain Dyer through Miss M. Dyer, 1965

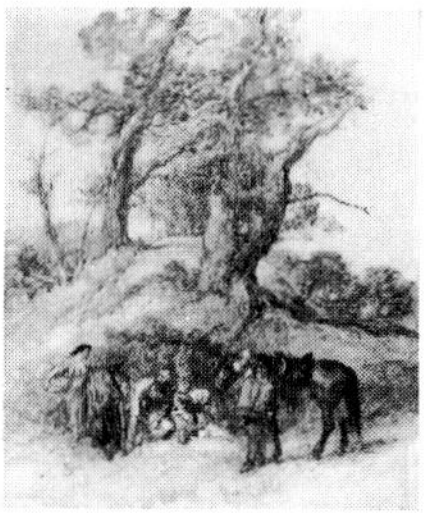

acc. no. 800
A Halt (1888)

watercolour: $14\frac{1}{4} \times 12$ in.
signed (mono): *JG* and dated: *March 1888*
Bequeathed by George Gilbert, 1903

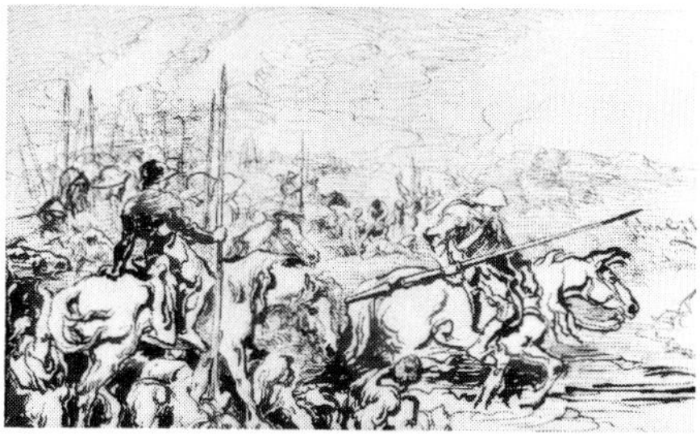

acc. no. 1704b
War: After the Battle (1888)

pen and ink: $8 \times 13\frac{1}{4}$ in.
signed and dated: *John Gilbert* / *1888* and inscribed and signed on verso: *Title* / *Size 4 feet × 2½ feet* / *Gilbert* / (59) / reduce to 5 inches long
Bequeathed by Captain Dyer through Miss M. Dyer, 1965

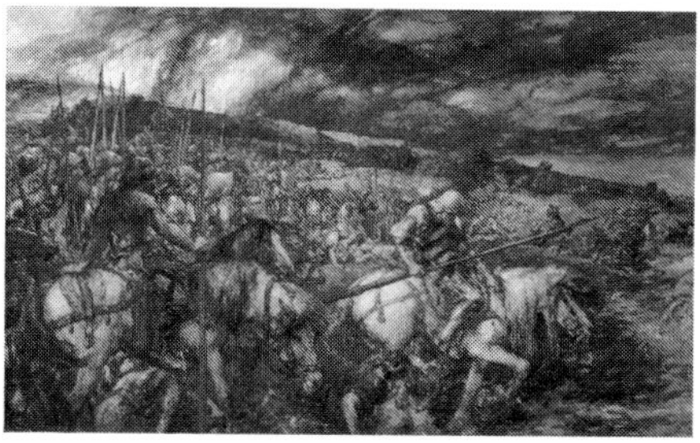

acc. no. 540
War: After the Battle (1888)

watercolour: 30×48 in.
signed and dated: *JG 1888*
Presented by the artist, 1893

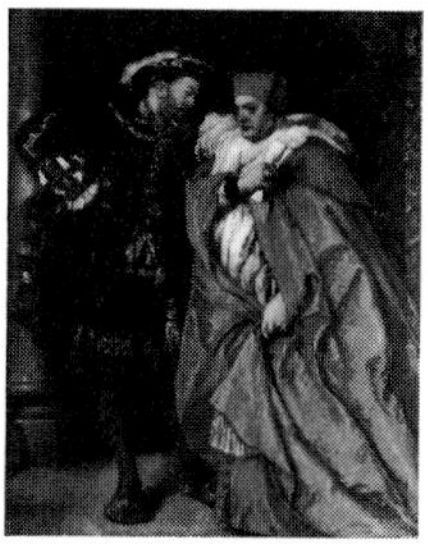

acc. no. 529
Ego et Rex Meus (1888)

oil on canvas: 63×41 in.
signed (mono) and dated: *JG* / *1888*
Presented by the artist, 1893

acc. no. 796
The Witch (1888)

watercolour: $9\frac{1}{2} \times 14\frac{1}{4}$ in.
signed (mono) and dated: *JG / 1888*
Bequeathed by George Gilbert, 1903

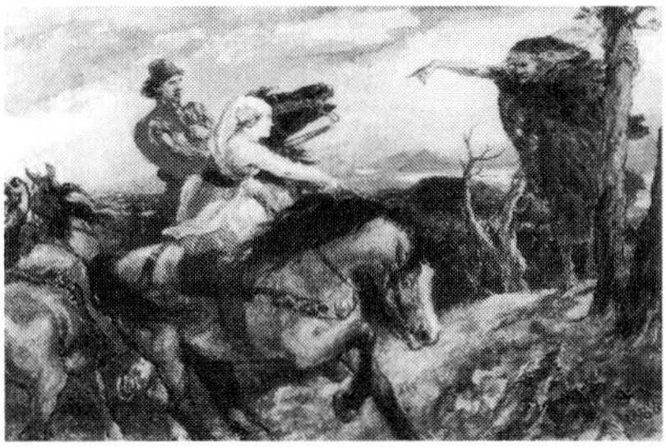

acc. no. 538
The Witch (1889)

watercolour: 24×36 in.
signed (mono) and dated: *JG 1889*
Presented by the artist, 1893

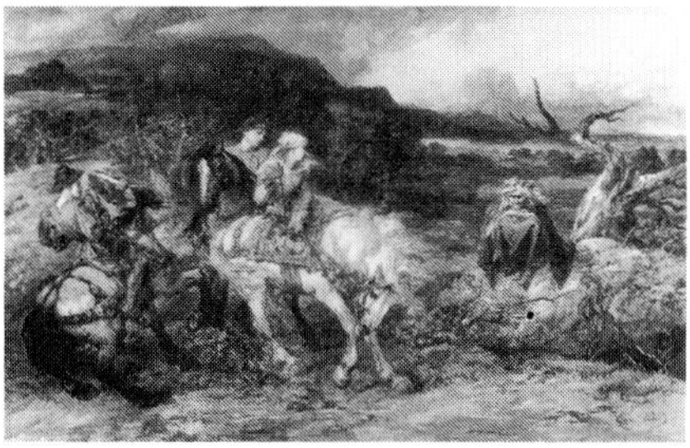

acc. no. 1704c
Study for 'Charcoal Burners' (1889)

pen and ink: $9 \times 6\frac{1}{4}$ in.
inscribed and signed on verso: *Charcoal Burners / 5 feet × 4 feet / John Gilbert* and *let it if possible fill the page of catalogue*
Bequeathed by Captain Dyer through Miss M. Dyer, 1965

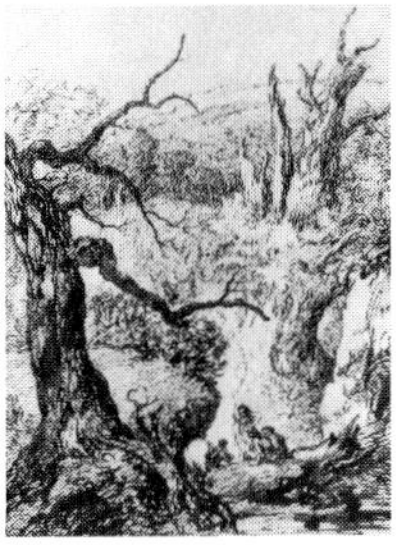

acc. no. 536
Charcoal Burners (1889)

watercolour: 68×48 in.
signed (mono) and dated: *JG / 1889*
Presented by the artist, 1893

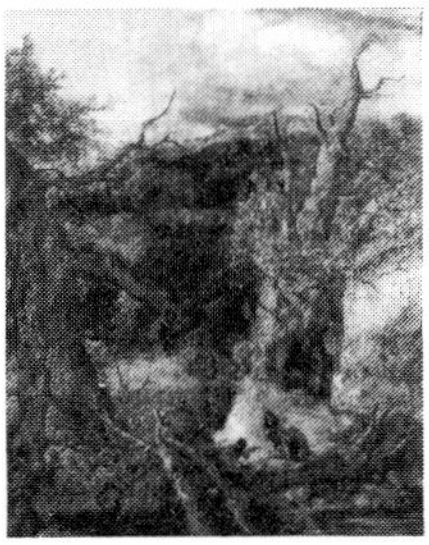

acc. no. 539
A Bishop (1889)

watercolour: $30 \times 21\frac{3}{4}$ in.
signed (mono) and dated: *JG / 1889*
Presented by the artist, 1893

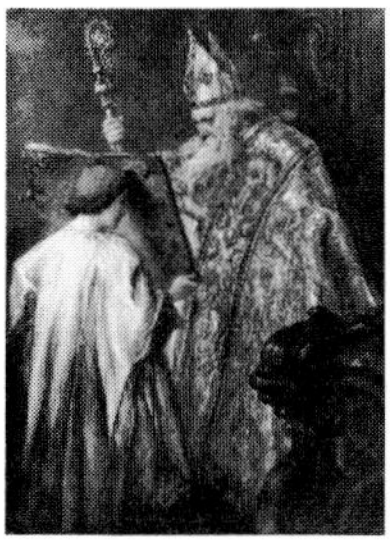

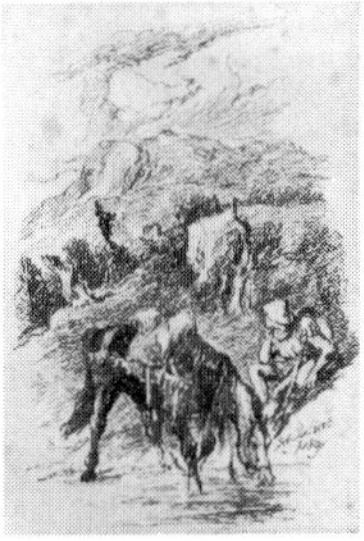

acc. no. 1704a
The Ford (1891)

pen and ink: $10\frac{3}{8} \times 7\frac{1}{4}$ in.
signed and dated: *John Gilbert / 1891*; inscribed on verso: *28 / reduce to 6 inches high*
Bequeathed by Captain Dyer through Miss M. Dyer, 1965

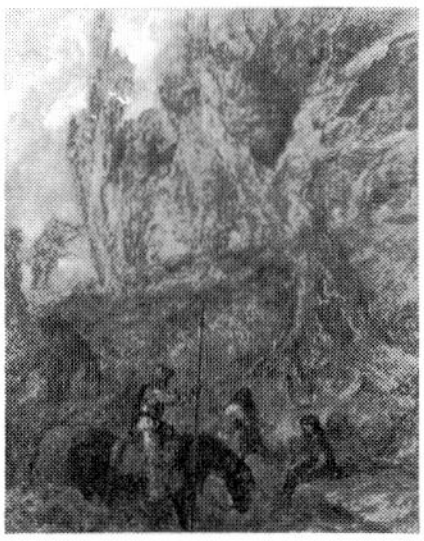

acc. no. 776
The Ford (1891)

oil on canvas: 36 × 28 in.
signed (mono) and dated: *JG 1891*
Bequeathed by George Gilbert, 1903

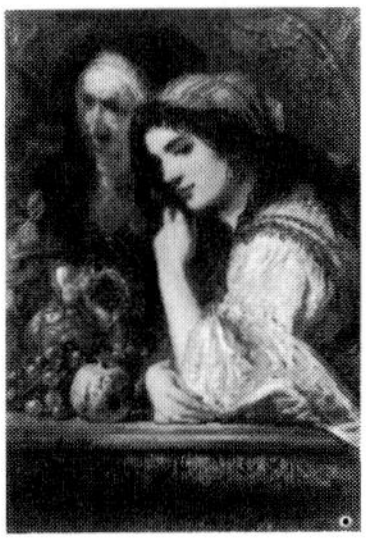

acc. no. 530
Don Quixote's Niece and Housekeeper (1891)

oil on canvas: 33 × 25 in.
signed (mono) and dated: *JG 1891*
Presented by the artist, 1893

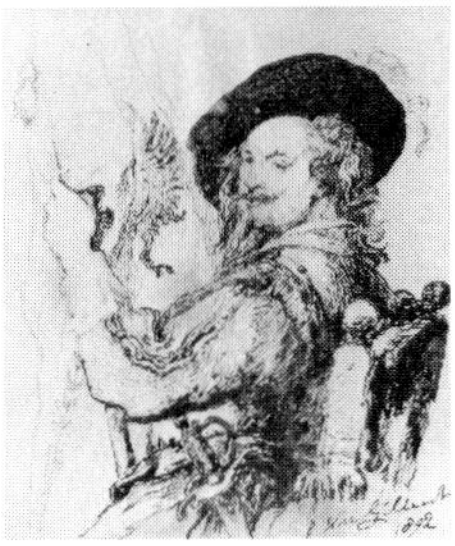

acc. no. 1705a
A Standard Bearer (1892)

pen and ink: $9\frac{1}{8} \times 8$ in.
signed and dated: *John Gilbert / 1892*; inscribed and signed on verso: (ti)*tle: A Standard Bearer / (s)ize – 18 in × 10 in / John Gilbert*
Bequeathed by Captain Dyer through Miss M. Dyer, 1965

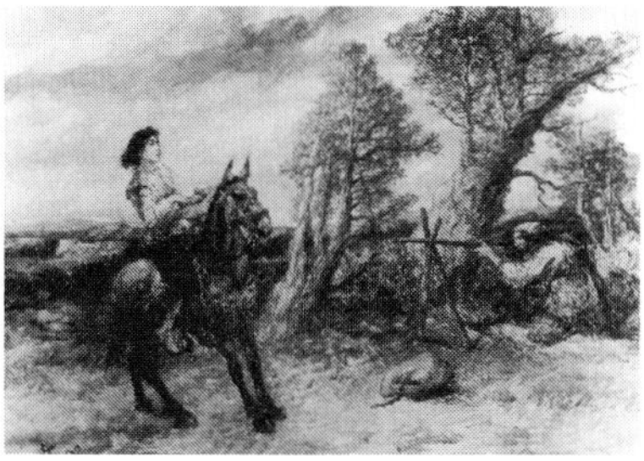

acc. no. 541
Gil Blas' First Adventure (1892)

watercolour: 20 × 26 in.
signed (mono) and dated: *JG / 1892*
Presented by the artist, 1893

acc. no. 542
Gil Blas Taken Prisoner (1893)
watercolour: 20 × 27 in.
signed (mono) and dated: *JG 1893*
Presented by the artist, 1893

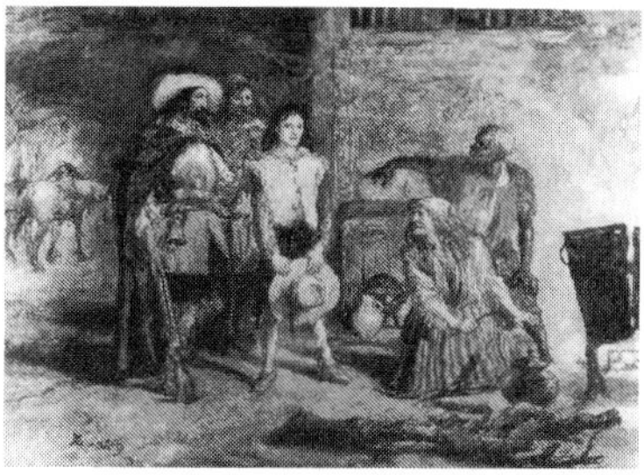

acc. no. 775
Landscape with Hunting Party (?1893)
oil on canvas: 29 × 47 in.
signed (mono) and dated: *JG 1893* (?)
Bequeathed by George Gilbert, 1903

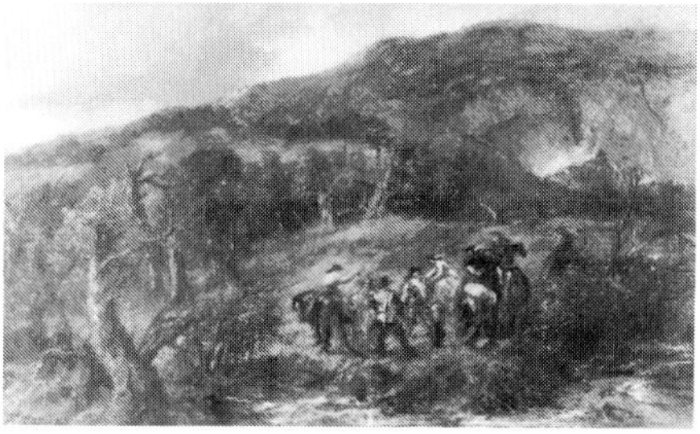

acc. no. 788
The Lost Route (1894)
watercolour: 29 × 24 in.
signed (mono) and dated: *JG/1894*
Bequeathed by George Gilbert, 1903

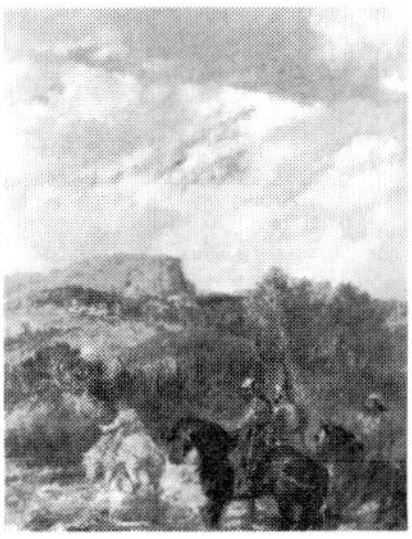

acc. no. 789
Don Quixote and Sancho Panza (1894)
watercolour: $20\frac{1}{4} \times 27\frac{1}{2}$ in.
signed (mono) and dated: *JG 1894*
Bequeathed by George Gilbert, 1903

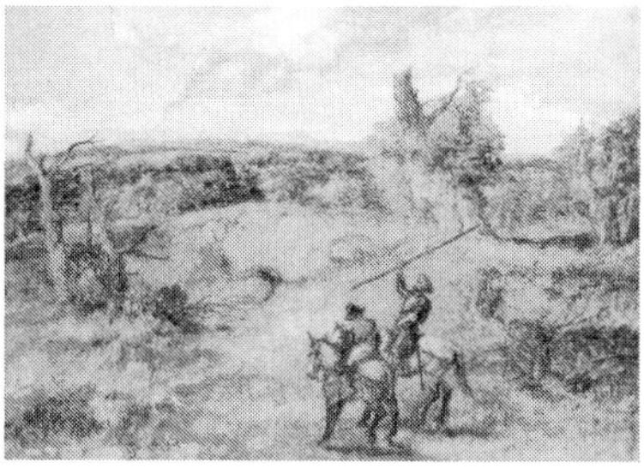

acc. no. 792
A Standard Bearer (1897)
watercolour: 47 × 29 in.
signed (mono) and dated: *JG 1897*
Bequeathed by George Gilbert, 1903

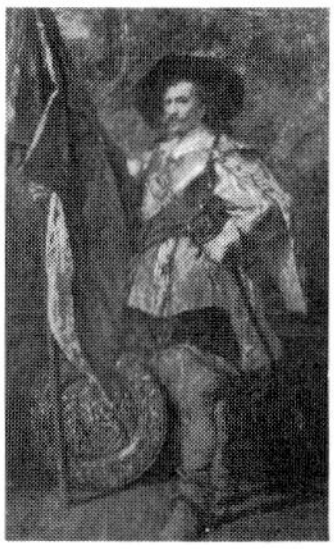

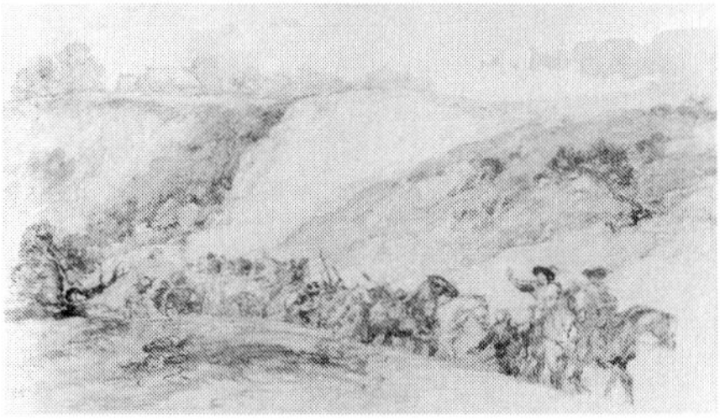

acc. no. 565
Army Waggons in a Ravine
watercolour: $8\frac{3}{4} \times 15\frac{1}{2}$ in. (sight)
signed (mono): *JG*; inscribed on verso: *has been Exhibited*
Presented by the artist, 1893

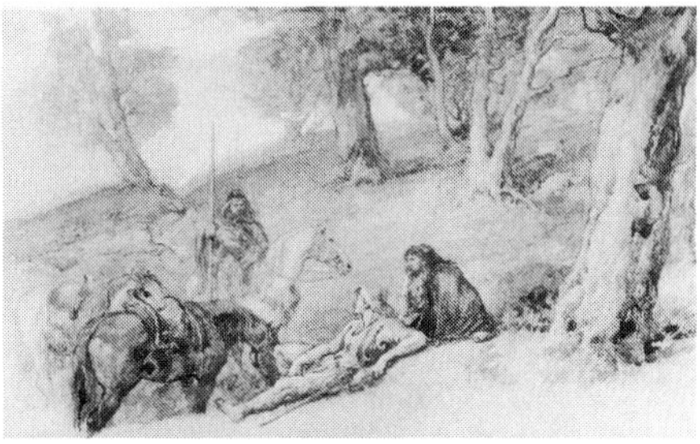

acc. no. 564
Warriors Resting
sepia wash: $9\frac{3}{4} \times 16\frac{1}{4}$ in.
signed (mono): *JG*; inscribed on verso: *Has been exhibited JG*
Presented by the artist, 1893

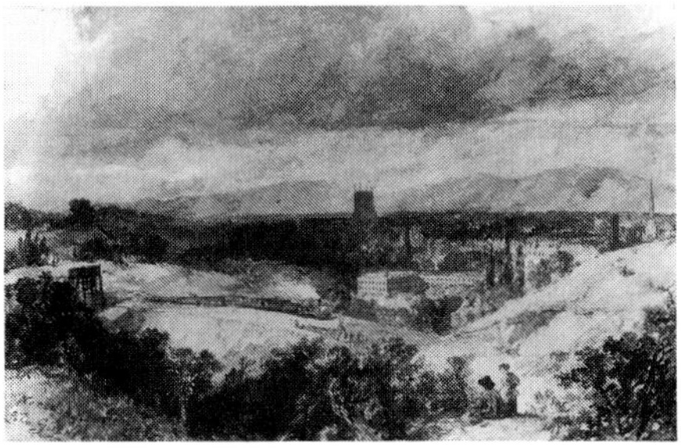

acc. no. 811
Worcester
watercolour over pencil, with gum: $13\frac{7}{8} \times 21$ in.
inscribed and signed: *Worcester./John Gilbert*
Bequeathed by George Gilbert, 1903

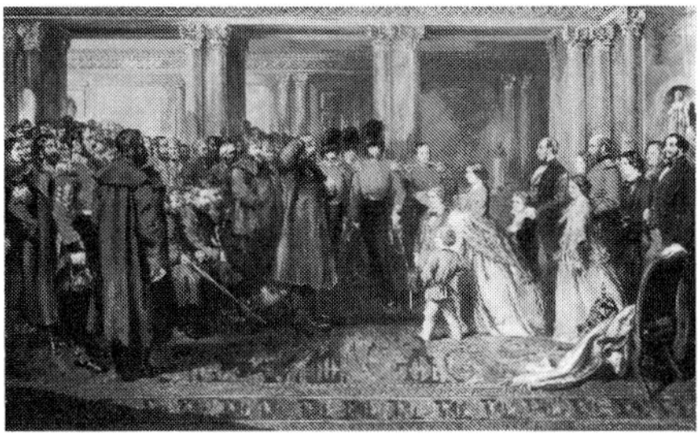

after Sir John Gilbert by W. Bunney (*fl.* 1853–9)

acc. no. 791
Queen Victoria Presenting Medals to the Guards after the Crimean War (1856)
chromolithograph: $21\frac{1}{4} \times 35\frac{7}{8}$ in.
signed in the plate: *John Gilbert 1856 / W. Bunney lith.*
Published by *VINCENT BROOKS CHROMO LONDON*
Bequeathed by George Gilbert, 1903

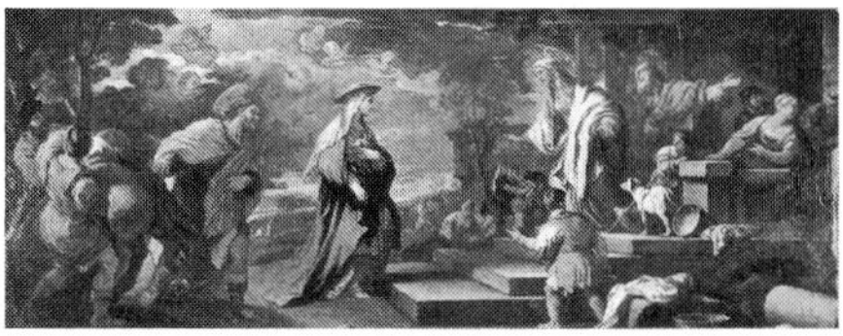

Luca Giordano (1632–1705)

acc. no. 2266
The Visit of the Virgin Mary to her Cousin Elizabeth
oil on canvas: 40×102 in.
Presented by the Government under Capital Transfer Law, 1981

attributed to Luca Giordano (1632–1705)

acc. no. 442
Night and Morning
oil on canvas: 32 × 26 in.
Bequeathed by William Dunnett, 1888

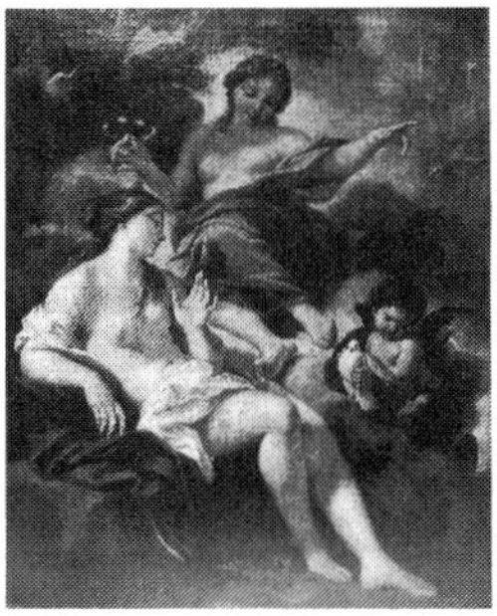

George F. Glennie (*fl.* 1861–82)

acc. no. 1732
Prisoners
watercolour: $7\frac{3}{4}$ × 15 in.
signed: *G.F. Glennie*
Bequeathed by Miss S. R. Field, 1966

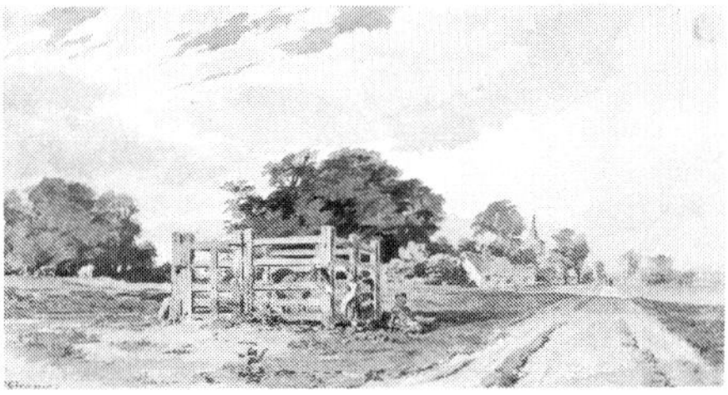

acc. no. 1733
Middlesex Landscape
watercolour: 9 × $13\frac{3}{4}$ in.
Bequeathed by Miss S. R. Field, 1966

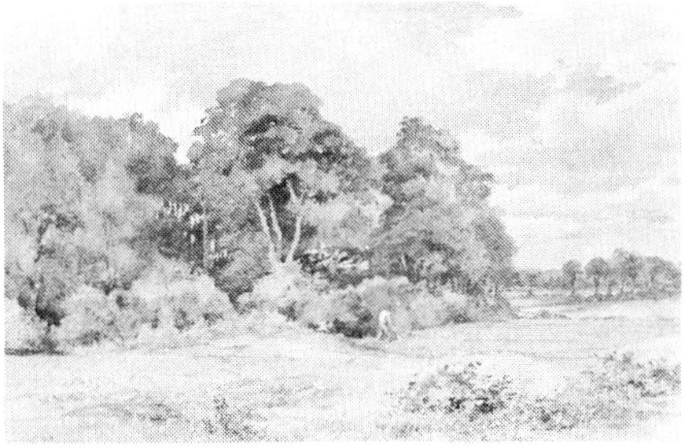

John William Godward (1861–1922)

acc. no. 981
The Betrothed (1892)
oil on canvas: 17 × 33 in.
signed and dated: *J.W. GODWARD. 1892.*
Presented by H. S. E. Vanderpant, 1916

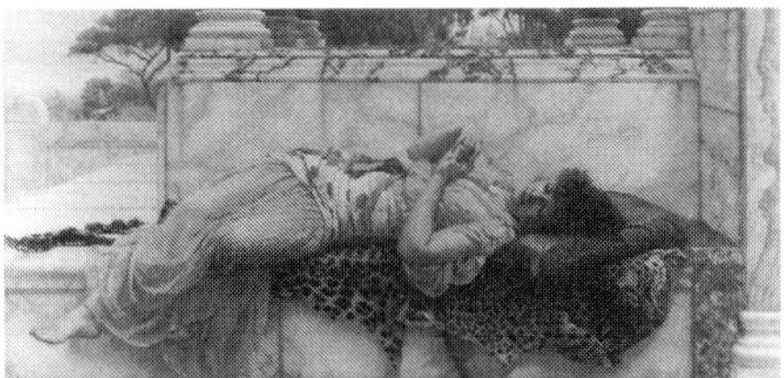

Sigismund Christian Hubert Goetze (1866–1939)

acc. no. 878
Sir Joseph Barnby (1893)
oil on canvas: 50 × 36 in.
signed and dated: *S.C.H.G. / 1893*
Presented by the sitter, 1909

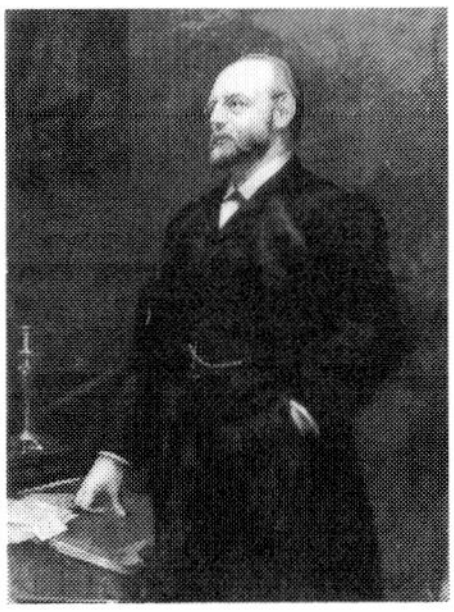

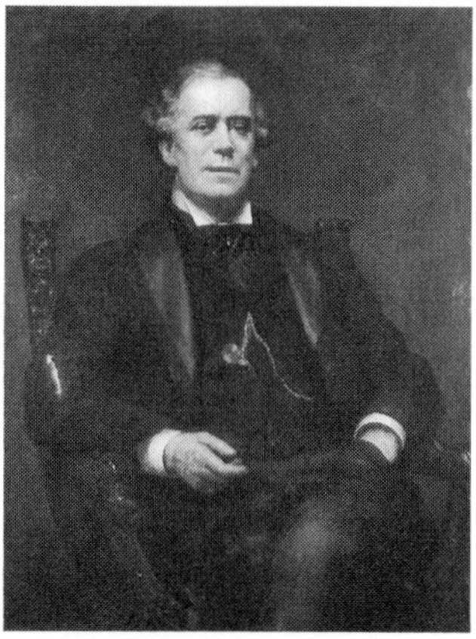

acc. no. 843
John Lawrence Toole
oil on canvas: 44 × 34 in.
Presented by the Executors of J. L. Toole, 1906

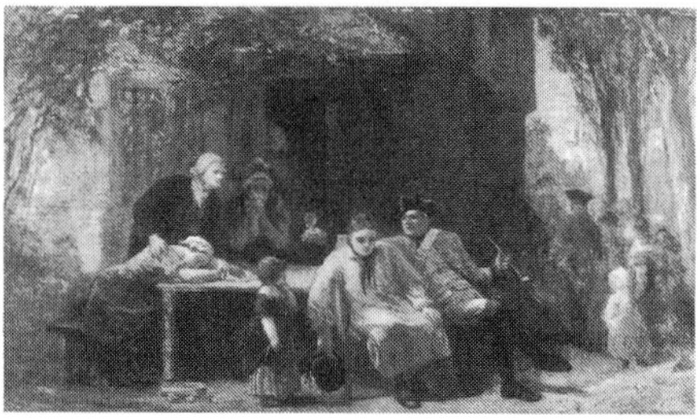

Frederick Goodall (1822–1904)

acc. no. 671
Conscription (1851)
oil on panel: 5 × 9 in.
signed and dated: *F. Goodall/1851*
Bequeathed by Charles Gassiot, 1902

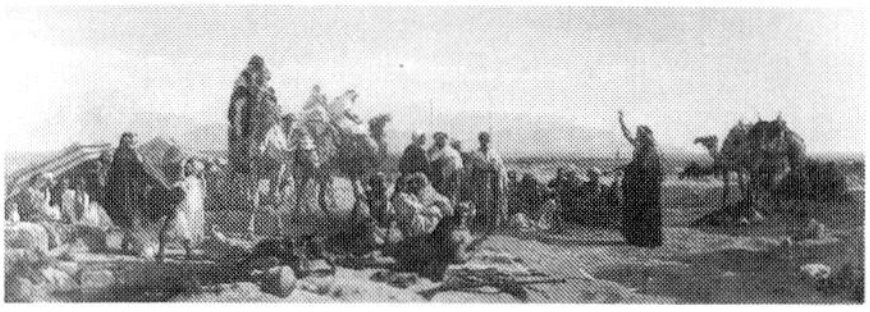

acc. no. 841
Early Morning in the Wilderness of Shur (1860)
oil on canvas: 42 × 120 in.
signed and dated: *Frederick Goodall 1860*
Presented by Charles T. Harris, 1906

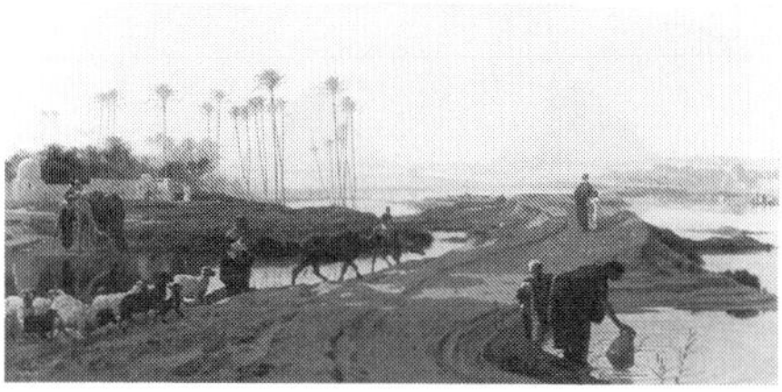

acc. no. 669
The Subsiding of the Nile (1873)
oil on canvas: 30 × 60 in.
signed (mono) and dated: *FG 1873*
Bequeathed by Charles Gassiot, 1902

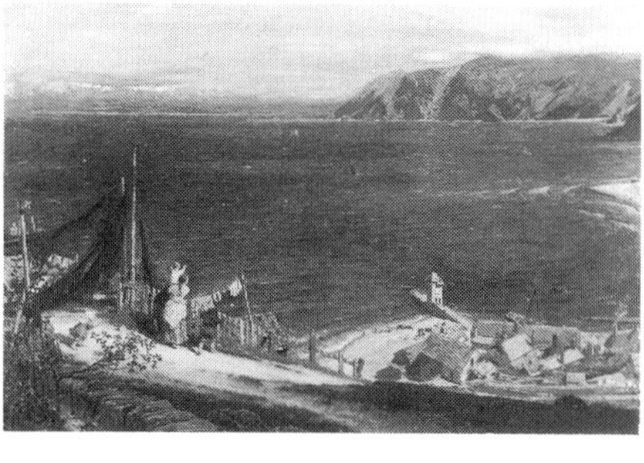

Albert Goodwin (1845–1932)

acc. no. 871
The Toilers' Return (1877)
oil on canvas: 38 × 56 in.
signed and dated: *Albert Goodwin /77*
Presented by Charles T. Harris, 1908

acc. no. 862
Durham Cathedral (1903)

pen and ink and watercolour: $10\frac{3}{4} \times 14\frac{3}{4}$ in.
inscribed: *Durham. / Half Church of God / Half Castle – 'gainst the Scot* and signed and dated: *1903/Albert Goodwin*
Presented by Miss Evelyn P. McGhee, 1908

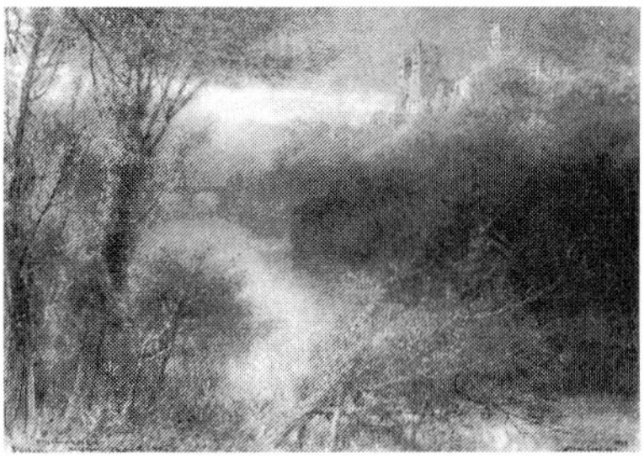

acc. no. 864
Venice, before the Campanile fell (1903–4)

watercolour: $9 \times 11\frac{1}{4}$ in.
inscribed: *Venice before the Tower fell* and signed and dated: *Albert Goodwin 1903/4*
Presented by Miss Evelyn P. McGhee, 1908

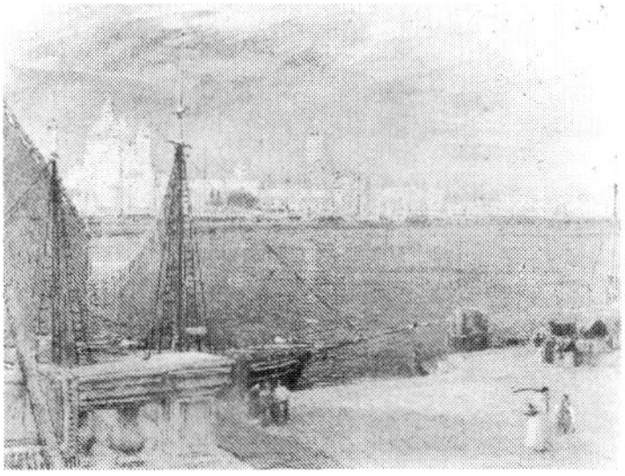

acc. no. 867
Woody Bay, North Devon (1905)

watercolour: $10 \times 14\frac{1}{4}$ in.
inscribed: *Woody Bay N. Devon* and signed and dated: *Albert Goodwin 1905*
Presented by Miss Evelyn P. McGhee, 1908

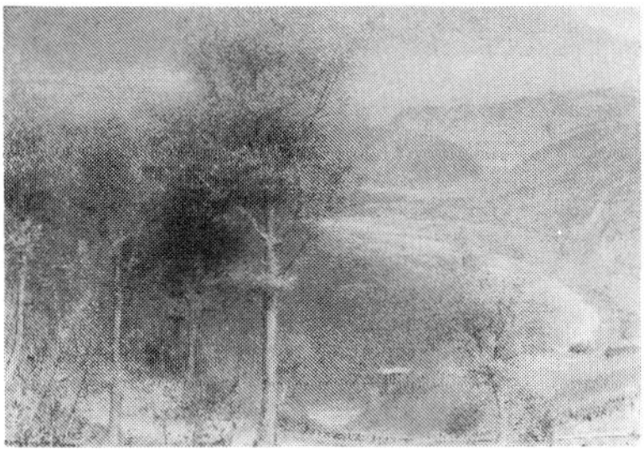

acc. no. 863
Locarno, Lake Maggiore (1905)

watercolour: $15 \times 10\frac{1}{2}$ in.
inscribed: *Locarno Lago Maggiore* and signed and dated: *Albert Goodwin 1905*
Presented by Miss Evelyn P. McGhee, 1908

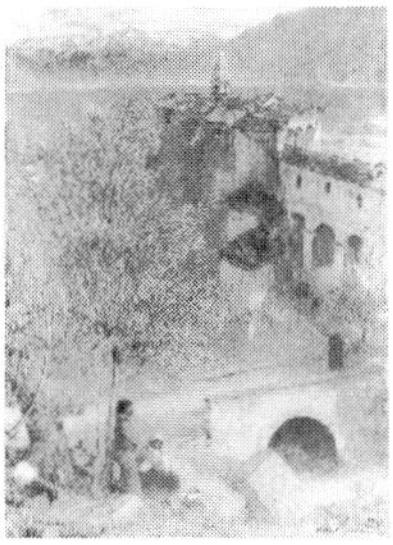

acc. no. 866
Westminster by Night (1905)

watercolour: $10\frac{1}{2} \times 14\frac{1}{2}$ in.
inscribed: *Westminster* and signed and dated: *Albert Goodwin. 1905*
Presented by Miss Evelyn P. McGhee, 1908

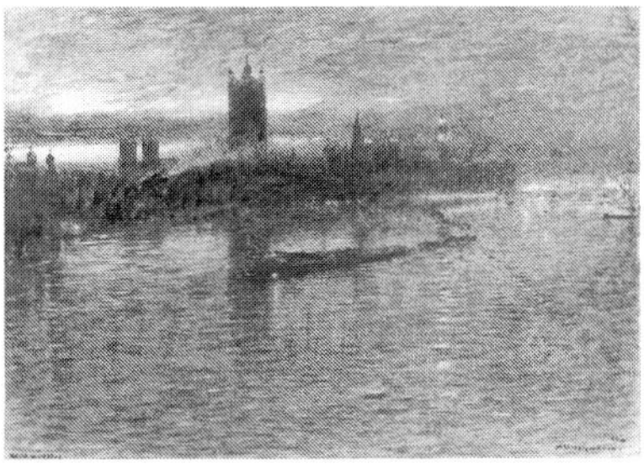

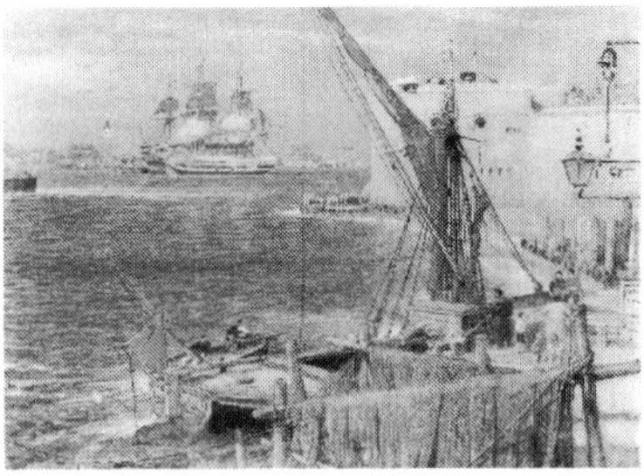

acc. no. 865
HMS 'The Victory' at Portsmouth (1907)

watercolour: $12 \times 15\frac{1}{4}$ in.
inscribed: *Portsmouth* and signed and dated: *Albert Goodwin 1907*
Presented by Miss Evelyn P. McGhee, 1908

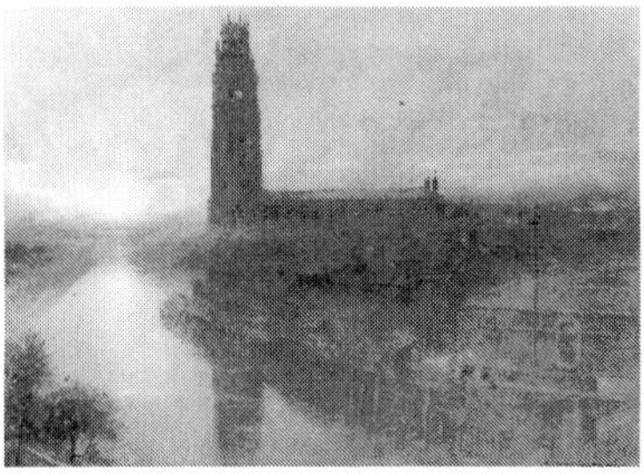

acc. no. 934
Boston (1907)

watercolour: $10\frac{5}{8} \times 14\frac{1}{2}$ in.
inscribed: *Boston* and signed and dated: *Albert Goodwin 1907*
Presented by Miss Evelyn P. McGhee, 1912

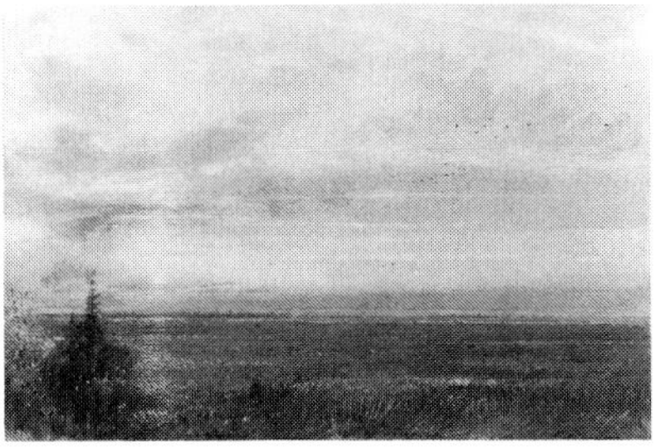

acc. no. 915
Venice, from the Mainland (1908)

watercolour: $10 \times 14\frac{1}{2}$ in.
inscribed, signed and dated: *Venice from the mainland The City in the Sea Albert Goodwin 1908*
Presented by Miss Evelyn P. McGhee, 1910

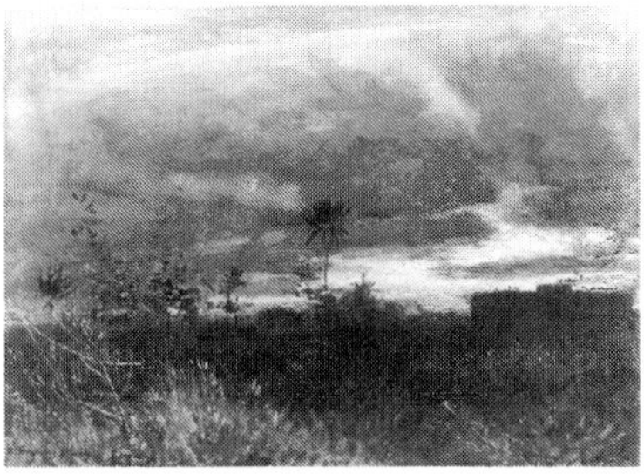

acc. no. 923
The Towers of Silence, Bombay (1909)

watercolour: $10\frac{1}{4} \times 14\frac{1}{4}$ in.
inscribed: *The Towers of Silence Bombay* and signed and dated: *Albert Goodwin 1909*
Presented by Miss Evelyn P. McGhee, 1911

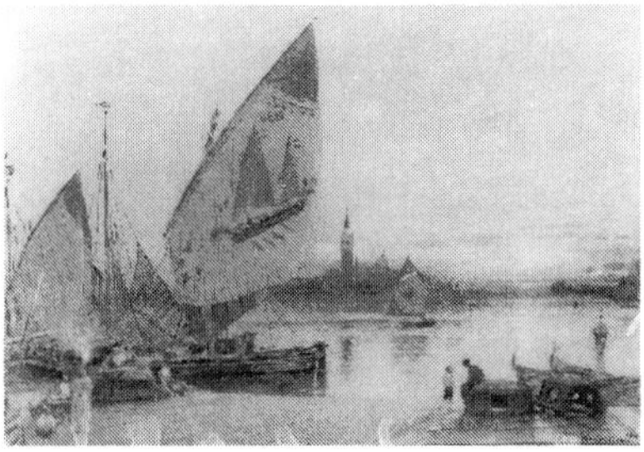

acc. no. 914
Venice (1910)

watercolour: 10×15 in.
signed and dated: *Albert Goodwin 1910*
Presented by Miss Evelyn P. McGhee, 1910

acc. no. 921
The Lagoons, Venice (1910)
watercolour: $10\frac{1}{4} \times 14\frac{1}{4}$ in.
inscribed: *The Lagoons, Venice* and signed and dated: *Albert Goodwin 1910*
Presented by Miss Evelyn P. McGhee, 1911

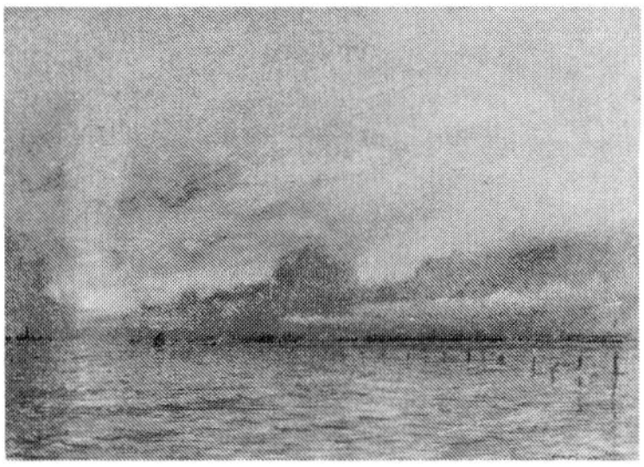

acc. no. 924
Cley, Norfolk (1910)
watercolour: $10 \times 14\frac{1}{2}$ in.
inscribed: *Cley Norfolk* and signed and dated: *Albert Goodwin 1910*
Presented by Miss Evelyn P. McGhee, 1911

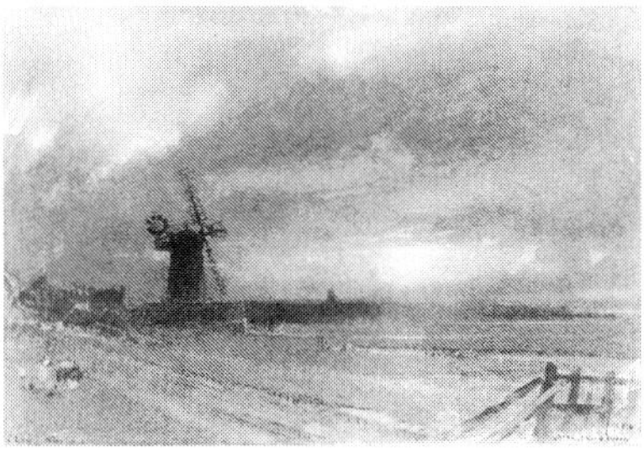

acc. no. 922
Stansstad and the Pilatus, Switzerland
watercolour: $10\frac{1}{2} \times 14\frac{1}{4}$ in.
Presented by Miss Evelyn P. McGhee, 1911

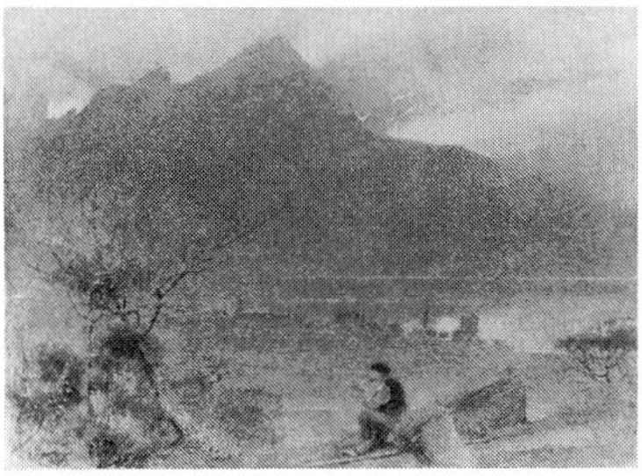

William Henry Gore (*c.*1864–1931)

acc. no. 672
'Listed (*c.* 1885)
oil on canvas: 36 × 24 in.
signed: *W. HENRY GORE*
Bequeathed by Charles Gassiot, 1902

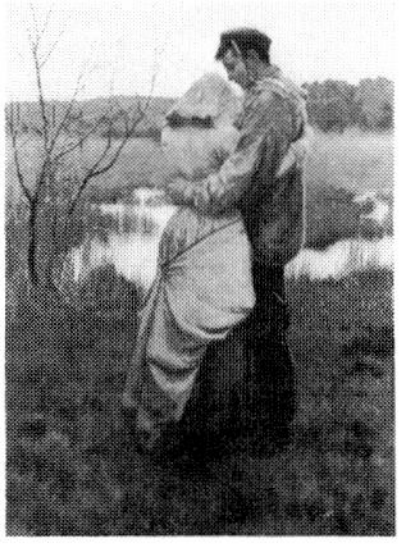

Andrew Carrick Gow (1848–1920)

acc. no. 613
Queen Victoria's Diamond Jubilee Service, June 22 1897 (1897–99)
oil on canvas: 56 × 96 in.
signed and dated: *A.C. GOW / 97–99*
Presented by Henry Clarke, 1899

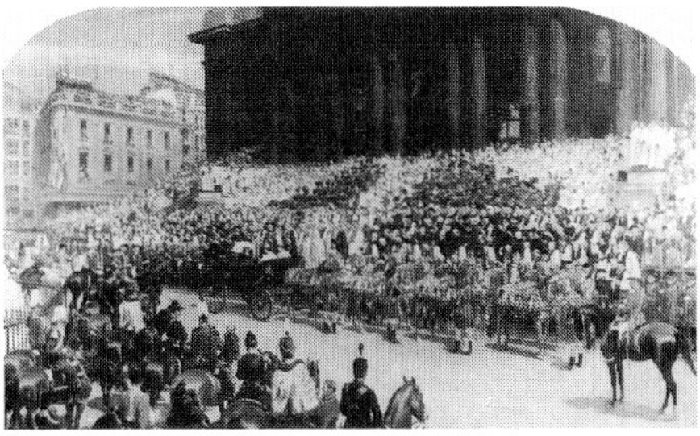

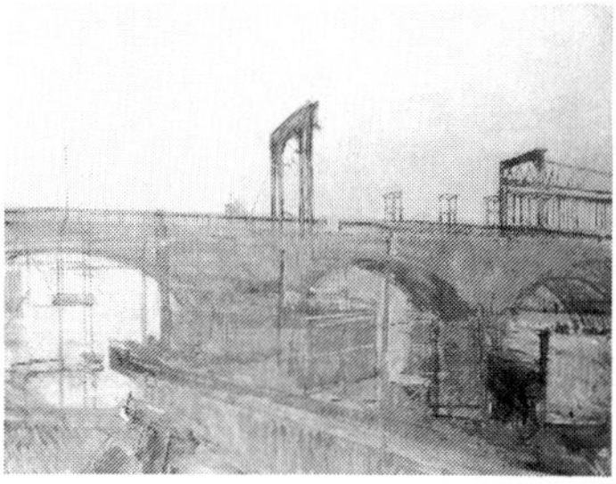

David Graham (b.1926)

acc. no. 1906
London Bridge to Arizona (1969)

oil on canvas: 34 × 44 in.
signed and dated: *David Graham 69* and again on verso with artist's address
Purchased from the artist, 1972

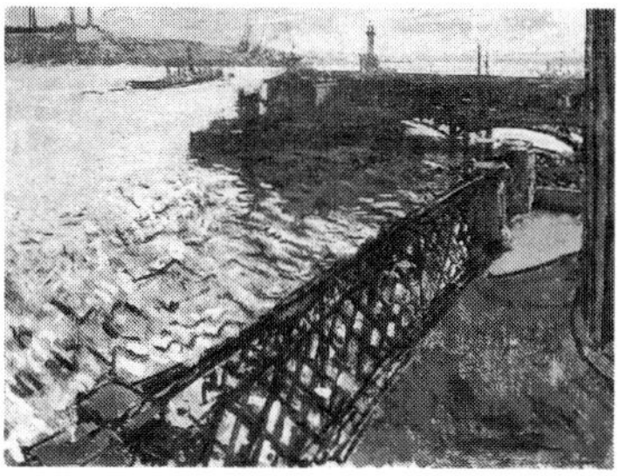

acc. no. 1907
River Thames at Gravesend

oil on canvas: 30 × 34 in.
signed: *David Graham*
Purchased from the artist, 1972

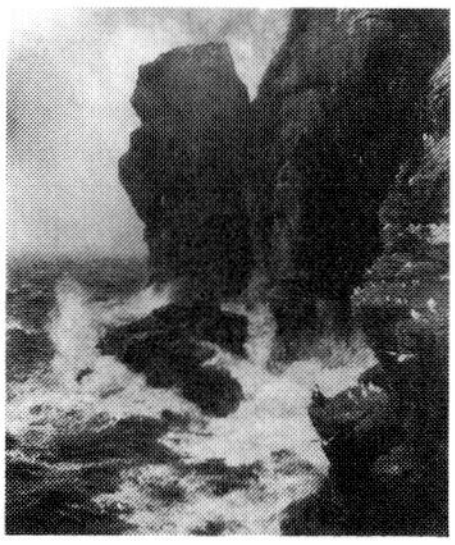

Peter Graham (1836–1921)

acc. no. 1045
Ribbed and Paled in by Rocks Unscaleable (1885)

oil on canvas: 62 × $52\frac{1}{2}$ in.
signed and dated: *Peter Graham / 1885*
Purchased, 1926

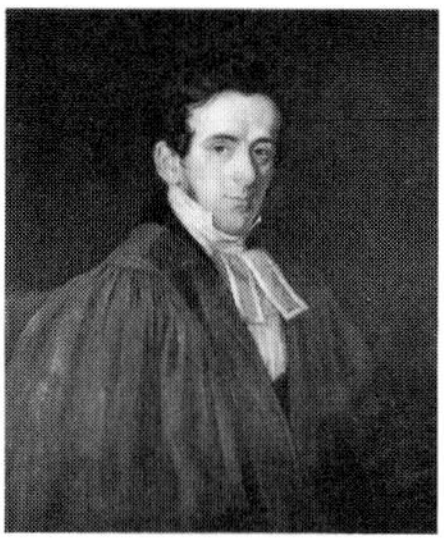

Charles Grant (*fl.* 1825–39)

acc. no. 1236
The Rev. John Allen Giles, Headmaster of the City of London School 1836–40

oil on canvas: 30 × 25 in.
Presented to the City of London School, source unknown, 1937

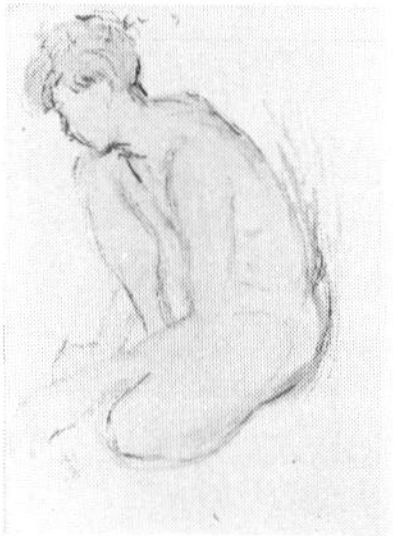

Duncan Grant (1885–1978)

acc. no. 2235
Nude Boy (1949)

pencil and wash: $14\frac{5}{8} \times 10\frac{3}{8}$ in.
signed and dated: *DG/49*
Presented by Miss Helen Guiterman, 1985

William James Grant (1829–66)

acc. no. 673
The Combat

oil on panel: 7 × 13 in.
Bequeathed by Charles Gassiot, 1902

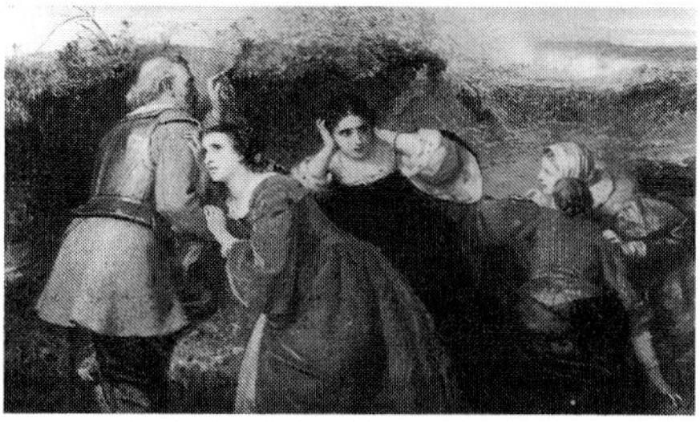

E. F. Green (*fl.* 1824–51)

acc. no. 848
Portrait of a Young Man (formerly thought to be William Hazlitt)

oil on canvas: $21\frac{1}{2} \times 18\frac{1}{2}$ in.
Presented by Lindo Myers, 1907

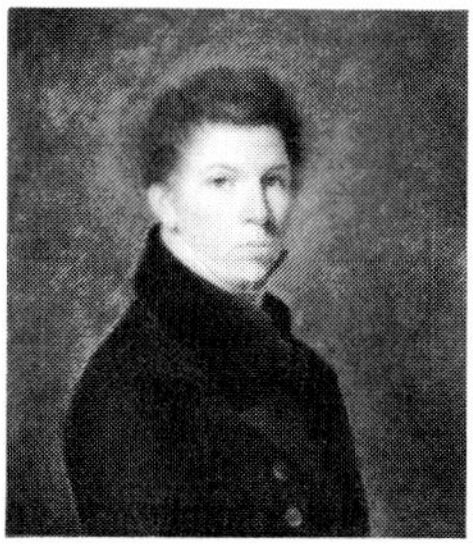

attributed to Frank R. Grey (19th C)

acc. no. 3561
An 18th Century Artist sketching in his Studio

pen and ink: $8\frac{3}{4} \times 6\frac{1}{4}$ in.
signed (mono): *FRG*
Presented by Miss Helen Guiterman, 1985

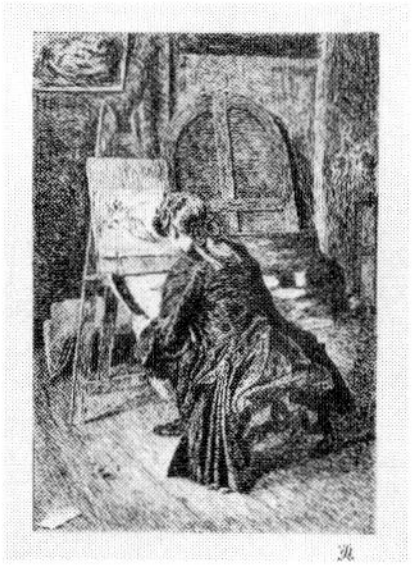

Jan Griffier the Younger (d. *c.*1750)

acc. no. 1706
The Thames during the Great Frost of 1739

oil on canvas: $18\frac{1}{2} \times 25\frac{1}{2}$ in.
signed and dated: *Jn. Griffier f 1739*
Purchased from Agnews', 1965

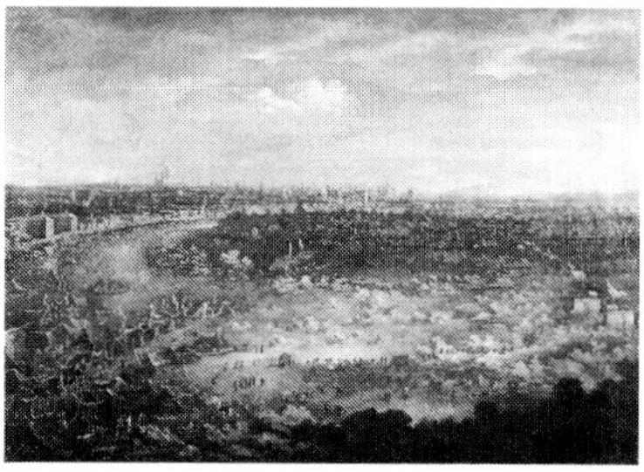

Frederick Griffin (b.1906)

acc. no. 1901
The Guildhall Reconstruction (*c.*1972)

oil on hardboard: $29\frac{1}{2} \times 39\frac{3}{4}$ in.
signed: *Frederick Griffin*
Purchased from the artist, 1972

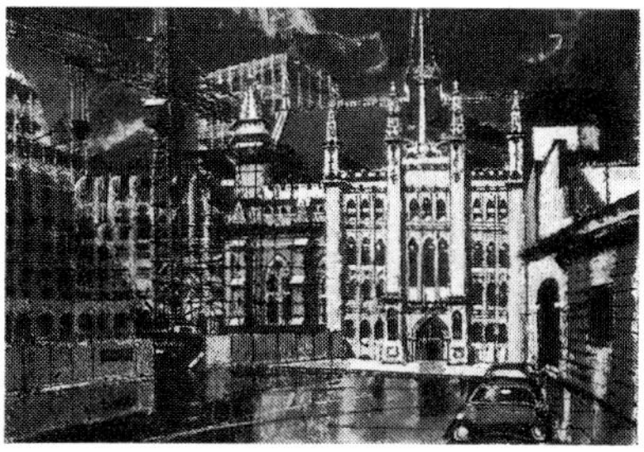

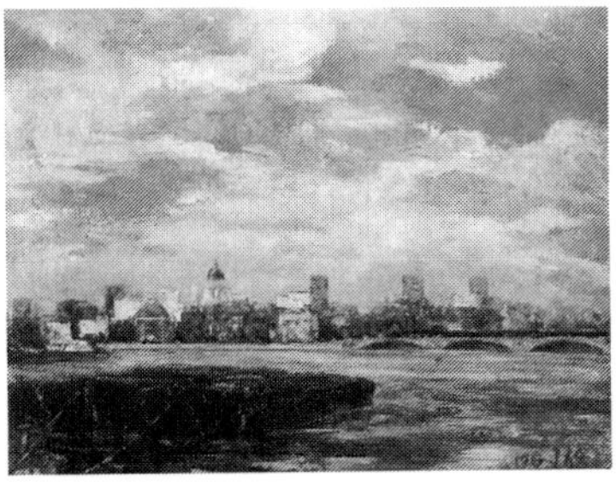

Mervyn Griffith-Jones (1909–79)

acc. no. 1824
St. Paul's from the South Bank (1968)

oil on canvas: 25 × 30 in.
signed and dated: *MGJ 68*
Purchased from the John Whibley Gallery, 1969

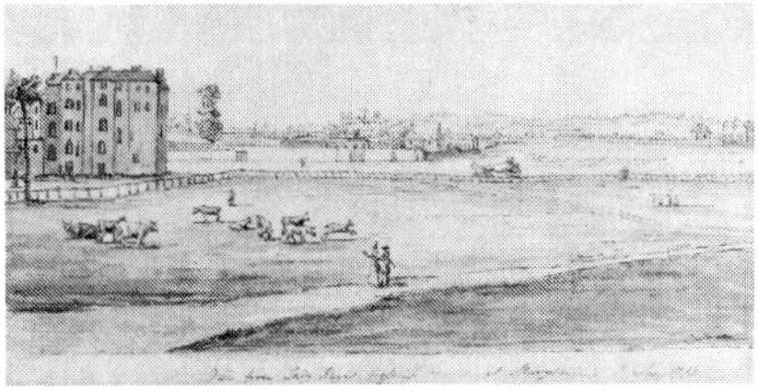

Samuel Hieronymus Grimm (1733–94)

acc. no. 2259
View from Lady Kaye's Dressing Room at Marylebone (1793)

pen and grey ink and wash: 4½ × 10 in.
inscribed and dated: *View from Lady Kaye's Dressing room at Marybone. May 1793*
Presented by Miss Helen Guiterman, 1985

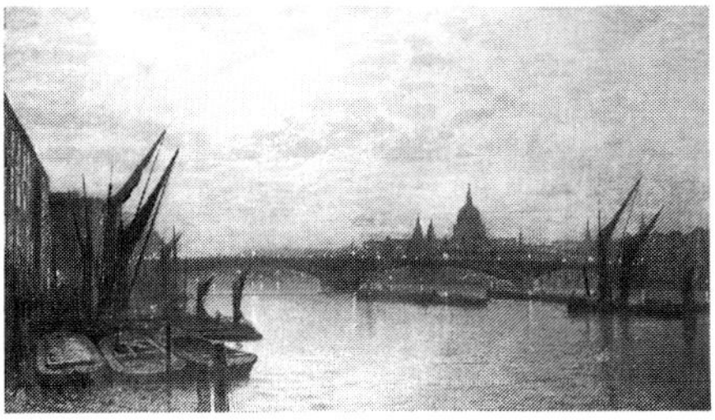

Atkinson Grimshaw (1836–93)

acc. no. 1781
The Thames by Moonlight with Southwark Bridge (1884)

oil on canvas: 29½ × 50 in.
signed and dated: *Atkinson Grimshaw 1884*
Purchased, 1967

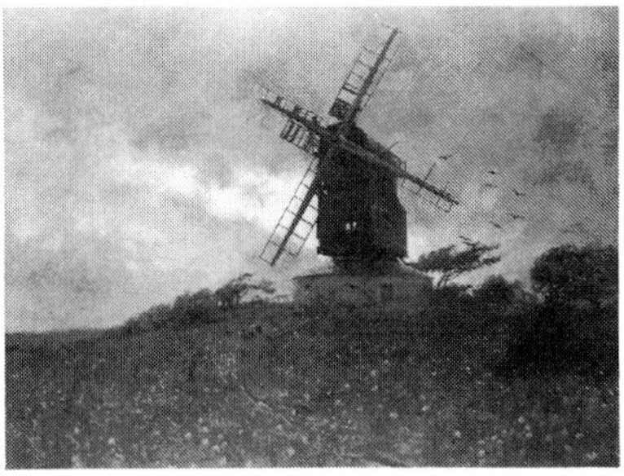

W. H. Murphy Grimshaw (*fl.* 1885–96)

acc. no. 578
The Haunted Mill (1893)

oil on canvas: 30 × 40 in.
Presented by the artist, 1893

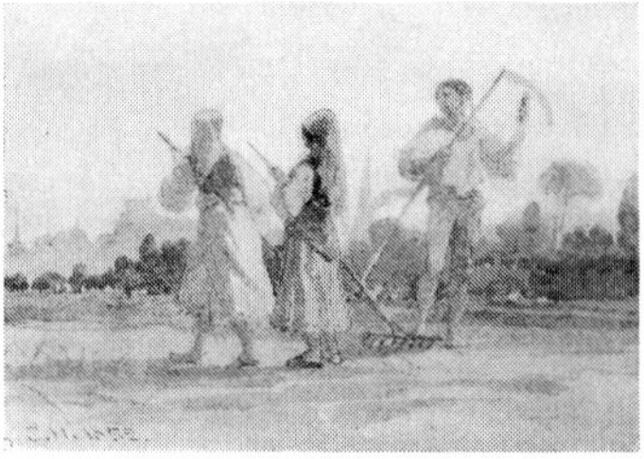

Carl Haag (1820–1915)

acc. no. 3566
Franconian Peasants near Würzburg (1852)

pencil and watercolour: 5 × 7 in.
signed and dated: *C.H. 1852*; inscribed on verso: *Franconian Peasants near Würzburg / 1852* and with an 8-line Scandinavian poem; and a pencil sketch of a young girl in profile
Presented by Miss Helen Guiterman, 1985

acc. no. 3566 (verso)

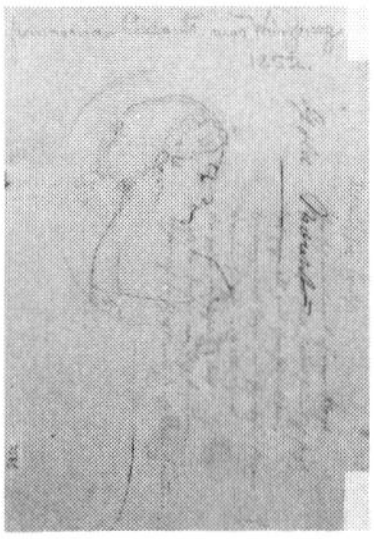

acc. no. 941
La Illah il Allah

watercolour: $20 \times 13\frac{3}{4}$ in.
signed and inscribed: *Carl Haag / ΙΛΛΟ*
Presented by Sir Edward Durning-Lawrence, 1913

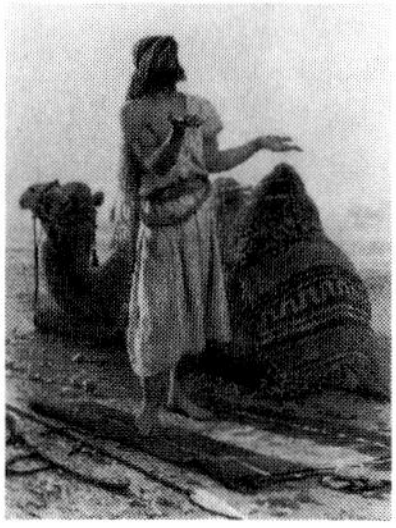

Karl Hagedorn (b.1889)

acc. no. 1802
All Hallows Barking by the Tower (1968)

watercolour: $15\frac{1}{2} \times 22$ in.
signed and dated: *Karl Hagedorn '68*
Purchased from the artist, 1969

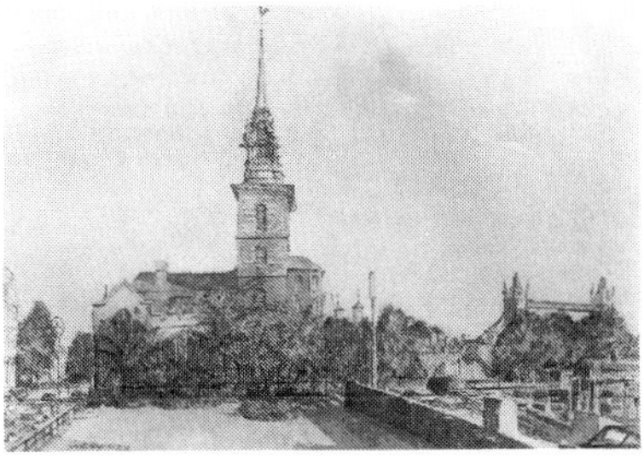

Edward Matthew Hale (1852–1924)

acc. no. 1058
Les Trois Princesses (1881)

oil on canvas: $52 \times 81\frac{1}{2}$ in.
signed and dated: *E. Matthew Hale / 1881*
Presented by Mrs. Henry Ladenburg, 1927

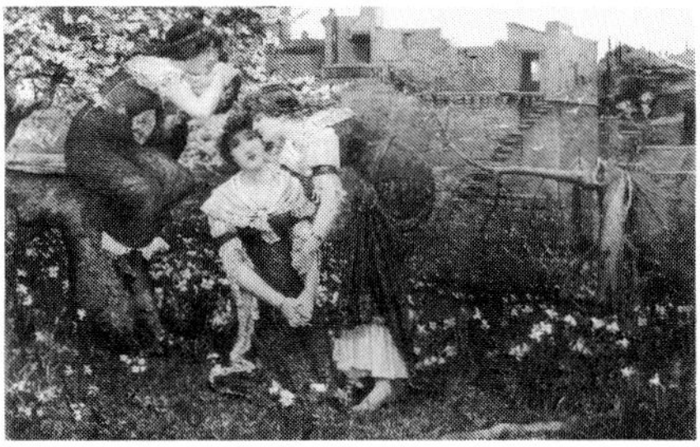

Oliver Hall (1869–1957)

acc. no. 1616
Bracelet Moor

oil on canvas: 13×18 in.
signed: *Oliver Hall*
Presented by Angus Butterworth, 1960

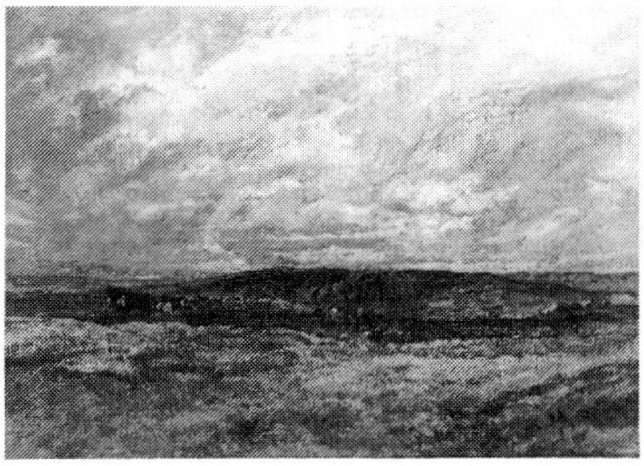

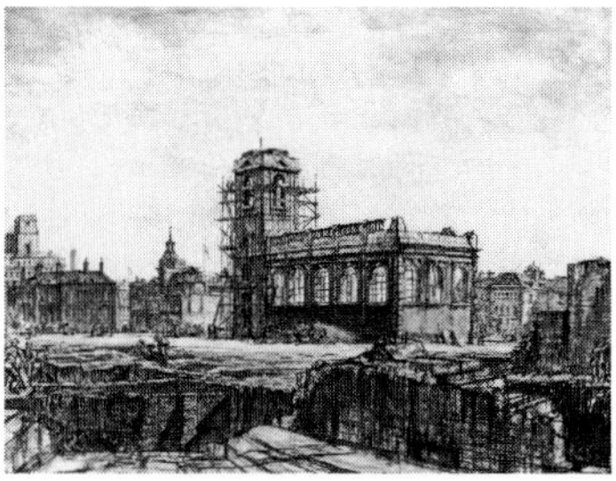

Patrick Hall (b.1906)

acc. no. 1257
St. Nicholas Cole Abbey (1943)

black chalk: 15 × 19¼ in.
signed and dated: *Patrick Hall 1943*
Purchased from the artist, 1943

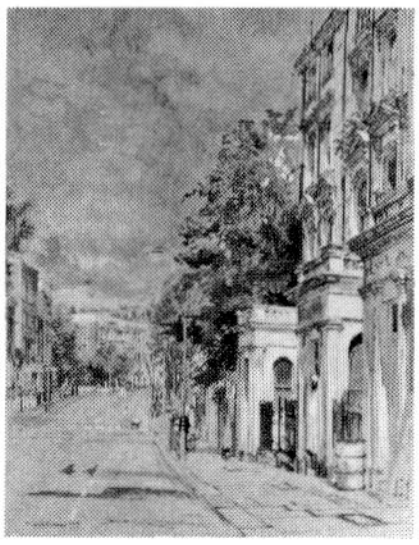

Charlotte Halliday (b.1935)

acc. no. 2203
Formosa Street Commune (1975)

watercolour: 16¼ × 13 in.
signed and dated: *Charlotte Halliday 1975*
Purchased from the artist, 1976

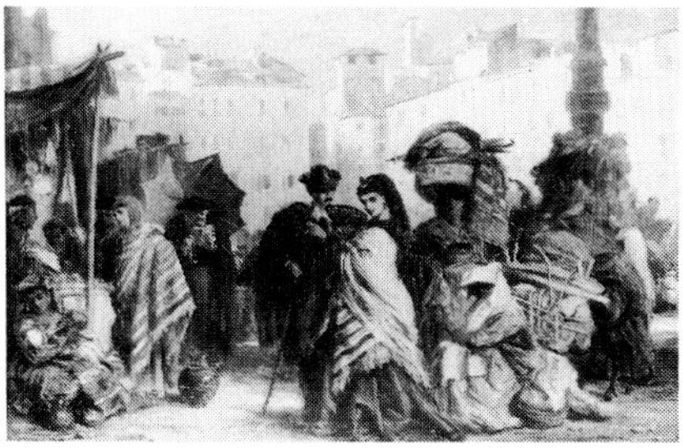

Keeley Halswelle (1832–91)

acc. no. 678
The Fan Seller (1869)

oil on canvas: 16 × 24 in.
inscribed and dated: *SKETCH OF FAN SELLER / Keeley Halswelle RA ROME 1869*
Bequeathed by Charles Gassiot, 1902

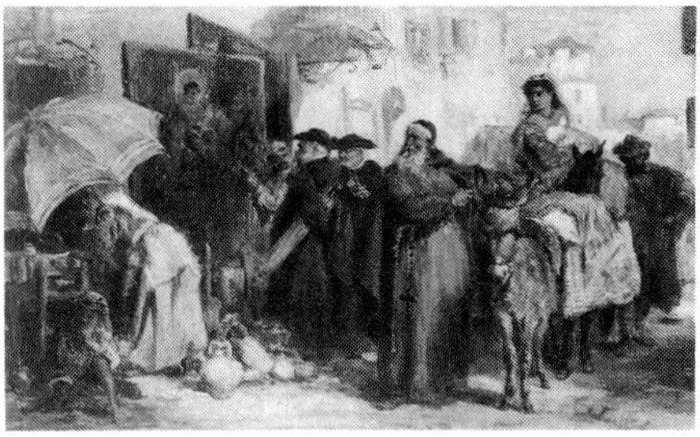

acc. no. 679
The Letter Writer (1869)

oil on canvas: 14½ × 24 in.
inscribed, signed and dated: *SKETCH Keeley Halswelle ROME / 1869*
Bequeathed by Charles Gassiot, 1902

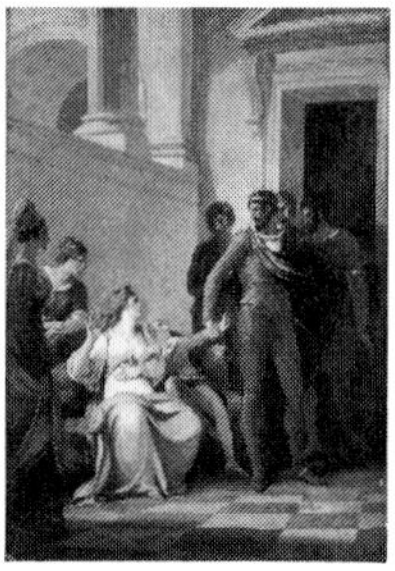

William Hamilton (1751–1801)

acc. no. 328
Scene from 'The Winter's Tale' (Act II scene i)

oil on canvas: 31 × 23 in.
Presented by Alderman Sir Francis Wyatt Truscott, 1886

Hermione Hammond (living)

acc. no. 1803
The Barbican (1963)

watercolour: $19\frac{1}{2} \times 14\frac{1}{4}$ in.
signed and dated: *Hermione Hammond 6/63*
Purchased from the artist, 1969

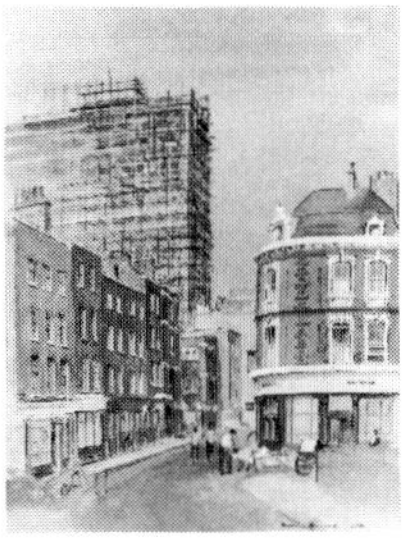

acc. no. 1694
St. Mary Aldermanbury (1964)

watercolour: $18\frac{5}{8} \times 24\frac{1}{2}$ in.
Purchased from the artist, 1964

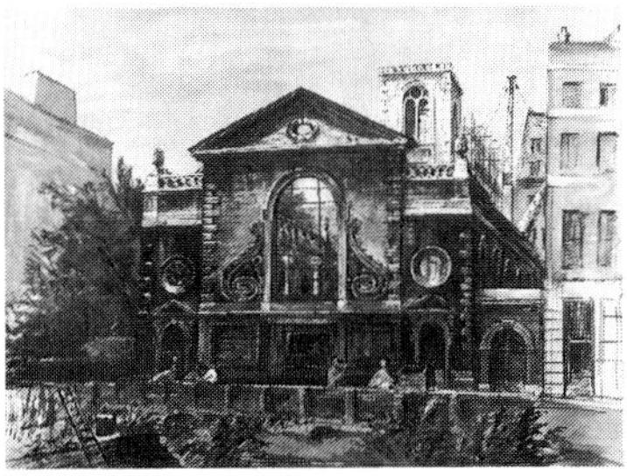

Samuel Harry Hancock (d.1932)

acc. no. 1633
Goldsmiths' Hall from Foster Lane (*c.*1913)

watercolour: $14\frac{3}{8} \times 10\frac{1}{8}$ in.
signed: *S H HANCOCK*
Presented by Mrs. E. Hancock, 1962

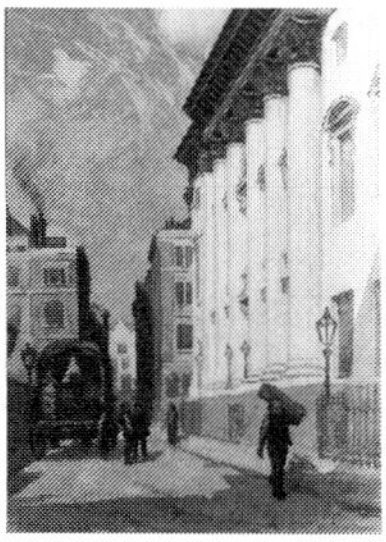

acc. no. 1631
The Lights of London, Cannon Street Station (*c.*1924)

oil on canvas: 10×14 in.
signed: *S H Hancock*
Presented by Mrs. E. Hancock, 1962

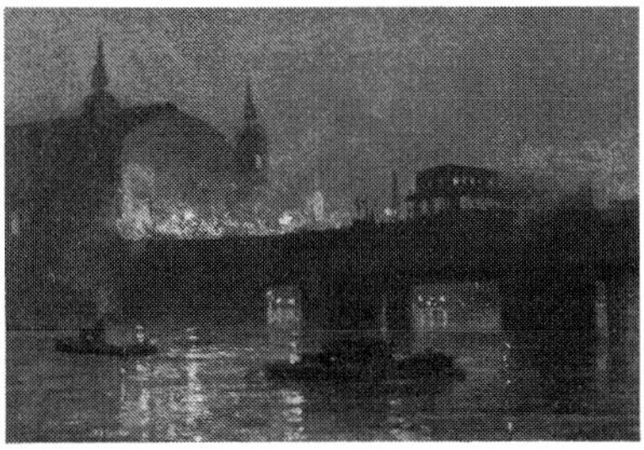

acc. no. 1628
Near Brewers' Quay (*c.*1930)

oil on panel: $13\frac{3}{4} \times 20$ in.
Presented by Mrs. E. Hancock, 1962

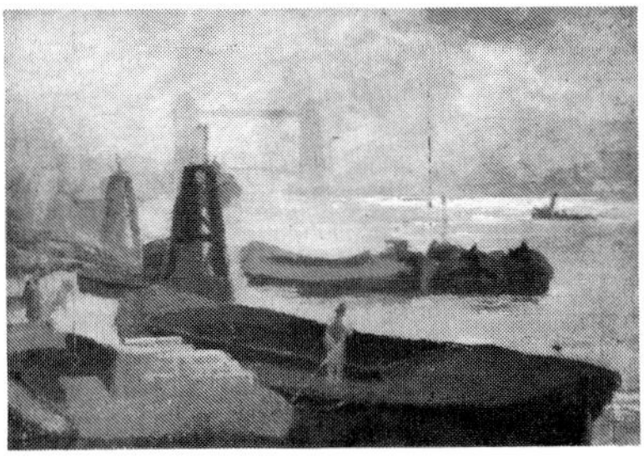

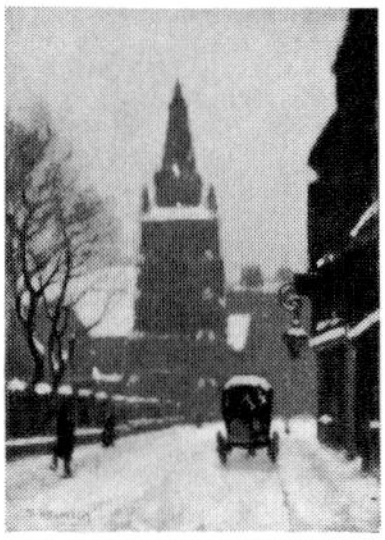

acc. no. 1629
Bunhill Row
oil on academy board: $13\frac{7}{8} \times 10$ in.
signed: *S H Hancock*
Presented by Mrs. E. Hancock, 1962

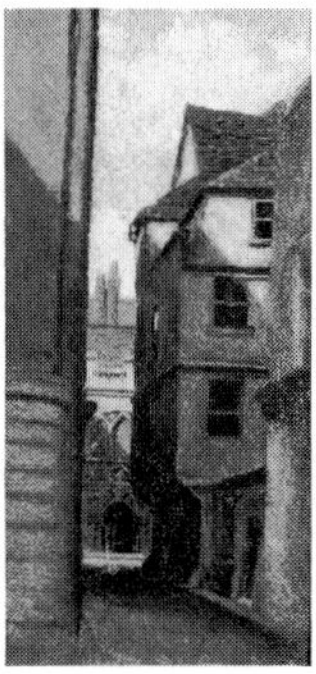

acc. no. 1630
Tudor House, Great St. Helens
oil on panel: $12\frac{1}{8} \times 5\frac{3}{4}$ in.
Presented by Mrs. E. Hancock, 1962

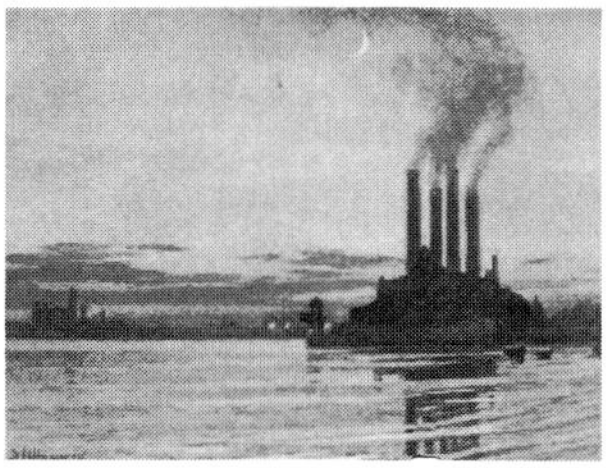

acc. no. 1632
Lots Road Power Station – Evening
watercolour: $9\frac{5}{8} \times 12\frac{5}{8}$ in.
signed: *S.H. HANCOCK*
Presented by Mrs. E. Hancock, 1962

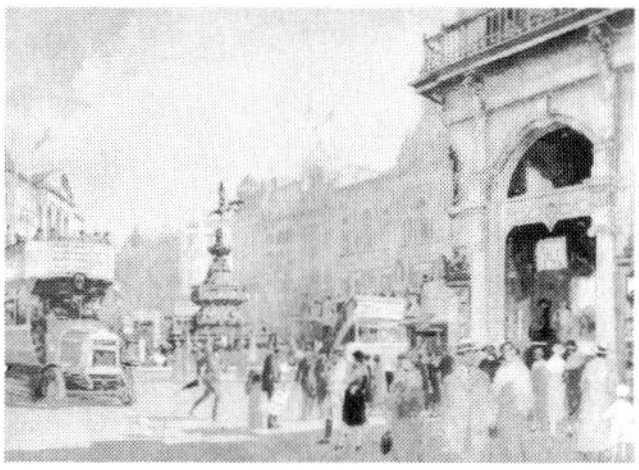

Edward Harry Handley-Read (1869–1935)

acc. no. 1569
Piccadilly Circus (1920)
watercolour: $21\frac{5}{8} \times 30\frac{1}{4}$ in.
signed: *E. Handley-Read*
Presented by Dr. E. Handley-Read, 1958

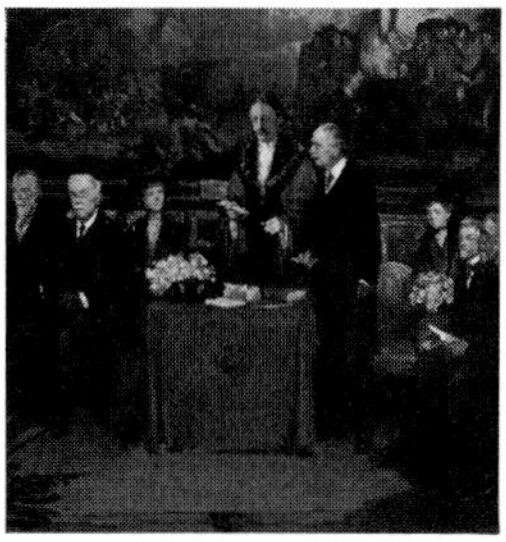

George Harcourt (1868–1947)

acc. no. 3514
Sir Thomas V. Bowater, Lord Mayor, speaking at the Royal Drawing Society's AGM at Guildhall Art Gallery, 16 January 1914
oil on canvas: $32\frac{3}{4} \times 31\frac{1}{4}$ in.
Purchased from Dennis Ewen, 1985

acc. no. 1956
Deputy Walter Bull (1923)

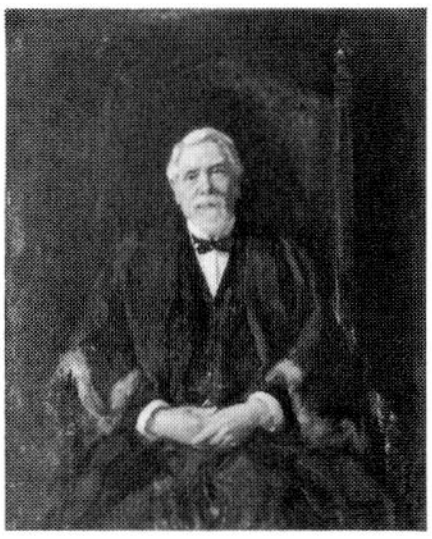

oil on canvas: 50 × 40 in.
signed: *Harcourt*
Presented by the National Pawnbrokers Association, 1973

acc. no. 1252
Amaryllis (1924)

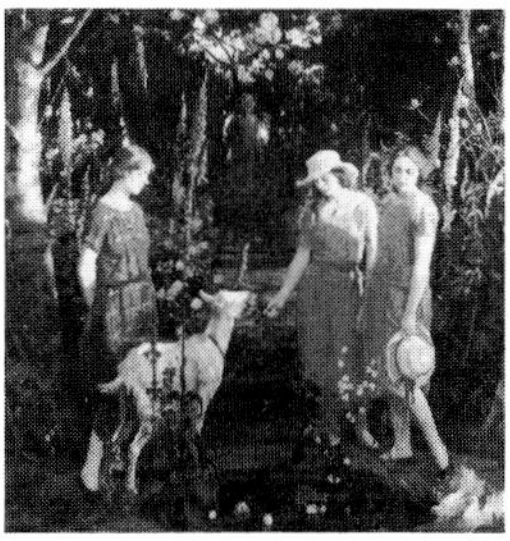

oil on canvas: $87\frac{1}{2} \times 84\frac{1}{2}$ in.
Presented by the artist, 1943

Charles E. Hardaker (20th C)

acc. no. 1770
Hawksmoor Baroque – St. Mary Woolnoth (*c.*1966)

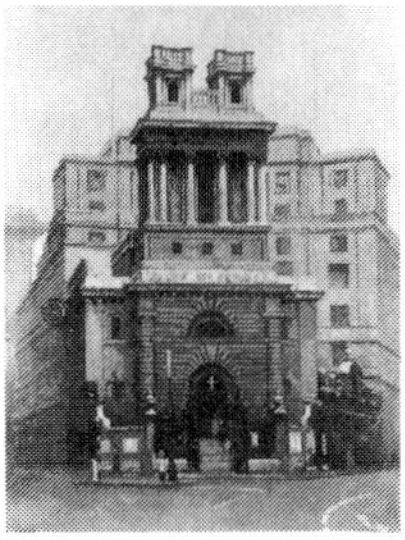

oil on canvas: $39\frac{3}{4} \times 30$ in.
signed: *Hardaker*
Purchased from the artist, 1967

acc. no. 1805
The City – Winter, 1968

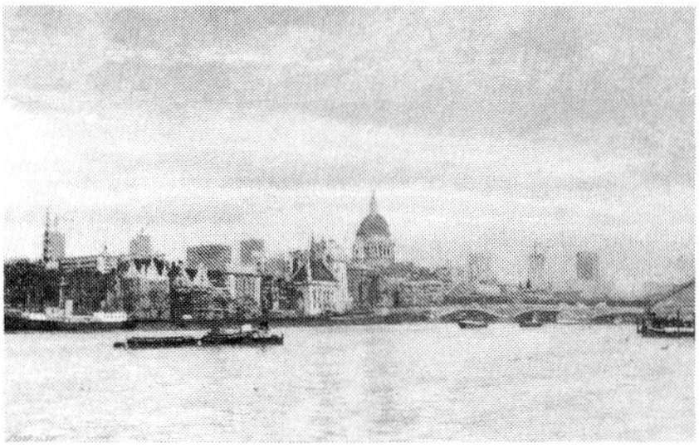

oil on canvas: 18 × 27 in.
signed: *Hardaker*
Purchased from the artist, 1969

acc. no. 1806
Removal of London Bridge, December 1968

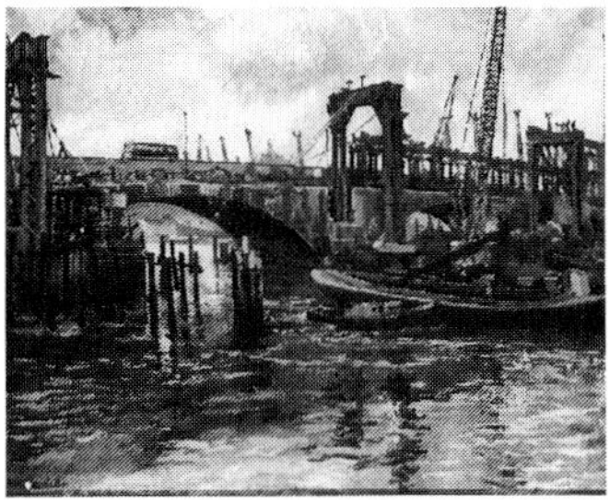

oil on canvas: 20 × 24 in.
signed: *Hardaker*
Purchased from the artist, 1969

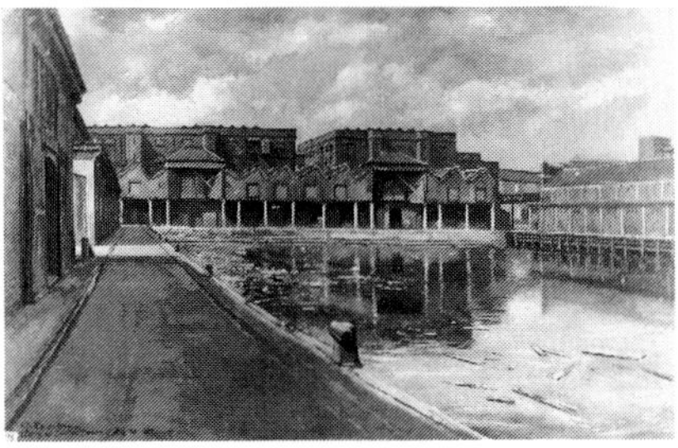

acc. no. 1835
The Closing of London Docks, May 9 1969

oil on canvas: $21\frac{3}{4} \times 34\frac{3}{4}$ in.
signed, inscribed and dated: *C.E. Hardaker / Closing of London Docks. May 9th. 1969.*
Purchased from the artist, 1970

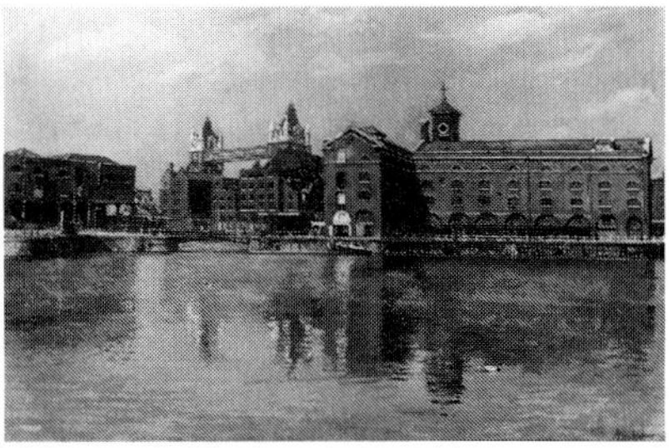

acc. no. 1833
St Katharine's Dock (1969)

oil on canvas: 20×30 in.
signed: *Hardaker*
Purchased from the artist, 1970

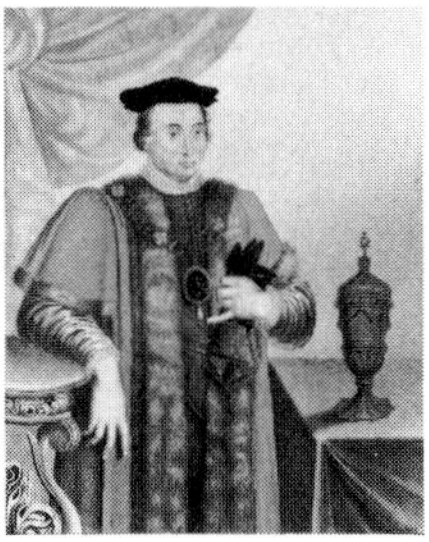

George Perfect Harding (b.1882) after an unknown 16th century artist

acc. no. 1786
Sir Martin Bowes

watercolour: $7\frac{1}{2} \times 6$ in.
signed: *G.P. Harding*
Purchased from R. J. Bulkeley, 1968

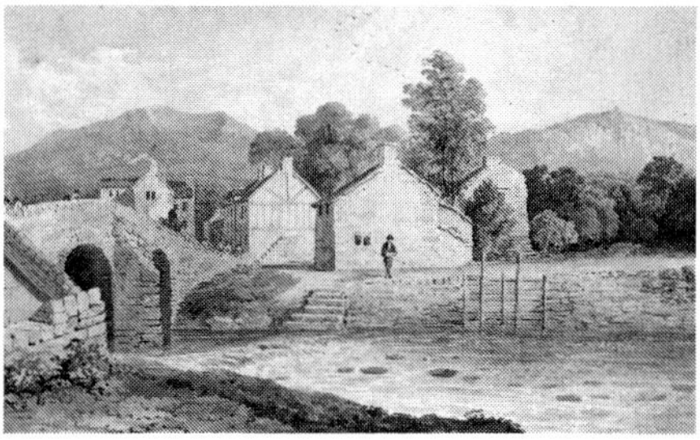

James Duffield Harding (1798–1863)

The following ten watercolours were presented by the Rev. A. A. D. Harding in 1957.

acc. no. 1550
Entrance into Keswick, Cumberland

watercolour: $8\frac{7}{8} \times 14$ in.
inscribed on verso: *Keswick Cumberland*

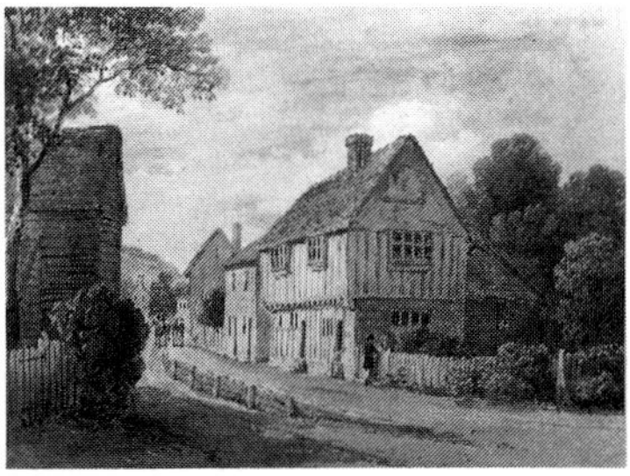

acc. no. 1551
At Otford, Kent

watercolour: 8×11 in.
inscribed on verso: *At Otford/Kent*

acc. no. 1554
Thirnham Church, near Maidstone, Kent
watercolour: 9 × 14 in.
inscribed on verso: *Thirnham Church near Maidstone*

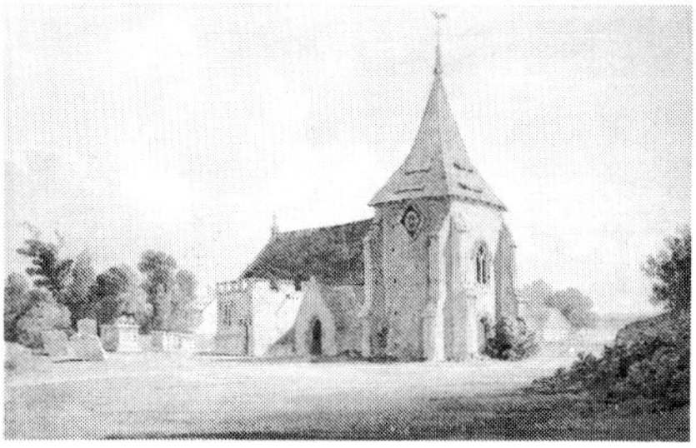

acc. no. 1556
Allington Castle, near Maidstone, Kent
watercolour: $11\frac{3}{8} \times 17\frac{1}{8}$ in.

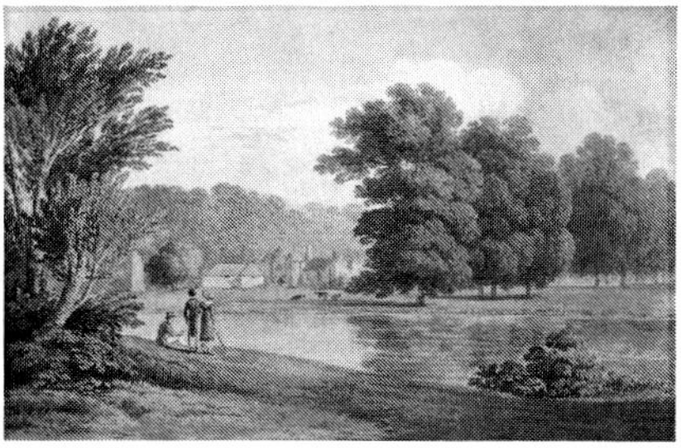

acc. no. 1557
Allington Castle, near Maidstone, Kent – Moonlight
watercolour: $8\frac{7}{8} \times 14$ in.

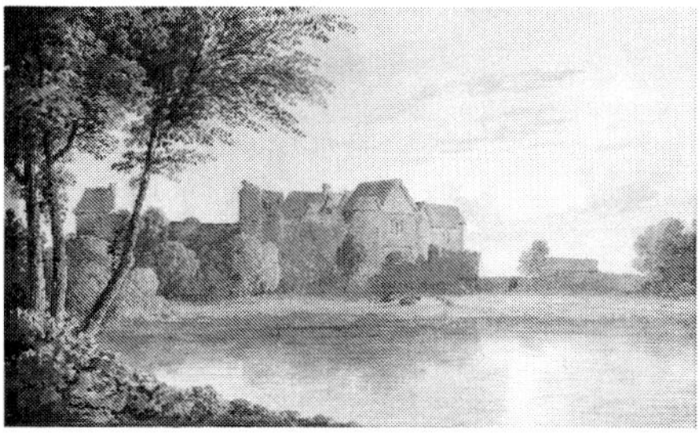

acc. no. 1558
Aylesford, near Maidstone, Kent
watercolour: $11\frac{7}{8} \times 17\frac{7}{8}$ in.
inscribed on verso: *Aylesford near Maidstone/Kent*

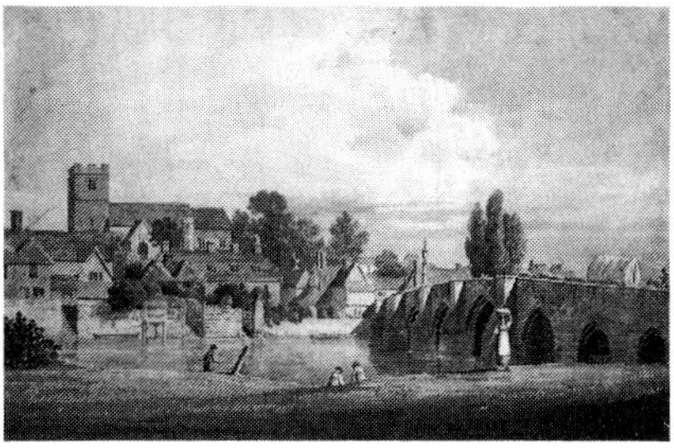

acc. no. 1559
A Church in Kent
watercolour: $9\frac{3}{4} \times 12\frac{5}{8}$ in.

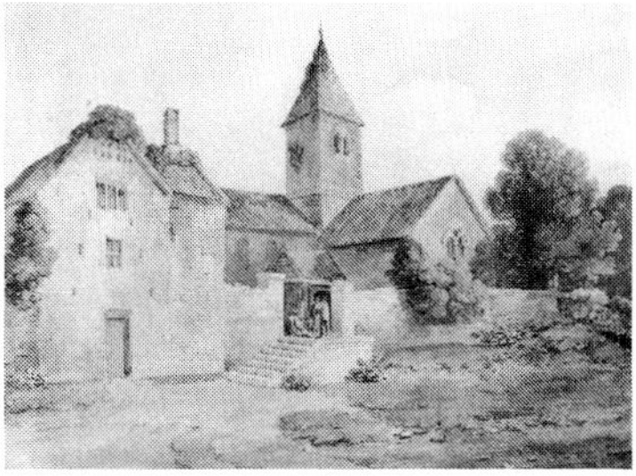

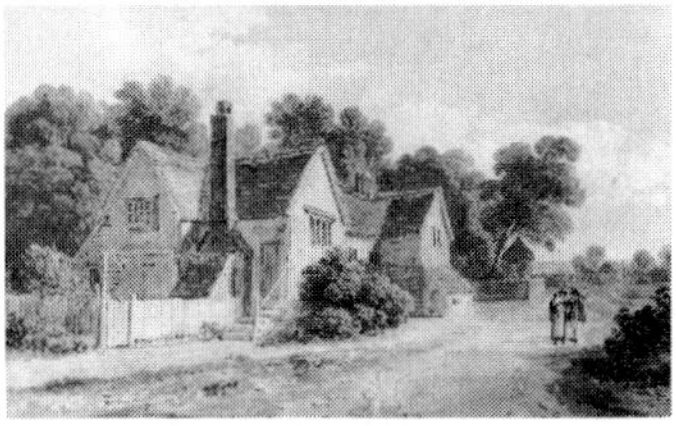

acc. no. 1552
View at Dorking, Surrey
watercolour: $7\frac{3}{4} \times 11\frac{1}{2}$ in.

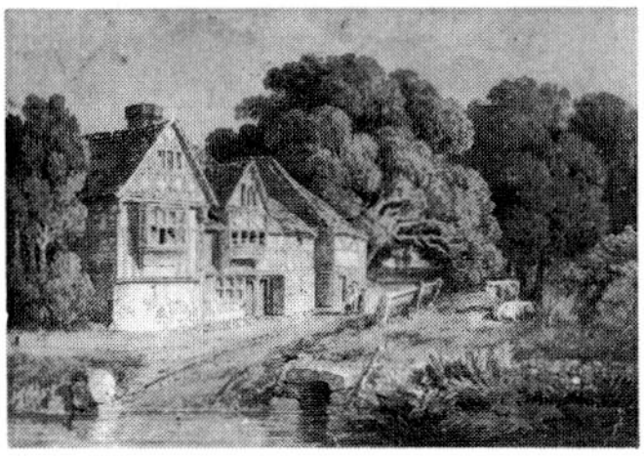

acc. no. 1553
The Ost House at Hastings, Sussex
watercolour: $9\frac{1}{4} \times 13\frac{1}{4}$ in.
inscribed on verso: *The Ost House at Hastings*

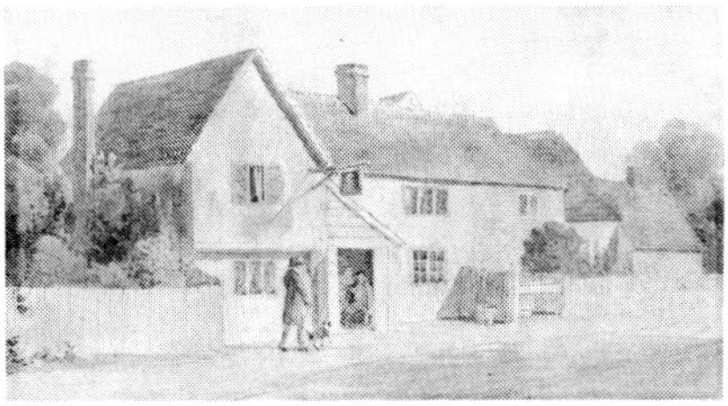

acc. no. 1555
Cottages at Chadwell, Essex
watercolour: $6\frac{3}{4} \times 10\frac{3}{8}$ in.
inscribed on background: *cottages at Chadwell, Essex* and signed: *James Harding*

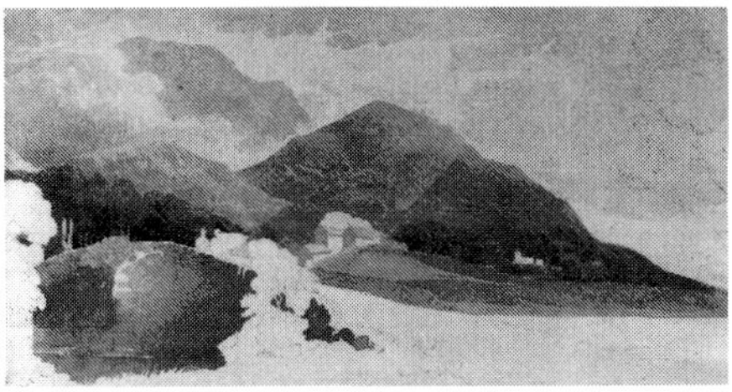

acc. no. 3648
Mountainous Landscape with a Stone Bridge
watercolour over pencil: $11\frac{1}{2} \times 17\frac{1}{4}$ in.
Removed from back of acc. no. 1556 during conservation, 1986

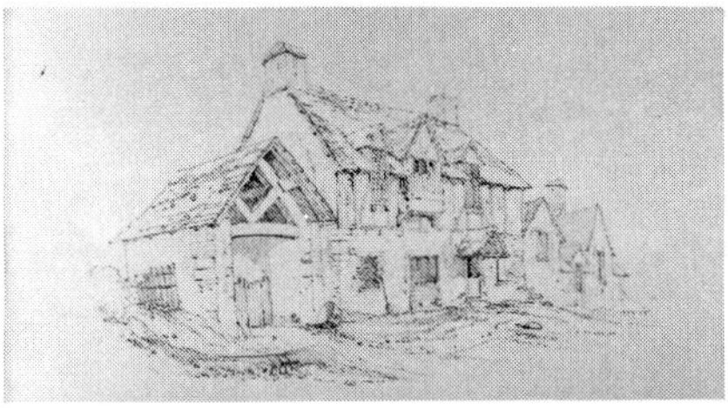

acc. no. 3649
A Cottage
lithograph: $9\frac{1}{8} \times 14$ in.
Removed from back of acc. no. 1550 during conservation, 1986

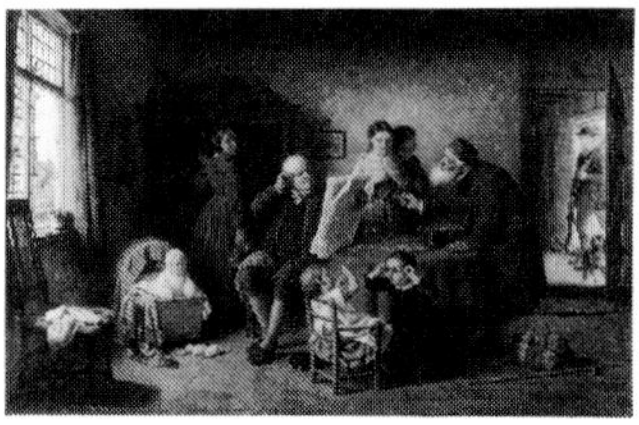

Frederick Daniel Hardy (1826–1911)

acc. no. 674
Try this Pair (1864)
oil on canvas: 11×16 in.
signed and dated: *F D Hardy 1864*
Bequeathed by Charles Gassiot, 1902

Heywood Hardy (1843–1933)

acc. no. 676
Duty (1880)

oil on canvas: $32\frac{1}{2} \times 46\frac{1}{2}$ in.
signed and dated: *Heywood Hardy / 1880*
Bequeathed by Charles Gassiot, 1902

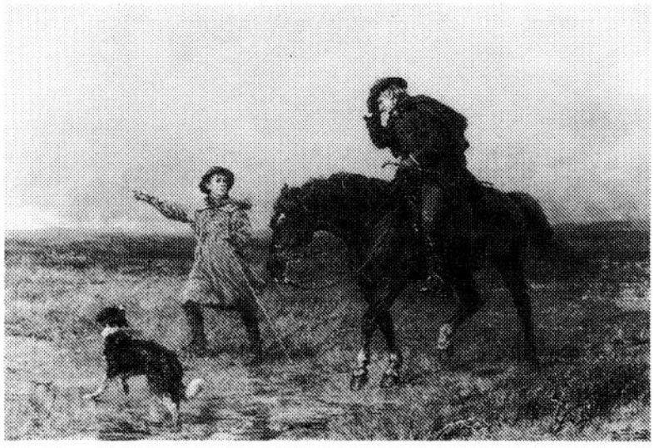

Thomas Hardy (1757–*c.*1805)

acc. no. 523
Brass Crosby, Alderman of Bread Street Ward (*c.*1787)

oil on canvas: 66 × 54 in.
Presented by the Hon. Irish Society, 1892

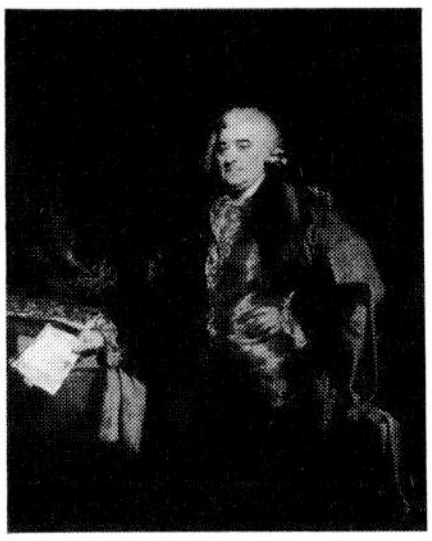

Augustus Hare (1834–1903)

acc. no. 3536
View of a Church Tower on a Hill

pencil and watercolour: 10 × 14 in.
Presented by Miss Helen Guiterman, 1985

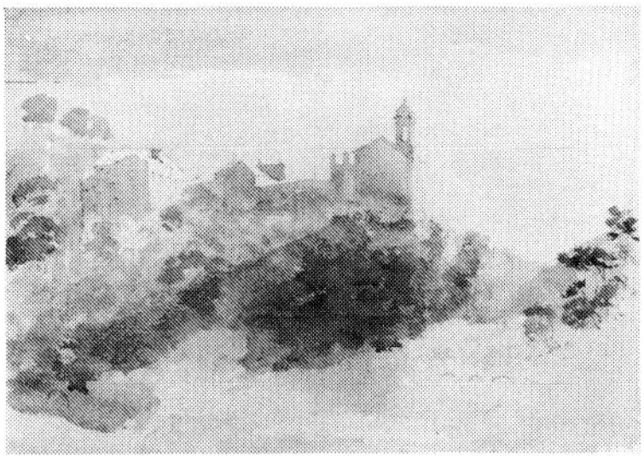

acc. no. 3557
Malcesina

pencil and watercolour: $8\frac{3}{4} \times 11\frac{7}{8}$ in.
Presented by Miss Helen Guiterman, 1985

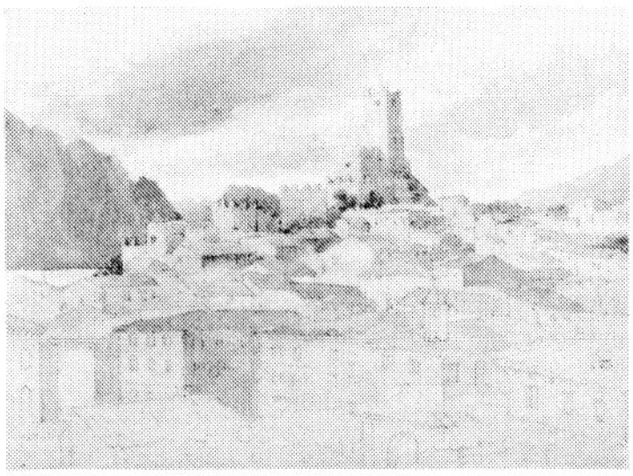

acc. no. 3559
Lakeland Scene

watercolour: $5\frac{7}{8} \times 10$ in.
Presented by Miss Helen Guiterman, 1985

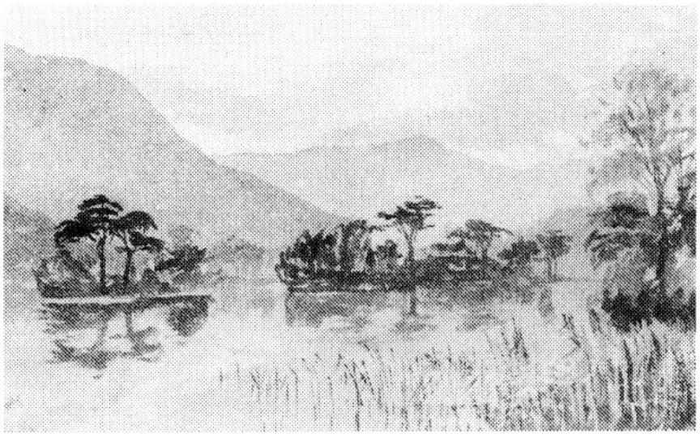

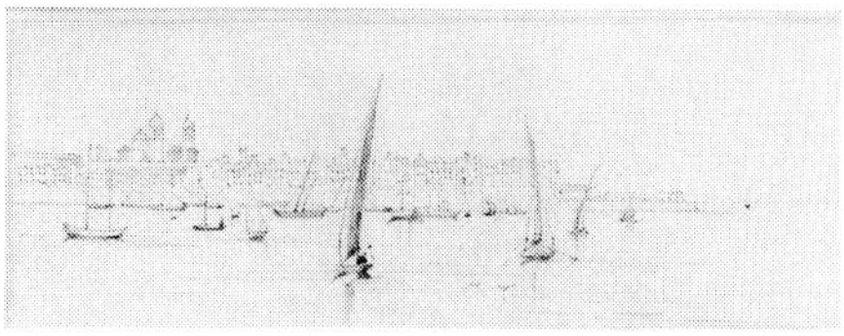

acc. no. 3560
Cadiz

pencil: 5 × 14 in.
Presented by Miss Helen Guiterman, 1985

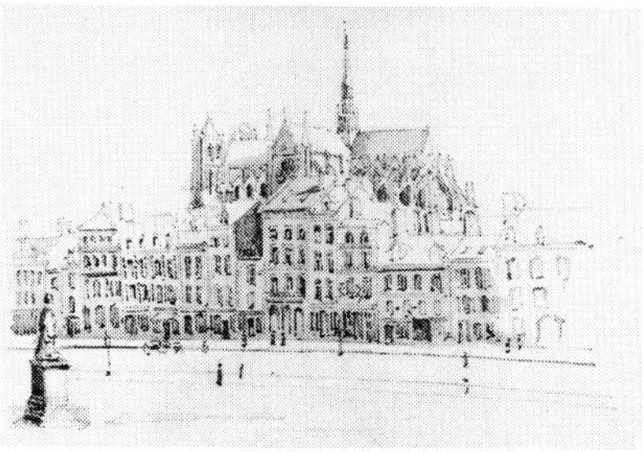

acc. no. 3545
Amiens

pencil and wash: 7 × 10 in.
Presented by Miss Helen Guiterman, 1985

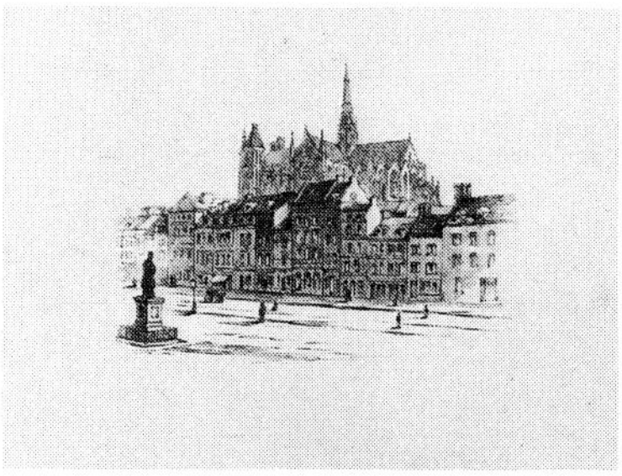

acc. no. 3544
Amiens

engraving: $6\frac{1}{8} \times 6\frac{5}{8}$ in.
inscribed: *Amiens*
Presented by Miss Helen Guiterman, 1985

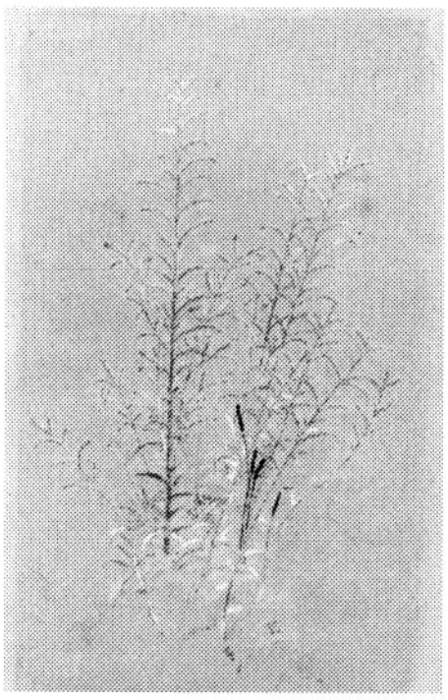

Edward Hargitt (1835–95)

acc. no. 3573
Study of Plant Fronds

pencil and watercolour: $8\frac{1}{2} \times 5\frac{1}{2}$ in.
Presented by Miss Helen Guiterman, 1985

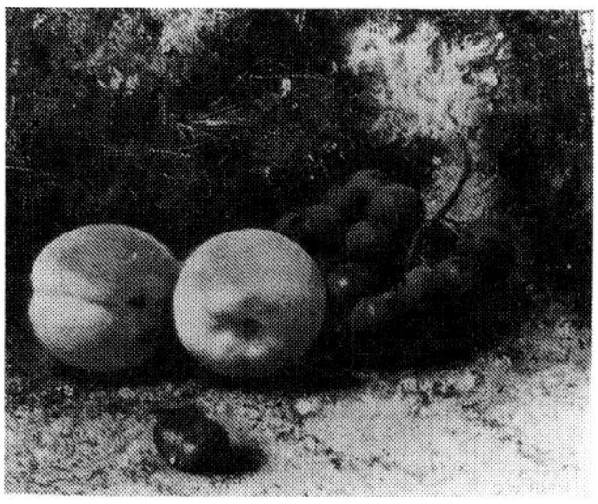

George Walter Harris (*fl.* 1864–93)

acc. no. 749
Peaches and Grapes (1864)

oil on canvas: 11 × 13 in.
signed and dated: *G.W. HARRIS / 1864*
Bequeathed by Charles Gassiot, 1902

Suzanne C. Harris (20th C)

acc. no. 1999
London Market, Camden Town (*c.*1974)
oil on canvas: $19\frac{1}{4} \times 23\frac{1}{4}$ in.
signed: *S.C. HARRIS*
Purchased from the artist, 1974

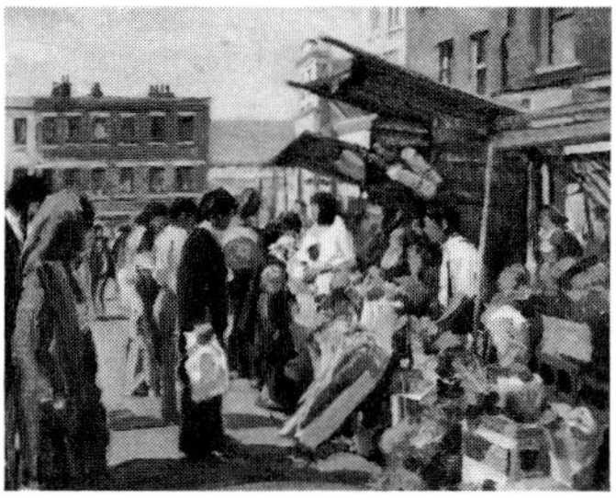

Solomon Alexander Hart (1806–81)

acc. no. 158
Sir David Salomons (*c.*1856)
oil on canvas cut down to: 36×28 in.
Presented by the sitter, 1856

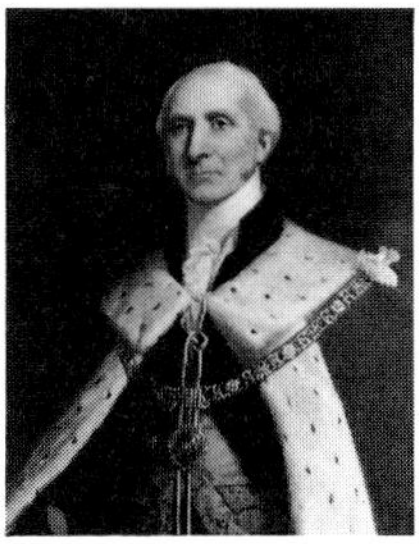

Ian Hay (20th C)

acc. no. 2191
Towpath to St. Pancras (exh. 1975)
conté: $17 \times 21\frac{5}{8}$ in.
signed: *Ian Hay*
Purchased from the artist, 1975

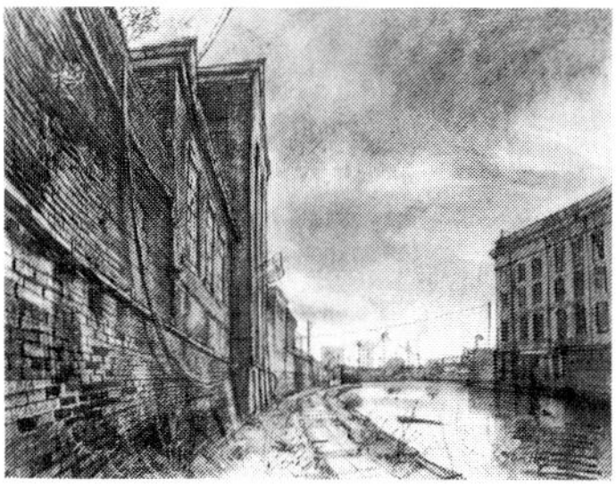

acc. no. 2192
Towards Tower Bridge (exh. 1975)
charcoal: $20\frac{1}{2} \times 21\frac{7}{8}$ in.
signed: *Ian Hay*
Purchased from the artist, 1975

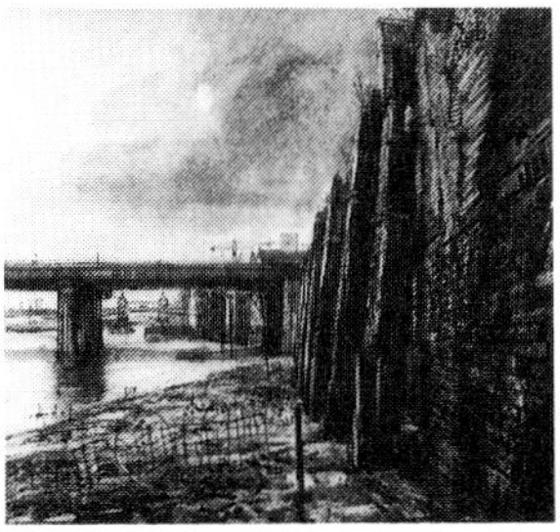

acc. no. 2202
Beachcombers at Blackfriars (exh. 1976)
watercolour: $16\frac{1}{2} \times 18\frac{1}{2}$ in.
signed: *Ian Hay*
Purchased from the artist, 1976

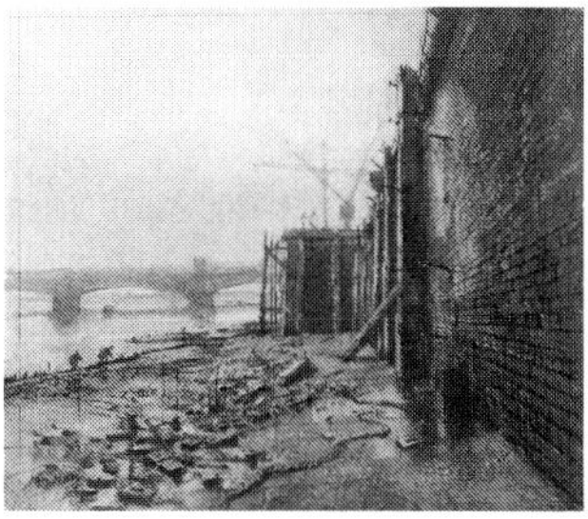

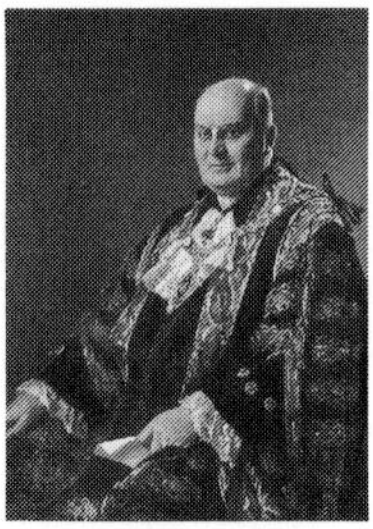

Peter Alexander Hay (1866–1952)

acc. no. 1515
Sir William Waterlow KBE (1931)

oil on canvas: 40 × 30 in.
signed and dated: *P.A. Hay / 1931*
Purchased from E. H. Stringer, 1954

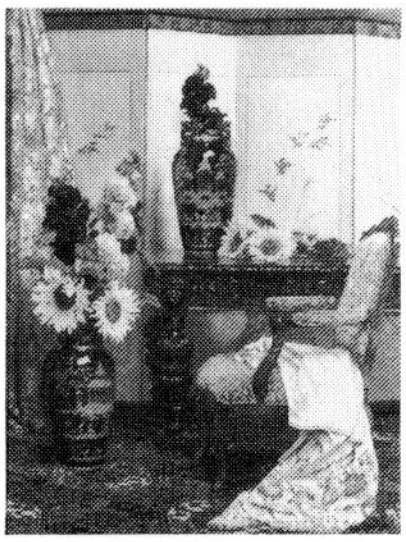

Kate Hayllar (*fl.* 1883–1900)

acc. no. 1662
Sunflowers and Hollyhocks (1889)

watercolour: $12\frac{1}{2} \times 9\frac{1}{2}$ in.
signed and dated: *Kate Hayllar / 1889*
Presented by John Byram, 1963

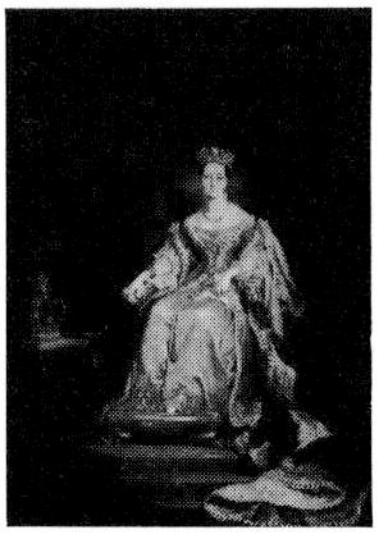

Sir George Hayter (1792–1871)

acc. no. 102
Queen Victoria seated on the Throne in the House of Lords (1838)

oil on canvas: 106 × 87 in.
signed and dated: *George Hayter 1838*
Commissioned by Queen Victoria and presented by her, 1839

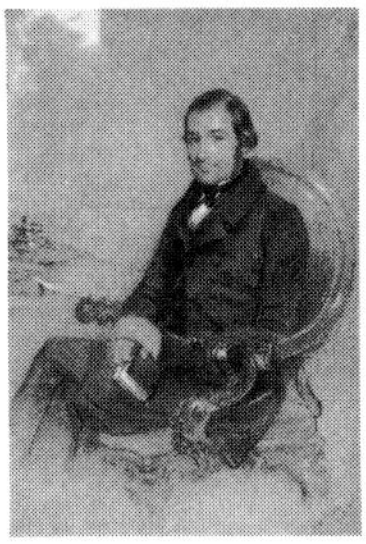

John Hayter (1800–91)

acc. no. 3599
Gentleman in an Armchair with a Book (1847)

coloured chalks: $18\frac{3}{8} \times 12\frac{1}{2}$ in.
signed and dated: *John Hayter / 1847 Oct.*
Presented by Miss Helen Guiterman, 1985

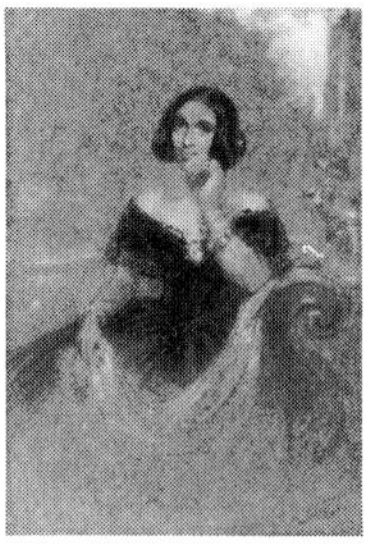

acc. no. 3601
Lady in a Black Dress (1847)

coloured chalks: $18\frac{1}{2} \times 12\frac{1}{2}$ in.
signed and dated: *John Hayter 1847 / Dec. 31*
Presented by Miss Helen Guiterman, 1985

acc. no. 3600
John Britten (1848)

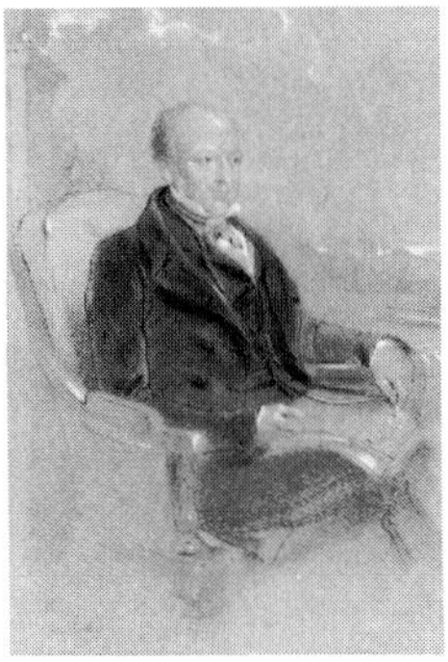

coloured chalks and bodycolour: $17\frac{1}{2} \times 11\frac{7}{8}$ in.
signed and dated: *John Hayter / 1848*
Presented by Miss Helen Guiterman, 1985

Edward Arthur Heffer (*fl.* 1857–1910)

acc. no. 480
Promptuarium, Chester Cathedral (1857)

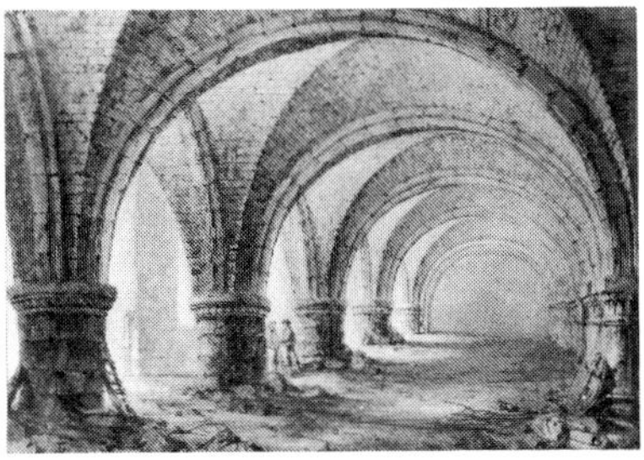

watercolour: $11\frac{7}{8} \times 16\frac{3}{4}$ in.
signed (mono) and dated: *EAh / 1857*
Presented by the artist, 1889

acc. no. 482
Rock Cut Temple, Ellora (1878)

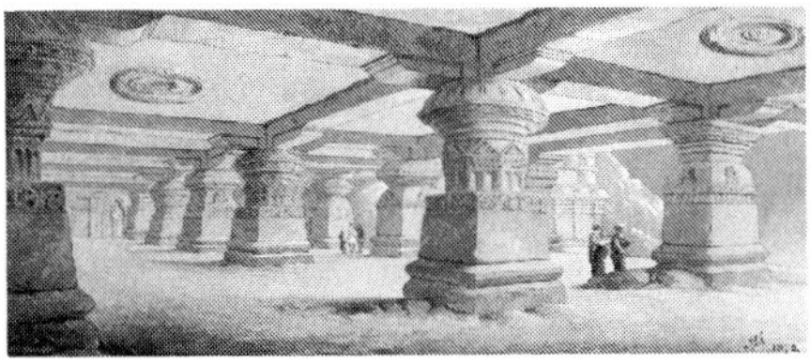

watercolour: $7 \times 15\frac{3}{4}$ in.
signed (mono) and dated: *EAh / 1878*; inscribed on verso: *N.º 3. Rock-Cut Temple. Ellora – / Edward Arthur Heffer / Dec = 1878* – and: *No 89 in book. / (own register).*
Presented by the artist, 1889

acc. no. 481
The Last Vestige of the River Fleet, in the Rear of Houses on the East Side of Fleet Road, Hampstead (1880)

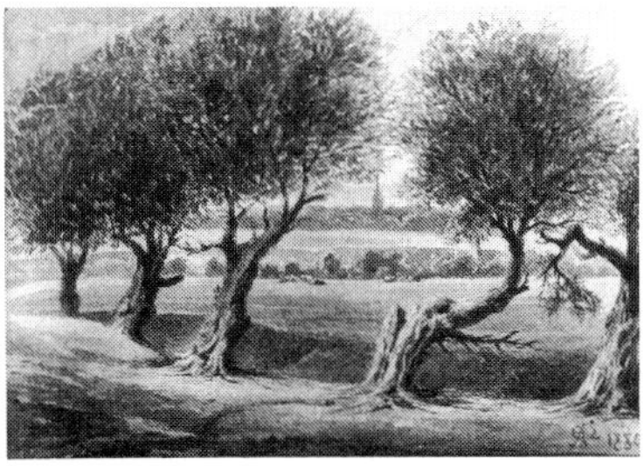

watercolour: 4×5 in.
signed (mono) and dated: *EAh 1880*
Presented by the artist, 1889

George Philip Helmsley (b.1933)

acc. no. 1713
The Holborn Viaduct (*c.*1965)

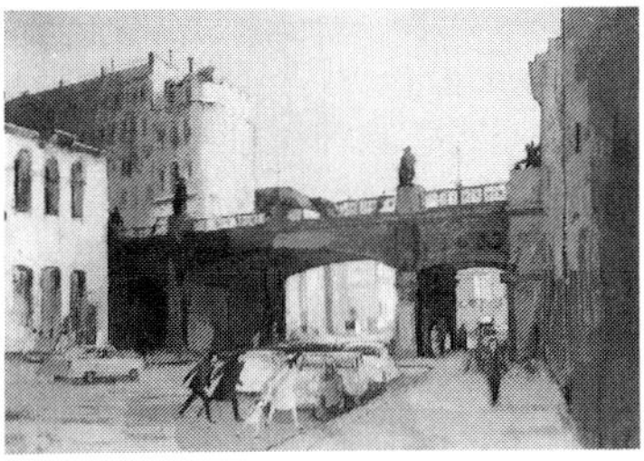

oil on hardboard: 36×48 in.
Purchased from the artist, 1965

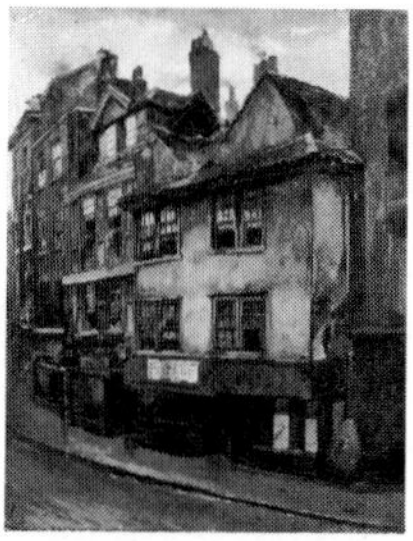

Joseph Henderson (1832–1908)

acc. no. 834a
The Cock and Magpie Tavern, Drury Lane (1890)
oil on canvas: 15 × 11 in.
signed (mono) and dated: *JH / 1890*
Presented by J. Seymour Lucas, 1904

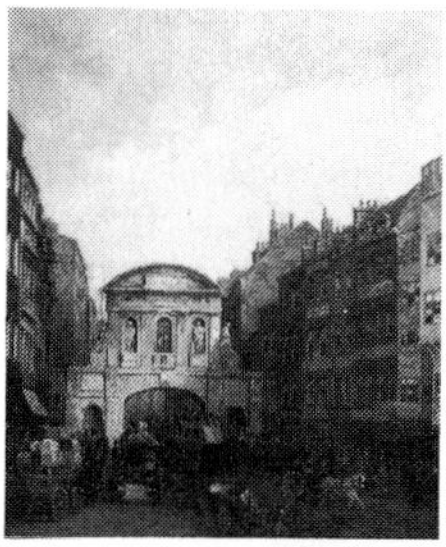

William Henry (pseud. of William Henry Haines, 1812–84)

acc. no. 1314
Temple Bar from the Strand (1878)
oil on canvas: 36 × 29 in.
signed and dated: *W Henry 1878*
Purchased from Leggatt Bros., 1944

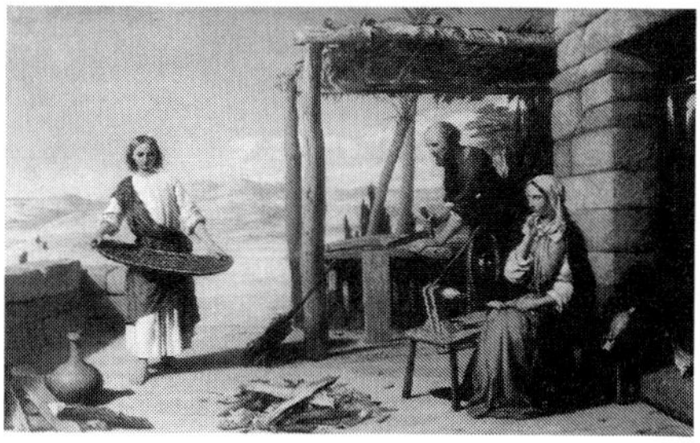

John Rogers Herbert (1810–90)

acc. no. 596
The Youth of our Lord (1847–56)
oil on canvas: 32 × 51 in.
signed and dated: *J.R.Herbert / London 1856*
Presented by Charles Gassiot, 1895

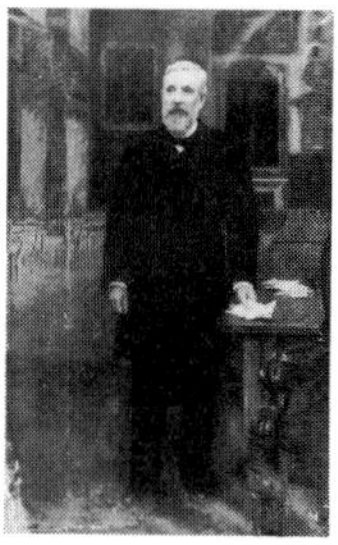

Sir Hubert von Herkomer (1849–1914)

acc. no. 2196
Sir Sydney Waterlow (1890)
oil on canvas: 94 × 57 in.
signed in monogram, mostly obliterated by damage
Presented by St. Bartholomew's Hospital, 1974

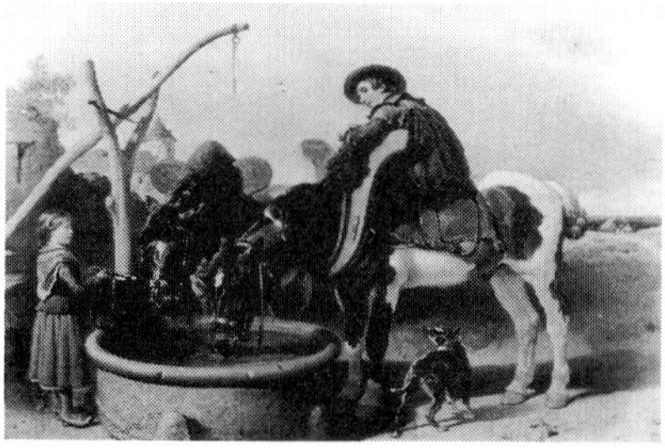

John Frederick Herring (1795–1865) and Henry Bright (1814–73)

acc. no. 680
Horses at a Well (1854–57)
oil on canvas: 24 × 36 in.
signed and dated: *J.F. Herring. Sen.r 1854 / H. Bright. 57*
Bequeathed by Charles Gassiot, 1902

Sir Wilhelm Ernst Hans Franz Heysen (1877–1968)

acc. no. 1623
White Gums in Morning Light (1961)
watercolour: $13 \times 16\frac{5}{8}$ in.
signed and dated: *HANS HEYSEN '61*
Presented by the Corporation of the City of Adelaide, 1961

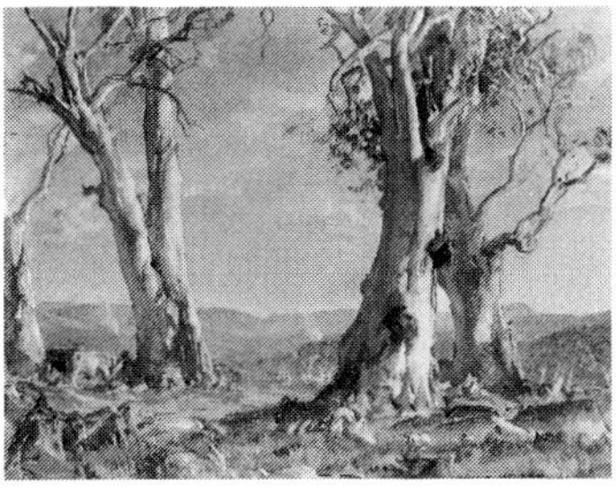

attributed to Miss Hibbert (*fl.* 1837–40)

acc. no. 1056
Sir John Cowan, Lord Mayor 1837 (?1838)
watercolour on ivory: 7×5 in.
Purchased, 1927

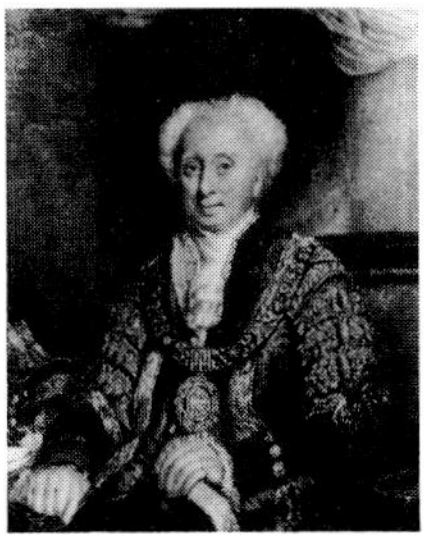

Jacqueline Hick (b.1920)

acc. no. 1850
Creek Bed
oil on hardboard: $25\frac{1}{2} \times 37$ in.
signed: *HICK*
Presented by the Corporation of the City of Adelaide, 1970

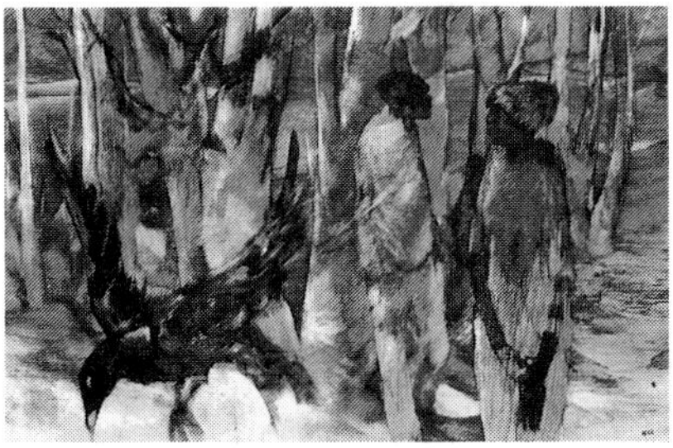

Joseph Highmore (1692–1780)

acc. no. 1561
Sir John Barnard, Lord Mayor 1737 (1738)
oil on canvas: $92\frac{3}{4} \times 56\frac{3}{4}$ in.
signed and dated: *J. Highmore 1738*
Presented by Edwina, Countess Mountbatten, 1957

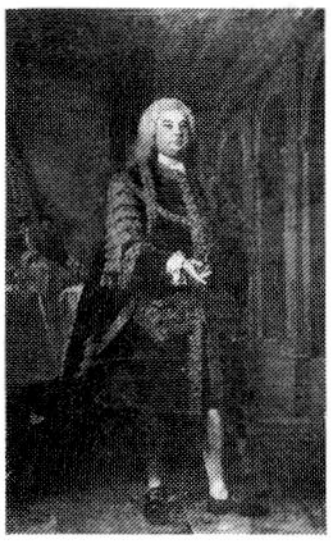

Frank Hoar (20th C)

acc. no. 1857
Rebuilding London Bridge (1970)
watercolour: $20 \times 28\frac{1}{2}$ in.
signed and dated: *FRANK HOAR AUG 70*
Purchased from the artist, 1971

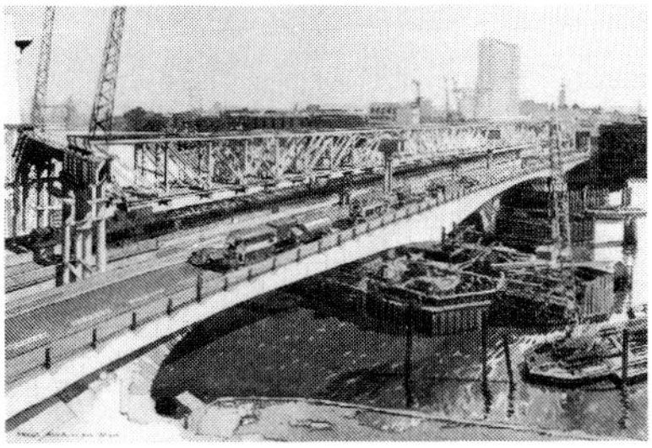

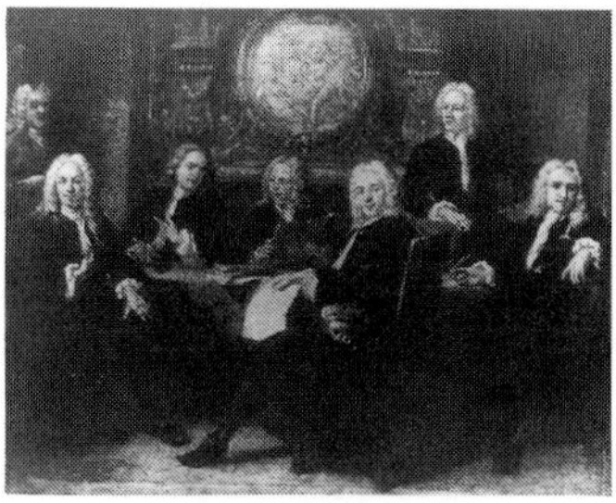

attributed to William Hogarth (1697–1764)

acc. no. 615
Portrait Group (thought to be Sir Theodore Janssen and his Five Sons)

oil on canvas: 20 × 16 in.
Bequeathed by Captain Carpenter, 1900

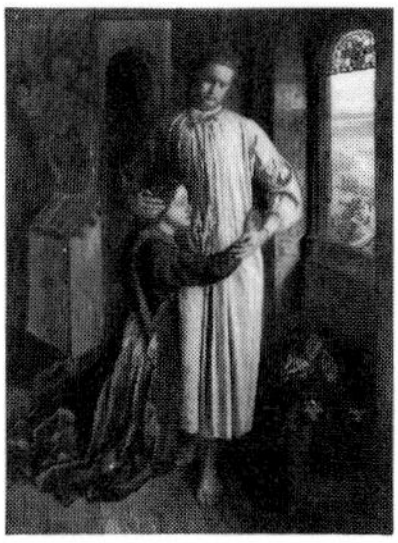

Henry Holiday (1839–1927)

acc. no. 970
The Burgesses of Calais (1859)

oil on canvas: 39 × 29 in.
Presented by R. W. Allars, 1914

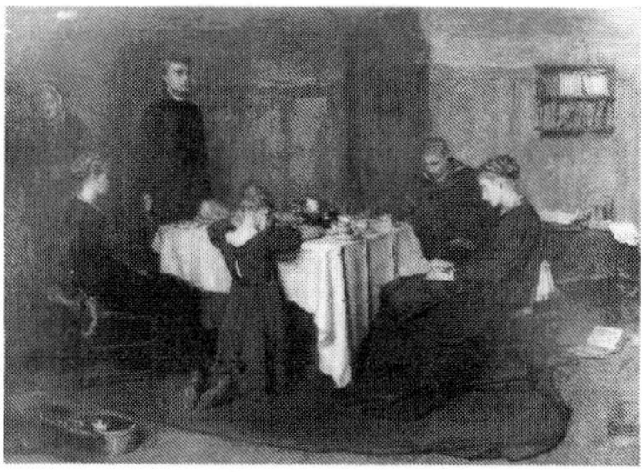

Frank Holl (1845–88)

acc. no. 975
The Lord Gave and the Lord Taketh Away – Blessed be the Name of the Lord (1868)

oil on canvas: 36 × 49 in.
Bequeathed by F. C. Pawle, 1915

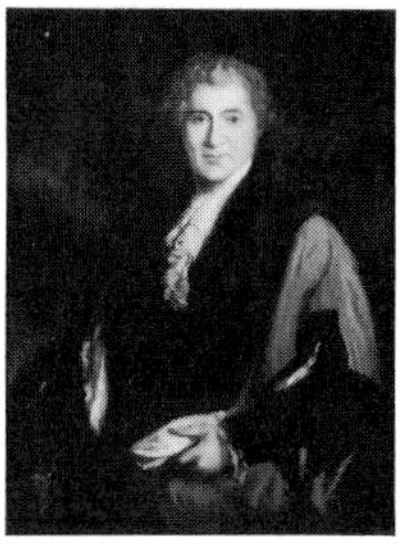

George Holloway (d.1843)

acc. no. 1079
Sir George Carroll

oil on canvas: 44 × 34 in.
Presented by Mary A. Holloway, 1931

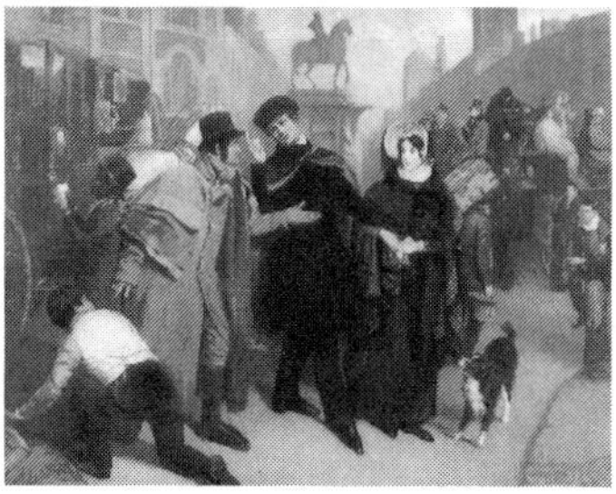

James Holmes (1777–1860)

acc. no. 1394
Charing Cross (1832)

oil on canvas: 28 × 36 in.
signed and dated: *J. HOLMES / 1832*
Purchased from A. Reader, 1950

Sir Charles Holroyd (1861–1917) after Arthur Stockdale Cope (1857–1940)

acc. no. 609
Rev. William Rogers, Chaplain in Ordinary to the Queen, Prebendary of St. Paul's (*c.*1895)
oil on canvas: 50 × 37 in.
Presented by the Earl of Rosebery on behalf of friends, 1897

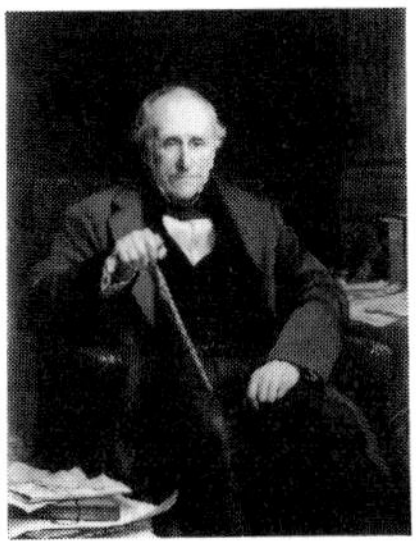

James Clarke Hook (1819–1907)

acc. no. 683
Sea Urchins (1861)
oil on canvas: 20 × 33 in.
signed (mono) and dated: *JCH 61*
Bequeathed by Charles Gassiot, 1902

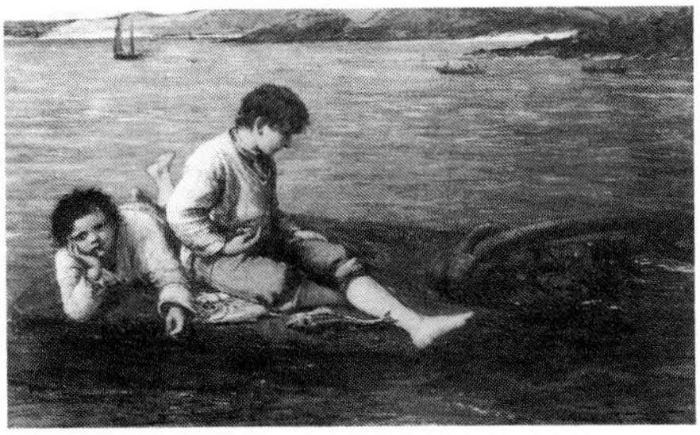

acc. no. 681
Caught by the Tide (1869)
oil on canvas: 27½ × 42½ in.
Bequeathed by Charles Gassiot, 1902

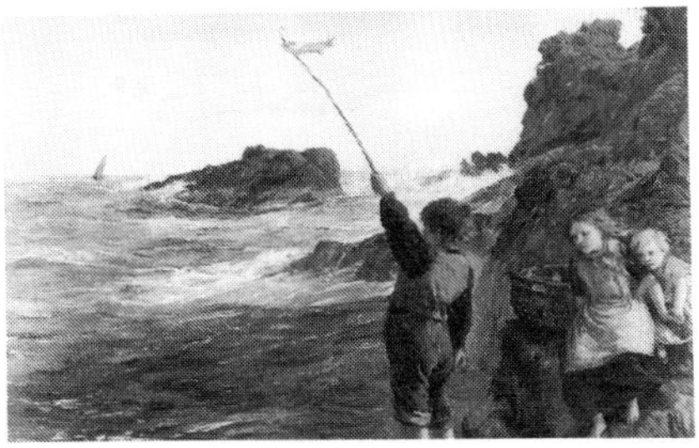

acc. no. 685
The Bonxie, Shetland (1873)
oil on canvas: 29 × 44 in.
Bequeathed by Charles Gassiot, 1902

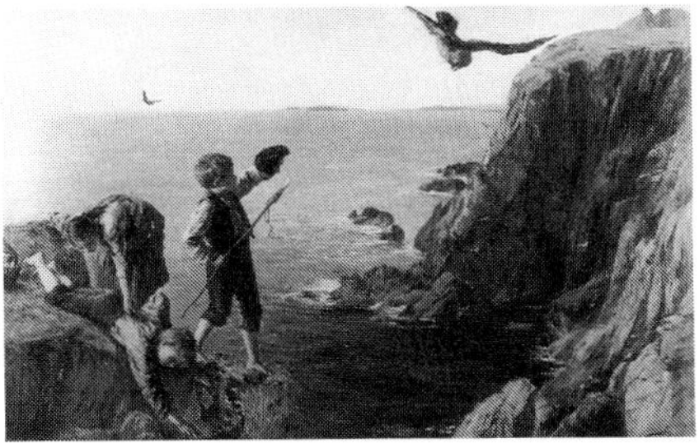

acc. no. 682
Word from the Missing (1877)
oil on canvas: 30½ × 51 in.
signed (mono) and dated: *JHC 77*
Bequeathed by Charles Gassiot, 1902

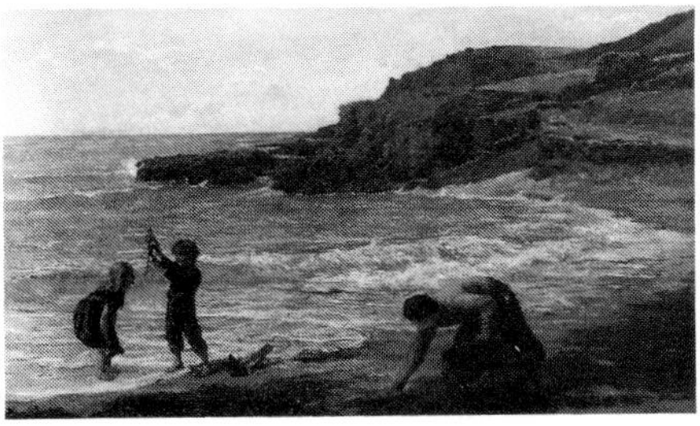

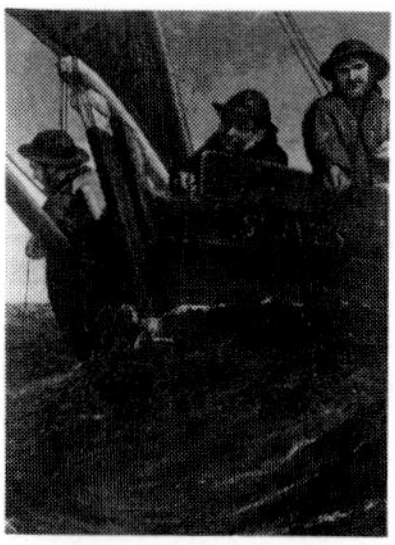

acc. no. 684
Deep Sea Fishing
oil on canvas: 33 × 24 in.
Bequeathed by Charles Gassiot, 1902

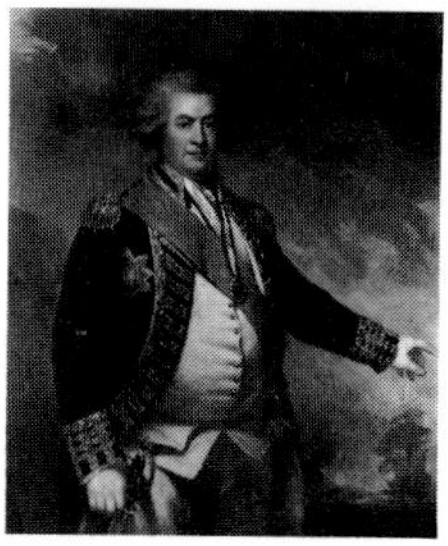

John Hoppner (1758–1810)
acc. no. 60
Admiral Lord Duncan
oil on canvas: 57 × 45 in.
Presented by Alderman Boydell, 1798

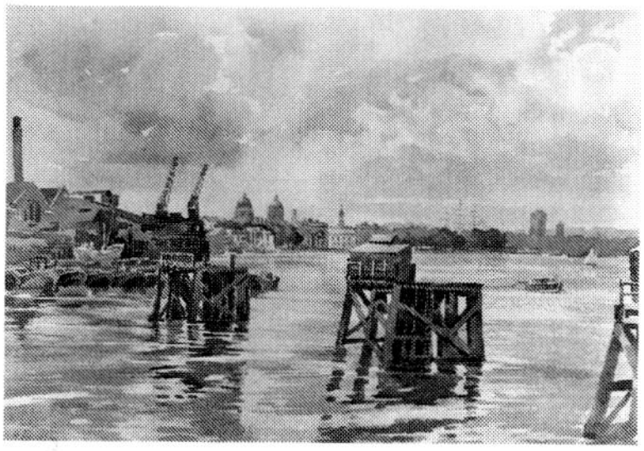

Albert Houghton (b.1906)
acc. no. 1842
From Blackwall Reach, Greenwich (1970)
watercolour: $14\frac{3}{8} \times 20\frac{1}{2}$ in.
Purchased from the artist, 1970

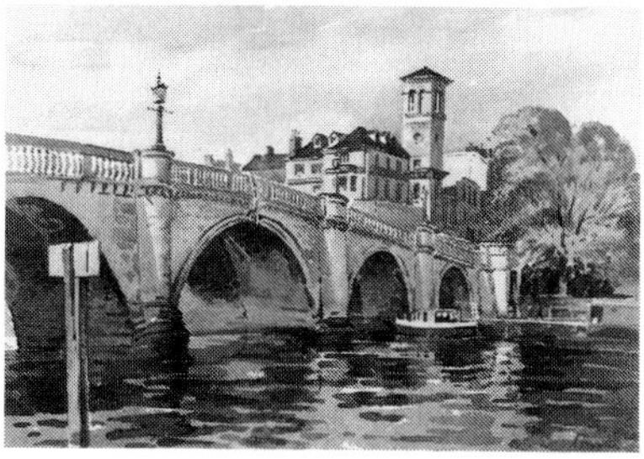

acc. no. 1843
Richmond Bridge (1970)
watercolour: $14\frac{3}{8} \times 20\frac{1}{2}$ in.
signed: *A. Houghton*
Purchased from the artist, 1970

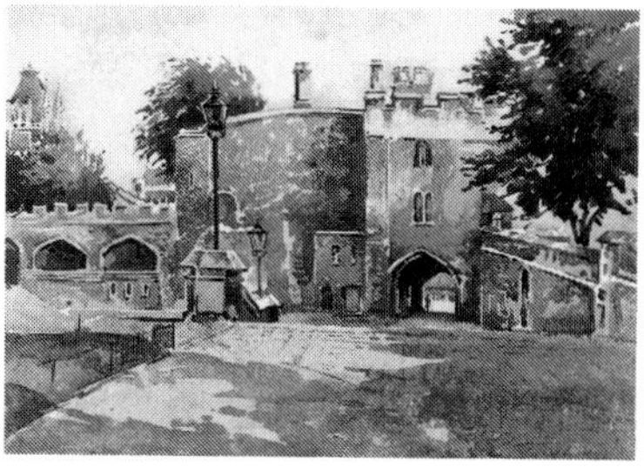

acc. no. 1844
Light and Shade, Tower of London (1970)
watercolour: $14\frac{3}{8} \times 20\frac{1}{2}$ in.
signed: *A. Houghton*
Purchased from the artist, 1970

Ken Howard (b.1932)

acc. no. 1636
Billingsgate Market (1962)
oil on canvas: 27 × 36 in.
signed and dated: *J.K. Howard / 62*
Purchased from the artist, 1962

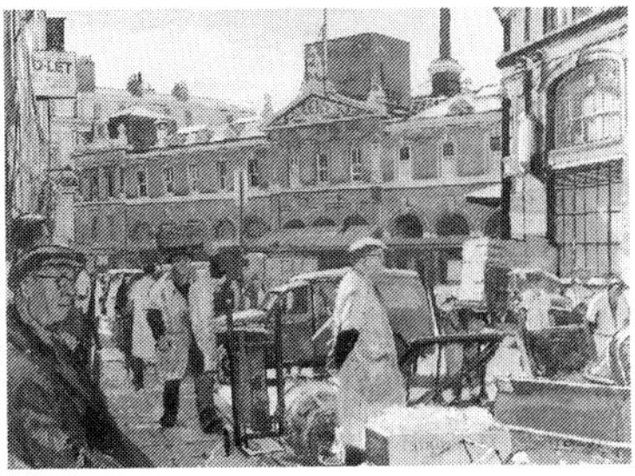

acc. no. 1712
The City from Rotherhithe (1965)
oil on canvas: 27 × 36 in.
signed: *KEN HOWARD*
Purchased from the artist, 1965

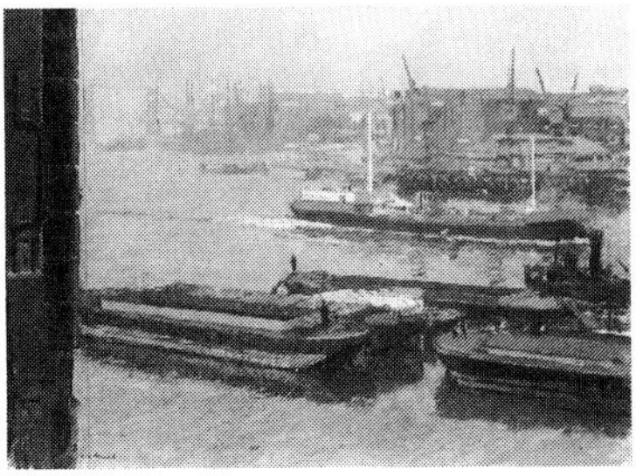

acc. no. 1809
The Royal Exchange (1969)
oil on canvas: 24 × 20 in.
signed: *Ken Howard*
Purchased from the artist, 1969

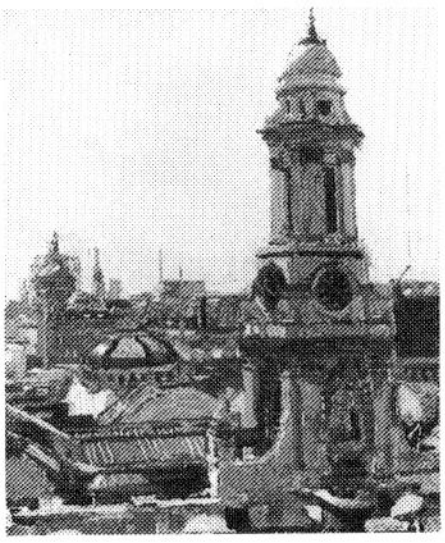

acc. no. 1894
Mansion House (*c.*1971)
oil on canvas: 20 × 24 in.
signed: *Ken Howard*
Purchased from the New Grafton Gallery, 1971

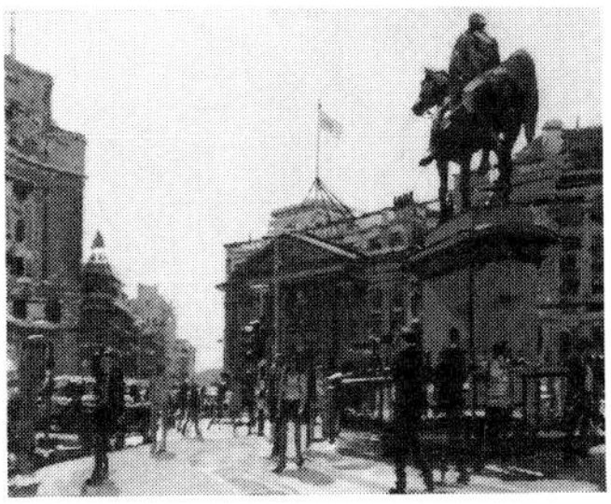

Henry Hughes (*fl.* 1859–?99)

acc. no. 582
Design for the Stained Glass Window in Memory of Prince Albert, formerly at the West End of Guildhall (1869)
watercolour: $51\frac{1}{2} \times 52$ in.
signed: *Henry Hughes / Ferd. Brand. / Comptroller.*; inscribed: *Agriculture., Industry., Commerce., Trades., Benevolence.*
Presented by H. Clifford Hughes, 1893

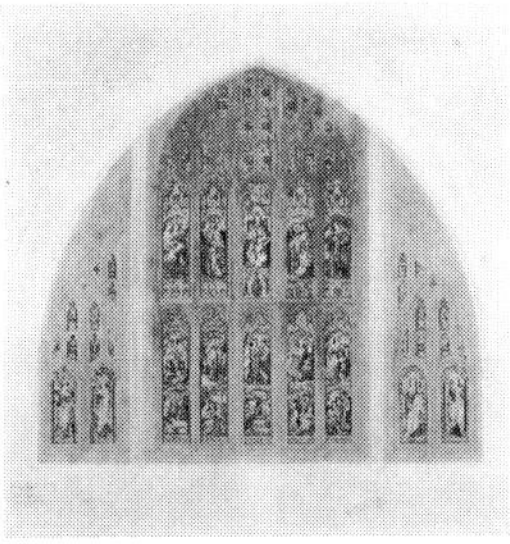

William Holman Hunt (1827–1910)

acc. no. 3631
Studies for 'The Eve of St Agnes' (or 'The Flight of Madeline and Porphyro during the Drunkeness attending the Revelry') (*c.*1847–48)

pencil and red chalk: 22 × 15 in.
signed three times in monogram; inscribed (by Gladys Holman Hunt): *Studies for the Eve of St Agnes / WHH*
Purchased with the aid of grants from the Victoria & Albert Museum and the N.A.-C.F., from Sotheby's sale 10.10.1985 (7)

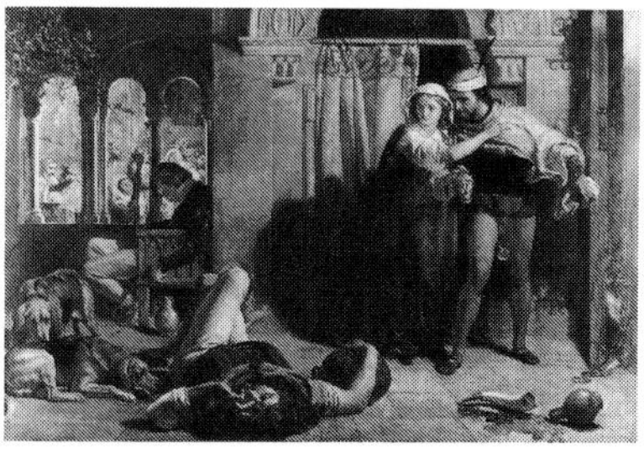

acc. no. 1033
The Eve of St Agnes (or 'The Flight of Madeline and Porphyro during the Drunkeness attending the Revelry') (1848)

oil on canvas: $30\frac{1}{2} \times 44\frac{1}{2}$ in.
signed: *WILLIAM H HUNT*
Presented by Sir Charles Wakefield, Sir George Touche and Sir Francis Agar, 1924

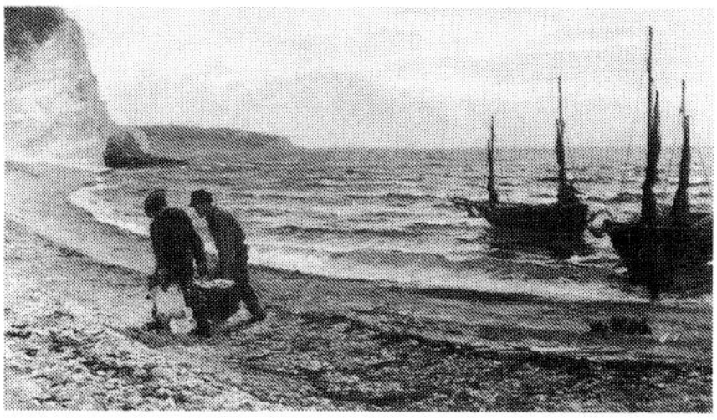

Colin Hunter (1841–1904)

acc. no. 1003
A Sea View (1879)

oil on canvas: $19\frac{3}{4} \times 34$ in.
signed and dated: *Colin Hunter 1879*
Presented by Sir Marcus Samuel, 1919

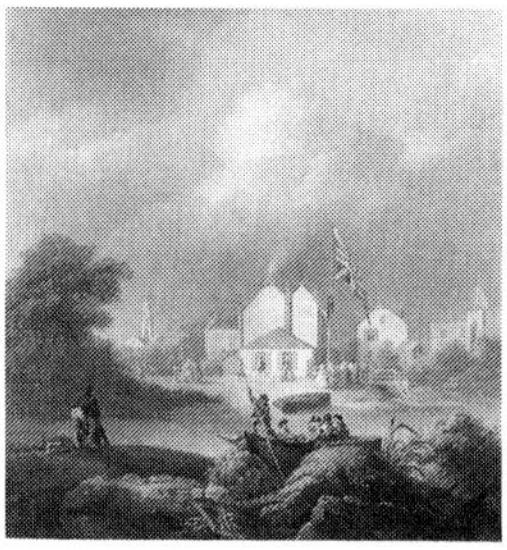

Julius Caesar Ibbetson (1759–1817)

acc. no. 1777
View Towards Deptford from across the Ravensbourne

oil on canvas: $23\frac{1}{2} \times 19\frac{1}{2}$ in.
Purchased from F. T. Sabin, 1967

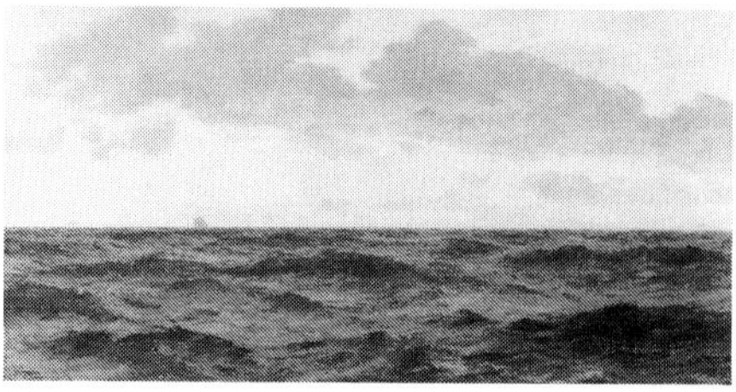

William Ayerst Ingram (1855–1913)

acc. no. 611
Evening (1898)

oil on canvas: $41 \times 71\frac{1}{2}$ in.
Presented anonymously, 1898

Eleanor Isle (early 20th C)

acc. no. 2261
The Albert Embankment
pencil and wash: $7\frac{3}{4} \times 12\frac{1}{4}$ in.
signed: *Eleanor Isle*
Presented by Miss Helen Guiterman, 1985

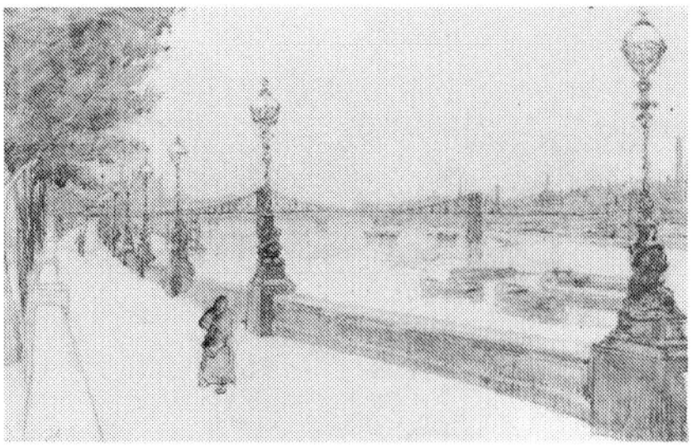

Gilbert Jackson (17th C)

acc. no. 1042
Sir Edward Coke, Recorder of London (1615)
oil on canvas: 50×40 in.
inscribed: *Sir/EDW*$^{D}_{R}$ *COKE/A*^{e}*66/A*^{o}*1615*
Purchased, 1925

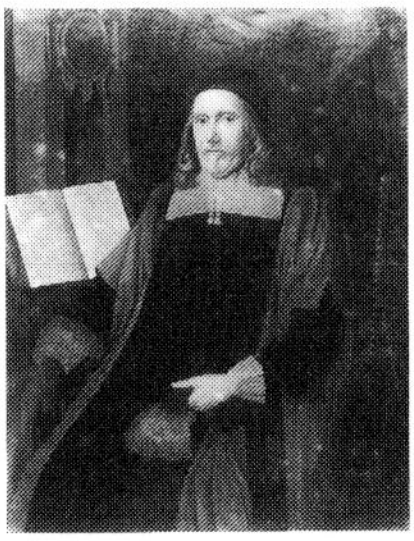

James Ranalph Jackson (1886–1975)

acc. no. 1626
Hills at Tallangatta, Victoria (1955)
oil on canvas: 20×24 in.
signed and dated: *JAMES R JACKSON / 55*
Presented by the City of Melbourne, 1962

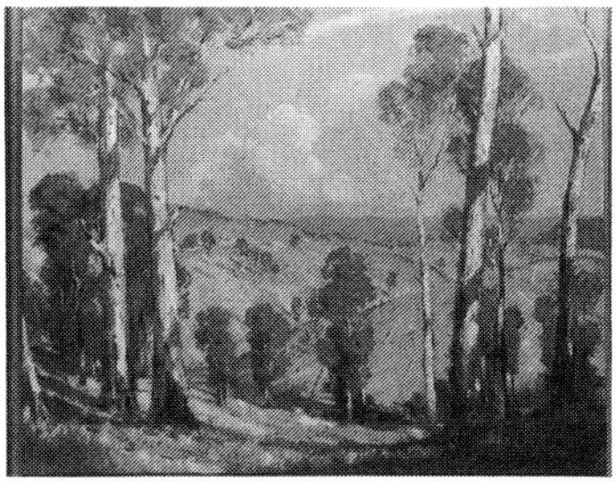

George Percy Jacomb-Hood (1857–1927)

acc. no. 1051
The Raising of Jairus's Daughter (1885)
oil on canvas: 48×63 in.
signed: *G.P. Jacomb-Hood*
Presented by the artist, 1926

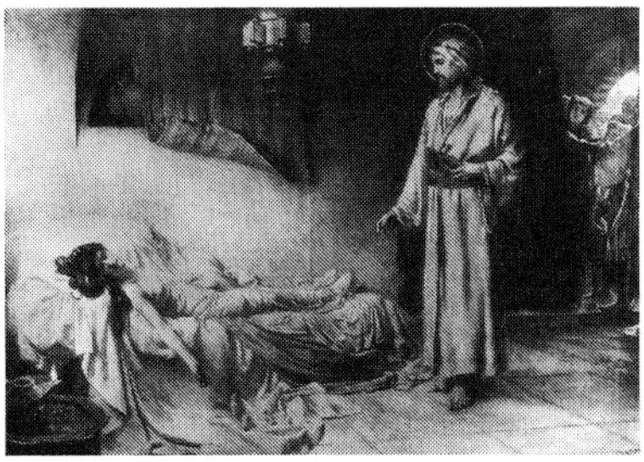

Dennis James (b. 1916)

acc. no. 1643
Temple Embankment (*c.*1962)
watercolour: $21 \times 14\frac{3}{8}$ in.
signed: *Dennis James*
Purchased from the artist, 1962

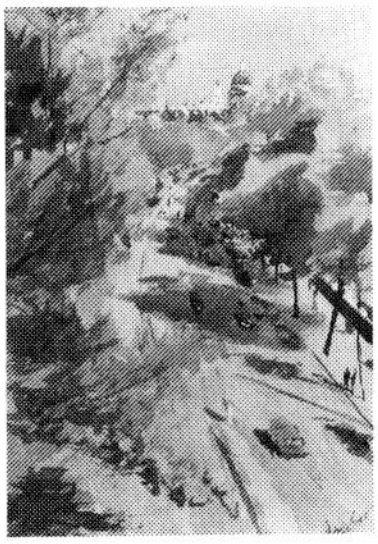

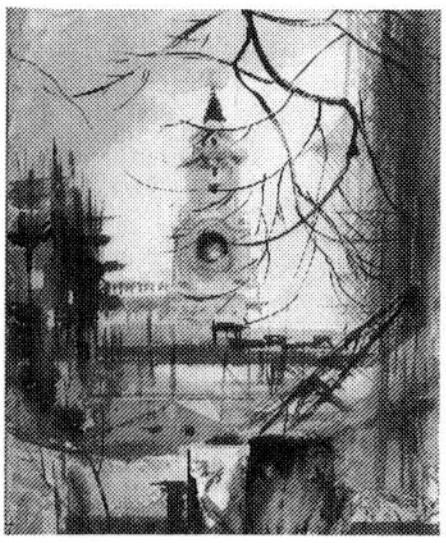

acc. no. 1695
Tom Tower (*c.* 1964)

watercolour: $27\frac{1}{2} \times 22\frac{1}{2}$ in.
signed: *Dennis James* and inscribed: *18 gns framed*

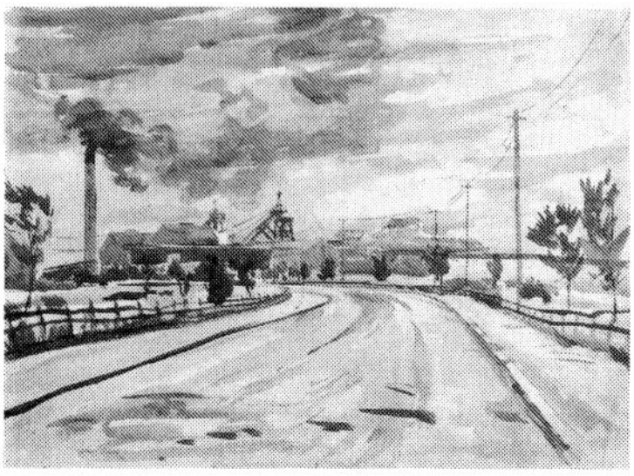

on verso: *Mining Scene* (1949)
watercolour: $22\frac{1}{2} \times 27\frac{1}{2}$ in.
signed and dated: *Dennis James / '49*
Purchased from the artist, 1964

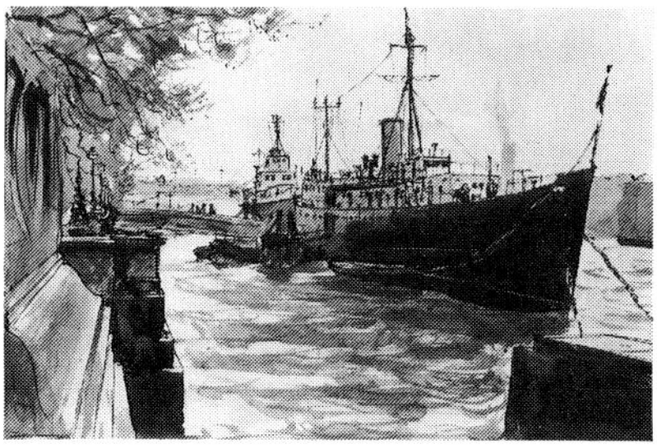

acc. no. 1900
'President' and 'Chrysanthemum' (1970)

watercolour: $15\frac{1}{4} \times 22\frac{1}{2}$ in.
signed and dated: *Dennis James / 1970*
Purchased from the artist, 1972

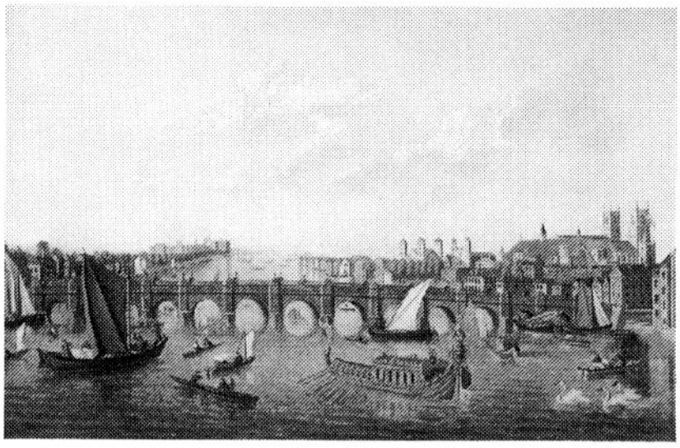

attributed to William James (*fl.* 1754–71)

acc. no. 575
Westminster Bridge looking Up-River

oil on canvas: 28 × 45 in.
Presented by Sir Reginald Hanson, 1893

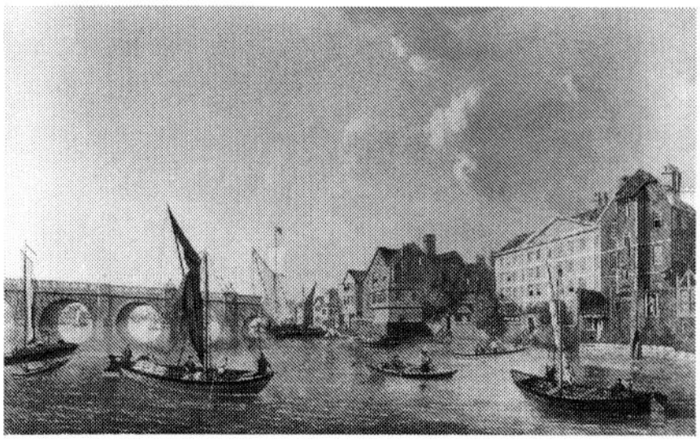

attributed to William James (*fl.* 1754–71) after Samuel Scott (1703–72)

acc. no. 576
Westminster Bridge with Neighbouring Houses

oil on canvas: 28 × 45 in.
Presented by Sir Reginald Hanson, 1893

Alexander Jamieson (1873–1937)

acc. no. 1234
The Mill, Weston Turville (1936)
oil on canvas: $47\frac{1}{2} \times 62\frac{1}{2}$ in.
signed and dated: *Alexander Jamieson / January 1936*
Purchased, 1939

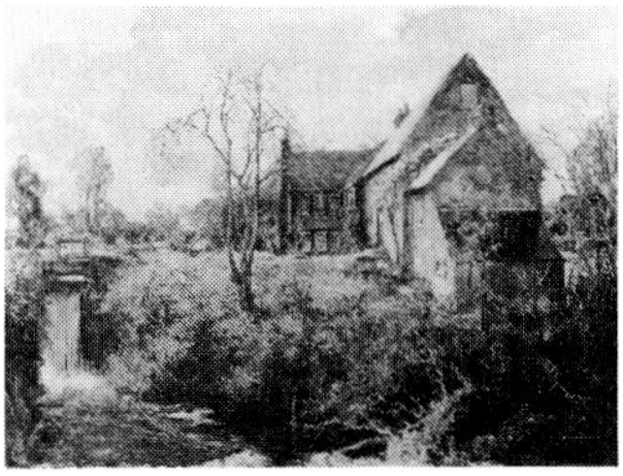

Norman Janes (1892–1980)

acc. no. 1848
The Thames at Greenwich (*c.*1970)
watercolour: $14\frac{1}{2} \times 19\frac{5}{8}$ in.
signed: *Norman Janes*
Purchased from the artist, 1970

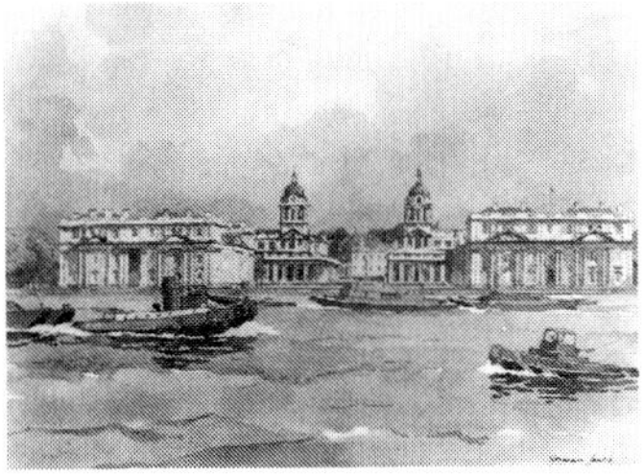

Charles Jervas (c.1675–1739)

acc. no. 31
King George II (*c.*1727–28)
oil on canvas: 93×57 in.
Commissioned by the Corporation, 1727

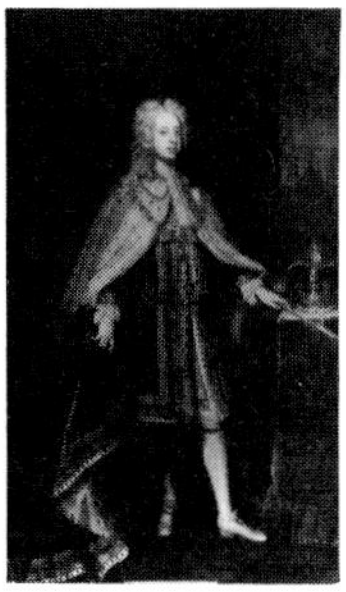

acc. no. 32
Wilhelmina Carolina of Brandenburg-Anspach, Queen Consort of George II (*c.*1727–28)
oil on canvas: 93×57 in.
Commissioned by the Corporation, 1727

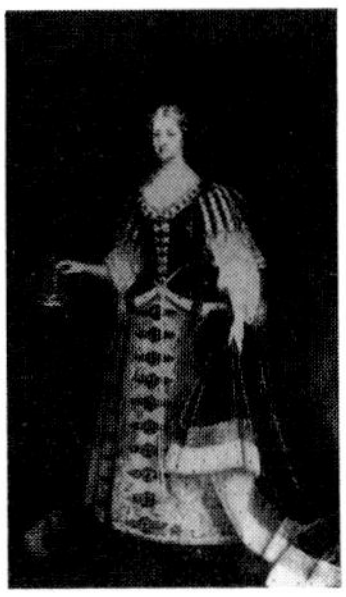

Robert Jobling (1841–1923)

acc. no. 1840
Middle Temple (1912)
watercolour: $6\frac{1}{2} \times 4\frac{5}{8}$ in.
signed: *R Jobling* over an earlier inscription and the date *1912*;
inscribed: *Middle Temple*
Purchased from John Oakes (Ariel Associates) 1970

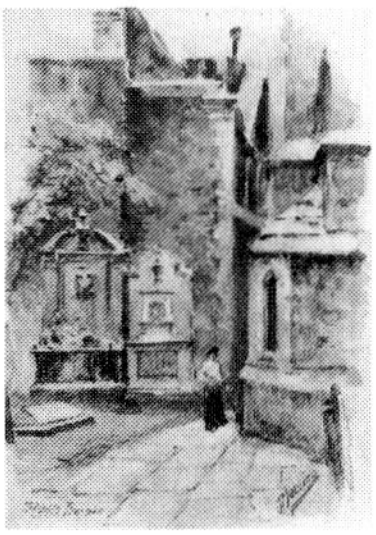

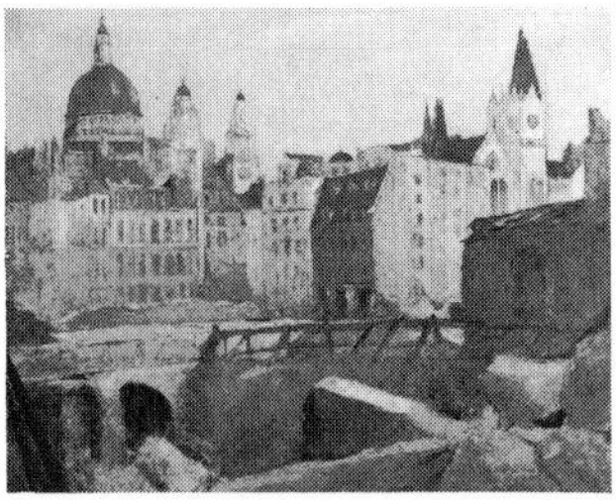

Ernest Borough Johnson (1866–1949)

acc. no. 1910
Ruins around St. Paul's (1945)

oil on canvas: 28 × 34 in.
signed, dated and inscribed: *Borough Johnson. 1945 / Ruins around St Pauls*
Presented by Mrs. Ellison-Rich, 1972

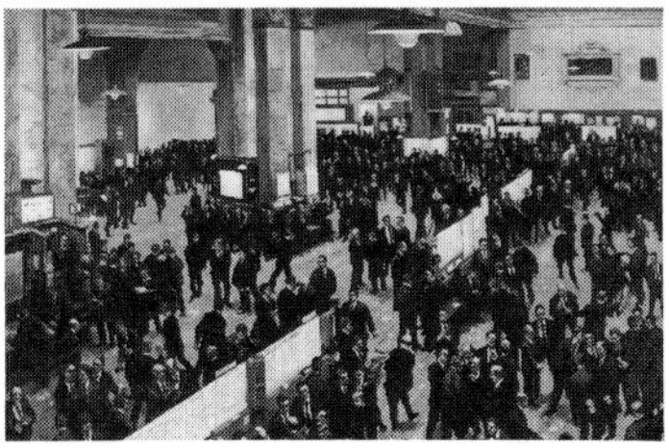

Roderick Jordan (b.1931)

acc. no. 1772
The Stock Exchange (1966/67)

oil on hardboard: 28 × 36 in.
Purchased from the artist, 1967

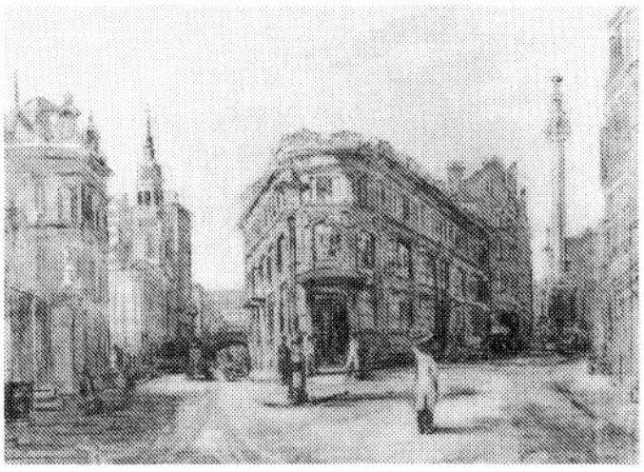

Amy Joseph (1876–1961)

acc. no. 2214
Billingsgate Market

pencil and watercolour: $12\frac{3}{8} \times 15\frac{3}{4}$ in.
Purchased from the City of Westminster Archives Department, 1978

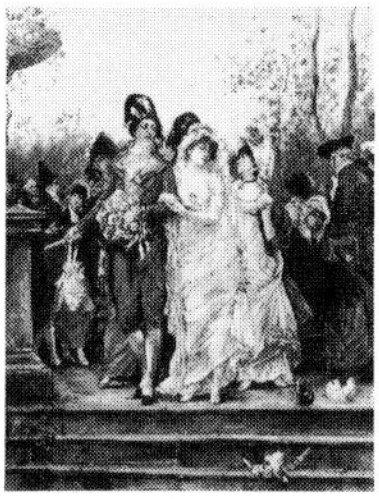

after Frederik Hendrik Kaemmerer (1839–1902)

acc. no. 446
The Revolutionist's Bride: Paris, 1799

oil over goupilgravure, laid on panel: 11 × 7 in.
with printed signature: *F.H. KAEMMERER.*
and stamp: *Goupil & Cie*
Bequeathed by William Dunnett, 1888

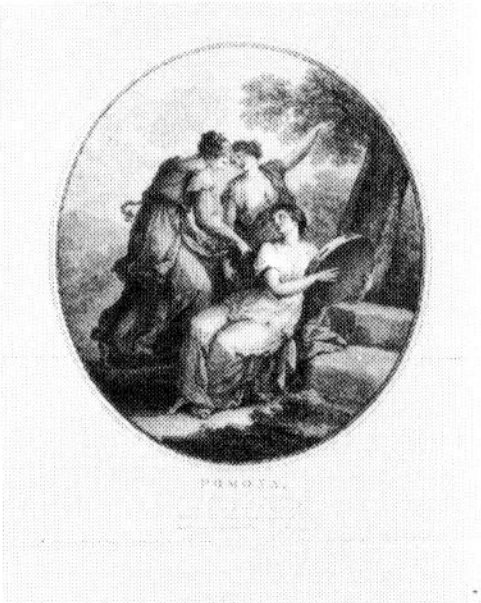

after Angelica Kauffman (1740–1807) by Francesco Bartolozzi (1725–1815)

acc. no. 458
Pomona

stipple engraving: $14\frac{1}{2} \times 12$ in. (plate)
lettered: *Angelica Kauffman delt F. Bartolozzi sculpt / POMONA / Bear me Pomona: to thy citron groves, / To where the lemon and the piercing lime, / With the deep orange glowing thro' the green, / Their lighter glories blend. / Thom. Summer / Publish'd as the Act directs April 15. 1782 by A. Torre No 44 Market Lane, London. A Paris Chez L Torre Porte St Antoine A.P.D.R.*
Bequeathed by William Dunnett, 1888

acc. no. 460
Ceres

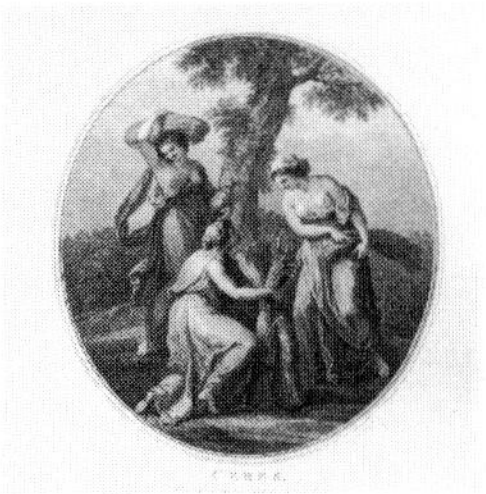

stipple engraving: $14\frac{1}{2} \times 12$ in. (plate)
lettered: *Angelica Kauffman del^{t} F. Bartolozzi sculp^{t} / CERES, / Crown'd with the Sickle and the wheaten sheaf, / While Autumn nodding o'er the yellow plain / Comes jovial on, the Doric reed once more / Well please'd I tune / Thom. Autumn / Publish'd as the Act directs April 15. 1782 by A. Torre N. 44 Market Lane, London. A Paris Chez L. Torre Porte St Antoine A.P.D.R.*
Bequeathed by William Dunnett, 1888

acc. no. 462
Winter

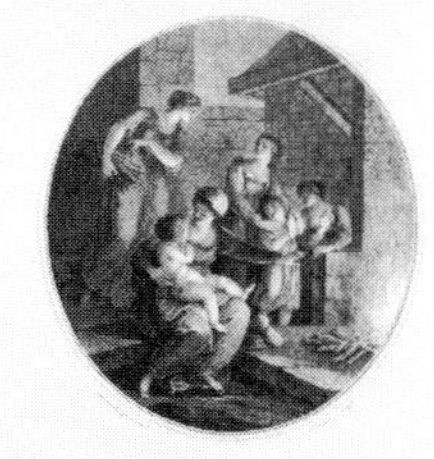

stipple engraving: $14\frac{1}{2} \times 12$ in. (plate)
lettered: *Angelica Kauffman pinx^{t} F. Bartolozzi sculp^{t} / WINTER / Publish'd as the Act directs July 1st 1782 by A. Torre N° 44 Market Lane London A Paris Chez L. Torre Porte St Antoine A.P.D.R.*
Bequeathed by William Dunnett, 1888

after Angelica Kauffman (1740–1807) by W. Wynne Ryland (1732–83)

acc. no. 463
Juno

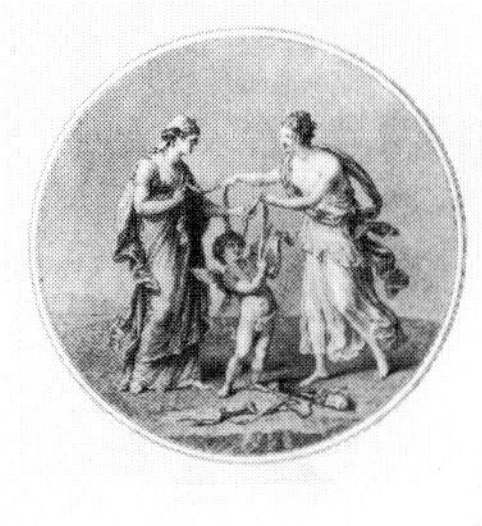

stipple engraving: $14\frac{3}{4} \times 12\frac{3}{4}$ in.
lettered: *Angelica Kauffman Pinx. William. Wynne Ryland Scul. / JUVΛO borrowing the Cestus, from VEVΛUS. / Published January 1. 1777 by W.W. Ryland in the Strand London.*
Bequeathed by William Dunnett, 1888

after Angelica Kauffman (1740–1807) by Gavrila Ivanovitch Scorodomoff (1755–92)

acc. no. 467
The Three Graces and Cupid

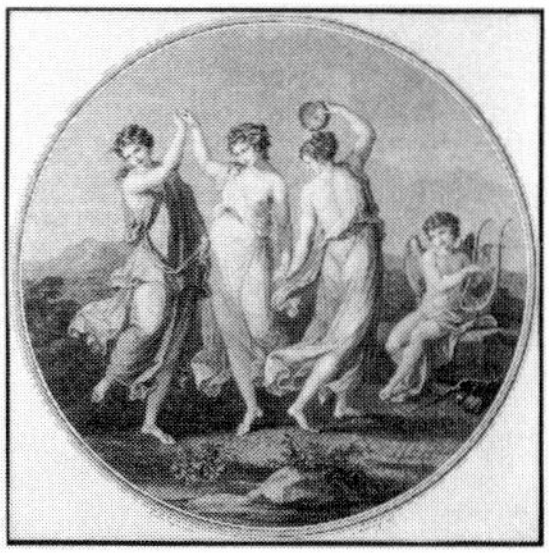

stipple engraving:
lettered: *Angelica Kauffman pinx. G. Scorodomoff sculp^{t}*
Bequeathed by William Dunnett, 1888

Charles Samuel Keene (1823–91)

acc. no. 3569
Elizabethan Soldier, Shot

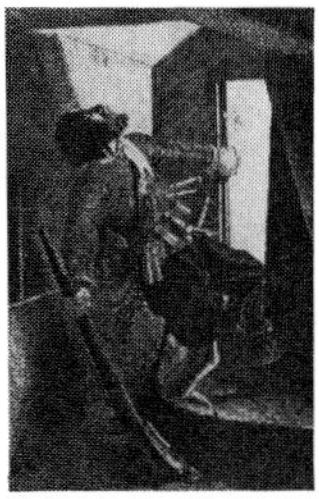

etching and drypoint: 6×5 in. (plate)
Presented by Miss Helen Guiterman, 1985

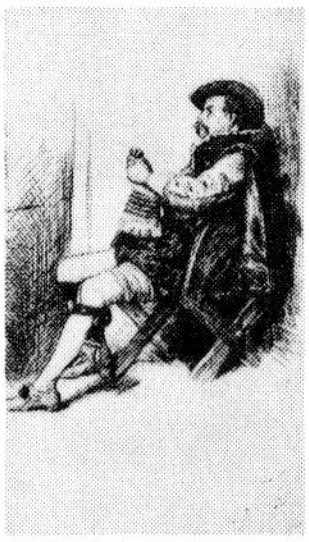

acc. no. 3570
Seated Man, in Doublet and Cloak
etching and drypoint: $7\frac{3}{8} \times 4\frac{1}{4}$ in. (plate)
Presented by Miss Helen Guiterman, 1985

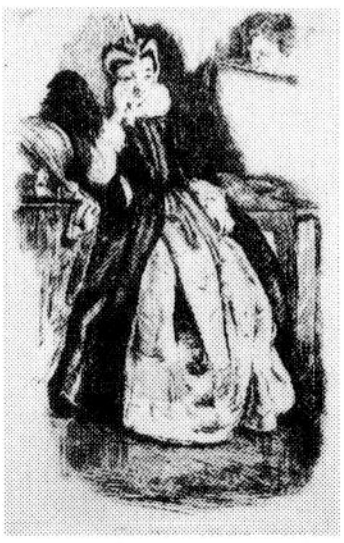

acc. no. 3571
Lady in Elizabethan Dress
etching and drypoint: $6\frac{1}{4} \times 4$ in. (plate)
signed (mono) in the plate: *C.K.*
Presented by Miss Helen Guiterman, 1985

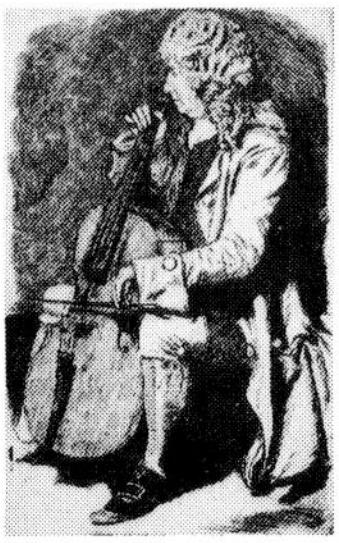

acc. no. 3572
Man in 18thC Dress, Playing the Violoncello
etching and drypoint: $5\frac{1}{8} \times 3\frac{1}{4}$ in.
signed (mono) in the plate: *C.K.*
Presented by Miss Helen Guiterman, 1985

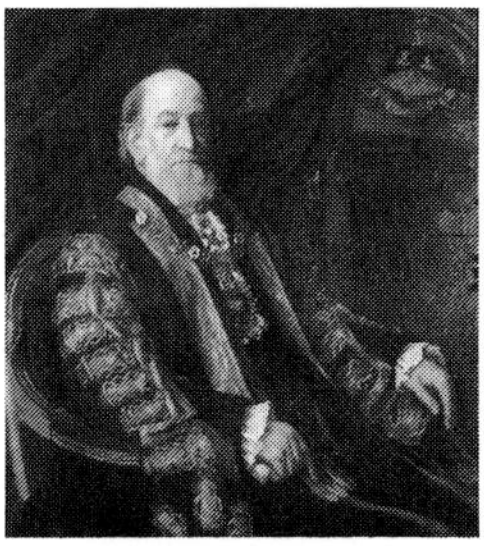

John Kelt-Edwards (*fl.* 1906–08)

acc. no. 1498
Sir William Vaughan Morgan, Lord Mayor 1905
oil on canvas: $41\frac{7}{8} \times 37\frac{7}{8}$ in.
signed and dated: *J. Kelt- Edwards / 1906*
Presented by J. Hornby Steer, 1953

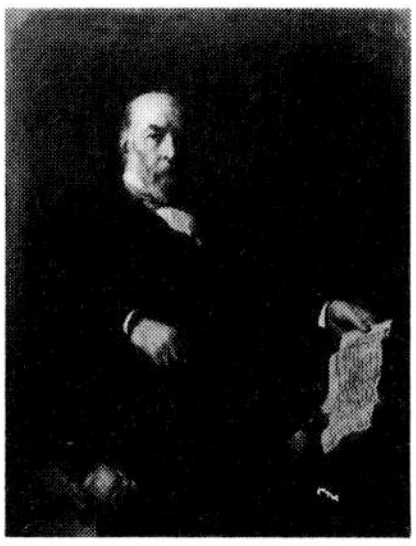

Charles H. M. Kerr (1858–1907)

acc. no. 591
R. Malcolm Kerr, Judge of the City of London Court (1894)
oil on canvas: 50×40 in.
signed and dated: *CHARLES KERR. / 1894*
Presented by the sitter's family, 1894

acc. no. 1078
The Rose-Coloured Gown (Miss Giles) (1896)

oil on canvas: $44\frac{1}{4} \times 34$ in.
signed: *CHARLES KERR*
Presented by the artist's wife, 1931

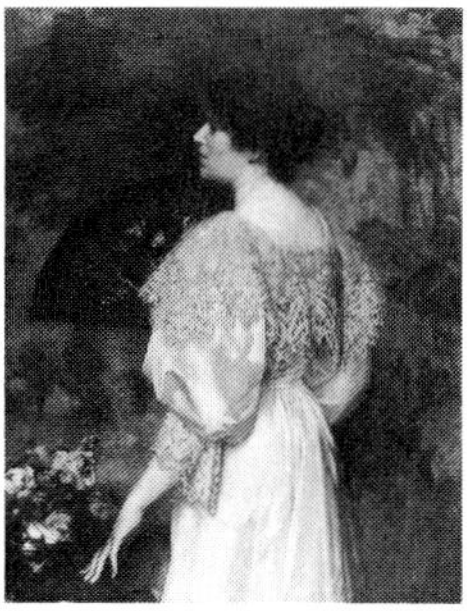

Charles H. M. Kerr (1858–1907) after W. C. J. Dobson (1817–98)

acc. no. 598
Charles Knight, the Publisher of Shakespeare's works

oil on canvas: 24×20 in.
Presented by R. Malcolm Kerr, 1895

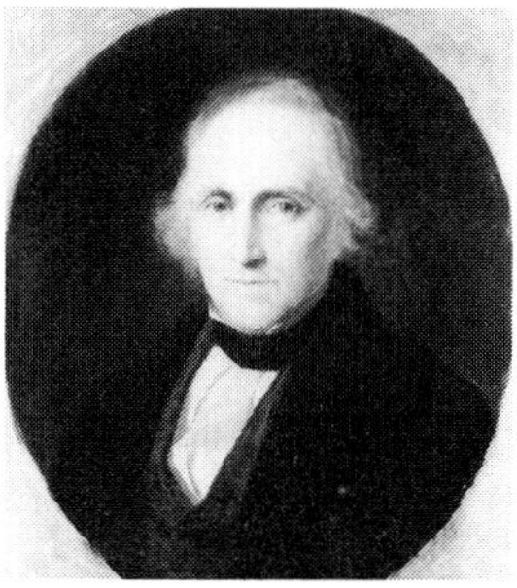

James Kerr-Lawson (1865–1939)

acc. no. 3574
Lady in a Pink Robe, seated by a Table

pencil and watercolour: $10\frac{1}{2} \times 9\frac{5}{8}$ in.
signed: *J.K.L.*
Presented by Miss Helen Guiterman, 1985

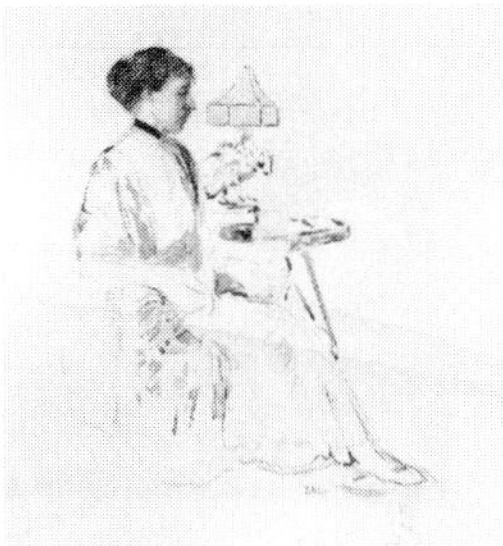

James A. Kirby (20th C)

acc. no. 1720
The Quay, Billingsgate Market (*c.*1965)

oil on canvas: 18×24 in.
signed: *James A. Kirby*
Purchased from the artist, 1965

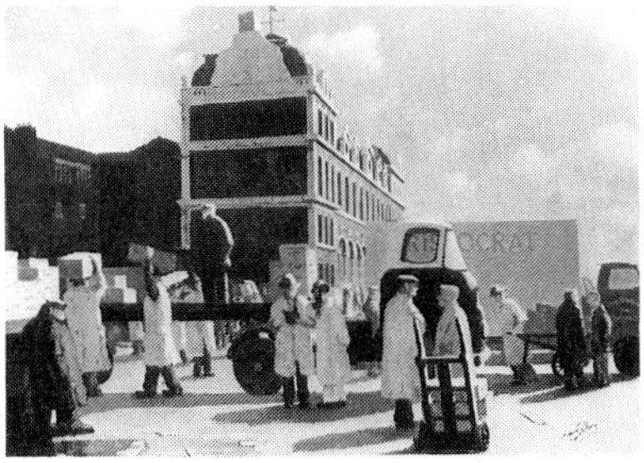

acc. no. 1727
Low Tide, Low Spirits (*c.*1966)

oil on hardboard: $16 \times 32\frac{1}{2}$ in.
signed: *James A. Kirby*
Purchased from the artist, 1966

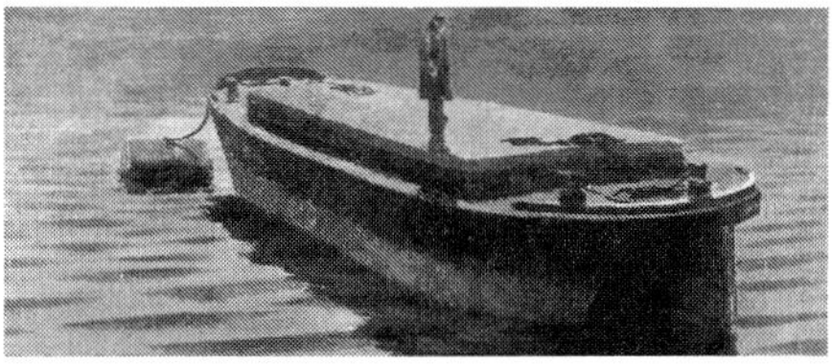

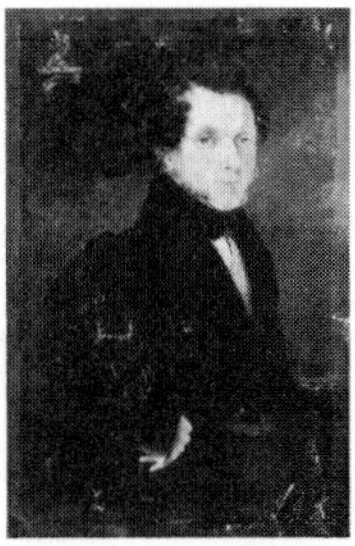

J . . . A . . . K . . . (*fl.* 1840)

acc. no. 3567
Portrait of a Gentleman (1840)

oil on canvas laid on panel: $12\frac{1}{2} \times 8\frac{1}{8}$ in.
signed: *J.A.K.* and signed and dated on verso: *J.A.K. Windsor 1840*
Presented by Miss Helen Guiterman, 1985

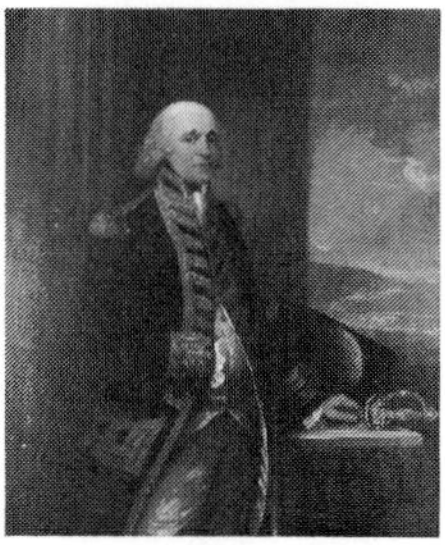

George Kirtland (*fl.* 1791–98) after Gainsborough Dupont (1754–97)

acc. no. 65
Admiral Lord Howe

oil on canvas: 56 × 47 in.
Commissioned by the Corporation, *c.*1800

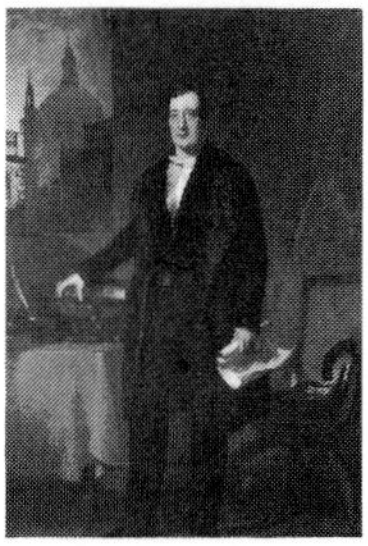

John Preston Knight (1803–81)

acc. no. 1902
James Bentley, Treasurer of St. Bartholomew's Hospital (1848)

oil on canvas: $94 \times 58\frac{1}{2}$ in.
Presented by St. Bartholomew's Hospital, 1972

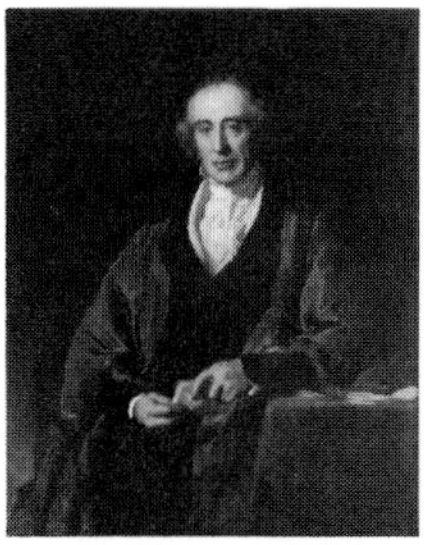

acc. no. 256
Thomas Corney, Deputy (1850)

oil on canvas: 50 × 40 in.
Presented by the Ward of Broad Street, 1879

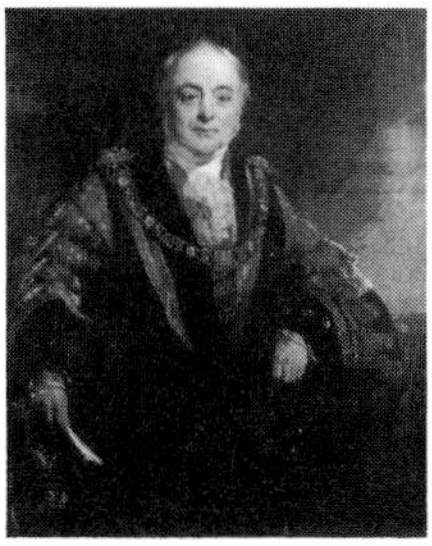

acc. no. 257
Sir John Musgrove, Bt., Lord Mayor 1851 (1852)

oil on canvas 50 × 43 in.
Presented by the Ward of Broad Street, 1879

acc. no. 1903
William Foster White, Treasurer of St. Bartholomew's Hospital (1865)

oil on canvas: 94 × 59 in.
signed (mono): *JPK / RA*
Presented by St. Bartholomew's Hospital, 1972

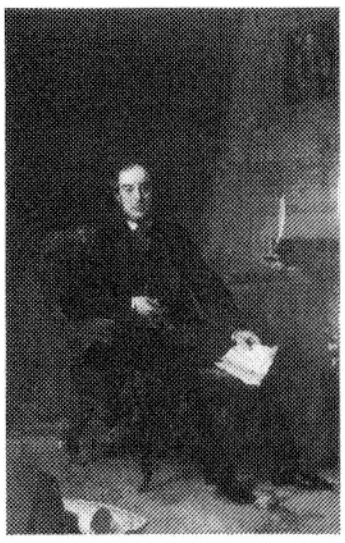

Hermanus Koekkoek (1815–1882)

acc. no. 688
A Calm (1852)

oil on canvas: 16 × 22 in.
signed and dated: *H Koekkoek 1852*
Bequeathed by Charles Gassiot, 1902

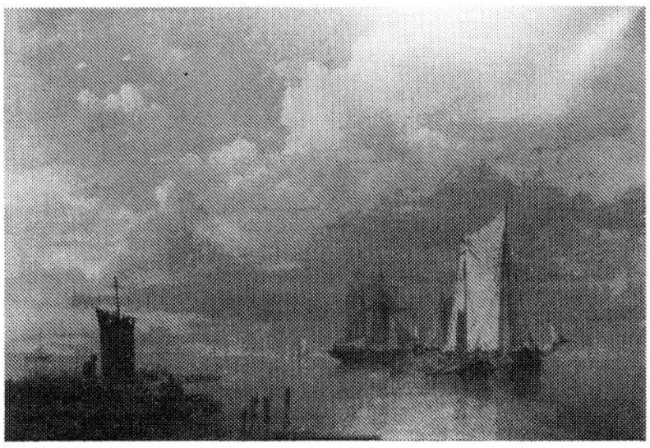

Willem Koekkoek (1839–95)

acc. no. 840
Winter Scene in Amsterdam

oil on canvas: 23½ × 17½ in.
signed: *W. Koekkoek*
Bequeathed by H. C. Richards, K.C., M.P., 1905

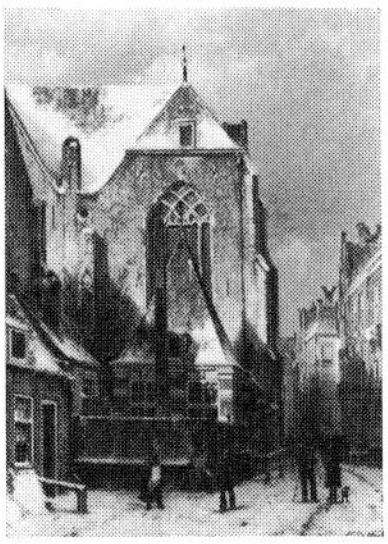

Sir Edwin Landseer (1802–73)

acc. no. 690
The Travelled Monkey (1827)

oil on canvas: 19 × 22 in.
Bequeathed by Charles Gassiot, 1902

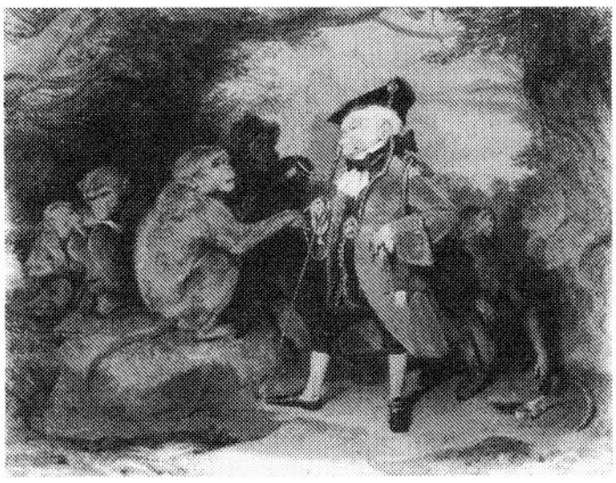

acc. no. 691
The First Leap: Lord Alexander Russell on his Pony 'Emerald' (1829)

oil on millboard: 16 × 18 in.
signed and dated: *E.L. 1829*
Bequeathed by Charles Gassiot, 1902

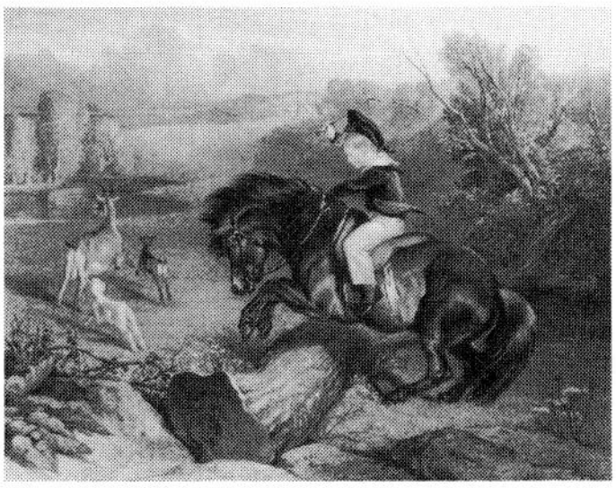

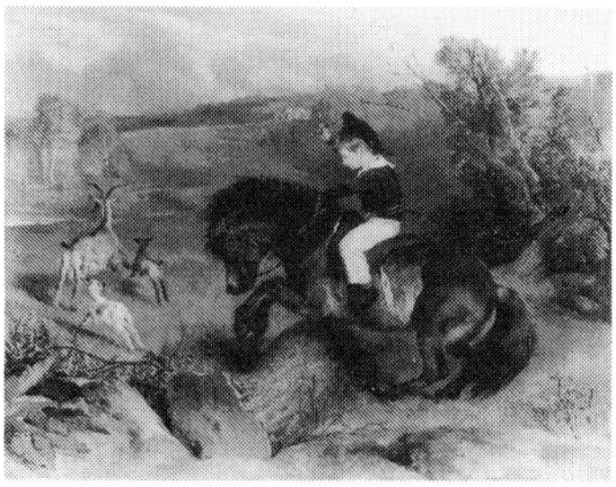

after Landseer by Charles George Lewis (1808–80)

acc. no. 3513
The First Leap (engraved 1857)

engraving: 23 × 28 in. (plate)
Purchased from Grosvenor Prints, 1985

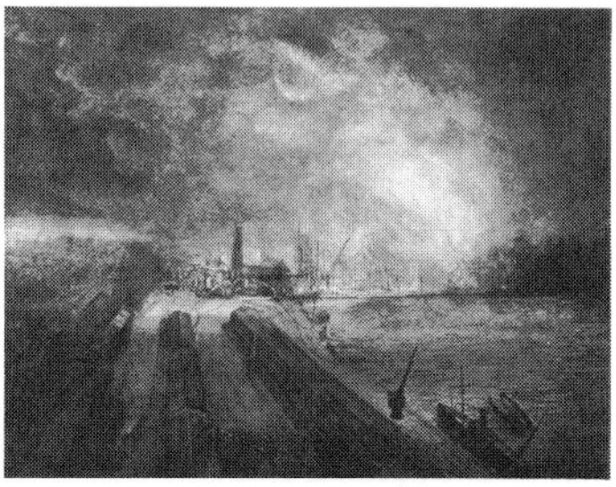

H. T. Lane (20th C)

acc. no. 1692
Royal Docks During Enemy Air Raid, 1940

watercolour: $8\frac{1}{4} \times 10\frac{5}{8}$ in.
signed: *H.T. Lane*
Presented by the artist, 1964

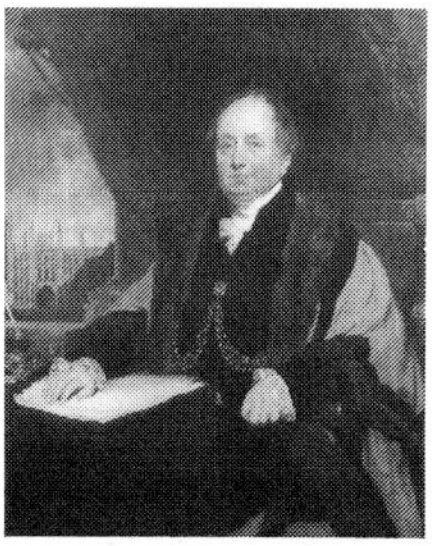

Samuel Lane (1780–1859)

acc. no. 2165
Alderman Anthony Brown (1844)

oil on canvas: $50 \times 39\frac{1}{2}$ in.
Purchased from the Knowle Gallery, 1975

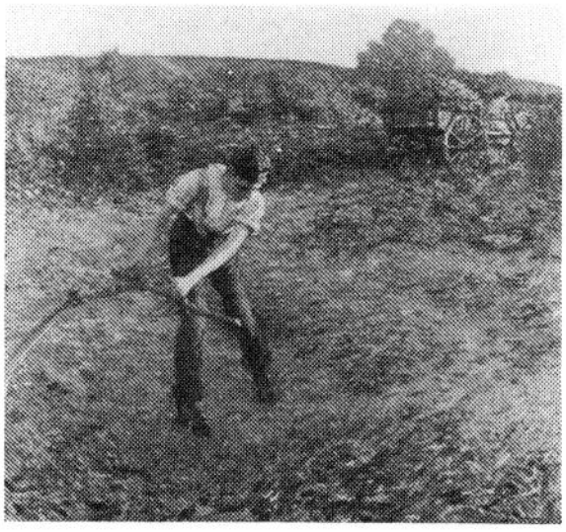

Henry Herbert La Thangue (1859–1929)

acc. no. 771
Mowing Bracken (1903)

oil on canvas: $51\frac{1}{2} \times 58$ in.
signed: *H.H. LA THANGUE*
Purchased from the artist, 1903

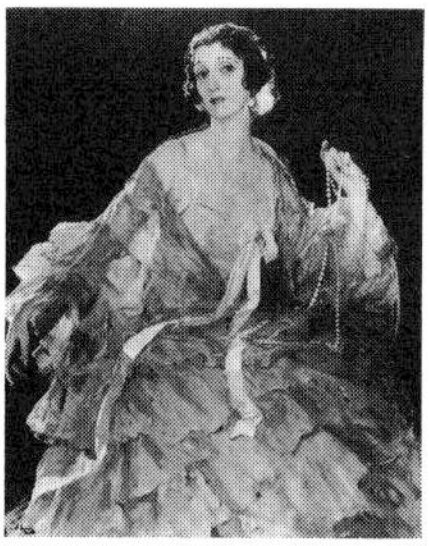

Sir John Lavery (1856–1941)

acc. no. 1027
Lady Lavery (1922)

oil on canvas: 50 × 40 in.
signed: *J. Lavery*
Presented by Lady Cunard, 1923

Sir Thomas Lawrence (1769–1830)

acc. no. 844
John Philip Kemble as Coriolanus (1798)
oil on canvas: 113 × 70½ in.
Presented by the Earl of Yarborough, 1906

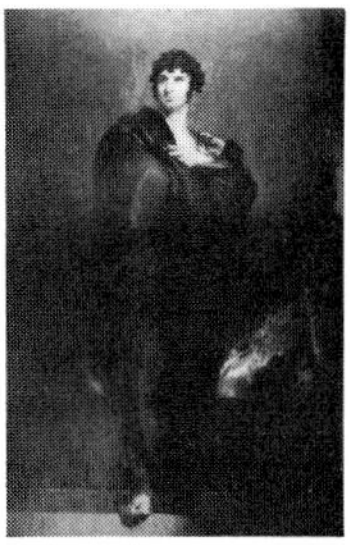

acc. no. 590
Sir William Grant, Master of the Rolls (*c.*1802)
oil on canvas: 30 × 25 in.
Presented by Sidney Young, 1894

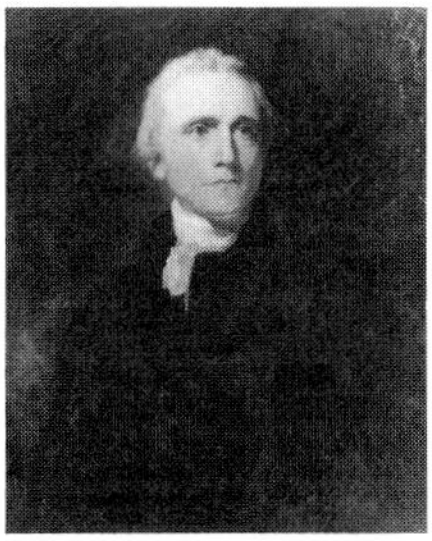

acc. no. 93
Richard Clark, Chamberlain of London (1825–27)
oil on canvas: 56 × 44 in.
Commissioned by the Corporation, 1825

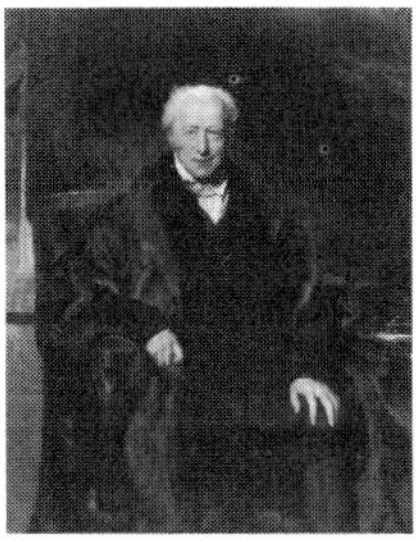

acc. no. 1516
George Dance the Younger
oil on canvas: 30 × 25¼ in.
Purchased from S. Frisell, 1955

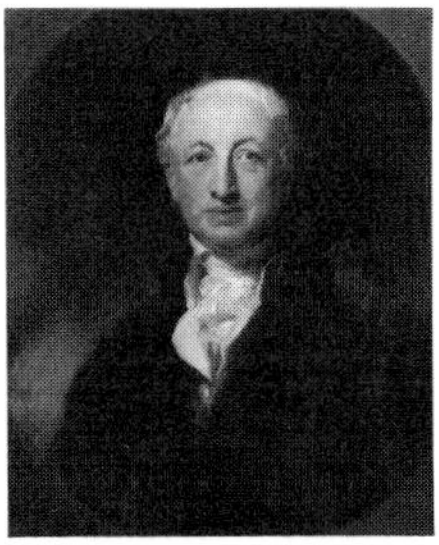

after Sir Thomas Lawrence (1769–1830)

acc. no. 1377
George Dance the Younger
watercolour: 4 × 2⅞ in. (sight)
Bequeathed by Miss M. S. Dance, 1948

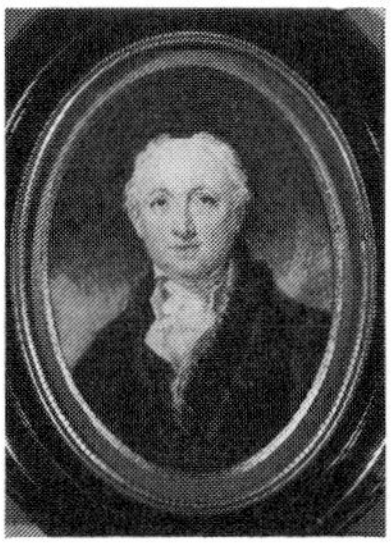

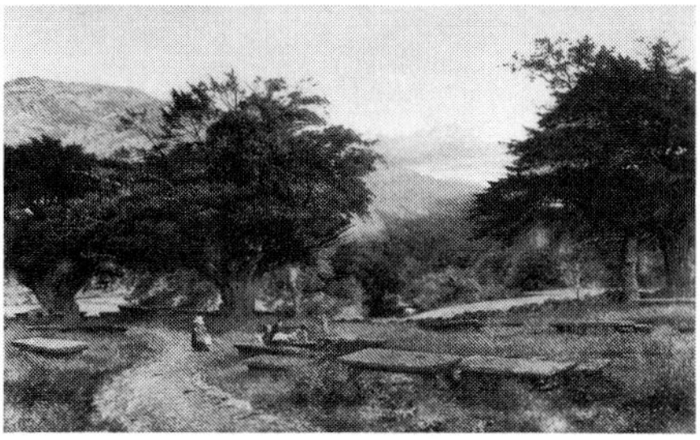

Benjamin Williams Leader (1831–1923)

acc. no. 692
The Churchyard, Bettws-y-Coed (1863)
oil on canvas: 32 × 53 in.
signed and dated: *B.W. Leader 1863*
Bequeathed by Charles Gassiot, 1902

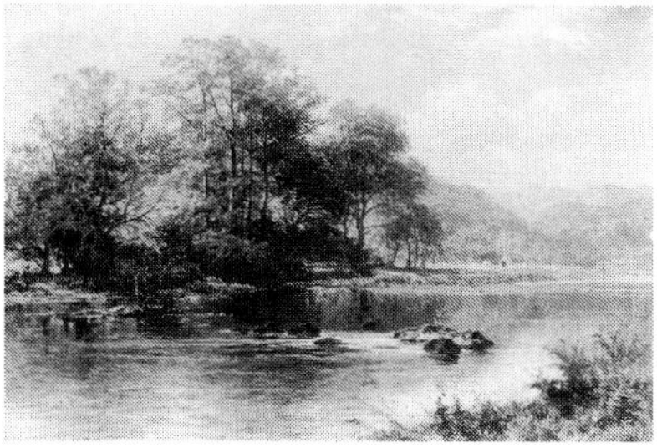

acc. no. 334
The Stream in Summertime (1887)
oil on canvas: 18 × 26 in.
signed and dated: *B.W. LEADER 1887*
Presented by the Worshipful Company of Drapers, 1887

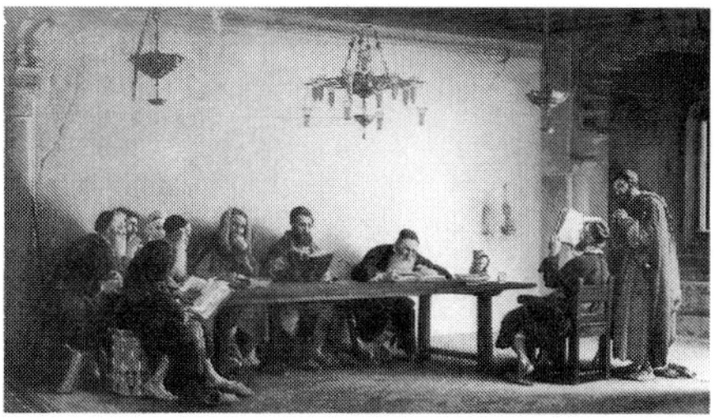

Jean Jules Antoine Lecomte du Noüy (1842–1923)

acc. no. 1040
The Reading of the Bible by the Rabbis – a Souvenir of Morocco (1882)
oil on canvas: 30 × 52 in.
signed and dated: *Lecomte du Nouÿ* (sic) *'82*
Presented by Adam Scott in Memory of his Sister, Janet-Mary Scott, 1925

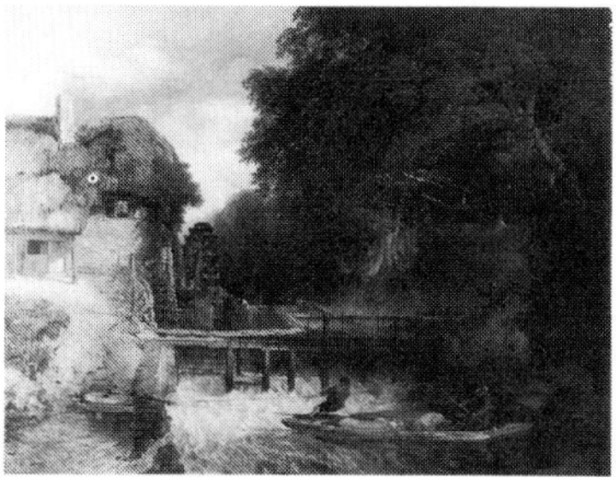

Frederick Richard Lee (1798–1879)

acc. no. 693
The Miller's Boat (1847)
oil on canvas: $34\frac{1}{2} \times 44\frac{1}{2}$ in.
signed and dated: *F.R. Lee R.A. 1847*
Bequeathed by Charles Gassiot, 1902

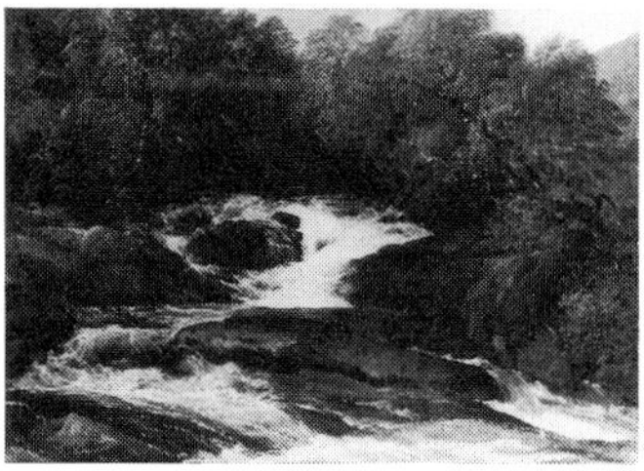

acc. no. 612
A Devonshire Stream (1860)
oil on panel: 18 × 24 in.
signed and dated: *F.R. Lee R.A. 1860*
Presented by J. H. Skilbeck, 1899

John Leech (1817–64)

acc. no. 1888
The Weinbrunnen, Schwalbach

watercolour: $12 \times 18\frac{1}{2}$ in.
signed: *JL* and inscribed: *The Weinbrunnen. Schwalbach*
Presented by Miss Helen Guiterman, 1985

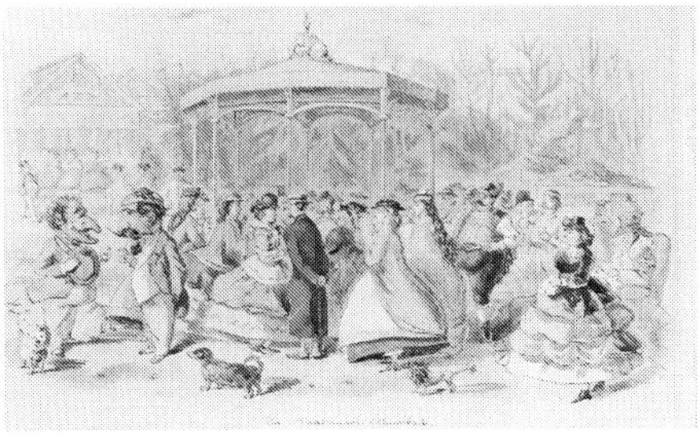

Geoffrey Lefever (20th C)

acc. no. 1718
Two Bridges (Cannon St. Railway Bridge and London Bridge) (1964)

oil on board: $24 \times 35\frac{7}{8}$ in.
signed and dated: *Lefever '64*
Purchased from the artist, 1965

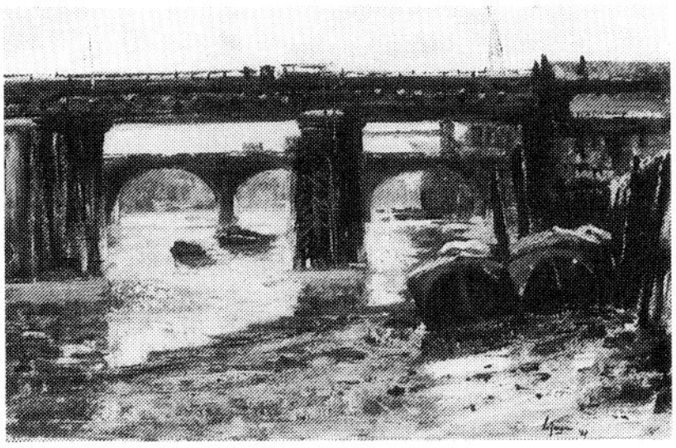

Alphonse Legros (1837–1911)

acc. no. 3540
Young Man with a Beard

black and red chalk: $13\frac{1}{2} \times 9\frac{3}{4}$ in.
signed: *A Legros*
Presented by Miss Helen Guiterman, 1985

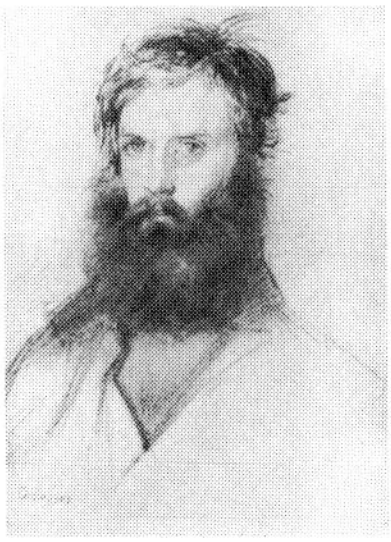

Frederick, Lord Leighton (1830–96)

acc. no. 1039
The Music Lesson (1877)

oil on canvas: $36\frac{1}{2} \times 37\frac{1}{2}$ in.
Presented by Lord Bearsted, 1925

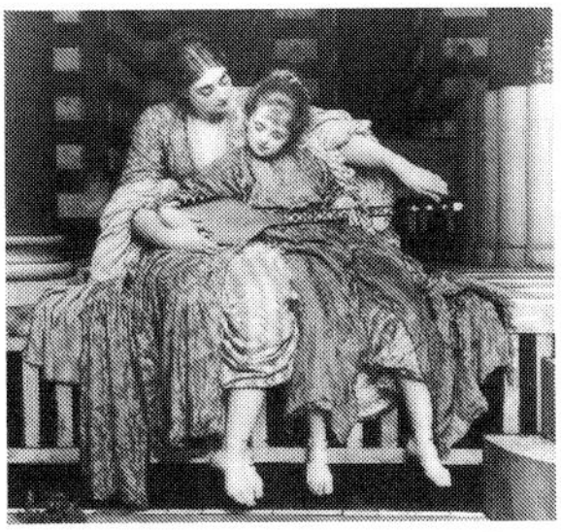

Sir Peter Lely (1618–80)

acc. no. 1289
Sir Edward Hales and His Family (?c.1656)

oil on canvas: 68×92 in.
signed (mono): *Pely*
Presented by Lady Wakefield, 1944

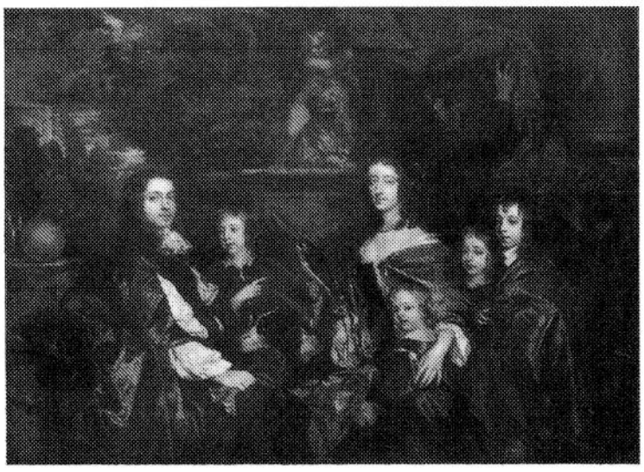

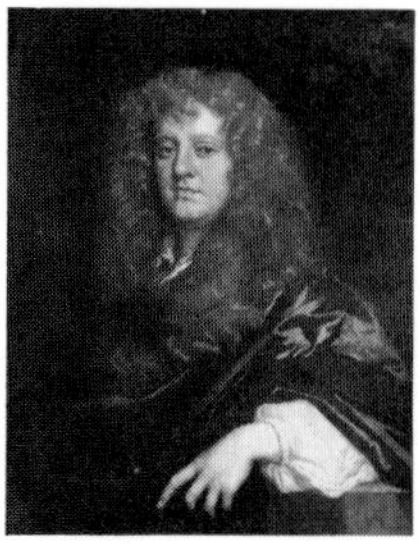

acc. no. 1312
Sir Ralph Bankes

oil on canvas: 30 × 25 in.
Presented by Lady Wakefield, 1944

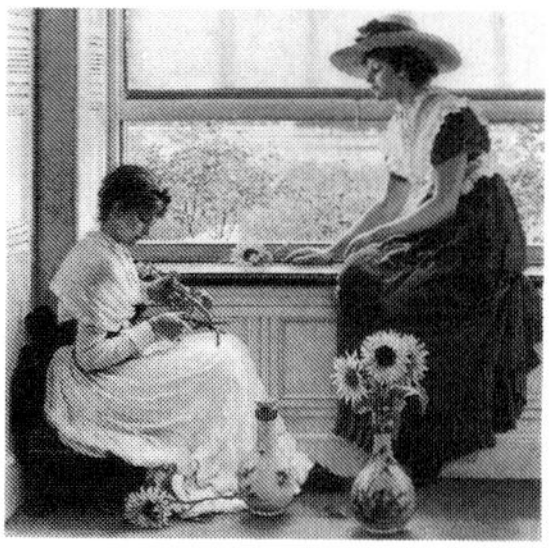

George Dunlop Leslie (1835–1921)

acc. no. 695
Sun and Moon Flowers (1889)

oil on canvas: $28\frac{1}{2} \times 28\frac{1}{2}$ in.
signed: *GDL*
Bequeathed by Charles Gassiot, 1902

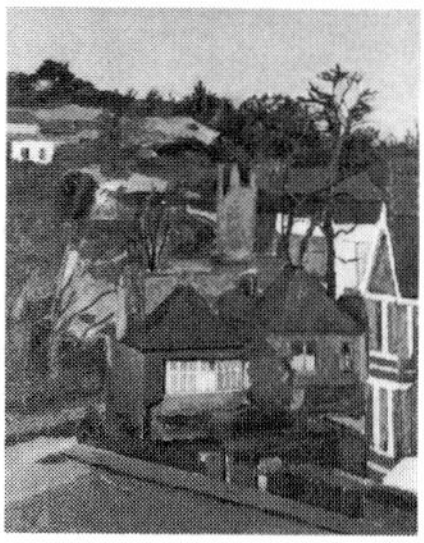

Ben Levene (b.1938)

acc. no. 1964
One Tree Hill, South London (1973)

oil on plywood: 30 × 24 in.
Purchased from the Thackeray Gallery, 1973

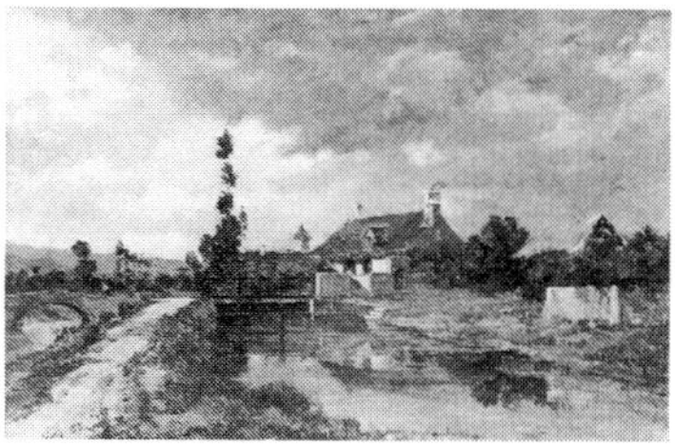

Maurice Levis (1860–1902)

acc. no. 982
A Canal in Belgium (1888)

oil on canvas: 15 × 21 in.
signed and dated: *M. Levis. – 88*
Presented by H. S. E. Vanderpant, 1916

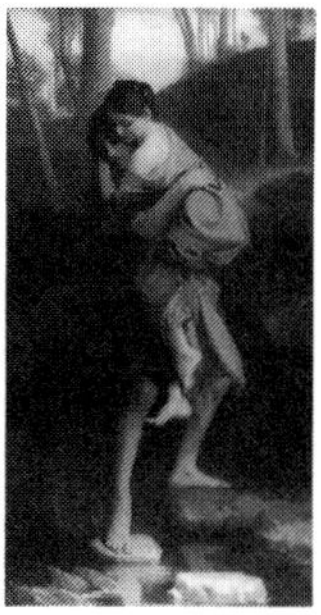

Emile Lévy (1826–90)

acc. no. 697
Paul et Virginie (1866)

oil on canvas: $22 \times 11\frac{1}{2}$ in.
signed and dated: *EMILY LEVY / 1866*
Bequeathed by Charles Gassiot, 1902

Sir Ernest Daryl Lindsay (b.1889)

acc. no. 1849
The Overseer, Northern Territory

oil on canvas: $12\frac{5}{8} \times 17$ in.
signed: *Daryl · Lindsay*
Presented by the Australian Capital Territory Advisory Council, 1970

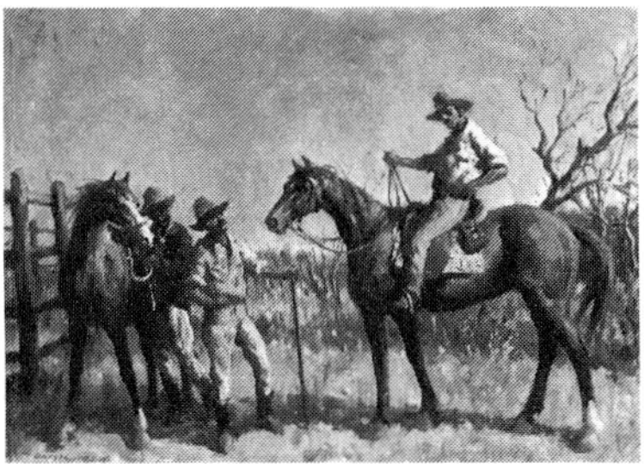

Mary Stella Ling (20th C)

acc. no. 3646
Sir Seymour Howard, Lord Mayor, 1954–5

oil on canvas: 72 × 50 in.
signed: *R. Ling* (sic)
Presented by the artist, 1956

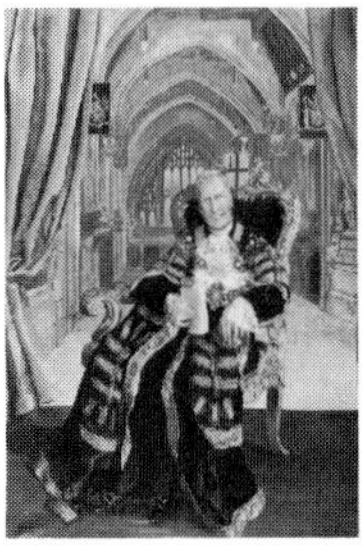

John Linnell (1792–1882)

acc. no. 699
Coast Scene (1860]

oil on panel: $6\frac{1}{2} \times 10\frac{1}{2}$ in.
signed and dated: *J LINNELL 1860*
Bequeathed by Charles Gassiot, 1902

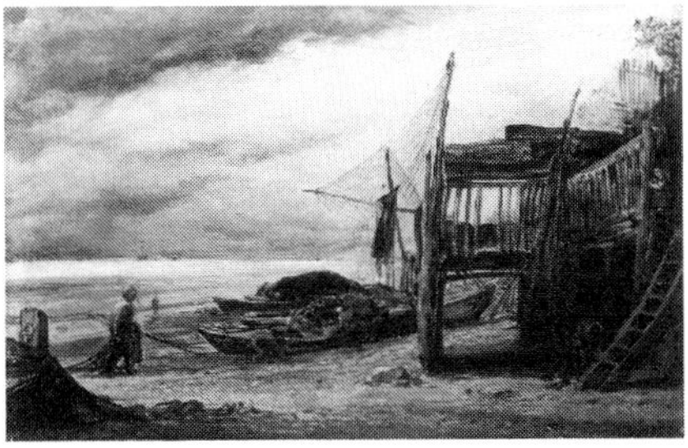

acc. no. 698
The Timber Waggon (1872)

oil on canvas: $40\frac{1}{2} \times 52$ in.
signed and dated: *J Linnell 1872*
Bequeathed by Charles Gassiot, 1902

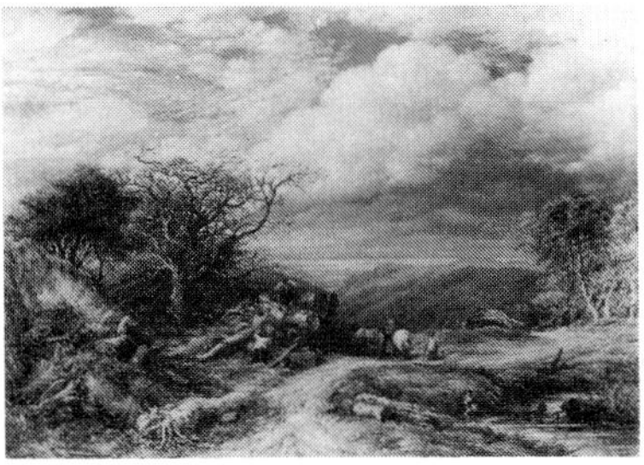

Flora Lion (1876–1958)

acc. no. 3549
Portrait of a Lady (1907)

oil on canvas: 24 × 20 in.
signed and dated: *Flora Lion / 07*
Presented by Miss Helen Guiterman, 1985

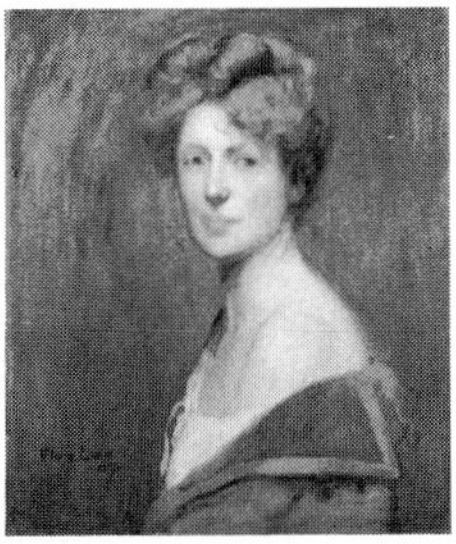

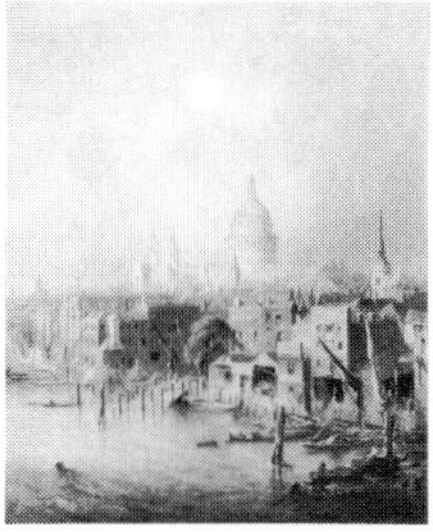

F. Lloyds (*fl.* 1858–61)

acc. no. 1233
Queenhithe – St. Paul's in the Distance

oil on canvas: 24 × 20 in.
Presented, source unknown, 1938 (?)

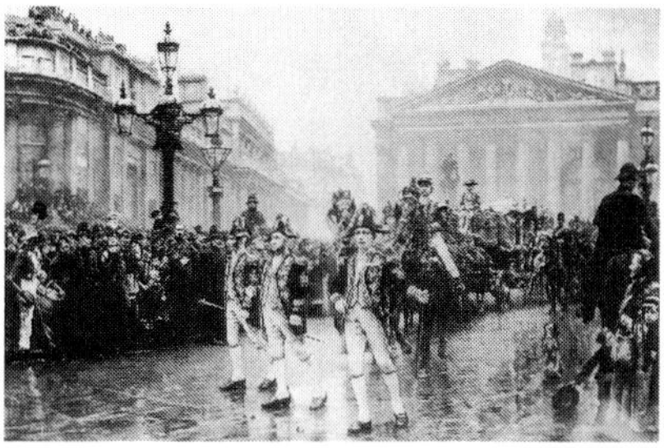

William Logsdail (1859–1944)

acc. no. 1091
The Ninth of November, 1888 (1890)

oil on canvas: $73\frac{3}{4} \times 107\frac{1}{4}$ in.
signed and dated: *WILLIAM LOGSDAIL 1890*
Purchased from the artist, 1933

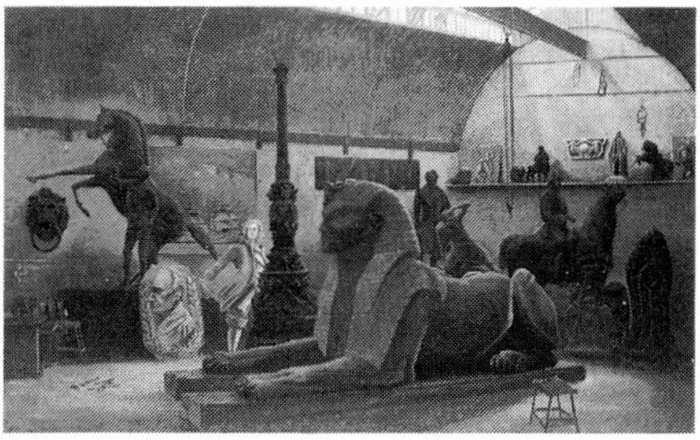

R. Lowry Lomax (19th C)

acc. no. 1851
Bronze Statue Chasing Shop – the Foundry of H.L. Young & Co. (1881)

oil on canvas: $23\frac{7}{8} \times 36$ in.
signed: *R Lowry Lomax / 1881*
Purchased from Mr. Deputy Douglas Young, 1970

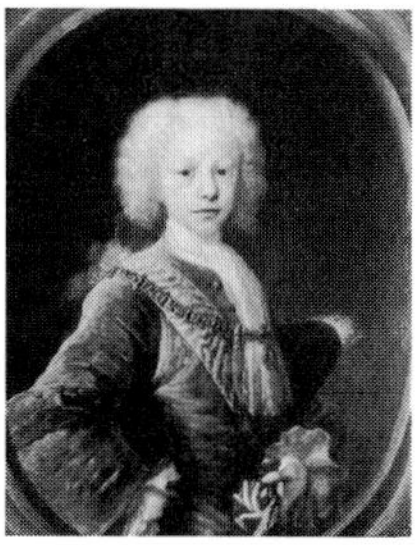

Alessandro Longhi (1733–1813)

acc. no. 1037
An Austrian Prince

oil on canvas: 33 × 25 in.
Presented by the Executors of the Estate of Sir Claude Phillips, 1925

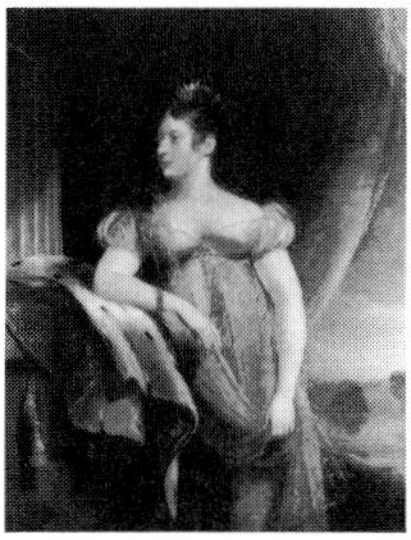

James Lonsdale (1777–1839)

acc. no. 91
Princess Charlotte (before 1817)

oil on canvas: 56 × 43 in.
Presented by Queen Caroline, 1820

acc. no. 873
John Reay, Sheriff of London 1814–1815 (?1819)
oil on canvas: 37 × 30 in.
Presented by the Rev. B. Reay, 1908

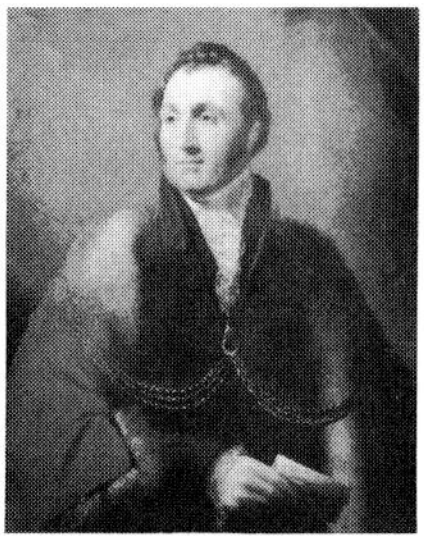

acc. no. 90
Caroline of Brunswick, Consort of George IV (1820)
oil on canvas: 56 × 44 in.
signed and dated: *Jas Lonsdale Sept. 1820*
Presented by Queen Caroline, 1820

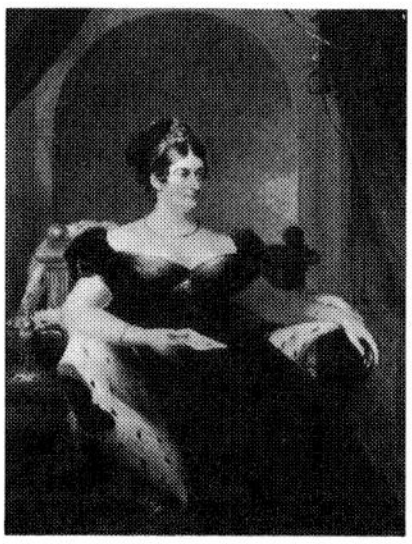

William Mouat Loudan (1868–1925)

acc. no. 1047
The Letter (1910)
oil on canvas: 42 × 31 in.
signed and dated: *MOUAT LOUDAN / 1910*
Purchased at Christie's 26.4.1926

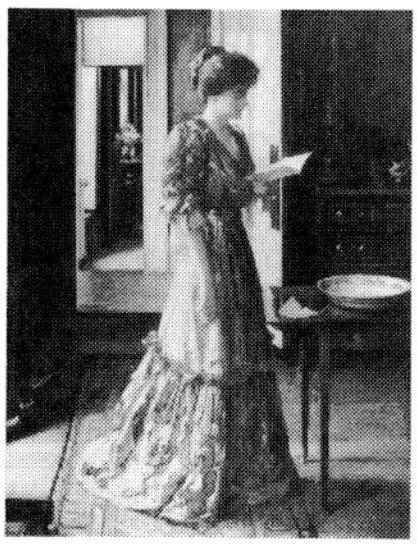

after Victor Louis (1731–1800) by (?) Jean-Nicholas Lerouge (b.1776)

acc. no. 2159
View of the Grand Theatre, Bordeaux
engraving: 13 × 22 in. (sight)
lettered: *Louis delinavit Lerouge sculpsit / VUE PERSPECTIVE, / Du grand Theatre de Bordeaux, construit sur les dessins de Mr. Louis, architecte du Roi / A Paris, chez Jean, Rue St. Jean de Beauvais, N. 10 Deposee a la Direction generale*
Presented by the City of Bordeaux, 1974

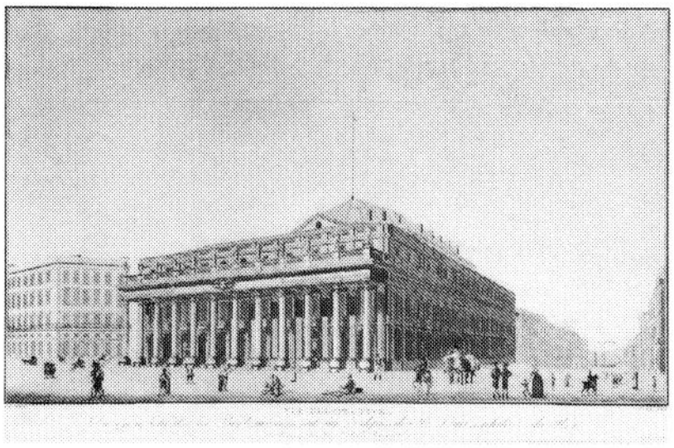

R. C. D. Lowry (b.1924)

acc. no. 1957
Low Tide, Deptford (1972)
oil on hardboard: 22 × 20 in.
signed: *RCD LOWRY*
Purchased from the artist, 1973

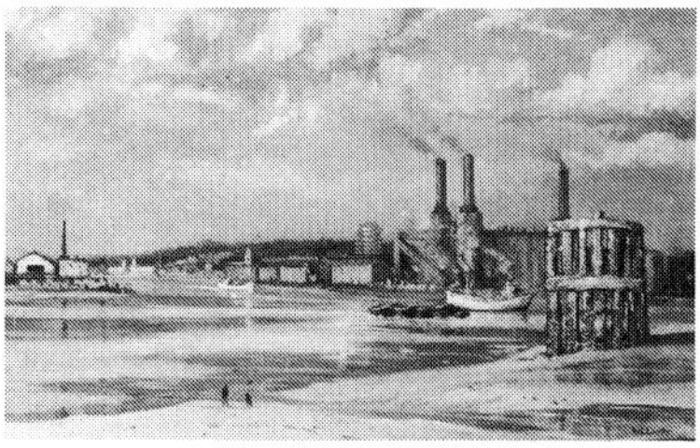

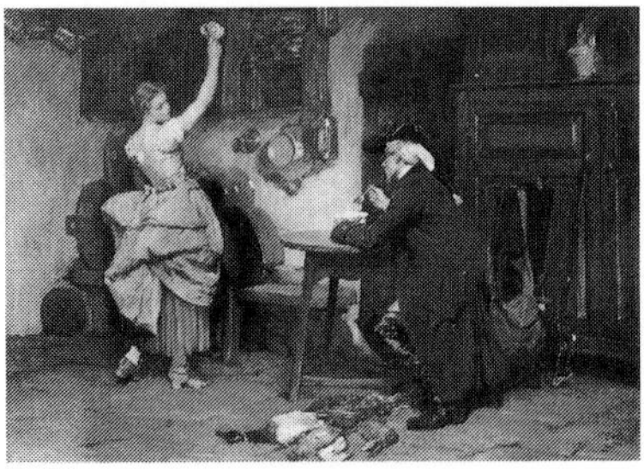

John Seymour Lucas (1849–1923)

acc. no. 297
Flirtation (1885)

oil on canas: 22 × 30 in.
signed and dated: *Seymour Lucas / 1885*
Presented by Henry Clarke, 1886

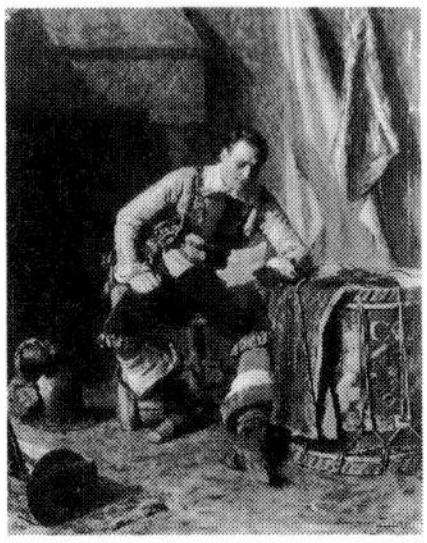

acc. no. 1229
The Standard Bearer (1903)

oil on canvas: $26\frac{3}{8} \times 20\frac{5}{8}$ in.
signed and dated: *Seymour Lucas. / 1903*
Presented by Henry J. Burgess, 1936

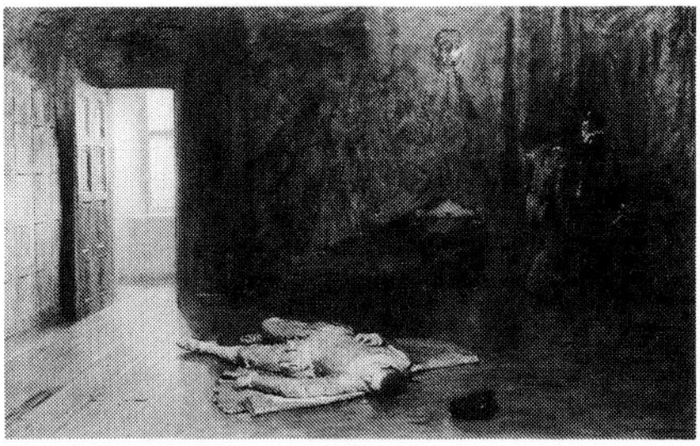

acc. no. 875
Silenced (1908)

oil on canvas: 35 × 56 in.
signed and dated: *Seymour Lucas 1908*
Presented by Alfred F. Bird, 1909

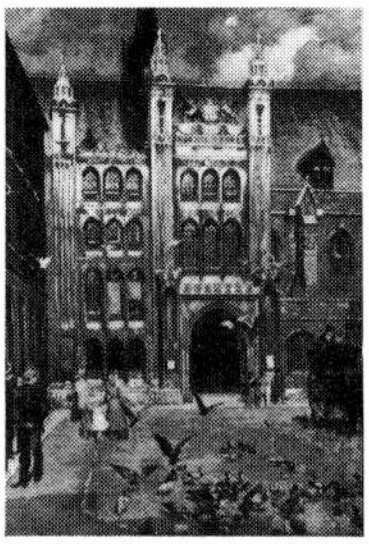

attributed to William Luker Jnr. (b.1867, *fl.* until 1892)

acc. no. 1785
Guildhall from the West Side of Guildhall Yard (*c.*1905)

oil on canvas: 34 × 24 in.
Purchased from R. Richards, 1968

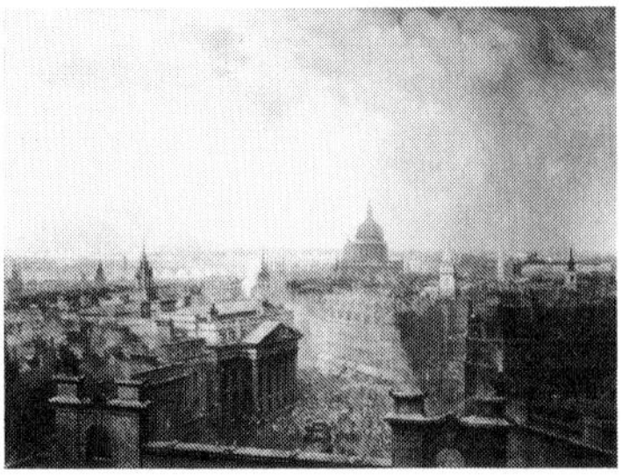

Niels Moeller Lund (1863–1916)

acc. no. 1029
The Heart of the Empire (1904)

oil on canvas: 54 × 72 in.
signed: *Niels M Lund* and signed and dated on verso: *Niels M. Lund pinx. / London 1904*
Bequeathed by Sir William Purdie Treloar, 1923

Robert Walker Macbeth (1848–1910)

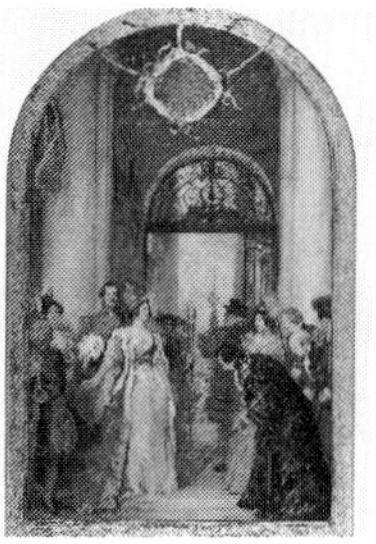

acc. no. 1571
Study for 'The Opening of the Royal Exchange by Queen Victoria, 1844' (*c.*1891)

oil on canvas: $23\frac{1}{8} \times 15\frac{3}{8}$ in.
inscribed: *No hot Iron to be used / in mounting or lining R.W.M.*
Presented by Gresham College, 1959

Charles McCall (b.1907)

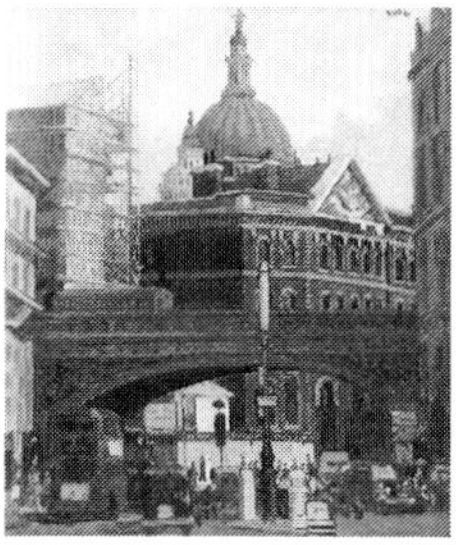

acc. no. 1639
Blackfriars (1962)

oil on canvas: 30 × 25 in.
signed and dated: *McCall '62*
Purchased from the artist, 1962

Andrew MacCallum (1821–1902)

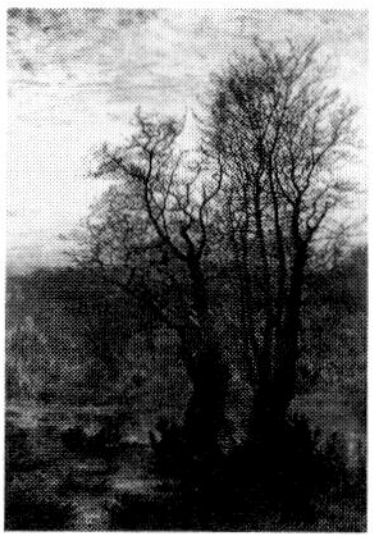

acc. no. 594
Burnham Beeches

watercolour: 51 × 35 in.
signed: *A. MacCallum*
Presented by the artist, 1894

William Alister Macdonald (1861–1948)

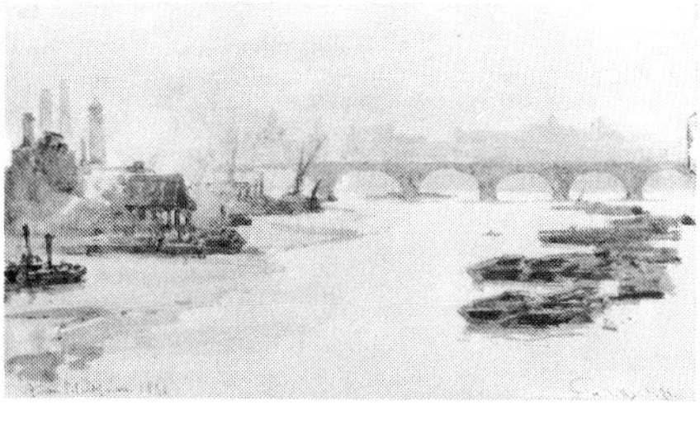

The following 121 watercolours were presented by Lord Wakefield in 1936.

acc. no. 1130
Looking Up-River from Blackfriars (1895)

watercolour over pencil: $5\frac{3}{8} \times 8\frac{3}{4}$ in.
signed and dated: *W.A.M. 1895* and inscribed: *from Blackfriars. 1895.*

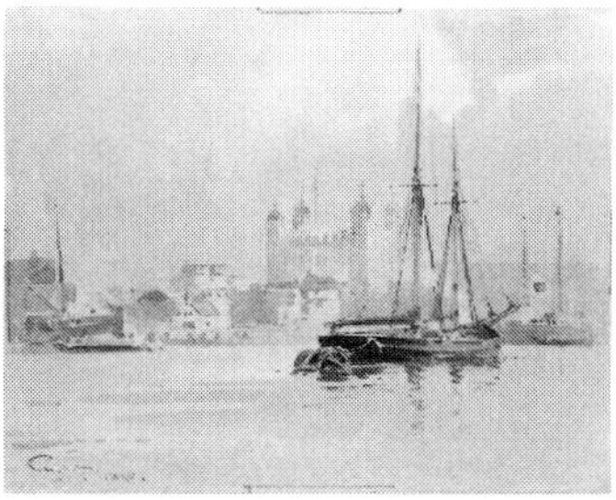

acc. no. 1214
Off the Tower (1895)

watercolour over pencil: $7 \times 8\frac{3}{4}$ in.
signed and dated: *W.A.M. 1895*

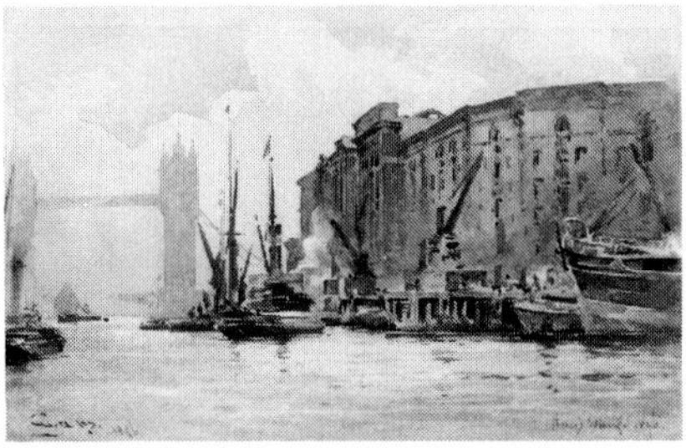

acc. no. 1213
Hay's Wharf (1896)

watercolour over pencil: $5\frac{7}{8} \times 9$ in.
signed and dated: *W.A.M. 1896* and inscribed: *Hay's Wharf. 1896.*

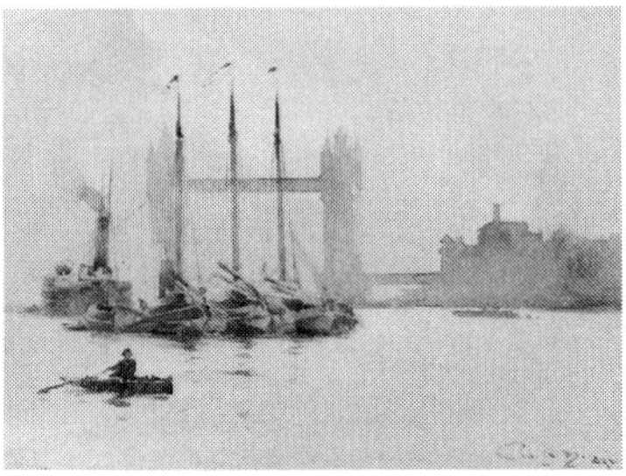

acc. no. 1221
Dutch Eel Boats off Billingsgate (1896)

pencil and watercolour on card: $6\frac{3}{4} \times 9$ in.
signed and dated: *W.A.M. 1896 and dated 1896*

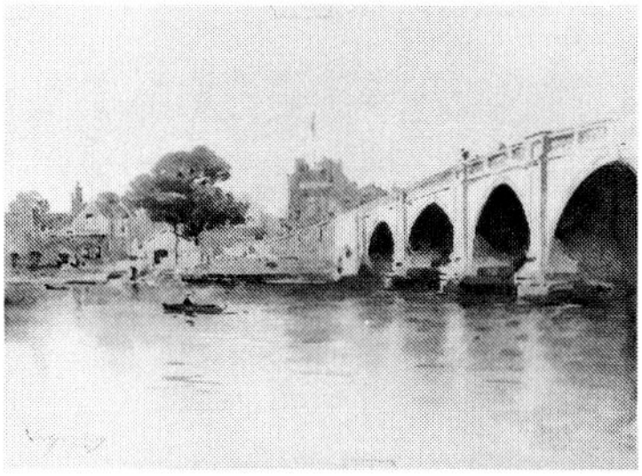

acc. no. 1113
Kew Bridge (1897)

watercolour over pencil: $6\frac{1}{2} \times 9\frac{1}{8}$ in.
signed and dated: *W.A. Macdonald / 97 –* and inscribed: *Kew Bridge / July 97 –*

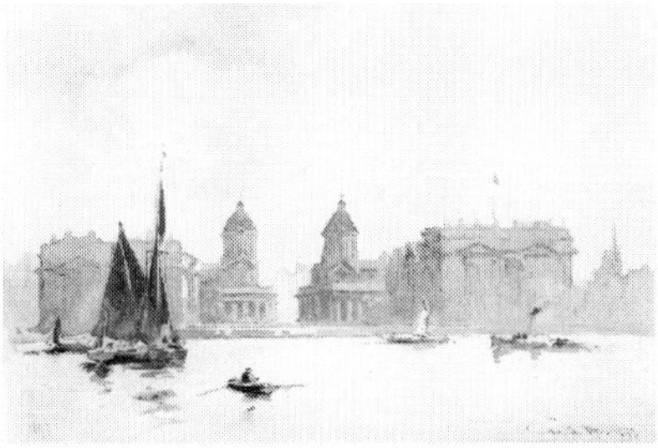

acc. no. 1208
Off Greenwich (1897)

watercolour over pencil: $6\frac{3}{8} \times 9\frac{1}{2}$ in.
signed and dated: *W.A.M. 1897* and dated again *1896*

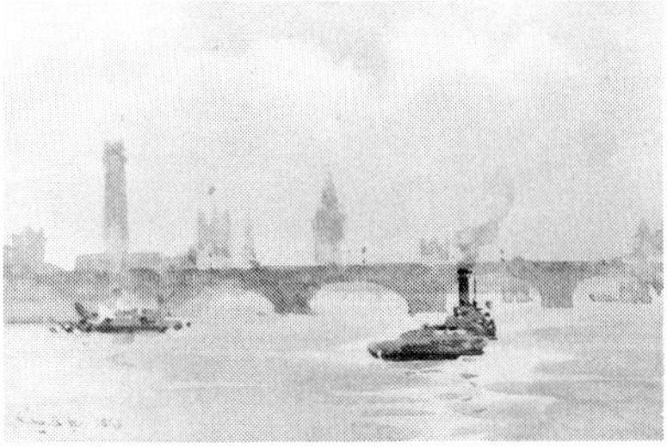

acc. no. 1111
Waterloo Bridge and the River (1898)

watercolour: $5\frac{1}{4} \times 7\frac{3}{8}$ in.
signed and dated: *W.A.M. 1898*

acc. no. 1201
Cannon Street Station from London Bridge (1898)
watercolour over pencil: $5\frac{1}{8} \times 8\frac{1}{4}$ in.
signed and dated: *W.A.M. 1898*; inscribed and dated: *From London Br. / June 23.98 –*

No photograph available

acc. no. 1162
Old Vauxhall Bridge (1898)
watercolour: $6\frac{5}{8} \times 9\frac{5}{8}$ in.
signed and dated: *W.ALISTER MACDONALD. 98*; inscribed on back of former mount: *By Vauxhall Bridge. / May 98* and *£i – ii – T.* (*sic*) and *Old Vauxhall Bridge. / 1898*

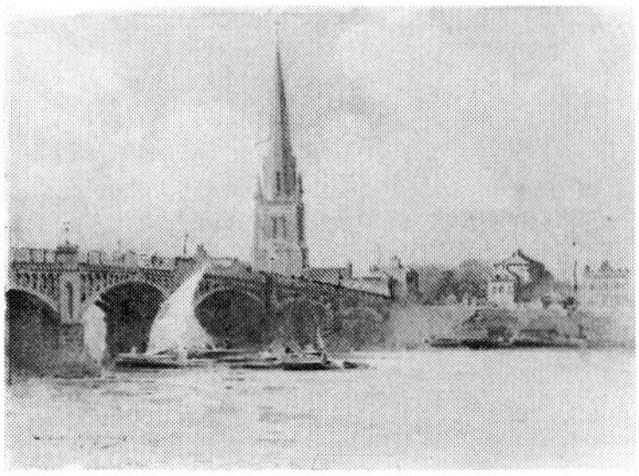

acc. no. 1153
Temporary Bridge, Vauxhall (1899)
watercolour: $9\frac{3}{4} \times 14$ in.
signed and dated: *W.A. Macdonald – / 1899 –* ; signed again and dated: *W.A.M. 1902. / W.A.M.* and inscribed: *Temporary Bridge. Vauxhall. 1902*

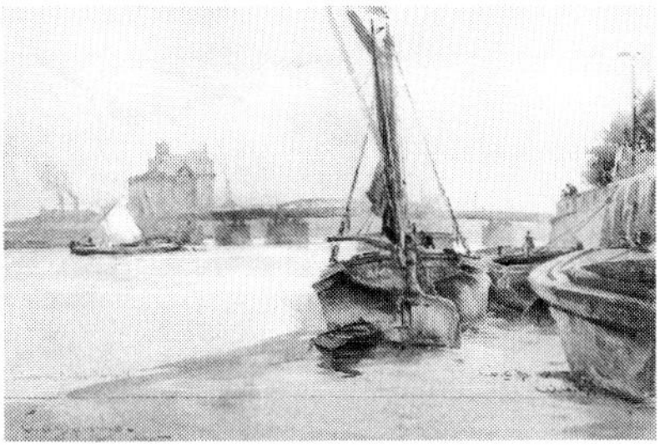

acc. no. 1198
Holywell Street, Strand (1899)
watercolour: $8\frac{1}{2} \times 5\frac{1}{2}$ in.
dated *1899*; signed and dated: *W.A.M. 1902*; inscribed: *Holywell St. 1902*

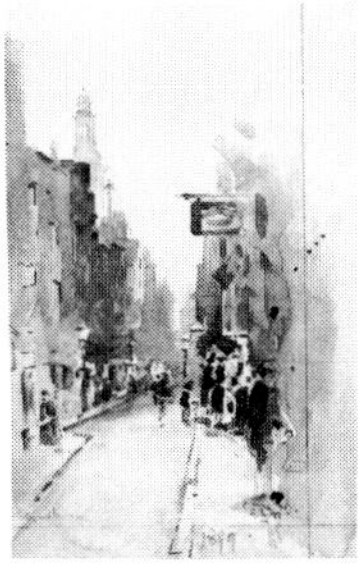

acc. no. 1203
Lincoln's Inn Fields (1899)
pencil and watercolour: $4\frac{3}{4} \times 8\frac{1}{8}$ in.
signed and dated: *W.A.M. 1899*; inscribed: *Lincolns Inn / Fields – Mar 99*

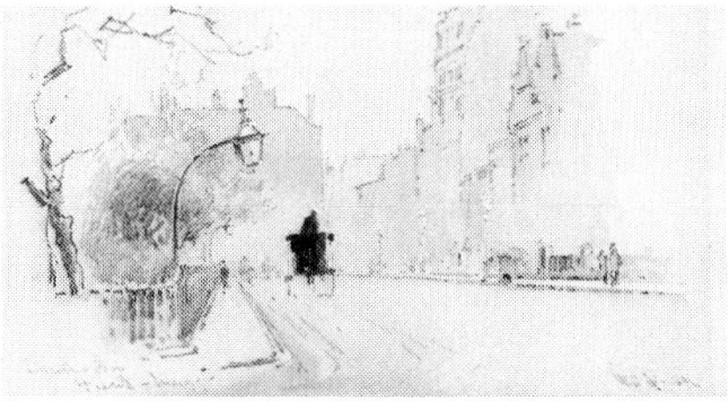

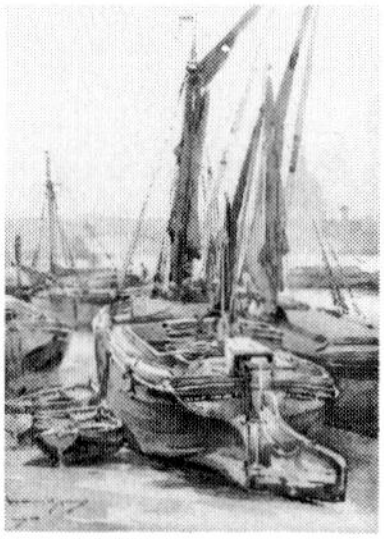

acc. no. 1192
Thames Barges, Low Tide, Bankside (1899)
watercolour: $9\frac{3}{4} \times 6\frac{3}{4}$ in.
signed and dated: *W. ALISTER MACDONALD / 1899–*; inscribed on back of former mount: *Thames Barges. / Low Tide / Bankside. / 1899*

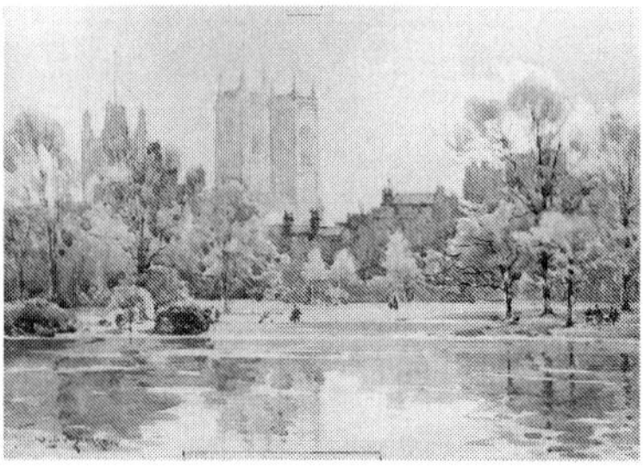

acc. no. 1156
Spring Time, St. James's Park (1900)
watercolour over pencil: $7\frac{1}{8} \times 10\frac{1}{2}$ in.
signed and dated: *W.A.M. 1900*

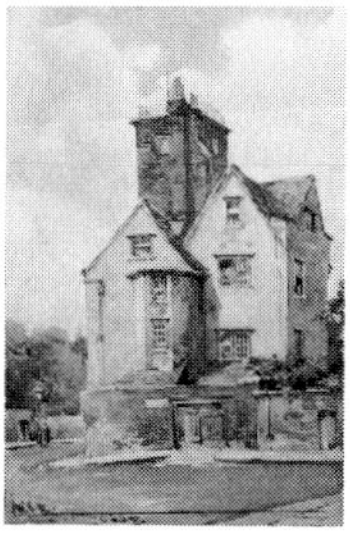

acc. no. 1195
Canonbury Tower, Islington (1900)
watercolour: $11 \times 7\frac{1}{8}$ in.
signed (twice): *W.A.M.* and inscribed: *Canonbury Tower*

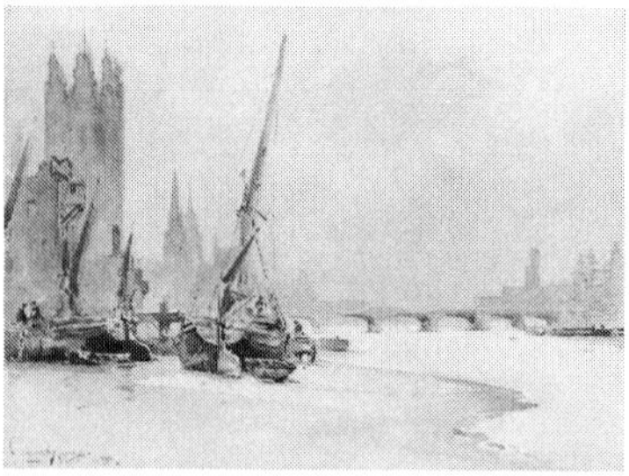

acc. no. 1123
Low Tide and Barges, Millbank (1901)
watercolour over pencil: $6\frac{3}{4} \times 9$ in.
signed and dated: *W. ALISTER MACDONALD. / 1901*

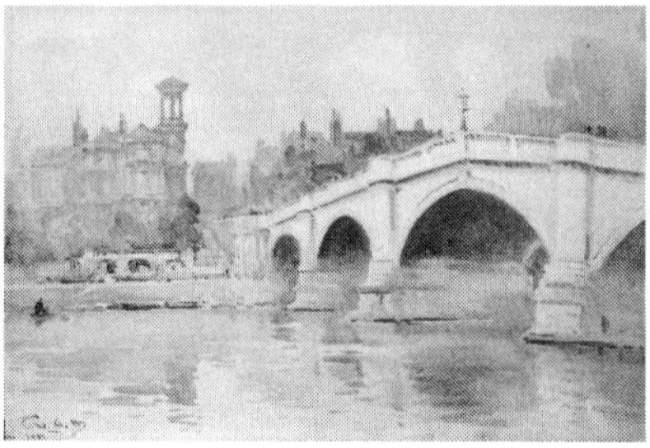

acc. no. 1128
Old Richmond Bridge (1901)
watercolour on card: $7\frac{1}{4} \times 10\frac{1}{2}$ in.
signed (over a faint earlier signature) and dated: *W.A.M. / 1901*; inscribed on verso: *£N.N.P.* and *Old Richmond Bridge / 1900* (*sic.*)

acc. no. 1138
St Mary at Hill and the Tower of St Margaret Pattens (1902)

watercolour: $10\frac{3}{4} \times 5$ in.
signed and dated (below level of former mount): *W. ALISTER MACDONALD / 1902*; second signature over this; signed and dated above level of former mount: *W.A.M. 1908* (?)

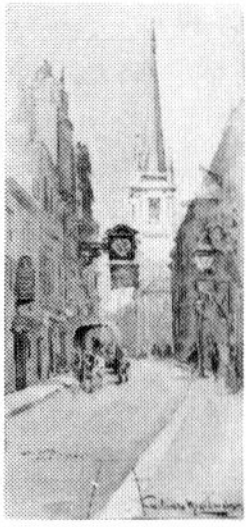

acc. no. 1180
The Pool of London and Tower Bridge from Cherry Garden Pier (1902)

watercolour over pencil: $7 \times 10\frac{1}{4}$ in.
signed and dated: *W.A.M. 1902* and inscribed: *The Pool. 1902.*

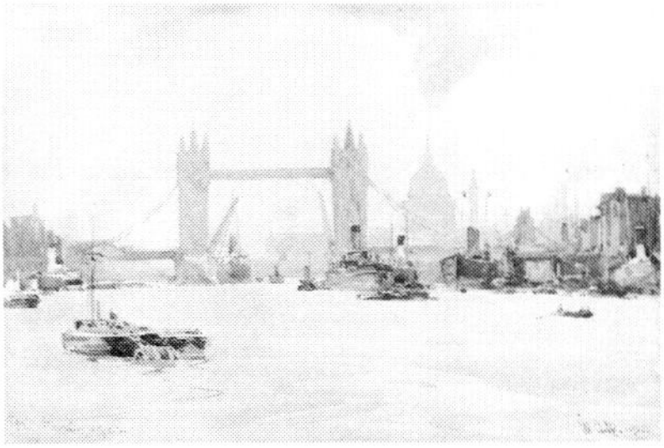

acc. no. 1223
Fleet Street (1902)

watercolour and pencil: $9\frac{1}{4} \times 5\frac{3}{4}$ in.
signed and dated: *W.A.M. / 1902* and inscribed: *Fleet St. 1902.*

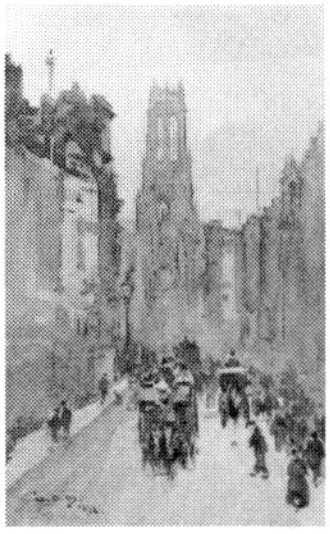

acc. no. 1152
Clifford's Inn (1903)

watercolour: $9\frac{1}{2} \times 7\frac{1}{4}$ in.
signed and dated: *W.A.M. 1903* and inscribed: *Cliffords Inn / 1903*

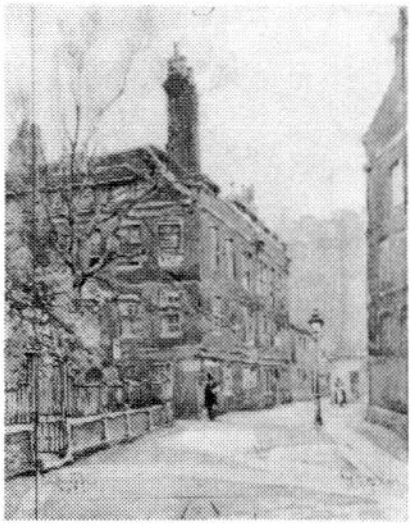

acc. no. 1164
Watergate, Buckingham Street (1903)

watercolour over pencil on Newman's Artist Drawing Tablet: $10\frac{1}{2} \times 7\frac{1}{4}$ in.
signed and dated: *W.A.M. / 1903*; inscribed: *Water Gate. / Buckingham St. / 1903.*; inscribed on verso: *Water Gate. Buckingham St Strand / 1903*

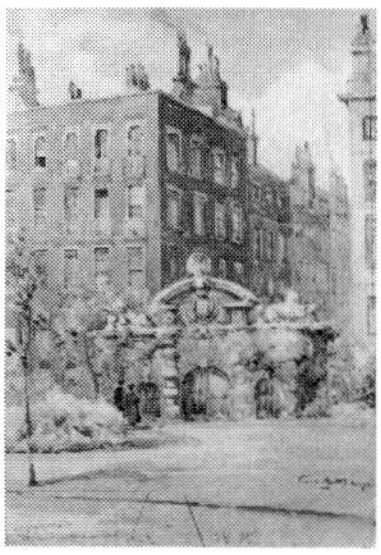

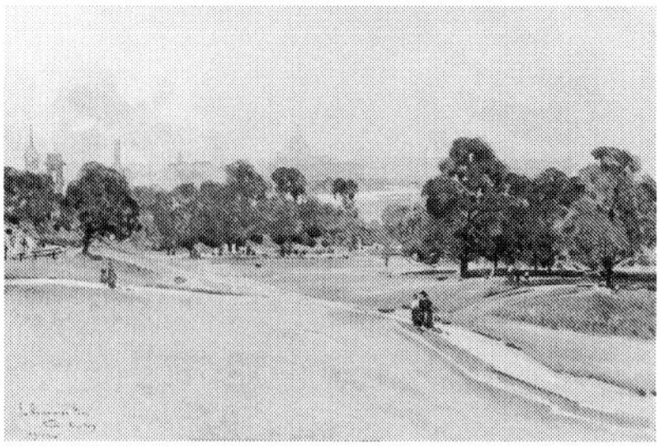

acc. no. 1170
London From Greenwich Park (1904)

watercolour: $6\frac{1}{8} \times 8\frac{7}{8}$ in.
inscribed, signed and dated: *In Greenwich Park. / W.A.M. / 1904*

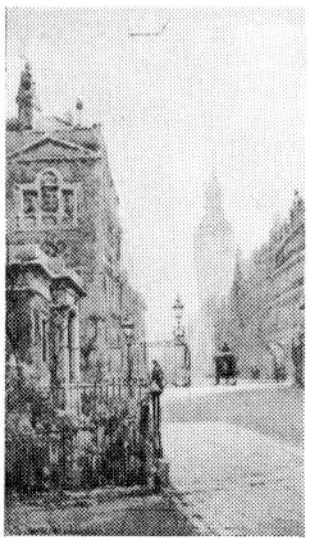

acc. no. 1135
Storey's Gate, Westminster (1904)

watercolour over pencil: $10\frac{3}{4} \times 6\frac{1}{4}$ in.
signed (below level of former mount) *W. Alister Macdonald*; signed and dated (above level of mount): *W.A.M. 1904.*

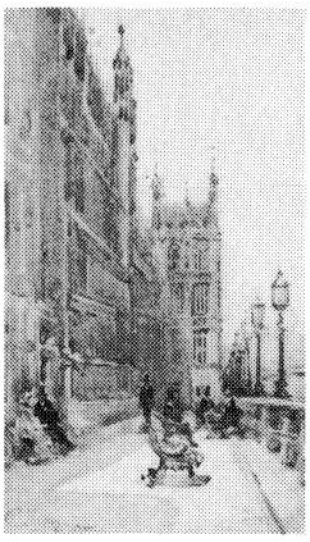

acc. no. 1163
The Terrace, House of Commons (1904)

watercolour: $7\frac{1}{2} \times 4\frac{1}{2}$ in.
signed and dated: *W.A.M. 1904.*

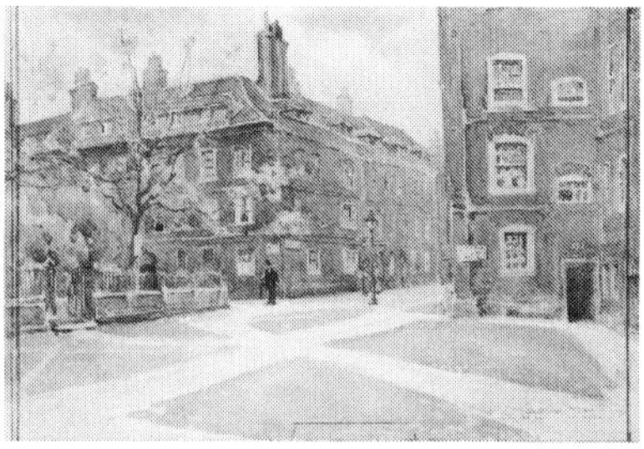

acc. no. 1143
Clifford's Inn, Fleet Street (1904)

watercolour over pencil: $7\frac{1}{8} \times 10\frac{3}{4}$ in.
signed, inscribed and dated: *W. ALISTER MACDONALD/Cliffords Inn 1904.*; inscribed partly trimmed, on border of mount: (Cli)*ffords Inn*

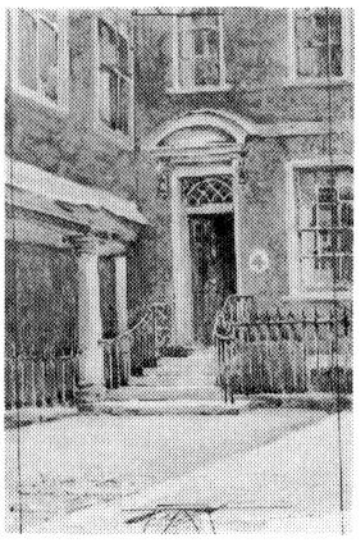

acc. no. 1200
Field Court, Gray's Inn (1904)

watercolour over pencil: $10\frac{3}{4} \times 7\frac{1}{8}$ in.
Inscribed, signed and dated: *Field Court. Grays Inn. / W. ALISTER MACDONALD 1904*

acc. no. 1209
Temple from the River (1904)

watercolour: $6\frac{5}{8} \times 9$ in.
signed and dated: *W.A.M. / 1904* and
inscribed: *Temple.from River / 1904*

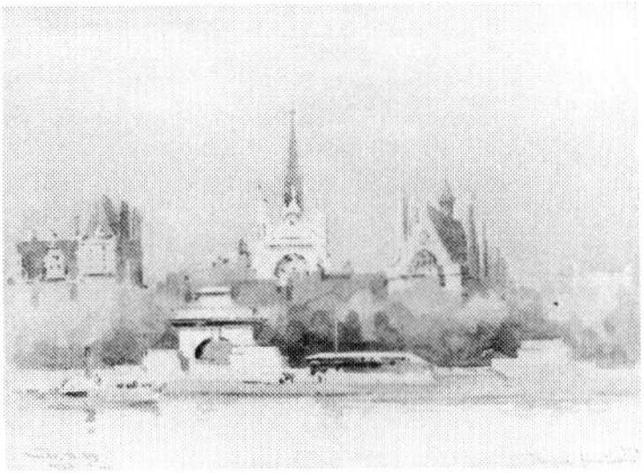

acc. no. 1206
In Middle Temple Lane (1904)

watercolour: $10\frac{1}{2} \times 7$ in.
signed and dated (below level of former mount): *W.A. MACDONALD / 1904. TEMPLE* and *W.A.M. 1904.*; signed and dated (above mount level): *W.A.M. / 1905* (*sic.*); inscribed on verso of mount (trimmed): (O)*ld London / . . .mple to Upper River*

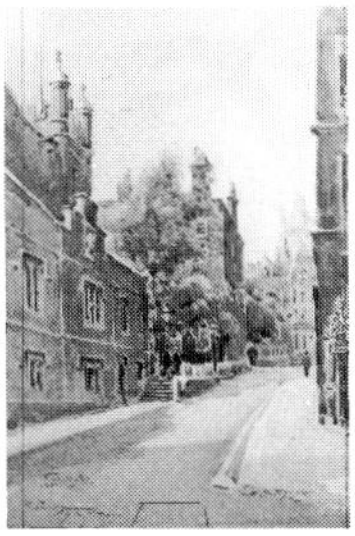

acc. no. 1107
The 'Steam Packet' Public House and Fish Street Hill (1904)

watercolour: $10 \times 6\frac{1}{4}$ in.
signed and dated: *W.A.M. 1904* and inscribed: *Fish St Hill. 1904*

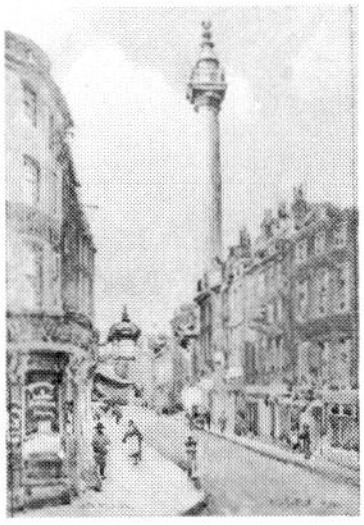

acc. no. 1216
Straw Barges, Bankside (1904)

watercolour on Newman's Artist Drawing Tablet: $14\frac{1}{2} \times 10\frac{1}{2}$ in.
signed and dated: *W. Alister Macdonald. 1904*

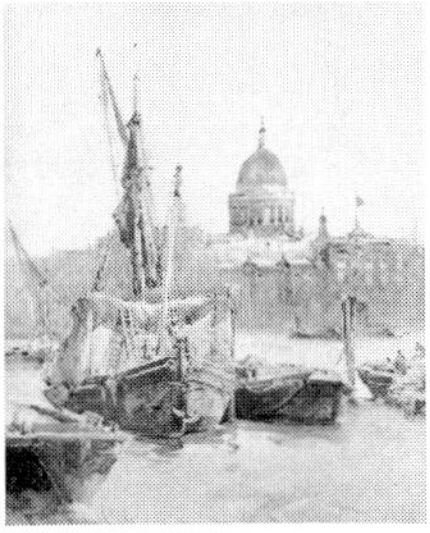

acc. no. 1191
St Paul's from Bankside (1904)

watercolour: $9\frac{3}{4} \times 6\frac{3}{4}$ in. (sight)
signed: *W.A.M.* and inscribed: *Bankside. 1904.*

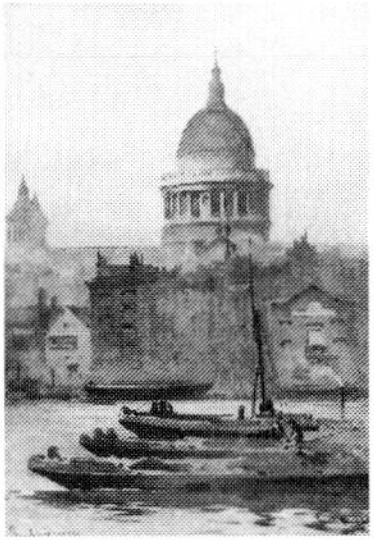

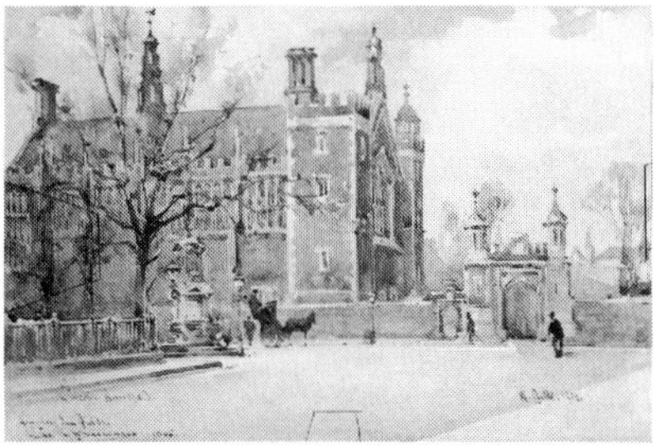

acc. no. 1173
Lincoln's Inn Hall and Gateway (1905)

watercolour over pencil: $6\frac{7}{8} \times 10\frac{1}{4}$ in.
inscribed, signed and dated (below level of former mount): *Lincoln's Inn Fields. / W.A. Macdonald 1905*; signed and dated (above mount level): *W.A.M. 1903* and inscribed: *Lincoln's Inn.1903*

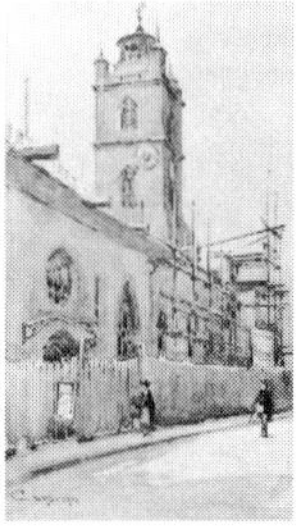

acc. no. 1211
Restoration of St. Giles Cripplegate (1905)

watercolour: $10 \times 5\frac{5}{8}$ in.
signed and dated: *W.A.M. 1905*

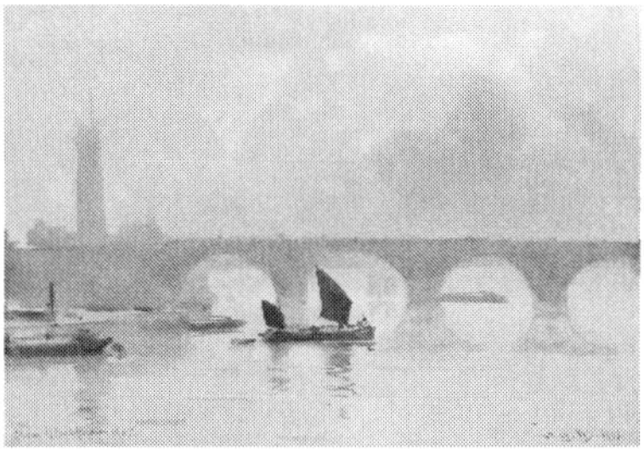

acc. no. 1142
Waterloo Bridge and Shot Tower from Blackfriars (1905)

watercolour: $7\frac{3}{8} \times 10\frac{3}{4}$ in.
signed and dated: *W.A.M. 1905* and inscribed: *From Blackfriars 1905*

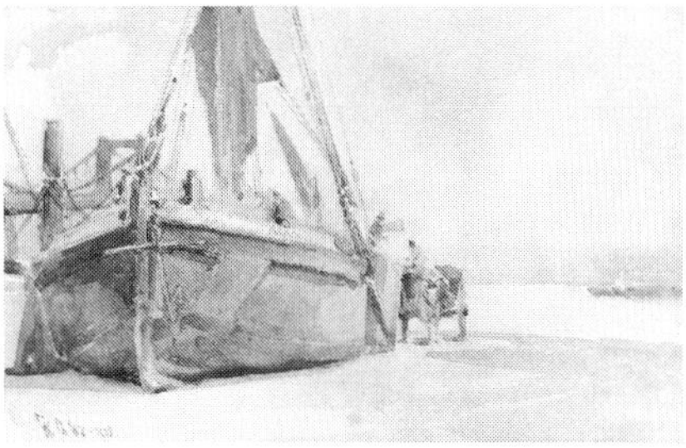

acc. no. 1217
The Barge 'Alacrity' unloading at Low Water (1905)

watercolour: $9\frac{1}{4} \times 12\frac{7}{8}$ in.
signed and dated: *W.A.M. 1905.*

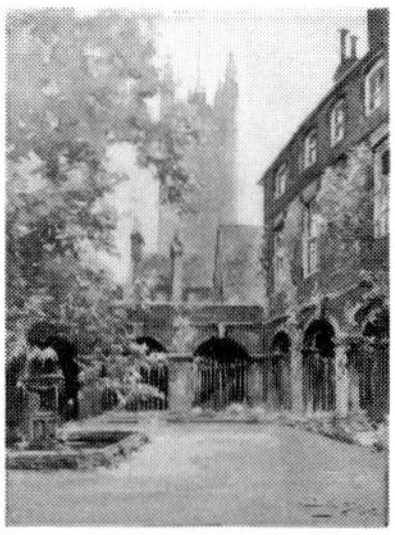

acc. no. 1227
Little Cloister, Westminster (1905)

watercolour: $12\frac{5}{8} \times 9\frac{1}{2}$ in.
signed and dated: *W.A.M. / 1905*; inscribed on verso of mount: *Little Cloister. / Westminster Abbey* and *£7*

acc. no. 1146
Foreshore by Westminster Bridge, Whitehall Court in the Distance (1905)

watercolour: $8 \times 12\frac{7}{8}$ in.
signed and dated: *W. Alister Macdonald. / 1905*; inscribed in verso of former mount: *Foreshore by Westr. Bridge – / Whitehall Court in distance / 1906* (*sic.*)

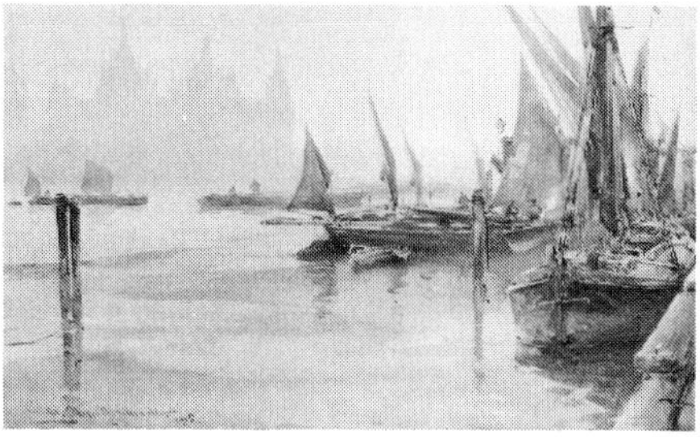

acc. no. 1121
Riverside at Westminster (1905)

watercolour: $8\frac{3}{4} \times 14\frac{1}{8}$ in.
signed and dated: *W. Alister Macdonald, 1905*

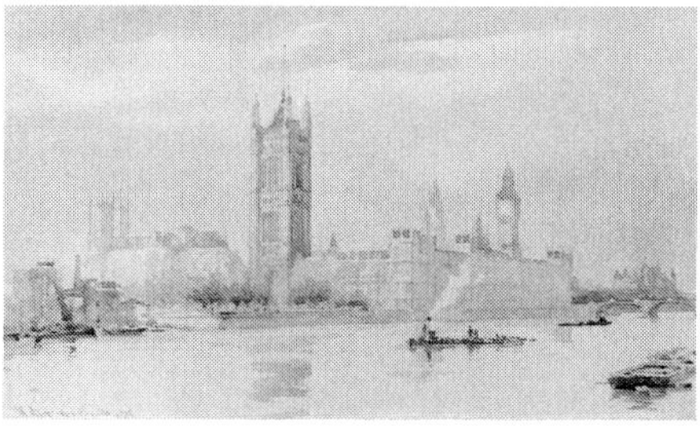

acc. no. 1134
Cloth Fair and 'Dick Whittington' Inn (1905)

watercolour: $11\frac{1}{4} \times 7\frac{1}{4}$ in.
signed: *W.A.M.* and inscribed and dated: *1905 Old Cloth Fair*

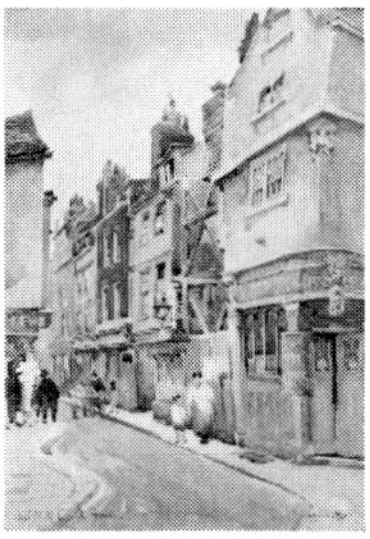

acc. no. 1186
Old Smithy Yard by St. Bartholomew's Church (1905)

watercolour: $14\frac{1}{8} \times 9\frac{7}{8}$ in.
signed and dated: *W.A.M. 1905* and inscribed: *Old yard. St Barts / & Smithy.*

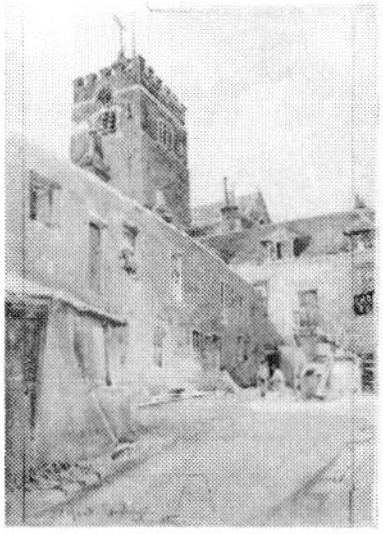

acc. no. 1215
Entrance to St Bartholomew the Great (1906)

watercolour: $7\frac{1}{8} \times 10\frac{1}{2}$ in.
signed and dated: *W. ALISTER MACDONALD.1906* and inscribed: *SMITHFIELD. 1906*

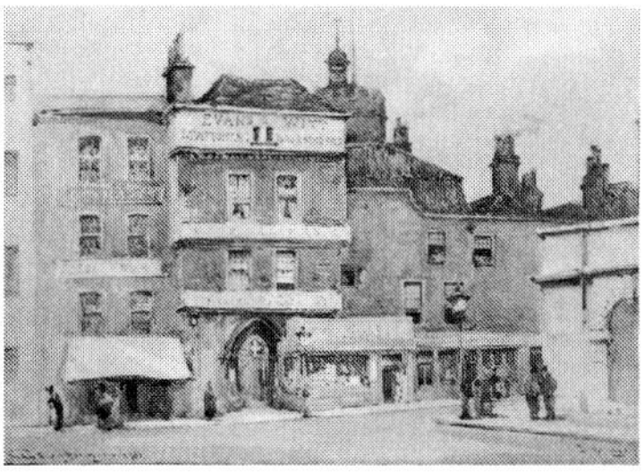

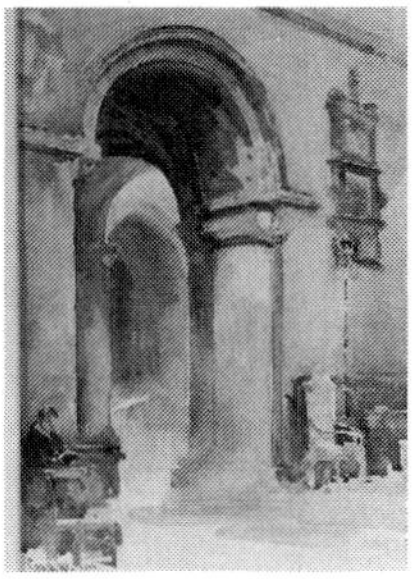

acc. no. 1120
In St. Bartholomew's Church (1906)

watercolour over pencil: 13 × 9 in.
signed and dated: *W.A.M. 1906.* and inscribed: *St. Barts – Smithfield.*

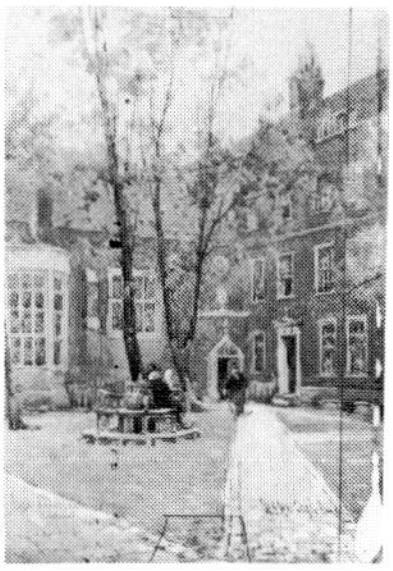

acc. no. 1137
Staple Inn Courtyard (1906)

watercolour: $11\frac{1}{4} \times 7\frac{3}{4}$ in.
signed: *W.A.M. Staple Inn* and dated: *Staple Inn.1906*

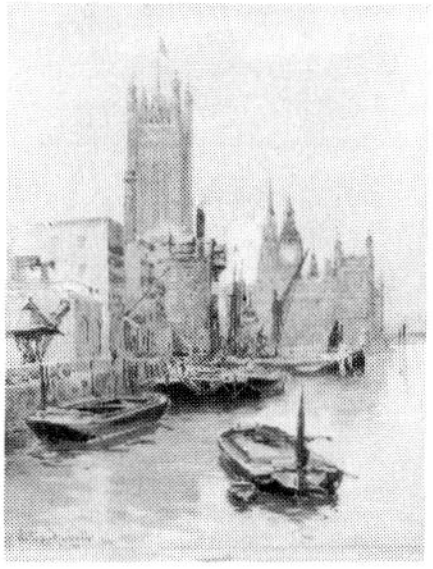

acc. no. 1122
Old Millbank (1906)

watercolour: $14\frac{1}{4} \times 10\frac{1}{2}$ in.
signed and dated: *W. Alister Macdonald. 1906.*

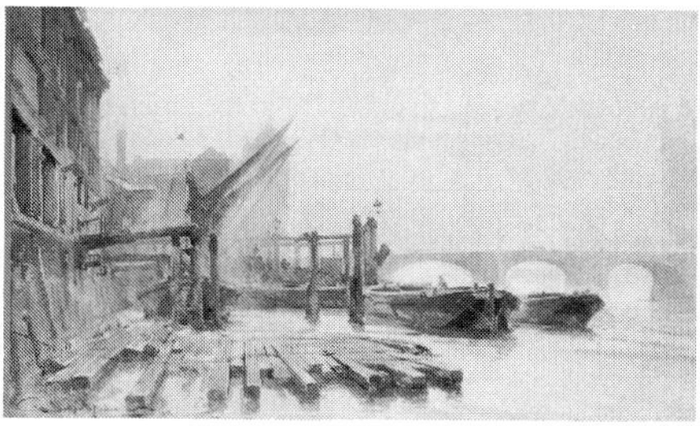

acc. no. 1148
Timber Wharf and Dust Shoot – Site of County Hall (1906)

watercolour: $9\frac{5}{8} \times 16$ in.
signed and dated: *W. Alister Macdonald. 1906*; inscribed on former mount: *by Old Westr. Bridge. (Site of new County Hall.)*; inscribed on back of former mount: *By Westminster Bridge.* (crossed out) *See list. / Site of new Lon. County Hall / 1906*

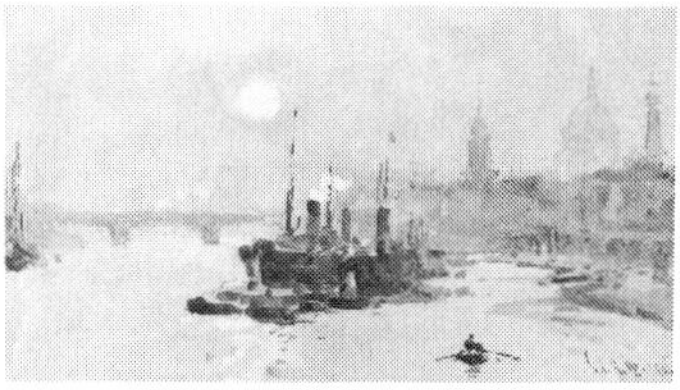

acc. no. 1220
The Upper Pool at Sunset (1906)

watercolour, bodycolour and pencil: $4\frac{1}{2} \times 7\frac{7}{8}$ in.
signed and dated: *W.A.M. 1906*

acc. no. 1155
Looking Down-River from Old Lambeth Bridge (1906)

watercolour: 9 × $14\frac{1}{8}$ in.
signed and dated: *W. Alister Macdonald / 1906.*

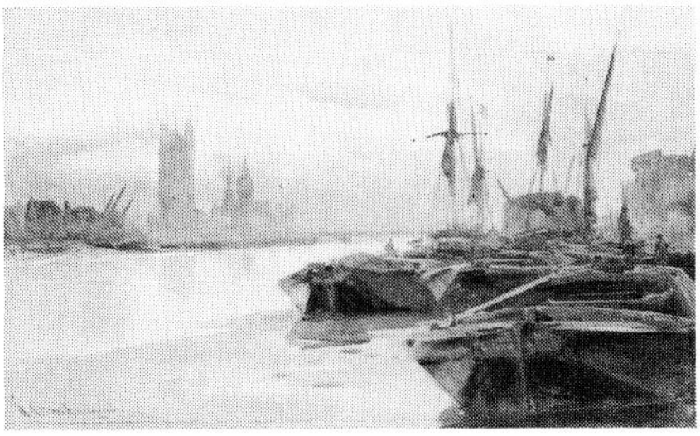

acc. no. 1168
Old Lambeth Bridge (1906?)

watercolour: $5\frac{1}{4}$ × $8\frac{7}{8}$ in.
signed: *W.A.M.* and dated: *Old Lambeth Bridge / 1906* (?)

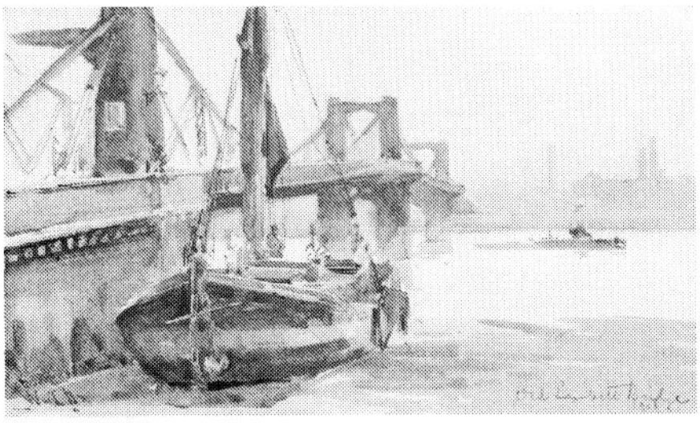

acc. no. 1183
Old Palace Yard, Westminster (1906)

watercolour: $9\frac{7}{8}$ × $7\frac{1}{2}$ in.
inscribed and signed: *Old Palace yard. Westr. / W. ALISTER MACDONALD.* and dated: *Mar. 1906*

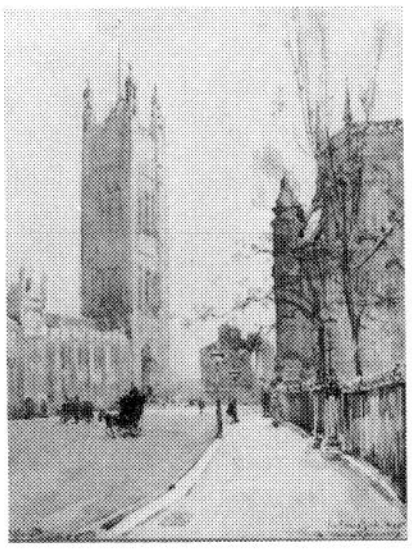

acc. no. 1222
Clifford's Inn, Fleet Street (1906)

watercolour on Newman's Artist Drawing Tablet: $10\frac{1}{2}$ × $7\frac{1}{4}$ in.
signed and dated: *W.A.M. / 1906* and inscribed and signed: *Cliffords Inn Fleet St. / 1906. / W. ALISTER MACDONALD*

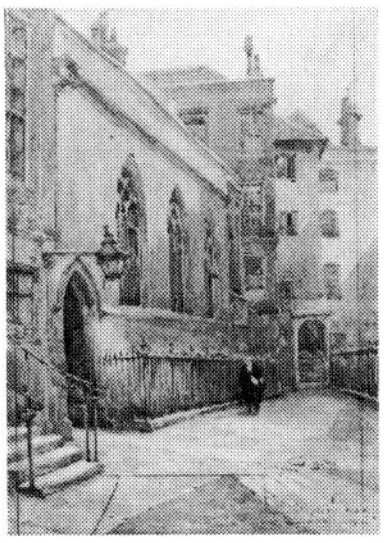

acc. no. 1154
Abingdon Street, Westminster (1907)

watercolour: $7\frac{5}{8}$ × $9\frac{3}{4}$ in.
signed: *W. Alister Macdonald* and inscribed and dated: *Old Abingdon St Westr. / 1907*; and again on back of former mount

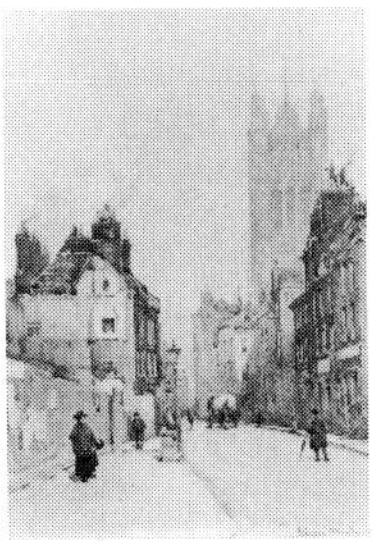

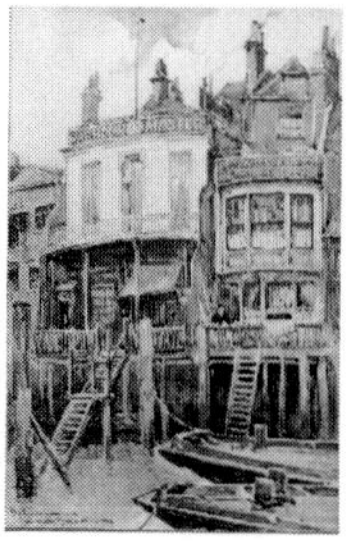

acc. no. 1133
Old Houses, Limehouse (1907)
watercolour: $9\frac{7}{8} \times 6\frac{1}{4}$ in.
signed, dated and inscribed: *Old Houses, Limehouse / W. Alister Macdonald. 1907*; inscribed on back of former mount: *Old Inn &c. / Bankside Limehouse / 1907*

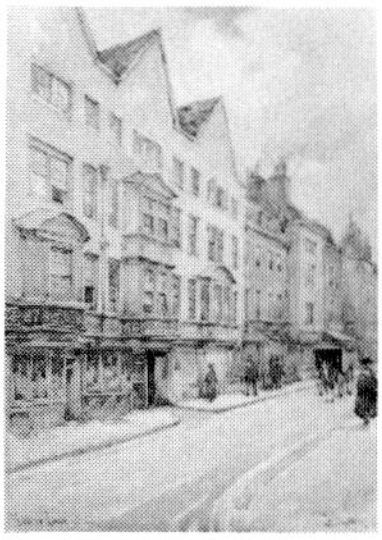

acc. no. 1108
Old Houses in Fetter Lane (1907)
watercolour: 10×7 in.
signed: *W.A.M.* and inscribed and dated: *Fetter Lane. E.C. / 1907*; inscribed on back of former mount: *Old Houses / Fetter lane. 1907 / Pulled down 1910*

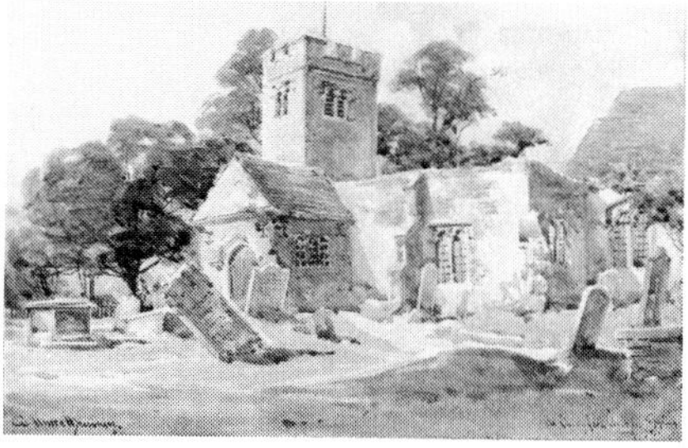

acc. no. 1116
Old Chingford Church (1907)
watercolour: $6\frac{1}{8} \times 9\frac{1}{2}$ in. (sight)
signed: *W. ALISTER MACDONALD.* and inscribed and dated: *Old Chingford Church. Epping. / Aug.1907*

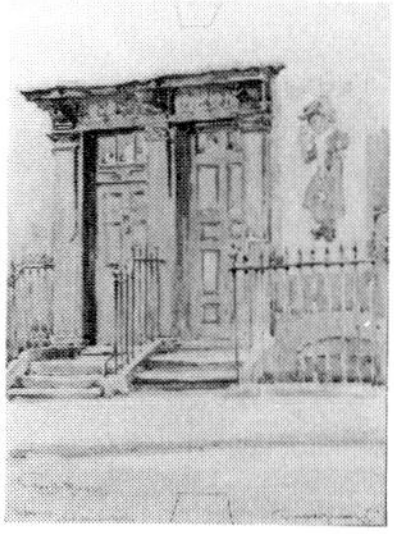

acc. no. 1176
Old Doorways, Little Britain (1907)
watercolour: $10\frac{3}{4} \times 7\frac{1}{2}$ in.
signed and dated: *W.A.M. 1907.* and *W. ALISTER MACDONALD. 1907.* and inscribed: *Old Doorways. / Little Britain. Smithfield*

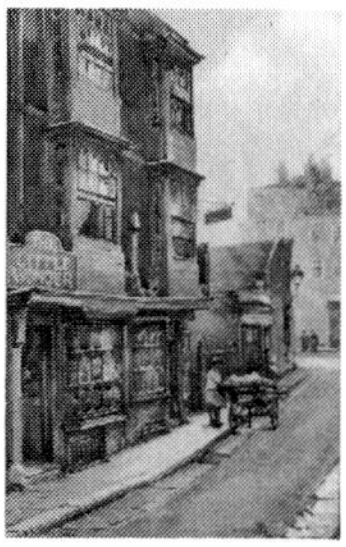

acc. no. 1129
The 'little Wonder' Eating House, Smithfield (1907)
watercolour: $10\frac{1}{2} \times 6\frac{5}{8}$ in. (sight)
signed: *W. Alister Macdonald* and inscribed and dated: *By Cloth Fair. / SMITHFIELD. 1907*

acc. no. 1136
St Bartholomew's Gate, Smithfield (1907)

watercolour: $11 \times 7\frac{1}{8}$ in.
signed and dated: *W.A.M. / 1907.* and
W. ALISTER MACDONALD. 1907. and
inscribed: *SMITHFIELD*

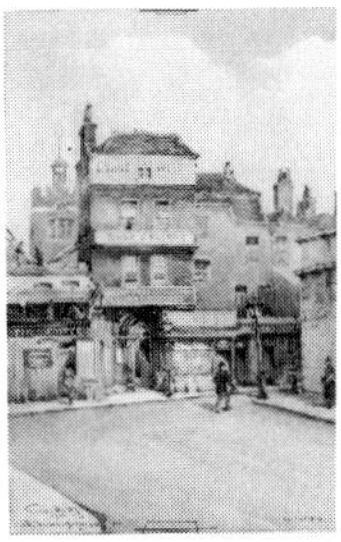

acc. no. 1193
Behind Cloth Fair and St Bartholomew the Great (1907)

watercolour: $10\frac{7}{8} \times 7\frac{1}{8}$ in.
signed: *W.A.M.* and dated: *1907.* and inscribed and dated: *Behind / Cloth Fair. & St Bart's Ch. / 1907.*

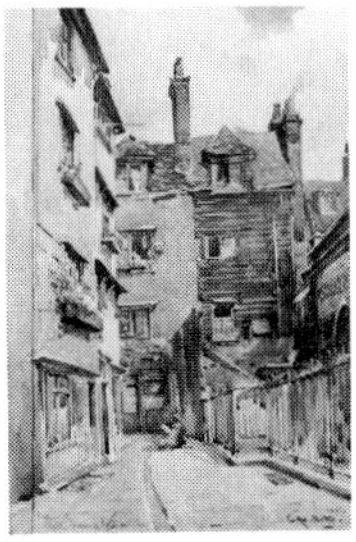

acc. no. 1105
Entrance to St. Bartholomew's Hospital, St Bartholomew the Great Beyond

watercolour: $9\frac{3}{8} \times 6\frac{3}{4}$ in. (sight)
signed and dated: *W.A.M. / 1908.* and: *W. Alister Macdonald.* and inscribed and dated: *Smithfield. / 1908.*; inscribed on verso: *Smithfield / 1908 and Old / London*

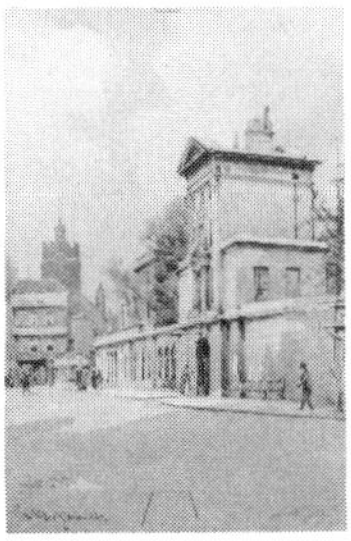

acc. no. 1117
St Bartholomew the Great and Old Cloth Fair (1908)

watercolour: $15 \times 10\frac{7}{8}$ in.
signed and dated: *W.A.M. / 1908* and inscribed: *St. Barts & Old Cloth Fair.*; inscribed on back of former mount: *St Bartholomew. / & Old Cloth Fair. / 1908*

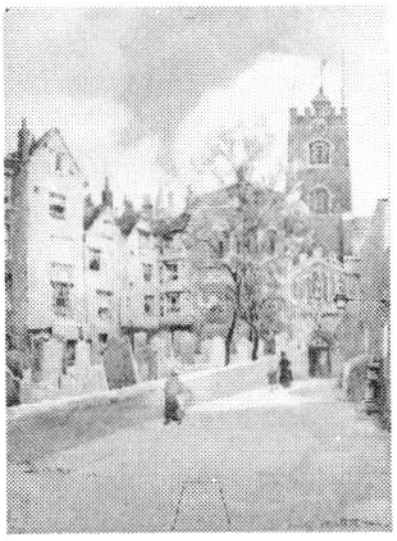

acc. no. 1149
Cloth Fair, Smithfield (1908)

watercolour: $9\frac{7}{8} \times 6\frac{1}{2}$ in.
signed and dated: *W.A.M. 1908* and inscribed and dated: *Cloth fair.1908.*

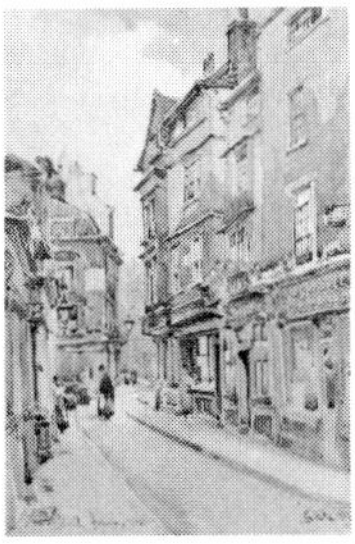

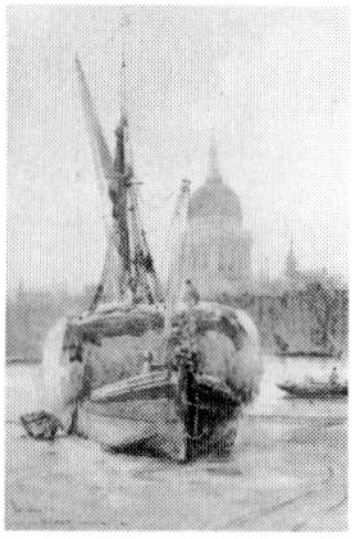

acc. no. 1104
Straw Barge, Bankside (1908)
watercolour on card: $9\frac{7}{8} \times 6\frac{3}{8}$ in.
inscribed, signed and dated: *Bankside. / W. Alister Macdonald. 1908.*; inscribed on verso: *Straw barge / on the mud – Bankside. / 1908.*

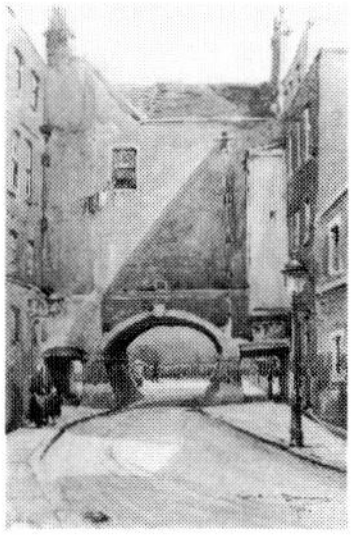

acc. no. 1126
Old Archway, Sardinia Street (1908)
watercolour: $10\frac{1}{2} \times 6\frac{3}{4}$ in. (sight)
signed and dated: *W. ALISTER MACDONALD. / 1908.*

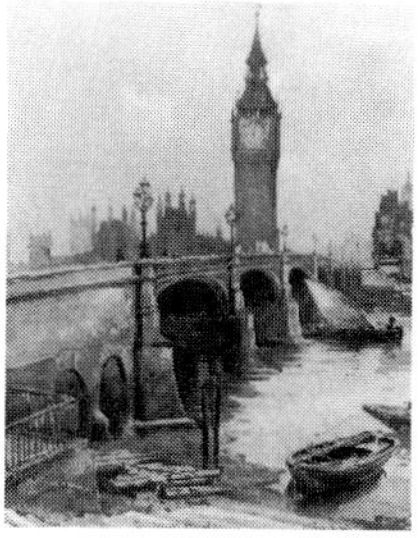

acc. no. 1184
By Westminster Bridge (1908)
watercolour on card: $12\frac{1}{4} \times 9\frac{1}{4}$ in. (sight)
signed and dated: *W.A.M. 1908.* and inscribed: *By Westr. Bridge. / 1908*

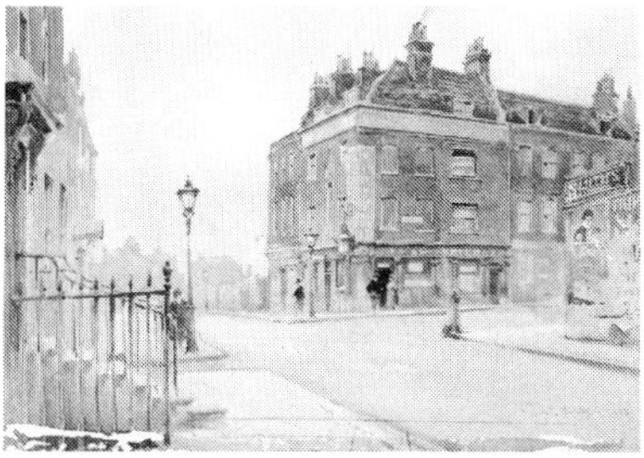

acc. no. 1144
The 'Jolly Miller' Public House, Millbank (1908)
watercolour on Newman's Artist Drawing Board: $9\frac{7}{8} \times 14\frac{1}{2}$ in.
signed and dated: *W.A.M. 1908.* and inscribed: *"The Jolly Miller"* and with measurements; inscribed on back of former mount: *The "Jolly Miller" – / & old Houses. Millbank 1908*

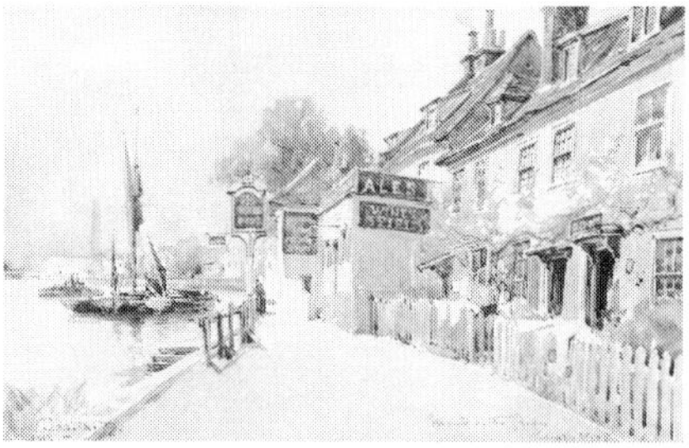

acc. no. 1160
Strand-on-the Green, Kew (1908)
watercolour: $6\frac{3}{4} \times 10\frac{1}{2}$ in. (sight)
signed and dated: *W.A.M. / 1908* – and inscribed and dated: *Strand on the Green / Kew – 1908* and again on back of former mount: *Strand on the Green. Kew. / 1908*

acc. no. 1224
Old Doorway, Crutched Friars (1908)
watercolour: $10\frac{1}{2} \times 5\frac{1}{4}$ in.
signed and dated: *W.A.M. / 1908*

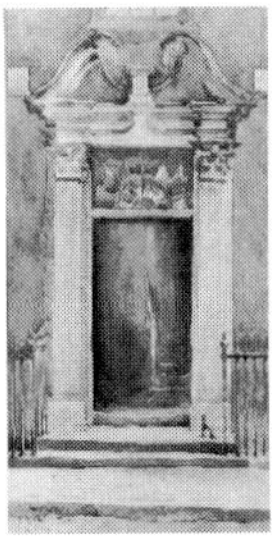

acc. no. 1165
Ludgate Hill, Bank Holiday Morning (1908)
watercolour: $10\frac{7}{8} \times 7$ in.
signed and dated: *W.A.M. / 1908.* and *W. Alister Macdonald* and inscribed: *Holiday morning / Ludgate Hill*; inscribed on back of former mount: *Holiday morning / Ludgate Hill – 1908*

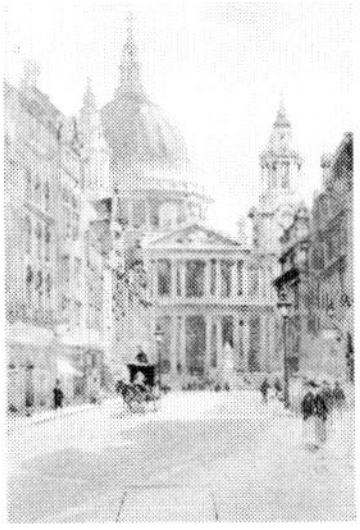

acc. no. 1188
Brick Court, Temple (1908)
watercolour: $11 \times 7\frac{1}{2}$ in.
signed: *W.A.M.* and inscribed and dated: *Brick Court. Temple. 1908.* and inscribed on back of former mount: *Middle Temple & Brick Court / Before restoration 1908*

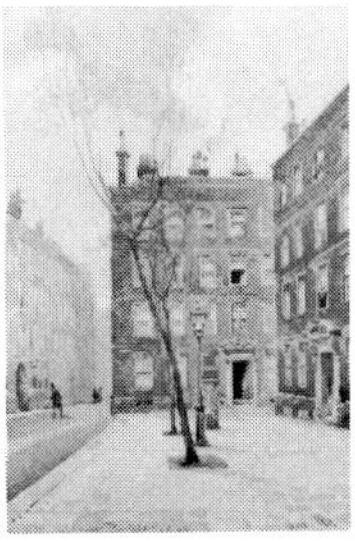

acc. no. 1161
The Shot Tower from Westminster Bridge (1908)
watercolour: $6\frac{1}{8} \times 9\frac{1}{4}$ in. (sight)
signed and inscribed: *from Westminster Bridge. / W. ALISTER MACDONALD.*

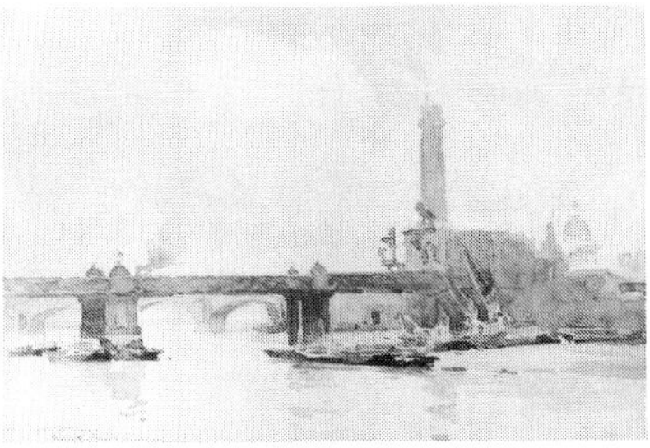

acc. no. 1175
Surrey End of Westminster Bridge, Looking Up-River (1908)
watercolour: $7\frac{1}{8} \times 9\frac{3}{4}$ in.
signed: *W. Alister Macdonald*

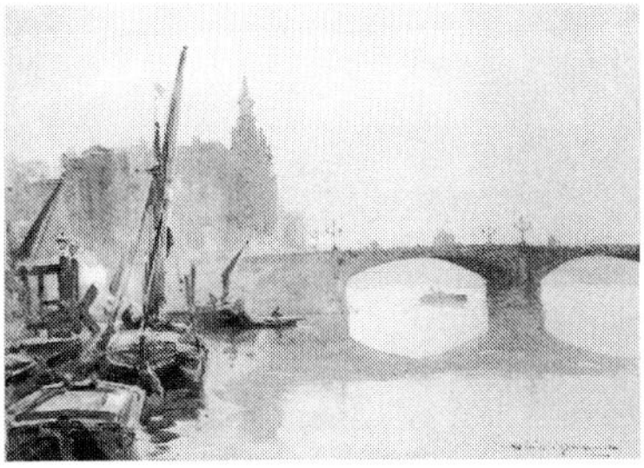

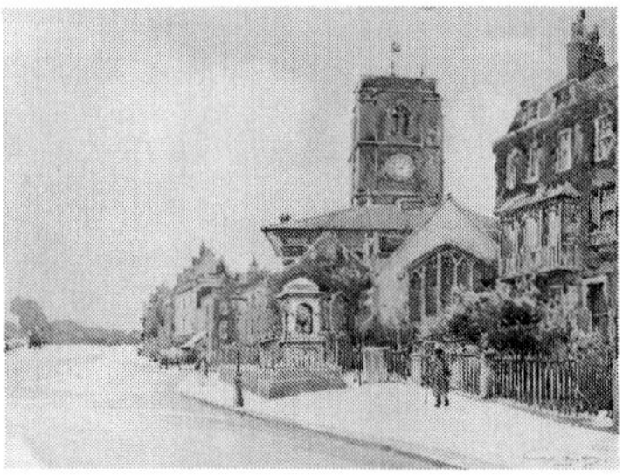

acc. no. 1178
Old Chelsea Church (1908)
watercolour: 10 × $12\frac{7}{8}$ in.
signed and dated: *1908. / W.A.M.*

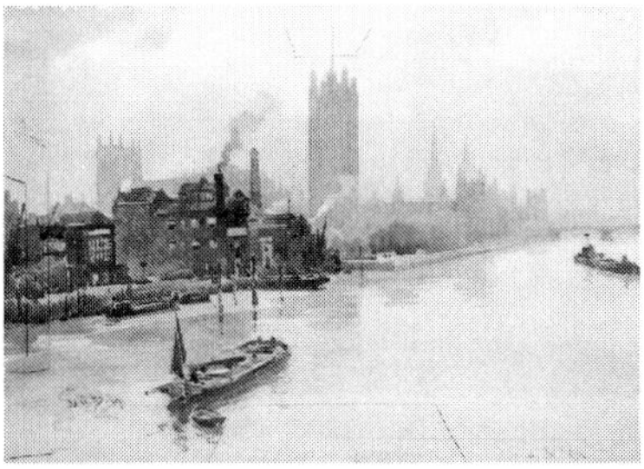

acc. no. 1140
Millbank from Old Lambeth Bridge (1909)
watercolour: $6\frac{1}{4}$ × 10 in. (sight)
signed and dated: *W.A.M. 1909*

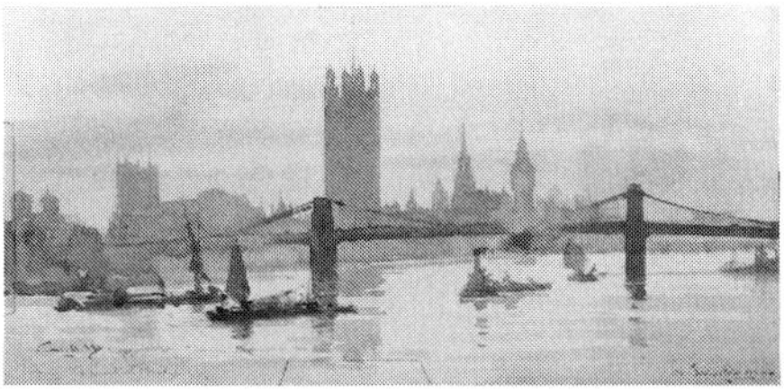

acc. no. 1159
Old Lambeth Bridge (1909)
watercolour: $6\frac{1}{2}$ × $14\frac{1}{2}$ in. (sight)
signed and dated: *W.A.M. 1909.* and signed: *W. Alister Macdonald* and inscribed: *Evening. Old Lambeth Bridge – 1909.*

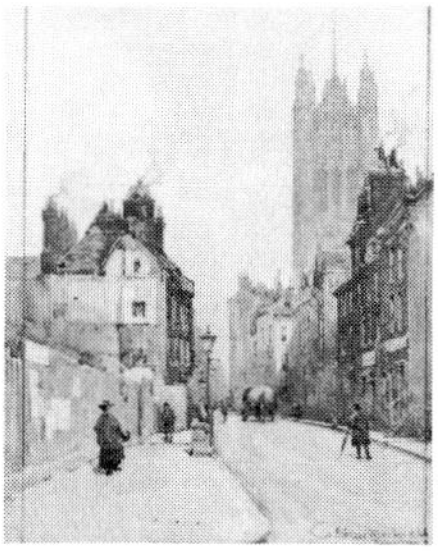

acc. no. 1189
Millbank (1909)
watercolour: 10 × $7\frac{1}{2}$ in.
signed: *W. Alister Macdonald*

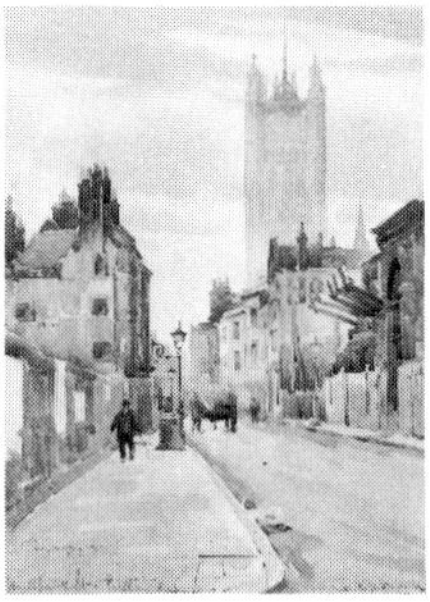

acc. no. 1179
Millbank (1910)
watercolour: $11\frac{1}{8}$ × $7\frac{7}{8}$ in.
signed and dated: *W.A.M. 1910* and signed: *W. Alister Macdonald* and inscribed: *Millbank St. Pulling down.1910*

acc. no. 1115
Houses of Parliament from Westminster Bridge (1910)

watercolour: 11 × $7\frac{1}{8}$ in.
signed and dated: *W. Alister Macdonald. / 1910* and inscribed on back of former mount: *from West.r Bridge / 1910.*

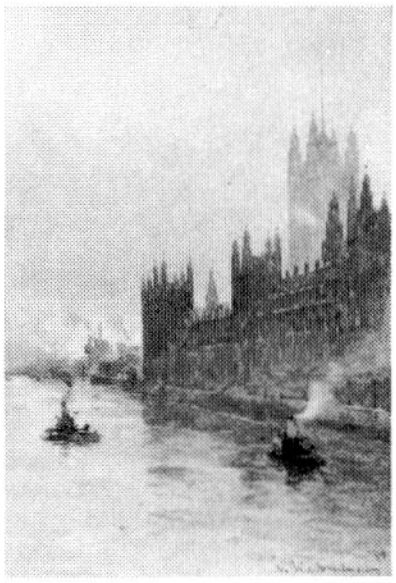

acc. no. 1151
Westminster Abbey and Houses of Parliament from Lambeth (1910)

watercolour: $9\frac{1}{8}$ × $19\frac{1}{8}$ in. (sight)
signed and dated: *W.A.M. 1910*

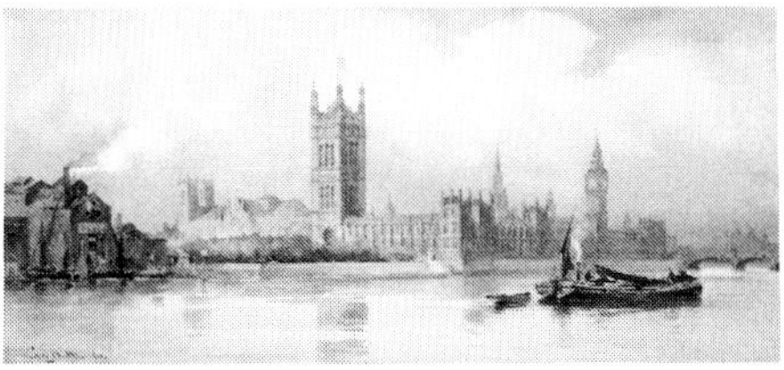

acc. no. 1118
Westminster Bridge and the Houses of Parliament, Evening (1910)

watercolour: $7\frac{3}{4}$ × $10\frac{5}{8}$ in.
signed: *W.A.M.*

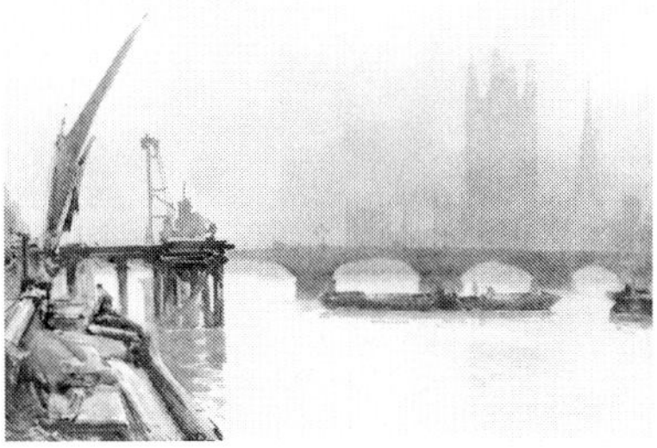

acc. no. 1124
Dean's Yard, Westminster (1910)

watercolour: $14\frac{1}{2}$ × $10\frac{1}{4}$ in.
signed and dated: *W.A.M. 1910.*; signed and inscribed below level of former mount: *W.A.M. Dean's Yard. Westminster.* and: *W. ALISTER MACDONALD. / 190* (. . .) and inscribed: *DEAN'S YARD. WESTR. / Convocation Morning.*

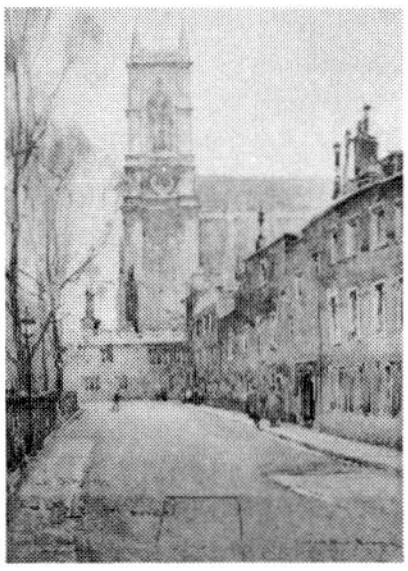

acc. no. 1177
Storey's Gate, Westminster (1910)

watercolour: $11\frac{1}{4}$ × $9\frac{1}{2}$ in. (sight)
signed and dated: *W. Alister Macdonald. 1910* and *W. Alister Macdonald*

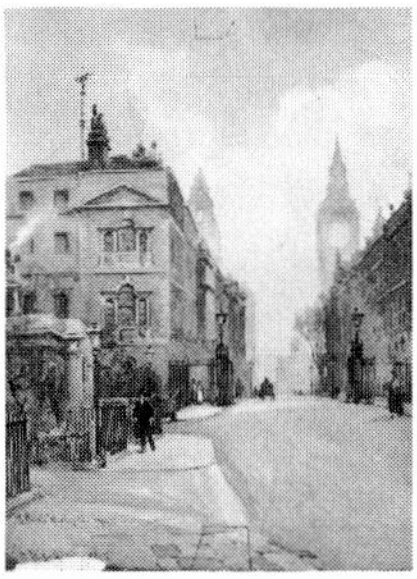

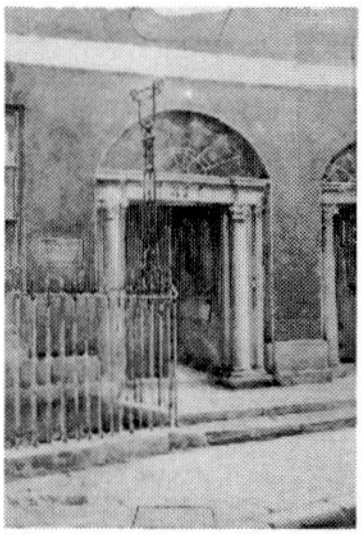

acc. no. 1225
Doorway, 37 Great George St., Westminster (1910)

watercolour: 11 × $7\frac{3}{4}$ in.
signed and dated: *1910 W.A.M.* and inscribed on back of former mount: *Doorways. / 37. Great George St West. / Pulled down March 1910.*

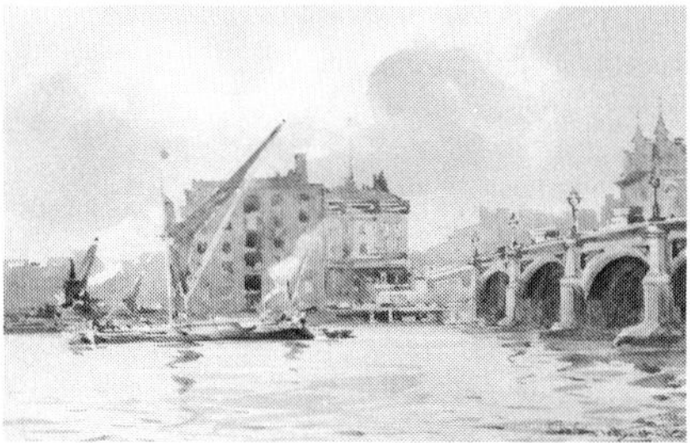

acc. no. 1145
Clearing the Site for the New County Hall (1910)

watercolour: $6\frac{3}{8} \times 9\frac{7}{8}$ in.
signed and dated: *W. Alister Macdonald. 1910.*; inscribed on back of former mount: *"Coronet"* (crossed out) *Clearing site for new Lond County Hall. / 1910.*

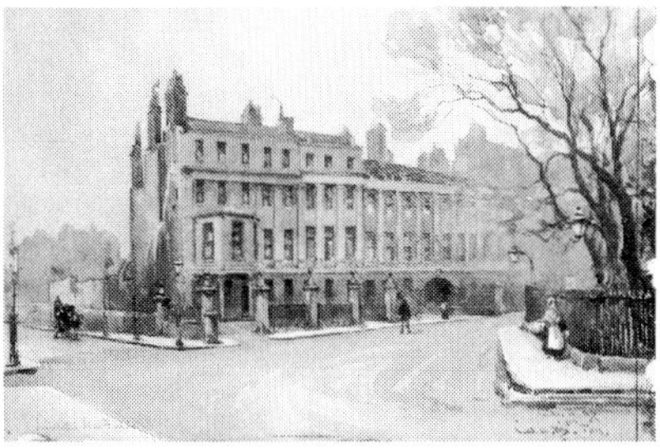

acc. no. 1204
Lincoln's Inn Fields (1910)

watercolour: $8\frac{7}{8} \times 12\frac{1}{8}$ in.
signed and dated: *W.A.M. / 1910* and *W.A.M. 1910* and inscribed: *"Lincoln's Inn Fields"*

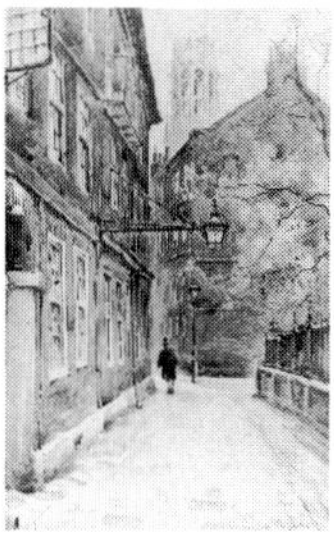

acc. no. 1119
Clifford's Inn (1910)

watercolour: $13\frac{3}{8} \times 8\frac{3}{4}$ in. (sight)
signed and dated: *W.A.M./1910* and inscribed: *Clifford's Inn*

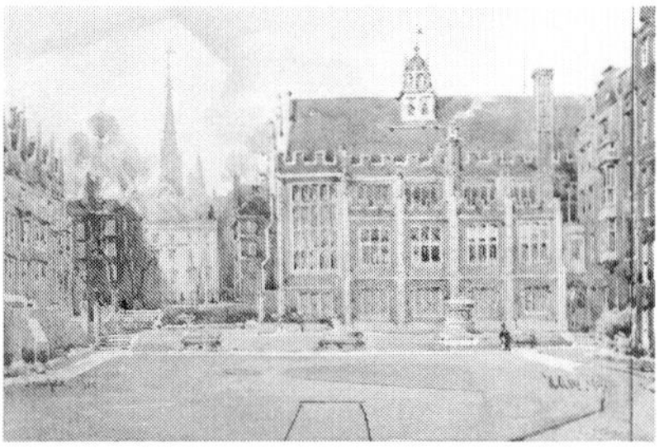

acc. no. 1182
Fountain Court and Middle Temple Gardens (1910)

watercolour: $6\frac{3}{4}$ × 10 in.
signed: *W.A.M.*; signed and dated: *W.A.M. 1910.*; inscribed: *Temple.1910* and inscribed on back of former mount: *Temple Gardens*

acc. no. 1218
Goldsmith's Grave, Temple (1910)

watercolour: $12\frac{3}{8} \times 8\frac{3}{4}$ in.
signed and dated: *W.A.M. 1910.*; inscribed over earlier inscription: *Goldsmith's G*(rave) / *1910 Temple*; inscribed on back of former mount: *Goldsmith's Grave – / Temple.*

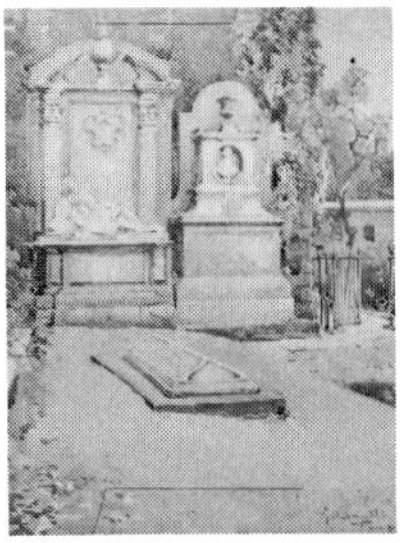

acc. no. 1125
Shackleton's 'Nimrod' at Temple Pier (1910)

watercolour over pencil: $6\frac{1}{2} \times 9\frac{1}{2}$ in. (sight)
signed: *W.A.M.*; inscribed and dated on mount: *Shackleton's "Nimrod" – at Temple Pier - 1910*

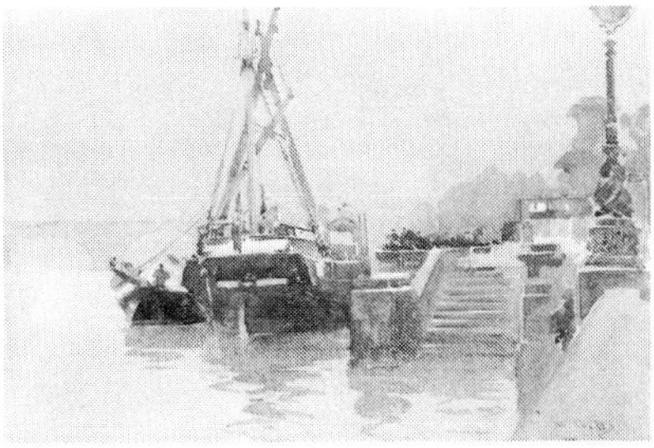

acc. no. 1190
Old Clifford's Inn and Record Office (1910)

watercolour: $9\frac{1}{2} \times 6\frac{5}{8}$ in. (sight)
signed and dated: *W.A.M. / 1910*

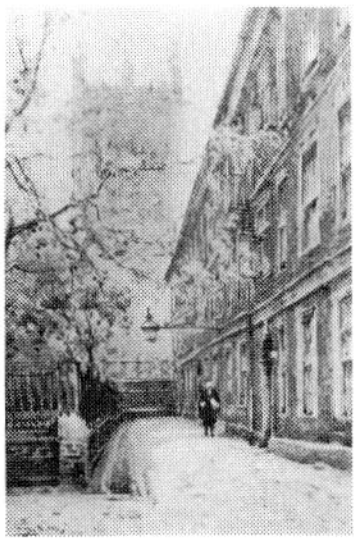

acc. no. 1106
Outer Gate, St Bartholomew the Great (1910)

watercolour: $10\frac{3}{4} \times 7\frac{1}{2}$ in.
signed, inscribed and dated: *W. Alister Macdonald / St. Bartholomew, Smithfield, 1910*

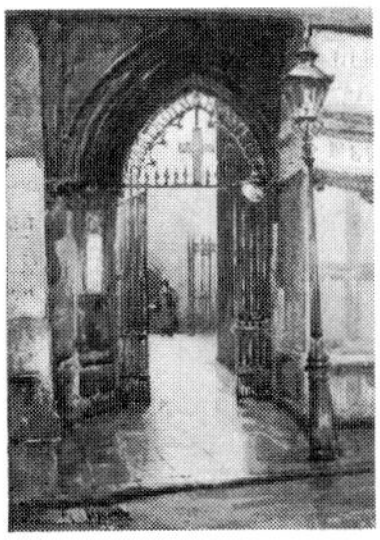

acc. no. 1197
Smithfield End of Cloth Fair (1910)

watercolour: $10\frac{3}{4} \times 7\frac{3}{4}$ in.
signed and dated: *W.A.M. 1910.* and inscribed and dated: *Cloth Fair. 1910.*

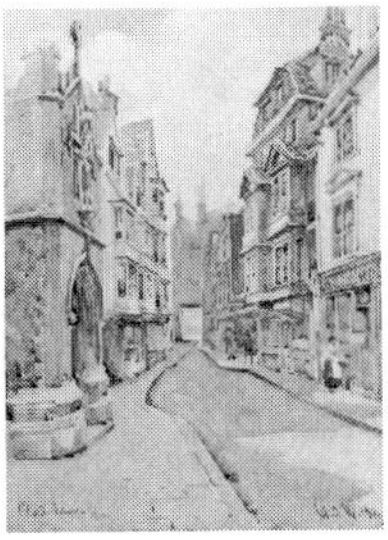

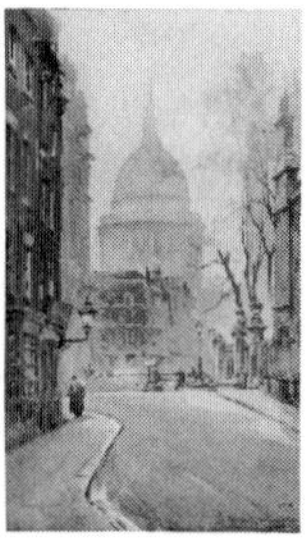

acc. no. 1131
Little Britain and the Gates of Bluecoat School (1910)

watercolour: $11\frac{1}{4} \times 6\frac{1}{2}$ in. (sight)
signed and dated: *1910 / W. Alister Macdonald*; inscribed on mount: *Little Britain.* and on verso: *Little Britain. E.C. / & Gates of Old Bluecoat School / 1910*

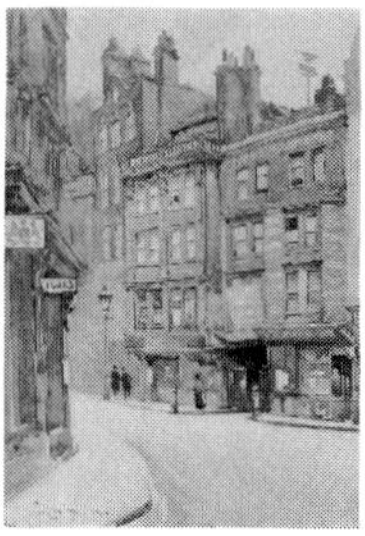

acc. no. 1210
Old Houses, Bishopsgate (1910)

watercolour: 11×8 in.
signed and dated: *W.A.M. 1910.*; inscribed on back of former mount: *Old Houses Bishopsgate. / EC. / 1910*

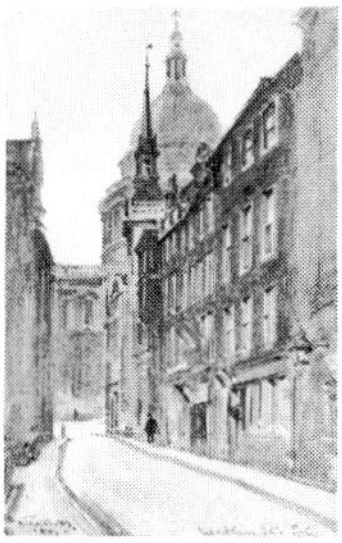

acc. no. 1207
Watling Street (1910)

watercolour: $10 \times 6\frac{3}{8}$ in.
signed and dated: *W.A.M. / 1910* and: *Watling St. EC. / 1910*

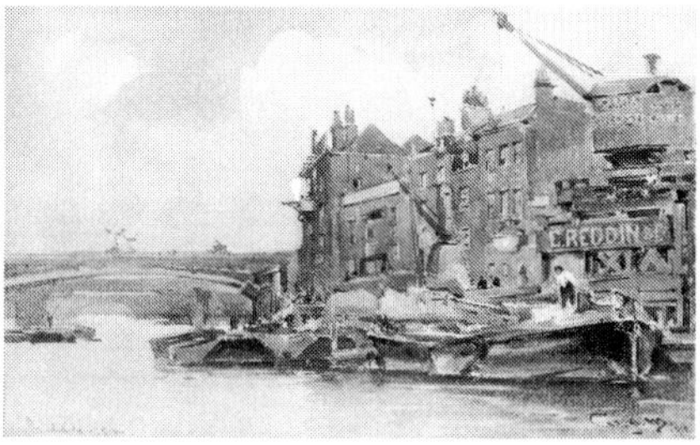

acc. no. 1139
Bankside and Old Southwark Bridge (1910)

watercolour: $6\frac{1}{2} \times 10$ in.
signed and dated: *W.A.M. / 1910* and inscribed and dated: *Bankside.1910*; inscribed on back of former mount: *Bankside & old Southwark Bridge / 1910*

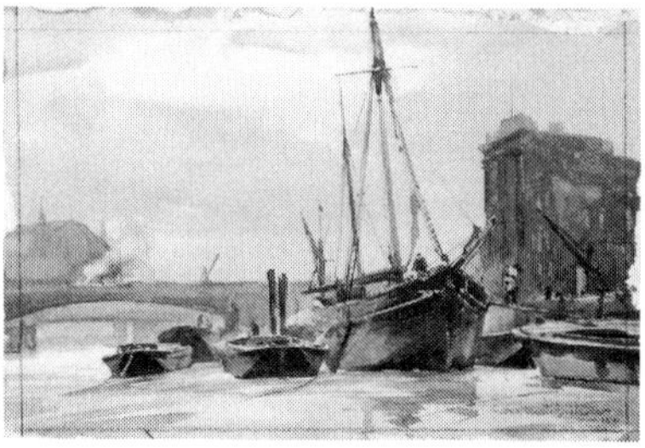

acc. no. 1141
Low Tide, Bankside, with Cannon Street Station in the Distance (1910)

watercolour: $8\frac{1}{8} \times 11\frac{3}{4}$ in.
inscribed, signed and dated: *Bankside / W. Alister Macdonald / – 1910.*

acc. no. 1171
Unloading a Straw Barge, Bankside (1910)

watercolour: $13\frac{3}{4} \times 10\frac{1}{2}$ in.
inscribed and signed: *Bankside. / W. Alister Macdonald.*

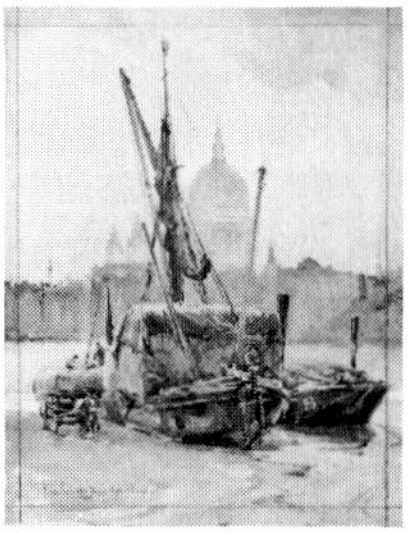

acc. no. 1199
Waterloo Bridge looking East (1910)

watercolour: $4 \times 7\frac{3}{4}$ in.
signed: *W. Alister Macdonald.*; inscribed on back of former mount: *Waterloo Bridge / Looking east / 1910*

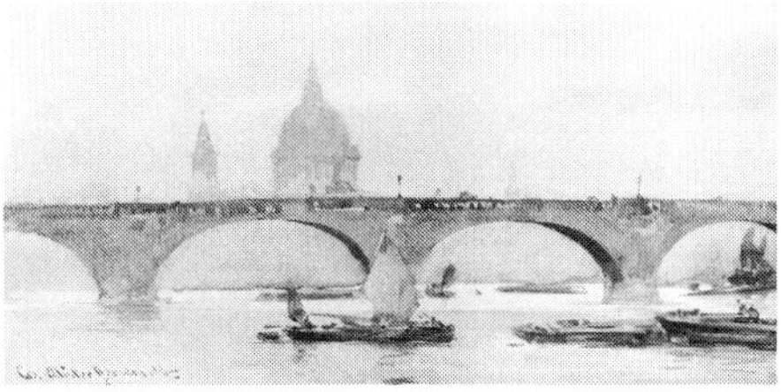

acc. no. 1196
By New Inn and St. Clement Danes (1910)

watercolour: $9\frac{3}{4} \times 6\frac{1}{2}$ in.
signed and dated: *W.A.M. 1910.*; inscribed: *Corner by St. Clements Dane / now Aldwych*

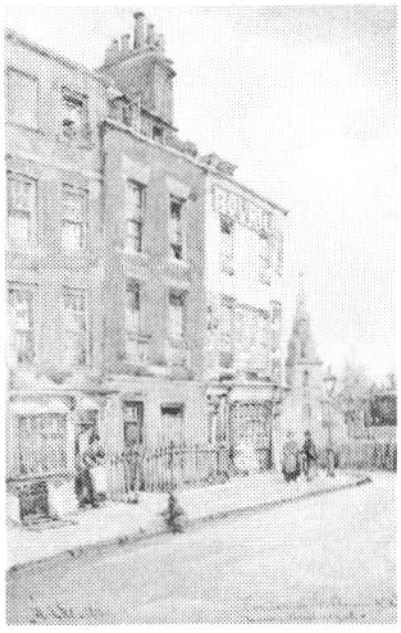

acc. no. 1205
The Old 'George' Inn, Borough (1910)

watercolour: $9\frac{1}{8} \times 7\frac{1}{2}$ in.
signed and dated: *W.A.M. / 1910.* and inscribed and dated: *George Inn – Borough*

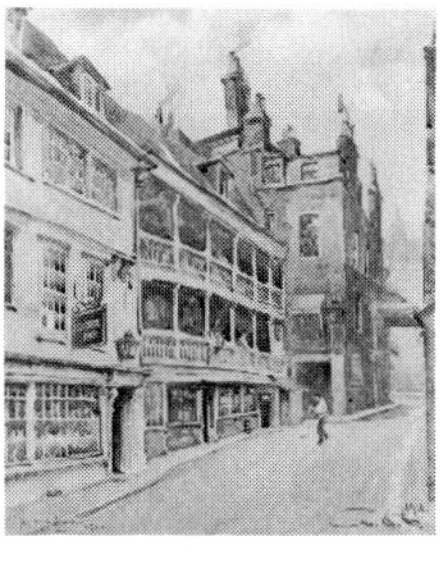

acc. no. 1157
Old Millbank (1911)

watercolour: $9\frac{1}{4} \times 11\frac{3}{4}$ in. (sight)
inscribed, signed and dated: *Old Millbank. / W. Alister Macdonald.1911.*; inscribed on mount: *Millbank. & Old Lambeth Bridge. 1911*

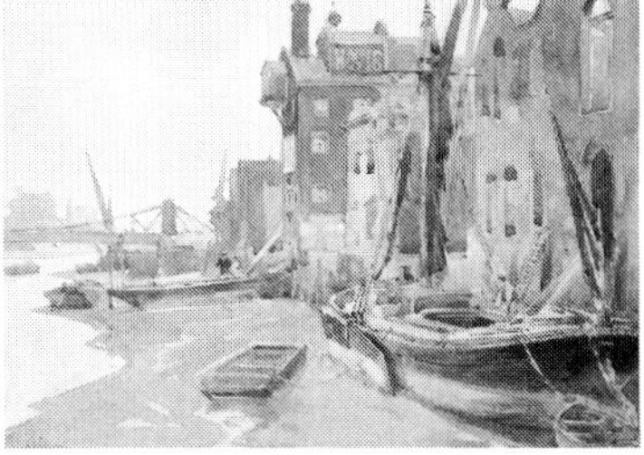

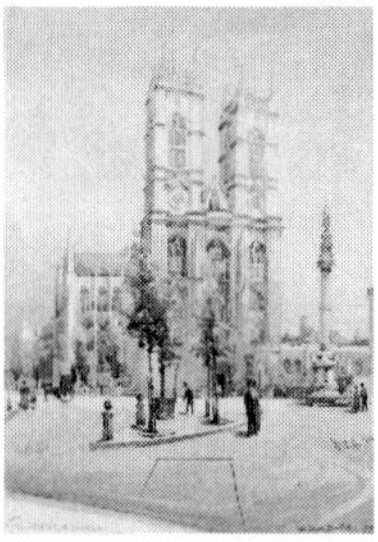

acc. no. 1172
Westminster Abbey (1911)

watercolour: 11 × $7\frac{3}{4}$ in.
signed below level of former mount: *W.Alister Macdonald* and inscribed and dated: *Westminster Abbey.1911*; signed and dated above level of former mount: *W.A.M. 1908* (*sic*) and inscribed: *Westr. 1908.* (*sic*)

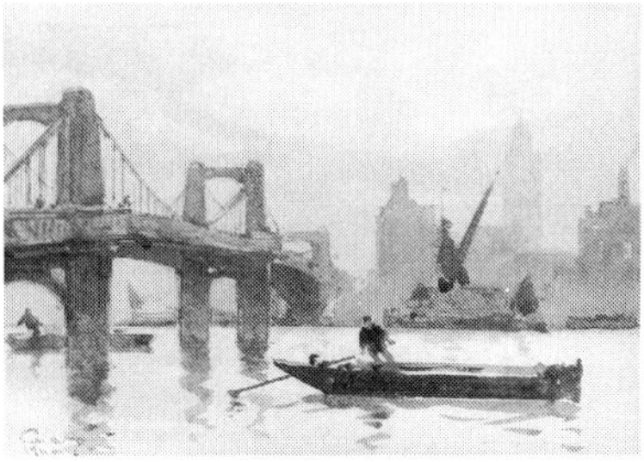

acc. no. 1185
Old Lambeth Bridge (1911)

watercolour: $5\frac{3}{8}$ × $7\frac{1}{2}$ in.
signed and dated: *W.A.M. / 1911*; inscribed on back of former mount: *Old Lambeth Bridge. Evening. / 1911*

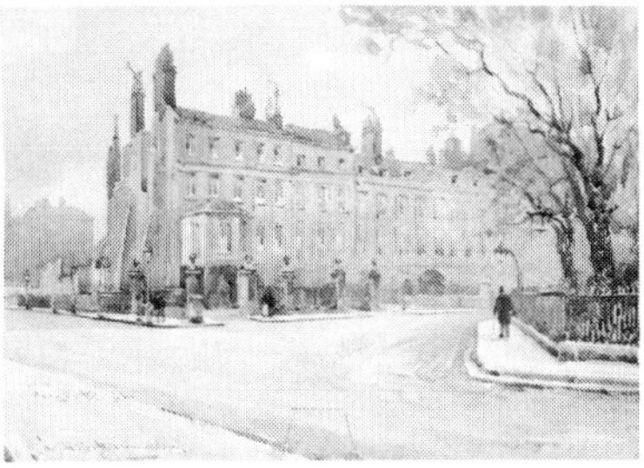

acc. no. 1158
Lincoln's Inn Fields (1912)

watercolour: $7\frac{3}{4}$ × 11 in.
signed and dated: *W.A.M. 1912.* and signed: *W. Alister Macdonald*

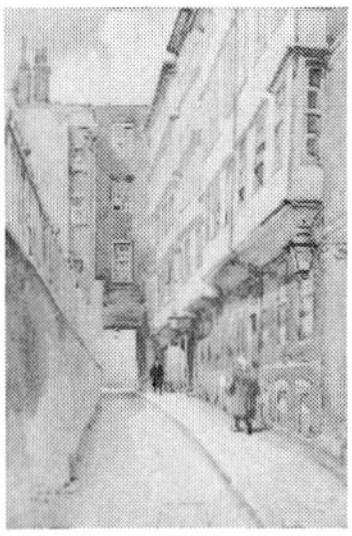

acc. no. 1167
Middle Temple Lane (1912)

watercolour: $9\frac{1}{2}$ × $6\frac{3}{4}$ in.
signed and dated: *W.A.M. / 1912.*; inscribed on former mount: *Middle Temple Lane 1912* and inscribed on back of former mount: *Middle Temple Lane. / 1912*

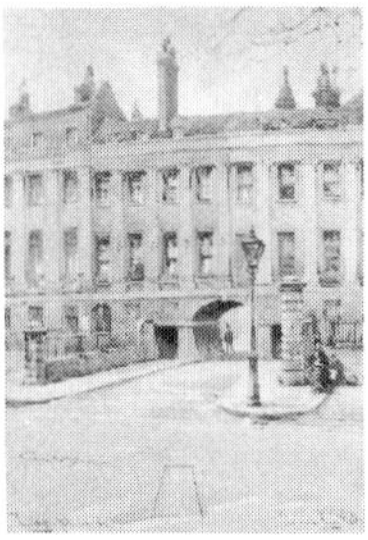

acc. no. 1109
Lincoln's Inn Fields and Archway into Sardinia Street (1912)

watercolour on card: $9\frac{1}{2}$ × $7\frac{1}{8}$ in. (sight)
signed and dated: *W.A.M. 1912.* and signed again: *W. Alister Macdonald* and inscribed: *Lincoln's Inn Fields*; inscribed on back of former mount: *Lincoln's Inn Fields. / & entrance to Sardinia St. / Demolished.1912*

acc. no. 1127
Houses at Corner of Lincoln's Inn Fields (1912)

watercolour: 11 × 7¾ in.
signed and dated: *W. Alister Macdonald.1912.*
and inscribed: *Lincoln's Inn Fields.*

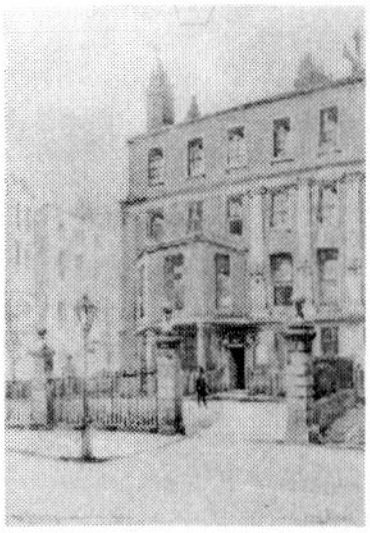

acc. no. 1112
The Old 'Coronet' Public House at the East Corner of Westminster Bridge (1912)

watercolour: 11⅛ × 7½ in.
signed and dated: *W.A.M. 1912.*; inscribed on back of former mount: *The Old Coronet Public House / by West^r Bridge. / 1912*

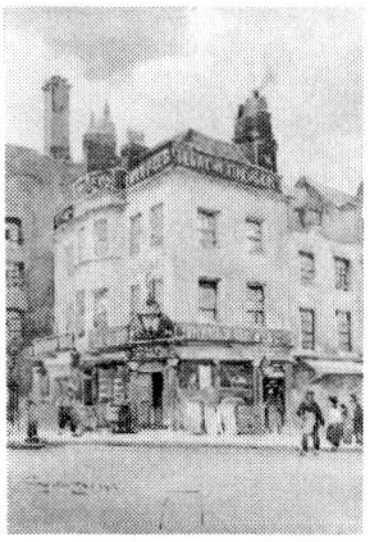

acc. no. 1187
Old Southwark Bridge (1912)

watercolour: 5⅞ × 10 in.
signed: *W. Alister Macdonald* and inscribed and dated: *Old Southwark Bridge / 1912*; inscribed on back of former mount: *Old Southwark Bridge. from Surrey Shore. / Pulled down & rebuilt 1912–14.*

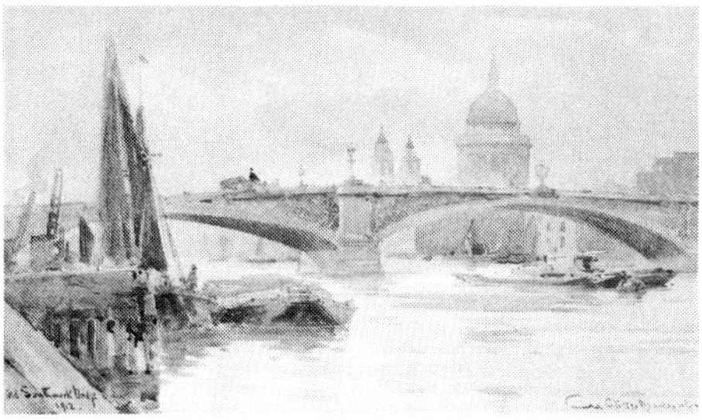

acc. no. 1212
Seething Lane and Entrance to Catherine Court (1912)

watercolour: 11¾ × 7⅜ in.
signed and dated: *W.A.M. / 1912* and signed: *W.A.M.*

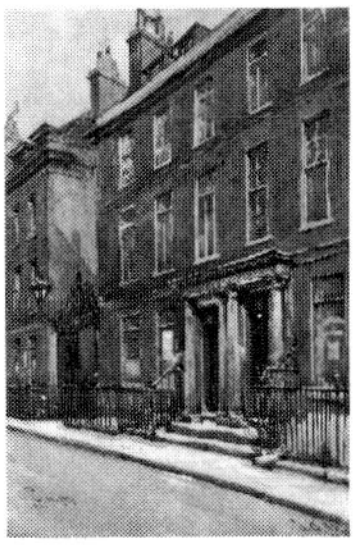

acc. no. 1174
Catherine Court, Trinity Square, Looking East (1912)

watercolour: 10¾ × 7½ in. (sight)
signed and dated: *W.A.M. / 1912*; inscribed on back of former mount: *Demolished.* and *Looking East* and: *Catherine Court / Trinity Square.E.C. / Looking East. Demolished / +el. 1913.*

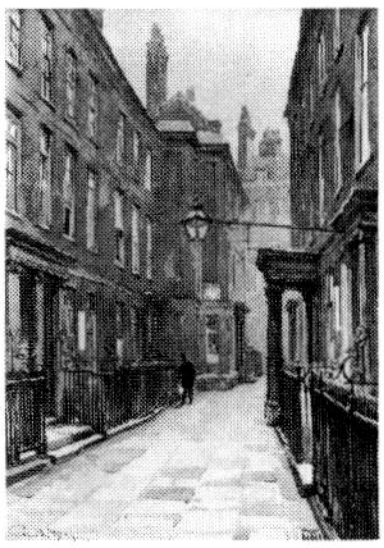

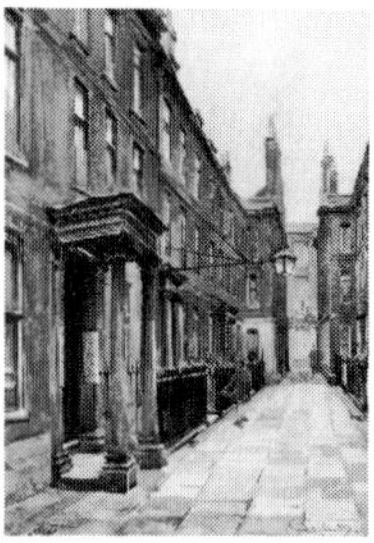

acc. no. 1181
Catherine Court, Trinity Square, Looking West (1912)

watercolour: $11 \times 7\frac{5}{8}$ in.
signed and dated: *W.A.M. / 1912*

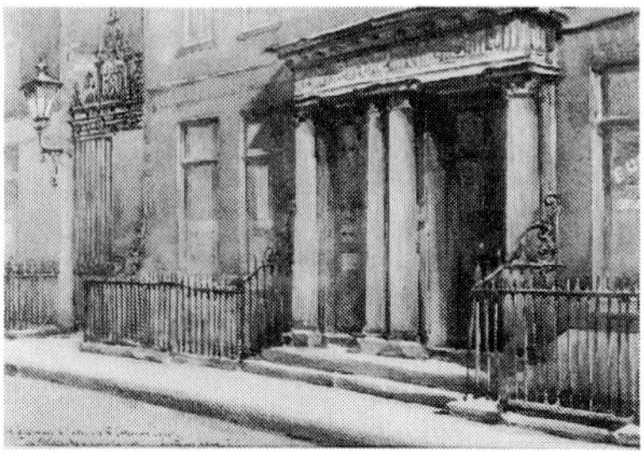

acc. no. 1194
Old Doorways and Entrance to Catherine Court (1913)

watercolour: $7\frac{3}{8} \times 10\frac{5}{8}$ in. (sight)
inscribed, signed and dated: *Old Doorways & Entrance to Catherine Court. / W. Alister Macdonald. 1913. Seething Lane. E.C.*; inscribed on back of mount: *Entrance to St Catherine's Court.E.C. / 1913*

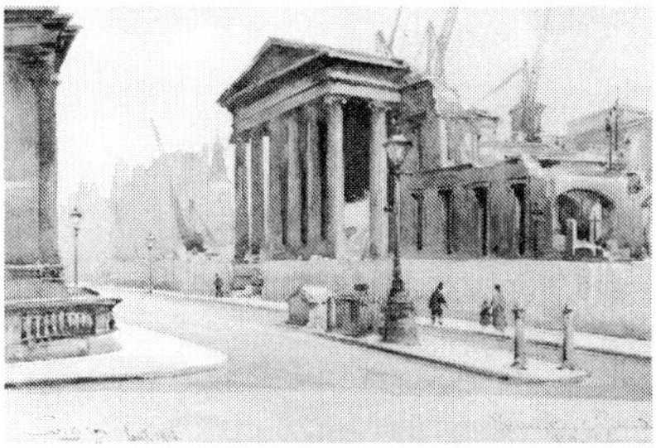

acc. no. 1219
Pulling down the General Post Office, St. Martin-le-Grand (1913)

watercolour: $7\frac{3}{4} \times 11$ in.
signed and dated: *W.A.M. Jan.y 1913.* and inscribed: *St. Martins le Grand – P.O – pulling down*

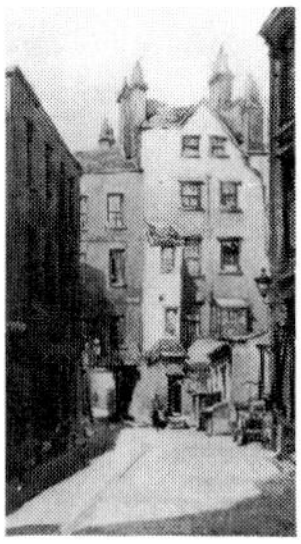

acc. no. 1110
Saracen's head Yard, Bishopsgate (1913)

watercolour: $11\frac{3}{8} \times 6\frac{1}{4}$ in.
signed and dated: *W. Alister Macdonald.1913.*

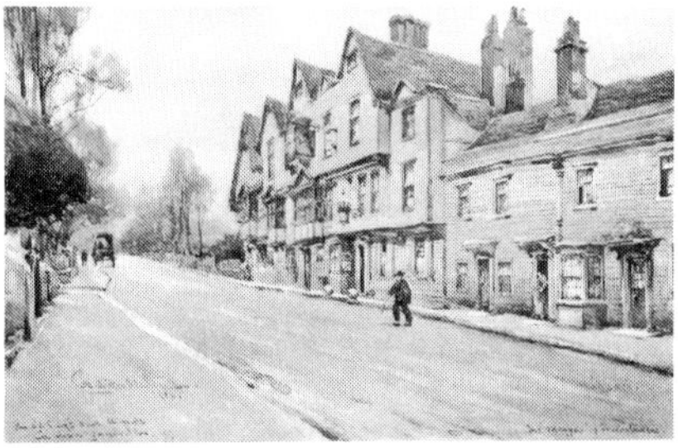

acc. no. 1147
The 'King's Head', Chigwell (1913)

watercolour: $7\frac{1}{8} \times 10\frac{7}{8}$ in.
signed and dated: *W. Alister Macdonald. / 1913.* and inscribed, signed and dated *The Old King's Head.Chigwell. / W. Alister Macdonald.1913* and inscribed: *Chigwell* and *The "Maypole" of Charles Dickens*; inscribed on back of mount: *The old King's Head / Chigwell – Epping – / Dickens' "Maypole"*

acc. no. 1150
Dean's Yard, Westminster (1913)
watercolour: $15 \times 10\frac{1}{2}$ in.
signed, inscribed and dated: *W. Alister Macdonald. / Dean's Yard. West: / 1913.*

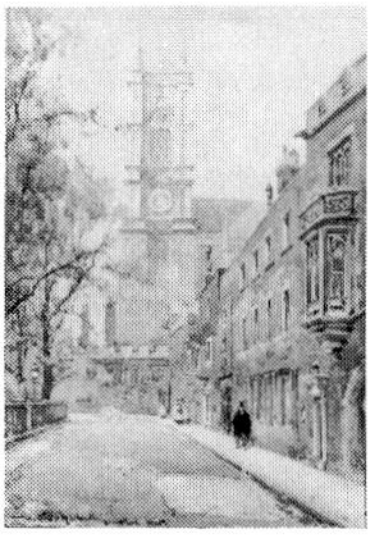

acc. no. 1166
Old Houses, Strand (1913)
watercolour: $9\frac{7}{8} \times 6\frac{1}{8}$ in.
signed and dated: *W. Alister Macdonald.1913*;
inscribed on back of former mount: *Old Houses. Strand – / demolished.1913*

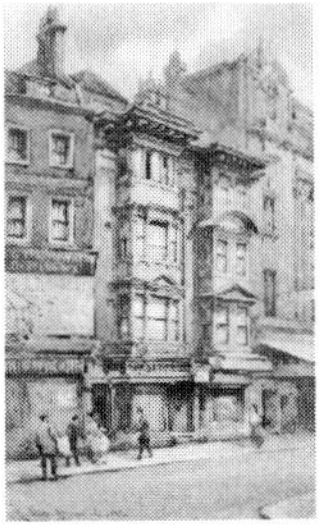

acc. no. 1226
Watergate, Essex Street, Strand (1913)
watercolour: $11 \times 7\frac{3}{4}$ in.
signed and dated: *W.A.M. / 1913.* and inscribed on former mount: *Essex Street – Watergate.1913.* and on back of former mount: *Water Gate. / Essex St Strand / 1913*

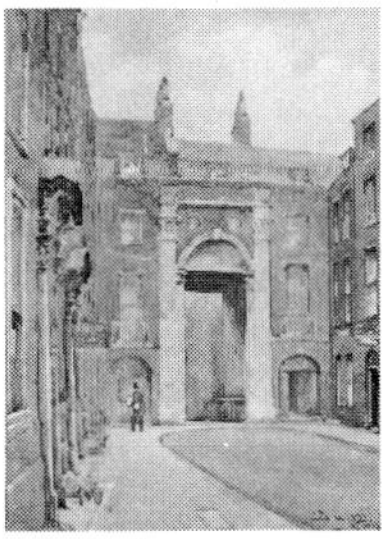

acc. no. 1132
St Bartholomew the Great Churchyard and Old Houses, Cloth Fair (1914)
watercolour: $9\frac{7}{8} \times 6\frac{3}{4}$ in.
signed and dated: *W.A.M. 1914.*

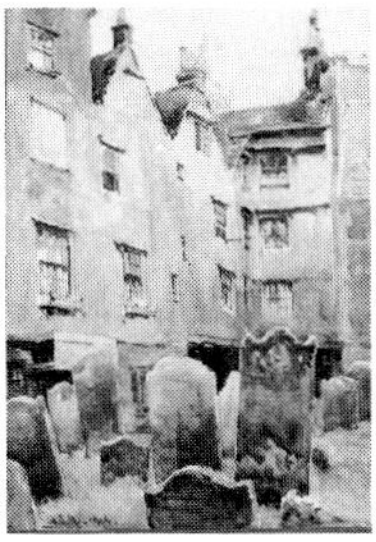

acc. no. 1613
The Pool of London Looking West (1914)
watercolour: $3\frac{1}{4} \times 4\frac{3}{8}$ in.
signed and dated: *W.A.M. 1914*
Presented by Lady Forbes, 1960

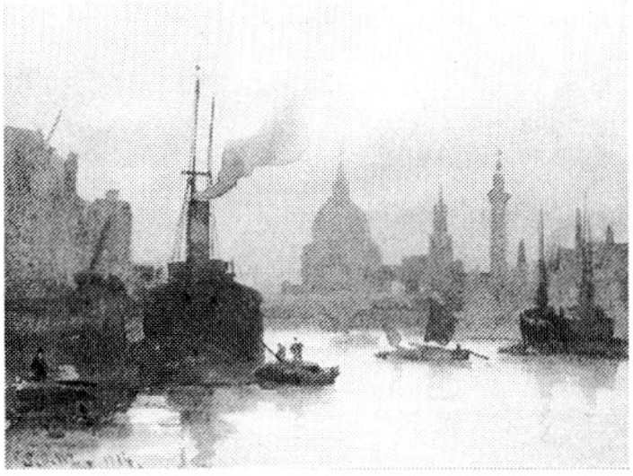

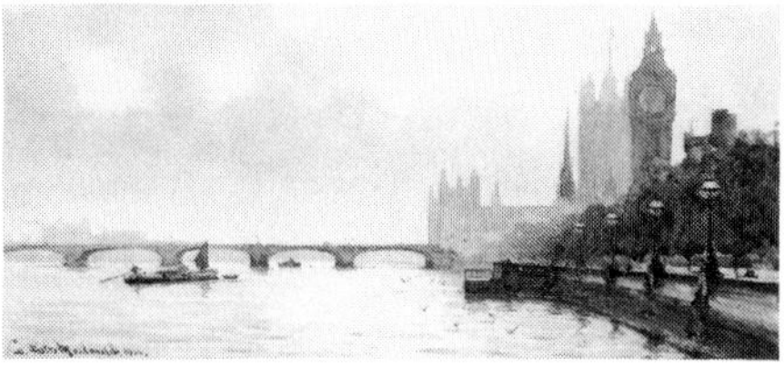

acc. no. 1611
Westminster Bridge from Hungerford Bridge (1914)

watercolour: $4\frac{5}{8} \times 10$ in.
signed and dated: *W. Alister Macdonald.1914.*
Presented by Lady Forbes, 1960

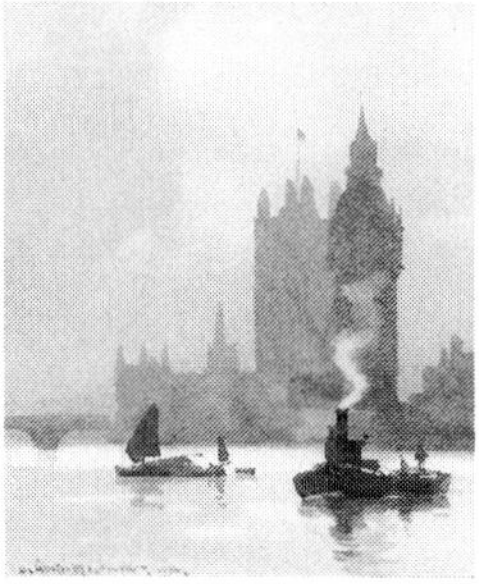

acc. no. 1612
The Houses of Parliament from across the River (1914)

watercolour: $4\frac{3}{8} \times 3\frac{5}{8}$ in.
signed and dated: *W. Alister Macdonald.1914*
Presented by Lady Forbes, 1960

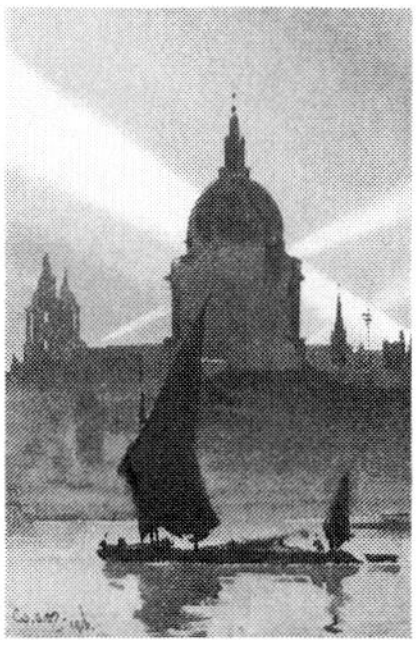

acc. no. 1202
St Paul's and the Thames with Searchlights (1916)

watercolour and ink on card: $4\frac{3}{4} \times 3\frac{1}{8}$ in. (sight)
signed and dated: *W.A.M. 1916*; dated on verso: *1915–1916*
Presented by Lord Wakefield, 1936

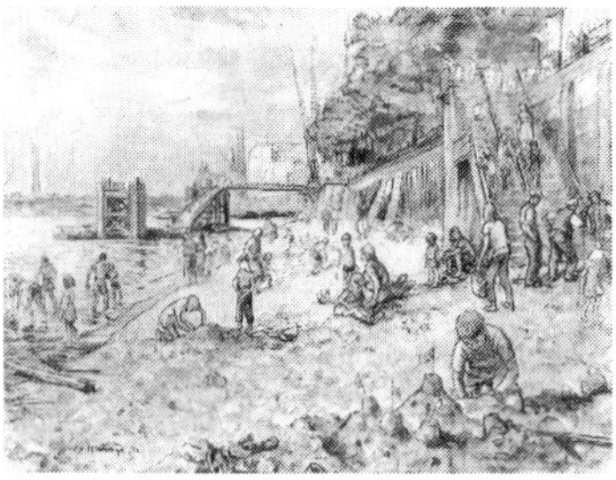

Constance V. Mackenzie (*fl.* 1924–62)

acc. no. 1642
The Children's Beach at the Tower (1962)

crayon and watercolour: $22\frac{3}{8} \times 29\frac{1}{2}$ in.
signed and dated: *C.V. Mackenzie / 62*
Purchased from the artist, 1962

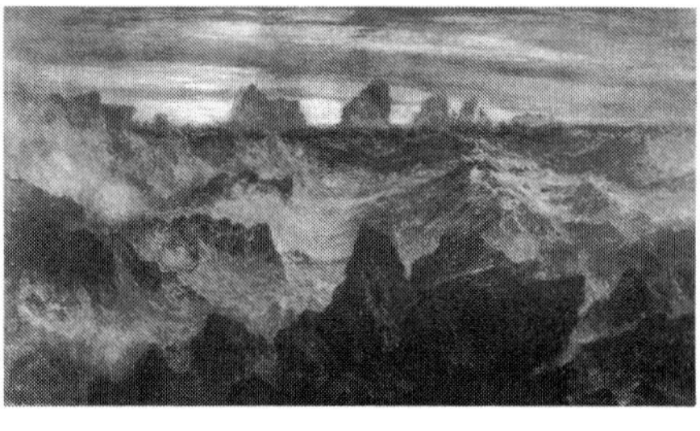

Thomas Hope McLachlan (1845–97)

acc. no. 610
The Isles of the Sea (1894)

oil on canvas: 28×50 in.
signed and dated: *Hope McLachlan / 1894*
Presented by the artist's Memorial Committee, 1898

Daniel Maclise (1806–70)

acc. no. 830
The Banquet Scene in 'Macbeth' (1840)
oil on canvas: 72 × 120 in.
Purchased from F. W. Cosens, 1904

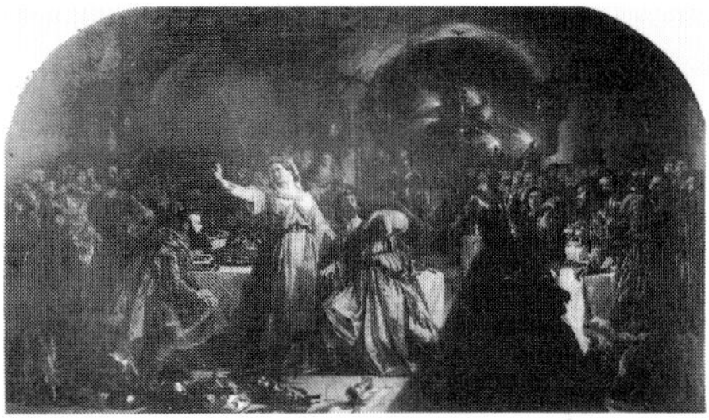

attributed to Daniel Maclise (1806–70)

acc. no. 601
The Trial of Sir William Wallace at Westminster
oil on canvas: 54 × 73 in.
Bequeathed by E. J. Brett, 1895

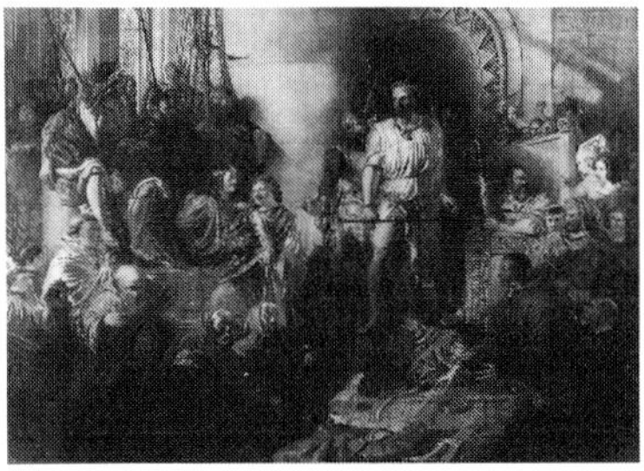

John MacWhirter (1839–1911)

acc. no. 1024
Scotch Firs, Rothiemurchus (1903)
oil on canvas: $50\frac{1}{4} \times 42\frac{1}{4}$ in.
signed: *MacW*
Presented by Mrs. Florence Solomon in memory of her husband, 1923

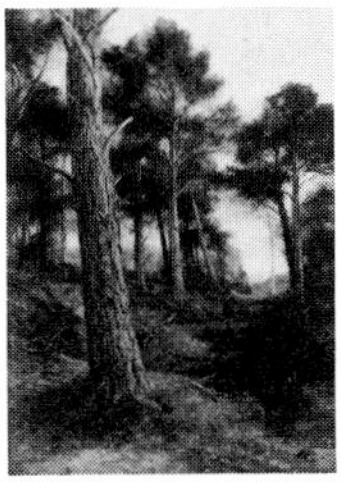

Willes Maddox (1813–53)

acc. no. 751
The Golden Age (1849)
oil on canvas: 34 × 44 in.
Bequeathed by Charles Gassiot, 1902

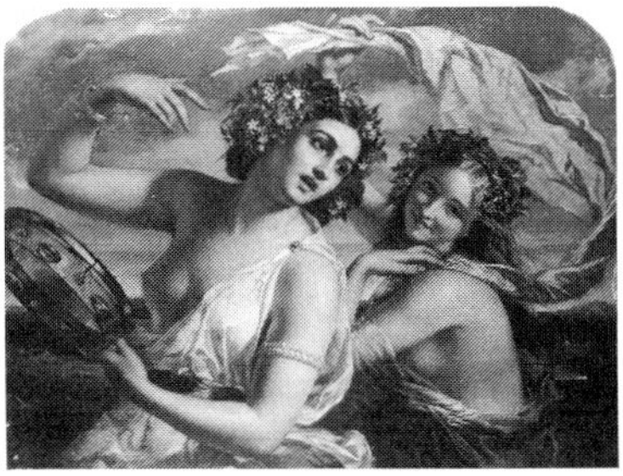

Nicolas Maes (1634–93)

acc. no. 1295
Colonel Charles Campbell (?)
oil on canvas: 24 × 20 in.
signed: *MAES*
Presented by Lady Wakefield, 1944

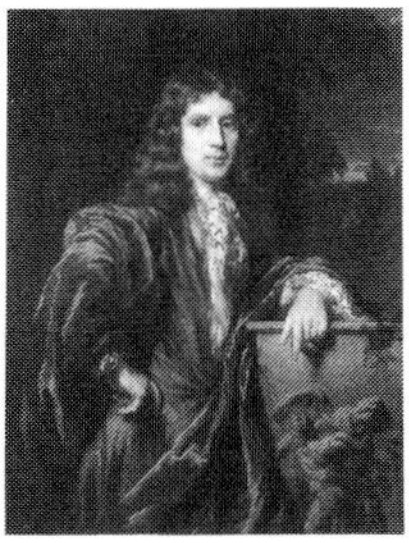

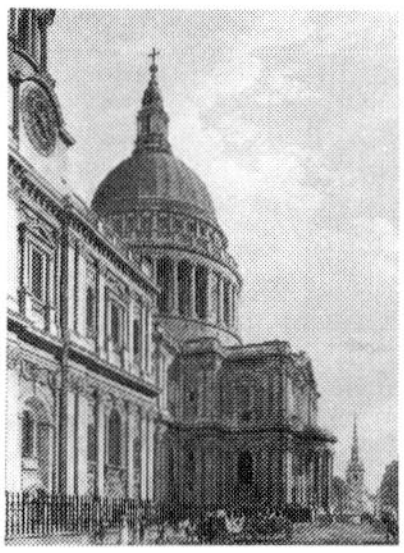

James Malton (*c.*1766–1803)

acc. no. 1258
South Side of St. Paul's Cathedral (1795)
watercolour: $23\frac{3}{4} \times 17\frac{3}{4}$ in.
signed and dated: *James Malton 1795*
Presented by Lady Wakefield, 1944

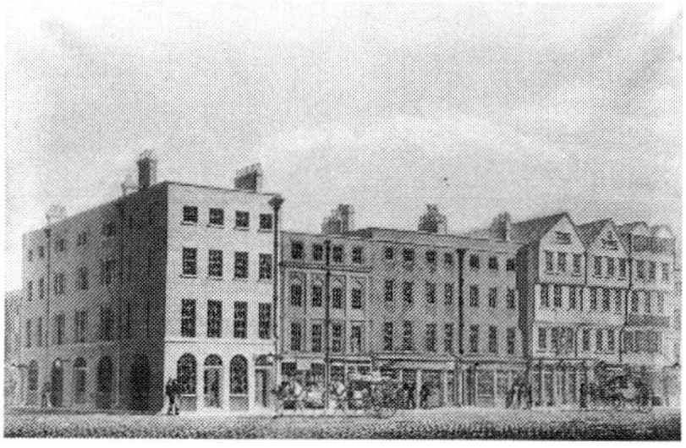

attributed to Thomas Malton (1748–1804)

acc. no. 1254
Leadenhall Street
pen, ink and watercolour over pencil, varnished, laid on linen: $23\frac{1}{2} \times 35\frac{1}{2}$ in.
Purchased from the Nicholson Gallery, 1943

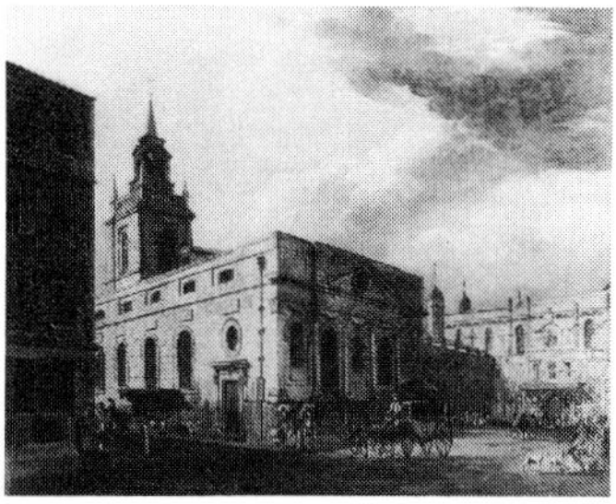

after Thomas Malton (1748–1804)

acc. no. 1028
St Lawrence Jewry and the Guildhall
oil on canvas: 25 × 30 in.
Presented by James Northcott, 1923

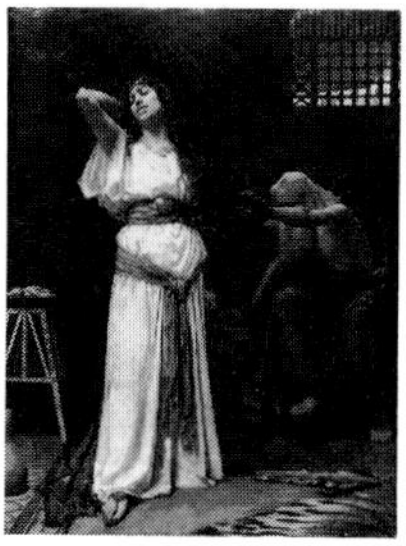

G. Grenville Manton (1855–1932)

acc. no. 514
The Wife of Jeroboam and the Blind Prophet (1888)
oil on canvas: 78 × 60 in.
signed: *G. Grenville Manton*
Presented by George Shaw, 1891

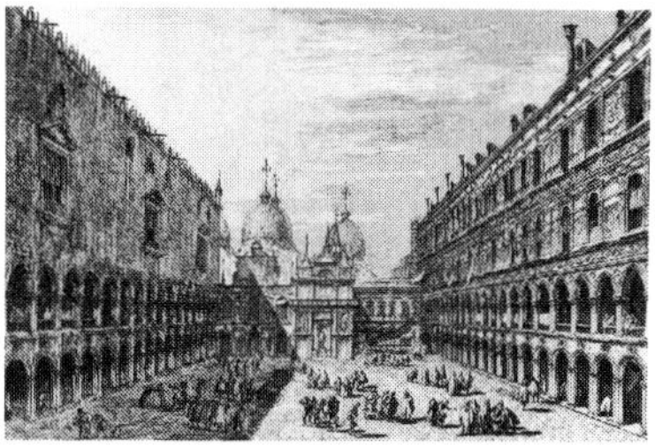

Michele Marieschi (1696–1743)

acc. no. 3605
St Mark's, Venice
etching and engraving: $12 \times 17\frac{5}{8}$ in.
lettered: *Magnificum Aedium Divalium impluvium varie, et eleganter exornatum, ac in eius extrema parte Testudines Basilicae D: Marci supereminentes. / Mich! Marieschi del! et inci!*
Presented by Miss Helen Guiterman, 1985

acc. no. 3606
The Grand Canal, Venice
etching and engraving: 12 × 17$\frac{5}{8}$ in.
lettered: *Pars Canalis mgni se extendens a laeva usque ad palatium familiae Valaressae; at e fronte caput Canalis regij, et ultra pontem Hebraeorum Domiciliam / Mich! Marieschi del! et inci!*
Presented by Miss Helen Guiterman, 1985

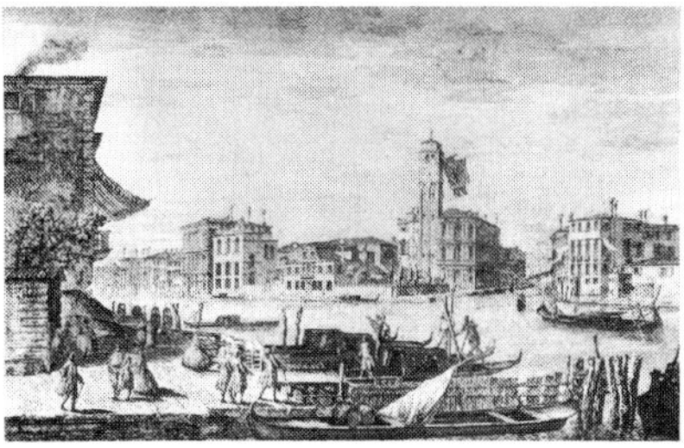

William Marlow (1740–1813)

acc. no. 1837
Fresh Wharf, near London Bridge (?c.1762)
oil on canvas: 38$\frac{1}{4}$ × 49$\frac{1}{2}$ in.
Purchased at Sotheby's 18.3.1970 (118)

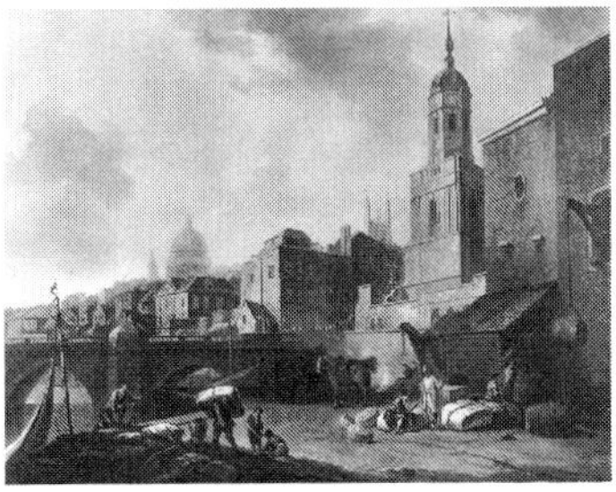

acc. no. 1368
Blackfriars Bridge and St. Paul's (?c.1774)
oil on canvas: 39 × 48 in. (oval)
signed: *W. Marlow*
Purchased from Captain E. Blake Budden, 1947

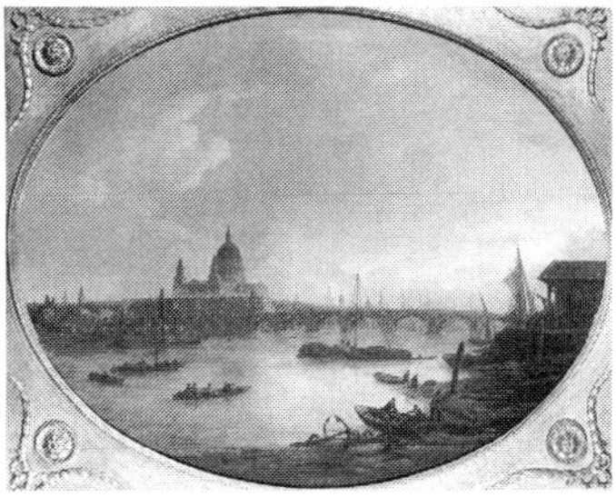

acc. no. 1369
Westminster Bridge (?c.1774)
oil on canvas: 39 × 48 in. (oval)
signed: *W. Marlow*
Purchased from Captain E. Blake Budden, 1947

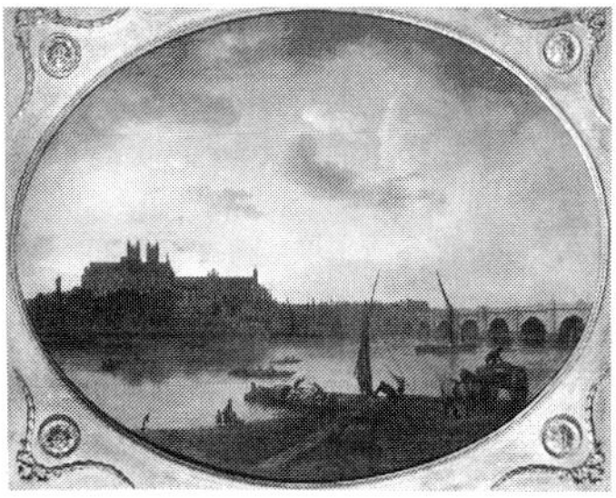

acc. no. 1543
The Waterworks at London Bridge on Fire, 1779
oil on canvas: 28 × 36 in.
signed: *W. Marlow*
Purchased from the Parker Gallery, 1956

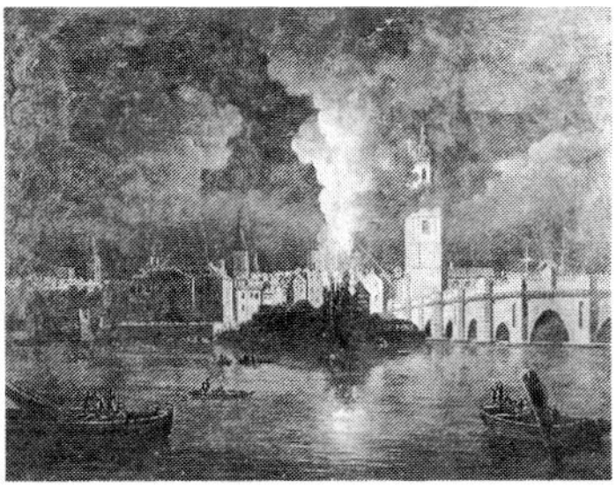

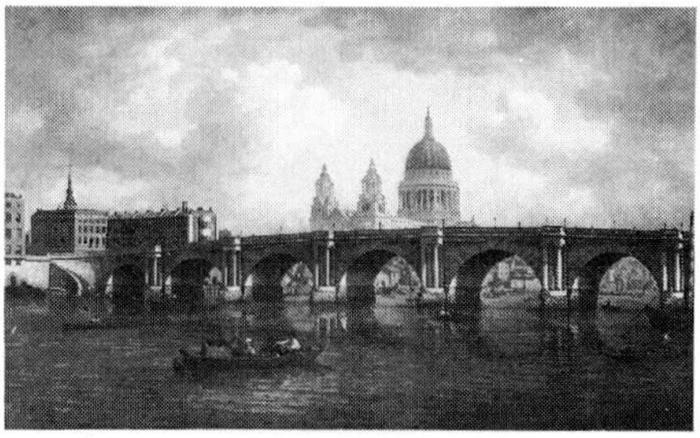

acc. no. 2185
Blackfriars Bridge and St. Paul's
oil on canvas: 41 × 66 in.
Presented by the Slater Foundation, 1975

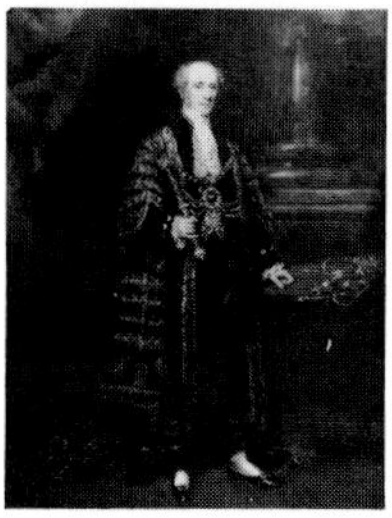

attributed to Charles Martin (1820–1906)

acc. no. 931
Colonel Samuel Wilson, Lord Mayor 1838
oil on canvas: 45 × 33 in.
signed (mono): *CM*
Presented by the family of Cornelius Lea Wilson, 1912

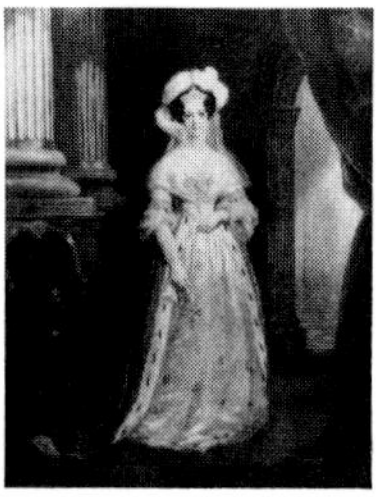

acc. no. 932
Mrs Wilson
oil on canvas: 45 × 33 in.
signed (mono): *CM*
Presented by the Family of Cornelius Lea Wilson, 1912

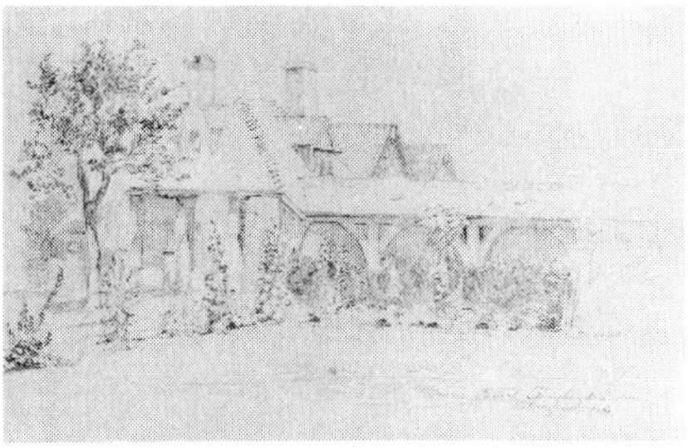

Anna Lea Merritt (1844–1930)

Drawings, watercolours, etchings and oil studies, presented through the Victoria & Albert Museum, 1963

acc. no. 3456
Great Tangley Manor, Surrey (1886)
pencil: $6\frac{1}{2}$ × 10 in.
inscribed and dated: *Great Tangley Manor / July 20 1886*

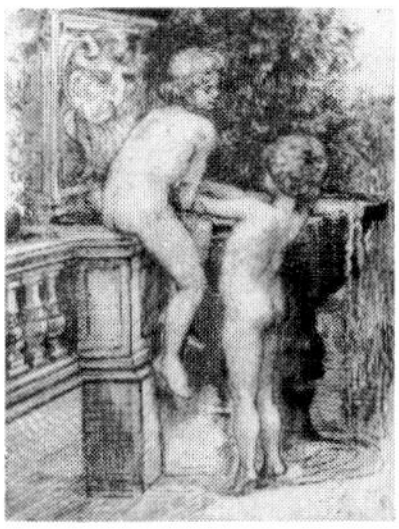

acc. no. 3487a
Two Boys at a Water Fountain (?1887)
etching: 9 × 7 in. (plate)
indistinctly signed and dated in the plate: *Anna Lea Merritt / 1887* (?)

acc. no. 3487b
a different state, signed in the plate *Anna Lea Merritt*; indecipherable inscription; inscribed on former mount: *on old paper – Good proof?*

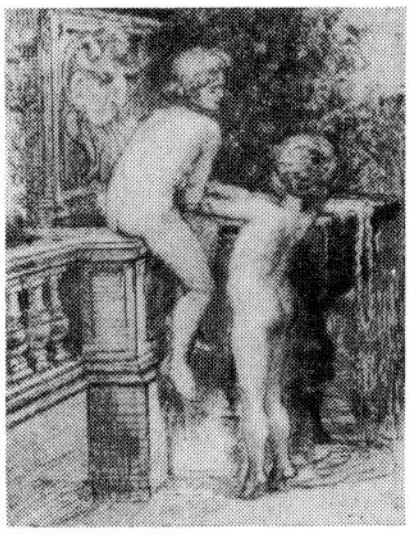

acc. no. 3487c
a different state, touched with purple pencil, signed *Anna Lea Merritt* and signed in the plate *Anna Lea Merritt*

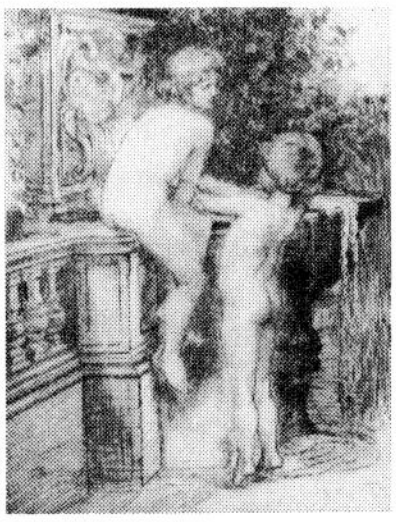

acc. no. 3491a
Small Girl feeding Doves (?1888)

etching: $11\frac{3}{4} \times 7$ in. (plate)
signed and dated in the plate: *Anna Lea Merritt / pinxt 1888* (?); indecipherable inscription

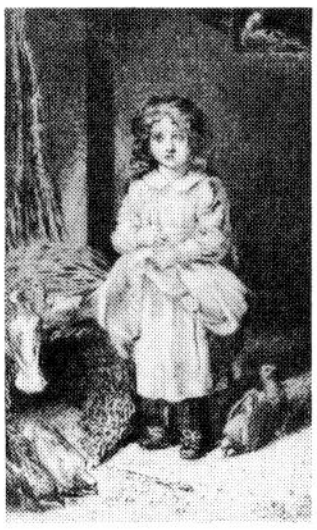

acc. no. 3491b
a different state, signed and dated in the plate as above

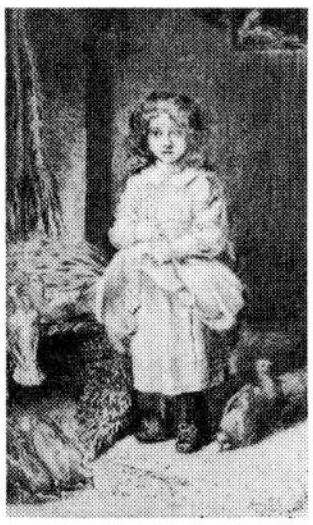

acc. no. 3482
Miss Mildred Carter – 'Grandmother's Boa' (1891)

etching: 9×7 in. (plate)
signed: *Anna Lea Merritt A.R.A.*

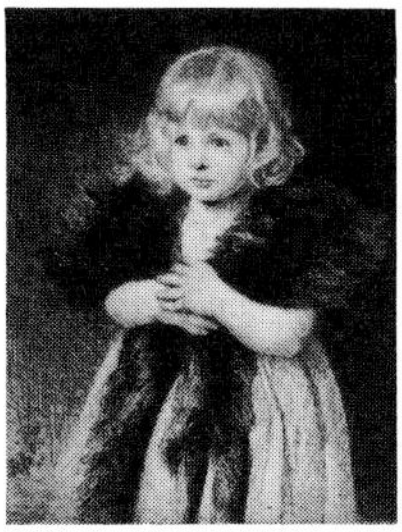

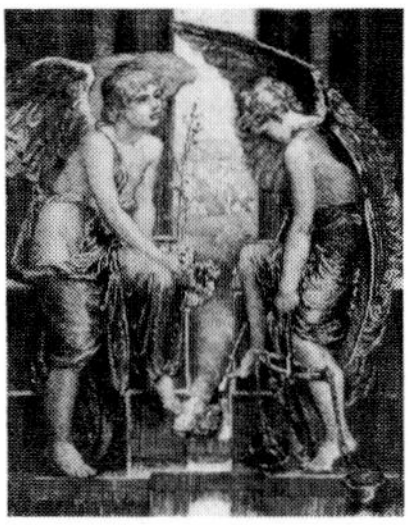

acc. no. 3494a
The Narrow Way (*c.*1894)

etching: 13¼ × 10¼ in. (plate)
signed: *Anna Lea Merritt pinxit et aqft* and again in reverse in the plate; inscribed: *The Narrow Way*

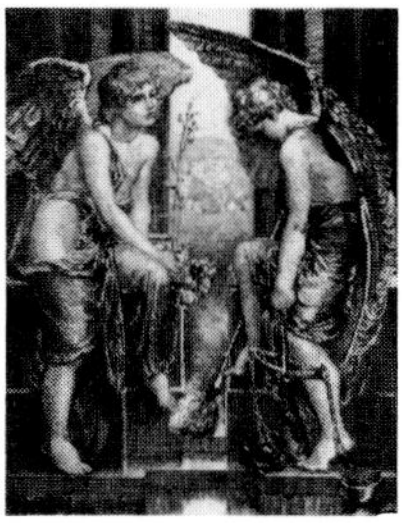

acc. no. 3494b
another impression, printed in brown, signed: *Anna Lea Merritt*

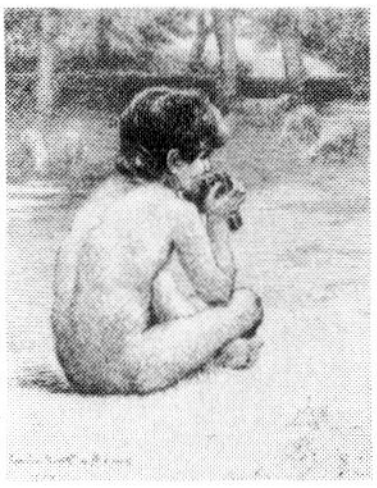

acc. no. 3485a
Piping Shepherd Boy (1904)

etching, remarque proof: 8 × 6¼ in. (plate)
signed: *Anna Lea Merritt*; signed and dated in the plate: *Anna Lea Merritt aq:ft & pinxt/1904*

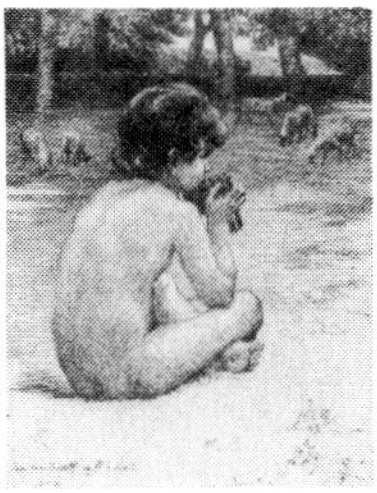

acc. no. 3485b
a different state, signed and dated in the plate as above

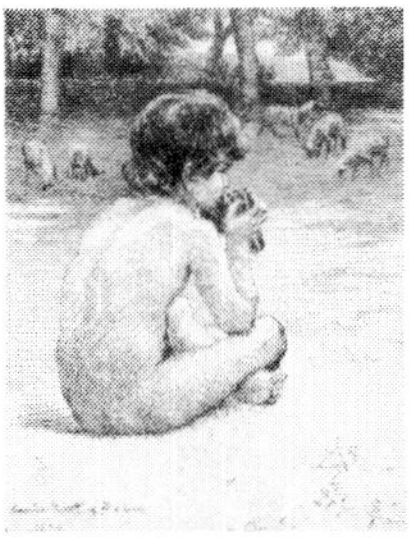

acc. no. 3485c
a different state, signed *Anna Lea Merritt* and inscribed: *A Piping Shepherd*; signed and dated in the plate as above

acc. no. 3492a
Cupid Bound (1908)

etching: 10 × $7\frac{3}{4}$ in. (plate)
signed: *Anna Lea Merritt* and inscribed: *Trial of 'Cupid Bound'*; signed and dated in the plate: *Anna Lea Merritt d e 2 aq (....) / 1908*

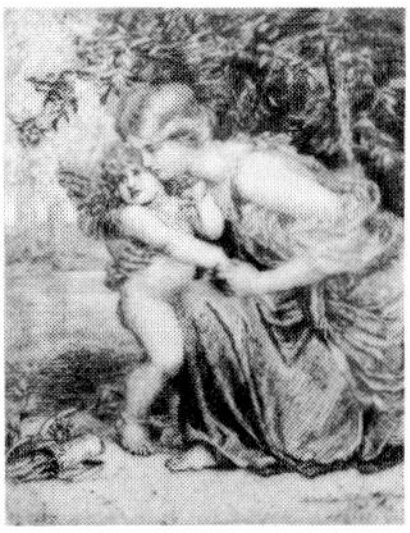

acc. no. 3492b
a different state, signed: *Anna Lea Merritt* and inscribed: *Trial*; signed and dated in the plate as above

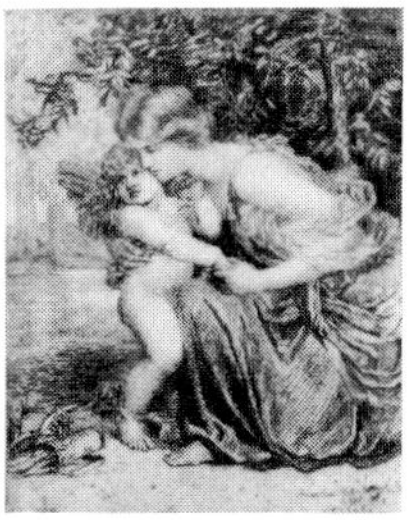

acc. no. 3492c
another impression, signed: *Anna Lea Merritt* and inscribed: *Trial* signed and dated in the plate as above

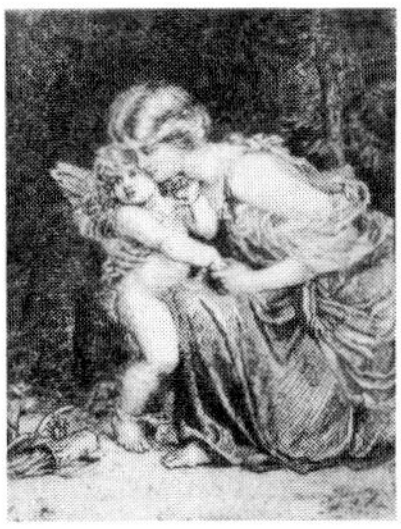

acc. no. 3492d
a different state, signed: *Anna Lea Merritt ARE*; signed and dated in the plate as above

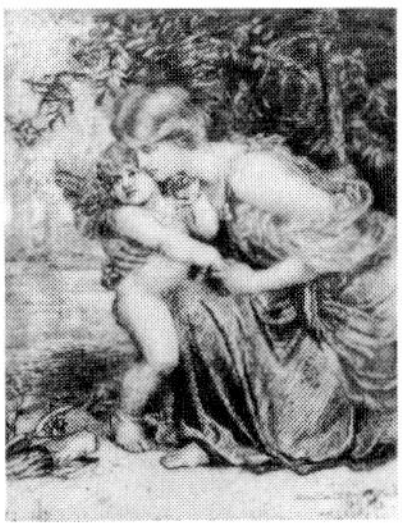

acc. no. 3483
Mother and Child (1911)

etching: 8 × 5 in. (plate)
inscribed: *Trial*

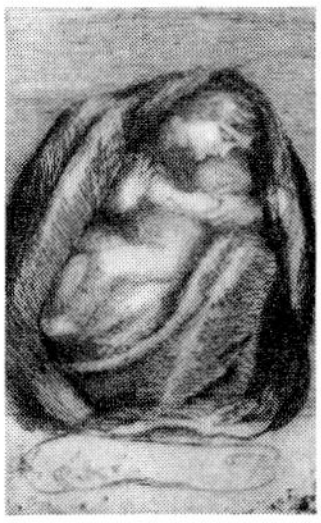

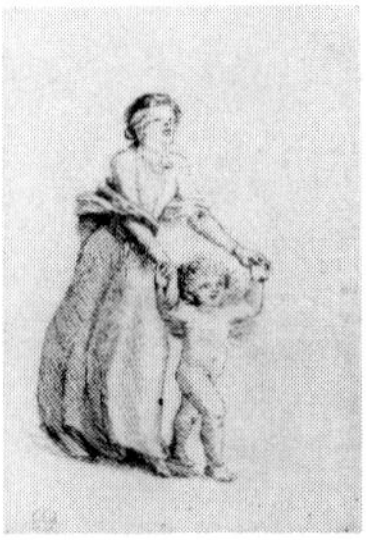

acc. no. 3486a
Cupid Leading a Blindfolded Girl (1912)

etching: 9 × 6 in. (plate)
signed (mono) and dated in the plate: *ALM / 1912*

acc. no.s 3486b – 3486i: a further eight impressions

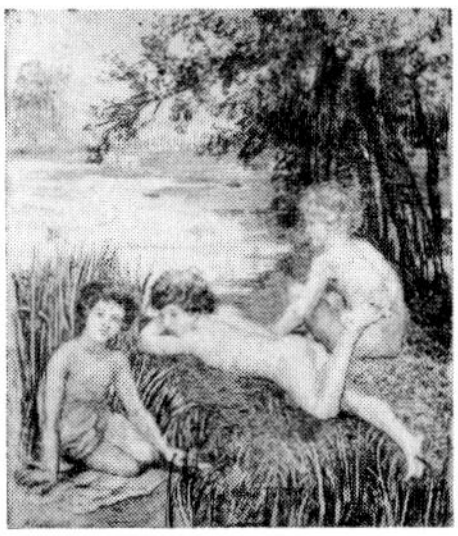

acc. no. 3495a
Wild Duck (1913)

etching: $11\frac{1}{2} \times 9\frac{1}{2}$ in. (plate)
inscribed: *Trial*; signed and dated in the plate: *A. Lea Merritt 1913*

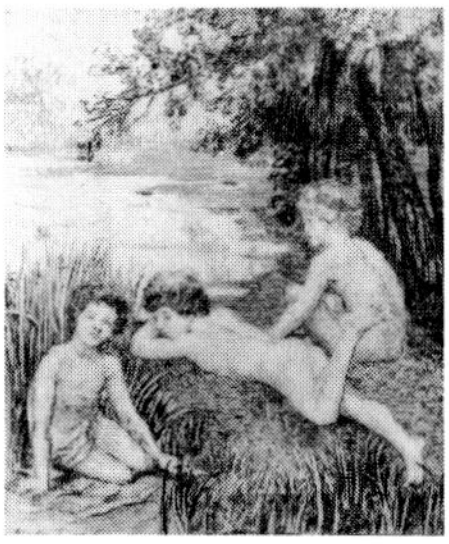

acc. no. 3495b
a different state, signed *Anna Lea Merritt* and inscribed: *Wild Duck*; signed and dated in the plate as above

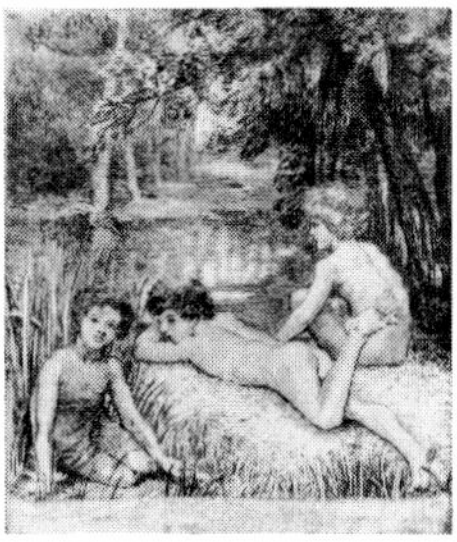

acc. no. 3495c
a different state, signed and dated in the plate as above; the bottom inch masked with white bodycolour

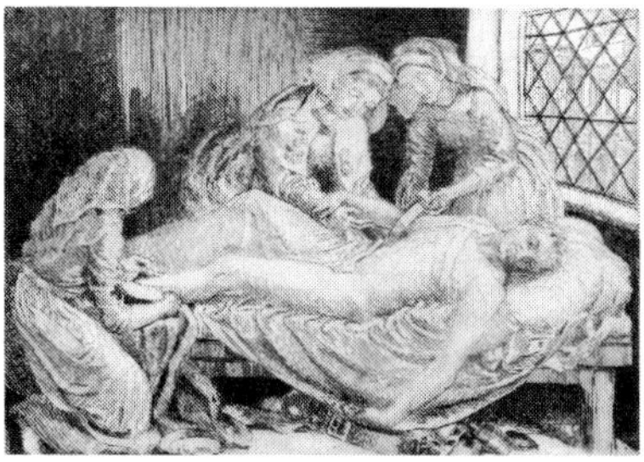

acc. no. 3488
Three Nurses tending a Wounded Soldier (1915)

etching: $8\frac{3}{4} \times 10\frac{3}{4}$ in. (plate)
signed and dated in the plate: *Anna Lea Merritt 1915*

acc. no. 3489
Three Nurses tending a Wounded Soldier (1915–16)
etching: 9¼ × 12¼ in. (plate)
signed (mono) and dated in the plate: *ALM / 1915* and *ALM / 1916*

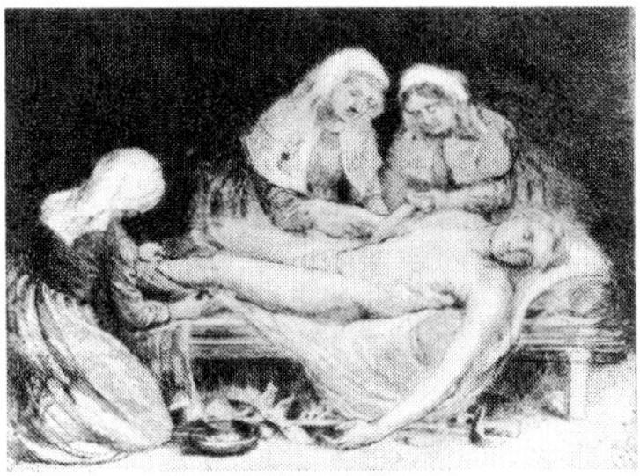

acc. no. 3464
Study for the Wounded Soldier (*c.*1915)
brown crayon: 5¼ × 9 in.

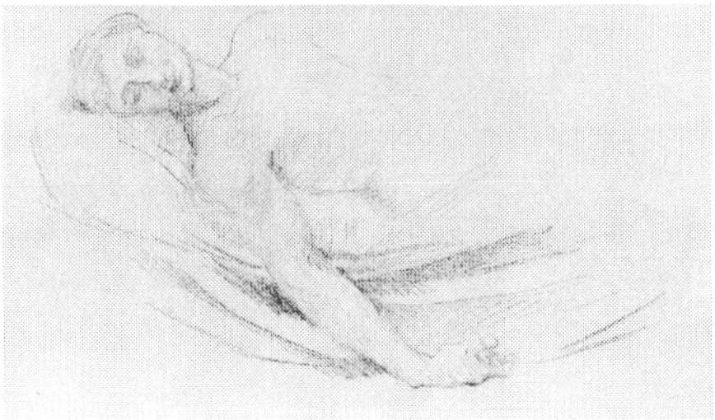

acc. no. 3490
Old Man in a Flat Cap (1916)
etching and drypoint on vellum: 11¾ × 7⅛ in. (plate)
signed: *Anna Lea Merritt*; signed and dated in the plate: *Anna Lea Merritt / 1916*

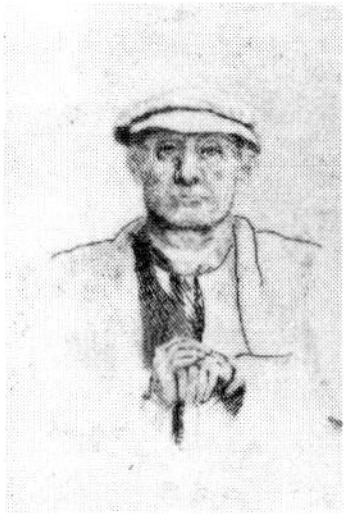

acc. no. 3496b
Pond with Trees (1917)
etching and drypoint: 4⅝ × 6⅜ in. (plate)
signed and dated: *Anna Lea Merritt ARE April / 1917*; signed (mono) in the plate: *ALM*

acc. no. 3496a
another impression – identical to 3496b

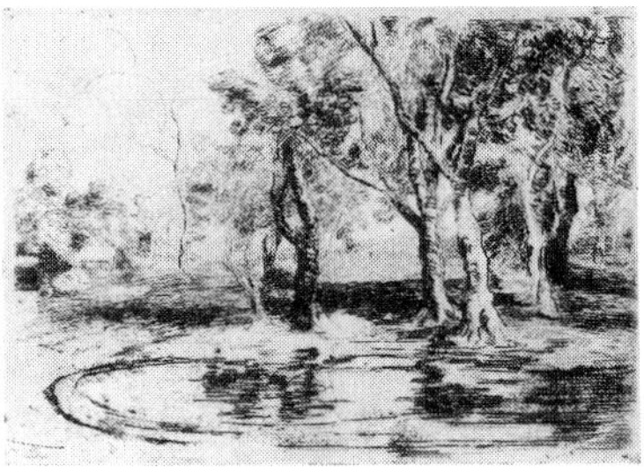

acc. no. 3484a
Two Boys on a Ledge
etching: 7⅝ × 5 in. (plate)
signed: *Anna Lea Merritt*; signed in the plate: *Anna Lea Merritt*

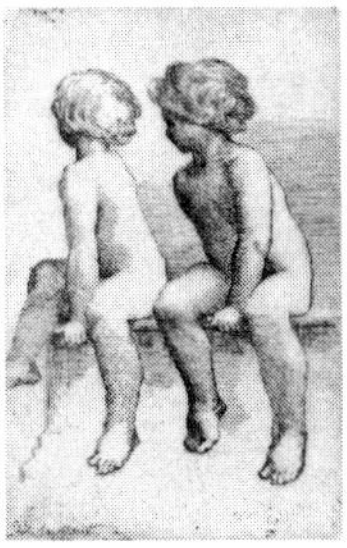

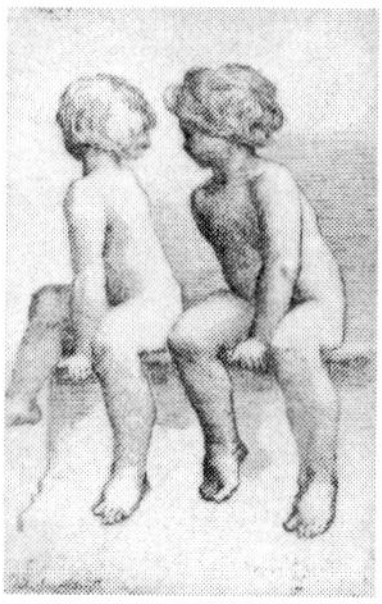

acc. no. 3484b
another impression, signed: *Anna Lea Merritt*

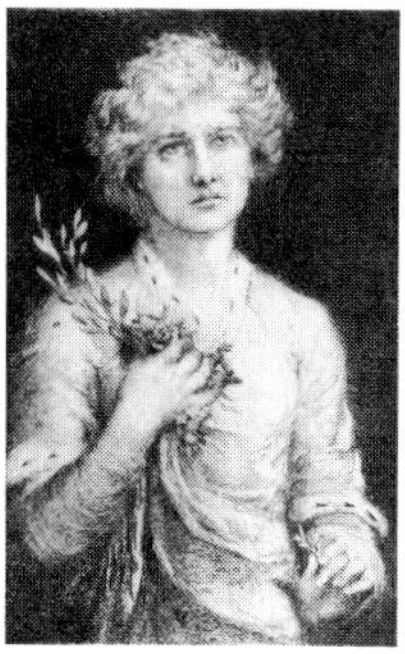

acc. no. 3493a
Lady in a Fur-Lined Robe
etching: $10\frac{3}{4} \times 6\frac{7}{8}$ in. (plate)
numbered in pencil: *3*

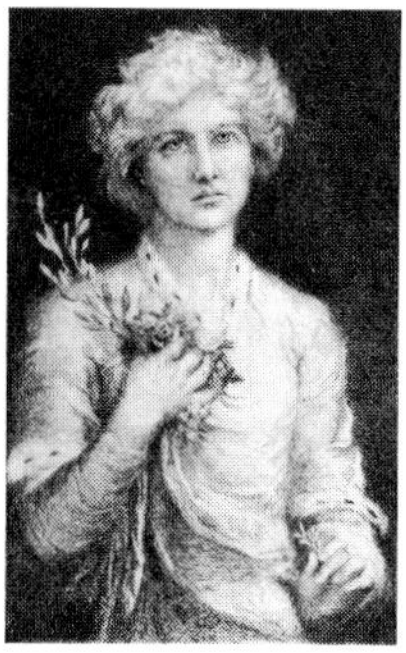

acc. no. 3493b
a different state

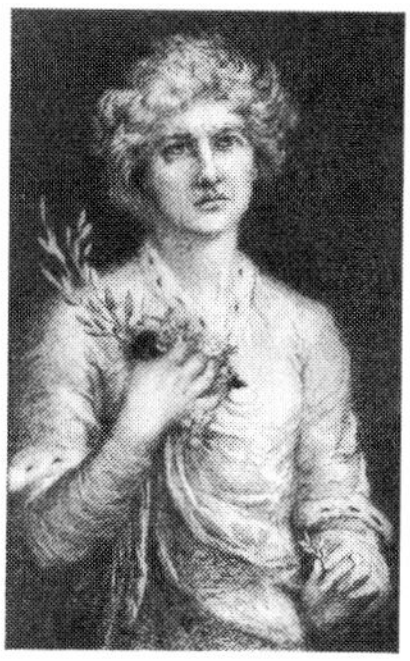

acc. no. 3493c
a different state

acc. no. 3416
Design for Stained Glass
watercolour and pencil: $15 \times 6\frac{1}{4}$ in.

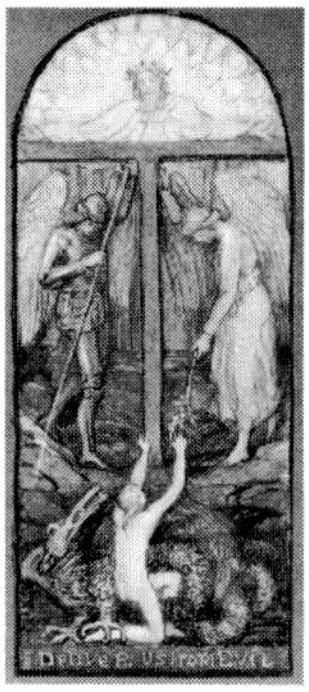

acc. no. 3417
A Woman in White writing at a Desk
watercolour: $9\frac{3}{4} \times 6\frac{7}{8}$ in.

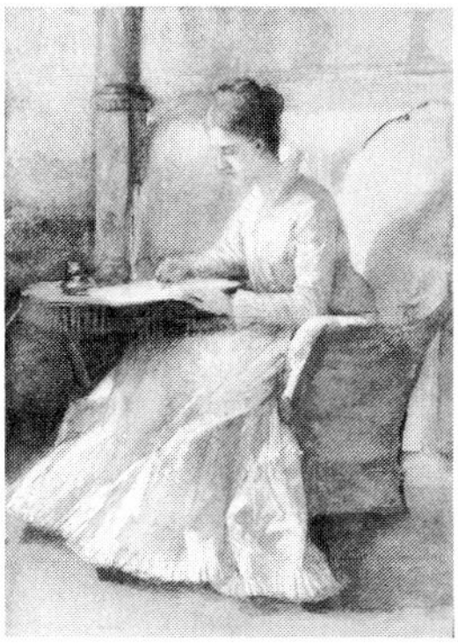

acc. no. 3418
Woman reading a Letter
watercolour and pencil: $10 \times 7\frac{1}{8}$ in.

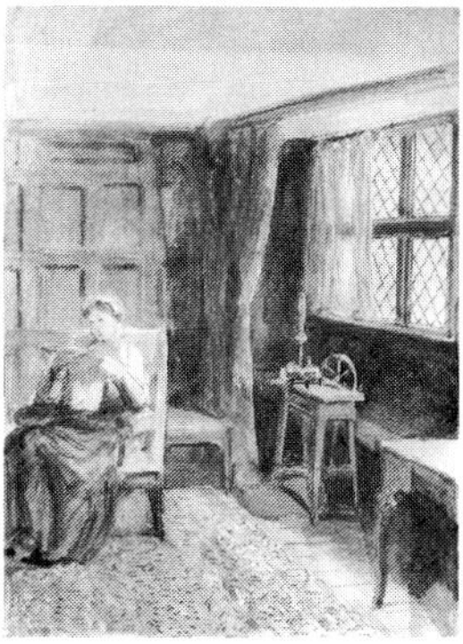

acc. no. 3419
A Lake with Sailing Boats
watercolour: 7×10 in.

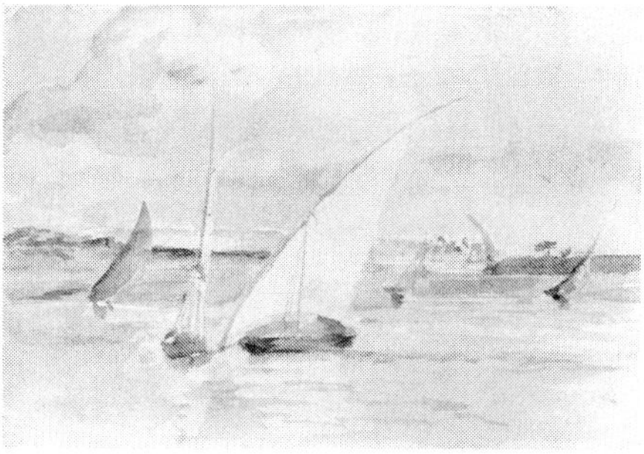

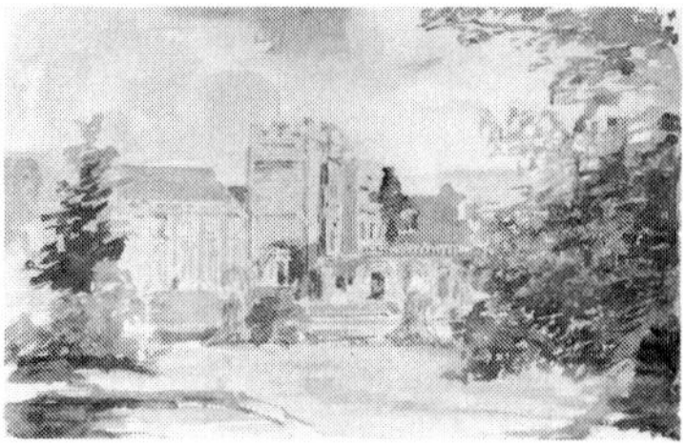

acc. no. 3420
Castle seen through Trees
watercolour: $6\frac{5}{8} \times 10$ in.

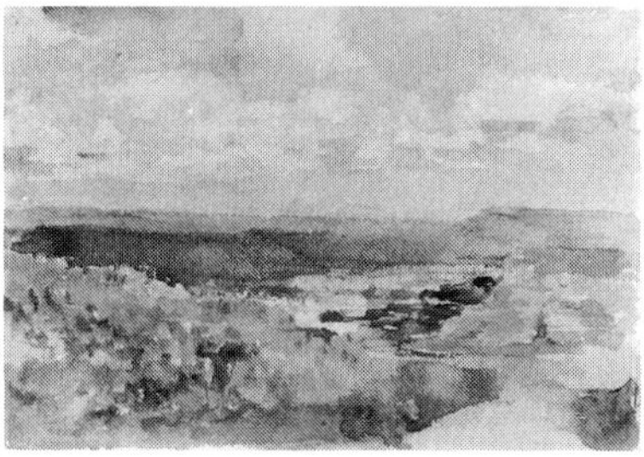

acc. no. 3421
Coastal Landscape
watercolour: $4\frac{7}{8} \times 7$ in.

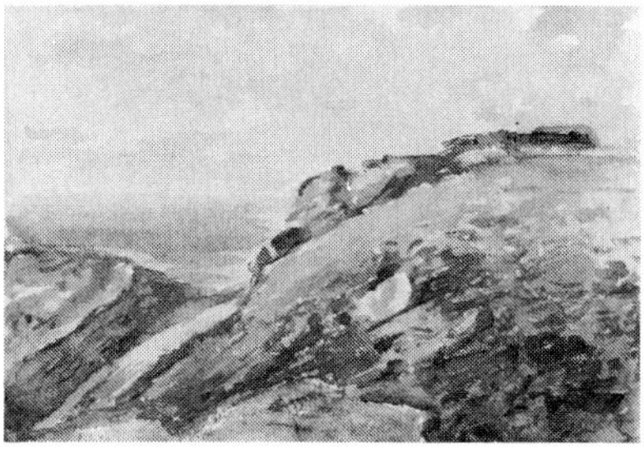

acc. no. 3422
Landscape with Cliffs and Sea
watercolour: $4\frac{7}{8} \times 7$ in.

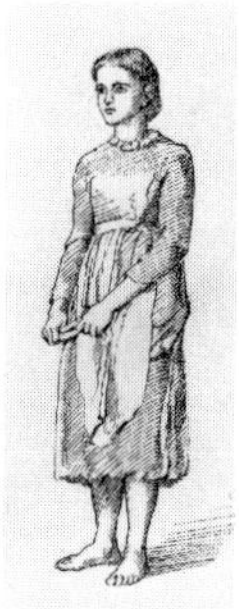

acc. no. 3423
A Beggar Maid
pen and ink over pencil: $11\frac{3}{4} \times 5\frac{1}{4}$ in.

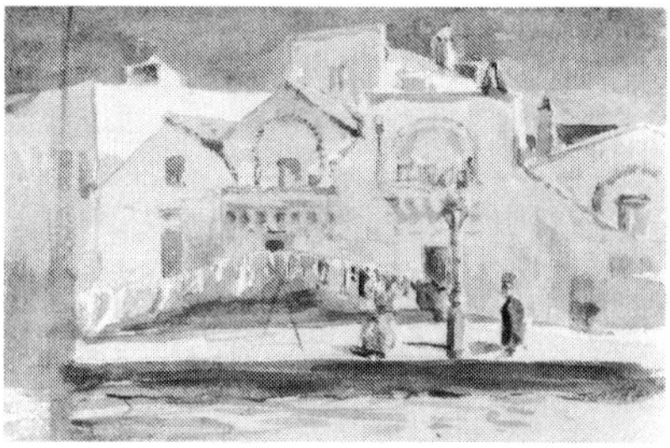

acc. no. 3424
Houses by a Canal with a Washing Line
watercolour over pencil: $7 \times 9\frac{7}{8}$ in.

acc. no. 3425
A Byzantine City
pen and ink over pencil: $9\frac{3}{4} \times 13\frac{1}{8}$ in.

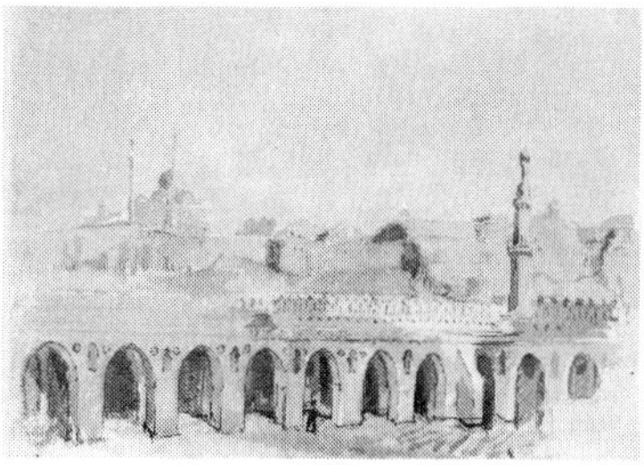

acc. no. 3426
In a Wood
watercolour: $7\frac{1}{8} \times 10$ in.

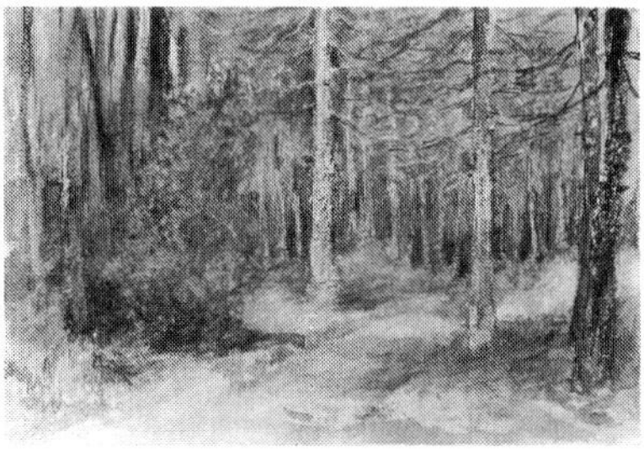

acc. no. 3427
River Scene
watercolour over pencil: 10×14 in.

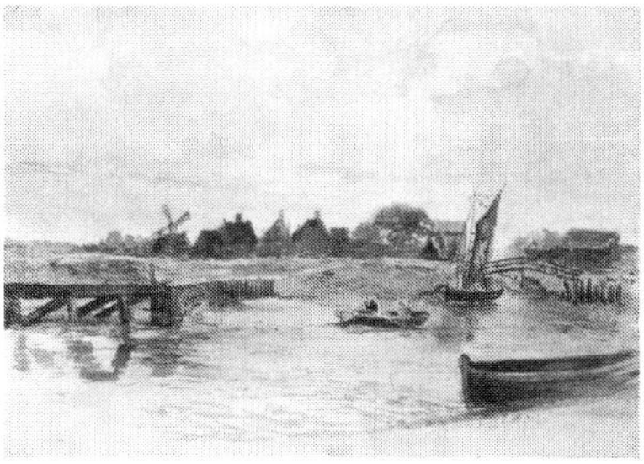

acc. no. 3428
Castle seen through Trees
watercolour: 10×14 in.

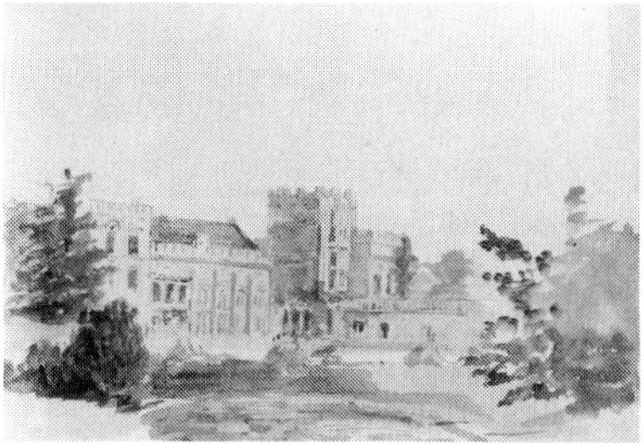

acc. no. 3429
Landscape
watercolour over pencil: $6\frac{3}{8} \times 10$ in.

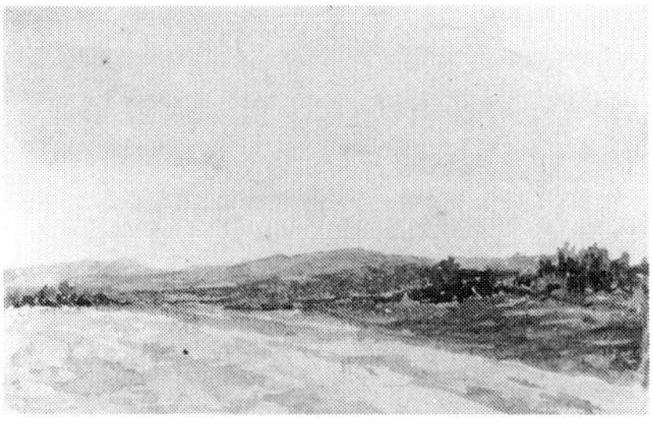

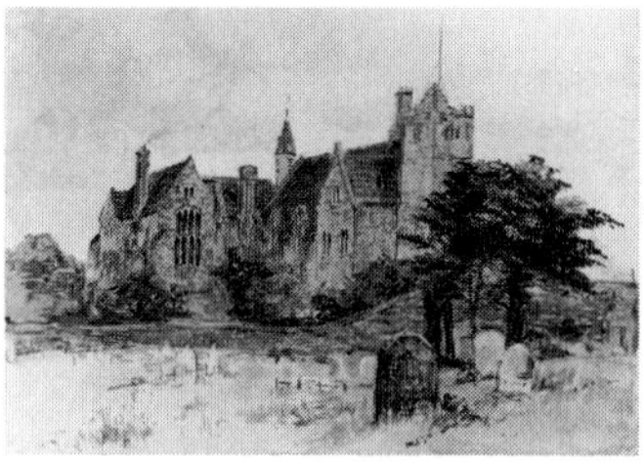

acc. no. 3430
Church with Rectory and Churchyard
watercolour over pencil: 10 × 14 in.

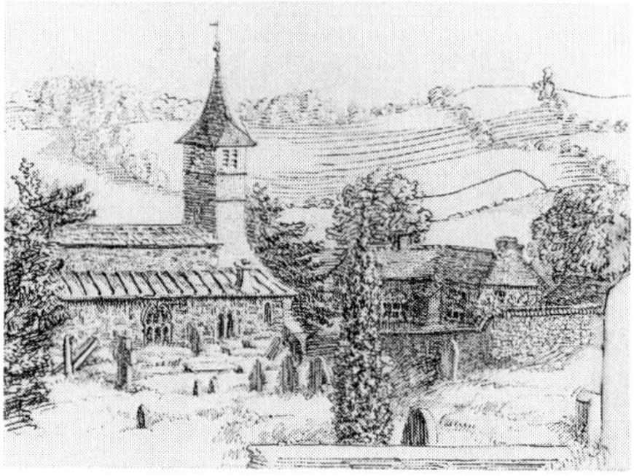

acc. no. 3471
Church with Rectory and Churchyard
pen and ink heightened with white, on board: $10\frac{5}{8} \times 14\frac{1}{2}$ in.
signed: *ALM*; inscribed: *The distant lines will fail to reproduce* (cancelled) and: *I have gone over the former / lines which were too faint / and consequently also in foreground. / Please say if a drawing retouched / like this would ever do well?* and, partially erased: (....) *impossible to use the pen on it afterwards / A.L.M.*

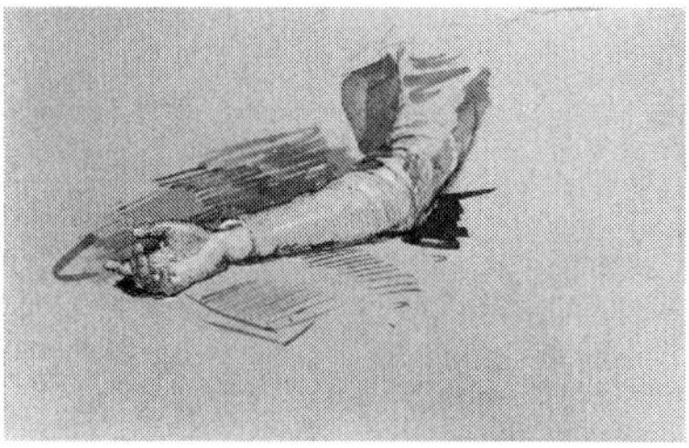

acc. no. 3431
Study of an Arm
pencil and watercolour: $6\frac{3}{4} \times 10\frac{1}{4}$ in.

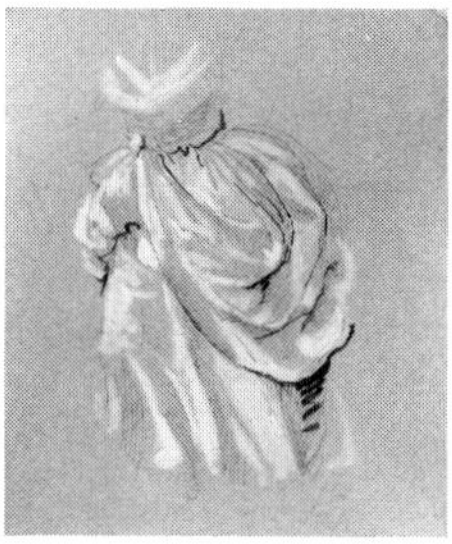

acc. no. 3432
Study of a Dress
pencil and watercolour on blue paper: $7\frac{5}{8} \times 6\frac{3}{8}$ in.

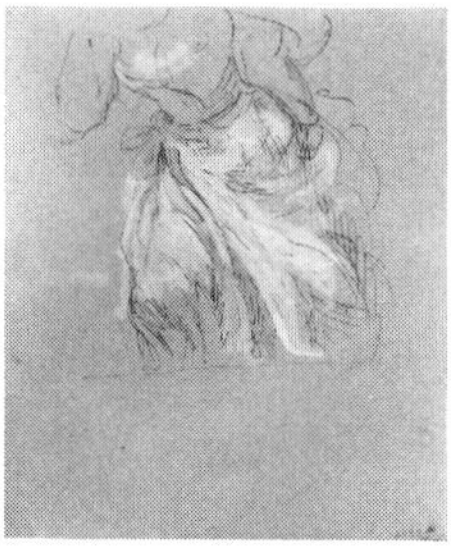

verso: *Female Figure with Flowing Drapery*
pencil and white bodycolour

acc. no. 3433
A Mediterranean Town
watercolour: $7 \times 9\frac{7}{8}$ in.

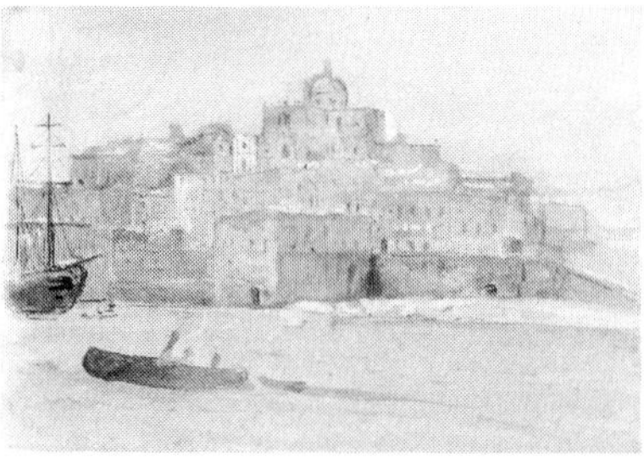

acc. no. 3434
Village Street with Tudor Houses
watercolour: $9\frac{3}{4} \times 13\frac{7}{8}$ in.

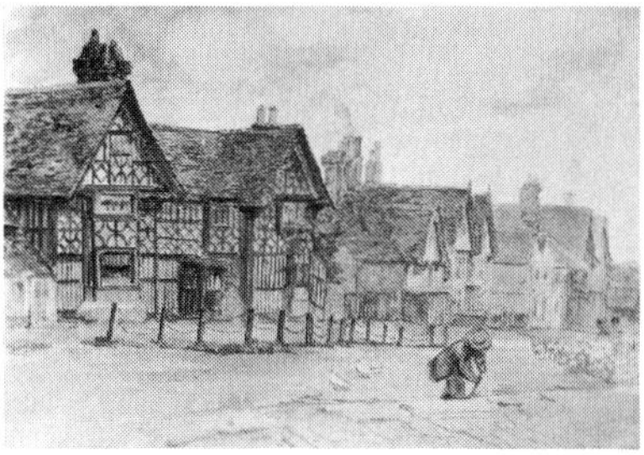

acc. no. 3435
Seated Woman and a Young Girl
watercolour: $13 \times 9\frac{5}{8}$ in.

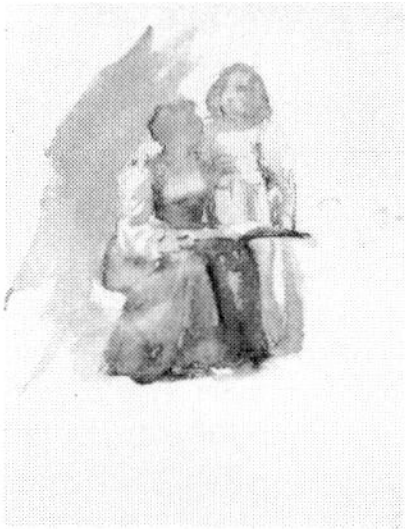

acc. no. 3436
Man and Woman on a River Bank
watercolour: 10×14 in.

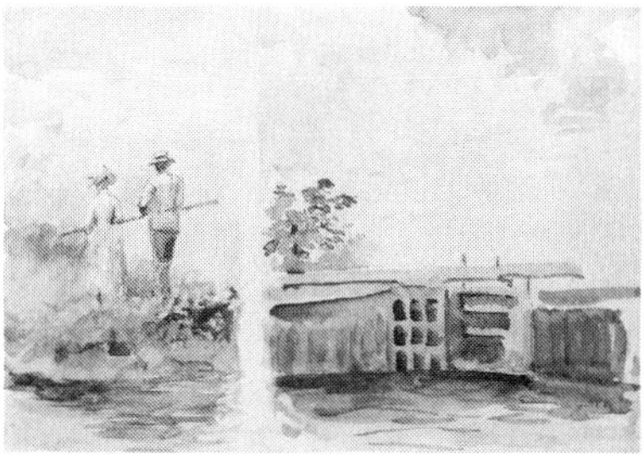

acc. no. 3437
Young Girl embracing a Woman
oil on canvas: $14 \times 9\frac{3}{4}$ in.

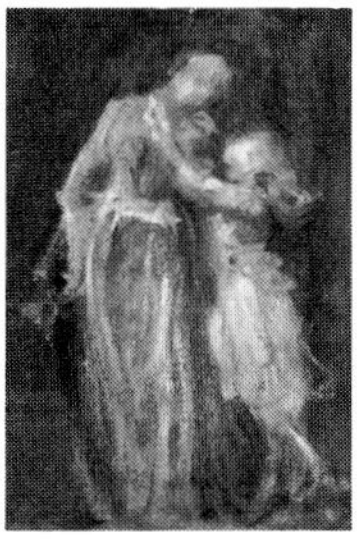

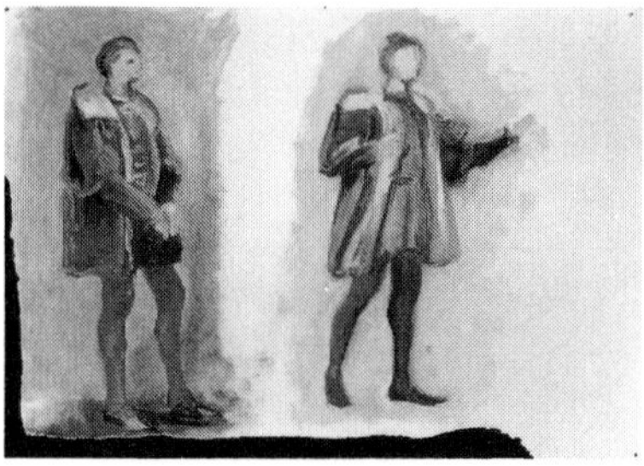

acc. no. 3438
Two Studies of a Man in 15thC Dress
oil on paper: 10 × 14 in.

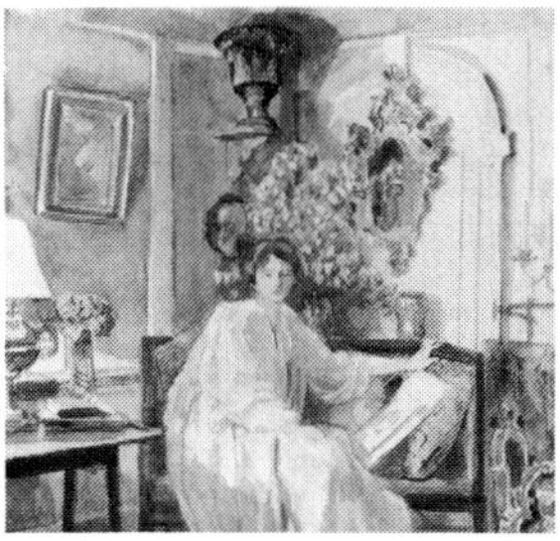

acc. no. 3439
Young Woman in White
watercolour and pencil: $12\frac{1}{4} \times 12$ in.

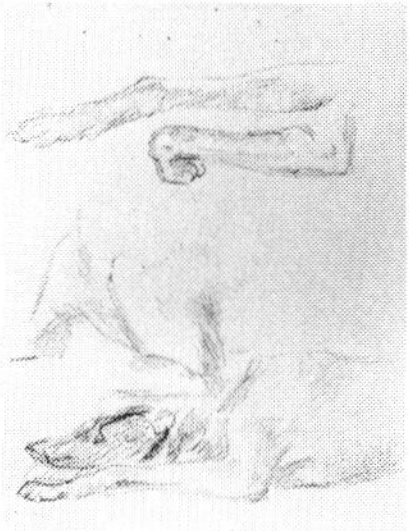

acc. no. 3440
Three Studies of a Greyhound
brown pencil on buff paper: $7\frac{1}{8} \times 5\frac{1}{2}$ in.

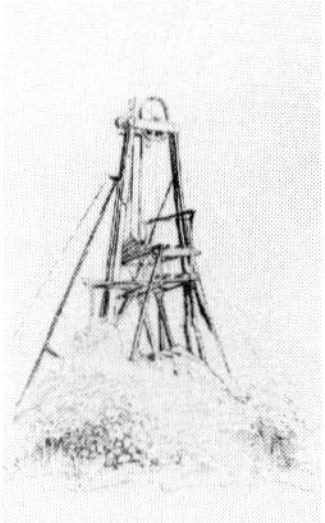

acc. no. 3441
A Colliery Winding Engine
pen and ink and pencil: $12\frac{1}{8} \times 7\frac{1}{2}$ in.

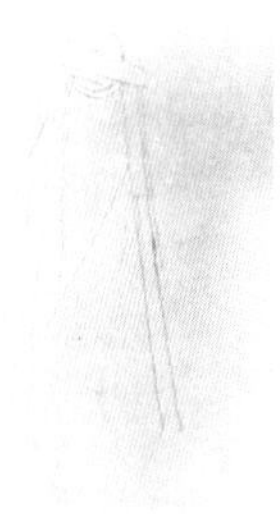

verso: *slight Study of a Winding Engine*
pencil

acc. no. 3480
A Colliery Winding Engine
pen and ink and pencil: 14 × 10 in.

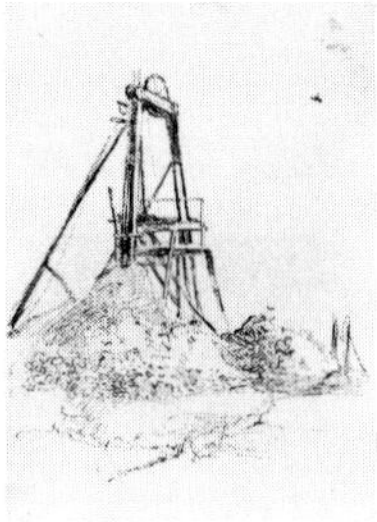

acc. no. 3442
Study of a Draped Figure
black, brown and white chalks on grey paper, laid on canvas: $14\frac{1}{8} \times 7\frac{1}{2}$ in.

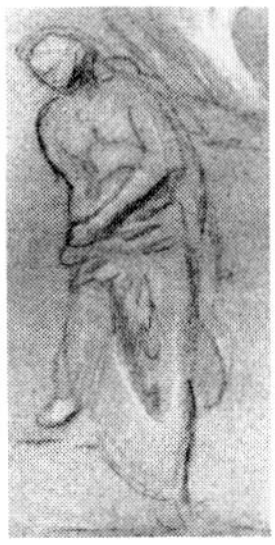

acc. no. 3443
Seated Woman with Cap and Shawl
grey wash and pencil on blue board: $11 \times 8\frac{1}{4}$ in.

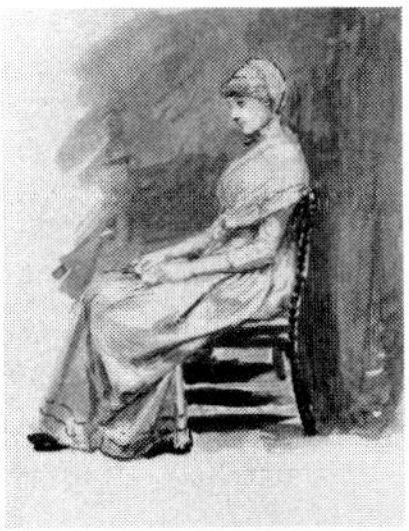

acc. no. 3444
Nude Study of a Seated Boy
pencil: $11 \times 7\frac{5}{8}$ in.

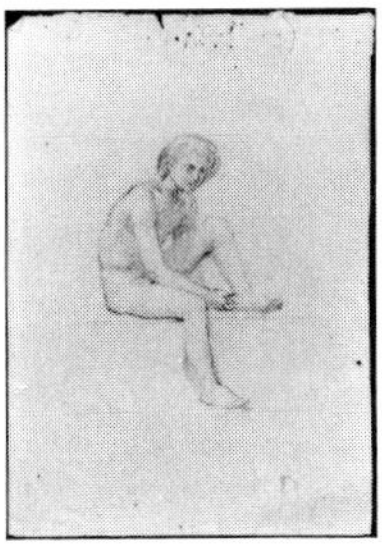

verso: *Nude Study of a Seated Boy (in reverse)*
pencil

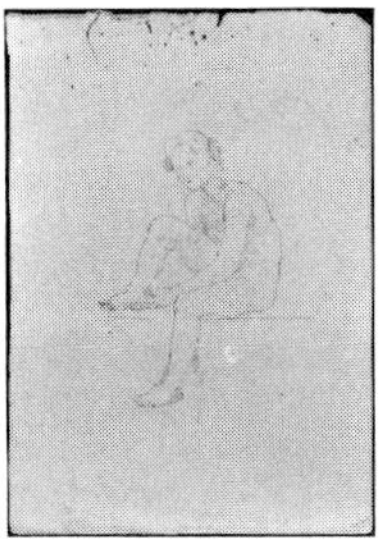

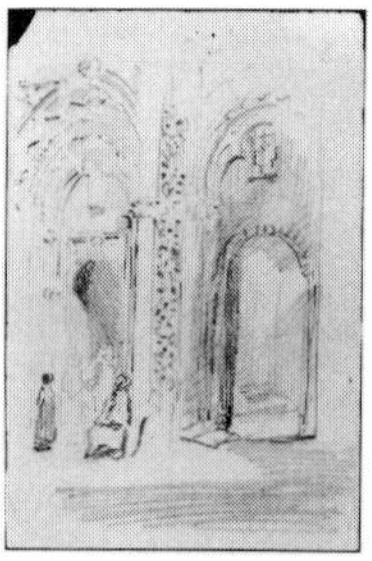

acc. no. 3445
Entrance to a Mosque
pencil: $7\frac{5}{8} \times 5$ in.

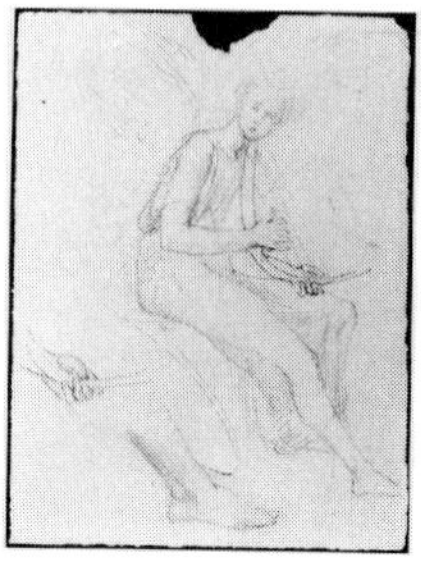

acc. no. 3446
Studies for a Seated Angel with a Harp
pencil: $7\frac{5}{8} \times 5\frac{3}{4}$ in.

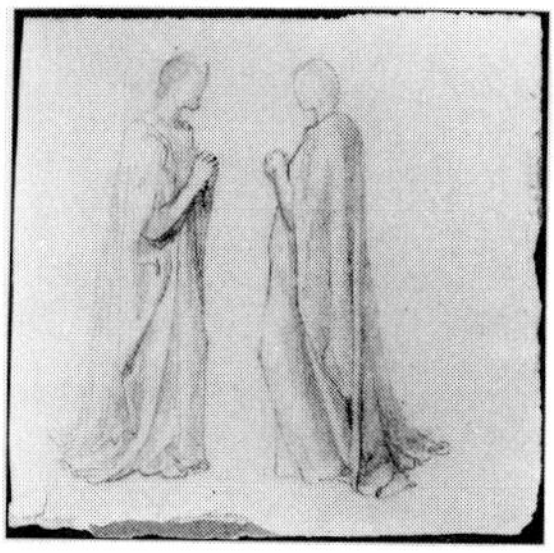

acc. no. 3447
Study of Two Robed Figures
pencil: $11 \times 11\frac{1}{4}$ in.

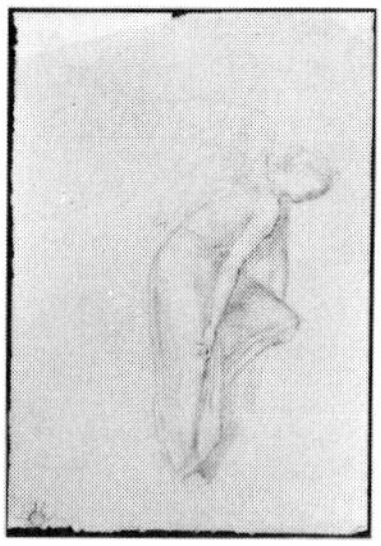

acc. no. 3448
Study of a Bending Angel
pencil: $11 \times 7\frac{5}{8}$ in.

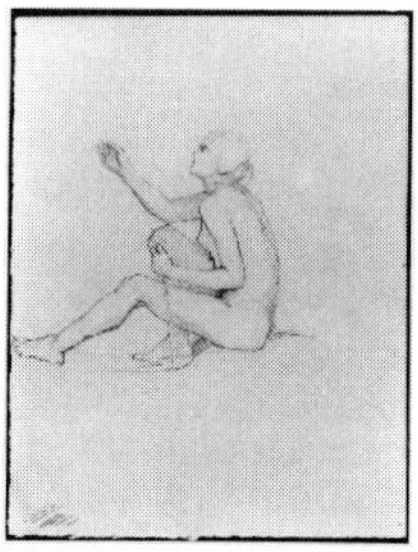

acc. no. 3449
Seated Nude with a Stick
pencil: $11\frac{1}{2} \times 8\frac{7}{8}$ in.

acc. no. 3450
Study of a Bending Woman
pencil: $11\frac{3}{8} \times 8\frac{3}{4}$ in.

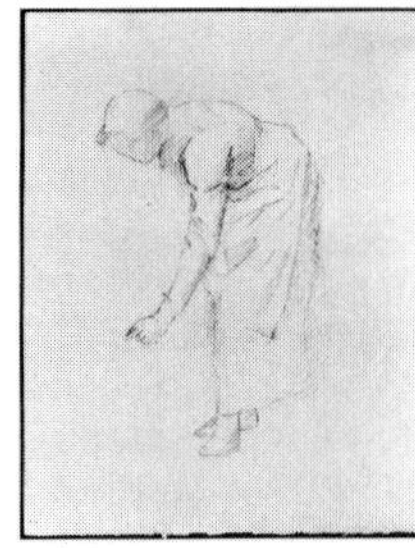

acc. no. 3451
Two Studies of Kneeling Woman, Arms Outstretched
pencil: $10\frac{7}{8} \times 12$ in.

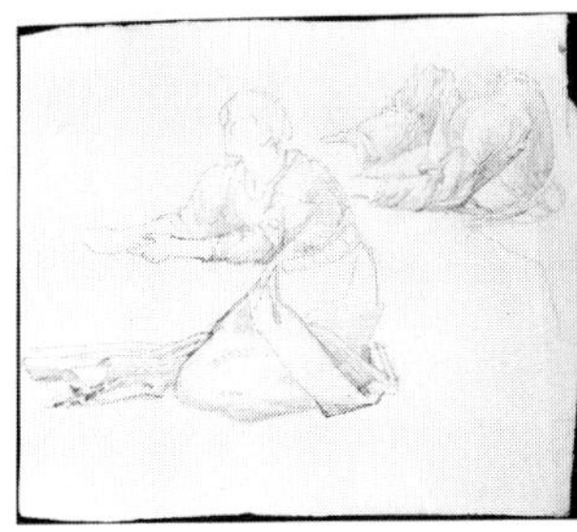

acc. no. 3452
Head of a Man
brown and white chalk on brown paper: $10 \times 8\frac{3}{4}$ in.

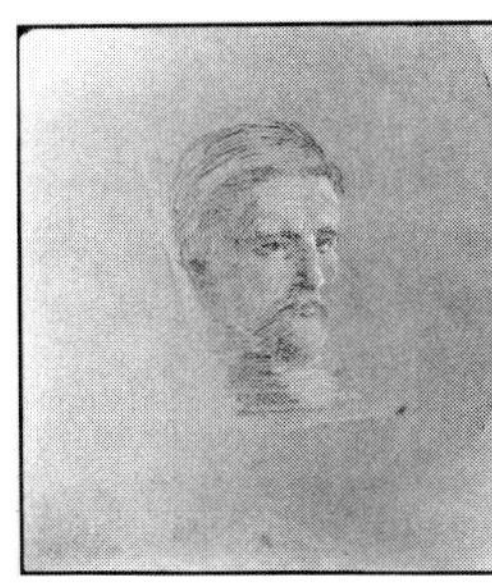

acc. no. 3453
Head of a Woman
brown chalk on brown paper: 10×9 in.

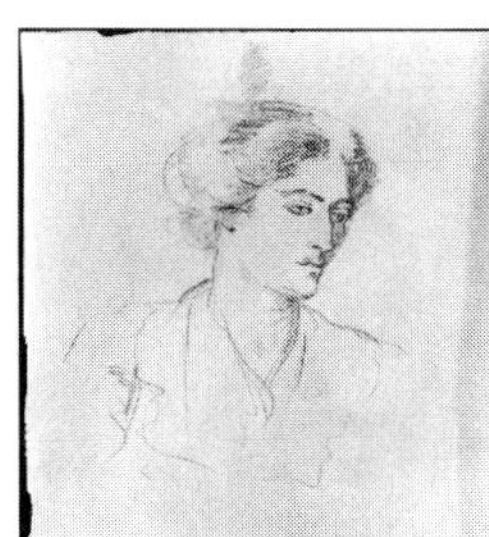

acc. no. 3477
Head of a Woman
pencil: $16\frac{3}{8} \times 11\frac{1}{8}$ in.
inscribed: *Good neck & arms / long hands*

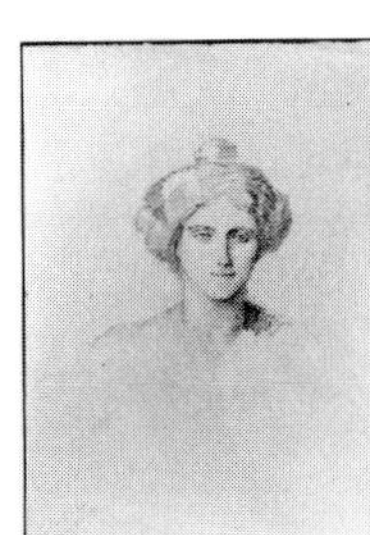

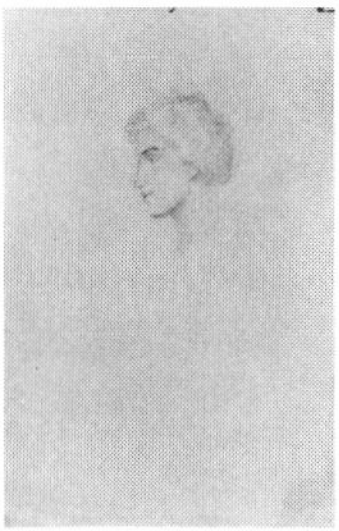

acc. no. 3478
Profile of a Woman
pencil: $16\frac{3}{8} \times 10\frac{1}{8}$ in.

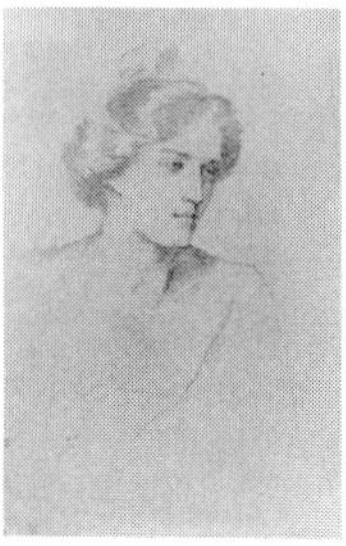

acc. no. 3479
Head of a Woman, Three-Quarters
pencil: $16\frac{1}{8} \times 10\frac{3}{8}$ in.

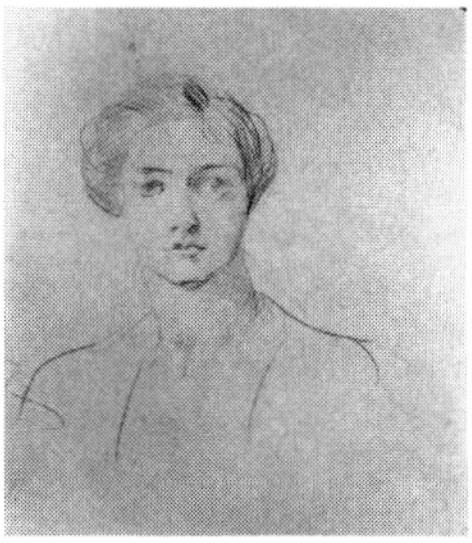

acc. no. 3454
Head and Shoulders of a Woman
brown chalk on brown paper: 10 × 9 in.

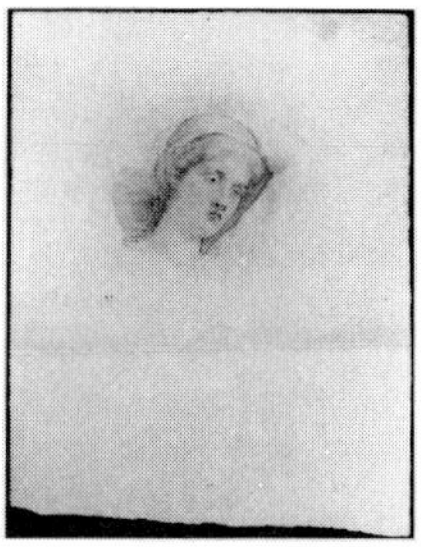

acc. no. 3455
Head and Arm of a Woman
pencil: $9\frac{1}{4} \times 11\frac{1}{8}$ in.

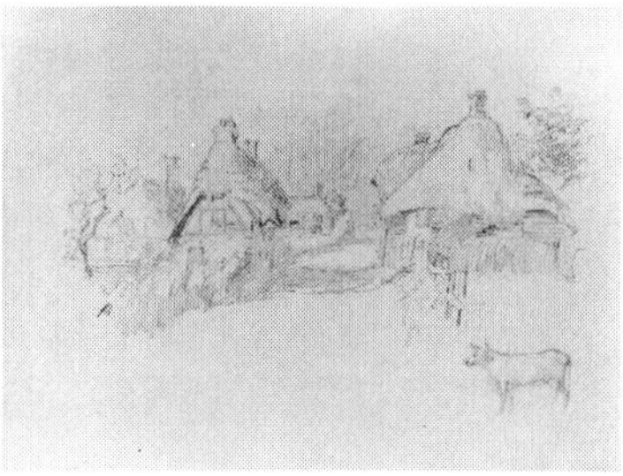

acc. no. 3457
Street with Thatched Cottages
pencil: $9\frac{1}{8} \times 11\frac{1}{8}$ in.

acc. no. 3458
Half Length Back View of a Nude Woman
pencil: $7\frac{1}{2} \times 5\frac{1}{2}$ in.

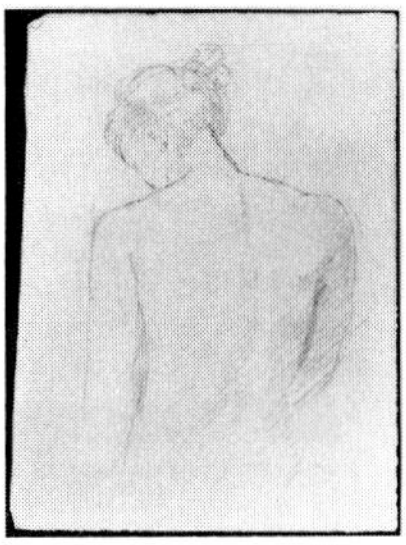

verso: *Standing Nude with a Pole*
pencil

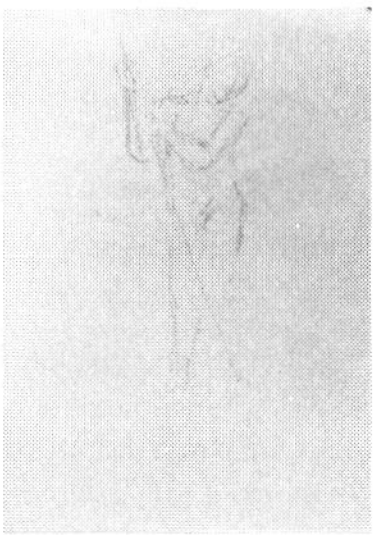

acc. no. 3459
Standing Nude Woman with a Harp
pencil: $7\frac{1}{4} \times 5\frac{1}{8}$ in.

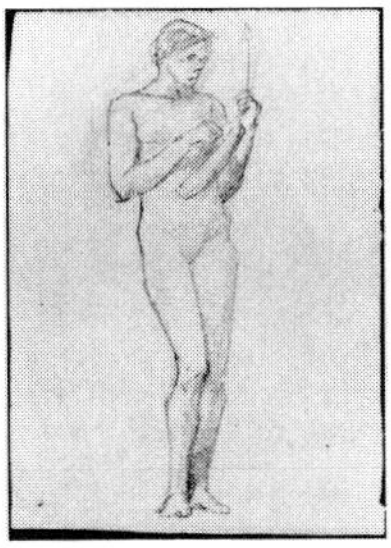

acc. no. 3460
Head of an Old Woman with a Cap
pencil: 10×7 in.

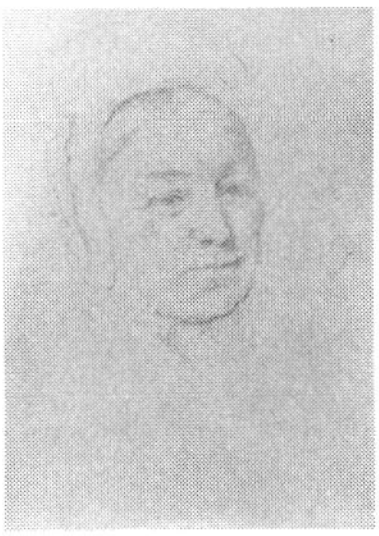

acc. no. 3461
Three Studies of a Cow
pencil: $7 \times 9\frac{3}{4}$ in.

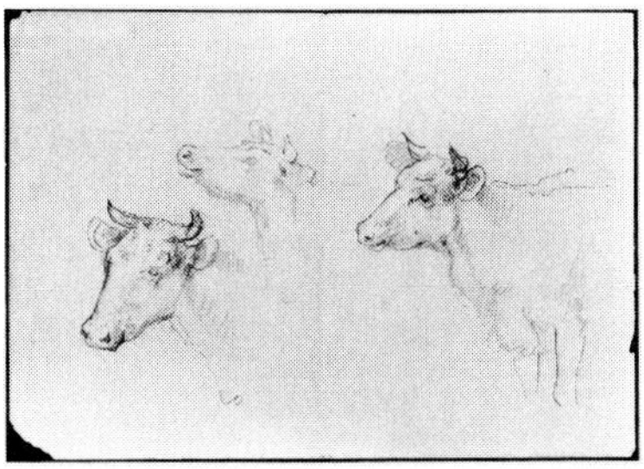

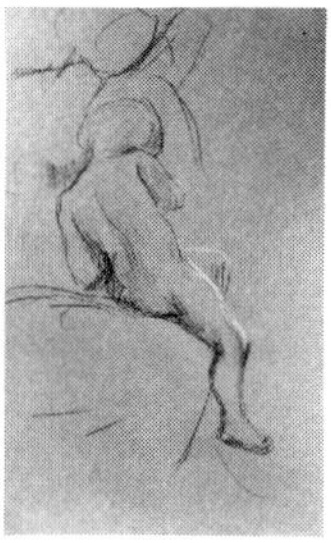

acc. no. 3462
Study of a Child on a Mother's Lap
brown and white chalk on brown paper: $10 \times 6\frac{7}{8}$ in.

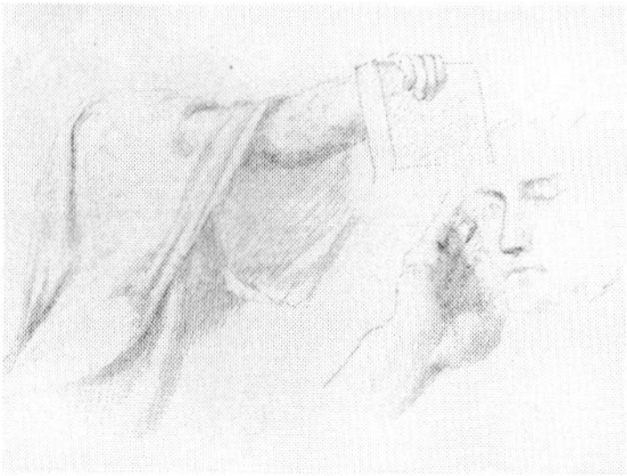

acc. no. 3463
Study of Robed Arm with Book Outheld; and Study of Man, Head in Hand
pencil: $7 \times 9\frac{3}{4}$ in.

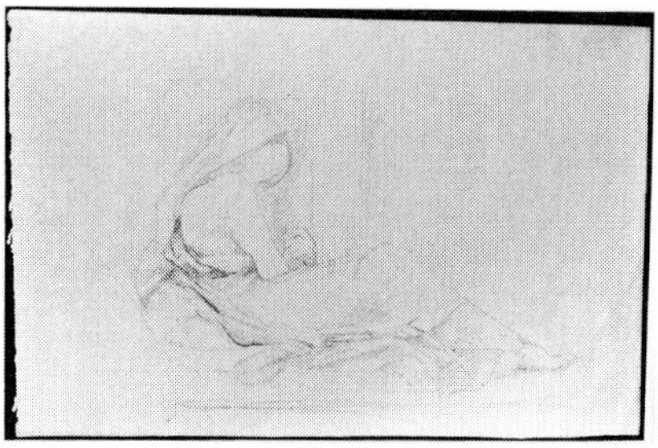

acc. no. 3465
Study of Reclining Figure wrapped in Drapery
brown crayon: $7\frac{3}{8} \times 11$ in.

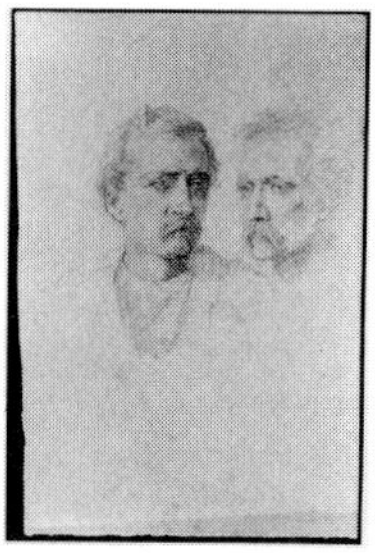

acc. no. 3466
Two Studies of a Man's head
pencil: $11 \times 7\frac{1}{8}$ in.

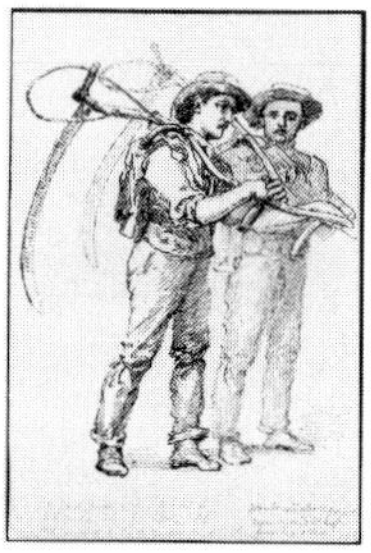

acc. no. 3468
Two Men with Scythes
pen, ink and pencil: $11 \times 7\frac{1}{2}$ in.
inscribed: *Would the above figure seem more distant than the other? – No, partly because the top part is so different in colour to the bottom the work in the top part is as dark as that of the other figure.*

acc. no. 3469
Man with Scythe, and a Study of his Head
pen, ink and pencil: $11\frac{1}{4} \times 7\frac{5}{8}$ in.

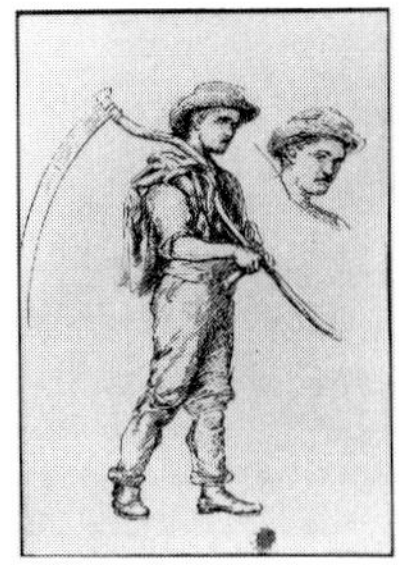

acc. no. 3470
Thatched Farm
pen and ink heightened with white on board: $10\frac{5}{8} \times 14\frac{1}{2}$ in.

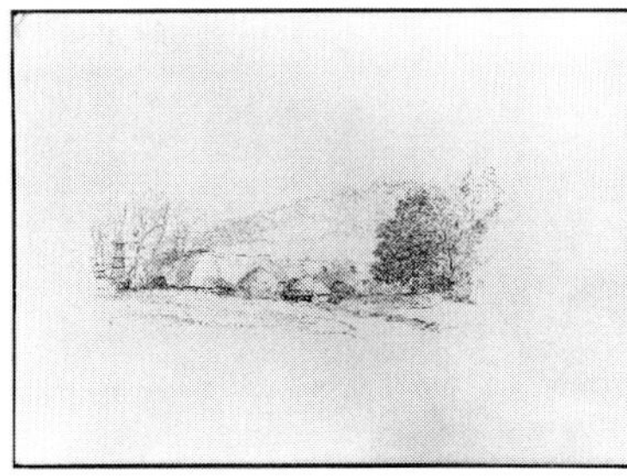

acc. no. 3472
Studies of an Old Woman in a Bonnet and of Hand clasping those of a Child
pencil: $12\frac{3}{4} \times 10\frac{7}{8}$ in.

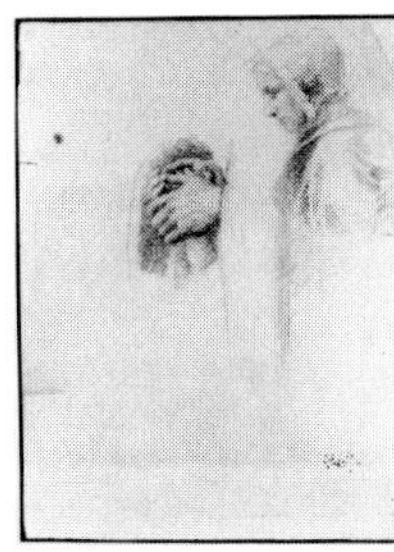

acc. no. 3473
Two Studies of a Pair of Figures
brown and white chalks on brown paper: $10 \times 16\frac{1}{8}$ in.

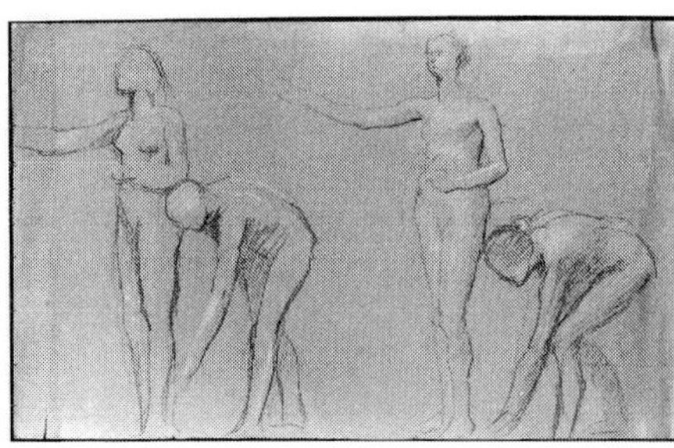

acc. no. 3474
Studies of Bending and Standing Figures
brown and white chalks on brown paper: $10 \times 16\frac{7}{8}$ in.

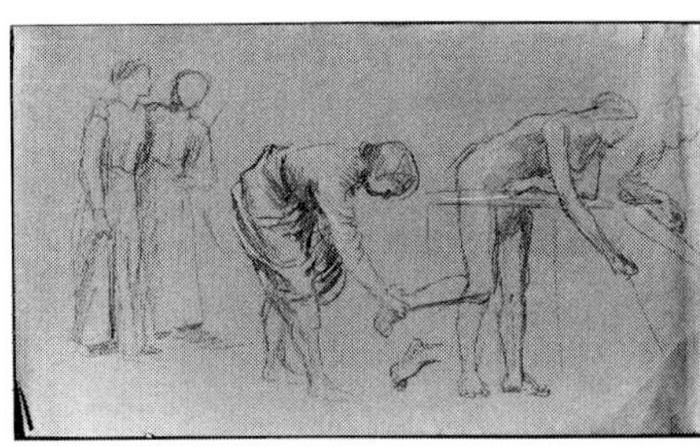

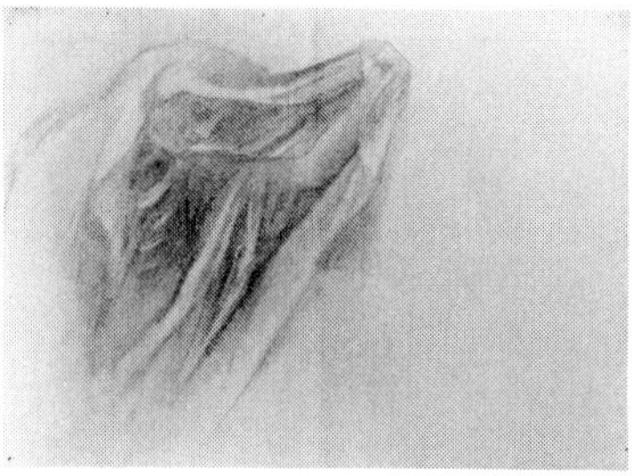

acc. no. 3475
Half Length Draped Figure
charcoal: $11\frac{1}{4} \times 14\frac{7}{8}$ in.

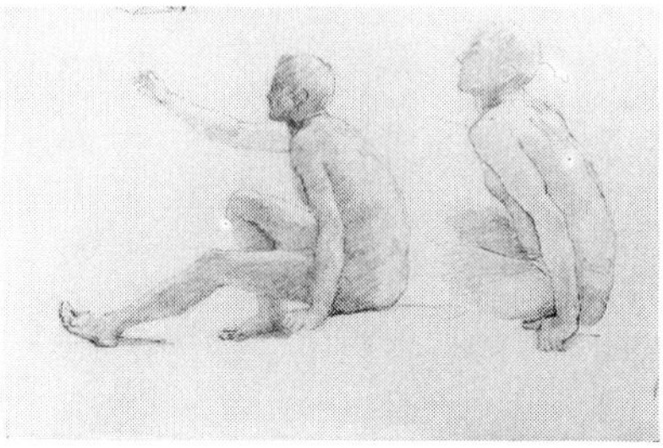

acc. no. 3476
Two Studies of a Seated Male Nude
pencil: $10\frac{1}{2} \times 15\frac{1}{2}$ in.

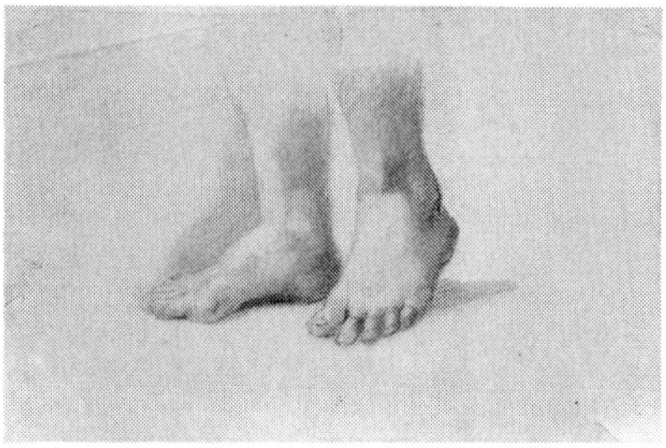

acc. no. 3481
Study of a Pair of Feet
red and brown chalks: 11 × 17 in.

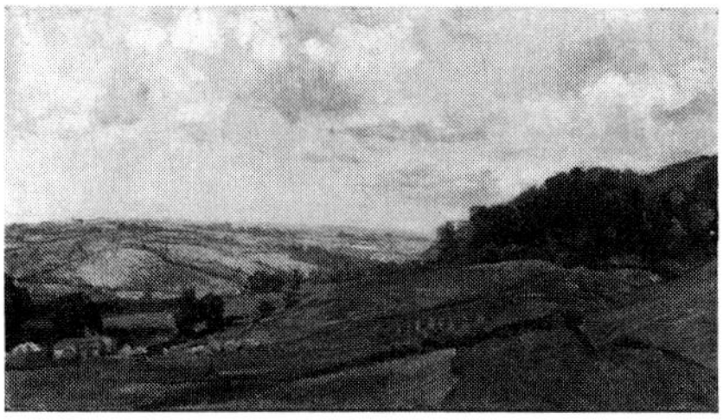

acc. no. 1655
Across the Valley
oil on canvas laid on hardboard: $14\frac{1}{2} \times 26$ in.

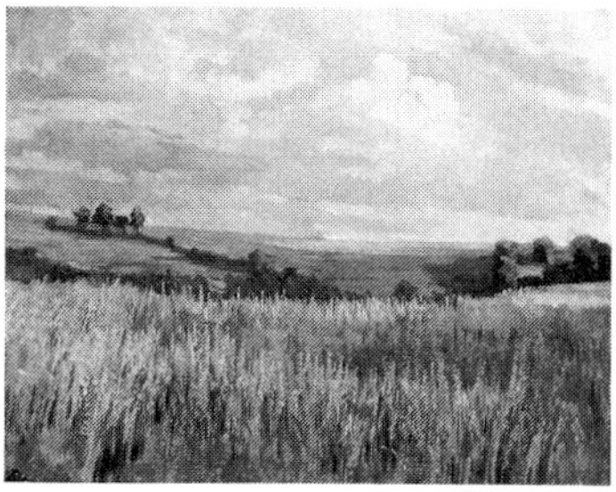

acc. no. 1656
The Cornfield
oil on canvas laid on hardboard: $16\frac{7}{8} \times 20\frac{7}{8}$ in.
signed (mono): *ALM*

acc. no. 1657
Landscape
oil on canvas laid on hardboard: 16⅞ × 20⅞ in.
signed (mono): *ALM*

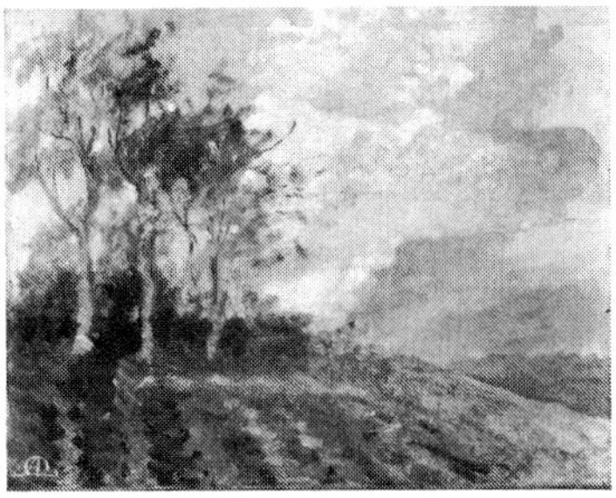

Lord Methuen (1886–1974)

acc. no. 2186
View from the Artist's Studio (1936)
watercolour: 10⅝ × 14½ in. (sight)
signed and dated: *Methuen / 1936* and inscribed: *view from my studio window at 12 Medway St* and *The County Council yard behind 12 Medway St with the Houses of Parliament in the Distance / after the removal of the Gasometers. 24 April 1936.* and *View from my studio 3 at 12 Medway St. over / Houses of Parliament* and with numerous measurements and calculations
verso: drawing of a child's head
red chalk
inscribed: *Carmen*
Purchased from Fieldborne Galleries, 1975

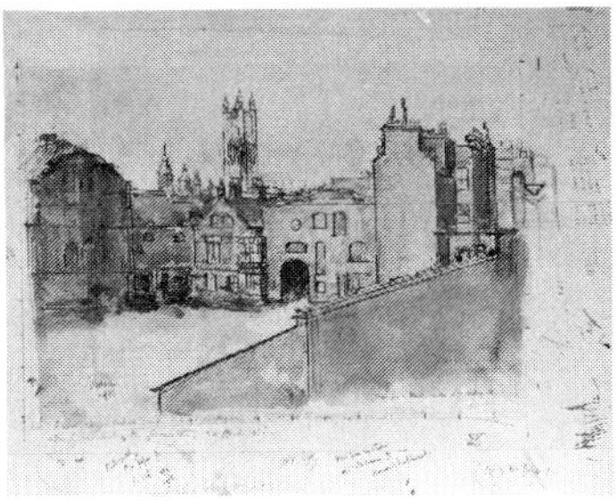

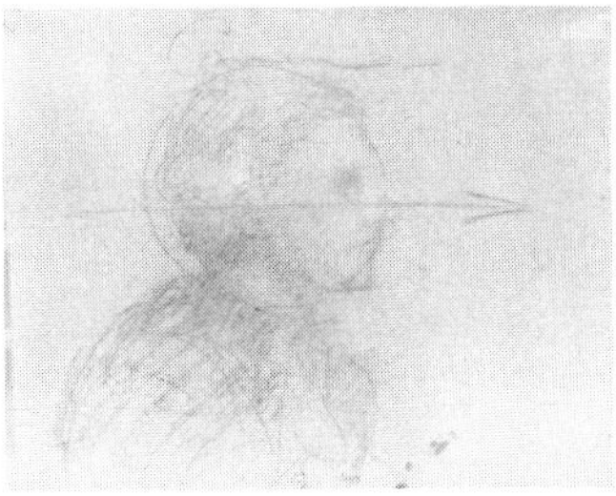

acc. no. 1954
St Paul's Cathedral, June 1940
oil on canvas: 40 × 34 in.
signed: *Methuen*
Purchased from Fieldborne Galleries, 1973

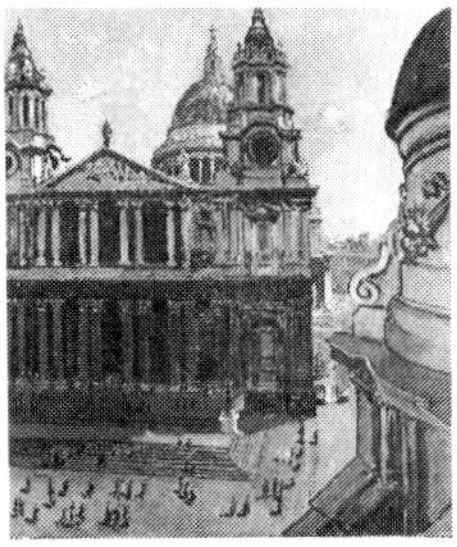

acc. no. 2199
View of the Thames from Whitehall Court (*c.*1950)
oil on canvas: 48 × 76 in.
signed: *Methuen*
Purchased from Fieldborne Galleries, 1975

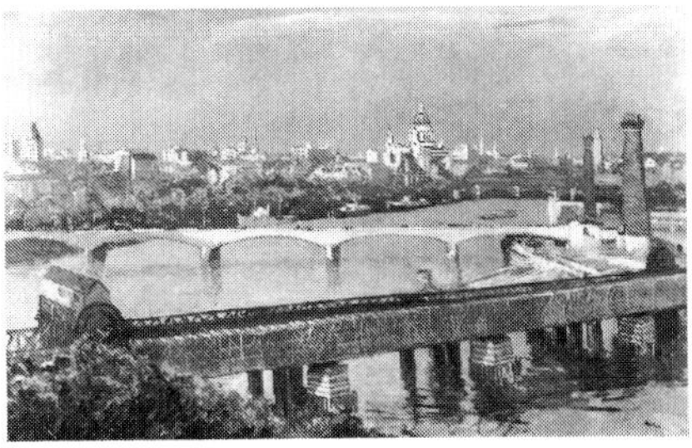

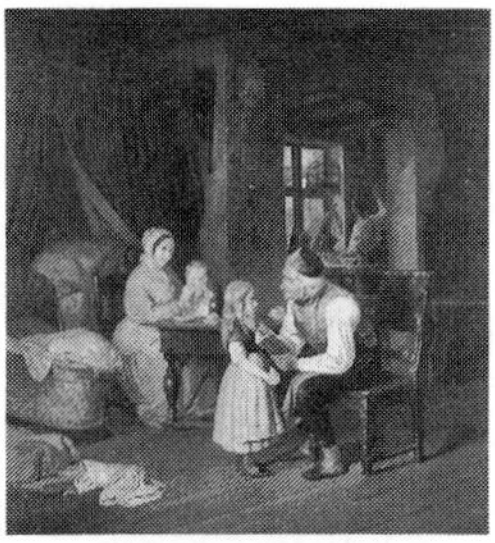

Freidrich Eduard Meyerheim (1808–79)

acc. no. 1659
Grandpapa's Favourite

oil on canvas: $16\frac{1}{4} \times 14\frac{1}{2}$ in.
Presented by John Byram, 1963

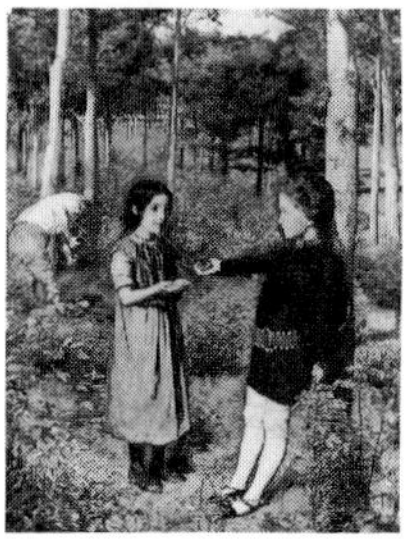

Sir John Everett Millais (1829–96)

acc. no. 1015
The Woodman's Daughter (1851)

oil on canvas: $35 \times 25\frac{1}{2}$ in.
signed and dated: *JMillais 1851*
Presented by Lord Bearsted, 1921

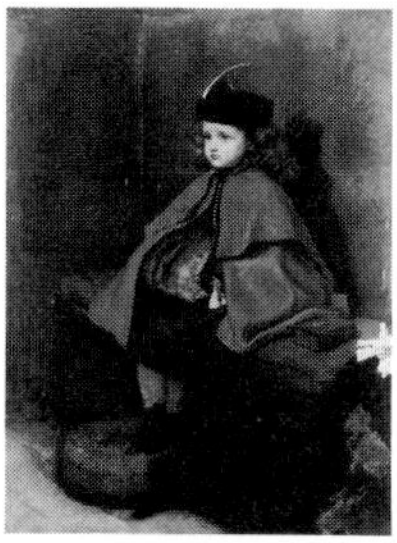

acc. no. 701
My First Sermon (1863)

oil on canvas: $36\frac{1}{4} \times 30\frac{1}{4}$ in.
signed (mono) and dated: *18 JM 63*
Bequeathed by Charles Gassiot, 1902

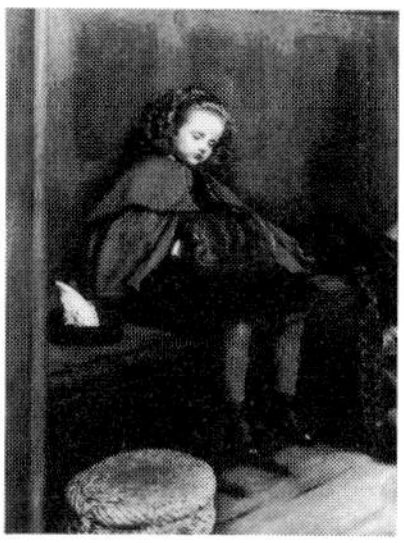

acc. no. 702
My Second Sermon (1864)

oil on canvas: $38\frac{1}{4} \times 28\frac{1}{4}$ in.
signed (mono) and dated: *18 JM 64*
Bequeathed by Charles Gassiot, 1902

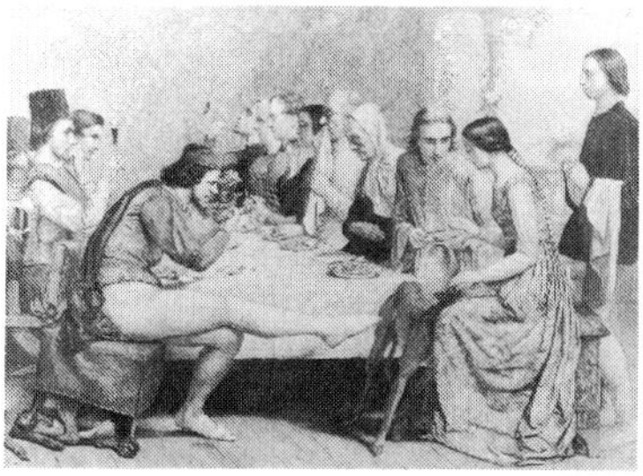

attributed to Sir John Everett Millais (1829–96)

acc. no. 1054
Lorenzo and Isabella

watercolour: $14\frac{1}{4} \times 20$ in.
Presented by Alderman Sir Charles (later Lord) Wakefield, 1927

William Miller (*c.*1740–*c.*1810)

acc. no. 55
The Ceremony of Administering the Mayoralty Oath to Nathaniel Newnham, November 8 1782

oil on canvas: 61 × 85 in.
Presented by Alderman John Boydell, 1792

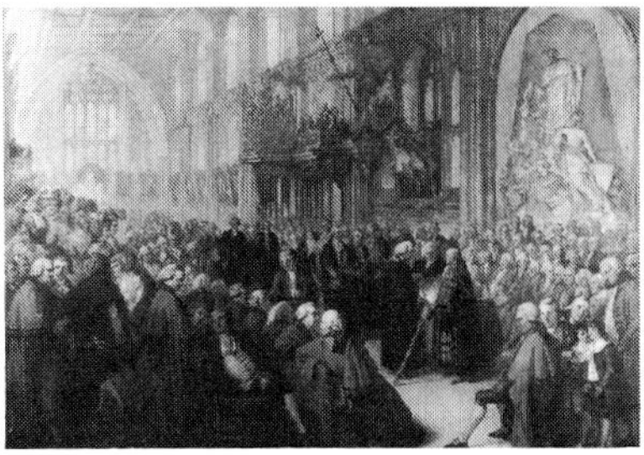

John Mogford (1821–85)

acc. no. 752
River Scene

oil on canvas: 26 × 38 in.
Bequeathed by Charles Gassiot, 1902

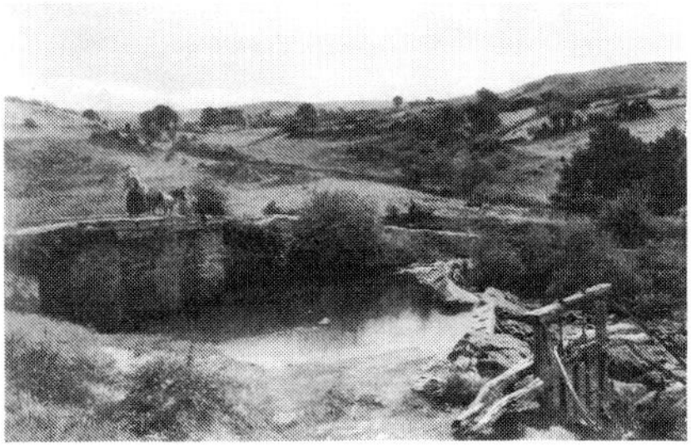

Edward Lobo Moira (1817–87)

acc. no. 1240
Henry Woods, Chairman of the Library Committee (1882)

watercolour: 3 × $2\frac{3}{8}$ in.
signed: *E. Moira.*
Presented by Miss Amy Woods, 1937

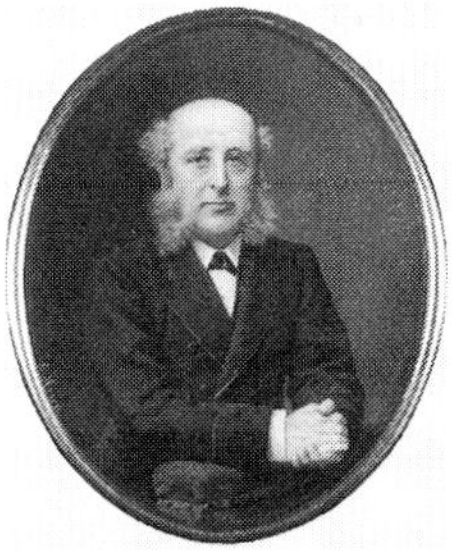

Francis Moltino (*fl.* 1847–67)

acc. no. 1800
The Thames Near London Bridge

oil on canvas: 24 × 36 in.
Purchased from Ashurst, Morris, Crisp & Co., 1969

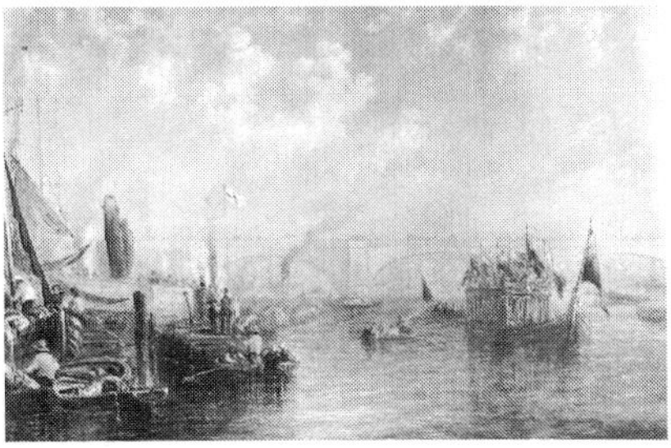

acc. no. 1801
The Thames at Westminster

oil on canvas: 24 × 36 in.
Purchased from Ashurst, Morris, Crisp & Co., 1969

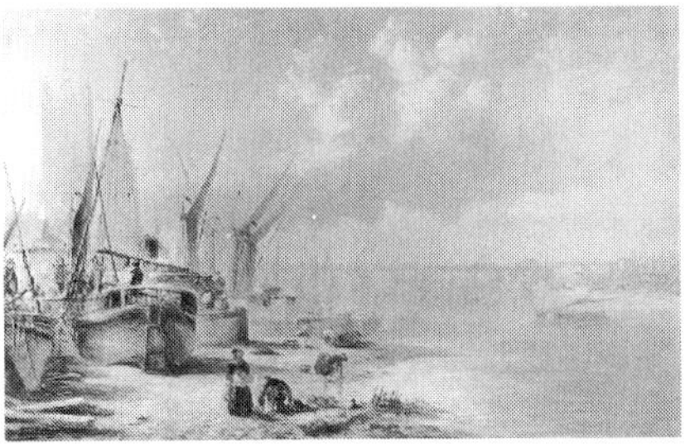

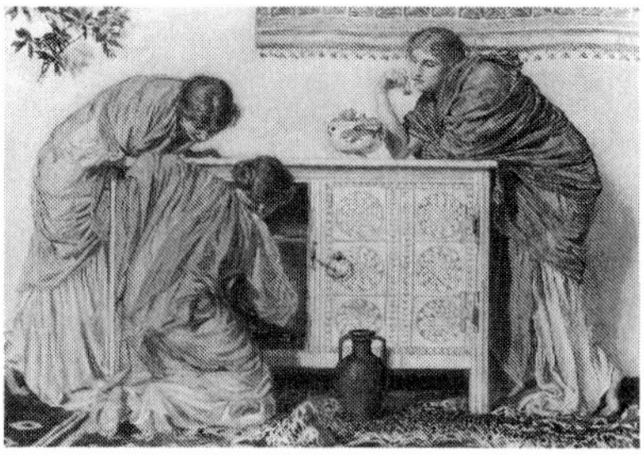

Albert Joseph Moore (1841–93)

acc. no. 1512
Pomegranates (1866)

oil on canvas: 10 × 14 in.
signed (mono): *AM*
Bequeathed by Cecil French, 1954

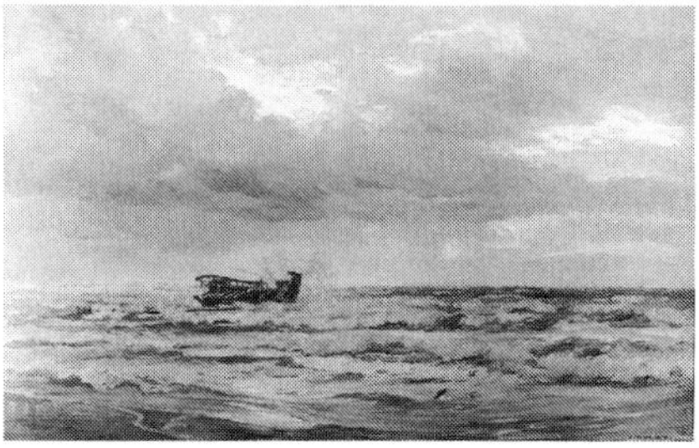

Henry Moore (1831–95)

acc. no. 885
The Wreck (1875)

oil on canvas: 17 × 26 in.
signed and dated: *H. Moore. 1875.*
Bequeathed by James Thomas Slater, 1909

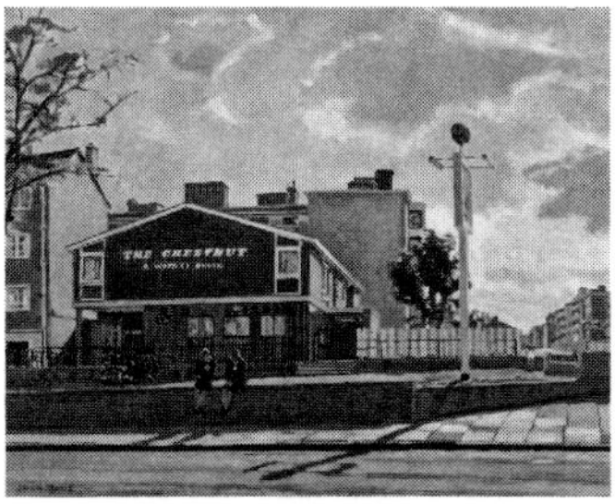

John Moore (b.1933)

acc. no. 1855
A Modern Estate, Tulse Hill (1970)

oil on hardboard: 24 × 30 in.
signed: *JOHN MOORE*
Purchased from the artist, 1971

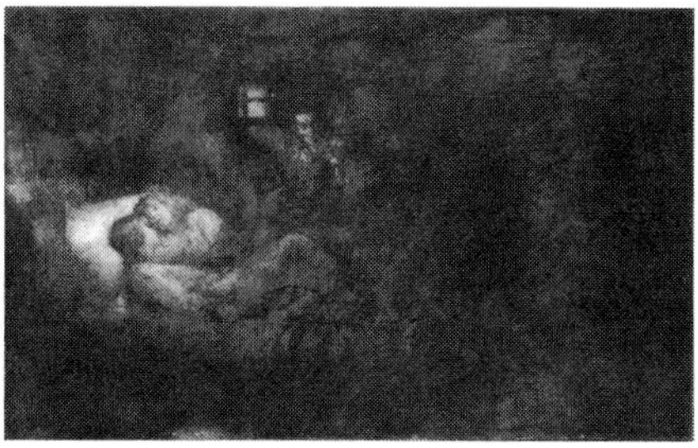

Joseph Mordecai (1851–1940)

acc. no. 1621
The Murder of the Princes in the Tower

oil on canvas: 46 × 72 in.
Presented by Mrs. Mordecai, 1961

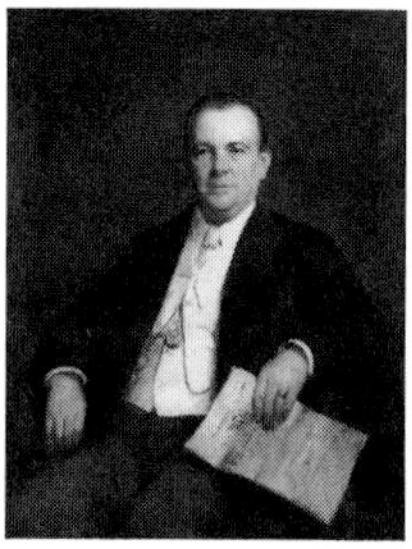

acc. no. 1730
John Lobb

oil on canvas: $44\frac{1}{4} \times 34\frac{1}{4}$ in.
signed: *J Mordecai*
Presented by Miss Dorothy Lobb, 1966

acc. no. 2265
Dorothy

oil on canvas: $23\frac{1}{4} \times 19\frac{1}{2}$ in.
signed: *Mordecai*
Presented by Miss Dorothy Lobb, 1981

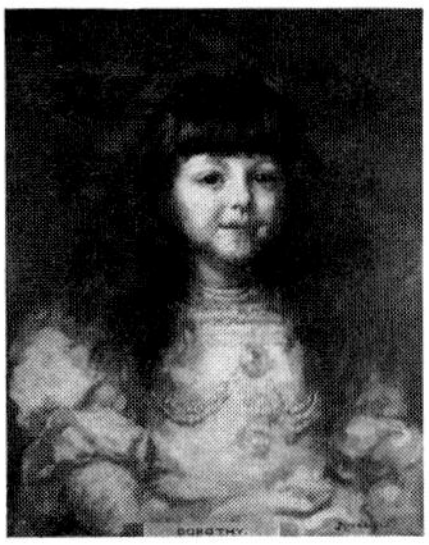

John Morgan (1823–86)

acc. no. 753
Gossip in the Hold

oil on canvas: 15 × 13 in.
signed: *J. Morgan.*
Bequeathed by Charles Gassiot, 1902

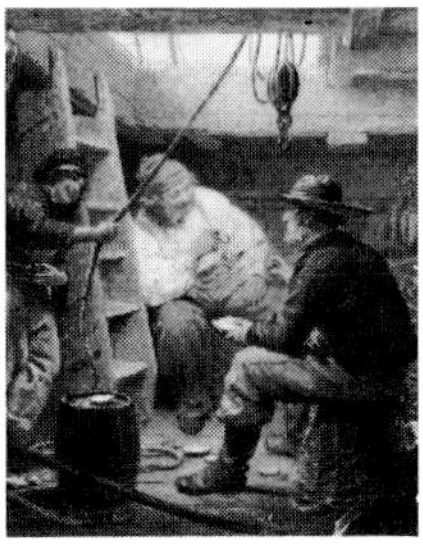

George Morland (1762–1804)

acc. no. 1298
Skating (1792)

oil on canvas: 27 × 36 in.
signed and dated: *G.M^d 1792*
Presented by Lady Wakefield, 1944

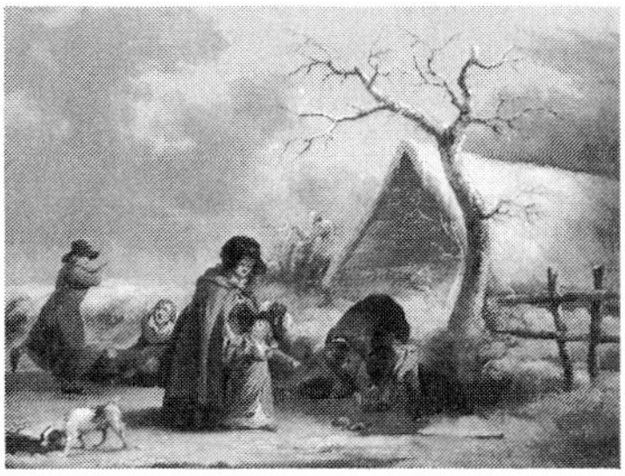

attributed to George Morland (1762–1804)

acc. no. 2324
The Gamekeeper

oil on canvas: $33\frac{1}{2} \times 28\frac{1}{2}$ in.
Presented by R. C. Deith, 1982

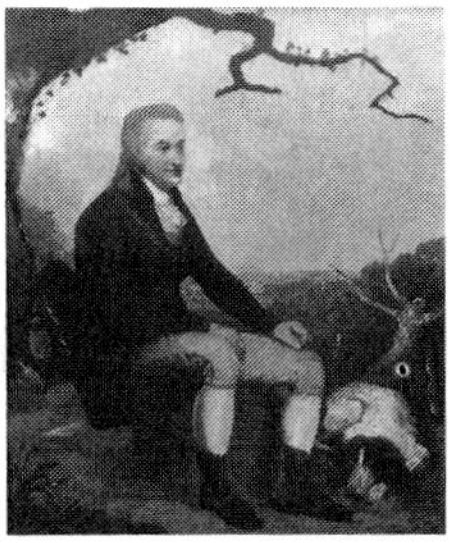

David Morris (living)

acc. no. 1771
Sunset over Cannon Street (1966)

oil on hardboard: $28\frac{1}{2} \times 36$ in.
Purchased from the artist, 1967

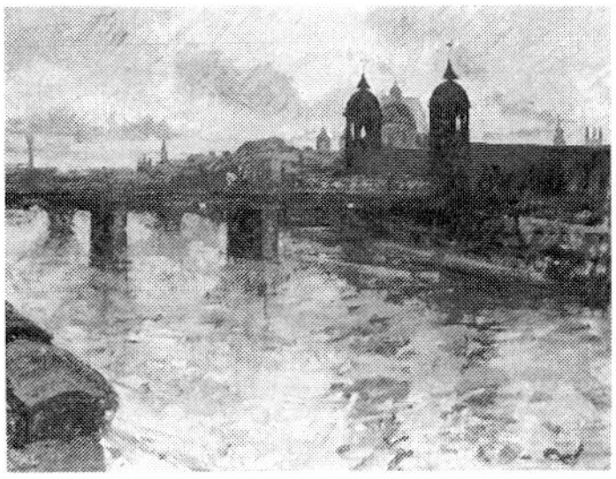

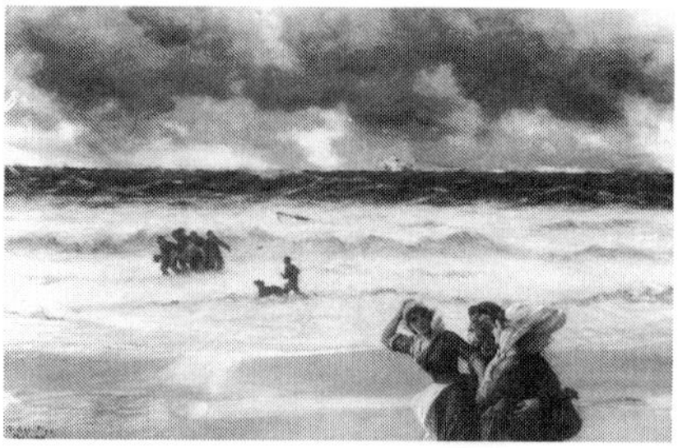

Philip Richard Morris (1838–1902)

acc. no. 476
Cardigan Bay

oil on canvas: 36 × 54 in.
signed and inscribed: *Cardigan Bay / Phil Morris*
Presented by the Worshipful Company of Salters, 1889

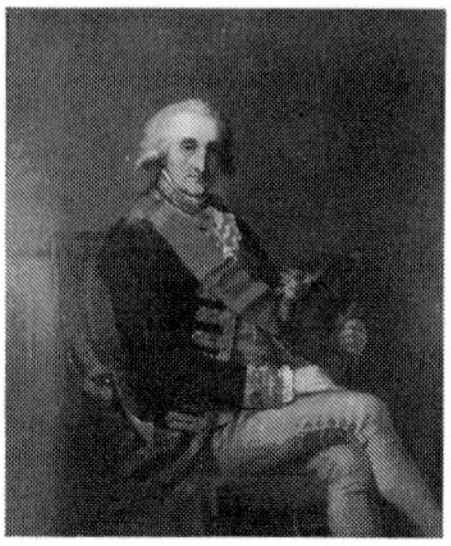

after Jean Laurent Mosnier (1743/4–1808)

acc. no. 64
Lord Rodney (*c.*1792)

oil on canvas: 57 × 45 in.
Presented by Alderman John Boydell, *c.*1793

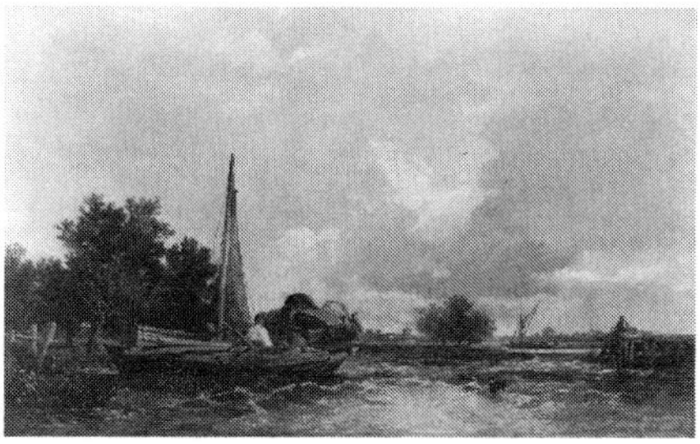

William James Müller (1812–45)

acc. no. 703
On the Medway

oil on canvas: $22\frac{1}{2}$ × 35 in.
signed: *W Müller*
Bequeathed by Charles Gassiot, 1902

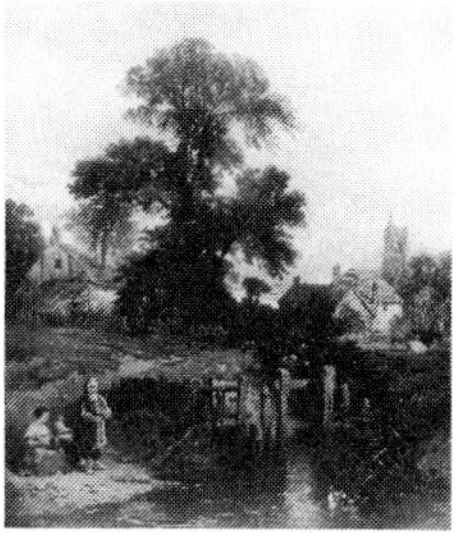

acc. no. 704
Gillingham on the Medway (1841)

oil on canvas: 42 × 34 in.
signed and dated: *W Müller / 41* (*sic*)
Bequeathed by Charles Gassiot, 1902

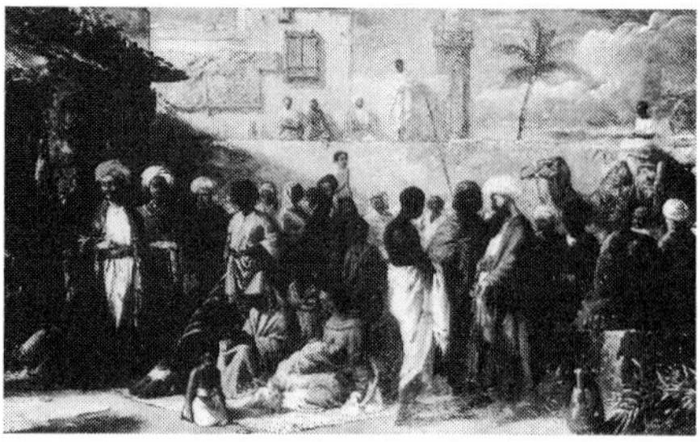

acc. no. 828
The Slave Market at Cairo (1841)

oil on canvas: 24 × 41 in.
signed and dated: *W J Muller Pinxt 1841*
Presented by Mrs. Mary Penrose, R. P. Walters and H. E. Walters in memory of their father, 1904

Augustus E. Mulready (*fl.* 1863–1905)

acc. no. 705
Remembering Joys that have passed away (1873)
oil on canvas: $15\frac{1}{2} \times 20\frac{1}{2}$ in.
signed and dated: *A.E. Mulready. / 1873.*
Bequeathed by Charles Gassiot, 1902

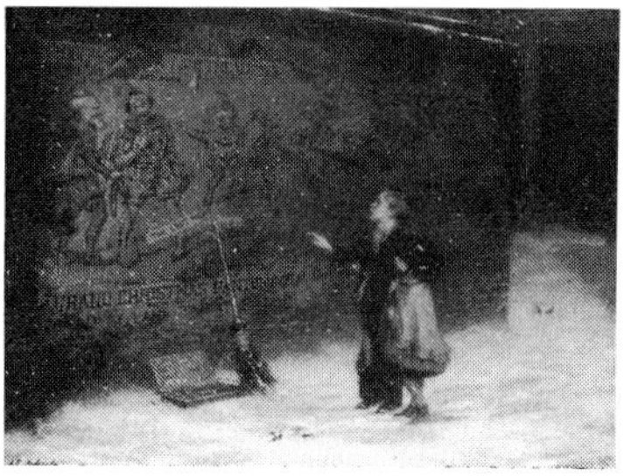

Henry James Munns (1832–98)

acc. no. 185
Sir Thomas Dakin, Lord Mayor 1870 (1871)
oil on canvas: 50×40 in.
signed and dated: *H.J. Munns / 1871*
Presented by the artist, 1871

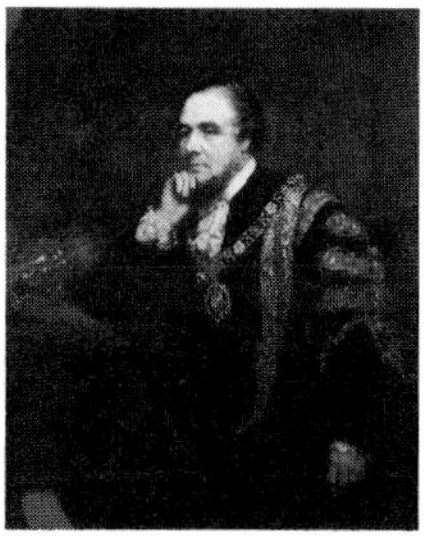

after Bartolome Esteban Murillo (1617–82)

acc. no. 3505
Flower Girl (19th C)
oil on canvas: 34×44 in.
Manner and date of acquisition unknown

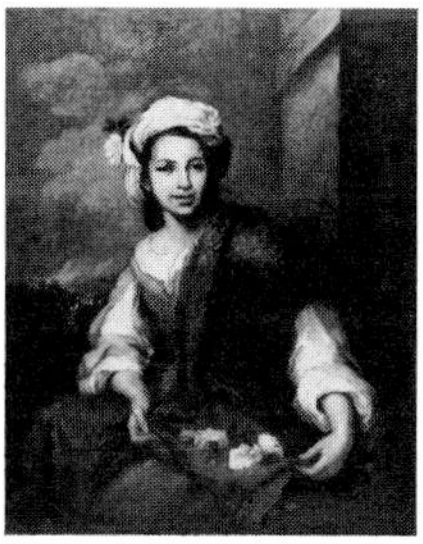

Andrew Murray (b.1917)

acc. no. 3650
View over the Lakeside Terrace. Barbican Centre, towards St. Giles Cripplegate (1982)
oil on canvas: 20×24 in.
signed: *Andrew Murray*
Purchased from the artist, 1986

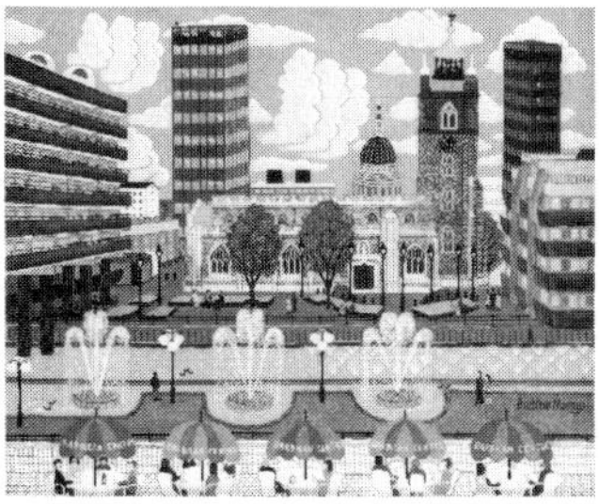

Sir David Murray (1849–1933)

acc. no. 951
Showery Weather (1907)
watercolour: $17\frac{1}{2} \times 11\frac{1}{2}$ in.
signed and dated: *David Murray. 1907*
Presented by Miss Evelyn P. McGhee, 1914

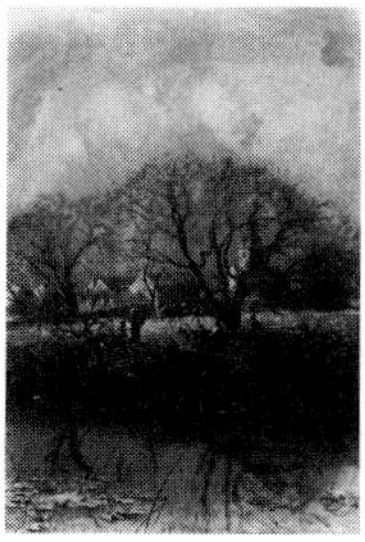

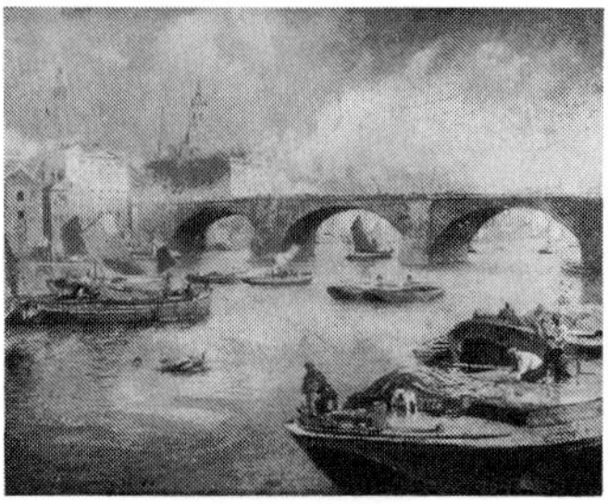

acc. no. 1097
London Bridge from Bankside (1915)

oil on canvas: $55\frac{1}{4} \times 66\frac{1}{4}$ in.
signed and dated: *David Murray.1915.*
Purchased, 1935

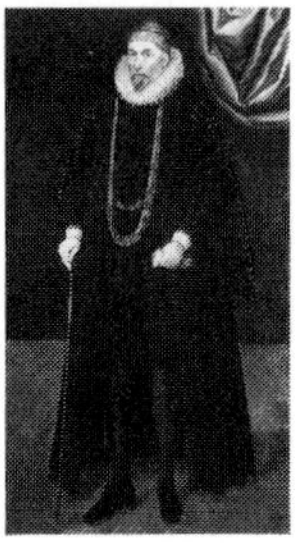

Daniel Mytens (1590–*c.*1648)

acc. no. 1578
Sir John Garrard (Lord Mayor 1601) (1618)

oil on canvas: $75\frac{1}{2} \times 43\frac{1}{2}$ in.
inscribed: *Anno 1618 / Ae 73*
Presented by Mrs. A. Cherry-Garrard, 1959

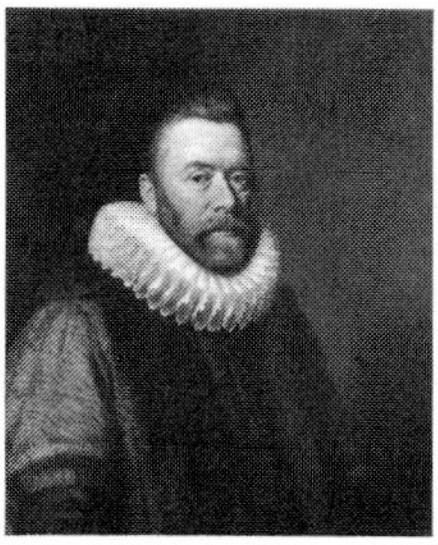

acc. no. 1423
Sir Clement Edmondes

oil on canvas: $29\frac{1}{2} \times 24\frac{3}{4}$ in.
inscribed: *Sir Clement Edmondes / Rememb:r of ye City of London / Clerk to Priv. Co.cl of JAMES 1.st*
Purchased from Spink & Son Ltd. 1951

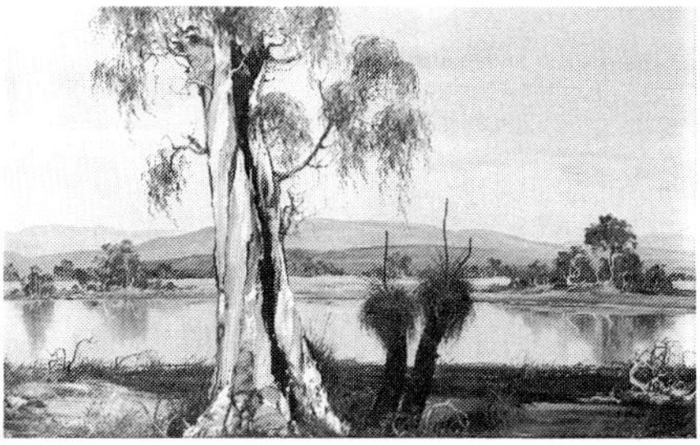

Nardino (20th C)

acc. no. 2195
Swan River Gums

oil on canvas: $17\frac{1}{2} \times 28$ in.
signed: *NARDINO*
Presented by the City of Perth, Western Australia, 1975

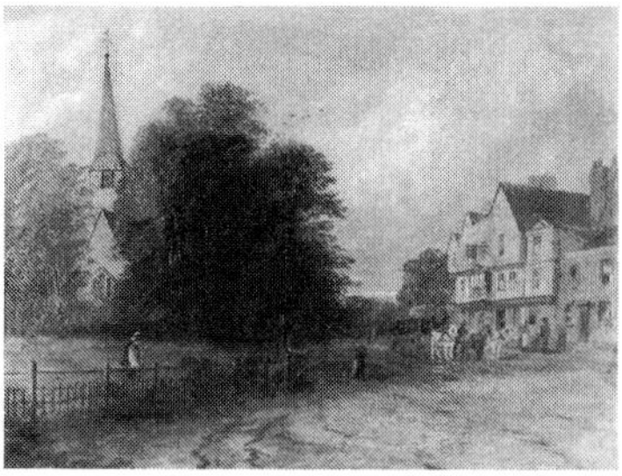

Joseph Nash (1808–78)

acc. no. 990
The King's Head, Chigwell

oil on canvas: 10×13 in.
signed: *J. Nash*
Presented by Deputy Walter Bull, 1918

Patrick Nasmyth (1787–1831)

acc. no. 707
View in Hampshire (1826)
oil on canvas: $27\frac{1}{2} \times 36$ in.
signed and dated: *Patk. Nasmyth. / 1826*
Bequeathed by Charles Gassiot, 1902

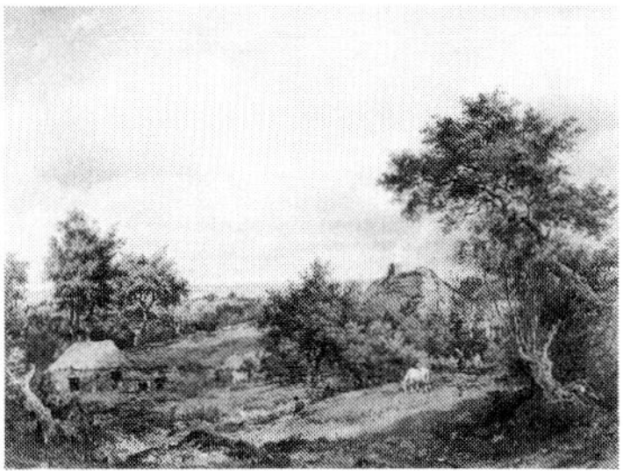

acc. no. 708
The Meeting of the Avon and Severn (1826)
oil on canvas: $27\frac{1}{2} \times 37$ in.
signed and dated: *Patk. Nasmyth / 1826.*
Bequeathed by Charles Gassiot, 1902

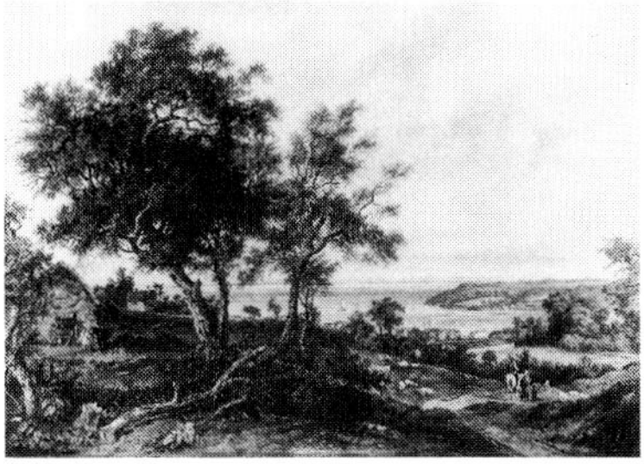

acc. no. 706
Watermill at Carshalton (1830)
oil on panel: $22\frac{1}{2} \times 28\frac{1}{2}$ in.
signed and dated: *Patk Nasmyth / 1830*
Bequeathed by Charles Gassiot, 1902

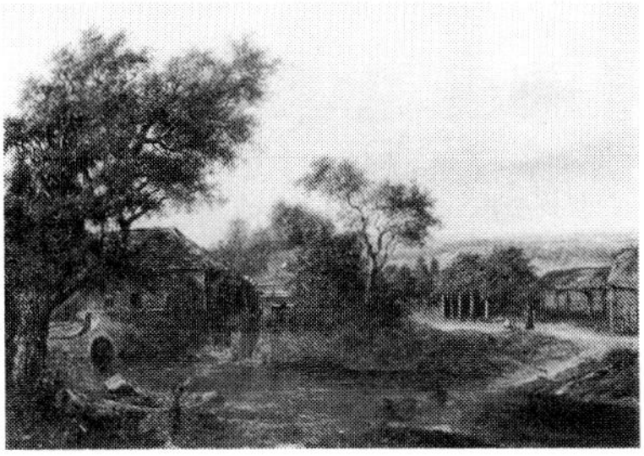

H. J. Neave (d.1971)

acc. no. 1635
The Stonemason's Yard, Moorgate (c.1962)
oil on canvas: $30\frac{3}{8} \times 40\frac{1}{4}$ in.
signed: *H.J. NEAVE*
Purchased from the artist, 1962

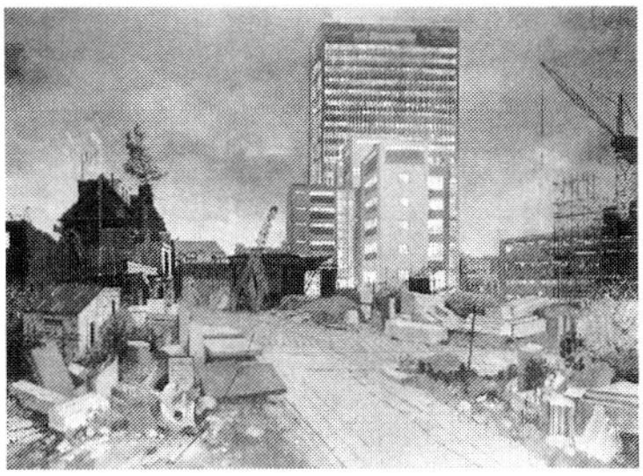

acc. no. 1728
Funeral of Sir Winston Churchill, St. Paul's Cathedral (1966)
watercolour on paper laid on board: 32×44 in.
signed and dated: *H J NEAVE. / 66*
Commissioned by the Corporation, 1965

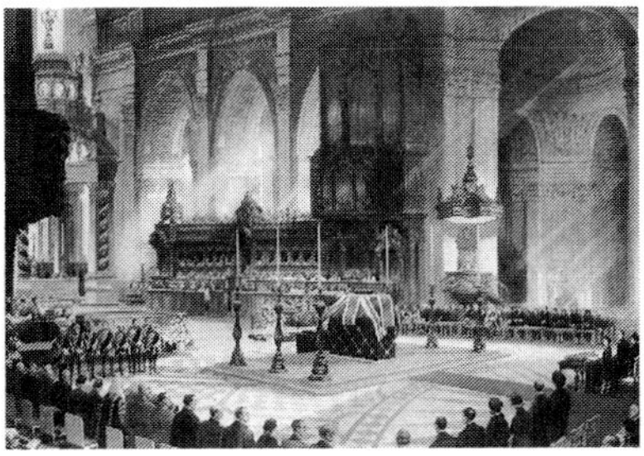

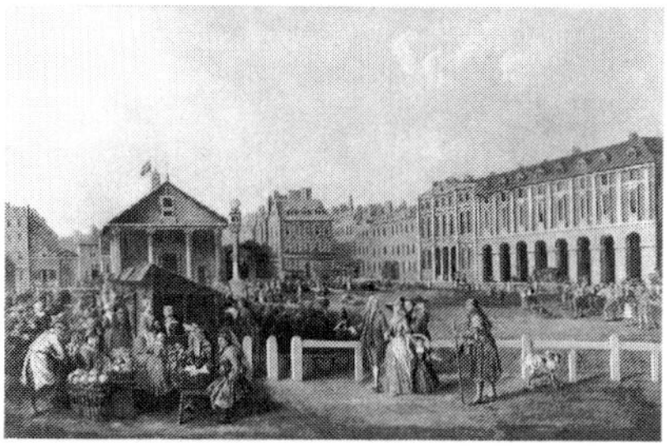

Balthazar Nebot (*fl.* 1730–62)

acc. no. 1348
Covent Garden Market and St. Paul's Church (*c.*1737)

oil on canvas: 48 × 31 in.
Presented by Chester Beatty, 1946

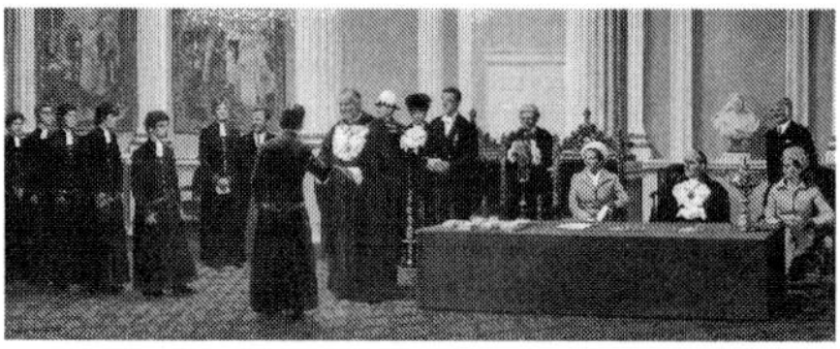

Edmund Hugh Nelson (b.1910)

acc. no. 2215
Presentation of the Lord Mayor's Bounty to the Boys of Christ's Hospital, St. Matthew's Day, 1976 (1977)

oil on canvas: 23 × 59 in.
signed and dated: *Edmund Nelson 1977*
Purchased from the artist, 1977

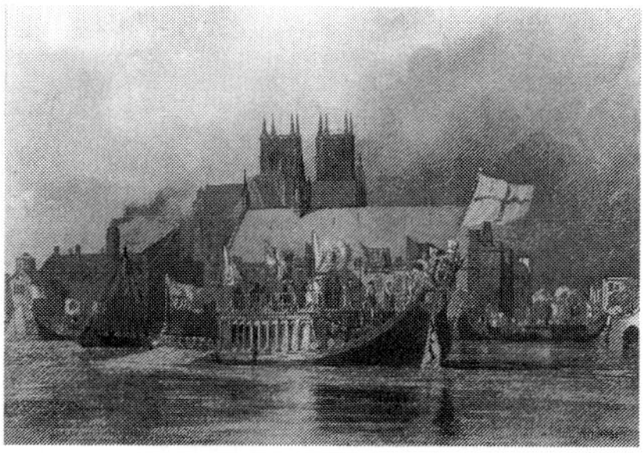

Richard Henry Nibbs (1816–93)

acc. no. 1239
Arrival of the Lord Mayor at Westminster (?1841)

watercolour: $10\frac{3}{4} \times 14\frac{5}{8}$ in.
Purchased from Mr. Dallas, 1937

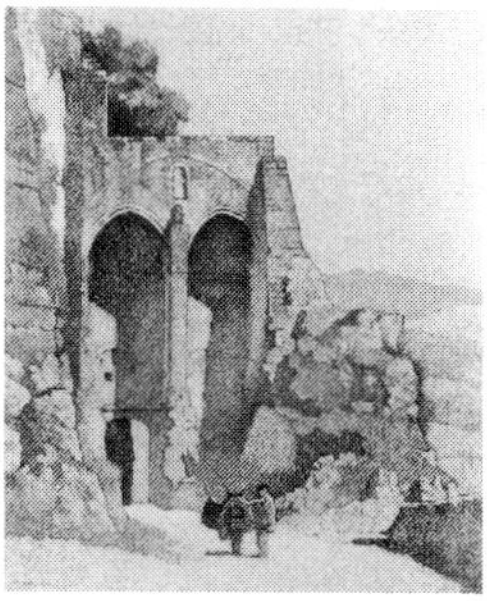

Bertram Nicholls (b.1883)

acc. no. 1049
Porto Rocco, Orvieto (1926)

oil on board: 15 × 13 in.
signed and dated: *Nicholls.1926*
Purchased, 1926

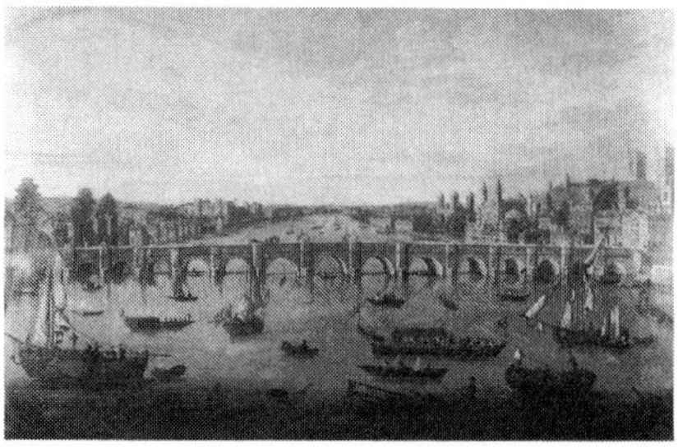

attributed to Joseph Nicholls (*fl.* 1730s)

acc. no. 238
Westminster Bridge

oil on canvas: 37 × 51 in.
Presented by J. O. Halliwell, 1872

John Henry Nixon (1808–*c.*1850)

acc. no. 258

Queen Victoria's Procession to Guildhall, November 9 1837 (1838)

oil on canvas: 44 × 56 in.
signed: *J H Nixon*
Purchased from F. H. Nixon, the artist's son, 1879

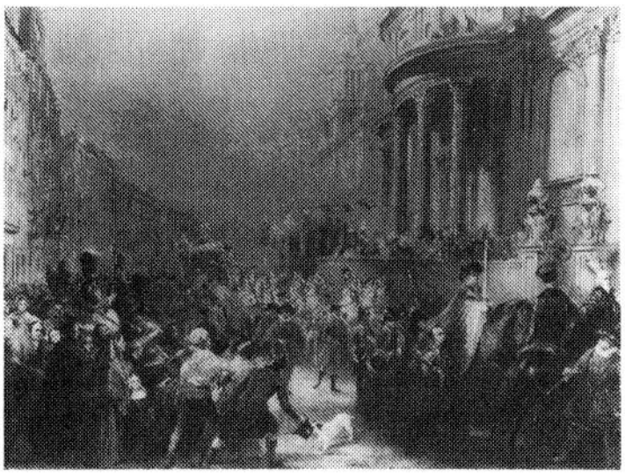

Michael Noakes (b.1933)

acc. no. 2000

The Royal Family (1972–1974)

oil on canvas: $42\frac{1}{2} \times 68$ in.
signed and dated: *Michael Noakes / 1972–74*
Commissioned by the Corporation, 1972

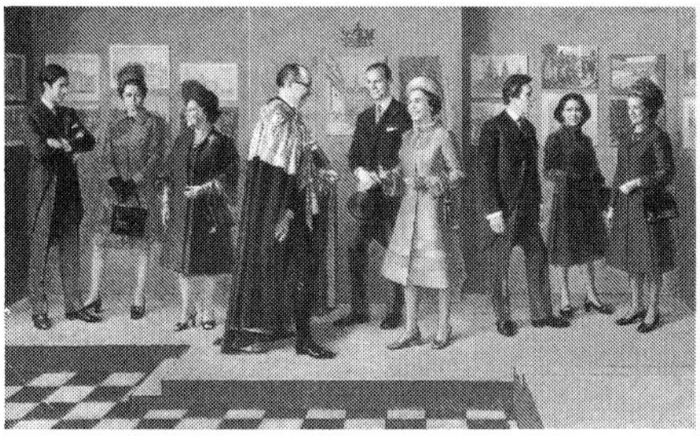

attributed to Orlando Norie (1832–1901)

acc. no. 3520

A North African Caravan outside a Town

pencil and watercolour heightened with white: $4 \times 6\frac{3}{8}$ in.
Presented by Miss Helen Guiterman, 1985

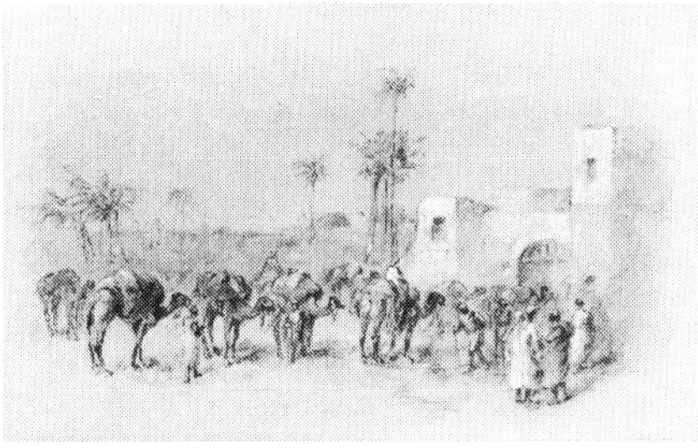

Philip Norman (1843–1931)

acc. no. 524

Staple Inn, Holborn (1887)

watercolour: 22 × 31 in.
signed and dated: *PHILIP NORMAN 1887*
Purchased, 1892

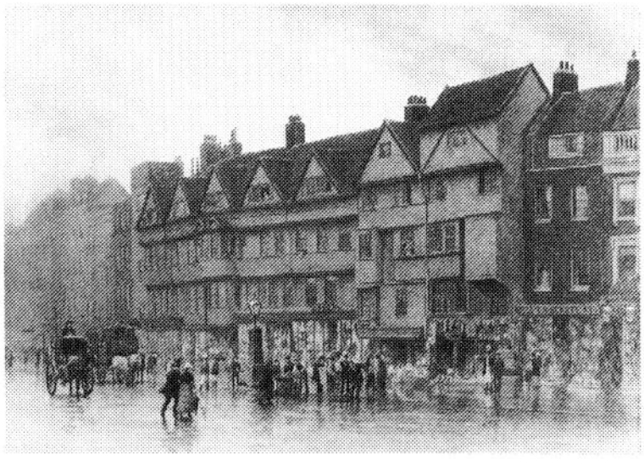

after James Northcote (1746–1831)

acc. no. 300

The Murder of the Princes in the Tower

oil on canvas: 33 × 24 in.
Presented by Alderman William Treloar, 1886

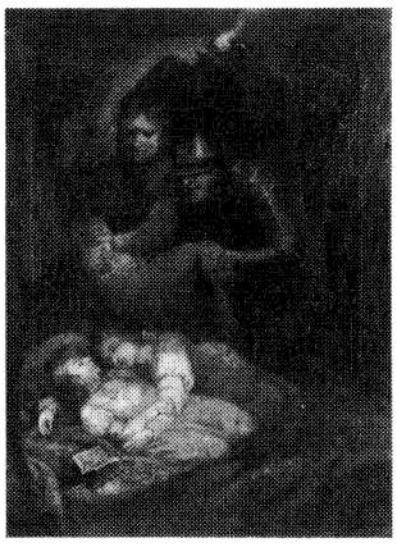

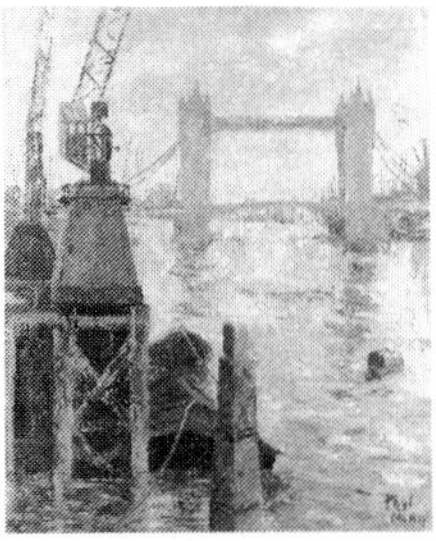

Phyllis Nunn (20th C)

acc. no. 1714
The Pool of London (*c.*1965)

oil on canvas: 24 × 20 in.
signed: *Phyl Nunn*
Purchased from the artist, 1965

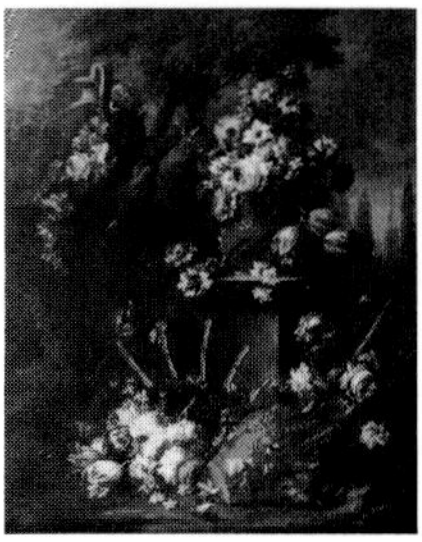

Mario Nuzzi (1603–73)

acc. no. 349
Vases and Flowers

oil on canvas: 50 × 40 in.
Bequeathed by William Dunnett, 1888

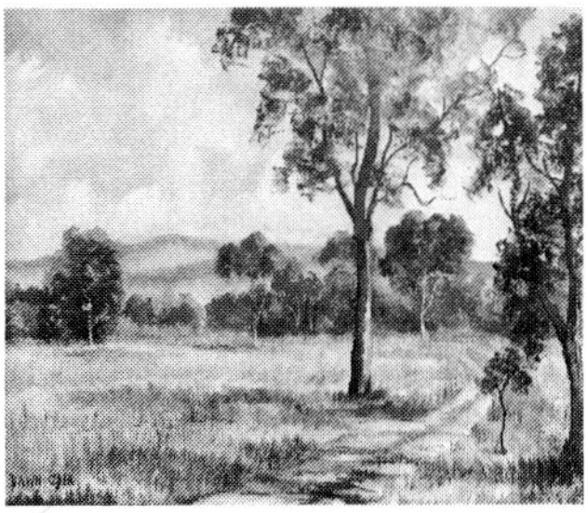

Dawn O'Dea (20th C)

acc. no. 2193
Australian Bush Scene

oil on hardboard: 12 × 14 in.
signed: *DAWN O'DEA*
Presented by the Australian Capital Territory Legislature Assembly, 1975

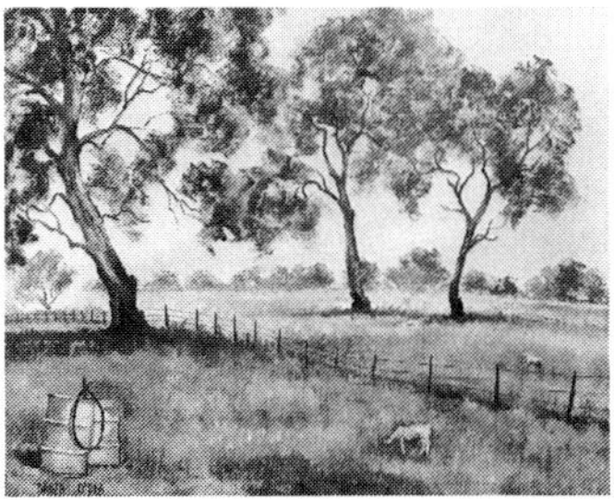

acc. no. 2194
Australian Bush Scene

oil on hardboard: 12 × 14 in.
signed: *DAWN O'DEA*
Presented by the Australian Capital Territory Legislature Assembly, 1975

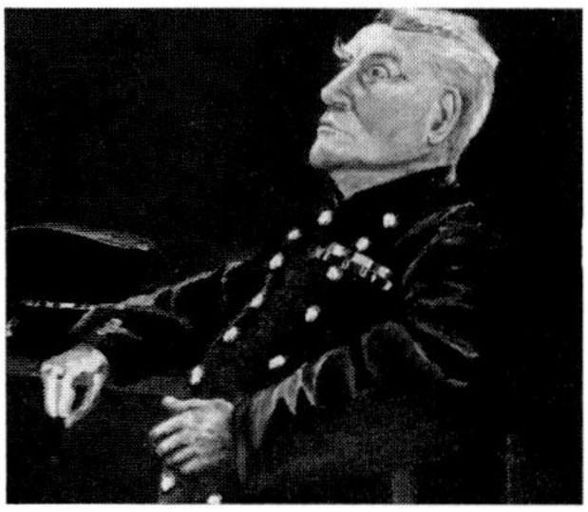

Winifred Oldak (20th C)

acc. no. 1958
A Chelsea Pensioner (1972)

oil on hardboard: $13\frac{1}{2} \times 16\frac{1}{4}$ in.
Purchased from the artist, 1973

John Edwin Oldfield (19th C)

acc. no. 1592
Waterloo Bridge looking down River
watercolour: $11\frac{5}{8} \times 16\frac{3}{4}$ in. (sight)
signed: *J.Oldfield*
Purchased from F. T. Sabin, 1960

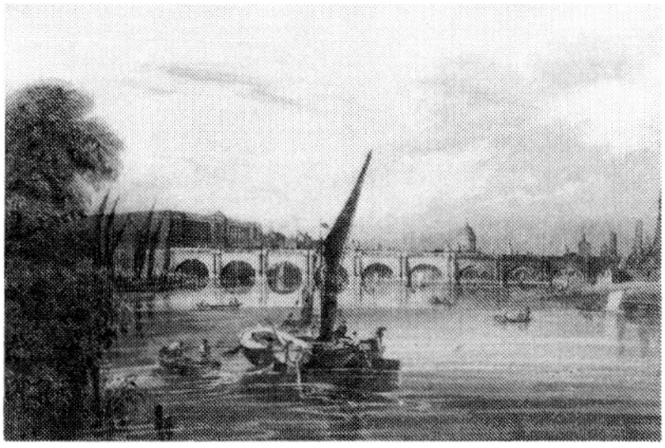

George Bernard O'Neill (1828–1917)

acc. no. 709
Gran's Treasures (1866)
oil on canvas: 14 × 11 in.
signed: *G.B.O'N.*
Bequeathed by Charles Gassiot, 1902

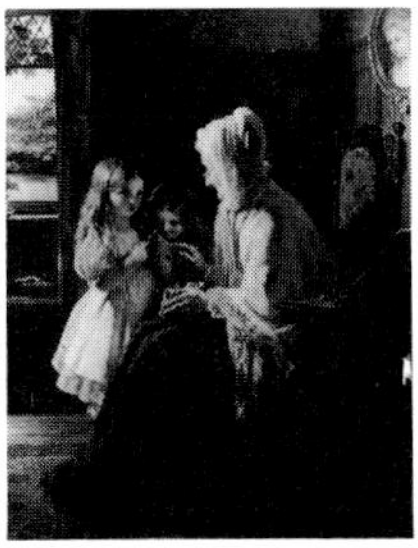

John Opie (1761–1807)

acc. no. 49
The Murder of Rizzio (1787)
oil on canvas: $94\frac{1}{2} \times 113\frac{1}{2}$ in. (after cutting down)
Presented by Alderman John Boydell, *c.*1793

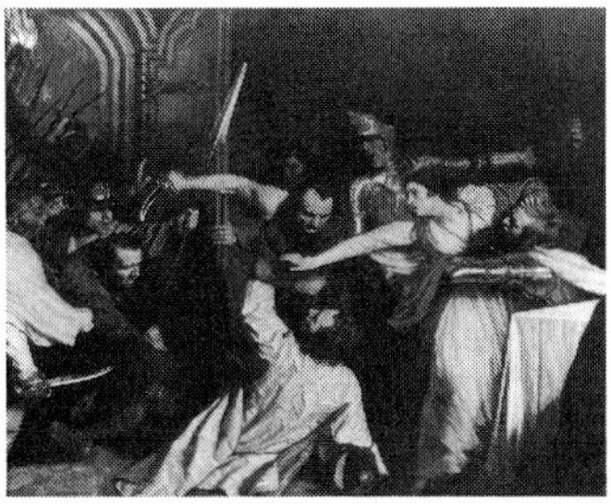

acc. no. 83
Daniel Pinder, Deputy
oil on canvas: 56 × 44 in.
Presented by several of his colleagues in the Corporation, 1807

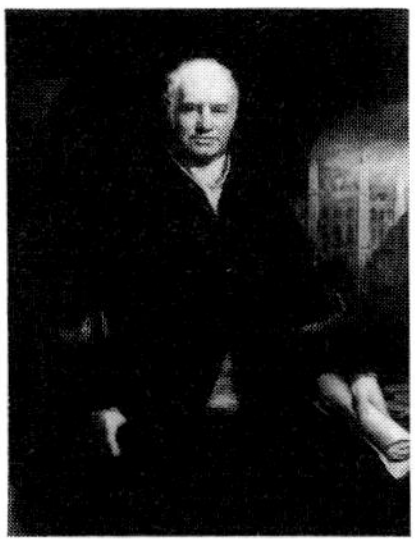

acc. no. 1301
Portrait of Lady (called 'Miss Holcroft')
oil on canvas: 29 × 24 in.
Presented by Lady Wakefield, 1944

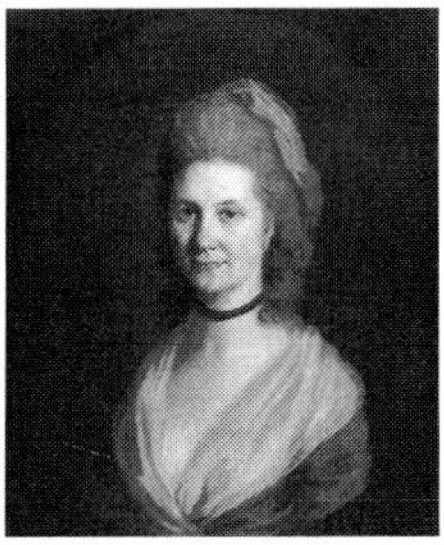

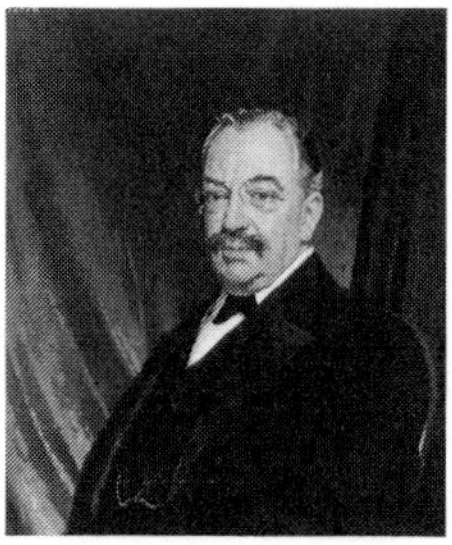

Sir William Orpen (1878–1931)

acc. no. 1019
Viscount Bearsted (1922)

oil on canvas: 30 × 25 in.
signed: *ORPEN*
Presented by Lady Bearsted, 1922

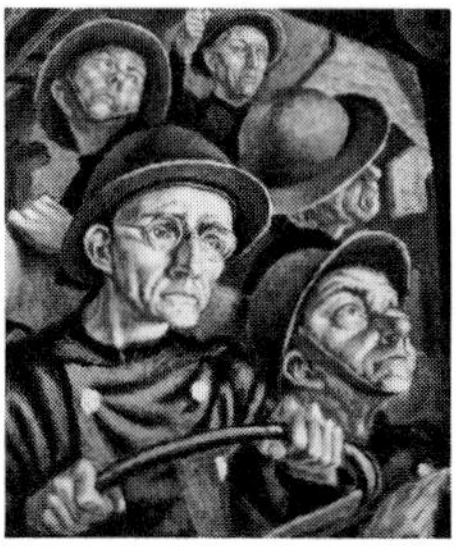

James Robert Wallace Orr (b.1907)

acc. no. 2327
London Firemen in the Blitz (1982)

oil on canvas: $29\frac{1}{2} \times 24\frac{1}{2}$ in.
signed and dated: *Wallace Orr / 1982*
Presented by the artist, 1983

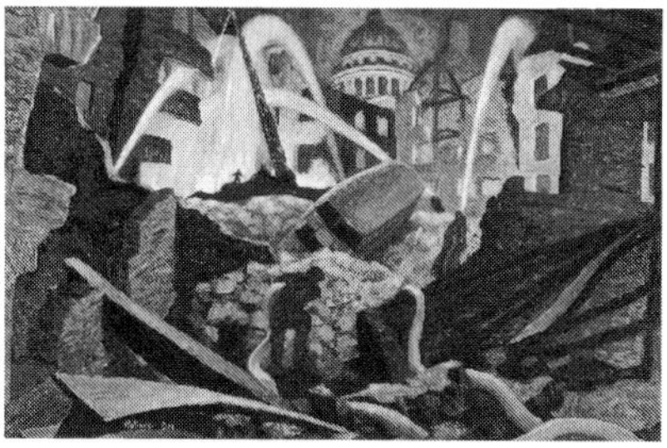

acc. no. 2328
Bombed Ruins near St Paul's

oil on canvas: $19\frac{1}{2} \times 29\frac{1}{2}$ in.
signed: *Wallace Orr*
Presented by the artist, 1983

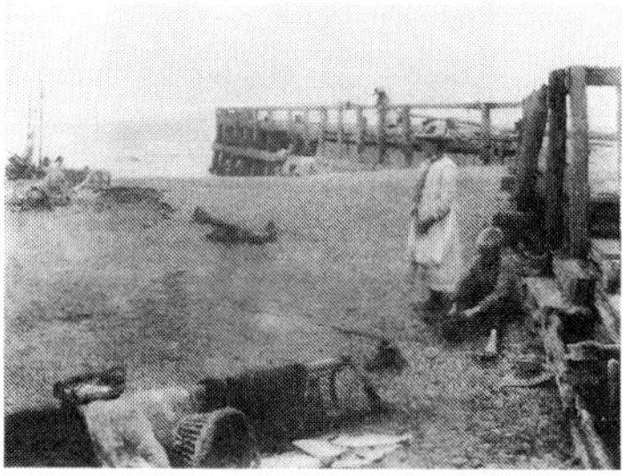

Walter Frederick Osborne (1859–1903)

acc. no. 829
An October Morning (1885)

oil on canvas: 28 × 36 in.
signed and dated: *WALTER OSBORNE / 1885*
Presented by the Artists' Cricket Club as a memorial to the artist, 1904

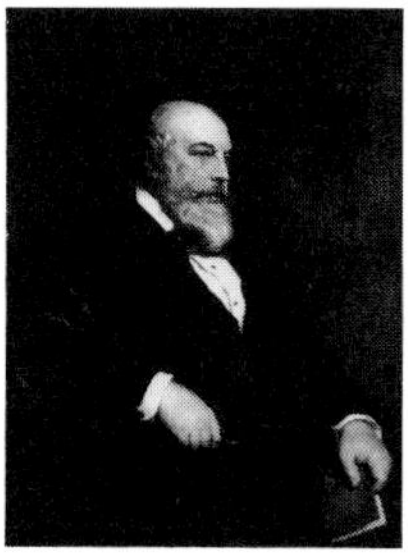

Walter William Ouless (1848–1933)

acc. no. 1832
Sir Horace Jones (1886)

oil on canvas: 45 × 35 in.
signed and dated: *W.W. Ouless 1886*
Bequeathed by Miss A. H. Jones, 1969

Cyril V. Parker (1897–1984)

acc. no. 1625
From Charing Cross to Blackfriars (1961)

watercolour: $15\frac{3}{4} \times 19\frac{7}{8}$ in.
signed: *C.V. PARKER*
Purchased from the artist, 1962

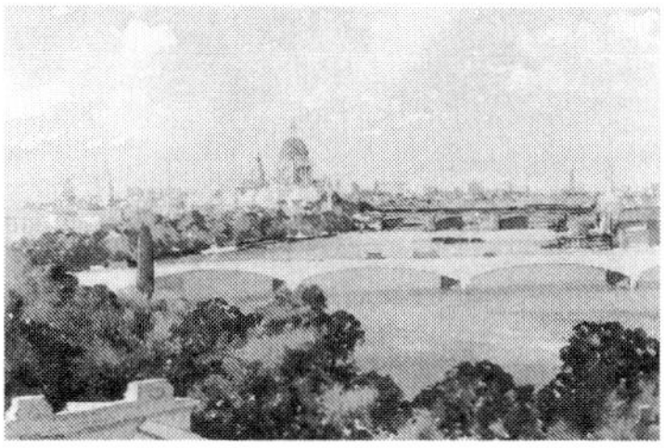

acc. no. 1890
Low Tide, Strand on the Green (*c.*1971)

watercolour: $15\frac{3}{8} \times 20\frac{3}{8}$ in.
signed: *C.V. PARKER*
Purchased from the artist, 1971

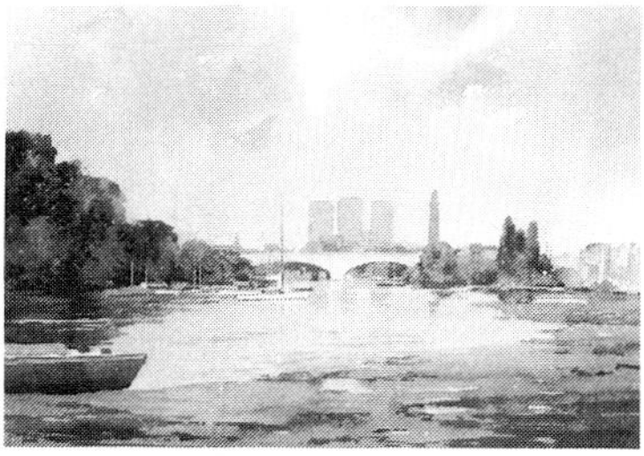

Edmund Thomas Parris (1793–1873)

acc. no. 1023
Queen Adelaide (1859)

oil on panel: $11\frac{7}{8} \times 10$ in.
signed and dated: *E.T. Parris / 1859*; inscribed on verso: *Her Majesty Queen Adelaide. died Dec 2. 1849 / Painted by E.T. Parris. Hist painter to Her Majesty / Painted partly from a drawing in crayons by G. Richmond / Jan. / 1859*
Presented by Miss Janet Scott in memory of her sister, Mary Scott, 1923

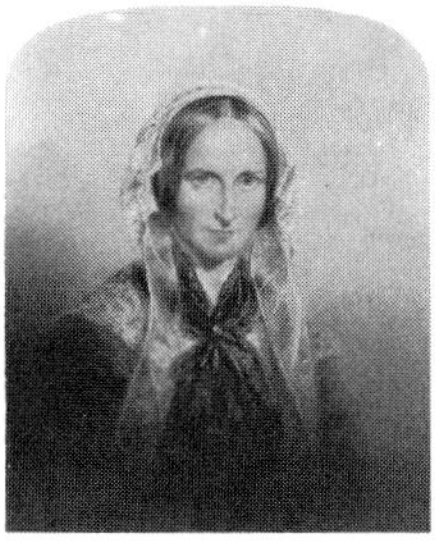

Daniel Pasmore (*fl.* 1829–65)

acc. no. 3415
St. Martin Outwich (1838)

oil on canvas: $21\frac{1}{4} \times 17$ in.
dated: *1838*
Purchased from the John Denham Gallery, 1984

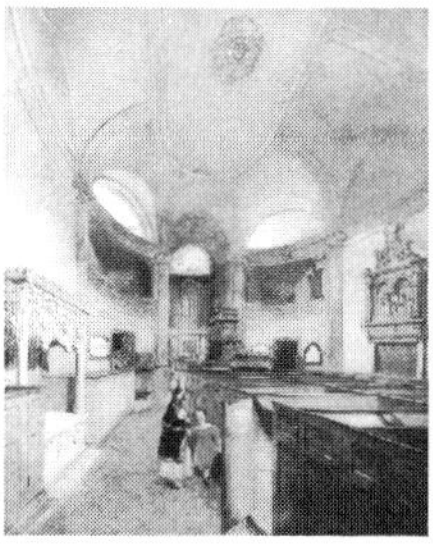

attributed to John F. Pasmore (19th C)

acc. no. 762
Two Children at Drawing Lessons

oil on panel: 15×12 in.
signed: *Passmore (sic)*
Bequeathed by Charles Gassiot, 1902

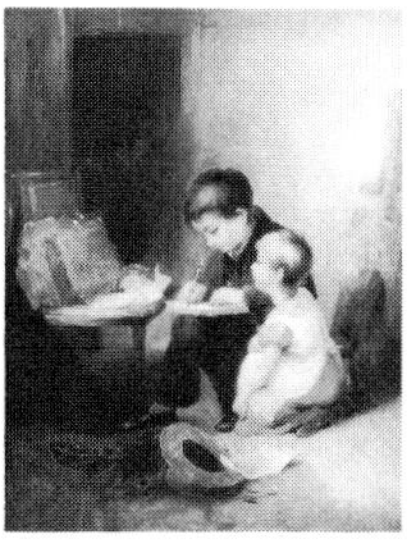

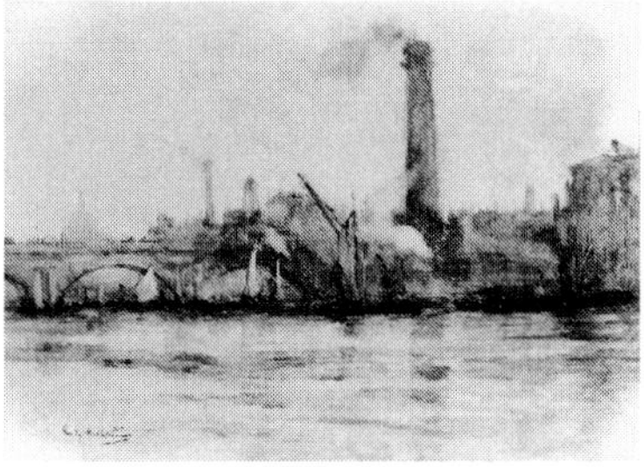

Emily Murray Paterson (1855–1934)

acc. no. 1093
Waterloo Bridge and St. Paul's from the Embankment
watercolour: $10\frac{3}{8} \times 14\frac{1}{2}$ in.
signed: *Emily M. Paterson*
Presented by the artist's family, 1934

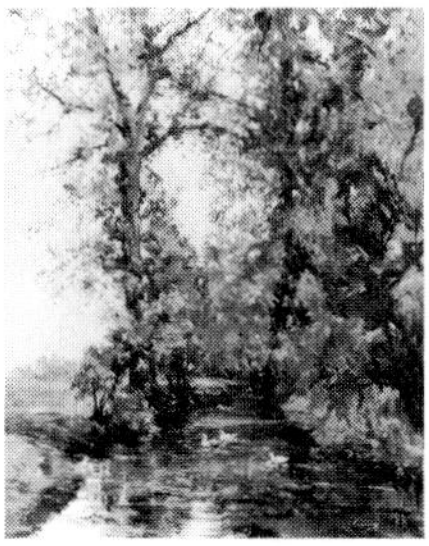

acc. no. 1094
The Silent Pool
watercolour: $38\frac{3}{4} \times 30\frac{3}{4}$ in.
signed: *Emily M. Paterson*
Presented by the artist's family, 1934

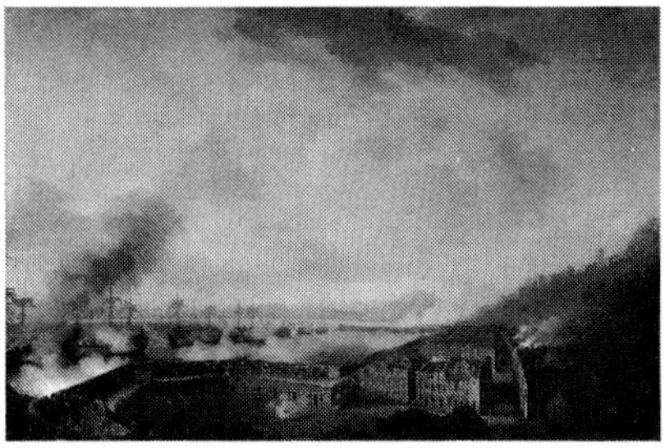

Richard Paton (1717–91)

acc. no. 68
The Defence of Gibraltar against the French and Spanish on the Afternoon of September 13, 1782
oil on canvas: 47 × 70 in.
Presented by Alderman John Boydell, 1792

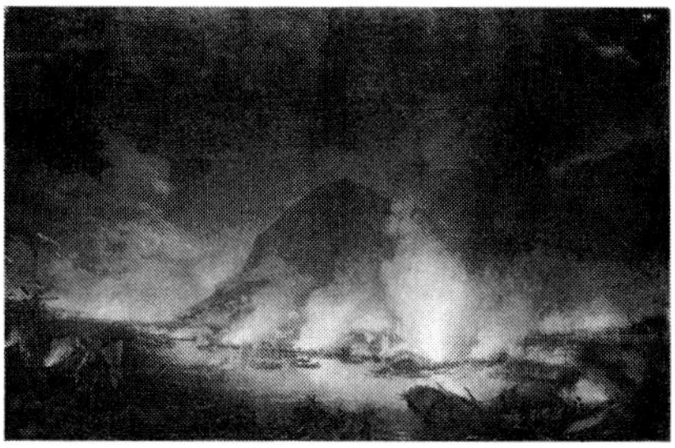

acc. no. 69
The Defence of Gibraltar on the Night of September 13 1782, with the Spanish Gunboats Ablaze
oil on canvas: 47 × 70 in.
Presented by Alderman John Boydell, 1792

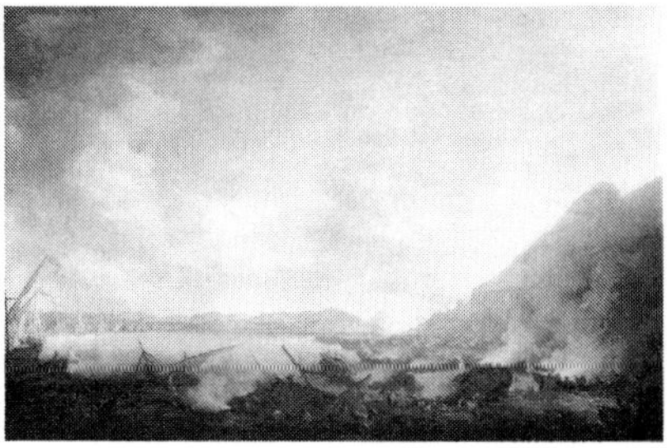

acc. no. 70
The Defence of Gibraltar, with the English taking up the Spanish and French Sailors in Distress, September 14 1782
oil on canvas: 47 × 70 in.
Presented by Alderman John Boydell, 1792

acc. no. 71
The Relief of Gibraltar, October 11 1782
oil on canvas: 47 × 70 in.
Presented by Alderman John Boydell, 1792

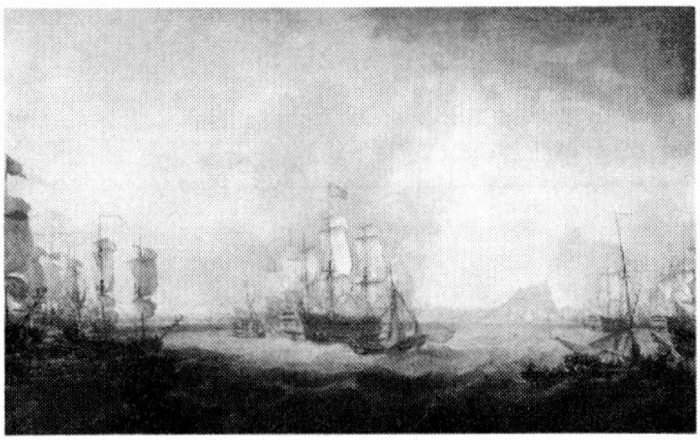

For acc. no. 54, *The Lord Mayor's Procession by Water to Westminster, 1789* see under **Wheatley**

George Patten (1801–65)

acc. no. 1061
Sir Matthew Wood, Lord Mayor 1815–1817 (1818)
oil on canvas: 30 × 25 in.
signed and dated: *G Patten 1818*
Purchased 1928

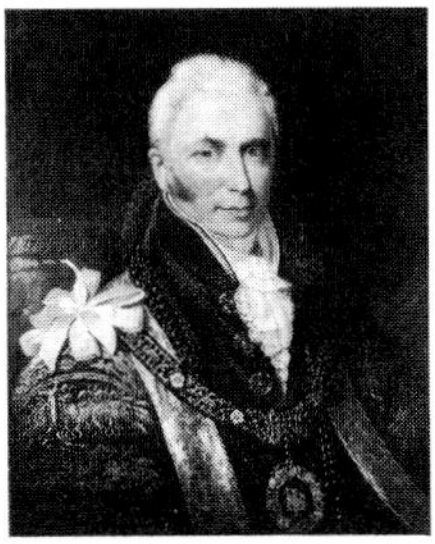

acc. no. 97
Alderman Robert Waithman
oil on canvas: 34 × 28 in.
Presented by the sitter's family, 1822

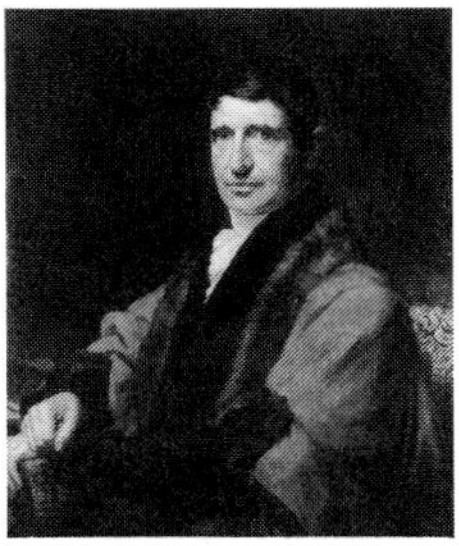

William Patten (d.1843)

acc. no. 599
Sir Edward Banks (1829)
oil on canvas: 38 × 32 in.
Presented by Sir Richmond Cotton, 1895

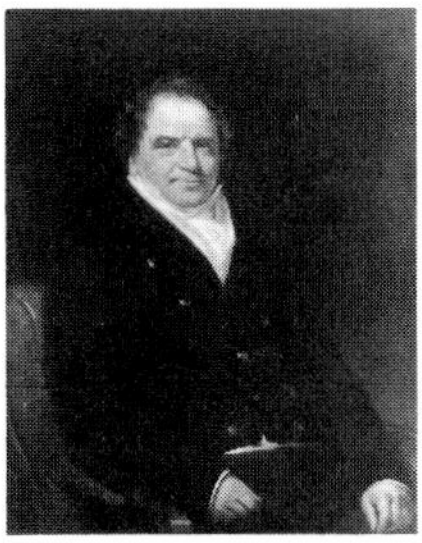

Charles Pears (1873–1958)

acc. no. 1563
The Pool of London During Dockland Air Raids, 1940
oil on canvas: 40 × 60 in.
signed: *CHAS. PEARS*
Presented by Mrs. Pears, 1958

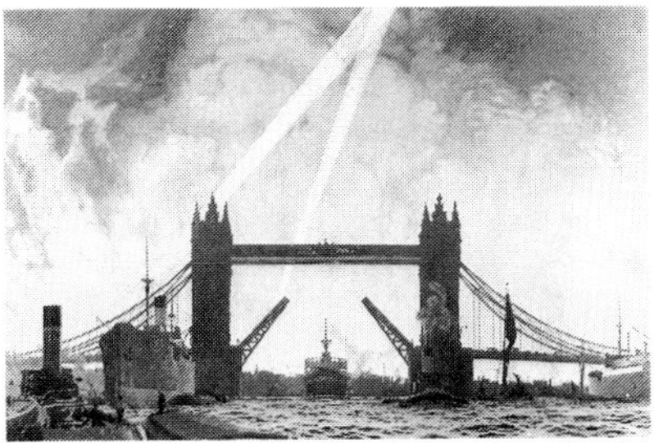

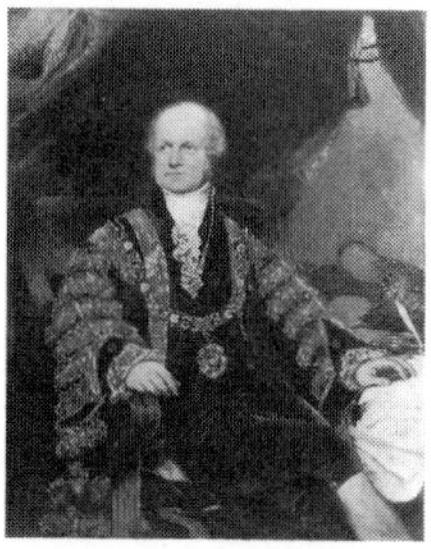

Mary Martha Pearson (*fl. c.*1814–44)

acc. no. 254
Samuel Birch, Lord Mayor 1814

oil on canvas: 58 × 47 in.
Presented by the sitter's grand-daughter, 1877

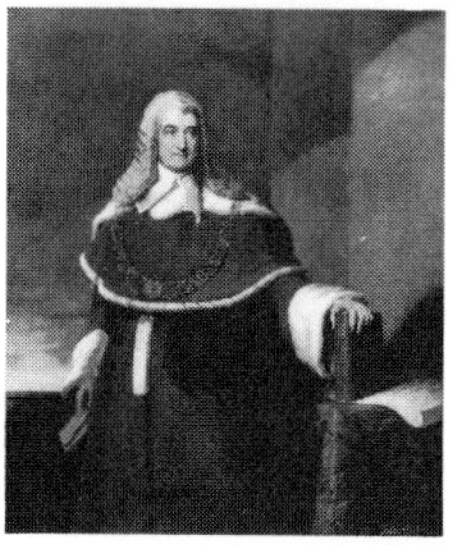

acc. no. 112
Lord Denman (?c.1832)

oil on canvas, cut down: 72 × 60 in.
Presented by the artist, 1844

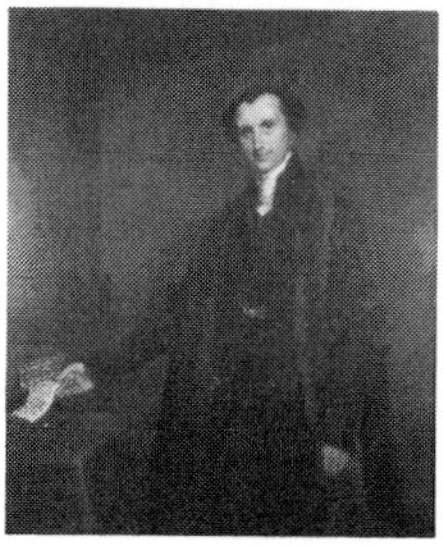

acc. no. 111
Sir James Shaw, City Chamberlain (1834)

oil on canvas, cut down: 60 × 50 in.
Presented by Sir James Shaw, 1843

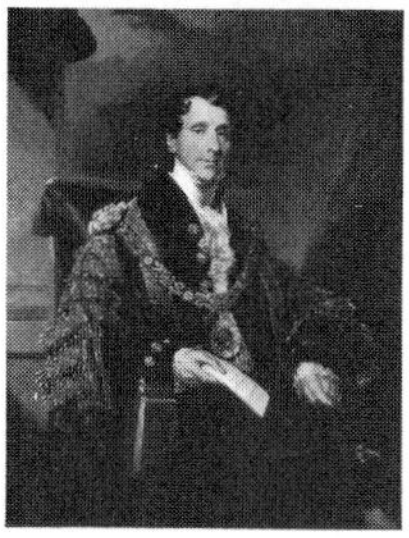

acc. no. 475
Sir Thomas Kelly, Lord Mayor 1836 (1837)

oil on canvas: 56 × 44 in.
Presented by a relative of the sitter, 1889

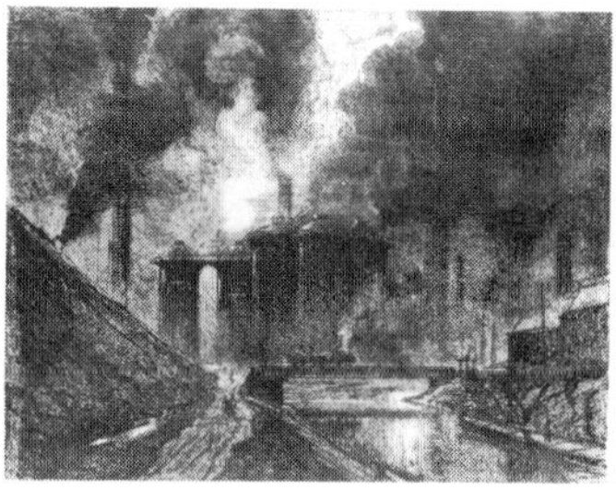

Joseph Pennell (1860–1926)

acc. no. 942
Ironworks in the Midlands

lithograph: 18 × 23 in.
signed: *J S Pennell*
Presented by Miss Evelyn P. McGhee, 1913

Abraham Pether (1756–1812)

acc. no. 574
Old Drury Lane Theatre on Fire, February 24 1809
oil on canvas: 29 × 42 in.
signed and dated: *A. Pether 1809*
Presented by J. L. Rutley, 1893

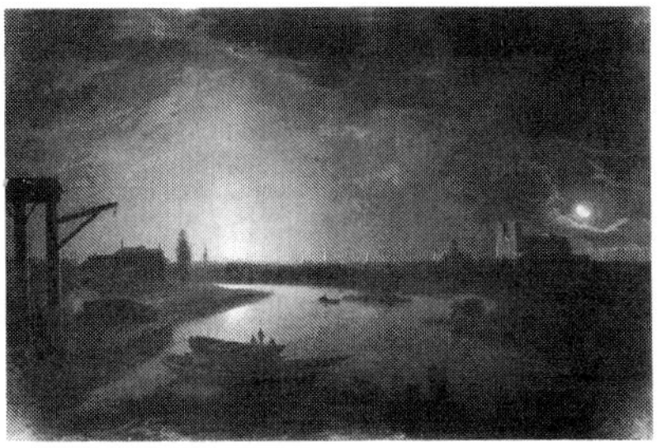

Henry Pether (1828–65)

acc. no. 1232
Gun Wharf, Tower of London
oil on canvas: $24\frac{1}{2} \times 36\frac{1}{2}$ in.
signed: *Henry Pether*
Presented by Lord Wakefield, 1938

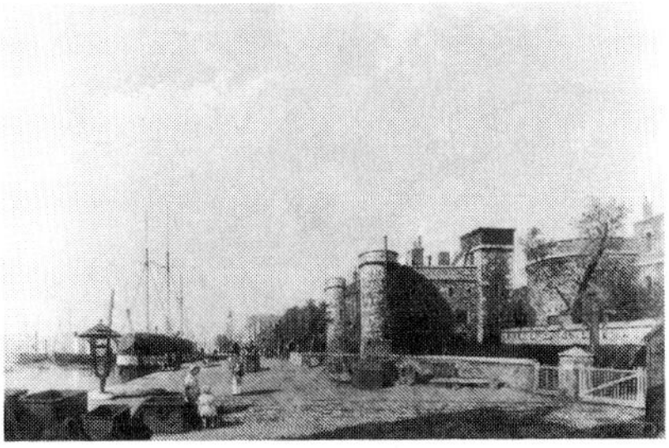

acc. no. 1315
Traitors' Gate, Tower of London
oil on canvas: 18 × 24 in.
Purchased from Leggatt & Co., 1944

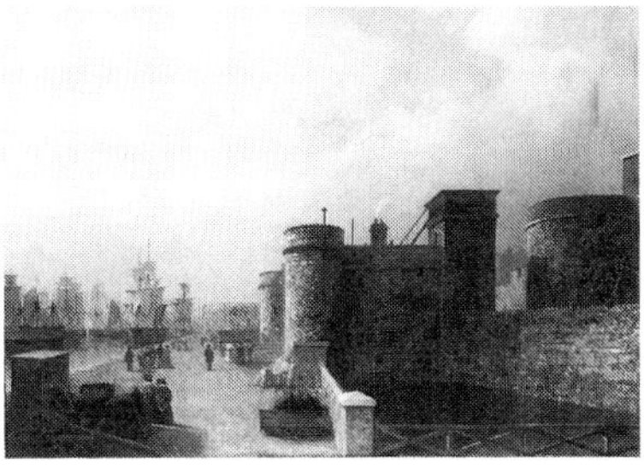

acc. no. 1830
The Custom House and Pool of London by Moonlight
oil on canvas: $23\frac{7}{8} \times 36$ in.
Purchased from Richard Green, 1969

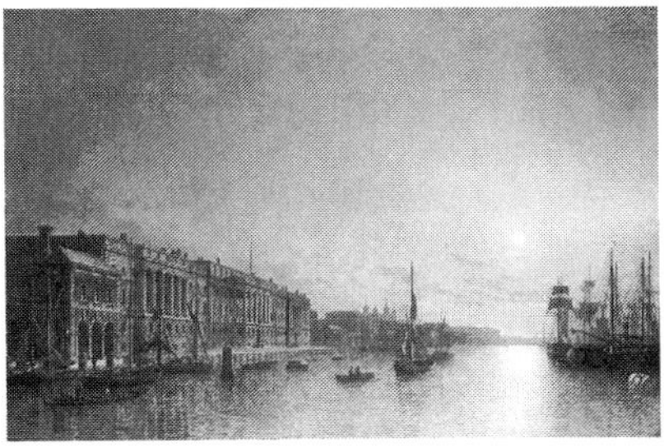

attributed to François Joseph Pfeiffer (1778–1835)

acc. no. 386
Peasants Merrymaking
oil on canvas: $19\frac{1}{4} \times 25\frac{3}{4}$ in.
signed: *P*
Bequeathed by William Dunnett, 1888

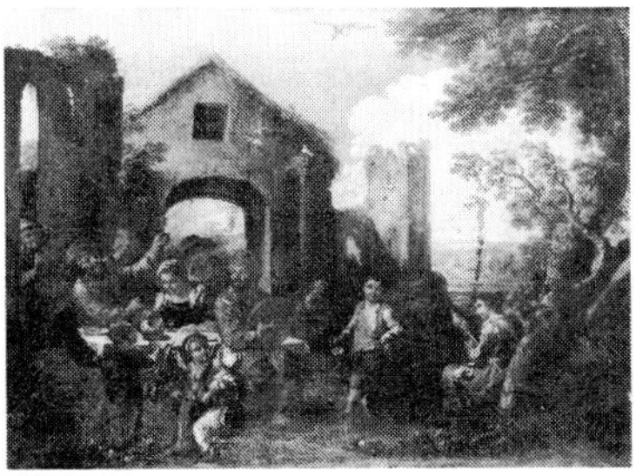

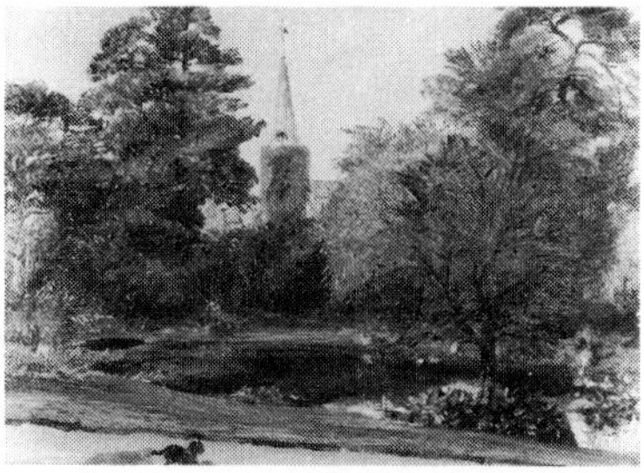

John Phillip (1817–67)

acc. no. 716
Near Chelmsford, Essex (1857)
oil on panel: 10 × 13½ in.
inscribed on verso: *Sketched in 1857 – background to a portrait of Mr. Parker*
Bequeathed by Charles Gassiot, 1902

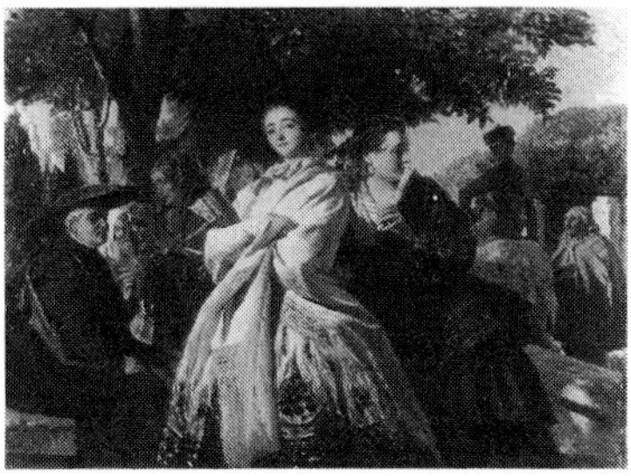

acc. no. 714
The Huff (1859)
oil on millboard: 10½ × 4 in.
signed and dated: *JP / '59*
Bequeathed by Charles Gassiot, 1902

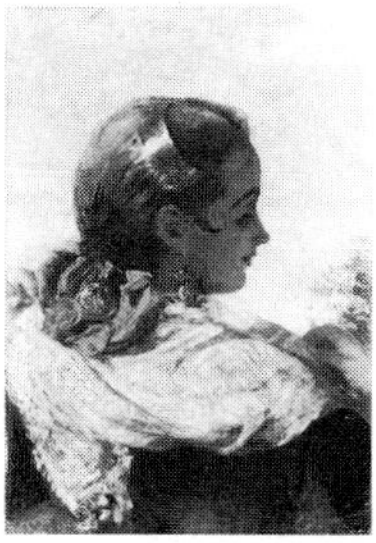

acc. no. 715
Head of a Spanish Girl (1860)
oil on panel: 9½ × 6½ in.
signed (mono) and dated: *18 JP 60*
Bequeathed by Charles Gassiot, 1902

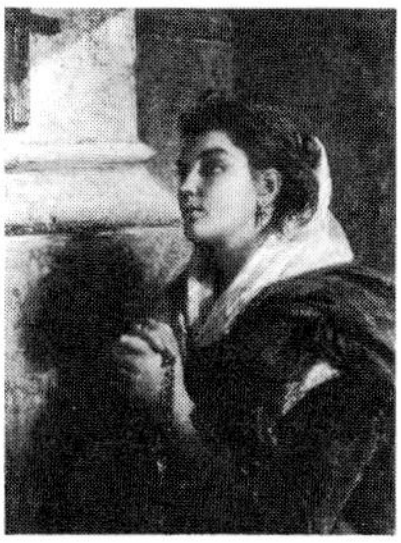

acc. no. 710
Faith (1864)
oil on canvas: 32 × 24 in.
signed (mono) and dated: *18 JP 64*
Bequeathed by Charles Gassiot, 1902

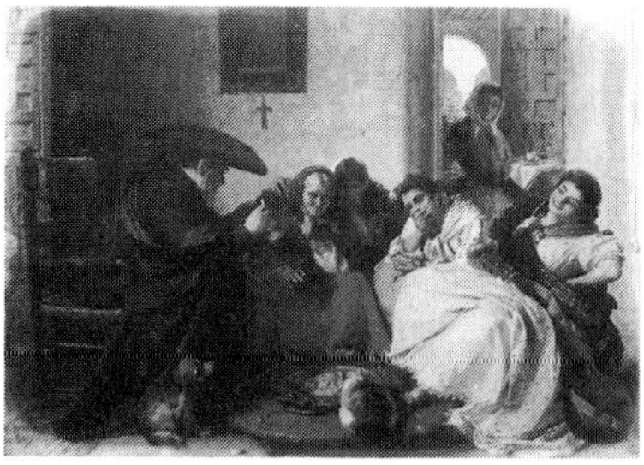

acc. no. 711
A Chat Round the Brasero (1866)
oil on canvas: 36 × 48 in.
signed and dated: *18 JP 66*
Bequeathed by Charles Gassiot, 1902

Thomas Phillips (1770–1845)

acc. no. 110
Sir Matthew Wood, Lord Mayor 1815–1817
oil on canvas: 30 × 25 in.
Presented by Mrs. Maria Weybridge, 1843

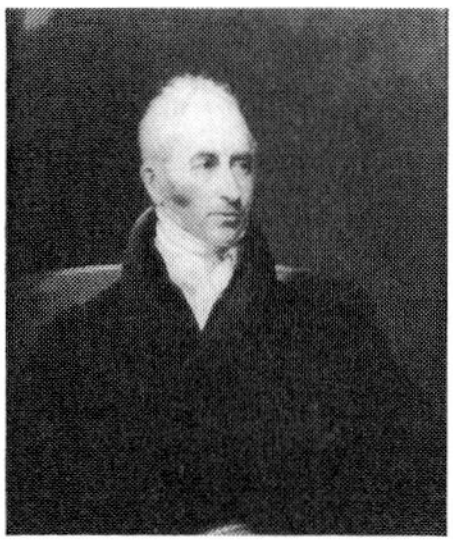

Frederick Richard Pickersgill (1820–1900)

acc. no. 755
On the Way to the Spring (*c.*1862)
oil on panel: $14\frac{1}{2} \times 12\frac{1}{2}$ in.
signed (mono) and dated: *FRP 186...* (last digit illegible)
Bequeathed by Charles Gassiot, 1902

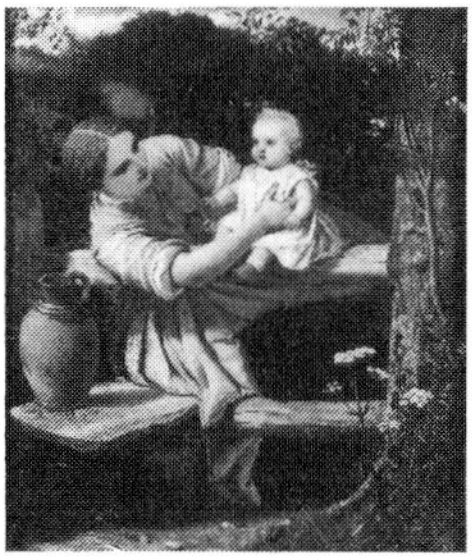

Henry William Pickersgill (1782–1875)

acc. no. 1064
Sir John Pirie Bt., Lord Mayor 1841–2
oil on canvas: 56 × 44 in.
Purchased from F. Syer & Sons, 1929

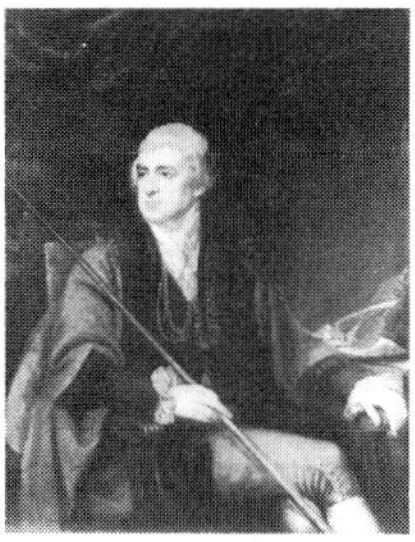

acc. no. 121
Henry Benjamin Hanbury Beaufoy (1848)
oil on canvas: 56 × 44 in.
Commissioned by the Corporation, 1848

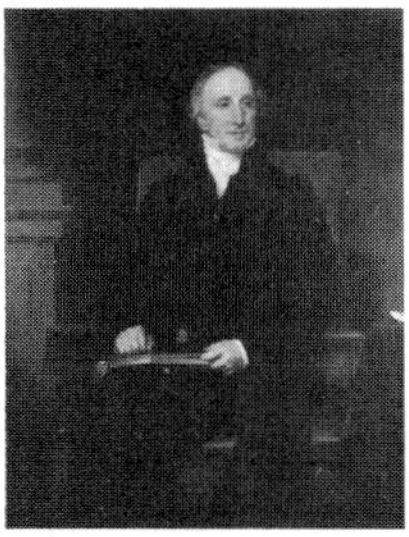

after Henry William Pickersgill (1782–1875) by Charles Fox (1794–1849)

acc. no. 1343
Henry Benjamin Hanbury Beaufoy (*c.*1848)
steel engraving: $13\frac{1}{4} \times 14\frac{1}{2}$ in.
Presented by H. M. Beaufoy, 1945

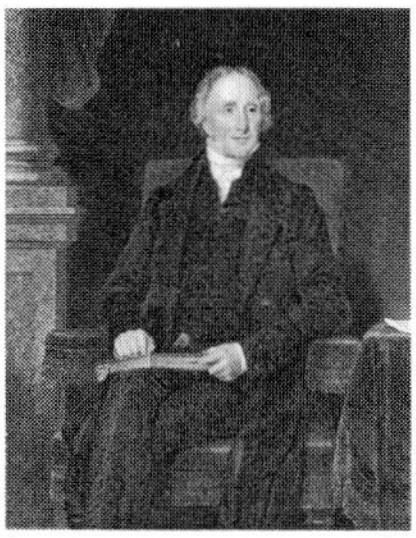

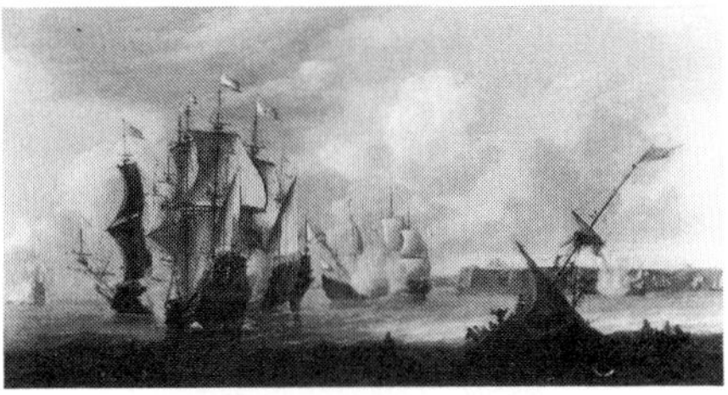

attributed to Jan Pieters (1624–1667/80)

acc. no. 383
Dutch Ships attacking a Portuguese Harbour
oil on panel: 19 × 36 in.
Bequeathed by William Dunnett, 1888

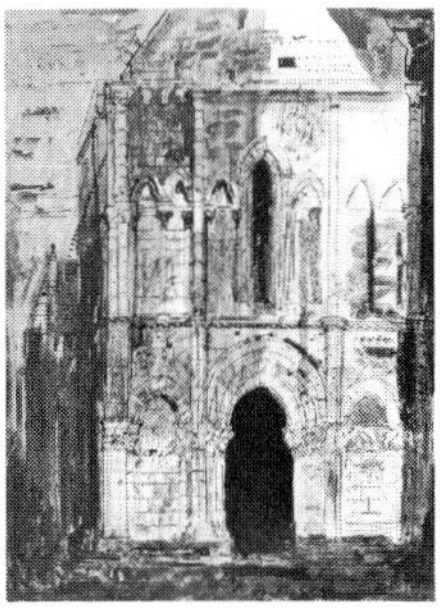

John Piper (b.1903)

acc. no. 1813
Montpellier, Charente (*c*.1969)
screenprint: 30 × 21¾ in. (image)
signed in the plate: *John Piper*; numbered in margin: *51/70*
Purchased from Marlborough Fine Art, 1969

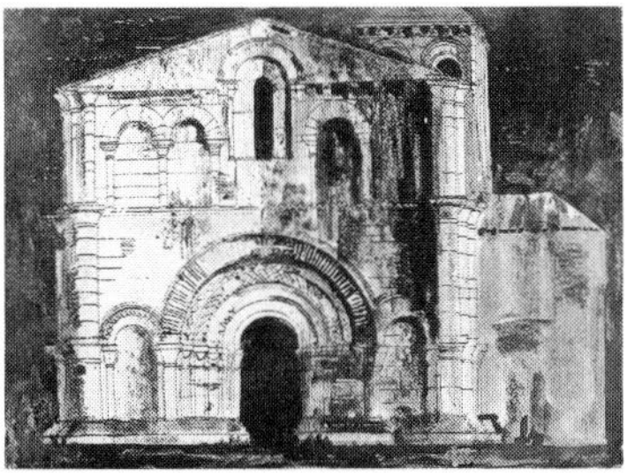

acc. no. 1814
Jazennes, Charente (*c*.1969)
screenprint: 22½ × 30½ in.
signed in the plate: *John Piper*; numbered in margin: *51/70* and inscribed: *Jonzac (not on list)*
Purchased from Marlborough Fine Art, 1969

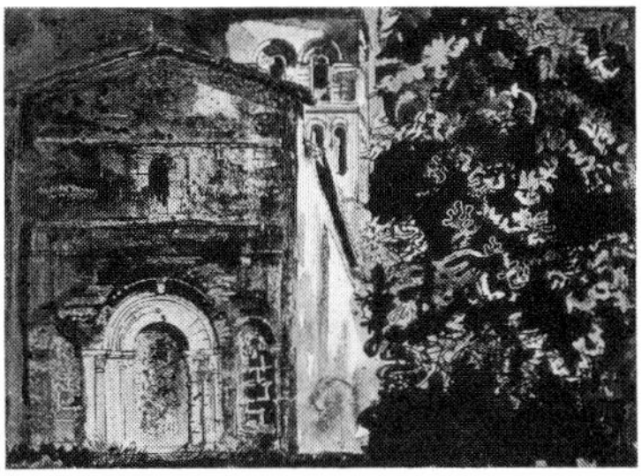

acc. no. 1815
La Chapelle de St Robert, Dordogne
screenprint: 22½ × 30½ in.
Purchased from Marlborough Fine Art, 1969

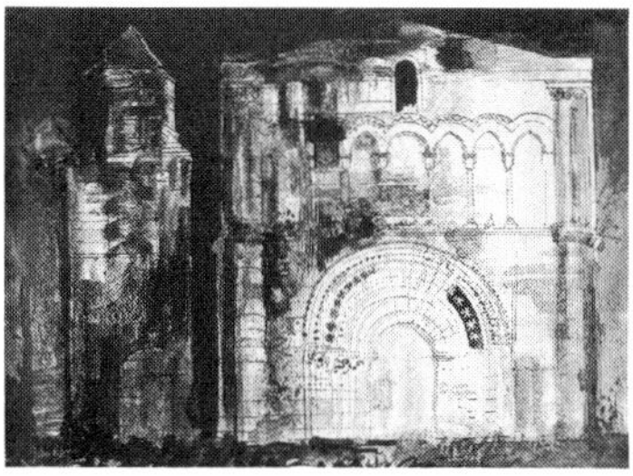

acc. no. 1816
S. Simon de Pelouaille, Charente
screenprint: 22½ × 30½ in.
signed in the plate: *John Piper*; numbered in the margin: *53/70* and inscribed on the verso: *ST. Simon*
Purchased from Marlborough Fine Art, 1969

acc. no. 1817
Besse, Dordogne

screenprint: 30½ × 22½ in.
signed in the plate: *John Piper*; numbered in the margin *53/70*
Purchased from Marlborough Fine Art, 1969

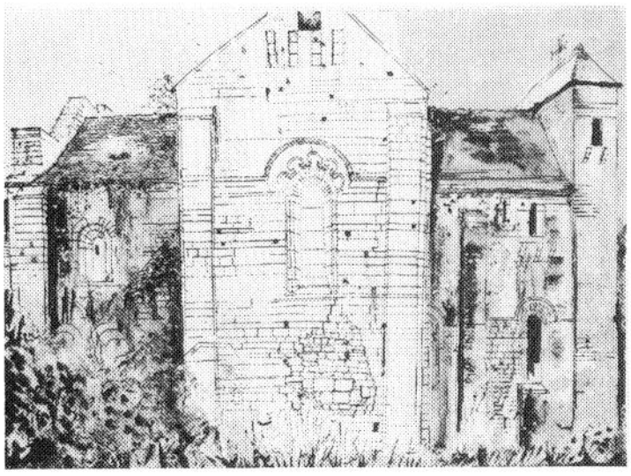

acc. no. 1818
S. Raphael, Dordogne

screenprint: 22½ × 30½ in.
signed in the plate: *John Piper*; numbered in the margin *13/70*; inscribed on the verso: *St Raphael*
Purchased from Marlborough Fine Art, 1969

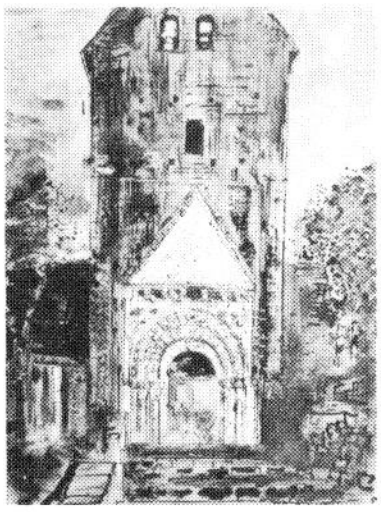

acc. no. 1819
S. Amand de Coly, Dordogne

screenprint: 30½ × 23 in.
signed in the plate: *John Piper*; numbered in the margin *52/70*; inscribed on the verso: *ST. Amand / ST AMAND DE COLY – DORDOGNE*
Purchased from Marlborough Fine Art, 1969

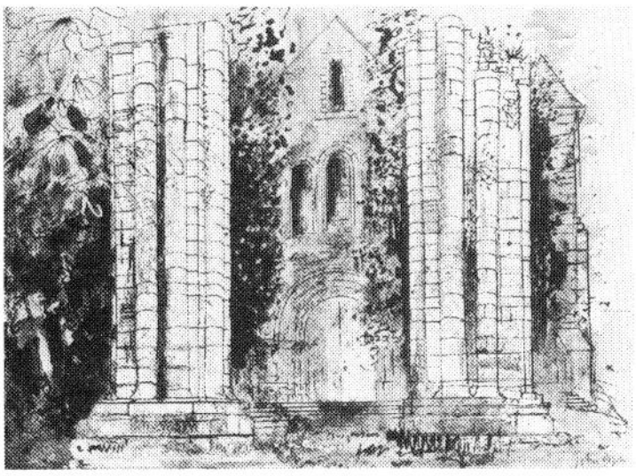

Jean Platteel (*fl.* 1839–67)

acc. no. 1660
The Letter (1853)

oil on panel: 17½ × 13½ in. (sight)
signed and dated: *J^n Platteel. f^t 1853*; label on verso signed *JP* and inscribed: (first line illegible) *Le tableau, qui represente "Une / "Jeune Dame lisant une lettre / "Qu'un Cavalier lui a* (*sic*) remis", est peint par lui. / Bruxelles le 16 aout 1800 cinquante trois / Jean Platteel
Presented by John Byram, 1963

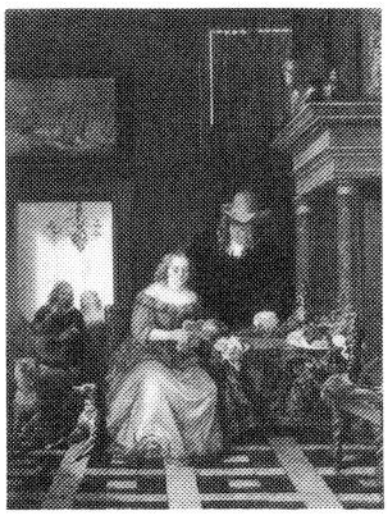

David Poole (b.1931)

acc. no. 2216
The Silver Jubilee Luncheon in Guildhall, June 7 1977 (1978)

oil on canvas: 82 × 142 in.
signed and dated: *David Poole 1978*
Commissioned by the Corporation, 1977

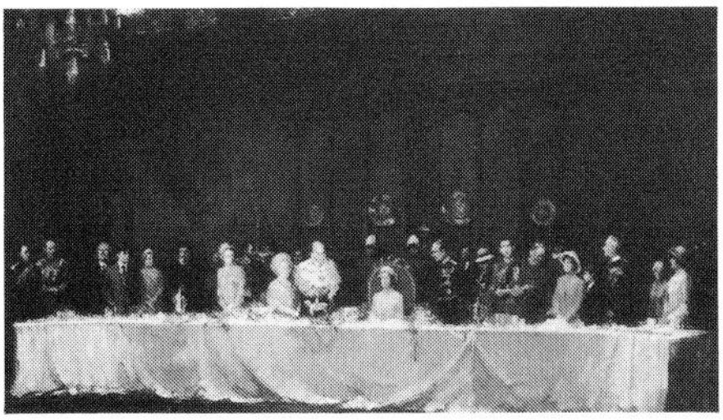

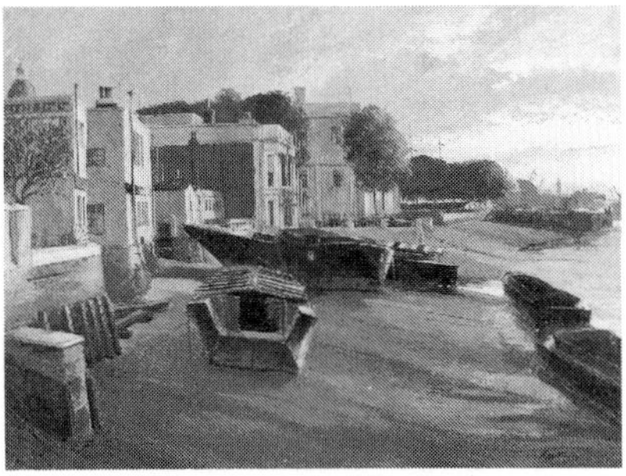

Jack Dennis Pountney (20th C)

acc. no. 1960
Evening – Greenwich (*c.*1973)
oil on hardboard: $23\frac{1}{4} \times 31\frac{5}{8}$ in.
signed: *Pountney*
Purchased from the artist, 1973

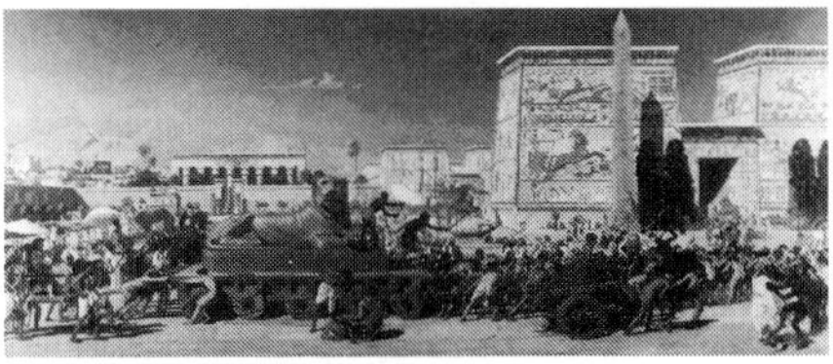

Sir Edward John Poynter (1836–1919)

acc. no. 1014
Israel in Egypt (1867)
oil on canvas: 54 × 125 in.
signed (mono) and dated: *18 EJP 67*
Presented by Sir George Touche, 1921

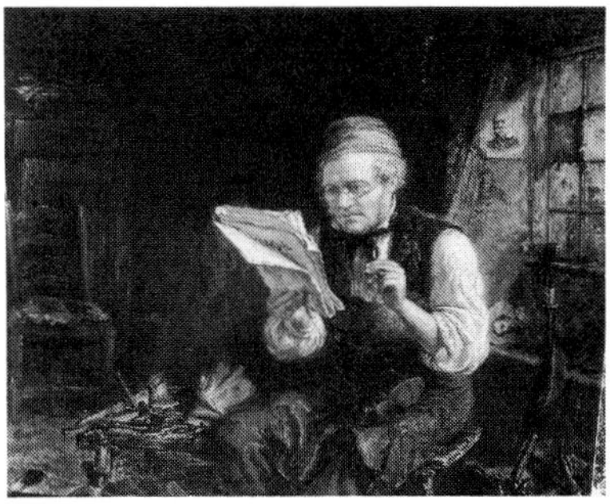

Jonathan Pratt (1835–1911)

acc. no. 757
The Politician (1871)
oil on canvas: 11 × 13 in.
signed and dated: *J. Pratt 1871*
Bequeathed by Charles Gassiot, 1902

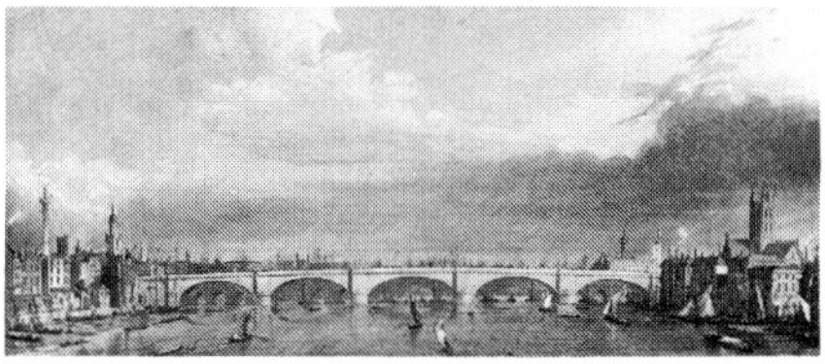

Augustus Charles Pugin (1762–1832)

acc. no. 1511
New London Bridge (1829)
watercolour: $17\frac{3}{8} \times 7\frac{5}{8}$ in.
Purchased from the Watkins Gallery, 1954

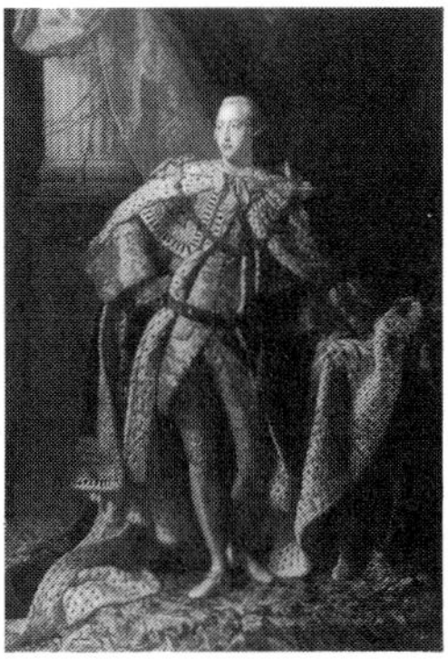

Allan Ramsay (1713–84)

acc. no. 38
King George III (*c.*1762–64)
oil on canvas: 97 × 64 in.
Presented by King George III, 1764

acc. no. 39
Queen Charlotte (*c.*1762–64)
oil on canvas: 97 × 64 in.
Presented by King George III, 1764

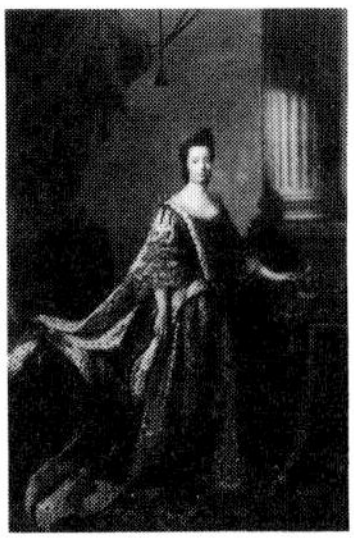

acc. no. 1296
Portrait of a Young Woman (called 'Flora Macdonald')
oil on canvas: 33 × 27 in.
Presented by Lady Wakefield, 1944

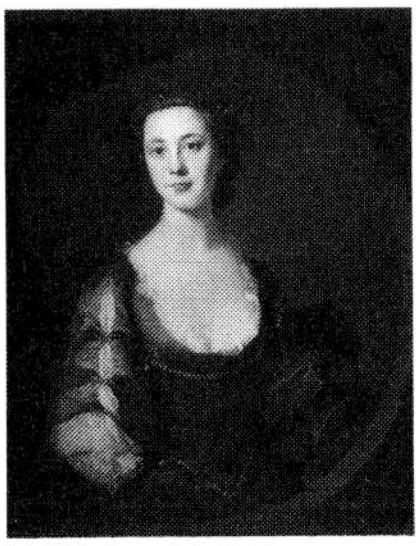

after Raphael (1483–1520)
acc. no. 358
The Holy Family
oil on canvas: 20 × 16 in.
Bequeathed by William Dunnett, 1888

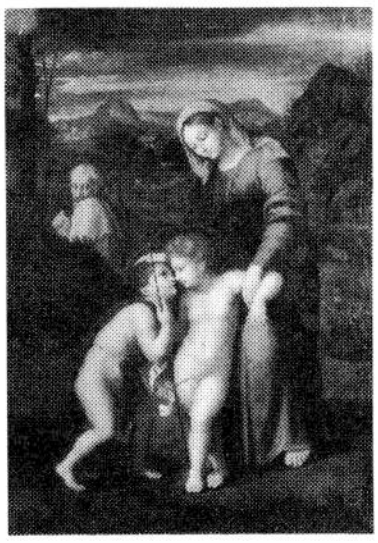

John Samuel Raven (1829–77)
acc. no. 589
Aspens in Spring Bud
oil on canvas: 43 × 71 in.
Presented by Mrs. Morris, 1894

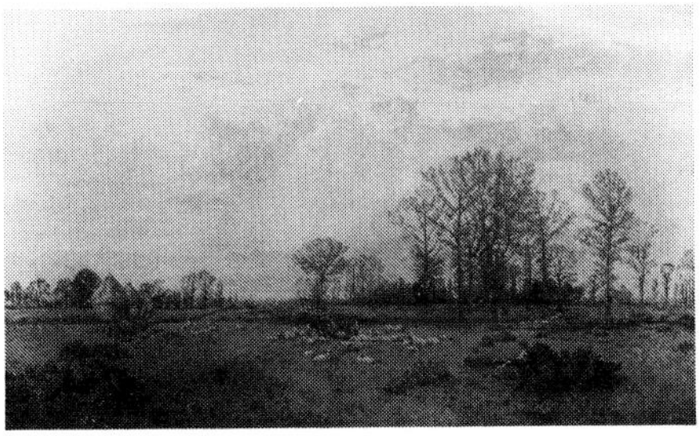

H. J. Reddell (20th C)
acc. no. 1841
The Old London Bridge from Tower Wharf
oil on canvas: 20 × 30 in.
signed: *REDDELL*
Purchased from the artist, 1970

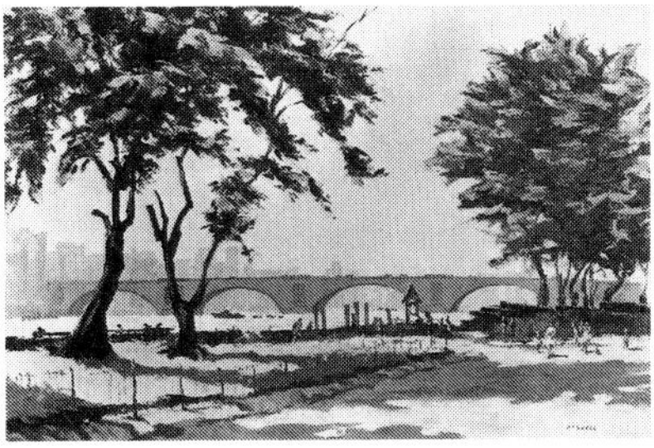

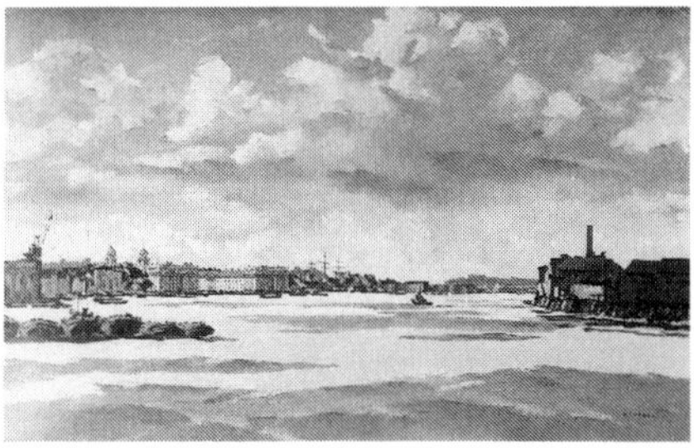

acc. no. 1893
Greenwich Reach
oil on canvas: $19\frac{1}{2} \times 29\frac{1}{2}$ in.
signed: *REDDELL*
Purchased from the artist, 1971

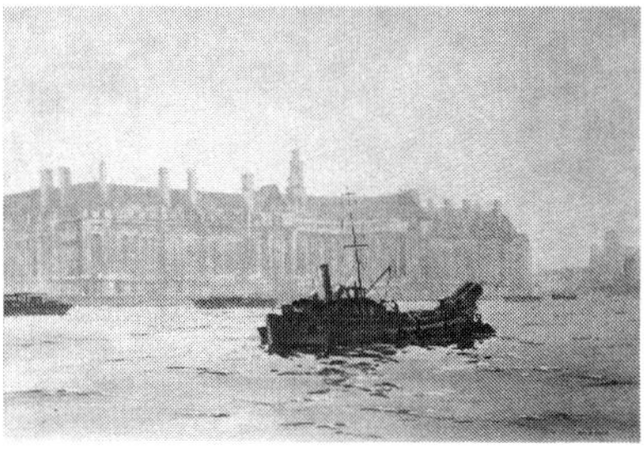

acc. no. 1961
County Hall in Morning Haze
oil on canvas: $15\frac{3}{4} \times 22$ in.
signed: *REDDELL*
Purchased from the artist, 1973

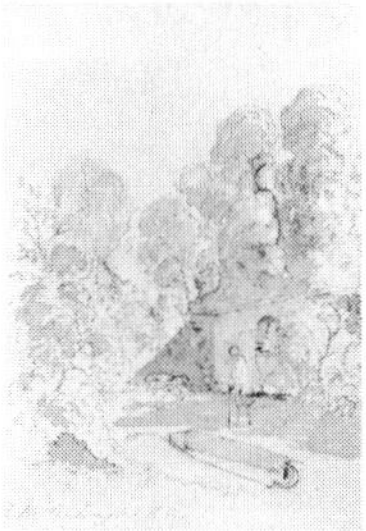

Ramsay Richard Reinagle (1775–1862)

acc. no. 2257
Landscape with an Open Grave (?)
pencil and wash: $6\frac{3}{8} \times 4\frac{3}{8}$ in.
signed: *R. R. Reinagle R.A.*
Presented by Miss Helen Guiterman, 1985

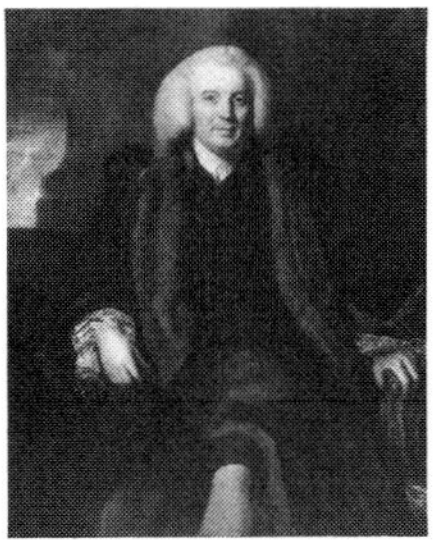

Sir Joshua Reynolds (1723–92)

acc. no. 1853
Sir Thomas Harrison, Chamberlain of London (1758)
oil on canvas: $49\frac{3}{4} \times 39\frac{3}{4}$ in.
Purchased from the Executors of Miss E. M. Harrison, 1971

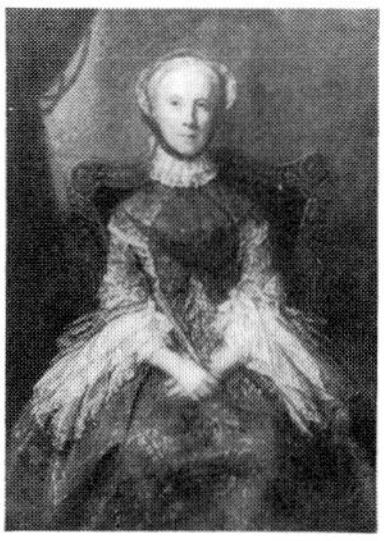

acc. no. 1854
Lady Dorothea Harrison (1758)
oil on canvas: $49\frac{3}{4} \times 39\frac{3}{4}$ in.
Purchased from the Executors of Miss E. M. Harrison, 1971

acc. no. 1305
Pope Paviarius (*c.*1770–75)

oil on canvas: 30 × 25 in.
Presented by Lady Wakefield, 1944

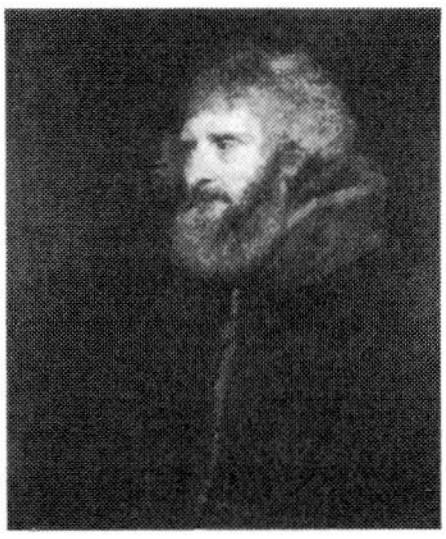

acc. no. 40
Sir Charles Pratt (1764)

oil on canvas, cut down: 48 × 40 in.
Commissioned by the Corporation, 1764

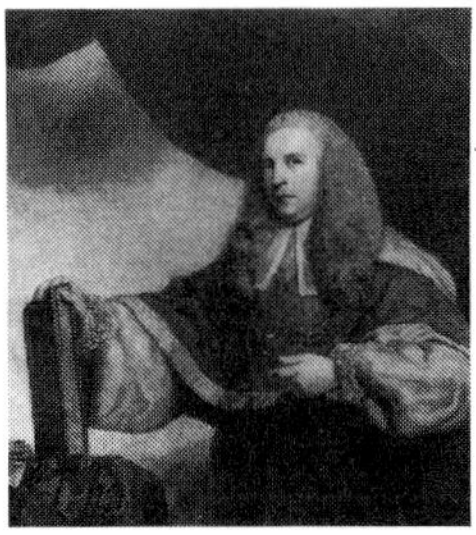

acc. no. 45
Thomas Tomkins (1789)

oil on canvas: 29 × 24 in.
Presented by the sitter, 1790

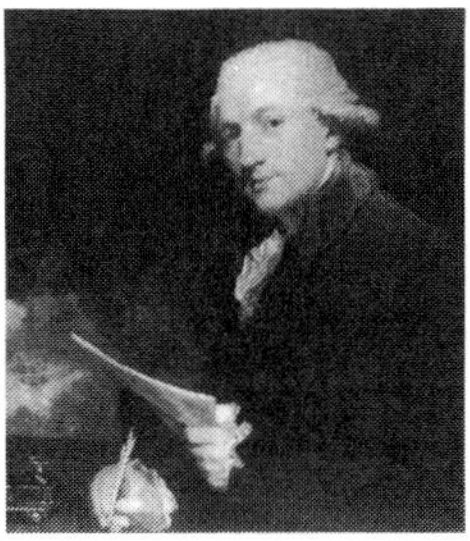

after Sir Joshua Reynolds (1723–92)

acc. no. 63
Lord Heathfield (*c.*1809)

oil on canvas: 56 × 44 in.
Presented by Josiah Boydell, *c.*1809

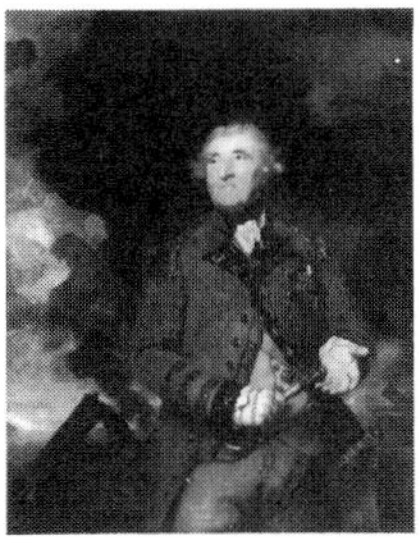

acc. no. 1310
The Marquis of Granby

oil on canvas: 30 × 25 in.
Presented by Lady Wakefield, 1944

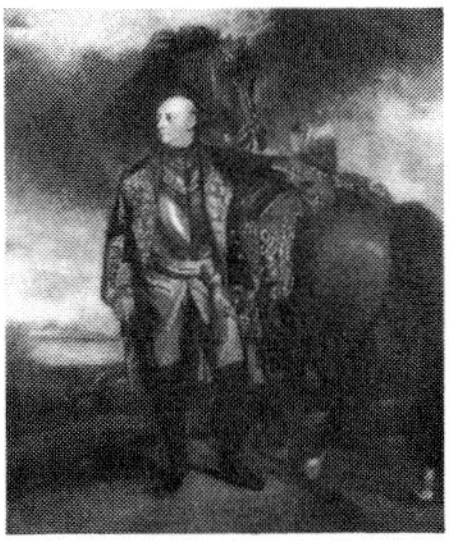

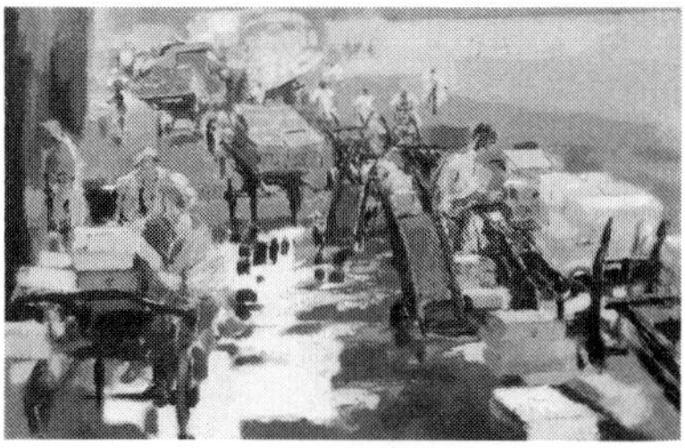

Ian Ribbons (b.1924)

acc. no. 3635
Billingsgate Market (1981)
oil on canvas: $19\frac{7}{8} \times 30\frac{1}{8}$ in.
signed and dated on stretcher: *Ian Ribbons 1981*
Purchased from the artist, 1985

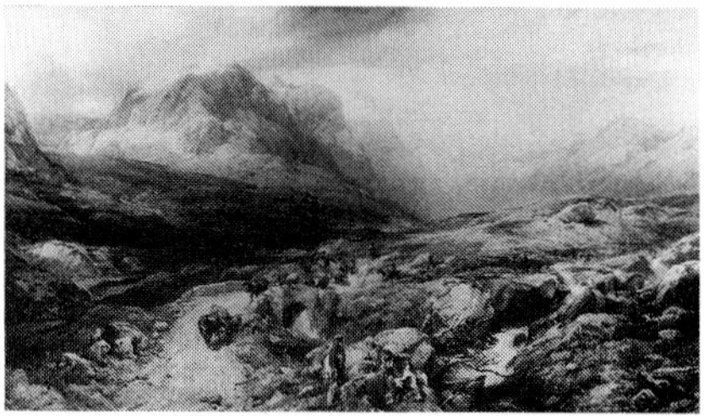

Thomas Miles Richardson jnr (1813–90)

acc. no. 1081
The Pass of Glencoe from Rannoch Moor (1884)
watercolour: 30 × 50 in.
signed and dated: *T.M. Richardson 1884*
Presented by Montrose Cloete, 1931

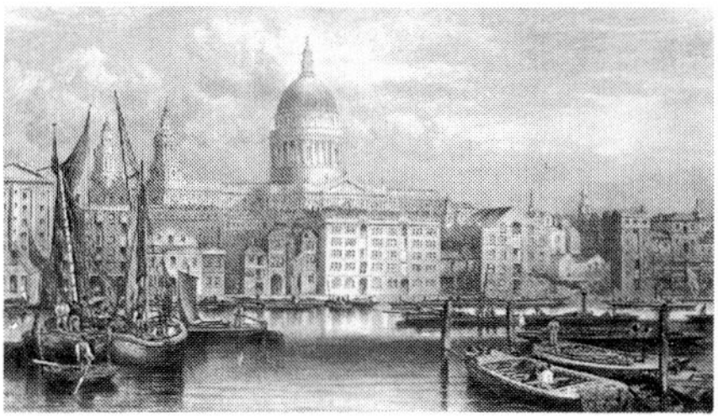

William Richardson (*fl.* 1842–83)

acc. no. 1776
St Paul's from Bankside, Southwark (1883)
watercolour: $17\frac{1}{2} \times 28\frac{1}{4}$ in.
signed and dated: *W. Richardson / 1883*
Purchased from F. T. Sabin, 1967

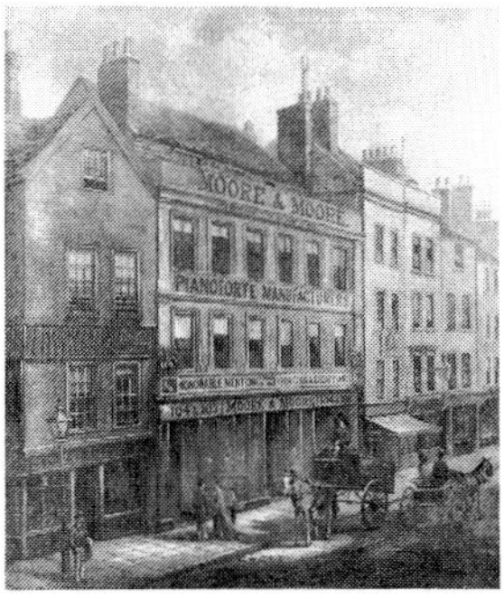

Walter Riddle (19th C)

acc. no. 1537
Bishopsgate in 1871 (1872)
oil on canvas: $24 \times 19\frac{3}{4}$ in.
signed, dated and inscribed on verso: *BISHOPSGATE IN 1871 / by / WALTER RIDDLE. / JULY – 1872* and: *caption / Hayward – Kings Arms / Moore and Moore / Gresham House Gateway / Bradshaw – Hosier / Baker – Coffee House / Yorkman – Confections / Barton – Fishmonger / Right*
Presented by Mrs. Moore on behalf of her husband, 1956

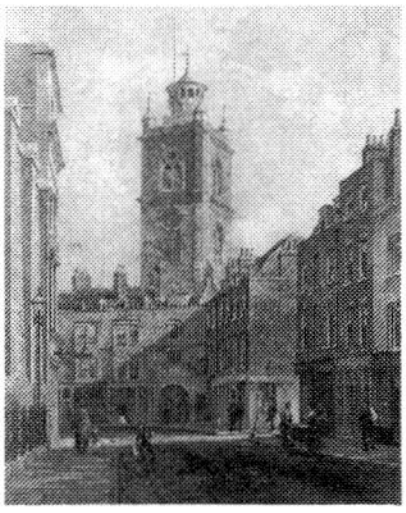

acc. no. 1538
Fore Street and St Giles Cripplegate (*c.*1880)
oil on canvas: 21 × 17 in.
Presented by Mrs. Moore on behalf of her husband, 1956

acc. no. 1539
Newnham's Place, Bishopsgate with Moore and Moore's Piano Factory (1890–91)

oil on canvas: 24 × 20 in.
dated, inscribed and signed on verso: *Sept. 1890 / NEWNHAM'S PLACE FACTORY, / by WALTER RIDDLE. / finished June 1891*
Presented by Mrs. Moore on behalf of her husband, 1956

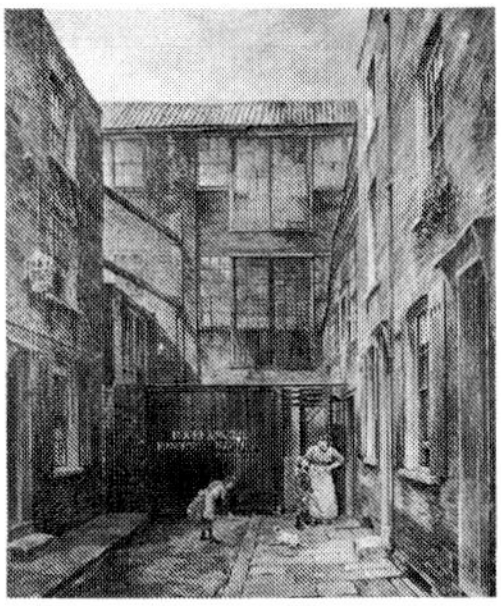

John Francis Rigaud (1742–1810)

acc. no. 1319
Happiness (1794)

oil on canvas: $19\frac{1}{2} \times 18\frac{1}{4}$ in.
signed and dated on verso: *J.F. Rigaud pinx. 1794*
Purchased from Miss La Touche, 1945

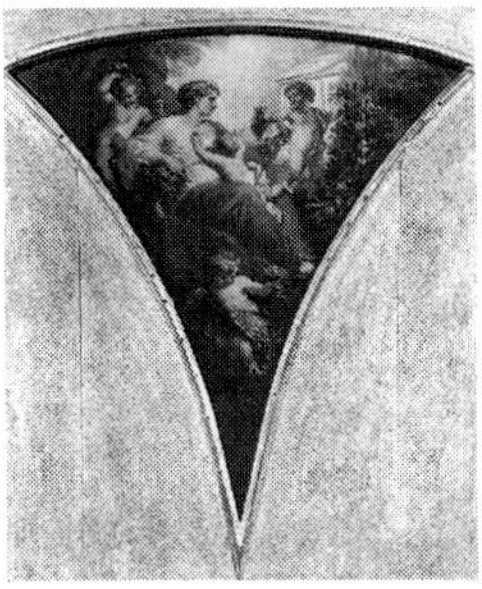

after John Francis Rigaud (1742–1810) by Thomas Burke (1749–1815)

acc. no. 73
Happiness (1799)

stipple engraving: 22 × 17 in.
lettered: *Painted by I.F. Rigaud R.A. Engraved by Thos. Burke. / HAPPINESS / from the Original Picture / presented to the City by ALD. BOYDELL / TO THEIR MOST EXCELLENT MAJESTIES KING GEORGE III & QUEEN CHARLOTTE / This Print is most humbly Dedicated by their most Dutiful and Loyal Subject / JN BOYDELL / Pub. Sept. 29, 1799, by J. & J. BOYDELL, Nº 90, Cheapside; & at the Shakspeare Gallery, Pall Mall, LONDON*
Presented by Alderman John Boydell, *c.*1799

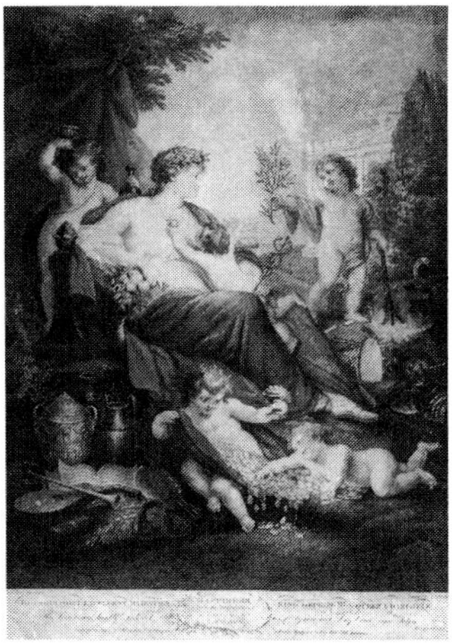

John Francis Rigaud (1742–1810)

acc. no. 1320
Innocence (1794)

oil on canvas: $19\frac{1}{2} \times 18\frac{1}{4}$ in.
signed and dated on verso: *J.F. Rigaud pinx. 1794*
Purchased from Miss La Touche, 1945

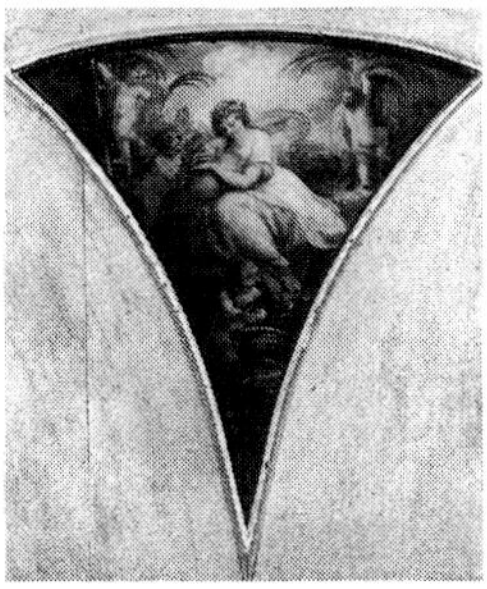

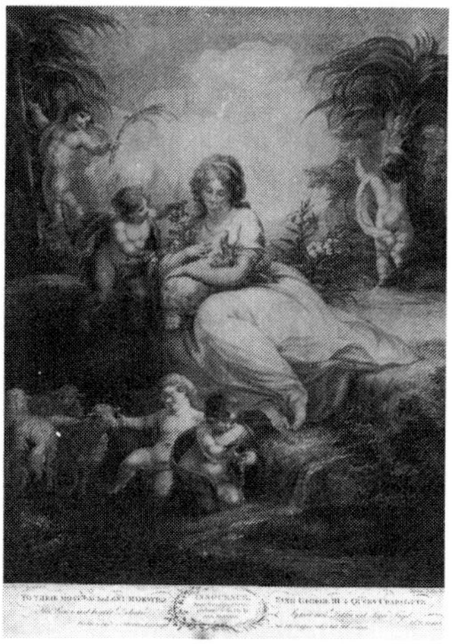

after John Francis Rigaud (1742–1810) by Benjamin Smith (d.1833)

acc. no. 74
Innocence (1799)

stipple engraving: 22 × 17 in.
lettered: *Painted by I.F. Rigaud RA Engraved by Benj. Smith / INNOCENCE / from the Original Picture / presented to the City by / ALD. BOYDELL / TO THEIR MOST EXCELLENT MAJESTIES KING GEORGE III & QUEEN CHARLOTTE. / This Print is most humbly Dedicated by their most Dutiful and Loyal Subject. / JNº BOYDELL / Pub. Sept. 29, 1799, by J. & J. BOYDELL, Nº 90, Cheapside; and at the Shakspeare Gallery, Pall Mall, LONDON.*
Presented by Alderman John Boydell, *c.*1799

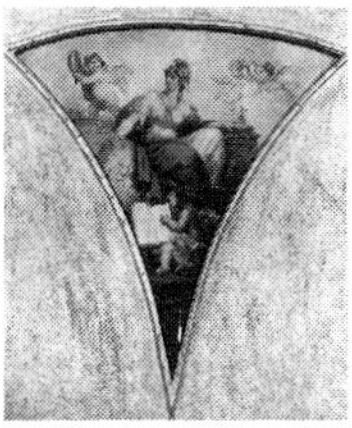

John Francis Rigaud (1742–1810)

acc. no. 1321
Wisdom (1794)

oil on canvas: $19\frac{1}{2} \times 18\frac{1}{4}$ in.
signed and dated on verso: *J.F. Rigaud pinx. 1794*
Purchased from Miss La Touche, 1945

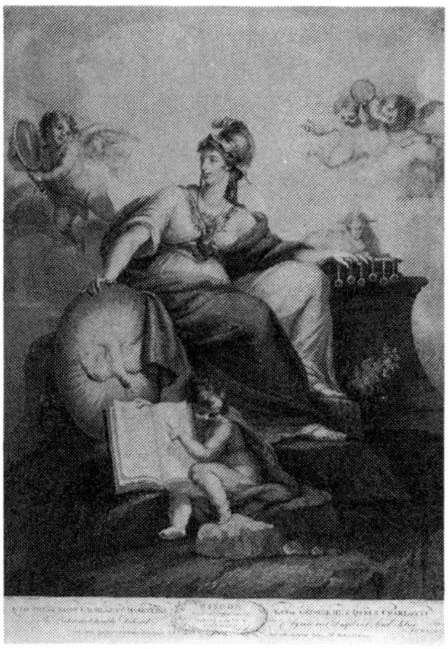

after John Francis Rigaud (1742–1810) by J. P. Simon (18th C)

acc. no. 72
stipple engraving: 22 × 17 in.
lettered: *Painted by I.F. Rigaud R.A. Engraved by I.P. Simon / WISDOM / From the Original Picture / presented to the City by / ALD. BOYDELL / TO THEIR MOST EXCELLENT MAJESTIES KING GEORGE III & QUEEN CHARLOTTE. / This Print is most humbly Dedicated by their most Dutiful and Loyal Subject, / JNº BOYDELL. / Pub. Sept. 29, 1799, by J. & J. BOYDELL, Nº 90, Cheapside; and at the Shakspeare Gallery, Pall Mall, LONDON.*
Presented by Alderman John Boydell, *c.*1799

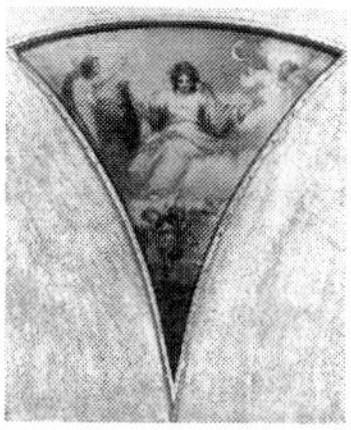

John Francis Rigaud (1742–1810)

acc. no. 1322
Providence (1794)

oil on canvas: $19\frac{1}{2} \times 18\frac{1}{4}$ in.
signed and dated on verso: *J.F. Rigaud pinx. 1794.*
Purchased from Miss La Touche, 1945

after John Francis Rigaud (1742–1810) by Benjamin Smith (d.1833)

acc. no. 75
Providence (*c.*1799)

stipple engraving: 22 × 17 in.
lettered: *Painted by I.F. Rigaud R.A. Engraved by B. Smith / PROVIDENCE / From the Original Picture / presented to the City by / ALD. BOYDELL. / TO THEIR MOST EXCELLENT MAJESTIES KING GEORGE III & QUEEN CHARLOTTE, This Print is most humbly Dedicated by their most Dutiful and Loyal Subject, / JNº BOYDELL. / Pub. Sept. 29, 1799, by J. & J. BOYDELL, Nº 90, Cheapside; and at the Shakspeare Gallery, Pall Mall, LONDON.*
Presented by Alderman John Boydell, *c.*1799

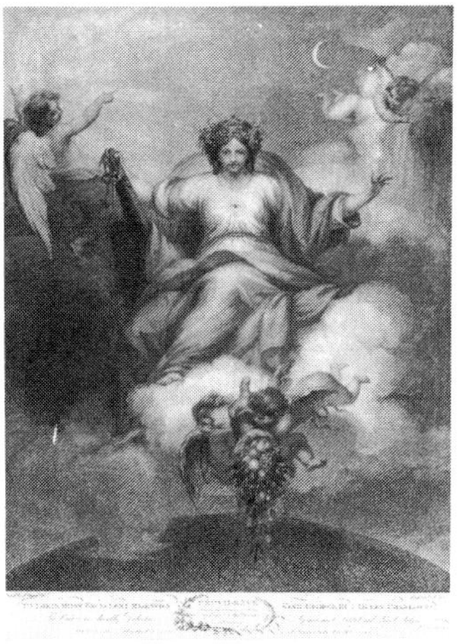

John Riley (1646–91)

acc. no. 96
Sir Robert Clayton, Lord Mayor, 1679

oil on canvas: 48 × 39 in.
Transferred from the London Workhouse, 1829

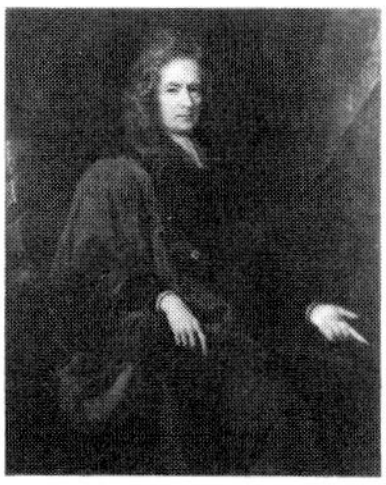

Briton Riviere (1840–1920)

acc. no. 717
The King Drinks (1875)

oil on canvas: 6 × 9 in.
signed and dated: *Briton Riviere 1875*
Bequeathed by Charles Gassiot, 1902

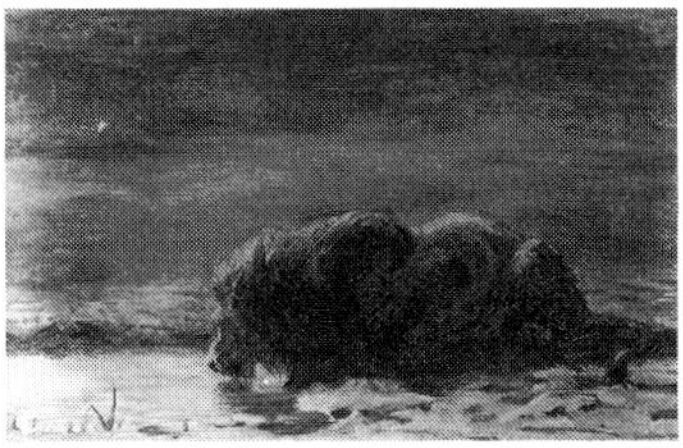

acc. no. 767
The Temptation in the Wilderness (1898)

oil on canvas: 46 × 74½ in.
signed and dated: *BR '98*
Presented by the artist, 1903

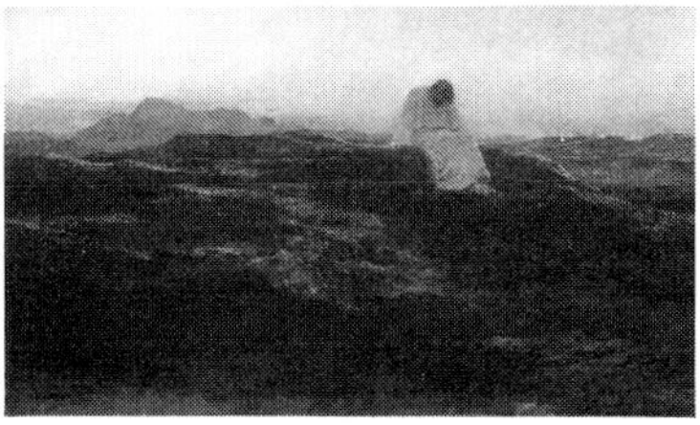

acc. no. 1009
On the Bank of an African River (1918)

oil on canvas: 29 × 51 in.
signed (mono) and dated: *19 BR 18*
Presented by the artist, 1920

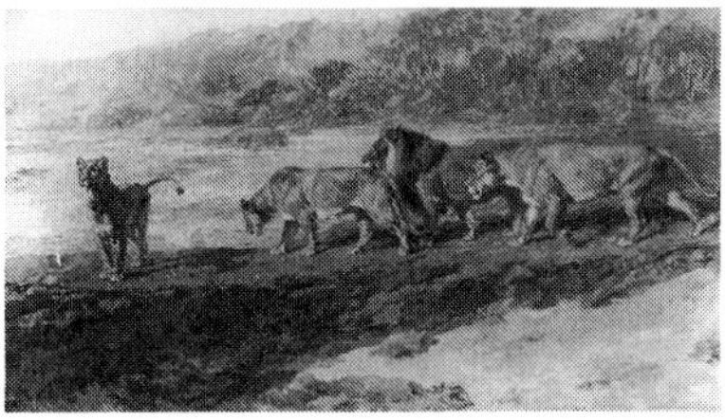

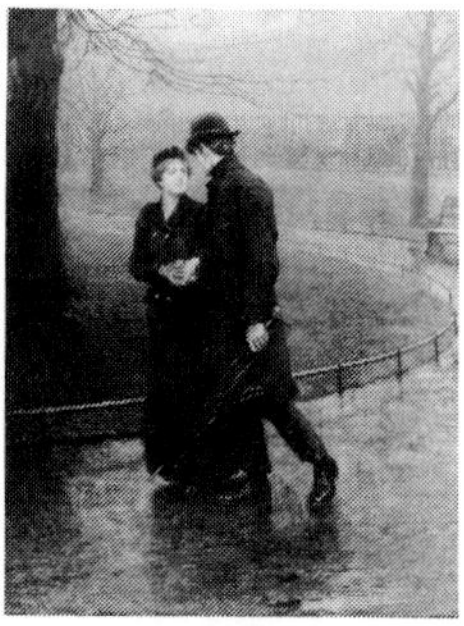

Hugh Goldwyn Riviere (1869–1956)

acc. no. 1057
The Garden of Eden (1901)

oil on canvas: $48\frac{1}{4} \times 37$ in.
signed and dated: *HRiviere. 1901*
Presented by Lady Cooper, 1927

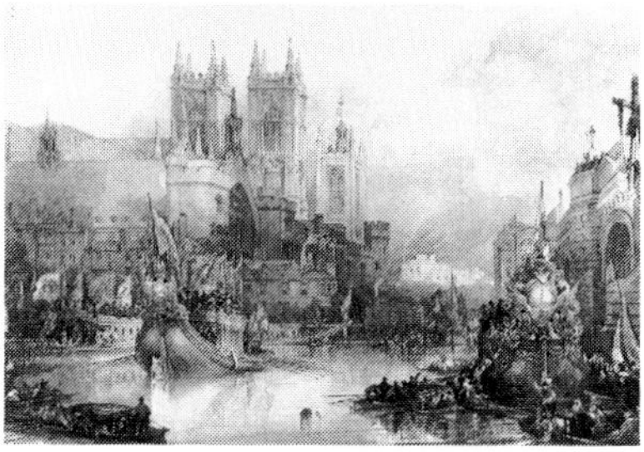

David Roberts (1796–1864)

acc. no. 1246
The Lord Mayor's Show at Westminster (1830)

watercolour: $12\frac{7}{8} \times 18\frac{1}{2}$ in.
signed and dated: *D. Roberts 1830*
Presented by Lord Wakefield, 1939

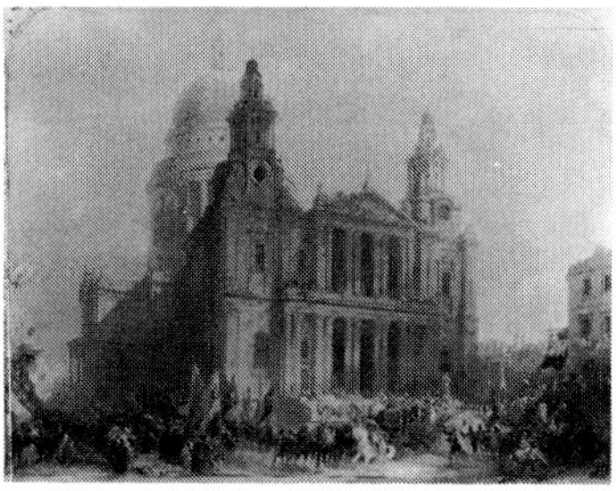

acc. no. 989
St Paul's Cathedral with the Lord Mayor's Procession (1837)

oil on panel: 24×30 in.
Bequeathed by Mrs. Pitman-Lovell, 1918

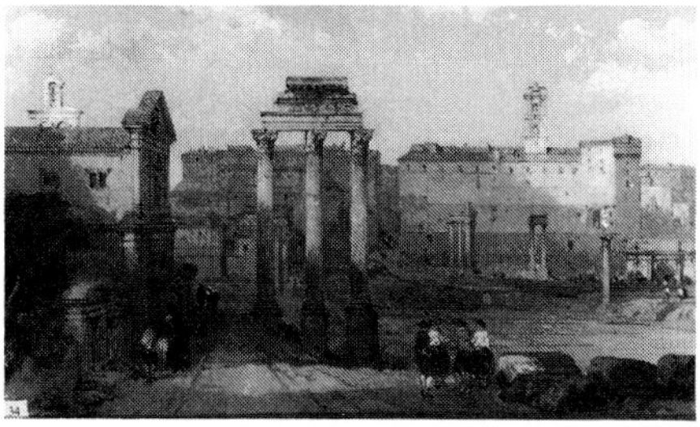

acc. no. 719
The Forum, Rome (1859)

oil on panel: $15 \times 24\frac{1}{2}$ in.
signed and dated: *David Roberts. R.A. 1859*
Bequeathed by Charles Gassiot, 1902

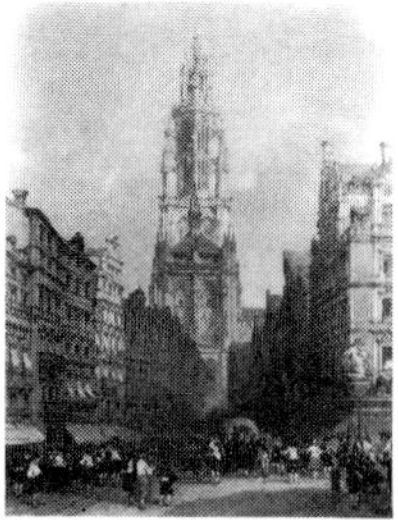

acc. no. 253
Antwerp Cathedral (1860)

oil on canvas: 37×25 in.
signed and dated: *David. Roberts. 1860.*
Presented by the Executors of Mrs. E. Bunning, 1877

acc. no. 718
SS Giovanni e Paolo, Venice (1861)

oil on canvas: 21 × 29½ in.
signed and dated: *David Roberts R.A. 1861.*;
inscribed on the verso: *To my dear Christie on her birthday 1861*
Bequeathed by Charles Gassiot, 1902

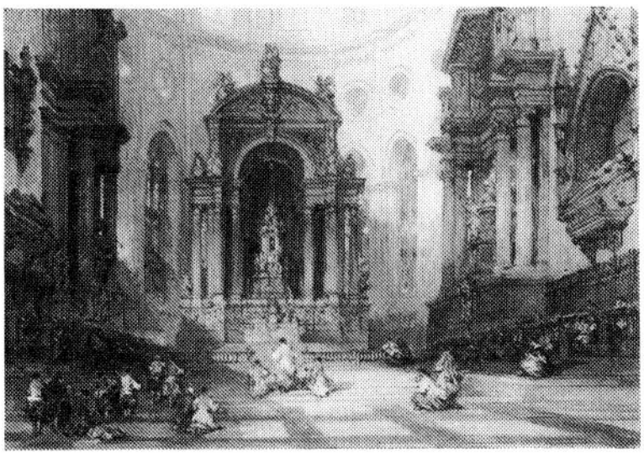

acc. no. 252
The Church of St Stephen, Vienna (1863)

oil on canvas: 37 × 25 in.
signed and dated: *David Roberts. R.A. 1863*
Presented by the Executors of Mrs. E. Bunning, 1877

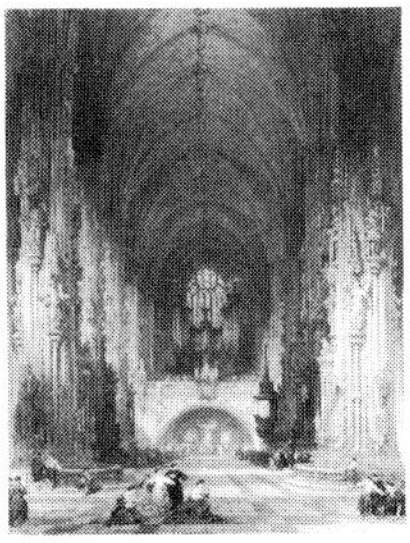

acc. no. 720
Edinburgh from the Calton Hill, looking West (1863)

oil on canvas: 20 × 30 in.
signed and dated: *David Roberts R.A. 1863*
Bequeathed by Charles Gassiot, 1902

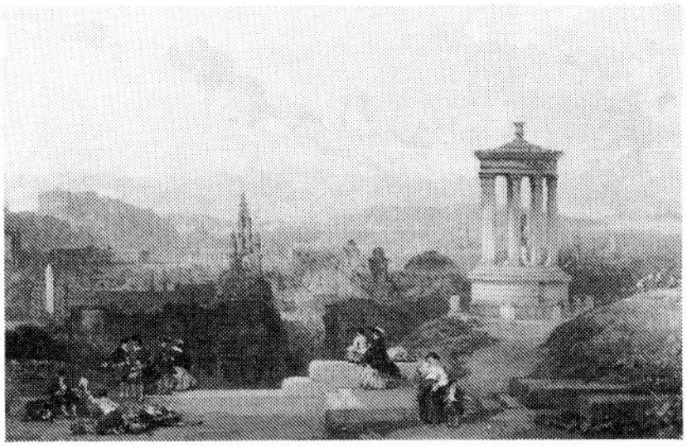

Fred Roe (1864–1947)

acc. no. 1290
Recruiting in the Guildhall by Sir Charles Wakefield (1919–1920)

oil on canvas: 45 × 71 in.
signed: *Fred Roe*
Presented by Lady Wakefield, 1944

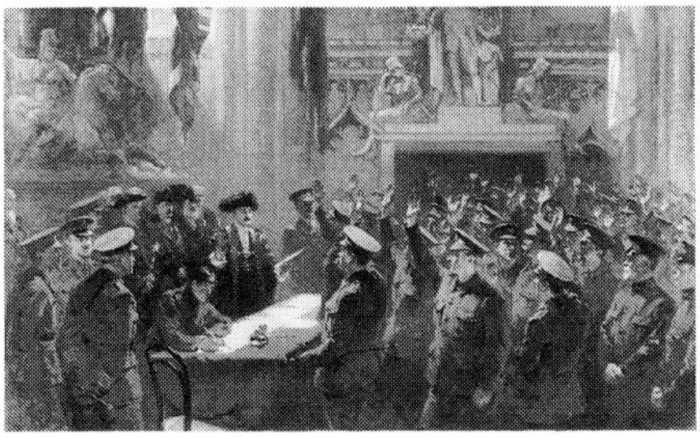

acc. no. 1291
The Passing of John Sargent (1925–1926)

oil on canvas: 41 × 64 in.
signed: *Fred Roe*
Presented by Lady Wakefield, 1944

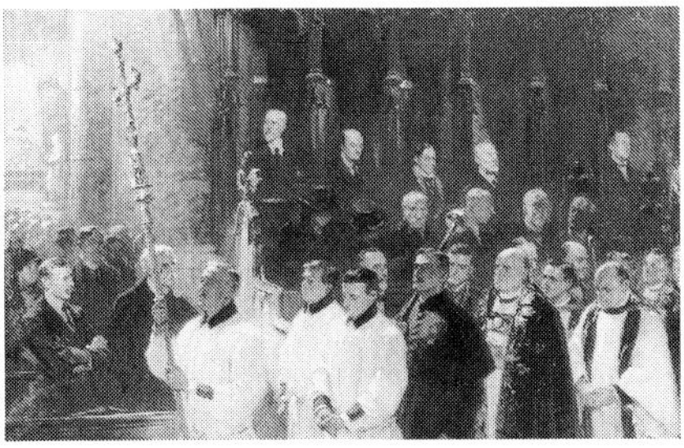

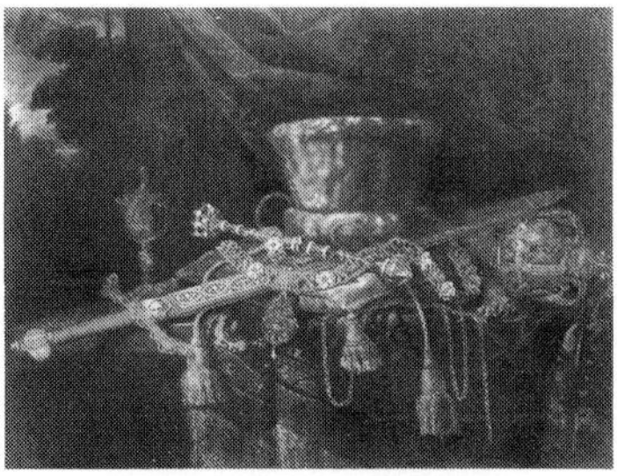

attributed to Pieter Gerritsz van Roestraten (1630–1700)

acc. no. 1256
The Insignia of the City of London
oil on canvas: 46 × 56 in.
Purchased from the Nicholson Gallery, 1943

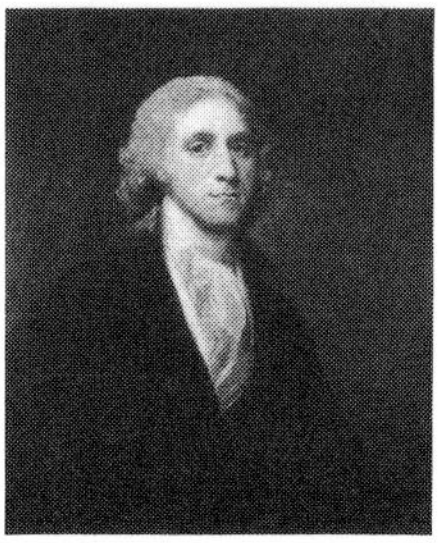

George Romney (1734–1802)

acc. no. 1303
Captain Arthur Forbes
oil on canvas: 30 × 25 in.
Presented by Lady Wakefield, 1944

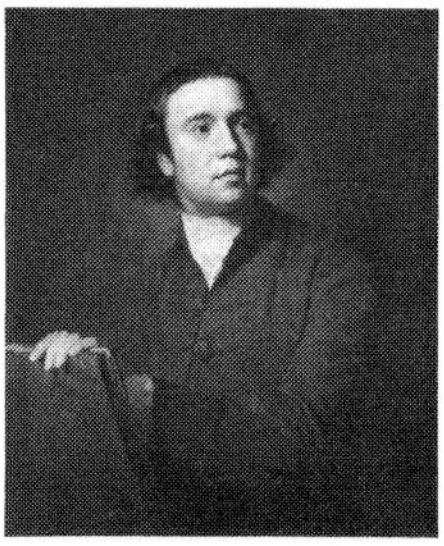

acc. no. 1311
Thomas Barrow (? *c.*1770)
oil on canvas: 30 × 25 in.
Presented by Lady Wakefield, 1944

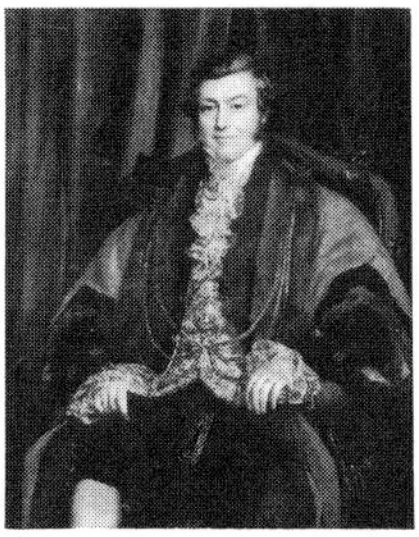

Thomas Roods (*fl.* 1833–67)

acc. no. 344
Thomas Quested Finnis, Sheriff of London 1849 (1850)
oil on canvas: 50 × 40 in.
Presented by Mrs. McLaughlin, 1888

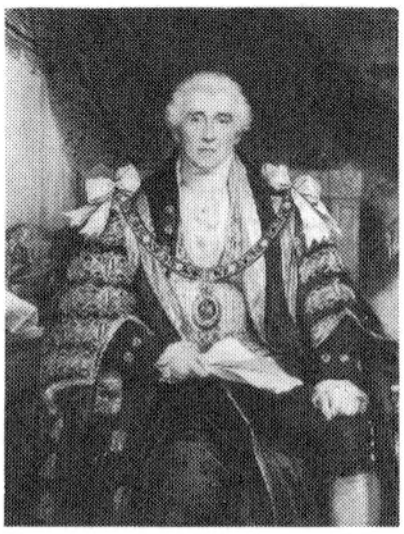

Sir William Charles Ross (1794–1860)

acc. no. 583
John Crowder, Lord Mayor 1829 (*c.*1829)
watercolour: 14 × 11 in.
Presented by John King-Farlow, 1893

Dante Gabriel Rossetti (1828–82)

acc. no. 1059
La Ghirlandata (1873)
oil on canvas: 49 × $33\frac{1}{2}$ in.
signed and dated: *D.G. Rossetti/1873*
Purchased from David Croal Thomson, 1927

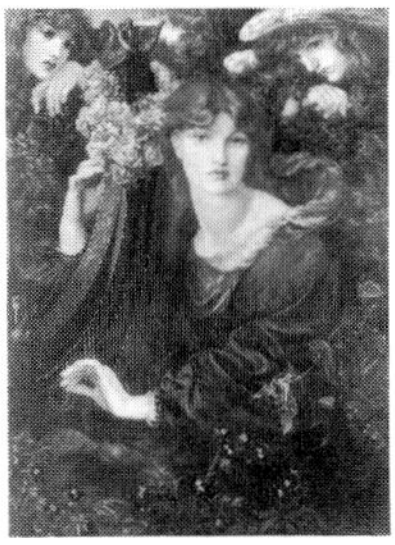

Jim Russell

acc. no. 1858
Cafe, Parma Crescent, London SW11 (1970)
watercolour: 21 × 17 in.
signed: *RUSSELL*
Purchased from the artist, 1971

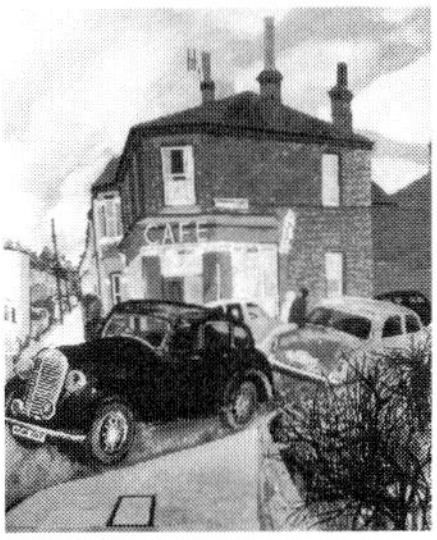

H... I... R...

acc. no. 3551
Mrs Beechey at the Card Table (1828)
pencil: $6\frac{5}{8}$ × 6 in.
signed and dated: *HIR. 1828*; inscribed on backboard: *Mrs Beechey / Aged 86 / 1828*
Presented by Miss Helen Guiterman, 1985

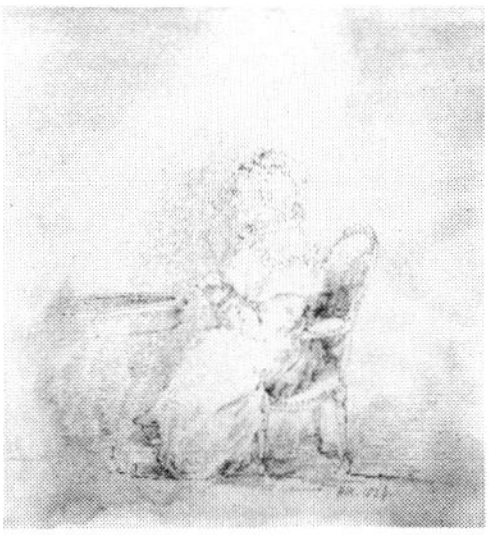

Walter Dendy Sadler (1854–1923)

acc. no. 1292
Sweethearts
oil on canvas: 34 × 26 in.
signed: *W. Dendy Sadler*
Presented by Lady Wakefield, 1944

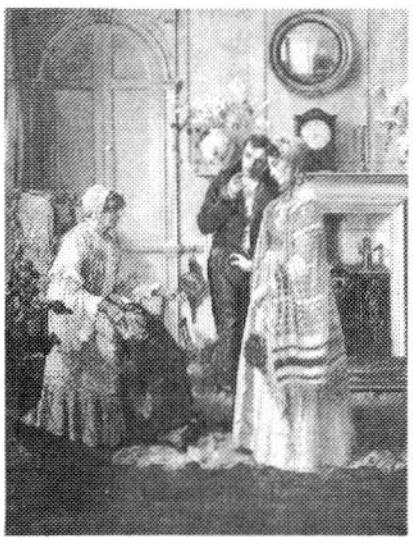

Frank Owen Salisbury (1874–1962)

acc. no. 1936
Sir Horace Brooks Marshall
oil on canvas: 49 × 39 in.
signed: *Frank O. Salisbury*
Purchased from Mr. D. Tildsley, 1972

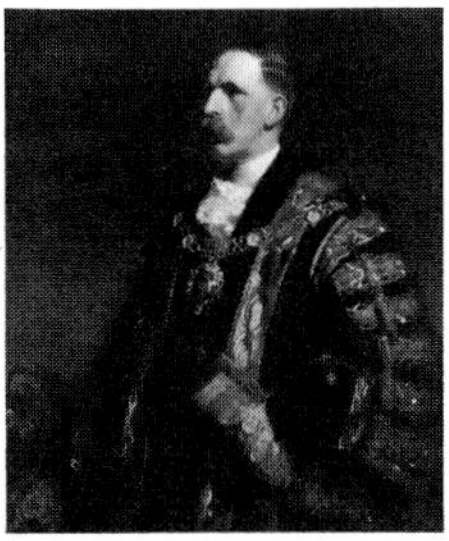

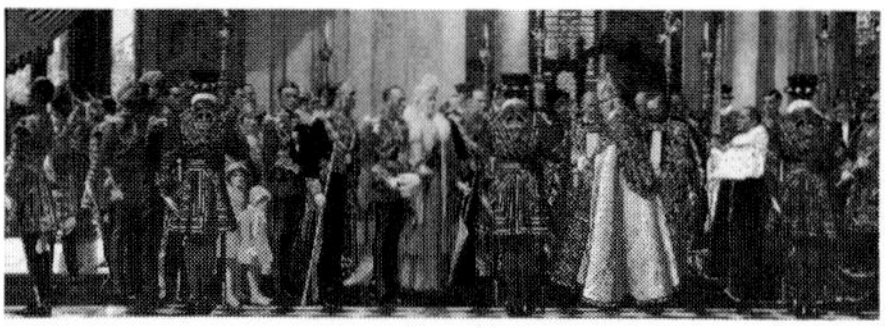

acc. no. 1228
Reception of King George V and Queen Mary at the West Door of St Paul's Cathedral, Jubilee Day, May 6 1935

oil on canvas: 60 × 168 in.
signed: *Frank O. Salisbury*
Purchased from the artist, 1936

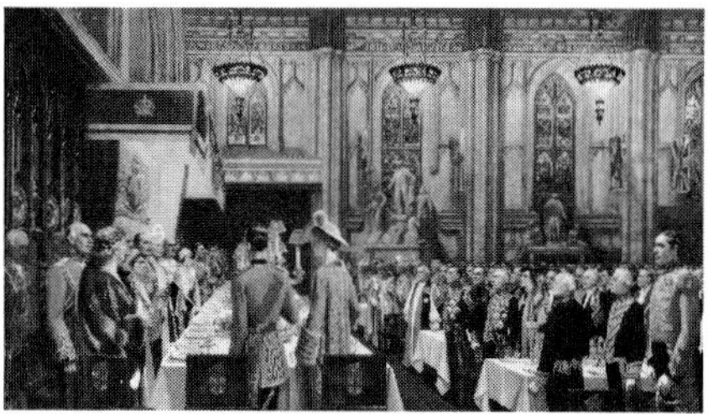

acc. no. 1235
The Coronation Luncheon at Guildhall, May 19 1937: the Toast to The King (1937–1938)

oil on canvas: 70 × 155 in.
signed and dated: *Frank O. Salisbury / 1938*
Presented by Lord Wakefield, 1939

Accession numbers 3608 to 3630 are rough sketches by Frank O. Salisbury for no. 1235, *The Coronation Luncheon at Guildhall*, mostly made on the spot on 19 May 1937. All were purchased at the sale of Salisbury's studio collection, Christies, 25 September 1985, lot 274.

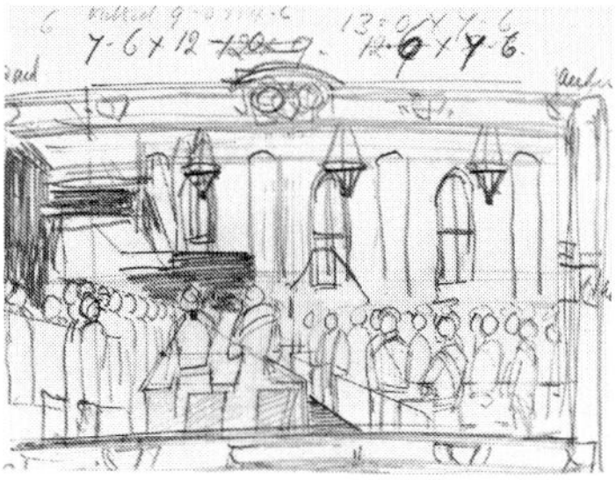

acc. no. 3608
Rough Sketch of the Toast to the King

pencil: 7 × 9 in.
inscribed with measurements

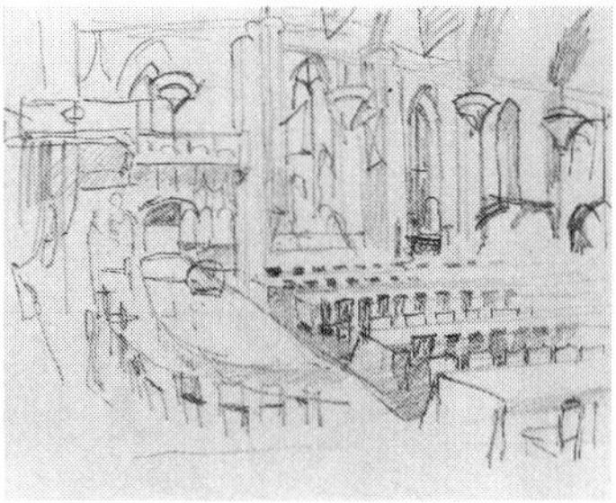

acc. no. 3609
Sketch of the Great Hall, with Chairs, Tables and the Dais

pencil: 8 × $9\frac{1}{4}$ in.

acc. no. 3610
The East End of the Great Hall, with the Dais and Canopy

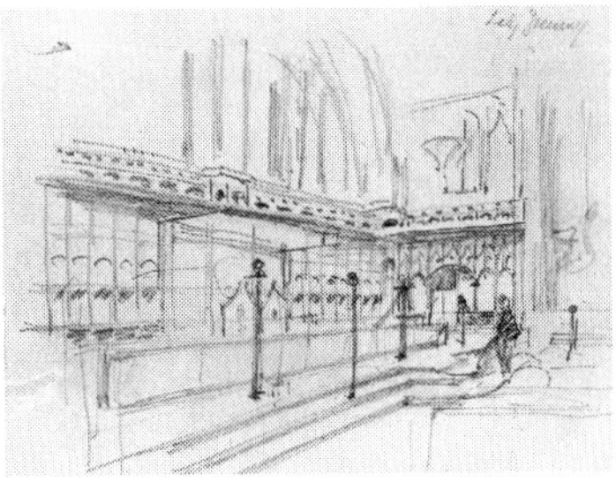

pencil: $8 \times 9\frac{3}{4}$ in.
inscribed illegibly; on verso, sketch of a table plan, inscribed with measurements and three illegible words

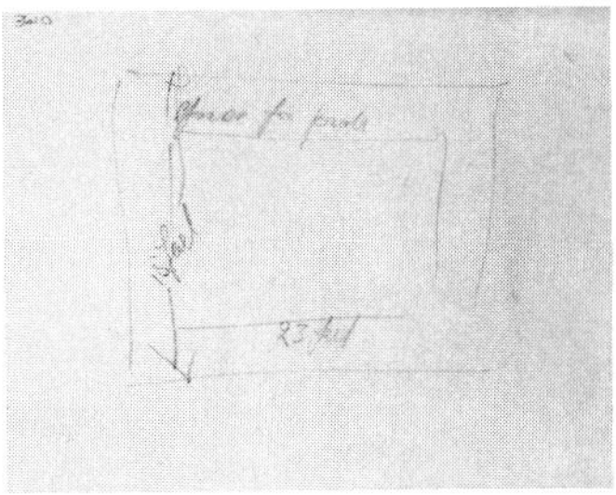

acc. no. 3611
Rough Sketch of the East End of the Great Hall, with the Dais and Canopy

pencil: $8 \times 9\frac{3}{4}$ in.

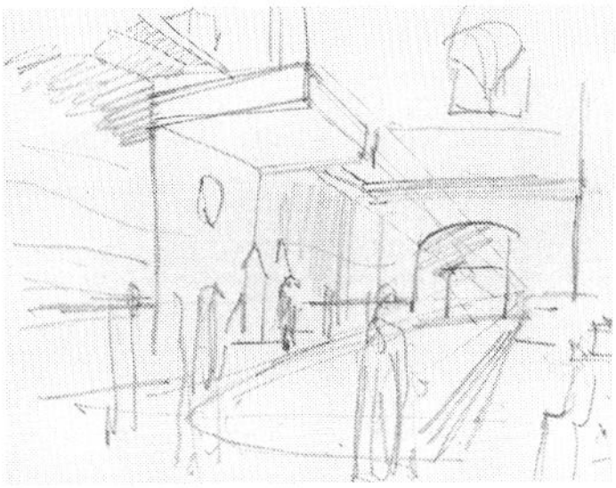

acc. no. 3612
Rough Sketch of the Candelabra and Flowers on the Royal Table

pencil: 8×10 in.
inscribed: *Red Shades* and *4 candles / etc*

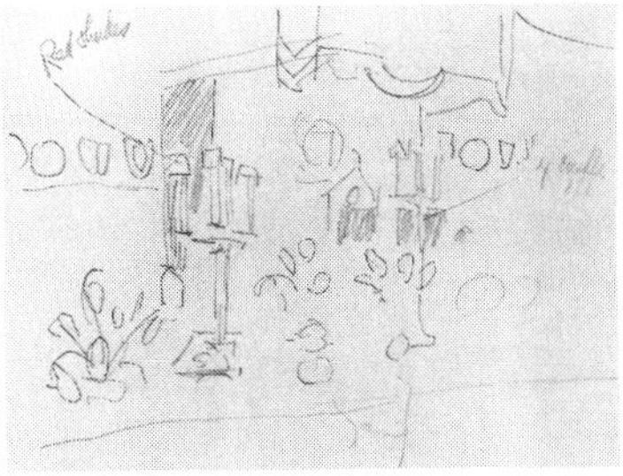

acc. no. 3613
Rough Sketch of Princess Alice

pencil: 10×8 in.
inscribed illegibly

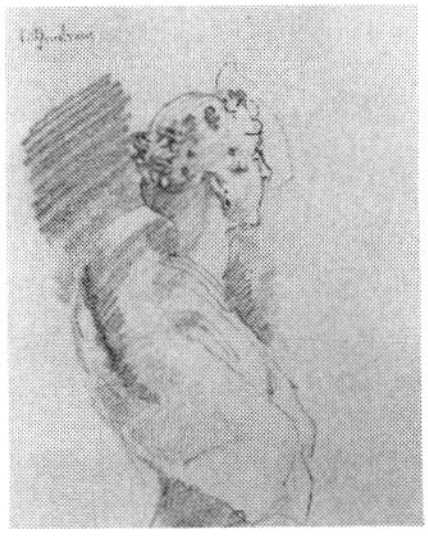

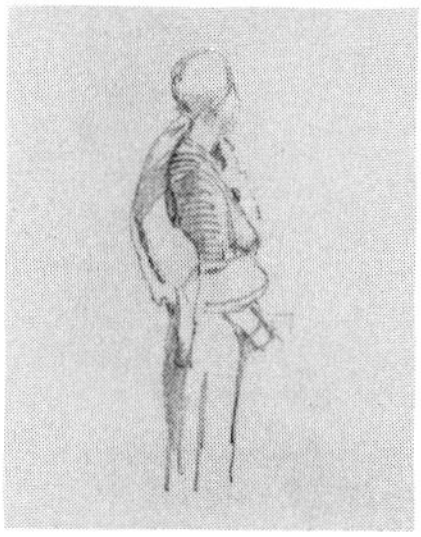

acc. no. 3614
Princess Alice
pencil: 10 × 8 in.

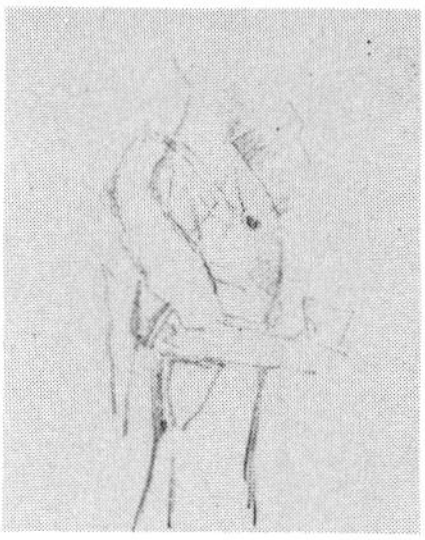

acc. no. 3615
Princess Alice
pencil: 10 × 8 in.

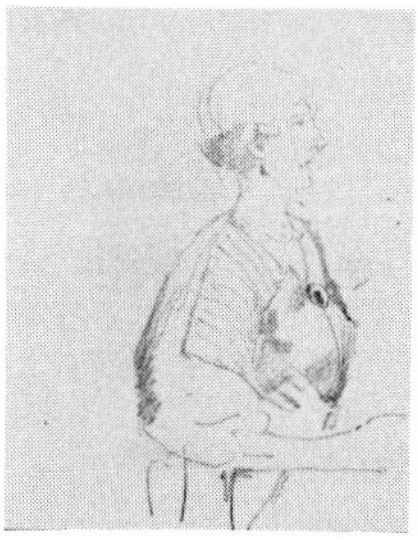

acc. no. 3616
Princess Alice
pencil: 10 × 8 in.

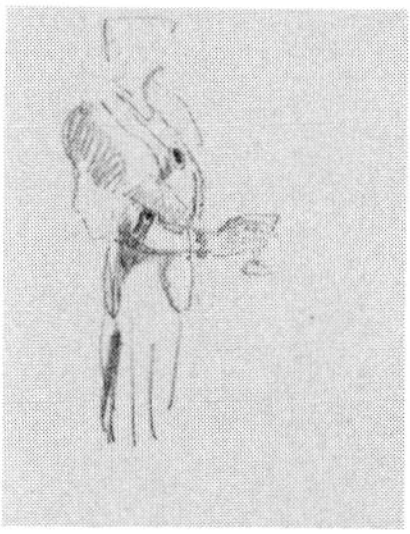

acc. no. 3617
Princess Alice, Holding a Glass
pencil: 10 × 8 in.

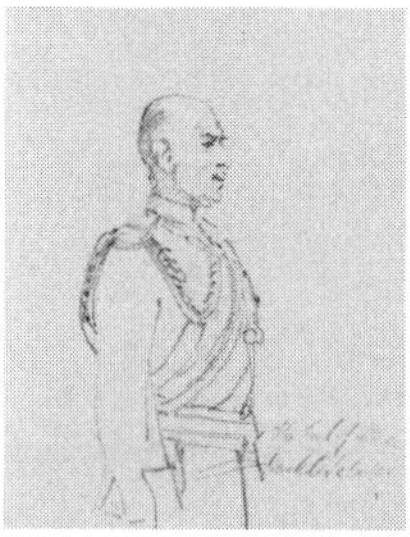

acc. no. 3618
The Earl of Athlone
pencil: 10 × 8 in.
inscribed and signed: *The Earl of Athlone / Frank O. Salisbury*

acc. no. 3619
Head and Shoulders of the Earl of Athlone

pencil: $9\frac{3}{4} \times 8$ in.
inscribed and signed: *The Earl of Athloun* (*sic*) / *Frank O. Salisbury*

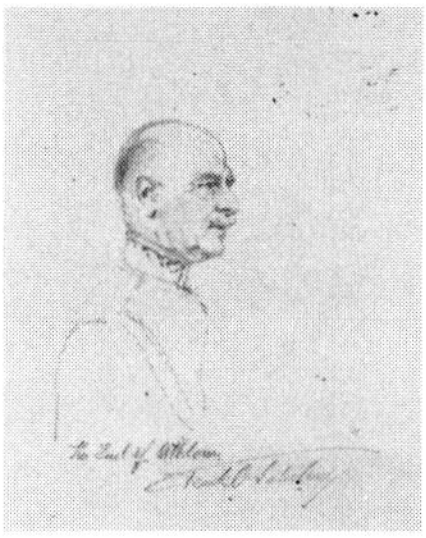

acc. no. 3620
Rough Sketch of a Lady, Half Length, with a Hat

pencil: 10×8 in.

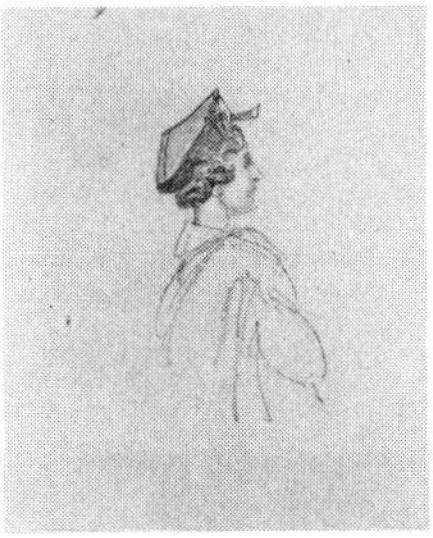

acc. no. 3621
Rough Sketch of the King and Queen, other Guests and Footmen at the Royal Table

pencil: 8×10 in.
inscribed with colour and other brief notes

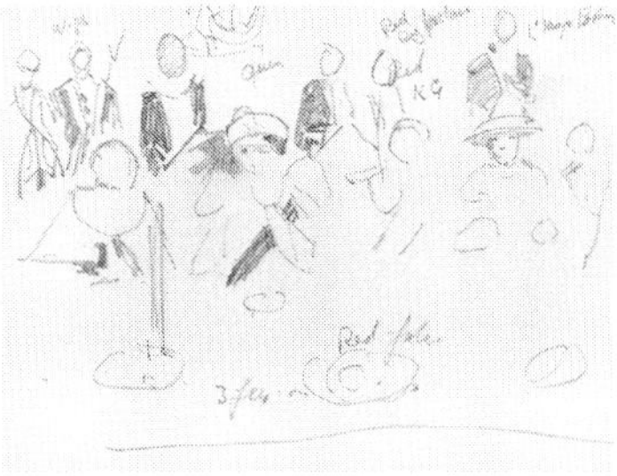

acc. no. 3622
Rough Sketch of Some of the Dignitaries seated at the First Table

pencil: 8×10 in.
inscribed: *1st* and *Hertzog* and *red lace / to sash* and *Ld Cragalan* (*sic*)

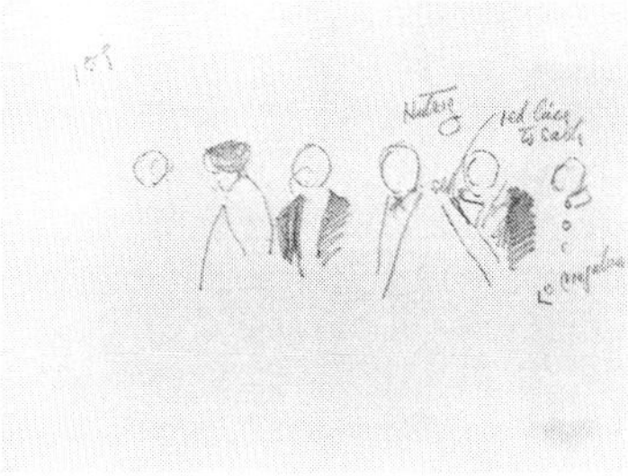

acc. no. 3623
Rough Sketch of Guests at the Second Table

pencil: 8×10 in.
inscribed: *2^d table* and *Canterbury* (?) and *Red Sash* (?) and *Next* (word illegible) / *in grey* and (illegible letter)*B* and *Brazil* and *Plumb* and *Bladen* and *Black* and *Bath / red*

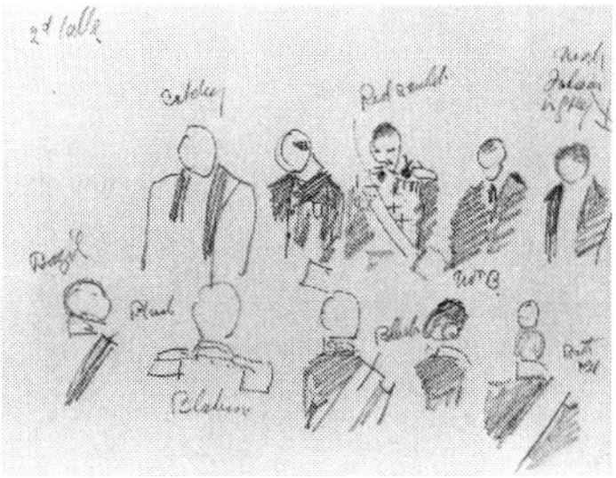

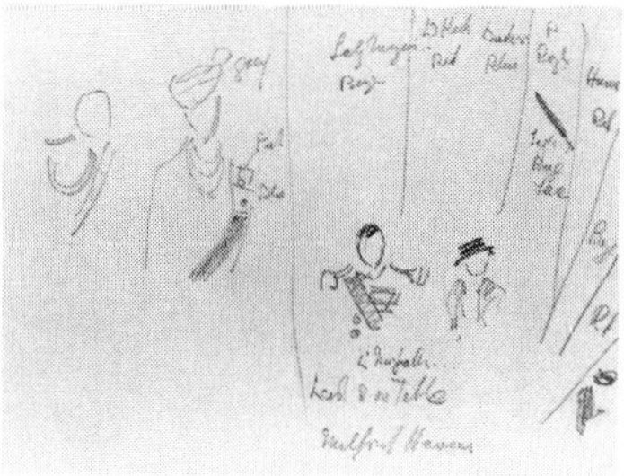

acc. no. 3624
Slight Sketches of Guests
pencil: 8 × 10 in.
inscribed: *grey/pink / blue* and with many other partly illegible names and colour notes

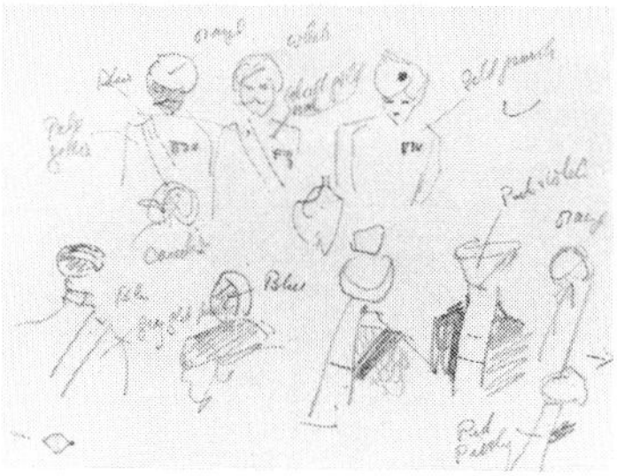

acc. no. 3625
Rough Sketch of Indian Princes and other Guests
pencil: 8 × 10 in.
inscribed with numerous colour notes

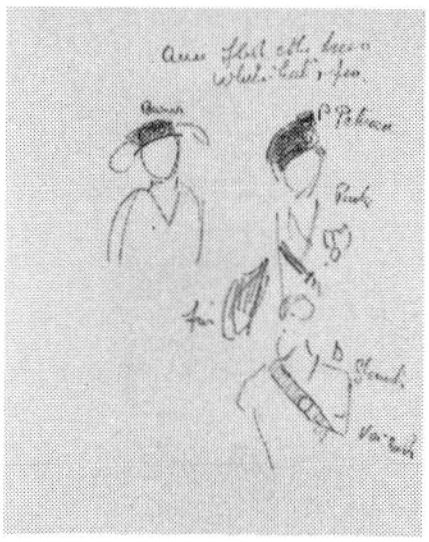

acc. no. 3626
Rough Sketch of Guests
pencil: 10 × 8 in.
inscribed: *Queen flesh colour dress / White hat and fur* and with other colour notes

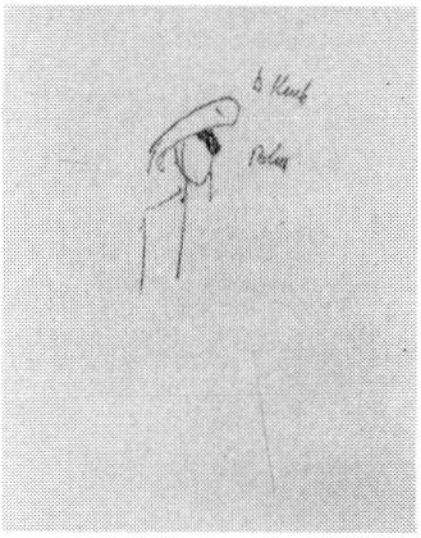

acc. no. 3627
Slight Sketch of a Female Guest
pencil: 10 × 8 in.
inscribed with two illegible notes

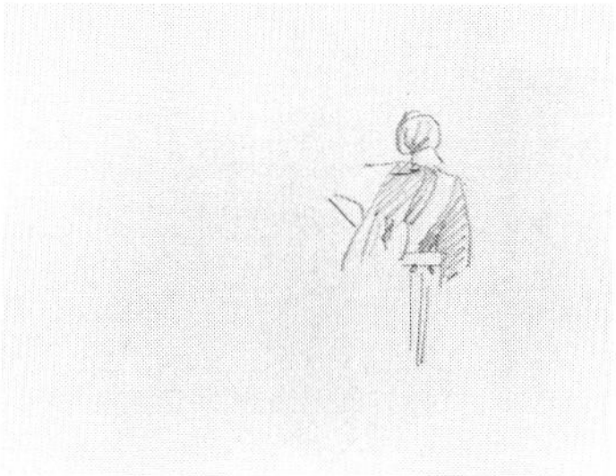

acc. no. 3628
Slight Sketch of a Uniformed Man from Behind (? the Marquess of Carisbrooke)
pencil: 8 × 10 in.

acc. no. 3629
A Standing Woman and a Head of an Indian Prince

pencil: 10 × 8 in.

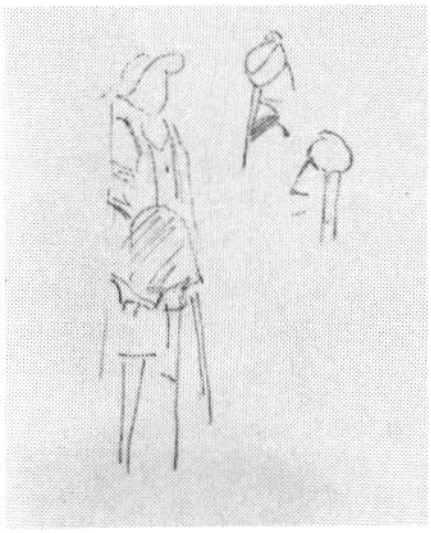

pencil: 10 × 8 in.
acc. no. 3630
A Group of Figures Standing and Sitting near the East End of the Great Hall

pencil: 10 × 8 in.

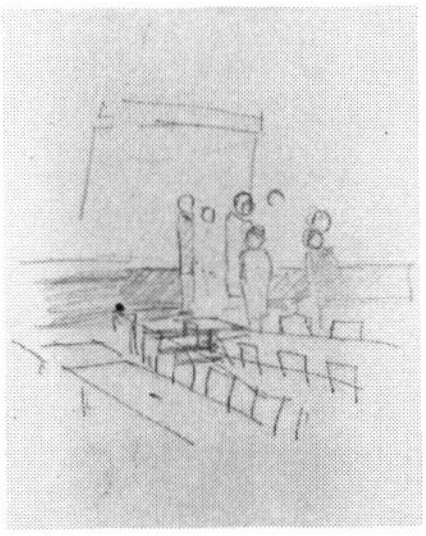

verso: *Sketch of a Bowl of Flowers,* inscribed: (word illegible) / *yellow* and *flowers on centre of table*

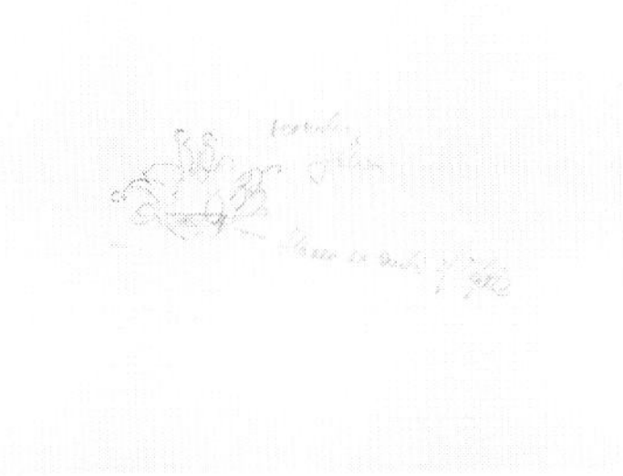

acc. no. 1316
Presentation of the Freedom of the City to Winston Churchill in Guildhall, June 30 1943

oil on canvas: 58 × 110 in.
signed: *Frank O. Salisbury*
Presented by Lady Joseph and Sir Keith Joseph, 1944

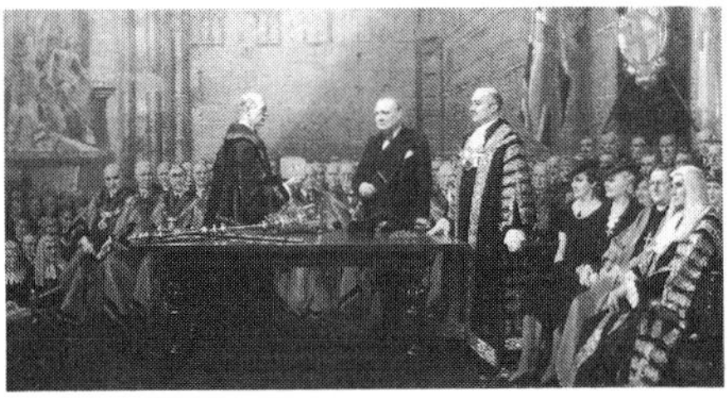

acc. no. 1374
Sir William Thomas

oil on canvas: 36 × 27½ in.
signed: *Frank O. Salisbury*
Presented by Miss Thomas on behalf of the late Sir William Thomas, 1947

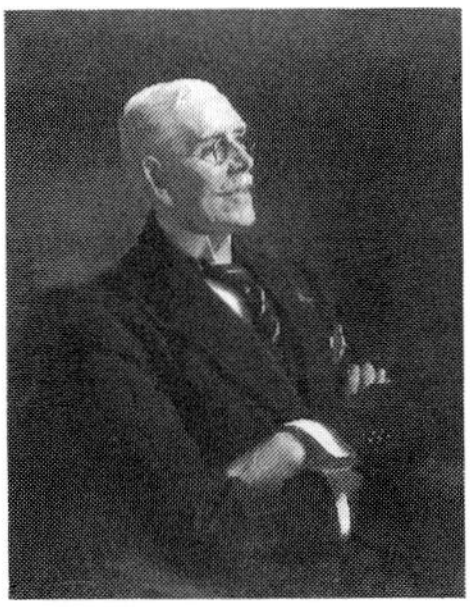

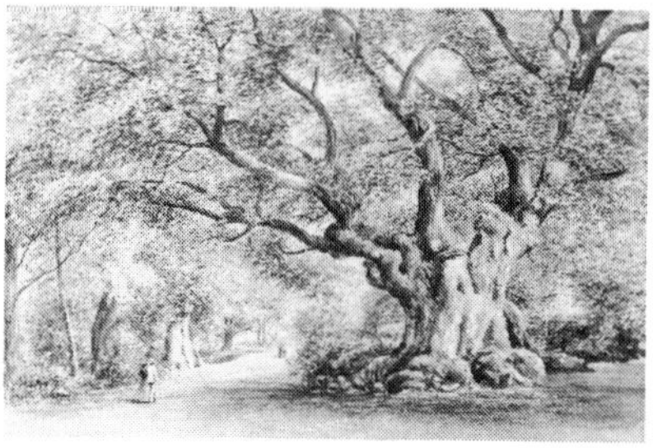

E. Salter (*fl.* 1903)

acc. no. 1775
Gray's, or Jenny Lind's, Beech, Burnham Beeches (1903)

watercolour: $12\frac{3}{4} \times 19\frac{1}{2}$ in. (sight)
signed and dated: *E. Salter / 1903*
Purchased from Travers King, 1967

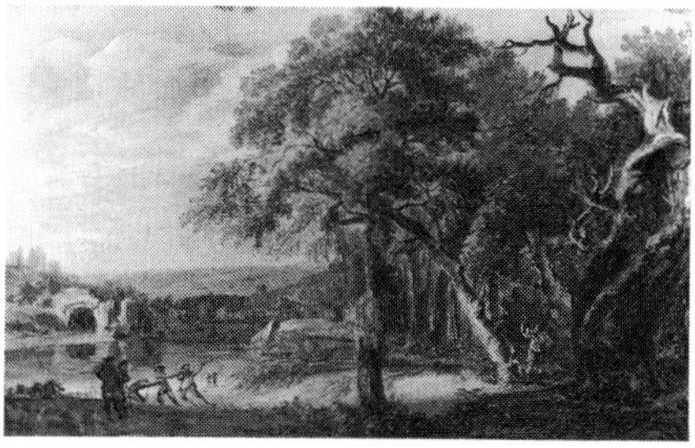

Paul Sandby (1730–1809)

acc. no. 836
Woodcutters near a River (? 1755)

watercolour and bodycolour: $15\frac{1}{4} \times 25$ in.
signed and dated: *P. Sandby 1755*
Bequeathed by W. A. Sandby, 1905

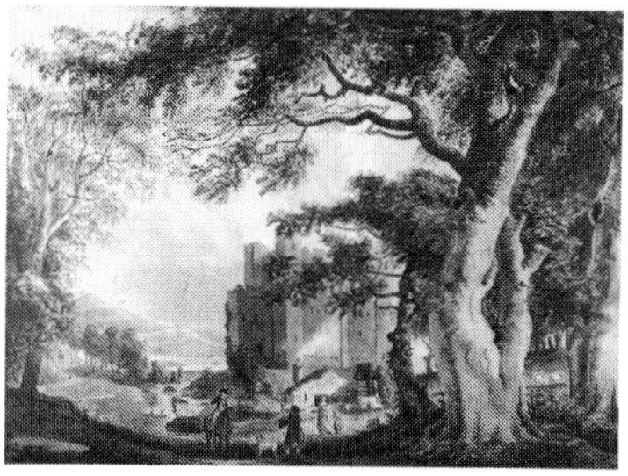

acc. no. 835
Landscape with Castle (? *c*1793)

watercolour: 19×25 in.
Bequeathed by W. A. Sandby, 1905

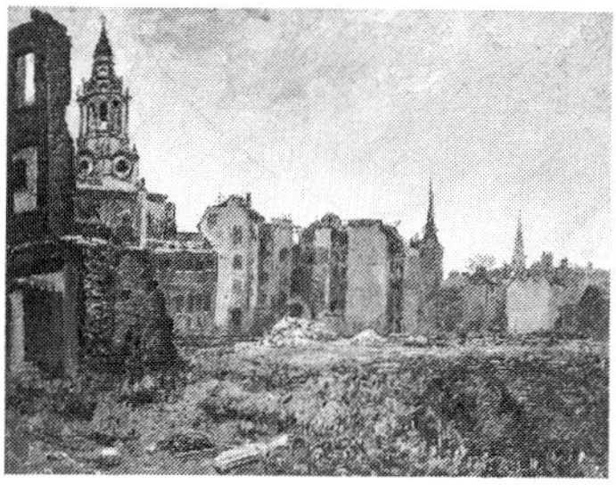

The following seven paintings by **Piero Sansalvadore (1892–1955)** were presented by G. M. Reeves in 1955

acc. no. 1522
A Bomb Site near St. Paul's (1946)

oil on panel: $13\frac{1}{2} \times 17\frac{1}{2}$ in.
signed and dated: *Piero Sansalvadore / 1946*; signed and inscribed on label attached to verso: *Piero Sansalvadore / London. A bomb site near St. Paul's. / 269*

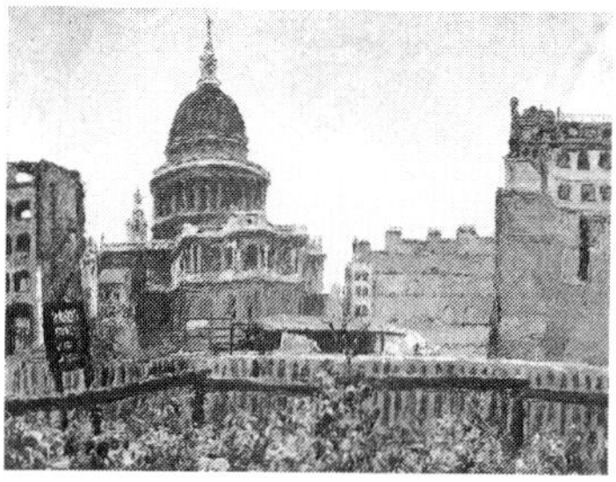

acc. no. 1523
St. Paul's Cathedral from St. Mary-le-Bow (1946)

oil on panel: $13\frac{1}{2} \times 17\frac{1}{2}$ in.
signed: *P. Sansalvadore*; signed, dated and inscribed on label attached to verso: *Piero Sansalvadore / London 1946: St Paul's Cathedral / from St. Mary-le-Bow. / 281*

acc. no. 1525
St. Mary-le-Bow (1946)
oil on panel: $15\frac{1}{2} \times 11\frac{3}{4}$ in.
signed and dated: *P. Sansalvadore / 1946*;
signed, dated and inscribed on label attached to verso: *Piero Sansalvadore / London 1946: St. Mary-le-Bow / 268*

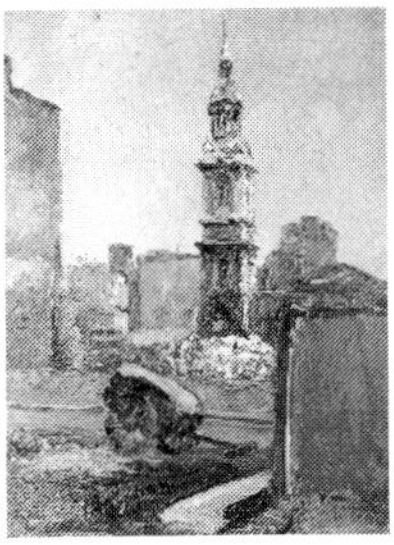

acc. no. 1528
St. Vedast, Foster Lane (1946)
oil on panel: $9\frac{1}{4} \times 7\frac{1}{8}$ in.
signed: *P. Sansalvadore*; signed, dated and inscribed on label attached to verso: *Piero Sansalvadore / London 1946: St Vedast Church / 287*

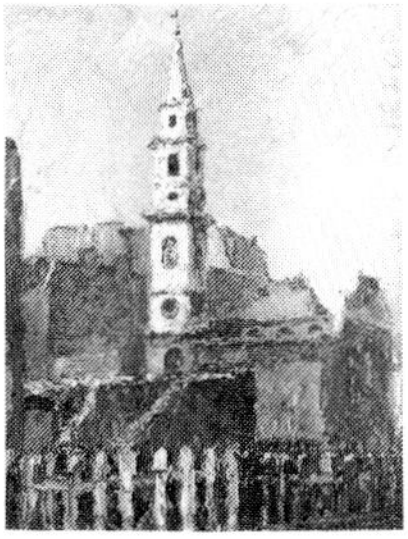

acc. no. 1526
A Winter Afternoon in Old Change (1946 or 1947)
oil on panel: $9\frac{3}{8} \times 7\frac{1}{8}$ in.
signed and dated: *Piero Sansalvadore 1947*;
signed, dated and inscribed on label attached to verso: *Piero Sansalvadore / London 1946: A Winter Afternoon in Old Change / 288*

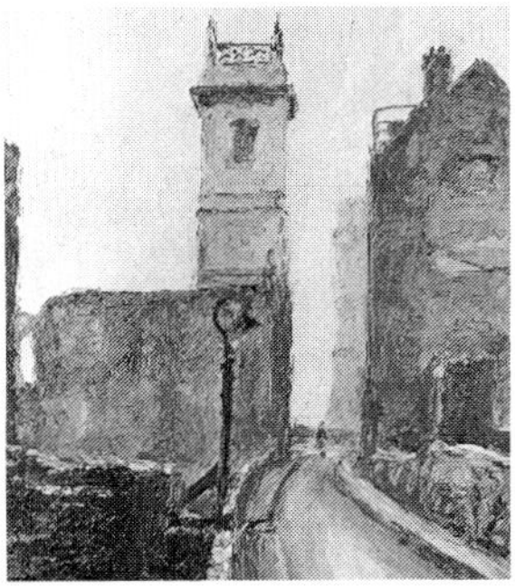

acc. no. 1524
The Tower of London from a Bombed Site (1947)
oil on panel: $13\frac{1}{2} \times 17\frac{1}{2}$ in. (sight)
signed and dated: *P. Sansalvadore / 1947*;
signed and inscribed on label attached to verso: *Piero Sansalvadore / The Tower of London / from the bombed Premises of / DENT, URWICK & YEATMAN 284*

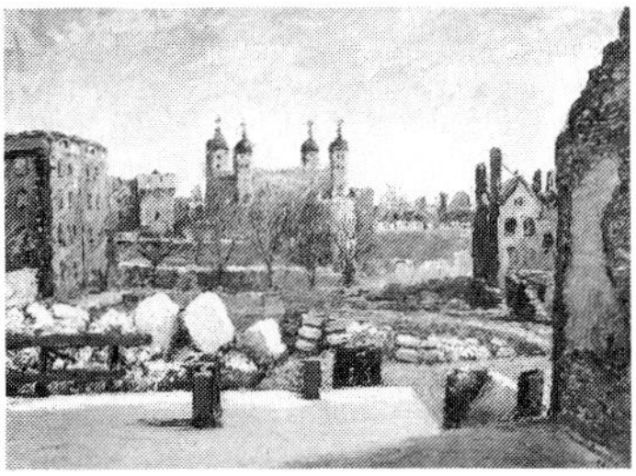

acc. no. 1527
St. Paul's Cathedral from Fetter Lane (1947)
oil on panel: $9\frac{1}{8} \times 7$ in.
signed and dated: *P. Sansalvadore / 1947*;
signed and inscribed on label attached to verso: *Piero Sansalvadore / London A glimpse of St Paul's / from a bombside in Fetter Lane / (Berbeck College) / 290*

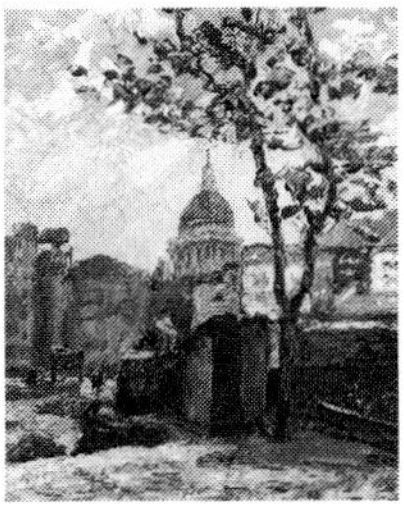

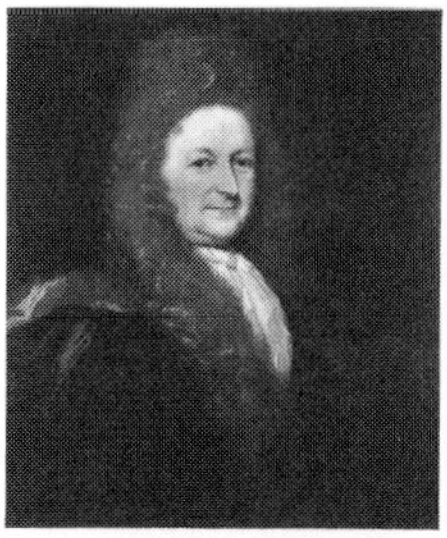

Godfried Schalken (1643–1706)

acc. no. 1393
Sir Richard Levitt (Lord Mayor, 1699)

oil on canvas: 30 × 25 in.
signed: *G. Schalken*
Purchased from Bourlet & Sons, 1949

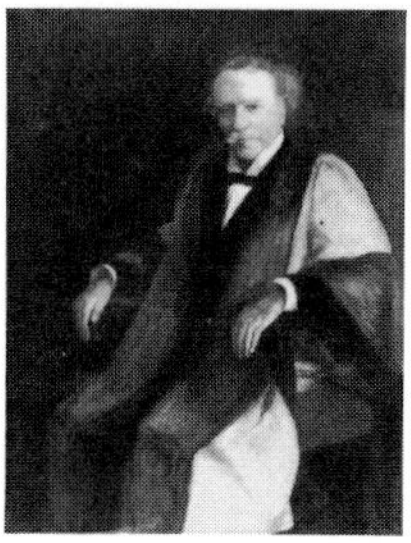

Betia Schebsman (*fl.* 1908–12)

acc. no. 879
Dr. William Hayman Cummings, Principal of the Guildhall School of Music, 1896–1910

oil on canvas: 54 × 40 in.
Presented by the sitter's friends, 1909

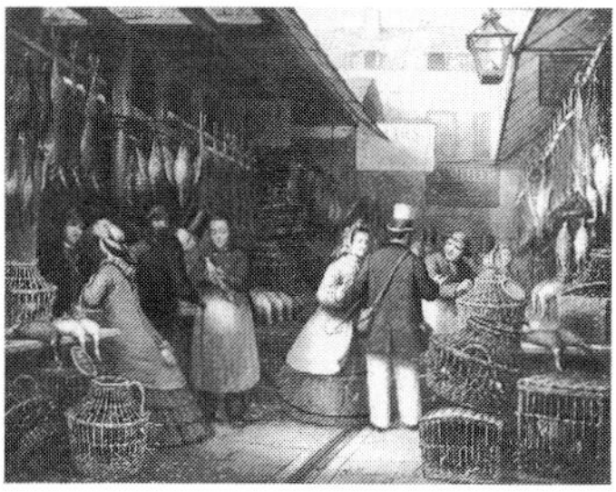

Andries Scheerboom (1832–80)

acc. no. 1519
Leadenhall Market (1865)

oil on canvas: 17 × $20\frac{7}{8}$ in.
signed and dated: *A. Scheerboom 65*
Presented by John Weir, 1955

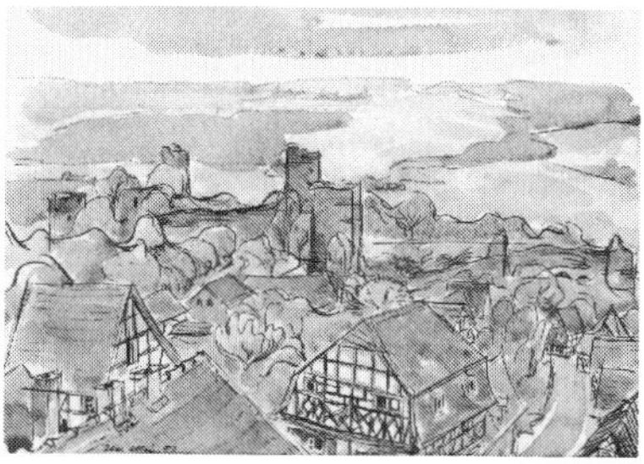

Ilse Mai Schlegel (20th C)

acc. no. 1560
View of Blankenberg, West Germany (1957)

watercolour: $11\frac{3}{4}$ × $15\frac{3}{4}$ in.
signed and dated: *Ilse Mai 57*
Presented by the Mayor of Blankenberg, 1957

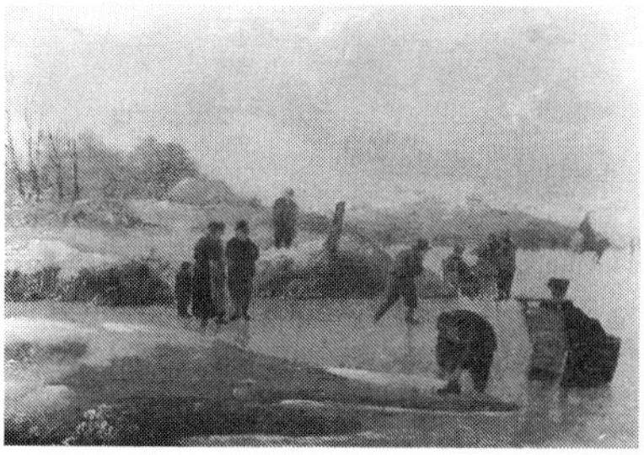

Heinrich Wilhelm Schweickhardt (1746–97)

acc. no. 357
Skating

oil on panel: 9 × 10 in.
Bequeathed by William Dunnett, 1888

Samuel Scott (1702–72)

acc. no. 1784
The Thames with Montagu House, from near Westminster Bridge (*c.*1749)
oil on canvas: 27 × 46½ in.
Purchased at Christie's sale, 22.3.1968 (111)

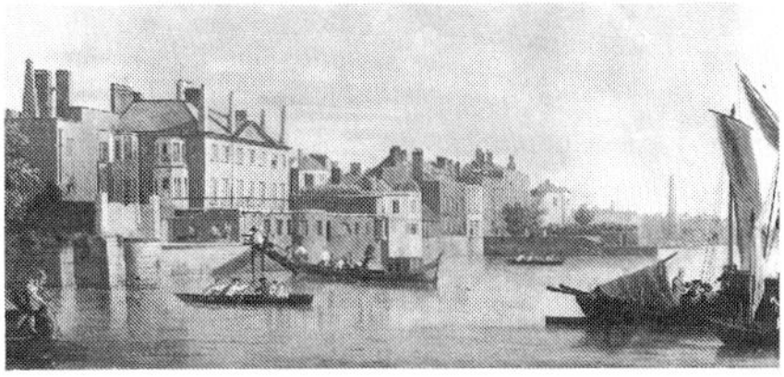

after Samuel Scott (1702–72)

acc. no. 47
Old London Bridge
oil on canvas: 22 × 48 in.
Acquired, source unknown, *c.*1793

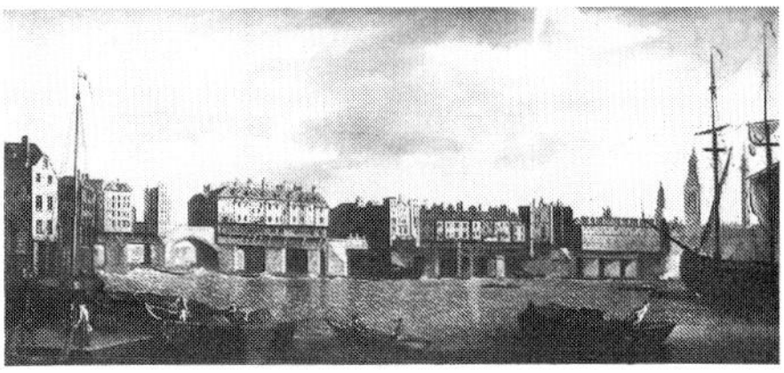

follower of Samuel Scott (18th C)

acc. no. 46
Entrance to the Fleet River
oil on canvas: 23 × 44 in.
Acquired, source unknown, *c.*1793

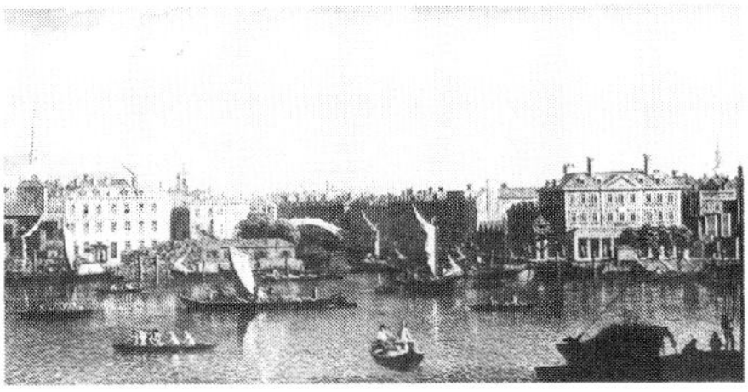

L. Scotti (18th/19th C)

acc. no. 414
Deposition (1805)
oil on panel: 9⅛ × 15¾ in.
signed and dated on verso: *L. Scotti inv. 1805*
Bequeathed by William Dunnett, 1888

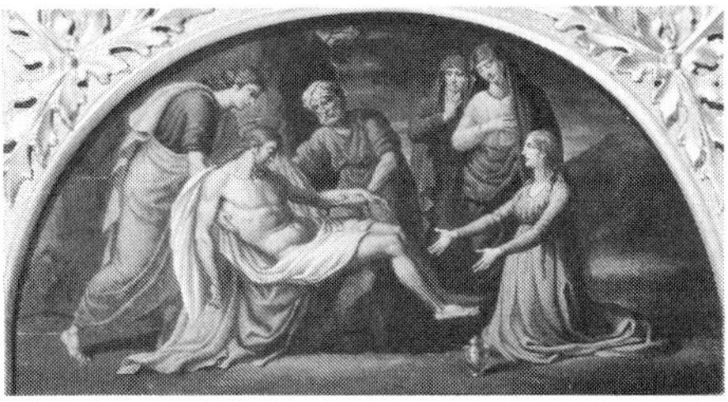

James Scouler (1741–87)

acc. no. 764
John Davis, the Proprietor of Bagnigge Wells
oil on canvas: 30 × 20 in.
Bequeathed by W. G. Wallis, 1902

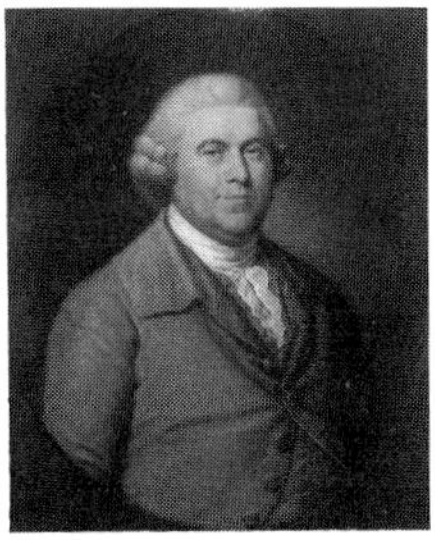

attributed to James Scouler (1741–87)

acc. no. 1542
John Hatchett, Master of the Clockmakers' Company, 1785
oil on canvas: 24 × 20 in.
Purchased from R. T. Hatchett, 1956

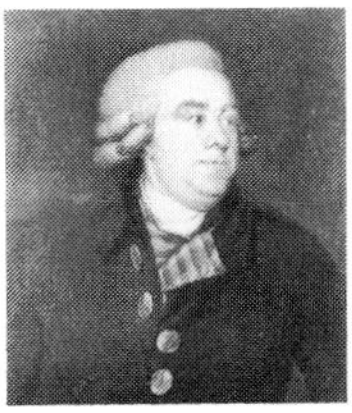

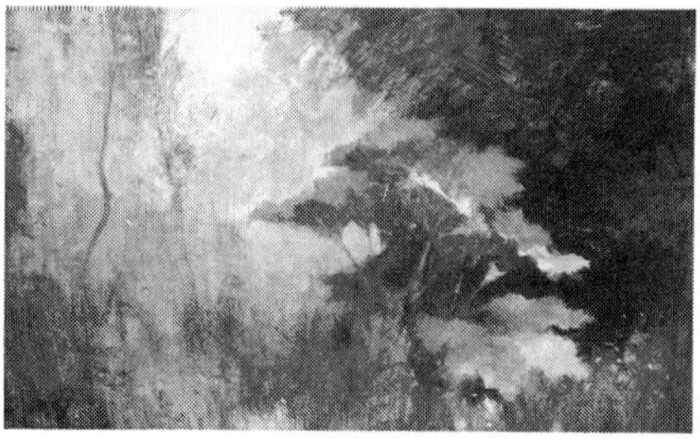

Edward Seago (1910–74)

acc. no. 1812
The Water Garden

oil on hardboard: 20 × 30 in.
Purchased from Marlborough Fine Art, 1969

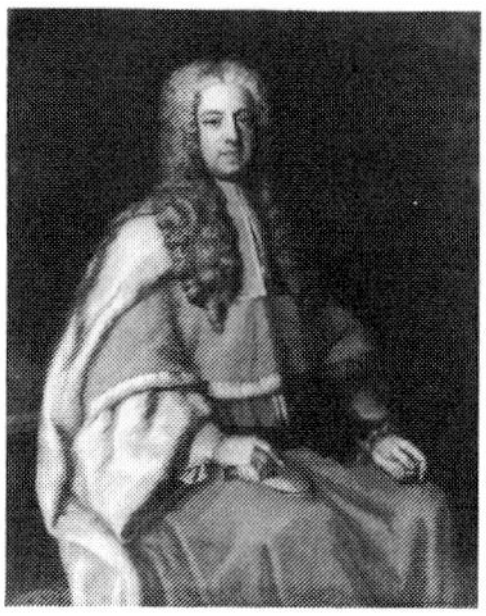

Enoch Seaman (1694–1744)

acc. no. 37
Sir William Thompson, Recorder of London, 1714–1739

oil on canvas: 50 × 40 in.
Bequeathed by Sir William Thompson, 1739

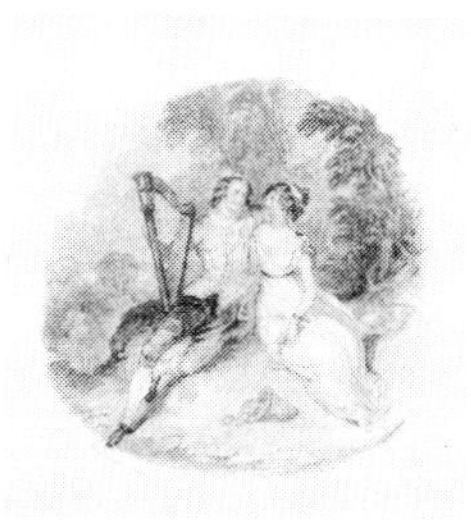

Henry Courtney Selous (or Slous) (1803–90)

acc. no. 507
Two Lovers on a Bank with a Harp

watercolour: $5\frac{1}{2} \times 4\frac{3}{4}$ in. (whole sheet)
signed: *H.C. SLOUS. DEL.*
Presented by Felix Joseph, 1890

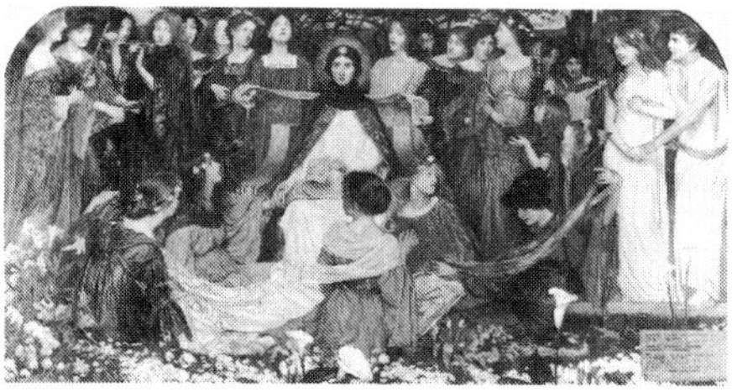

John Byam Liston Shaw (1872–1919)

acc. no. 1055
The Blessed Damozel (1895)

oil on canvas: 37 × 71 in.
signed and dated: *BYAM SHAW ' 95*
Purchased from N. Mitchell, 1927

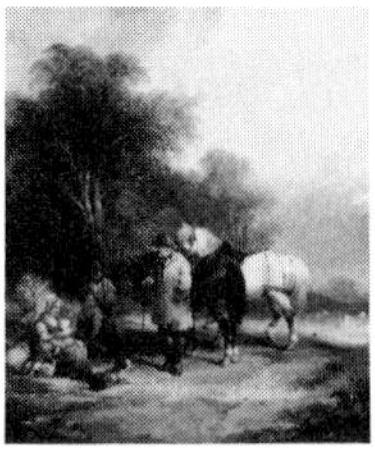

William Shayer (1787–1879)

acc. no. 354
Harvest Time

oil on canvas: 14 × 12 in.
signed: *W. Shayer*
Bequeathed by William Dunnett, 1888

acc. no. 1089
Milking Time
oil on canvas: 24 × 20 in.
signed: *Wm. Shayer*
Purchased, 1932

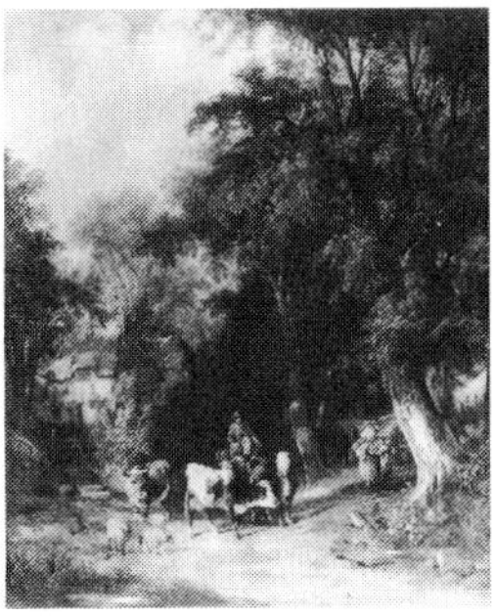

David Shepherd (b.1931)

acc. no. 1567
December 30 1940 – again tonight? (1958)
oil on canvas: 30 × 40 in.
signed: *David Shepherd.*
Purchased from the artist, 1958

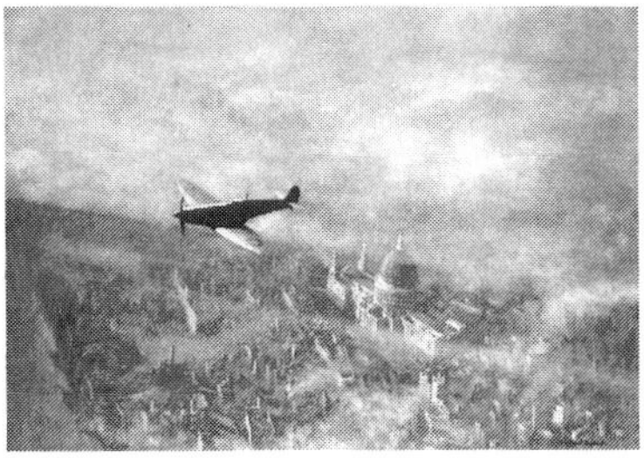

George Sidney Shepherd (*fl.* 1830, d.1858)

acc. no. 1564
The Old General Post Office and St. Martins-le-Grand (1835)
oil on panel: $9\frac{3}{4} \times 13$ in.
dated: *1835*
Purchased from F. T. Sabin, 1958

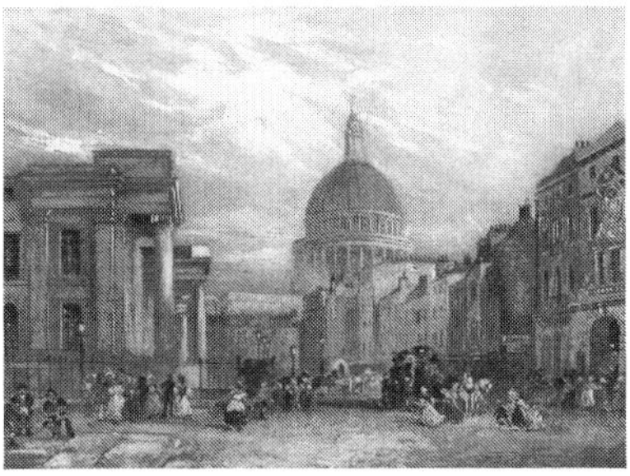

Reginald Shepherd (living)

acc. no. 1931
Squid Jigging
screenprint: $13\frac{1}{2} \times 21\frac{1}{2}$ in.
signed: *Reginald Shepherd*
Presented by the Mayor of St. John's, Newfoundland, 1972

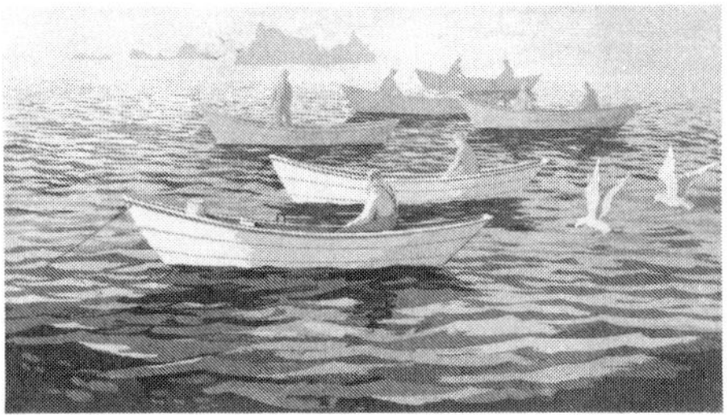

Thomas Hosmer Shepherd (1792–1864)

acc. no. 2250
Hungerford Market (1832)
pen and ink and sepia wash: $2\frac{3}{4} \times 5\frac{1}{8}$ in.
signed: *T. HOSMER SHEPHERD* and dated: *Orig Aug 1832*; inscribed on verso: *Hungerford Market*
Presented by Miss Helen Guiterman, 1985

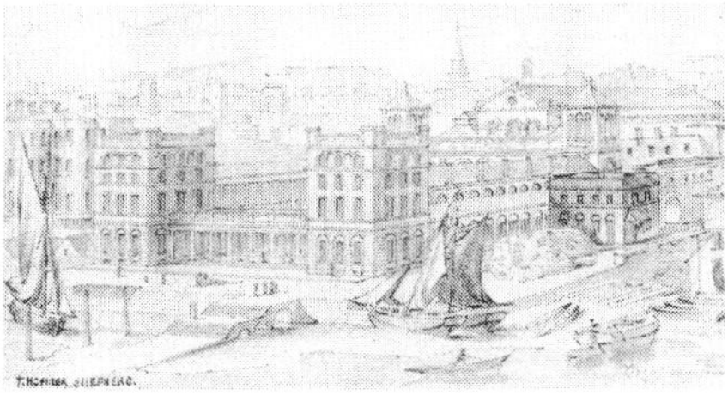

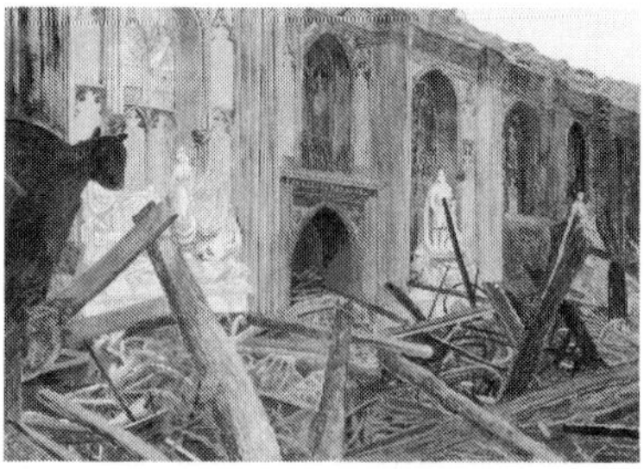

A. A. Simco (20th C)

acc. no. 3636
Guildhall: Inside the Great Hall after Bombing (1941)

watercolour: $12\frac{1}{4} \times 17$ in.
signed and dated: *A.A. SIMCO / 1941* and inscribed: *GUILDHALL LONDON*; inscribed on verso: *The Guildhall / London. / after bombing / A.A. Simco*
Purchased from G. S. Harrison, 1985

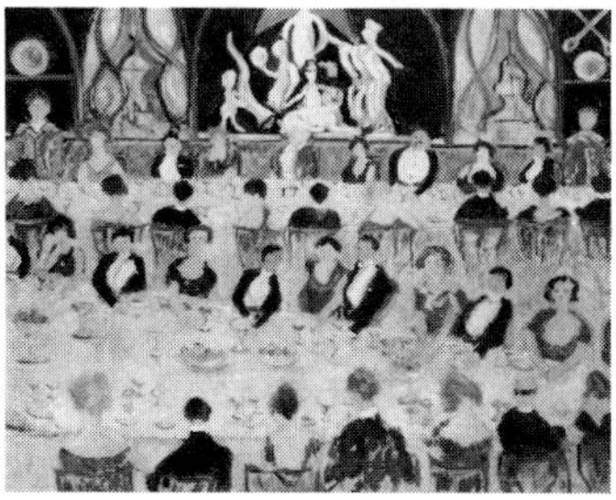

Ronald Montagu Simon (d.1971)

acc. no. 2223
The Banquet (1965)

oil on canvas: $19\frac{3}{4} \times 23\frac{3}{4}$ in.
signed and dated: *Simon 65*
Presented by Mr. Deputy Dyer, 1980

after William Simpson (1833–99)
The following eight lithographs were presented by Miss Helen Guiterman in 1985

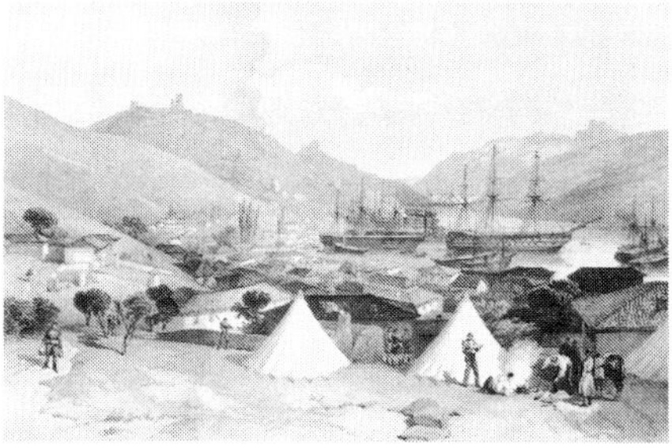

by W. Walton (19th C)

acc. no. 3593
Balaklava Looking Towards the Sea (1855)

lithograph: $14 \times 21\frac{3}{4}$ in.
lettered: *W Simpson del. W. Walton Lith. Published Jany 15th 1855 by Paul & Dominic Colnaghi & Co., 13 & 14 Pall Mall East, Publishers to Her Majesty Day & Son. Lith^rs to the Queen. / BALAKLAVA, LOOKING TOWARDS THE SEA. / DEPOSE / Paris, Goupil & Cie / COLNAGHI'S AUTHENTIC SERIES.*

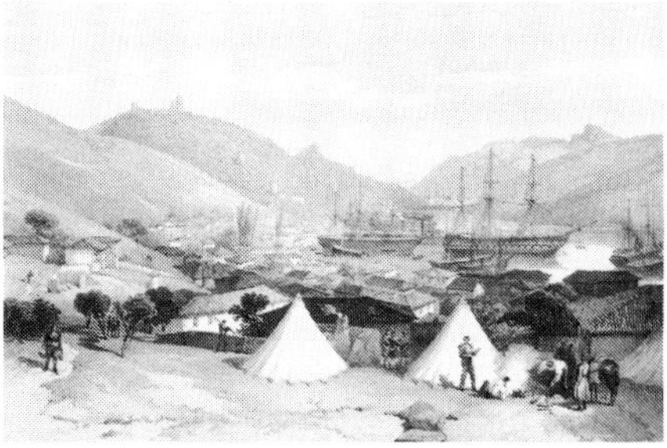

acc. no. 3594
another impression, lettered as above

acc. no. 3595
another impression, lettered: *W Simpson del. W. Walton Lith. Published Jany 15th 1855 by Paul & Dominic Colnaghi & Co., 13 & 14 Pall Mall East, Publishers to Her Majesty Day & Son. Lithrs to the Queen. / BALAKLAVA LOOKING TOWARDS THE SEA. / DÉPOSÉ / Paris, Goupil & Cie / COLNAGHI'S AUTHENTIC SERIES / LEIPZIG – OTTO WEIGEL / PLATE 3.*

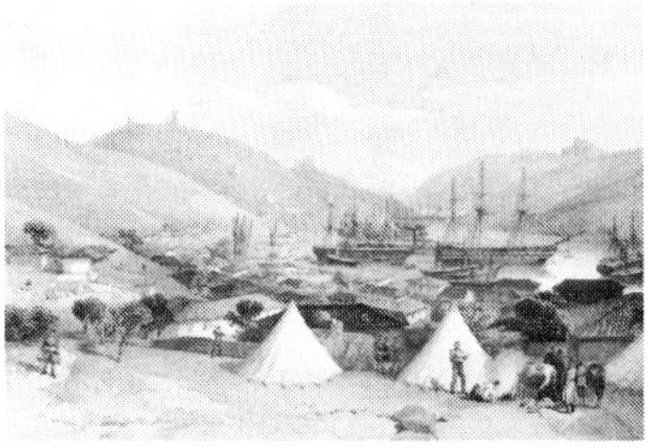

by an unknown hand

acc. no. 3591
Excavated Church in the Caverns at Inkermann, Looking West (1855)

lithograph: $14 \times 13\frac{3}{4}$ in.
lettered: *W Simpson, del. Published May 22nd 1855, by Paul & Dominic Colnaghi & Co. 13 & 14 Pall Mall, East – Publishers to Her Majesty Day & Son Lithrs to The Queen. / EXCAVATED CHURCH IN THE CAVERNS AT INKERMANN. / LOOKING WEST. / DÉPOSÉ / Paris, Goupil & Cie COLNAGHI'S AUTHENTIC SERIES.*

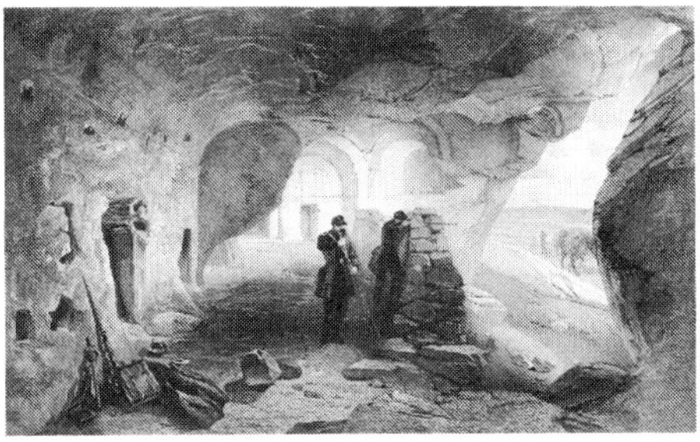

by T. G. Dutton (*fl.* 1842–73)

acc. no. 3596
The Lighthouse at Cape Chersonese, Looking South (1855)

lithograph: $13\frac{7}{8} \times 21\frac{3}{4}$ in.
lettered: *W. Simpson, delt – T.G. Dutton, lith. Published June 15th 1855, by Paul & Dominic Colnaghi & Co. 13 & 14 Pall Mall East. – Publishers to Her Majesty. Day & Son, Lithrs to the Queen. / THE LIGHTHOUSE AT CAPE CHERSONESE. / LOOKING SOUTH. / COLNAGHI'S AUTHENTIC SERIES. / DÉPOSÉ / Paris, Goupil & Cie.*

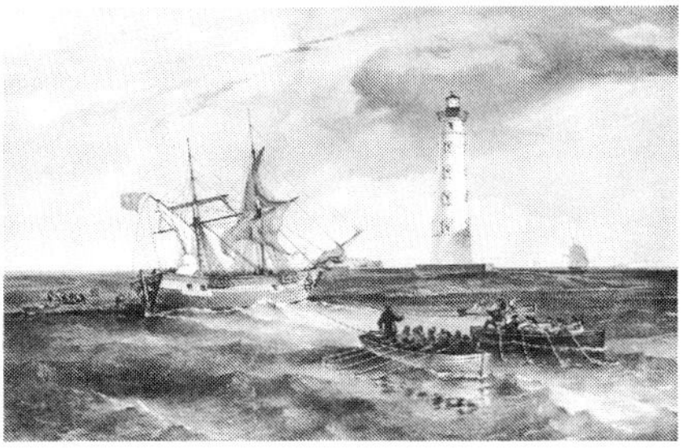

by E. Walker (*fl.* 1850s)

acc. no. 3592
Disembarkation of the Expedition to Kertch at Kamish Bournou (1855)

lithograph: $14\frac{1}{4} \times 21\frac{5}{8}$ in.
lettered: *W Simpson del. – E Walker lith. Published Augt 3rd 1855, by Paul & Dominic Colnaghi & Co. 13 & 14 Pall Mall East, – Publishers to Her Majesty Day & Son Lithrs to the Queen. / DISEMBARKATION OF THE EXPEDITION TO KERTCH AT KAMISH BOURNOU. / AND THE BLOWING UP OF ST PAUL'S BATTERY. / DÉPOSÉ / Paris, Goupil & Cie / LEIPZIG, OTTO WEIGEL / COLNAGHI'S AUTHENTIC SERIES / PLATE 1.*

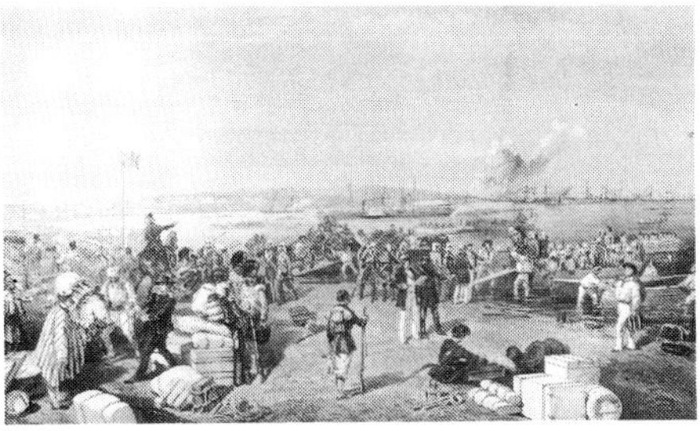

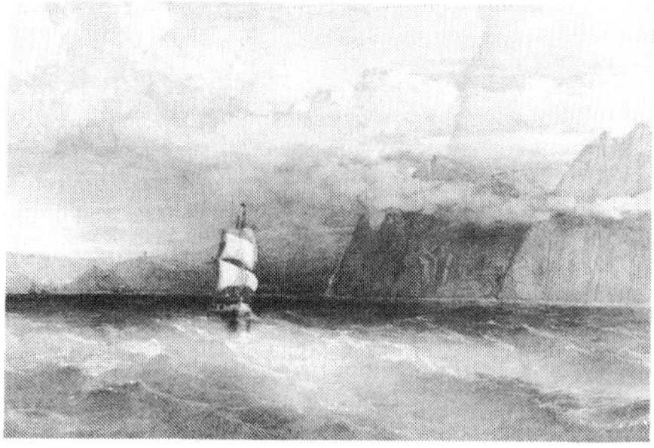

by an unknown hand

acc. no. 3597
Cape Aiya, Looking North Towards Balaklava (1855)
lithograph: $14\frac{1}{8} \times 21\frac{5}{8}$ in.
lettered: *W. Simpson, del. Published Octr 15th 1855, by Paul & Dominic Colnaghi & Co. 13 & 14 Pall Mall East. – Publishers to Her Majesty. Day & Son, Lith[rs] to The Queen. / CAPE AIYA. / LOOKING NORTH, TOWARDS BALAKLAVA. / PLATE 17. / DÉPOSÉ / Paris, Goupil & Cie / LEIPZIG, OTTO WEIGEL / COLNAGHI'S AUTHENTIC SERIES*

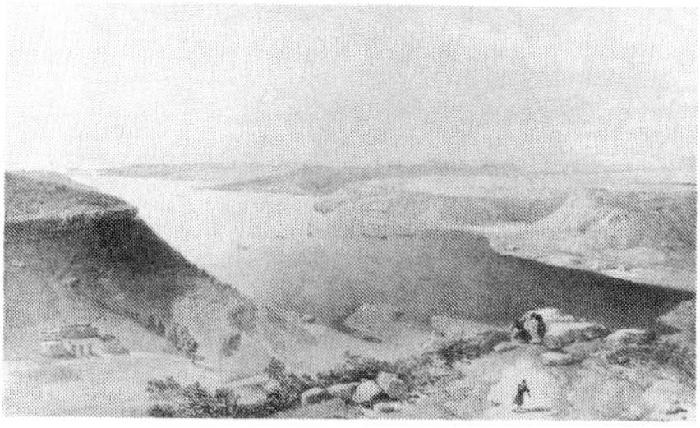

by Jonathan Needham (*fl.* 1850–74)

acc. no. 3604
The North Side of the Harbour at Sebastopol, 22 June 1855
lithograph: $13\frac{1}{4} \times 20$ in.
lettered: *W. Simpson, del – J. Needham, lith. Published Octr 25th 1855, by Paul & Dominic Colnaghi & Co. 13 & 14, Pall Mall East. – Publishers to Her Majesty. Day & Son, Lith[rs] to the Queen. / THE NORTH SIDE OF THE HARBOUR OF SEBASTOPOL. / FROM THE TOP OF THE HARBOUR – 22ND JUNE 1855. / COLNAGHI'S AUTHENTIC SERIES / DÉPOSÉ / Paris. Goupil & Cie / LEIPZIG, OTTO WEIGEL. PLATE 24.*

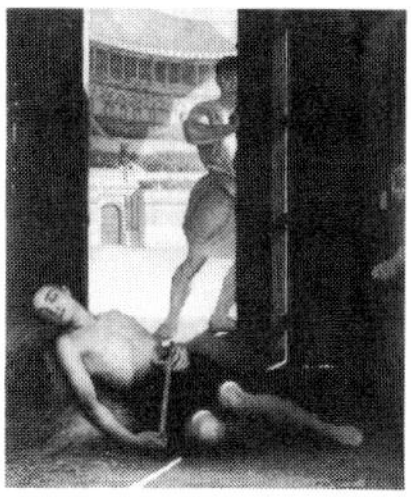

Ernest Slingeneyer (1830–94)

acc. no. 727
A Christian Martyr (1863)
oil on panel: $21 \times 18\frac{1}{2}$ in.
signed and dated: *Ernest Slingeneyer. 1863.*
Bequeathed by Charles Gassiot, 1902

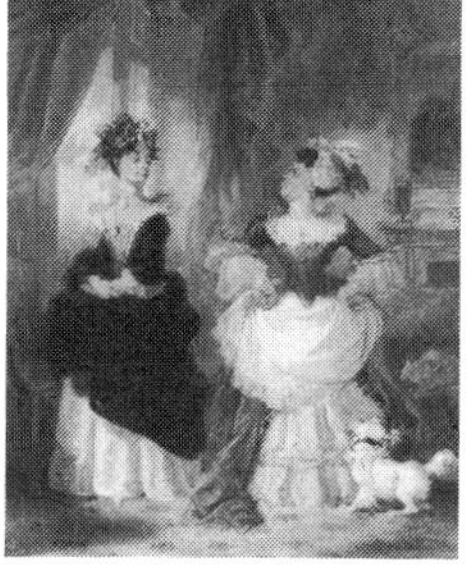

Robert Smirke (1752–1845)

acc. no. 588
The Rivals (from 'Tom Jones' by Henry Fielding) (? *c.*1827)
oil on panel: 8×7 in.
Presented by J. L. Rutley, 1894

acc. no. 3515
King Lear (?)

oil on paper: $2\frac{3}{4} \times 1\frac{3}{4}$ in.
Presented by Miss Helen Guiterman, 1985

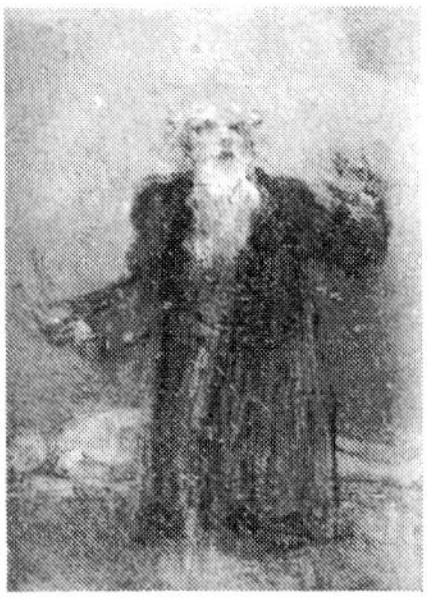

acc. no. 3516
A Mermaid

pen and brown ink with bodycolour, varnished: $2 \times 2\frac{7}{8}$ in.
Presented by Miss Helen Guiterman, 1985

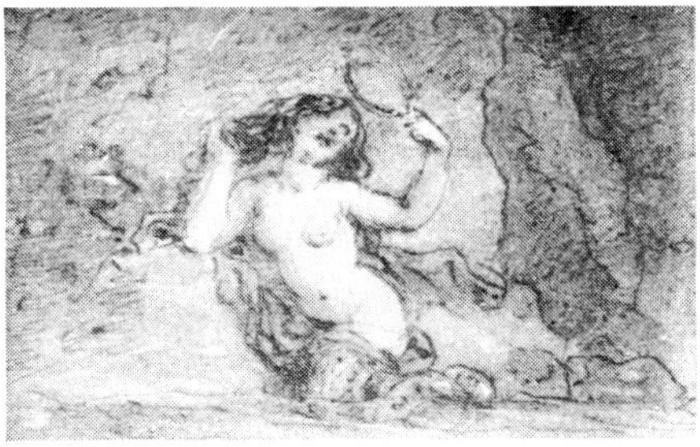

acc. no. 3517
Ulysses and Nausicaa

oil on paper: $2\frac{7}{8} \times 4$ in.
Presented by Miss Helen Guiterman, 1985

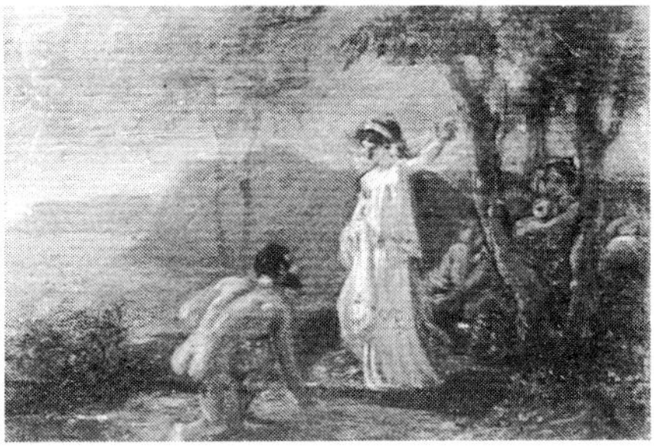

attributed to Francis Smith (*fl.* 1764–1802) after Canaletto (1697–1768)

acc. no. 1664
London Bridge and the City from the Terrace of Somerset House

oil on canvas: $16 \times 39\frac{1}{2}$ in. (sight)
Purchased from Leggatt Bros., 1963

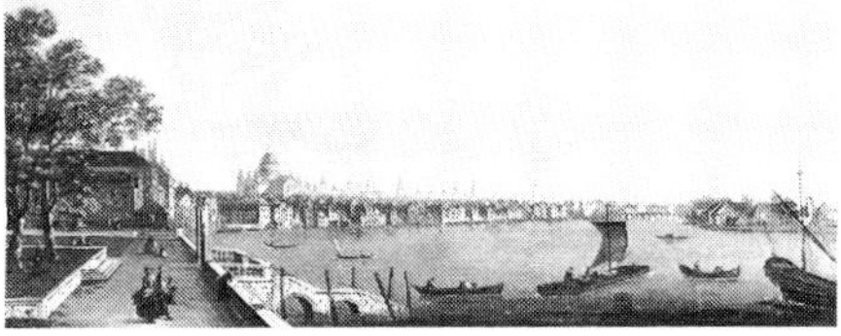

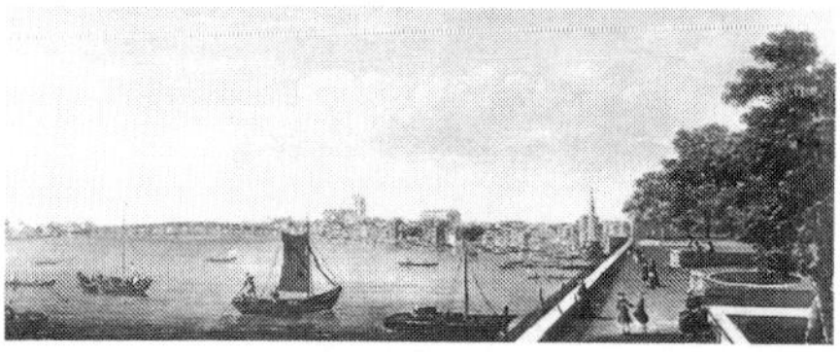

acc. no. 1665
Westminster Bridge from the Terrace of Somerset House

oil on canvas: 16 × 39½ in. (sight)
Purchased from Leggatt Bros., 1963

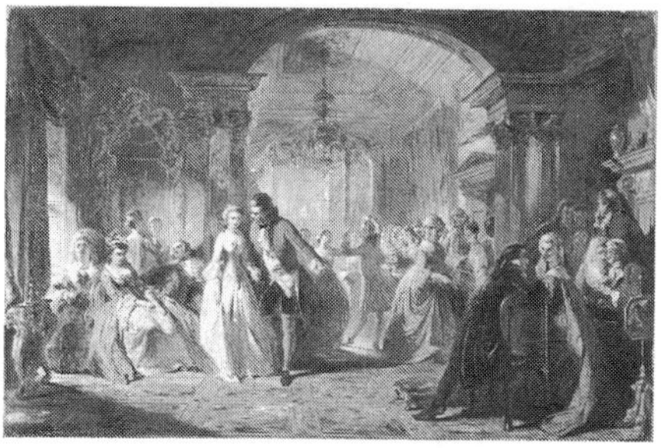

Abraham Solomon (1823–62)

acc. no. 758
A Ballroom in the Year 1760 (1848)

oil on canvas: 15 × 21 in.
signed and dated: *A. Solomon 184*(8)
Bequeathed by Charles Gassiot, 1902

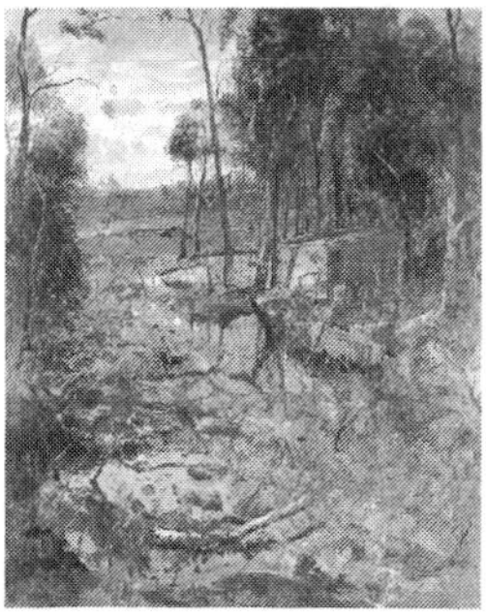

Lance Solomon (b.1913)

acc. no. 1845
By the Pump Shed – the Billabong (*c.*1966)

oil on hardboard: 36 × 30 in.
signed: *L. SOLOMON*
Presented by the Corporation of Sydney, New South Wales, 1970

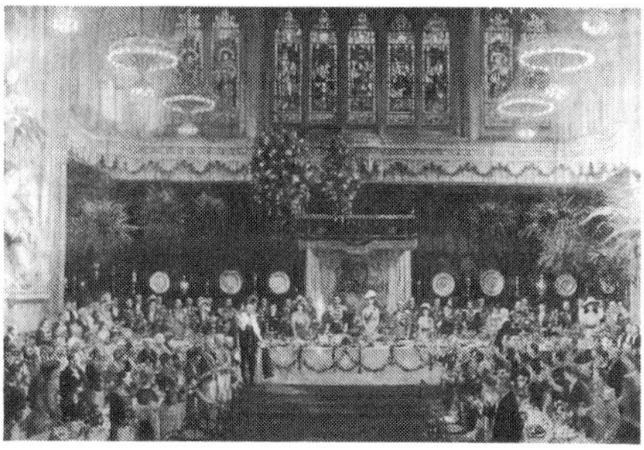

Solomon Joseph Solomon (1860–1927)

acc. no. 1021
The Coronation Luncheon to King George V and Queen Mary in Guildhall, June 29 1922 (1914–1922)

oil on canvas: 85 × 125 in.
Presented by John Wanamaker, 1922

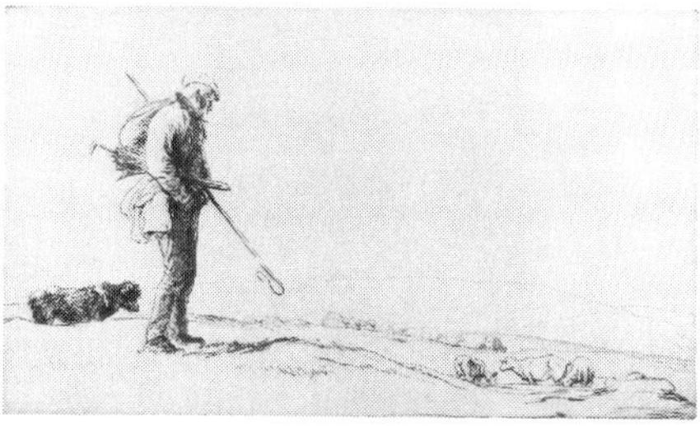

George Soper (1870–1942)

acc. no. 2268
Southdown Shepherd

etching: 5 × 8¾ in.
signed: *George Soper.*
Bequeathed by F. A. Cooke, 1981

Joseph Frédéric Charles Soulacroix (1825–*c.*1900)

acc. no. 1663
The Embrace

oil on canvas: $34\frac{1}{2} \times 20$ in.
signed: *F. Soulacroix.*
Presented by John Byram, 1963

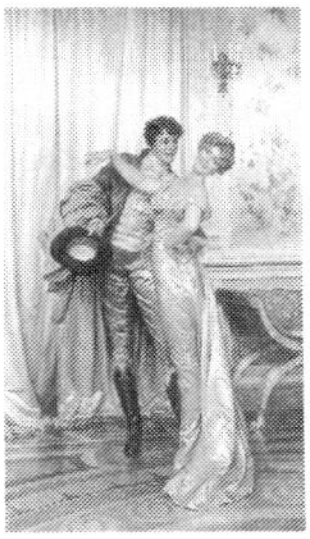

Robert Spence (1871–1964)

acc. no. 2270
Illustration to 'The Legend of St. Cuthbert' (*c.*1896)

etching and drypoint: $13\frac{1}{4} \times 9\frac{1}{4}$ in.
signed: *Robert Spence* and inscribed: *1st. State*
Bequeathed by F. A. Cooke, 1981

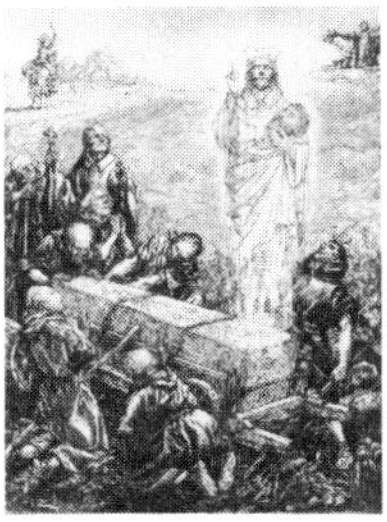

acc. no. 2269
Illustration to 'George Fox, His Journal'

etching and drypoint: $7\frac{3}{4} \times 5$ in.
signed: *Robert Spence* and inscribed: *With Christmas Greetings*
Bequeathed by F. A. Cooke, 1981

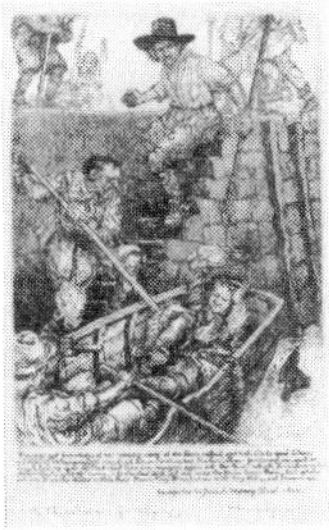

Benjamin Walter Spiers (1845–94)

acc. no. 1661
The Search for the Will (1890)

watercolour: $10\frac{1}{2} \times 20$ in. (sight)
signed and dated: *B.W. Spiers. 1890*
Presented by John Byram, 1963

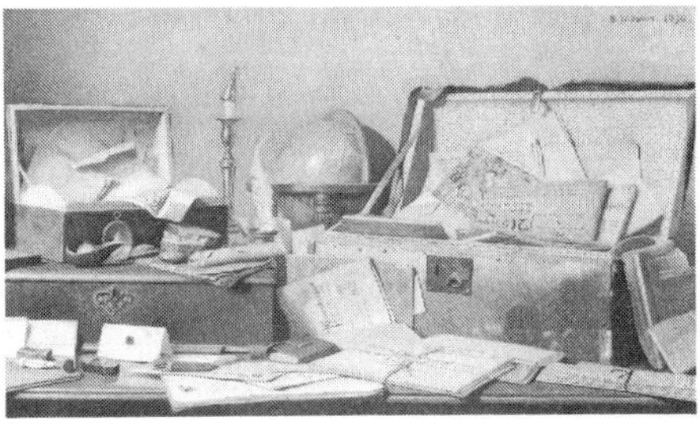

Effie Spring-Smith (b.1907)

acc. no. 3552
A Fleet Street Warden (1945)

oil on canvas: 24×20 in.
signed: *E SPRING- / SMITH* and inscribed: *"A Fleet Street Warden" / Exhib. R.B.A. 1945*
Purchased from the John Denham Gallery, 1985

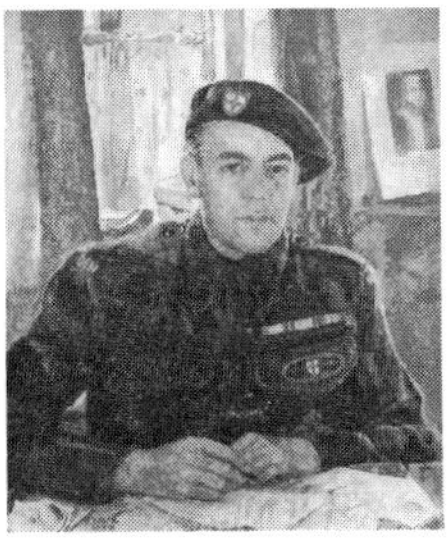

Clarkson Stanfield (1793–1867)

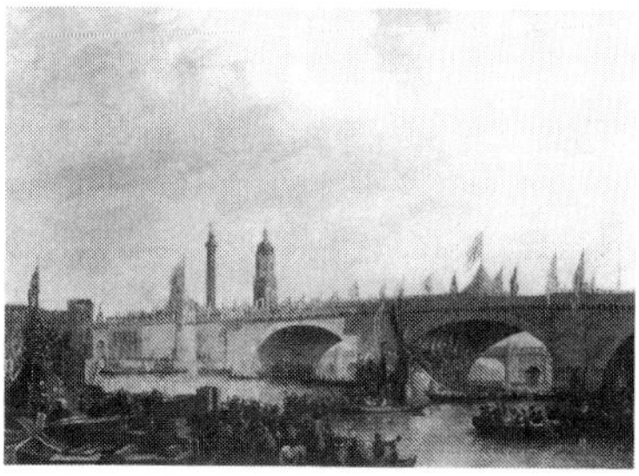

acc. no. 1260
The Opening of London Bridge by William IV, August 1 1831
oil on canvas: 28 × 36 in.
Presented by Lady Wakefield, 1943

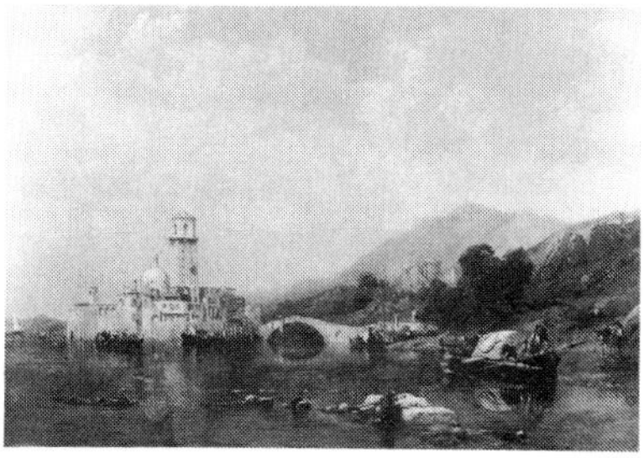

acc. no. 730
In the Gulf of Venice (1848)
oil on canvas: 28 × 40 in.
signed and dated: *C Stanfield R.A. 1848*
Bequeathed by Charles Gassiot, 1902

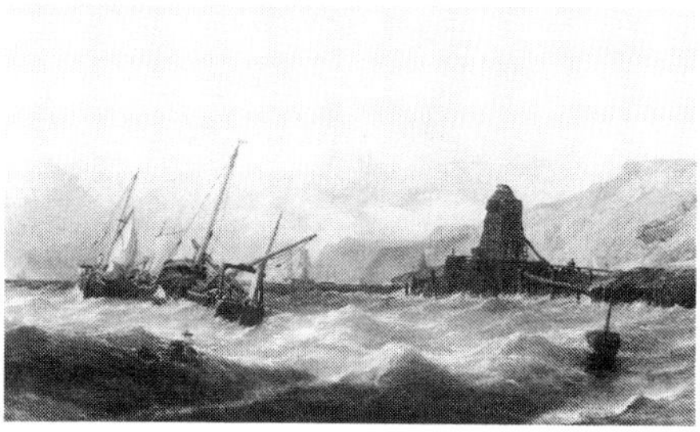

acc. no. 732
Oxwich Bay, South Wales (1851)
oil on canvas: 29 × 49 in.
signed and dated: *C Stanfield RA. / 1851*
Bequeathed by Charles Gassiot, 1902

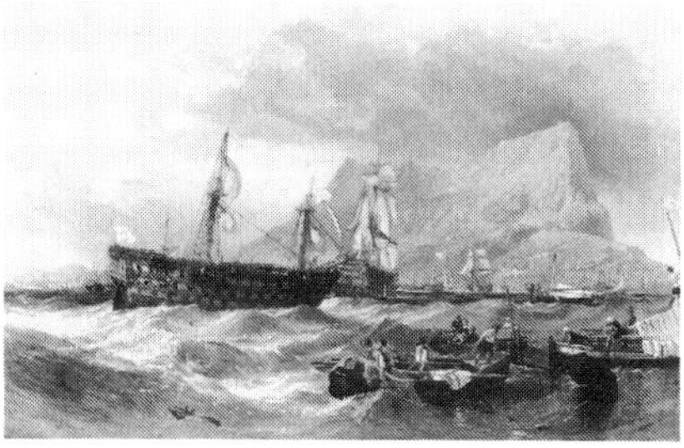

acc. no. 734
The 'Victory' Towed into Gibraltar (1854)
oil on panel: 18 × $27\frac{1}{2}$ in.
signed and dated: *C Stanfield RA. / 1854*
Bequeathed by Charles Gassiot, 1902

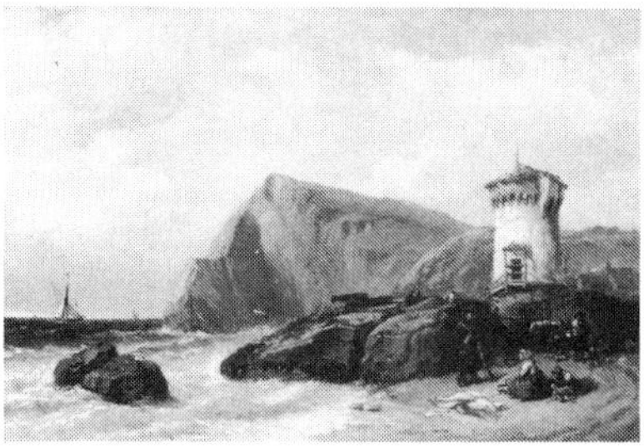

acc. no. 735
Terracina Tower (1854)
oil on panel: 14 × 20 in.
signed and dated: *C. Stanfield / R.A. 1854*
Bequeathed by Charles Gassiot, 1902

acc. no. 731
Men-of-War off Portsmouth (1855)

oil on canvas: $18\frac{1}{2} \times 30\frac{1}{2}$ in.
signed and dated: *C. Stanfield R.A. 1855*
Bequeathed by Charles Gassiot, 1902

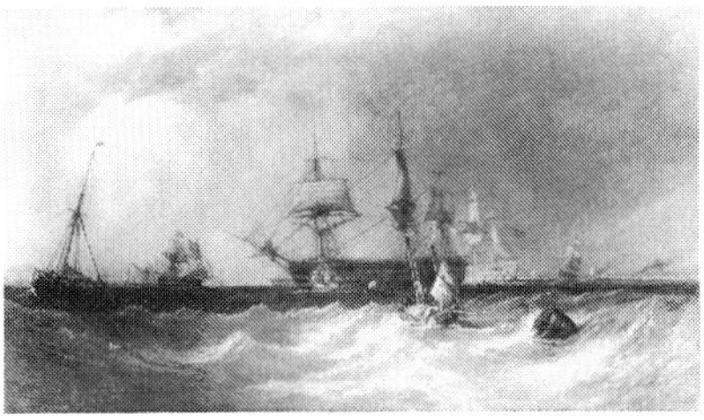

acc. no. 733
On the Texel (1856)

oil on canvas: 24 × 36 in.
signed and dated: *C Stanfield R.A. 1856*
Bequeathed by Charles Gassiot, 1902

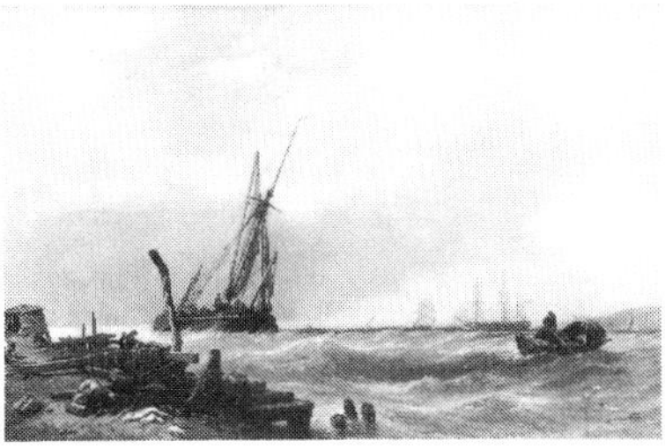

acc. no. 729
Old Holland (1858)

oil on canvas: 48 × 42 in.
signed and dated: *C. Stanfield R.A. 1858*
Bequeathed by Charles Gassiot, 1902

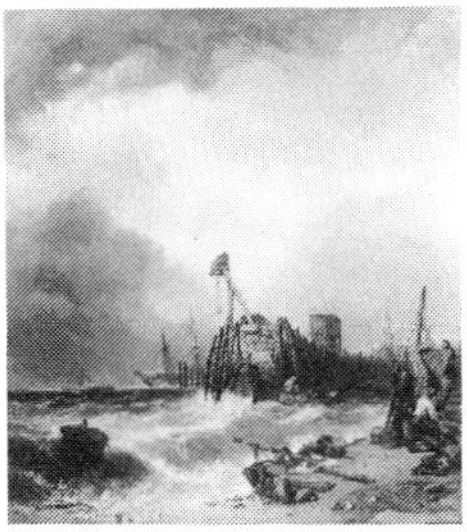

Jacqueline Stanley (20th C)

acc. no. 1810
Leadenhall Market (1968)

oil on hardboard: 42 × 36 in.
signed: *STANLEY*
Purchased from the artist, 1969

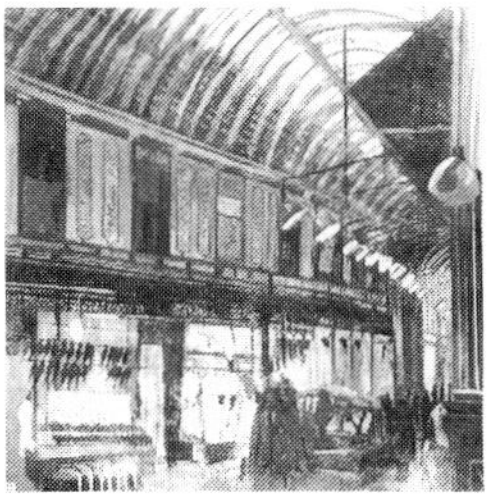

Alfred Stevens (1823–1906)

acc. no. 723
Spring (? *c.*1876)

oil on canvas: 30 × 10 in.
signed: *A Stevens*
Bequeathed by Charles Gassiot, 1902

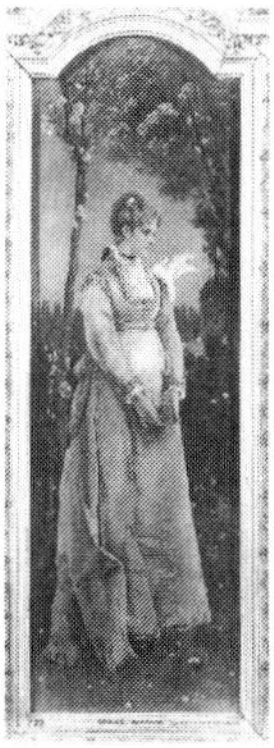

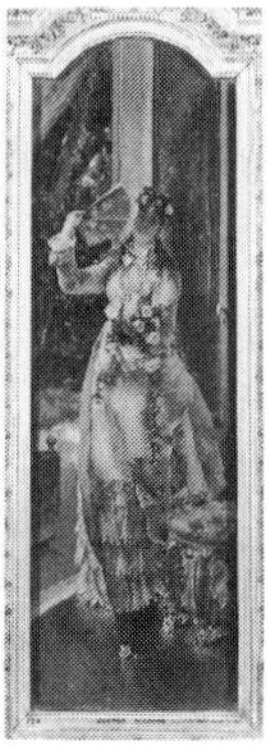

acc. no. 724
Summer (? *c.*1876)
oil on canvas: 30 × 10 in.
signed: *A Stevens*
Bequeathed by Charles Gassiot, 1902

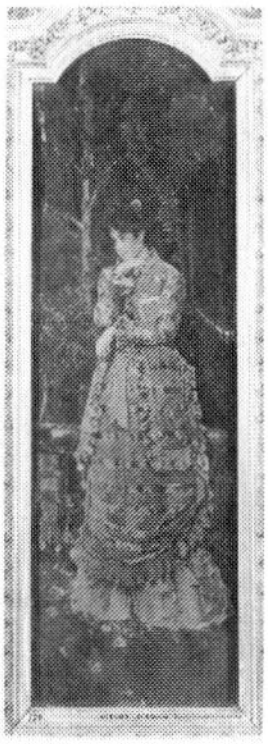

acc. no. 725
Autumn (? *c.*1876)
oil on canvas: 30 × 10 in.
signed: *A Stevens*
Bequeathed by Charles Gassiot, 1902

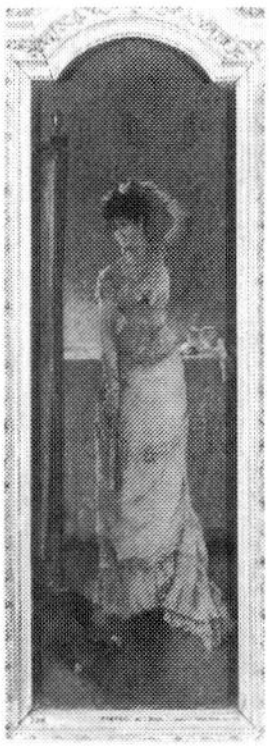

acc. no. 726
Winter (? *c.*1876)
oil on canvas: 30 × 10 in.
signed: *A Stevens*
Bequeathed by Charles Gassiot, 1902

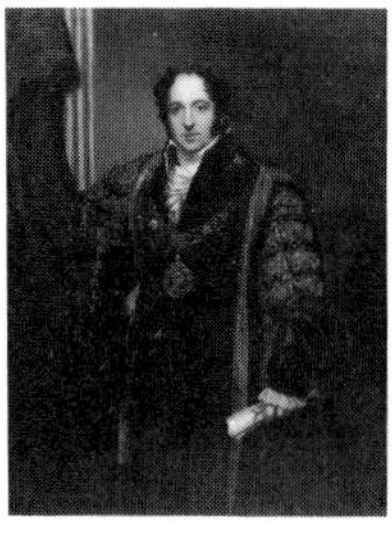

Thomas Stewardson (1781–1859)

acc. no. 891
John Garratt, Lord Mayor 1824 (1825)
oil on canvas: 53 × 41 in.
Presented by W. F. H. Garratt, 1909

Christian Stocklin (1741–95)

acc. no. 350
Interior of a Church (1781)
oil on panel: 15 × 13 in.
signed: *C. Stocklin f* and dated: *1781*
Bequeathed by William Dunnett, 1888

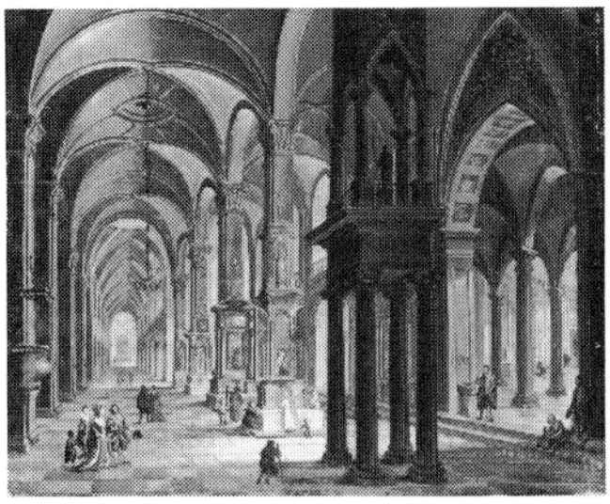

Adrian Stokes (1854–1936)

acc. no. 953
Wild Cherry Trees in the South Tyrol (*c.*1909)
oil on canvas: 25 × 29½ in.
signed: *Adrian Stokes*
Presented by T. L. Devitt, 1914

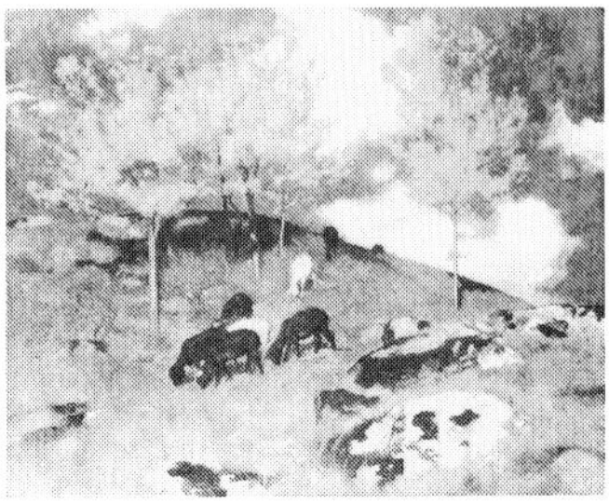

Marianne Stokes (1855–1927)

acc. no. 954
The Net Mender
oil on canvas: 26 × 29 in.
signed: *MS*
Presented by T. L. Devitt, 1914

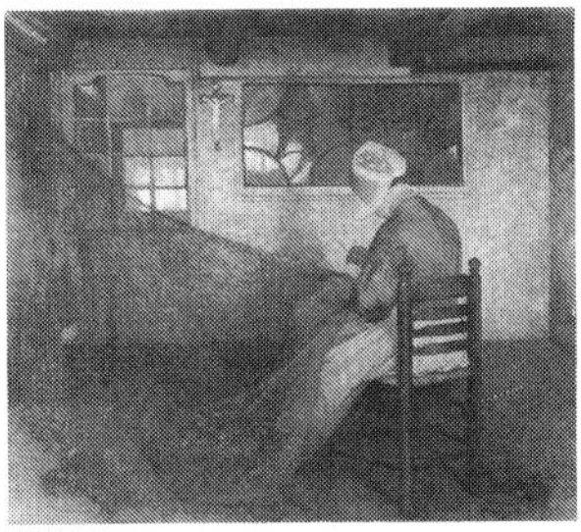

Marcus Stone (1840–1921)

acc. no. 721
Claudio, Deceived by Don John, Accuses Hero ('Much Ado about Nothing') (1861)
oil on panel: 11½ × 15 in.
signed (mono) and dated: *MS 61*
Bequeathed by Charles Gassiot, 1902

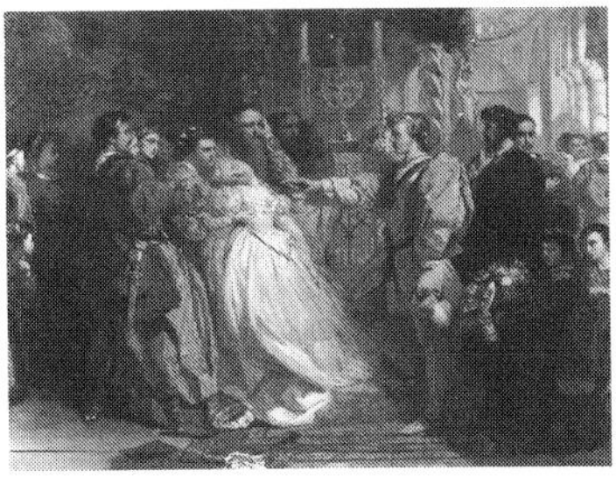

acc. no. 722
On the Road from Waterloo to Paris (1863)
oil on canvas: 44 × 60 in.
signed: *MARCUS STONE*
Bequeathed by Charles Gassiot, 1902

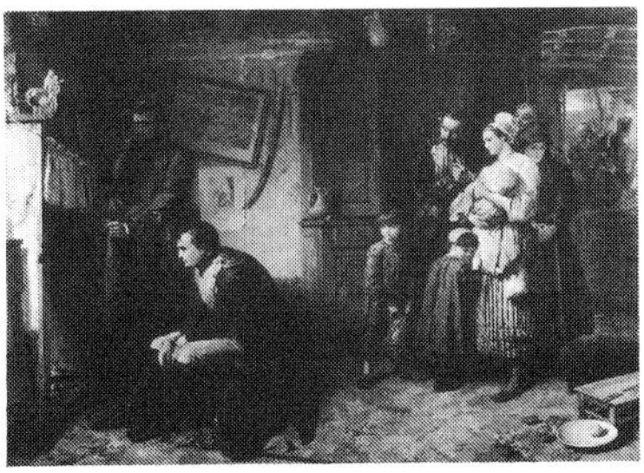

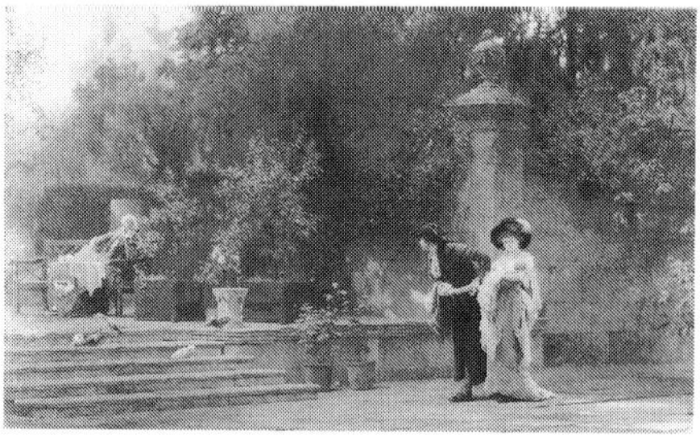

acc. no. 858
Married for Love (1882)

oil on canvas: $38\frac{1}{2} \times 48$ in.
signed and dated: *MARCUS STONE 1882*
Presented by the Executors of Henry Callcott Brunning, 1908

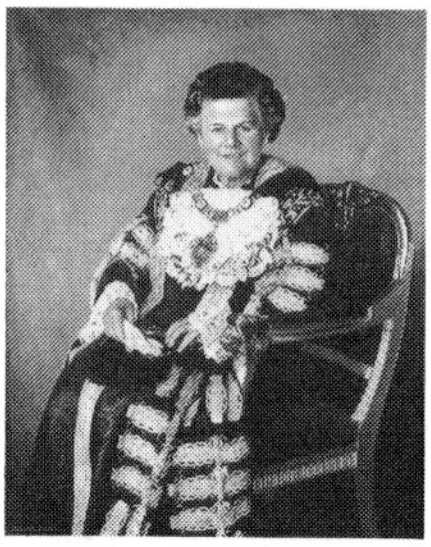

Richard Stone (b.1951)

acc. no. 3512
Dame Mary Donaldson, Lord Mayor 1983/4 (1985)

oil on canvas: 50×40 in.
signed: – *RICHARD STONE* –
Commissioned by the Corporation, 1985

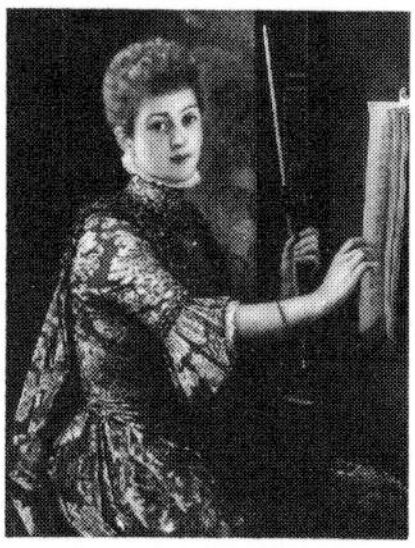

George Adolphus Storey (1834–1919)

acc. no. 473
The Violinist (1886)

oil on canvas: 36×28 in.
signed (mono) and dated: *GAS / 1886*
Presented by the Worshipful Company of Goldsmiths, 1888

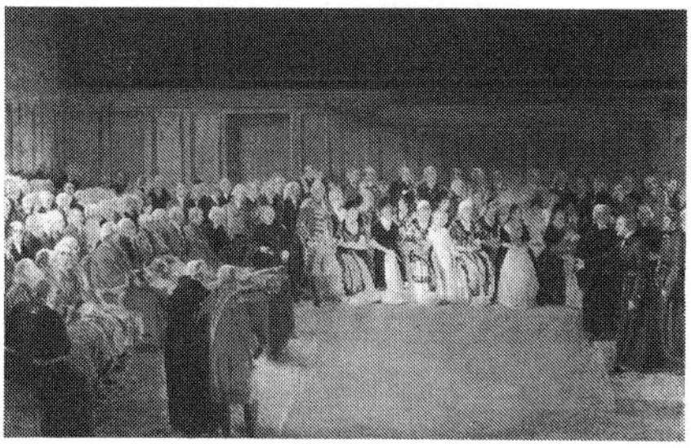

Thomas Stothard (1755–1834)

acc. no. 1231
Christ's Hospital, St. Matthew's Day, 1798

oil on canvas: $16\frac{1}{2} \times 25\frac{3}{4}$ in.
inscribed on label on stretcher: *Christ's Hospital / St Matthew's Day 1798 / Painted by T Stothard / RA.*
Presented by Lord Bearsted, 1937

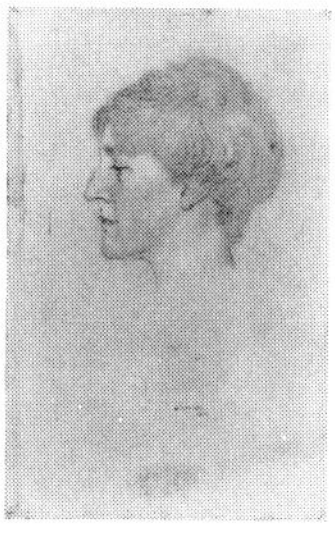

William Strang (1859–1921)

acc. no. 3602
Woman's Head in Profile (1909)

pencil and coloured chalk: $16\frac{3}{8} \times 10\frac{1}{2}$ in.
signed and dated: *W. STRANG / 1909.*
Presented by Miss Helen Guiterman, 1985

François Stroobant (1819–1916)

acc. no. 250
Hotel de Ville, Brussels (1870)

oil on canvas: 55 × 45 in.
signed and dated: *F. STROOBANT / BRUXELLES 1870*
Presented by Alderman Robert Besley, 1877

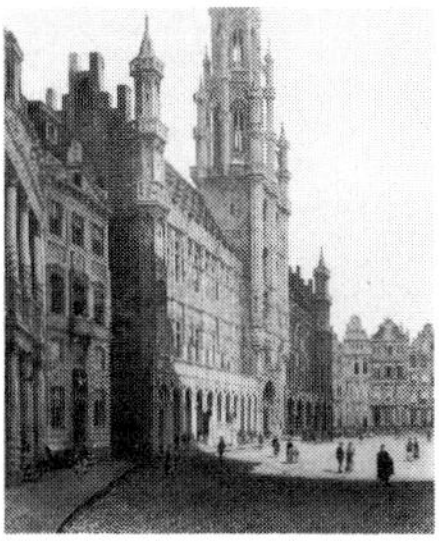

acc. no. 606
The Old Bishop's Palace, Liege (1870)

oil on canvas: 55 × 45 in.
signed and dated: *F. STROOBANT / BRUXELLES 1870*
Presented by Sir Edwin Lawrence, 1897

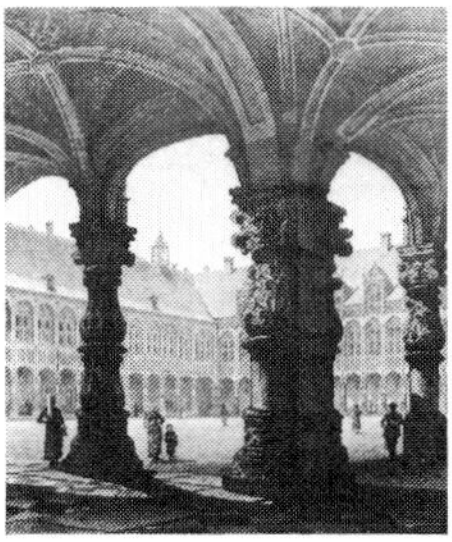

Samuel John Stump (*c.*1783–1863)
The following seven miniatures were bequeathed by F. W. Daniels in 1882.

acc. no. 268
Madame Giulia Grisi

watercolour on ivory: 6 × 5 in.

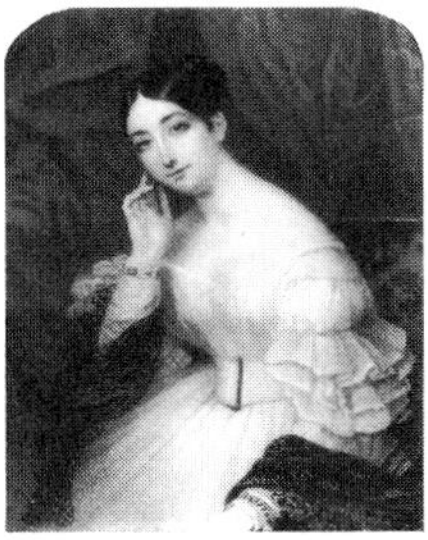

acc. no. 270
Maria Foote, Countess of Harrington

watercolour on ivory: $6\frac{1}{2} \times 5\frac{1}{2}$ in.
signed: *Stump pinx^t*; inscribed on verso: *S.J. Stump Pinxt. / N° 7 Cork Street / Burlington Gardens*

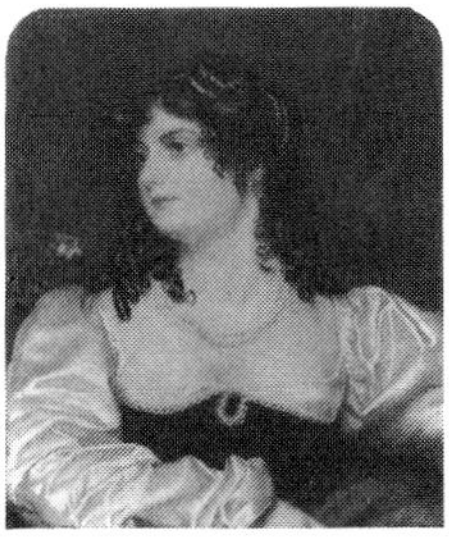

acc. no. 273
Self-Portrait

watercolour on ivory: $6\frac{5}{8} \times 5$ in.

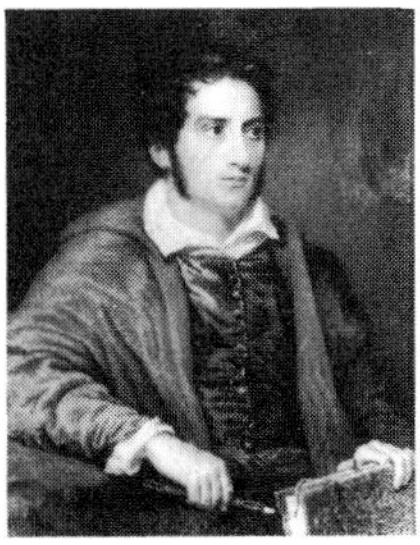

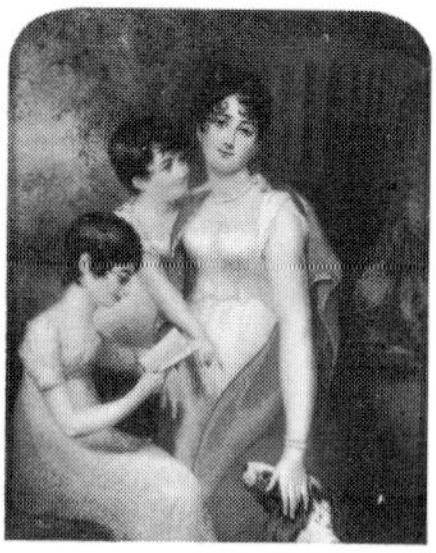

acc. no. 274
Three Girls and their Dog
watercolour on ivory: $7 \times 5\frac{1}{2}$ in.
signed: *Stump pinxt*

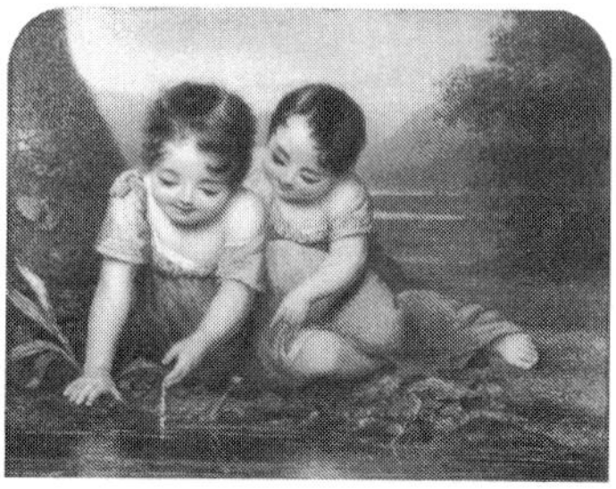

acc. no. 275
Two Children at a Stream
watercolour on ivory: $5\frac{3}{4} \times 7\frac{1}{2}$ in.
signed: *Stump / pinxt*

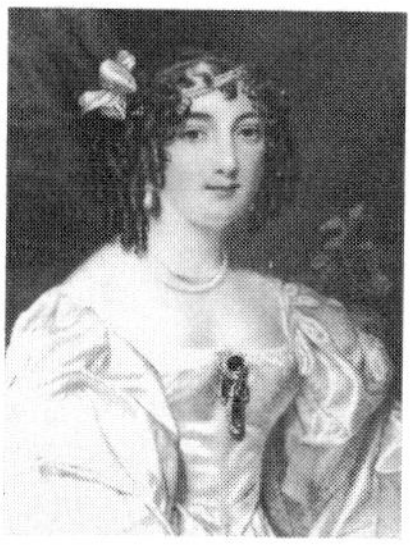

acc. no. 276
A Young Woman
watercolour on ivory: 7×5 in.
signed: *Stump / pinxt*; signed and inscribed on label attached to backboard: *N° 1 / S J Stump Pinxt / N° 7 Cork Street / Burlington Gardens*

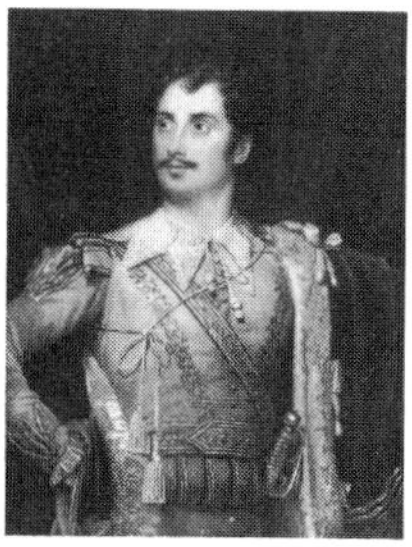

acc. no. 277
A Young Man in Costume
watercolour on ivory: $7\frac{3}{8} \times 5\frac{1}{4}$ in.
signed: *Stump / pt*; inscribed on mount: *N° 7*; inscribed on verso: *S J Stump Pinxt / N° 7 Cork Street/ Burlington Gardens*

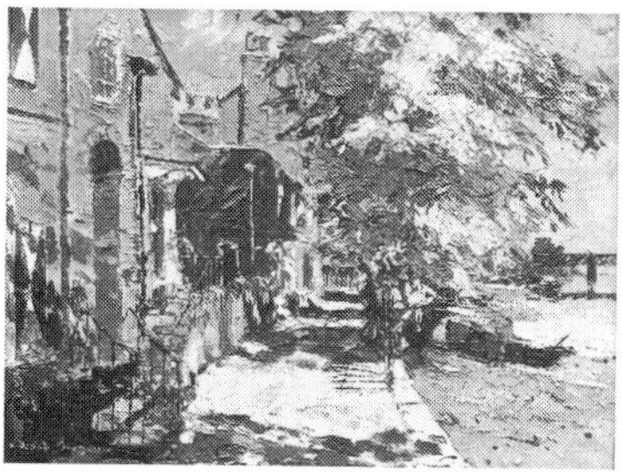

Josiah Sturgeon (20th C)

acc. no. 1962
Strand on the Green (1973)
oil on board: 16×20 in.
signed: . *Josiah Sturgeon.*
Purchased from the artist, 1973

John Macallan Swan (1847–1910)
The following 18 drawings were purchased with a fund raised by public subscription in 1910.

acc. no. 895
Lioness

watercolour: 14 × 21 in.
inscribed on backboard: *"Lioness watching" / painted by John M. Swann / Authenticity vouched by Mary Swann / 5 May 1910*

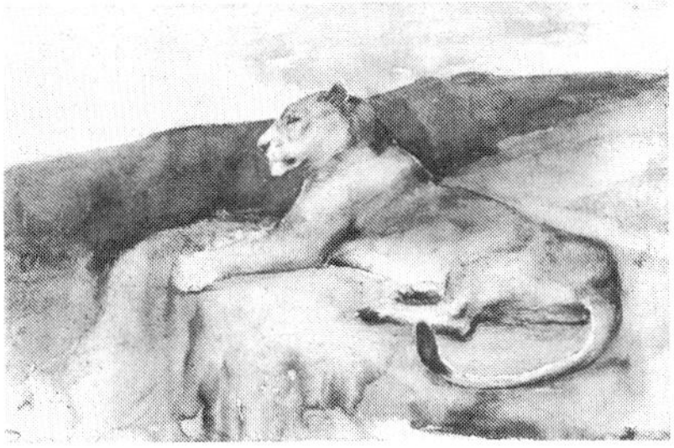

acc. no. 896
Wreckage

watercolour: 11 × 18 in.
signed: *J.M. SWAN.*

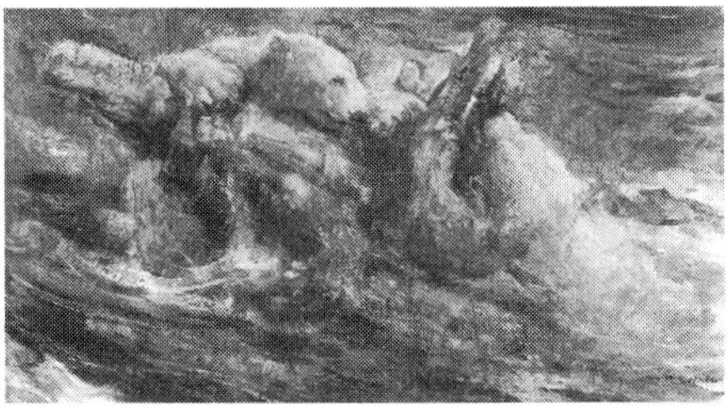

acc. no. 897
St Maldonata

pastel: 15 × 13½ in.
signed: *John M. Swan*

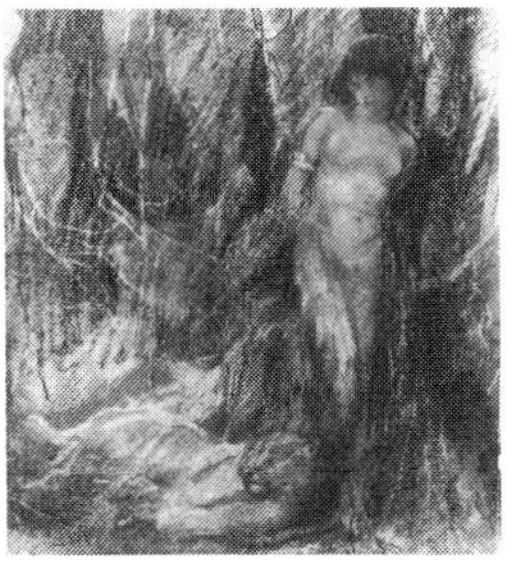

acc. no. 898
A Lioness

watercolour: 14 × 21 in.

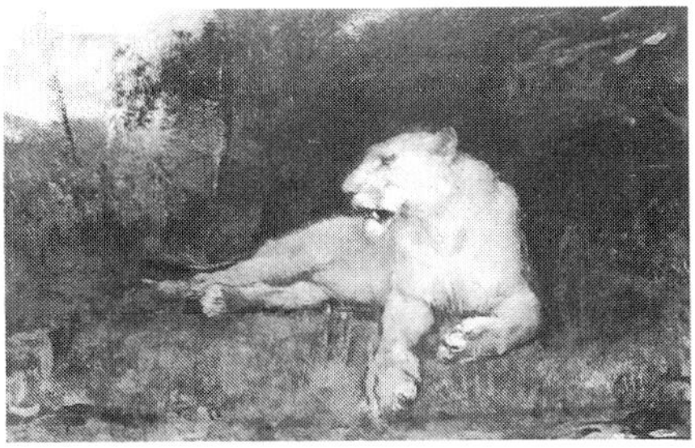

acc. no. 899a
A Lion

brown and white chalk on blue paper: 12 × 15 in.

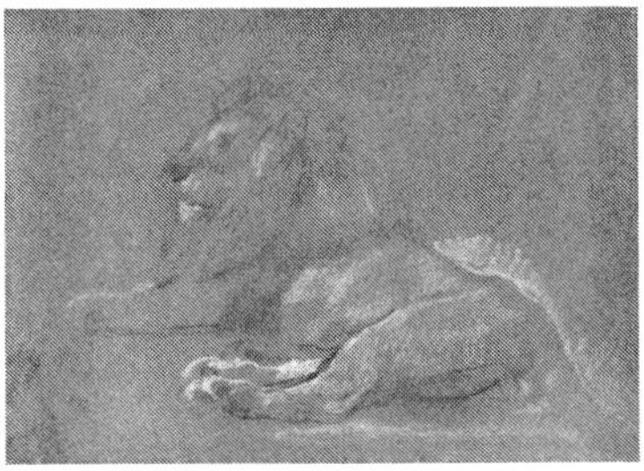

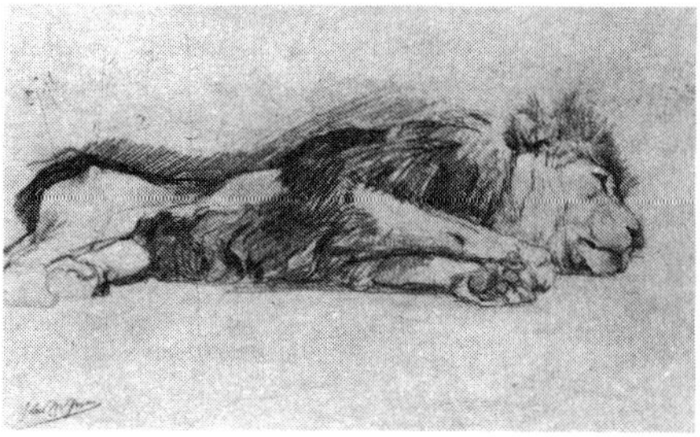

acc. no. 899b
A Lion Sleeping

black chalk on brown paper: 9 × 14⅜ in.
signed: *John M Swan* and inscribed with numbers

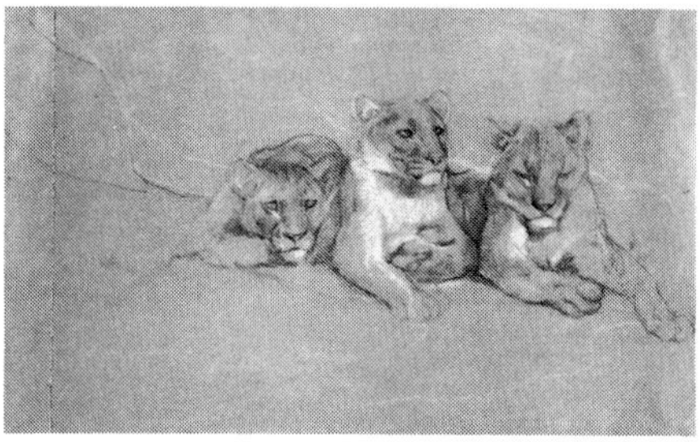

acc. no. 899c
Tom, Dick and Harry

black and white chalk on brown paper: 11 × 17 in.

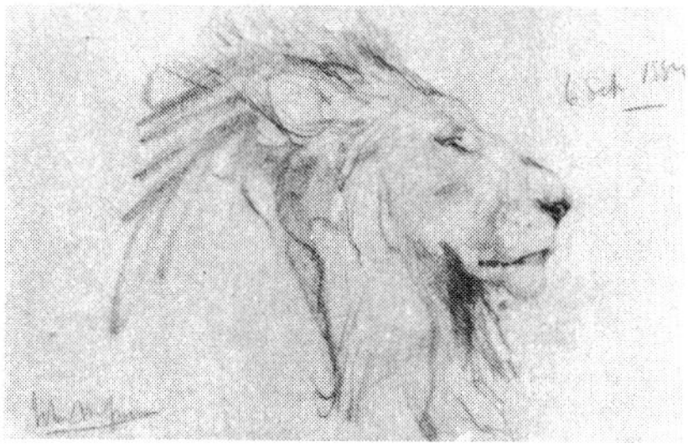

acc. no. 899d
Head of a Lion (1889)

black chalk on brown paper: 6 × 9 in.
signed: *John M Swan* and dated *6 Sept 1889*

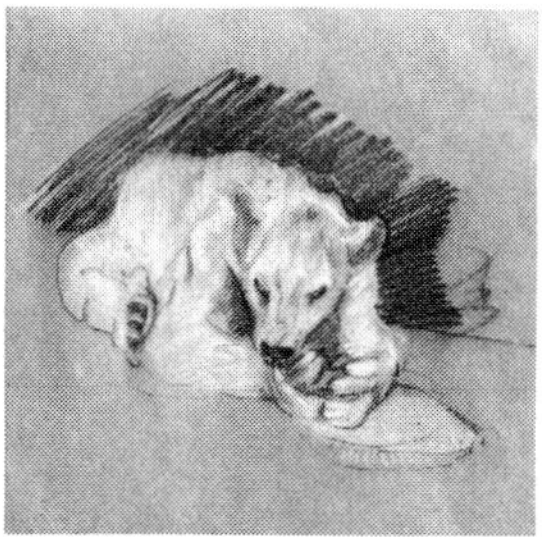

acc. no. 899e
Barbara Eating a Fish

black and white chalk on brown paper: 13¾ × 8¾ in.
signed: *John M Swan*

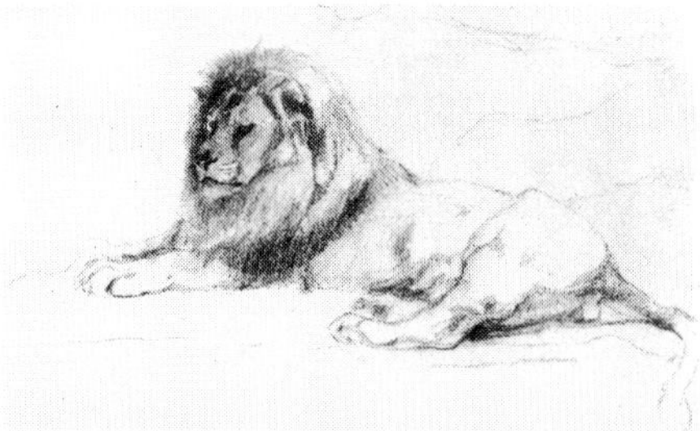

acc. no. 899f
A Lion Lying Down

black and grey chalks on brown paper: 10 × 16⅝ in. (sight)

acc. no. 899g
A Tiger Gnawing a Bone

black and white chalk on blue paper: $8\frac{1}{4} \times 12\frac{1}{2}$ in.
signed: *JOHN.M. SWAN*

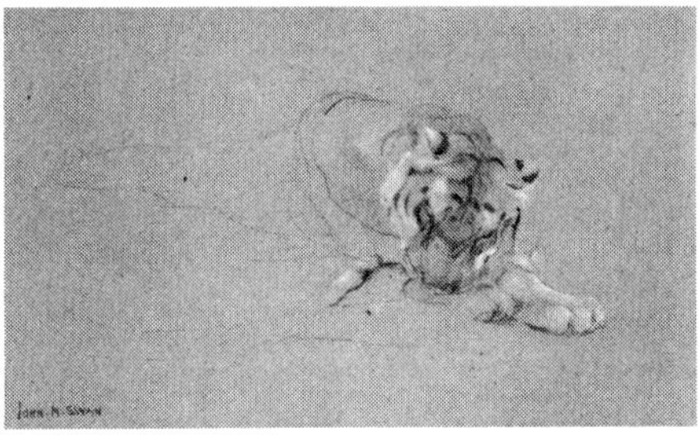

acc. no. 900a
A Tiger Drinking

coloured chalks on brown paper: $9\frac{1}{8} \times 14\frac{3}{8}$ in. (sight)
signed: *John M Swan*

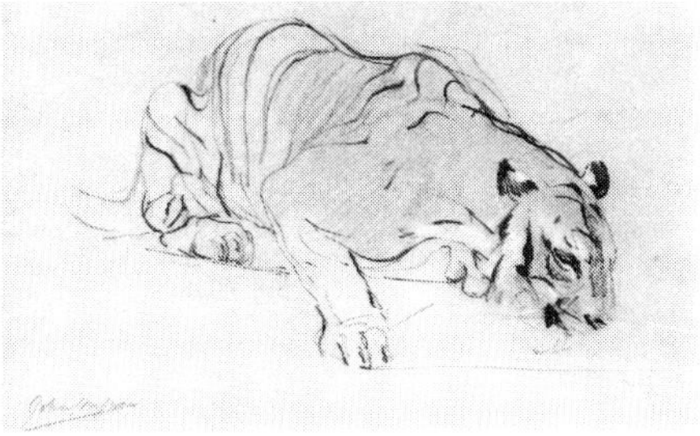

acc. no. 900b
A Clouded Tiger Cat

black and brown chalks on brown paper: $9\frac{1}{4} \times 14\frac{1}{2}$ in. (sight)
signed: *John M Swan*

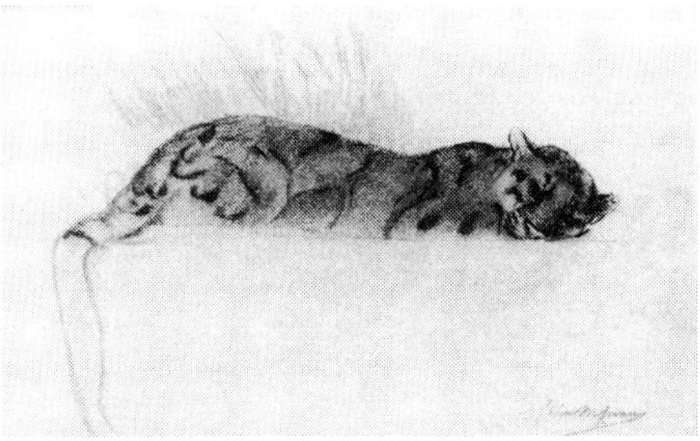

acc. no. 900c
A Tiger Lying Down – 'Chamundi'
coloured chalks on brown paper: $9 \times 12\frac{3}{4}$ in.
signed: *John M Swan*

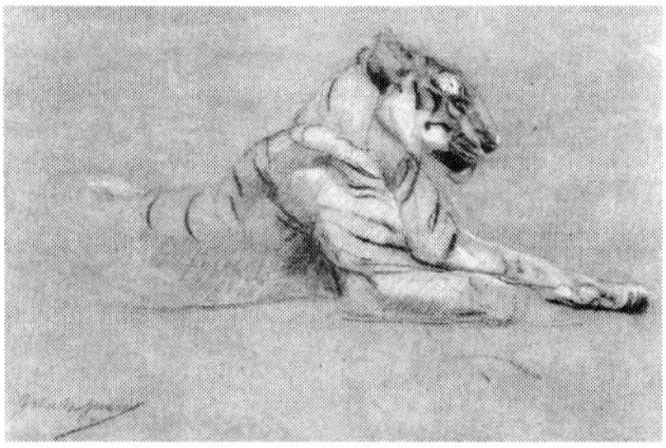

verso: *study of the head and paw of a polar bear*
black chalk

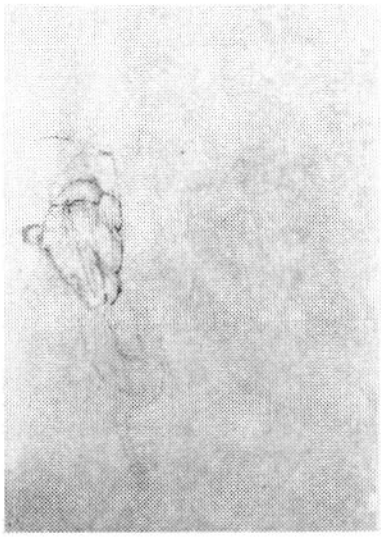

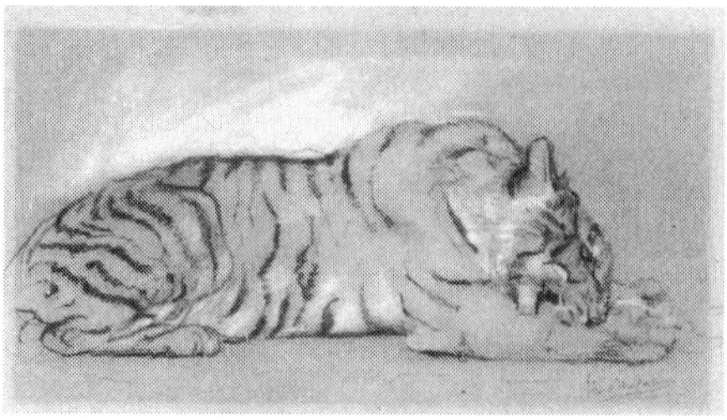

acc. no. 900d
A Tiger Feeding
coloured chalks on brown paper: $6\frac{3}{4} \times 11\frac{7}{8}$ in.
signed: *John M Swan*

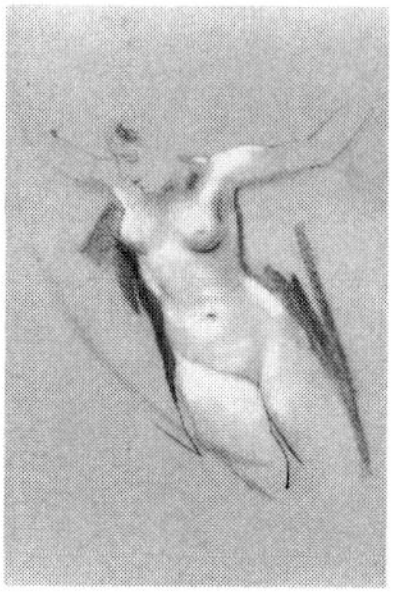

acc. no. 900e
Female Nude
coloured chalks on green paper: $15 \times 9\frac{3}{4}$ in.

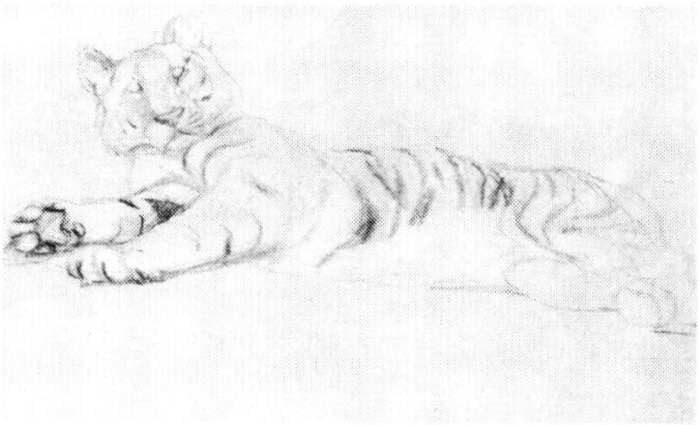

acc. no. 900f
A Tiger Resting
coloured chalks on brown paper: $8\frac{1}{2} \times 13\frac{1}{2}$ in.

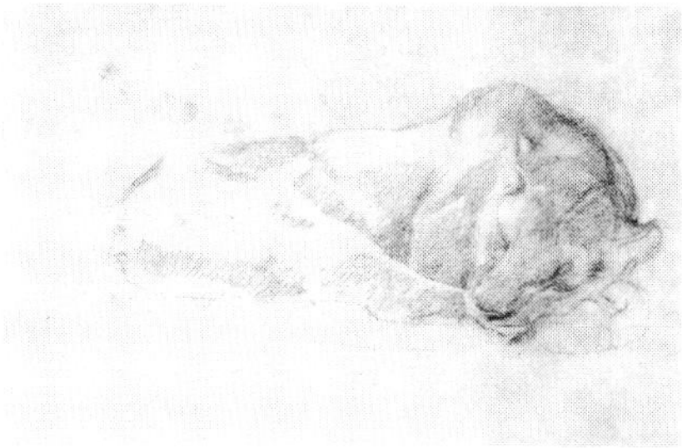

acc. no. 900g
A Lioness Asleep
black chalk on brown paper: $8\frac{3}{8} \times 12$ in.

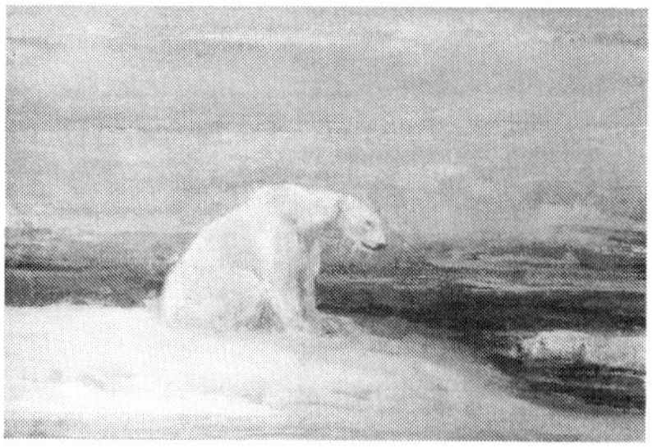

acc. no. 917
Polar Bears Watching for Seals at an Ice Hole
watercolour: 14×20 in.
Presented by J. C. J. Drucker and Friends, 1911

Robert M. Swan (20th C) after Terence Cuneo (b. 1907)

acc. no. 1895
St. Paul's: Awaiting the Funeral Procession of Sir Winston Churchill, February 1965
oil on canvas: 72 × 54 in.
Presented by Alderman Sir James Miller, 1972

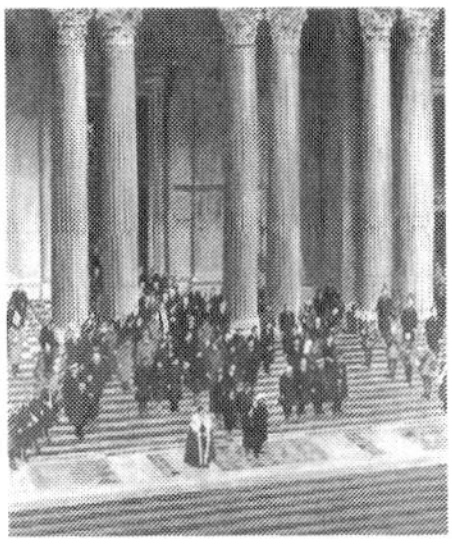

Aubrey Sykes (20th C)

acc. no. 2156
Turk's Boat Yard, Kingston (1974)
oil on canvas board: 24 × 19$\frac{7}{8}$ in.
signed: *Sykes*
Purchased from the artist, 1974

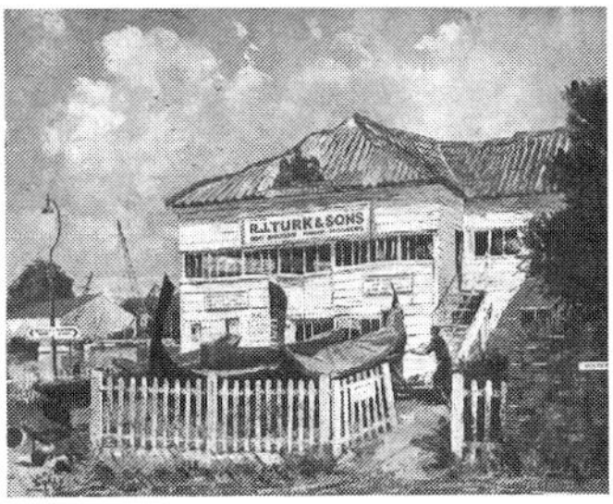

acc. no. 2198
Low Water, Strand on the Green (1975)
oil on canvas board: 19$\frac{1}{4}$ × 29$\frac{1}{4}$ in.
signed: *Sykes*
Purchased from the artist, 1975

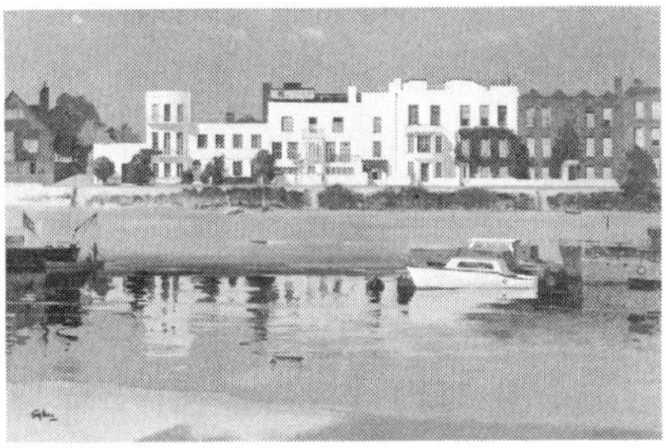

J... W... S... (?)

acc. no. 515
Demolition of London Bridge
oil on canvas: 21 × 31 in.
signed (mono): *JWS* (?)
Presented by J. W. Oxley, 1891

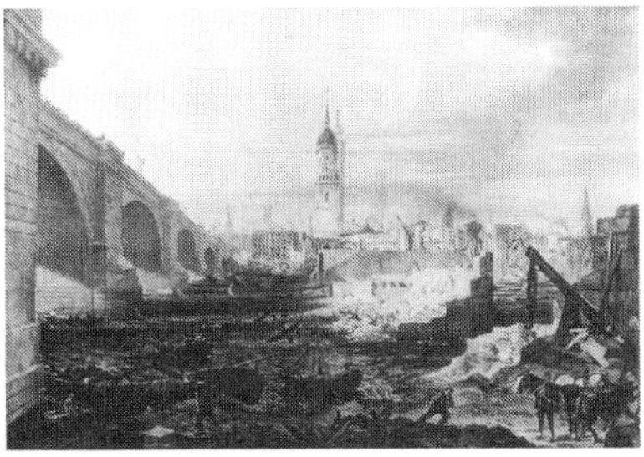

Albert Chevallier Tayler (1862–1925)

acc. no. 1006
Field Marshall the Earl Haig (1920)
oil on canvas: 50 × 40 in.
signed and dated: *A. Chevallier Tayler 1920*
Presented by William Lund, 1920

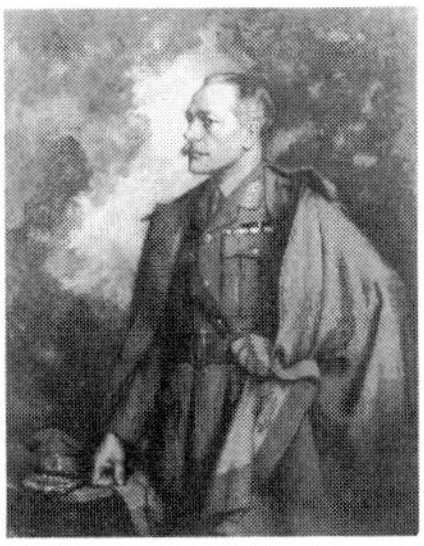

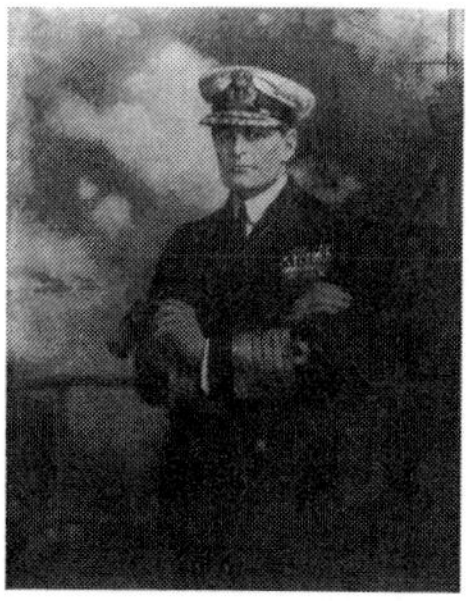

acc. no. 1007
Admiral of the Fleet, the Earl Beatty (1920)
oil on canvas: 50 × 40 in.
signed and dated: *A. Chevallier Tayler 1920*
Presented by William Lund, 1920

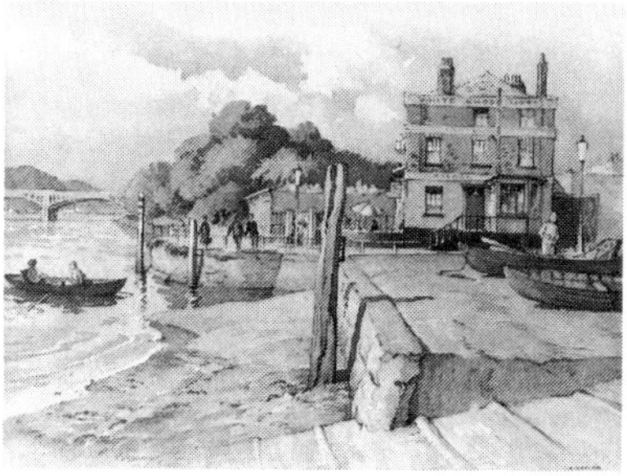

Albert Taylor (20th C)

acc. no. 1891
White Cross Hotel, Richmond (1971)
watercolour: $14\frac{1}{2} \times 18\frac{1}{4}$ in.
signed: *A. TAYLOR*
Purchased from the artist, 1971

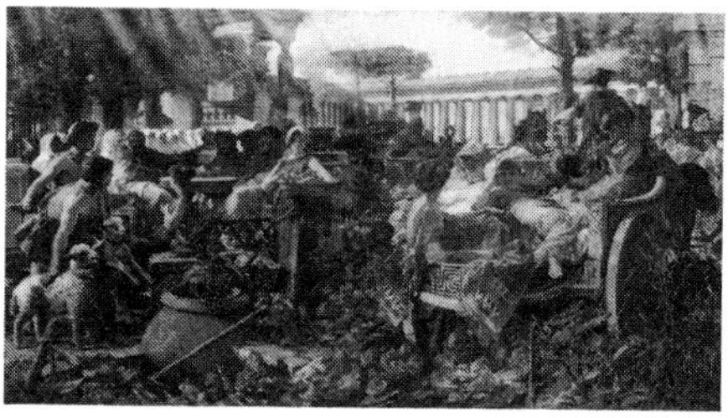

Michele Tedesco (1834–1917)

acc. no. 581
A Pythagorean School Invaded by Sybarites (1887)
oil on canvas: 108 × 195 in.
signed and dated: *Tedesco 1887*
Presented by the Italian Ambassador, Sig. P. Tornelli, 1894

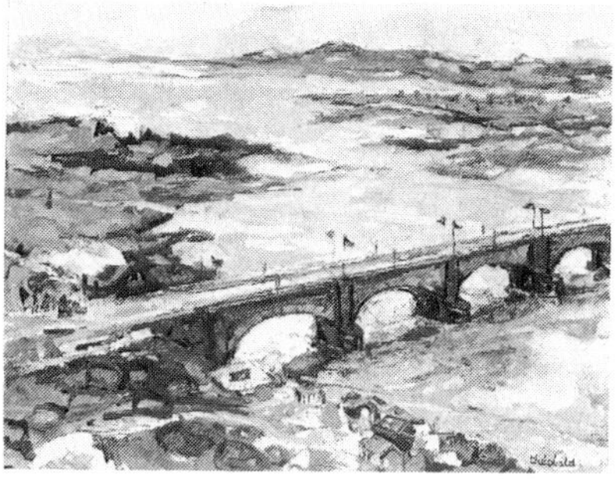

Renée Théobald (b.1926)

acc. no. 1937
London Bridge in Arizona (1972)
oil on canvas: $28\frac{3}{4} \times 36\frac{1}{4}$ in.
signed: *théobald*
Purchased from Emile Walter, 1972

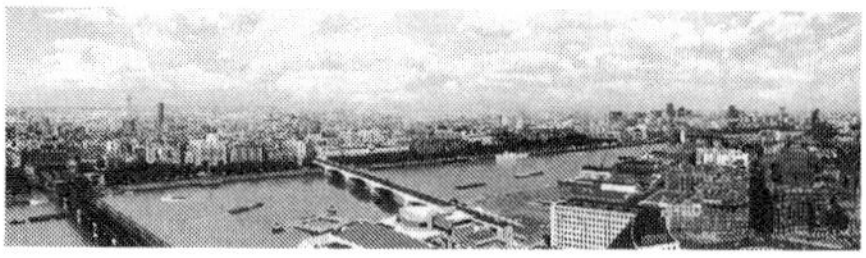

David Thomas (b.1916)

acc. no. 1788
London from the Top of the Shell Centre (1968)
oil on canvas: 54 × 192 in.
signed: *DAVID THOMAS.*
Purchased from the artist, 1968

Edith E. Thomas (*fl.* 1921–39)
The following 21 watercolours were presented by Professor C. A. Pannett in 1943.

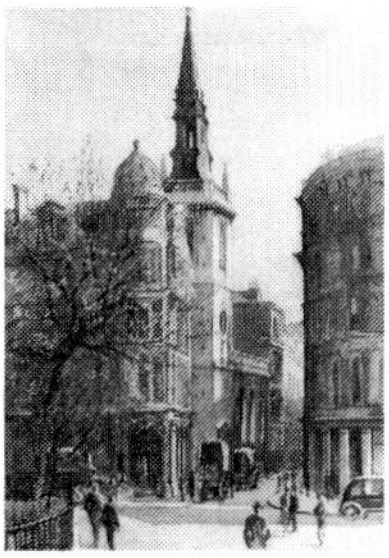

acc. no. 1261
St. Augustine, Old Change (1939)
watercolour: $14\frac{1}{8} \times 10$ in.
signed: *Edith E. Thomas*

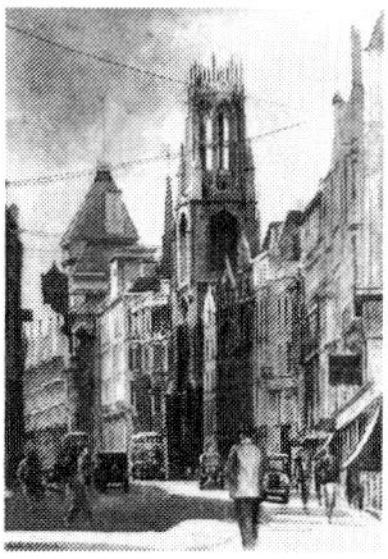

acc. no. 1262
St Dunstan in the West (1939)
watercolour: $14\frac{1}{8} \times 10$ in.
signed: *Edith E. Thomas*

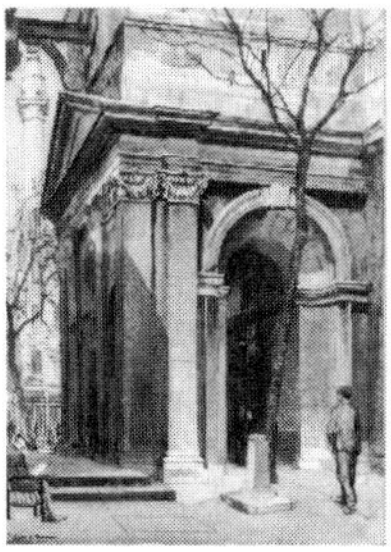

acc. no. 1263
St. Magnus the Martyr, London Bridge (1939)
watercolour: $14\frac{1}{8} \times 10$ in.
signed: *Edith E. Thomas*

acc. no. 1264
St Nicolas Cole Abbey (1939)
watercolour: $14\frac{1}{8} \times 9\frac{3}{4}$ in.
signed: *Edith E. Thomas*

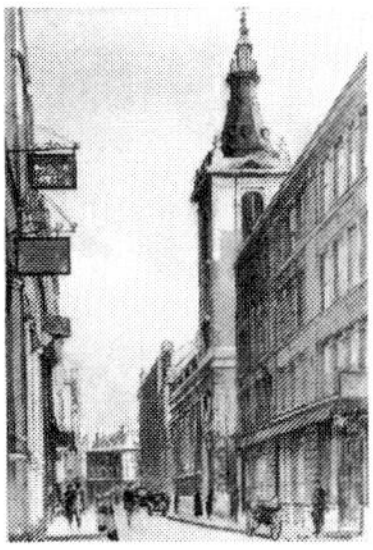

acc. no. 1265
St Vedast Foster Lane (1939)
watercolour: $14\frac{1}{8} \times 10$ in.
signed: *Edith E. Thomas*

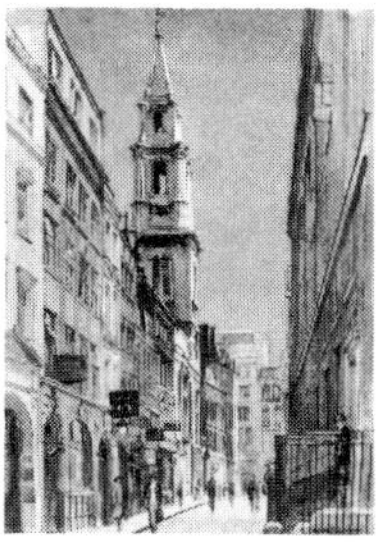

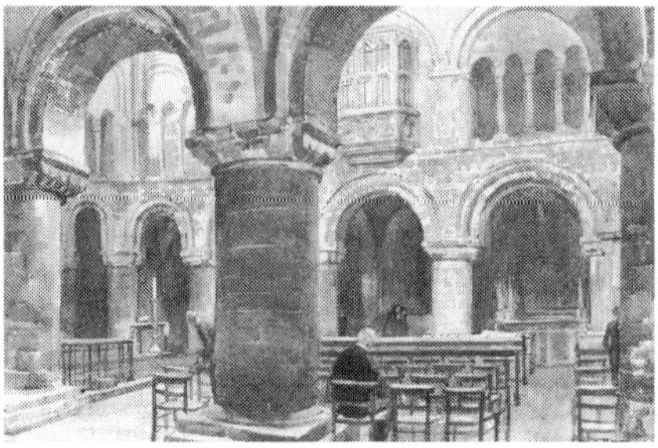

acc. no. 1266
Interior of St Bartholomew the Great (1939)

watercolour: $9\frac{3}{4} \times 14\frac{1}{8}$ in.
signed: *Edith E. Thomas*; inscribed on verso: *S. BARTHOLOMEW THE GREAT / (Smithfield) / 1143 / Clerestory re-instated 15th Cent. / Built as a vow by one Rahere – courtier / of Henry I. / Restored by.DANCE 1788.* and *In 1939*

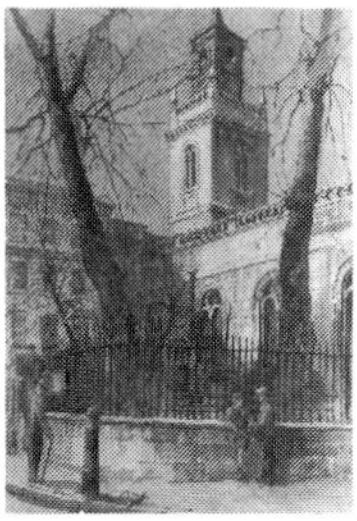

acc. no. 1267
St Mary the Virgin, Aldermanbury (1939)

watercolour: $13\frac{7}{8} \times 9\frac{3}{4}$ in.
signed: *Edith E. Thomas*

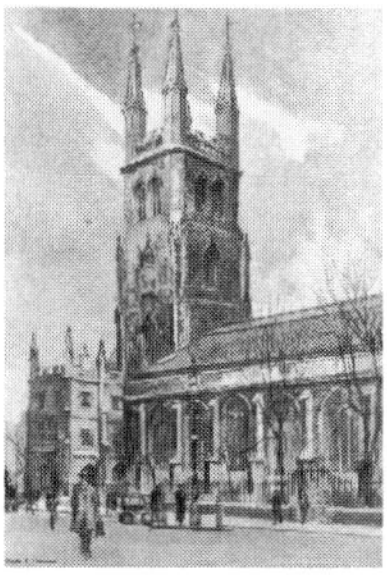

acc. no. 1268
St Sepulchre, Holborn Viaduct (1939)

watercolour: $13\frac{7}{8} \times 9\frac{3}{4}$ in.
signed: *Edith E. Thomas*; inscribed on verso: *CHURCH OF THE HOLY SEPULCHRE. / "S. Sepulchre". / Newgate. / Mainly destroyed in G.F, re-built 1670* [*WREN ?*] */ Body of church re-built in 1880 / Largest area of any City church.* [*150′ by 62′*] *Tolled for executions* and: *In 1939*

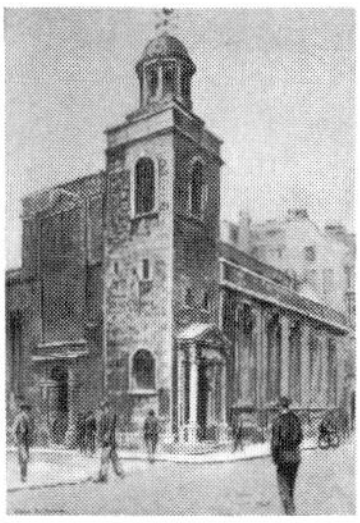

acc. no. 1269
St Katharine Cree, Leadenhall Street (1939)

watercolour: $14\frac{1}{8} \times 10$ in.
signed: *Edith E. Thomas*

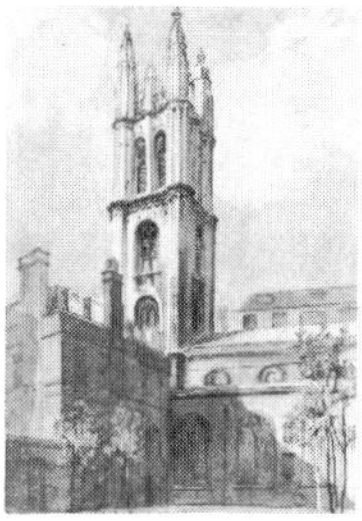

acc. no. 1270
St Michael Cornhill (1939)

watercolour: $14\frac{1}{8} \times 10$ in.
signed: *Edith E. Thomas*

acc. no. 1271
Interior of St Peter Upon Cornhill (1939)

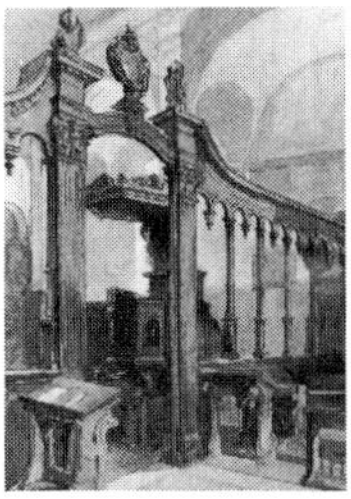

watercolour: $14\frac{1}{8} \times 10$ in.
signed: *Edith E. Thomas*; inscribed on verso: *S. PETER UPON CORNHILL / WREN 1680 / Screen with Charles II's Coat of Arms.* and *(Painted in Sept–Oct. 1939.)*

acc. no. 1272
Christchurch, Greyfriars (1939)

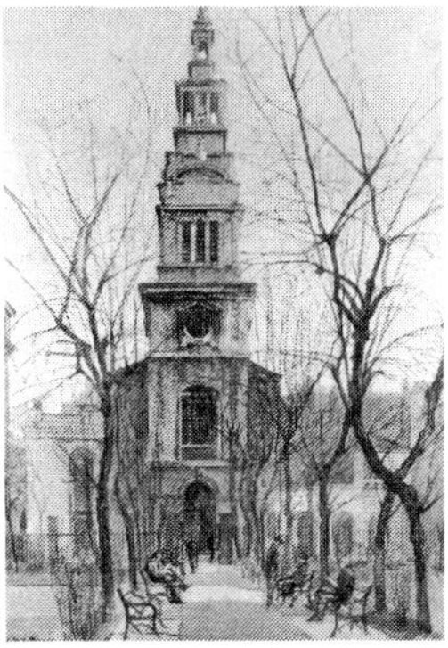

watercolour: $13\frac{7}{8} \times 9\frac{3}{4}$ in.
signed: *Edith E. Thomas*; inscribed on verso: *CHRIST CHURCH GREYFRIARS. / (Newgate Street) / WREN 1687 / On site of church founded by Franciscans / Choir stalls made partly from ship of / Spanish Armada. / Some of the paving from the Greyfriars' ch. / Attended by Christ's Hosp. boys. & still / done so once a year.* and *In 1939*

acc. no. 1273
St Botolph Aldgate (1939)

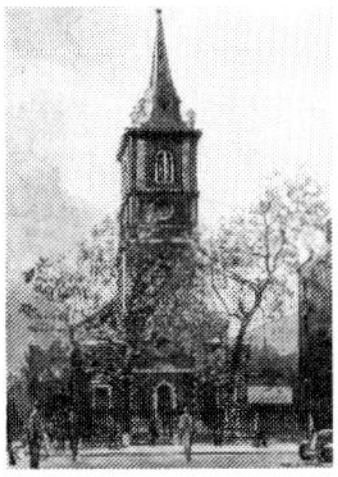

watercolour: $14\frac{1}{8} \times 10$ in.
signed: *Edith E. Thomas*

acc. no. 1274
St James Garlickhithe (1939)

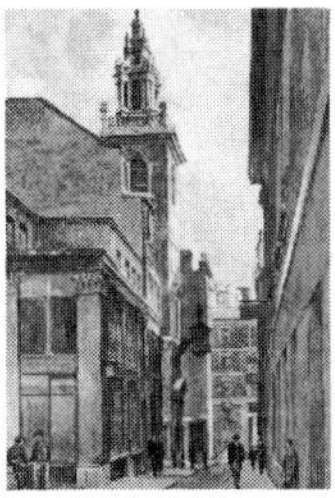

watercolour: $14\frac{1}{8} \times 9\frac{3}{4}$ in.
signed: *Edith E. Thomas*; inscribed on verso: *S. JAMES GARLICKHITHE / (Garlick Hill) / WREN 1682* and *In 1939*

acc. no. 1275
All Hallows, Barking by the Tower (1939)

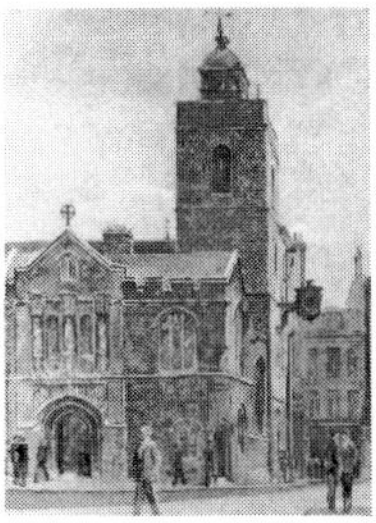

watercolour: $14\frac{1}{8} \times 9\frac{3}{4}$ in.
signed: *Edith E. Thomas*; inscribed on verso: *ALL HALLOWS BARKING / or / All Hallows-by-the-Tower. / Mark Lane. / Survived the G.F. / foundation 675? / Architect unknown / In Lady Chapel central shrine of "Toc H."*

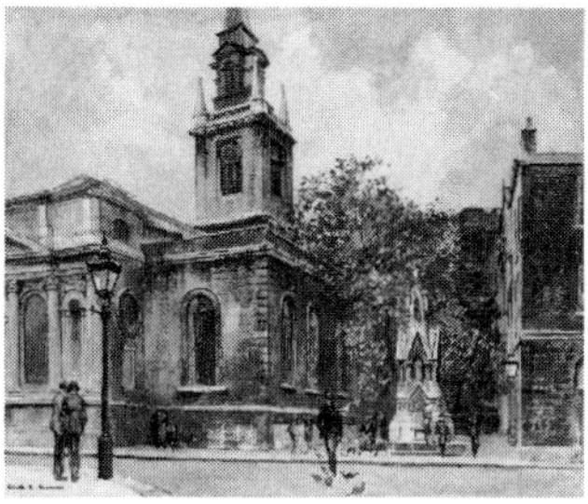

acc. no. 1276
St Lawrence Jewry (1939)

watercolour: $10\frac{7}{8} \times 12\frac{7}{8}$ in.
signed: *Edith E. Thomas*; inscribed on verso: *S. LAWRENCE JEWRY / (Gresham Street) / WREN 1680* and *In 1939*

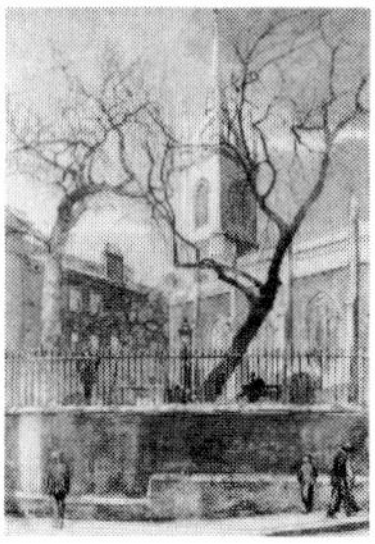

acc. no. 1277
St Dunstan in the East (1939)

watercolour: $13\frac{3}{4} \times 9\frac{3}{4}$ in.
signed: *Edith E. Thomas*; inscribed on verso; *S DUNSTAN-IN-THE-EAST. / (Lower Thames Street) / WREN 1699 / steeple re-built in 1821 by David Laing / A Fish Festival held here annually / In 1939*

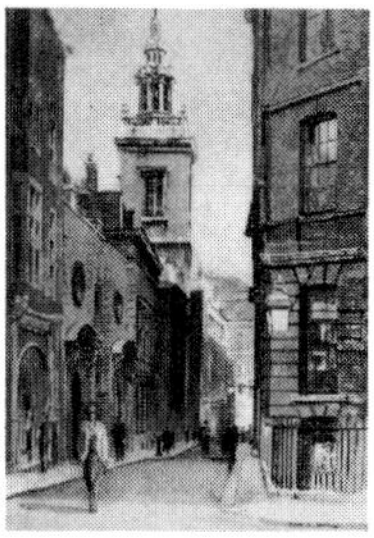

acc. no. 1278
St Michael Paternoster Royal (1939)

watercolour: $13\frac{7}{8} \times 10$ in.
signed: *Edith E. Thomas*

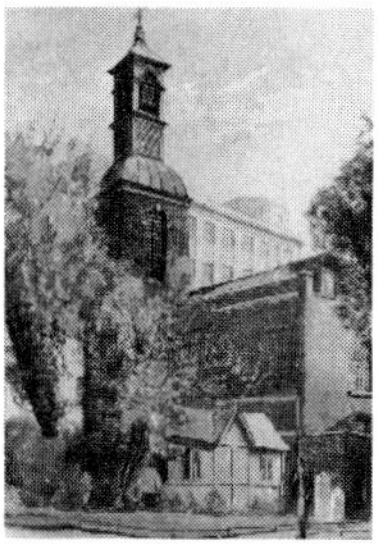

acc. no. 1279
St Botolph, Aldersgate Street (1939)

watercolour: $14\frac{1}{8} \times 10$ in.
signed: *Edith E. Thomas*; inscribed on verso: *S. BOTOLPH without ALDGATE / (Aldersgate Street.) / Dance. 1744. / In 1939*

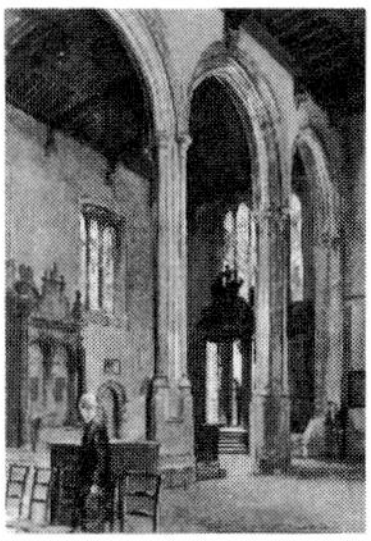

acc. no. 1280
Interior of St. Helen Bishopsgate (1939)

watercolour: $14\frac{1}{8} \times 10$ in.
signed: *Edith E. Thomas*; inscribed on verso: *S. HELEN. / (Bishopsgate) / XV. Cent. / "The Westminster Abbey of the City for / Ancient Tombs Has a Nun's grille.* and *In 1939*

acc. no. 1281
St Giles Cripplegate (1939)

watercolour: $14\frac{1}{8} \times 10$ in.
inscribed on verso: *S. GILES. CRIPPLEGATE. / Rebuilt in 1624. & / since many times restored / John Milton. / John Foxe. / Sir Martin Frobisher. buried here. Oliver Cromwell married.* and *Painted hurriedly & unfinished. / Nov. 1939.*

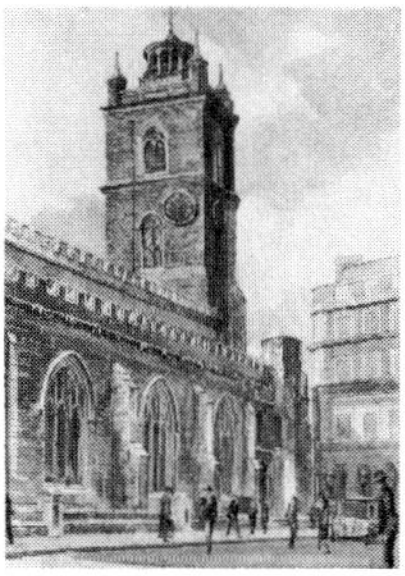

acc. no. 1415
St Margaret Pattens (1939)

watercolour: $13\frac{3}{4} \times 9\frac{5}{8}$ in.
signed: *Edith E. Thomas*; inscribed on verso: *S. MARGARET PATTENS / (Eastcheap.) / From Billingsgate / WREN 1687 / Spire 200 ft.*
Presented by Professor C. A. Pannett, 1950

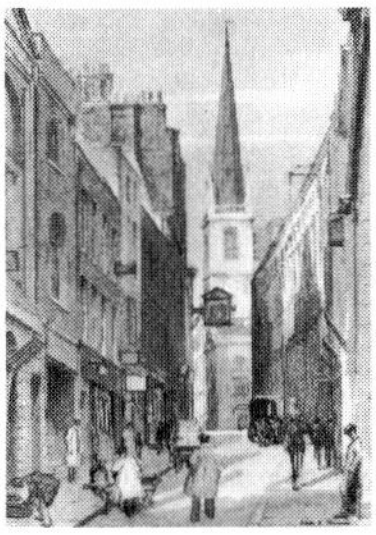

after Henry Thomson (1773–1843) by William Say (1768–1834)

acc. no. 1293
Crossing the Brook (*c.*1803)

mezzotint: $23\frac{1}{2} \times 15$ in.
lettered: *Painted by H. Thomson A. Engraved by W. Say / CROSSING the BROOK / To. Sir John. Fleming Leicester Bar.t this Print is respectfully inscribed by his most obedient & devoted humble Servant*
Presented by Lady Wakefield, 1944

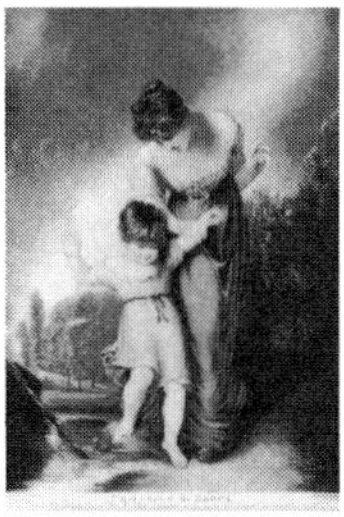

Sir James Thornhill (1675–1734)

acc. no. 1506
Sir Samuel Garrard, Lord Mayor 1709

oil on canvas: $29\frac{7}{8} \times 25$ in.
Presented by the Hon. Justice Holroyd Pearce, 1953

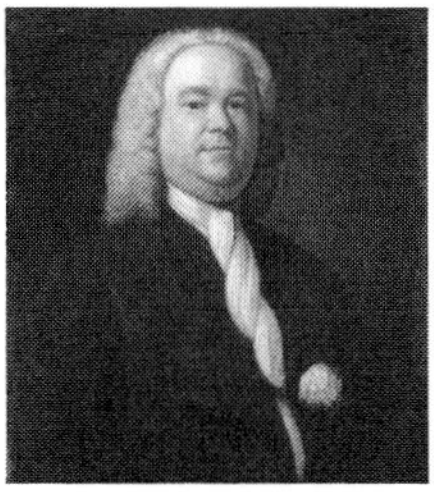

acc. no. 34
Allegory of London: London, Pallas Athene, Peace and Plenty (1725–7)

oil on canvas: 72 × 113 in. (oval)
Presented by the artist for the ceiling of the Aldermen's Court Room, 1727

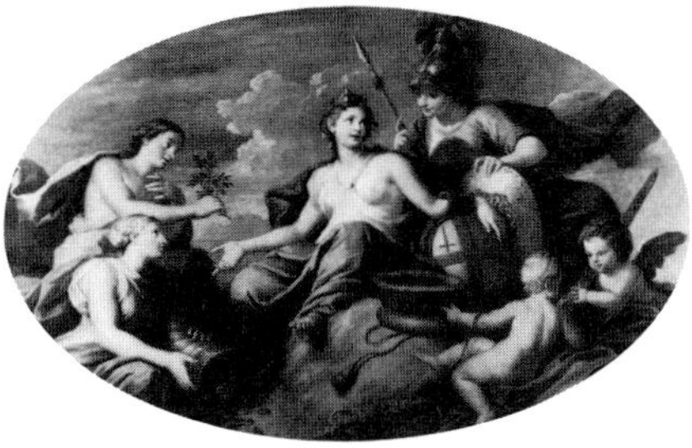

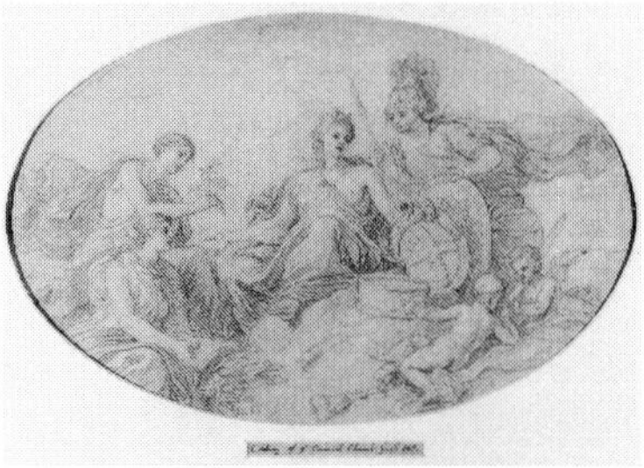

acc. no. 2329
Study for 'London, Pallas Athene, Peace and Plenty'

red chalk heightened with white: $12\frac{1}{4} \times 18$ in.
inscribed: *ceiling of ye Council Chamb. Guild Hall*
Purchased at Sotheby's Sale, 7 July 1983 (99)

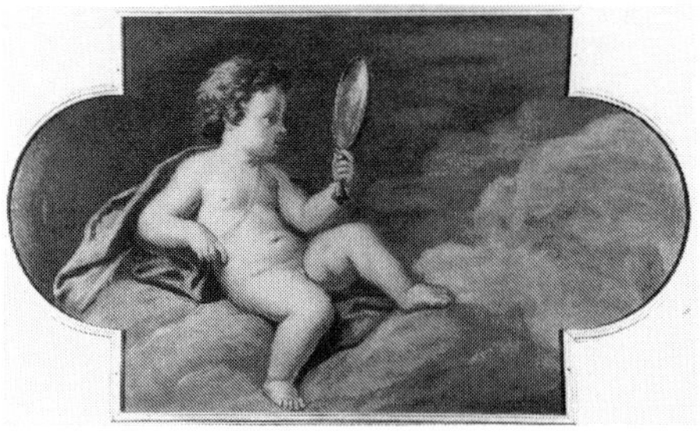

acc. no. 34a
Prudence (1725–7)

oil on canvas: 32×56 in.
Presented by the artist for the ceiling of the Aldermen's Court Room, 1727

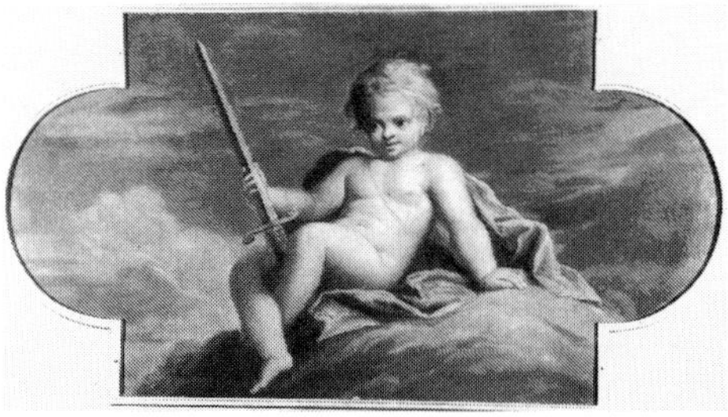

acc. no. 34b
Justice (1725–7)

oil on canvas: 32×56 in.
Presented by the artist for the ceiling of the Aldermen's Court Room, 1727

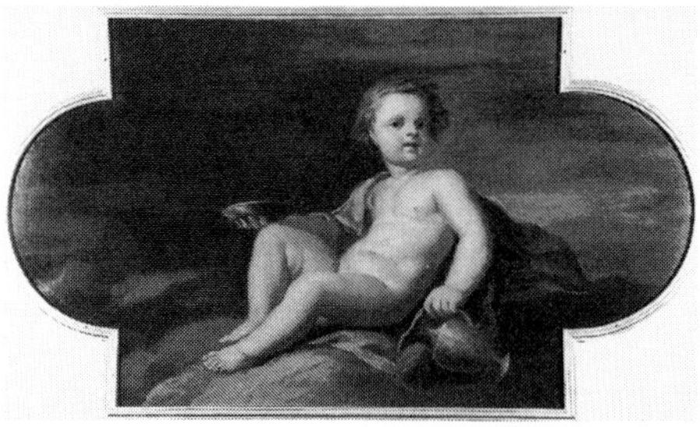

acc. no. 34c
Temperance (1725–7)

oil on canvas: 32×56 in.
Presented by the artist for the ceiling of the Aldermen's Court Room, 1727

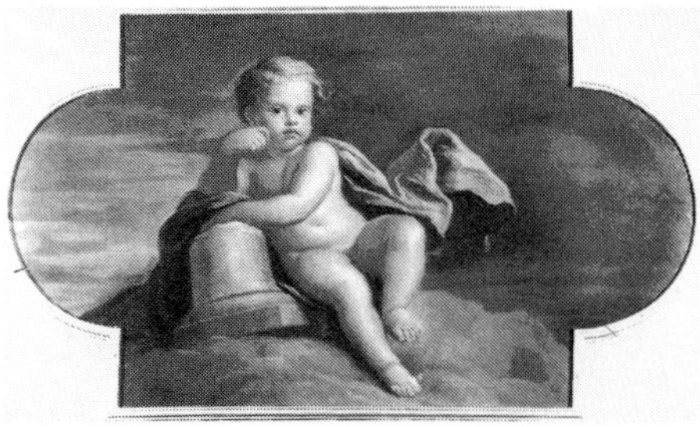

acc. no. 34d
Fortitude (1725–7)

oil on canvas: 32×56 in.
Presented by the artist for the ceiling of the Aldermen's Court Room, 1727

William Eric Thorp (b.1901)

acc. no. 1640
Thames Barges (1962)
oil on hardboard: 14 × 18 in.
signed: *W ERIC THORP*
Purchased from the artist, 1962

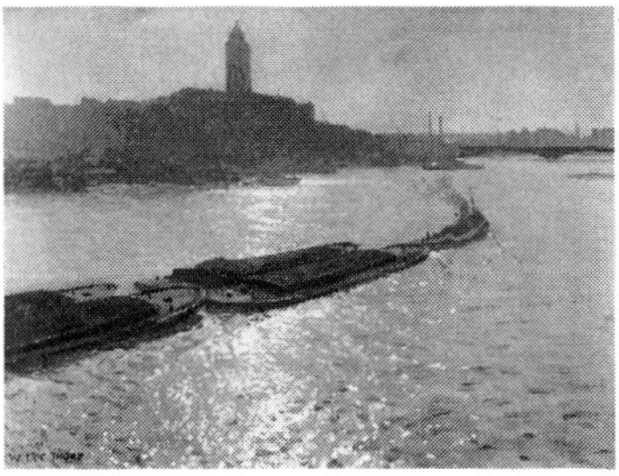

acc. no. 1825
The S.S. Katharine leaving the Pool of London (1969)
oil on hardboard: $18\frac{1}{4}$ × 26 in.
signed: *W ERIC THORP*
Purchased from the artist, 1969

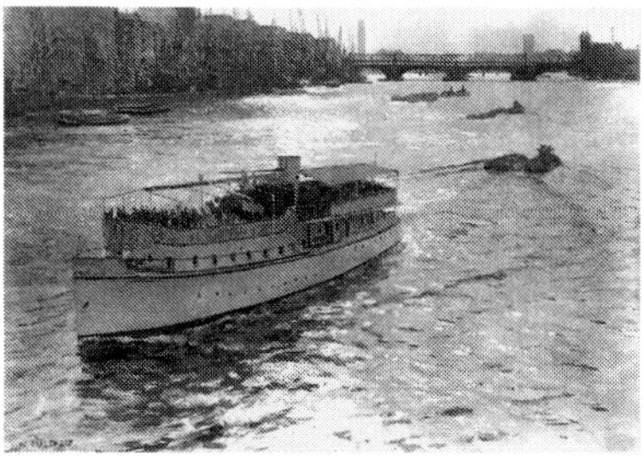

acc. no. 2157
Thames Barges (1974)
oil on hardboard: 28 × 36 in.
signed: *W.ERIC THORP*
Purchased from the artist, 1974

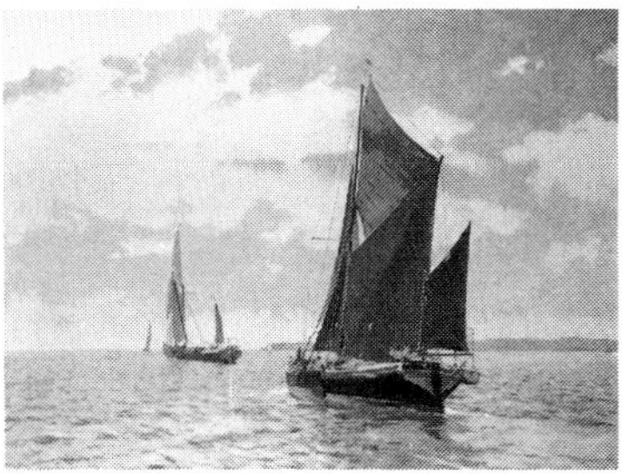

John Thurston (1774–1822)

acc. no. 510
The Stolen Lyre
pencil and watercolour: $3\frac{3}{8}$ × $2\frac{3}{4}$ in.
Presented by Felix Joseph, 1890

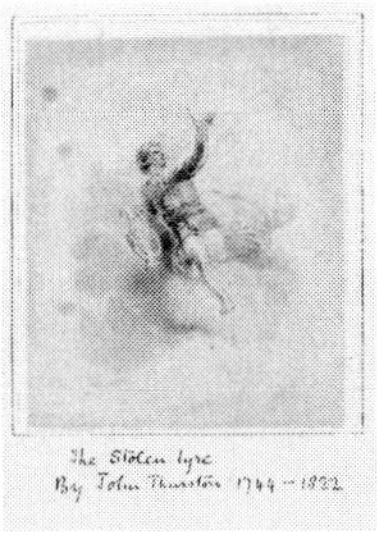

H. E. Tidmarsh (*fl.* 1880–1925)

acc. no. 1339
Fleet Street Looking East (1898)
watercolour: $30\frac{1}{2}$ × $19\frac{3}{4}$ in.
signed and dated: *H.E. TIDMARSH / 1898*
Presented by Frederick E. Tidmarsh, 1945

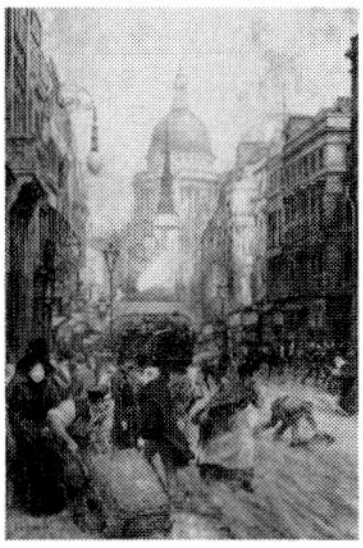

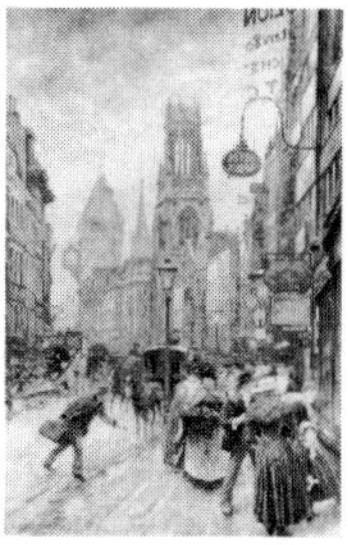

acc. no. 1340
Fleet Street Looking West (1899)

watercolour: $30\frac{1}{2} \times 19\frac{3}{4}$ in.
signed and dated: *H.E. TIDMARSH / 1899*
Presented by Frederick E. Tidmarsh, 1945

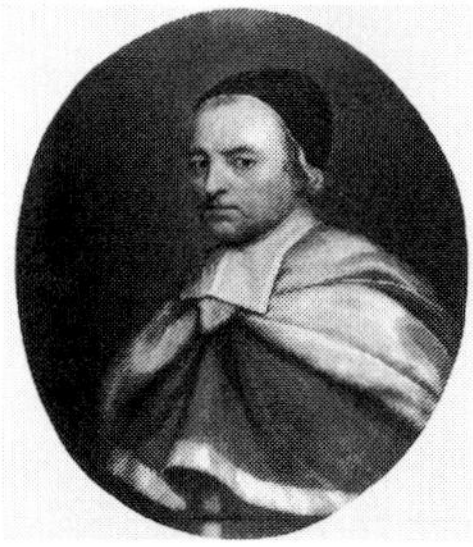

Henry Tilson (1659–1695)

acc. no. 107
Sir William Dolben, Recorder of London 1676

oil on canvas: 30 × 25 in. (oval)
signed very indistinctly
Presented by Sir William Heygate, 1843

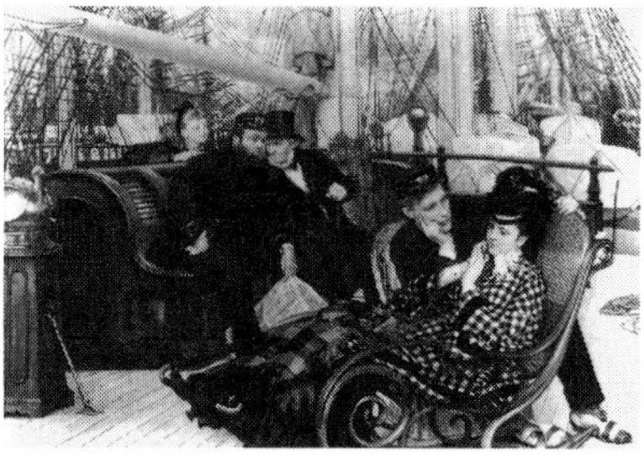

James Jacques Joseph Tissot (1836–1902)

acc. no. 737
The Last Evening (1873)

oil on canvas: $28\frac{1}{2} \times 40\frac{1}{2}$ in.
signed and dated: *f. 1873 J.J. Tissot*
Bequeathed by Charles Gassiot, 1902

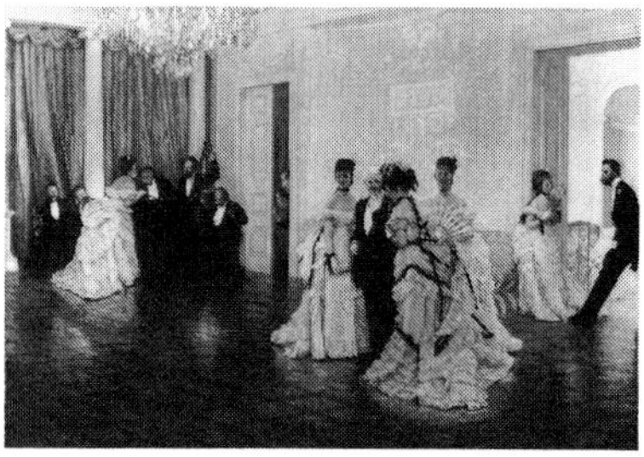

acc. no. 738
Too Early (1873)

oil on canvas: 28 × 40 in.
signed and dated: *J.J. Tissot / f. 1873*
Bequeathed by Charles Gassiot, 1902

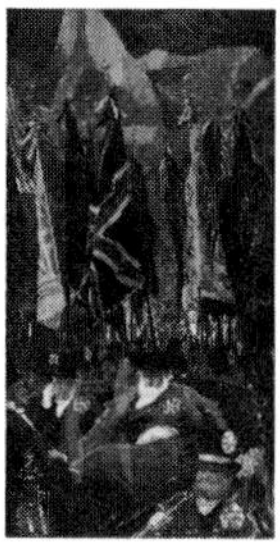

acc. no. 1909
The Lord Mayor's Procession (? *c.*1879)

oil on canvas: $84\frac{1}{2} \times 43$ in.
Purchased from Mme. Léonce Bénédite, 1972

Charles Tomkins (1757–1823)

acc. no. 2260
Three Cranes Wharf (1801)

pen and ink and watercolour: $5 \times 7\frac{7}{8}$ in.
signed and dated: *C Tomkins 1801*
Presented by Miss Helen Guiterman, 1985

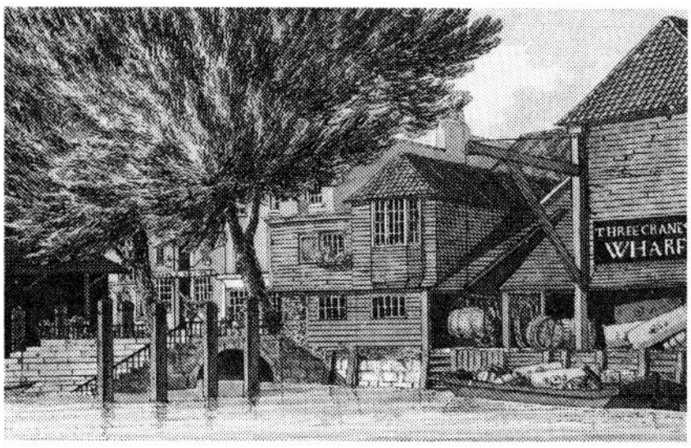

Francis William Topham (1808–77)

acc. no. 520
The Shepherd's Meal (1844)

watercolour: 30 × 25 in.
signed and dated: *F W Topham / 1844*
Bequeathed by John Kirchner, 1891

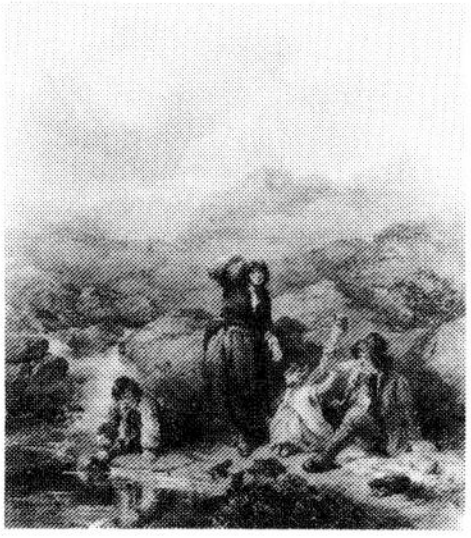

Frank William Warwick Topham (1838–1929)

acc. no. 999
Rescued from the Plague (1898)

oil on canvas: 72 × 45 in.
signed and dated: *Frank W. W. Topham 1898*
Presented by the artist, 1919

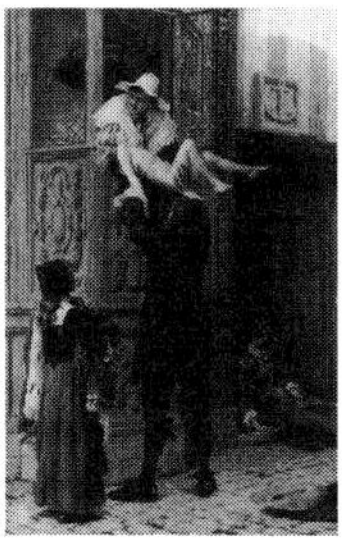

Feliks Topolski (b.1907)

acc. no. 1358
Home Guards versus Canadians (1941)

watercolour: 22 × 30 in.
signed, inscribed and dated: *Feliks Topolski / City of London "invasion" final / Home Guards v Canadians Summer 1941*
Allocated by the War Artists Advisory Committee, 1947

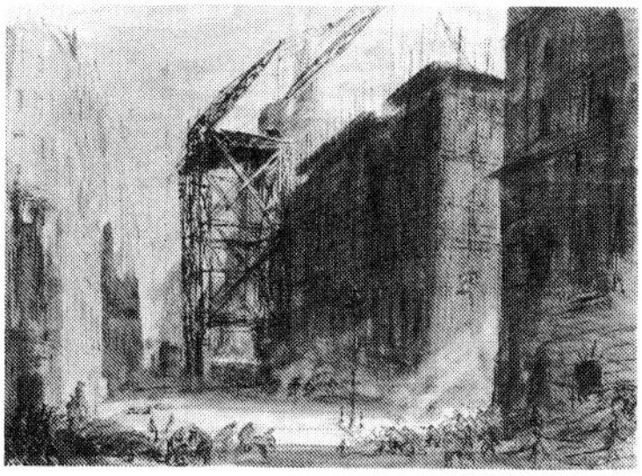

William Townsend (1909–73)

acc. no. 3506
St Mary Aldermanbury (1947)

oil on canvas: 17 × 15 in.
Purchased from Mrs. Mary Townsend, 1984

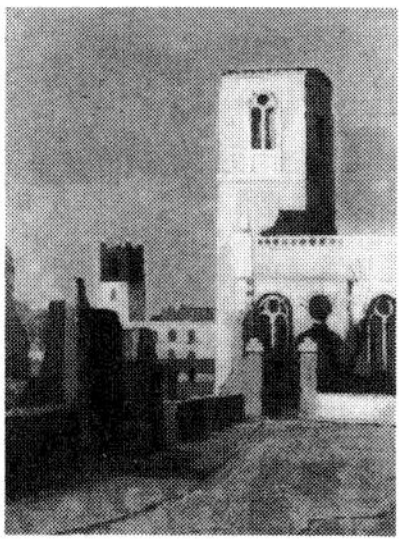

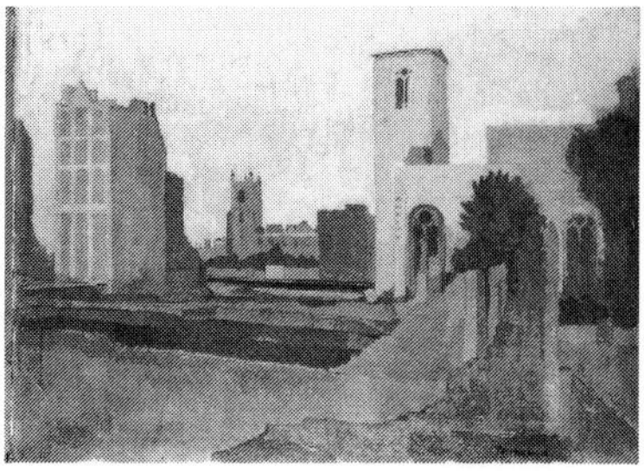

acc. no. 3507
City Churches – St Mary Aldermanbury and St Alban Wood Street (1947)

oil on canvas: 18 × 24 in.
Purchased from Mrs. Mary Townsend, 1984

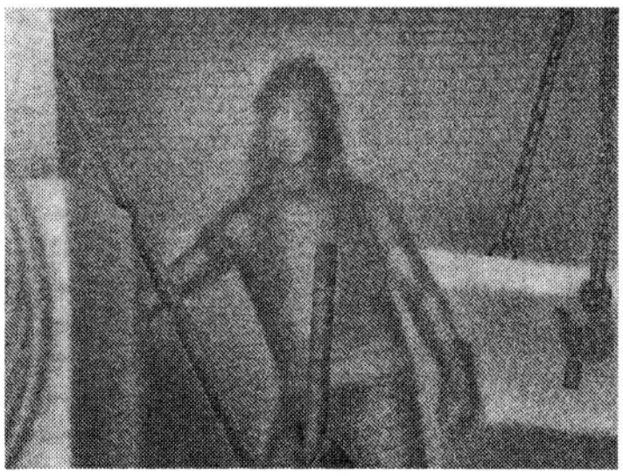

Claudio Tozu (20th C)

acc. no. 2262
Steelworker (1978)

liquitex on canvas: 31 × 39¾ in.
signed and dated: *Clau Tozu / 78*; inscribed on verso: *Operario – Aço 1978 80 × 102 cms Liquitex s/tela / Clau Tozu / 78 / Claudio Tozu São Paulo 1978*
Presented by the City of São Paulo, 1978

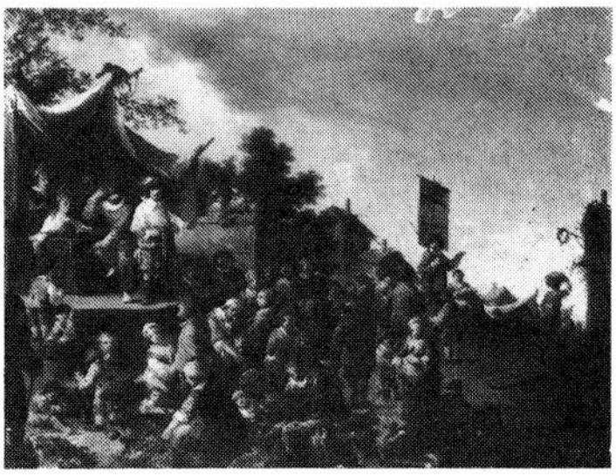

attributed to Johann Georg Trautmann (1713–69)

acc. no. 379
Village Merrymaking (1763)

oil on copper: 12 × 16 in.
signed (mono) and dated: TM 1763
Bequeathed by William Dunnett, 1888

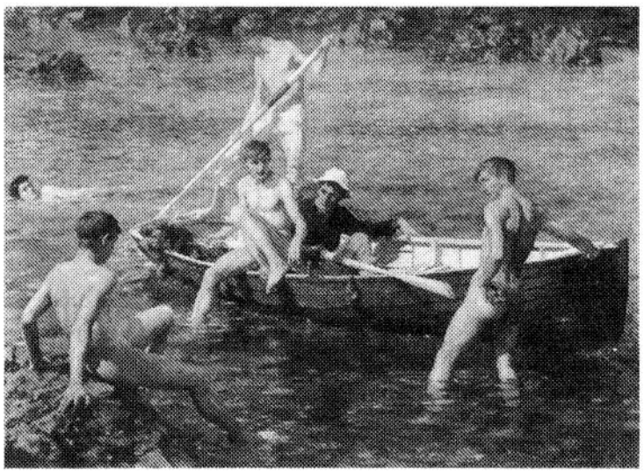

Henry Scott Tuke (1858–1929)

acc. no. 635
Ruby, Gold and Malachite (1902)

oil on canvas: 46 × 62½ in.
signed and dated: *H.S. Tuke 1902*
Purchased from the artist, 1902

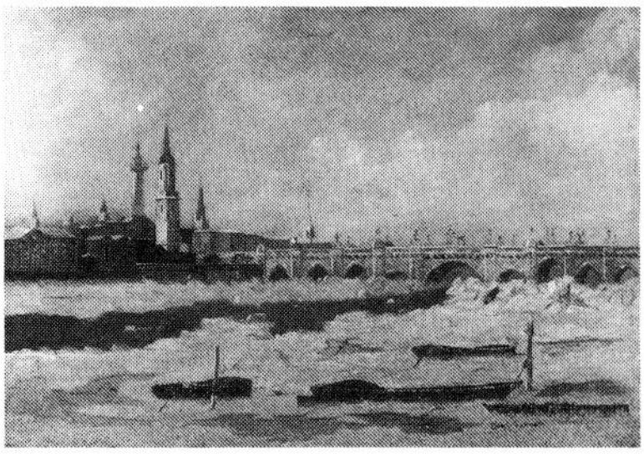

Daniel Turner (*c.*1775–1815)

acc. no. 859
London Bridge during the Frost of 1795–1796

oil on panel: 8¾ × 12¾ in.
signed: *DAN^{L} TURNER*
Presented by George and J. B. Hilditch, 1908

acc. no. 1096
Blackfriars from Southwark

oil on canvas: $11\frac{1}{2} \times 19\frac{3}{4}$ in.
Presented by F. W. Hubbard, 1935

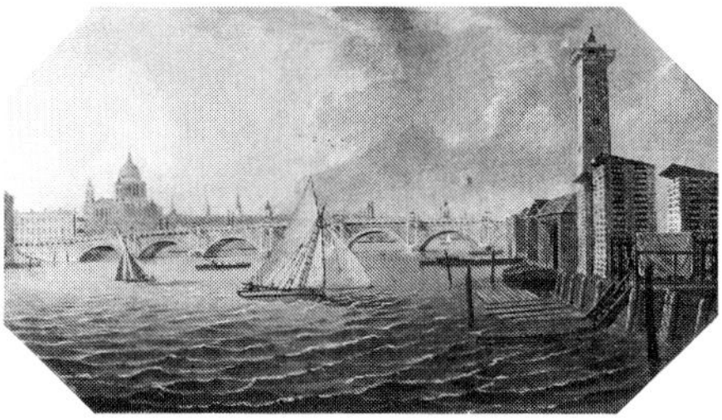

acc. no. 1829
The procession of Barges attending Lord Nelson's Body from Greenwich Hospital, January 8 1806

oil on panel: $18\frac{1}{2} \times 26\frac{1}{2}$ in.
signed: *DAN^L. TURNER*
Purchased from the Leger Gallery, 1969

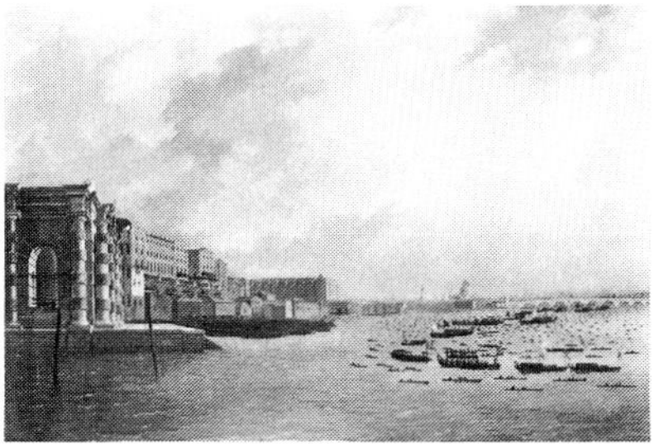

acc. no. 1799
Adelphi Terrace and York Watergate

oil on canvas: $27\frac{1}{2} \times 35\frac{3}{4}$ in.
signed: *D. Turner*
Purchased from the Leger Gallery, 1968

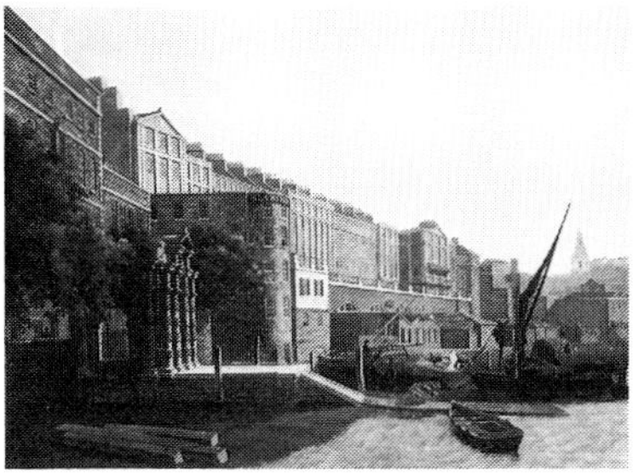

Joseph William Mallord Turner (1775–1851)

acc. no. 1259
Hythe, Kent (1824)

watercolour: $5\frac{1}{2} \times 9$ in.
Presented by Lady Wakefield, 1943

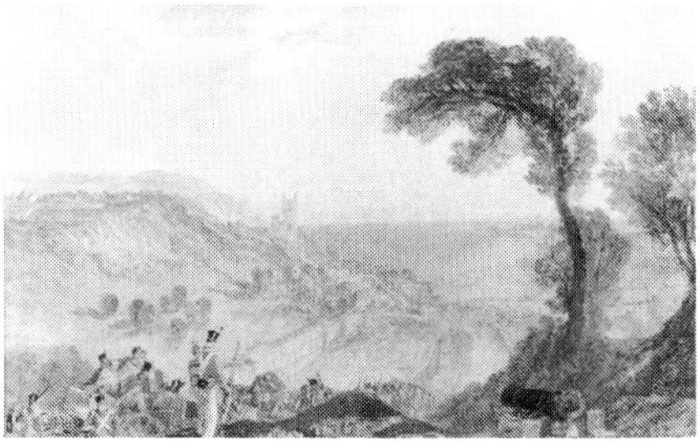

W. Turner (19th C)

acc. no. 3539
Man with a Top Hat (1851)

pen and ink: $11\frac{1}{8} \times 8$ in.
signed and dated: *W. Turner 1851.*
Presented by Miss Helen Guiterman, 1985

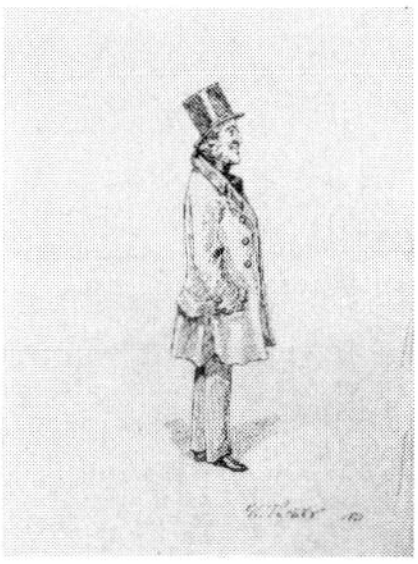

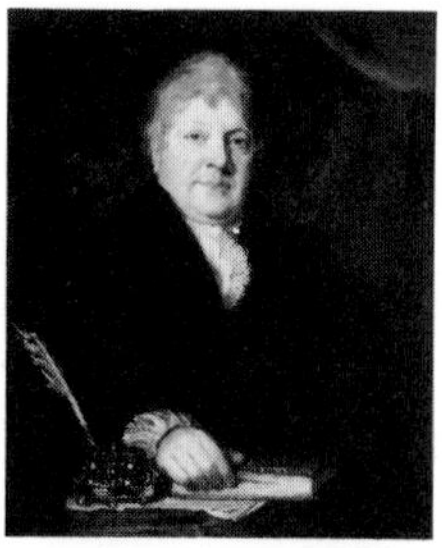

Works by **Unknown artists**
arranged by order of accession

acc. no. 101
Henry Woodthorpe, Town Clerk 1801–25
oil on canvas: 29 × 25 in.
Presented by the sitter's son, Henry Woodthorpe, 1837

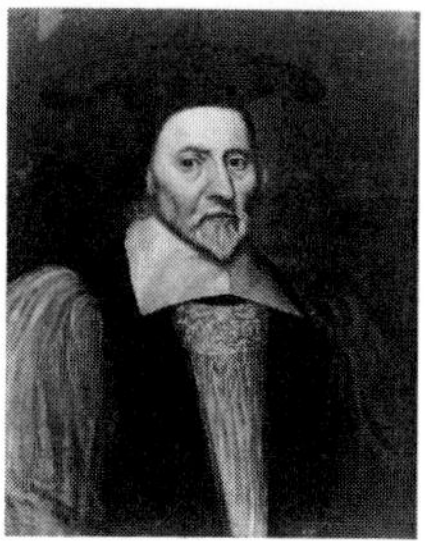

acc. no. 123
Robert Sanderson, Bishop of Lincoln
oil on canvas: 26 × 20 in.
Presented by Miss Beata Elizabeth Macaulay, 1850

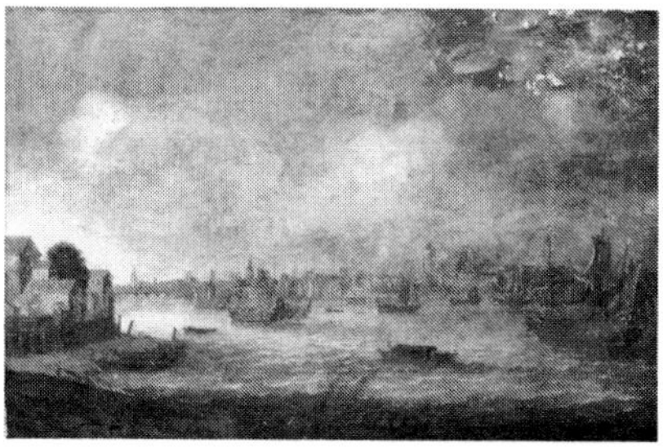

acc. no. 159
The Thames from Dockhead
oil on canvas: 24 × 36 in.
Presented by Francis Fuller, 1856

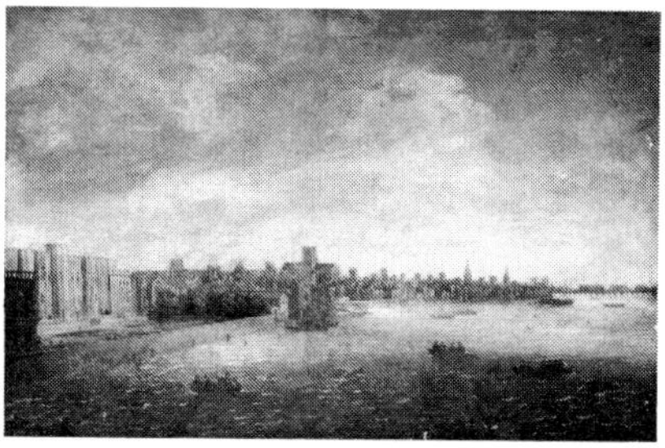

acc. no. 160
The Thames from Bankside, showing Bridewell and the Entrance to the River Fleet
oil on canvas: 24 × 36 in.
Presented by Francis Fuller, 1856

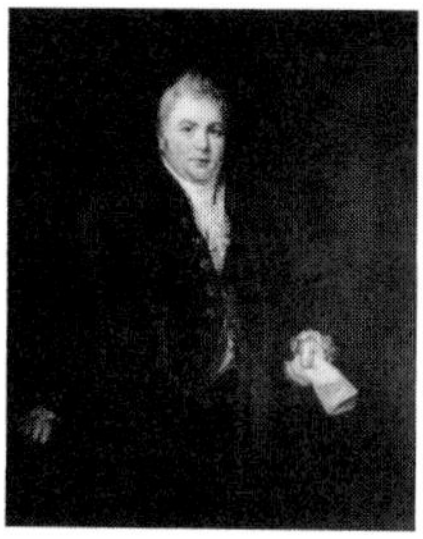

acc. no. 285
Sir Richard Phillips, Sheriff, 1807
oil on canvas: 50 × 40 in.
Presented by the Rev. G. E. Phillips, 1885

acc. no. 287
Inside the Debtors Prison, Whitecross Street
oil on paper laid on board: $8\frac{3}{4} \times 9\frac{3}{4}$ in.
inscribed on verso: *The Property of James Ward CC 1853–4 for / the ward of Aldersgate*
Presented by Miss Ward, 1885

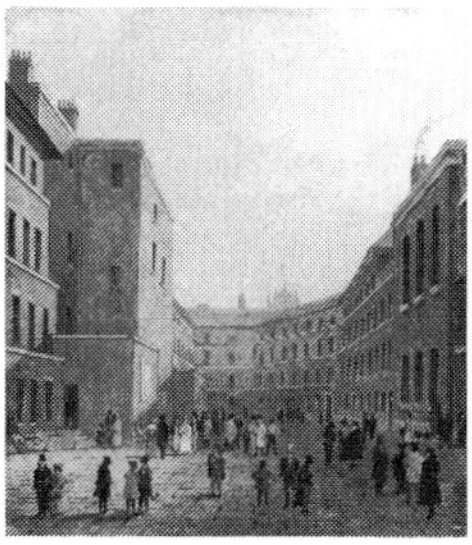

acc. no. 288
Mansion House, c.1750
oil on canvas: 32 × 39 in.
Purchased, 1885

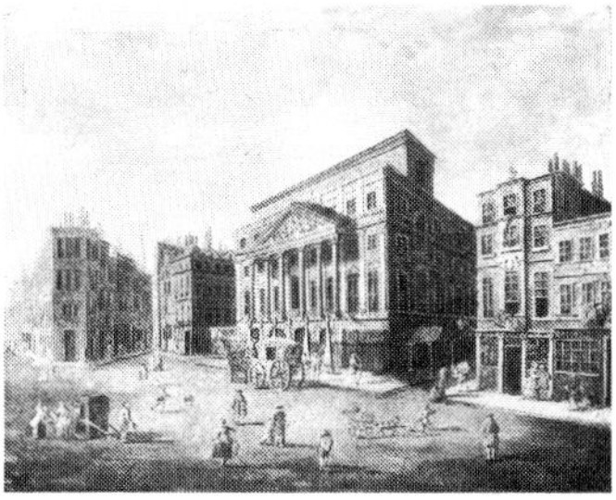

acc. no. 362
Diana in the Chase
oil on canvas: 39 × 71 in.
Bequeathed by William Dunnett, 1888

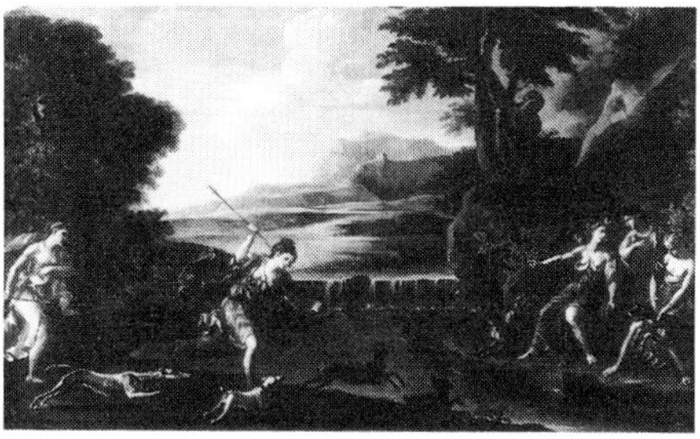

acc. no. 376
The Annunciation
oil on panel: 8 × 10 in.
Bequeathed by William Dunnett, 1888

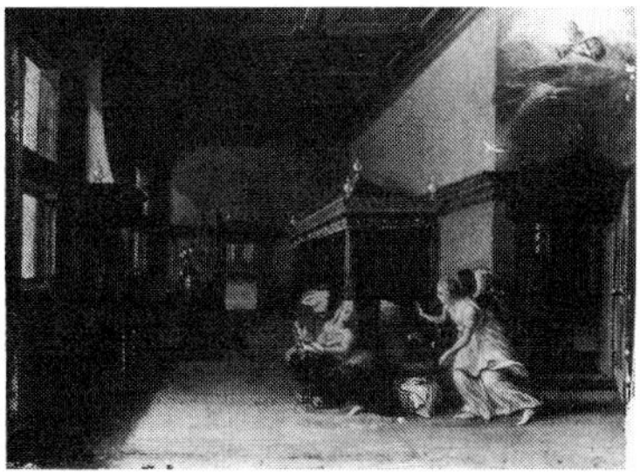

acc. no. 378
The Ferry by Moonlight
oil on panel: 9 × 13 in.
Bequeathed by William Dunnett, 1888

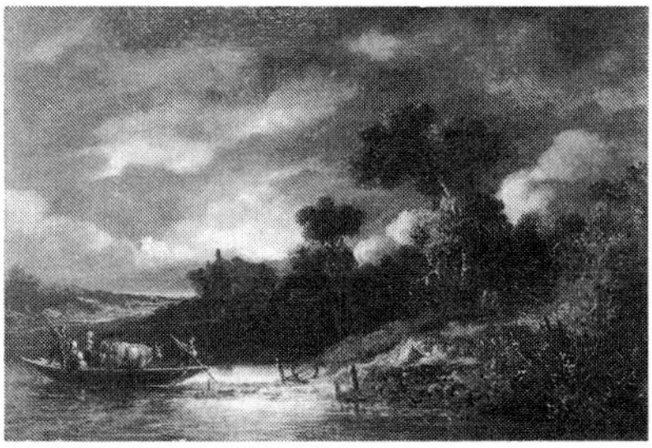

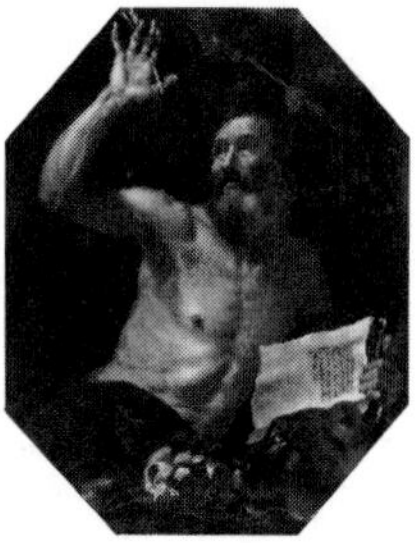

acc. no. 387
St Jerome
oil on canvas: 44 × 35 in.
Bequeathed by William Dunnett, 1888

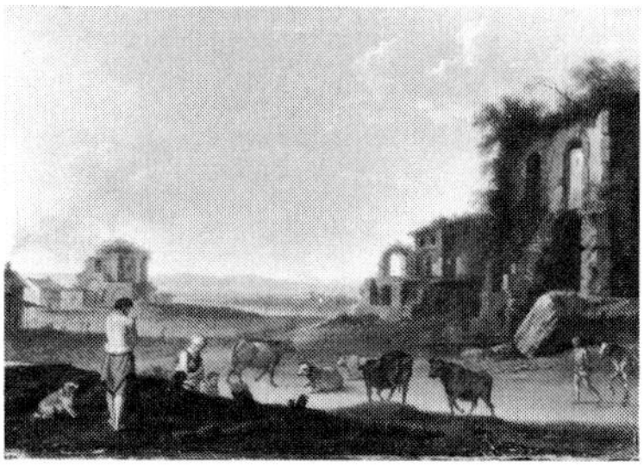

acc. no. 393
Landscape with Cattle
oil on panel: 8 × 11 in.
Bequeathed by William Dunnett, 1888

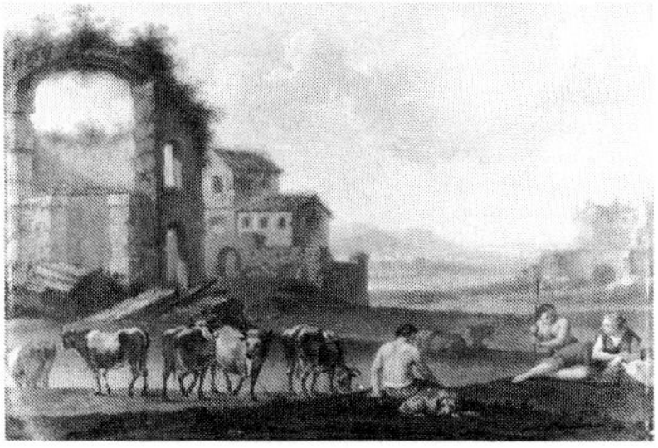

acc. no. 396
Landscape with Cattle
oil on panel: 8 × 12 in.
Bequeathed by William Dunnett, 1888

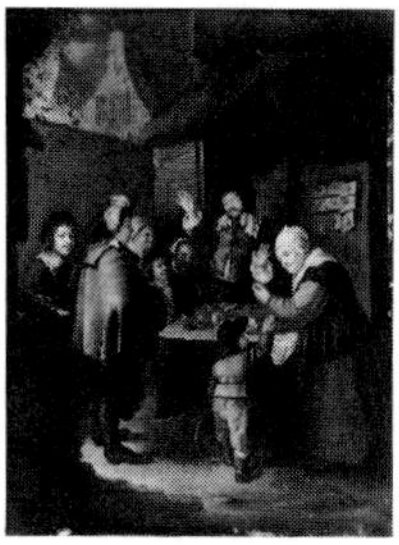

acc. no. 400
The Charlatan
oil on canvas: 18 × 13 in.
Bequeathed by William Dunnett, 1888

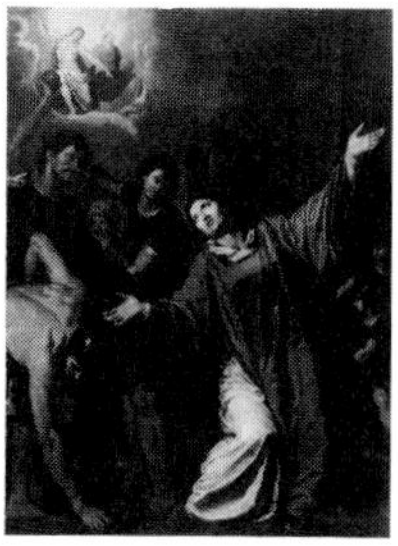

acc. no. 416
The Stoning of St Stephen
oil on canvas: 58 × 44 in.
Bequeathed by William Dunnett, 1888

acc. no. 419
King David
oil on canvas: 37 × 50 in.
Bequeathed by William Dunnett, 1888

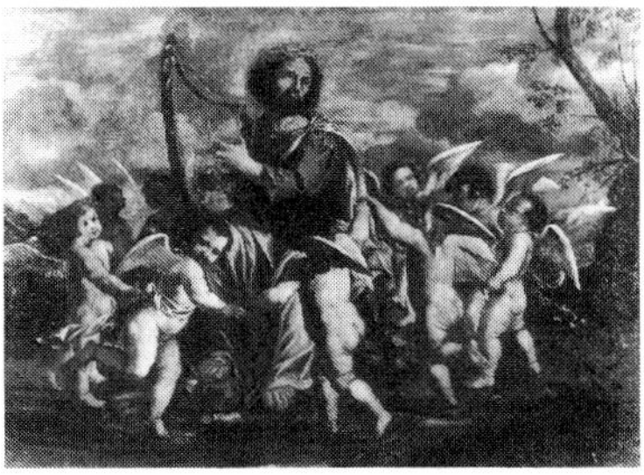

acc. no. 430
Three Putti playing by a Stream
watercolour: 9 × 12 in.
inscribed on mount: *Albano*
Bequeathed by William Dunnett, 1888

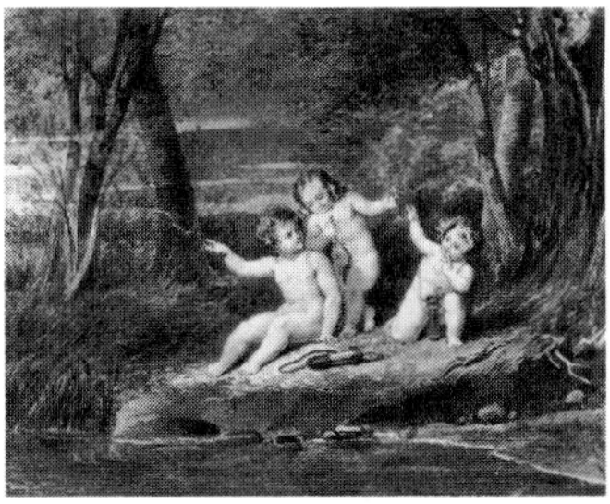

acc. no. 519
Banquet in the Guildhall
oil on copper: 7 × 9 in.
Presented by the Rev. A. E. Clementi-Smith, 1891

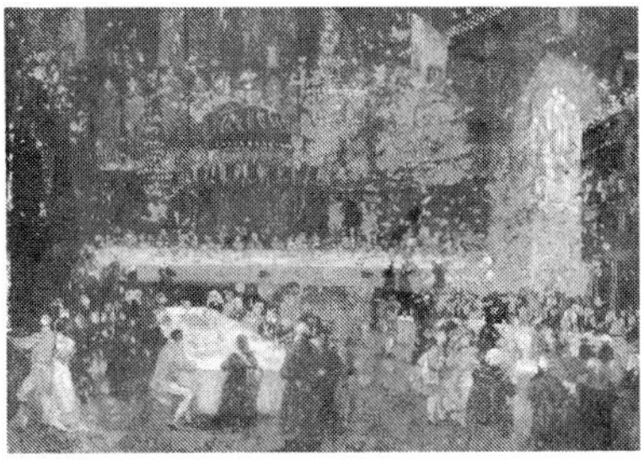

acc. no. 622
Gregory Fiennes, 10th Lord Dacre
oil on panel: 23 × 20 in.
dated: *1590* and inscribed: AE^{T} *50*
Presented by the Emanuel Hospital Committee, 1900

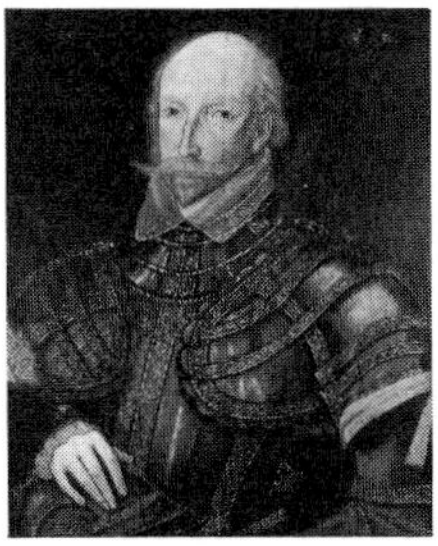

acc. no. 984
John Strange Williams and Sarah Ann Williams
oil on canvas: 60 × 45 in.
Presented by Mrs. Brand, 1917

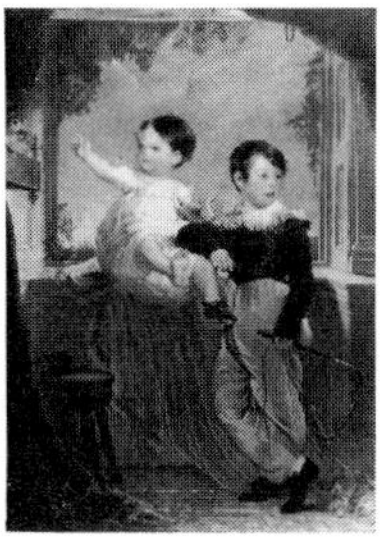

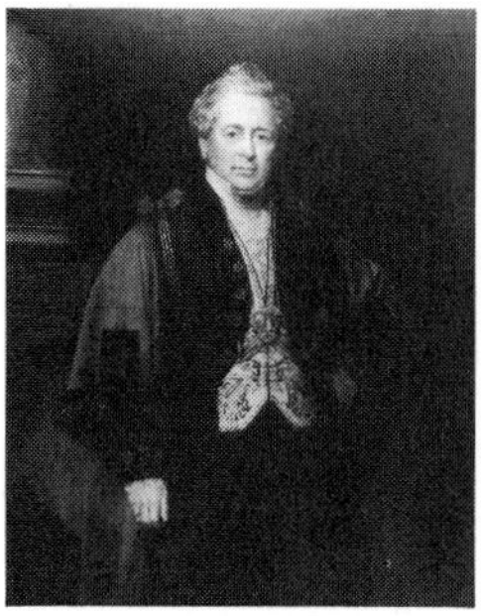

acc. no. 985
William Hunter, Lord Mayor 1852
oil on canvas: 50 × 40 in.
Presented by Mrs. Brand, 1917

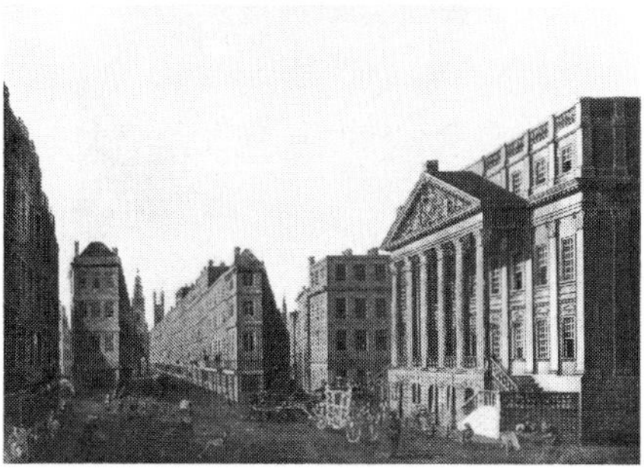

acc. no. 1065
The Mansion House, Lombard Street and Cornhill
oil on canvas: $19 \times 24\frac{1}{4}$ in. (sight)
Presented by Sir Abe Bailey, 1929

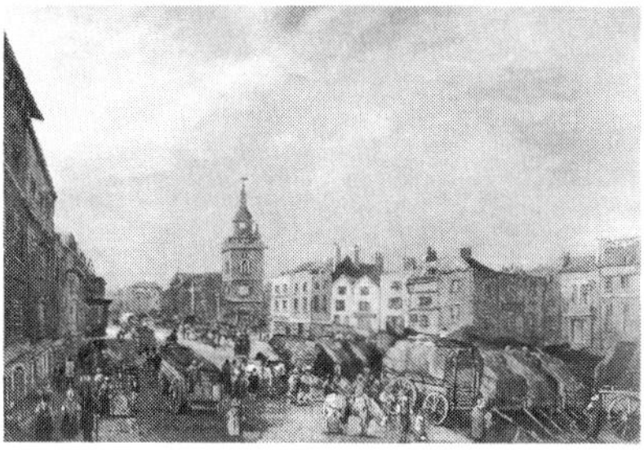

acc. no. 1071
The Hay Market, Whitechapel, Looking East (*c.*1835)
oil on panel: 15 × 23 in.
Purchased, 1930

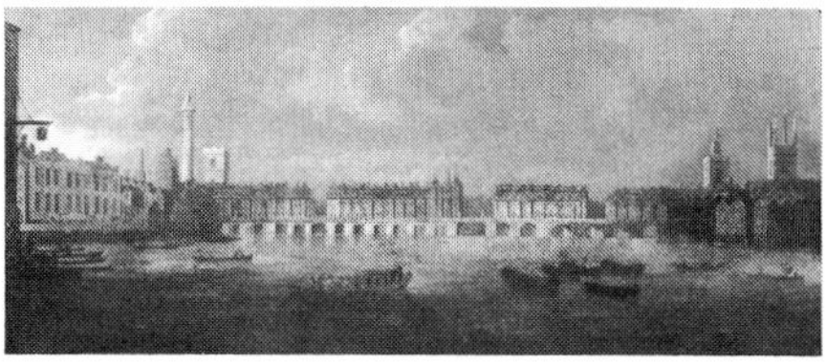

acc. no. 1077
West Side of Old London Bridge
oil on canvas: $57\frac{1}{2} \times 26\frac{1}{2}$ in.
Presented by John Newman, 1931

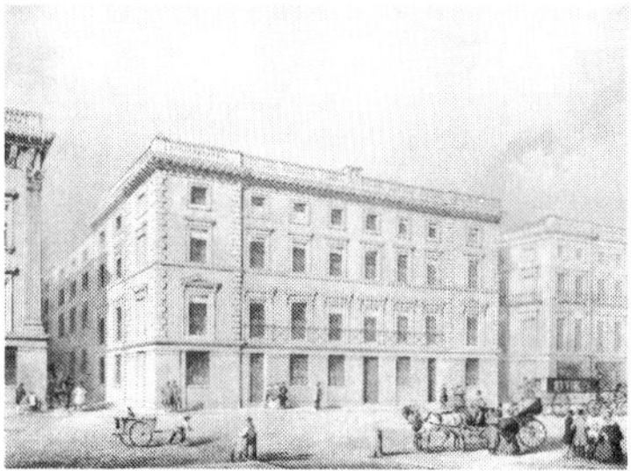

acc. no. 1101
West End of Moorgate Street (*c.*1840)
watercolour: 25 × 33 in.
Purchased, 1935

acc. no. 1245
Sir Robert Carden, Lord Mayor 1857
oil on canvas: 40 × 30 in.
Purchased from G. N. Jameson, 1932

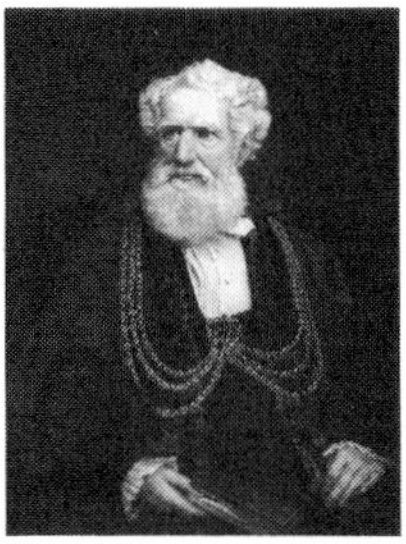

acc. no. 1299
Portrait of a lady, called 'The Countess of Ossory'
oil on canvas: 50 × 40 in.
Presented by Lady Wakefield, 1944

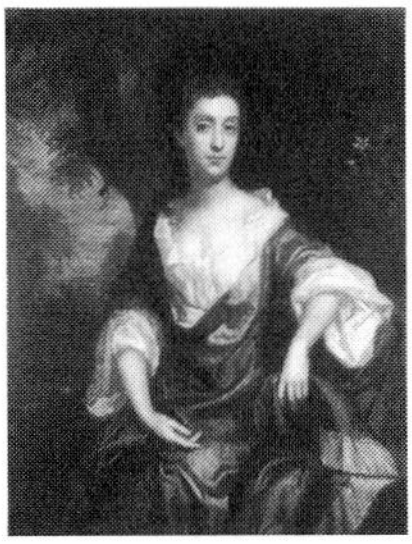

acc. no. 1302
Henry, 8th Viscount Dillon
oil on canvas: 50 × 40 in.
Presented by Lady Wakefield, 1944

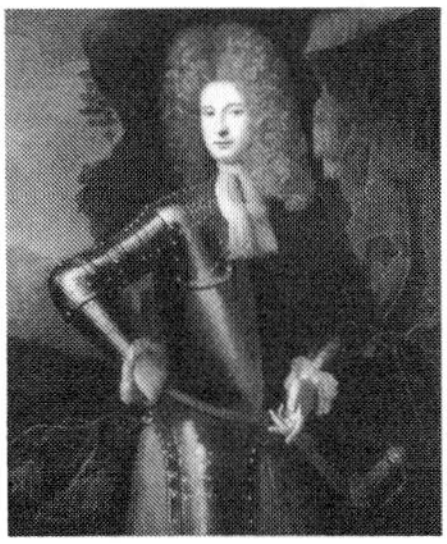

acc. no. 1304
Portrait of a Lady
oil on canvas: 46 × 36 in.
Presented by Lady Wakefield, 1944

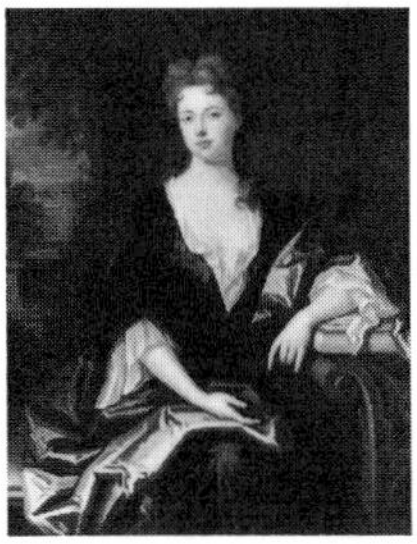

acc. no. 1323
Sir Christopher Clitherow, Lord Mayor 1635
oil on canvas: 30 × 25 in.
Purchased from C. Howes, 1945

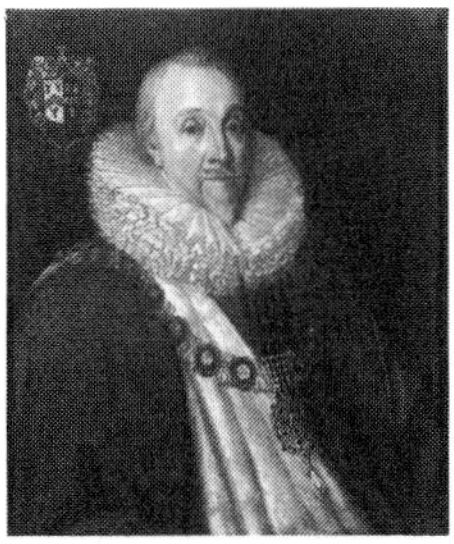

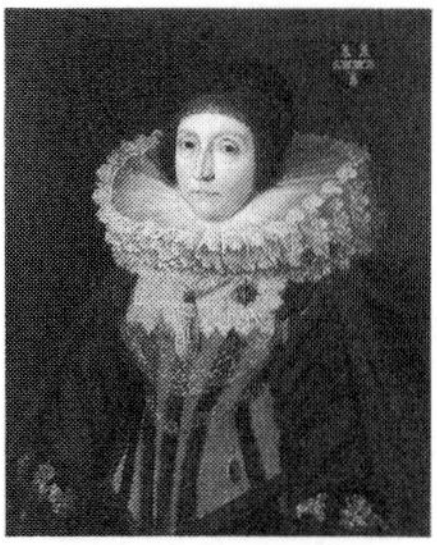

acc. no. 1324
Lady Mary Clitherow
oil on canvas: 30 × 25 in.
Purchased from C. Howes, 1945

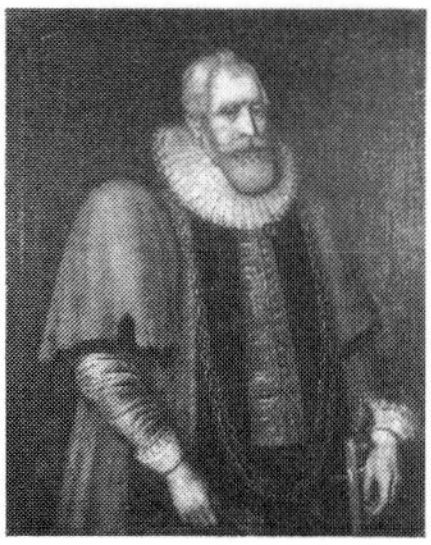

acc. no. 1345
Sir Thomas Myddleton, Lord Mayor 1613
oil on canvas: 45 × 35 in.
Presented by Sir John Lawes, 1979

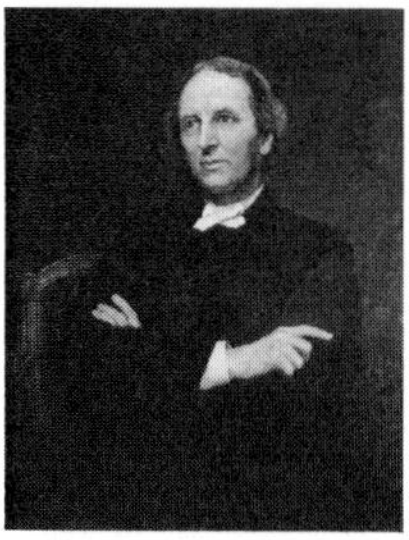

acc. no. 1350
E. A. Abbott
oil on canvas: 36 × 30 in.
Presented by old pupils and friends to the City of London School, date unknown

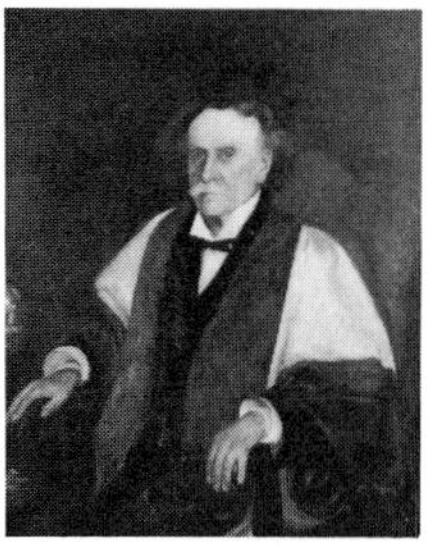

acc. no. 1376
Dr. William Hayman Cummings, Principal of the Guildhall School of Music 1896–1910
oil on canvas: 41 × 32½ in.
Presented to the Guildhall School of Music by the Incorporated Society of Musicians, 1948

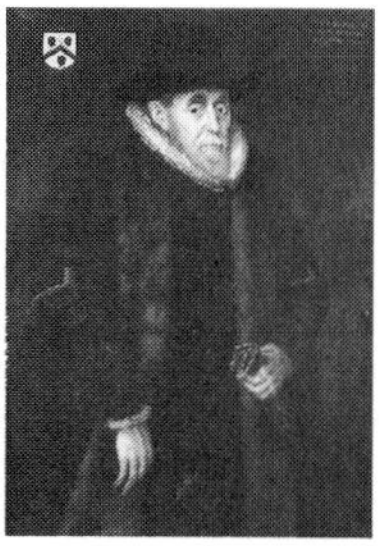

acc. no. 1494
Edmund More (1610)
oil on panel: 45 × 31⅝ in.
inscribed: *AETATIS SUAE 80 ANNO DOMMINI 1610*
Presented by A. C. Borrett in Memory of Major A. C. J. Borrett, 1953

acc. no. 1495
Sir Allen Cotton, Lord Mayor 1624
oil on panel: 44 × 33½ in.
inscribed: *AE^ts 68 / 1627* over an earlier inscription: *AETAT. SUA. 55 / ANO DOMI 1612* and: *Allen. / Cotton.*
Presented by A. C. Borrett in memory of Major A. C. J. Borrett, 1953

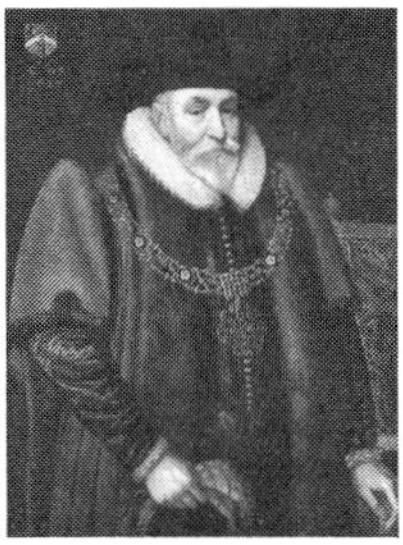

acc. no. 1496
Margaret Cotton
oil on panel: 45 × 32⅝ in.
inscribed: *Margaret / Cotton*
Presented by A. C. Borrett in memory of Major A. C. J. Borrett, 1953

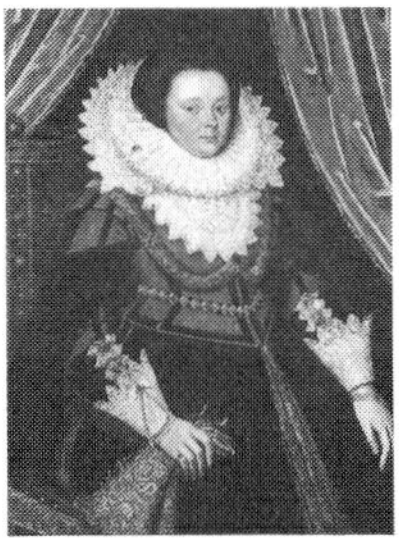

acc. no. 1517
John Charles Kitching, Last Tide Carpenter of London Bridge
oil on canvas: 30 × 25 in.
Presented by Miss Clare Rose, 1955

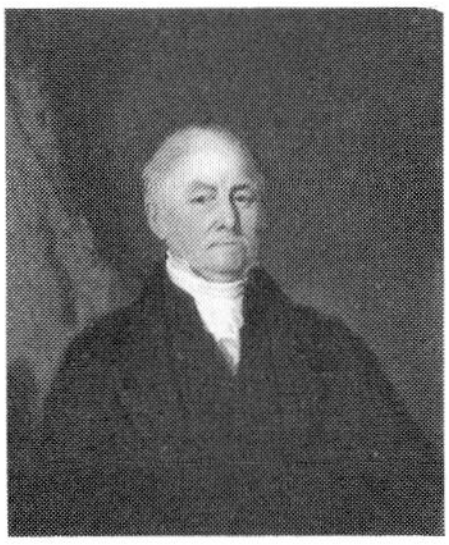

acc. no. 1535
Sir William Gore, Lord Mayor 1701
oil on canvas: 49¼ × 39¾ in.
inscribed: *Sr Wm Gore / Ld Mayor of London / d. Jan 1707*
Purchased from Appleby Brothers, 1956

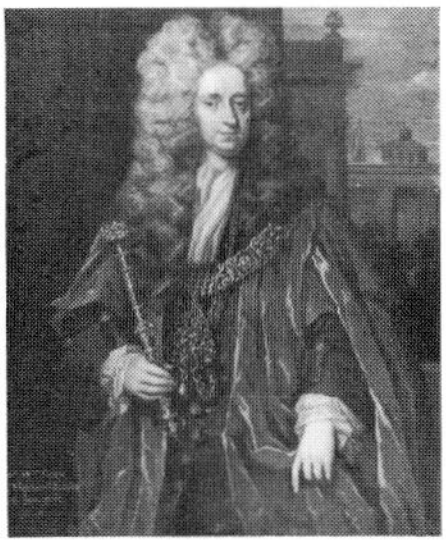

acc. no. 1536
Lady Gore
oil on canvas: 49½ × 39¾ in.
inscribed: *Eliz^th D^r of Walter Hampton / & Maria Mellish of Sandersted / Wife of Sr Wm Gore / d. Mar. 1705.*
Purchased from Appleby Brothers, 1956

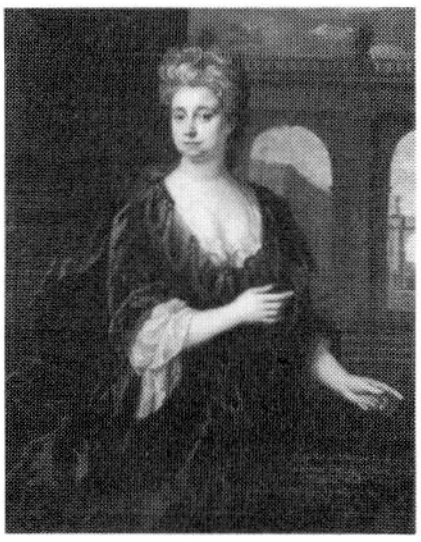

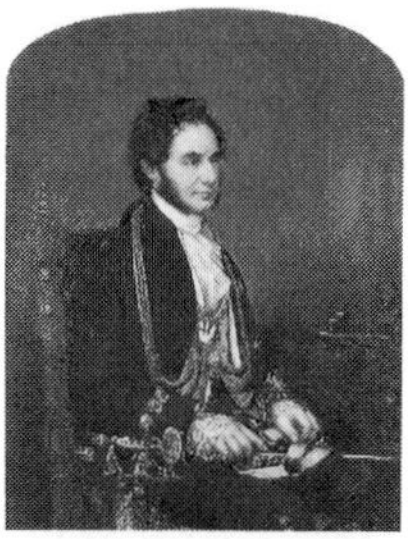

acc. no. 1540
Thomas Cotterell, Sheriff 1851
watercolour over photographic process on card: $7\frac{7}{8} \times 5\frac{7}{8}$ in.
Presented by Sir L. Thulford, 1956

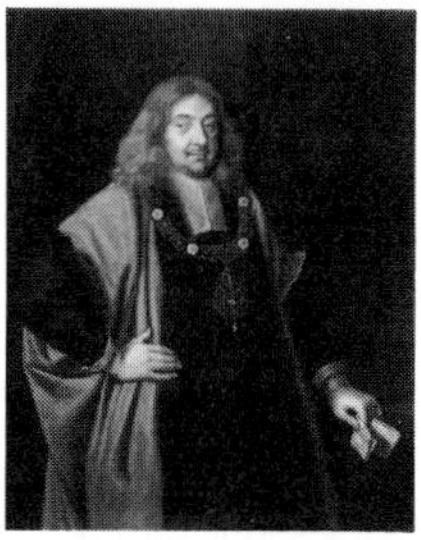

acc. no. 1548
Sir William Hooker, Lord Mayor 1673
oil on canvas: $50 \times 40\frac{1}{4}$ in.
Purchased from W. J. Goldsmith, 1957

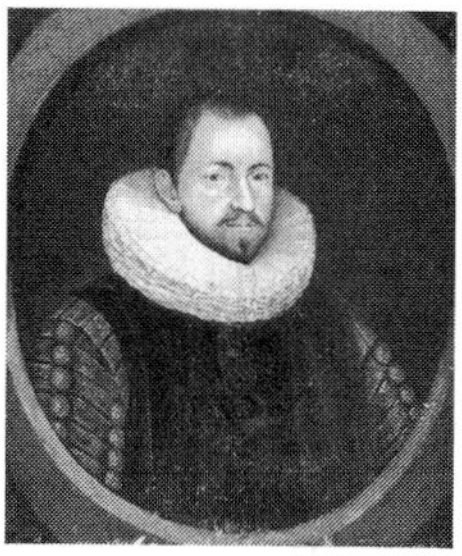

acc. no. 1562
William Holyday, Alderman of Cripplegate
oil on canvas: $29\frac{7}{8} \times 25$ in.
inscribed: *Gul Holyday / Ald'rms Londinfs*
Purchased from N. C. E. Ashton, 1958

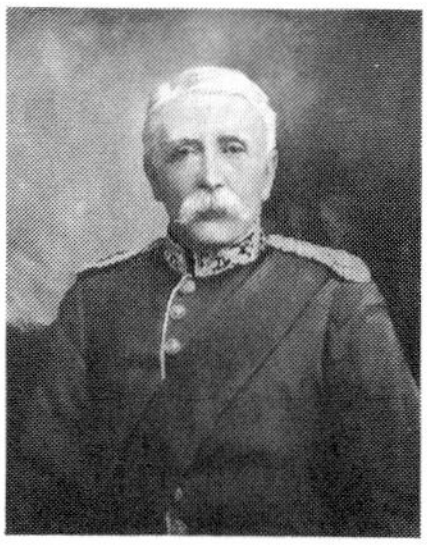

acc. no. 1570
Alderman Charles Jones Cuthbertson
oil on canvas: 30×25 in.
Presented by Mrs. M. Savill, 1959

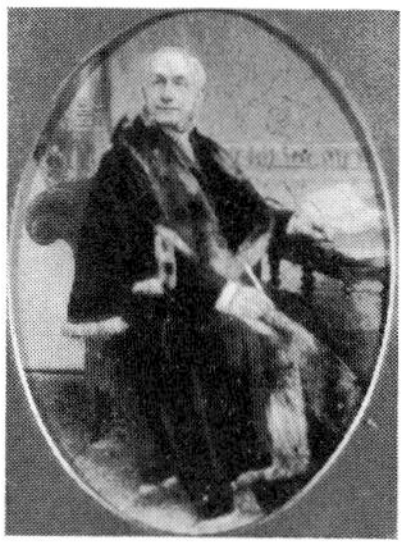

acc. no. 1572
Frederick Kent, Member of the Court of Common Council, 1868–1877
oil over photograph: $7\frac{3}{4} \times 5\frac{3}{4}$ in.
Presented by Mrs. K. Kent, 1959

acc. no. 1573
Sir William Farmer, Sheriff of London 1890
oil on canvas: 45 × 32 in.
Presented by C. F. M. Burnside, 1959

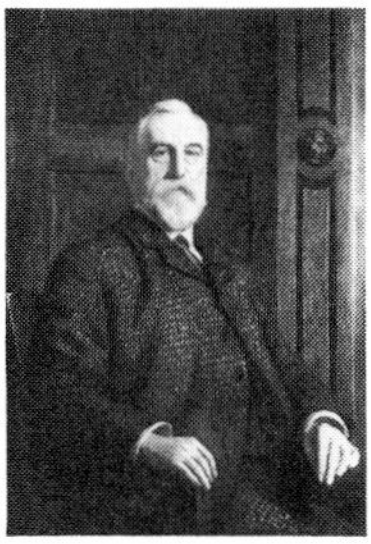

acc. no. 1576
Sir Edward Clarke, Lord Mayor 1696
oil on canvas: $87\frac{1}{2} \times 51\frac{1}{2}$ in.
Purchased from John McMaster, 1959

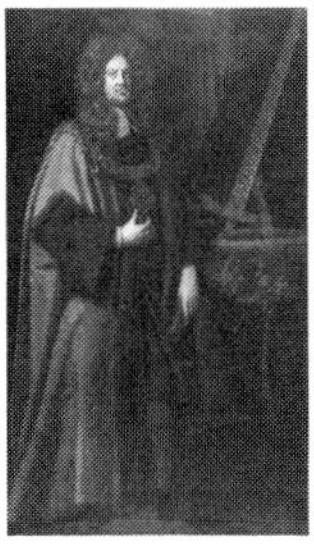

acc. no. 1577
Sir William Garrard, Lord Mayor 1555
oil on canvas: $32\frac{1}{2} \times 25\frac{3}{4}$ in.
inscribed: *An. 1568.* and *Aet^e 62.*
Presented by Mrs. A. Cherry-Garrard, 1959

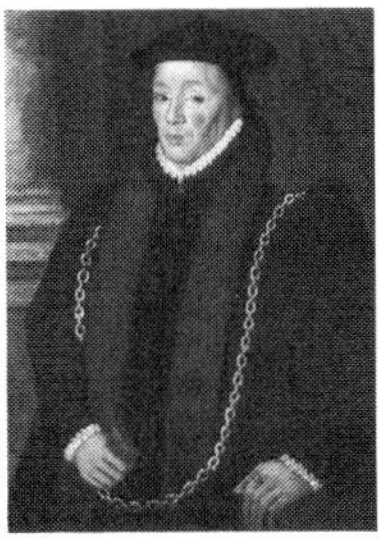

acc. no. 1627
Laying the Foundation Stone of the Royal Exchange, 1842
oil on canvas: $12\frac{1}{2} \times 17\frac{1}{2}$ in.
Purchased from B. Stewart, 1962

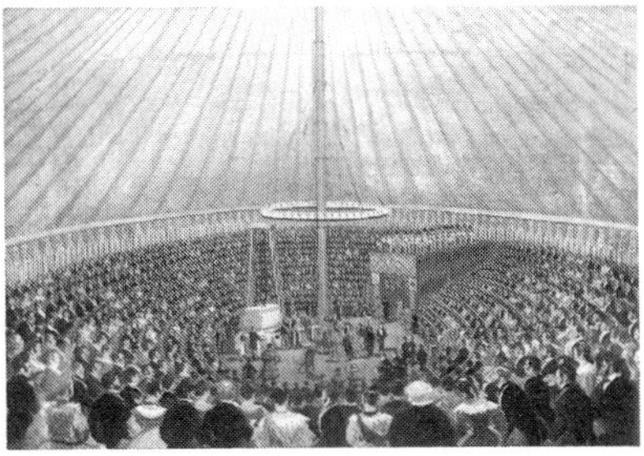

acc. no. 1645
Sir Charles Peers, Lord Mayor 1715, and his Grand-Daughter
oil on canvas: $94\frac{1}{4} \times 58$ in.
Presented by C. J. Peers, 1963

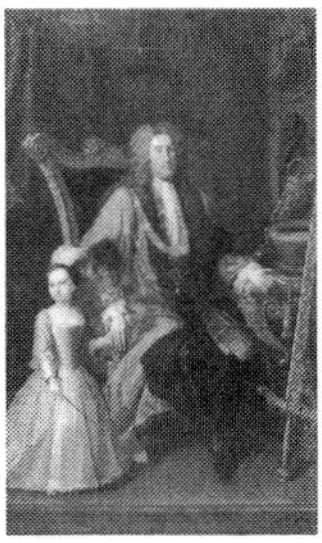

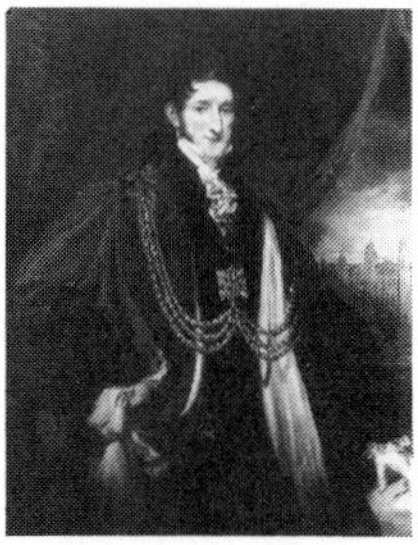

acc. no. 1708
Sir William Henry Poland, Sheriff 1831

oil over photograph: $19 \times 15\frac{1}{2}$ in.
inscribed: *S Wm Po...*
Purchased, 1965

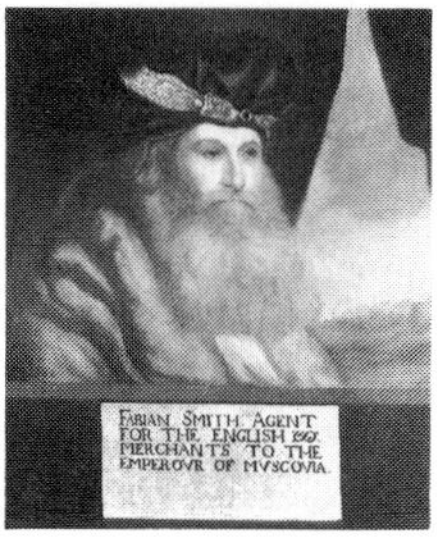

acc. no. 1725
Fabian Smith, Agent for the English Merchants to the Emperor of Muscovia, Ambassador to Russia, 1630

oil on canvas: 30×25 in.
Presented by the Russia Company, 1966

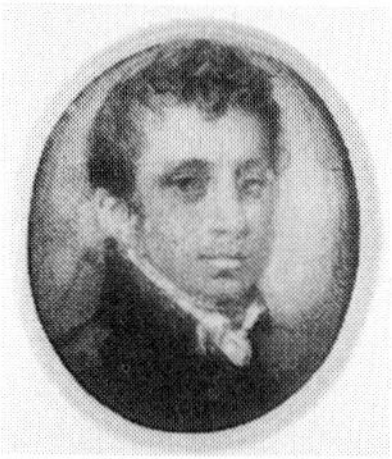

acc. no. 1778
Sir George Faudel-Phillips, Lord Mayor 1896

watercolour: $1\frac{3}{8} \times 1\frac{1}{4}$ in.
Presented by G. F. Booker, 1967

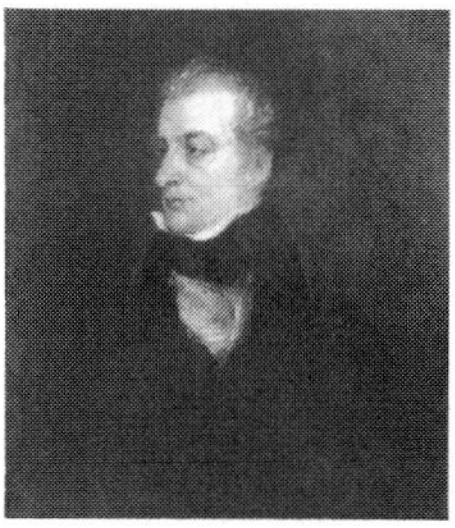

acc. no. 1838
Daniel Whittle Harvey (*c.*1830)

oil on canvas: 30×25 in.
Purchased from W. J. Goldsmith, 1970

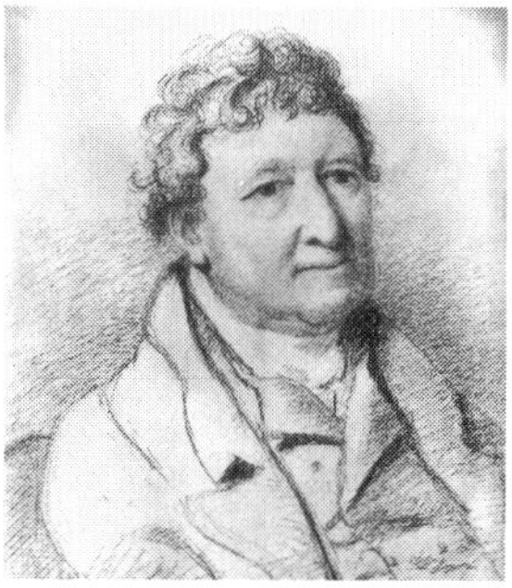

acc. no. 1939
Z. W. Vincent, Barber-Surgeon

black and white chalk: $9 \times 7\frac{1}{4}$ in.
Presented by A. R. Martin, 1973

acc. no. 1940
Edward Baker III, Astronomical Instrument Maker
oil on panel: $5\frac{3}{4} \times 4\frac{7}{8}$ in.
Presented by A. R. Martin, 1973

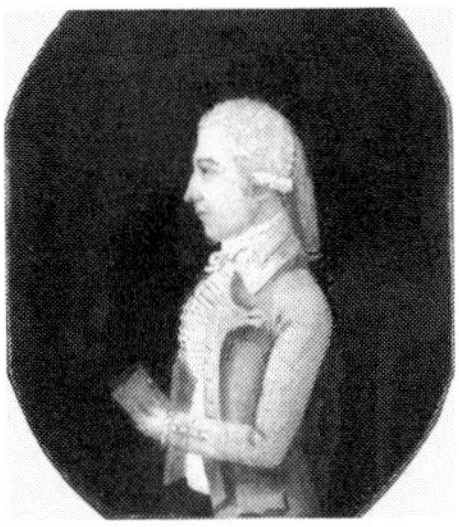

acc. no. 2001
Badge of the Union Assurance Society
oil on panel: $14\frac{1}{2} \times 27\frac{1}{2}$ in.
Presented by Commercial Union Assurance Society, 1974

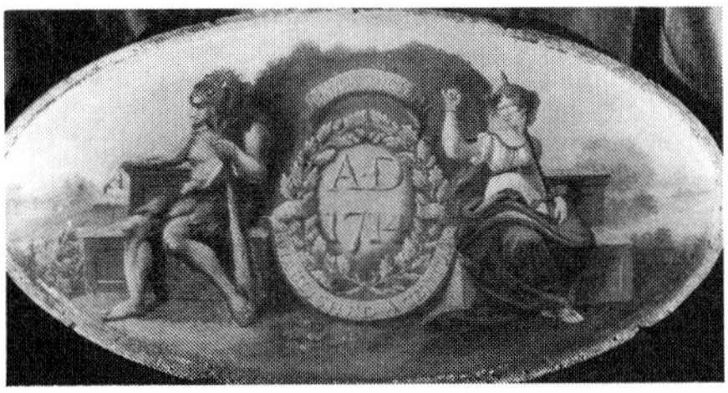

acc. no. 2158
Joseph Lardner, Poor Rate Collector in the Parish of St Bartholomew the Great (1869)
oil on canvas: 36 × 28 in.
Presented by Miss E. Lardner, 1974

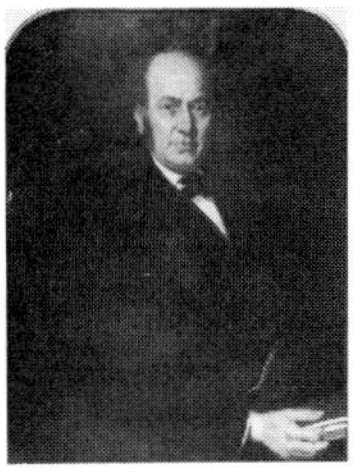

acc. no. 2218a
Henry John Purkiss, Principal of the Royal College of Naval Architecture (*c.*1865)
oil on canvas: $20\frac{1}{4} \times 13\frac{1}{4}$ in.
Presented, source unknown, to the City of London School and accessioned 1978

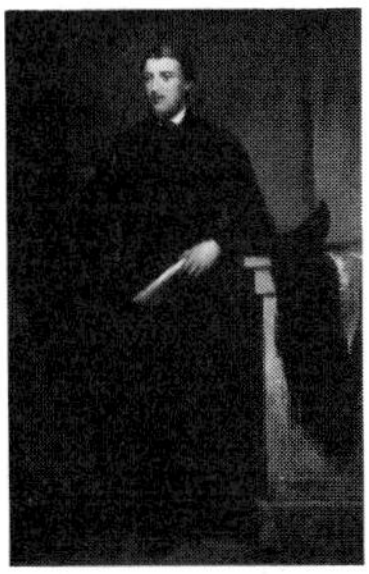

acc. no. 2218b
Henry John Purkiss
oil on canvas: $20\frac{1}{4} \times 13\frac{1}{4}$ in.
Found in store, source unknown, 1983

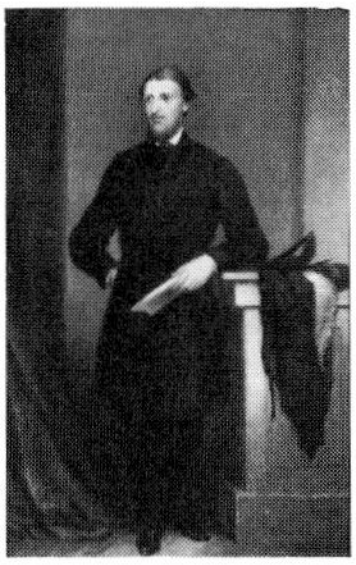

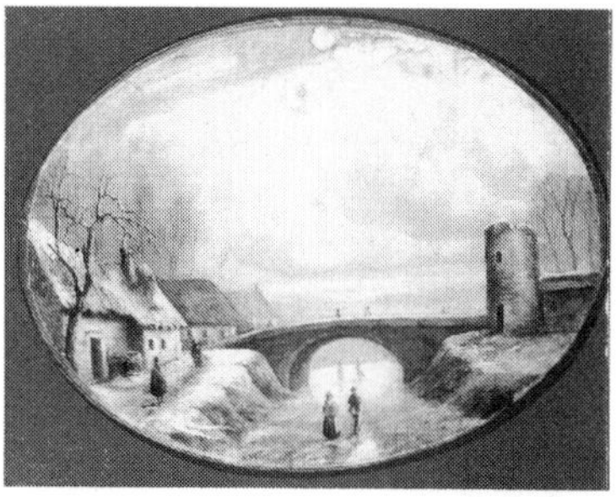

The following 22 items were presented by Miss Helen Guiterman in 1985.

acc. no. 3521
Winter Scene
oil on canvas: $6\frac{1}{4} \times 7\frac{3}{4}$ in. (oval)

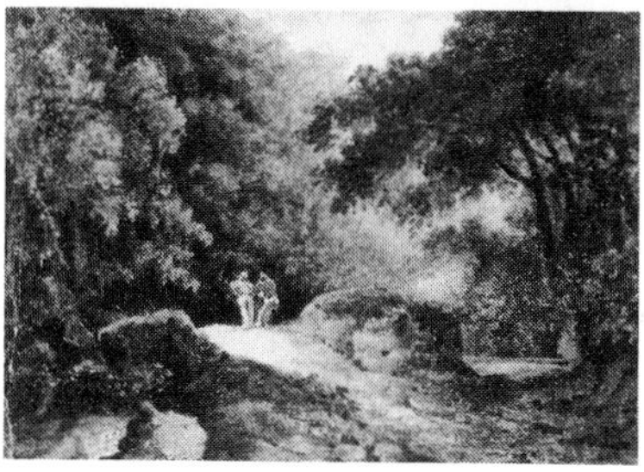

acc. no. 3523
Two Figures on a Woodland Path
watercolour with varnish: $4\frac{3}{8} \times 6\frac{1}{8}$ in.

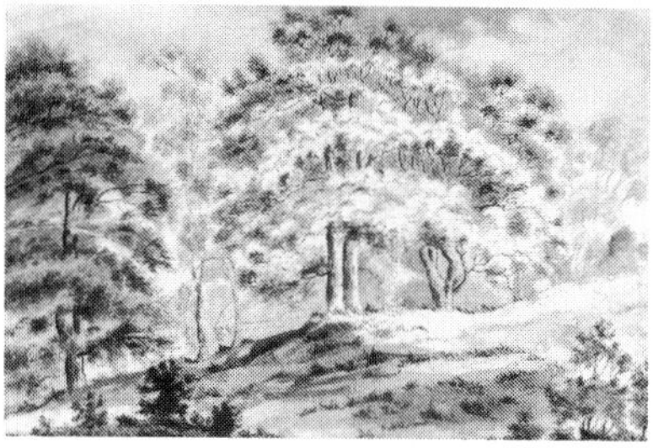

acc. no. 3524
Trees in a Meadow
wash over pencil: $13\frac{1}{8} \times 18\frac{3}{4}$ in.

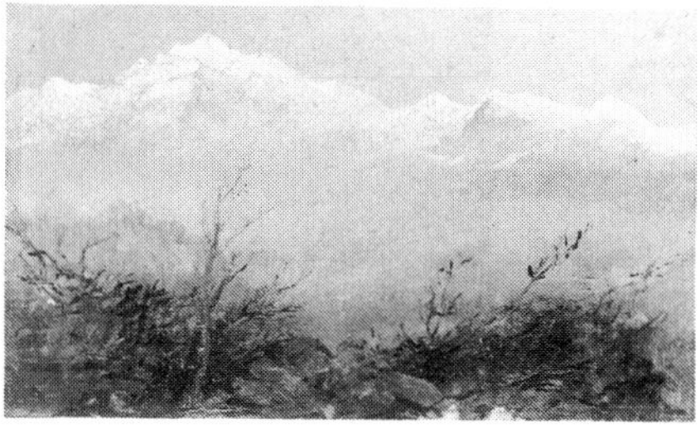

acc. no. 3525
The Alps
oil on Rowney's Academy Board: 5×8 in.

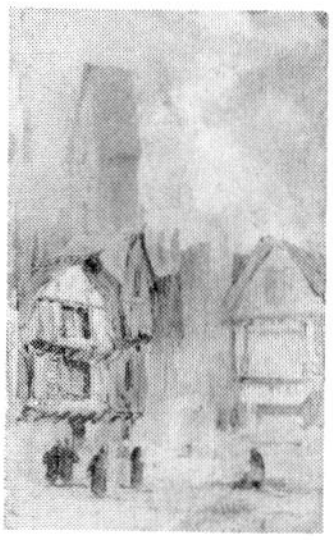

acc. no. 3526
Alpine Village with Figures
oil on Rowney's Academy Board: $8\frac{1}{8} \times 5$ in.

acc. no. 3527
Alpine House
oil on Rowney's Academy Board: $6 \times 5\frac{1}{8}$ in.

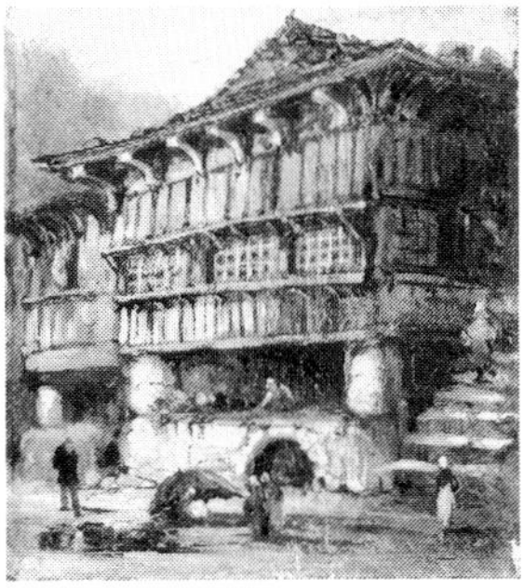

acc. no. 3528
Market Place with Figures
oil on Rowney's Academy Board: $6 \times 5\frac{1}{8}$ in.

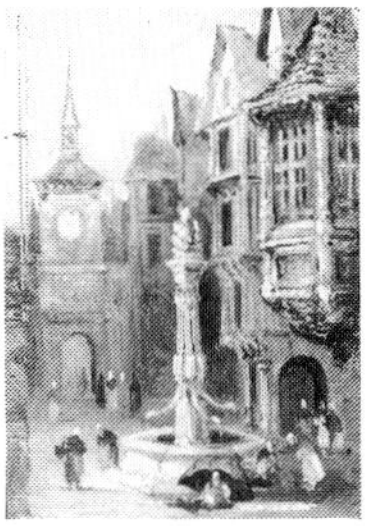

acc. no. 3529
View of the Alps
oil on Rowney's Academy Board: $3\frac{1}{2} \times 3\frac{5}{8}$ in.
signed or inscribed on label attached to verso: *Irving Morta*

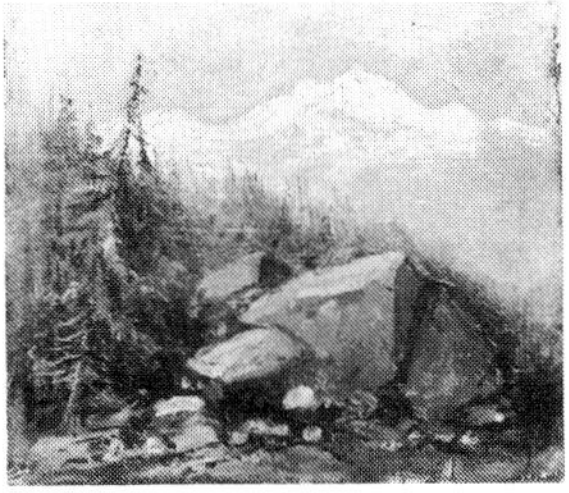

acc. no. 3530
View of the Alps
oil on Rowney's Academy Board: $4\frac{1}{2} \times 2\frac{3}{8}$ in.

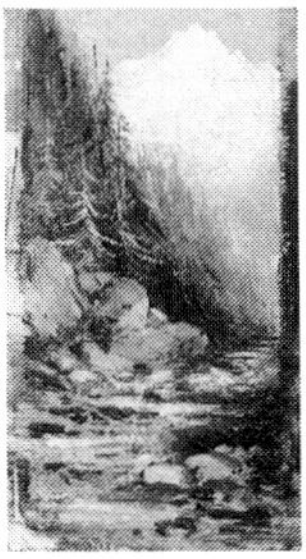

acc. no. 3532
View of Arles (1861)
pencil and watercolour: $10\frac{5}{8} \times 14\frac{3}{4}$ in.
inscribed on verso: *Arles Feb 15 – 1861*

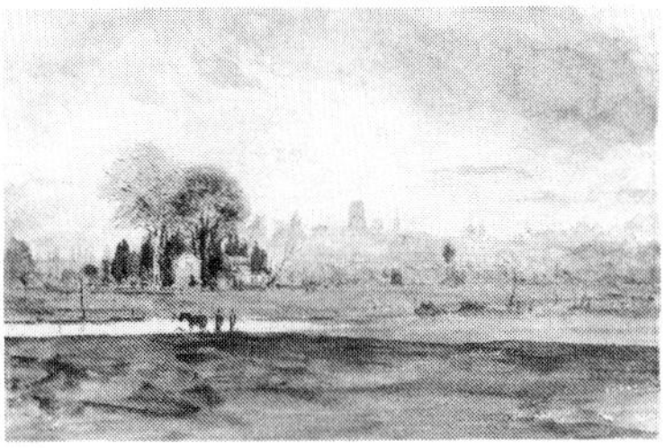

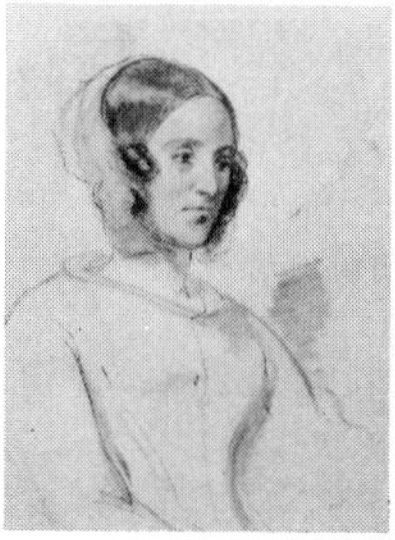

acc. no. 3537
Portrait of a Lady in a Cap
pastel on grey paper: $9\frac{1}{8} \times 7\frac{3}{4}$ in.

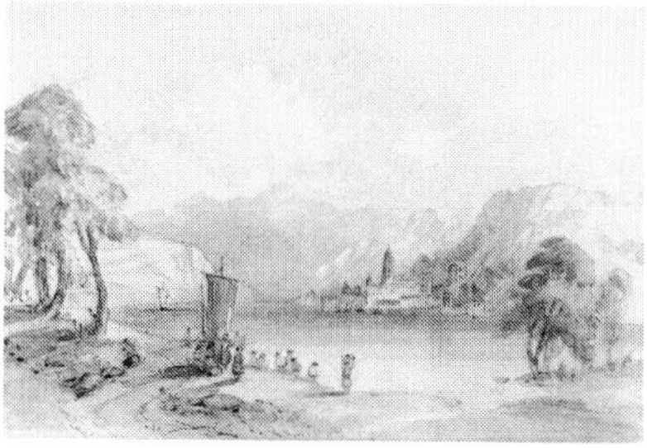

acc. no. 3542
Lakeside Scene
brown ink and watercolour: $5\frac{1}{4} \times 7\frac{1}{2}$ in.

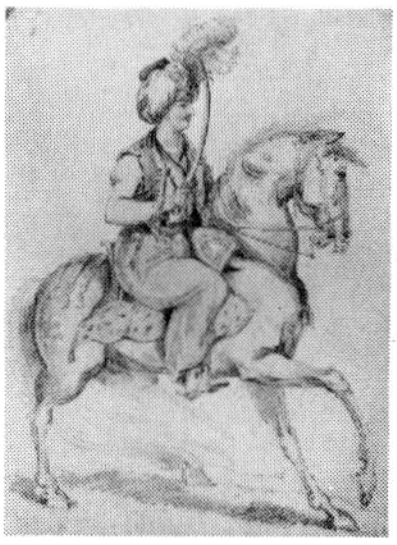

acc. no. 3543
Mameluke Commander of the Emperor's Bodyguard
watercolour: $14\frac{1}{2} \times 10\frac{1}{2}$ in.
inscribed on verso (partly illegible): 20/– / (.....) *Mameluke M(.....) shot / (.....) mander of the Emperor's Body Guard / (.....)*

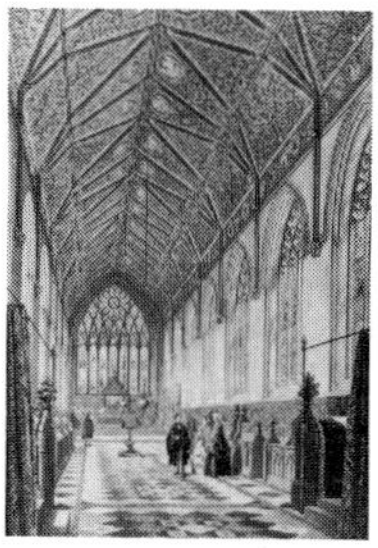

acc. no. 3546
Interior of a Chapel, with Figures
lithograph: $17\frac{1}{4} \times 11\frac{7}{8}$ in.

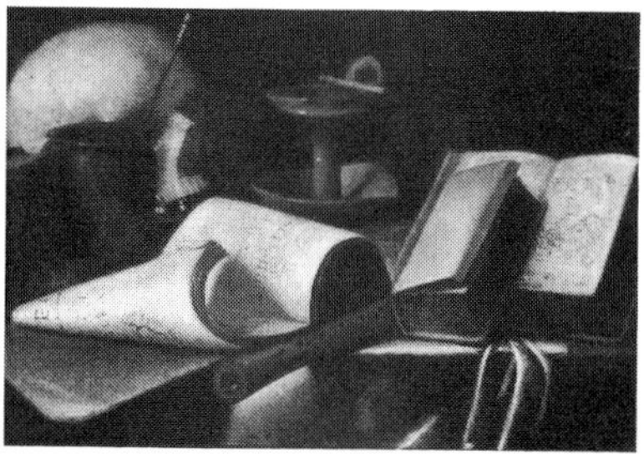

acc. no. 3548
Skull, Candlestick and Books
oil on canvas: $15\frac{1}{2} \times 12\frac{1}{2}$ in.

acc. no. 3550
A Sleeping Woman
steel engraving, hand coloured: $4\frac{1}{2} \times 3\frac{3}{8}$ in.
signed with initials: *H.F.V.*

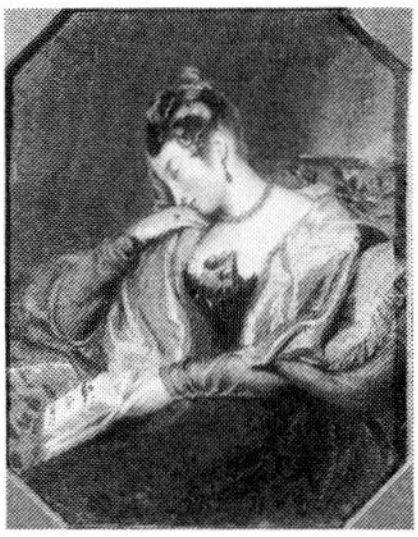

acc. no. 3554
River Running through a Meadow
black chalk and watercolour: $7 \times 11\frac{1}{4}$

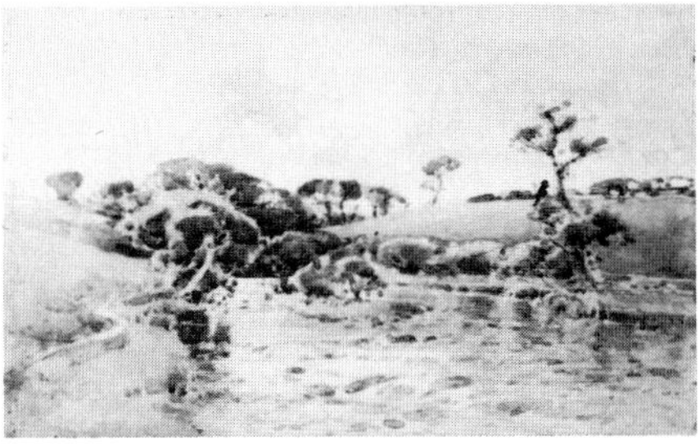

acc. no. 3562
A Market Place in the Near East
pencil and watercolour: $4\frac{1}{2} \times 7\frac{7}{8}$ in.

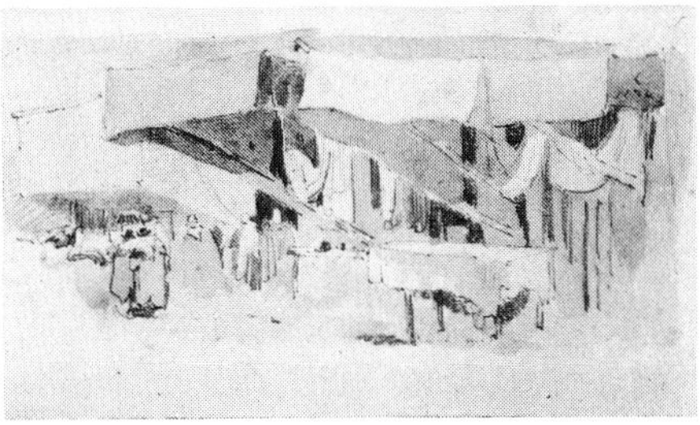

acc. no. 3565
Greek Fishermen and the Temple of Poseidon, Sounion Cape, Attica
watercolour: $5\frac{7}{8} \times 9$ in.

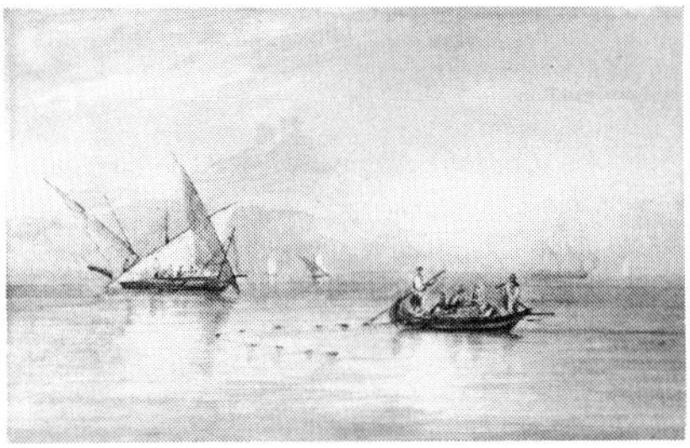

acc. no. 3575
Sketches of Guests at the Chelsea Arts Ball
pen and brown ink on Goodall's Bristol Board: $12\frac{1}{2} \times 15\frac{1}{4}$ in.
inscribed: *Reduce to* $\frac{3}{4}$ *of all width, others to come with it* (....) *Black* (?); and: *S. Jacomb Hood, P.W. Steer, Miss Jennie Lee, G.P. Jacomb-Hood, W.H. Trood, Miss Norreys, C.P. Sainton, Miss Roche, Miss Mappin, Bernard Sickert, Miss E. Nias*

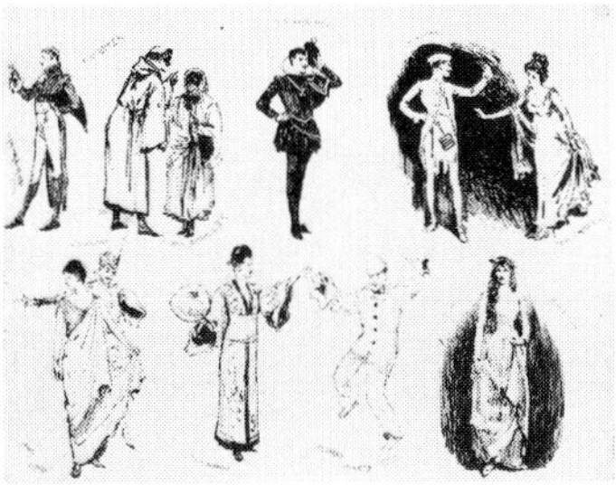

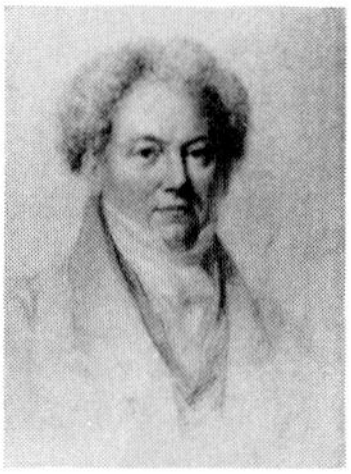

acc. no. 3598
Gentleman in a High Collar
crayon: $22\frac{1}{8} \times 16\frac{1}{4}$ in.

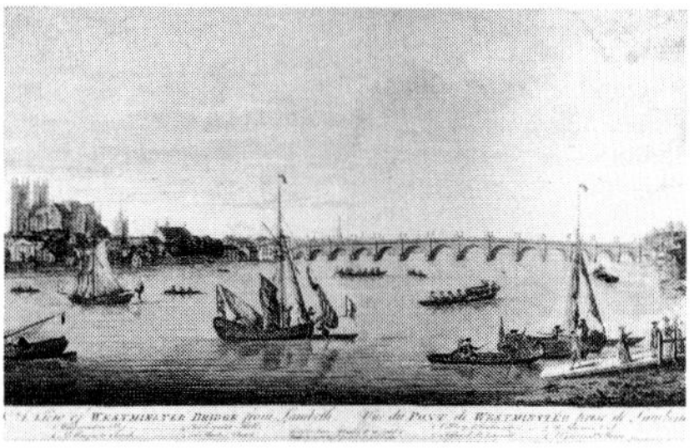

acc. no. 3607
Westminster Bridge from Lambeth

engraving, hand-coloured with watercolour: $10\frac{7}{8} \times 16\frac{1}{2}$ in. (plate)
lettered: *A View of WESTMINSTER BRIDGE from Lambeth. Vue du PONT de WESTMINSTER prise de Lambeth. / Printed for Robert Wilkinson, No 58 Cornhill, & Bowles & Carver 69 St Pauls Church Yard London*; and with the following buildings identified in English and French: Westminster Abbey, St Margaret's Church, Westminster Hall, St Martin's Church.

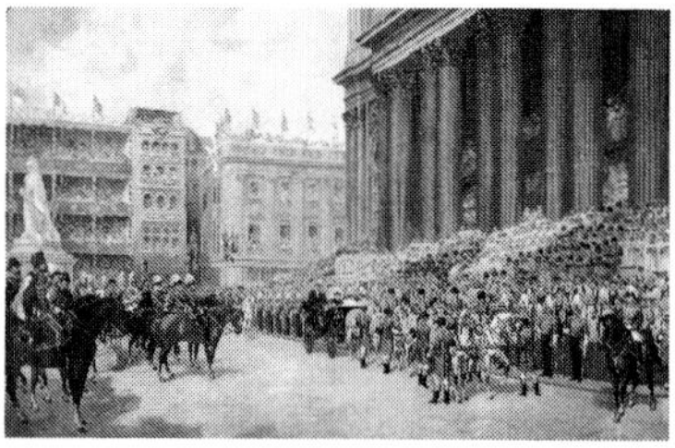

acc. no. 3632
St Paul's: Queen Victoria's Diamond Jubilee, 1897

chromolithograph: $25 \times 34\frac{1}{8}$ in.
proof copy with colour bars identified in reverse with the names of the colours
Presented by Alfred Twigg, 1985

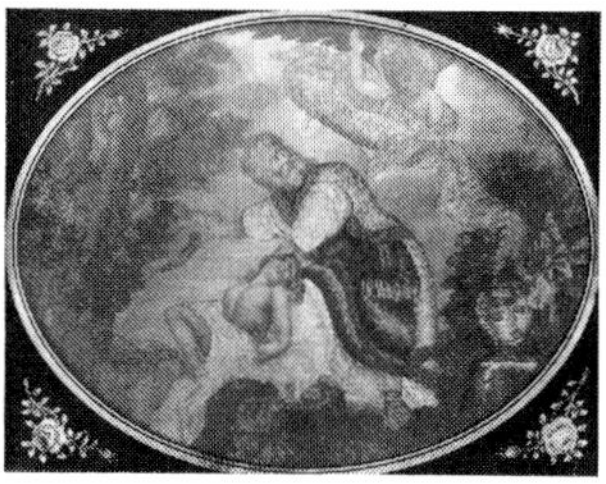

acc. no. 3634
Abraham and Isaac

wool and silk embroidered on to painted silk: $14\frac{1}{2} \times 18\frac{1}{2}$ in.
Presented by Mrs. Charlotte Sanders, 1880

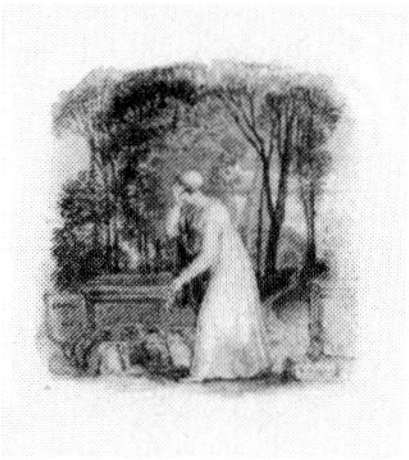

Thomas Uwins (1782–1857)
The following five drawings were presented by Felix Joseph in 1890.

acc. no. 502
Constantia at the Grave of Theodosius
watercolour: $4 \times 3\frac{3}{8}$ in.

acc. no. 503
Cupid and a Lover Lamenting the Death of a Loved One

watercolour: $6\frac{1}{8} \times 4\frac{1}{4}$ in.
signed: *Thos. Uwins / Del.*

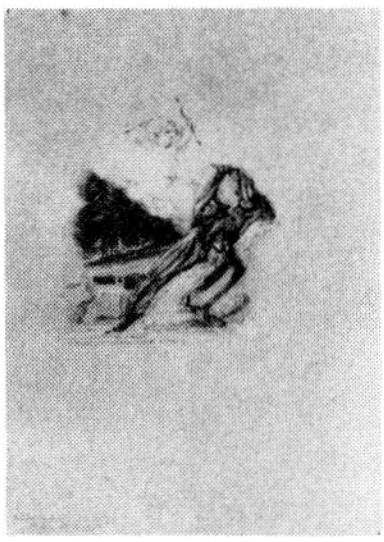

acc. no. 504
The Broken Bridge

pen and ink and watercolour: $3\frac{5}{8} \times 3$ in.
signed indistinctly: *Thos. Uwins*

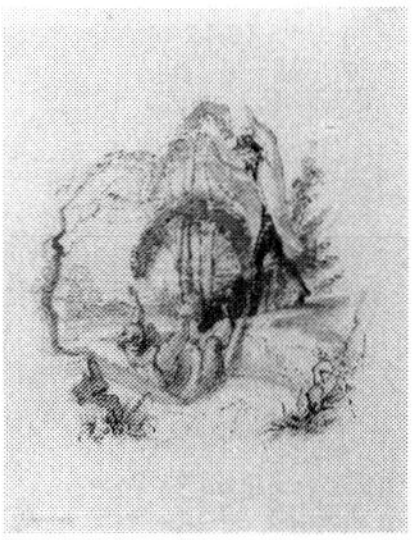

acc. no. 505
Jerome and his Grandchildren

pen and ink and watercolour: $5 \times 3\frac{3}{8}$ in.

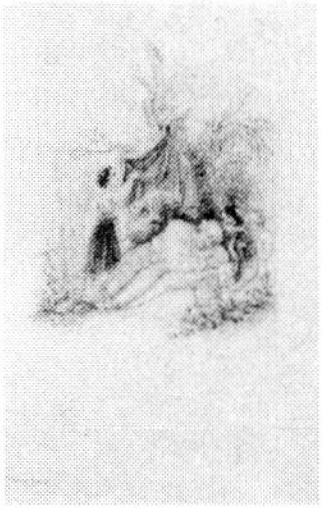

acc. no. 506
The Origin of Song

pen and ink and watercolour: $4\frac{1}{4} \times 3\frac{3}{4}$ in.

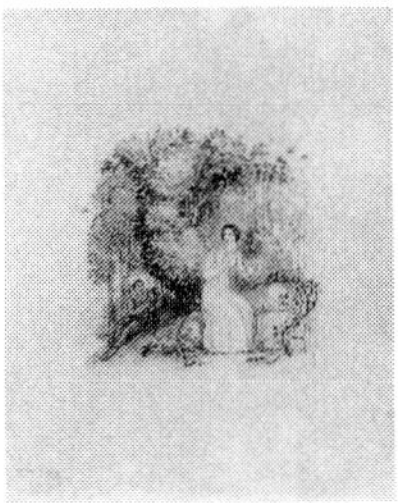

Jan van der Vaardt (1647–1721)

acc. no. 26
King William III

oil on canvas: 95×60 in.
Purchased from R. Hayes, Citizen and Painter, 1690

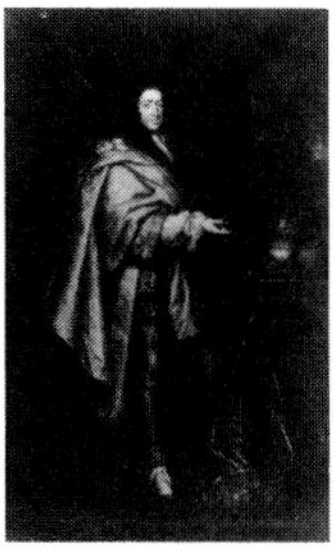

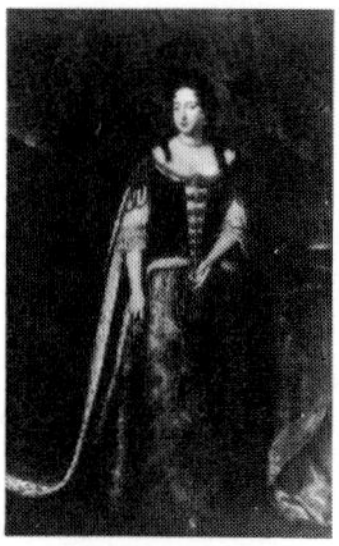

acc. no. 27
Queen Mary

oil on canvas: 95 × 60 in.
Purchased from R. Hayes, Citizen and Painter, 1690

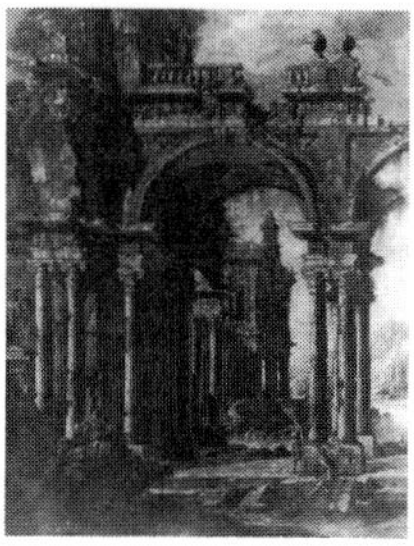

Gaspare Vanvitelli (or Gaspare/ Kaspar van Vitelli/ van Wittel) (1653–1736)

acc. no. 360
Architectural Cappriccio

oil on canvas: 29 × 24 in.
Bequeathed by William Dunnett, 1888

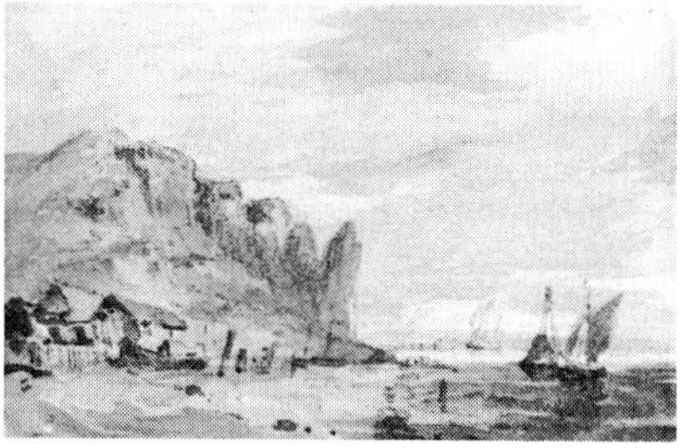

John Varley (1778–1842)

acc. no. 3518
Coastal Scene

pencil and watercolour: $2\frac{1}{4} \times 3\frac{1}{2}$ in.
inscribed on verso: *Constable*
Presented by Miss Helen Guiterman, 1985

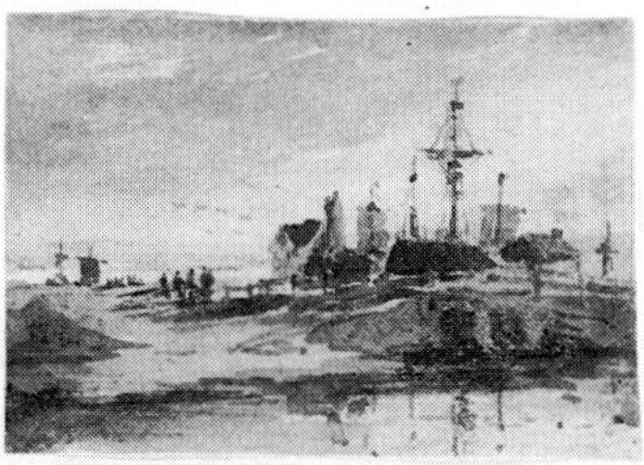

acc. no. 3519
Coastal Scene

pencil and watercolour: $2 \times 2\frac{7}{8}$ in.
Presented by Miss Helen Guiterman, 1985

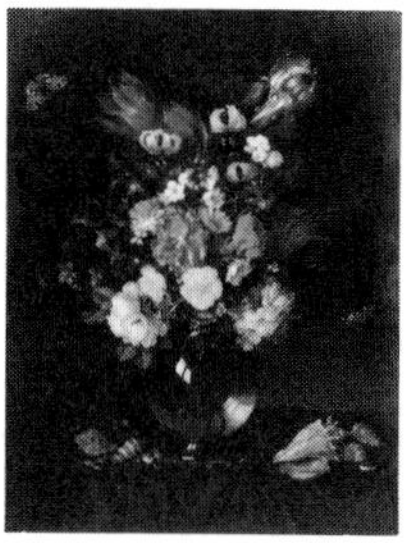

Pieter van de Venne (d.1657)

acc. no. 347
Vase and Flowers (1655)

oil on canvas: 26 × 20 in.
signed and dated: *P.v.d. Venne 1655*
Bequeathed by William Dunnett, 1888

Harman Verelst (*c.*1643–1702)

acc. no. 1568
A Young Man of the Dashwood Family, probably Sir Francis Dashwood (? 1683)

oil on canvas: 37 × 31 in. (oval)
signed and dated: *H Verelst / 168(?)*
Presented by Joseph Hayward, 1958

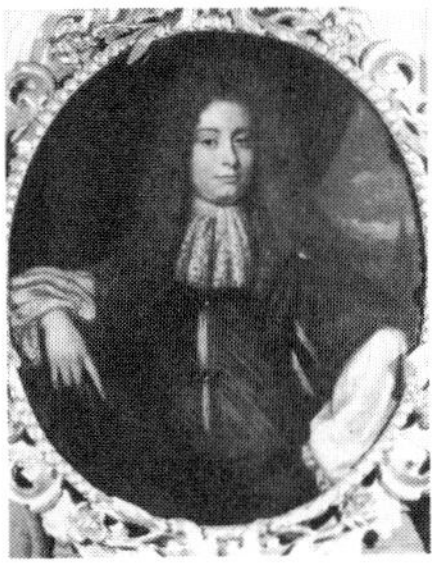

N. A. Verrall (20th C)

acc. no. 1898
Fountains, Trafalgar Square (1971)

pastel: $11\frac{1}{4}$ × 19 in.
Purchased from the artist, 1972

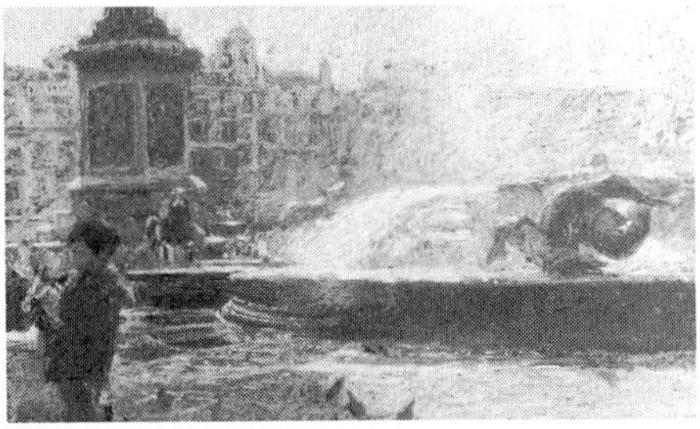

Alfred Vickers (1786–1868)

acc. no. 739
Near Wilford, Nottinghamshire (1864)

oil on canvas: 9 × 12 in.
signed and dated: *Vickers / 64*
Bequeathed by Charles Gassiot, 1902

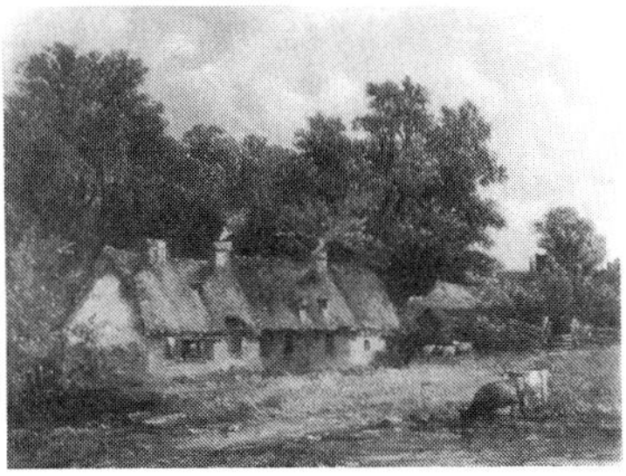

acc. no. 740
Corwen, North Wales

oil on canvas: 12 × 17 in.
Bequeathed by Charles Gassiot, 1902

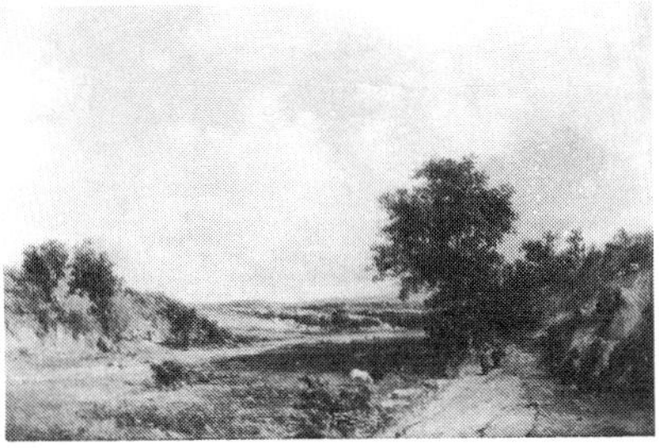

acc. no. 741
Haddon Hall

oil on canvas: 9 × 15 in.
signed: *A Vickers*
Bequeathed by Charles Gassiot, 1902

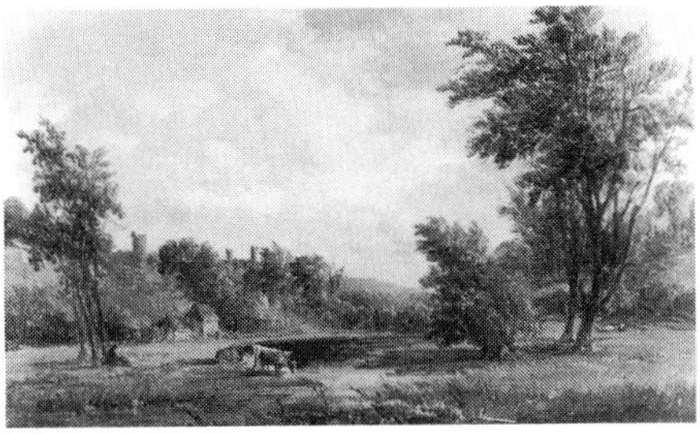

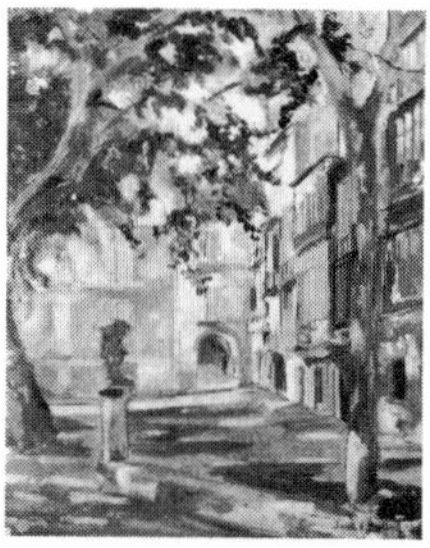

John A Videan (20th C)

acc. no. 2162
Inner Temple (1953)

oil on canvas: 24 × 20 in.
signed and dated: *JOHN A VIDEAN 53*
Purchased from the artist, 1975

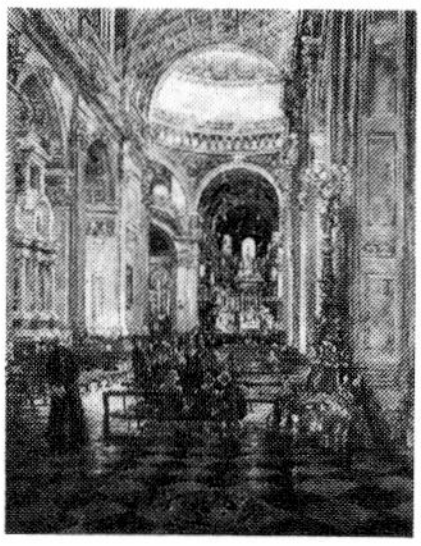

Joseph William Topham Vinall (1873–1953)

acc. no. 1250
Interior of St. Paul's Cathedral (*c.*1930)

oil on canvas: $35\frac{1}{2} \times 27\frac{1}{2}$ in.
signed: *J.W.T. VINALL*
Presented by the artist, 1941

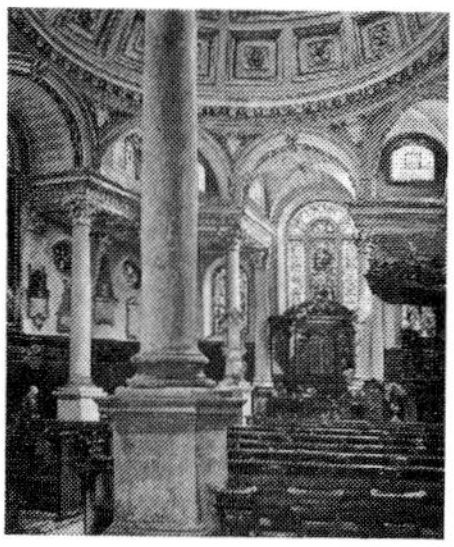

acc. no. 1249
Interior of St. Stephen's Walbrook (1936)

oil on canvas: $29\frac{1}{2} \times 24\frac{1}{2}$ in.
signed: *J.W.T. Vinall*
Presented by the artist, 1941

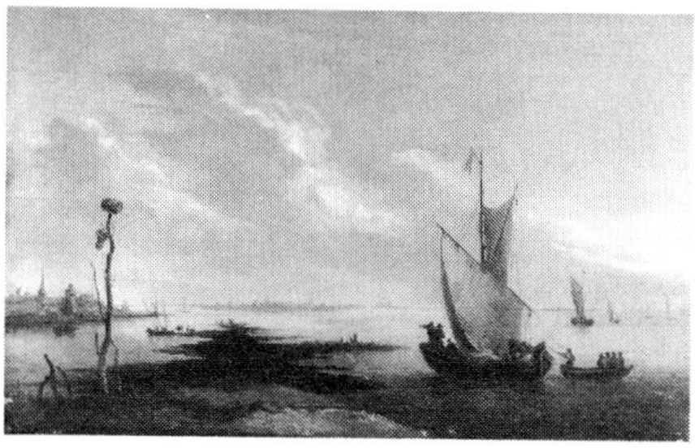

attributed to Simon de Vlieger (*c.*1600–1653)

acc. no. 382
Estuary Scene

oil on panel: 8 × 12 in.
signed indistinctly: *Vlieger* (?)
Bequeathed by William Dunnett, 1888

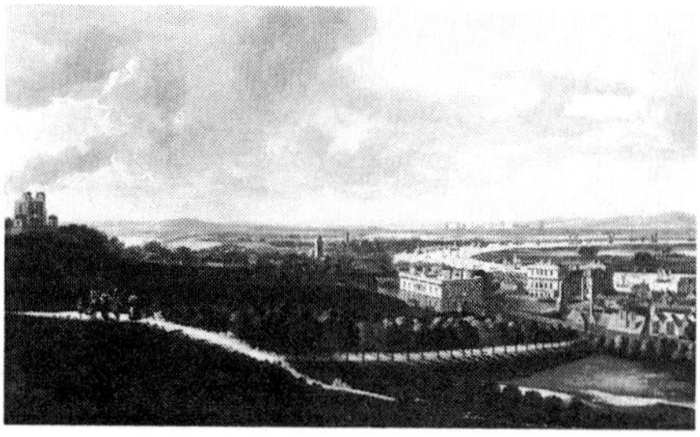

Jan Vorsterman (1643–99)

acc. no. 1769
London from Greenwich Hill (*c.*1680)

oil on canvas: $42\frac{1}{2} \times 71\frac{1}{2}$ in.
Purchased at Christie's sale 18.11.1966 (49)

after Waggoner (17th C)

acc. no. 1379
The Great Fire of London, 1666

oil on canvas: $18\frac{1}{2} \times 28\frac{1}{2}$ in.
Purchased from the Appleby Gallery, 1948

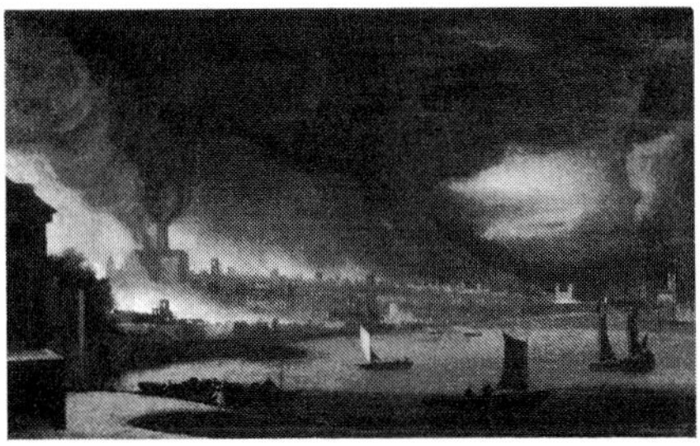

William Walcot (1874–1943)

acc. no. 892
The Trojan Horse (1909)

watercolour: 23 × 32 in.
signed and dated: *W. WALCOT / 1909*
Presented by Miss Evelyn P. McGhee, 1910

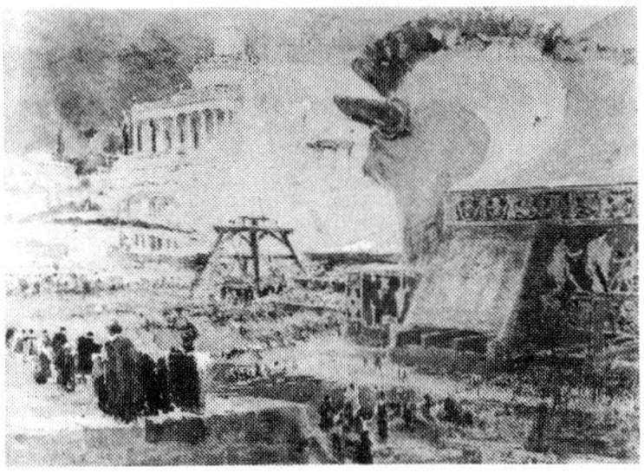

acc. no. 925
Church on the Grand Canal, Venice

watercolour: $17\frac{1}{4} \times 21\frac{1}{2}$ in.
signed: *W. WALCOT*
Presented by Miss Evelyn P. McGheee, 1911

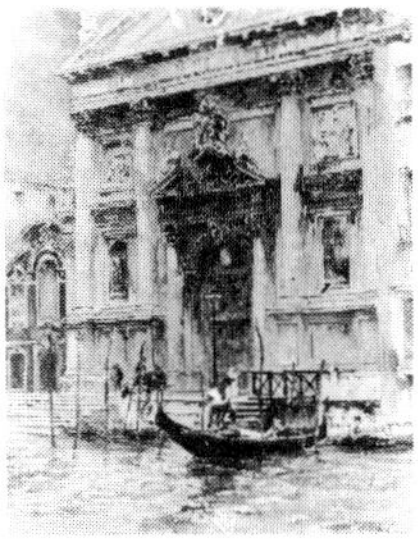

Frederick Walker (1840–75)

acc. no. 3568
A Mediaeval Scene

pen and ink over traces of pencil: $4\frac{3}{8} \times 5$ in.
Presented by Miss Helen Guiterman, 1985

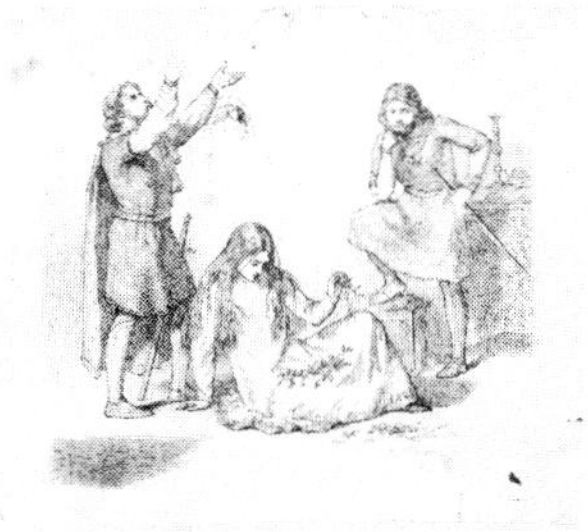

Henry Walter (1786–1849)

acc. no. 2263
Near Battersea (1818)

watercolour: 12 × 19 in.
Presented to the Corporation by Brisbane City Council, 1980

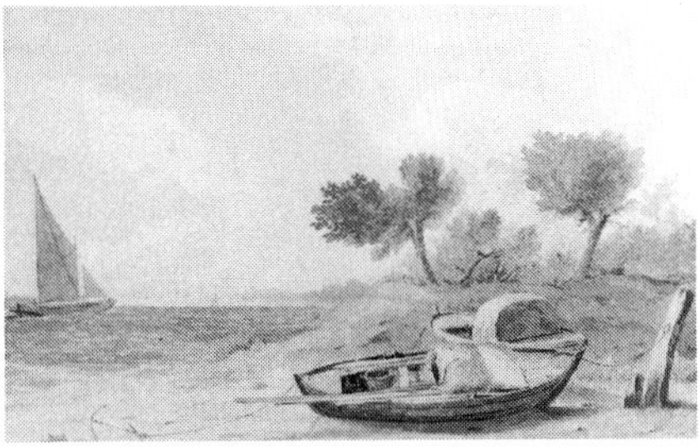

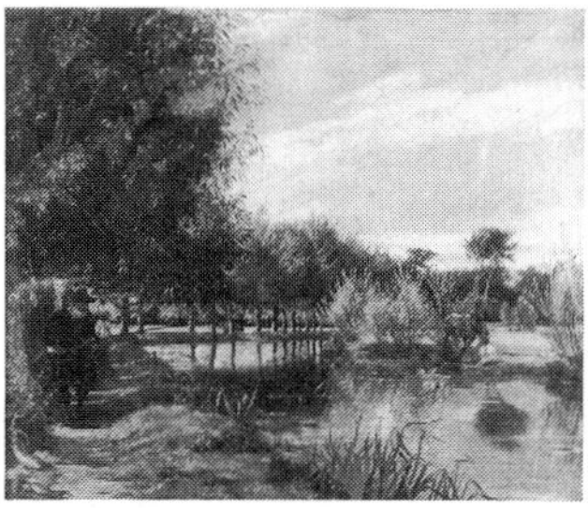

Edward Matthew Ward (1816–79)

acc. no. 1385
Izaak Walton Fishing (1850)

oil on canvas: $23 \times 27\frac{3}{4}$ in.
signed and dated: *E M WARD / 1850*
Presented by F. J. Nettlefold, 1948

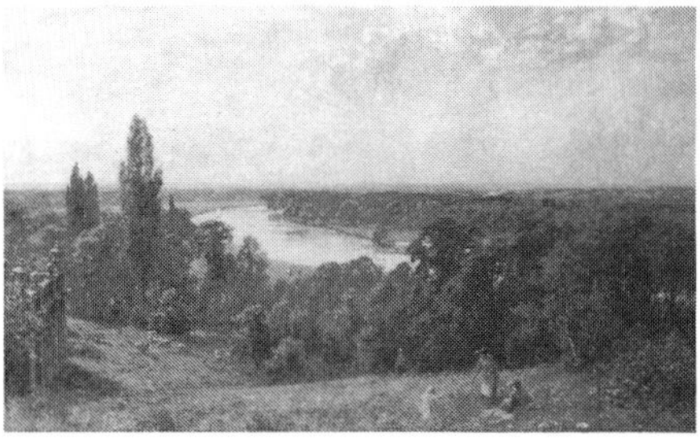

Sir Ernest Albert Waterlow (1850–1919)

acc. no. 1008
The Thames from Richmond Hill (1905)

oil on canvas: 54×84 in.
signed: *E A Waterlow*
Presented by Lady Waterlow, 1920

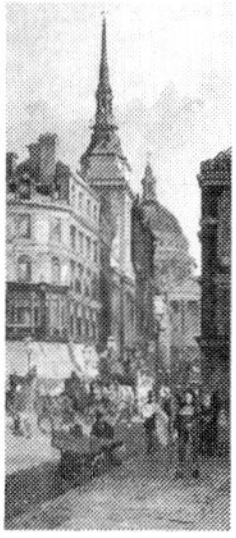

Charles John Watson (1846–1927)

acc. no. 1251
Ludgate Hill (1884)

oil on canvas: $35\frac{1}{2} \times 15\frac{1}{4}$ in.
signed and dated: *CHARLES J WATSON / 1884*
Purchased, 1943

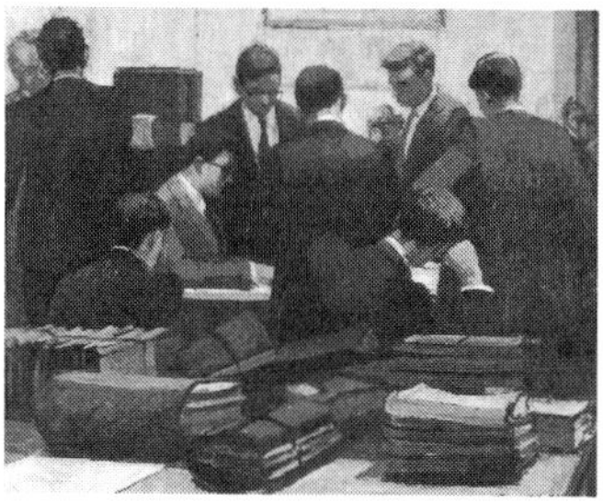

Frances Watt (20th C)

acc. no. 1710
Interior of Lloyd's (1963)

oil on hardboard: 20×24 in.
signed and dated: *Frances Watt 1963*
Purchased from the artist, 1965

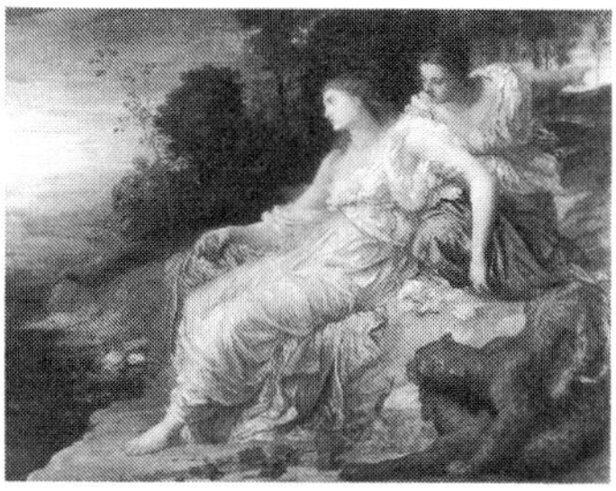

George Frederick Watts (1817–1904)

acc. no. 986
Ariadne in Naxos (1875)

oil on canvas: $29\frac{1}{2} \times 37$ in.
signed and dated: *G.F.W. 1875*
Presented by Sir Marcus Samuel through the N.A.–C.F., 1918

James Webb (1825–95)

acc. no. 1062
Mont St. Michel (1868)

oil on canvas: $53\frac{1}{2} \times 69$ in.
signed and dated: *J. Webb / 68*
Presented by James Northcott, 1929

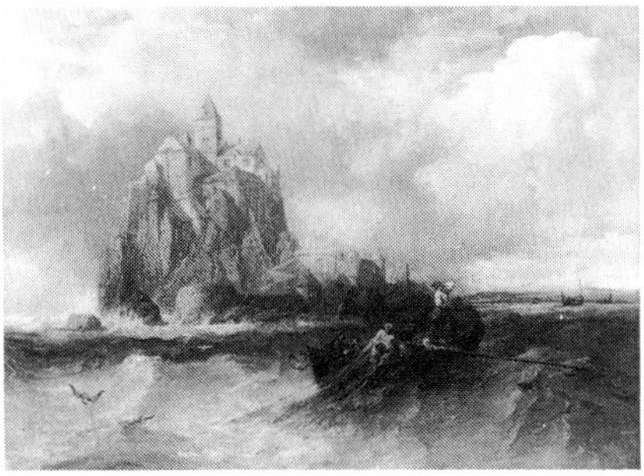

A. C. Webster (20th C)

acc. no. 3522
South Coast Beach (1959)

oil on card: 4×7 in.
signed: *a.c. webster 59*
Presented by Miss Helen Guiterman, 1985

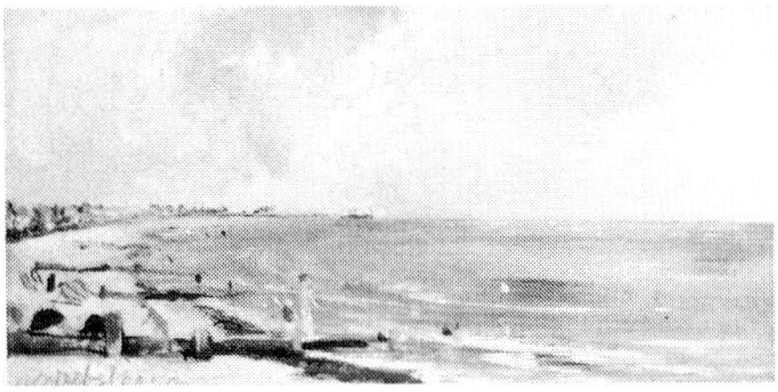

Thomas Webster (1800–86)

acc. no. 745
The Smile (1842)

oil on panel: $12\frac{1}{2} \times 25$ in.
signed and dated: *T. Webster 1842*
Bequeathed by Charles Gassiot, 1902

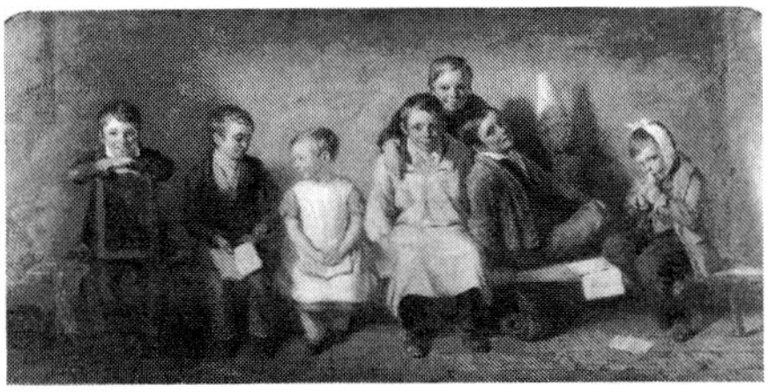

acc. no. 746
The Frown (1842)

oil on panel: $12\frac{1}{2} \times 25$ in.
signed and dated: *T. Webster 1842*
Bequeathed by Charles Gassiot, 1902

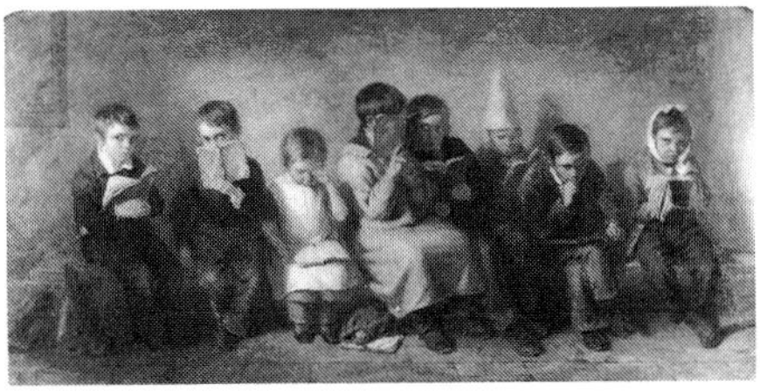

acc. no. 743
The See-Saw (1849)

oil on panel: $6\frac{1}{2} \times 10\frac{1}{2}$ in. (sight)
signed and dated: *TWebster 1849*
Bequeathed by Charles Gassiot, 1902

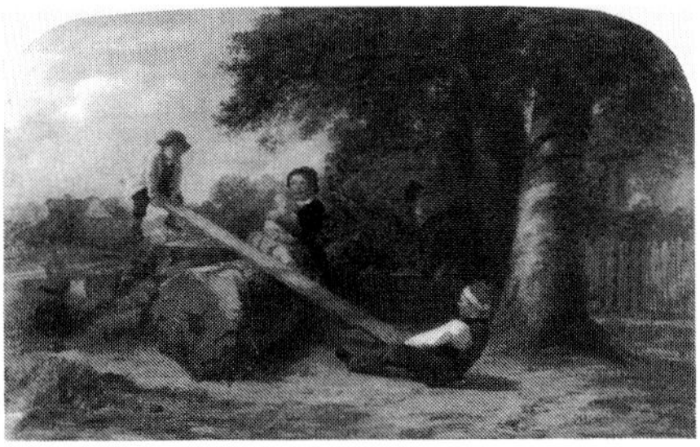

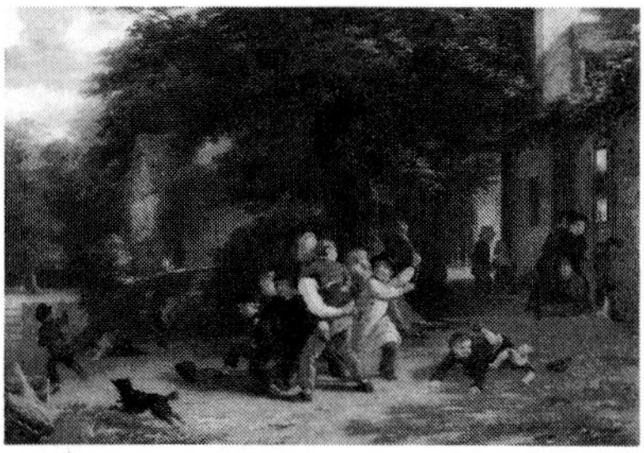

acc. no. 744
The Playground (*c.*1852)

oil on panel: $10\frac{1}{2} \times 13\frac{1}{2}$ in. (sight)
signed (mono): *TW*
Bequeathed by Charles Gassiot, 1902

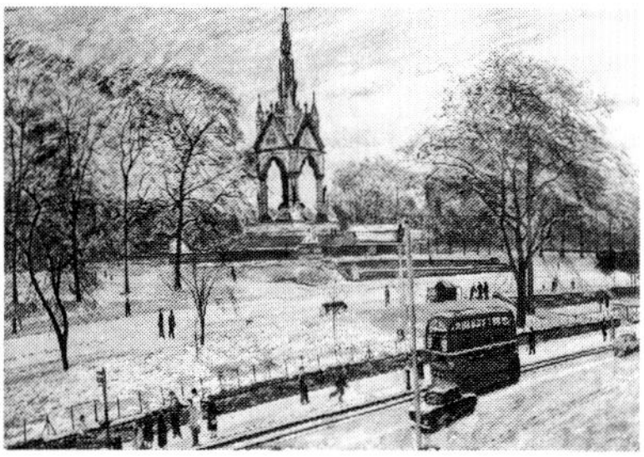

Carel Weight (b.1908)

acc. no. 2187
The Albert Memorial (1970)

oil on canvas: $33\frac{3}{4} \times 48$ in.
signed: *Carel Weight*
Purchased from Fieldborne Galleries, 1975

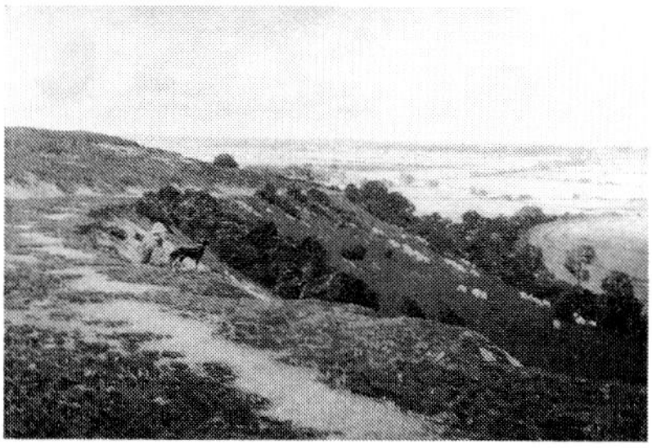

Jose Weiss (1859–1919)

acc. no. 1090
Bury Hill and Village with a View of the North Downs

oil on canvas: $32\frac{1}{2} \times 48\frac{1}{2}$ in.
signed: *Jose Weiss*
Presented by the Rev. St. Barte Sladen, 1932

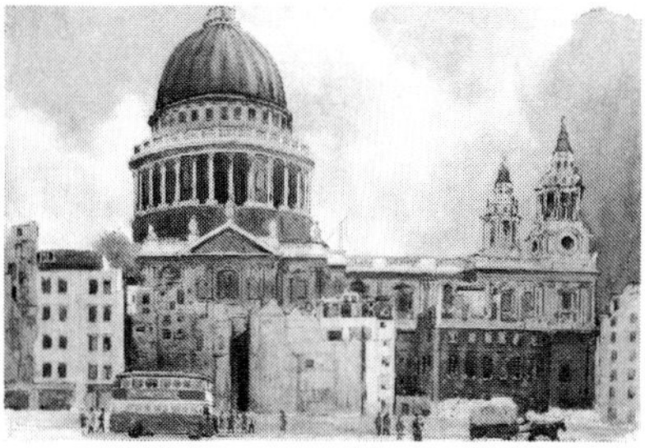

Denys G. Wells (1881–1973)

acc. no. 3638
St Paul's Cathedral (*c.*1930s)

pen and ink and watercolour: $15\frac{1}{4} \times 22\frac{1}{8}$ in.
signed: *Denys G. Wells*
Purchased from the artist's daughter, Mrs K. Karen, 1985

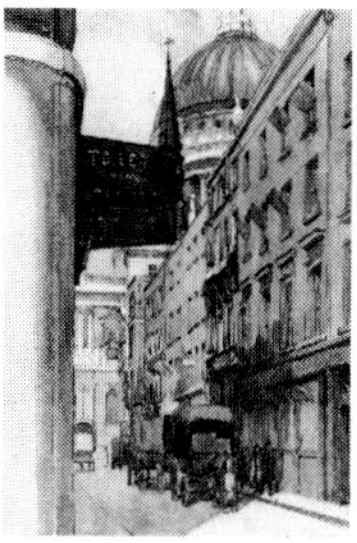

acc. no. 2166
St Paul's from Friday Street (1935)

pencil and watercolour: $17\frac{1}{2} \times 11\frac{5}{8}$ in.
signed: *Denys G. Wells*
Presented by the artist's daughter, Mrs K. Karen, 1975

acc. no. 2167
The Admiralty (*c*.1938)

pen and ink and watercolour: $14\frac{1}{2} \times 21\frac{1}{2}$ in.
Presented by the artist's daughter, Mrs K. Karen, 1975

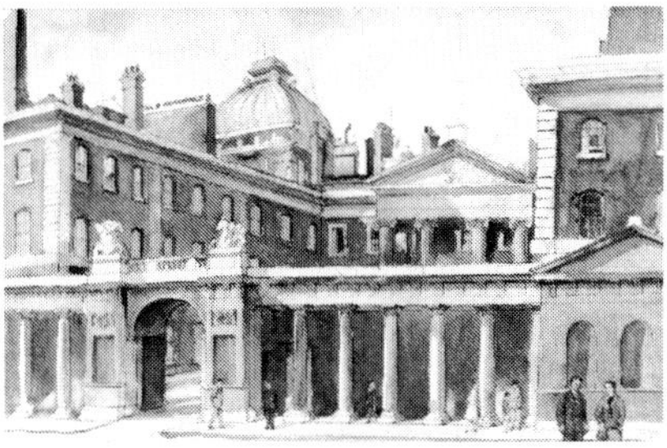

acc. no. 2219
The Old Bailey (*c*.1930s)

pencil and watercolour: 19 × 12 in.
signed: *D G Wells*
Purchased from the artist's daughter, Mrs K. Karen, 1978

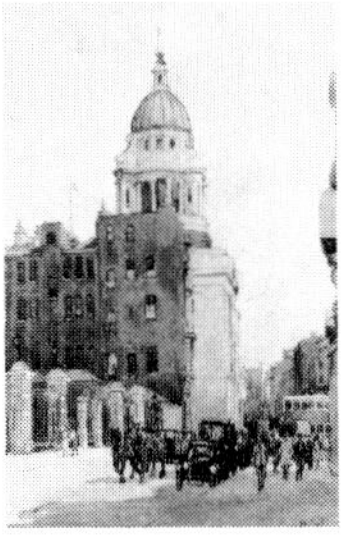

acc. no. 3642
St. Bride's Fleet Street (1941)

pencil and watercolour: $18\frac{1}{8} \times 11\frac{1}{4}$ in.
Purchased from the artist's daughter, Mrs K. Karen, 1985

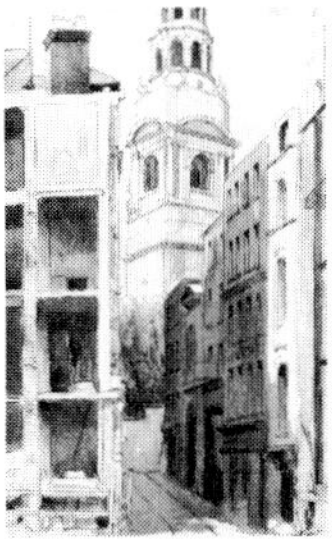

acc. no. 3644
St. Paul's from Queen Victoria Street (1941)

pencil, pen and ink and watercolour: $18\frac{1}{2} \times 11\frac{1}{2}$ in.
signed and dated: *D.G. Wells 1941*
Purchased from the artist's daughter, Mrs K. Karen, 1985

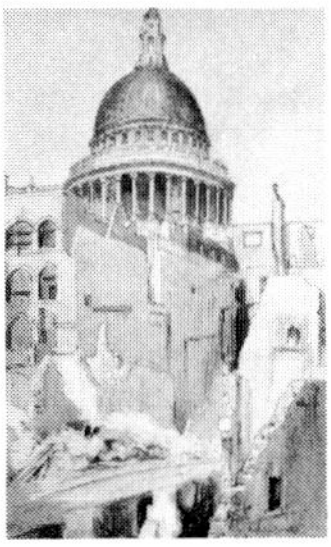

acc. no. 2171
Marble Arch (1947)

pen and ink and watercolour: $13\frac{7}{8} \times 21\frac{1}{4}$ in.
signed and dated: *Denys. G. Wells – 47*
Presented by the artist's daughter, Mrs K. Karen, 1975

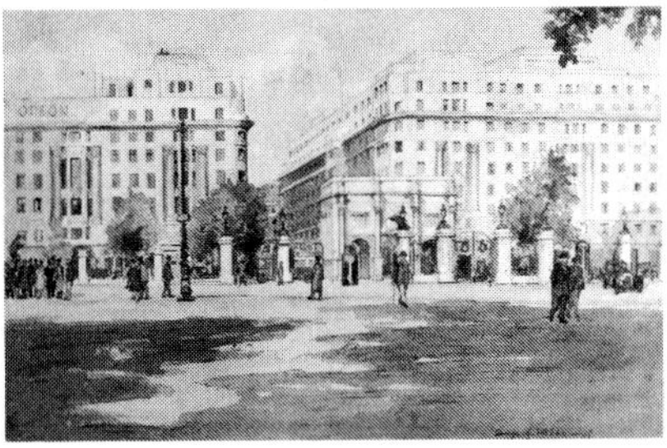

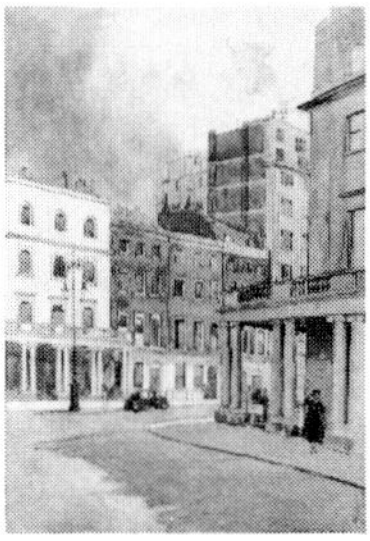

acc. no. 2175
Portland Place (1948)

pen and ink and watercolour: $21\frac{1}{2} \times 14\frac{1}{2}$ in.
signed and dated: *Denys G. Wells – 48*
Presented by the artist's daughter Mrs K. Karen, 1975

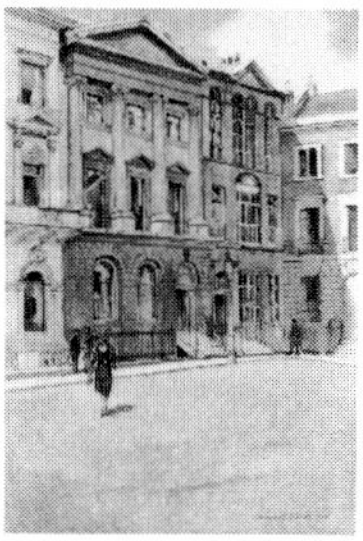

acc. no. 2178
St. James's Square (1948)

pen and ink and waterecolour: $21\frac{1}{2} \times 14\frac{1}{2}$ in.
signed and dated: *Denys. G. Wells – 48*
Presented by the artist's daughter, Mrs K. Karen, 1975

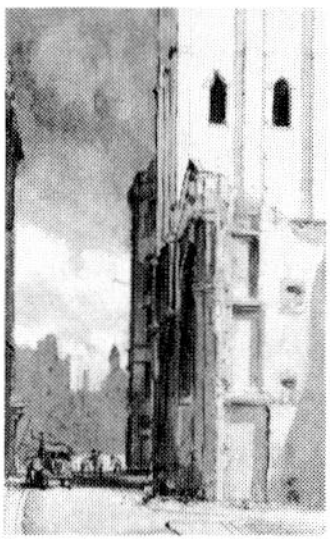

acc. no. 3641
St Alban Wood Street (*c.*1940s)

pencil and watercolour: $18\frac{1}{2} \times 11\frac{3}{8}$ in.
signed: *Denys Wells*
Purchased from the artist's daughter, Mrs K. Karen, 1985

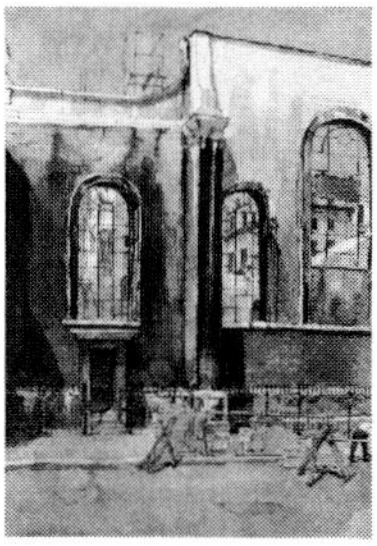

acc. no. 3640
Christ Church, Newgate Street (*c.*1950)

pen and brown ink and watercolour: $21\frac{7}{8} \times 15$ in.
signed: *D.G. Wells*
Purchased from the artist's daughter, Mrs K. Karen, 1985

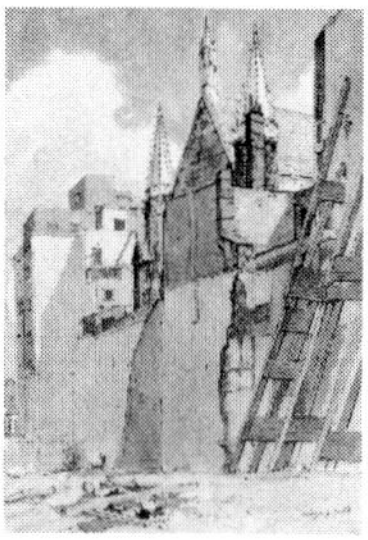

acc. no. 3637
The West End of Guildhall (*c.*1950)

pen and ink and watercolour: 22 × 15 in.
signed: *Denys.G. Wells*
Presented by the artist's daughter, Mrs K. Karen, 1985

acc. no. 2179
India office, Whitehall (1955)

pen and ink and watercolour: $21\frac{1}{2} \times 14\frac{1}{2}$ in.
signed and dated: *Denys. G. Wells 1955*
Presented by the artist's daughter, Mrs K. Karen, 1975

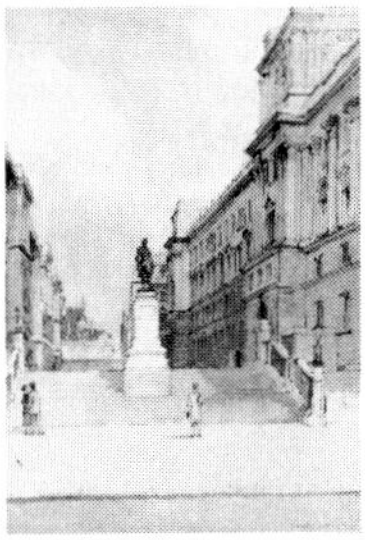

acc. no. 2169
St Martin, Ludgate Hill (*c.*1958)

pen and ink and watercolour: $21\frac{1}{2} \times 14\frac{1}{2}$ in.
Presented by the artist's daughter, Mrs K. Karen, 1975

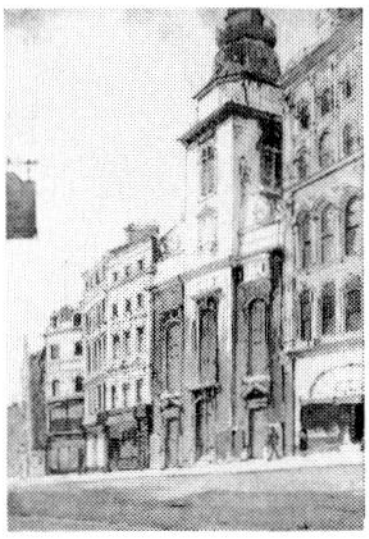

acc. no. 2170
St Martin in the Fields (1959)

pen and ink and watercolour: $14\frac{1}{2} \times 21\frac{1}{2}$ in.
signed and dated: *Denys. G. Wells – 59*
Presented by the artist's daughter, Mrs K. Karen, 1975

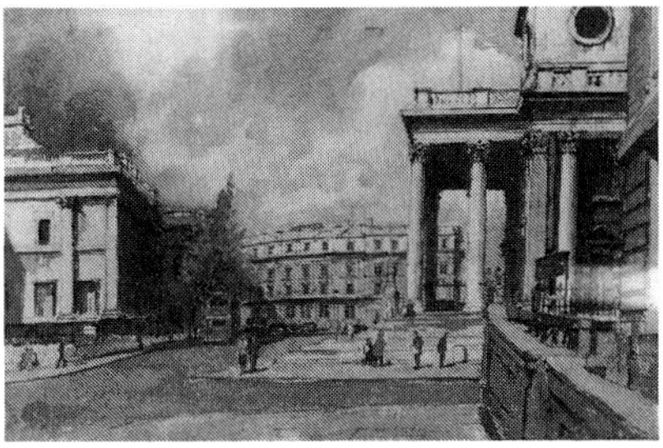

acc. no. 2173
Post Office, King Edward Street (1959)

pen and ink and watercolour: $21\frac{1}{2} \times 14\frac{1}{2}$ in.
signed and dated: *Denys.G. Wells – 59*
Presented by the artist's daughtere, Mrs K. Karen, 1975

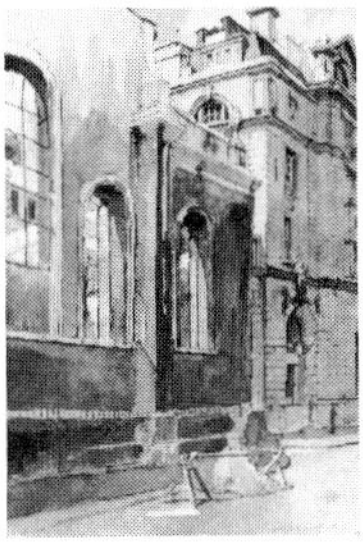

acc. no. 3643
A View of St. Bride's Fleet Street (*c.*1950s)

pencil and watercolour: $17\frac{3}{4} \times 12\frac{1}{8}$ in.
signed: *D.G. Wells*
Purchased from the artist's daughter, Mrs K. Karen, 1985

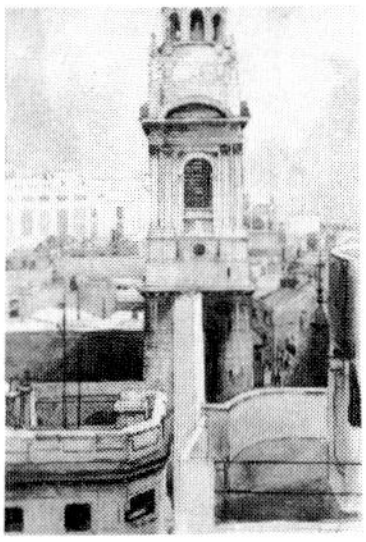

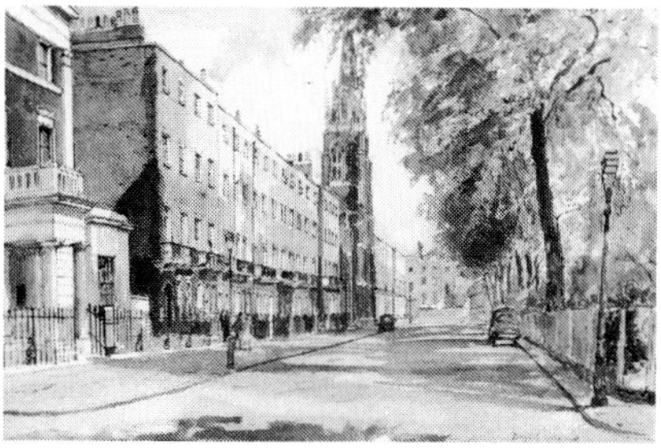

acc. no. 2176
Gordon Square (1960)

pen and ink and watercolour: $14\frac{1}{2} \times 21\frac{1}{2}$ in.
signed and dated: *Denys.G. Wells – 60*
Presented by the artist's daughter, Mrs K. Karen, 1975

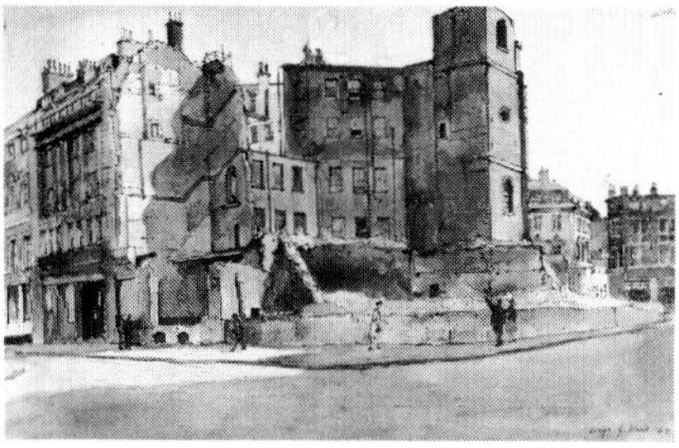

acc. no. 3639
Devastation in the City (1964)

pen and ink and watercolour: $14\frac{7}{8} \times 22\frac{1}{2}$ in.
signed and dated: *Denys.G. Wells – 64*
Purchased from the artist's daughter, Mrs K. Karen, 1985

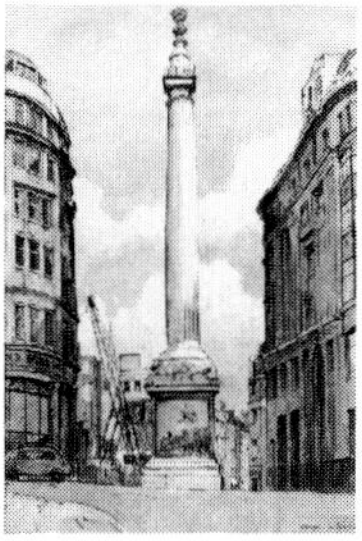

acc. no. 2174
The Monument (1965)

pen and ink and watercolour: $21\frac{1}{2} \times 14\frac{1}{2}$ in.
signed and dated: *Denys.G.Wells – 65*
Presented by the artist's daughter, Mrs K. Karen, 1975

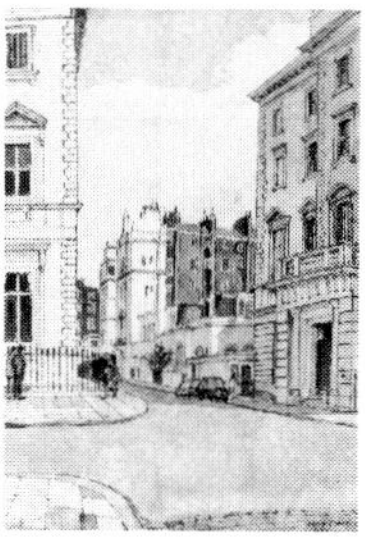

acc. no. 2172
Belgravia (1968)

pen and ink and watercolour: $21\frac{1}{2} \times 14\frac{1}{2}$ in.
signed and dated: *Denys G Wells – 68*
Presented by the artist's daughter, Mrs K. Karen, 1975

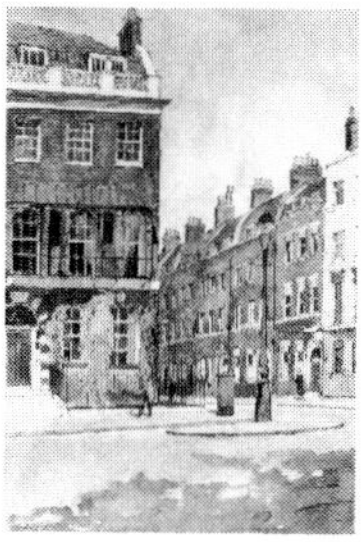

acc. no. 2168
Bedford Place, Bloomsbury (*c.*1968)

pen and ink and watercolour: $21\frac{1}{2} \times 14\frac{1}{2}$ in. (sight)
Presented by the artist's daughter, Mrs K. Karen, 1975

acc. no. 3645
The West End of St Lawrence Jewry and the Corner of Gresham Street and Aldermanbury (*c.*1960s)

pen and ink and watercolour: 21 × 14¼ in.
signed: *D.G. Wells*
Purchased from the artist's daughter, Mrs K. Karen, 1985

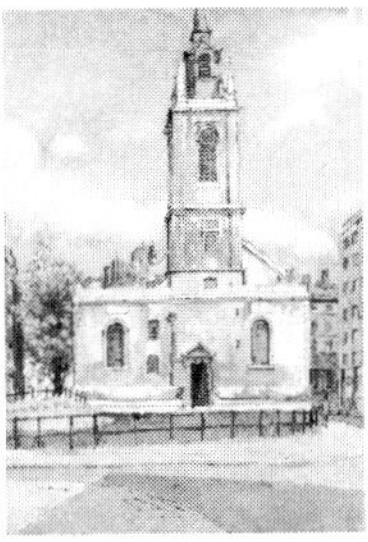

acc. no. 2177
St James's Place (1970)

pen and ink and watercolour: 14½ × 21½ in. (sight)
signed and dated: *Denys.G. Wells – 70*
Presented by the artist's daughter, Mrs K. Karen, 1975

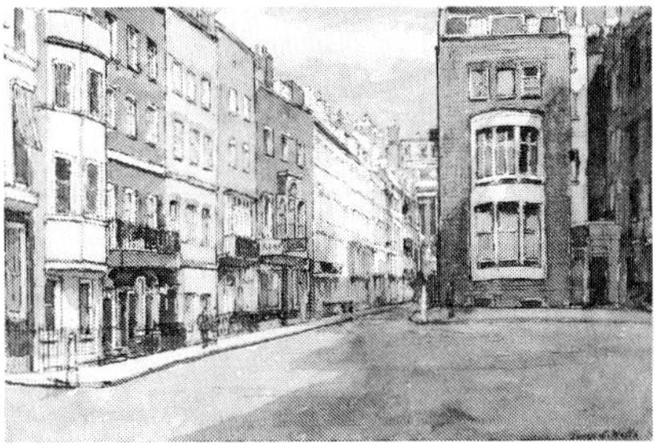

acc. no. 2180
Brompton Oratory (*c.*1970)

pen and ink and watercolour: 21½ × 14½ in. (sight)
Presented by the artist's daughter, Mrs K. Karen, 1975

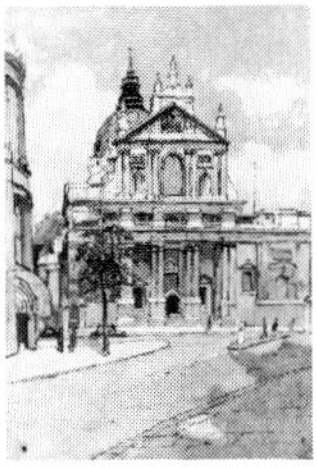

acc. no. 2181
Westminster Abbey Behind Houses

pen and ink and watercolour: 14½ × 21½ in. (sight)
Presented by the artist's daughter, Mrs K. Karen, 1975

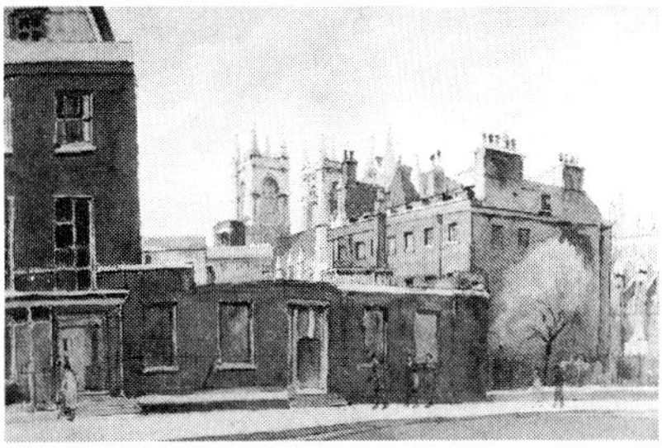

Henry Tanworth Wells (1828–1903)

acc. no. 773
Quarrymen of Purbeck (1885)

oil on canvas: 56 × 85 in.
signed: *Harry T Wells*
Presented by the artist's daughters, Mrs A. E. Street and Mrs W. J. Hadley, 1903

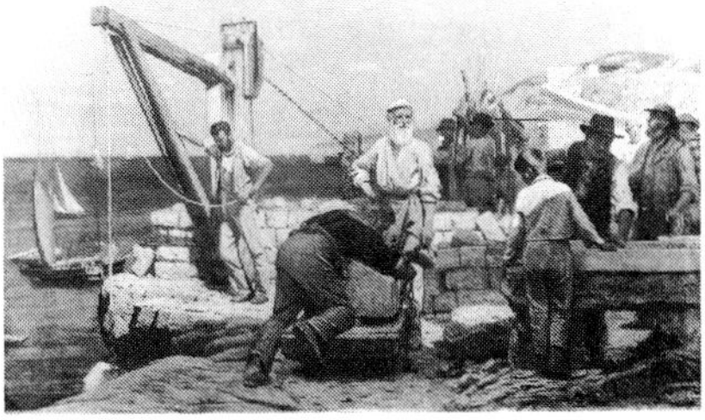

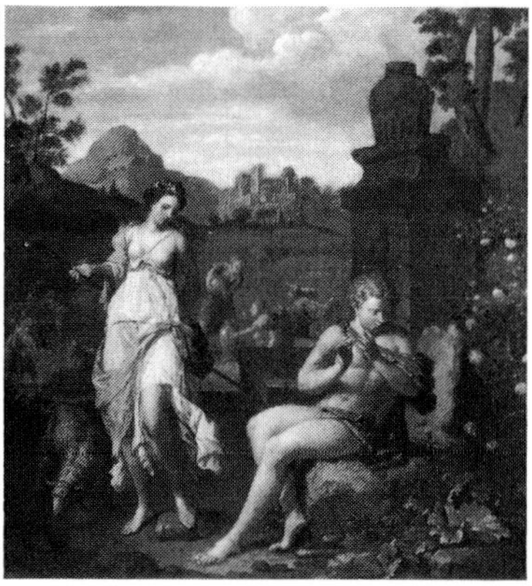

attributed to Adriaan van der Werff (1659–1722)

acc. no. 380
Shepherd Piping and Nymph Dancing
oil on panel: 18 × 14 in.
Bequeathed by William Dunnett, 1888

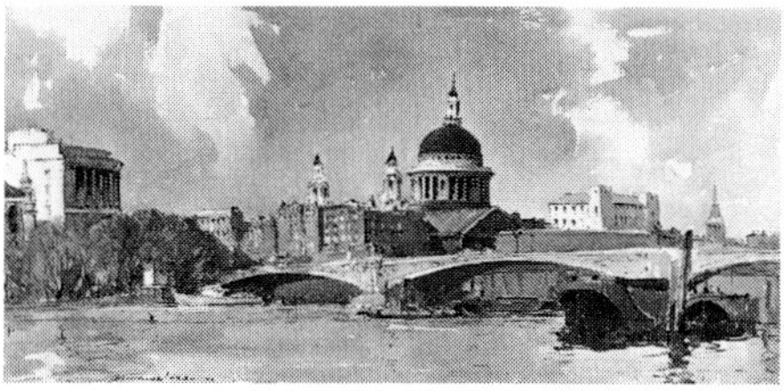

Edward Wesson (b.1910)

acc. no. 1779
Above Blackfriars (*c.*1967)
watercolour: $13\frac{5}{8} \times 27\frac{5}{8}$ in.
signed: *Edward Wesson*
Purchased from the artist, 1967

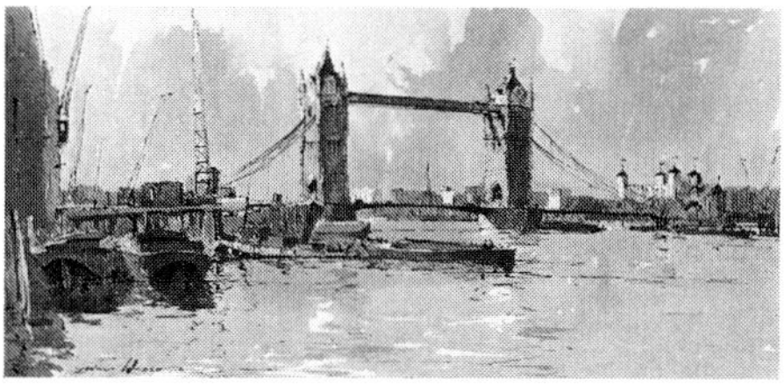

acc. no. 1780
Below the Pool (*c.*1967)
watercolour: $13\frac{1}{2} \times 27\frac{5}{8}$ in.
signed: *Edward Wesson*
Purchased from the artist, 1967

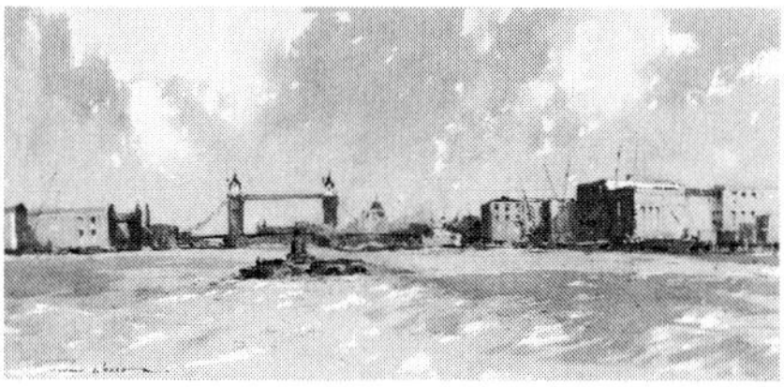

acc. no. 1791
Making for the Pool (*c.*1968)
watercolour: $13\frac{1}{4} \times 27\frac{1}{2}$ in.
signed: *Edward Wesson*
Purchased from the artist, 1968

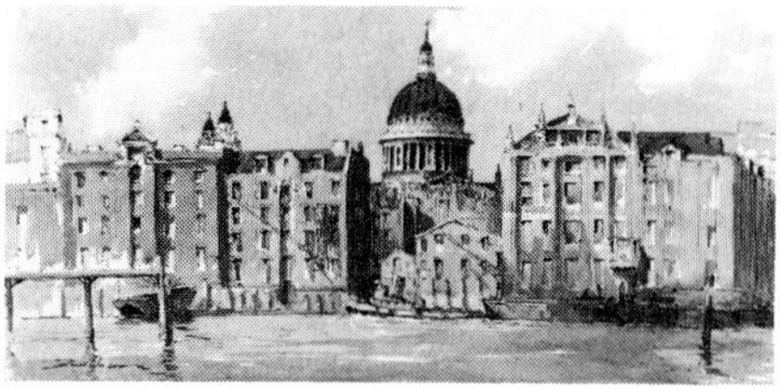

acc. no. 1792
The Thames from Bankside (*c.*1968)
watercolour: $13\frac{3}{8} \times 27\frac{3}{8}$ in.
signed: *Edward Wesson*
Purchased from the artist, 1968

William Westall (1781–1850)

acc. no. 508

The River Dee and St. John's Church

pencil and watercolour: $3\frac{1}{2} \times 5\frac{3}{4}$ in.

Presented by Felix Joseph, 1890

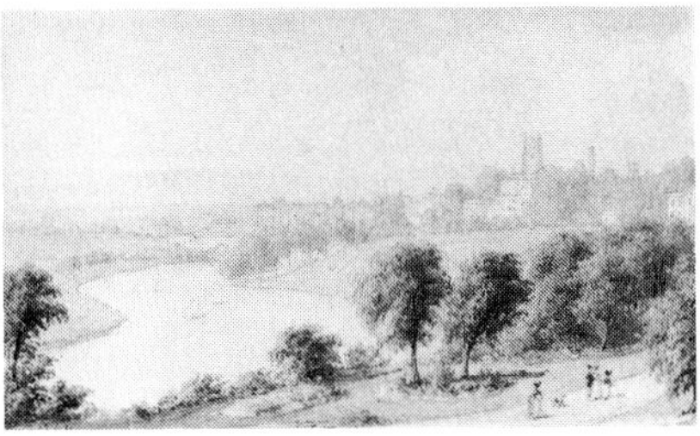

acc. no. 509

Hythe Church and Martello Tower

pencil and watercolour: $3\frac{7}{8} \times 5\frac{5}{8}$ in.

Presented by Felix Joseph, 1890

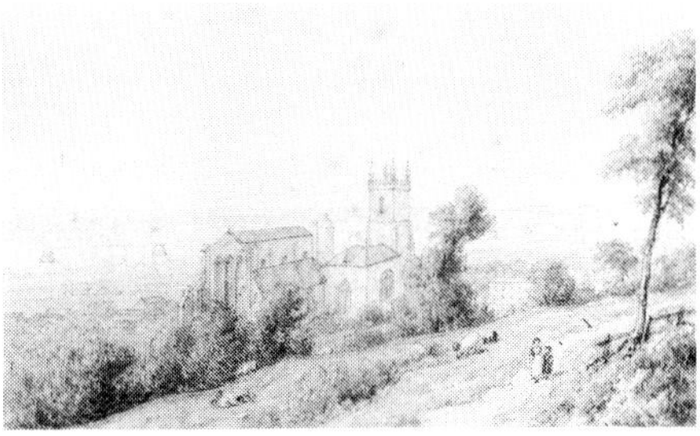

Francis Wheatley (1747–1801) and Richard Paton (1717–91)

acc. no. 54

The Lord Mayor's Procession by Water to Westminster, November 9 1789

oil on canvas: 61 × 85 in.

Presented by Alderman John Boydell, 1792

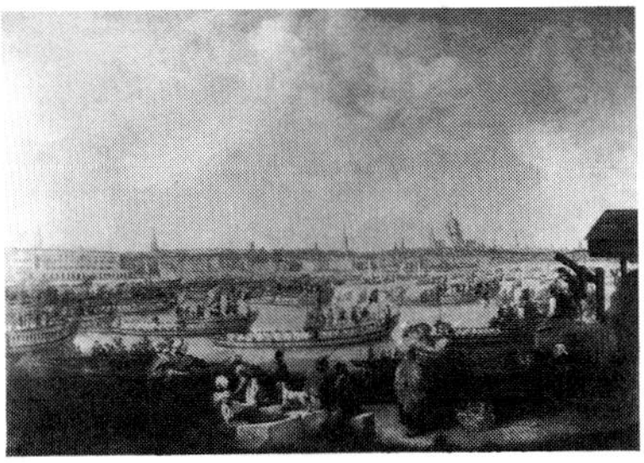

after Francis Wheatley (1747–1801)

acc. no. 1294

The Benevolent Cottager

oil on canvas: 30 × 25 in.

Presented by Lady Wakefield, 1944

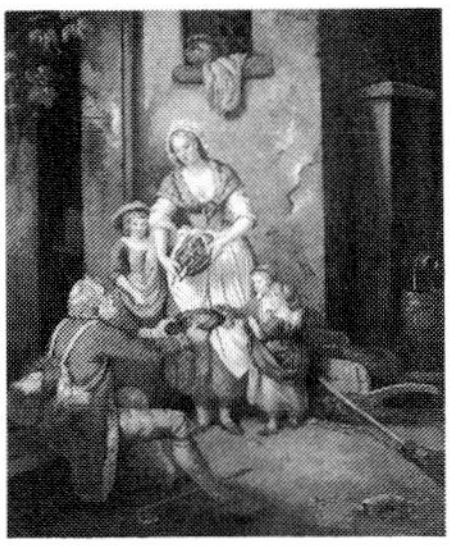

Robert P. Whellock (*fl.* 1877–1903)

acc. no. 2182

Wellington's Monument in St. Paul's Cathedral (1877)

watercolour: $39\frac{1}{8} \times 25\frac{3}{4}$ in.

signed and dated: *R.P. Whellock. Pinx. / 1877.*

Presented by Miss A. M. Young, 1975

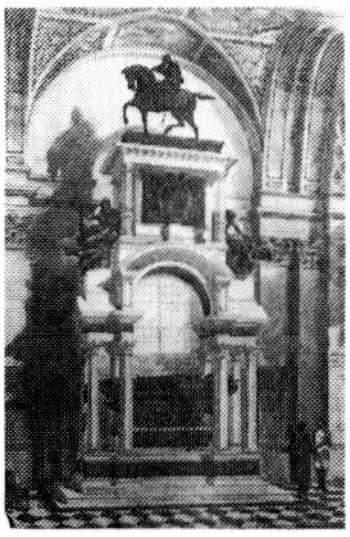

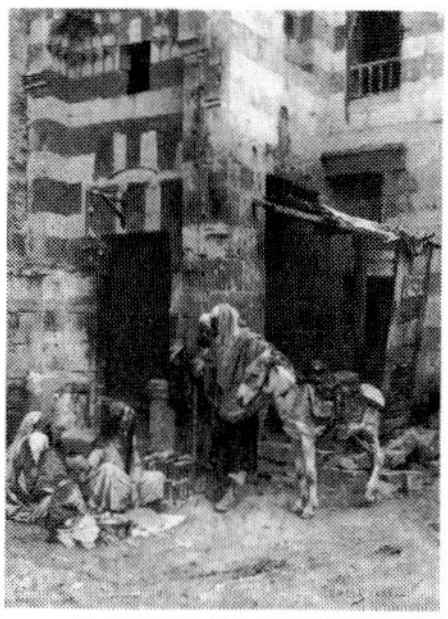

Charles H. Wilda (1854–1907)

acc. no. 747
Fortune Telling (1887)
oil on canvas: 37 × 28 in.
signed and dated: *C H. WILDA CAIRO. 1887*
Bequeathed by Charles Gassiot, 1902

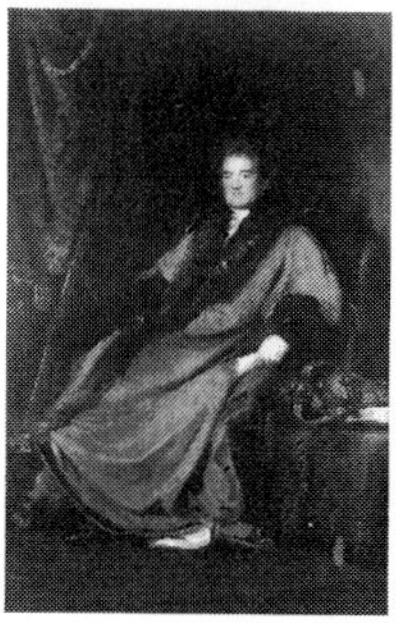

Sir David Wilkie (1785–1841)

acc. no. 1905
Matthias Prime Lucas, Lord Mayor 1827 and President of St. Bartholomew's Hospital (1838)
oil on canvas: 94 × 58½ in.
signed and dated: *David Wilkie / 1.5.38*
Presented by the Governors of St. Bartholomew's Hospital, 1972

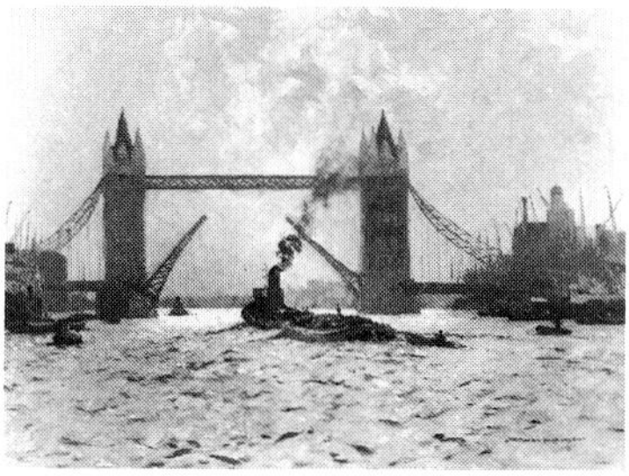

Norman Wilkinson (1878–1971)

acc. no. 1638
Towing Past the City (*c.*1962)
oil on canvas: 24 × 32 in.
signed: *NORMAN WILKINSON*
Purchased from the artist, 1962

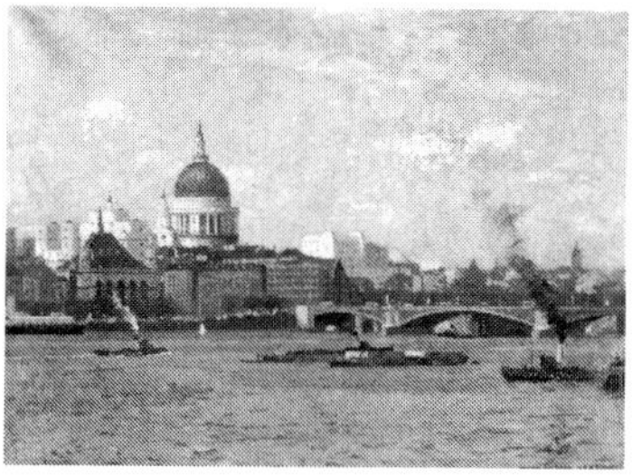

acc. no. 1889
St. Paul's and Blackfriars Bridge (*c.*1971)
oil on canvas: 24 × 32 in.
signed: *NORMAN WILKINSON*
Purchased from the artist, 1971

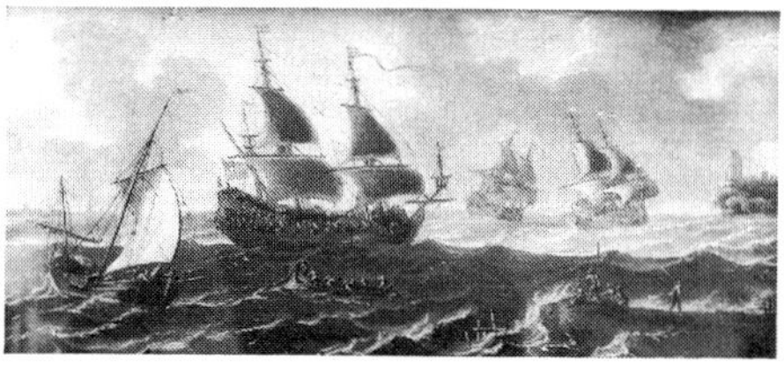

attributed to Adam Willaerts (1577–1669)

acc. no. 384
Dutch Naval Battle
oil on canvas: $8\frac{3}{4} \times 18\frac{3}{4}$ in.
Bequeathed by William Dunnett, 1888

acc. no. 385
Dutch Naval Battle
oil on canvas: $8\frac{3}{4} \times 18\frac{3}{4}$ in.
Bequeathed by William Dunnett, 1888

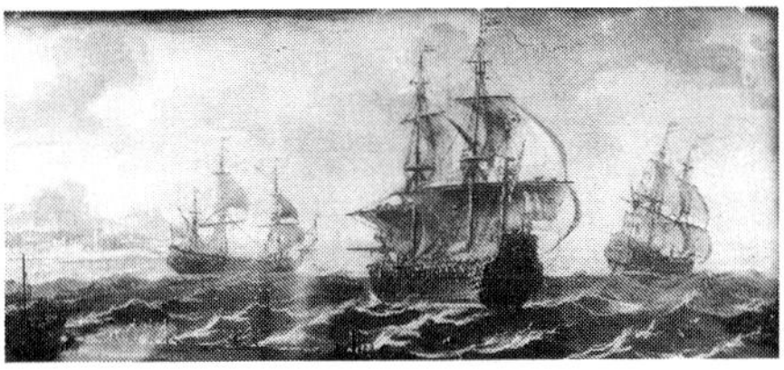

Alyn Williams (1865–1941)

acc. no. 837
King Edward VII (1904)
watercolour on ivory: $3\frac{3}{4} \times 2\frac{7}{8}$ in. (oval)
signed and dated: *– Alyn Williams – / 1904*
Presented by Sir A. Reynolds, 1904

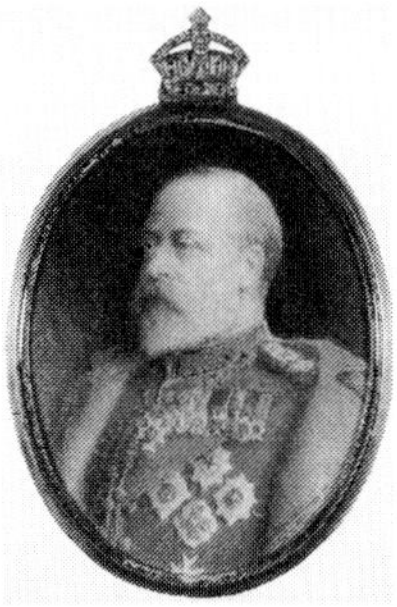

John Edgar Williams (*fl.* 1846–83)

acc. no. 1080
Sir Sills John Gibbons, Lord Mayor 1871 (1872)
oil on canvas: 30 × 25 in.
Presented by F. A. Garrett, 1931

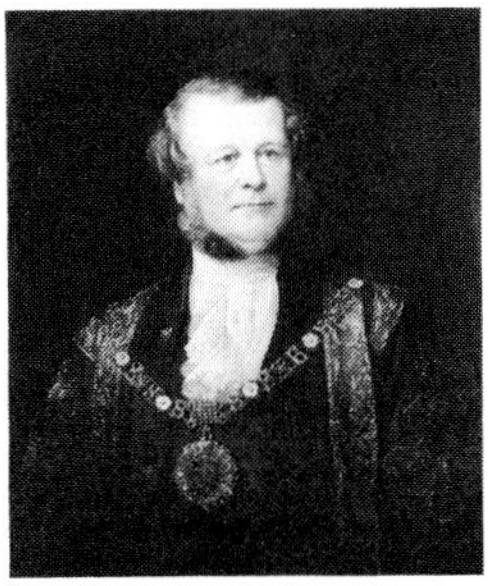

acc. no. 255
Robert Besley, Lord Mayor 1869 (1874)
oil on canvas: 56 × 45 in.
signed and dated: *J. EDGAR WILLIAMS / 1874*
Bequeathed by Robert Besley, 1877

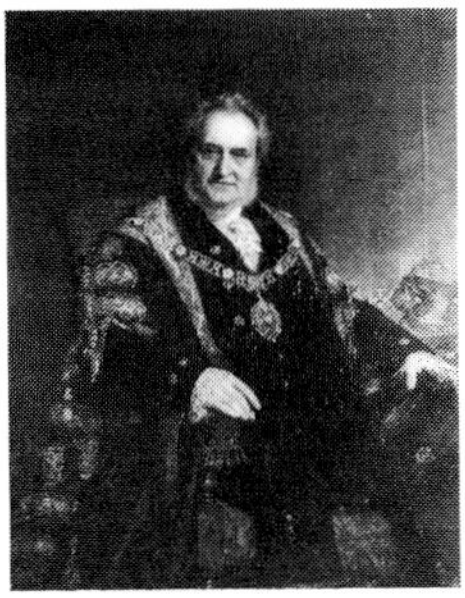

Eduard Willmann (1820–1877)

acc. no. 2154
Baden Baden
steel engraving: $13\frac{5}{8} \times 20\frac{7}{8}$ in.
signed: *ED. WILLMANN DEL ET SCULPT*
Presented by the Burgomeister of Baden Baden, 1974

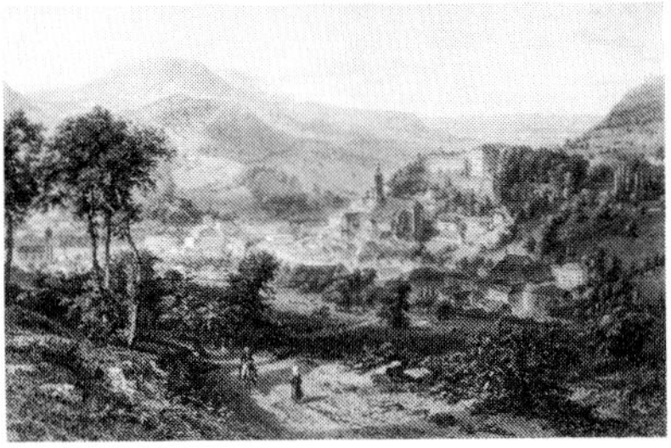

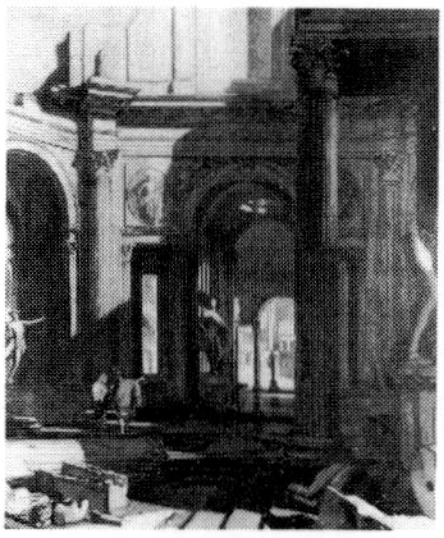

Emanuel de Witte (1617–92)

acc. no. 580
Roman Ruins

oil on canvas: 36 × 31 in.
Presented by Wyatt Papworth, 1893

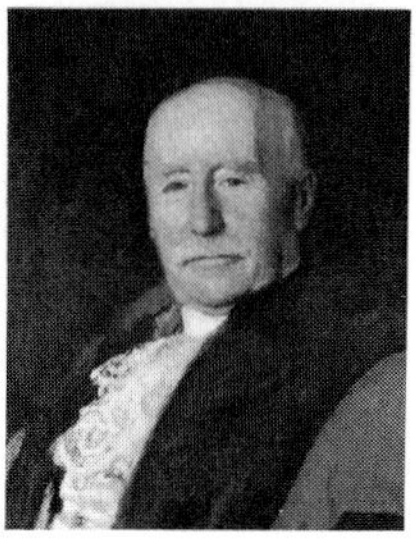

Charles Haigh Wood (1856–1927)

acc. no. 880
Sir Frederick Prat Alliston (*c.*1908)

oil on canvas, cut down to: $21\frac{1}{2} \times 16\frac{3}{4}$ in.
Presented by Sir Frederick Prat Alliston, 1909

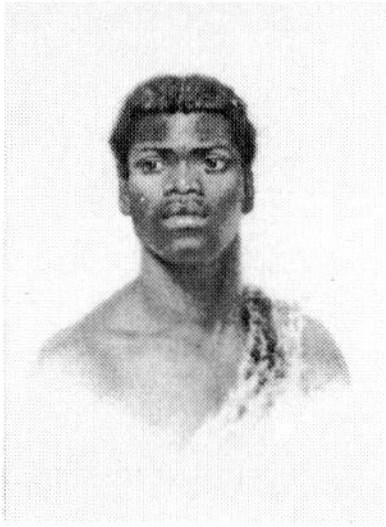

Constance Wood (*fl.* 1880)

acc. no. 1575
Head of a Zulu (1881)

watercolour: 20 × 12 in.
inscribed with initials: *E.B.K.*
Presented by the artist's daughter, Miss Collingridge, to the City of London Freemen's School, 1959

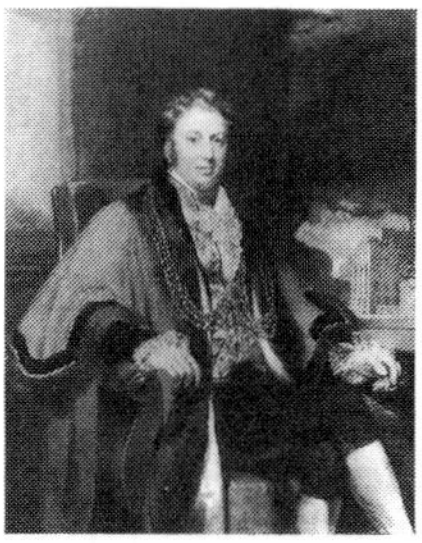

John Wood (1801–70)

acc. no. 1505
John Humphery, Sheriff 1832–3 (*c.*1833)

oil on canvas: 56 × 44 in.
Presented by Lady de la Bere, 1953

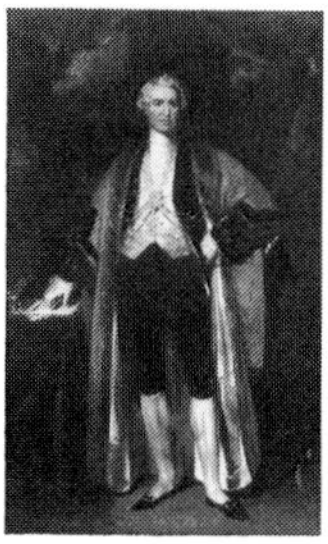

acc. no. 1904
Sir George Carroll, Sheriff 1837–8 (1838)

oil on canvas: 94 × 58 in.
signed and dated: *JOHN WOOD / 1838*
Presented by the Governors of St. Bartholomew's Hospital, 1972

Geoffrey Wright (20th C)

acc. no. 1938
The Woolwich Ferry (1971)

oil on hardboard: 18 × 30 in.
signed and dated: *Geoffrey Wright / 1971*
Purchased from the artist, 1972

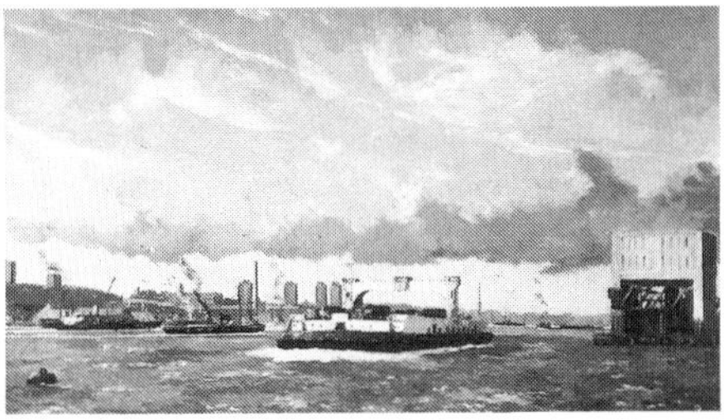

John Michael Wright (*c.*1617–94)

acc. no. 1836
Sir John Robinson, Lord Mayor 1662

oil on canvas: 53 × 45 in.
inscribed: *Sir John Robinson, Bart, / Gov.r of the Tower, Vcr / of Farming Woods, / Northamptonshire* and *Painted by / J Michael Wright* (over an earlier inscription with the name *Sir Peter L...*)
Purchased from John Harvey, 1970

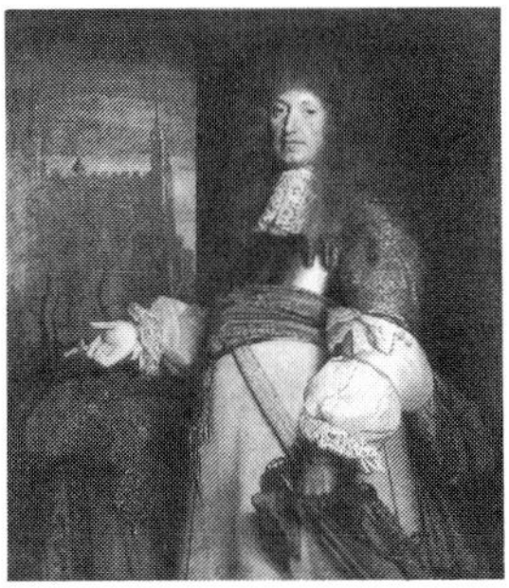

acc. no. 10
Sir Matthew Hale, Chief Justice of the King's Bench

oil on canvas: 87 × 60 in.
Commissioned by the Corporation, 1670

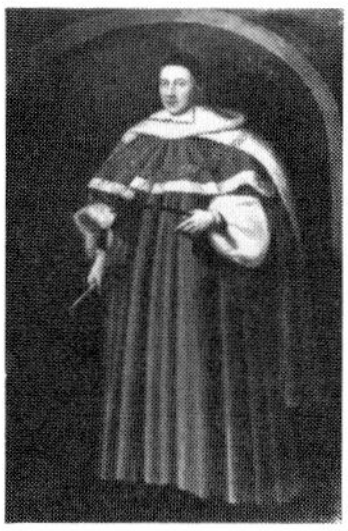

acc. no. 24
Sir Hugh Wyndham, Judge of the Common Pleas

oil on canvas: 87 × 60 in.
Commissioned by the Corporation, 1670

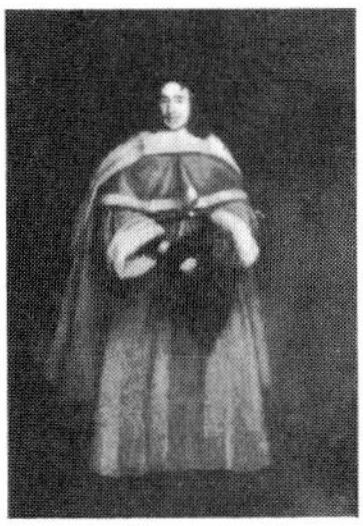

H. W. Wright (b.1912)

acc. no. 2220
St. Katharine's Dock (*c.*1979)

oil on canvas: $19\frac{1}{2} \times 23\frac{1}{2}$ in. (sight)
signed: *H W Wright*
Purchased from the artist, 1979

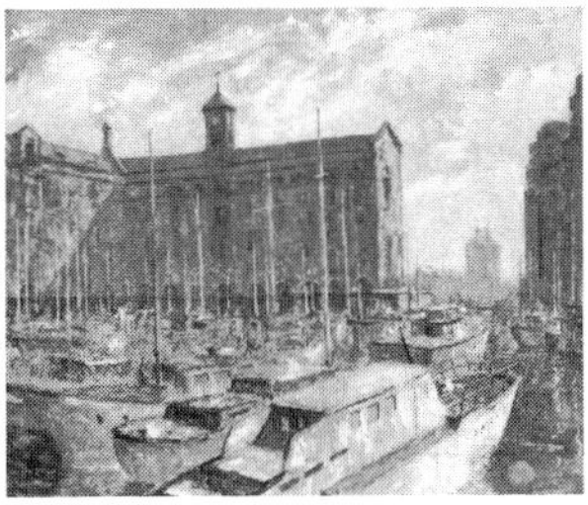

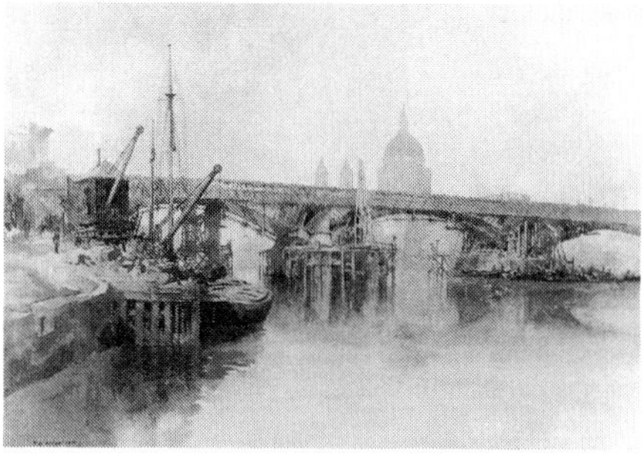

Richard Henry Wright (1857–1930)

acc. no. 1095
Southwark Bridge in Course of Demolition (1915)
watercolour: $10 \times 14\frac{1}{2}$ in.
signed and dated: *R.H. Wright 1915*
Presented by Mrs. Wright, 1935

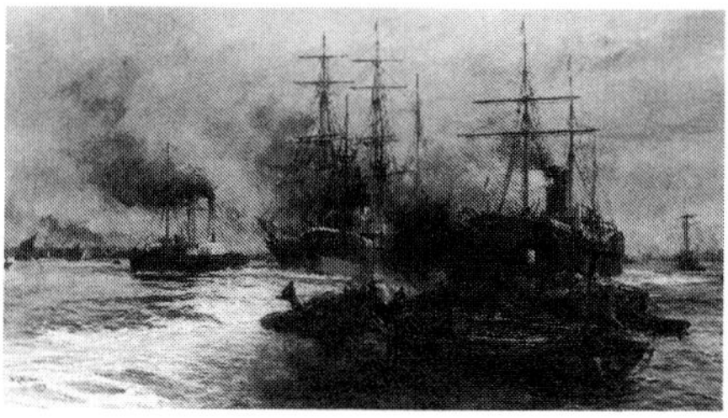

William Lionel Wyllie (1851–1931)

acc. no. 884
Scene on the Lower Thames (1884)
oil on canvas: 18×32 in.
signed and dated: *W L Wyllie. / 1884*
Bequeathed by James Thomas Slater, 1909

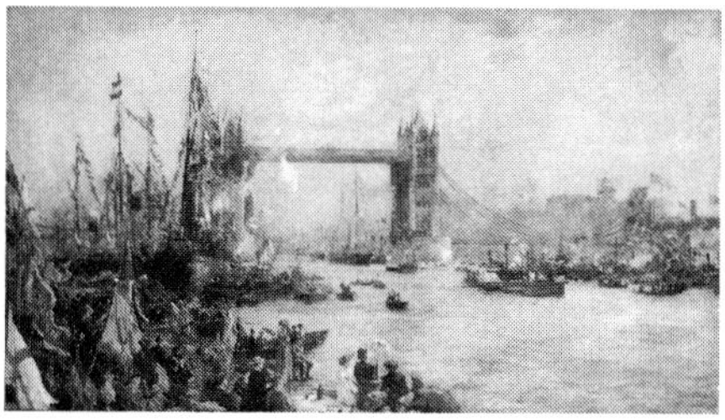

acc. no. 1721
The Opening of Tower Bridge (1894–5)
oil on canvas: 48×84 in.
signed: *W.L. Wyllie*
Purchased from Colonel Harold Wyllie, 1965

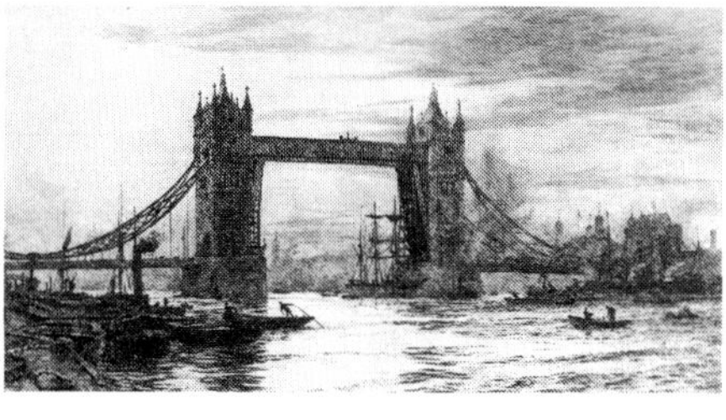

acc. no. 1617
Tower Bridge
etching: $13 \times 21\frac{1}{2}$ in. (plate)
signed: *W.L. Wyllie*
Purchased from Mrs. Reynell Wreford, 1960

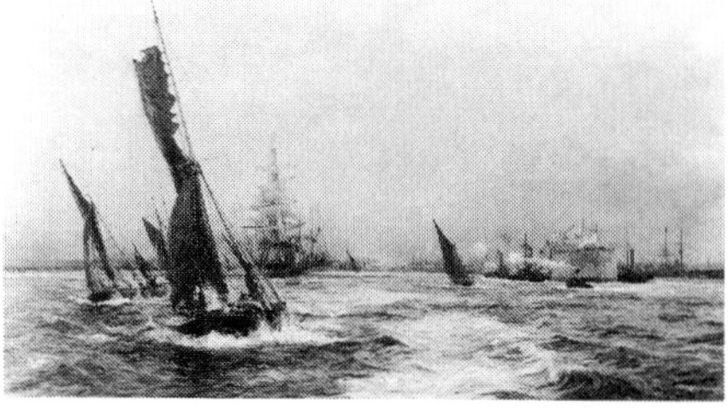

acc. no. 616
Commerce and Sea Power (1898)
oil on canvas: 36×60 in.
signed: *W.L. Wyllie*
Presented by Charles T. Harris, 1900

Lisa Zirner (living)

acc. no. 3498
World's End (1958)

oil on hardboard: $23\frac{1}{4} \times 47\frac{1}{4}$ in.
signed: *LIZA ZIRNER*
Purchased from the artist, 1984

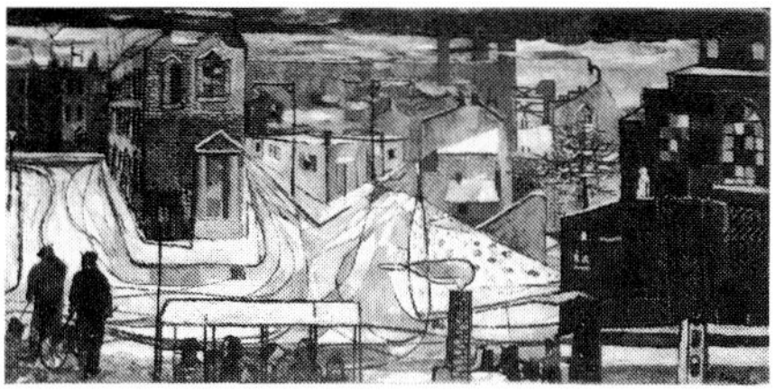

Sculpture

Jaroslaw Giercarz Alfer (b.1936)

acc. no. 2221
Head of Chopin (1978)

plaster: 22 × 11 × 11 in.
Presented by the Byron Society, the Anglo-Polish Society and the Chopin Society, 1978

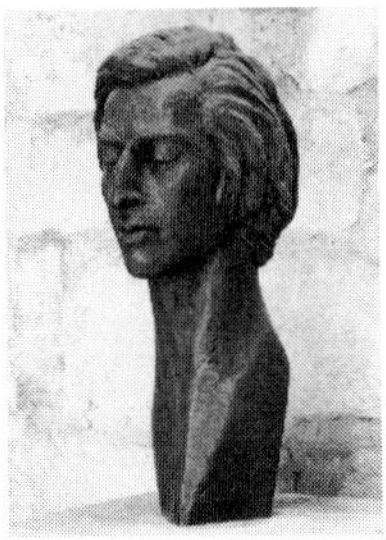

Charles Bacon (1821–*c.*1885)

acc. no. 180
Warren Stormes Hale

marble: 33 × 22 × 12 in.
Presented by the sitter to the City of London School, 1866

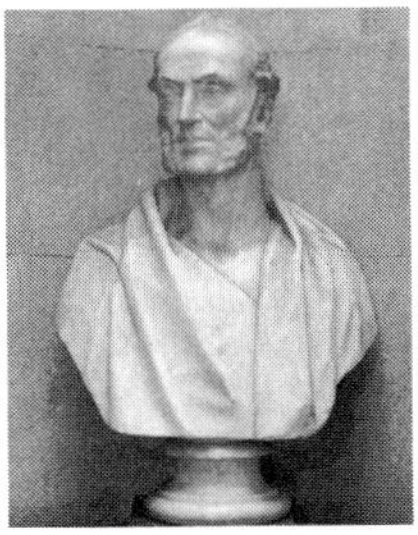

acc. no. 267
Dr. G.F.W. Mortimer (1866)

marble: 30 × 22 × 10 in.
Presented by Mrs. Mortimer to the City of London School, 1882

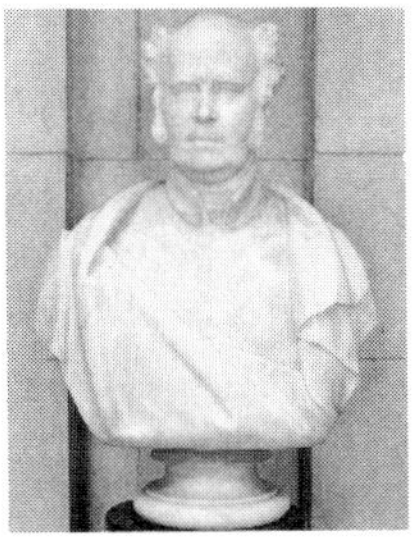

John Bacon (1740–99)

acc. no. 42
Monument to William Pitt, Earl of Chatham (1783)

marble: 170 × 175 × 50 in.
Commissioned by the Corporation, 1779

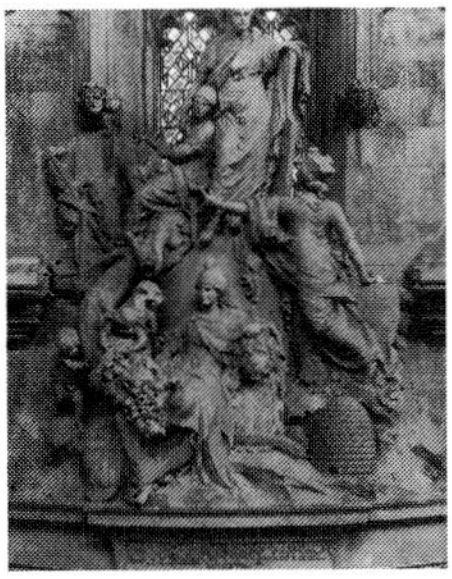

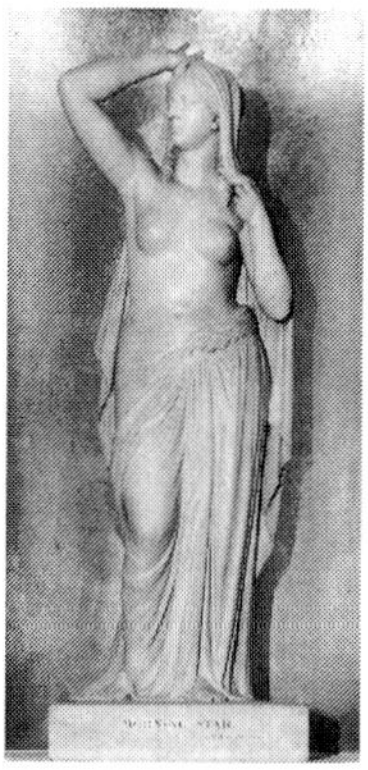

Edward Hodges Baily (1788–1867)

acc. no. 144
The Morning Star (1854)

marble: 79 in. high
Commissioned by the Corporation for the Mansion House, 1853

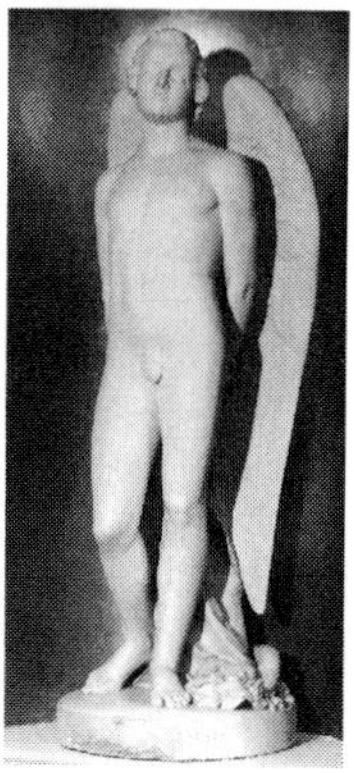

acc. no. 135
The Fate of Genius (1856)

marble: 68 in. high
Commissioned by the Corporation for the Mansion House, 1856

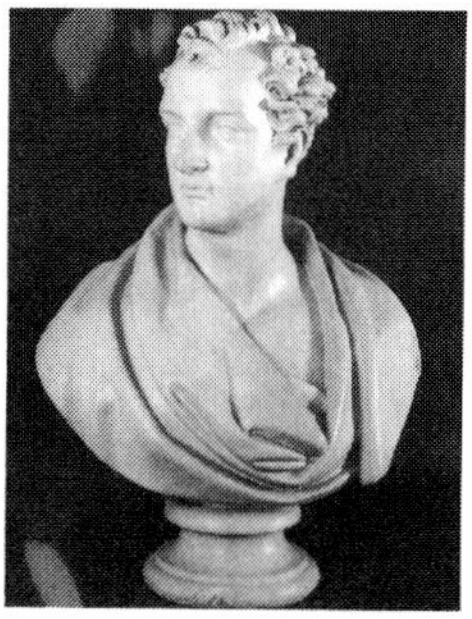

after Edward Hodges Baily (1788–1867)

acc. no. 170
Byron

plaster: 28 in. high
Acquired *c.*1860, source unknown

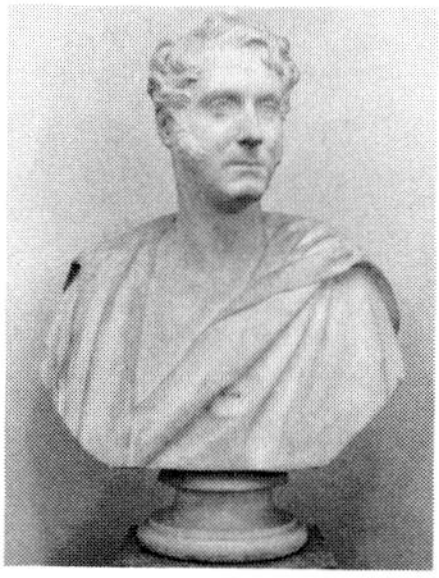

William Behnes (1795–1864)

acc. no. 1861
Sir David Salomons, Lord Mayor 1855 (1855)

marble: 30 in. high
Presented by R. H. Taylor, Salomons Trustees, to the City of London School, 1971

acc. no. 168
Sir David Salomons (1858)

marble: 29 × 23½ × 12 in.
Commissioned by the Corporation, 1858

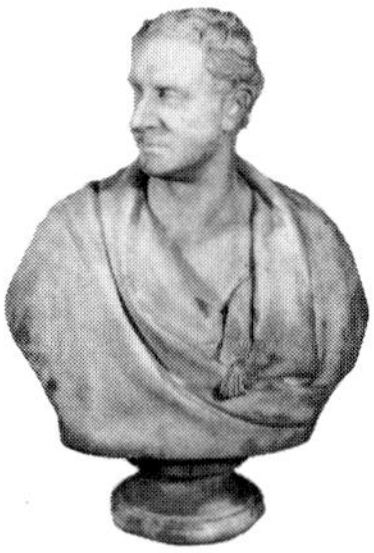

acc. no. 167
Major-General Sir Henry Havelock (1858)

marble: 26¾ × 22 × 9½ in.
Commissioned by the Corporation, 1858

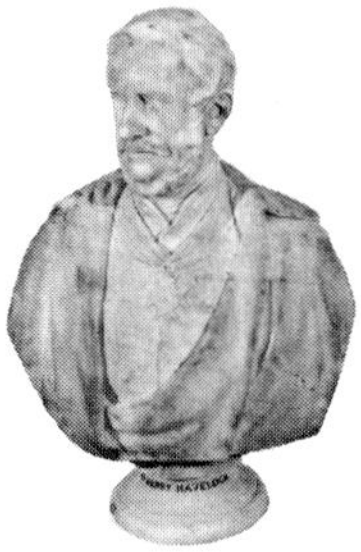

John Bell (1812–95)

acc. no. 154
Monument to the Duke of Wellington

marble: 165 × 165 × 45 in.
Commissioned by the Corporation, 1854

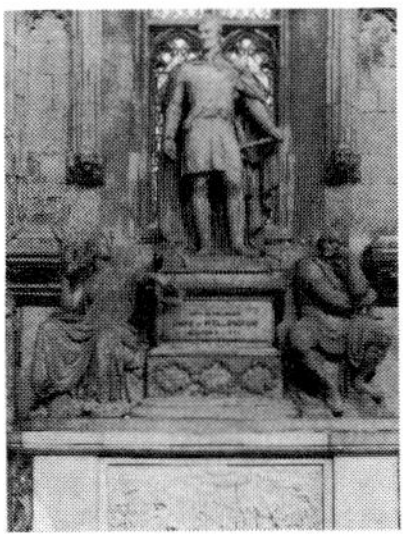

Charles Bell Birch (1832–93)

acc. no. 1521
Sir Francis Wyatt Truscott, Lord Mayor 1879 (1881)

marble: 20 × 25½ × 13 in.
Purchased, 1955

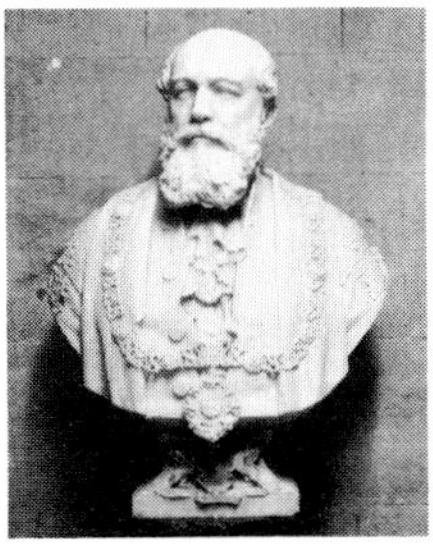

acc. no. 1831
Sir Horace Jones, City Architect (1886)

marble: 20½ × 15½ × 11 in.
Bequeathed by the sitter's daughter, Miss A. C. Jones, 1969

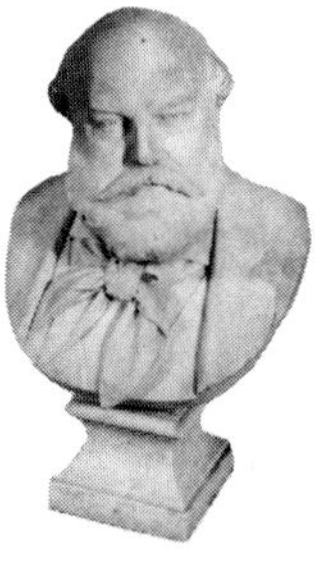

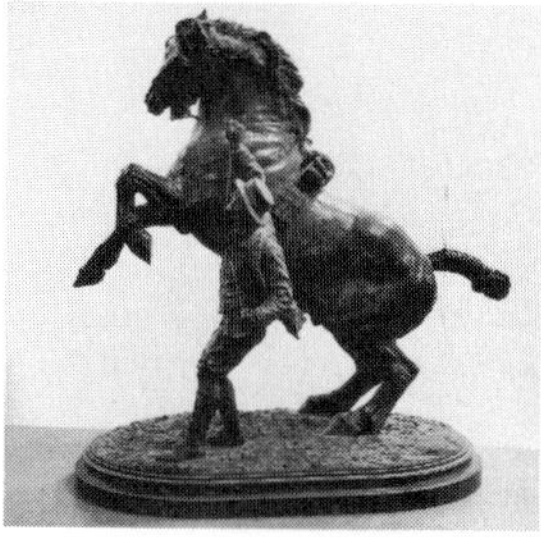

Sir Joseph Edgar Boehm (1834–90)

acc. no. 2184
Cart Stallion with Groom (1869)

bronze: 23 × 20 in.
signed: *BOEHM*
Presented by Miss A. M. Young, 1975

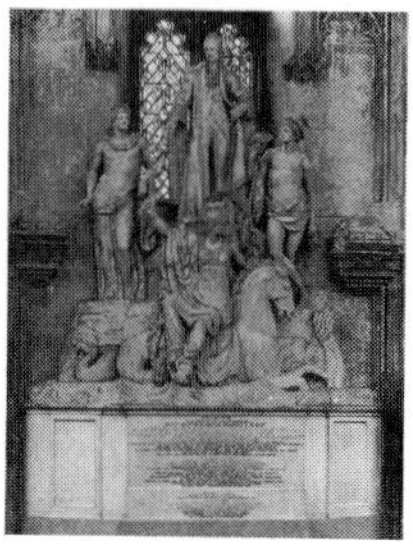

James George Bubb (1782–1853)

acc. no. 85
Monument to William Pitt (1813)

marble: 155 × 180 × 48 in. approx.
Commissioned by the Corporation, 1807

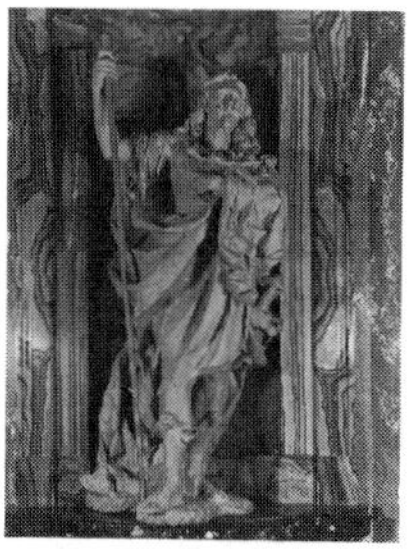

John Bushnell (d.1701)

acc. no. 963
King Charles I

purbeck stone: 84 × 38 × 28 in.
Removed from the Royal Exchange, 1838

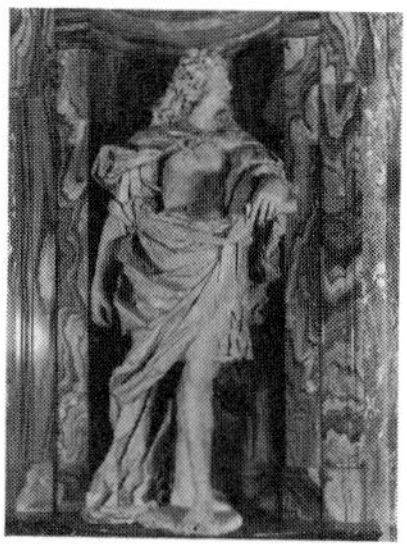

acc. no. 964
King Charles II

purbeck stone: $83\frac{1}{2}$ × 40 × 34 in.
Removed from the Royal Exchange, 1838

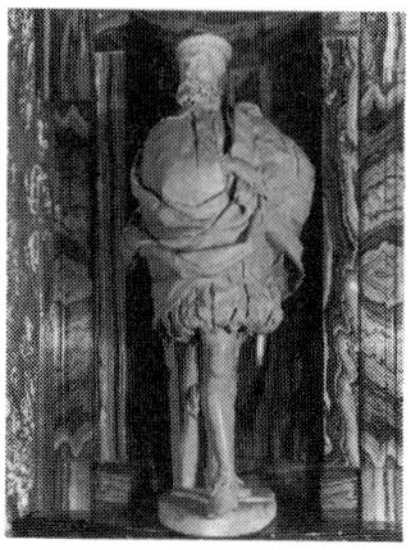

acc. no. 965
Sir Thomas Gresham

purbeck stone: 83 × 32 × 25 in.
Removed from the Royal Exchange, 1838

Emma-Marie Cadwallader-Guild (b.1843)

acc. no. 1286
Dr Joseph Joachim (1877)

bronze: $30 \times 25 \times 21\frac{1}{2}$ in.
Presented to the Guildhall School of Music by Dame Nellie Melba, 1923

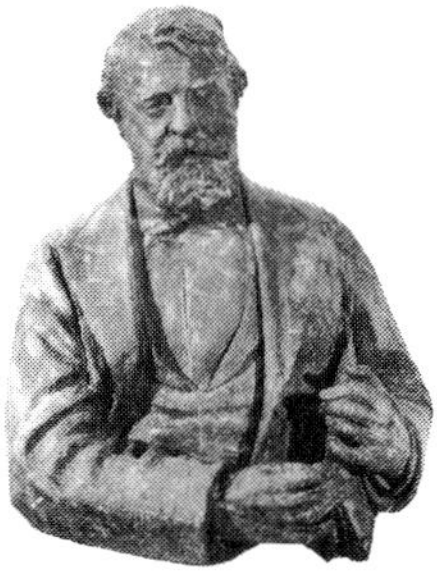

Giorgio Castiglioni (20th C)

acc. no. 1722
St. George and the Dragon (1965)

bronze: $11\frac{1}{2} \times 7\frac{1}{2}$ in.
Presented by the City of Milan, 1965

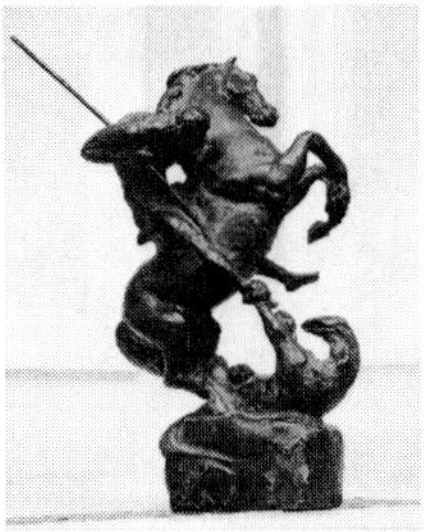

after Sir Francis Legatt Chantrey (1781–1841)

acc. no. 169
Sir Walter Scott

plaster: 28 in. high
Acquired, method and source unknown, *c.*1860

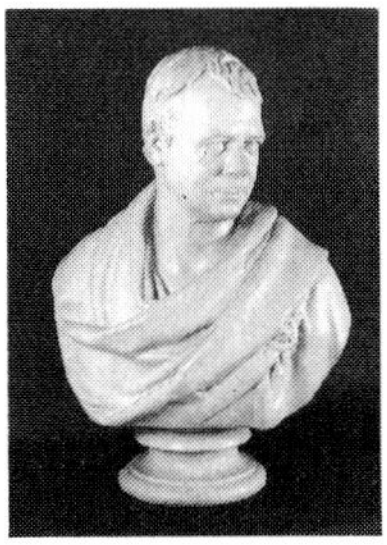

Robert Colton (1869–1922)

acc. no. 1030
Field Marshall the Earl Roberts of Kandahar

bronze: 14×10 in.
Purchased by the Corporation, 1924

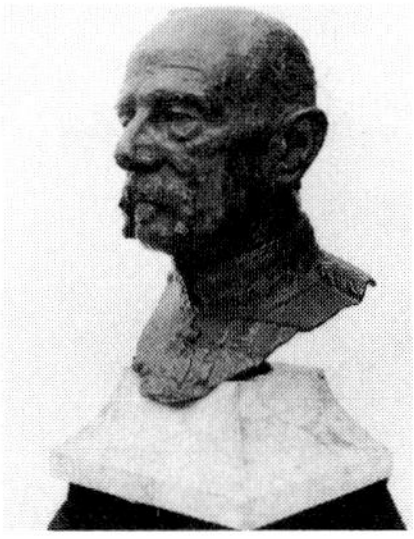

John D. Crittenden (*fl.* 1853–78)

acc. no. 993
Ferdinand Brand, City Comptroller (1859)

plaster: $25 \times 18 \times 10\frac{1}{2}$ in.
Presented by the sitter's daughter, Mrs. J. E. Turner, 1917

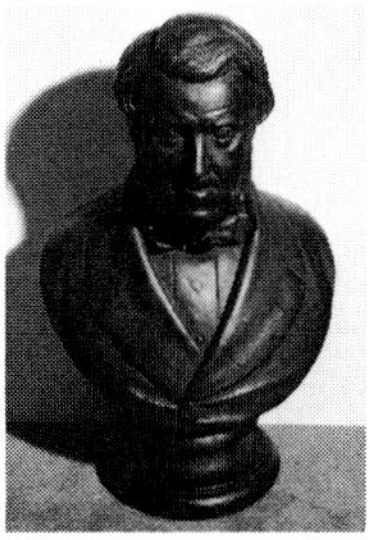

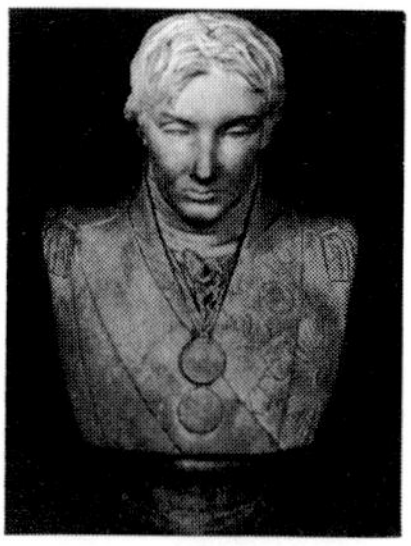

Anne Seymour Damer (1749–1828)
acc. no. 81
Horatio, Viscount Nelson (*c.*1797)
marble: 24 × 20 × 12½ in.
Presented by the artist, 1797

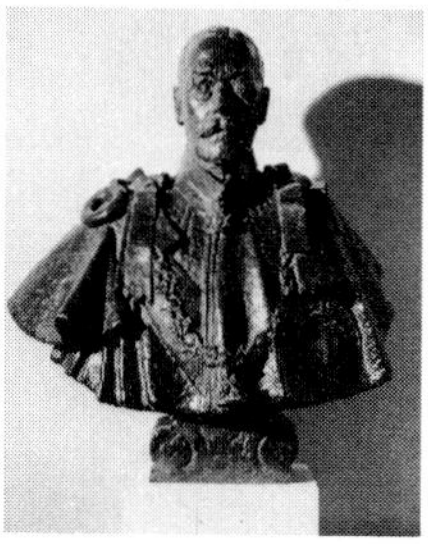

Sir William Reid Dick (1879–1961)
acc. no. 1509
King George V
bronze: 31 in. high
Presented by Sir Maurice Jenks, 1954

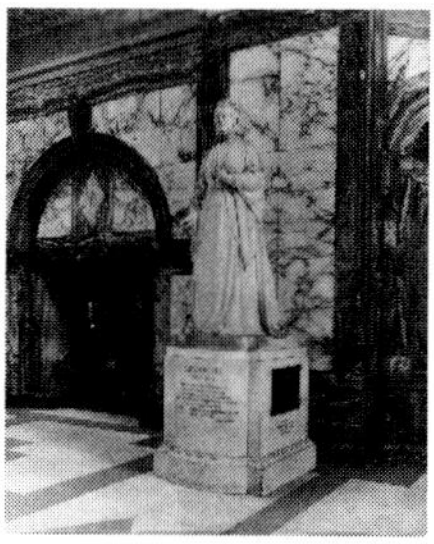

Alfred Drury (1857–1954)
acc. no. 955
Elizabeth Fry (1913)
marble: 90 × 39 × 49 in.
Presented by Miss P. J. Fletcher, 1914

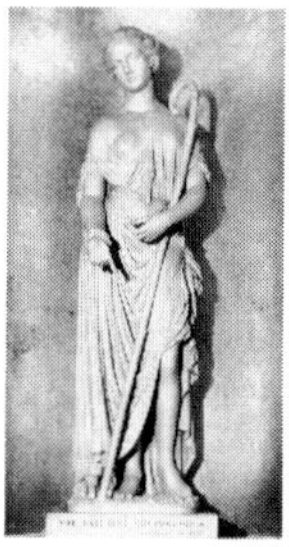

Susan Durant (d.1873)
acc. no. 143
The Faithful Shepherdess (1863)
marble: 78 in. high
Commissioned by the Corporation for the Mansion House, 1861

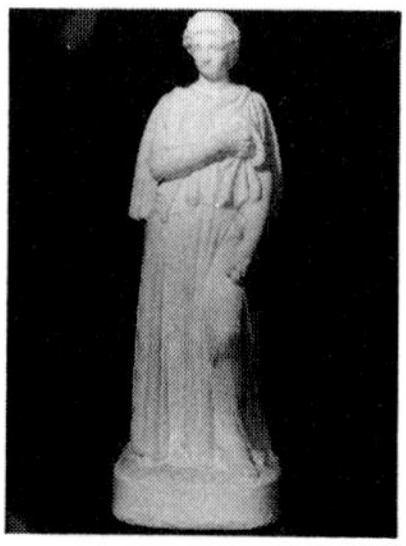

Joseph Durham (1814–77)
acc. no. 138
Maquette for 'Hermione' (*c.*1855)
plaster: 27 in. high
Submitted *c.*1855

acc. no. 137
Hermione (1856)

marble: 73 in. high
Commissioned by the Corporation for the Mansion House, 1856

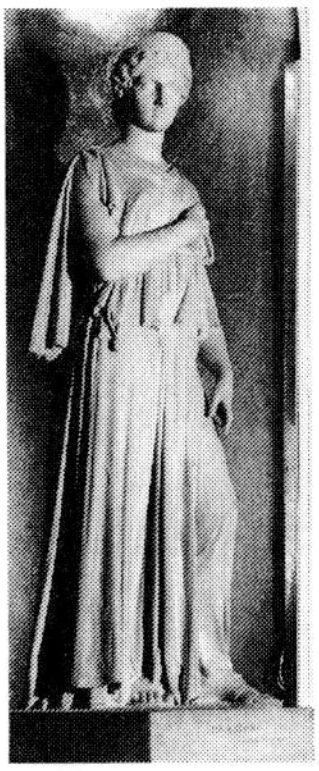

acc. no. 125
Alastor (1864)

marble: 87 in. high
Commissioned by the Corporation for the Mansion House, 1861

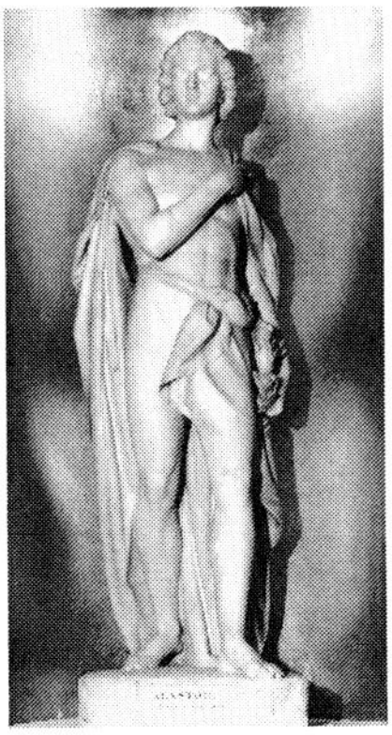

acc. no. 585
Waiting His Innings (1866)

marble: 34 × 38 × 20 in.
Presented by Basil E. Lawrence, 1893

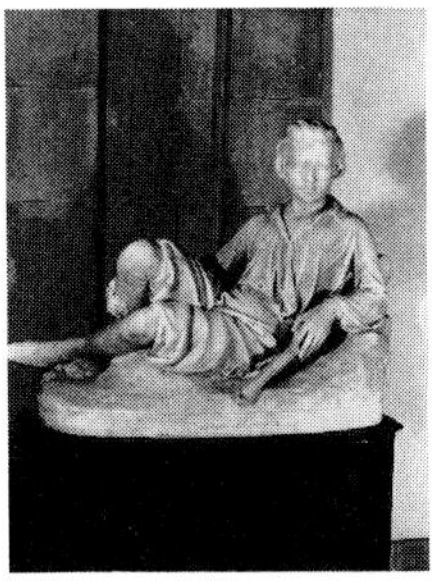

David Evans (b.1895)

acc. no. 1499
Gog (1953)

painted wood: 114 in. high
Presented by Sir George Wilkinson, 1953

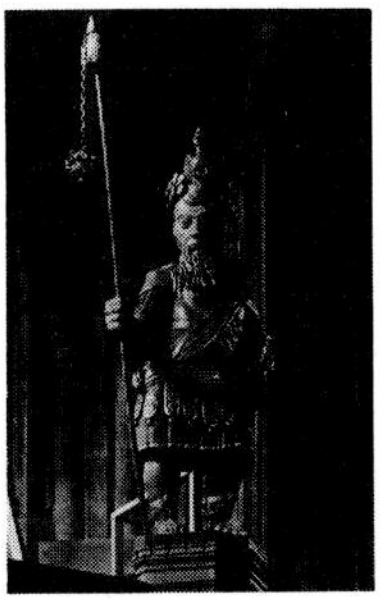

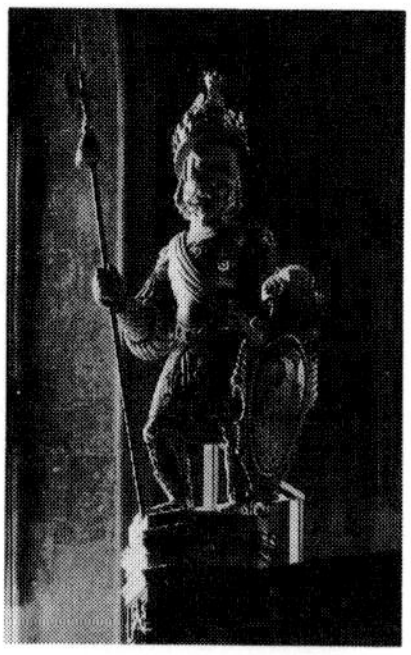

acc. no. 1500
Magog (1953)

painted wood: 114 in. high
Presented by Sir George Wilkinson, 1953

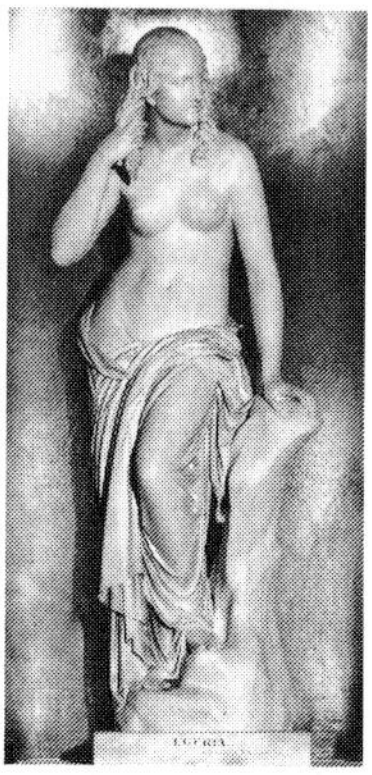

John Henry Foley (1818–74)

acc. no. 131
Egeria (1855)

marble: 82 in. high
Commissioned by the Corporation for the Mansion House, 1853

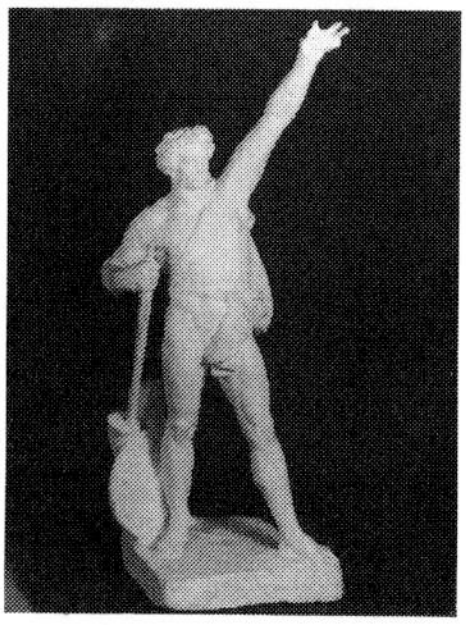

acc. no. 134
Maquette for 'Caractacus' (1856)

plaster: 27 in. high
Submitted 1856

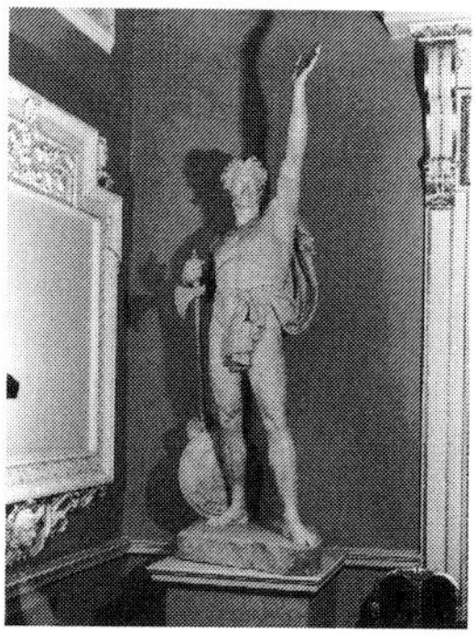

acc. no. 133
Caractacus (1859)

marble: 112 in. high
Commissioned by the Corporation for the Mansion House, 1856

Edward Onslow Ford (1852–1901)

acc. no. 511
Sir Henry Irving as Hamlet (*c.*1885)
marble: 55 × 36 × 44 in.
Presented by the artist, 1890

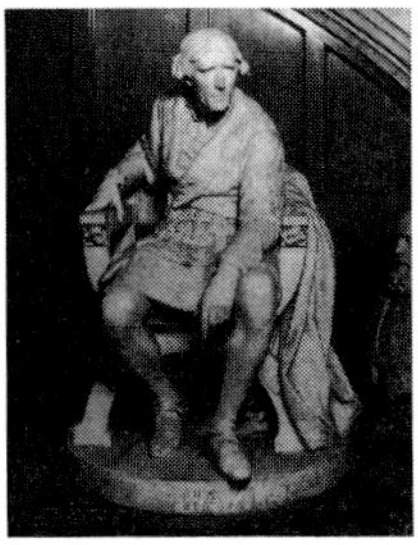

acc. no. 632
Queen Victoria (1898)
marble: 32 × 27 × 19 in.
Presented by George Paul Ernst, 1900

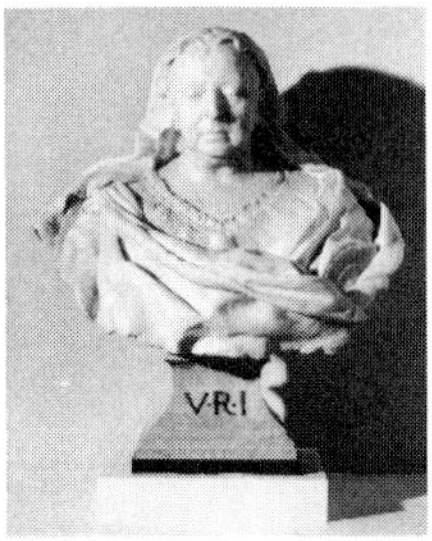

acc. no. 1035
George Swan Nottage, Lord Mayor 1884 (*c.*1884)
marble: $26\frac{1}{2} \times 24 \times 16\frac{1}{2}$ in.
Presented by the sitter's daughter, Lady Palmer, 1925

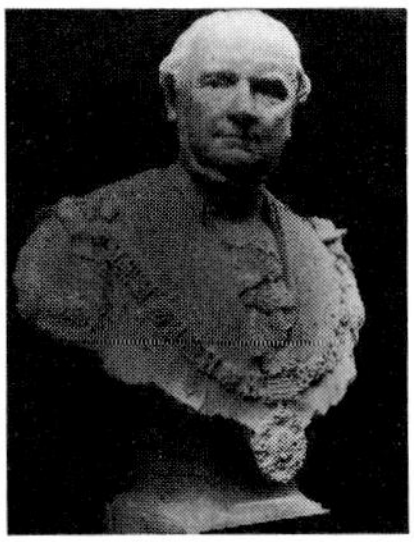

James Nesfield Forsyth (*fl.* 1885–1903)

acc. no. 602
Head of a Boy (? 1891)
bronze: $12\frac{3}{4} \times 6\frac{1}{4} \times 7$ in.
Presented by the artist, 1895

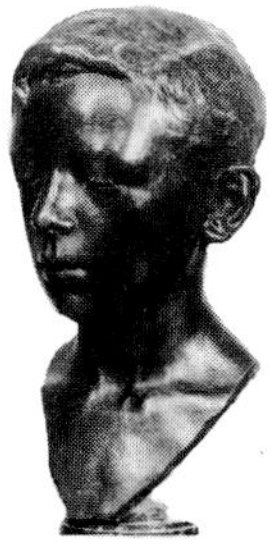

acc. no. 832
Robert Malcolm Kerr, Judge of the City of London Court (1896)
marble: $20\frac{1}{2} \times 18 \times 9\frac{1}{2}$ in.
Presented by the sitter's daughter, Elizabeth Malcolm Kerr, 1904

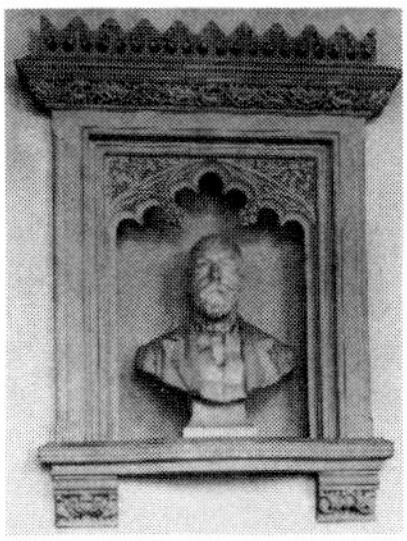

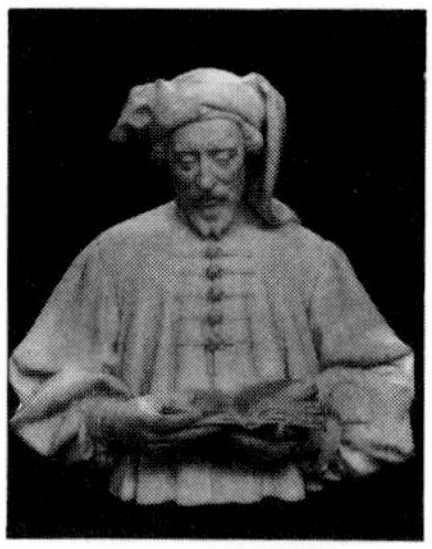

Sir George James Frampton (1860–1928)

acc. no. 765
Chaucer (1902–3)
marble: 30 × 25 × 20 in.
Presented by Alderman Sir Reginald Hanson, 1903

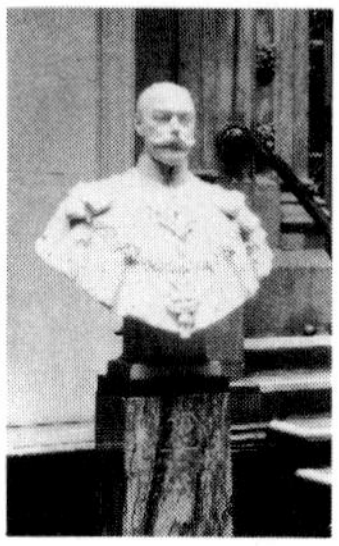

acc. no. 966
King George V (1914)
marble: 34 × 32 × 16 in.
Presented by Alderman Sir Edward E. Cooper, 1914

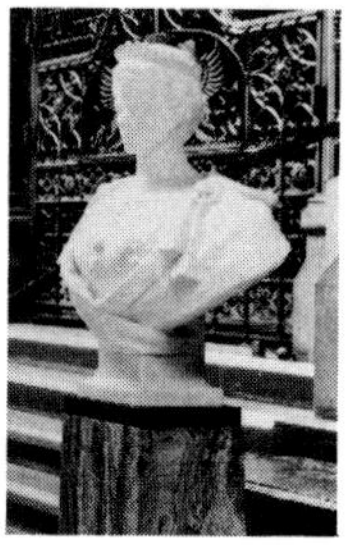

acc. no. 967
Queen Mary (1914)
marble: 36 × 28 × 16 in.
Presented by Sir Charles (later Lord) Wakefield, 1914

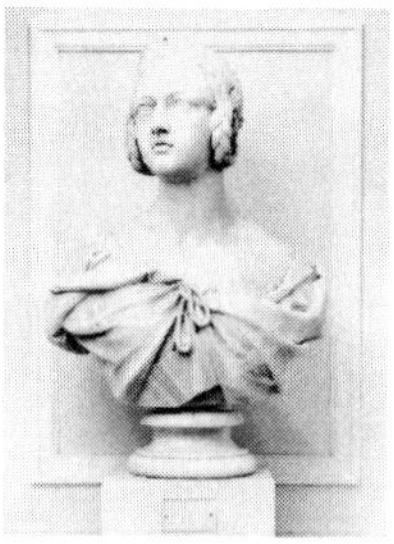

John Francis (1780–1861)

acc. no. 100
Queen Victoria (1837)
marble: 28 × 21 × 13 in.
Purchased, 1852

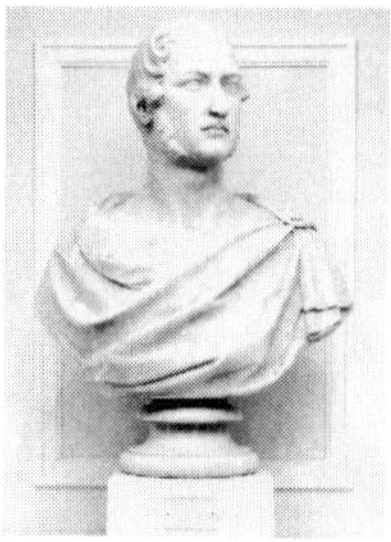

acc. no. 105
Prince Albert (1840)
marble: $30 \times 24\frac{1}{2} \times 14$ in.
Purchased, 1852

John Hancock (1825–69)

acc. no. 140
Maquette for 'Penserosa' (*c*.1861)
plaster: 27 in. high
Submitted, 1861

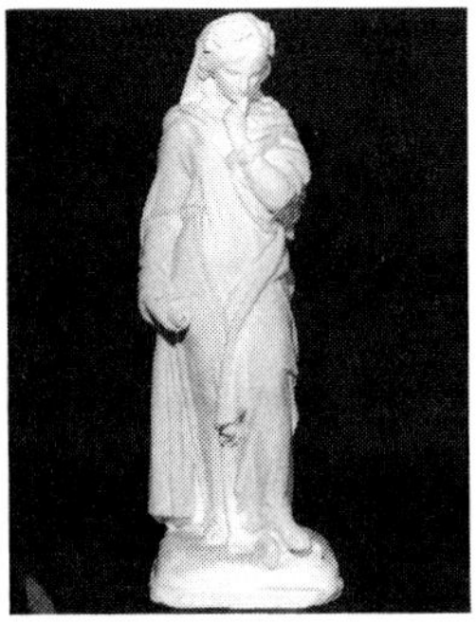

acc. no. 139
Penserosa (1862)
marble: 73 in. high
Commissioned by the Corporation for the Mansion House, 1861

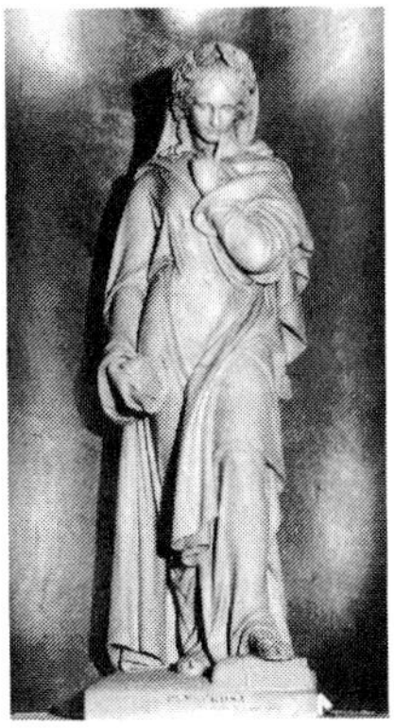

Charles Leonard Hartwell (1873–1951)

acc. no. 1016
Edward, Prince of Wales (1921)
marble: 28 × 19 × 10 in.
Presented by the Rt. Hon. Alderman Lord Marshall, 1921

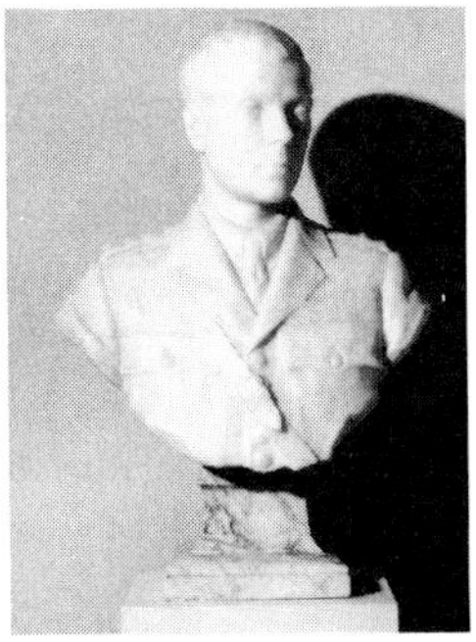

acc. no. 1351
Henry Herbert Asquith, 1st Earl of Oxford and Asquith (1930)
bronze: $27\frac{1}{2} \times 21\frac{1}{2} \times 12$ in.
Commissioned by the Corporation for the City of London School, 1929

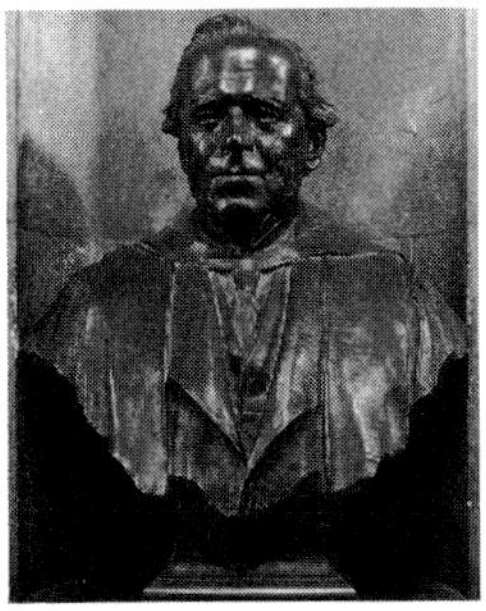

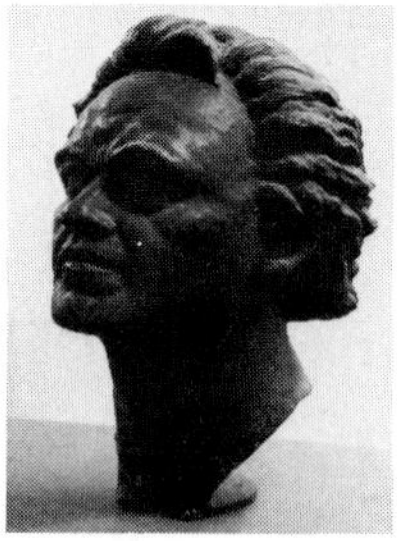

Alexander Jaray (b.1870)

acc. no. 1282
Beethoven

bronze: 18 × 15 × 9 in.
Presented by Mrs. M. Fischer-Ledenice, 1943

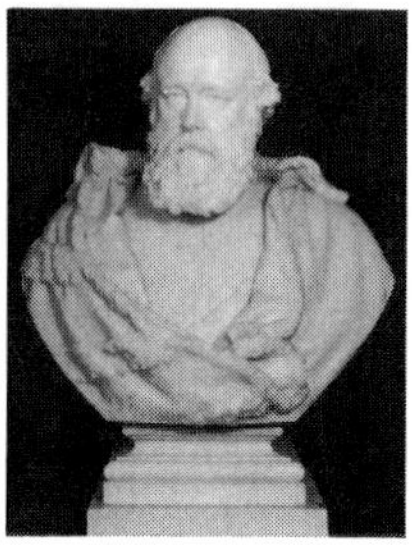

Albert Bruce Joy (1843–1924)

acc. no. 295
The Marquess of Salisbury (1886)

marble: 30 in. high
Purchased by public subscription, 1886

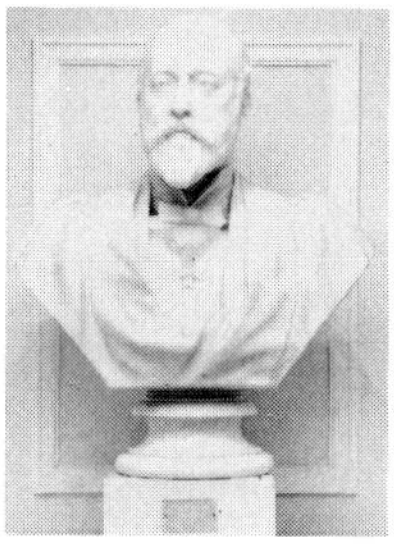

acc. no. 1053
King Edward VII

marble: 29 × 25 × 15 in.
Presented by Sir Charles (later Lord) Wakefield, 1927

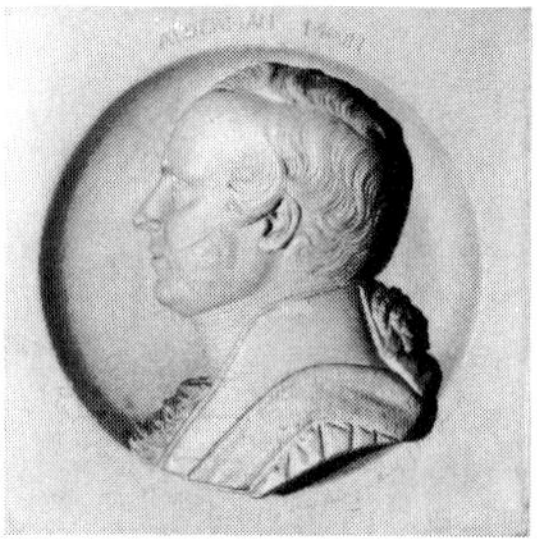

Claude François Lequine (19th C)

acc. no. 2222
Alderman Moon (1845)

plaster: $12\frac{3}{4} \times 12\frac{3}{4} \times 1\frac{3}{4}$ in.
inscribed and signed: *ALDERMAN MOON / 'The Original in the possession of his Majesty Louis Phillippe King of the French. / Fr. Lequine ft. Londres 1845'*
Presented by Bruce Clarke, 1979

John Graham Lough (1798–1876)

acc. no. 130
Maquette for 'Comus' (*c.*1852)
plaster: 27 in. high
Submitted, 1853

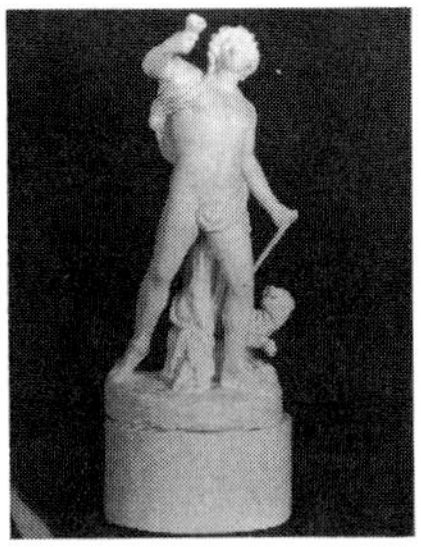

acc. no. 129
Comus (1856)
marble: 88 in. high
Commissioned by the Corporation for the Mansion House, 1853

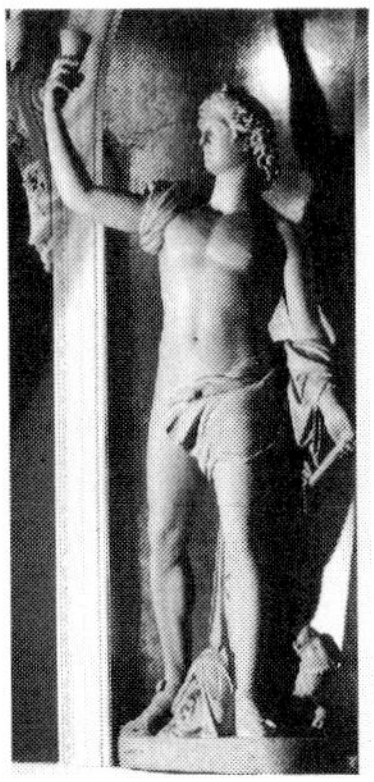

Hamilton Patrick MacCarthy (*fl.* 1875–84)

acc. no. 1338
The Rt. Hon. Russell Gurney, Recorder of London (1879)
marble: 23 × 19 × 14 in.
Presented by the sitter's great-nephew, E. W. Forham, 1945

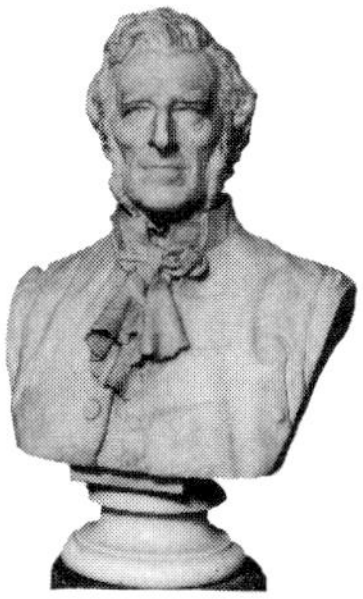

Patrick MacDowell (1799–1870)

acc. no. 141
Lea, One of the Daughters of Men (from Moore's 'Loves of the Angels', 1822) (1855)
marble: 76 in. high
Commissioned by the Corporation for the Mansion House, 1853

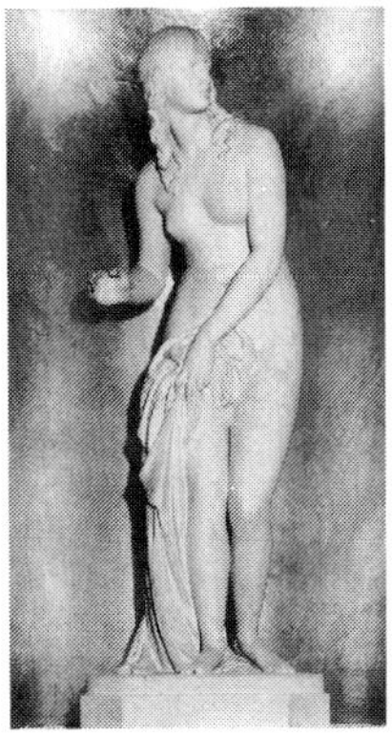

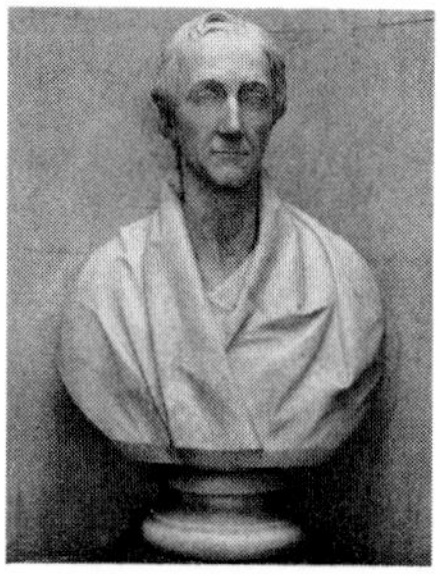

William Calder Marshall (1813–94)

acc. no. 114
H.B.H. Beaufoy (1852)

marble: 30 × 20 × 12 in.
Commissioned by the City of London School Committee, 1844

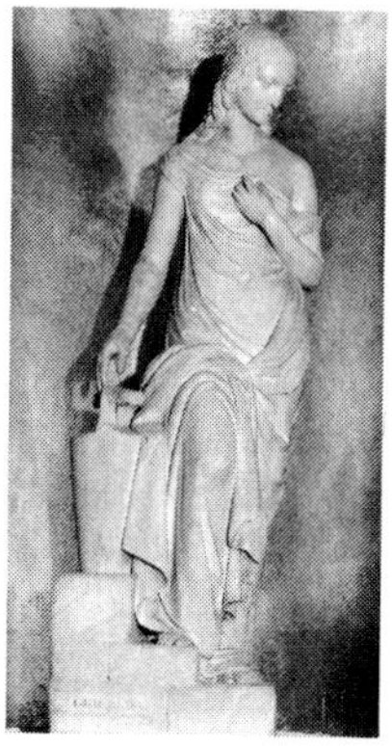

acc. no. 136
Griselda (1855)

marble: 79 in. high
Commissioned by the Corporation for the Mansion House, 1853

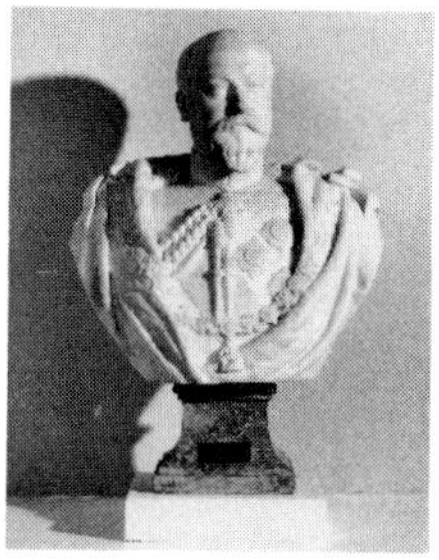

Walter Merrett (*fl.* 1873–1911)
acc. no. 633
King Edward VII (1902)

marble: 34 in. high
Presented by Alderman Sir T. Vansittart Bowater, 1902

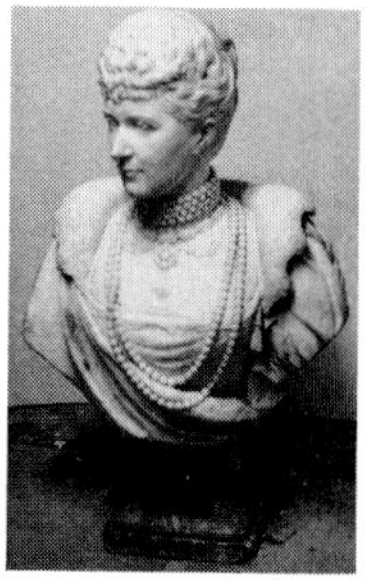

acc. no. 833
Queen Alexandra (1904)

marble: $27\frac{1}{2}$ × 23 × 13 in.
Presented by Alderman Sir T. Vansittart Bowater, 1904

acc. no. 936
Florence Nightingale (1912)
marble: 37 × $10\frac{1}{2}$ × 15 in.
Purchased, 1912

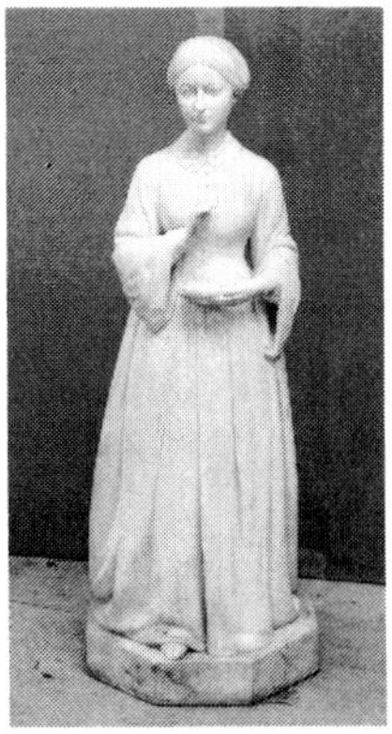

acc. no. 1287
Samuel Heilbuth (1914)
marble: 23 × $18\frac{1}{2}$ × 11 in.
Probably presented by the sitter's son, G. H. Heilbuth, to the Guildhall School of Music, *c.*1914

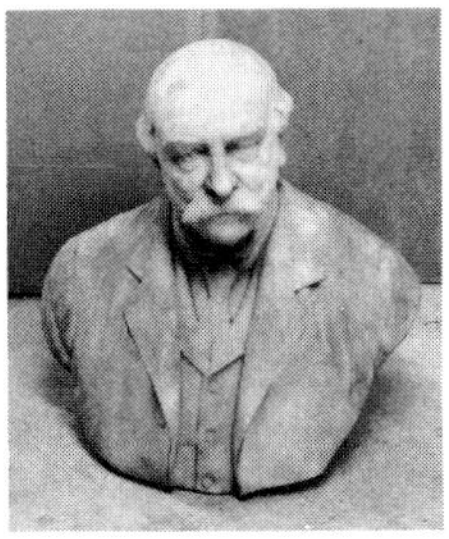

John Francis Moore (d.1809)

acc. no. 41
Monument to William Beckford, Lord Mayor 1762
marble: 100 × 135 × $20\frac{1}{2}$ in.
Commissioned by the Corporation, 1770

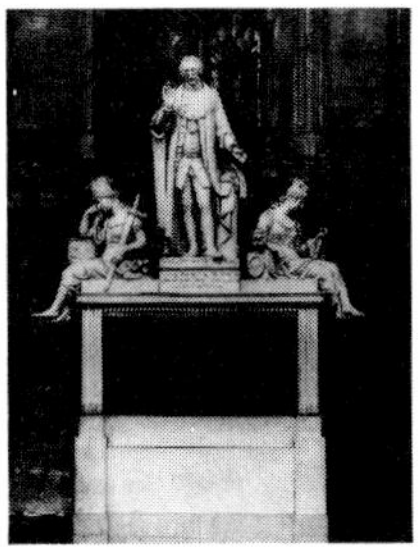

Oscar Nemon (b.1906)

acc. no. 1533
Sir Winston Churchill (1955–9)
bronze: 60 × 60 × 36 in.
Commissioned by the Corporation, 1955

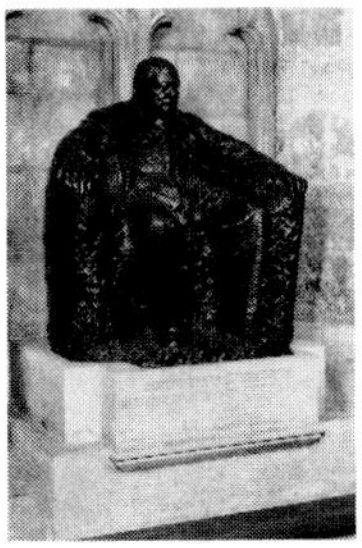

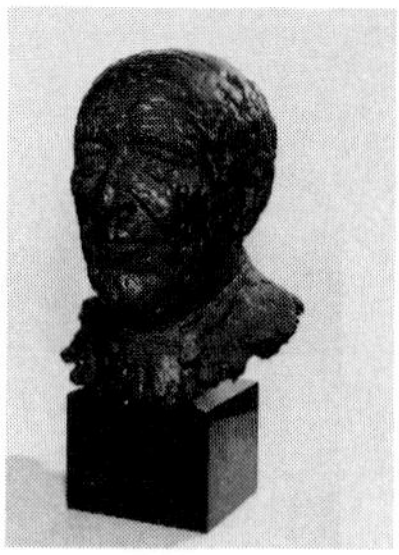

Karen Newman (20th C)

acc. no. 1952
Head of Eric Wilkins C.B.E. (1972)

bronze: 17 in. high
Commissioned by the sitter's friends, 1972

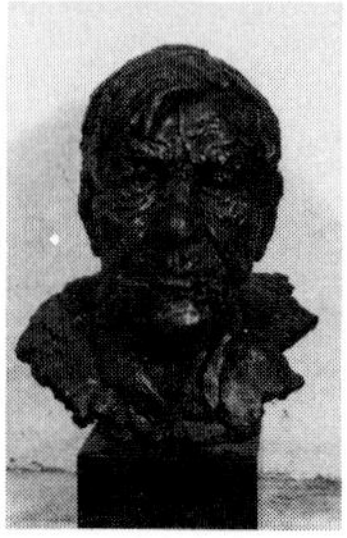

acc. no. 1953
Head of W.H. Auden

bronze: 13 in. high
Presented by G. M. Vine C.B.E., 1973

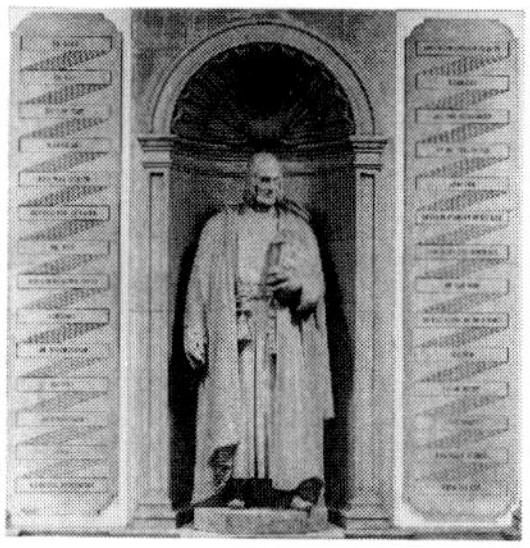

Samuel Nixon (1803–54)

acc. no. 113
John Carpenter, Town Clerk and Founder of the City of London School

marble: 72 in. high approximately
Erected at the cost of the Corporation, 1844

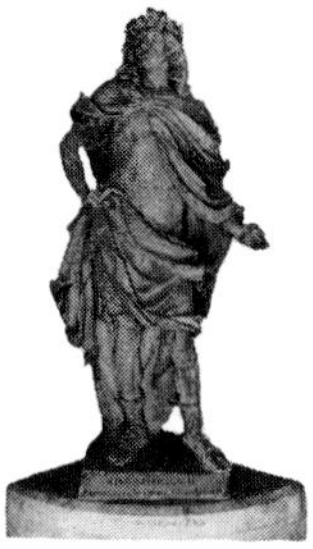

Arnold Quellin (1653–86)

acc. no. 1087
Charles II

limestone: $86\frac{1}{2}$ in. high
Removed from the College of Physicians, Warwick Lane, 1873, and presented by A. W. H. and E. B. Taylor

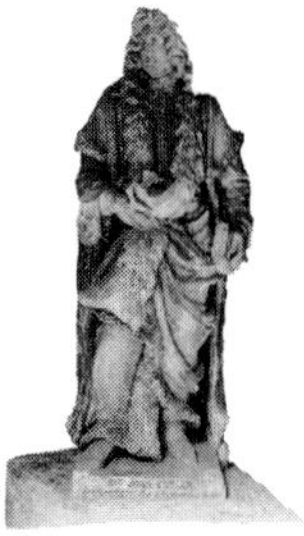

acc. no. 1088
Sir John Cutler

limestone: 79 in. high
Removed from the College of Physicians, Warwick Lane, 1873, and presented by A. W. H. and E. B. Taylor

Louis Francois Roubiliac (1705–62)

acc. no. 1098
John Wilkes (*c.*1761)

marble: 29 in. high
Presented by the Duke of St. Albans, 1935

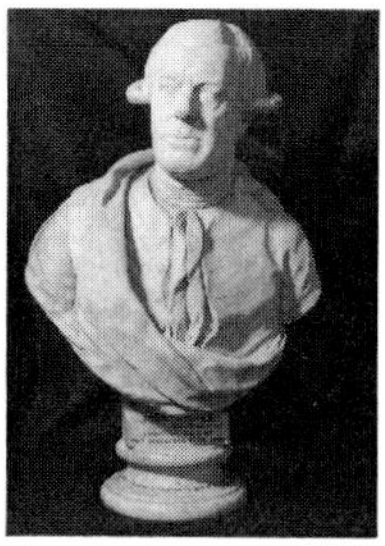

Sava (20th C)

acc. no. 1285
Sir Landon Ronald, Principal of the Guildhall School of Music

bronze:
Presented to the Guildhall School of Music by Lady Ronald, 1938

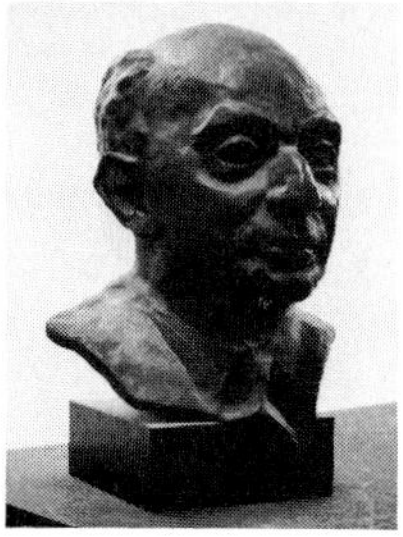

Kathleen Shaw (1870–1958)

acc. no. 1390
Colonel the Earl of Albemarle (1901)

plaster: $25\frac{1}{2} \times 23 \times 14$ in.
Presented by the sitter, 1949

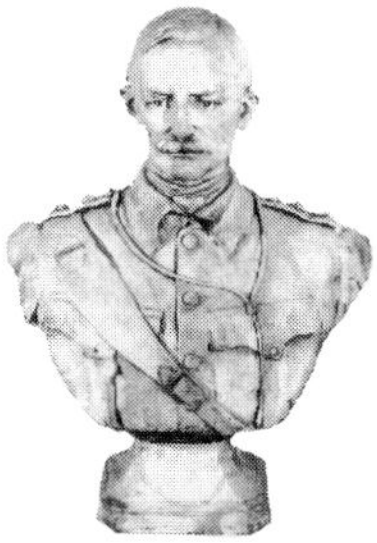

Robert William Sievier (1794–1865)

acc. no. 1375
Sir John Silvester, Recorder of London 1803–1822

marble: $27 \times 24 \times 12\frac{1}{2}$ in.
Presented by J. C. S. Davies, 1948

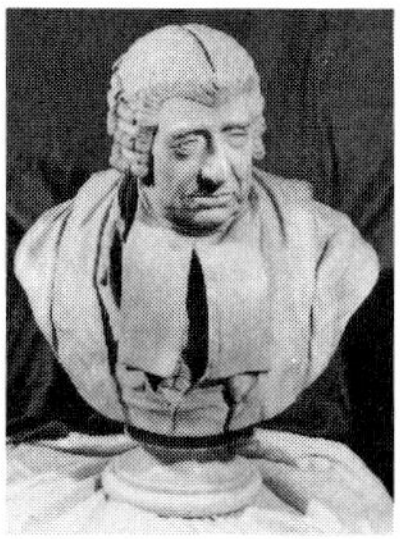

acc. no. 1375a
Sir John Silvester

plaster: $26 \times 24 \times 12\frac{1}{2}$ in.
Source and date of acquisition unknown

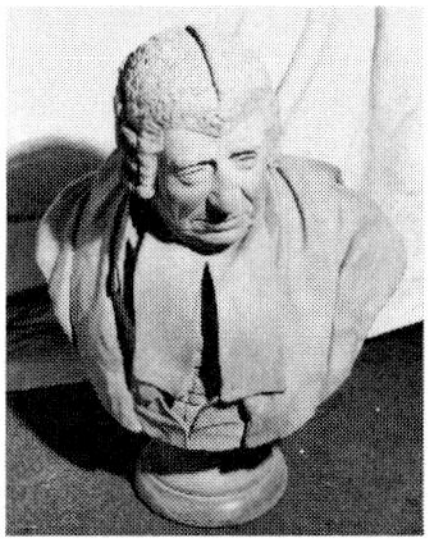

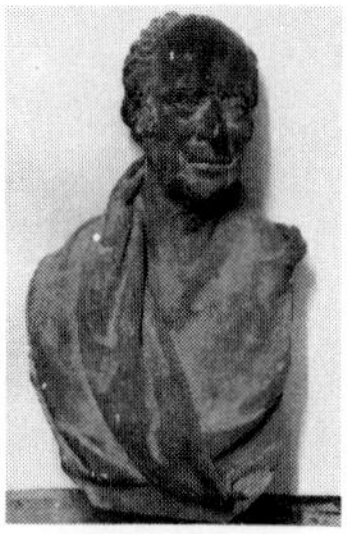

acc. no. 95
Richard Clark, Chamberlain of London (1829)
marble: 23 × $15\frac{1}{2}$ × 10 in.
Presented by Officers of the Corporation, 1829

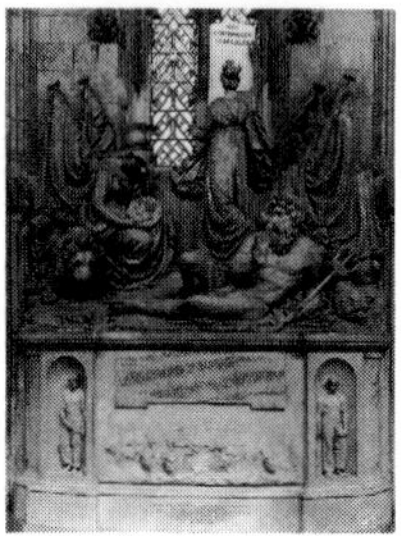

James Smith (1775–1815)

acc. no. 84
Monument to Horatio, Viscount Nelson (1810)
marble: 150 × 165 × 37 in.
Commissioned by the Corporation, 1807

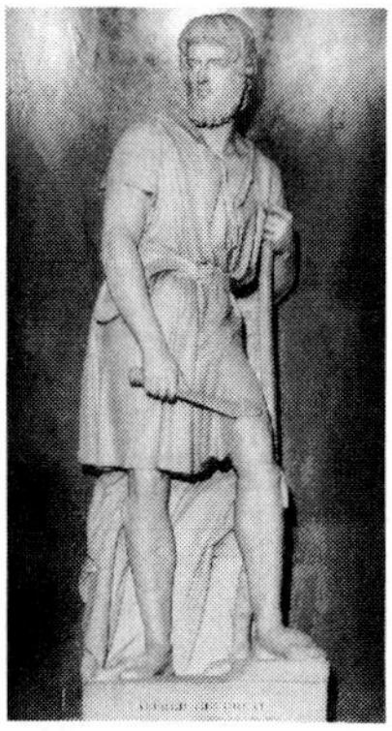

Edward Bowring Stephens (1815–82)

acc. no. 127
Alfred the Great in the Neatherd's Cottage (1863)
marble: 80 in. high
Commissioned by the Corporation for the Mansion House, 1861

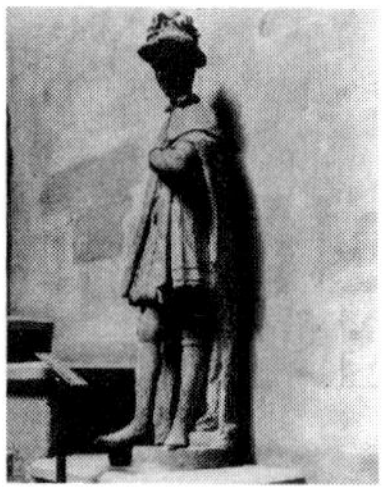

Nicholas Stone (1586–1647)

acc. no. 1
King Edward VI (1623)
stone: 78 × 26 × 18 in.
Commissioned by the Corporation for Guildhall Chapel, 1623

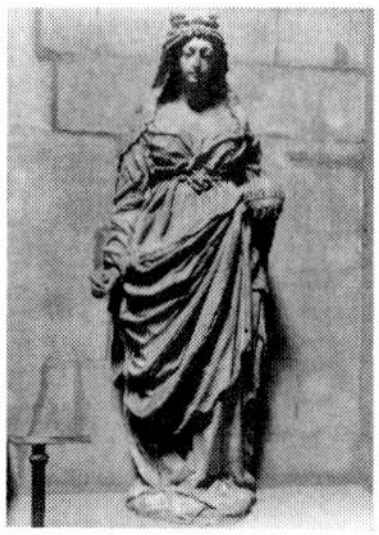

acc. no. 2
Queen Elizabeth I (1623)
stone: 70 × 29 × $19\frac{1}{2}$ in.
Removed from the Royal Exchange to Guildhall Chapel, *c.*1625

John Macallan Swan (1848–1910)

acc. no. 918
A Tiger

bronze: $4\frac{3}{4} \times 12\frac{3}{4} \times 4\frac{1}{2}$ in.
Presented by J. C. J. Drucker and others, 1911

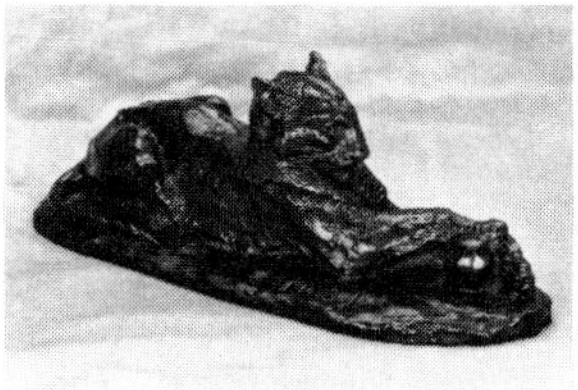

Joseph William Swynnerton (1848–1910)

acc. no. 619
Lord Brampton

marble: 33 × 38 × 18 in.
Presented by Lady Brampton, 1900

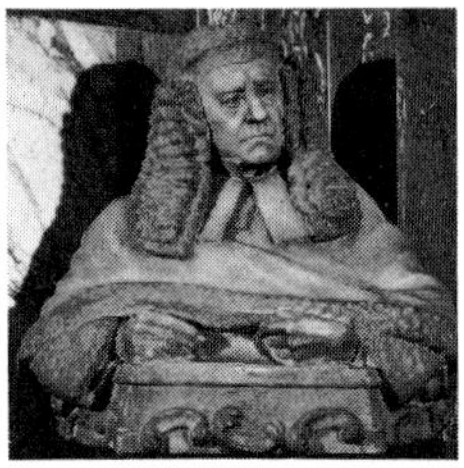

William Theed (1804–91)

acc. no. 148
The Welsh Bard (1858)

marble: 85 in. high
Commissioned by the Corporation for the Mansion House, 1856

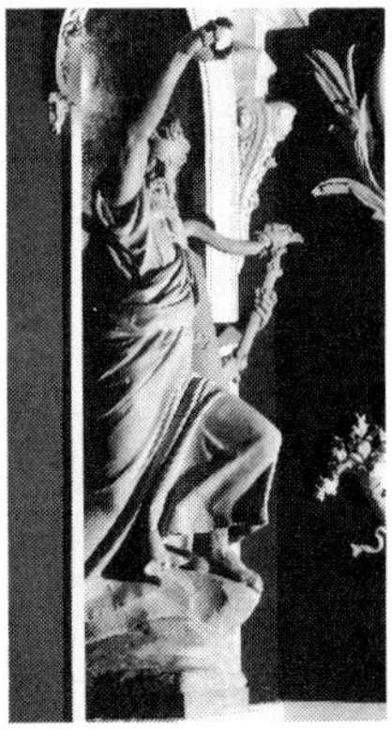

acc. no. 291
General Gordon (1886)

marble: $27\frac{3}{4} \times 25\frac{1}{2} \times 12$ in.
Commissioned by the Corporation, 1886

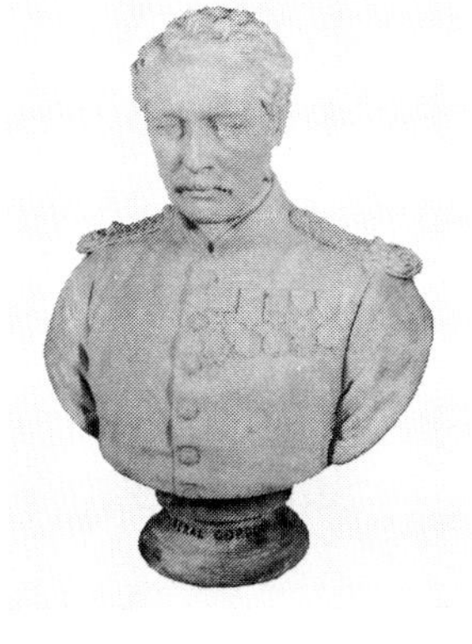

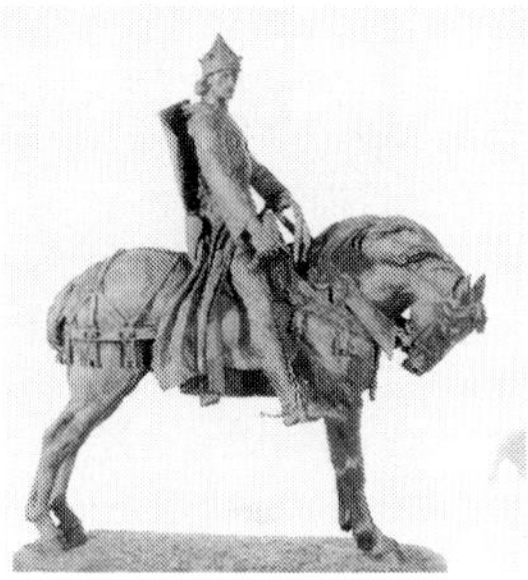

Sir William Hamo Thornycroft (1850–1925)

acc. no. 1048
King Edward I ('Longshanks') (1894)
bronze: 37 × 30 × 14 in.
Purchased, 1926

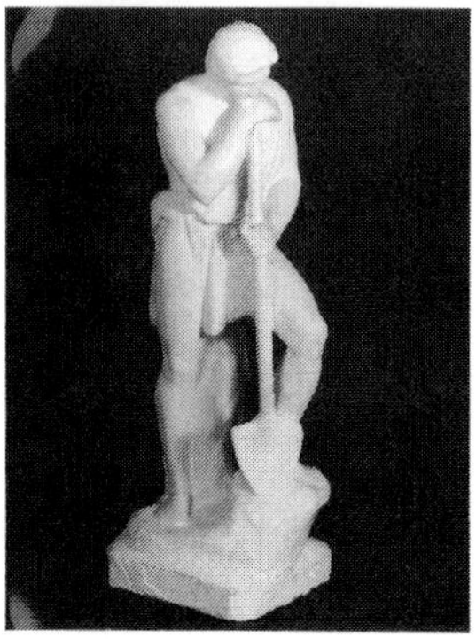

Frederick Thrupp (1812–95)

acc. no. 147
Maquette for 'Timon of Athens' (*c*.1853)
plaster: 27 in. high
Submitted, 1853

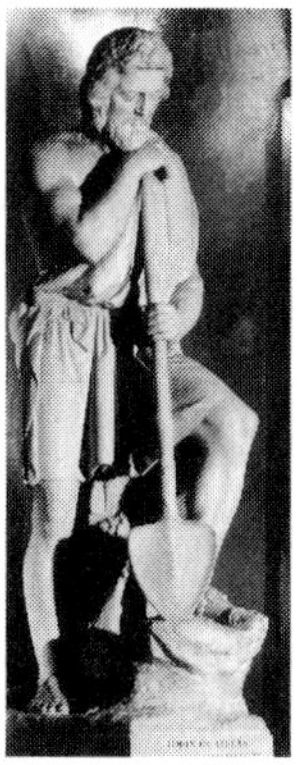

acc. no. 146
Timon of Athens (1855)
marble: 79 in. high
Commissioned by the Corporation for the Mansion House, 1853

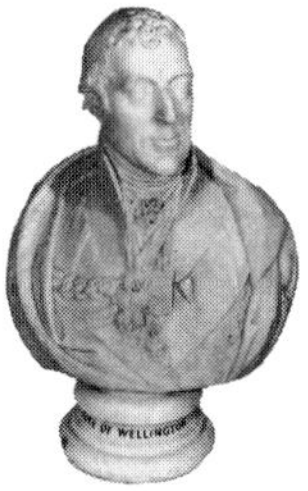

Peter Turnerelli (1774–1839)

acc. no. 89
Arthur Wellesley, Duke of Wellington (1814)
marble: $23\frac{1}{2} \times 21\frac{1}{2} \times 9$ in.
Purchased from the artist, 1814

Works by **Unknown Sculptors**

arranged in order of date of acquisition

acc. no. 3
Charles I

stone: 78 × 28 × 19 in.
Commissioned before 1660 for Guildhall Chapel; removed from Guildhall Chapel *c.* 1820

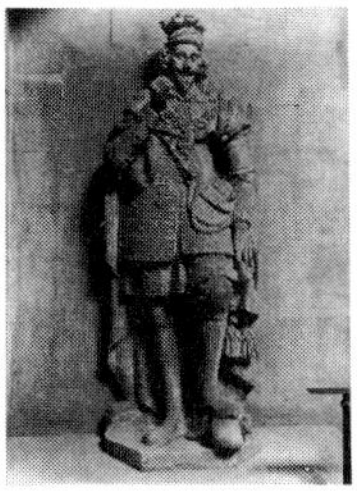

acc. no. 1288
Dr. William Hayman Cummings, Principal of the Guildhall School of Music

plaster: 28 × 25 × 16 in.
Date, method and source of acquisition by the Guildhall School of Music unknown

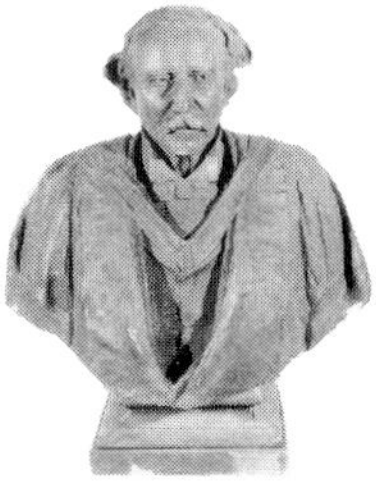

acc. no. 1615
'Sir John Silvester'

plaster: 23 × $17\frac{3}{4}$ × 14 in.
Transferred, provenance unknown, from the Guildhall Museum, 1960

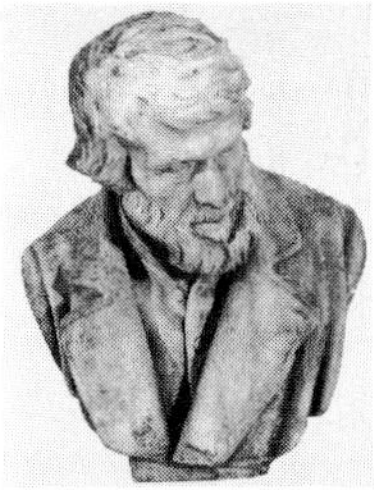

acc. no. 1932
Eskimo Child

black marble: $6\frac{1}{2}$ × 6 × $5\frac{1}{2}$ in.
Presented by the Mayor of Ottawa, 1972

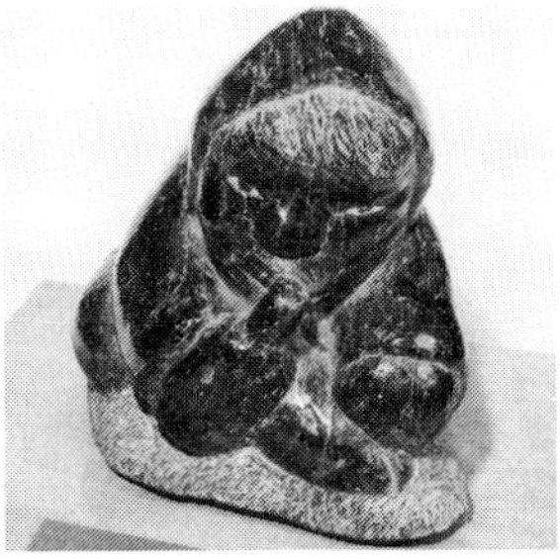

George Frederick Watts (1817–1904)

acc. no. 995
Clytie (1878)

marble: 28 × 24 × 17 in.
Presented by Lady Battersea, 1919

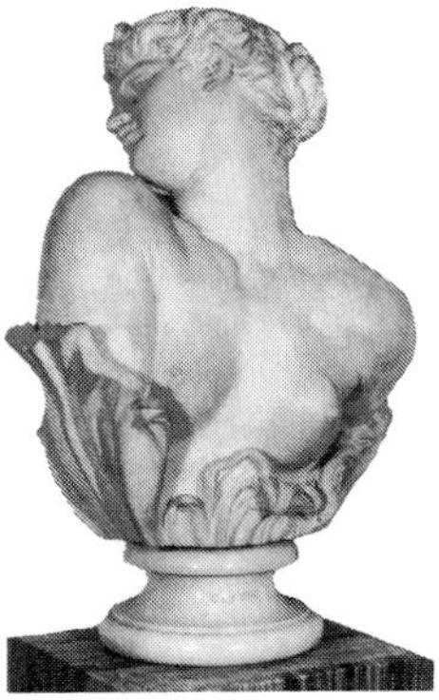

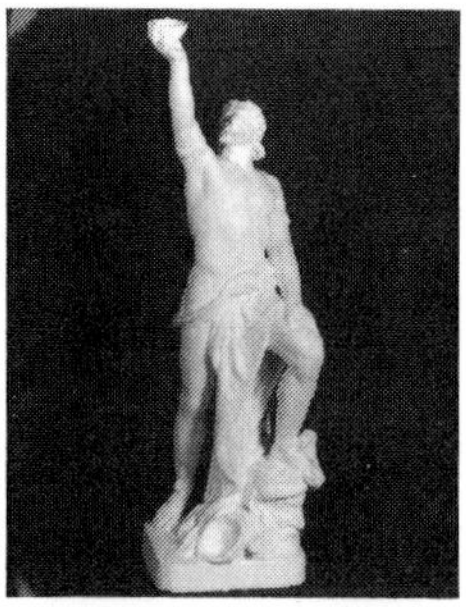

Henry Weekes (1807–77)

acc. no. 151
Maquette for 'Sardanapalus' (*c.*1856)

plaster: 27 in. high
Submitted, 1856

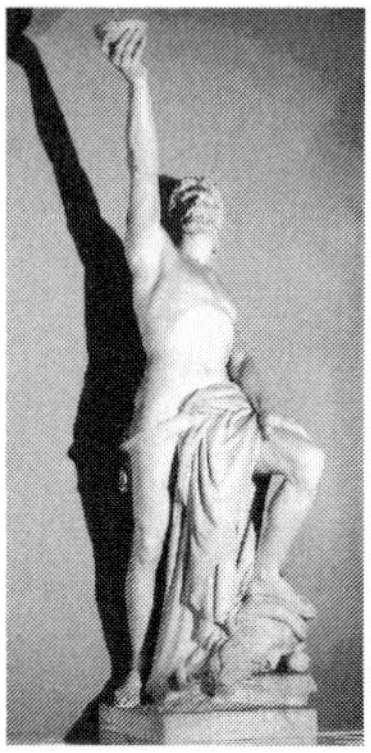

acc. no. 150
Sardanapalus (1861)

marble: 103 in. high
Commissioned by the Corporation for the Mansion House, 1856

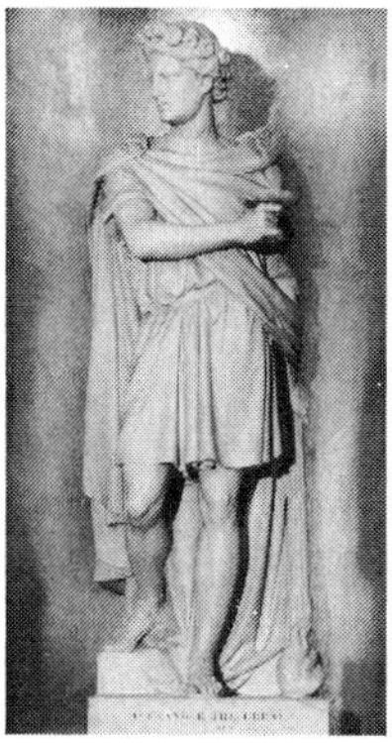

James Sherwood Westmacott (1823–1900)

acc. no. 126
Alexander the Great (1863)

marble: 85 in. high
Commissioned by the Corporation for the Mansion House, 1861

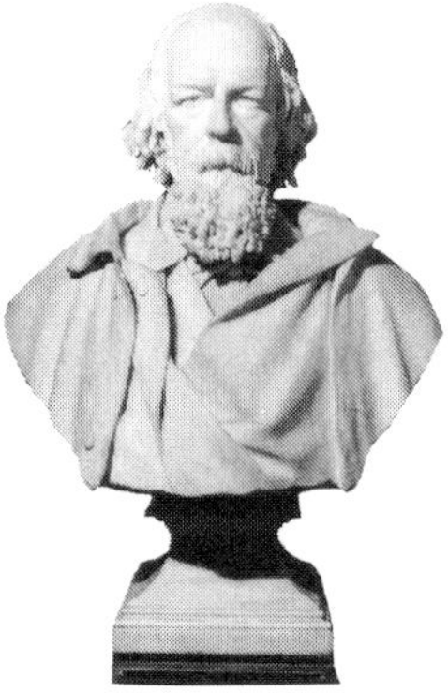

Francis John Williamson (1833–1920)

acc. no. 584
Alfred, Lord Tennyson (1893)

marble: $27 \times 25\frac{1}{2} \times 17$ in.
Commissioned by the Corporation, 1893

acc. no. 607
The Duke of Cambridge (1898)
marble: 26 × 21 × 13 in.
Commissioned by the Corporation, 1897

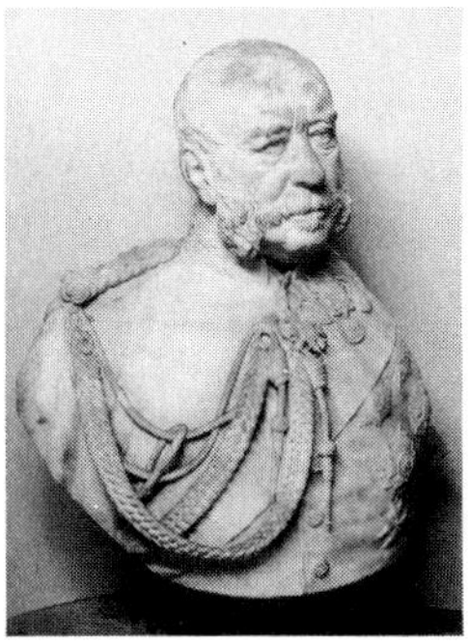

David Wynne (b.1926)
acc. no. 1828
Charles, Prince of Wales (1969)
bronze: 23 in. high
Purchased from the artist, 1969

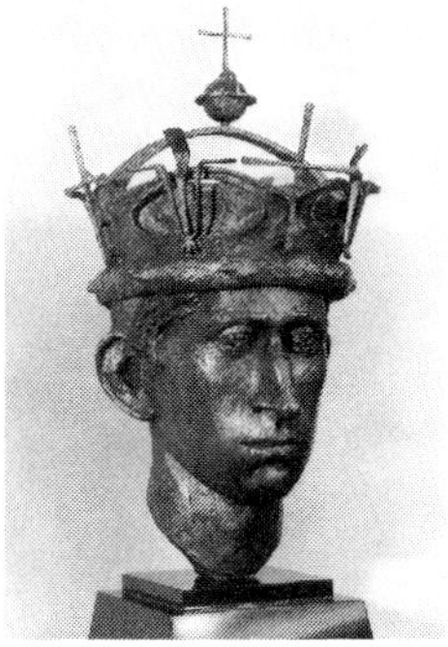

acc. no. 1955
Embracing Lovers
marble: 24 × 24 × 24 in.
Presented by Alderman Neville Burston, 1973

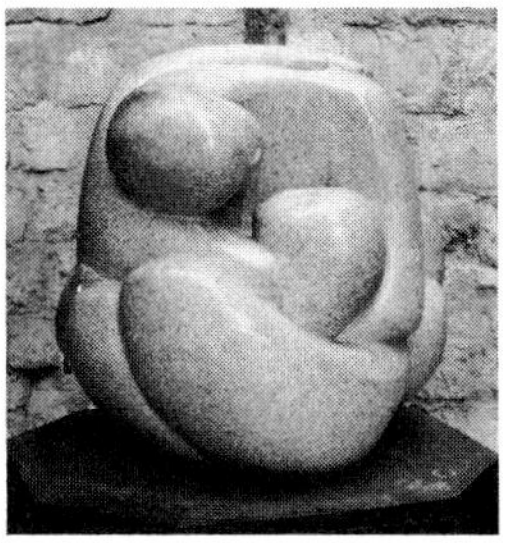

Edward William Wyon (1811–85)
acc. no. 128
Britomartis (from Spenser's 'Faerie Queene') (1861)
marble: 80¾ in. high
Commissioned by the Corporation for the Mansion House, 1856

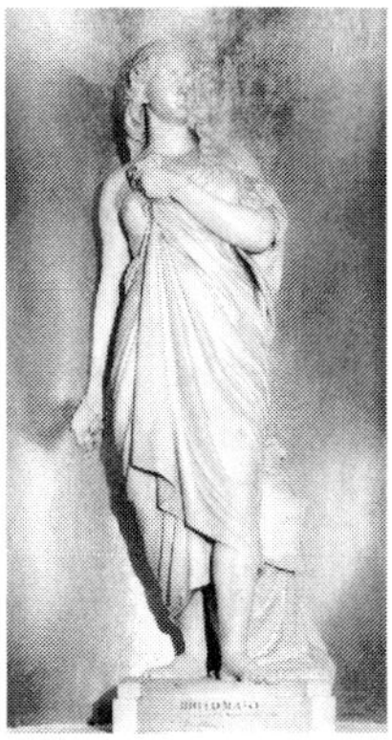

Index of Artists, Sculptors, Donors and Subjects

Note: Roman numerals refer to artists and sculptors; **bold** numerals refer to subjects; and *italic* numerals refer to donors.

D

H

M

N

Index of Places